Microsoft® Office 2010

ADVANCED

by Sandra Cable and Connie Morrison

Microsoft® Office 2010

ADVANCED

by Sandra Cable and Connie Morrison

Sandra Cable, Ed. D.
Texas A&M University

Connie Morrison, M.A.
Consultant, Encore Training, Inc

COURSE TECHNOLOGY
CENGAGE Learning™

Australia • Brazil • Japan • Korea • Mexico • Singapore • Spain • United Kingdom • United States

Microsoft Office 2010 Advanced
Sandra Cable, Connie Morrison

Executive Editor: Donna Gridley

Product Manager: Allison O'Meara McDonald

Development Editors: Ann Fisher, Karen Porter

Associate Product Managers: Amanda Lyons; Tricia Coia

Editorial Assistant: Kim Klasner

Senior Content Project Manager: Catherine DiMassa

Associate Marketing Manager: Julie Schuster

Director of Manufacturing: Denise Powers

Text Designer: Shawn Girsberger

Photo Researcher: Abigail Reip

Manuscript Quality Assurance Lead: Jeff Schwartz

Manuscript Quality Assurance Reviewers: Green Pen QA, Susan Pedicini, Marianne Snow, Susan Whalen, John Freitas, Serge Palladino, Jeff Schwartz, Danielle Shaw

Copy Editor: Michael Beckett

Proofreader: Green Pen Quality Assurance

Indexer: Sharon Hilgenberg

Art Director: Faith Brosnan

Cover Designer: Hannah Wellman

Cover Image: © Neil Brennan / Canopy Illustration / Veer

Compositor: GEX Publishing Services

Library of Congress Control Number: 2011922322

Hardcover:
ISBN-13: 978-0-538-48129-8
ISBN-10: 0-538-48129-3

Hard spiral:
ISBN-13: 978-0-538-48142-7
ISBN-10: 0-538-48142-0

Softcover:
ISBN-13: 978-0-538-48143-4
ISBN-10: 0-538-48143-9

Course Technology
20 Channel Center Street
Boston, Massachusetts 02210
USA

Cengage Learning is a leading provider of customized learning solutions with office locations around the globe, including Singapore, the United Kingdom, Australia, Mexico, Brazil, and Japan. Locate your local office at: **international.cengage.com/region**

Cengage Learning products are represented in Canada by Nelson Education, Ltd.

To learn more about Course Technology, visit **www.cengage.com/coursetechnology**

To learn more about Cengage Learning, visit **www.cengage.com**

To access additional course materials [including CourseMate], please visit www.cengagebrain.com. At the CengageBrain.com home page, search for the ISBN of your title (from the back cover of your book) using the search box at the top of the page. This will take you to the product page where these resources can be found.

Printed in the United States of America
1 2 3 4 5 6 7 15 14 13 12 11

ABOUT THIS BOOK

Microsoft Office 2010 Advanced is designed for beginning users of Microsoft Office 2010. Students will learn to use the application through a variety of activities, simulations, and case projects. *Microsoft Office 2010 Advanced* demonstrates the tools and features for this program in an easy-to-follow, hands-on approach.

This self-paced, step-by-step book with corresponding screen shots makes learning easy and enjoyable. End-of-lesson exercises reinforce the content covered in each lesson and provide students the opportunity to apply the skills that they have learned. It is important to work through each lesson within a unit in the order presented, as each lesson builds on what was learned in previous lessons.

Illustrations provide visual reinforcement of features and concepts, and sidebars provide notes, tips, and concepts related to the lesson topics. Step-by-Step exercises provide guidance for using the features. End-of-lesson projects concentrate on the main concepts covered in the lesson and provide valuable opportunities to apply or extend the skills learned in the lesson, and instructors can assign as many or as few of the projects at the end of the lesson as they like.

The lessons in the **Word Unit** introduce students to details and special features that will help them achieve a higher level of expertise in word processing skills. Students learn how to customize styles, themes, tables, and charts. To improve productivity, there is full coverage of creating merge documents for letters, envelopes, labels, emails, and directories. Students learn how to protect documents and restrict access when sharing documents. To work more efficiently, students learn to create citations and bibliographies for research papers, and also how to create indexes, tables of contents, tables of figures, and tables of authorities for long documents. Students also learn to create macros for repetitive tasks and to customize the Word application settings.

The lessons in the **Excel Unit** teach students advanced spreadsheet features; how to apply advanced formats to worksheets; how to use advanced chart features; how to improve data accuracy; how to create PivotTables and PivotCharts; how to use advanced functions such as VLOOKUP and HLOOKUP; how to create macros; how to protect, share, and track data; and how to import and export data.

The lessons in the **Access Unit** teach students enhanced table design that helps with data entry accuracy; how to create professional queries using different search data each time the query is opened; how to develop advanced forms with command buttons and themes; how to add sub-reports and charts to reports; how to create embedded macros; how to develop navigation forms to be used as menus for the database; and how to write functions and procedures for programming in Access.

The lessons in the **PowerPoint Unit** build on the skills and features introduced in the Introductory PowerPoint unit. The lessons emphasize the importance of clarity in a presentation and how to use PowerPoint features to create a presentation that will effectively deliver a message. The exercises provide extensive practice working with tables and charts, using visual and sound objects, and customizing slide designs and slide layouts. The unit also provides comprehensive coverage and practice importing and exporting information to other applications and sharing and delivering presentations in a business or professional environment.

To complete all lessons and End-of-Lesson material, this book will require approximately 70 hours.

Start-Up Checklist

Hardware

- Computer and processor 500-megahertz (MHz) processor or higher
- Memory: 256 megabytes (MB) of RAM or higher
- Hard disk: 3.5 gigabyte (GB) available disk space
- Display 1024 × 768 or higher-resolution monitor

Software:

- Operating system: Windows XP with Service Pack 3, Windows Vista with SP1, or Windows 7

INSIDE THIS BOOK

Step-by-Step Exercises offer "hands-on practice" of the material just learned. Each exercise uses a data file or requires you to create a file from scratch.

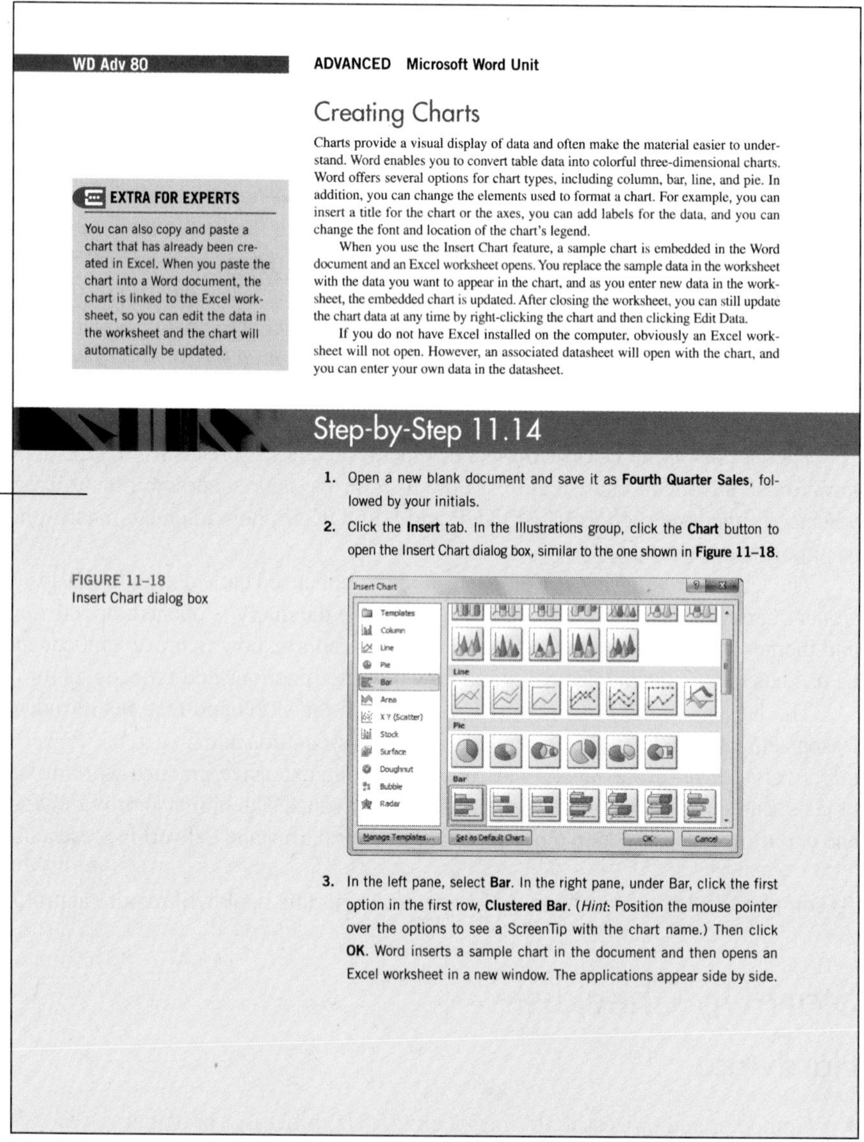

WD Adv 80

ADVANCED Microsoft Word Unit

Creating Charts

Charts provide a visual display of data and often make the material easier to understand. Word enables you to convert table data into colorful three-dimensional charts. Word offers several options for chart types, including column, bar, line, and pie. In addition, you can change the elements used to format a chart. For example, you can insert a title for the chart or the axes, you can add labels for the data, and you can change the font and location of the chart's legend.

When you use the Insert Chart feature, a sample chart is embedded in the Word document and an Excel worksheet opens. You replace the sample data in the worksheet with the data you want to appear in the chart, and as you enter new data in the worksheet, the embedded chart is updated. After closing the worksheet, you can still update the chart data at any time by right-clicking the chart and then clicking Edit Data.

If you do not have Excel installed on the computer, obviously an Excel worksheet will not open. However, an associated datasheet will open with the chart, and you can enter your own data in the datasheet.

EXTRA FOR EXPERTS

You can also copy and paste a chart that has already been created in Excel. When you paste the chart into a Word document, the chart is linked to the Excel worksheet, so you can edit the data in the worksheet and the chart will automatically be updated.

Step-by-Step 11.14

1. Open a new blank document and save it as **Fourth Quarter Sales**, followed by your initials.
2. Click the **Insert** tab. In the Illustrations group, click the **Chart** button to open the Insert Chart dialog box, similar to the one shown in **Figure 11–18**.

FIGURE 11–18
Insert Chart dialog box

3. In the left pane, select **Bar**. In the right pane, under Bar, click the first option in the first row, **Clustered Bar**. (*Hint*: Position the mouse pointer over the options to see a ScreenTip with the chart name.) Then click **OK**. Word inserts a sample chart in the document and then opens an Excel worksheet in a new window. The applications appear side by side.

Lesson opener elements include the **Objectives, Suggested Completion Time**, and **Vocabulary Terms**.

End of Lesson elements include the **Summary**, **Vocabulary Review**, **Review Questions, Lesson Projects**, and **Critical Thinking Activities**.

Instructor Resources Disk

ISBN-13: 978-0-538-47523-5
ISBN-10: 0-538-47523-4

The Instructor Resources CD or DVD contains the following teaching resources:

- The Data and Solution files for this course.
- ExamView® tests for each lesson.
- Instructor's Manual that includes lecture notes for each lesson and references to the end-of-lesson activities and Unit Review projects.
- Answer Keys that include solutions to the end-of- lesson and unit review questions.
- Critical thinking solution files that provide possible solutions for critical thinking activities.
- Copies of the figures that appear in the student text.
- Suggested Syllabus with block, two quarter, and 18-week schedule.
- Annotated Solutions and Grading Rubrics.
- PowerPoint presentations for each lesson.
- Spanish glossary and Spanish test bank.
- Appendices that include models for formatted documents, an e-mail writing guide, and a letter writing guide.
- Proofreader's Marks.

ExamView®

This textbook is accompanied by ExamView, a powerful testing software package that allows instructors to create and administer printed, computer (LAN-based), and Internet exams. ExamView includes hundreds of questions that correspond to the topics covered in this text, enabling students to generate detailed study guides that include page references for further review. The computer-based and Internet testing components allow students to take exams at their computers, and save the instructor time by grading each exam automatically.

Online Companion

This book uses an Online Companion Web site that contains valuable resources to help enhance your learning.

- Student data files to complete text projects and activities
- Key terms and definitions for each lesson
- PowerPoint presentations for each lesson
- Additional Internet boxes with links to important Web sites
- Link to CourseCasts

CourseCasts

CourseCasts—Learning on the Go. Always Available…Always Relevant.

Want to keep up with the latest technology trends relevant to you? Visit our site to find a library of podcasts, CourseCasts, featuring a "CourseCast of the Week," and download them to your mp3 player at http://coursecasts.course.com.

Our fast-paced world is driven by technology. You know because you're an active participant—always on the go, always keeping up with technological trends, and always learning new ways to embrace technology to power your life.

Ken Baldauf, a faculty member of the Florida State University Computer Science Department, is responsible for teaching technology classes to thousands of FSU students each year. He knows what you want to know; he knows what you want to learn. He's also an expert in the latest technology and will sort through and aggregate the most pertinent news and information so you can spend your time enjoying technology, rather than trying to figure it out.

Visit us at http://coursecasts.course.com to learn on the go!

SAM 2010 SAM

SAM 2010 Assessment, Projects, and Training version 1.0 offers a real-world approach to applying Microsoft Office 2010 skills. The Assessment portion of this powerful and easy to use software simulates Office 2010 applications, allowing users to demonstrate their computer knowledge in a hands-on environment. The Projects portion allows students to work live-in-the-application on project-based assignments. The Training portion helps students learn in the way that works best for them by reading, watching, or receiving guided help.

- SAM 2010 captures the key features of the actual Office 2010 software, allowing students to work in high-fidelity, multi-pathway simulation exercises for a real-world experience.
- SAM 2010 includes realistic and explorable simulations of Office 2010, Windows 7 coverage, and a new user interface.
- Easy, web-based deployment means SAM is more accessible than ever to both you and your students.
- Direct correlation to the skills covered on a chapter-by-chapter basis in your Course Technology textbooks allows you to create a detailed lesson plan.
- SAM Projects offers live-in-the-application project-based assignments. Student work is automatically graded, providing instant feedback. A unique cheating detection feature identifies students who may have shared files.
- Because SAM Training is tied to textbook exams and study guides, instructors can spend more time teaching and let SAM Training help those who need additional time to grasp concepts

Note: This textbook may or may not be available in SAM Projects at this time. Please check with your sales representative for the most recent information on when this title will be live in SAM Projects.

About the Authors

Sandra Cable, Texas A&M University – Commerce

Sandra Cable received her doctorate in Education from Texas A&M University—Commerce in 2003. In addition to working as an adjunct professor, she teaches computer classes at corporations that want to enhance the computer skills of their employees. Sandra also volunteers at schools and not-for-profit organizations, giving seminars that demonstrate simple approaches to using computer applications.

I would like to thank the great team at Course Technology: Donna Gridley, Executive Editor; Allison O'Meara McDonald, Product Manager; Cathie DiMassa, Senior Content Project Manager. This team is truly the best group of individuals with whom I have worked! I would also like to give special thanks to Ann Fisher, the Developmental Editor. Thank you so much for all of your great work, coordination efforts, and incredible sense of humor. You are truly wonderful to work with. To the thousands of students and clients that I have taught over the years, many thanks for your encouragement and for all you have taught me. Finally, I am very grateful to my family, Keith and Meridith Albright, for their enduring support.— **Sandra Cable**

Connie Morrison, M.A.Consultant, Encore Training, Inc.

Connie Morrison has more than 35 years of combined experience in education and educational publishing. She began her career teaching business education at the high school and college levels, and then becamean education consultant in the publishing industry. Connie currently works as a consultant for Encore Training, Inc., providing staff training and professional development.

This book represents a true team effort, and it was a pleasure working with everyone. My appreciation goes to all the members of the team who made this book possible. I owe special thanks to the following individuals: Donna Gridley, Allison O'Meara McDonald, and Cathie DiMassa for their direction and support in the development of this book; Karen Porter, for her meticulous editing and valuable input; and my family, Gene, Al, Amy, and Chris, for their continued support. — **Connie Morrison**

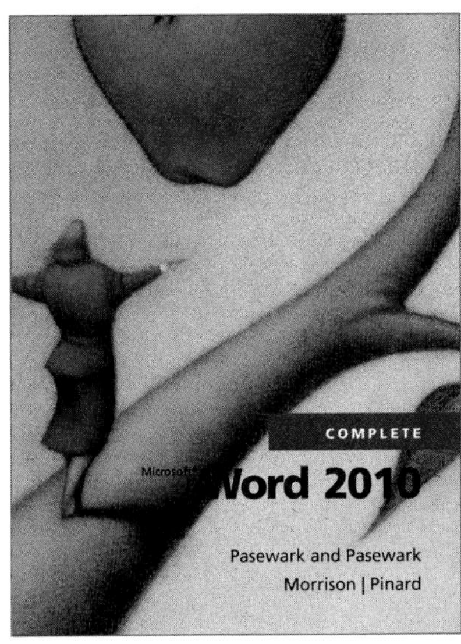

Microsoft® Word 2010 Complete
Hardcover
ISBN-13: 978-1-111-52951-2

Microsoft® Excel® 2010 Complete
Hardcover
ISBN-13: 978-1-111-52952-9

Microsoft® Access® 2010 Complete
Hardcover
ISBN-13: 978-1-111-52990-1

Microsoft® PowerPoint® 2010 Complete
Hardcover
ISBN-13: 978-1-111-52953-6

CONTENTS

LESSON 11
Improving Data Accuracy EX Adv 53

LESSON 12
Creating PivotTables and PivotCharts EX Adv 79

LESSON 13
Using Powerful Excel Functions EX Adv 105

LESSON 14
Creating and Using Macros EX Adv 125

LESSON 15
Working with Auditing and Analysis Tools EX Adv 149

LESSON 16
Protecting, Tracking, and Sharing Workbooks EX Adv 171

LESSON 11
Creating and Running Macros AC Adv 109

LESSON 12
Automating Database Processes AC Adv 133

LESSON 13
Programming in Access AC Adv 157

LESSON 14
Creating Database Security and Documentation AC Adv 177

ADVANCED MICROSOFT POWERPOINT 2010 UNIT

LESSON 5
Editing and Formatting Slide Content PPT Adv 3

LESSON 6
Working with Tables and Charts PPT Adv 27

PASEWARK OFFICE 2010 ADVANCED DATA FILES GRID

APPLICATION	LESSON	DATA FILE	SOLUTION FILE
INTRODUCTION	1	Class Descriptions.docx	Final Spectrum Follow-up.docx
		Clients.accdb	First Qtr Sales.xlsx
		Historic Preservation.pptx	Historic Housing.pptx
		January Sales.xlsx	JC's Updated Data.mdb
		JC's Data.accdb	Revised Sales Report.xlsx
		Sales Report.xlsx	Updated Class Descriptions.docx
		Spectrum Follow-up.docx	Updated Clients.accdb
WORD	9	Get Fit.docx	Enhanced Get Fit 1.docx
		Invitation.docx	Enhanced Get Fit 2.docx
		Lead Out.docx	Enhanced Get Fit 3.docx
		Plastic.docx	Enhanced Get Fit 4.docx
		Recycling symbol.jpg	Enhanced Invitation.docx
		Trees.docx	Enhanced Lead Out 1.docx
			Enhanced Lead Out 2.docx
			Enhanced Plastic 1.docx
			Enhanced Plastic 2.docx
			Enhanced Plastic 3.docx
			Enhanced Plastic 4.docx
			Enhanced Trees.docx
WORD	10	Agenda.docx	Agenda Template.dotx
		Certificate.docx	Certificate Template.dotx
		Credit Letter.docx	Final Events.docx
		Events.docx	Final Flyer.docx
		Flyer.docx	Final Waste.docx
		LCCU Building Blocks.docx	November Agenda.docx
		Pharmacy.docx	Pharmacy 1.docx
		Quick Parts.docx	Pharmacy 2.docx
		Waste.docx	Pharmacy 3.docx
			Pharmacy 4.docx
			Updated Credit Letter.docx
			Weber Certificate.docx
			Your Name Template.dotx

APPLICATION	LESSON	DATA FILE	SOLUTION FILE
WORD	11	Accounts Receivable.docx	Balances Due 1.docx
		Employee.docx	Balances Due 2.docx
		Expenses.xlsx	Countries.xlsx
		Green Bucket.docx	Country Requests.docx
		Rates.docx	Employee Data 1.docx
		Rates.xlsx	Employee Data 2.docx
		Sales.xlsx	Employee Data 3.docx
			First Quarter Expenses.xlsx
			First Quarter Report.docx
			Fourth Quarter Sales.docx
			Green Bucket Letter.docx
			Monthly Sales 1.docx
			Monthly Sales 2.docx
			New Members.docx
			New Rates.docx
			Past Due Accounts 1.docx
			Past Due Accounts 2.docx
			Past Due Accounts 3.docx
			Payroll.docx
			Products 1.docx
			Products 2.docx
			Purchase Order.docx
			Quarterly Sales.xlsx
			Recycling Rate.docx
			Regional Sales.xlsx
			Sales Report 1.docx
			Sales Report 2.docx
			Sales Report 3.docx

APPLICATION	LESSON	DATA FILE	SOLUTION FILE
WORD	12	Account Holders.docx	Account Holders Data Source.docx
		Catalog.docx	Catalog Main Document.docx
		Clients.docx	Client Envelopes Main Document.docx
		Course Catalog.docx	Clients Data Source.docx
		Courses.docx	Courses Catalog Main Document.docx
		Customers.docx	Courses Data Source.docx
		Donation Letter.docx	Customer Labels Main Document.docx
		Order Confirmation.docx	Customers Data Source.docx
		Orders Shipped.docx	Donation Letter Main Document.docx
		Orders.docx	Membership Contacts Data Source.mdb
		Overdraft Letter.docx	Merged Client Envelopes.docx
		Products.docx	Merged Customer Labels.docx
		Prospects.docx	Merged Donation Letters.docx
		Shipped Message.docx	Merged Order Confirmations.docx
		Sponsors Letter.docx	Merged Overdraft Labels.docx
		Staff.docx	Merged Overdraft Letters.docx
			Merged Product Catalog.docx
			Merged Prospects Envelopes.docx
			Merged Shipped Messages.docx
			Merged Sponsors Letters.docx
			Merged Spring Courses Catalog.docx
			Merged Staff Messages.docx
			Order Confirmation Main Document.docx
			Orders Data Source.docx
			Orders Shipped Data Source.docx
			Overdraft Labels Main Document.docx
			Overdraft Letter Main Document.docx
			Products Data Source.docx
			Prospects Data Source.docx
			Prospects Envelopes Main Document.docx
			Selian Letter.docx
			Shipped Message Main Document.docx
			Sponsors Data Source.mdb
			Sponsors Letter Main Document.docx
			Staff Data Source.docx
			Staff E-mail Main Document.docx

APPLICATION	LESSON	DATA FILE	SOLUTION FILE
WORD	13	Bill of Sale.docx	Certified Employee Evaluation.docx
		Board Minutes RD.docx	Certified Employee Evaluation.xps
		Board Minutes RE.docx	Completed Challenge.docx
		Board Minutes.docx	Confidential Employee Evaluation.docx
		Challenge.docx	Final Bill of Sale.docx
		Completed Employee Evaluation.docx	Final Board Minutes.docx
		Consultation Call.docx	Final Emergency Contacts.docx
		Emergency Contacts 1.docx	Final Employee Evaluation.docx
		Emergency Contacts 2.docx	Final Job Description.docx
		Employee Evaluation.docx	Protected Consultation.docx
		Job Description RA.docx	Restricted Consultation Call.docx
		Job Description RB.docx	Restricted Employee Evaluation 1.docx
		Jones.jpg	Restricted Employee Evaluation 2.docx
		Sales Goal.docx	Restricted Employee Evaluation 3.docx
		Will Draft 1.docx	Revised Board Minutes 1.docx
		Will Draft 2.docx	Revised Board Minutes 2.docx
			Revised Board Minutes 3.docx
			Revised Board Minutes 4.docx
			Revised Board Minutes 5.docx
			Revised Sales Goal.docx
			Signed Bill of Sale.docx
			Updated Will.docx
WORD	14	Apollo 11.docx	Apollo 11 Revised.docx
		Apollo 12.docx	Family Disaster Plan.docx
		Apollo 13.docx	Final Lease.docx
		Apollo Resources.docx	Final Soil.docx
		Extreme Heat.docx	Journeys to the Moon 1.docx
		Family Disaster Plan.docx	Journeys to the Moon 2.docx
		Floods.docx	Journeys to the Moon 3.docx
		Landslides.docx	Journeys to the Moon 4.docx
		Lease.docx	Journeys to the Moon 5.docx
		Mission Highlights.docx	Journeys to the Moon 6.docx
		Moon Missions.docx	Journeys to the Moon 7.docx
		Natural Disasters Sources.docx	Journeys to the Moon 8.docx
		Returning Home.docx	Journeys to the Moon 9.docx

APPLICATION	LESSON	DATA FILE	SOLUTION FILE
WORD	14	Soil.docx	Journeys to the Moon 10.docx
		Tornadoes.docx	Journeys to the Moon 11.docx
			Journeys to the Moon 12.docx
			Journeys to the Moon Readability.docx
			Preparing for Natural Disasters 1.docx
			Preparing for Natural Disasters 2.docx
WORD	15	Apollo Missions 11-17.docx	Apollo Missions 1.docx
		Calories.docx	Apollo Missions 2.docx
		Disaster Index Entries.docx	Apollo Missions 3.docx
		Financial Review.docx	Apollo Missions 4.docx
		Fohey Case.docx	Apollo Missions 5.docx
		Foreign Trade.docx	Apollo Missions 6.docx
		Freedman Case.docx	Apollo Missions 7.docx
		Index Entries.docx	AutoMark Index Entries.docx
		Natural Disasters.docx	Fohey Case Summary.docx
		Nutrition Facts.docx	Freedman Case Summary.docx
			Revised Financial Revew.docx
			Revised Foreign Trade.docx
			Revised Natural Disasters 1.docx
			Revised Natural Disasters 2.docx
			Revised Nutrition Facts.docx
			Updated Disaster Index Entries.docx
WORD	16	Investment Club.docx	Final Resume.docm
		Profile.docx	Final Resume.xps
		Registrations.docx	Investment Club Agreement 1.docx
		Resume.docx	Investment Club Agreement 2.docx
		Revised Profile 1.docx	Personal Template 2.dotm
			Personal Template 3.dotm
			Quick Access Toolbar Screenshot.docx
			Revised Profile 1.docx
			Revised Profile 2.docx

APPLICATION	LESSON	DATA FILE	SOLUTION FILE
WORD	16		Updated Registrations 1.docm
			Updated Registrations 2.docm
			Updated Registrations 3.docm
			Updated Registrations 4.docm
WORD	17	LLDPE Blends and Coextrusions.docx	Custom Ribbon Screenshot.docx
		Member Directory.docx	Custom Ribbon Settings.exportedUI
			Members.dic
			Personal Template 4.dotx
			Revised LLDPE Blends and Coextrusions.docx
			Revised Member Directory.docx
			Toolbar Screenshot.docx
			Ultratech.dic
			Word Customizations.exportedUI
WORD	Unit Review	Home Remedies Entries.docx	Envelopes Main Document.docx
		Home Remedies.docx	Final Home Remedies.docx
		Kick City.docx	Final Kick City.docx
		Managers.docx	Final Kick City.xps
		Pet Travel 1.docx	Final Pet Travel.docx
		Pet Travel 2.docx	Final Sales Letter.docx
		Pyramid.JPG	Marketing.dic
		Sales Letter.docx	Merged Sales Letter 1.docx
		Ski Club.docx	Merged Sales Letter 2.docx
			Merged Sales Letter Envelopes 1.docx
			Merged Sales Letter Envelopes 2.docx
			Personal Template 5.dotm
			Quarterly Sales Chart.docx
			Revised Sales Letter.docx
			Sales Letter Main Document.docx
			Ski Club Flyer.docx
			Ski Club Flyer.xps
			Updated Managers 1.docx
			Updated Managers 2.docx
EXCEL	9	Bakery.xlsx	AppliedThemes2.xlsx
		Budget.xlsx	AppliedThemes.xlsx
		Coach Assignment.xlsx	BakerySales.xlsx
		Customer.xlsx	CoachAssignmentInformation.xlsx
		Employee.xlsx	CustomerList.xlsx

APPLICATION	LESSON	DATA FILE	SOLUTION FILE
EXCEL	9	Home Sales.xlsx	EmployeeList.xlsx
		StoreLeaseDates.xlsx	HomeSales-2014.xlsx
		Team - Revised.xlsx	ProposedBudget.xlsx
		Team.xlsx	StoreLeaseDatesInformation.xlsx
		Themes.xlsx	TeamAssignments.xlsx
		Tool.xlsx	TeamList.xlsx
		Trendy Resort.xlsx	ToolSales.xlsx
			TrendyResortProjectedSales.xlsx
EXCEL	10	Byars Pizza.xlsx	Byars Pizza Sales.xlsx
		College Book.xlsx	College Book Sales.xlsx
		College Clothing.xlsx	College Bookstore.xlsx
		College.xlsx	CollegeClothing Sales.xlsx
		Donation.xlsx	Donation Goal.xlsx
		GMRE Real Estate.xlsx	GMRE Real Estate Listings.xlsx
		Income.xlsx	Income Statement.xlsx
		Pie Sales.xlsx	Pie Sales First Quarter 2013.xlsx
		Projected Earnings.xlsx	Projected Earnings by Department.xlsx
		Rain Totals.xlsx	Rain Totals Change.xlsx
		University Expenses.xlsx	University Expenses Chart.xlsx
EXCEL	11	Arts&Crafts.xlsx	Arts & Crafts Inventory.xlsx
		CollegeBookSales.xlsx	College Book Sales and Expenses.xlsx
		ComputerTrainingStudents.xlsx	Computer Training Students List.xlsx
		Employees.xlsx	Employees List.xlsx
		FanFair.xlsx	Fan Fair Inventory - 2.xlsx
		LocalDeptSales.xlsx	Fan Fair Inventory.xlsx
		NewLock.xlsx	Household Inventory.xlsx
		PacificSales.xlsx	Local Dept Sales and Expenses.xlsx
		Pharmacy.xlsx	New Lock Sales.xlsx
			Pacific Sales by Employee.xlsx
			Pharmacy Refills.xlsx
			Watch Window.xlsx
EXCEL	12	Discount Internet.xlsx	Discount Internet Sales.xlsx
		Division Sales.xlsx	Division Sales for Hawaii.xlsx
		Electricity.xlsx	Electricity Usage.xlsx
		P K Industries.xlsx	P K Industries Analysis.xlsx
		Spelling Bee.xlsx	Spelling Bee Groups.xlsx
		Student Loans.xlsx	Student Loans - 2014.xlsx
		Virginia Sales.xlsx	Virginia Sales by Region.xlsx

APPLICATION	LESSON	DATA FILE	SOLUTION FILE
EXCEL	13	AntiqueClass.xlsx	Antique Class Enrollment.xlsx
		Bonus.xlsx	Bonus for Sports.xlsx
		Booth.xlsx	Booth Sales.xlsx
		ChineseClass.xlsx	Chinese Class Enrollment.xlsx
		ClassEnrollment.xlsx	Class Enrollment Totals.xlsx
		LibraryVolunteers.xlsx	Library Volunteers - June 2014.xlsx
		PCISales.xlsx	PCI Sales Bonuses.xlsx
		Sales.xlsx	Sales Commissions.xlsx
		SpanishClass.xlsx	Spanish Class Costs.xlsx
		StudentGymnastics.xlsx	Student Gymnastics - Paid.xlsx
EXCEL	14	Arts and Crafts.xlsx	Arts and Crafts Expenses.xlsm
		College Book.xlsm	College Book Sales.xlsm
		College Budget.xlsx	College Budget - Annual.xlsm
		Month End.xlsm	Month End Budget.xlsm
		Pet Store.xlsm	Pet Store Inventory.xlsm
		Project Sales.xlsx	Project Sales Totals.xlsm
		School Budget.xlsx	School Budget First Year.xlsm
EXCEL	15	Auto Parts.xlsx	Auto Parts Sales.xlsx
		Blooming Yards.xlsx	Blooming Yards Income and Expenses.xlsx
		Book Sales.xlsx	Coastal Sales - First Quarter.xlsx
		Coastal Sales.xlsx	College Fund Goal.xlsx
		Credit Card.xlsx	Credit Card Payoff.xlsx
		Grades.xlsx	Down Payment Goal.xlsx
		International Sales.xlsx	History Grades.xlsx
		Supplies.xlsx	International Sales Financials.xlsx
		Trees and Landscaping.xlsx	Office Supplies.xlsx
			Payoff.xlsx
			Trees and Landscaping Financials.xlsx
			Yearly Book Sales.xlsx
EXCEL	16	Airline Rates.xlsx	Airline Rates Shared.xlsx
		Best Diamonds.xlsx	Best Diamonds List.xlsx
		Cost and Sale.xlsx	Cost and Sales Prices.xlsx
		Employee.xlsx	Employee List - Revised.xlsx
		Hobby Store.xlsx	Employee List.xlsx
		New York College.xlsx	Hobby Store Inventory.xlsx
		State College.xlsx	New York College Sports.xlsx
		Water Usage.xlsx	State College Inventory.xlsx
			Water Usage by Department.xlsx

APPLICATION	LESSON	DATA FILE	SOLUTION FILE
EXCEL	17	Angelina Tarrant signature.tif	A&C Imported File.xlsx
		Arts and Crafts.txt	Access Import.xlsx
		Customer.accdb	Computer Students.pdf
		Doctors.accdb	Computer Students.xlsx
		Household.xlsx	Doctors Import.xlsx
		Income.xlsx	Household Addresses.pdf
		Pacific Sales.txt	Income Statement for Verification.xlsx
		Regional Managers.xlsx	Income Statement.xlsx
		Students.xlsx	Regional Managers Weekly Sales.xlsx
			Text Import.xlsx
EXCEL	Unit Review	Corporate.xlsx	Corporate Tees.xlsx
		DiscountInterior.xlsx	Discount Interior Inventory.xlsx
		Imports.xlsx	Imports Unlimited.xlsx
		LawSchool.xlsx	Law School Budget.xlsm
		NewWestern.xlsx	New Western Sales.xlsx
		TripPlanning.xlsx	Trip Planning Estimates.xlsx
ACCESS	7	Division Sales.accdb	Division Sales Database.accdb
		Internet Sales.accdb	Internet Sales Database.accdb
		P & K Industry.accdb	P & K Industry Database.accdb
		Pacific Sales.accdb	Pacific Sales Database.accdb
		Pet Sales.accdb	Pet Sales Database.accdb
		Sales.accdb	Sales Database.accdb
		Student Teams.accdb	Student Teams Database.accdb
ACCESS	8	Atlantic Sales.accdb	Atlantic Sales Database.accdb
		Book Sales.accdb	Book Sales Database.accdb
		Healthcare Training.accdb	Healthcare Training Database.accdb
		Pet Supplies.accdb	Pet Supplies Database.accdb
		Regional Sales.accdb	Regional Sales Database.accdb
		Teams.accdb	Teams Database.accdb
ACCESS	9	Animal Supply Industry.accdb	Animal Supply Industry Database.accdb
		Book Sales.accdb	Book Sales Database.accdb
		Coastal Sales.accdb	Coastal Sales Database.accdb
		Healthcare Training.accdb	Healthcare Training Database.accdb
		Internet Sales Logo.tif	Internet Sales Database.accdb

APPLICATION	LESSON	DATA FILE	SOLUTION FILE
ACCESS	9	Internet Sales.accdb	My Form.accdb
		Pets Unlimited.accdb	Pets Unlimited Database.accdb
ACCESS	10	Book Sales.accdb	Book Sales Databsae.accdb
		Computer Sales.accdb	Computer Sales Database.accdb
		Pacific Sales.accdb	Pacific Sales Database.accdb
		Pet Supplies.accdb	Pet Supplies Database.accdb
		Regional	Regional Sales Database.accdb
		Sales.accdb	
ACCESS	11	Book Sales.accdb	Book Sales Database.accdb
		Computer Sales.accdb	Computer Sales Database.accdb
		Internet Sales.accdb	Internet Sales Database.accdb
		Regional Sales.accdb	Regional Sales Database.accdb
		Supplies for Happy Pets.accdb	Supplies for Happy Pets Database.accdb
ACCESS	12	Book Sales Logo.tif	Book Sales Database.accdb
		Book Sales.accdb	Coastal Sales Database.accdb
		Coastal Sales.accdb	Online Sales Dtabase.accdb
		Online Sales Logo.tif	Pets Database.accdb
		Online Sales.accdb	Region Sales Database.accdb
		Pets.accdb	
		Region Sales.accdb	
ACCESS	13	End of Year Sales.accdb	End of Year Sales Database.accdb
		Epic Internet Sales.accdb	Epic Internet Sales Database.accdb
		National Events.accdb	National Events Database.accdb
		New Sales.accdb	New Sales Database.accdb
		Wholesale International Sales. accdb	Wholesale International Sales Database.accdb
ACCESS	14	Book Sales.accdb	Book Sales Database.accdb
		Coach Files.accdb	Book Sales Database_2014-09-20.accdb
		Coastal Sales.accdb	Coach Files Database.accdb
		Employee Sales.accdb	Coastal Sales Database.accdb
		Happy Pets.accdb	doc_rptObjects - Student Teams.pdf
		Student Teams.accdb	doc_rptObjects.pdf
			Employee Sales Database 2.accdb
			Employee Sales Database 2_2014-09-18.accdb
			Employee Sales Database.accdb
			Happy Pets Database.accdb
			Student Teams Database.accdb

APPLICATION	LESSON	DATA FILE	SOLUTION FILE
ACCESS	Unit Review	New Book Sales.accdb	New Book Sales Database.accdb
		New Generation.accdb	New Generation Database.accdb
		Pet Supplies.accdb	Pet Supplies Database.accdb
		Revelation Sales.accdb	Revelation Sales Database.accdb
		West Coast Sales.accdb	West Coast Sales Database.accdb
		Winter Sales.accdb	Winter Sales Database.accdb
			doc_rptObjects - West Coast Sales.pdf
POWERPOINT	5	1950 Paint.docx	AEP.dic
		Coasting.pptx	Before 1950.docx
		Employee Manual.pptx	Coaster Terms.docx
		Lead Poisoning.pptx	ET.dic
		Lightning.pptx	Final Lead Poisoning.pptx
		RRP.docx	Revised Coasting 1.pptx
		Terms.docx	Revised Coasting 2.pptx
			Revised Coasting 3.pptx
			Revised Coasting 4.pptx
			Revised Coasting 5.pptx
			Revised Coasting 6.pptx
			Revised Coasting 7.pptx
			Revised Coasting 8.pptx
			Revised Employee Manual.pptx
			Revised Lightning.pptx
			RRP Rule.docx
POWERPOINT	6	Byron Chart.pptx	Q1 Expenses.xlsx
		Coaster History.pptx	Rate of Loss.xlsx
		Deer Creek Inn.pptx	Revised Byron Chart.pptx
		Expenses.xlsx	Revised Coaster History 1.pptx
		Financial Review.pptx	Revised Coaster History 2.pptx
		Loss Rate.xlsx	Revised Coaster History 3.pptx
		Next Year.xlsx	Revised Coaster History 4.pptx
		Organization.pptx	Revised Organization.pptx
		Wetlands.pptx	Revised Wetlands.pptx
			The Year Ahead.xlsx
			Updated Deer Creek Inn 1.pptx
			Updated Deer Creek Inn 2.pptx
			Updated Deer Creek Inn 3.pptx
			Updated Deer Creek Inn 4.pptx
			Updated Deer Creek Inn 5.pptx
			Updated Financial Review.pptx

APPLICATION	LESSON	DATA FILE	SOLUTION FILE
POWERPOINT	7	A perfect catch!.jpg	Final Motocross.pptx
		Blue.jpg	Hawaiian Sunsets.pptx
		Bright horizon.jpg	Pet Photo Album.pptx
		Charlie.jpg	Pet Photo Album.wmv
		Cuddles.jpg	Revised Dynamic Park.pptx
		Dynamic Park.pptx	Revised Dynamic Park.wmv
		Focus.jpg	Revised Happy Tails 1.pptx
		Frisbee fun.wmv	Revised Happy Tails 2.pptx
		Happy Tails.pptx	Revised Happy Tails 3.pptx
		Kylie.jpg	Revised Happy Tails 4.pptx
		Let's play!.jpg	Revised Happy Tails 5.pptx
		Motocross.pptx	Revised Happy Tails 6.pptx
		Motocross.wmv	Revised Happy Tails 7.pptx
		MX Finish.jpg	Revised Happy Tails 8.pptx
		MX Jump.jpg	Revised Happy Tails 9.pptx
		MX Start.jpg	Revised Service.pptx
		Nap time.jpg	
		Pink horizon.jpg	
		Run fast.jpg	
		Service.pptx	
		Sunset fog.jpg	
		Sunset high waves.jpg	
		Sunset silhouette.jpg	
		Sunset trees.jpg	
		Sunset waves.jpg	
		Taffy.jpg	
		Yellow sunset.jpg	
POWERPOINT	8	Building Renovation.pptx	Building Renovation Design.potx
		Grand Canyon.jpg	Custom Template yn.potx
		National Parks.pptx	Final Building Renovation.pptx
		Time Management.pptx	Final Time Management.pptx
			National Parks Draft 1.pptx
			National Parks Draft 2.pptx
			National Parks Draft 3.pptx
			National Parks Draft 4.pptx
			National Parks Draft 5.pptx
			National Parks Draft 6.pptx
			National Parks Draft 7.pptx
			National Parks Draft 8.pptx
			National Parks Draft 9.pptx
			National Parks Draft 10.pptx
			National Parks Draft 11.pptx

APPLICATION	LESSON	DATA FILE	SOLUTION FILE
POWERPOINT	8		National Parks Handout.docx
			Organized Five Rules.pptx
POWERPOINT	9	Blood Drive.pptx	Community Service Outline.rtf
		Community Service.pptx	County Parks Outline.rtf
		County Parks.pptx	Final Preserving Wetlands.pptx
		Donations.xlsx	Revised Community Service 1.pptx
		Food Bank.pptx	Revised Community Service 2.pptx
		Items.docx	Revised Community Service 3.pptx
		Long-Term Care.docx	Revised Community Service 4.pptx
		Park Visitors.xlsx	Revised Community Service 5.pptx
		Participation.xlsx	Revised Community Service 6.pptx
		Popular County Parks.accdb	Revised Community Service 7.pptx
		Preserving Wetlands.pptx	Revised Community Service 8.pptx
		Visitor Centers.docx	Revised County Parks 1.pptx
		Volunteer Participation.accdb	Revised County Parks 2.pptx
		Wetlands Outline.docx	Revised Long-Term Care.docx
			Revised Park Visitors.xlsx
			Revised Volunteer Participation.accdb
			Title Slide.jpg
			Updated Donations.xlsx
			Updated Items.docx
			Updated Participation.xlsx
			Wetland Losses.jpg
POWERPOINT	10	Festival Reviewer A.pptx	Festival CD (folder with Presentation Package folder, AUTORUN.INF, and Revised Festival 7.pptx)
		Festival.pptx	Final Karate (folder with Presentation Package folder, AUTORUN.INF, and Revised Karate 2.pptx)
		Karate 1.pptx	Revised Festival 1.pptx
		Karate 2.pptx	Revised Festival 2.pptx
		Karate Reviewer A.pptx	Revised Festival 3.pptx
		Scarecrow 1.pptx	Revised Festival 4.odp
		Scarecrow 2.pptx	Revised Festival 4.ppsx
			Revised Festival 4.pptx
			Revised Festival 4.xps
			Revised Festival 5.pptx
			Revised Festival 6.pptx
			Revised Festival 7.pptx
			Revised Festival 8.pptx
			Revised Festival 9.pptx
			Revised Festival Picture.pptx

APPLICATION	LESSON	DATA FILE	SOLUTION FILE
POWERPOINT	10		Revised Karate 1.pptx
			Revised Karate 2.pptx
			Revised Karate 3.pptx
			Revised Scarecrow 1.pdf
			Revised Scarecrow 1.pptx
			Revised Scarecrow 2.pptx
POWERPOINT	Unit Review	1 meter.avi	Current Client Survey.xlsx
		3 meter.avi	Diving Videos.pptx
		10 meter.avi	Guide.jpg
		Buffalo.jpg	Revised Cabins.pptx
		Cabins.pptx	Revised Codes.pptx
		Client Survey.xlsx	Revised Fire Instructions.pptx
		Codes.pptx	Revised Insurance 1.pptx
		Diving.pptx	Revised Insurance 2.pptx
		Elephant.jpg	Revised Insurance 3.pptx
		Fire Instructions.pptx	Revised Insurance 4.pptx
		Insurance Overview.docx	Revised Insurance 5.pptx
		Leopard.jpg	Revised Insurance 6.pptx
		Lion.jpg	Revised Insurance 6.wmv
		New Insurance.pptx	Revised Insurance 6.xps
		Rhinoceros.jpg	S-P Template.potx
			The Big 5a.pptx
			The Big 5b.pptx
			The Big 5c.pptx
			The Big 5d.wmv
			WWCR.dic
OUTLOOK	4	Kylie.bmp	Out of Office.oft
			Your Name Template.oft
	5	Elliott Logo.jpg	
	6		My Calendar.msg
			My Outlook.pst
			My Tasks.docx
			Next Month Calendar 1.msg
			Next Month Calendar 2.docx
			Study Group Invite.msg

APPLICATION	LESSON	DATA FILE	SOLUTION FILE
CAPSTONE		AlexanderPharm.accdb	AlexanderPharamaceutical.accdb
		CS Job 1a.docx	Alexander Merged Letters.docx
		CS Job 1b.docx	Job 2 Message.docx
		CS Job 1c.docx	Job 2 Task.docx
		CS Job 4.xlsx	Proposal Letter Main Document.docx
		CS Job 6.xlsx	
		CS Job 7.xlsx	Proposal.docx
		CS Job 11.docx	Technology Proposal Workbook 2.xlsx
			Technology Proposal Workbook.xlsx
			Technology Proposal.pptx
			Technology Upgrade Report.rtf

Estimated Time for Unit: 2 hours

ADVANCED

INTRODUCTION

LESSON 1 **2 HRS.**

Microsoft Office 2010 and the Internet

Estimated Time: 2 hours

LESSON 1

Microsoft Office 2010 and the Internet

OBJECTIVES

Upon completion of this lesson, you should be able to:

- Apply basic Microsoft Word, Excel, Access, PowerPoint, and Outlook features.
- Search for information on the World Wide Web.
- Evaluate Web sites.
- Bookmark favorite Web sites.
- Manage the history of the Web sites visited.

VOCABULARY

bookmark
browser
hits
keywords
search engine
wildcard

Microsoft Office 2010 is a complete set of computer applications that equips you with the tools you need to produce a variety of documents and files, and to help streamline your everyday computing activities. This course focuses on the more complex and advanced capabilities of the Word, Excel, Access, PowerPoint, and Outlook applications.

This lesson provides a review of basic application features and will help you refresh your application skills. In this lesson, you will also learn more about how to access resources on the World Wide Web.

Applying Word Features

As you know, Microsoft Word is a powerful, full-featured word processor with comprehensive writing tools. You've already learned many of the basic features that enable you to complete common word-processing documents. The Word lessons in this course will introduce you to features that will enable you to further enhance the appearance of your documents and save time preparing and editing documents. Developing a document often involves multiple team members, and Word offers several tools to help you share documents and effectively collaborate on projects.

However, before you begin to explore these and other advanced features in Word, complete the following Step-by-Step, which provides a review of many basic Word skills.

Step-by-Step 1.1

1. Launch Word and then open the **Class Descriptions.docx** file from the drive and folder where your Data Files are stored. Save the document as **Updated Class Descriptions**, followed by your initials.
2. Edit the document as shown in **Figure 1–1**.

FIGURE 1–1
Edits for document in Step-by-Step 1.1

Health and Nutrition Class Descriptions

For many months we have anticipated the opening of the new Family Fitness Facility in Columbus, and we are now counting down the days for our grand opening on October 1.

As we approach our grand opening day, I am finalizing the class schedule. You will recall that when we met last week we discussed several health and nutrition classes. Before I finalize the class schedule, I would like for you to reveiw the updated class descriptions shown below and respond to the questions on the following page.

Weight Management will help individuals identify their recommended weight. The focus will be on sound advise for exercise and diet programs that will help individuals acheive ideal body weight.

Cooking for Good Health will provide information on selecting and preparing food. Participants will learn about the nutritional benefits of a variety of foods from organic products to frozen dinners. The focus will be on making good choices, cooking foods properly, and creating wholesome menus.

Reading Food Labels will be a short class defining the information included in food labels and explaining its relevance to diet.

Value of Vitamins will explore the advantages and disadvantages of supplementing diets with vitamins. The benefits of a variety of vitamins will be described.

Strengthening Your Immune System will explore how regular exercise, a healthy diet, and reduce emotional stress help strengthen the immune system.

Please email me your responses to these questions by the end of the day tomorrow.

Regarding the proposed health and nutrition lasses:

- Does each class description adequately describe the objectives of the class?
- Are these classes necessary, and will they complement our instruction on physical training?
- Do you think our family members will be interested in these classes?
- Should we offer more than one class on cooking and design the instruction for specific age groups?
- Do you have suggestions for any other health and nutrition classes that you think we should offer?

3. Center and bold the title, and then change the font to Arial 18 point. Change the title text to all uppercase.
4. Select the paragraphs that describe the five classes and format all the paragraphs with a left indent of 0.5" and a right indent of 5.5" (0.5" from the right margin).
5. Select the list of bulleted questions at the end of the document and apply the number format (1., 2., 3.) to create an enumerated list.
6. Position the insertion point anywhere in the first numbered paragraph and add space after the paragraph. Then use the Format Painter feature to copy the new paragraph format to the other paragraphs in the numbered list.
7. Search for the word *email* and replace it with **e-mail**.

8. Change the document margins to **Office 2003 Default** setting (1" top and bottom and 1.25" left and right).
9. Position the insertion point in front of the paragraph that begins *Regarding the proposed...* and insert a page break.
10. Create a header for only the second page of the document. Use the Blank (Three Columns) format for the header, and then type the title **Health and Nutrition Classes** in the center of the header.
11. Check the document for spelling and grammar and make any necessary corrections. The spelling checker doesn't catch mistypes if they are the same as correctly spelled words.
12. Save the changes. Close the document, and then exit Word.

Applying Excel Features

Excel is the spreadsheet application in the Office suite. As you've discovered, spreadsheets are used for entering, calculating, and analyzing data. You should now be familiar with the basic features for creating, editing, and formatting worksheet information. Excel's advanced features enable you to perform complex calculations and in-depth analysis that you'd normally leave up to an economist or mathematician! With Excel's data analysis tools, you can generate reports, charts, and tables that are every bit as professional looking and accurate as those created by the experts. In this course, you'll also learn how to share workbooks with colleagues.

Before you venture into the advanced features of Excel, complete the following Step-by-Step, which provides a review of the Excel basic skills.

Step-by-Step 1.2

1. Launch Excel and then open the **Sales Report.xlsx** file from the drive and folder where your Data Files are stored. Save the workbook as **Revised Sales Report**, followed by your initials.
2. Go to cell M5 and type the column heading **TOTAL**.
3. Go to cell M6 and enter a formula to calculate the sum of the numbers in cells B6:L6. Fill the formula down through cell M12.
4. Go to cell A14 and type the row heading **TOTAL**.
5. Go to cell B14 and enter a formula to calculate the sum of the numbers in cells B6:B13. Fill the formula across through cell M14.

6. Insert a new column to the left of the *TOTAL* column. In the new column, type the heading **Dec**, and then enter the following data in the new column:

   61258

   50211

   61858

   50212

   61855

   50215

   61852

7. Copy the formula in cell L14 and paste it in cell M14.
8. Merge and center the title *Division Sales Report* over cells A1:N1. Format the title text bold and italic, and change the font size to 14 point.
9. Delete rows 2 and 3.
10. Format the column and row headings bold, and then center the column headings.
11. Apply a currency format to all the numeric data, with no decimal points. If necessary, automatically adjust the column widths.
12. Create a 3-D pie chart on a new sheet, using only the data in the cell ranges A4:A10 and N4:N10. Add the title **Total Sales by Division** to the chart and apply a chart style of your choice.
13. Format the worksheet to fit on one page in landscape orientation.
14. Save the changes. Close the file, and then exit Excel.

Applying Access Features

Access is the database application in the Office suite that is used for storing and organizing information. Databases are made up of objects, including tables, queries, forms, and reports. You now should be familiar with the basic techniques for creating these objects. In the advanced lessons, you will learn about features that give you even more control over how database records are viewed, edited, and professionally analyzed. You'll learn how to streamline data entry and editing and to present the data in an attractive, reader-friendly manner.

Before you begin exploring advanced features in Access, walk through the following Step-by-Step to review the application's basic features.

Step-by-Step 1.3

1. Launch Access and open the **JC's Data.accdb** file from the drive and folder where your Data Files are stored. Save the database as **JC's Updated Data**, followed by your initials.
2. Open the EMPLOYEE table in Design View. Between the *Employee ID* and *Last Name* fields, insert a new field titled **Department**. Define the field data type as **Text**.
3. Save the changes to the table and then switch to Datasheet View.
4. Sort the table alphabetically by last name and then update the records to include the department name in which each employee works:

   Dominquez: **Marketing**
   Gonzalez: **Administrative**
   Keplinger: **Sales**
   Mann: **Accounting**
   Pullis: **Accounting**
   Thomsen: **Sales**
   Ti: **Marketing**
   Wong: **Sales**

5. Sort the table by Employee ID, and then add a new record to the table and enter the following information:

   Employee ID: **9**
   Department: **Sales**
   Last Name: **Barkin**
   First Name: **Dave**
   Salary: **$145,000**
   Home Phone: **608-555-5121**
   Date Hired: **3/24/13**

6. Adjust the column widths to show all the data, and then show the table in Print Preview.
7. Change the page layout to **Landscape** and close Print Preview. Save the changes and close the table.
8. Open the PRODUCTS table and filter the data to show only those products with a price greater than $10. The filter should produce eleven records. Remove the filter and close the table. When prompted, save the changes.

9. Use the Form Wizard to create a form based on the EMPLOYEE table.
   a. Include all the fields in the form.
   b. Select the **Columnar** layout.
   c. Name the form **EMPLOYEE FORM**.
10. Use the Report Wizard to create a report based on the EMPLOYEE table.
   a. Include all the fields except *Salary* and *Date Hired*.
   b. Group the records by **Department**.
   c. Sort the records in ascending order by **Last Name**.
   d. Apply the **Stepped** layout and **Portrait** orientation.
   e. Name the report **EMPLOYEE TELEPHONE REPORT**.
11. Close the report and the form, and then exit Access.

Applying PowerPoint Features

PowerPoint is a presentation graphics program that enables you to create presentation materials for a variety of audiences, including slide shows using a projector and online presentations that everyone on a network can view. In the PowerPoint unit, you will explore some of its more advanced features. To make your presentations more interesting and effective, PowerPoint provides tools to add multimedia effects to your slides. The many customizing features PowerPoint offers enable you to create your own color schemes, backgrounds, and design templates. When preparing for your final presentation, PowerPoint has many options for distributing your slide show, including sharing via e-mail or presenting it remotely over a Web page or network.

Before you explore these advanced PowerPoint features, complete the following Step-by-Step to review your PowerPoint skills.

Step-by-Step 1.4

1. Launch PowerPoint, and then open the **Historic Preservation.pptx** file from the drive and folder where your Data Files are stored. Save the presentation as **Historic Housing**, followed by your initials.
2. On the title slide, replace *Your Name* with your own first and last names.
3. Add a new slide after the title slide, using the **Two Content** layout for the new slide.
4. In the title placeholder, type **Stabilization**. In the text placeholder on the left, type the following two lines of text. The text should automatically be formatted with bullets.

   Reestablish structural stability.

   Maintain essential form.
5. Move slide #5 (with the title *Resources)* so it is the last slide in the presentation.

6. Add graphics to slides 2–9. If possible, search Office.com for the graphics. *Hint*: Try search terms such as *house, fix, historic, tools,* and *blueprints.*
7. Apply a built-in design, and, if desired, change the color theme and/or fonts.
8. Apply a transition to all slides in the presentation. Adjust the timing of the transitions as needed.
9. Apply custom animations to the text and graphics on slides 2–10 to control when and how the objects appear.
10. Run the slide show and observe your transitions and animations, and make any necessary changes.
11. Save your changes. Close the presentation, and then exit PowerPoint.

Applying Outlook Features

Outlook is a desktop information management application. As you already know, using Outlook helps you keep track of e-mail messages, appointments, meetings, contact information, and tasks you need to complete. In this course, you will explore some of Outlook's more advanced features. You will learn about features that make it even easier to manage contact information, manage e-mails, and communicate with others. You will also learn about many features and tools that make it easier for you to schedule events and track progress on tasks.

Before you explore Outlook's advanced features, complete the following Step-by-Step to review the basic skills and features for Outlook.

Step-by-Step 1.5

1. Launch Outlook. Open a new journal entry and enter the information below. Then start the timer and leave the journal entry open.

   Subject: **Step-by-Step 1.5**

   Entry type: **Task**
2. Open the Contacts folder. Create a new contact group and name the group **Fitness Trainers**.
3. Add the following contacts to the new group and save the group.

   Name: **Sharon McKee**

   E-mail: **smckee@familyfit.xyz**

   Name: **Ronald DeVilliers**

   E-mail: **rdevillers@familyfit.xyz**

   Name: **Alisa Mandez**

   E-mail: **amandez@familyfit.xyz**

4. Create a new e-mail message. Send the message to the Fitness Trainers group, and type **Health and Nutrition Classes** in the Subject box. Then type the following in the message area:

   Please review the attached document and give me your feedback by the end of the day tomorrow.
5. Attach your solution file **Updated Class Descriptions.docx** to the e-mail message, and save the e-mail message as a draft. Do not attempt to send the e-mail.
6. Create the following two notes:

   Upload the health and nutrition class descriptions to the Web site.

   Confirm yoga class schedule with Bonnie.
7. Open the Calendar and show the calendar for a week from the current date. Create an appointment with your dentist for 10 a.m. and set a reminder. The appointment should last 45 minutes.
8. Open the Tasks folder and create the following new task. Give the task high priority and specify that it be completed within a week.

   Gather information for dental bills to submit for insurance.
9. Delete the dentist appointment.
10. Delete the contact group and contacts you created, and then delete the e-mail draft.
11. Delete the insurance task.
12. Delete the two notes.
13. Return to the journal entry and pause the timer. Make note of how much time you spent on this activity, and then delete the journal entry.
14. Exit Outlook.

Accessing Internet Resources

Microsoft Office 2010 is designed to give you quick and easy access to the World Wide Web, regardless of which Office application you are currently using. A ***browser*** is a program that connects you to remote computers and gives you the capability to access, view, and download data from the Web. Microsoft's browser program is Microsoft Internet Explorer.

VOCABULARY
browser

Searching for Information and Evaluating Web Sites

Each day, millions of people use the World Wide Web to find information. To get the information they're looking for, they must navigate through an enormous amount of data. As a result, even with high-speed connections and powerful search engines, searching for specific information can be very time consuming.

VOCABULARY
search engine
keywords
hits
wildcard

A ***search engine***, such as Microsoft's Bing, is a tool designed to find information on the Web. When you enter ***keywords***, words that describe the information you are seeking, the search engine generates a list of Web sites that potentially match the search criteria. These search results (the best matching Web sites) are often referred to as ***hits***. Searches often produce a long list of hits; if you wish to narrow the search results, you need to be more specific in the keywords that you provide. **Table 1–1** describes several options for refining a search so you can find information quickly and effectively.

TABLE 1–1 Options for refining searches

SEARCH OPTIONS	DESCRIPTION
Capitalization	If you want the results to include occurrences of both upper and lowercase letters, enter the keywords using all lowercase letters. However, if you want to narrow your results to words that begin with capital letters (such as Central Intelligence Agency) or all capital letters (such as CIA), enter the keywords with the same capitalization.
Plurals	Most search engines consider singular keywords as both singular and plural. For example, results for the keyword *agent* will include hits with the word *agents*. If you want the results to include only hits with a plural word, be sure the keyword is plural.
Phrases	Search for a group of words by including quotation marks before and after the sequence of words. With the quotation marks, only hits with all of the words in the exact same sequence will appear in the results. Without the quotation marks, the results will include hits that contain all or most of the words anywhere within a Web site.
Operators	Narrow or broaden the search using operators including *+*, *&*, *and*, *-*, *not*, and *or*. For example, if you are searching for information about international exchange students, use the following keywords in the search engine to exclude hits for currency exchange rates: **+international +exchange +students -currency** or **international and exchange and students not currency**
Related pages	Many search engines provide options to include hits for Web pages with similar information. Look for links such as *Similar pages*, *Also try*, or *Related searches*.
Truncation	Some search engines support the use of a symbol, sometimes referred to as a ***wildcard***, that allows for variations in the spelling of words. When an asterisk (*) symbol is used in a word, the search results include hits with alternate spellings for the word at the point that the asterisk appears. For example, *extra** generates hits for Web pages with *extra*, *extras*, *extract*, and *extraordinary*.
Domains	You can limit search results to a specific domain, such as an educational institution or a government Web site. For example, to find information about environmental research at an educational institution, in the search engine, enter the following keywords: **+domain:edu +environmental +research** or **domain:edu and environmental and research**

When the search results appear, read the information carefully before clicking any of the links. You can determine the validity of some of the hits by looking at the URLs. For example, if you're looking for information about deadlines for filing forms for personal income taxes, you want to click a link that includes IRS in the URL. Also, domain name extensions help to identify the type of entity. **Table 1–2** shows common domain extensions and the type of entity related to them.

EXTRA FOR EXPERTS

Most search engines include links that provide information about advanced search features. Be sure to access these links to learn how to make your searches more effective.

TABLE 1–2 Common domain extensions

DOMAIN EXTENSIONS	DESCRIPTIONS
.com	Commercial business
.edu	Educational institution
.gov	Governmental institution
.org	Nonprofit organization
.mil	Military site
.net	Network site
.us	Abbreviation that indicates a country; for example: .us (United States), .ja (Japan), .uk (United Kingdom), .ca (Canada), and .hk (Hong Kong)

TIP

Clicking a link on a Web site can distract you and take you off task. Before you click a link, try to determine if the link will take you where you want to go. If you click a link and see that the target is not what you expected, click the Back button to return to the previous Web page and stay on task.

Just about anyone can publish information on the Web—often for free, and usually unmonitored. So how do you know if you can trust the information that you find? When you depend on the Web for sources of information, it is your responsibility to determine the integrity and validity of the information and its source. **Table 1–3** provides questions that will guide you through an evaluation process.

TABLE 1–3 A guide for evaluating information on the Web

QUESTIONS TO ASK	WHAT TO CONSIDER
Is the information relevant to my query?	The information should help you to accomplish your goals and objectives. Make sure you analyze the information and determine if it meets your needs.
Is the information current?	Check for a date on the Web page that indicates when the information was last updated.
Is the Web site published by a company or an entity, or is it a personal Web site?	The URL often includes a company name. If you are familiar with the company or entity, consider whether you trust information from this source. If you are not familiar with the company, or the individual, look for links such as *About Us*, *Background*, or *Biography*.
What is the purpose of the Web site?	Use the domain name to identify the type of Web site. For example: a domain name ending with .com is a business, and the intent of the Web site is to sell or promote a product or service.
Who is the author?	Look for information that explains who the author is and how the author is connected to the subject. Verify that the author is qualified to address the subject. Individuals sometimes falsify their credentials, so research the author's background and confirm that the author is credible. For example, if information at the Web site indicates that the author is a professor at a university, go to the university Web site and check the faculty roster.
Is the author biased in his/her opinion?	When looking for facts, be sure the author provides objective viewpoints and cites information with credible sources.
Is the Web site presented professionally?	Information should be well organized and presented accurately, free from spelling and grammar errors.
Are the links legitimate and credible?	Confirm that links are up to date. Links to a credible Web site, such as a business or an organization, do not mean that the business or organization approves of or supports the content on the linked Web page.

Step-by-Step 1.6

1. If necessary, log onto the Internet and open your browser.
2. In the address bar, type **www.bing.com** and then press **Enter** to open the Bing search engine.
3. In the Bing search box, type **lake tahoe ski** and then click the **Search** button, or press **Enter**.
4. Note that the number of hits is indicated at the top of the search results. Scroll down and review the first set of results. Each link provides a brief preview of the Web page content, and the keywords are highlighted in the preview. Occurrences of the word *skiing* may also appear highlighted in the previews.
5. Edit the text in the search box to read **+lake +tahoe +ski -water**. Click the **Search** button, or press **Enter**. Scroll down through the first set of results. Note that the number of hits is greatly reduced, and the word *water* is not found in any of the previews.
6. Edit the text in the search box to read **"lake tahoe water ski"** and then click the **Search** button, or press **Enter**. Note that the number of hits is considerably less because adding more keywords often narrows the search.
7. Delete the text in the search box and then type **domain:org and tahoe and ski**. Click the **Search** button, or press **Enter**. Scroll down through the first set of results. Notice every URL has a .org extension.
8. Type **www.nasa.gov** in the address bar and then press **Enter**. The NASA home page opens.
9. Navigate the Web site and find the following information:
   a. the date when the site was last updated
   b. NASA locations
   c. blogs
   d. the names of the authors of the site's articles and blogs
   e. any available information about the authors' backgrounds
   f. information for contacting NASA
10. Return to the home page for the NASA Web site.
11. Leave the NASA Web site open for the next Step-by-Step.

Revisiting Web Sites

As you rely more and more on the Web as a primary source of information on any topic, you'll find that there are sites you visit frequently or that you know you'll want to access again. You can create a bookmark for quick and easy access to a Web page. A ***bookmark*** is a link that navigates you to the Web page, and it is saved in a Favorites folder. You can create additional folders inside the Favorites folder to keep the list of sites organized.

VOCABULARY
bookmark

Your browser keeps track of the sites you have visited, so you can also quickly revisit a site by selecting the Web site from the History list. The History list can be organized by date, site, most visited, and the order the sites were visited on the current day. You can easily delete the History list, as well as temporary Internet files, cookies, form data, and passwords.

Step-by-Step 1.7

The following steps describe bookmarking Web pages using Internet Explorer features. If you are not using Internet Explorer as your browser, you can still explore the features for creating the bookmarks, but these steps will not exactly describe your browser features.

1. If necessary, log onto the Internet, open your Internet Explorer browser, and open **www.nasa.gov**. Or navigate to the NASA home page, if necessary.
2. Click the **Favorites** button on the Command bar in the upper-left corner of the screen, as shown in **Figure 1–2**.

FIGURE 1–2
Favorites button on the Internet Explorer browser

Favorites button

3. If necessary, click the **Favorites** tab to show a list of your favorite sites. Your favorites list will be different than the one shown in **Figure 1–3**.

FIGURE 1–3
Folders on the Favorites tab

History tab

Favorites list

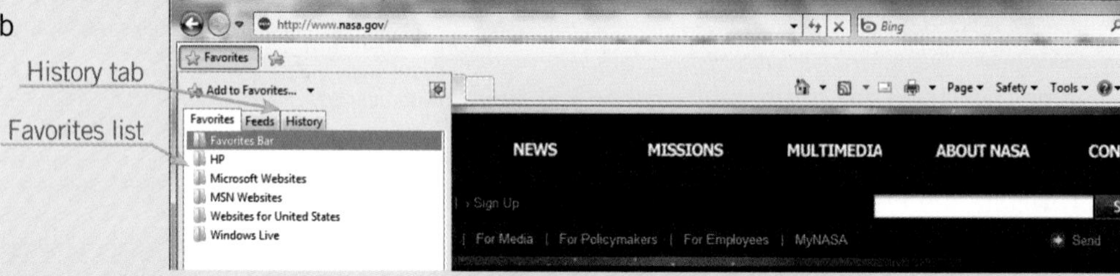

4. Click the **Add to Favorites** button to open the Add a Favorite dialog box shown in **Figure 1–4**.

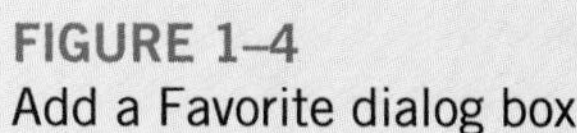

FIGURE 1–4
Add a Favorite dialog box

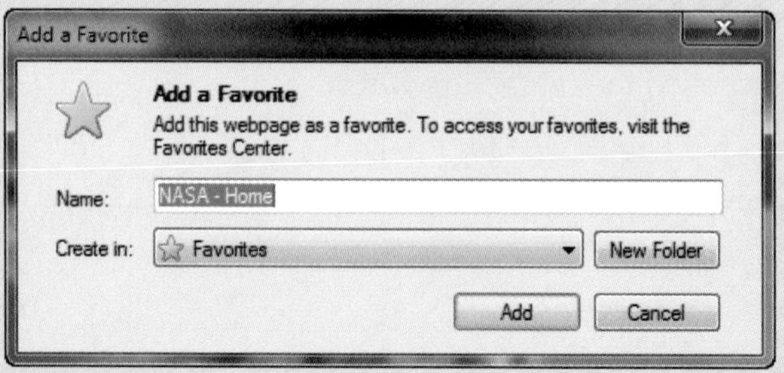

5. In the Name text box, *NASA - Home* appears. Leave the name as is and click **New Folder** on the dialog box. The Create a Folder dialog box similar to the one shown in **Figure 1–5** opens. In the Folder Name text box, type **Research** and then click **Create**. The Add a Favorite dialog box is still open. Click **Add**.

TIP

You can also quickly add Web sites to the Favorites folder using the shortcut keys Ctrl+D.

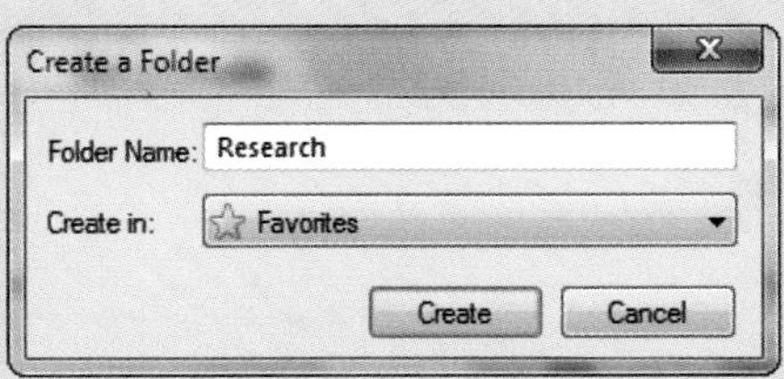

FIGURE 1–5
Create a Folder dialog box

6. Click the **Favorites** button to show your list of favorites. Click the new folder **Research** and you will see the *NASA - Home* site. You can move favorites into folders by dragging the site name to the desired folder.
7. Click the **History** tab on the Favorites pane. Click the **View By...** button at the top of the History list, and then click **View By Order Visited Today**. Notice that the NASA Web page is included in the list of documents and Web sites accessed today. Click the **View By...** button at the top of the History list again, then click **View By Most Visited**. The list is rearranged.
8. Right-click one of the Web sites in this list, click **Delete** in the shortcut menu, and then click **Yes** to confirm the deletion.
9. Click the **Favorites** button, and on the History tab, click any one of the site names on the History list. The Web page opens.
10. Click the **list arrow** at the right side of the address bar in the browser, as shown in **Figure 1–6**. A history of accessed Web sites is displayed, as well as a list of favorite sites. Click anywhere outside the History list to close it.

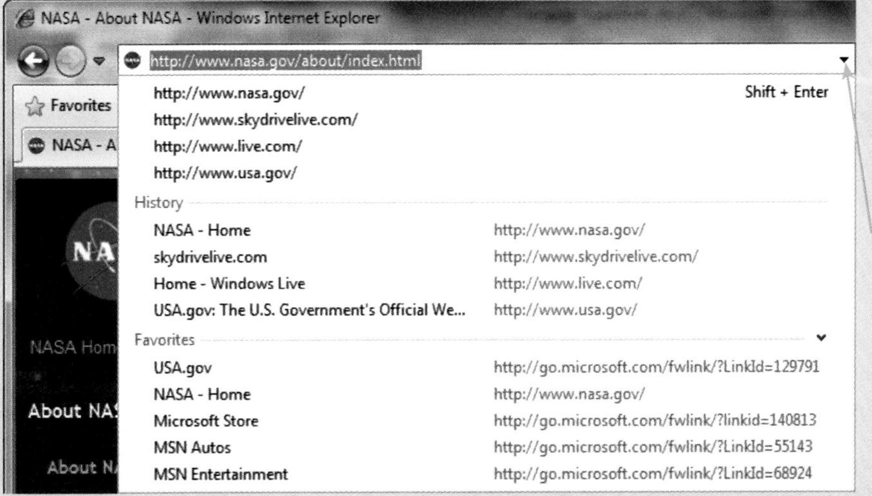

FIGURE 1–6
History and Favorites lists on the address bar

11. Click the **Safety** button on the browser toolbar, as shown in **Figure 1–7**.

FIGURE 1–7
Safety button on browser toolbar

12. Click **Delete Browsing History** to open the dialog box in **Figure 1–8**. If necessary, change the settings so they match those shown in the figure, and then click **Delete**.

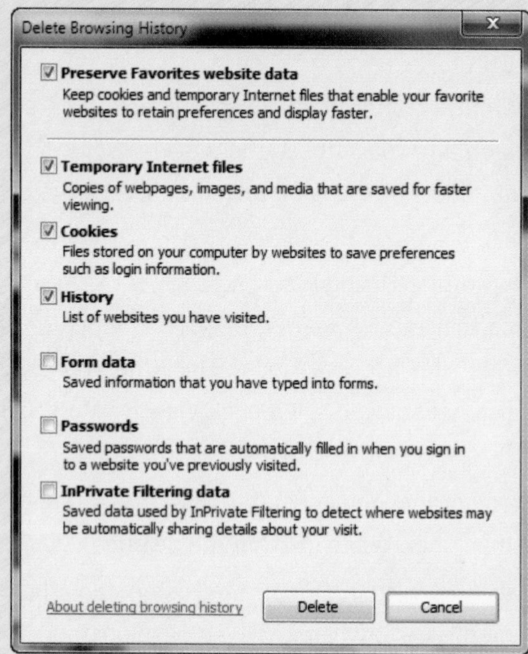

FIGURE 1–8
Delete Browsing History dialog box

13. Click the **Favorites** button. Click the **Favorites** tab, and in the Favorites list, right-click the **Research** folder, and then click **Delete** in the shortcut menu. Click **Yes** to confirm the deletion.
14. Close Internet Explorer.

SUMMARY

In this lesson, you learned:

- Microsoft Word is a powerful, full-featured word processor. Its advanced features enable users to further enhance the appearance of documents and save time preparing and editing documents. Developing a document often involves multiple team members, and Word offers several tools to help you share documents and effectively collaborate on projects.
- Excel is the spreadsheet application in the Microsoft Office suite. Spreadsheets are used primarily for calculating and analyzing data, and Excel's advanced features enable you to perform complex calculations and in-depth analysis. Excel includes many features that enable you to generate accurate and professional-looking reports, charts, and tables.
- Access is the database application in the Office suite. Databases are used for storing and organizing information. The advanced features in Access give you more control over how database records are viewed, edited, and professionally analyzed. Effectively designed forms and reports help to streamline data entry and editing.
- Microsoft PowerPoint is a presentation graphics program that enables you to create materials for presentations of many kinds. Its advanced features include several tools for customizing slide designs and using multimedia effects to enhance your content. Remote publishing features in PowerPoint enable you to share presentations over the Internet or a network.

- Microsoft Outlook is a desktop information management program that provides several tools for scheduling appointments and meetings, managing and delegating tasks, and communicating with others. Advanced features help you customize the tools to fit your needs.
- An enormous amount of information is available on the World Wide Web. Effective search strategies not only save you time, but they also lead you to more relevant sources.
- When you depend on the Web for sources of information, it is your responsibility to determine the integrity and validity of the information and its source.
- You can bookmark Web sites that you visit frequently and save the links to the Favorites folder. You can create additional folders to organize your Favorites list.
- You can also quickly revisit a site by selecting the Web site from the History list, which can be organized by date, site, most visited, and the order the sites were visited on the current day.

VOCABULARY REVIEW

Define the following terms:

bookmark
browser
hits
keywords
search engine
wildcard

REVIEW QUESTIONS

MATCHING

Match the most appropriate application in Column 2 to the application described in Column 1.

Column 1

_____ 1. A graphics application with multimedia capabilities that can be used to create materials to present and share information with others

_____ 2. An application designed for entering, calculating, and analyzing data

_____ 3. An application used for storing and organizing information

_____ 4. A desktop information management application

_____ 5. An application that provides comprehensive writing tools for sharing information with others

Column 2

A. Microsoft Outlook

B. Microsoft PowerPoint

C. Internet Explorer

D. Microsoft Word

E. Microsoft Excel

F. Microsoft Access

MULTIPLE CHOICE

Select the best response for the following statements.

1. A _______________ is a program that gives you the capability to access, view, and download data from the Web.

   A. search engine C. browser
   B. Web page D. tracking device

2. _______________ are used to broaden or narrow an online search.

   A. Keywords C. Operators
   B. Phrases D. all of the above

3. Non-profit organizations commonly use the _______________ extension in the domain name.

   A. .net C. country abbreviation
   B. .org D. .com

4. ______________ are the results generated by a search engine.

   A. Hits
   B. Domains
   C. Wildcards
   D. Quick links

5. You can organize your Internet Explorer History list based on ______________.

   A. the date sites were accessed
   B. the names of the sites
   C. the order in which sites were visited today
   D. all of the above

WRITTEN QUESTIONS

1. Explain how the search results are affected when you include quotation marks before and after a group of words when entering keywords in a search engine.

2. Explain how the domain name can help you identify the purpose of a Web site.

3. Give an example of when you would include operators with the keywords in a search engine.

4. How can you validate that a Web site author has credibility?

5. Name some examples of related pages options provided by some search engines.

PROJECTS

If you have a SAM 2010 user profile, your instructor may have assigned an autogradable version of the indicated project. If so, log into the SAM 2010 Web site at *www.cengage.com/sam2010* to download the instruction and start files.

PROJECT 1–1

1. Launch Word, then open the **Spectrum Follow-up.docx** data file from the drive and folder where your Data Files are stored. Save the document as **Final Spectrum Follow-up**, followed by your initials.
2. Make the edits indicated in **Figure 1–9**.
3. Change the left and right margins to 1.25 inches.
4. Justify the alignment of the paragraphs in the body of the letter.
5. Indent the bulleted list .5 inches from the left margin.
6. Adjust the paragraph spacing as needed to fit the entire document on one page.
7. Proofread and check for spelling and grammar errors, and make any necessary corrections.
8. Save the changes and leave the document open for the next project.

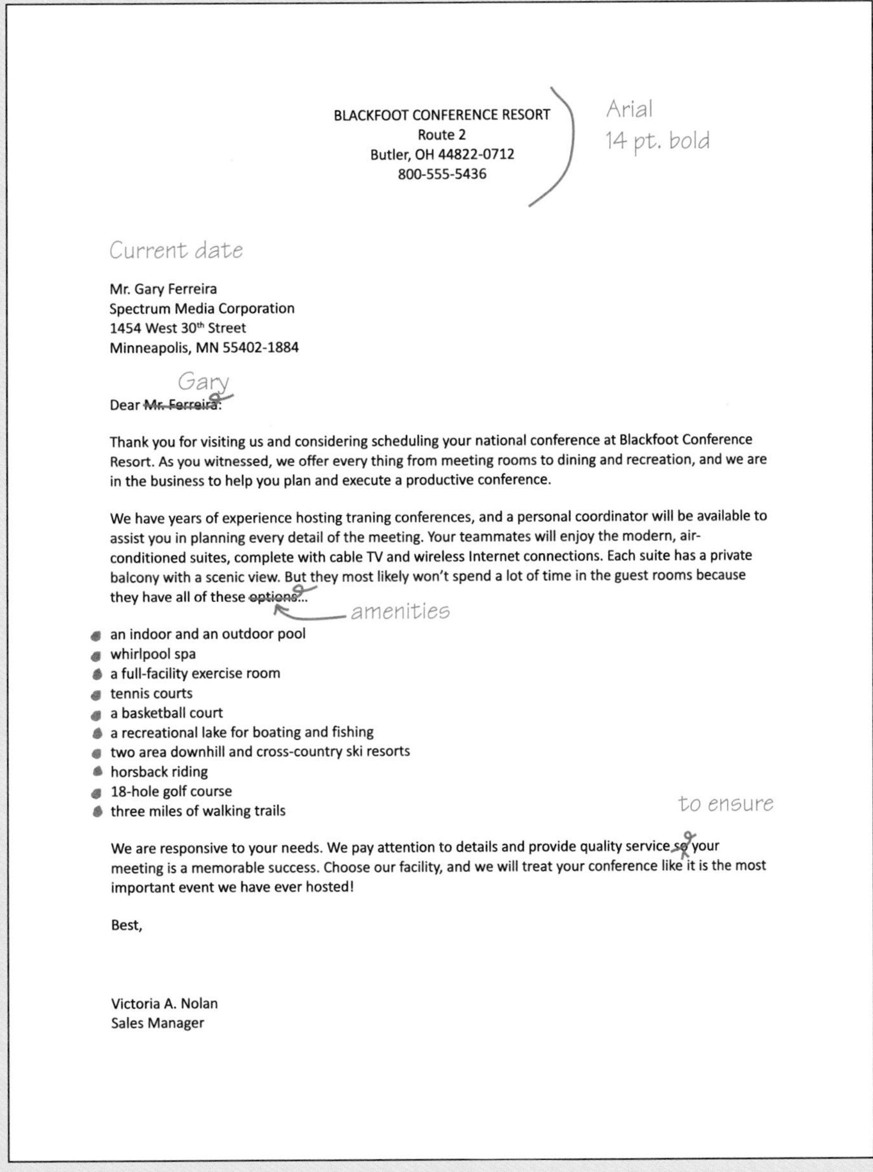

BLACKFOOT CONFERENCE RESORT
Route 2
Butler, OH 44822-0712
800-555-5436

Arial
14 pt. bold

Current date

Mr. Gary Ferreira
Spectrum Media Corporation
1454 West 30th Street
Minneapolis, MN 55402-1884

Gary
Dear ~~Mr. Ferreira~~:

Thank you for visiting us and considering scheduling your national conference at Blackfoot Conference Resort. As you witnessed, we offer every thing from meeting rooms to dining and recreation, and we are in the business to help you plan and execute a productive conference.

We have years of experience hosting traning conferences, and a personal coordinator will be available to assist you in planning every detail of the meeting. Your teammates will enjoy the modern, air-conditioned suites, complete with cable TV and wireless Internet connections. Each suite has a private balcony with a scenic view. But they most likely won't spend a lot of time in the guest rooms because they have all of these ~~options~~...

amenities

- an indoor and an outdoor pool
- whirlpool spa
- a full-facility exercise room
- tennis courts
- a basketball court
- a recreational lake for boating and fishing
- two area downhill and cross-country ski resorts
- horsback riding
- 18-hole golf course
- three miles of walking trails

to ensure

We are responsive to your needs. We pay attention to details and provide quality service ~~so~~ your meeting is a memorable success. Choose our facility, and we will treat your conference like it is the most important event we have ever hosted!

Best,

Victoria A. Nolan
Sales Manager

FIGURE 1–9 Edits for the Word document in Project 1–1

SAM PROJECT 1–2

1. Launch PowerPoint and open a new presentation. Save the presentation as **Blackfoot Resort**, followed by your initials.
2. Create a slide show highlighting the guest amenities described in the Blackfoot Conference Resort letter in Project 1-1. This presentation will be distributed on the Internet to promote the resort.
3. Add pictures and graphics to help viewers visualize the amenities.
4. Add a creative title slide at the beginning of the presentation, and add a slide for closure at the end of the presentation.
5. Apply an appropriate design or background colors to the slides.
6. Add transitions to the slides, animations to the text, and objects on the slides to produce special effects and keep the viewer's attention.
7. Save the changes and exit PowerPoint.

PROJECT 1–3

1. If necessary, log onto the Internet and open your browser.
2. In the address bar, type **www.bing.com** and press Enter.
3. Enter the keywords **Conference Resorts Ohio** to search for Ohio-based conference resort sites that offer options for guests that are similar to the options described in the Blackfoot Conference Resort document you edited in Project 1-1.
4. When you find at least two Web sites promoting a conference center similar to the Blackfoot Conference Resort, save the sites to your Favorites list in a Conference Resort folder. *Hint*: Several hits may be sites that showcase multiple resorts, and you will need to navigate to the individual resort pages to get the required information.
5. Evaluate the Web sites and answer the following questions about each Web site.
   a. Were you able to find relevant information to compare resorts?
   b. Is the information at the site current?
   c. When was the site last updated?
   d. Is the site organized well, and is the information presented accurately and professionally?
   e. Does the site provide background information about the resort?
   f. Can you easily access information to contact the resort?
   g. Would you recommend this resort? Explain the reasons for your answer.
6. Close the browser.

PROJECT 1–4

1. Launch Excel and open the **January Sales.xlsx** file from the drive and folder where your Data Files are stored. Save the workbook as **First Qtr Sales**, followed by your initials.
2. In cell C1, type the column heading **February**. In cell D1, type the column heading **March**. In cell E1, type the column heading **Total**. In cell A7, type the row heading **Total**.
3. Enter the following data in the new columns.

	February	March
Byron Store	**23112**	**42109**
Fenton Store	**38432**	**41002**
Holly Store	**31902**	**48111**
Howell Store	**27656**	**39202**
Linden Store	**29211**	**43007**

4. Proofread the data entries to make sure you entered the numbers correctly.
5. Apply the Accounting number format to all the cells with numbers and remove the decimal places.
6. Enter a formula to calculate the sum of the cell range B2:D2 in cell E2, then fill the formula down through cell E6.
7. Enter a formula to calculate the sum of the cell range B2:B6 in cell B7, then fill the formula across through cell E7.
8. Create a 3-D column chart on the same sheet showing total sales by store. Apply a design of your choice.
9. Add a centered overlay title and type **First Qtr. Sales**. Turn off the legend options.
10. Reposition the chart on the sheet so you can see the sales data in the worksheet.
11. Save the changes and close the document.

PROJECT 1–5

1. Launch Access and open the **Clients.accdb** file from the drive and folder where your Data Files are stored. Save the database as **Updated Clients**, followed by your initials.
2. Open the CLIENTS table in Datasheet View.
3. Delete the record for Daniel Warner.
4. Update the address for Helen Sanderson. Her street address is now **709 Vienna Woods Drive, Cincinnati, OH 45211**.
5. In Design View, add a new field named **Mobile Phone**. Save the changes to the table and then switch back to Datasheet View.
6. Delete the home phone number for Paula Trobaugh and add her mobile phone number, **513-555-4465.**
7. Add two new clients:

   Penelope Rausch

   5074 Signal Hill

   Cincinnati, OH 45244

   Home Phone 513-555-0133

   Mobile Phone 513-555-0899

   Roger Williamson

   722 Red Bud Avenue

   Cincinnati, OH 45229

   Mobile Phone 513-555-1055
8. Save and close the database, then exit Access.

 CRITICAL THINKING

ACTIVITY 1–1

Excel and Access have some similarities because both applications are used to organize data. If possible, look at two computer screens, side by side. On one computer, open an Excel worksheet. On the other computer, open an Access database table in Datasheet View. Compare the two screens, and create a list of similarities and differences between the worksheet and the database table. You should point out at least four similarities and four differences.

ACTIVITY 1–2

Open your browser and go to *www.bing.com.* Search for the keywords *Top Ten Search Engines*. Find the most current information available, and confirm that the sources are credible. Then, from the two sources, choose two search engines that you have never used and explore the features in each. Write a brief description of the features you like and why you would use them.

Estimated Time for Unit: 17 hours

ADVANCED

MICROSOFT WORD UNIT

Estimated Time: 2 hours

LESSON 9

Enhancing Documents

OBJECTIVES

Upon completion of this lesson, you should be able to:

- Modify the document background color and effects.
- Apply shading and borders to text, paragraphs, and pages.
- Create a watermark.
- Format drop caps.
- Create a sidebar and a pull quote using text boxes.
- Repeat text box contents on multiple pages.
- Change the orientation of text in text boxes.
- Modify and create document themes.

VOCABULARY

chain
drop cap
gradient fill
pull quote
sans serif fonts
serif fonts
serifs
sidebar
story
watermark

Word offers several features that you can use to add visual interest to your documents, as well as make them more useful. You can use these features to emphasize the content in newsletters and flyers, and you can also create sophisticated and professional-looking documents such as formal invitations.

Formatting Document Backgrounds

You can make the appearance of documents more interesting by modifying the page background. The colors and special effects can be added to the entire document, or to sections within the document. The formats you apply will depend on how you plan to distribute the document. Color highlights and shading are most effective when the recipient of the document reviews the document online or on a color printout. If the document is to be printed in black and white, light colors and shading patterns work best.

Modifying the Document Background Color and Effects

VOCABULARY
gradient fill

Changing the page background in a document can make the document easier to read, especially if the document is going to be published as a Web page, posted online, or attached to an e-mail message. Several formats are available, including gradients, textures, and patterns. A ***gradient fill*** is a gradual blending together of two or more fill colors. You can use built-in gradient fills, or you can create your own. You can also use pictures for the page background.

A page background looks great on the screen, but when you print the document, the page background colors and effects will not print. Saving the document in PDF or XPS format also saves the background effects, and they will print. However, sometimes the background effects change when the file is converted to PDF or XPS format, and the backgrounds don't look the same as they do in Word. And, depending on the printer, any border area around the background might not print.

Step-by-Step 9.1

1. Launch Word and then open the **Plastic** file from the drive and folder where your Data Files are stored. Save the document as **Enhanced Plastic 1**, followed by your initials.
2. On the Ribbon, click the **Page Layout** tab. In the Page Background group, click the **Page Color** button.
3. Move the mouse pointer over the color options to see live previews of the options. Then, under Theme Colors, in the second row of colors, fifth column, click the **Blue, Accent 1, Lighter 80%** color. The page is filled with a background color.

4. Click the **Page Color** button again, then click **More Colors** to open the Colors dialog box shown in **Figure 9–1**. Because you already applied a background color, the Custom tab appears, and you can customize the setting.

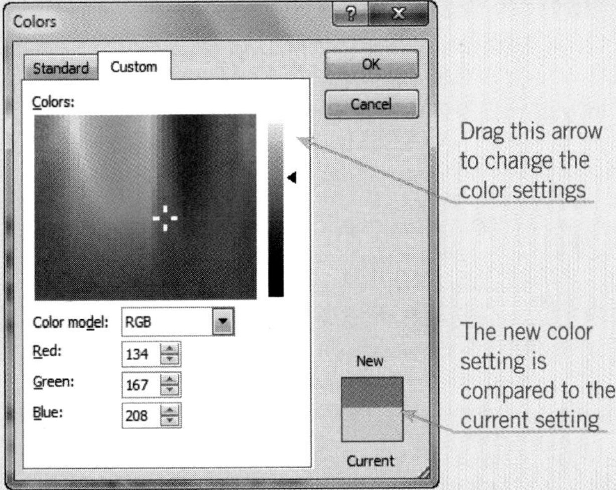

FIGURE 9–1
Colors dialog box

5. Drag the arrow to the right of the vertical bar to change the color. Notice as you drag the arrow, the new and current colors both show at the bottom of the dialog box, so you can compare the colors. Also, as you drag the arrow, you will see that the number references for the RGB (Red, Green, Blue) settings change.
6. Click the **Standard** tab and then click a light blue color in the middle of the diagram. Compare the new and current colors at the bottom of the dialog box. When you are satisfied with the new color choice, click **OK** to apply the change to the background color.
7. Click the **File** tab and then click **Print**. Notice that the background color you applied does not show in Print Preview. The page color background will not print. Click the **File** tab to close the Print Preview.

EXTRA FOR EXPERTS

If you know the exact RGB settings, you can manually change them. You can also click the Color model list arrow and select HSL (Hue, Saturation, Luminosity) to view and change those settings.

8. In the Page Background group, click the **Page Color** button, and then click **Fill Effects**. The Fill Effects dialog box shown in **Figure 9–2** opens. On the Gradient tab, under Colors, click the **Preset** option and then click the **Preset colors** list arrow. Click some of the options to view the built-in gradient fills.

FIGURE 9–2
Fill Effects dialog box

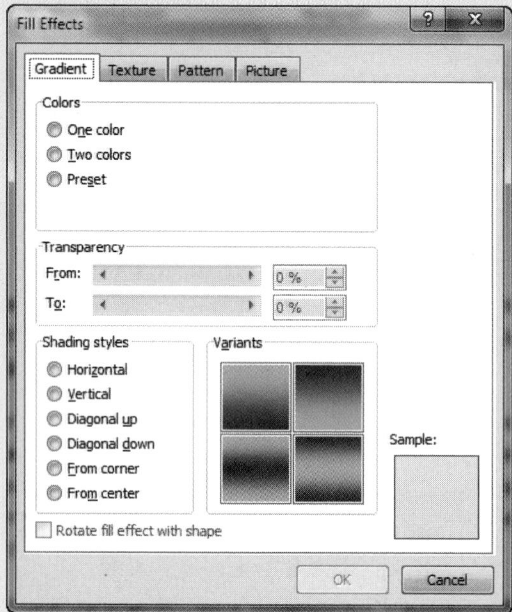

9. Under Colors, click the **Two colors** option. Leave the color setting in the Color 1 box as is. Click the **Color 2** list arrow and select a darker blue color.
10. Under Shading styles, click the **Diagonal down** option, and then under Variants, click each of the four samples. Each time you click a different variant, the Sample in the dialog box will reflect the change. Click the variant in the lower-right corner, then click **OK** to apply the custom gradient fill.
11. Click the **Page Color** button, click **Fill Effects**, and then click the **Pattern** tab. Under Pattern, click any one of the options. Click the **Foreground** list arrow, and select a dark blue color. Click the **Background** list arrow, and select a light blue color. Notice that the Sample previews your selections. Click **OK** to replace the two-color gradient background with the new customized patterns background.
12. Click the **Page Color** button, click **Fill Effects**, and then click the **Picture** tab. Click **Select Picture** to open the Select Picture dialog box. Navigate to the Data Files, select the file **Recycling Symbol.jpg**, click **Insert**, and then click **OK**. Several images of the picture appear in the background.

13. Click the **Page Color** button, click **Fill Effects**, and then click the **Texture** tab. Scroll down to view the options. Click the texture in the fourth row, third column. The texture name *Parchment* will appear in the text box just below the options. Click **OK**. The picture background is replaced with the new texture background.
14. Save the changes, and keep the document open for the next Step-by-Step.

Applying Shading and Borders to Text, Paragraphs, and Pages

You can set apart sections of a document by applying shading and borders. You can add shading and borders to an entire page, to a paragraph or group of paragraphs, and to a letter, word, or group of words. Border options include many line styles and colors as well as a variety of graphics. A page border is a section format, and the border prints on all pages in the section formatted with a page border. The border can be formatted for any or all sides of each page in a document, for pages in a section, for the first page only, or for all pages except the first page.

Step-by-Step 9.2

1. If necessary, open **Enhanced Plastic 1** from your solution files. Save the document as **Enhanced Plastic 2**, followed by your initials.
2. Click anywhere within the title *Recycled Plastic is Fantastic!*. Click the **Home** tab, and in the Paragraph group, click the **Shading** button arrow to open a menu containing the color palette. Select a tan (light brown) color. The shading is applied to the entire paragraph. Triple-click the title to select the entire paragraph, and then increase the font size to **36** point.
3. Position the insertion point at the end of the document and type your first and last names, press **spacebar**, and then enter the current date. Select your first and last names, and then click the **Shading** button to apply the same tan color you applied to the title paragraph. The shading is applied only to the selected text.
4. Click anywhere within the third paragraph of text that begins *PET (PETE)*. Click the **Shading** button arrow again to open the color palette. Under Theme Colors, select an olive green color.

TIP

To apply shading to multiple paragraphs, select all the paragraphs before choosing a color.

5. Click anywhere within the title, then click the **Borders** button arrow. At the bottom of the menu, click **Borders and Shading** to open the dialog box shown in **Figure 9–3**. The settings in the dialog box will vary depending on the formats recently applied.

FIGURE 9–3
Borders tab in the Borders and Shading dialog box

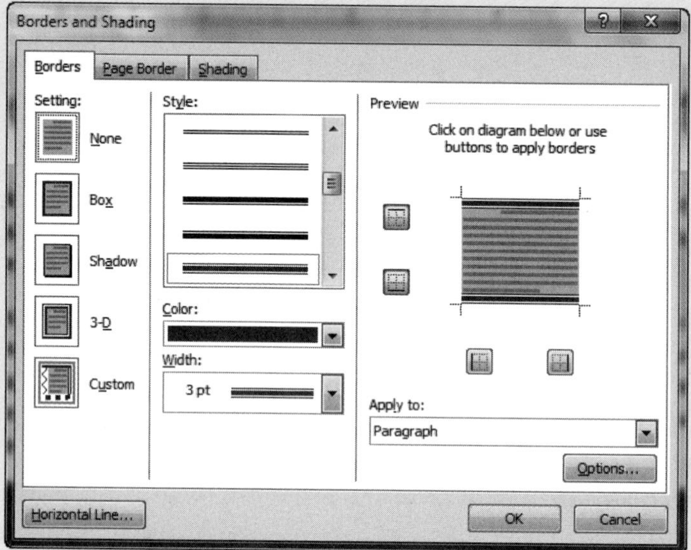

6. Select the border settings:
   a. Under Style, scroll down and select the style with three lines, as shown in Figure 9–3. (The middle line is thick, and the top and bottom lines are thin.)
   b. Under Color, select a dark olive green color.
   c. If necessary, under Width, select **3 pt**.
7. Select where the border will be applied:
   a. Under Setting, click the **None** setting to clear all settings.
   b. In the Preview pane, click at the top of the sample paragraph in the diagram. A new border line will appear above the paragraph.
   c. Click at the bottom of the sample paragraph to apply a border line below the paragraph.
   d. Click **OK**.
8. Click the **Borders** button arrow and then click **Borders and Shading** to reopen the dialog box. Under Color, select a dark tan (brown) color. Notice that the colors in the Preview pane are still green. Click the top and bottom borders in the diagram to update the color settings. Then click **OK** to apply the new format.
9. At the end of the document, select the current date that you entered. Click the **Borders** button arrow, and then click **Outside Borders**. The most recent border settings (style, color, and weight) are applied to all sides of the selected text. Click **Undo**.

10. With the date still selected, click the **Borders** button arrow. Then click **Borders and Shading** to reopen the dialog box. All the default settings appear. Under Setting, click the **Box** setting, then click **OK**. The new border style is applied to the selected text.
11. Click the **Page Layout** tab, and in the Page Background group, click the **Page Borders** button to open the Borders and Shading dialog box. If necessary, click the **Page Border** tab in the dialog box. Under Setting, click the **Box** setting. Under Color, select the dark tan (brown) color you chose for the title paragraph border. Under Art, scroll down about halfway through the list and select the border shown in **Figure 9–4**. Change the width to **30 pt**. When your dialog box settings match those in Figure 9–4, click **OK**.

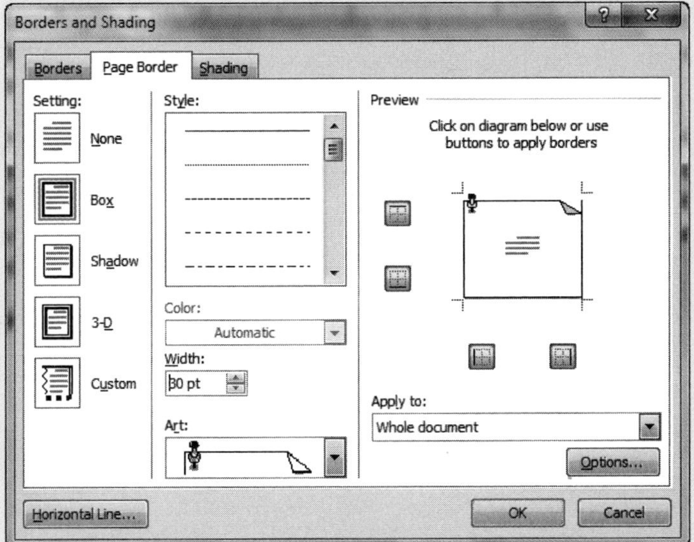

FIGURE 9–4
Page Border tab in the Borders and Shading dialog box

12. On the Page Layout tab, in the Page Setup group, click the **Dialog Box Launcher** to open the Page Setup dialog box. Click the **Layout** tab. Under Page, click the **Vertical alignment** list arrow, select **Center**, and then click **OK**. The document content is centered vertically on the page.
13. Click the **File** tab and then click **Print**. Note that the borders and the shading will print, but the texture background will not print. Click the **File** tab to close Print Preview.
14. Save the changes and keep the document open for the next Step-by-Step.

Creating a Watermark

VOCABULARY
watermark

A ***watermark*** is a ghost image that appears behind the content of a document. Watermarks traditionally have been used to print logos or text, such as *CONFIDENTIAL*, on company stationery. A watermark can be created from text or a graphic and printed in the background of a document. A watermark image can also be created by impressing text or a graphic image in the paper when the paper is manufactured. An impressed watermark is visible when the paper is held to the light.

Word offers several options for creating watermarks in documents that are to be distributed in hard copies and onscreen. To see a watermark in a Word document on screen, you must view the document in Print Preview or in Print Layout or Full Screen Reading view. The watermark will appear in the printed document.

When you create a watermark, the formats for the text or image are stored within the header and footer panes. Therefore, to edit a watermark (resize, recolor, reposition, and so on), you must access the watermark content in the header or footer. This does not mean, though, that a watermark must appear at the top or bottom of the page. A watermark can be positioned anywhere on the document page.

Step-by-Step 9.3

1. If necessary, open **Enhanced Plastic 2** from your solution files. Save the document as **Enhanced Plastic 3**, followed by your initials.
2. Click the **View** tab. In the Zoom group, click the **One Page** button.
3. Click the **Page Layout** tab, and in the Page Background group, click the **Watermark** button to show the built-in watermark options. Under Confidential, click the **DO NOT COPY 1** watermark. Then switch to Full Screen Reading view to clearly see the watermark in the document. Close Full Screen Reading view.
4. On the Page Layout tab, click the **Watermark** button again, and this time click **Custom Watermark** to open the Printed Watermark dialog box shown in **Figure 9–5**.

WARNING

The screen resolution settings affect the Full Screen Reading view. If your screen resolution is set low, the watermark image may not appear in Full Screen Reading view.

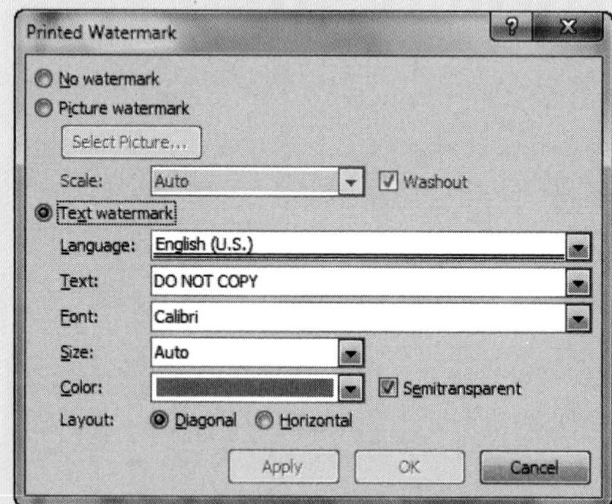

FIGURE 9–5
Printed Watermark dialog box

5. If necessary, click to enable the **Text watermark** option. Click the **Text** list arrow, scroll down, and select **TOP SECRET**. Click **Apply**. The dialog box remains open, and the watermark text changes. Select the text in the Text box and type **Eco Friends** to create your own custom text. Then change the text formats as follows:
   Font: **Cambria**
   Size: **48**
   Color: a dark olive green
   Layout: **Diagonal**
6. Click **Apply**. The dialog box remains open. If necessary, reposition the dialog box so you can see the watermark in the document. Change the size to **72**, click **Apply**, and then click **Close**.
7. Double-click in the margin area above the document title to open the header pane. On the Header & Footer Tools Design tab, in the Options group, click **Show Document Text** to disable the option. This will make it easier for you to work with the watermark image.
8. In the body of the document, move the mouse pointer over the watermark text, and when the pointer changes to a four-headed arrow, click to select the image. The image is selected when you see eight object handles around the text. Drag the watermark text upward and to the left so that the watermark is positioned in the upper-left corner on the page.
9. A watermark is created as a WordArt graphic, so when you select the watermark object, the Ribbon adapts. Click the **WordArt Tools Format** tab. In the Word Art Styles group, click the **WordArt Shape Fill** button arrow and select a light olive green color. Then click the **WordArt Shape Outline** button arrow and select a slightly darker color.
10. Click the **Header & Footer Tools Design** tab, then click the **Close Header and Footer** button. Click the **File** tab, then click **Print** to preview the document as it will print.
11. Click the **Page Layout** tab, and in the Page Background group, click the **Watermark** button and then click **Custom Watermark**.
12. Click to enable the **Picture watermark** option, then click **Select Picture** to open the Insert Picture dialog box. Navigate to the data files, select the file **Recycling symbol.jpg**, and click **Insert**. Click **Apply** and then click **Close**.
13. The white background in the picture covers the texture format. On the Page Layout tab, in the Page Background group, click the **Page Color** button, and then click **No Color**. Then click anywhere in the third paragraph. Click the **Home** tab. In the Paragraph group, click the **Shading** button arrow and then click **No Color**.
14. Save the changes and leave the document open for the next Step-by-Step.

TIP

When you create the watermark, it is anchored in the header pane. When you reposition the watermark image, the anchor may move to the footer pane. So, if you cannot access the image through the header pane, try opening the footer pane.

Formatting Drop Caps

VOCABULARY
drop cap

TIP

Sometimes drop caps are referred to as *initials*.

A ***drop cap*** is a letter or word at the beginning of a paragraph that is larger than the rest of the text. Drop caps are used to draw attention to the content, such as the beginning of a magazine article or the beginning of a chapter in a book. The drop cap format can be added to the first letter in the first word of a paragraph, or it can be added to the entire first word. You can position a drop cap to appear in the paragraph or in the margin. However, a drop cap cannot be positioned in the margin when the text is formatted in columns.

Step-by-Step 9.4

1. If necessary, open **Enhanced Plastic 3** from your solution files. Save the document as **Enhanced Plastic 4**, followed by your initials.
2. Position the insertion point anywhere in the first paragraph of text, which begins with *The promise.* Click the **Insert** tab. In the Text group, click the **Drop Cap** button. Position the mouse pointer over the **Dropped** option. A live preview of the format will show in the document.
3. Position the mouse pointer over the **In margin** option, and a new live preview shows the first letter of the paragraph formatted in the margin to the left.
4. Go back up in the list and click the **Dropped** option. The first letter in the paragraph is formatted as a drop cap with the default settings, positioned in the upper-left corner of the paragraph.
5. Position the insertion point in the second paragraph of text, and click the **Repeat** button on the Quick Access Toolbar (or press **F4**) to repeat the drop cap edit.
6. With the insertion point still positioned in the second paragraph, click the **Drop Cap** button, and then click **None** to remove the drop cap format. Then position the insertion point in the first paragraph and click the **Repeat** button on the Quick Access Toolbar (or press **F4**) to repeat the edit.
7. Select the first word *The* in the first paragraph of text. Click the **Drop Cap** button, and then click **Drop Cap Options** to open the Drop Cap dialog box shown in **Figure 9–6**.

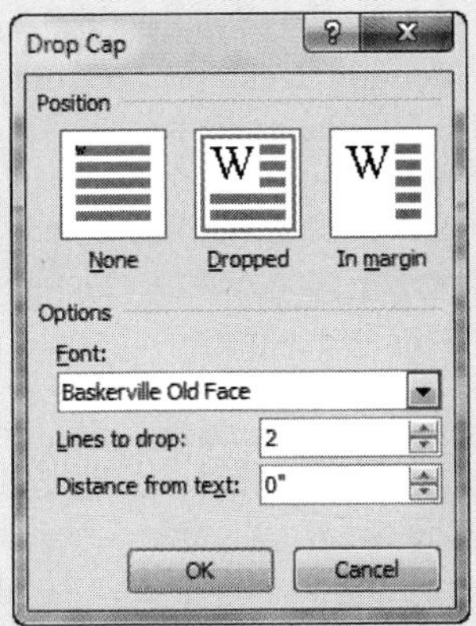

FIGURE 9–6
Drop Cap dialog box

8. Change the settings for the drop cap format:
   a. Under Position, select the **Dropped** option.
   b. Under Options, click the **Font** list arrow, scroll down, and then select **Baskerville Old Face**.
   c. In the Lines to drop setting, click the **down arrow** once to change the setting to **2**. This setting specifies the height of the drop cap in lines of text.
   d. Leave the Distance from text setting as is. This setting controls the amount of space between the drop cap and that text that follows it.
9. When the settings match those shown in Figure 9–6, click **OK**. The entire word is formatted as a drop cap in a frame in the upper-left corner of the paragraph.
10. In the drop cap frame, select just the letter *h*. Using the Mini toolbar, change the font size to **26** point. Then, select the letter *e* in the drop cap frame, and change the font size to **20** point.
11. Save the changes and close the document.

Formatting Text Boxes

Many types of documents include special sections of text relating to the subject matter that are formatted differently from the rest of the document. For example, newsletters and magazine articles often include sections that summarize the contents of the article, highlight specific text, and draw the reader's attention to specific content.

You can use text boxes to position these special sections of text and to apply various formats, such as shading, font styles, line fills, and shadows. You can adjust the text box size so that the content fits, and you can change the alignment of text inside the text box.

Creating a Sidebar

A ***sidebar*** is distinct, supplemental text added to a document such as a magazine or newspaper article to highlight the main text. For example, a sidebar can be used

VOCABULARY
sidebar

to list the names of officers in a club newsletter, or it can be used to summarize the contents of a magazine article. Sidebars are usually formatted in a boxed area with effects to draw the reader's attention. If the sidebar content is extensive, you can link text boxes so the content can continue on another page.

Sidebars are formatted in text boxes, so they can be positioned anywhere on the pages. The Text Box gallery in Word's Building Blocks Organizer provides several preformatted text boxes, especially designed for sidebars. Of course, you can modify these built-in text box formats to fit your needs.

VOCABULARY
story
chain

The text contained within a text box is called a ***story***. When you create a link between two or more text boxes, you create a ***chain***, which is a series of links that lets the story flow from one text box to the next, enabling you to continue the story elsewhere in the document. The chain can move either forward or backward, and one document can contain several stories, each with a chain of links. However, all the linked text boxes must be contained in the same document. When linking text boxes, the new box that you are adding to the chain must be empty.

Step-by-Step 9.5

1. Open the **Get Fit** file from the drive and folder where your Data Files are stored. Save the document as **Enhanced Get Fit 1**, followed by your initials.
2. Position the insertion point in the second paragraph of text. Click the **Insert** tab. In the Text group, click the **Quick Parts** button, and then click **Building Blocks Organizer** to open the Building Blocks Organizer dialog box shown in **Figure 9–7**.

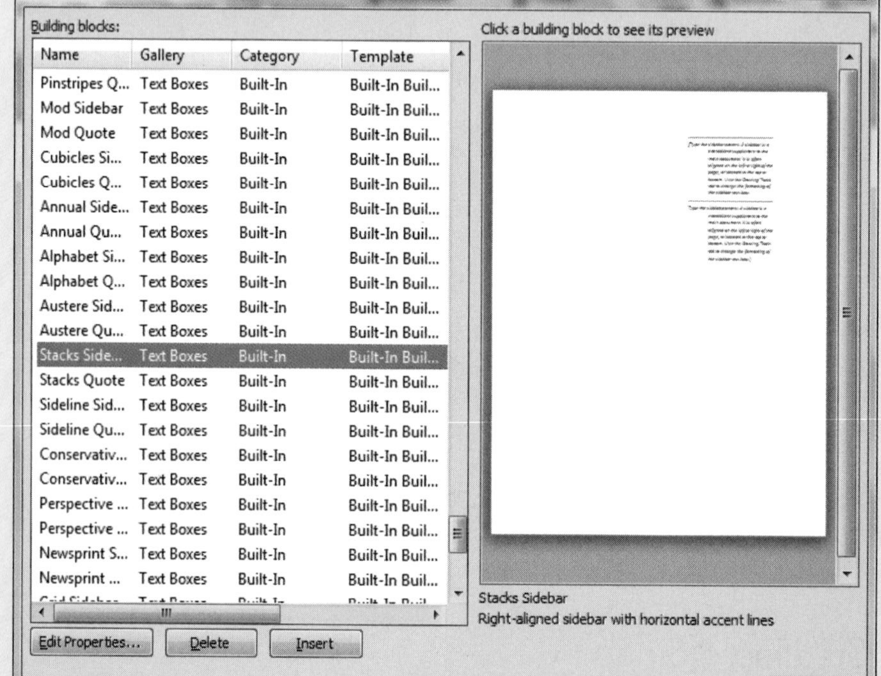

FIGURE 9–7
Building Blocks Organizer dialog box

3. Scroll down to the Text Boxes gallery, and in the Name column, click **Stacks Sidebar** (near the end of the list). Click **Insert**, and the preformatted text box is inserted in the document. The text box is already formatted for text wrapping.
4. The text box should be selected, and the Drawing Tools Format tab should show on the Ribbon. If necessary, click the Size button to the right of the Arrange group to show the options in the Size group. In the Size group, change the Height setting to **3.25"**. Drag the text box to reposition it in the lower-left corner of the page, next to the last two paragraphs in the section under the heading *Eat Smart*. (*Hint*: Point to a border of the text box. When the mouse pointer changes to a four-headed arrow, drag the text box.)
5. Click the placeholder in the text box and then type **Power-Packed Foods**. Press **Enter**. Each time you press Enter in the text box placeholder, Word automatically formats a line to divide the paragraphs.
6. Continue to enter the sidebar content by typing the following text.

   Asparagus - High in B vitamins; also a good source of Vitamins A and C and iron.

   Bananas - High in fiber, low in sodium, and fat-free; a good source of Vitamins B6 and C and potassium.
7. Position the insertion point in the first paragraph on the second page of the document. Insert a **Stacks Sidebar** text box. If necessary, click anywhere in the text box to select the placeholder. Press **Delete**. To link text boxes, the text box must be empty.
8. Select the text box on the first page. On the **Drawing Tools Format** tab in the Text group, click the **Create Link** button. The mouse pointer changes to an upright pitcher.
9. Scroll to the second page and position the mouse pointer over the new text box. The mouse pointer changes to a pouring pitcher. Click to add the text box to the chain. Now the text from the previous text box in the chain can flow into this text box.

10. Position the insertion point at the end of the text in the text box on the first page. Press **Enter** and type the following. As you enter the new text, it will flow to the text box on the second page.

    Broccoli – Ounce for ounce, twice as much Vitamin C as oranges; low in sodium; a great source of potassium, calcium, and fiber.

    Brussels sprouts - An excellent source of Vitamin C and iron; rich in Vitamin B and potassium.

    Carrots - Rich in potassium and calcium; more Vitamin A than any other vegetable.

    Citrus fruits - A prime source of Vitamin C, fiber, and potassium; low in calories and sodium-free.

    Lima beans - High in iron, B vitamins, and calcium; excellent source of potassium.

    Spinach - Low in sodium and fat, and cholesterol-free; a great source of iron, calcium, potassium, and Vitamin A.

    Strawberries - Naturally sweet and sodium-free; an excellent source of Vitamin C and fiber.

    Sweet potatoes - Second only to carrots as a source of Vitamin A; also very high in Vitamin C.

11. Select the heading in the sidebar text box on the first page. Right-click and, using the Mini toolbar, change the font size to **12** point and center the line of text. Then select all the remaining text in that text box and change the font size to **11** point. You'll notice that some of the newly formatted text flows to the next text box. Select all the text in the text box on the second page and change the font size to **11** point.

> **TIP**
>
> To remove the link between text boxes, select the text box from which the text is flowing and then click the Break Link button in the Text group on the Drawing Tools Format tab.

12. Select the text box on the first page. The Drawing Tools Format tab appears on the Ribbon. Click the tab to show the groups and commands. Format the fill color and border:
    a. In the Shape Styles group, click the **Shape Fill** button arrow and then click the **Blue, Accent 1** color.
    b. Select all the text in the sidebar text box, right-click and, on the Mini toolbar, change the font color to **White**.
    c. In the Shape Styles group, click the **Shape Outline** button arrow and select the **Olive Green, Accent 3** color. Click the **Shape Outline** button arrow again, and change the border weight to **2 ¼** point.
    d. Click anywhere in the text box on the second page, and apply the same fill and border formats as the text box on the first page.
    e. Select all the text in the second text box. Using the Mini toolbar, change the font color to **White**.

13. Select the text box on the first page. Drag the sizing handles on the top or bottom of the text box to adjust the size of the text box on the first

page so that all the information about the first three foods (asparagus, bananas, and broccoli) appears in that text box. Then adjust the size of the second text box to eliminate extra blank space at the bottom.

14. Save the changes, and leave the document open for the next Step-by-Step.

Creating a Pull Quote

A ***pull quote*** is a line or phrase excerpted from the main text and used to draw attention. Pull quotes are often used in magazine and newsletter articles to highlight specific text included within the article. A pull quote is usually positioned on the same page and close to where it is referenced. The pull quote text is often formatted in a different font style, size, or color to add emphasis.

Like sidebars, pull quotes are formatted in text boxes. Word's Building Blocks Organizer also provides several preformatted text boxes that are especially designed for pull quotes. After inserting the building block, you can enter the pull quote text. If you are pulling a lot of text for the pull quote, you can copy the text in the document and then paste the content into the pull quote text box.

VOCABULARY
pull quote

Step-by-Step 9.6

1. If necessary, open **Enhanced Get Fit 1** from your solution files. Save the document as **Enhanced Get Fit 2**, followed by your initials.
2. Position the insertion point in the first paragraph under the heading *Eat Smart* to anchor the pull quote text box to this paragraph.
3. Click the **Insert** tab. In the Text group, click the **Quick Parts** button, and then click **Building Blocks Organizer**.
4. Scroll down to the Text Boxes gallery, and in the Name column, select **Sticky Quote**. Click **Insert**, and the preformatted text box is inserted in the document. The text box is already formatted for text wrapping.
5. The text box should be selected, and the Drawing Tools Format tab should show on the Ribbon. If necessary, click the **Size** button to expand the Size group. Change the height to **1.5"** and the width to **2"**.
6. Drag the text box to reposition it. Align the text box in the middle of the paragraph beginning with *Experts agree*, with the right side of the text box aligned with the right margin.
7. Click the placeholder in the text box and type the following:

   Nutritionists recommend that not more than 30 percent of the total daily calories you consume come from fat.
8. Select the pull quote text box. The Drawing Tools Format tab shows on the Ribbon. In the Shape Styles group, click the **Shape Fill** button arrow and select the **Blue, Accent 1, Lighter 40%** color.
9. Save the changes and leave the document open for the next Step-by-Step.

TIP

To select the text box, position the mouse pointer over the object border. When the pointer changes to a four-headed arrow, click and drag the box to reposition it.

Repeating Text Box Contents and Changing the Text Direction

You can repeat text box contents on every page of a document or section of a document by inserting a text box item in a header or footer and positioning the text box where you want the contents to print.

The default setting for text boxes is to show the text in a horizontal orientation. However, you can easily change the text format to a vertical orientation. For example, you may want to print a title in the left margin on each page of a document. You can format the text to read from bottom to top or from top to bottom.

Step-by-Step 9.7

1. If necessary, open **Enhanced Get Fit 2** from your solution files. Save the document as **Enhanced Get Fit 3**, followed by your initials.
2. Click the **View** tab, and in the Zoom group, click the **One Page** button.
3. Double-click in the margin at the top of the document to access the header pane. The Ribbon will adapt and show the Header & Footer Tools Design tab.
4. Click the **Insert** tab. In the Text group, click the **Text Box** button and then select the **Simple Text Box** option. A text box with a placeholder for a quote is inserted, and the text box is anchored in the header pane.
5. If necessary, click the placeholder in the text box. Type **Healthy Living**. Word automatically adjusts the height of the text box.
6. Click the **Header & Footer Tools Design** tab, then click the **Close Header and Footer** button. Scroll down to the second and third pages, and you'll see that the text box also appears in the header on those pages. Press **Ctrl+Home** to return to the top of the document.
7. Double-click in the top margin of the document to access the header pane. Select the text box, and then click the **Drawing Tools Format** tab on the Ribbon. In the Text group, click the **Text Direction** button, and then click **Rotate all text 90°**.
8. Drag the text box down to the document and position it in the right margin, about halfway down the page. (*Hint*: Click a text box border. When the pointer changes to a four-headed arrow, drag the box to reposition it.)
9. Triple-click inside the text box to select all the text. You may see only a shading color and no text, or you may see no color at all. Use the Mini toolbar to increase the font size to **26** point. The size of the text box will adjust, and you still probably won't be able to see the text.
10. Click a border on the text box to select it, and then drag a handle at the top or bottom of the box to make the box taller so that the text fits on one line in the text box.

11. Triple-click in the text box again to select all the text. Use the Mini toolbar to change the font color to **Blue, Accent 1**, to match the blue fill in the sidebar text box.
12. With the text box still selected, click the **Drawing Tools Format** tab. In the Shape Styles group, click the **Shape Outline** button arrow, then click **No Outline.**
13. Double-click anywhere in the body of the document to close the header pane. Your page should now look similar to the one shown in **Figure 9–8.**

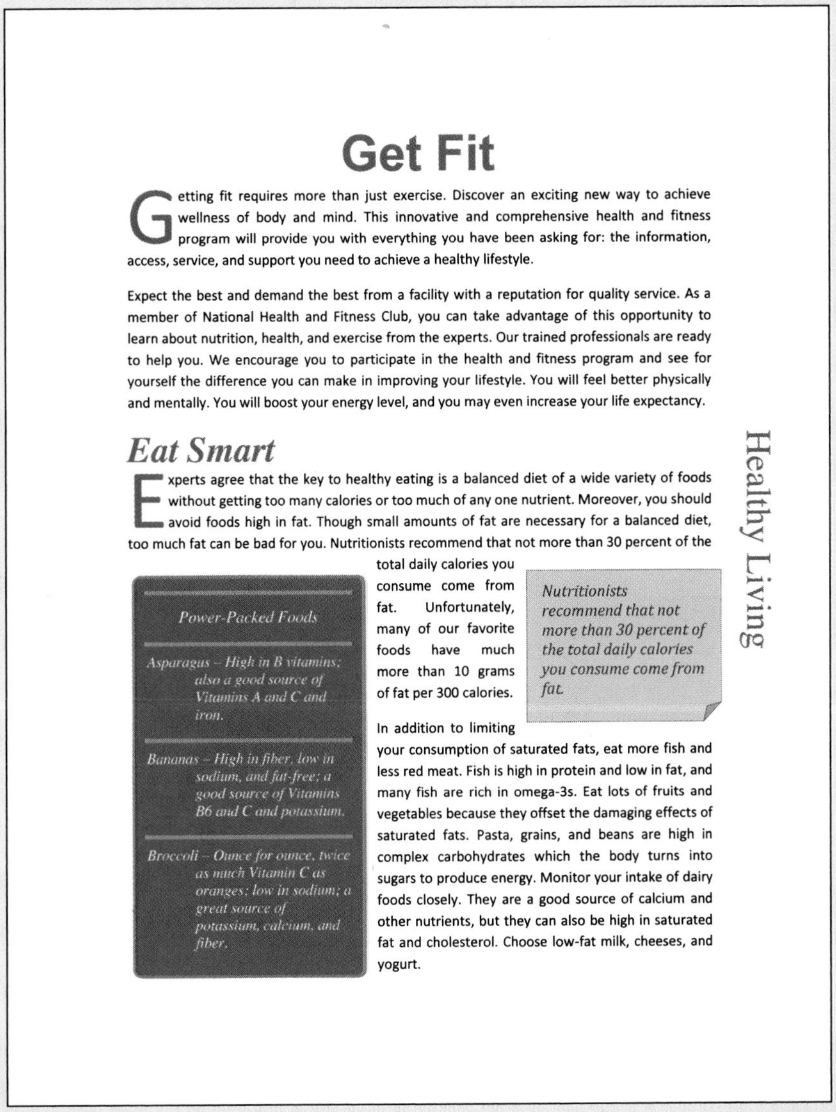

Get Fit

Getting fit requires more than just exercise. Discover an exciting new way to achieve wellness of body and mind. This innovative and comprehensive health and fitness program will provide you with everything you have been asking for: the information, access, service, and support you need to achieve a healthy lifestyle.

Expect the best and demand the best from a facility with a reputation for quality service. As a member of National Health and Fitness Club, you can take advantage of this opportunity to learn about nutrition, health, and exercise from the experts. Our trained professionals are ready to help you. We encourage you to participate in the health and fitness program and see for yourself the difference you can make in improving your lifestyle. You will feel better physically and mentally. You will boost your energy level, and you may even increase your life expectancy.

Healthy Living

Eat Smart

Experts agree that the key to healthy eating is a balanced diet of a wide variety of foods without getting too many calories or too much of any one nutrient. Moreover, you should avoid foods high in fat. Though small amounts of fat are necessary for a balanced diet, too much fat can be bad for you. Nutritionists recommend that not more than 30 percent of the total daily calories you consume come from fat. Unfortunately, many of our favorite foods have much more than 10 grams of fat per 300 calories.

Power-Packed Foods

Asparagus – High in B vitamins; also a good source of Vitamins A and C and iron.

Bananas – High in fiber, low in sodium, and fat-free; a good source of Vitamins B6 and C and potassium.

Broccoli – Ounce for ounce, twice as much Vitamin C as oranges; low in sodium; a great source of potassium, calcium, and fiber.

Nutritionists recommend that not more than 30 percent of the total daily calories you consume come from fat.

In addition to limiting your consumption of saturated fats, eat more fish and less red meat. Fish is high in protein and low in fat, and many fish are rich in omega-3s. Eat lots of fruits and vegetables because they offset the damaging effects of saturated fats. Pasta, grains, and beans are high in complex carbohydrates which the body turns into sugars to produce energy. Monitor your intake of dairy foods closely. They are a good source of calcium and other nutrients, but they can also be high in saturated fat and cholesterol. Choose low-fat milk, cheeses, and yogurt.

FIGURE 9–8
Enhanced Get Fit 3 document

14. Save the changes, and keep the document open for the next Step-by-Step.

Modifying Document Themes

Themes help you quickly change the appearance of a document and make it look professional. Word provides many built-in themes, and each has a specific look and feel. You can consistently apply formats to multiple documents because the same themes are also available in Excel and PowerPoint. For example, you can use the same theme to format a report in Word, a chart in an Excel spreadsheet, and slides in a PowerPoint presentation.

When you apply a theme, the new formats show up in headings, charts, picture borders, and tables. If you don't find a built-in theme that fits your needs, you can find additional themes online, you can modify the existing themes, or you can create your own themes. Office 2010 provides many built-in themes, and each theme defines three document elements: colors, fonts, and effects.

VOCABULARY
serif fonts
serifs
sans serif fonts

Several research studies and extensive discussions have been conducted to determine if the typeface can make text easier to read. ***Serif fonts*** have ***serifs*** (small lines or curls) at the ends of characters. The serifs are an embellishment for the font character. Some argue that the serifs help guide the eye along a line of text and connect the characters in a word. ***Sans serif fonts*** do not include the serifs, and some believe that sans serif typefaces are more difficult to read. Typically, sans serif fonts are used for headings and captions, and serif fonts are used for large blocks of text. Many people think serif fonts are easier to read on screen, but the research is still inconclusive. **Table 9–1** lists commonly used serif and sans serif fonts.

TABLE 9–1 Commonly used serif and sans serif fonts

SERIF FONTS	SANS SERIF FONTS
Cambria	Arial
Courier	Calibri
Garamond	Franklin Gothic
Georgia	Helvetica
Rockwell	Trebuchet MS
Times New Roman	Verdana

Step-by-Step 9.8

1. If necessary, open **Enhanced Get Fit 3** from your solution files. Save the document as **Enhanced Get Fit 4**, followed by your initials.
2. Change the zoom to **35%**, so you can view all three pages in the document side by side.
3. Click the **Page Layout** tab. In the Themes group, click the **Themes** button to show the available built-in themes. The current theme for the document is the default, *Office*.

4. Slowly move the mouse pointer over several of the options. Notice in the live previews that the formats in the headings, text boxes, and table change. Not only do the colors change, but the flow of text is sometimes rearranged because the font styles and sizes change.
5. Select the **Grid** theme. Click the pull quote text box. Then click the Drawing Tools Format tab, and in the Shape Styles group, click the **Shape Fill** button arrow and change the fill color to a darker tan. Your edit affected the document, but no changes were made to the theme settings. When you apply this theme to another document, the fill color will show the lighter tan.
6. Click the **Page Layout** tab. In the Themes group, click the **Theme Colors** button. The Theme Colors gallery opens. At the bottom of the list, click **Create New Theme Colors**. The Create New Theme Colors dialog box shown in **Figure 9–9** opens. A theme has a combination of twelve colors: four colors for body text and backgrounds, six accent colors for headings and tables, and two colors for new and used hyperlinks.

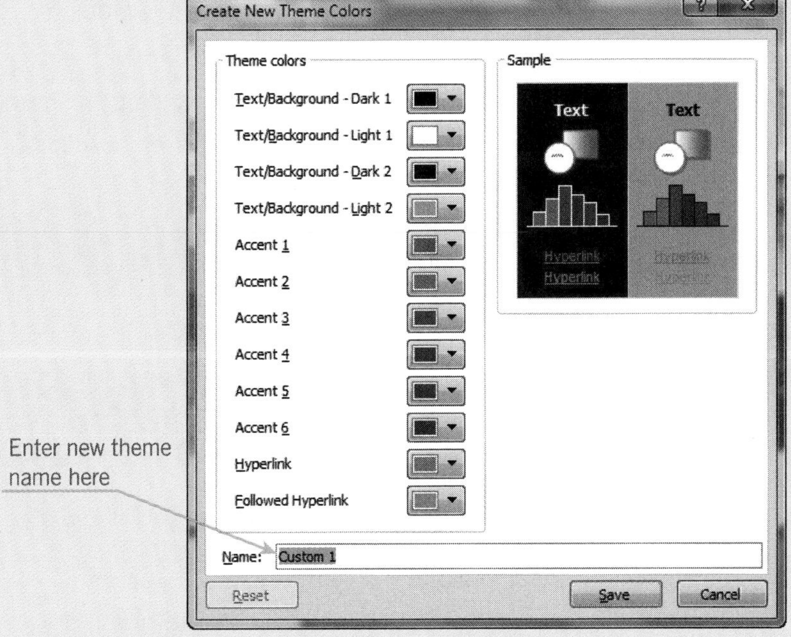

FIGURE 9–9
Create New Theme Colors dialog box

7. Click the **Accent 1** list arrow and then select a darker tan color. Notice that the Name box shows a proposed new theme name, such as *Custom 1*. Enter your first and last name followed by the number 1. Click **Save**. The changes are updated in the document, and the revised theme is saved under a new theme name.

8. In the Themes group, click the **Theme Fonts** button. The Theme Fonts gallery opens. Scroll down and click the **Flow** option. The font changes are reflected in the document, but the theme settings are not altered.
9. In the Themes group, click the **Theme Effects** button. The Theme Effects gallery opens. Click the **Concourse** option. You will notice a slight difference in the effects for the SmartArt object on the third page. Twenty effects are available for themes, including shadows, lines, and 3D.
10. In the Themes group, click the **Themes** button. At the bottom of the menu, click **Save Current Theme**. The Save Current Theme dialog box opens. In the File name box, enter your first and last name followed by the number 1. Click **Save**.
11. Click the **Themes** button again. Your new theme appears at the top of the list under the heading *Custom*. Right-click your custom theme and then click **Delete**. When prompted about deleting the theme, click **Yes**.
12. In the Themes group, click the **Themes Color** button. Right click the custom theme with your name, then click **Delete**. When prompted about deleting the theme colors, click **Yes**.
13. With the theme changes, the content may have shifted in the document. Review each page, and adjust the text flow as needed so that content layout looks good.
14. Save the changes and close the document.

SUMMARY

In this lesson, you learned:

- Changing document backgrounds can enhance the appearance of a document and make the document easier to read.
- Shading and borders enable you to set apart sections of a document.
- Watermarks are often used to print logos or text on company stationery. A watermark can be created from text or a graphic and formatted to appear behind the document content, or the image can be impressed in the paper when the paper is manufactured.
- Drop caps are used to draw attention to the content in a document.
- Sidebars and pull quotes are used to highlight content in a document. Several Quick Parts are available to help you quickly create professional text boxes to format these features.
- You can repeat text box contents on every page or section of a document by inserting a text box in a header or footer.
- You can change the direction of text in a text box so that the text reads from top to bottom or from bottom to top.
- You can override formats within the many built-in themes for a single document, or you can modify the formats and then save the changes using a new theme name.

VOCABULARY REVIEW

Define the following terms:

chain
drop cap
gradient fill
pull quote
sans serif fonts
serif fonts
serifs
sidebar
story
watermark

REVIEW QUESTIONS

TRUE / FALSE

Circle T if the statement is true or F if the statement is false.

T F 1. The drop cap format can be added to only the first letter of a word.

T F 2. Even though document background colors will not print, a document background texture or pattern will print.

T F 3. All linked text boxes must be in the same document.

T F 4. Changing the background color in a document can make it easier to read if the document is going to be distributed online.

T F 5. Watermark formats are stored in the header and footer panes.

FILL IN THE BLANK

Complete the following sentences by writing the correct word or words in the blanks provided.

1. A(n) ________________ is a ghost image that appears behind the document content.
2. The ________________ is the content in a text box.
3. When two or more text boxes are connected, it is referred to as a(n) ________________.
4. The lines or curls added to the ends of font characters are referred to as ________________.
5. ________________ fonts are often used to format headings and captions.

MULTIPLE CHOICE

Select the best response for the following statements.

1. If a document is to be printed in black and white, ________________.
   A. light colors and shading patterns are most effective
   B. gradients and textures are most effective
   C. color highlights are most effective
   D. background colors are most effective
2. Shading can be applied to ________________.
   A. an entire page
   B. a paragraph or a group of paragraphs
   C. a letter, a word, or a group of words
   D. all of the above

3. Themes define three elements in a document: ______________.
   A. colors, fonts, and page layout
   B. colors, fonts, and effects
   C. fonts, margins, and page layout
   D. colors, page backgrounds, and patterns
4. Borders can be applied to any or all sides of ______________.
   A. a page or a section
   B. only the first page of a document
   C. all pages except the first page of a document
   D. all of the above
5. A sidebar ______________.
   A. is used to format headings and captions
   B. emphasizes a passage from a document, such as a magazine article
   C. is supplemental text added to a magazine or newspaper article
   D. none of the above

PROJECTS

If you have a SAM 2010 user profile, your instructor may have assigned an autogradable version of the indicated project. If so, log into the SAM 2010 Web site at *www.cengage.com/sam2010* to download the instruction and start files.

PROJECT 9–1

The company you work for has asked you to format a banquet invitation that is to be distributed online. It is a formal banquet, so you need to create a classy, professional-looking document. The primary color in the company logo is burgundy, but you do not have to use that color.

1. Open the **Invitation** file from the drive and folder where your Data Files are stored. Save the document as **Enhanced Invitation**, followed by your initials. This file includes all the information that needs to be included on the invitation.
2. Format the document to create an attractive one-page invitation. Consider applying the following formats: backgrounds, page borders, paragraph borders and shading, font styles, font colors, and paragraph alignment. (You do not have to use all of those formats.) Adjust the spacing between lines of text as needed.
3. Format the document so it is centered vertically on the page.
4. Save the changes and close the document.

SAM PROJECT 9–2

Your boss asked you to format content for a flyer that will be distributed in the local community. To be effective, the flyer needs to be attractive and easy to read.

1. Open the **Trees** file from the drive and folder where your Data Files are stored. Save the document as **Enhanced Trees**, followed by your initials.
2. Center the title and change the font style and font size so that the title is much bigger, but not so big that it wraps to a second line.
3. Change the title to a serif font. (*Hint*: See Table 9–1.)
4. Format a box border around the title text, using a line style and color of your choice. Then add a shade to the paragraph, using a color that complements the border color. If necessary, change the font color of the title text so it complements the shading and border.
5. Format the first word in the first paragraph as a drop cap, using the dropped option. Adjust the number of drop lines to **2** and change the distance from the text to **.2"**. Change the drop cap font to a font style of your choice (a serif font is recommended), and then change the font color so it complements the colors in the title.
6. Repeat the drop cap formats for the first word in each of the two remaining paragraphs.
7. Format the last paragraph with an outline border, using a border style and color of your choice.
8. This document needs approval before it is published and distributed, so you need to make sure anyone who sees it knows that it is a draft copy. Choose a text watermark from the built-in options, or create your own custom watermark.
9. Position the watermark near the bottom of the document, and apply a shape outline to make the watermark more noticeable.
10. Save the changes and close the document.

PROJECT 9–3

1. Open the **Lead Out** file from the drive and folder where your Data Files are stored. Save the document as **Enhanced Lead Out 1**, followed by your initials.
2. Click anywhere in the second paragraph and insert the Motion Sidebar text box from the Building Blocks Organizer.
3. Format the sidebar text box so the height is 3.5" and the width is 2". Position the text box in the lower-right corner of the first page.
4. Copy the text box to the Clipboard, click anywhere in the middle of the second page of the document, and paste the text box.
5. Link the text box on the first page so the text will flow to the text box on the second page. Be sure to delete the content in the text box placeholder before you create the link.
6. Cut the entire first paragraph to the Clipboard, then paste the text in the sidebar text box. The story will flow to the second text box.
7. Deselect the text boxes, then select the text box on the second page and adjust the height so it is big enough to show the entire story. Position the text box in the upper-left corner of the second page, and if necessary, adjust the font size and font color.
8. Click in the first sentence of the second paragraph under the heading *Health Risks*. Open the Building Blocks Organizer and insert the Exposure Quote text box. Format the text box size so that it is approximately 1" high and 2" wide.
9. Position the text box where it fits best near the heading *Health Risks*. Type the following excerpt in the text box. Adjust the text box size if necessary so that all the pull quote text fits. If necessary, adjust the font size and font color.

   Lead poisoning is the most common environmental illness in children.
10. At the end of the document, select the heading *Prevention of Lead Poisoning* and all of the bulleted items below the heading. Apply a paragraph shading and an outside border that complements the color theme for the sidebars and the pull quote.
11. Apply a border to the title at the top of the document using a border setting, style, and color of your choice. If desired, add a shading format to the title. If necessary, or if it makes the document attractive, adjust the font size and font color.
12. Check to make sure all the text in the sidebar text boxes and the pull quote text box are visible. If necessary, adjust the height of the text boxes. Check the flow of text from one page to the next. Make sure the headings stay with the first paragraph below them, and make line spacing adjustments as needed to keep content together so that it is easier to read.
13. Save the changes, and leave the document open for the next project.

PROJECT 9–4

1. If necessary, open **Enhanced Lead Out 1** from your solution files. Save the document as **Enhanced Lead Out 2**, followed by your initials.
2. Change the margin settings to 1" top and bottom and 1.25" left and right.
3. Format a text box in the header pane so it will appear on every page. In the text box, type **HEALTH WATCH**. Change the font size to 28 point and change the font color to one that fits in with the current theme colors.
4. Change the text orientation so that the text reads from bottom to top, then resize the text box to show all of the text. The width of the text box should be no more than .7".
5. Position the text box about halfway down the page in the left margin. Remove the outline from the text box shape.
6. Apply a new theme to the document.
7. Modify one or more color formats in the document, such as changing shading to a darker color. Do not make any changes to an existing theme, and do not create a new theme.
8. Check to make sure all the text in the sidebar text boxes and the pull quote text box are visible. If necessary, adjust the height of the text box. Check the flow of text from one page to the next. Make sure the headings stay with the first paragraph below them, and make line spacing adjustments as needed to keep content together so that it is easier to read. Also check that the *Health Watch* text box is visible on all pages.
9. Save the changes and close the document.

CRITICAL THINKING

ACTIVITY 9–1

Open a new blank document. Type **=rand(2,2)** and then press Enter to create some sample text. Select the first paragraph of text and apply a serif font. Then select the second paragraph of text and apply a sans serif font. (*Hint*: See Table 9–1.) If necessary, increase the font sizes of both paragraphs of text so you can compare the ends of the characters. Describe the differences you see in the two types of fonts. Also comment on which font type you prefer and whether you find one font type easier to read than the other.

ACTIVITY 9–2

Word provides shortcuts that enable you to insert a horizontal line by typing only a few characters. The horizontal lines are automatically formatted for page width. Search the Help screens to learn about these shortcuts. When you find the information, practice the shortcuts, then make a list of the shortcuts and describe how to insert the horizontal lines with just a few taps on the keyboard. Include a few sentences about which shortcut you like most, and describe when you would find that shortcut useful.

Estimated Time: 2 hours

LESSON 10

Working with Templates and Styles

OBJECTIVES

Upon completion of this lesson, you should be able to:

- Create a custom document template.
- Create a new document based on a document template.
- Attach a template to a document and make a template global.
- Apply and change styles.
- Create and modify styles.
- Copy, edit, and delete styles.
- Reveal and clear formats.
- Use a template to share building blocks.

VOCABULARY

boilerplate text
document template
global template
Normal template
style
style sheet
template

When you open a new blank document, do you ever think about all the predefined formats that are part of the document? It is easy to take for granted the default settings that affect the page layout, margin settings, paragraph spacing, and font styles. As you work with a document, you often change those default settings. You can predefine your own set of formats to help you save time and effort and ensure consistency when formatting your documents.

Working with Templates

VOCABULARY

template

document template

global template

Normal template

boilerplate text

Every Microsoft Word document is based on a ***template***, a file that affects the basic structure of a document and contains document settings such as fonts, line spacing, margins, and page layout. Using templates increases the speed and efficiency of your work since you do not need to spend time formatting page layouts and font formats. Templates also help you maintain consistency in the documents you create.

Word has two basic types of templates. A ***document template*** contains document settings, content, and styles that are available only to documents based on that template. A ***global template*** contains document settings that are available to all documents. Word's default global template is the ***Normal template*** (Normal.dotm), and it shares styles with all open documents. To run Word, you must have a Normal template. If the Normal template is deleted, Word will create a new one using the factory defaults.

You can create additional global templates so that you can store customized styles, formats, and AutoText, and then make them available to all documents. Although you can only use one document template to create a document, you can use multiple global templates. For example, you can open a document that is based on the global template Normal, and then you can also access the styles and formats in another global template.

TIP

Depending on your Word installation, many document templates may already be installed, but if you can't find what you need, hundreds more are available at the Microsoft Web site.

Creating a Custom Document Template

Microsoft provides a variety of document templates to help you quickly create a new document, such as a resume, brochure, fax cover sheet, or business cards. A document template can include headers and footers, AutoText, pictures and graphics, styles and themes, and more. Standard text that is reusable in documents, such as contracts and correspondence, is referred to as ***boilerplate text***. At any time, you can edit the template contents.

If you frequently create a particular document, such as an agenda for monthly meetings, you can make a customized document template and then use that template each time you need to prepare an agenda. You can make a customized document template by opening a blank document or by modifying an existing document or an existing template.

EXTRA FOR EXPERTS

The default location for saving templates varies depending on the version of Word. You can see (and modify) the default location from the File tab. Click Options, and in the Word Options dialog box that opens, click Advanced. Scroll to the end of the Advanced options list, and under General, click File Locations. In the File Locations dialog box, under File types, click User templates. The location is indicated to the right.

Step-by-Step 10.1

1. Launch Word and then open the **Agenda** file from the drive and folder where your Data Files are stored. Note that the document is already formatted and contains boilerplate text and graphics that can be used in future documents.

2. Click the **File** tab, and then click **Save As** to open a Save As dialog box similar to the one shown in **Figure 10–1**.

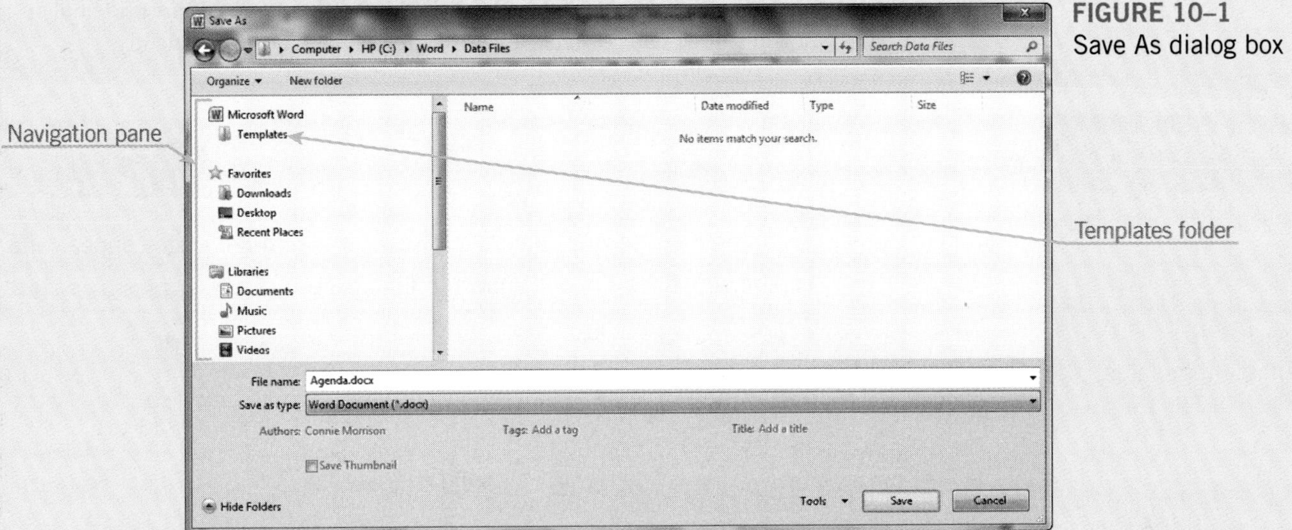

FIGURE 10–1
Save As dialog box

3. In the File name box, change the filename to **Agenda Template**, followed by your initials. In the Save as type box, select **Word Template (*.dotx)**.
4. Navigate to the folder where you save your solution files, and then click **Save** to save the template file in that folder.
5. In the Paragraph group, click the **Show/Hide ¶** button ¶ to show nonprinting characters in the document.
6. Make the following changes to the template, taking care not to change the formatting:
   a. In the lower-right corner of the document heading, replace the date *October 14, 2014* with ***Date***.
   b. In the column to the right of *PLEDGE OF ALLEGIANCE*, delete *Eagle Scout Eric Chapman*.
   c. Under *APPROVAL OF MINUTES*, delete the date *September 16, 2014*.
   d. Under *OPEN ISSUES*, in the left column, delete the two entries of text, but be sure to leave all formatting symbols. This will maintain the formats and make it easy for you to create new entries for future documents.
   e. In the right column under *OPEN ISSUES*, delete the two occurrences of *Patrick Carmody*.
   f. Under *NEW BUSINESS*, in the left column, delete the one entry of text, but leave the nonprinting formatting symbol. In the right column, delete *Superintendent Brad Jones*.
7. Save the changes and close the document.

EXTRA FOR EXPERTS

If the template contains macros (which you will learn about in Lesson 16), you would select the Word Macro-Enabled Template (*.dotm) file type.

Creating a New Document Using a Custom Template

Just as you use the installed templates and those available at www.office.com to create a new document, you can also use your new custom template. Your template won't include any field placeholders like those provided in the Microsoft templates, but you will still be able to create a new document quickly and efficiently.

Step-by-Step 10.2

1. Click the **File** tab, and then click **New**. Available templates appear in a screen similar to the one shown in **Figure 10–2**.

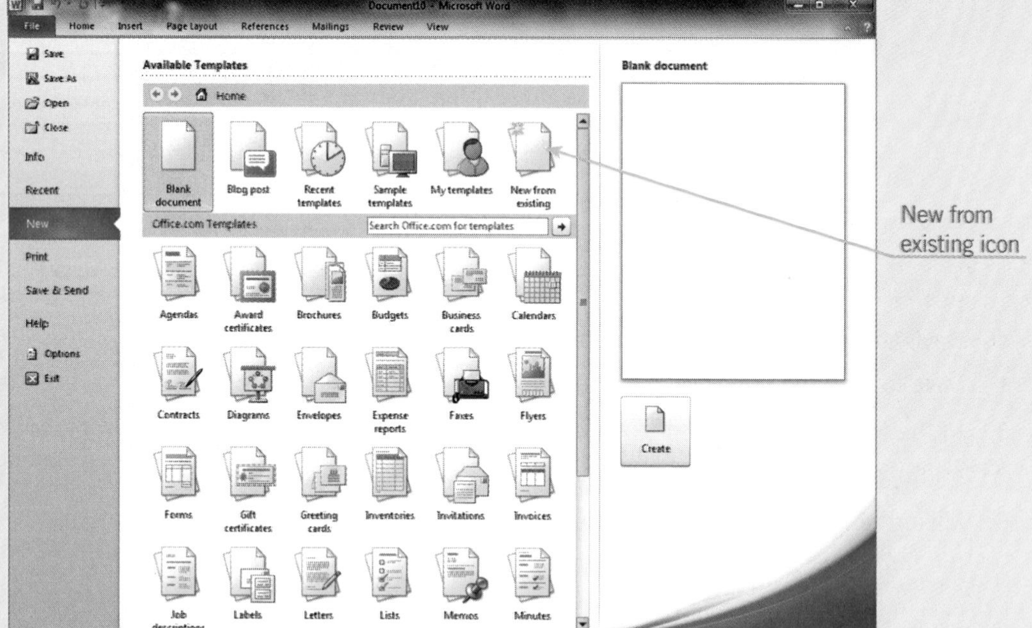

FIGURE 10–2
Available templates

2. In the Home section, click the **Sample templates** icon and review the types of document templates available. Above the first row of sample templates, click **Home** to return to the Available Templates.
3. Click the **New from existing** icon. Navigate to the folder where you save your solution files and then click **Agenda Template.dotx**. Click **Create New**. A new document opens and shows the template boilerplate text.
4. Click the **File** tab, click **Save As**, and navigate to the folder where you save your solution files. Name the document **November Agenda**, followed by your initials. Click **Save**. Note that the file is saved as a new document and the template is no longer open, so as you make changes, the changes will be saved to the document and not to the template.
5. In the lower-right corner of the heading, replace *Date* with ***November 18, 2014***.

6. Click in the column to the right of *PLEDGE OF ALLEGIANCE* and type **Eagle Scout Aidan Rivera**.
7. Under *APPROVAL OF MINUTES*, position the insertion point after the word *of* and type the date **October 14, 2014**.
8. In the left column under *OPEN ISSUES*, position the insertion point to the right of the tab symbol. Type **Dunham Road, street lighting**. Delete the ¶ symbol and the tab symbol because you do not need to use the blank line below.
9. Click in the right column next to *Dunham Road, street lighting* and type **Ethan Brzezinski**. Delete the ¶ symbol to remove the blank line below.
10. Under *NEW BUSINESS*, in the left column, type **Interlocal agreement with Wilson Township for ambulance service**. Click in the right column and type **Les Hanes**.
11. Save the changes and then close the document.

Creating a Personal Template

By default, Word stores styles and building blocks in the Normal template. All users of the computer have access to the Normal template. Because you may share a computer with learners in other classes, you will create a personal template so you can store the new styles and building blocks that you create in this lesson. That way you can also copy the template and use it on other computers.

TECHNOLOGY TIMELINE

Before electric typewriters and computers, manual typewriters were used to create formal documents. The manual typewriters used monospaced fonts (also referred to as fixed-width fonts), so all characters were the exact same width. For example, the amount of horizontal space provided for the letter *i* was the same as the amount of horizontal space provided for the letter *w*. It was common practice to create two blank spaces at the end of a sentence because the extra blank space made it easier to see the break between sentences. Today's word-processing applications include proportional fonts, which means the character widths vary depending on the shape of the characters. Proportional fonts are easier to read because there is no excess blank space between characters. Also, the blank spaces between sentences are more obvious, so you need only enter one blank space between sentences.

Although proportional fonts are easier to read, monospaced fonts have not vanished. They are especially useful when aligning text in columns. Computer programmers use monospaced fonts to increase the readability of source code.

Step-by-Step 10.3

1. Open a new blank document.
2. Click the **File** tab, and then click **Options.** In the left pane of the Word Options dialog box, click **Advanced**. Scroll down to the Save section shown in **Figure 10–3**.

FIGURE 10–3
Save options in the Advanced options for working with Word

Option to prompt before saving

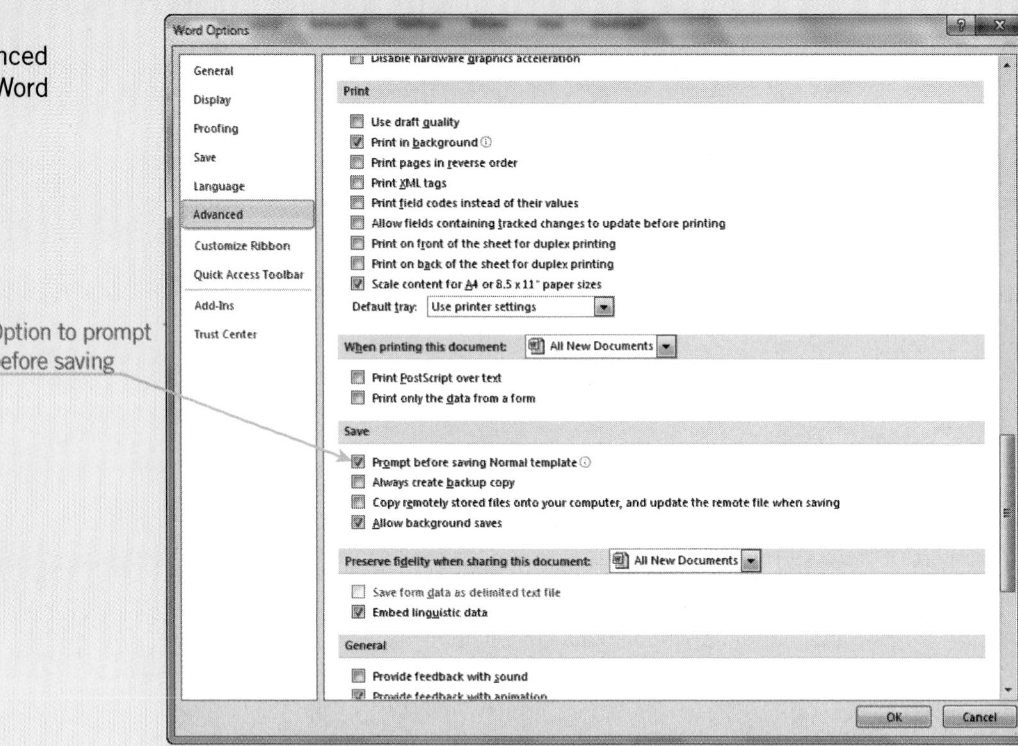

3. If necessary, enable the **Prompt before saving Normal template** option, and then click **OK**. Turning on this prompt will prevent you from accidentally saving changes to the Normal template, and Word will also prompt you to save changes to your personal template.
4. Click the **File** tab, and then click **Save As** to open the Save As dialog box. Navigate to the folder where you save your solution files.
5. In the File name box, type your first and last names, type **Template**, and then type your initials.
6. In the Save as type box, select **Word Template (*.dotx)**.
7. Click **Save**. Your personal template contains all the styles provided in the Normal template, and you can add additional styles to the template.
8. Close the template.

WARNING

If prompted to save changes to the global Normal template upon exiting Word, click No.

Attaching a Template and Making a Template Global

By default, Word attaches the Normal template to a new blank document. If you want to use styles or formats from a different template, you can attach additional templates to the document. When you attach a template to a document, it gives you access to the styles in the newly attached template. The styles in the attached template are only available to that one document.

You can make the template temporarily global to all open documents and all new documents that you create during the Word session. However, when you restart Word, the template will no longer be global. To make a template permanently global, you can store it in Word's startup folder, and then the template will be loaded as an add-in every time you start Word. Do not save any global templates on a classroom computer unless you have permission.

EXTRA FOR EXPERTS

If you move the document or template to a different folder or to a different computer, the attachment between the document and the template will be broken. The existing styles and formats in the document will not change, but unless you reattach the template or make the template global, you will not be able to apply additional formats and styles from the template.

Step-by-Step 10.4

1. Open the **Pharmacy** file from the drive and folder where your Data Files are stored. In the folder where you save your solution files, save the document as **Pharmacy 1**, followed by your initials.
2. Click the **File** tab, and then click **Options**. In the left pane in the Word Options dialog box, click **Add-Ins**. The Word Options screen opens with information and options for Add-ins, as shown in **Figure 10–4**.

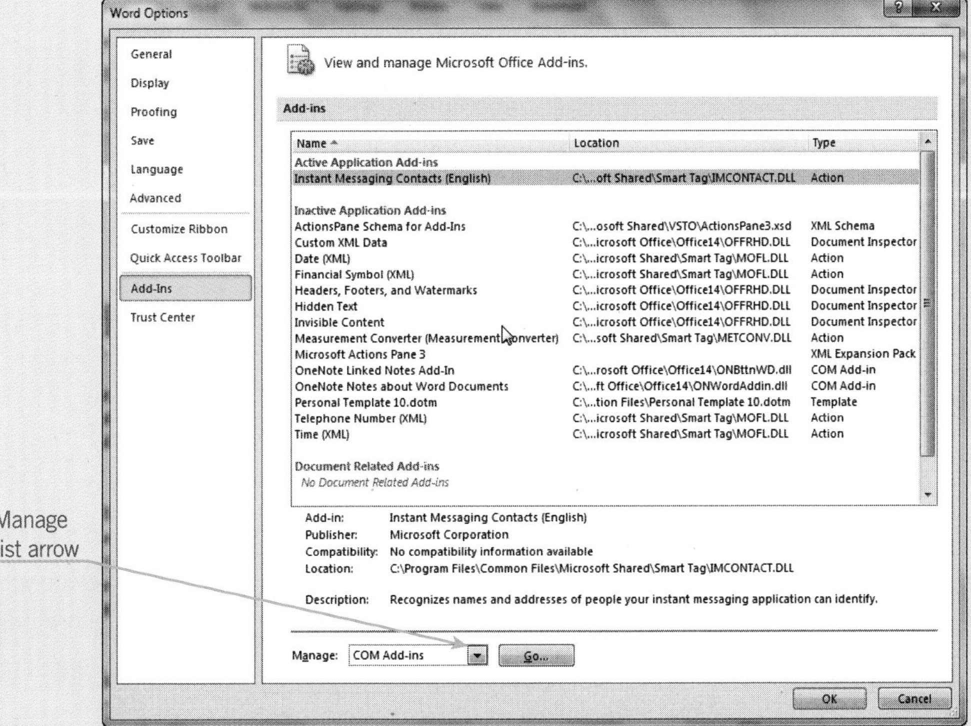

FIGURE 10–4 Information and options to manage Microsoft Office Add-ins

3. Click the **Manage** list arrow, click **Templates**, and then click **Go**. The Templates and Add-ins dialog box shown in **Figure 10–5** opens, and the Normal template name appears in the Document template box.

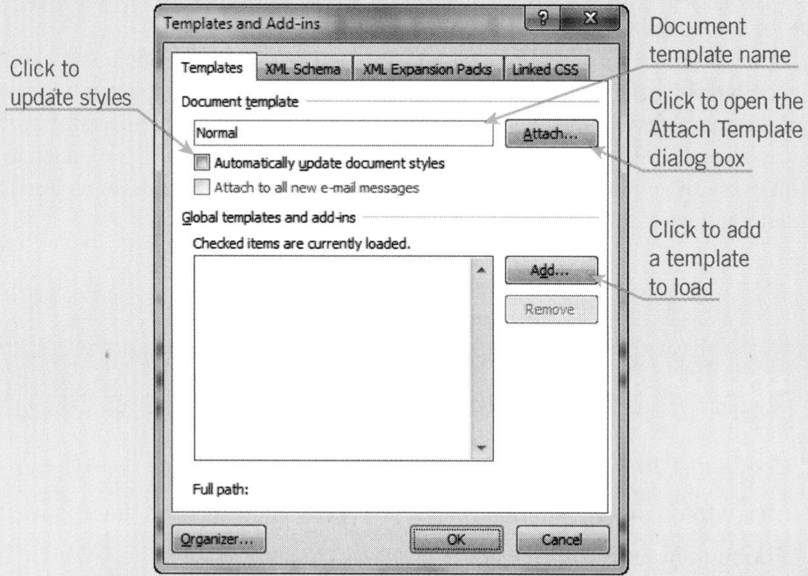

FIGURE 10–5
Templates and Add-ins dialog box

4. Click **Attach** to open the Attach Template dialog box shown in **Figure 10–6**. Your folders and filenames may differ.

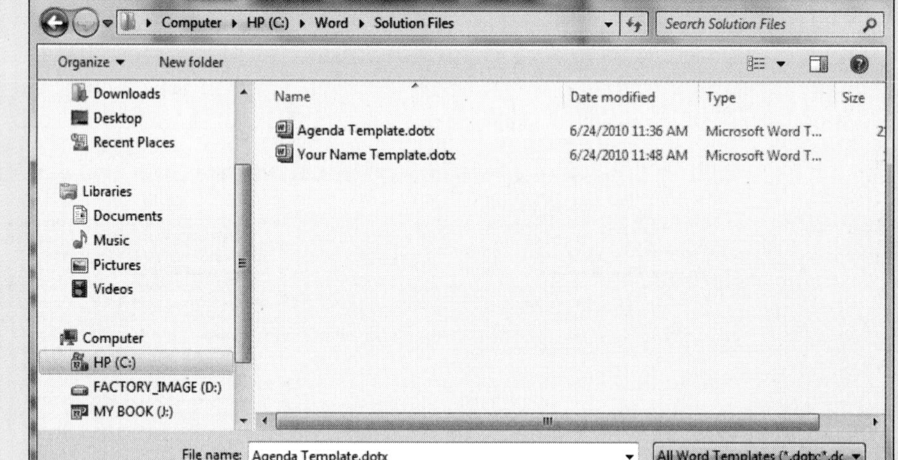

FIGURE 10–6
Attach Template dialog box

5. Navigate to the folder where you save your solution files. Select your personal template and then click **Open**. Now the name of your personal template will appear in the Document template box in the Templates and Add-ins dialog box.

6. Under Global templates and add-ins, click **Add**. Navigate to your solutions folder, select your personal template, and then click **OK**.
7. Under *Checked items are currently loaded*, your personal template now appears in the list. Make sure the check box next to your personal template file is enabled. Click **OK**.
8. Leave the document open for the next Step-by-Step.

Working with Styles

A ***style*** is a set of predefined formats you can apply to characters, paragraphs, tables, and numbered and bulleted lists. When you apply a style, you apply a whole group of formats in one simple step. For example, instead of taking multiple steps to change the font, font size, font color, and alignment for heading text, you can achieve the same results in one step by applying a title style. When a paragraph is moved or copied, the styles are moved or copied with the text and they do not need to be reapplied.

By applying styles to text, you can make sure that parts of your document, such as headings, are formatted consistently throughout the document. Styles are included in templates, and several styles are available in the Normal template. You can also create your own styles. When you save the styles in a template, they are available when the template is attached to a document. By saving styles in a template, you can ensure formatting consistency across multiple documents.

VOCABULARY
style

Applying and Changing the Formatting of Styles

To apply a new style, you must identify the text or content you want to format. When applying a paragraph format, you need only position the insertion point anywhere within the paragraph. However, when applying a character format, you must select all of the text to which you want to apply the style.

You can modify a style by changing one or more of the style formats. For example, after applying a heading style, you can select the text and change the font size. The other formats will remain unchanged. When you modify a style in a document, the changes are applied only to the current selected content, and the settings for the original style are not affected. When a paragraph is moved or copied within a document, the text retains the style.

When working with styles, you can open the Styles pane, which lists the styles available in the template that is attached to the document. An alternative to opening the Styles pane is to open the Apply Styles pane. The Apply Styles pane is smaller and shows only the current style, but you can scroll through all the available styles and apply, update, and modify them.

Step-by-Step 10.5

1. If necessary, open the **Pharmacy 1** document from your solution files.
2. On the Home tab, in the Styles group, click the **Dialog Box Launcher** to open the Styles pane shown in **Figure 10–7**.

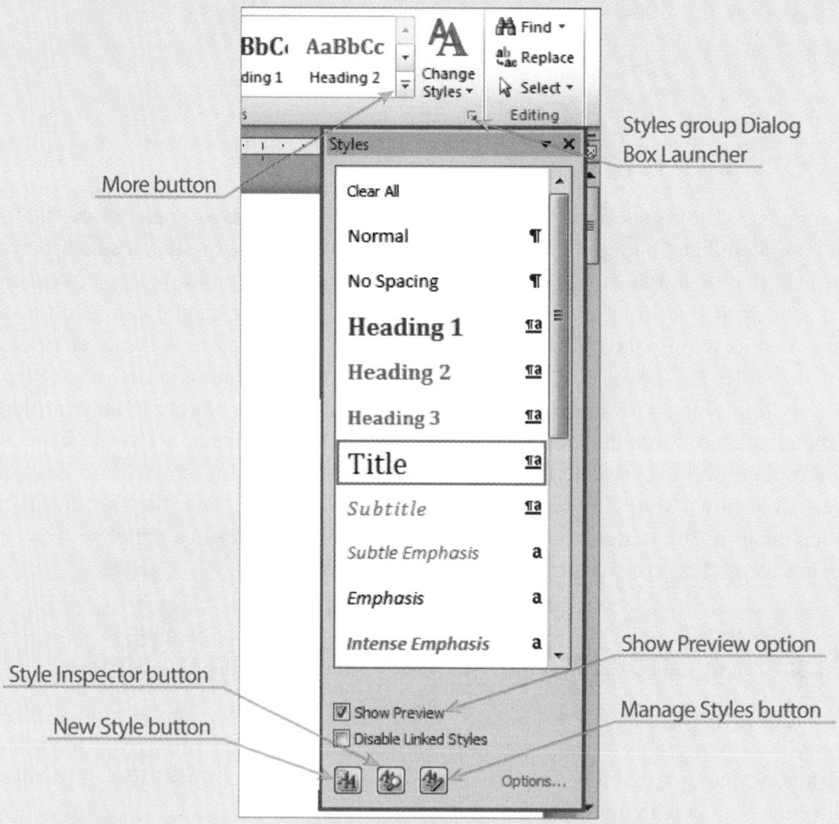

FIGURE 10–7
Styles pane

3. Note that the styles listed in the Styles pane are the same as the styles available in the Styles group on the Home tab. If necessary, enable the option **Show Preview** to see what the styles look like in the Styles pane.
4. If necessary, click anywhere within the title *Pharmacy*. Note that in the Styles pane (and also in the Styles gallery on the Ribbon), the style *Title* is selected, indicating that the style is applied.
5. Select the title text and change the font size to **24** point. Then, change the font color to a dark red or burgundy color. Change the paragraph alignment to **Center**.
6. Deselect the text, and then position the insertion point anywhere in the title *Pharmacy*. Reapply the Title style by clicking **Title** in the Styles pane. Even though you changed the formats where the style was applied in the document, the Title style settings were not changed.

7. Click the **More** button in the Styles group (see Figure 10–7), and then click **Apply Styles** to open the Apply Styles pane, shown in **Figure 10–8**. The style name Title appears in the Style Name box.

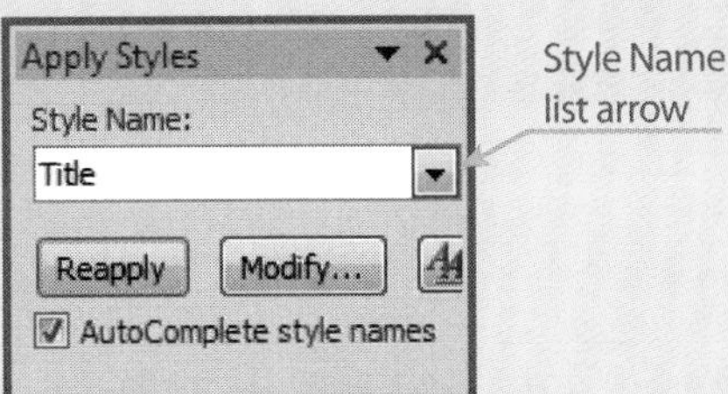

FIGURE 10–8
Apply Styles pane

8. Click the title bar of the Apply Styles pane and drag the pane to the left side of the document. You can reposition the pane anywhere on the screen. (If you drag the pane to the edge of the window, it will expand. Drag the pane back toward the center of the screen to reduce its size.)
9. Triple-click anywhere in the paragraph under the title *Pharmacy* to select the entire paragraph.
10. Click the **Style Name** list arrow in the Apply Styles pane. Scroll down and select the style **Intense Emphasis**. Because the style is a character format, it is applied to only the selected characters.
11. Click anywhere within the heading *Course of Study*. Apply the style **Heading 2**. The new style replaces the original style. Because the style contains both paragraph and character settings, all the formats were applied to the entire heading paragraph.
12. Save the changes and leave the document open for the next Step-by-Step.

Creating Styles Based on Formatted Text

You can create your own styles for characters, paragraphs, tables, and lists. You can quickly create a style based on formatted text. In this course, you will store the custom styles that you create in your personal template so that you do not alter the Normal template.

Step-by-Step 10.6

1. If necessary, open **Pharmacy 1** from your solution files. Save the document as **Pharmacy 2**, followed by your initials. Your personal template is already attached to the document, and if you did not close Word, the template is still temporarily global.
2. If necessary, open the **Styles** pane. (*Hint*: On the Home tab, in the Styles group, click the Dialog Box Launcher.) If necessary, open the **Apply Styles** pane. (*Hint*: On the Home tab, in the Styles group, click the More button.)

3. Select all the text in the document title. Change the font color to **Red, Accent 2**.
4. With the text still selected, at the bottom of the Styles pane, click the **New Style** button. The Create New Style from Formatting dialog box opens, as shown in **Figure 10–9**.

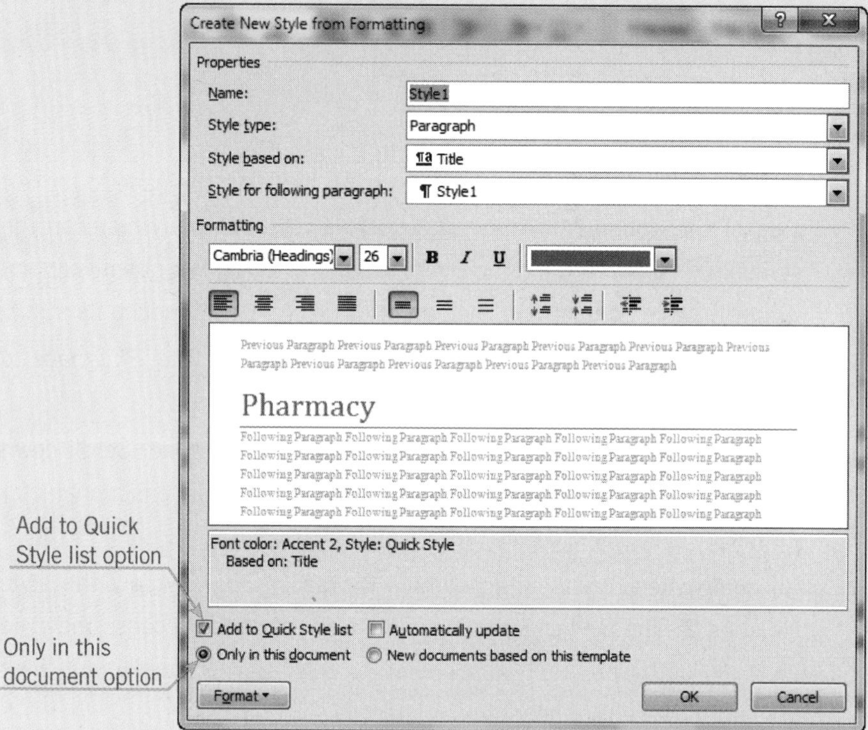

FIGURE 10–9
Create New Style from Formatting dialog box

5. In the Name box, replace *Style1* with **Title1**, followed by your initials.
6. Leave the Style type and Style based on settings as is. Make sure the options **Add to Quick Style list** and **Only in this document** are enabled.
7. Click **OK** to save the new style and close the dialog box. The new style appears in the Styles gallery on the Ribbon, in the Styles pane, and in the Apply Styles pane.
8. Close the Apply Styles pane.
9. Save the changes and leave the document open for the next Step-by-Step.

Creating Styles Using Commands and Existing Styles

You can also create a style using formatting commands, or you can base a style on an existing style. When you base a new style on an existing style, the new style inherits the characteristics of the existing style. This can save you a lot of time when creating a new style.

Step-by-Step 10.7

1. If necessary, open **Pharmacy 2** from your solution files. Save the document as **Pharmacy 3**, followed by your initials. If necessary, open the **Styles** pane.
2. Position the insertion point in the heading *Introduction*. Click the **New Style** button in the Styles pane to open the Create New Style from Formatting dialog box.
3. In the Name box, replace *Style1* with **Side Heading 1**, followed by your initials. In the Style type box, leave the setting *Paragraph* as is.
4. Click the **Style based on** list arrow, scroll to the top, and then click **(no style)**. This will allow you to create the style without using previous format settings.
5. In the Style for following paragraph box, select **Normal**. The paragraph immediately following this style will have the Normal character and paragraph formats.
6. Define the character and paragraph formats for the new style:
    a. Click **Format** in the lower-left corner of the dialog box, and then click **Font**. If necessary, click the **Font** tab.
    b. Change the font to **Calibri**, and change the point size to **16** point. Change the font color to **Dark Blue, Text 2, Darker 25%**, and then click **OK**.
    c. Click **Format** and then click **Paragraph**. If necessary, click the **Indents and Spacing** tab, and then under Spacing, set Before to **6 pt** and After to **6 pt**.
    d. Click **OK** twice to close both dialog boxes.
7. Using the Styles pane, apply your new **Side Heading 1** style to the headings *Education*, *Licenses*, *Opportunities*, *Benefits*, and *Conclusion*.
8 Position the insertion point anywhere in the heading *Course of Study*. Apply your new **Side Heading 1** style.
9. In the Styles pane, click the **New Style** button to open the Create New Style from Formatting dialog box. In the Name box, replace *Style 1* with **Side Heading 2**, followed by your initials.
10. In the Create New Style from Formatting dialog box, leave the Style type and the Style based on settings as is. You will create the new style settings based on the Side Heading 1 style you just created.
11. In the Formatting section, change the font size to **14** point and also click the **Italic** button. Click **OK** to close the dialog box.

TIP

You must set capitalization options in the Font dialog box if you want them to be part of the style.

12. Using the Styles pane, apply your new **Side Heading 2** style to the headings *Internships, Residencies, and Fellowships* and *Skills.*
13. Save the changes and leave the document open for the next Step-by-Step.

Copying Styles from Other Templates or Documents

Styles can also be moved between templates and documents. You can show the styles for documents and templates in panes side by side, and then you can copy the styles from one pane to the other. You can copy styles from a document to a template, and from a template to a document. You can also copy styles between two templates or between two documents.

Step-by-Step 10.8

1. If necessary, open **Pharmacy 3** from your solution files. If necessary, open the **Styles** pane.
2. At the bottom of the Styles pane, click the **Manage Styles** button. The Manage Styles dialog box opens, as shown in **Figure 10–10**.

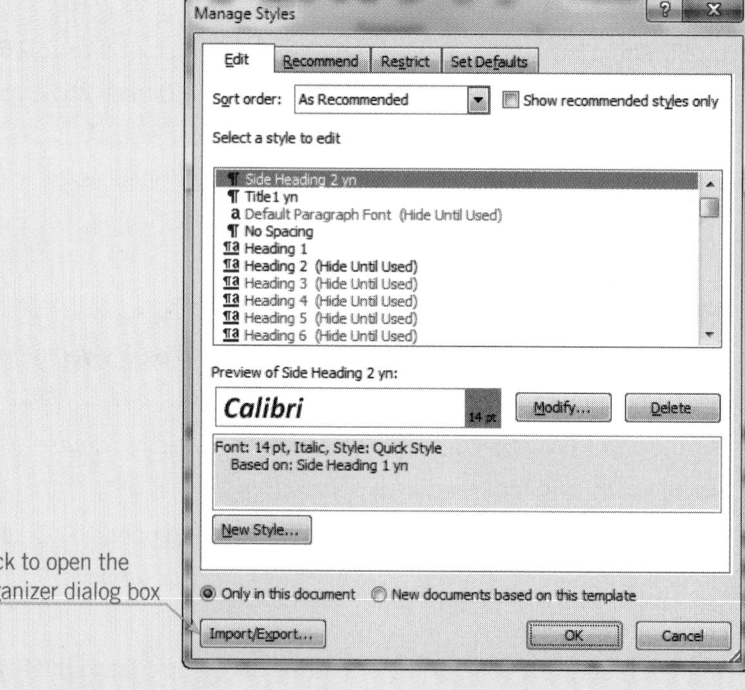

FIGURE 10–10
Manage Styles dialog box

3. Click **Import/Export** to open the Organizer dialog box shown in **Figure 10–11**. Note that the styles in the Normal template appear on the right, and your new styles are not available in the Normal template. However, if you scroll down through the list on the left, you will see that your new styles are stored in the document.

TIP

You can also access the Organizer dialog box by clicking Organizer in the Templates and Add-ins dialog box.

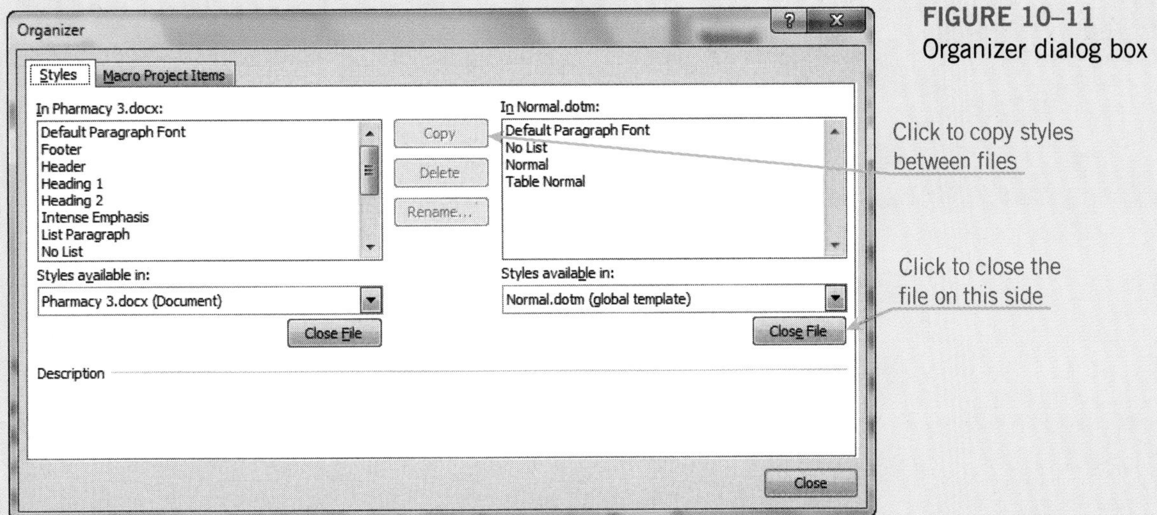

FIGURE 10–11
Organizer dialog box

4. On the right, under the Styles available in box for the Normal.dotm template, click **Close File**. The list of Normal template styles is removed from the pane.
5. Click **Open File**. In the navigation pane of the Open dialog box, navigate to the folder where you save your solution files, select your personal template, and then click **Open**. The styles available in your personal template now appear on the right.
6. In the Pharmacy 3.docx style list on the left, click your new style **Side Heading 1** (followed by your initials). Then click **Copy** to copy the style to your personal template.
7. Scroll down to show the remainder of the style list for Pharmacy 3.docx. Select your new **Side Heading 2** (followed by your initials). Hold down **Ctrl** and then click your new style **Title1** (followed by your initials). Click **Copy** to copy both styles to your personal template.
8. Click **Close** to close the dialog box. Now when you attach your personal template to a document, these three new styles will be available.
9. Leave the document open for the next Step-by-Step. (If you close the document, you will be prompted to save the changes to your personal template. Click Save.)

Editing and Deleting Styles

After you create a style, you can easily modify it. You can change the style name and/or the formatting options. You can also remove styles from a template.

Step-by-Step 10.9

1. If necessary, open **Pharmacy 3** from your solution files. Save the document as **Pharmacy 4**, followed by your initials. Click Yes if prompted to save changes to the document template. If necessary, open the **Styles** pane.
2. Position the insertion point in the title *Pharmacy*. In the Styles pane, point to the style name **Title1** (followed by your initials) and then click the **list arrow** that appears next to the style name. In the menu that opens, click **Modify** to open the Modify Style dialog box shown in **Figure 10–12**.

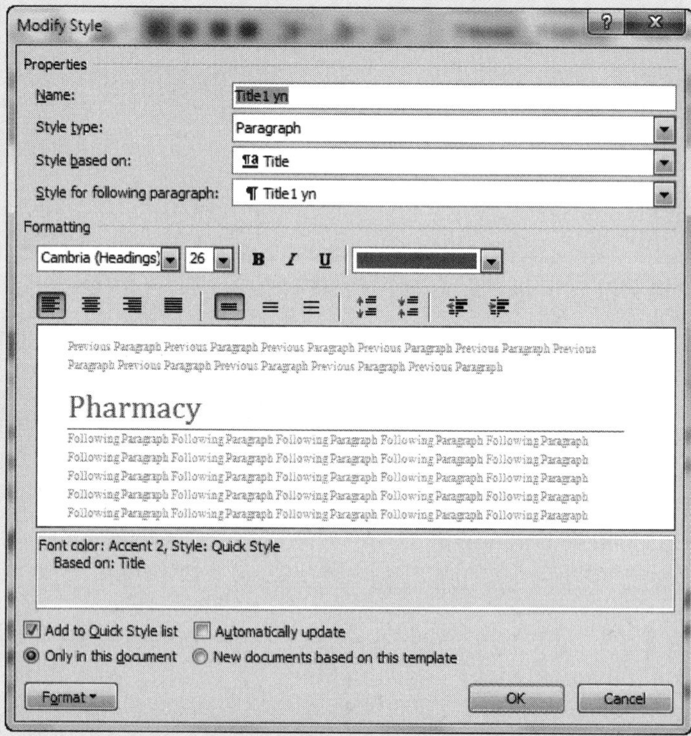

FIGURE 10–12
Modify Style dialog box

3. In the lower-left corner of the dialog box, click **Format** and then click **Font**. In the Font dialog box, under Effects, enable the **All caps** option. Click **OK** to close the Font dialog box.
4. In the Name box of the Modify Style dialog box, change the style name to **Title2**, followed by your initials, and then click **OK**. All the characters in the title are now formatted in all caps.
5. In the Styles pane, click the **Manage Styles** button to open the Manage Styles dialog box. Click **Import/Export** to open the Organizer dialog box. On the right side, click **Close File** to close the Normal global template. Then click **Open File** and navigate to and select your personal template file. Click **Open**.

6. In the Pharmacy 4 document styles list on the left, scroll down and select your new style **Title2** (followed by your initials). Click **Copy** to save the style to your personal template.
7. You can also easily delete styles from a template. In the list of styles on the right, select the **Title2** style. Click **Delete**. When prompted to delete the style, click **Yes**. Deleting the style from the template does not affect the style stored in the document. Close the Organizer dialog box.
8. Save the changes to the document, and if prompted to save changes to the document template, click Yes. Leave the document open for the next Step-by-Step.

Revealing and Clearing Formats

A ***style sheet*** is a list of all styles that are used in a document or available in a template. Style sheets are automatically saved with each Word document. Therefore, if you open the document on a different computer, the style sheet is automatically loaded and the styles you applied are still available.

Many people prefer to show the descriptions of the styles and formats as they work with documents. The Style Inspector pane shows the currently applied paragraph- and text-level formatting, and it offers options for creating a new style or modifying the currently applied style. For more detail, you can open the Reveal Formatting pane to show paragraph settings including alignment, indentation, spacing, and tabs. This enables the user to verify the existing formats and quickly edit the formats if desired.

You can easily remove some or all styles from formatted content and restore the content to the Normal document style by using the Clear All option on the Styles pane or the Style Inspector pane.

VOCABULARY
style sheet

EXTRA FOR EXPERTS

To print a list of all the styles used in a document (including a description of each style), click the File tab and then click Print. Under Settings, click Print All Pages. Under Document Properties, click Styles, and then click the Print button at the top of the center pane.

Step-by-Step 10.10

1. If necessary, open **Pharmacy 4** from your solution files. If necessary, open the **Styles** pane.
2. Position the insertion point in the title. Click the **Style Inspector** button at the bottom of the Styles pane. The Style Inspector pane opens and displays the styles for the current paragraph, as shown in **Figure 10–13**.

FIGURE 10–13
Style Inspector pane

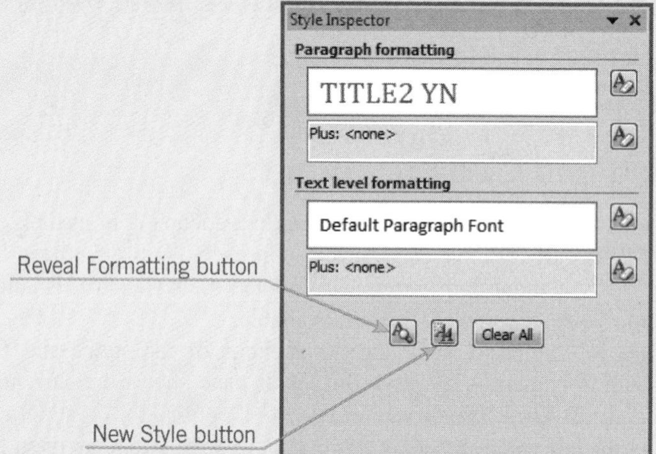

3. Click the title bar in the Style Inspector pane and drag the pane to position it away from where you are working in the document window. Position the mouse pointer over the buttons in the pane to view the ScreenTip and see the options available.
4. Position the insertion point in the first paragraph below the title. Note that the information in the Style Inspector pane changes.
5. Click the **Reveal Formatting** button at the bottom of the Style Inspector pane. A new pane similar to the one shown in **Figure 10–14** opens in the upper-right corner of the document window. (You may have to move or close the Styles pane to see the Reveal Formatting pane.)

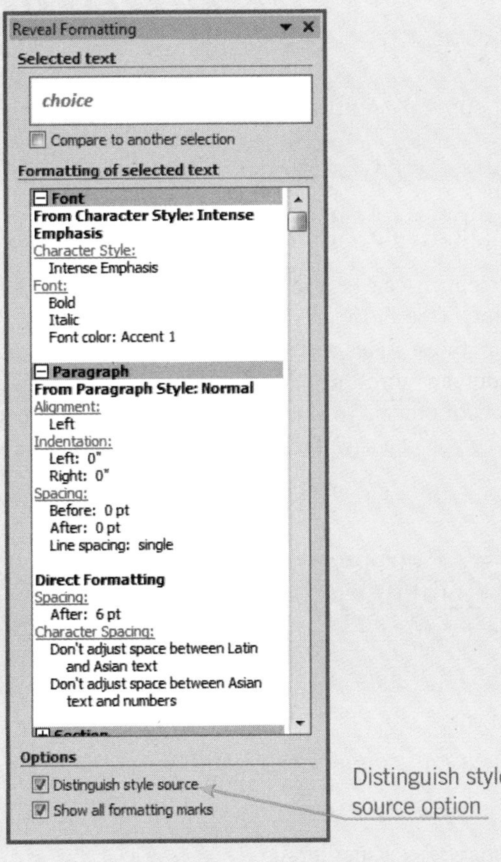

FIGURE 10–14
Reveal Formatting pane

6. In the Reveal Formatting pane, under Options, enable the **Distinguish style source** option. Notice that the pane now shows information about the source of the style, and you can determine whether the style is based on another style source.
7. Close the Reveal Formatting pane.
8. Click anywhere in the title. In the Style Inspector pane, click **Clear All**. The paragraph and character formats are removed, and the paragraph is now formatted with the default Normal style.
9. Click the **Undo** button to restore all the paragraph and character formats. Close the Style Inspector pane. If necessary, show the **Styles** pane.
10. Select any word in the first paragraph below the title. In the Styles pane, scroll to the top of the list of styles and click **Clear All**. Only the current word is affected because the Intense Emphasis style that is applied to this paragraph is a character style. To remove the style from the entire paragraph, you would need to first select the entire paragraph.
11. Click the **Undo** button to restore the character formats.
12. In the document window, select the entire document. In the Styles pane, click **Clear All** in the task pane. All the style formats are removed, and the entire document is formatted with the Normal style.

TIP

To quickly remove styles, select the text and then press the shortcut key combination Ctrl+Shift+N.

13. Click the **Undo** button to restore all the styles in the document. Close the Styles pane.
14. Close the document and the application without saving any changes.

Using a Template to Share Building Blocks

In a team environment, it can be useful for everyone to use the same styles and settings in documents. One of the advantages of using templates is that it makes it easy for you to share those styles and settings. For example, if you create your own building blocks, you can store them in your personal template, and then you can share the template with others. To share the template, you can distribute the file to all team members, or you can save the file in a central location, such as on a shared network drive.

Step-by-Step 10.11

1. Launch Word and then open the **Quick Parts** file from the drive and folder where your Data Files are stored. Note that the document contains boilerplate text and graphics that can be used in future documents.
2. Since this is a new Word session, you need to attach your personal template and make sure it is global.
   a. Click the **File** tab, click **Options**, and then, in the Word Options dialog box, click **Add-Ins**.
   b. Click the **Manage** list arrow, click **Templates**, and then click **Go**.
   c. Click **Attach**, open your solutions folder and select your personal template, and then click **Open**.
   d. If necessary, under Global templates and add-ins, add your personal template to the list. Make sure there is a check mark to the left of the filename, and then click **OK**.
3. Triple-click in the first paragraph to select the entire paragraph.
4. Click the **Insert** tab. In the Text group, click the **Quick Parts** button, and then click **Save Selection to Quick Part Gallery**. The Create New Building Block dialog box opens, similar to the one shown in **Figure 10–15**.

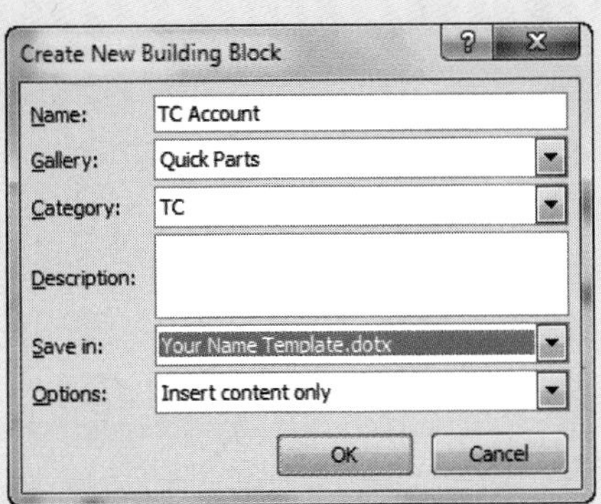

FIGURE 10–15
Create New Building Block dialog box

5. In the Name box, type **TC Account**. Leave the Gallery setting as *Quick Parts*.
6. Click the **Category** list arrow and then click **Create New Category**. In the Create New Category dialog box, type **TC**. Click **OK**.
7. Click the **Save in** list arrow and select your personal template. When the options in your dialog box match those in Figure 10–15, click **OK** to save the building block to your personal template.
8. Click anywhere on the company logo to select it. Click the **Quick Parts** button and then click **Save Selection to Quick Part Gallery**.
9. In the Name box, type **TC Logo**. Click the **Category** list arrow and then select **TC**.
10. Click the **Save in** list arrow and then click your personal template. Then, click **OK**.
11. Close the document, but do not close Word. When prompted to save the changes to the document, click **Don't Save**. Then when prompted to save changes to your personal template, click **Save**.
12. Open a new blank document. Click the **Insert** tab. In the Text group, click the **Quick Parts** button. You should see the two new building blocks you created and stored in the TC category. Scroll down if necessary.
13. Click the **TC Logo** building block to insert it in the document.
14. Close the document without saving the changes, and then close Word.

TIP

If you do not see the building blocks you just created, your personal template may not be global. Repeat Step 2 above.

SUMMARY

In this lesson, you learned:

- You can create a customized document template by opening a blank document or by modifying an existing document or an existing template.
- When you attach a template to a document, you have access to the styles and building blocks stored in the template. When you make a template temporarily global to all open documents, the template is available to all new documents you work with during that Word session.
- Word's Normal template provides many styles, but you can create your own styles. Using styles helps you format documents consistently.
- You can change document formats by applying new styles. When you override style formats in a document, the changes apply only to the selected content, but the original style settings are unaffected.
- Styles can be copied from documents to templates, and vice versa.
- Revealing formats enables you to view them as you work with a document. You can see the style information in the Style Inspector pane. More details about the style settings are provided in the Reveal Formatting pane.
- The Clear All option on the Styles pane and the Style Inspector pane enables you to remove applied styles quickly and restore the document text to the Normal style.
- Templates make it easy for you to share styles and building blocks with others.

VOCABULARY REVIEW

Define the following terms:

boilerplate text
document template
global template
Normal template
style
style sheet
template

REVIEW QUESTIONS

TRUE / FALSE

Circle T if the statement is true or F if the statement is false.

T F **1.** If the Normal template is deleted, Word will automatically create a new template using the factory defaults.

T F **2.** A style can contain both paragraph and character formats.

T F **3.** You must save all template files in the Microsoft Word Templates folder.

T F **4.** When a paragraph is moved or copied, you must reapply the style.

T F **5.** When you clear a style in a document, the text is formatted with the Normal style.

FILL IN THE BLANK

Complete the following sentences by writing the correct word or words in the blanks provided.

1. A(n) ________________ is a set of predefined formats you can apply to characters, paragraphs, tables, and numbered and bulleted lists.
2. The ________________ is Word's default global template.
3. Standard text that is reusable in various documents is referred to as ________________.
4. A(n) ________________ is a file that affects the basic structure of a document and contains document settings.
5. A(n) ________________ is a list of all styles that are used in a document or available in a template.

WRITTEN QUESTIONS

Write a brief answer to the following questions.

1. List ten examples of document templates that Word provides.

2. Describe how to change the Word settings so that you do not accidently save changes to the Normal template.

3. Describe how to attach a template to a document.

4. Describe how to make a template global.

5. Describe how to copy styles from a document to a template file.

PROJECTS

If you have a SAM 2010 user profile, your instructor may have assigned an autogradable version of the indicated project. If so, log into the SAM 2010 Web site at *www.cengage.com/sam2010* to download the instruction and start files.

PROJECT 10–1

1. Launch Word and open the **Certificate** file from the drive and folder where your Data Files are stored.
2. Save the document as a template in your solutions folder. Name the template **Certificate Template**, followed by your initials.
3. Remove the variable text from the template:
   a. Select the name *Elizabeth H. Kasper* and type **Name**.
   b. Select *25* and type **XX**.
4. Leave the rest of the boilerplate text. Save the changes and close the template file.
5. Open a new document based on the new certificate template you just created. Save the document to your solutions folder as **Weber Certificate**, followed by your initials.
6. Enter the variable data:
   a. Replace *Name* with **Alexander E. Weber**.
   b. Replace *XX* with **30**.
7. Save the changes and close the document.

SAM PROJECT 10–2

1. Open the **Flyer** file from the drive and folder where your Data Files are stored. Save the document as **Final Flyer**, followed by your initials.
2. Position the insertion point in the paragraph that begins *Hours*. Create a new style by defining the formats:
   a. Name the style Hours.
   b. Set the style type for Paragraph, and base the style on no other style.
   c. Set the style format for the following paragraph to the Normal style.
   d. Change the font style to Georgia, change the font size to 14 point, and change the font effects to Small caps.
   e. Apply the style only in the current document.
3. Select the text *WINTER INVITE*. Change the font color to a dark red to match the star in the logo.
4. With *WINTER INVITE* still selected, create a new style using the existing formats:
   a. Name the style Action Heading.
   b. Format the style type setting for Character.
   c. Save the style only in the current document. Do not add the new style to the Quick Style list.
5. In the Styles pane, click the Manage Styles button. Click Import/Export to open the Organizer dialog box. Then open your personal template file in the right pane.
6. Copy the two new styles (*Action Heading* and *Hours*) from the Final Flyer document to your personal template. Save the changes to your personal template.
7. Save the changes and close the document.
8. Open **Events** from the Data Files and save the document as **Final Events**, followed by your initials.
9. Attach your personal template to the document, and make the template global. Also enable the option to automatically update document styles.
10. Apply the Action Heading style to the text *UPCOMING EVENTS*.
11. Format the list of upcoming events with a 1/2" left indent.
12. Save the changes and close the document.

PROJECT 10–3

1. Open the **Waste** file from the drive and folder where your Data Files are stored. Save the document as **Final Waste**, followed by your initials.
2. Open the Styles pane and clear all the styles in the title and the headings.
3. Select the title text and apply the Title style.
4. From the Styles pane, open the Modify Style dialog box to modify the Title style. With the title text still selected, increase the font size to 16 point and change the font style to Georgia. Also, change the font color to Olive green, Accent 3, Darker 50%.
5. Apply the Subtitle style to the first heading *REDUCE WASTE.*
6. From the Styles pane, open the Modify Styles dialog box to modify the Subtitle style. Change the font color to Olive green, Accent 3, Darker 50%, and add the bold format.
7. Use the Styles pane to apply the modified Subtitle style to the remaining headings in the document: *CONVERT WASTE*, *RECYCLE IN BUSINESS*, *RECYCLE ALUMINUM*, and *RECYCLE PLASTICS*.
8. Save the changes and close the document.

PROJECT 10–4

1. Open the **LCCU Building Blocks** file from the drive and folder where your Data Files are stored.
2. If necessary, make your personal template file global. Also, check the Word settings to make sure that you will be prompted before any changes are made to the Normal template.
3. Select the first paragraph and save the text in the Quick Parts gallery:
   a. Name the building block Privacy.
   b. Leave the Gallery setting as Quick Parts.
   c. Create a new category LCCU and save the building block in the new category.
   d. Save the new building block in your personal template.
4. Select the second paragraph and save the text as a building block in the Quick Parts gallery. Name the building block Cards, and save it to the Quick Parts gallery in the LCCU category. Be sure to save the building block in your personal template.
5. Select the third paragraph and save the text as a building block in the Quick Parts gallery. Name the building block Report, and save it to the Quick Parts gallery in the LCCU category. Be sure to save the building block in your personal template.
6. Close the LCCU Building Blocks document, without saving any changes. If prompted to save the changes to your personal template, click **Save**.
7. Open the file **Credit Letter** from the Data Files. Save the document as **Updated Credit Letter**, followed by your initials.
8. Position the insertion point in front of the second paragraph in the body of the letter. Insert the building block **Cards**.
9. Position the insertion point at the end of the letter. First insert the building block Privacy. Press Enter, and then insert the building block Report.
10. Correct any spacing issues between paragraphs.
11. Save the changes and close the document. (If you close Word, click **Save** when prompted to save the changes to your personal template.)

CRITICAL THINKING

ACTIVITY 10–1

One of the installed templates provided in Word 2010 is the Blog post template. To learn more about creating a blog post in Word, go to the Microsoft Web site and search the keywords *blogging with Word*. After you have explored Word's blogging features, open a new Word document and write a brief summary describing the advantages of using the Blog post template. Also, comment on whether you feel the Blog post template will be useful to you now or in the future. Cite the sources of your information by including the URLs for the Web pages where you found the most useful information.

ACTIVITY 10–2

If you are sharing files with users who have older versions of Word software, you can save a Word .docx file as a Word 97–2003 document (with a .doc extension). When converting documents to the older format, you often lose some of the features. For example, some formats and graphics become static and you are unable to edit them. Search the Help screens and gather information about whether styles can be successfully converted to the older version and whether or not you can open Word 2010 templates using 97–2003 versions of Word. Write a brief summary of your findings.

Estimated Time: 2 hours

LESSON 11

Customizing Tables and Creating Charts

OBJECTIVES

Upon completion of this lesson, you should be able to:

- Rearrange the rows and columns in a table.
- Sort table data.
- Adjust column and row spacing, modify table styles, and split a table.
- Draw a table and split table cells.
- Change text alignment in table cells and align a table.
- Calculate sums and create other formulas in a table.
- Embed worksheet data into, or link worksheet data to, a Word document.
- Create and modify a chart.

VOCABULARY

caption

destination file

embedded object

gridlines

import

linked object

source file

Tables are very effective for organizing and presenting data. Word offers some powerful features to help you customize the table layout and design. And to illustrate data, you can quickly and easily create charts.

Rearranging Table Contents

After a table is created, you often need to rearrange the contents. You can move, copy, and paste the contents in a table the same way you move, copy, and paste text in a document.

Step-by-Step 11.1

1. Launch Word and then open the **Accounts Receivable** file from the drive and folder where your Data Files are stored. Save the document as **Balances Due 1**, followed by your initials.
2. Position the mouse pointer above the column heading *Balance Due*. When the pointer changes to a down arrow, click to select all cells in the column. Then click the **Cut** button (or press **Ctrl+X**). Position the insertion point anywhere in the heading *Date Due* above the first column. Click the **Paste** button (or press **Ctrl+V**). The *Balance Due* column is inserted to the left of the *Date Due* column.
3. Select the *Balance Due* column and then drag the mouse to the left to select the *Date Due* column. Then drag the selected columns to the right until the mouse pointer is positioned anywhere in the *Customer* heading cell, then release the mouse button to drop the two selected columns to the right of the *Customer* column.
4. In the middle of the table, select the three rows that show a due date of *12-15*. Position the insertion point to the left of the *R. Johnson* row. When the pointer changes to a right-pointing arrow, click to select all the cells in the row and then drag the pointer down to include the *W. Diaz* and *C. Featherhold* rows.
5. Click the **Table Tools Layout** tab. In the Rows & Columns group, click the **Insert Below** button. Three new rows are inserted below the selected rows.
6. Enter the following new data in the *Customer* and the *Balance Due* columns.

   Jonathon Latham 15,678.11

   Caroline Johnson 10,009.85

   Wendy Evans 12,433.66
7. Select the **12-14** due date in the third column, just below the new table rows. Copy the content to the Clipboard, and then click each of the empty cells in the *Date Due* column and paste the due date in each of those cells.

WARNING

If you select a range of cells by dragging across the cells (instead of selecting the entire row by clicking to the left of the first cell in the row), when you paste the selected data in another cell range, it will replace the existing data. So, be sure you select the entire row when you want to move data.

8. Select the bottom row (W. Grisham) and then cut the row to the Clipboard. Position the insertion point anywhere in the *Abby Johnson* cell just below the *Customer* heading, and then paste the row. The entire *W. Grisham* row is moved to a new position above the row where the insertion point is positioned.
9. Select the last two rows in the table (E. Diaz and A. Perez). With the rows selected, position the mouse pointer over the first selected cell. Press **Esc** to hide the Mini toolbar, and then drag the selected rows to the top of the table. When the insertion point is positioned anywhere in the *Jessi Smith* cell near the top of the *Customer* column, release the mouse button to drop the selected rows in the new position. The two rows are inserted above the *Jessi Smith* row.
10. Save the changes and leave the document open for the next Step-by-Step.

TIP

If you dropped the rows in the wrong location, click the Undo button and try the move again.

Sorting Table Contents

To reorder the contents of a table, you can use the Sort feature. You can choose to sort a single column without rearranging the data for the remaining columns, or you can sort all the data based on a specified column. Sorts can be based on as many as three criteria in multiple columns. Furthermore, you can sort by multiple words contained within a single table column. For example, if the column contains both first and last names, you can sort by either the last name or the first name.

Step-by-Step 11.2

1. If necessary, open the **Balances Due 1** file from your solution files. Save the document as **Balances Due 2**, followed by your initials.
2. To sort only the data in the first column of the table:
   a. Select the first column in the table. Note that the first data row shows the customer *Weston Grisham*. The account balance is *2,802.11* and the due date is *12-04*.

b. Click the **Home** tab, and in the Paragraph group, click the **Sort** button to open the dialog box shown in **Figure 11–1**. Your dialog box settings will be different.

FIGURE 11–1
Sort dialog box

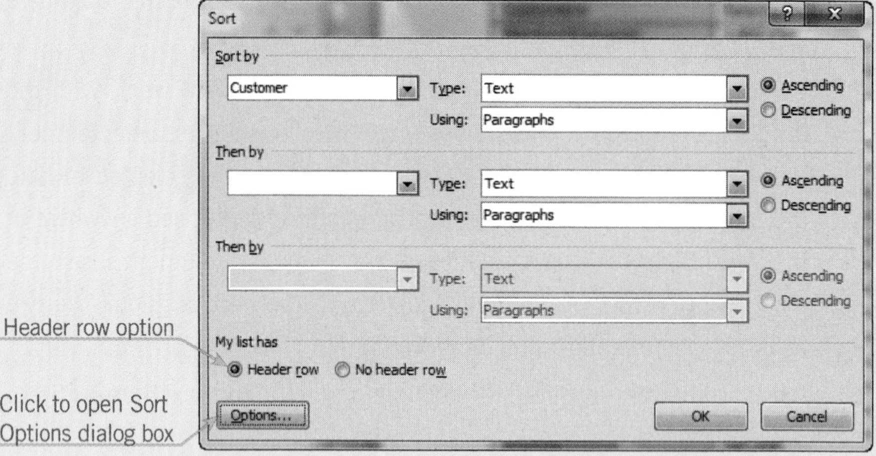

c. Under My list has, enable the **Header row** option. When this option is enabled, Word does not include the table column headings in the sort. Make sure your settings match those in Figure 11–1.

d. Click **Options** to open the Sort Options dialog box shown in **Figure 11–2**.

FIGURE 11–2
Sort Options dialog box

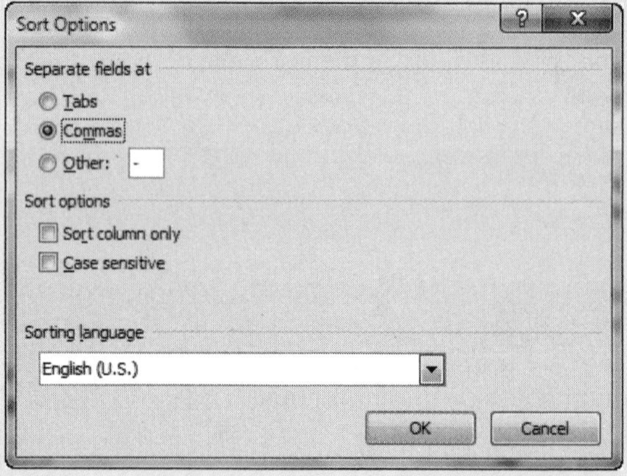

EXTRA FOR EXPERTS

When turned on, the Case sensitive option sorts text so words beginning with the same letter are arranged so that lowercase letters appear before uppercase letters.

e. Under Sort options, enable the **Sort column only** option, and then click **OK**.

f. Click **OK** in the Sort dialog box. The first column data is sorted in alphabetical order by first name, but the data in the other two columns did not sort.

3. Because the data is no longer accurate, click the **Undo** button to undo the sort.

4. To sort by multiple words within a single column:

   a. Click anywhere in the table to deselect the first column. Then, drag the mouse pointer over all the cells with customer names to select those cells. (Do not select the column heading *Customer*.)

b. Click the **Sort** button. Under My list has, make sure the **No header row** option is enabled. If necessary, in the Sort by box, select **Column 1**, and in the first Type box, select **Text**. Also, make sure the **Ascending** option is enabled.

c. Click the **Options** button. In the Sort Options dialog box, under Separate fields at, enable the **Other** option.

d. Click and drag the mouse pointer across the **Other** text box to select the contents (even if the box appears blank). If any content is in the text box from a previous sort, such as a blank space or a hyphen, the content will be highlighted in blue. Press the **spacebar** to enter a blank space.

e. Under Sort options, disable the **Sort column only** option. This will ensure that all the data in a row will stay together. Then click **OK**.

f. In the Sort dialog box, click the **list arrow** to the right of the first Using box, and then click **Word 2**, as shown in **Figure 11–3**.

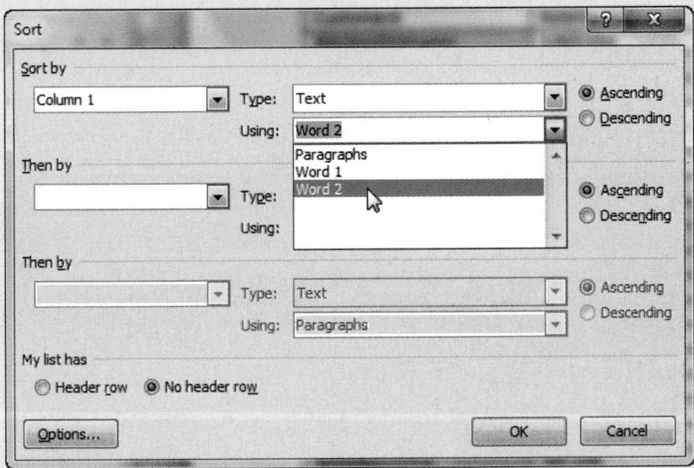

FIGURE 11–3
Using options in the Sort dialog box

g. Under the first Then by, select **Column 1**, and for the Using box, click **Word 1**. Click **OK**. The table content is sorted first based on the second word (or last name) in the first column. Then the content is sorted by the first word in the first column, and all the data remains intact.

5. To sort the table content based on criteria from multiple columns:

   a. Click anywhere in the table to deselect the table cells. Then click the **Sort** button.

   b. Under My list has, enable the **Header row** option.

   c. Under Sort by, select **Date Due**. The Type setting will automatically change to *Date*. To the right of the Type setting, make sure the **Ascending** option is enabled.

   d. Under the first Then by, click **Balance Due**. The Type setting will automatically change to *Number*. To the right of the Type setting, enable the **Descending** option.

e. Click **OK**. The rows are rearranged, first by the due date and then by the balance due. For accounts with the same due dates, the account with the highest balance due appears first in the order.

6. Click anywhere inside the table to deselect the rows.
7. Save the changes and leave the document open for the next Step-by-Step.

Modifying Table Structure and Formats

Word offers some powerful features to help you customize the layout and design for your tables. Not only can the layout and design make a table look professional, but using the right layout and design can also make the table easier to read.

Adjusting Column and Row Spacing

Generally, when you need to adjust the width of a column, you can simply drag a column border. But Word offers several other ways for you to automatically control column width. In certain instances, you may want rows or columns to be spaced evenly throughout the table. In the following steps, you will experiment with features that give you more control over column and row spacing.

Step-by-Step 11.3

1. If necessary, open the **Balances Due 2** file from your solution files. Save the document as **Past Due Accounts 1**, followed by your initials. If the ruler is not displayed above your document, click the View tab and in the Show group, select Ruler.
2. Select the **Customer** column. On the left side of the Ruler, click the **tab selector** until the Left Tab icon displays. Then click 1/4-inch to the right of the margin on the Ruler to set a left-aligned tab stop, as shown in **Figure 11–4**.

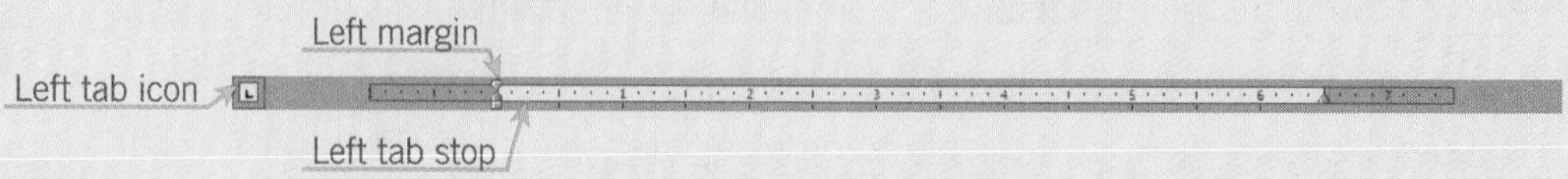

FIGURE 11–4 Left-aligned tab stop on the Ruler

3. Position the insertion point after *Emanuel Diaz* in the second row. Press **Enter** to create a second line in the cell. Then hold down **Ctrl** and press **Tab** to create a paragraph indent inside the cell. Then type the company name **A-1 Construction**.

4. Repeat Step 4 to add company names below the following customer names. The text will automatically wrap as needed to fit within the cell.

   Weston Grisham **Grisham Construction**

   Abby Johnson **ADCO Foundations**

   Jonathon Latham **Latham-Guenther Developers**

   Robert Johnson **R & S Builders**

5. Position the mouse pointer over the right border for the *Customer* column. When the pointer changes to a horizontal double-headed arrow, hold down the **Alt** key and drag the right column border. As you drag the column border, the column size displays on the horizontal ruler just below the Ribbon. Set the column width at **2.16"**.

6. Select the first row. Position the mouse pointer over the bottom border of the first row. When the pointer changes to a vertical double-headed arrow, hold down the **Alt** key and drag the border down to increase the height of the row. As you drag the row border, the row height displays on the vertical ruler at the left side of the document window. Set the row height to **0.5"**.

7. Select the second, third, and fourth rows (E. Diaz, S. Smith, and S. Diaz) in the table. Click the **Table Tools Layout** tab. In the Cell Size group, click the **Distribute Rows** button. The height for all the selected rows is adjusted so that they are the same height.

8. Select all the rows in the table except for the first row, and then click the **Distribute Rows** button to evenly adjust the height of all the rows in the table except the first row.

9. Select all three columns in the table. In the Cell Size group, click the **Distribute Columns** button. The width of the table remains the same, but the column widths are automatically adjusted to equal width.

10. Position the insertion point anywhere within the table. In the Cell Size group, click the **AutoFit** button, and then click **AutoFit Contents**. The column widths adjust to the longest line in each column.

11. Select the *Date Due* column. In the Rows & Columns group, click the **Insert Right** button. Click in the first row of the new column and type **Late Fee**. The width of the new column automatically adjusts to show all of the new text.

12. With the insertion point anywhere within the table, click the **AutoFit** button and then click **AutoFit Window**. The widths of the columns widen, and the table fills the document window and extends from the left margin to the right margin. This is the default setting that is applied when you first create a table in a document. Click the **Undo** list arrow and then click **Insert Column Right** to switch the table to its previous size and remove the new column.

TIP

You can double-click the right border of a column to resize a column quickly to accommodate the longest entry in the column. In some tables, however, you may have to narrow one or more columns before you can double-click to widen another.

13. Position the insertion point anywhere in the table. Click the **AutoFit** button, and then click **Fixed Column Width**. You will not see any changes in the column widths. Position the insertion point in the *Date Due* column, and then insert a new column to the right. The new column is the exact same width as the *Date Due* column. Type the heading **Late Fee**.
14. Save the changes and leave the document open for the next Step-by-Step.

Modifying Table Styles and Creating a New Table Style

In most cases, the default ½-point single-line border will be appropriate for the tables you create. However, sometimes you might want to customize the border and add shading to some or all of the table cells to make the content easier to read. Word offers many built-in table styles that are already formatted with borders, shading, and color. The six table style options are described in **Table 11–1**. You can easily toggle these style options on and off.

TABLE 11–1 Descriptions of table style options

OPTION	RESULT
Header Row	The first row is given special formatting, which is good for highlighting the column headings.
Total Row	The last row is given special formatting.
Banded Rows	Odd rows are formatted differently than even rows; for example, all the even rows have shading, which makes it easier to read the table contents.
First Column	The first column is given special formatting.
Last Column	The last column is given special formatting.
Banded Columns	Odd and even columns are formatted differently.

VOCABULARY
gridlines
caption

As you apply and modify table styles, you may choose to remove some or all cell borders. So that you can tell where the table cells begin and end, you can display the table ***gridlines***, the lines that distinguish the cell boundaries. Although gridlines are visible on your screen, they do not print. When you apply a cell border, the gridlines for the cell are no longer visible.

Most tables include captions, especially when more than one table appears in a document. A ***caption*** is a label that identifies or describes an illustration, a table, or a picture. You can easily add captions to tables, and if you choose to add numbers to the table captions, Word will automatically update the table numbers for you.

Step-by-Step 11.4

1. If necessary, open the **Past Due Accounts 1** file from your solution files. Save the document as **Past Due Accounts 2**, followed by your initials.

2. Position the insertion point anywhere within the table. Click the **Table Tools Design** tab. In the Table Styles group, click the **More** button to show the gallery of built-in table styles. If necessary, scroll to the bottom and, in the last row, click the **Colorful Grid – Accent 1** table style.
3. To view the cell borders as you work with the table, click the **Table Tools Layout** tab. In the Table group, click the **View Gridlines** button to toggle the option on to show the cell borders.
4. Click the **Table Tools Design** tab. Explore the options in the Table Style Options group, as follows:
   a. Click the **Header Row** option to toggle the setting off. The shading format in the first row changes, and the header row is formatted with the same shading as all the other rows in the table. Click the **Header Row** option again to toggle the setting back on.
   b. Click the **Banded Rows** option to toggle the setting off. The shading format is the same for all rows in columns 2, 3, and 4.
   c. Click the **First Column** option to toggle the setting off. The shading format in the first column changes, and the column does not stand out as much. Click the **First Column** option again to toggle the setting back on.
   d. Click the **Last Column** option. The shading format in the last column is now the same as in the first column. Click the **Last Column** option again to toggle the setting off.
   e. Click the **Banded Columns** option. The shading format changes for the second and fourth columns.

5. Create a new table style by modifying an existing style:
   a. In the Table Styles group, click the **More** button. Click **Modify Table Style** to open the dialog box shown in **Figure 11–5**. Your dialog box settings will be different.

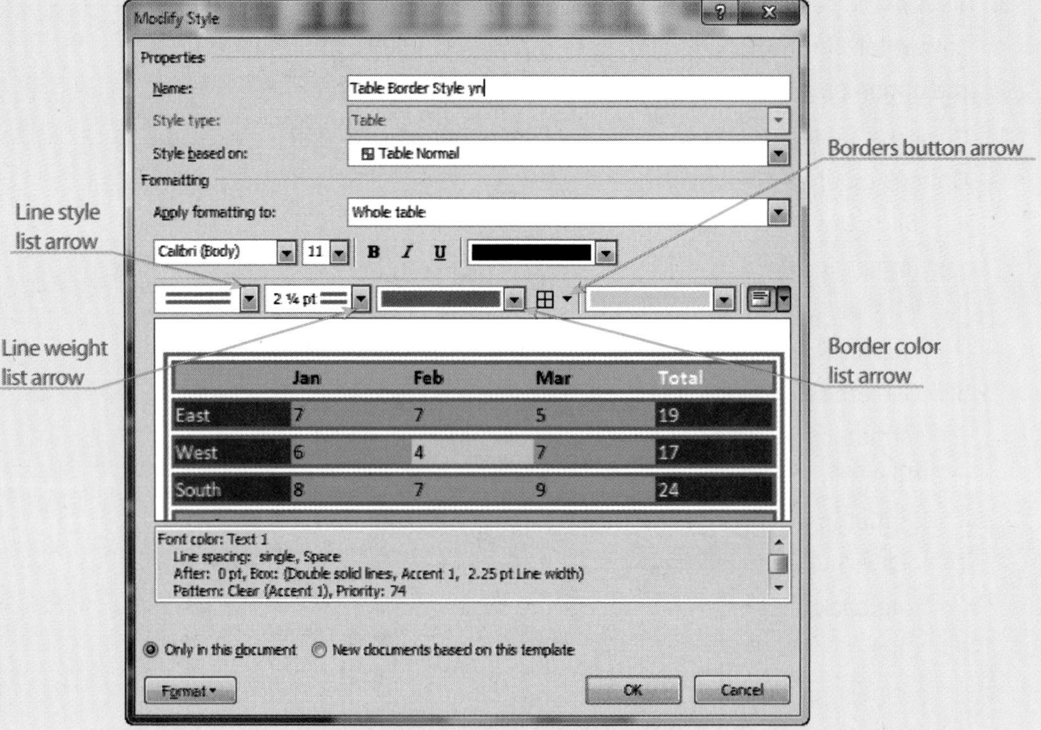

FIGURE 11–5
Modify Style dialog box

   b. In the Name box, replace the current style name with **Table Border Style**, followed by your initials.
   c. Click the **Line Style** list arrow and then click the first double-line style (the 7th line style).
   d. Click the **Line Weight** list arrow and then select **2 ¼ pt**.
   e. Click the **Border Color** list arrow and then select the **Blue, Accent 1** theme color.
   f. Click the **Borders** button arrow and then select **Outside Borders**. Your sample preview should look like the preview in Figure 11–5. Adjust the border settings if necessary.
   g. Make sure the **Only in this document** option is enabled, and then click **OK**. The new table style is added to the Table Styles gallery.

6. In the Table Styles group, click the **More** button. If necessary, scroll to the top of the Table Styles gallery. Under Custom, you will see the new table style you created. Position the mouse pointer over the new table to show the style name. Click anywhere in the document window to close the Table Styles gallery.

EXTRA FOR EXPERTS

If you enable the option *New documents based on this Template,* the new style will be saved to the attached template and available for future documents.

7. With the insertion point positioned anywhere in the table, click the **References** tab. In the Captions group, click the **Insert Caption** button to open the Caption dialog box shown in **Figure 11–6**.

FIGURE 11–6
Caption dialog box

8. Click the **Label** list arrow to view the built-in labels: *Equation*, *Figure*, and *Table*. Click the arrow again to avoid making any changes. Click the **Position** list arrow, and then click **Below selected item**. Click **OK**. The caption *Table 1* is inserted below the table.

TIP

To customize the caption text, click New Label in the Caption dialog box and then enter text for the label.

9. Click the **Insert Caption** button, and then click **AutoCaption** to open the AutoCaption dialog box, as shown in **Figure 11–7**. Under Add caption when inserting, scroll down and enable the **Microsoft Word Table** option. Click **OK**.

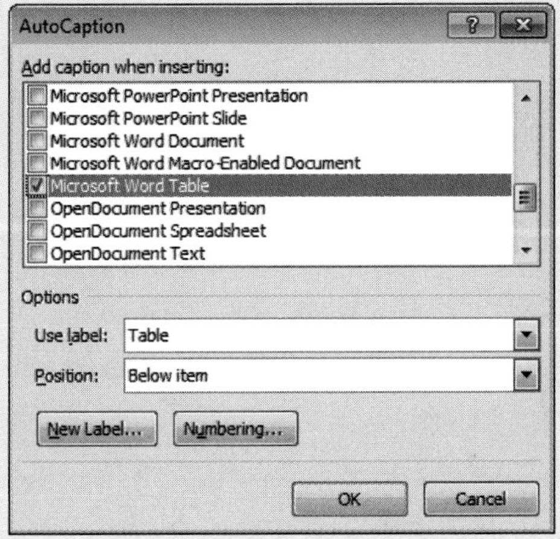

FIGURE 11–7
AutoCaption dialog box

10. Double-click below the *Table 1* caption to insert a new paragraph. Press **Ctrl+Enter** to insert a page break.
11. Insert a new table with 8 rows and 4 columns. Notice that the caption *Table 2* automatically appears below the table.
12. Apply your new custom table style to the new table.
13. Save the changes and leave the document open for the next Step-by-Step. If you are ending your Word session, follow Step 13 in Step-by-Step 11.5, to turn off the AutoCaption feature.

Splitting a Table

Sometimes the contents in a table grow and the number of table rows grows. Often a big table won't fit on one page, and when the table wraps to the next page, it does not include header rows. Or maybe you decide you want to divide the table content into two or more separate tables. Word provides features that can help you format long tables.

Step-by-Step 11.5

1. If necessary, open the **Past Due Accounts 2** file from your solution files. If necessary, enable the **AutoCaption** feature. (See Step-by-Step 11.4, Step 9.)
2. Select all of Table 1. (*Hint*: Click the **Table Select** button at the upper-left corner of the table.) Then copy the table to the Clipboard.
3. Open a new blank document and paste the table. The caption *Table 1* appears below the table because you enabled the AutoCaption setting. Save the new document as **Past Due Accounts 3**, followed by your initials.
4. Position the insertion point in front of the word *Customer* in the first cell at the top of the table. Press **Enter** twice to insert two blank lines above the table.
5. Switch to the Past Due Accounts 2 document. Select Table 2 and copy it to the Clipboard. Then switch to the Past Due Accounts 3 document. Position the insertion point in the first blank paragraph at the top of the document, and then paste the second table at this location. The new table is labeled *Table 1*, and the second table is now labeled *Table 2*.
6. Scroll down to the end of the second table. You will see that the table has wrapped to the next page. Position the insertion point in the first row of Table 2. Click the **Table Tools Layout** tab. In the Table group, click the **Properties** button. Click the **Row** tab to access the options, as shown in **Figure 11–8**.

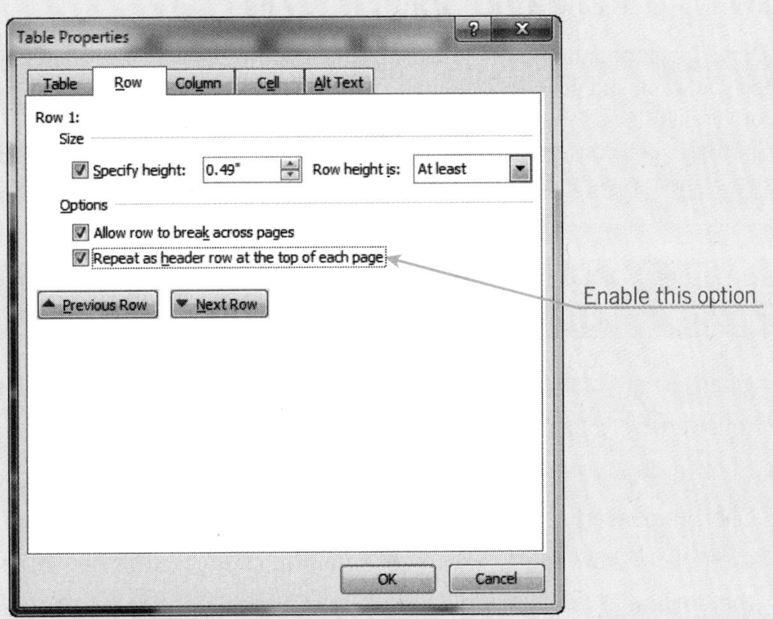

FIGURE 11–8
Row tab in the Table Properties dialog box

7. Enable the **Repeat as header row at the top of each page** option. Click **OK**. The header row for Table 2 now appears at the top of the table, and it also appears above the first row of the table on the second page.
8. Scroll back to Table 2 on the first page. Position the insertion point in the *Abby Johnson* cell. On the Table Tools Layout tab, in the Merge group, click the **Split Table** button. Notice that the header row is not repeated in the second table (instead, the *Abby Johnson* row is formatted as a header), and the first table does not have a caption.
9. Position the insertion point anywhere in what is now the second table in the document. Click the **References** tab. In the Captions group, click the **Insert Caption** button. Leave the settings as they are in the dialog box, and click **OK**. The new table is labeled *Table 2*, and the caption for the table below changes to *Table 3*.
10. With the insertion point after the caption *Table 2*, enter a blank space and then type **- 30 days past due**. Position the insertion point after the caption *Table 3*. Enter a blank space and then type **- 15 days past due**.
11. Select the header row in Table 2 and copy it to the Clipboard. Then position the insertion point at the beginning of the first cell in Table 3 and paste the contents. The new header row appears at the top of Table 3.
12. Scroll down to see the rest of Table 3 on the next page. The header row also appears at the top of the table on the next page, because the header row you pasted was formatted to repeat the header row.
13. Turn off the AutoCaption feature. Click the **References** tab, and in the Captions group, click the **Insert Caption** button. In the Caption dialog box, click **AutoCaption**, disable the **Microsoft Word Table** option, and click **OK**.
14. Save the changes and close both documents.

Drawing a Table and Splitting Cells

The Draw Table tool allows you to use a pen pointer to draw a table boundary just the size you want, and then draw column and row lines within the boundary, creating cells of various sizes.

Splitting a cell converts a single table cell into multiple cells. You can split a cell into two or more rows and/or into two or more columns.

Step-by-Step 11.6

1. Open a new blank document and save the document as **Products 1**, followed by your initials. If necessary, click the **View** tab, and in the Show group, enable the **Ruler** option.
2. Click the **Insert** tab. In the Tables group, click the **Table** button and then click **Draw Table**. The mouse pointer changes to a pen and, if the document is displayed in Draft or Outline view, Word automatically changes to Print Layout view.
3. Use the Draw Table tool to create the table shown in **Figure 11–9**. Follow these simple steps:

FIGURE 11–9
Table grid for Step 3

TIP

If the pointer does not show the Draw Table pen, click the Table Tools Design tab and, in the Draw Borders group, click the Draw Table button.

a. Position the pointer at the left edge of the screen. Click and drag down and to the right as if you were using the Rectangle drawing tool. Use the rulers at the top and left edges of the window to estimate the size. Release when the table (box) is approximately 5 inches wide by 4 inches high.

b. If the new table border is a double line, the formats for the border style you created earlier in the lesson are still active. On the Table Tools Design tab, in the Draw Borders group, change the Line Style to a single line, the Line Weight to 1/2 pt, and the Pen Color to Automatic.

c. Position the Draw Table tool near the top border of the table, at about the ½-inch mark on the horizontal ruler. Then click and drag the tool down to create the first vertical line. Word completes the line for you and automatically makes it straight.

d. Position the Draw Table tool near the top border of the table, at about the 3½-inch mark on the horizontal ruler. Click and drag the tool down to create the second vertical line.

e. Position the Draw Table tool near the first vertical line, at about the 1¼-inch mark on the vertical ruler. Click and drag the tool to the right to create the first horizontal line. Draw a second horizontal line at about the 2¾-inch mark on the vertical ruler.

f. Press **Esc** to toggle off the Draw Table pen.

4. Position the insertion point in the second column of the first row. Click the **Table Tools Layout** tab. In the Merge group, click the **Split Cells** button to open the dialog box shown in **Figure 11–10**. Your dialog box settings will be different.

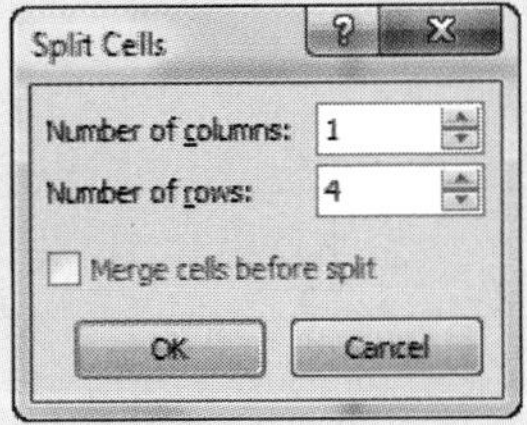

FIGURE 11–10
Split Cells dialog box

5. Change the number of columns to **1**, and change the number of rows to **4**. Click **OK**.

6. Position the insertion point in the second column of the second row. Split the cells by changing the number of columns to **1** and the number of rows to **3**.

7. Position the insertion point in the second column of the third row. Split the cells by changing the number of columns to **1** and the number of rows to **4**.

8. Position the insertion point anywhere in the top row. In the Rows & Columns group, click the **Insert Above** button.

9. Your table should look like the one shown in **Figure 11–11**. Click the **Table Tools Design** tab, and in the Draw Borders group, click the **Eraser** button. The mouse pointer changes to an eraser. Click the cell borders identified in Figure 11–11, and the targeted borders are removed.

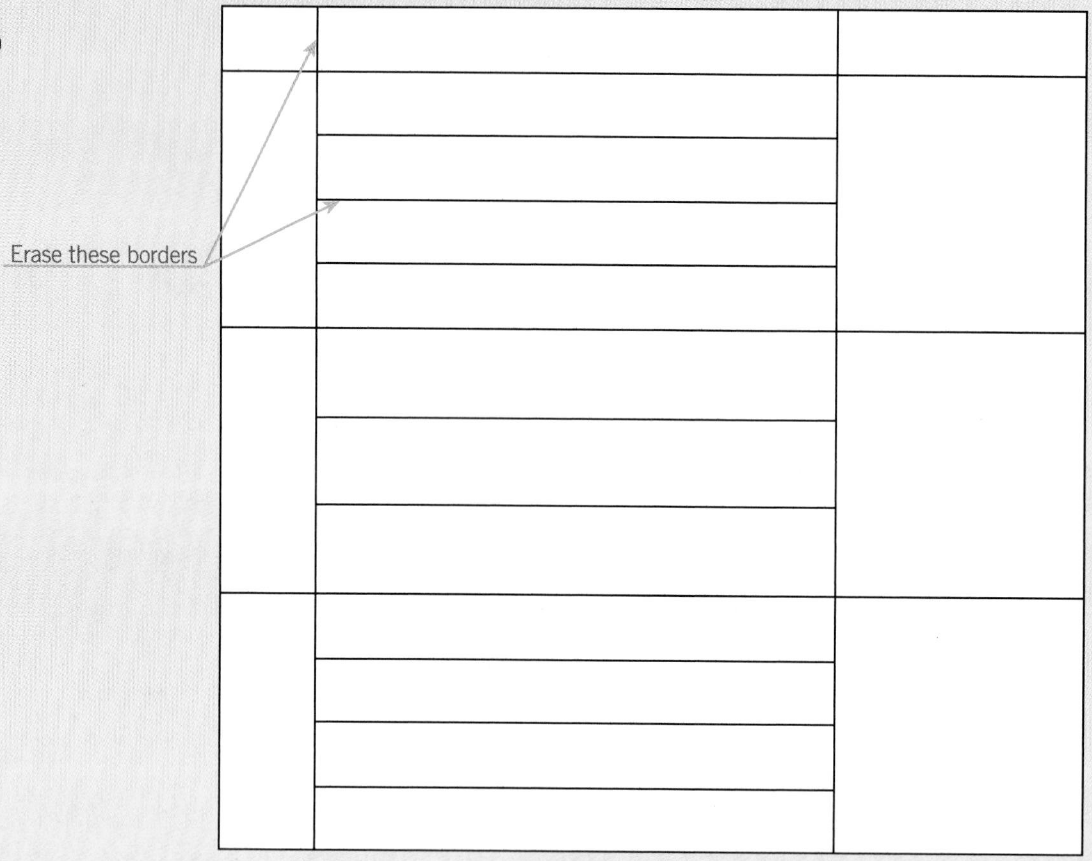

FIGURE 11–11
Table grid for Step 9

Erase these borders

10. Click the **Eraser** button to toggle off the Table Eraser tool. Select all but the first row in the second column. Click the **Table Tools Layout** tab. In the Cell Size group, click the **Distribute Rows** button.
11. Complete the table by entering the data shown in **Figure 11–12**.

Product		Recycled Material
Indoor	Glass tiles	Glass
	Flooring	
	Countertops	
Attire	Jewelry	Plastic
	T-shirts	
	Jackets	
Outdoor	Motor oil	Rubber
	Playground surfaces	
	Asphalt road repair	
	Roofing	

FIGURE 11–12
Table data for Step 11

12. Save the changes and leave the document open for the next Step-by-Step.

Changing Alignment and Rotating Text

Text can be aligned within a cell in a number of different ways. Word provides several settings for both horizontal and vertical alignment of the contents within a cell. You can also change the direction of text in a table cell by rotating the text.

Not only can you change the alignment of the content within a cell, but you can also change the alignment of the table, which affects where the table is positioned on the page. You can reposition the table anywhere in the document by dragging the table to a new location. You can also change the table alignment settings so the position of the table is relative to a paragraph, the margin, or the page.

Step-by-Step 11.7

1. If necessary, open the **Products 1** file from your solution files. Save the document as **Products 2**, followed by your initials.
2. Select the **Product** and **Recycled Material** cells. If necessary, click the Table Tools Layout tab. In the Alignment group, click the **Align Center** button, as shown in **Figure 11–13**.

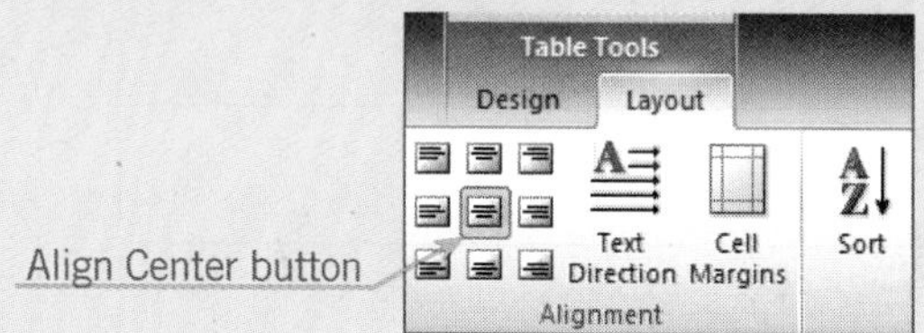

FIGURE 11–13
Options in the Alignment group on the Table Tools Layout tab

3. Select the **Glass**, **Plastic**, and **Rubber** cells, and then click the **Repeat** button on the Quick Access Toolbar to repeat the edit. Then select the **Indoor**, **Attire**, and **Outdoor** cells and repeat the edit.
4. Position the insertion point in the *Indoor* cell. In the Alignment group, click the **Text Direction** button twice to rotate the text so it can be read from the bottom to the top. The Text Direction button changes to show an image of rotated text. Also, the direction of the alignment option buttons changes.
5. Select the **Attire** cell and then click the **Repeat** button twice. Select the **Outdoor** cell and repeat the rotations.
6. Select the **Product** and **Recycled Material** cells. Click the **Table Tools Design** tab. In the Table Styles group, click the **Shading** button arrow and then select the **Orange, Accent 6, Darker 50%** color. With the cells still selected, change the font color to **White**.
7. Click anywhere in the *Indoor* cell. Click the **Shading** button arrow and then select the **Orange, Accent 6, Lighter 80%** color. Then repeat the edit in the *Glass tiles*, *Flooring*, *Counter tops*, and *Glass* cells.
8. Click anywhere in the *Attire* cell and apply the **Orange, Accent 6, Lighter 60%** color. Then repeat the edit for all the cells in the same row.
9. Click anywhere in the *Outdoor* cell and apply the **Orange, Accent 6, Lighter 40%** color. Then repeat the edit for all the cells in the same row.
10. Click the **View** tab, and in the Zoom group, click the **One Page** button. Point to the upper-left corner of the table. When the Table Move Handle appears, click the handle and drag the table down to the bottom of the page.

11. Click the **Table Tools Layout** tab. In the Table group, click the **Properties** button. If necessary, click the **Table** tab to open the Table Properties dialog box shown in **Figure 11–14**.

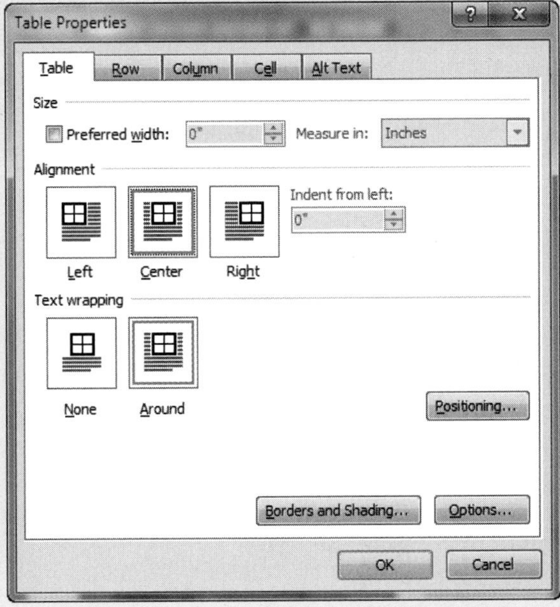

FIGURE 11–14
Table Properties dialog box

12. Under Alignment, click the **Center** option. Under Text wrapping, click the **Around** option. Then click **Positioning** to open the Table Positioning dialog box shown in **Figure 11–15**. Your dialog box settings will be different.

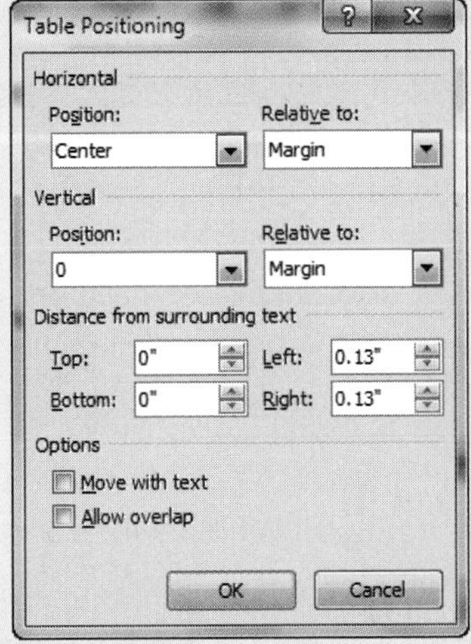

FIGURE 11–15
Table Positioning dialog box

13. Under Vertical Position, change the setting to **0**. Make any other necessary changes so your settings match those in Figure 11–15. Click **OK** twice to close the dialog boxes. The table is repositioned near the top of the document.

14. Save the changes and close the document.

TIP

When the Move with text option is enabled, the table will move with the paragraph if the paragraph is moved in the document.

Using Quick Tables

If you want to create a professional-looking table, but you don't have time to fuss with the table structure and the table styles, you can use a Quick Table. Word provides several table templates, including calendars. Choose a table that provides the structure and style you need, and then replace the boilerplate text with your own content.

Step-by-Step 11.8

1. Open a new blank document. Save the document as **Sales Report 1**, followed by your initials. If necessary, click the **View** tab and change the zoom to 100%.
2. Click the **Insert** tab. Click the **Table** button and then point to **Quick Tables**. The Built-In dialog box opens. Scroll down to view the Tabular List and With Subheads quick tables, as shown in **Figure 11–16**.

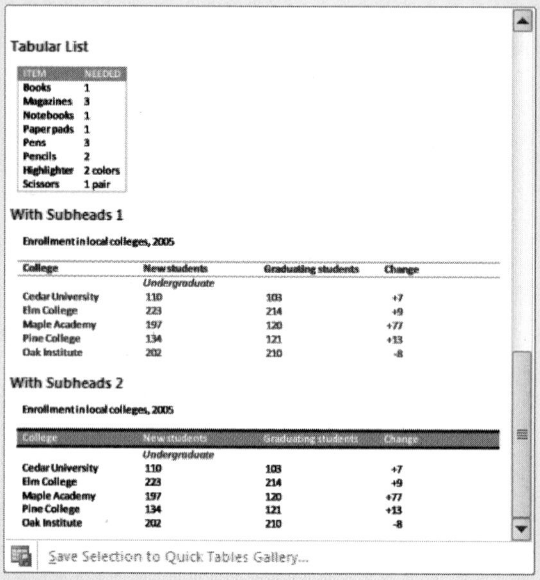

FIGURE 11–16
Built-In quick tables

Tabular List

ITEM	NEEDED
Books	1
Magazines	3
Notebooks	1
Paper pads	1
Pens	3
Pencils	2
Highlighter	2 colors
Scissors	1 pair

With Subheads 1

Enrollment in local colleges, 2005

College	New students	Graduating students	Change
	Undergraduate		
Cedar University	110	103	+7
Elm College	223	214	+9
Maple Academy	197	120	+77
Pine College	134	121	+13
Oak Institute	202	210	-8

With Subheads 2

Enrollment in local colleges, 2005

College	New students	Graduating students	Change
	Undergraduate		
Cedar University	110	103	+7
Elm College	223	214	+9
Maple Academy	197	120	+77
Pine College	134	121	+13
Oak Institute	202	210	-8

Save Selection to Quick Tables Gallery...

3. Select the **With Subheads 2** quick table. A new table with boilerplate text is inserted in the document. Notice the table has a custom caption.
4. Delete the text above the table, and then replace the boilerplate column headings with the following:

   Sales Representative **April** **May** **June**
5. Delete the words *Undergraduate* and *Graduate*.

6. Replace the boilerplate text in rows 3 through 7 with the following data. Row 2 will have no data. The *June* column will not have data, so delete the boilerplate text in that column.

Mari Colace	**51,342**	**62,005**
Michelle Fracassa	**48,254**	**49,807**
Jeff Guetle	**57,654**	**58,009**
Rita Homminga	**62,350**	**63,242**
William Jamison	**41,078**	**43,209**

7. Select rows 8–13 (all remaining rows except the *Total* row). Right-click the selected rows, and then click **Delete Rows**.
8. Leave the word *Total* in the last row of Column 1, but delete the numbers in Columns 2, 3, and 4.
9. Select and delete the caption.
10. Save the changes and leave the document open for the next Step-by-Step.

Performing Math Calculations

Word provides a calculation feature that enables you to add numbers in text and in tables. To perform a calculation in a table, position the insertion point in the cell where the result (such as a total) is to appear, and then enter a formula. You can also specify number formats or choose a function from the list of frequently used functions in Word.

Calculating Sums in Tables

When calculating sums in a table, Word provides an easy shortcut to total the columns and/or rows. You can calculate a sum by inputting a SUM formula using the Formula button. The SUM formula adds numbers in cells above the cell containing the insertion point or in cells to the left of the cell containing the insertion point.

After creating formulas to perform calculations, you may discover that you need to change the data in the cells. Word does not automatically update calculations as does a spreadsheet program such as Excel. However, Word does provide a shortcut that enables you to recalculate an entire table quickly. When you use the Formula button, Word inserts hidden fields for each total. To recalculate, you simply select the cells containing those fields and update the fields.

Step-by-Step 11.9

1. If necessary, open the **Sales Report 1** file from your solution files. Save the document as **Sales Report 2**, followed by your initials.
2. Insert a new column to the right of the *June* column. (*Hint*: Position the insertion point in the *June* column, and then click the **Table Tools Layout** tab. In the Rows and Columns group, click the **Insert Right** button.) Add the column heading **Total**.
3. Calculate the total for the *Mari Colace* row:
   a. Position the insertion point in the last cell in the *Mari Colace* row.
   b. Click the **Table Tools Layout** tab. In the Data group, click the **Formula** button. The Formula dialog box opens with the proposed formula =SUM(LEFT), as shown in **Figure 11–17**.

FIGURE 11–17
Formula dialog box

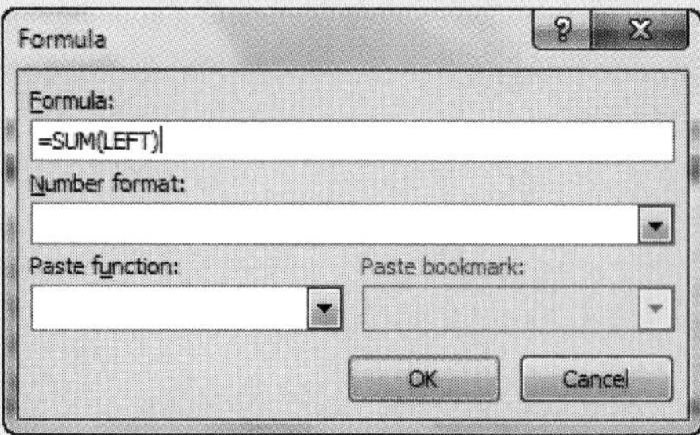

   c. Click **OK** to accept the proposed formula. The result (sum) of *113,347* is automatically inserted in the active cell.
4. To quickly insert the same formula in the other cells of the *Total* column, click in each cell and then click the **Repeat** button on the Quick Access Toolbar (or use the shortcut keys **Ctrl+Y**). Do not insert a formula for the *Total* row.
5. Calculate the total of the *April* column:
   a. Position the insertion point in the last cell in the *April* column.
   b. Click the **Formula** button. Word proposes the formula =SUM(ABOVE).
   c. Click **OK**. The total *260,678* is inserted in the active cell.
6. Repeat the formula to calculate the total for the *May*, *June*, and *Total* columns. Even though the *June* column has no numbers, you can still enter the formula for the column total. The result will be *0*.
7. Enter the following amounts in the *June* column:

Colace	**69,804**
Fracassa	**73,168**
Guetle	**92,544**
Homminga	**79,007**
Jamison	**47,996**

WARNING

When it is possible to add from either direction, the SUM formula may not choose the direction you want. Therefore, always check the accuracy of the result when using the SUM formula or any formula from the Formula button.

8. Select the entire table. Note that the current result in the *Total* column is *536,950.*
9. Press **F9**, the Update Field key. All sums are automatically recalculated. Click anywhere in the table to deselect the rows. Note that the new result in the *Total* column is now *899,469.*
10. Save the changes and leave the document open for the next Step-by-Step.

Creating Other Formulas in a Table

You can also perform other complex math calculations in tables, such as subtracting, multiplying, dividing, averaging, and calculating a percentage. For calculations, Word assigns letters to columns and numbers to rows, as in an Excel worksheet. Cells are named for their intersecting rows and columns. For example, A2 would be the intersection of the first column (A) and the second row (2); B3 would be the intersection of the second column (B) and third row (3); and so on.

Some basic symbols for operators in a formula are described in **Table 11–2**. Word also calculates results for functions such as AVERAGE, COUNT, MIN, and MAX by referencing the table cells. To learn about the operators and the available functions, search the Help screens for the keywords *formula*, *field*, *codes*, *operators*, and *functions*.

TABLE 11–2 Symbols for operators in formulas

SYMBOLS	OPERATORS
plus sign (+)	addition
hyphen (-)	subtraction
asterisk (*)	multiplication
forward slash (/)	division

Step-by-Step 11.10

1. If necessary, open the **Sales Report 2** file from your solution files. Save the document as **Sales Report 3**, followed by your initials.
2. Insert a new column between the *June* and *Total* columns. Type the heading **Average Sales.**
3. Calculate the average sales for Mari Colace:
   a. Position the insertion point in the *Average Sales* column for the *Mari Colace* row.
   b. Click the **Formula** button.
   c. Word proposes the formula =SUM(LEFT). If you accepted this formula, the results would be the sum of the *April*, *May*, and *June* amounts.

d. In the Formula text box, delete the proposed formula. To create your own formula, type **=(B3+C3+D3)/3**. This formula instructs Word to first add the amounts in the third row of Columns B, C, and D and then to divide that sum by 3 to find the average.

e. Under Number format, click the **list arrow** and select **#,##0**.

f. Click **OK**. The result *61,050* appears in the active cell.

4. You cannot use the Repeat Formula command because the cell references must change for each row. Create a new formula for row 4 **=(B4+C4+D4)/3**, following the actions in Step 3. Don't forget to change the number format to **#,##0**.
5. You can calculate averages quickly by pasting in a predefined function. Click cell **E5** (the Average Sales column for Jeff Guetle). Click the **Formula** button.
6. In the Formula text box, delete all except the equal sign in the proposed formula. Under Paste function, click the **list arrow** and then click **AVERAGE**.
7. The insertion point is positioned between the two parentheses in the Formula text box. Type **B5:D5**. This formula instructs Word to calculate the average of the amounts in cells B5 through D5.
8. Change the number format to **#,##0**, and then click **OK**. The result *69,402* is inserted in the active cell.
9. Create formulas to calculate the average sales for the remaining two sales reps.
10. Click in the last cell in the *Average Sales* column. Enter a formula to calculate the average for cells E3:E7, in the same format as the rest of the data.
11. Save the changes and close the document.

TIP

If the formula does not produce any results, check to make sure that the equal sign precedes the word AVERAGE in the formula.

Integrating Word and Excel

You have seen that Word tables can become fairly sophisticated. However, at times you might need a more complex table, or you may wish to include Excel data or an Excel chart in a Word document. If you want the additional functionality of an Excel worksheet, you can insert an Excel worksheet into your Word document. If you want your Word document to include data that is already in an Excel worksheet, you do not need to retype all the data. You can ***import*** the data, which means you bring the data into a document from another compatible application. To import Excel data into a Word document, you can copy and paste worksheet data, or you can integrate the worksheet into the Word document as a linked or embedded object.

VOCABULARY
import

Inserting an Excel Worksheet in a Word Document

The easiest way to create a complex table in which you can calculate and instantly recalculate and update numbers in your Word document is to insert an Excel worksheet into your Word document. Then you have access to all of the data formatting and calculation options from Excel, and you also have access to all Word features.

Step-by-Step 11.11

1. Open a new blank document and save the document as **Purchase Order**, followed by your initials.
2. Click the **Insert** tab. In the Tables group, click the **Table** button, and then click **Excel Spreadsheet**. A worksheet is inserted in the document, and the Excel Ribbon replaces the Word Ribbon.
3. Enter the data below in the worksheet cells.

Item #	**Qty.**	**Price**
11-356	**4**	**29.99**
11-358	**1**	**54.99**
11-067	**2**	**37.59**
Total		

4. Click anywhere outside the worksheet. The worksheet data appears in an embedded table, and the Word Ribbon appears.
5. Double-click the table, and the Excel Ribbon appears again.
6. Click cell **C5**. On the Excel Home tab, in the Editing group, click the **Sum** button Σ to calculate the total for cells C2:C4 and then press **Enter**.
7. Click anywhere outside of the worksheet.
8. Save the changes and close the document.

Copying Worksheet Data into a Word Document

The simplest way to import Excel data is to copy it in Excel and then paste it into a Word document. When copied and pasted into a Word document, the worksheet data is converted to a table. Then, you can edit and format the data as you would any other Word table data.

Step-by-Step 11.12

1. Open the **Rates** file from the drive and folder where your Data Files are stored. Save the document as **New Rates**, followed by your initials.
2. Launch Excel, navigate to the Data Files folder, and open the file **Rates.xlsx**.

3. Select the range **A1:D4**. (*Hint*: Click in cell A1, then drag the mouse pointer to the right and down to cell D4.)
4. Click the **Copy** button (or press **Ctrl+C**) to copy the worksheet data to the Clipboard.
5. Switch to the Word document. Position the insertion point in the blank paragraph after the paragraph of text. Click the **Paste** button (or press **Ctrl+V**) to paste the worksheet data.
6. Select the entire table. Click the **Table Tools Layout** tab. In the Cell Size group, click the **AutoFit** button and then click **AutoFit Contents.**
7. Click the **Table Tools Design** tab, and then apply a table style of your choosing.
8. Save the changes, and then close the Word document and the Excel document. Leave both applications open.

Embedding and Linking a Worksheet in a Word Document

VOCABULARY

source file

destination file

embedded object

linked object

EXTRA FOR EXPERTS

Another way to embed or to link worksheet data into a document is to use the Object command on the Insert tab. This command enables you to create a new object, or to link or embed an object that already exists in an earlier version of Excel.

If the Excel data you would like to include in your Word document is going to be updated regularly, you can import the worksheet data into your Word file as either an embedded object or a linked object. When importing data from one application to another, the document file from which you are transferring data is called the ***source file***. The document to which you are transferring the data is called the ***destination file***. For example, you can import sales data from an Excel worksheet (the source file) into a report created in Word (the destination file) and have access to the most recent data.

An ***embedded object*** becomes part of the destination file and can be edited in the destination file. For example, if you embed worksheet cells for the sales data into a Word document, you can double-click the cells and then use Excel commands to modify the sales data. To save file space in the destination file, you can choose to insert the source file as a linked object. A ***linked object*** is inserted as a static object and accesses data stored in the source file, so you cannot update the linked data in the destination file. However, if the destination file is open when the data is modified in the source file, the data is automatically updated in the destination file. If the destination file is not open when the source file is updated, the next time you open the destination file, a dialog box will open, prompting you to update the document with the data from the linked file. If the source file has been renamed or moved to a new location, the data will not be updated when you reopen the destination file.

Step-by-Step 11.13

1. In Word, open a new blank document and save it as **Monthly Sales 1**, followed by your initials.
2. In Excel, navigate to the Data Files folder and open the file **Sales.xlsx**. Save the worksheet as **Regional Sales**, followed by your initials.

3. Select the range **A1:E7**. Then click the **Copy** button (or press **Ctrl+C**) to copy the data to the Clipboard.
4. Switch to the Word document. Position the insertion point at the beginning of the document. On the Home tab, in the Clipboard group, click the **Paste** button arrow and then click **Paste Special**.
5. The Paste option is enabled. Under As, select **Microsoft Excel Worksheet Object**. Click **OK**. The selected cells from the worksheet are inserted in the document.
6. Press **Enter** two times. Then click the **Paste** button arrow again, click **Paste Special**, and this time enable the **Paste link** option. Under As, select **Microsoft Excel Worksheet Object** and then click **OK**. The worksheet appears in the Word document again, but this time it is not embedded. All the data is still stored in the Excel file.
7. Switch to the Excel worksheet. Press **Esc** and then enter the following numbers for June:

   138,911

   145,001

   133,041

   149,210
8. Save the changes to the Regional Sales Excel worksheet, and then switch to the Word document. Notice that the linked table is updated with the June data. However, the embedded worksheet does not include the June data.
9. Save the changes to the Word document, and close the document.
10. Switch the Excel worksheet. Use the Sum button to calculate the totals in the *TOTAL* column and the *TOTAL* row. Save the changes, and then close the worksheet and exit Excel.
11. Open your **Monthly Sales 1** Word document. When prompted to update, click **Yes**. Note that the linked table is updated, even though the Excel spreadsheet file is not open.
12. Save the Monthly Sales 1 document as **Monthly Sales 2**, followed by your initials.
13. To break the link, right-click the second (linked) Word table, point to **Linked Worksheet Object**, and then click **Links**. In the Links dialog box, click **Break Link**. When prompted to break the link, click **Yes**. Now when the worksheet data is updated, the Word table will not be updated.
14. Save the changes and close the Word document.

Creating Charts

Charts provide a visual display of data and often make the material easier to understand. Word enables you to convert table data into colorful three-dimensional charts. Word offers several options for chart types, including column, bar, line, and pie. In addition, you can change the elements used to format a chart. For example, you can insert a title for the chart or the axes, you can add labels for the data, and you can change the font and location of the chart's legend.

When you use the Insert Chart feature, a sample chart is embedded in the Word document and an Excel worksheet opens. You replace the sample data in the worksheet with the data you want to appear in the chart, and as you enter new data in the worksheet, the embedded chart is updated. After closing the worksheet, you can still update the chart data at any time by right-clicking the chart and then clicking Edit Data.

If you do not have Excel installed on the computer, obviously an Excel worksheet will not open. However, an associated datasheet will open with the chart, and you can enter your own data in the datasheet.

EXTRA FOR EXPERTS

You can also copy and paste a chart that has already been created in Excel. When you paste the chart into a Word document, the chart is linked to the Excel worksheet, so you can edit the data in the worksheet and the chart will automatically be updated.

Step-by-Step 11.14

1. Open a new blank document and save it as **Fourth Quarter Sales**, followed by your initials.
2. Click the **Insert** tab. In the Illustrations group, click the **Chart** button to open the Insert Chart dialog box, similar to the one shown in **Figure 11–18**.

FIGURE 11–18
Insert Chart dialog box

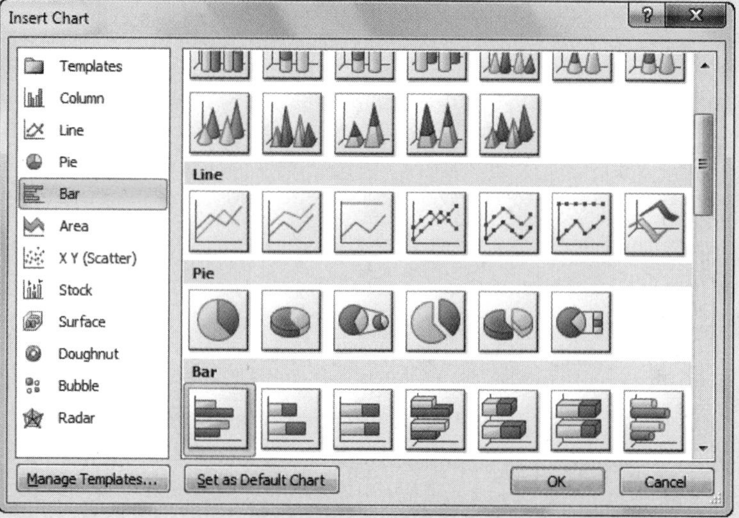

3. In the left pane, select **Bar**. In the right pane, under Bar, click the first option in the first row, **Clustered Bar**. (*Hint*: Position the mouse pointer over the options to see a ScreenTip with the chart name.) Then click **OK**. Word inserts a sample chart in the document and then opens an Excel worksheet in a new window. The applications appear side by side.

4. In the Excel worksheet, replace the sample data with the data below. The chart in Word is linked to the worksheet, so as you enter the data in the worksheet, the chart is automatically updated. (If you don't have Excel installed on your computer, enter the data in the datasheet.)

Sales Representative	October	November	December	Total
Colace, M.	36,443	42,775	45,982	
Fracassa, M.	43,907	44,168	46,561	
Guetle, J.	38,856	40,125	42,213	
Homminga, R.	41,006	21,766	53,447	
Jamison, W.	37,226	51,112	44,487	

5. Use the **Sum** button to calculate the totals in the *Total* column. Note that the SUM formula references table column headings instead of cells. Make sure only data in Columns B, C, and D are included in the SUM formula.
6. Change the chart type:
   a. In the Word document, click anywhere within the chart to select it. (*Hint*: When the chart is selected, the drawing canvas border appears around the chart.)
   b. On the Chart Tools Design tab, in the Type group, click the **Change Chart Type** button. The Change Chart Type dialog box opens.
   c. Under Column, click the second option in the second row, **Stacked Cylinder**. Click **OK**. The chart in the Word document adapts to the style change.
7. In the worksheet, click anywhere outside the range border. Then point to the lower-right corner of the range border. When the mouse pointer changes to a double-headed arrow ⤡, drag the border to the left one column to exclude the Total column from the selected range. Now that the monthly figures are stacked, it is not necessary to include the total data.
8. In the Word document, click the **Chart Tools Layout** tab. In the Labels group, click the **Chart Title** button and then click **Above Chart**. A text box with *Chart Title* is inserted above the chart. Select the text *Chart Title* and replace the text with **Fourth Quarter Sales**.
9. In the Labels group, click the **Axis Titles** button, point to **Primary Horizontal Axis Title**, and then click **Title Below Axis**. A new text box is inserted below the chart. Change *Axis Title* to **Sales Representatives**.
10. In the Labels group, click the **Axis Titles** button, point to **Primary Vertical Axis Title**, and then click **Rotated Title**. Replace *Axis Title* with **Sales Volume**. Then, in the Labels group, click the **Legend** button and click **Show Legend at Right**. The legend labels are inserted on the right side of the chart.

TIP

As you enter the *Total* column heading and the last row of data, the blue range border line will extend to include the additional data.

11. Save the Excel worksheet as **Quarterly Sales**, followed by your initials. Close the worksheet and exit Excel.
12. In the Word document, if necessary, click the **Chart Tools Layout** tab. In the Labels group, click the **Data Table** button and then click **Show Data Table with Legend Keys**. The data table appears below the chart.
13. Position the mouse pointer over the middle handle at the bottom border of the drawing canvas. When the pointer changes to a double-headed arrow, drag the border down to resize the chart and table to a height of 5½". Then drag the text box for the horizontal axis label to reposition the label below the chart.
14. Save the changes to the Word document, and then close the document.

SUMMARY

In this lesson, you learned:

- To rearrange table contents, you can copy and paste data, drag and drop rows and columns, and sort data.
- Word offers several ways for you to control column and row spacing.
- Sorting can be based on as many as three criteria at a time, and when sorting a single column, the data in the other table columns is not reordered.
- If a table gets too big and cannot fit on a page, you can repeat the header rows when the table wraps to the next page. Or, you can split the table content into separate tables.
- The Draw Table tool and the Draw Eraser tool enable you to create custom tables with cells of various sizes.
- Word provides several options for aligning text within a table cell, and you can also specify the alignment of the entire table.
- The Formula button enables you to perform math calculations in tables, such as adding, subtracting, multiplying, dividing, and averaging.
- You can insert data from an Excel worksheet into a Word document and then edit and format the data in the Word document.
- You can easily create charts in Word using an Excel worksheet to enter the chart data.

VOCABULARY REVIEW

Define the following terms:

caption
destination file
embedded object
gridlines
import
linked object
source file

REVIEW QUESTIONS

TRUE / FALSE

Circle T if the statement is true or F if the statement is false.

T F 1. When copied and pasted into a Word document, Excel worksheet data is converted to a table.

T F 2. When you open a Word document with linked data in an Excel worksheet, the worksheet must also be open to update the table data.

T F 3. Gridlines appear in a printed document.

T F 4. You can move rows and columns in a table the same way you move text in a document.

T F 5. A linked object saves file space.

FILL IN THE BLANK

Complete the following sentences by writing the correct word or words in the blanks provided.

1. A(n) ________________ is a label that describes an illustration, table, or picture.
2. When you link an object, you create a connection between the destination file and the ________________.
3. A(n) ________________ file becomes part of the destination file.
4. When you ________________ data, you bring data into a document from another compatible application.
5. When adjusting column widths, if you want the table to fill the document window and extend from the left margin to the right margin, click the AutoFit button and choose the ________________ option.

WRITTEN QUESTIONS

Write a brief answer to the following questions.

1. If you want to create a professional-looking table but you don't have a lot of time, describe the fastest way to create the table.

2. Describe how to rotate text in a table cell.

3. Describe how to quickly recalculate formulas after updating data in a Word table.

4. Explain how the Banded Rows or Banded Columns options affect the formatting of table styles.

5. What symbols can you use as operators in formulas for addition, subtraction, multiplication, and division?

PROJECTS

If you have a SAM 2010 user profile, your instructor may have assigned an autogradable version of the indicated project. If so, log into the SAM 2010 Web site at *www.cengage.com/sam2010* to download the instruction and start files.

PROJECT 11–1

1. Open the Employee file from the drive and folder where your Data Files are stored. Save the document as **Employee Data 1**, followed by your initials.
2. Insert a new paragraph above the table and enter the title **COMPANY EMPLOYEES**. Center the title.
3. Change the order of the columns so that the columns appear in the following order from left to right: *Name*, *Department*, *Title*, and *Date Hired*.
4. Sort by department in ascending order, and then by the date hired in ascending order.
5. Save the changes to the document. Then save the document as **Employee Data 2**, followed by your initials.
6. Near the top of the marketing department, for the employee *Pfeifer*, change the department to **Human Resources** and change the title to **Assistant Director**. Then move the row up in the table so that it is positioned before employee *Foster-Hale* in the Human Resources department.
7. Enter the following new employees in the table so they appear at the end of the Legal department employees. Complete the row data. All three new employees are in the Legal department, and their job title is Paralegal. They were all hired on 11-12-2013.

   Giroux, Jason
   Morris, Adam
   Torres, Tracey
8. Create a custom caption below the table. For the caption text, type **Current Employees**. Edit the caption by removing the number "1" at the end.
9. Format the header row to repeat at the top of the second page.
10. Select all the employee names in the first column, but do not select the column headings. Sort the table data based on the last and then the first names of the employees. (*Hint*: Open the Sort dialog box and then open the Sort Options dialog box. Under Separate fields at, select Commas and click OK. Then in the Sort dialog box, select a Sort by of Column 1 with Field 1 in the Using box, and a Then by of Column 1 with Field 2 in the Using box.)
11. Save the changes to the document, and then save the document as **Employee Data 3**, followed by your initials.
12. Remove the caption below the table. Click in the table and then sort the table content in ascending alphabetical order based on the *Department* column.
13. Split the table so that each department is in a separate table. Then copy and paste the header row into each of the new tables.
14. Save the changes and close the document.

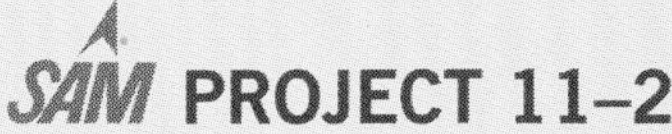

PROJECT 11–2

1. Open a new blank document and save it as **Payroll**, followed by your initials.
2. Create the table shown in **Figure 11–19**.
3. Insert formulas to calculate the earnings for each employee by multiplying the regular hours times the hourly rate. Apply the **$#,##0.00** format for the results.
4. Insert formulas to calculate the sums for the *Regular Hours* and *Earnings* columns.
5. Insert a new row at the end of the table. In the first column, type **AVERAGE**.
6. Insert a formula to calculate the average for rows 2 through 7 in the *Regular Hours* column. Apply the **#,##0.00** format for the results.
7. AutoFit the table to the contents.
8. Apply a table style to make the data easier to read. Modify the table style borders and shading to customize the style, and then save the modified table style as Payroll Table Style, followed by your initials. When you save the new style, be sure to enable the Only in this document option.
9. Save the changes and close the document.

Employee	Regular Hours	Hourly Rate	Earnings
Beintez, L.	40	14.00	
Daniel, K.	36	15.50	
Huang, M.	39.5	12.50	
O'Neil, A.	40	16.00	
Parker, N.	34.5	14.00	
Kennedy, N.	40	12.50	
TOTAL			

FIGURE 11–19 Table data for Project 11–2

PROJECT 11–3

1. Open a new blank document and save it as **Recycling Rate**, followed by your initials.
2. Use the Draw Table tool to create the table shown in **Figure 11–20**. The table is approximately 6 inches wide by 3 inches high.
3. Add shading and border formats to enhance the appearance of the table and make it easier to read.
4. Save the changes to the document.
5. Open the Green Bucket file from the folder where your Data Files are stored. Save the document as **Green Bucket Letter**, followed by your initials.
6. Switch to the Recycling Rate document and copy the table to the Clipboard.
7. Switch to the Green Bucket Letter document. Position the insertion point at the beginning of the paragraph below the bulleted list, and then paste the table.
8. AutoFit the table to the contents.
9. Format the table so that it is aligned at the right side of the paragraph and the text wraps around the paragraph. (*Hint:* Open the Table Properties dialog box. Under Alignment, select Right, and under Text wrapping, select Around.)
10. Save the changes and close both documents.

Recycling Rate			
PET	Soft drink bottles	55%	59%
	Vegetable oil bottles	15%	24%
HDPE	Milk jugs	33%	40%
	Bleach and laundry detergent bottles	19%	27%

FIGURE 11–20 Table data for Project 11–3

PROJECT 11–4

1. Open a new blank document and save it as **New Members**, followed by your initials.
2. Use a Quick Table to create the table shown in **Figure 11–21**. Modify the table structure as needed so it has the right number of columns and rows, and then replace the boilerplate text with the data shown in Figure 11–21.
3. Select the table and change the font to Calibri, 14 point.
4. Adjust the column widths to AutoFit the contents.
5. Save the changes and close the document.

Member #	Last Name	First Name	Address	ZIP
24561	Sautter	Arthur	6443 West Brandt	44904-2304
24562	Cole	George	1102 South Elm	44906-3941
24563	Takamoto	Li	256 North Diamond	44904-2855
24564	Dierks	Barbara	650 Wayne	44904-3027
24565	Fitzpatrick	Lorraine	747 Lenox Avenue	44906-0462
24566	Barry	David	162 North Murray	44906-3609
24567	Tolzmann	Agnes	202 Third Street	44906-2742

FIGURE 11–21 Table data for Project 11–4

PROJECT 11–5

1. Open a new blank document and save it as **First Quarter Report**, followed by your initials.
2. Launch Excel, navigate to the Data Files folder, and open the file Expenses.xlsx. Save the worksheet as **First Quarter Expenses**, followed by your initials.
3. Select the range A1:D9 and copy the data to the Clipboard.
4. Switch to the Word document, and paste the worksheet data into the document as a linked Microsoft Excel Worksheet Object.
5. Switch to the Excel worksheet and enter the following expense data in the *March* column:

   4250
   995
   250
   421
   1992
6. Save the changes to the worksheet.
7. Switch to the Word document. Save the changes, and then close the document.
8. In the Excel worksheet, edit the Miscellaneous Expense for March so that it shows 429 instead of *421*.
9. Save the changes to the worksheet, and then close Excel.
10. In Word, open the First Quarter Report.docx document. When prompted, click Yes to update the linked data.
11. Save the changes and close the document.

PROJECT 11–6

1. Open a new blank document and save it as **Country Requests**, followed by your initials.
2. Insert a column chart.
3. In the Excel worksheet, replace the boilerplate text in Columns A–C with the following data. Delete the boilerplate data in Column D, and adjust the range border to include only the information shown in **Figure 11–22**.

Country	Year One	Year Two
Austria	85	144
Germany	110	175
Italy	98	143
Switzerland	78	133

FIGURE 11–22 Table data for Project 11-6

4. Save the worksheet as **Countries**, followed by your initials.
5. Switch to the Word document, and create the chart title **Requests by Country** above the chart.
6. Insert a vertical axis title on the left side of the chart, and change the axis title to **# of Requests**. The text should be rotated so you can read it from bottom to top.
7. If necessary, show the legend at the right.
8. Save the changes to the Word document, and then close both the Word document and the Excel worksheet. Exit both applications.

CRITICAL THINKING

ACTIVITY 11–1

Create a formula to calculate the number of items in the first column in **Figure 11–23**. Note that the first row is a header row. To find information in the Help screens, search for the keywords *formula functions*.

Item#	Qty. in Stock
11-4508	542
29-545	10
33-090	54
33-091	98

FIGURE 11–23 Data for Activity 11-1

ACTIVITY 11–2

You create a newsletter each month in Word. The newsletter includes an update on the status of a fundraiser project. Data on the fundraising progress is provided in a table. You have several options for creating the newsletter table each month. Describe how you would create the table, and explain whether you would embed or link the data and why.

Estimated Time: 2 hours

LESSON 12

Creating Mail Merge Documents

OBJECTIVES

Upon completion of this lesson, you should be able to:

- Identify a main document and a data source.
- Insert merge fields into the main document.
- Preview, merge, and print merged documents.
- Create a new data source.
- Edit, sort, and filter data source records.
- Prepare mail merge documents for mass mailing labels and envelopes.
- Create a main document for mass e-mails.
- Use mail merge features to create catalogs and directories.

VOCABULARY

data source

field

field name

filter

MAPI (Messaging Application Programming Interface)

main document

merge field

record

switch

Word's mail merge feature enables you to personalize and customize letters, envelopes, labels, and e-mail messages for group or mass mailings. You can also use mail merge features to create a single document, such as a catalog or a membership directory.

Creating Mail Merge Documents

VOCABULARY

main document

data source

field

field name

record

The merge process combines boilerplate text with variable information, such as names and addresses. To begin the process, you must identify a main document and a data source. The ***main document*** is a file that contains the boilerplate text and formats that remain constant during the merge process, such as the body of a letter or the standard text for a catalog. The ***data source*** is a collection of variable information to be used in a merge. In the merge process, the variable information from the data source is merged into the main document. For example, the data source can be an Outlook file with contacts' names and addresses that can be merged into a letter. Another example of a data source is an Excel worksheet or an Access database that contains product data that can be merged into a catalog.

Identifying the Main Document and the Data Source

The first step in the merge process is to select the main document type. The options available include letters, e-mail messages, envelopes, labels, or a directory.

The second step is to select the starting (or main) document. You can use the current document, or you can start from a template or an existing document.

The third step in the mail merge process is to select the recipients. You must first locate or create the data source. The data source stores information in a ***field***, which is one or more characters that create a piece of information, such as a first name, last name, or telephone number. The ***field name*** is a label that identifies a field in a data source. When you identify a Word table or an Excel spreadsheet as the data source, Word uses the column headings for the field names. A ***record*** is a group of related fields, or a single field, treated as a unit in a data source, such as all the contact information for one individual. Once you identify the data source, you then identify the recipients (or records) you want to include in the merge.

If you are inexperienced at creating merges, you will find that the Mail Merge Wizard feature makes the process very easy. The wizard guides you through six basic steps to complete the merge process. Step-by-Steps 12.1, 12.2, and 12.3 cover the six steps for the Mail Merge Wizard. If you are unable to complete all six wizard steps in one session, you can save the changes to the main document and continue with the remaining steps later. Word will retain the data source and field information, and when you reopen the main document, you can continue the merge process at the point where you stopped.

Step-by-Step 12.1

1. Launch Word and open the **Orders** file from the drive and folder where your Data Files are stored. Save the document as **Orders Data Source,** followed by your initials, and close the document.
2. Open the **Order Confirmation** file from the drive and folder where your Data Files are stored. Save the document as **Order Confirmation Main Document**, followed by your initials.

3. Review the document, and you will notice that the letter is incomplete—it has no inside address or salutation. These elements will be determined by the variable information in a data source. The letters *XX* in the first paragraph of the body of the letter indicate locations where you will insert fields to merge additional variable information.
4. Click the **Mailings** tab. In the Start Mail Merge group, click the **Start Mail Merge** button, and then click **Step-by-Step Mail Merge Wizard**. The Mail Merge task pane shown in **Figure 12–1** opens. You can drag the Mail Merge task pane to reposition it on the screen.

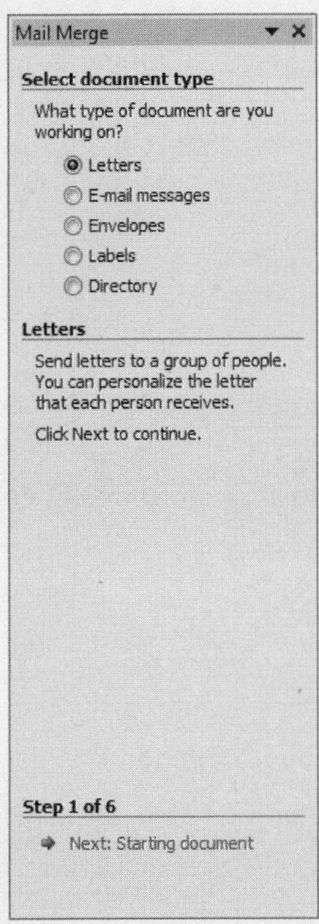

FIGURE 12–1
Step 1 of 6 in the Mail Merge task pane

5. If necessary, under Select document type, enable the **Letters** option. At the bottom of the task pane, click **Next: Starting document**. Under Select starting document, the option Use the current document is already enabled.
6. At the bottom of the task pane, click **Next: Select recipients**. Under Select recipients, the option Use an existing list is already enabled.
7. Under Use an existing list, click **Browse**. The Select Data Source dialog box opens. Navigate to your solutions folder, select the file **Orders Data Source**, and then click **Open**.

8. The Mail Merge Recipients dialog box shown in **Figure 12–2** opens. Notice that a check mark appears to the left of each record in the second column of the data source.

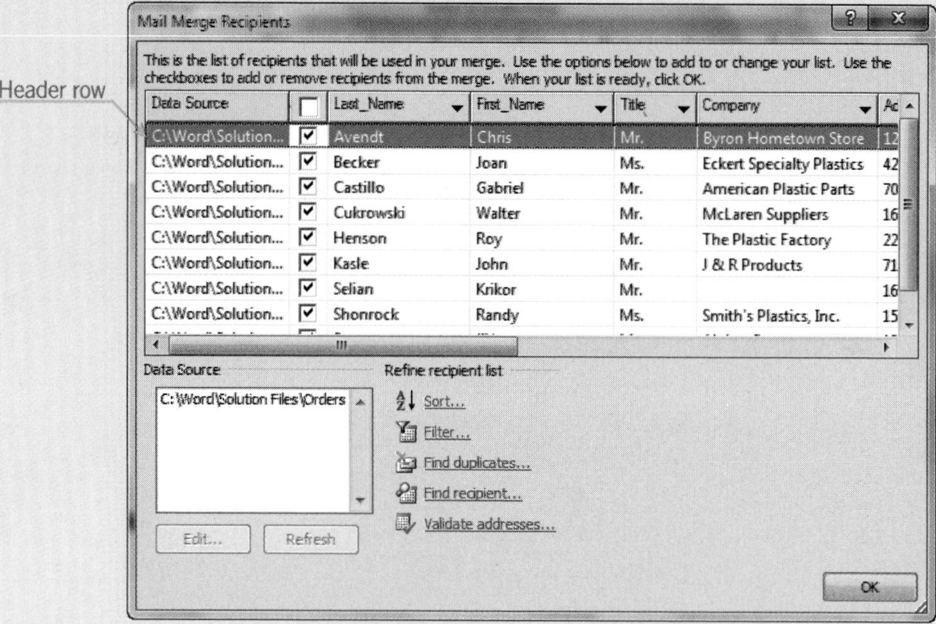

FIGURE 12–2 Mail Merge Recipients dialog box

9. Click the **check box** to the right of *Data Source* in the header row. A check mark is added to the box. Click the **check box** again, and all the check marks are removed. Deselecting all the records is useful when the list is extensive and you want to include only a few records in the merge.
10. Click the same **check box** again. All the records are again selected and all the recipients will be included in the merge.
11. Click the **check box** to the left of the last name *Cukrowski*. The check mark is removed, which means the record will be excluded from the merge.
12. Click the **check box** next to *Cukrowski* again to include the record in the merge. This method of adding/removing recipients to and from the merge is most useful when the list of records is short.
13. Click **OK** in the Mail Merge Recipients dialog box to close it.
14. Leave the main document and the Mail Merge task pane open for the next Step-by-Step.

Inserting Merge Fields into the Main Document

The fourth step in the merge process is to add merge fields to the main document. The ***merge field*** is a placeholder in the main document that instructs Word to find and insert the corresponding information from the data source. The merge field shows the field name surrounded by chevrons (e.g., *«LastName»*), which helps to distinguish the field from the regular text. Word simplifies the process of inserting merge fields by providing composite fields that group a number of fields together. For example, Word provides a preformatted address block with fields for the recipient's title, name, and address. You can use these composite fields to save time, and you can customize them as needed.

VOCABULARY
merge field

Step-by-Step 12.2

1. If necessary, open the **Order Confirmation Main Document** file from your solution files. Because the data source file is already linked to the main document, you will be prompted to place data from the data source. Click Yes.
2. If necessary, click the **Mailings** tab, click the **Start Mail Merge** button, and then click **Step by Step Mail Merge Wizard**. At the bottom of the Mail Merge task pane, if necessary, advance to Step 3 of 6.
3. At the bottom of the Mail Merge task pane, click **Next: Write your letter**.
4. If the nonprinting formatting characters are not visible, click the Home tab, toggle on the Show/Hide ¶ button, and then return to the Mailings tab. Position the insertion point in the second blank paragraph below the date line.
5. In the Mail Merge task pane, under Write your letter, click **Address block**. The Insert Address Block dialog box opens, as shown in **Figure 12–3**. Because the record for Walter Cukrowski was selected in the data source, a preview of that address appears in the preview pane of the dialog box.

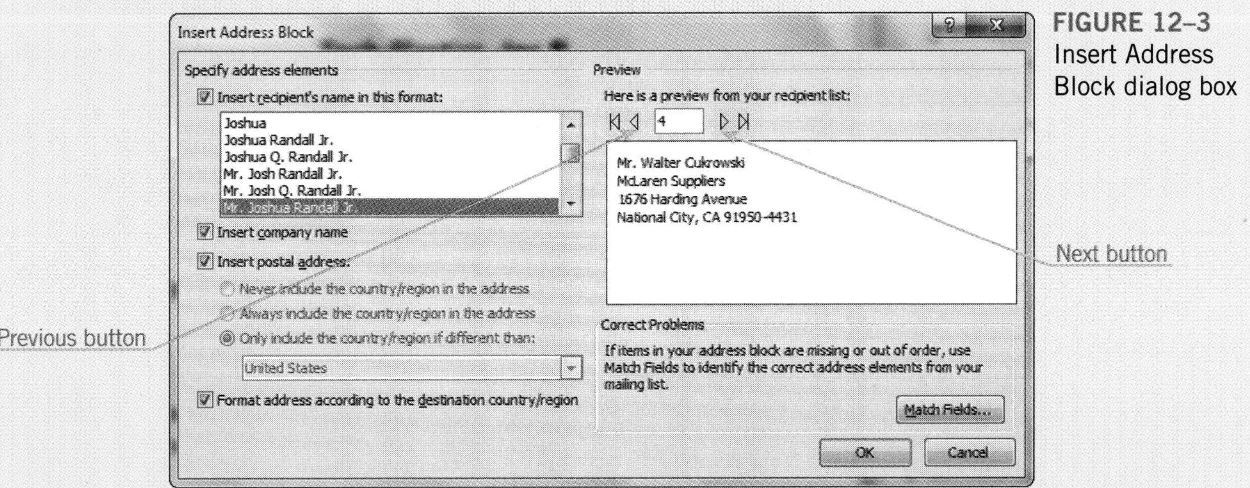

FIGURE 12–3
Insert Address Block dialog box

6. In the Preview section, click the **Previous** and **Next** arrows to view the proposed address blocks for the other records in the data source.
7. Click **OK** to accept the proposed recipient information in the address block. The merge field *«AddressBlock»* is inserted in the main document.
8. In the Write & Insert Fields group on the Ribbon, click the **Highlight Merge Fields** button. In addition to the chevrons, the highlight will make it easy to quickly identify the merge fields in the document.
9. Press **Enter** twice. Then click **Greeting line** in the Mail Merge task pane to open the Insert Greeting Line dialog box shown in **Figure 12–4**. If the greeting line is formatted to read Dear *«FirstName»* and the merged record doesn't include a first name, Word will automatically insert "Dear Sir or Madam" instead.

> **TIP**
>
> If the merge fields appear inside braces { } instead of chevrons « », Word is displaying field codes instead of merge fields. Right-click the field codes inside the braces, and then click Toggle Field Codes on the shortcut menu.

FIGURE 12–4
Insert Greeting Line dialog box

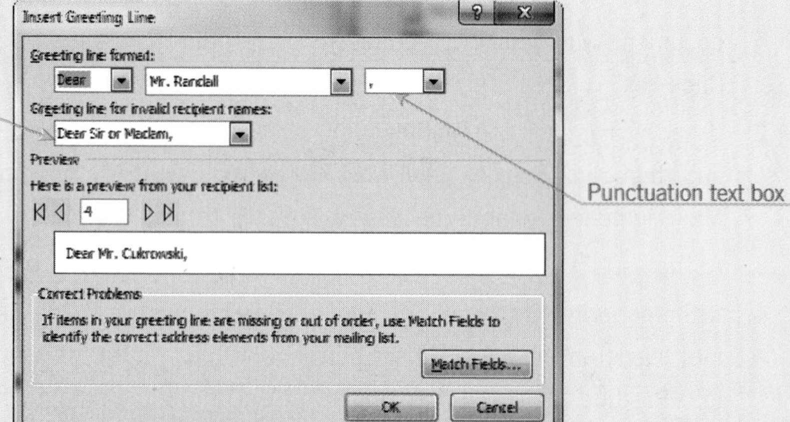

10. Click the **list arrow** in the Punctuation text box, and select **:** (a colon). Click **OK**. The GreetingLine merge field is inserted into the main document.
11. Delete **XX** after the # sign in the first sentence of the first paragraph. With the insertion point positioned just to the right of the # sign, click **More items** in the Mail Merge task pane. The Insert Merge Field dialog box opens, as shown in **Figure 12–5**.

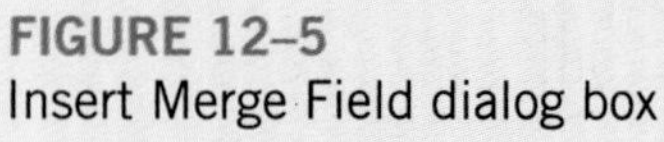

FIGURE 12–5
Insert Merge Field dialog box

12. Under Fields, select **Order**, and then click **Insert**. The merge field *«Order»* is inserted in the main document. Click **Close** in the Insert Merge Field dialog box.
13. Delete the next occurrence of **XX** in the same paragraph and repeat Step 12, inserting the **Total_Amount** field.
14. Save the changes to the main document, and leave the document and the Mail Merge task pane open for the next Step-by-Step.

Previewing, Merging, and Printing the Merged Documents

The fifth step in the process allows you to preview the merged data in the main document. If you are not satisfied with the preview results, you can click the Previous link at the bottom of the Mail Merge task pane to go back to Step 4 and edit the main document.

The sixth and final step in the process is to complete the merge. You can send the merged results directly to the printer, with options to print some or all of the merged records. Or, you can choose to save the merged results in a new document. The benefit of creating a new document is that you can print this document later, as you would any other Word document. For example, if you merged data to create labels or envelopes for a bulk mailing, you can save the merged results and then use the document in the future to print another set of labels or envelopes. You can also edit the results in the new document without altering the main document or the data source. For example, you can personalize the greeting line in one of several merged letters.

Step-by-Step 12.3

1. If necessary, open the **Order Confirmation Main Document** file from your solution files. And, if necessary, open the **Mail Merge** task pane to Step 4 of 6.
2. Click **Next: Preview your letters** at the bottom of the Mail Merge task pane. The main document is updated and shows the letter with a merged record. The merge fields are replaced with the variable data for Walter Cukrowski.
3. In the task pane, under Preview your letters, click the **Previous** button to view the merged letter to Recipient 3 (Castillo). Click the **Next** button twice to view the letter to Recipient 5 (Henson). Go to the letter addressed to Mr. Krikor Selian (Recipient 7).

TIP

If a merged document shows unexpected spaces or punctuation, you may have typed unnecessary spaces or punctuation in the data source records. Click *Previous: Write your letter* at the bottom of the task pane to return to Step 4. Make any necessary corrections to the data source, then click *Next: Complete the merge.*

4. To quickly locate a specific record, click **Find a recipient** in the Mail Merge pane. The Find in Field dialog box opens, as shown in **Figure 12–6**.

FIGURE 12–6
Find in Field dialog box

5. In the Find What box, type **J & R Products**. Click the **In Field** list arrow, and then click **Company**. Click **Find first**. When prompted to continue searching at the beginning of the database, click **Yes**. The merged document to John Kasle at J & R Products is displayed. Click **Close**.
6. In the task pane, under Make changes, click **Exclude this recipient**. The merged document is deleted, and the merged document for Krikor Selian is displayed.
7. Click **Next: Complete the merge** to show the final step in the process. Under Merge, click **Edit individual letters**. In the Merge to New Document dialog box, select the **Current record** option, then click **OK**. Word opens a new document titled *Letters1*. The new document contains only the merged letter for Krikor Selian.
8. In the greeting line, select **Mr. Selian** and then type **Krikor**. This makes the greeting less formal, which is appropriate when you know the recipient personally.
9. Save the new document as **Selian Letter**, followed by your initials. Close the document. The main document and the Mail Merge task pane should still be open, and the Selian letter is still part of the merged results.
10. At the bottom of the task pane, click **Previous: Preview your letters**. With the original Selian letter in the document window, click **Exclude this recipient** because you have saved a customized version of the letter as a separate document.
11. At the bottom of the task pane, click **Next: Complete the merge**. Under Merge, click **Print**. In the Merge to Printer dialog box, select **From** and then type **5** in both text boxes. Click **OK**. A Print dialog box opens. If you choose to print, only the merged letter for the specified record will print. Click **Cancel** in the Print dialog box.
12. Click **Edit individual letters**. In the Merge to New Document dialog box, select the **All** option, and then click **OK**. A new document, *Letters2*, opens. Save the new document as **Merged Order Confirmations**, followed by your initials.

13. Click the **File** tab and then click **Print**. The merged document appears in the Preview pane. You can view all seven pages of merged letters by clicking the Next and Previous buttons, using the vertical scroll bar on the right, or moving the wheel on the mouse.
14. Close the merged document. Close the main document, and when prompted to save the changes, click **Save**.

Creating and Editing Data Sources

As you have learned, the data source used for a mail merge can be created in a variety of applications. If the data source does not already exist, you can use the Mail Merge feature to help guide you through the process of creating a new data source. During the mail merge process, you can also edit and organize the records.

Creating a Data Source Using the Mail Merge Feature

Your first step in creating a data source is to identify the field names to be used. Although fields do not need to be in a particular order in the data source, for convenience, you may want to arrange the list so the fields are in an order that will make entering the data more expedient. Multiple merge documents can share the same data source. Some of the merge documents will use more fields than others. Therefore, when creating a data source, you must be sure to include all possible fields so the data can be used for a variety of merge documents.

Now that you are familiar with the mail merge process, you do not have to use the Wizard to guide you. Instead, you can use the buttons on the Mailings tab to complete the process. The advantage of using the Ribbon is that more options are available. When using the buttons on the Ribbon, you must perform the same basic tasks that you complete for all other merged documents. The buttons are arranged in a sequence that corresponds with the steps in the Mail Merge Wizard.

Step-by-Step 12.4

1. Open a new blank Word document.
2. Click the **Mailings** tab. In the Start Mail Merge group, click the **Start Mail Merge** button, and then click **Letters**.

3. In the Start Mail Merge group, click the **Select Recipients** button, and then click **Type New List**. The New Address List dialog box shown in **Figure 12–7** opens and shows common field names for addresses, which are frequently used in merged letters.

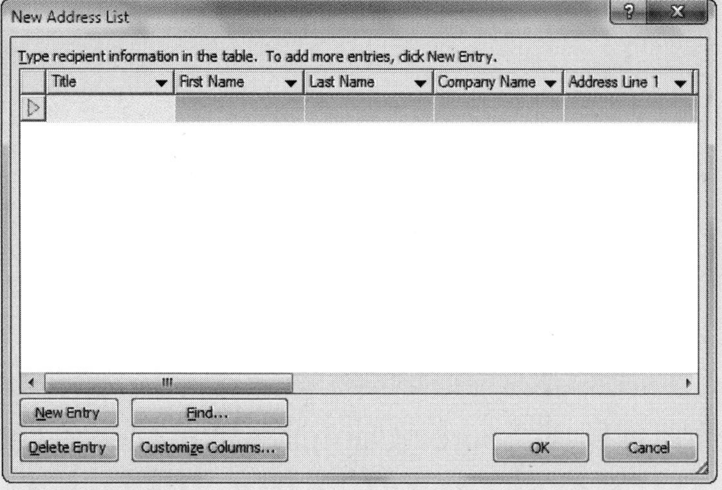

FIGURE 12–7
New Address List dialog box

4. Click **Customize Columns** at the bottom of the dialog box to open the Customize Address List dialog box shown in **Figure 12–8**.

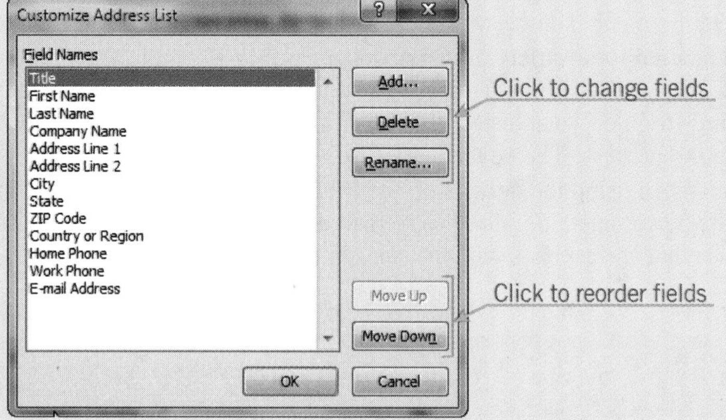

FIGURE 12–8
Customize Address List dialog box

5. Under Field Names, click **Company Name**, and then click **Delete** in the dialog box. When prompted to confirm the deletion, click **Yes**. Delete the following field names: **Address Line 2**, **Country or Region**, and **Work Phone**.
6. Click the field name **Address Line 1**, and then click **Rename**. In the To box, type **Address**, and then click **OK**.
7. Click the field name **E-mail Address**, and then click **Move Up** once to rearrange the order of the field names.
8. In the dialog box, click **Add**. In the Add Field dialog box, type **Contribution**, and then click **OK**. Click **Move Down** to make *Contribution* the last field name in the list. Click **OK** to close the dialog box.

9. The New Address List dialog box should still be open. Type the following data in the appropriate fields, pressing **Tab** to advance to the next field. To show more fields, enlarge the dialog box by dragging the dialog box borders.
   Title: **Mrs.**
   First Name: **Patsy**
   Last Name: **Stump**
   Address: **2237 Pinehurst Court**
   City: **Sterling Hts.**
   State: **MI**
   ZIP Code: **48310-7106**
   E-mail Address: **pstump@gateway.xyz**
   Home Phone: **248-555-8907**
   Contribution: **$500**
10. Click **New Entry** (or you can press Tab) to show a new row for the next record. Enter each of the following records. Do not be concerned when information such as contributions or e-mail addresses is not available. Just leave the fields blank.

Mr. Matt Caulfield
2650 Biddle Street
Wyandotte, MI 48192-5235
mc34@tools.xyz
734-555-8976

Ms. E. Moya
23761 Edward Street
Dearborn, MI 48128-1276
313-555-8767

Ms. Sharon Miller
6644 Norwood Avenue
Allen Park, MI 48101-2439
samiller@cool.xyz
313-555-9087
$100

Mr. Lane Sumners
15420 Meyer Avenue
Allen Park, MI 48101-2690
313-555-2323
$250

Ms. Eloisa Moya
23761 Edward Street
Dearborn, MI 48128-1276
moya331@tir.xyz
313-555-8767
$750

11. Click **OK** to close the New Address List dialog box. The Save Address List dialog box opens. Navigate to your solution folder, and in the File name box, type **Membership Contacts Data Source**, followed by your initials. Note in the Save as type box that the document type is Microsoft Office Address Lists. Click **Save**.
12. Close the document without saving changes.

Editing Data Source Records

As you work in the mail merge process, you can edit or delete existing entries and add new entries in the data source. If the data source is saved in an Access table, you can edit the data source in the Mail Merge Recipients dialog box by clicking the Edit button. However, if the data source was created in a Word table or in an Excel spreadsheet, the Edit button may not be available. When you close the Mail Merge Recipients dialog box, the data source is updated automatically to reflect the changes you made.

You should always check to make sure the fields in the data source correspond to the merge fields you have selected for the main document. The Match Fields command helps you identify fields from your data source that correspond with the required field. You should also check to make sure you do not have duplicate records.

Step-by-Step 12.5

1. Open the **Donation Letter** file from the drive and folder where your Data Files are stored. Save the document as **Donation Letter Main Document**, followed by your initials.
2. Click the **Mailings** tab. In the Start Mail Merge group, click the **Start Mail Merge** button, and then click **Letters**.
3. In the Start Mail Merge group, click the **Select Recipients** button, and then click **Use Existing List**. Navigate to and open your solution file **Membership Contacts Data Source**.

4. In the Start Mail Merge group, click the **Edit Recipient List** button. The Mail Merge Recipients dialog box opens, as shown in **Figure 12–9**.

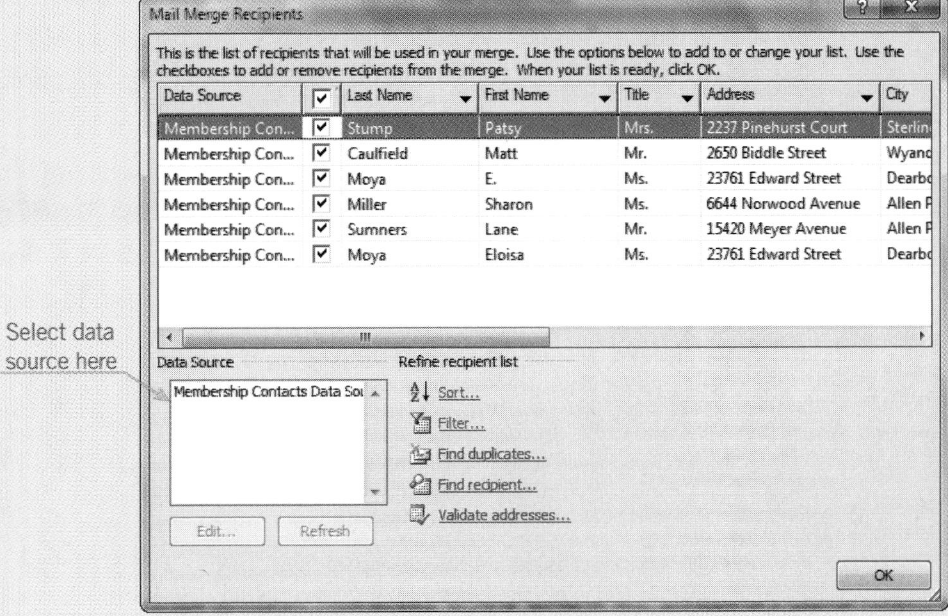

FIGURE 12–9
Mail Merge Recipients dialog box

5. Under Data Source, select **Membership Contacts Data Source**. Click the **Edit** button**.** The Edit Data Source dialog box opens, as shown in **Figure 12–10**.

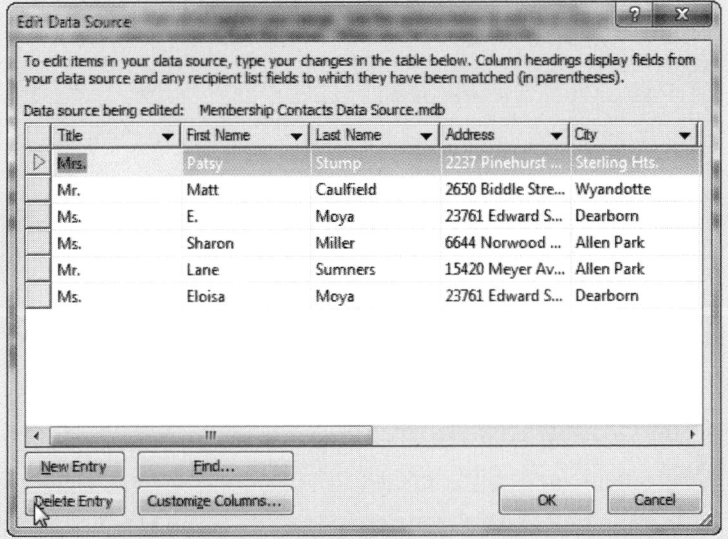

FIGURE 12–10
Edit Data Source dialog box

6. Select the record for **Sharon Miller**, and then scroll to the right end of the record to show the Contribution field. Change the contribution amount to **$900**.

7. Scroll back to the left. In the first record, *Patsy Stump*, change the last name to **Marquez**.
8. Click **OK** to close the dialog box. When prompted to save the changes to the recipient list and the data source, click **Yes**. The Mail Merge Recipients dialog box is still open. Notice that the records in the dialog box reflect the changes you just made.
9. Click **Find duplicates**. The Find Duplicates dialog box shown in **Figure 12–11** opens, identifying two records with similar data. Deselect the first record, and then click **OK** to close the dialog box. The first Moya record will not be included in the merge. Click **OK** again to close the Mail Merge Recipients dialog box.

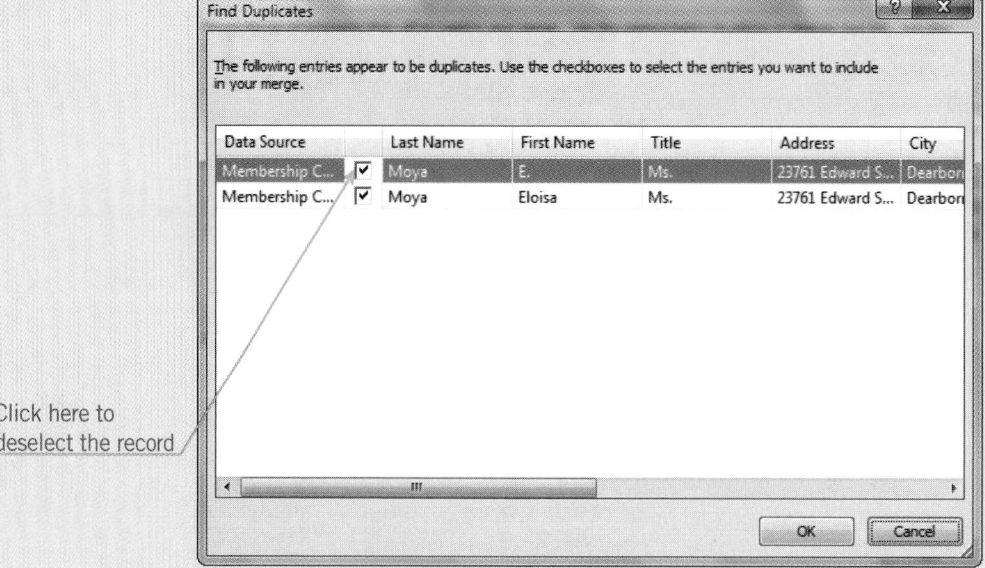

FIGURE 12–11
Find Duplicates dialog box

10. In the main document, delete the first set of XXs under the date line. Leave the insertion point positioned in the blank line. In the Write & Insert Fields group, click the **Address Block** button. The Insert Address Block dialog box opens.
11. In the Correct Problems section, click **Match Fields**. The Match Fields dialog box shown in **Figure 12–12** opens. Notice that the *Address* field in the data source is matched to the *Address 1* field in the Address Block. Word automatically matched the fields, but when necessary, you can manually match a field by clicking the list arrow and selecting a field name. Click **OK** twice to close the dialog boxes.

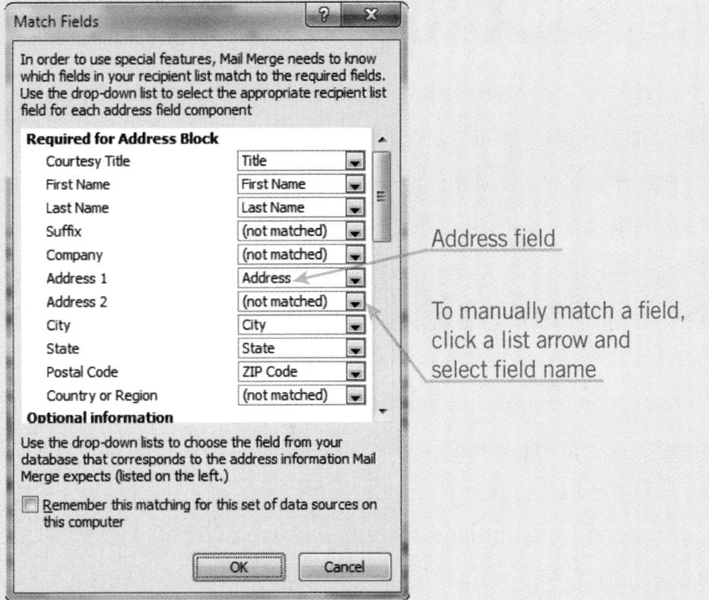

FIGURE 12–12
Match Fields dialog box

12. In the main document, delete the next occurrence of XX. In the Write & Insert Fields group, click the **Greeting Line** button. Change the punctuation to a colon, and then click **OK**.
13. Save the changes to the main document and leave it open for the next Step-by-Step.

Sorting and Filtering Data Source Records

If you want the merged documents to be organized in alphabetic or numeric order, you can sort the data source records before completing the merge. The records can be sorted in ascending or descending order by up to three fields in the records. For example, businesses can get a discount on postage rates by presorting the envelopes by postal code. By sorting the records before completing the merge, the envelopes will printed in the required order.

A ***filter*** screens records by identifying criteria that must be met before the records are included in a merge. Suppose, for example, you want to merge records only for people who live in the state of Michigan. To add additional criteria to the filter, you can use the And operator. For example, you might want to merge all records of individuals who live in the city of Dearborn and have the last name Smith. Only records that meet all three of these conditions will be merged. You can use the Or operator to filter for two different conditions. For example, you can specify a merge for records where the person lives in Bay City or Saginaw. This filter would merge all records for both cities.

VOCABULARY
filter

Step-by-Step 12.6

1. If necessary, open the **Donation Letter Main Document** file from your solution files. When prompted to place data from the data source file, click **Yes**.
2. In the Start Mail Merge group on the Mailings tab, click the **Edit Recipient List** button. The Mail Merge Recipients dialog box opens. Resize the dialog box to show all the fields, or as many fields as possible.
3. Click the **Last Name** column heading. The records are sorted in ascending alphabetic order by last name. Click the **Last Name** column heading again. The records are sorted in descending alphabetic order by last name.
4. If necessary, scroll to the right to view the E-mail Address field. Click the **list arrow** in the E-mail Address column heading, and then select **(Blanks)**. The E. Moya and Lane Sumners records, which have blank e-mail address fields, are displayed. Notice that the list arrow in the E-mail Address column heading changes color to indicate that the field has been filtered.
5. After you specify filter options for a data source, the options remain in effect until you change them. To remove the filter options, click the **list arrow** in the E-mail Address column heading, and then select **(All)** to show all the records in the E-mail Address field.
6. If necessary, scroll to the left to show the *City* field. Click the **list arrow** in the City column heading, and then select **Allen Park**. Only records of those contacts living in Allen Park are displayed. Click the **list arrow** in the City column heading, and then select **(All)** to show all the records again.
7. Click the **list arrow** in the City column heading, and then select **(Advanced...)**. The Filter and Sort dialog box opens.
8. Filter the records using multiple criteria:
   a. In the first row, click the **list arrow** in the Field box, and then select **City**.
   b. Make sure Equal to appears in the Comparison box.
   c. In the Compare to text box, type **Allen Park**.
   d. In the first text box of the second row, *And* should already be selected.
   e. In the second row, click the **list arrow** in the Field box, scroll down, and then select **Contribution**. Click the **list arrow** in the Comparison box, and then select **Greater than or equal**. In the Compare to text box, type **$500**.

f. The filter criteria should match that shown in **Figure 12–13**.

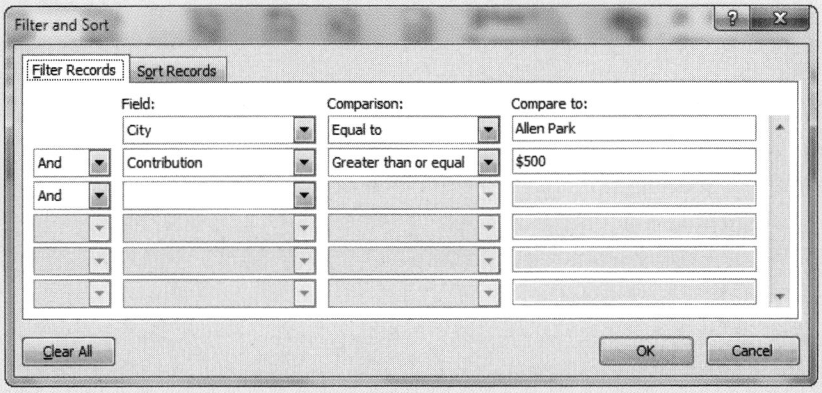

FIGURE 12–13
Filter and Sort dialog box

9. Click **OK** to close the Filter and Sort dialog box. The record for Sharon Miller is the only record that meets both criteria.
10. Click the **list arrow** in any column heading, and then select **(Advanced...)**. The Filter and Sort dialog box reopens. Click **Clear All** to remove all filters, and then click **OK**. All of the records should appear again in the Mail Merge Recipients dialog box.
11. Click **OK** to close the Mail Merge Recipients dialog box.
12. Save the changes to the main document, and leave it open for the next Step-by-Step.

Inserting Fields with Conditions

The Rules button provides special fields that set conditions for performing an action during the merge process. When you insert these special fields in a main document, you set parameters that Word uses to make a decision. For example, you can insert a rule in the main document for adding a paragraph of text under certain conditions. During the merge process, Word compares the specified field criteria to the merged field data. If the referenced merged field data meets the specified criteria, Word includes the additional paragraph in the merged letter. On the other hand, if the merged field data does not meet the specified field criteria, the additional paragraph does not appear in the merged letter for that record.

Table 12–1 describes each of the field rules.

TABLE 12–1 Field rules

RULE NAME	DESCRIPTION OF THE RULE
Ask	Instructs Word to show a message to prompt the user to respond. Use this field to repeat the same information in more than one place in a document. For example, you can set a rule to show a prompt when a name appears in a document for the second time. When prompted about the second occurrence, the user can choose to use only the first name for all occurrences after the first occurrence.
Fill in	Instructs Word to show a message to prompt the user to insert information. Use this field to insert information only once. For example, you can set the rule so that Word will prompt the user to enter the current date.
If...Then...Else...	Instructs Word to take action for set conditions. For example, if the merged record data includes a specified postal code, the letter will include a sentence about the location of a store.
Merge Record #	Instructs Word to insert the ordinal position of the merged data record, which reflects any sorting or filtering before the merge. For example, you can set a rule such that an applicant's entry number will appear in the document.
Merge Sequence #	Instructs Word to count the number of records in the merged document. The number is not visible in the merged document until the merge is completed. For example, the main document includes a sentence about the number of individuals attending an event. When the merge is completed, the number in the sentence will reflect the number of merged records.
Next Record	Instructs Word to insert the next data record into the current document without starting a new document. For example, this field is used when Word creates a full page of labels so that multiple records appear on the same page.
Next Record If	Instructs Word to determine whether the next data record should be merged into the current document or into a new document. For example, if two contacts have the same last name and address, both names can be inserted in the same document to eliminate mailing the same letter twice to the same address.
Set Bookmark	Instructs Word to refer to specific information stored in a bookmark. For example, the date for an event may appear several times throughout the document. Each occurrence of the date in the letter is cross-referenced to the bookmark. If the date changes, you simply change the content in the bookmark field and then all occurrences of the date in the document will be updated.
Skip Record If	Instructs Word to exclude records from the merge if conditions are not met. For example, if the contact has an out-of-state address, the record is not included in the merge.

Step-by-Step 12.7

1. If necessary, open the **Donation Letter Main Document** file from your solution files. When prompted to place data from the data source file, click **Yes**.
2. Position the insertion point in front of the second sentence in the first paragraph of the body of the letter. In the Write & Insert Fields group on the Mailings tab, click the **Rules** button, and then click **If...Then...Else....** The Insert Word Field: IF dialog box opens, as shown in **Figure 12–14**.

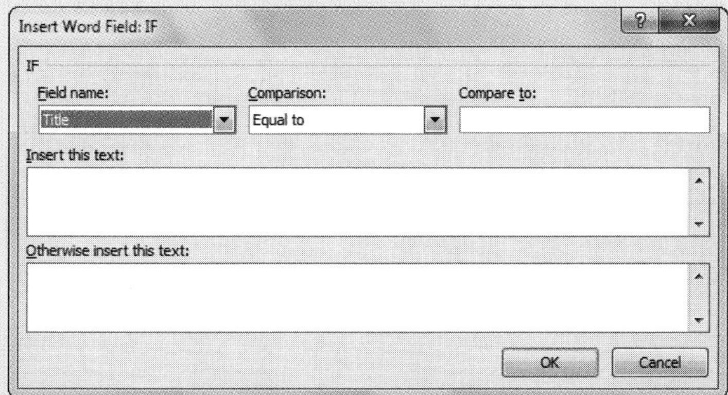

FIGURE 12–14
Insert Word Field: IF dialog box

3. Click the **Field name** list arrow, scroll down, and then select **Contribution**.
4. Click the **Comparison** list arrow, then select **Greater than or equal**.
5. In the Compare to text box, type **$500**.
6. In the Insert this text box, type **Your donation is very generous.**, and then press the **spacebar** to create a blank space after the sentence. Leave the next text box empty. Click **OK**.
7. In the Preview Results group, click the **Preview Results** button. Use the Next Record and Previous Record buttons, shown in **Figure 12–15**, to navigate through the merged documents. You will see that the merged documents for Recipients 2, 4, and 5 include the extra sentence. Recipient 3 does not appear in the preview because that record was not included in the merge.

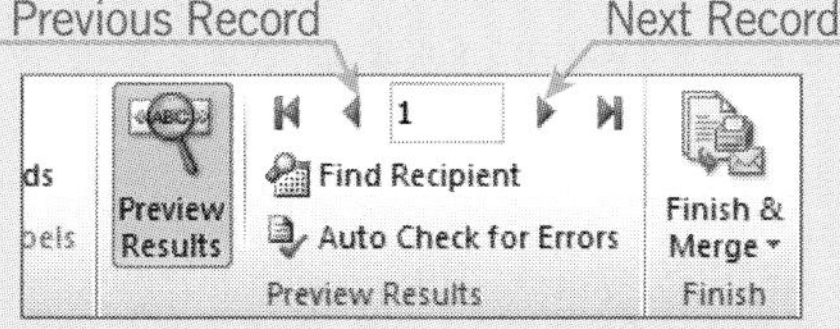

FIGURE 12–15
Preview Results group on the Mailings tab

8. Go to a letter containing the new sentence (Recipients 2, 4, or 5). Notice that the font style and size for the additional sentence does not match the font or format for the rest of the paragraph. Select the first paragraph, then right-click to open the Mini toolbar. Change the font style to **Calibri** and the font size to **11** point.
9. Click the **Next Record** and **Previous Record** buttons. The variable text should now match the boilerplate text in all letters. Click the **Preview Results** button to toggle off the preview.
10. In the Finish group, click the **Finish & Merge** button, and then click **Edit Individual Documents**. If necessary, select the **All** option in the Merge to New Document dialog box. Click **OK**.
11. A new document (such as *Letters3*) is opened. Save the new merged document as **Merged Donation Letters**, followed by your initials.
12. Click the **File** tab and then click **Print** to view the merged document in Preview pane. Navigate through all the pages in the document to view all five letters. At this point you could print one or all of the merged letters.
13. Close the merged document and the main document. When prompted to save the changes to the main document, click **Save**.

Preparing Mailing Labels and Envelopes

The processes for merging data to create envelopes and labels are similar to those used for creating mail merge letters. As with other merges, you can use data from an existing data source or you can create a new data source. Just as you can edit individual letters and print letters for selected records, you can edit individual labels or envelopes for selected records.

TIP

Note that the Envelopes and Labels buttons in the Create group are used only for individual envelopes or labels. These buttons are not used in mail merge documents.

Preparing Mailing Labels

Label options include more than just mailing labels. You can also merge records to create labels for name badges, business cards, postcards, folder labels, and more. When you select the Labels document type, Word automatically inserts the Next Record field rule, which propagates the first label to the other labels on the same page.

You can preview the merged records before you print. You may want to print a sample of labels on plain paper to compare the plain sheet sample with the sheet of labels. Then you can check to see if you need to position the sheet of labels differently in the printer or if you need to adjust your main document settings (margins, page length, and column width).

Step-by-Step 12.8

1. Open the **Customers** file from the drive and folder where your Data Files are stored. Save the document as **Customers Data Source**, followed by your initials, and then close the document.
2. Open a new blank Word document and save it as **Customer Labels Main Document**, followed by your initials.
3. Click the **Mailings** tab. In the Start Mail Merge group, click the **Start Mail Merge** button, and then select **Labels**. The Label Options dialog box opens, as shown in **Figure 12–16**. The options shown in the dialog box vary depending on the type of printer you use.

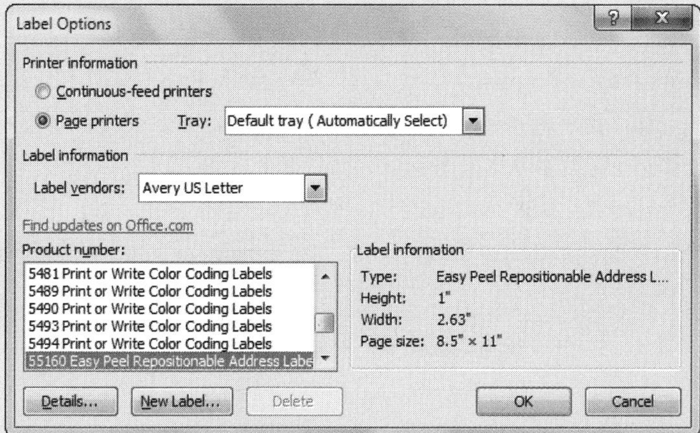

FIGURE 12–16
Label Options dialog box

4. Under Printer information, make sure the **Page printers** option is enabled. Under Label information, in the Label vendors box, select **Avery US Letter**. Under Product number, select **55160 Easy Peel Repositionable Address Labels**. A description of the label height and width is provided at the right.
5. Make sure your settings match those shown in Figure 12–16 (your Tray information may differ), and then click **OK**. If the gridlines for your label placement in the document are not visible, click the Table Tools Layout tab, and in the Table group, click the View Gridlines button, then click the Mailings tab.
6. In the Start Mail Merge group, click the **Select Recipients** button. Click **Use Existing List**, navigate to the folder where you save your solution files, select **Customers Data Source**, then click **Open**. The first label is still blank, but the other labels contain the merge field *Next Record*.

TIP

Labels come in a variety of sizes. Be sure to use the correct product number in the Label Options dialog box. The product number is generally provided on the label package.

7. The insertion point should be positioned in the first label. In the Write & Insert Fields group, click the **Address Block** button to open the Insert Address Block dialog box. Use the Next and Previous buttons in the Preview pane to view the data source addresses. You'll see that Recipients 3 and 11 require more than four lines; there won't be enough space to print all the lines on these labels. Return to Recipient 1 and click **Cancel**.
8. Format the address fields manually:
   a. In the Write & Insert Fields group, click the **Insert Merge Field** button arrow. Click **Title**. The merge field is entered in the first label. Press the **spacebar** to enter a blank space after the merge field.
   b. Click the **Insert Merge Field** button arrow, click **FirstName**, and then press the **spacebar**.
   c. Insert the **LastName** field, and then press **Enter**.
   d. Insert the **Company** field, and then press **Enter**.
   e. Insert the **Address1** field, and then press the **spacebar**. Insert the **Address2** field, and then press **Enter**.
   f. Insert the **City** field, type **,** (a comma), and then press the **spacebar**. Insert the **State** field, press the **spacebar**, and then insert the **PostalCode** field.
9. Select all the merge fields in the first label. Right-click to open the Mini toolbar, and then change the font size to **10** point. With the merge fields still selected, click the **Home** tab. In the Paragraph group, click the **Line and Paragraph Spacing** button and then click **Remove Space Before Paragraph**.
10. Click the **Mailings** tab. In the Write & Insert Fields group, click the **Update Labels** button to propagate the address fields for each label on the sheet. Word inserts the merge fields, with the 10-point font format, on all the other labels in the document. Do not be concerned that the first line of merge fields wraps to the next line.
11. In the Preview Results group, click the **Preview Results** button to view the merged data. You will notice that many of the labels on the page are blank, because the data source did not contain enough records to fill the page of labels. Click the **Preview Results** button again to toggle off the feature.
12. In the Finish group, click the **Finish & Merge** button, and then click **Edit Individual Documents**. Confirm that the All option is selected, then click **OK**. All records are merged into a single document.
13. Save the new merged labels document as **Merged Customer Labels**, followed by your initials. Click the **File** tab, and then click **Print** to view the document in the Preview pane.

14. Close the merged document, and then close the main document. When prompted to save the changes to the main document, click **Save**.

Preparing Envelopes Using the Mail Merge Feature

You can also use the Mail Merge feature to prepare addressed envelopes for a group or mass mailing. The process for preparing envelopes is very similar to the process you just completed to create mailing labels. However, instead of specifying label options, you specify options for the envelope size. You must also set the printing options to indicate how the envelopes are fed into the printer. Word will automatically insert a return address derived from the user information stored on your computer. You can replace this return address with a new one, or you can delete the return address if you are using envelopes with preprinted return addresses.

EXTRA FOR EXPERTS

Microsoft offers an add-in product that enables you to validate the existence and accuracy of addresses. This validation software is available for a fee. If you have the address validation software installed, you can use the Validate option in the Mail Merge Recipients dialog box to verify the recipients' addresses.

Step-by-Step 12.9

1. Open the **Clients** file from the drive and folder where your Data Files are stored. Save the document as **Clients Data Source**, followed by your initials, and then close the document.
2. Open a new blank Word document, and save it as **Client Envelopes Main Document**, followed by your initials. If necessary, toggle on **Show/Hide ¶** to display nonprinting formatting characters.
3. Click the **Mailings** tab. In the Start Mail Merge group, click the **Start Mail Merge** button, and then click **Envelopes**. The Envelope Options dialog box opens, as shown in **Figure 12–17**.

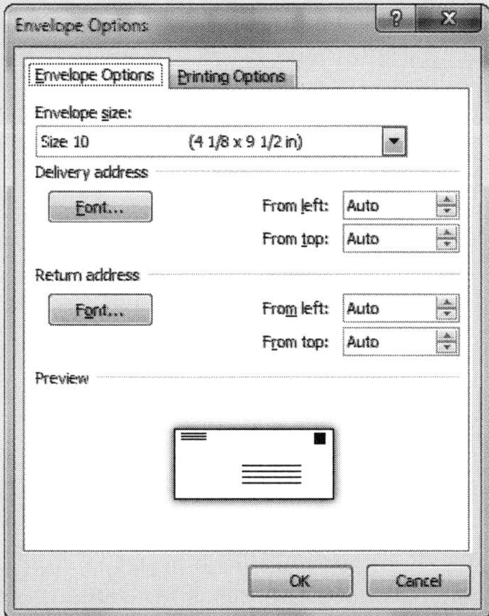

FIGURE 12–17
Envelope Options tab in the Envelope Options dialog box

4. On the Envelope Options tab, make sure the Envelope size is set for **Size 10**. The Size 10 envelope is commonly used for mailing business documents.
5. Click the **Printing Options** tab to display options similar to those shown in **Figure 12–18**. Options vary depending on the type of printer you use. This tab includes feed method settings, which are dependent on your currently selected printer. Under Feed method, Word suggests how to place the envelope in the tray. Click **OK** to close the dialog box. The document changes to landscape orientation.

FIGURE 12–18
Printing Options tab in the Envelope Options dialog box

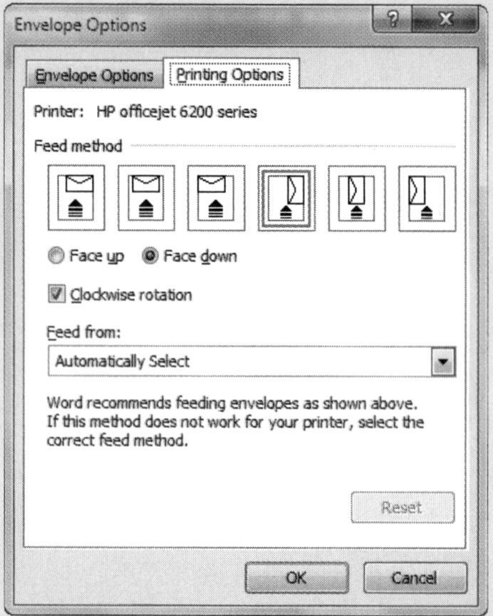

6. In the Start Mail Merge group, click the **Select Recipients** button, and then click **Use Existing List**. Navigate to and select your solution file **Clients Data Source**. Click **Open**.
7. Click near the paragraph mark in the middle of the envelope where you want the delivery address to appear. A cross-hatched border appears to indicate a preformatted text box.
8. In the Write & Insert Fields group, click the **Address Block** button. Click **OK**, and the AddressBlock merge field is inserted in the text box.
9. If necessary, show the nonprinting formatting characters. Click in the first blank paragraph in the upper-left corner. Type the following return address:
   MAPPS Investments
   259 Madison Avenue
   New York, NY 10016-2401
10. In the Preview Results group, click the **Preview Results** button to view the merged data. Navigate through the merged documents, and then click the **Preview Results** button again to close the preview.

11. In the Start Mail Merge group, click the **Edit Recipient List** button. In the Mail Merge Recipients dialog box, under Refine recipient list, click **Find duplicates**. Uncheck one of the records for *Garverich*, then click **OK** twice to close both dialog boxes.
12. In the Finish group, click the **Finish & Merge** button, and then click **Edit Individual Documents**. Confirm that the All option is selected, then click **OK**. All records are merged into a single document.
13. Save the new merged envelopes document as **Merged Client Envelopes**, followed by your initials. Scroll down through the document and you will see that one page has been created for each record.
14. Close the new merged document and main document. When prompted to save the changes to the main document, click **Yes**.

Creating a Main Document for Mass E-Mails

The merge feature also enables you to create group or mass mailings for personalized e-mail messages. You can use Outlook or another MAPI-compliant e-mail program. ***MAPI (Messaging Application Programming Interface)*** is a Windows programming interface that provides applications with a standard way to communicate when sending e-mail. This interface enables Word to share information during the merge process with one of the many MAPI-compliant e-mail programs.

VOCABULARY
MAPI (Messaging Application Programming Interface)

For the data source, you can use the contact information in your e-mail program, and in some cases, such as a customer or client list, the list of recipients may already be saved in a contacts subfolder. You can also access data files in Word, Excel, or Access, which are all MAPI-compliant.

The merge process for sending e-mails is similar to that for creating a merged letter. After you finalize the e-mail message in the main document, however, you send the messages using your e-mail program instead of printing the merged results.

To create a mass e-mail merge, you must use the same versions of Outlook and Word, such as Outlook 2010 and Word 2010. Also note that you cannot designate a recipient in the Cc line in the e-mail header, and you cannot attach files to the message.

Step-by-Step 12.10

1. Open the **Orders Shipped** file from the drive and folder where your Data Files are stored. Save the document as **Orders Shipped Data Source**, followed by your initials, and then close the document.
2. Open the **Shipped Message** file from the drive and folder where your Data Files are stored. Save the document as **Shipped Message Main Document**, followed by your initials. If necessary, toggle on **Show/Hide ¶** to display nonprinting formatting characters.

3. Click the **Mailings** tab. In the Start Mail Merge group, click the **Start Mail Merge** button, and then click **E-mail Messages**. The document view changes to Web Layout view.
4. Click the **Select Recipients** button, and then click **Use Existing List**. Navigate to and select your solution file **Orders Shipped Data Source**. Click **Open**.
5. Click the **Edit Recipient List** button. Scroll to the right to show the last column, *Shipped*. Click the **list arrow** in the Shipped column heading, and then click **Yes**. Click **OK** to close the dialog box.
6. With the insertion point in the first blank paragraph of the document, click the **Greeting Line** button in the Write & Insert Fields group. Click **OK** to accept the settings.
7. Delete the **XX**s in the second sentence of the message. Click the **Inset Merge Field** button arrow, and then click **Order**. The Order field is inserted following the # sign.
8. In the Preview Results group, click the **Preview Results** button. Review some of the messages to make sure the greeting line looks appropriate and the product number is inserted correctly. Click the **Preview Results** button again to close the preview.
9. In the Finish group, click the **Finish & Merge** button, and then click **Send E-mail Messages**. The Merge to E-mail dialog box opens, as shown in **Figure 12–19**.

FIGURE 12–19
Merge to E-mail dialog box

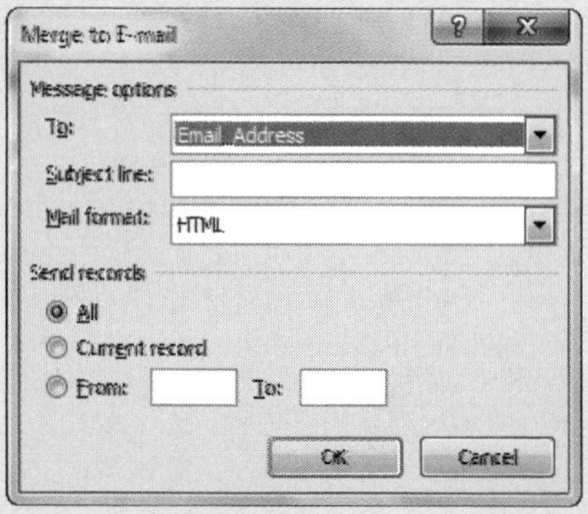

10. If necessary, click the **list arrow** in the To box and then select **Email_Address**. In the Subject line text box, type **Your order has shipped!**.
11. The next step would be to click OK, which would send all the e-mails in your default e-mail program. Instead, click **Cancel**.
12. Click the **Finish & Merge** button, and then click **Edit Individual Documents**. Click **OK** to accept that all records will be merged.

13. Scroll down through the document. You will see the message repeated several times, and each message is formatted on its own page with a Next Page section break. So that your instructor can see that you have completed all the steps, save the document as **Merged Shipped Messages**, followed by your initials.
14. Close the merged document and the main document. When prompted to save the changes to the main document, click **Save**.

Creating Catalogs and Directories

The merge feature is also convenient for creating a catalog or a price list. For example, a company may release a product price list at the beginning of each month. If the product information is stored in a data source, the information can easily be updated and merged into a Directory type main document.

Before the merge, you can edit a directory main document and data source in the same way you edit main documents and data sources for other types of merges. You can update the data source records, add or delete records, and sort and filter the records.

When you apply formats to the merge fields in the main document, the formats are applied to the variable data when the records are merged. Another way to format merged data is to add a formatting switch to the field code. A ***switch*** is a special instruction that modifies a field result. For example, if the data source includes the price of a product (55.95), but the information does not include dollar signs, you can create a switch to control the number format. The following is a merge field with a switch to add the dollar sign and the number format: { Price \# $#,###.00 }. In this switch, *Price* refers to the name of the field; *\#* indicates the switch is to format numbers; *$* is the character to be added in front of the field results; *#, ###* specifies the maximum number of digits; and *.00* indicates the decimal place and the number of digits to follow the decimal.

VOCABULARY
switch

Table 12–2 shows a few more switches that are commonly used. You can find additional switches by searching the keywords "field codes" in the Word Help screens, and then looking for a specific field name, such as *Date*. Then you can see if switches are available for that field.

TABLE 12–2 Common switches

SWITCH	TYPE	EXAMPLES	DESCRIPTION OF THE SWITCH
*	Capitalization	{ State * Upper }	The results for the field *State* will display all letters capitalized.
\@	Date/Time	{ Date \@, "dddd, MMMM d" } { Time \@, "hh:mm AM/PM" }	The results for the field *Date* will display in the format *Monday, April 11*. The results for the field *Time* will display in the format *10:30 AM*.
\#	Number	{ Phone \# ###'-' ###'-'#### }	The results for the field *Phone* will display with hyphens.
\p	Path	{ Filename \p }	The results for the field *Filename* will display the file location, or path, after the filename.

Step-by-Step 12.11

1. Open the **Products** file from the drive and folder where your Data Files are stored. Save the document as **Products Data Source**, followed by your initials, and then close the document.
2. Open the **Catalog** file from the drive and folder where your Data Files are stored. Save the document as **Catalog Main Document**, followed by your initials. If necessary, toggle on **Show/Hide ¶** to display nonprinting formatting characters.
3. Click the **Mailings** tab. In the Start Mail Merge group, click the **Start Mail Merge** button and then select **Directory**.
4. Click the **Select Recipients** button, and then click **Use Existing List**. Navigate to and select your solution file **Products Data Source**, and then click **Open**.
5. Click the **Edit Recipient List** button. Under Data Source, click the data source filename, **Products Data Source**, and then click **Edit**. The Data Form dialog box opens, as shown in **Figure 12–20**.

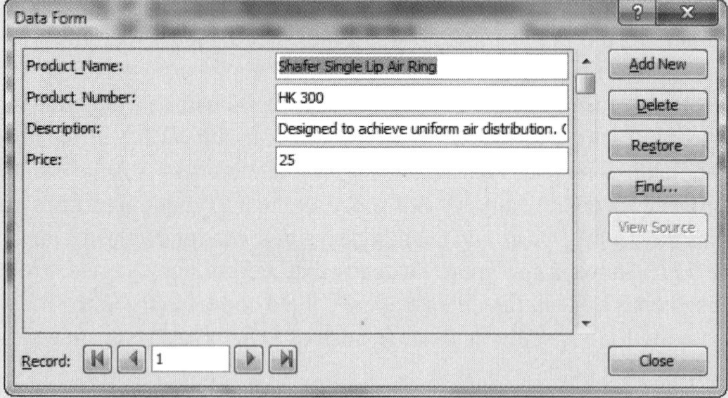

FIGURE 12–20
Data Form dialog box

6. Click **Find**. Drag the Find in Field dialog box that opens so you can see the Data Form dialog box. In the **Find what** text box, type **Shafer**, and then click **Find First**. Click **Find Next** to go to the next occurrence.
7. The *Shafer Internal Bubble Cooling System, IBC 150* appears in the Data Form dialog box. Close the Find in Field dialog box.
8. In the Data Form dialog box, change the price from *495* to **575**. Click **Close**, and then click **OK** to close the Mail Merge Recipients dialog box.
9. Insert the merge fields into the main document:
   a. Position the insertion point in the main document after *Item #:* and press the **spacebar**.
   b. In the Write & Insert Fields group, click the **Insert Merge Field** button arrow, and then click **Product_Number**.

c. Position the insertion point after *Product:*. Press the **spacebar** and insert the merge field **Product_Name**.

d. Position the insertion point in the blank paragraph just below *Product:*. Insert the merge field **Description**.

e. Position the insertion point in the main document after *List Price:*. Press the **spacebar** and insert the merge field **Price**.

10. Right-click the **Price** field, and then click **Edit Field**. The Field dialog box opens. In the lower-left corner, click **Field Codes**. The dialog box changes to display the options shown in **Figure 12–21**.

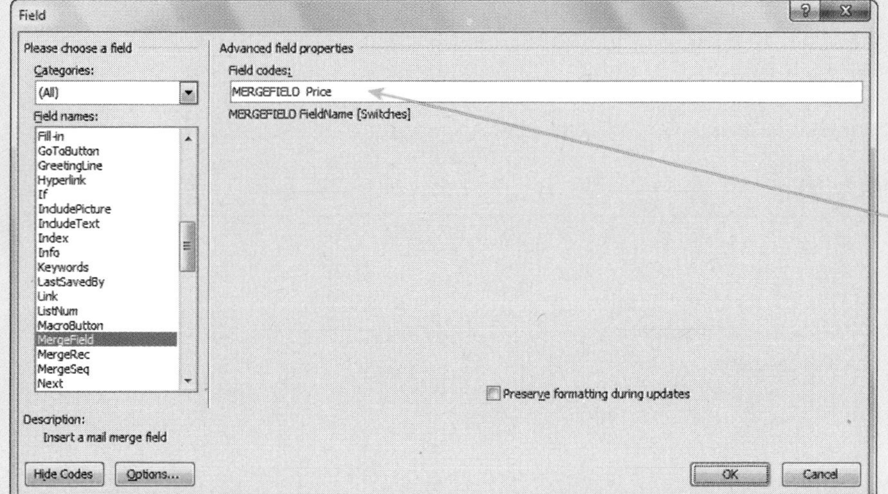

FIGURE 12–21
Field code options in the Field dialog box

11. Click to the right of *Price* in the Field codes text box and type **\# $#,###.00**. Then click **OK**.

12. In the Preview Results group, click the **Preview Results** button. A $ appears before each price, and the numbers are formatted with commas and decimals. Click the **Preview Results** button again to toggle off the feature.

13. In the Finish group, click the **Finish & Merge** button, and then click **Edit Individual Documents**. Click **OK** to merge all the records to a new document. Save the new merged document as **Merged Product Catalog**, followed by your initials.

14. Close the merged document, and then close the main document. When prompted to save changes to the data source file, click **Yes**. When prompted to save the changes to the main document, click **Save**.

SUMMARY

In this lesson, you learned:

- You can use the mail merge feature to create personalized and customized form letters, mailing labels, and envelopes.
- The mail merge process involves combining a main document with variable information from a data source.
- To create the main document, you can use the current document, or you can start from a template or an existing document.
- For the variable data, you can use an existing data source or you can create a new data source.
- You insert fields into the main document to merge the variable data from the data source.
- Data records can be sorted and edited before you merge them with a main document, and you can apply rules to the fields, which set parameters for the variable content.
- You can preview merge results before you complete a merge, and you can edit individual merged records.
- You can use the mail merge process to personalize an e-mail message to be sent to multiple recipients.
- You can use the mail merge process to create catalogs and directories.

VOCABULARY REVIEW

Define the following terms:

data source
field
field names
filter
MAPI (Messaging Application Programming Interface)
main document
merge fields
record
switch

REVIEW QUESTIONS

TRUE / FALSE

Circle T if the statement is true or F if the statement is false.

T F 1. If the data source does not already exist, you can create a new data source during the merge process.

T F 2. When the merge process is completed for a letter document type, you can choose to print all letters, the letter for the current record, or the letters for a range of records.

T F 3. The Ribbon provides more options for the mail merge process than the Mail Merge Wizard.

T F 4. Fields must be arranged in a specific order in the data source before the records can be merged into the main document.

T F 5. During the mail merge process, you can update and add or delete records.

MATCHING

Match the correct term in Column 2 to its description in Column 1.

Column 1

_____ 1. one or more characters that create a piece of information

_____ 2. a collection of variable information to be used in a merge

_____ 3. a label identifying a field

_____ 4. a placeholder in the main document

_____ 5. a group of related fields

Column 2

A. record

B. field name

C. main document

D. field

E. data source

F. filter

G. merge field

MULTIPLE CHOICE

Select the best response for the following statements.

1. The mail merge feature enables you to personalize and customize ______________ for mass mailings.

   A. letters

   B. e-mail messages

   C. envelopes and labels

   D. all of the above

2. The ______________ contains the variable information used in the merge process.

   A. field name

   B. main document

   C. merge field

   D. data source

3. The ______________ command helps you identify fields from your data source that correspond with the required field.

   A. Match Fields

   B. Highlight Merge Fields

   C. Auto Check for Errors

   D. Find Recipient

4. The ______________ button provides special fields that set conditions for performing an action during the merge process.

   A. Address Block

   B. Select Recipients

   C. Rules

   D. Insert Merge Field

5. The ______________ rule instructs Word to show a message to prompt the user to insert information.

   A. If...Else...

   B. Fill in

   C. Next Record If

   D. Set Bookmark

PROJECTS

If you have a SAM 2010 user profile, your instructor may have assigned an autogradable version of the indicated project. If so, log into the SAM 2010 Web site at *www.cengage.com/sam2010* to download the instruction and start files.

PROJECT 12–1

1. Open the **Sponsors Letter** file from the drive and folder where your Data Files are stored. Save the document as **Sponsors Letter Main Document**, followed by your initials.
2. Begin the merge process and create a merge document for letters. The current document is the main document.
3. Create a new data source with the following field names: **Title**, **First Name**, **Last Name**, **Company Name**, **Address**, **City**, **State**, and **ZIP Code**.
4. Enter the following records in the data source:
   Mr. Erik Stein
   Shannon Auto Sales
   954 West State Street
   Trenton, OH 45067-9690

   Mrs. Jennifer O'Brian
   Time for You
   3569 Radabaugh Road
   Trenton, OH 45067-2046

   Ms. Patti Ruiz
   Trenton Heating & Cooling
   5301 Kennedy Road
   Trenton, OH 45067-9436

   Dr. Barry Grossman
   McCormick Health Center
   607 Wayne Madison Road
   Trenton, OH 45067-9665
5. Save the data source as **Sponsors Data Source**, followed by your initials.
6. Complete the letter by inserting the appropriate fields for the inside address and the greeting. This letter will be printed on stationery that includes the Chamber name and address at the top of the page.
7. Add one more record to the data source:
   Mrs. Becky Laws
   Trenton Grocery and Pharmacy
   519 Holland Drive
   Trenton, OH 45067-9704
8. Sort the records in ascending order by the company name.
9. Preview the merged documents, and merge all the records to a new document. Save the new document as **Merged Sponsors Letters**, followed by your initials.
10. In Backstage view, preview how the Merged Sponsors Letters document will print.
11. Close the merged document and the main document. Save the changes to the main document.

SAM PROJECT 12–2

1. Open the **Account Holders** file from the drive and folder where your Data Files are stored. Save the file as **Account Holders Data Source**, followed by your initials. This data source contains account balance data that is updated daily. Close the data source file.
2. Open the **Overdraft Letter** file from the folder where your Data Files are stored. Save the document as **Overdraft Letter Main Document**, followed by your initials.
3. Begin the merge process by identifying the document type as **Letters**. Identify the data source as **Account Holders Data Source**.
4. Insert fields for the recipient's address and fields for the greeting line. Use appropriate punctuation in the greeting line.
5. In the first paragraph, insert fields for the account number and the current account balance. Edit the Account_Balance merge field by adding the switch **\# -$#,###.00**. This will format the field results so that a minus sign and a $ will appear in front of the number data.
6. Edit the data source. Add the title **Ms.** for Recipient 2, and add the title **Mr.** for Recipient 7.
7. Filter the records using the data in the Account_Balance field. In the Comparison box, select Less than. In the Compare to text box, type **0** (the number zero).
8. Preview the results. Go back and edit steps if necessary. Then complete the merge. You should have five merged letters. Save the merged letters as a single new document, and name the document **Merged Overdraft Letters**, followed by your initials.
9. Close the merged document and the main document. Save the changes to the data source and to the main document.
10. Open a new Word document and create mailing labels for the Avery US letter, **55160 Easy Peel Repositionable Address Labels**. Save the document as **Overdraft Labels Main Document**, followed by your initials.
11. Select the recipients from the **Account Holders Data Source**. You will need to repeat Step 7 above to filter the records.
12. Insert the Address Block in the first label, and then update the labels to propagate the fields for the remaining labels. Preview the merged results. You should have five labels.
13. Save the merged labels as a single new document, and name the document **Merged Overdraft Labels**, followed by your initials.
14. Close the new merged document, and then close the main document. Save the changes to the main document.

PROJECT 12–3

1. Open the **Prospects** file from the drive and folder where your Data Files are stored. Save the file as **Prospects Data Source,** followed by your initials. Close the data source file.
2. Open a new blank Word document, and save the document as **Prospects Envelopes Main Document**, followed by your initials.
3. Start the process to create envelopes for a mass mailing. Accept the default Size 10 setting for the envelope size.
4. Select the data source Prospects Data Source.
5. Exclude the record for Brad Jackson from the merge.
6. In the first paragraph, enter the following return address:
   New England Medical Association
   Two Federal Street
   Boston, MA 02110-2012
7. Insert the address fields in the preformatted text box. Format the fields so that the Address1 and Address2 data appear on the same line, separated with a blank space. Change the font size to 14 point.
8. Preview the merged envelopes and make any necessary corrections.
9. Complete the merge and saved the merged envelopes as the document **Merged Prospects Envelopes**, followed by your initials.
10. Close the merged document and the main document. Save the changes to the main document.

PROJECT 12–4

1. Open the **Staff** file from the drive and folder where your Data Files are stored. Save the document as **Staff Data Source**, followed by your initials, and then close the document.
2. Open a new blank Word document, and then start the mail merge process by creating an e-mail message. Save the document as **Staff E-mail Main Document**, followed by your initials.
3. Identify the data source as **Staff Data Source**.
4. Edit the data source by adding the following new staff member:
   John Georgakopalous
   Physician
   j_georgakopalous@fhc.xyz
5. Insert the First_Name field at the beginning of the document, and then type a comma after the merge field. Press Enter and type the following message.
   The staff meeting has been rescheduled for Thursday at 7:30 a.m.
6. Press Enter and type your initials.
7. Preview the merged results and make any necessary changes. Do not send the e-mail messages. Instead, save the merged results to a new document. Save the new document as **Merged Staff Messages**, followed by your initials.
8. Close the merged document and the main document. Save the changes to the data source and to the main document.

PROJECT 12–5

1. Open the **Courses** file from the drive and folder where your Data Files are stored. Save the document as **Courses Data Source**, followed by your initials. This data source contains information about all the community education course offerings. Close the document.
2. Open the **Course Catalog** file from the drive and folder where your Data Files are stored. Save the document as **Courses Catalog Main Document**, followed by your initials.
3. Begin the merge process to create a directory. Use the current document, and identify the file **Courses Data Source** as the data source.
4. Insert the merge fields in the main document as follows:
   a. Delete the first occurrence of xxx, and insert the **Course_Name** field.
   b. Delete the second occurrence of xxx, and insert the **Description** field.
   c. After *Class Begins*, replace xxx with the **Date_Beginning** field.
   d. After *Days*, replace xxx with the **Days** field.
   e. After *# of Times Class Meets*, replace xxx with the **Sessions** field.
   f. After Fee, replace xxx with the **Fee** field.
5. Filter the records for all classes offered at the Western campus for the spring term, which begins 3/26. (*Hint*: Filter the Location field for records equal to Western Campus and the Date Beginning field for records Greater than or equal to 3/26.)
6. Sort the records in ascending alphabetic order by Course Name.
7. Preview the merged results. Twelve courses should appear in the catalog.
8. Complete the merge process by saving the merged results as a new document.
9. Insert the following title at the top of the new document: **WESTERN CAMPUS SPRING COURSE OFFERINGS.** Center and bold the title, and change the font size to **16 point.**
10. Save the new merged document as **Merged Spring Courses Catalog**, followed by your initials.
11. In Backstage view, preview how the catalog pages will print.
12. Close the merged document and the main document. Save the changes to the main document.

CRITICAL THINKING

ACTIVITY 12–1

Click the File tab, and then click New. Under Office.com Templates, click the Letters folder. Search Office.com for a business thank you letter template. Download the template file and then open it. Explain how this template file would save you time when creating a mass mailing.

ACTIVITY 12–2

Henry works for a large distribution company. His company recently printed custom-sized address labels with preprinted information that included the company's address and logo. Henry is setting up the main document to print new mailing labels, but he cannot find a label in the Product Number box that matches the dimensions and layout of the new address labels. How can Henry create custom labels for the merge process? Use the Help feature and search for the keywords "set up labels" to find the answer.

Estimated Time: 2 hours

LESSON 13

Sharing Documents

OBJECTIVES

Upon completion of this lesson, you should be able to:

- Track changes and add comments.
- Merge revisions from multiple documents.
- Review and accept or reject changes.
- Compare documents.
- Restrict access to a document.
- Inspect documents to prepare for electronic distribution.
- Attach a digital signature to a document.
- Upload files to the Web.

VOCABULARY

case-sensitive
comment
digital signature
document workspace site
encryption
markup
metadata
Portable Document Format (PDF)
read-only document
revision bar
XML Paper Specification (XPS)

Many team members are often involved in the development of a document. If you collaborate with others to create or edit a document, Word offers many features that will help you and your teammates make the development process easier and more efficient.

Revising Documents

Team members commonly collaborate to develop a document. Often the document is reviewed by several individuals before the final version is prepared. As team members review the document, they edit the content, add new content, change formats, and share their thoughts. Word offers many features that make it easy for workgroups to track the changes, add comments, and compare revisions.

Tracking Changes in a Document

VOCABULARY
markup
revision bar

The Track Changes feature enables you to review suggested changes and feedback from reviewers. Word uses revision marks to indicate changes such as insertions, deletions, and formatting changes. Reviewers can also provide feedback in annotations without changing the content in the document. These revision marks and annotations that Word places in a document are called ***markup***.

When the Track Changes feature is toggled on, edits and annotations appear as the changes are made. The revisions are easy to recognize because the edits appear in different font colors and with strikethrough and underline effects, and annotations appear in the document margin. In addition, a vertical line referred to as a ***revision bar*** appears in the left margin and indicates a tracked change or comment related to the paragraph. Tracked changes can appear on the screen and in printed documents.

Word assigns a different markup color for up to eight reviewers. For example, one reviewer's edits appear in red and another reviewer's edits appear in blue. Using a unique color for each reviewer helps to distinguish the revisions that each reviewer contributes. If the more than eight reviewers edit the document, Word reuses the colors.

Each user can customize the Track Changes feature by enabling options and/or specifying specific colors. For example, you can choose to change the settings so that all moved text appears in yellow and all format changes appear in green. You can also choose to show formatting changes in the right or left margins.

Step-by-Step 13.1

1. Launch Word and open the **Board Minutes** file from the drive and folder where your Data Files are stored. Save the document as **Revised Board Minutes 1,** followed by your initials.
2. Click the **Review** tab. In the Tracking group, click the **Track Changes** button arrow and then click **Change User Name**. The Word Options dialog box opens, as shown in **Figure 13–1**.

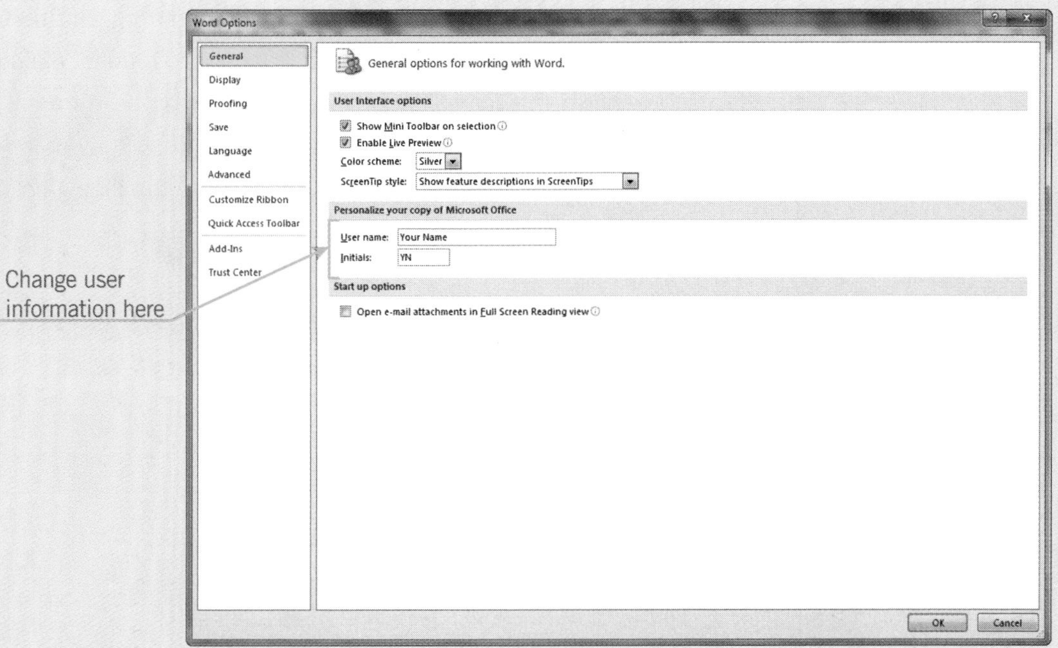

FIGURE 13–1 Word Options dialog box

3. Make note of the User name and the Initials text boxes. Then change the User name to **Reviewer A**, and change the Initials to **RA**. Click **OK** to accept the changes and close the dialog box.

4. In the Tracking group, click the **Track Changes** button arrow, and then click **Change Tracking Options**. The Track Changes Options dialog box opens, as shown in **Figure 13–2**. Your settings may be different. Compare your settings, and if necessary make changes so they match the settings shown in the figure. Then click **OK** to close the dialog box.

FIGURE 13–2
Track Changes Options dialog box

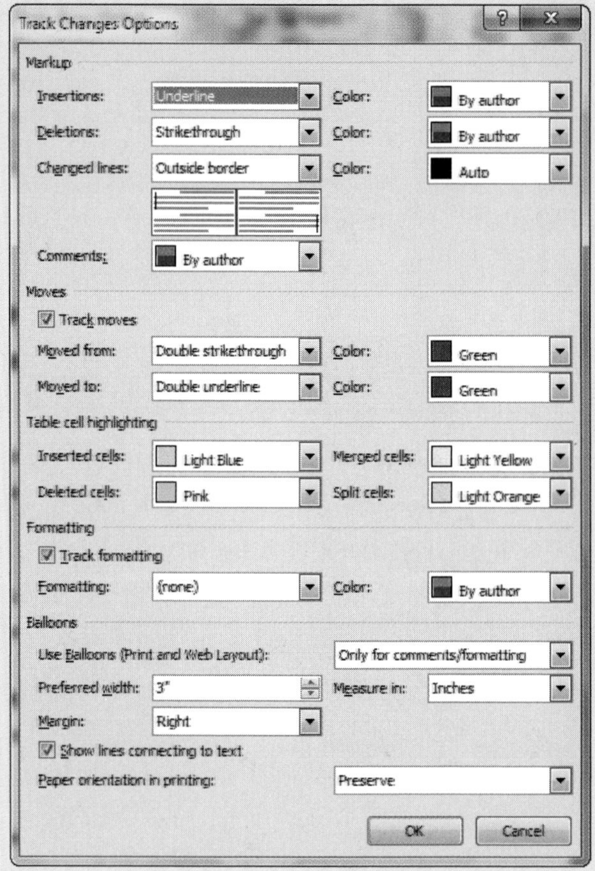

TIP

You can also use the shortcut keys Ctrl+Shift+E to toggle on and off the Track Changes feature.

5. Click the upper half of the **Track Changes** button to toggle on the feature. The feature is on when the button has an orange highlight, as shown in **Figure 13–3**.

FIGURE 13–3
Tracking group on the Review tab

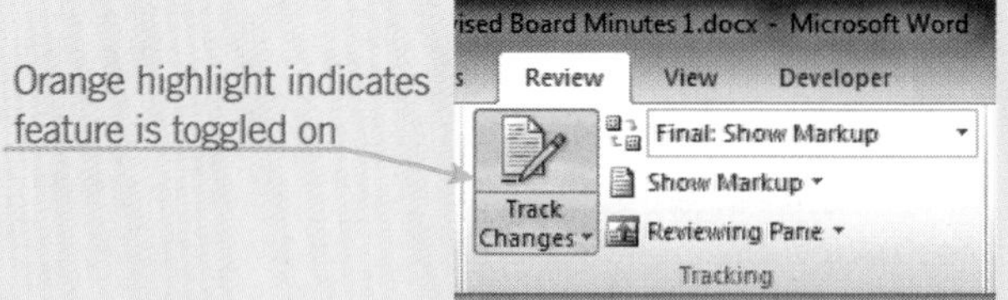

6. In the document, under the heading *ROLL CALL*, delete the second occurrence of *Janice Stork* and the comma and blank space following the name. The deleted text remains in the document, but it now appears in a different font color with a strikethrough effect. The revision bar in the left margin of the document indicates the lines of text that contain revisions.

7. In the document, under the heading *APPROVAL OF MINUTES FROM LAST MEETING*, position the insertion point at the end of the sentence. Press the **spacebar** and type **The minutes were approved as read.**. The new text is identified with an underline, and it also appears in the same font color as the deleted text above.
8. Scroll down to the heading *NEW BUSINESS*, select the three paragraphs beginning with *Finance*, *Production*, and *Sales*. Then click the **Home** tab, and in the Paragraph group, click the **Bullets** button. Deselect the text.
9. If necessary, scroll up to view the first selected paragraph. Notice that the document window adjusts to show both the text and the markup area (the shaded column on the right) using the same page orientation. Balloons appear in the markup area and describe the format changes. The color of the balloon borders matches the color for the markup related to the current reviewer.
10. Position the mouse pointer over a balloon in the markup area. A ScreenTip appears showing the user name *Reviewer A*, the current date and time, and a description of the format change.
11. Position the mouse pointer over the text connected to the balloon, and the same ScreenTip appears.
12. Scroll up to the heading *ROLL CALL*. Position the mouse pointer over the deleted text. The information about the reviewer and the date and time is displayed in a ScreenTip. The deleted text also is shown in the ScreenTip.
13. Save the changes and leave the document open for the next Step-by-Step. (If you are ending your Word session, click the **Track Changes** button arrow, click **Change User Name**, and restore the user name and initials to what you noted in Step 3 above.)

TIP

If the reviewer information does not appear in a ScreenTip, click the File tab, and then click Options. In the Word Options dialog box, click Display. Under Page display options, enable the Show document tooltips on hover option.

Adding Comments to a Document

A ***comment*** is an annotation that is added within a document by the author or reviewer. Comments provide an easy way for reviewers to share their ideas and suggestions without changing the content of the document. Word automatically assigns numbers to comments as they are inserted in the document. The numbers are sequential, regardless of the user name.

Like revision marks, comments can appear on the screen and in printed documents. Comments can be formatted to appear in balloons in the markup area, and you can also view the comments in ScreenTips above selected text in the document. You can insert comments even when the Track Changes feature is toggled off.

The Reviewing Pane offers an alternate way to show markup and provides a summary of tracked changes. You can work with the pane open, and you can choose to position the pane at the left side of the document or at the bottom of the screen.

VOCABULARY

comment

EXTRA FOR EXPERTS

If you have a Tablet PC, you can create handwritten notes in a comment balloon or in the Reviewing Pane.

Step-by-Step 13.2

1. If necessary, open the **Revised Board Minutes 1** file from your solution files. Save the document as **Revised Board Minutes 2,** followed by your initials.
2. Click the **Review** tab. Click the **Track Changes** button arrow, and then click **Change User Name**. Change the User name to **Reviewer B** and change the Initials to **RB**, and then click **OK**.
3. In the document, under the heading *OLD BUSINESS*, in the second paragraph, position the insertion point after the amount *$1,375,000*, press the **spacebar**, and then type **higher**. The inserted text appears in a different color to indicate a new reviewer.
4. Select the amount **$1,375,000**. On the Review tab, in the Comments group, click the **New Comment** button. The selected text is shaded, and a new balloon, formatted in the new color, appears in the right margin with the reviewer initials and the number 1. Type **Should this be $1,372,000?**.
5. Click anywhere outside the balloon to deselect it. To edit the comment, click the balloon to make it active again. Position the insertion point after the word *Should* and type **n't**.
6. On the Review tab, in the Tracking group, click the **Reviewing Pane** button arrow and then click **Reviewing Pane Vertical**. The Reviewing Pane opens on the left side of the document, as shown in **Figure 13–4**. If you do not see the markup summary details at the top of the Reviewing Pane, click the **Detailed Summary** button so that your Reviewing Pane matches Figure 13–4.

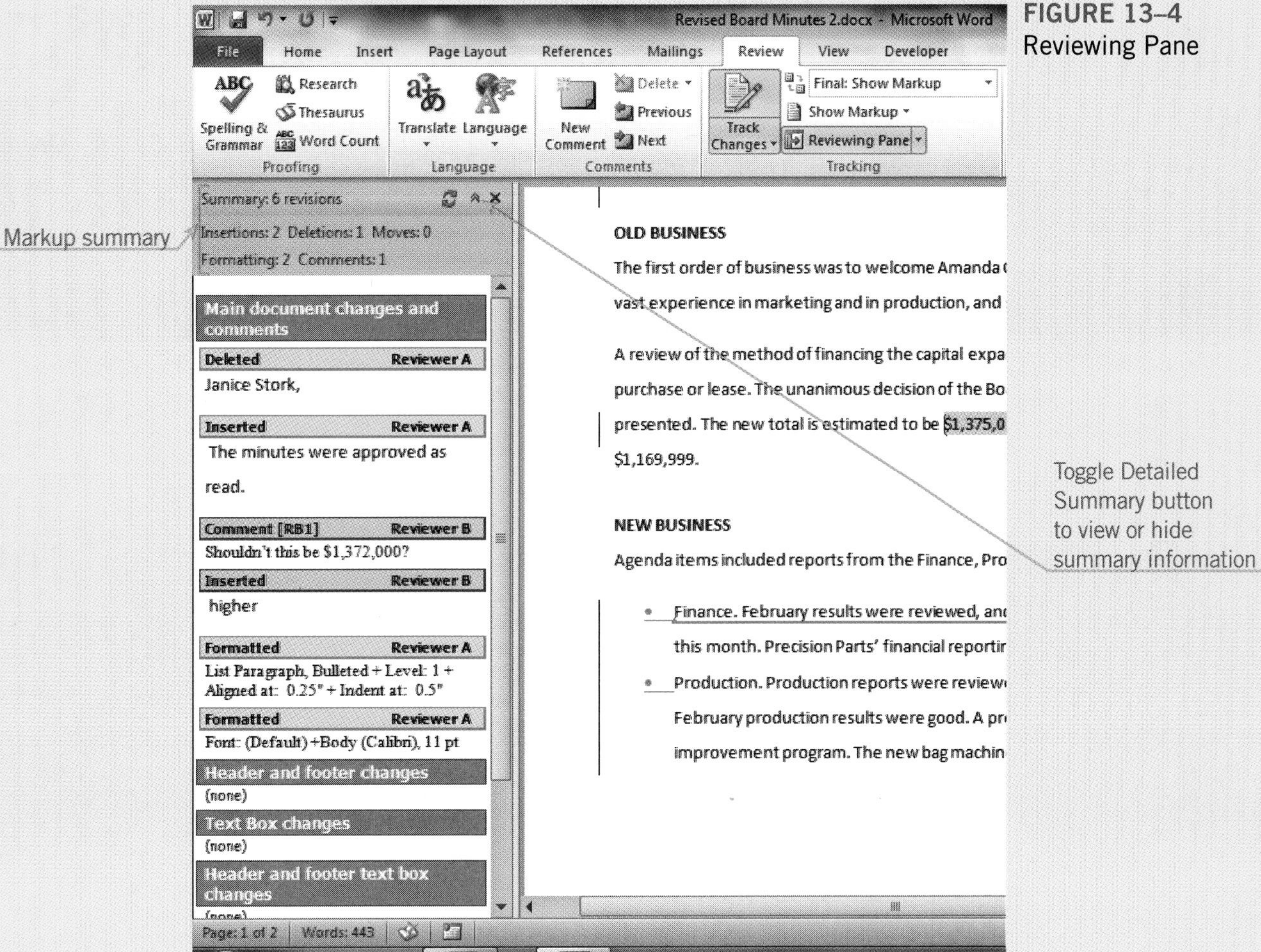

FIGURE 13–4
Reviewing Pane

7. In the Reviewing Pane, click the text of the insertion made by Reviewer B. Delete the blank space and the word *higher*. As you edit the tracked change in the Reviewing Pane, the edit is updated in the document window. When you finish deleting all of the inserted text, the tracked change is removed from the Reviewing Pane.
8. On the Review tab, in the Tracking group, click the **Reviewing Pane** button arrow and then click **Reviewing Pane Horizontal**. The Reviewing Pane is moved to the bottom of the screen. Click the **Close** button in the upper-right corner of the pane.

9. On the Review tab, in the Tracking group, click the **Track Changes** button arrow and then click **Change Tracking Options**. Under Balloons, in the list box next to *Use Balloons (Print and Web Layout)*, click the **list arrow** and then select **Never**, as shown in **Figure 13–5**. Click **OK** to apply the changes and close the dialog box.

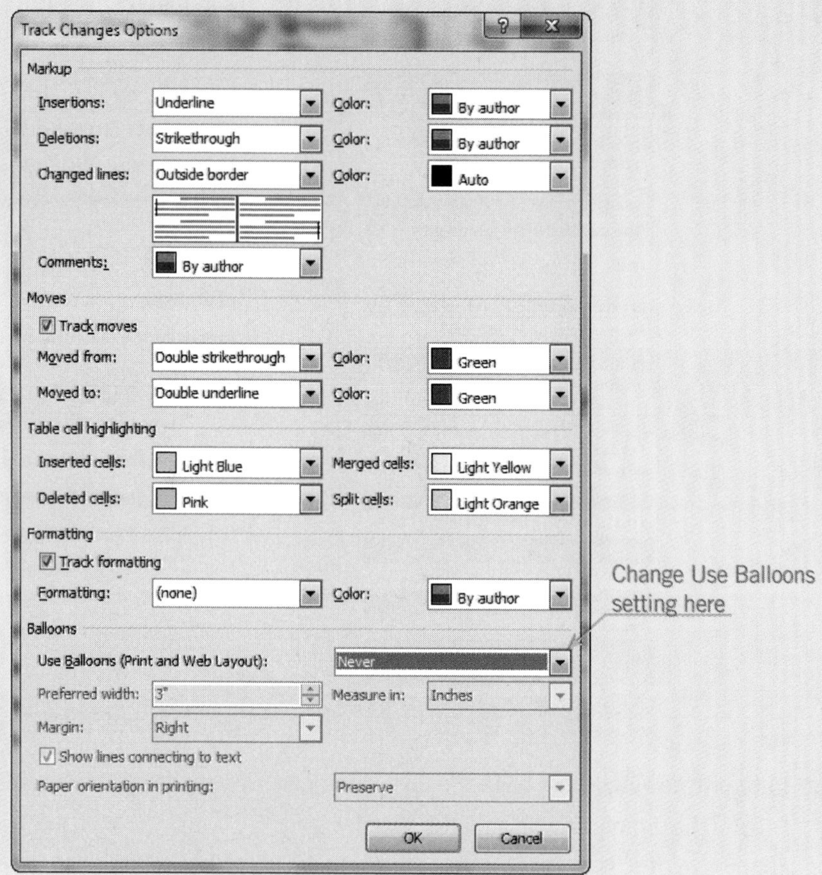

FIGURE 13–5
Track Changes Options dialog box

10. In the document, under the heading *ROLL CALL*, select the name **Rufenacht** at the end of the paragraph. On the Review tab, in the Comments group, click the **New Comment** button. A new comment box opens in the Reviewing Pane at the bottom of the screen. In the comment box, type **Make sure name is spelled correctly.**, and then click the **Close** button to close the pane. The reviewer's initials and the number 1 appear in brackets to the right of the selected word, and the comment will appear in a ScreenTip. The other comment, which appears below this comment, is now number 2.

11. Under the heading *ROLL CALL*, select the entire last sentence. Drag and drop the sentence to position it at the top of the document. When the text is moved or copied, the comment stays with the text. (If the text is deleted, the comment is also deleted.)

12. Notice, too, that the new position of the text appears with an underline to show it is new text. The text in the original position appears with a strikethrough effect to show it has been deleted. Click the **Undo** button to undo the edit.
13. On the Review tab, in the Tracking group, click the **Show Markup** button and then point to **Balloons**. In the menu that opens, enable the **Show Only Comments and Formatting in Balloons** option. Then click the **Track Changes** button arrow and click **Change User Name**. Restore the user name and initials to what you noted in Step 3 of Step-by-Step 13.1, above. Click **OK**.
14. Save the changes and leave the document open for the next Step-by-Step.

Showing and Hiding Markup

Word does not limit the number of reviewers for a document. When multiple reviewers add comments and make revisions to the document, it can be difficult to read the content and visualize the effect of all the revisions. You can choose from several options to control the markup that is shown in a document. For example, you can show markup for only specified types of edits or for specific reviewers. Even though the markup does not appear on the screen, it remains in the document until you accept or reject the changes.

If the markup shows on your screen when you send the document to the printer, then the markup will also appear in the printed document. If you want the document to print without the markup, you must first hide the markup.

Step-by-Step 13.3

1. If necessary, open the **Revised Board Minutes 2** file from your solution files. Save the document as **Revised Board Minutes 3,** followed by your initials.
2. If necessary, click the **Review** tab. In the Tracking group, click the **Show Markup** button. In the menu that opens, all markup types that are set to show in the document are indicated with check marks.

3. Point to **Reviewers** to show the names of the reviewers and their associated colors, as shown in **Figure 13–6**. The default setting will show all reviewer comments and changes in the document.

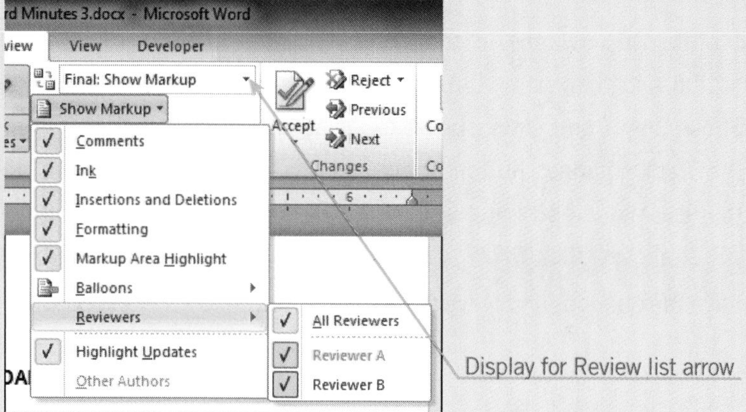

FIGURE 13–6
Show Markup options with the names of the reviewers

4. Click **Reviewer A** to uncheck the reviewer name. Now only markup made by Reviewer B will be shown in the document. However, even though the markup will not be visible, Reviewer A's changes are still saved in the document.
5. Click the **Show Markup** button, point to **Reviewers**, and then click **All Reviewers** to show changes for all reviewers.
6. Click the **Show Markup** button, and then click **Formatting** to uncheck the option. Under the heading *NEW BUSINESS*, the balloons describing the bullet format are no longer shown in the document. However, the bullets are shown as inserted characters.
7. Click the **Show Markup** button, and then click **Formatting** to enable the option again.
8. In the Tracking group, next to the list box containing the setting *Final: Show Markup*, click the **Display for Review** list arrow, as indicated in Figure 13–6, and then click **Final**. The document is shown on the screen with all the revisions accepted and the comments hidden. The markup has not been accepted or removed from the document; it just doesn't appear on the screen.
9. Click the **Display for Review** list arrow again, and then click **Final: Show Markup**.
10. Click the **File** tab, and then click **Print**. The Print preview pane confirms that the revision marks and the comments will print. The document is reduced in size so that the comments can be printed on the same page.
11. In the center pane, under Settings, click **Print All Pages** to open a menu with the options shown in **Figure 13–7**. Notice that the option Print Markup is selected. This is the default setting.

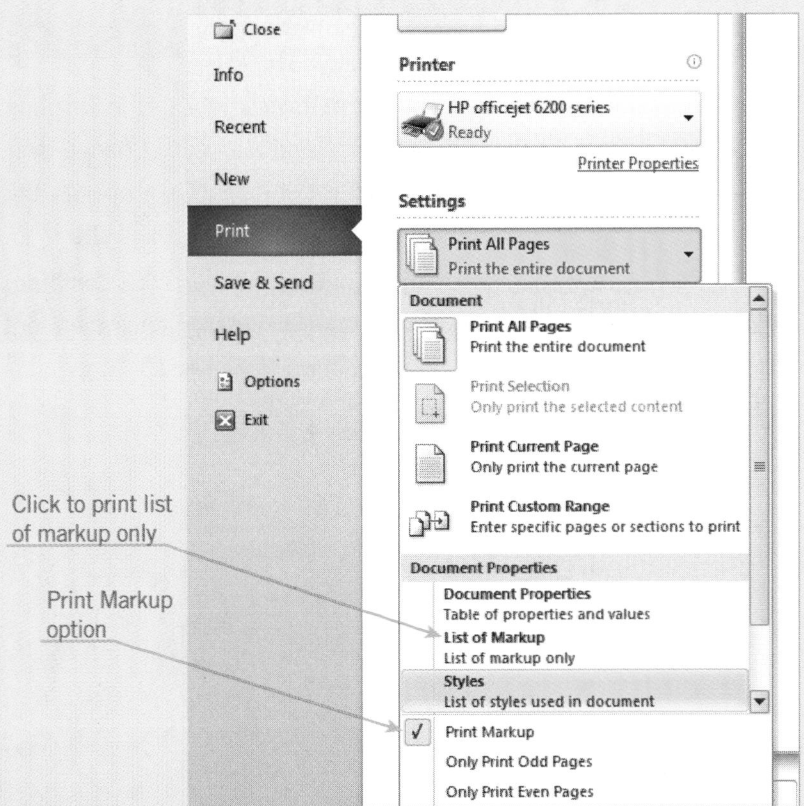

FIGURE 13–7
Document Properties printing options

12. Under Document Properties, click **List of Markup**. The menu closes. If you were to click the Print button, the document would not print; only the information in the Reviewing Pane would print.
13. Under Settings, click **List of Markup**. Click **Print All Pages** to restore the default setting, and then click the **Home** tab to close the print options.
14. Close the document without saving any changes.

Combining Revisions from Multiple Documents

Sometimes reviewers will make changes to their own copy of the same document, creating different versions of the document. Word lets you combine all the changes into one document. You can merge all the changes into the original document, or you can create a new document to show the combined revisions. Once combined, changes from each reviewer will appear in a unique color to differentiate the changes made by each reviewer. Reviewer identity is also revealed in a ScreenTip that shows above revision marks.

Step-by-Step 13.4

1. Open a new blank document and click the **Review** tab. In the Tracking group, click the **Track Changes** button arrow and then click **Change User Name**. Make note of the user name and the initials. Then change the User name to **Reviewer C** and change the Initials to **RC**. Click **OK**.
2. In the Compare group, click the **Compare** button and then click **Combine**. The Combine Documents dialog box opens. If necessary, click the **More** button to reveal the comparison options shown in **Figure 13–8**.

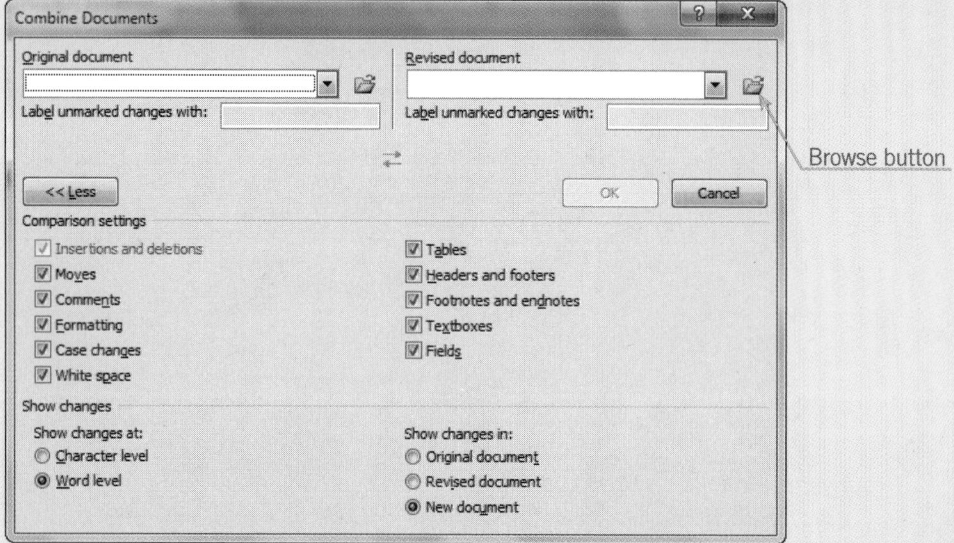

FIGURE 13–8
Combine Documents dialog box

3. Click the **Original document** list arrow. Recently opened documents appear in the list. Scroll down and click **Revised Board Minutes 3**.
4. Click the **Browse** button next to the Revised document list box. Navigate to the Data Files folder, select **Board Minutes RD**, and then click **Open**. Click **OK**.
5. A prompt appears stating that only one set of formatting changes can be merged. Make sure the Revised Board Minutes 3 document is selected and then click **Continue with Merge**. A new combined document opens showing the revisions from both documents.
6. If, in addition to the new combined document, the original document (Revised Board Minutes 3) and the revised document (Board Minutes RD) also appear, and the Reviewing Pane is open, skip to step 7. If not, then in the Tracking group, click the **Reviewing Pane** button to open the Reviewing Pane. In the Compare group, click the **Compare** button, point to **Show Source Documents**, and then click **Show Both**.
7. Scroll through the new document or the Reviewing Pane. You will see revisions from Reviewers A, B, and D.

8. The combined document is the active document. Save the combined document to your solutions folder as **Revised Board Minutes 4**, followed by your initials. Close the document. The Revised Board Minutes 3 and Board Minutes RD document windows also close.
9. In a new blank document, on the Review tab, in the Compare group, click the **Compare** button, and then click **Combine**.
10. In the Original document list box, select **Revised Board Minutes 4**. Next to the Revised document list box, click **Browse**. Navigate to the Data Files folder, select **Board Minutes RE**, and click **Open**. Click **OK**. Then click **Continue with Merge**.
11. If necessary, click the **Reviewing Pane** button in the Tracking group to show the Reviewing Pane. Scroll through the Reviewing Pane and you will see changes from five reviewers.
12. Close the Reviewing Pane. Save the new combined document to your solutions folder as **Revised Board Minutes 5**, followed by your initials.
13. Close the Revised Board Minutes 5 document. If the Revised Board Minutes 4 and Board Minutes RE documents are open, they will close, too. Click the **Track Changes** button arrow, click **Change User Name**, and restore the user name and initials to what you noted in Step 1 above.

Reviewing Revisions

The next step is to review the revisions and decide whether to accept or reject the proposed changes. Buttons on the Ribbon make it easy to navigate to revisions and comments. You can accept or reject the changes individually, or you can accept several or all changes at once. And you can easily remove the comments.

EXTRA FOR EXPERTS

You can also navigate to the next comment by clicking the Select Browse Object button on the vertical scroll bar and then clicking Browse by Comment. To go to a specific reviewer's comments, double-click the page number on the status bar. The Go To tab in the Find and Replace dialog box will open. Under Go to what, select Comment and then under Enter reviewer's name, select the reviewer. Click Next or Previous to move to that reviewer's comments.

Step-by-Step 13.5

1. Open the **Revised Board Minutes 5** file from your solution files. Save the document as **Final Board Minutes**, followed by your initials.
2. Position the insertion point at the top of the document. Click the **Review** tab. In the Comments group, click the **Next Comment** button. The first comment in the document is highlighted. Click the **Next Comment** button again to move to the second comment in the document. The Next Comment button moves the insertion point only to comments in the document.
3. Position the insertion point at the top of the document. On the Review tab, in the Changes group, click the **Next Change** button. The first comment is highlighted. Click the **Next Change** button again. The first revision showing deleted text is highlighted. The Next Change button moves the insertion point to the next tracked change or comment.
4. On the Review tab, in the Changes group, click the **Accept** button arrow, and then click **Accept and Move to Next**. The text *Janice Stork* is removed, and the next change in the document, a comment, is highlighted.
5. In the last sentence under the heading *APPROVAL OF MINUTES FROM LAST MEETING*, right-click anywhere in the new text and then click **Accept Change**. The change is accepted, but the next change is not highlighted. Choosing the Accept Change option is useful when you want to review the accepted changes before you move on to the next change.
6. In the Changes group, click the **Next Change** button. Under *OLD BUSINESS*, the first change in the set of numbers is highlighted. Click the upper half of the **Accept** button. The change is accepted and the next change, a deletion, is highlighted.
7. Click the **Next Change** button two times. The three bulleted items under the heading *NEW BUSINESS* are highlighted, and the balloon describing the format changes is highlighted. In the Changes group, click the **Reject** button arrow, and then click **Reject Change**. The bullet formats are removed. Click the **Undo** button. Deselect the paragraphs.
8. Show the Reviewing Pane. In the Reviewing Pane, delete the text for the first comment. (*Hint*: You cannot delete the ending paragraph mark.) Note that deleting all the text in the Reviewing Pane or in a comment balloon does not remove the comment mark in the document pane. You must delete the comment mark in the document pane to remove a comment.

9. The insertion point is in the comment box in the Reviewing Pane. The comment balloon is highlighted in the margin area. In the Comments group, click the **Delete Comment** button. The comment is removed from the margin area and from the Reviewing Pane.
10. In the document pane, scroll down and over, if necessary, and select the first paragraph with the bullet format. Right-click the selected paragraph and click **Accept Change**. All the selected changes are accepted.
11. If necessary, scroll to the bottom of the Reviewing Pane. Under Header and footer changes, click the Page number insertion by Reviewer E. Right-click the title bar for the change, and then click **Reject Insertion**. Click anywhere in the document pane.
12. In the Changes group, click the **Accept** button arrow and then click **Accept All Changes in Document**. All remaining changes in the document are accepted, but the comments are not removed. In the Tracking group, click the upper half of the **Track Changes** button to toggle off the feature.
13. In the Comments group, click the **Delete** button arrow, and then click **Delete All Comments in Document**. All comments are removed from the document. Close the Reviewing Pane.
14. Save the changes and close the document.

Comparing Documents

Sometimes you might want to compare the current version of a document with another version of the same document. For example, if a team member edited a copy of your document, but did not track the changes, you could compare the team member's version with a current version to review the edits. To compare the two documents, you can open the revised document and the original document and view them side by side.

If the documents you are comparing are long, it would be very time consuming to compare everything in both documents in order to identify the differences. The Compare feature in Word offers a simpler way to identify the differences. When you use the Compare feature, nothing will change in either of the documents you are comparing. The differences in the two documents will appear as tracked changes in a new third document. If either of the compared documents contains tracked changes, those changes are accepted before the documents are compared.

Step-by-Step 13.6

1. Open two blank documents. Then open the **Emergency Contacts 1** file from the drive and folder where your Data Files are stored. If necessary, maximize the document window and use the zoom controls to set the zoom level to 100%.
2. Open the **Emergency Contacts 2** file from the drive and folder where your Data Files are stored. Make sure the document window is maximized and the zoom level is set to 100%.
3. The Emergency Contacts 2 document should be the active document. Click the **View** tab. In the Window group, click the **View Side by Side** button. The Compare Side by Side dialog box opens, showing all the open files except the active document. (If only two Word documents are open, this dialog box will not open.)
4. Click the filename **Emergency Contacts 1**, and then click **OK**. The two documents appear side by side on the screen.
5. In the Emergency Contacts 2 document window on the left, drag the vertical scroll bar up and down. As you scroll through the document on the left, the page in the window on the right will also move.
6. Switch to the Emergency Contacts 1 document window on the right, and then click the **View** tab. If necessary, click the **Window** button to expand the Window group to access the group buttons, as shown in **Figure 13–9**. Note that both the View Side by Side and Synchronous Scrolling buttons are highlighted. Click the **Synchronous Scrolling** button to toggle off the feature. Then drag the vertical scroll bar in the window on the right and in the window on the left. The documents are no longer synchronized.

FIGURE 13–9
Window group on the View tab

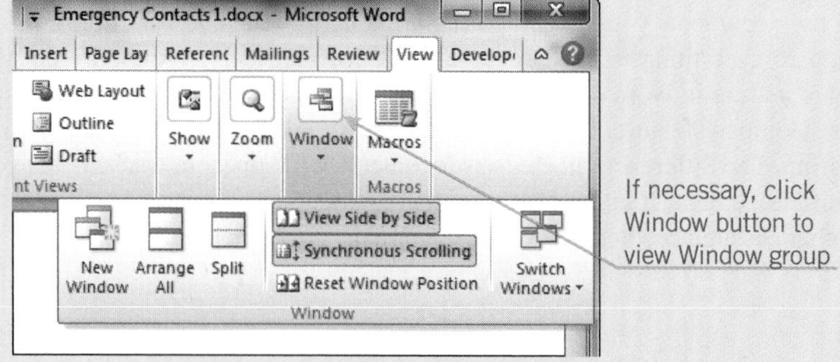

7. If necessary, expand the Window group in the document in the right pane. Click the **View Side by Side** button. The documents are no longer shown side by side. The Emergency Contacts 1 document should be the active document.

8. Switch to the Emergency Contacts 2 document. Click the **Review** tab. In the Compare group, click the **Compare** button, and then click **Compare**. The Compare Documents dialog box, which is very similar to the Combine Documents dialog box, opens.
9. Click the **Original document** list arrow and select **Emergency Contacts 1**. Then click the **Revised document** list arrow and select **Emergency Contacts 2**. Click **OK**. A compared document with merged tracked changes opens. The original document (Emergency Contacts 1) and the revised document (Emergency Contacts 2) are also still open. If it is not open, show the Reviewing Pane.
10. Save the merged results document as **Final Emergency Contacts**, followed by your initials. Close the Emergency Contacts 1 and Emergency Contacts 2 documents.
11. In the Final Emergency Contacts document window, click the **Review** tab, if necessary. In the Changes group, click the **Accept** button arrow and then click **Accept All Changes in Document**.
12. Save the changes to the Final Emergency Contacts document, and then close the document and any other open documents.

Preparing Documents for Electronic Distribution

The majority of the information we work with is now generated by electronic files. Instead of printing documents, it is common to exchange information using electronic files. When sharing files, you may want to consider saving the document as a read-only document. Users are able to open and read a ***read-only document***, but they are not able to save any changes to the document. To save changes, users will need to save the file in a different folder or use a different filename. When you use the Mark as Final command, you imply that the status of the document is final. Word saves the file as a read-only document, but the content is not secure. If a user wants to make edits, they can easily toggle off the Mark as Final feature.

VOCABULARY
read-only document

You can also protect a document by setting controls to restrict access, allowing only specified individuals to open the document. And for those individuals who are able to open the document, you can restrict formatting and edits.

Before distributing a document, you might want to ensure that the document is compatible with other platforms and Word versions. You also might want to prevent others from seeing some of the properties, such as personal information and document statistics. To help validate the authenticity of a document, you can embed a digital ID into the document. You can also personalize a document by adding your signature in a digital format.

Restricting Access

VOCABULARY
encryption
case-sensitive

WARNING

If you forget a password, you cannot access a document. Write down passwords and keep them in a secure location, or use a password management application.

To restrict access to a document, you can assign a password to it so that only users who know the password can open the document. To secure additional protection, you can encrypt the document so that it is unreadable without a password. ***Encryption*** is a standard method for encoding data. When assigning passwords in Word, you can use up to 15 characters in any combination of letters, numerals, spaces, and symbols. A strong password has at least eight characters in a combination of text, numbers, and symbols. The password is ***case-sensitive***, which means that when entering a password to open a document, the upper and lower casing of the letters must be identical to the casing of the letters in the assigned password. If the casing of the letters differs, the file will not open.

Step-by-Step 13.7

1. Open the **Employee Evaluation** file from the drive and folder where your Data Files are stored. Save the document as **Restricted Employee Evaluation 1**, followed by your initials.
2. Click the **File** tab, and in the center pane, click the **Protect Document** button. Click **Mark as Final**, and then click **OK** when prompted to confirm that the document will be marked as final. Click **OK** again, and the document is saved as a read-only document.
3. Click the **Home** tab. Notice that a yellow bar appears at the top of the window and the Mark as Final icon appears in the status bar. In the yellow bar at the top of the window, click **Edit Anyway**. You have just toggled off the Mark as Final feature, and the yellow bar no longer appears at the top of the document. You can make changes to the document.
4. Click the **File** tab, click the **Protect Document** button, and then click **Encrypt with Password**. In the Password text box, type **aem1116PS!** and then click **OK**. Type the password again and click **OK**. The document is encrypted, and users will need to enter that password to open the document.
5. Close the document. When prompted to save changes to the document, click **Save**. Reopen the document **Restricted Employee Evaluation 1** from your solution files. When prompted, type the password **aem1116PS!** and then click **OK**.
6. Save the document as **Restricted Employee Evaluation 2**, followed by your initials. Even though the filename has changed, the encryption still applies. Close the document. Then reopen the document. When prompted to enter a password, type **aem1116PS**! and then click **OK**.

7. To remove the encryption, click the **File** tab. Notice in the center pane, next to the Protect Document button, a Permission note appears indicating that a password is required. Click **Save As**. The Save As dialog box opens. At the bottom of the dialog box, next to Save, click **Tools** and then click **General Options**. The General Options dialog box opens, as shown in **Figure 13–10**.

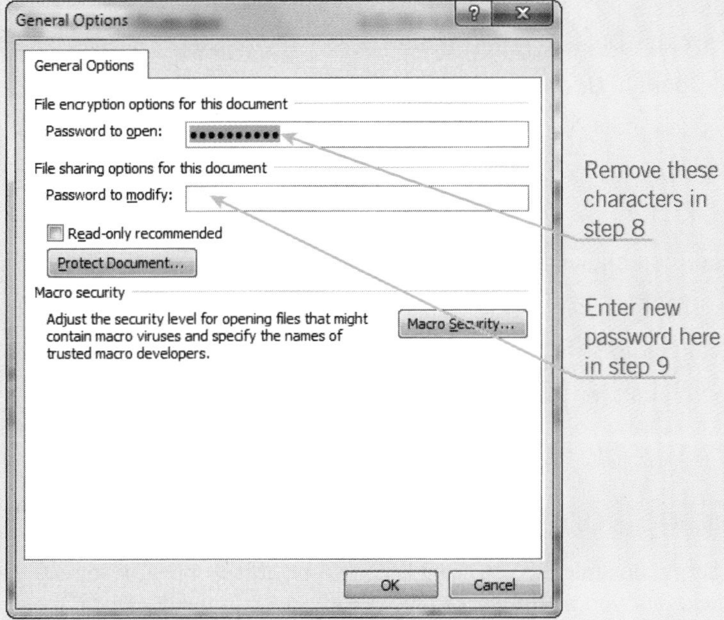

FIGURE 13–10
General Options dialog box

8. Remove all the characters in the Password to open text box. Click **OK** and then click **Save**. Close the document and then reopen it. The encryption is removed and the document opens without a password.
9. Click the **File** tab and then click **Save As**. Click **Tools** and then click **General Options**. In the Password to modify text box, type **CAM#54mxA+**. Click **OK**. When prompted, reenter the password. Click **OK** to close the General Options dialog box. Click **Save** to save the changes and close the Save As dialog box, and then close the document.
10. Reopen the **Restricted Employee Evaluation 2** document from your solution files. In the Password dialog box, click the option to **Read Only**. Notice that the document title in the title bar includes *[Read-Only]*. Click the **File** tab. Notice the Read-Only note in the center pane next to the Save As button. Although you can edit the document, you will not be able to save the changes without assigning a new filename or a new path. Close the document.

11. Reopen the **Restricted Employee Evaluation 2** document from your solution files. When prompted to open as read only again, click **No**. Then when prompted to enter a password, type **CAM#54mxA+** and then click **OK**. The document opens and the read-only feature is disabled so you can save changes to the document.
12. Position the insertion point to the right of *Date:* in the second row of the table in the right column. Click the **Insert** tab. In the Text group, click the **Date & Time** button. Select the XX/XX/XX format and enable the option **Update automatically**. Click **OK**. Save the changes to the document.
13. Remove the password. Click the **File** tab, and then click **Save As**. Click **Tools** and then click **General Options**. Delete the password characters, and then click **OK**.
14. In the File name box, change the filename to **Restricted Employee Evaluation 3**, followed by your initials. Click **Save** and leave the document open for the next Step-by-Step.

Restricting Formatting and Editing

When sharing documents, you want others to be able to open, read, and even edit a document, but you might want to restrict the areas in the document that they can change. You can designate certain parts of the document to be unrestricted but grant permission for specific individuals only to modify other restricted sections.

Step-by-Step 13.8

1. If necessary, open the **Restricted Employee Evaluation 3** file from your solution files.
2. Click the **Review** tab. In the Protect group, click the **Restrict Editing** button. The Restrict Formatting and Editing task pane opens.
3. Under Editing restrictions, click to enable the option **Allow only this type of editing in the document**. Exceptions options now appear in the task pane, as shown in **Figure 13–11**. These options enable you to make exceptions and allow specified reviewers to edit all or part of the document.

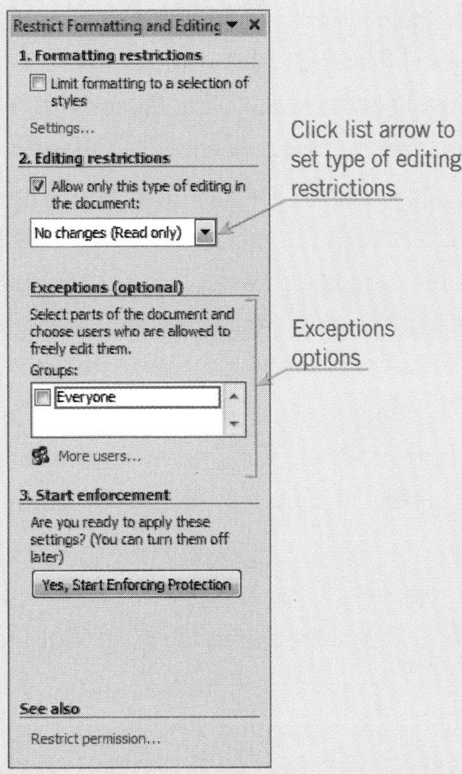

FIGURE 13–11
Restrict Formatting and Editing task pane

4. Under Editing restrictions, the current setting is *No changes (Read only)*. Click the **list arrow** in the setting box, and then click **Tracked changes**. Notice that the Exceptions options no longer appear. Users can make changes and add comments throughout the entire document.
5. Under Editing restrictions, click the **list arrow**, and then click **Comments**. The Exceptions are again available. You can specify reviewers and limit their access to the document.
6. Under Editing restrictions, click the **list arrow**, and then click **Filling in forms**. The exceptions are not available, and users cannot track changes or add comments.
7. Under Editing restrictions, click the **list arrow**, and then click **No changes (Read only)**.
8. Select the row with the heading *ACHIEVEMENTS, ACCOMPLISHMENTS, AND RESPONSIBILITIES*. Hold down **Shift** and then click anywhere in the row below the selected heading. In the task pane, under Exceptions (optional), enable the **Everyone** option.
9. Select the row with the heading *STRENGTHS AND AREAS FOR DEVELOPMENT*. Hold down **Shift** and then click anywhere in the blank row below *GOALS AND OBJECTIVES FOR NEXT EVALUATION PERIOD*. In the task pane, enable the **Everyone** option.

10. Click some of the other rows in the table. Note that as you click some of the other rows, the check mark does not appear next to the Everyone option. The option is only available in the rows you selected; users can edit only those rows in the document.
11. Under Start enforcement, click **Yes, Start Enforcing Protection**. In the first password text box, type the password **99$a*61820***. Reenter the password in the second password text box. Click **OK**. Users cannot change these settings unless they have the password. The areas in the document that can be edited by everyone are highlighted with a light yellow color.
12. Close the document. When prompted to save the changes, click **Save**. Reopen the **Restricted Employee Evaluation 3** document from your solution files.
13. Type the following data in the form:
    a. In the row under the heading *ACHIEVEMENTS, ACCOMPLISHMENTS, AND RESPONSIBILITIES*, position the insertion point at the end of the third paragraph.
    b. Press **Enter** and then type the following paragraph:
    Started a safety training program and developed a new recordkeeping system so that accidents and work-related injuries are documented and recorded accurately.
    c. In the blank row under the heading *CAREER DEVELOPMENT PLAN*, type the following three paragraphs:
    Complete requirements to attain certification in production and inventory management.
    Gain more experience to advance to the position of Senior Production Manager.
    Interested in working at an international plant.
14. Save the changes and close the document.

TIP

To remove the restriction from a document, click the Stop Protection button at the bottom of the Restrict Formatting and Editing task pane. You will need to enter the password to complete the task.

Inspecting the Document

The Backstage view offers several features to help you prepare for the distribution of your Word documents. In the right pane of the Info options, you will see a summary of document properties. The properties listed include when the document was created, the document size, the number of pages, and when the document was last modified. To aid in searching for documents, you can add additional information to the document properties, such as the subject matter and keywords in the document. Protecting a document, however, also means protecting your personal information. ***Metadata***—data that describes other data—is stored in the files that you create. Some of the metadata contains personal information that you might not want others to see. For example, the properties in Word documents include information about the author, the date and time the document was created, and the last person who modified the document.

VOCABULARY
metadata

The Inspect Document command checks the file for personal information, such as names and dates. For example, you may have hidden the markup to review the file, and you've forgotten that the document still contains comments and tracked changes. The markup includes a lot of personal information, including the reviewer name, date, and time for each revision and comment. Headers and footers also contain personal information, such as company names, addresses, and dates. Completing an inspection before sharing a document will help you search the document for this type of information, and then you can decide if you want to remove some of the personal data.

You can also quickly check for compatibility to determine if some features in the document are not supported by earlier versions of Word. This check is especially useful when you are sharing documents with users who are working with previous versions of Word.

Step-by-Step 13.9

1. Open the **Completed Employee Evaluation** file from the drive and folder where your Data Files are stored. In the password dialog box, type **jck@554E5** and click **OK**. Save the document as **Final Employee Evaluation**, followed by your initials. Note that the document has a header and two comments from Reviewer C.
2. In the first cell of the second row, position the insertion point in front of *Zurla*, type **James**, and press the **spacebar**. In the cell below, position the insertion point in front of *Schroeder*, type **R.**, and then press the **spacebar**. Save the changes to the document.
3. Click the **File** tab. The properties for the document appear on the right pane. The properties include information about the document size, number of pages, number of words, personal information such as the author, when the document was last modified, and the total editing time.
4. To update the information, click **Properties** at the top of the right pane, and then click **Show Document Panel**. The Document Properties panel opens, as shown in **Figure 13–12**. Your Location setting will be different.

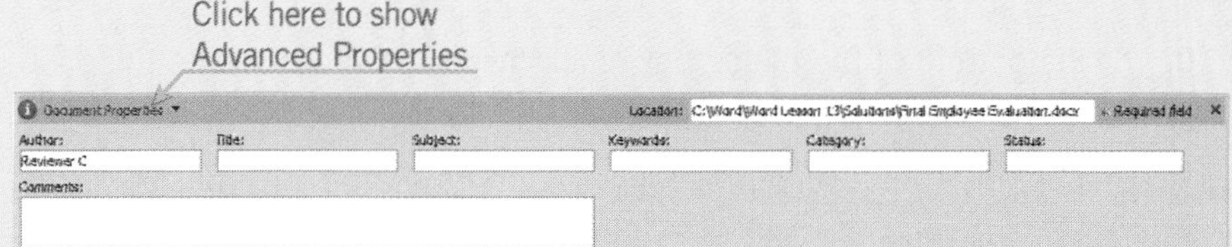

FIGURE 13–12 Document Properties panel

5. Click the **Title** text box, and then type **Adam Zurla**. In the Subject text box, type **Employee Evaluation**. In the Keywords text box, type **achievements, accomplishments, responsibilities, evaluation, strengths, goals**. Save the changes to the document.

6. At the top of the Document Properties panel, click **Document Properties** and then click **Advanced Properties**. The Properties dialog box for this document opens.
7. Click the **Statistics** tab. Notice that this includes information about when the document was created, the number of times the document has been revised, and the total editing time. Click **OK** to close the dialog box. Then click the **Close** button in the upper-right corner of the Document Properties panel.
8. Save the changes to the document. Then save the document as **Confidential Employee Evaluation**, followed by your initials.
9. Click the **File** tab. In the center pane, click the **Check for Issues** button, and then click **Inspect Document**. The Document Inspector dialog box shown in **Figure 13–13** opens, showing features that can be inspected.

FIGURE 13–13
Document Inspector dialog box

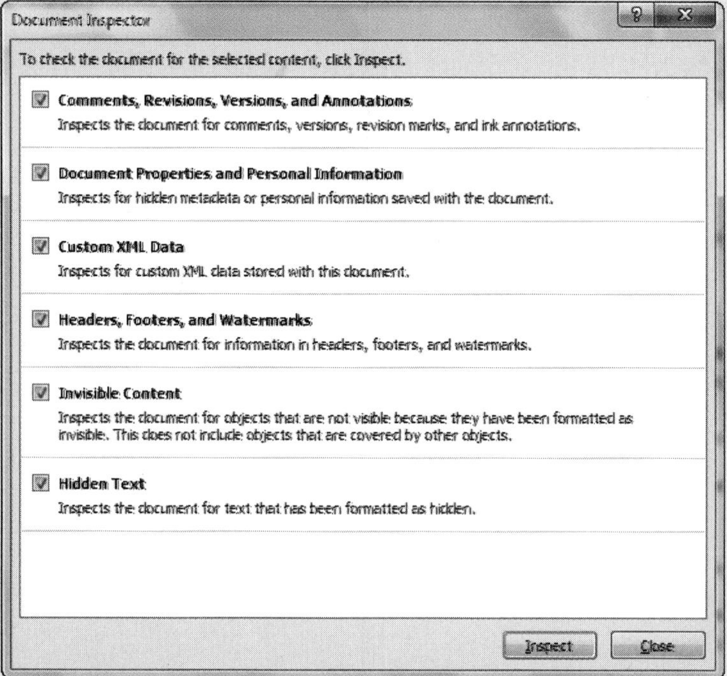

10. At the bottom of the dialog box, click **Inspect**. Word inspects the document and displays the results. You do not want to remove the comments from the document, so ignore the first Remove All button. In the Document Properties and Personal Information section, click **Remove All**. In the Headers, Footers, and Watermarks section, click **Remove All**. Close the Document Inspector dialog box.
11. Close the document, saving the changes. Then reopen the document. In the Password dialog box, type **jck@554E5** and click **OK**. Notice that the header has been removed from the document.

12. Notice, too, that the initials in the comment balloons have been replaced with *A1* and *A2*. Position the mouse pointer over the comment. The name of the reviewer is now *Author*, and there is no date or time. Because the personal information was removed from the document, the comments are now anonymous.
13. Click the **File** tab. Notice in the right pane that all the personal information has been removed from the properties. In the right pane, click **Properties** and then click **Advanced Properties**. Much of the data in the Statistics tab is still available, but the name of the last user to access the file and the total editing time has been removed. Click **OK** to close the dialog box.
14. In the center pane, click the **Check for Issues** button and then click **Check Compatibility**. The Microsoft Word Compatibility Checker dialog box opens and indicates that no issues were found. Close the dialog box. Save the changes, close the document, and then exit Word.

Attaching a Digital Signature

A ***digital signature*** is an attachment to a file or e-mail message that certifies that the infor mation in the file is authentic and safe. The digital signature is embedded in the document, and although it is not visible, recipients of the document can see that the document has been digitally signed. Signed files are marked as final and remain signed until the file is changed. If the document is edited, the signature is removed. You can embed multiple digital signatures in the same document.

Digital signatures are easy to create using the SelfCert.exe tool. However, when you use this program, you create a self-signed digital certificate, which does not verify your identity and, therefore, is appropriate only for personal use. The SelfCert.exe tool is used in this lesson to demonstrate how to attach a digital signature to a document. If you need an authenticated certificate, you must secure a service from a third-party vendor. Several commercial certification authority services are compatible with Office applications.

VOCABULARY
digital signature

Step-by-Step 13.10

To complete this Step-by-Step, the SelfCert.exe file must be installed.

1. Click the **Start** button on the taskbar and navigate to the folder where the Windows file SelfCert.exe is saved. The file is usually found in the c:\Program Files\Microsoft Office\Office14 folder. If necessary, use the Search feature to locate the file. Double-click the filename **SelfCert.exe**.
2. The Create Digital Certificate dialog box opens. Read the instructions, then type your first and last names and click **OK**.

3. A message box appears indicating that a new certificate has been successfully created. Click **OK**. If necessary, close the Search dialog box.
4. Launch Word and open the **Confidential Employee Evaluation** file from your solution files. In the Password dialog box, type **jck@554E5** and click **OK**. Save the document as **Certified Employee Evaluation**, followed by your initials.
5. Click the **File** tab. In the center pane, click the **Protect Document** button, and then click **Add a Digital Signature**. A message box appears explaining that Microsoft does not warrant a digital signature's legal enforceability. Click **OK**. The Sign dialog box opens, as shown in **Figure 13–14**. Your settings may be different.

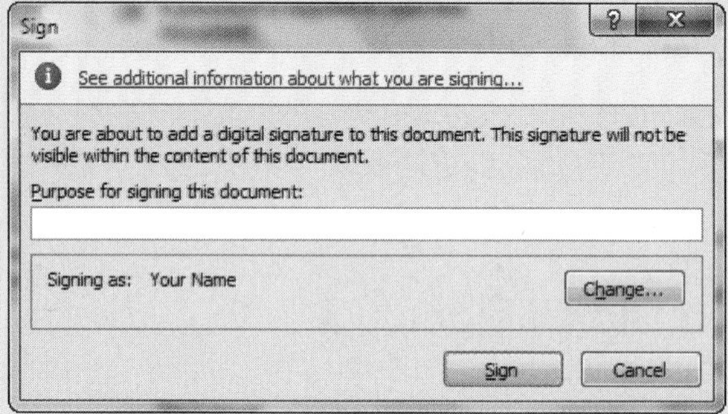

FIGURE 13–14
Sign dialog box

6. Click **See additional information about what you are signing**. The Additional Information dialog box shows more information that is being saved with the document. Click **OK**.
7. In the Sign dialog box, under Purpose for signing this document, type **To confirm the validity of the information in this document.**.
8. If your name does not appear after Signing as, click **Change**, select your certificate, and then click **OK**. Click **Sign**. If a message box appears indicating that the certificate cannot be verified, click **Yes**. (This is because it is a self-signed certificate.) A message box opens confirming that the signature has been successfully saved with the document. If any changes are made to the document, the signature will be invalid. Click **OK**.

9. An Invalid Signatures warning appears in the center pane, as shown in **Figure 13–15**. The signature is invalid because it is a self-signed certificate and the certificate was not issued by a trusted certificate authority.

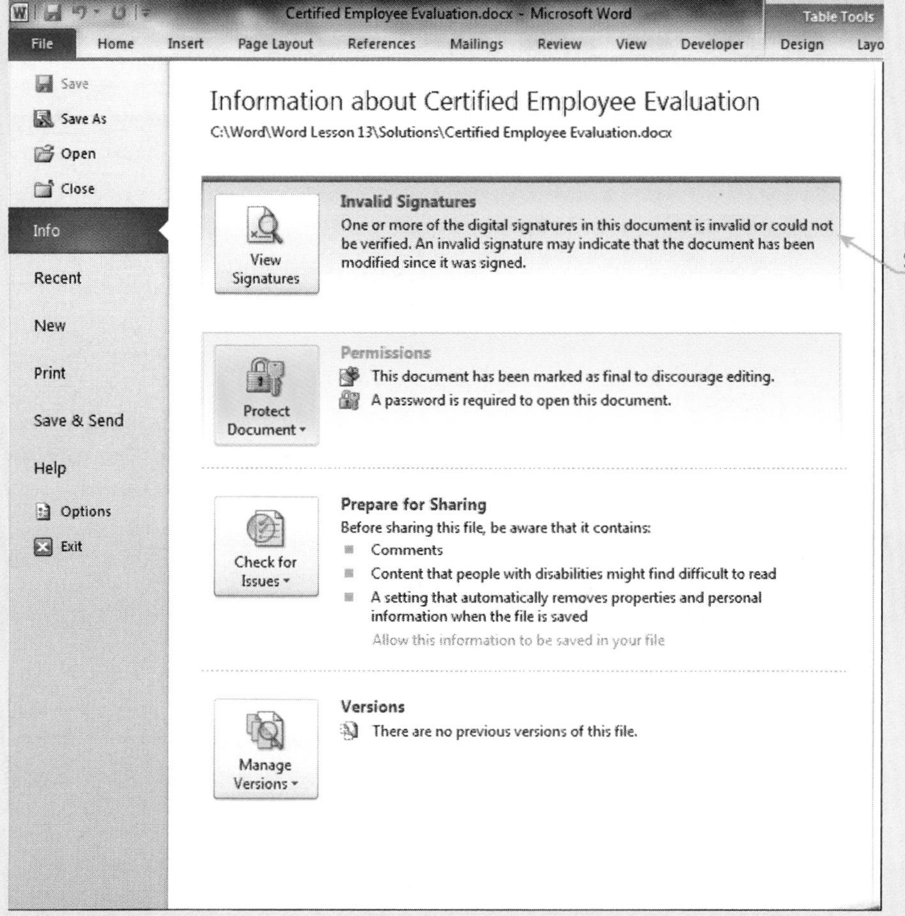

FIGURE 13–15
Invalid Signatures warning

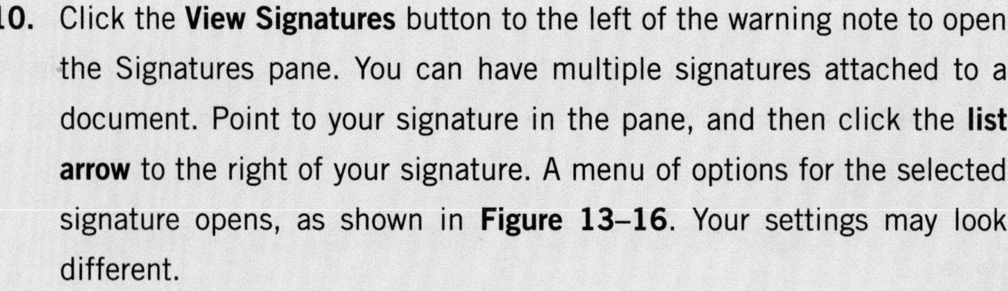

10. Click the **View Signatures** button to the left of the warning note to open the Signatures pane. You can have multiple signatures attached to a document. Point to your signature in the pane, and then click the **list arrow** to the right of your signature. A menu of options for the selected signature opens, as shown in **Figure 13–16**. Your settings may look different.

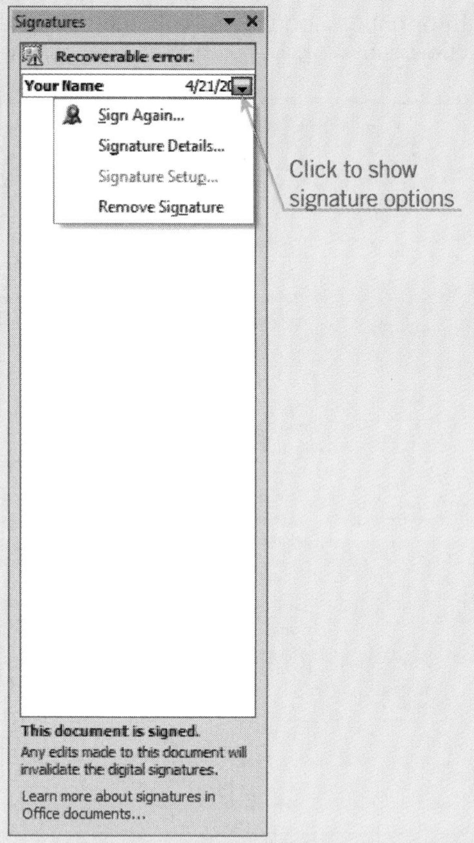

FIGURE 13–16
Signatures pane showing options for a signature

11. Click **Signature Details**. The dialog box shown in **Figure 13–17** opens.

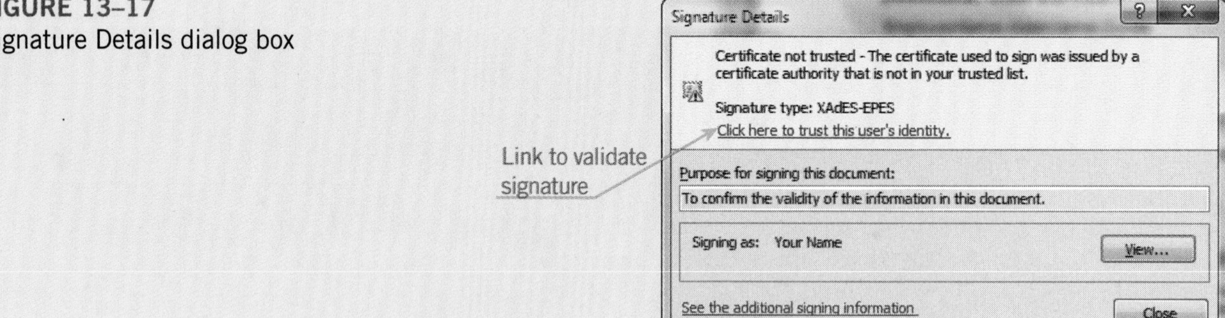

FIGURE 13–17
Signature Details dialog box

12. Click the link **Click here to trust this user's identify**. The signature is now valid. Close the Signature Details dialog box.

13. A yellow bar at the top of the document window shows that the document has been marked as final. The Signatures icon appears in the status bar and indicates that the document contains a signature.
14. The signature was automatically saved with the document. Close the document.

Creating a Signature Line

Word offers a feature that enables you to create a signature line in documents. The signature line looks like a typical signature placeholder, but it is actually more than just a placeholder. The signature line specifies information about the intended signer, and you can even provide instructions for the signer. When the signer receives the document, he or she can choose how to add their signature. If the signer receives an electronic copy of the document, they can choose to type a signature, insert a digital image of his or her signature, or write a signature using the inking feature on a Tablet PC. When a digital image of a signature is added to the document, a digital signature is added simultaneously to authenticate the identity of the signer. As is true with all digitally signed documents, the document will become read-only to prevent edits to the content.

Step-by-Step 13.11

1. Open the **Bill of Sale** file from the drive and folder where your Data Files are stored. Save the document as **Final Bill of Sale**, followed by your initials.
2. Position the insertion point at the end of the document. Click the **Insert** tab. In the Text group, click the **Signature Line** button. A dialog box opens showing a disclaimer stating that Microsoft cannot warrant the legal enforceability of a digital signature. Click **OK** to open the Signature Setup dialog box, as shown in **Figure 13–18**.

FIGURE 13–18
Signature Setup dialog box

3. In the first text box, type **Trevor Jones**. In the second text box, type **Seller**. Under Instructions to the signer, edit the text to read "Before signing this document, verify that the **dollar amount and the model number are** correct." Note that the option to show the sign date in the signature line is enabled. Click **OK**. The signature placeholder is inserted.
4. Press **Enter**. In the Text group, click the **Signature Line** button. Click **OK** to accept the disclaimer statement. The Signature Setup dialog box opens.
5. In the first text box, type **Jared Mancini**. In the second text box, type **Buyer**. Then enable the option **Allow the signer to add comments in the Sign dialog**. Click **OK**. A second signature placeholder is inserted.
6. Save the changes to the document. Close the document and reopen it. Note that a yellow bar at the top of the document indicates that the document needs to be signed. When the receiver opens the document, this note will prompt them to sign the document.
7. Save the document as **Signed Bill of Sale**, followed by your initials.
8. Right-click the first signature placeholder, and then in the shortcut menu, click **Sign**. Click **OK** to accept the disclaimer. The Sign dialog box opens, as shown in **Figure 13–19**.

FIGURE 13–19
Sign dialog box

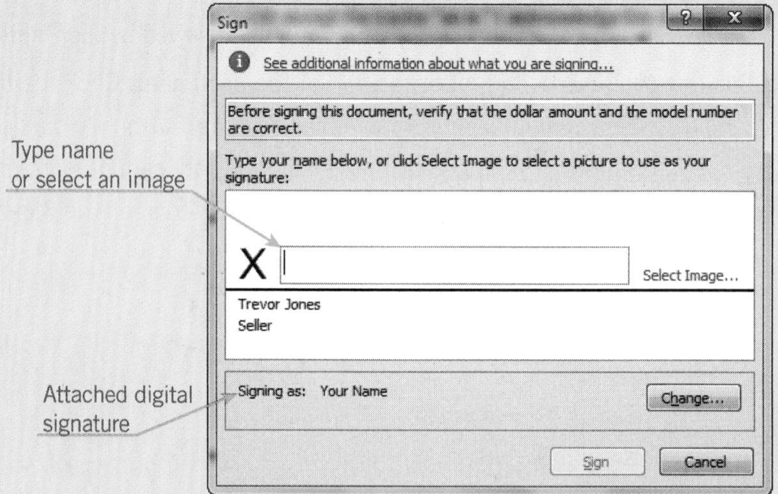

9. Note that the instructions at the top of the dialog box include the note you edited telling the signer to verify the dollar amount and model number. You can type your name in the box or select an image. Also note that your digital signature is automatically attached. If a digital signature for Trevor Jones was available on file, you could click Change and select that signature.

10. Click the link **Select Image**. Navigate to the drive and folder where your Data Files are stored. Select the filename **Jones.jpg** and then click **Select**. The digital image of the signature is inserted in the placeholder.
11. Click **Sign** and then click **OK** to confirm the signature. The digital image and the current date are both included in the signature placeholder.
12. Right-click the second signature placeholder, and then click **Sign**. Click **OK**, and in the Sign dialog box, type **Jared Mancini**. Click **Sign**, and then click **OK**. The typed signature and the current date are added to the signature placeholder.
13. Note that a yellow bar at the top of the document indicates that the document is marked as final. Close the document. The signatures have already been automatically saved. Leave Word open for the next Step-by-Step.

Sending Documents

Now that the document is protected, it is ready for distribution. You have several options for sending the document. You can send the file via e-mail or in a fax message. Obviously, to send the file via e-mail, you must have a network or Internet connection, and you must have sufficient bandwidth (the speed of data transfer) for transferring the file. Publishing to a blog is another alternative.

If you know the recipient of the file is working with a previous version of Office, you can convert the document to an earlier version of Word. If you're not sure what applications, platforms, or operating systems the recipient is using, you should consider saving the document in PDF or XPS format. The ***Portable Document Format (PDF)*** was created by Adobe Systems in 1993. Microsoft first offered the ***XML Paper Specification (XPS)*** format in Office 2007. Both the PDF and XPS document formats are designed to preserve the visual appearance and layout of each page and enable fast viewing and printing. PDF and XPS formats are especially useful for resumes, newsletters, and forms such as applications and invoices, because you can trust that when the receiver opens the document it will look and print exactly as intended.

VOCABULARY

Portable Document Format (PDF)

XML Paper Specification (XPS)

WARNING

A computer must be properly configured to send or receive and open documents in PDF and XPS formats. If your computer is unable to use these formats, you can download a free add-in from Microsoft.

Step-by-Step 13.12

1. Open the **Certified Employee Evaluation** file from your solution files. The password is **jck@554E5**.
2. Click the **File** tab, and then click **Save and Send**. In the center pane, click **Create PDF/XPS Document**, and then, in the right pane, click the **Create PDF/XPS** button. The Publish as PDF or XPS dialog box opens.
3. In the File name box, the same filename appears, but the document extension is changed to .pdf or .xps. If necessary, click the **Save as type** box, and then click XPS Document (*.xps).
4. Click **Publish**. When prompted to save in a format other than a Word document, click **Yes**. The document is no longer password protected.
5. The document opens in XPS format in Internet Explorer, your default browser, or the XPS Viewer. Drag across some text to select it, then press **Delete**. Because the XPS format is a read-only format, you cannot edit the document. Close the browser or viewer.
6. Click the **File** tab. Click **Save and Send**, and then, in the center pane, click **Change File Type**. The available document file types appear in the right pane. In the pane at the left, click **Close** to close the Certified Employee Evaluation document.
7. Open the **Final Board Minutes** document from your solution files. Click the **File** tab, and then click **Save and Send**. If necessary, click **Send Using E-mail** in the center pane. Then, in the right pane, click the **Send as Attachment** button. If Outlook is your default e-mail application, a new message window will open. If a different e-mail application is set as the default, a new message window will open in that application.
8. Note that the document is already attached to the e-mail message. At this point you would complete the header information and type a message. Close the message document window without saving any changes.
9. Click the **File** tab, and then click **Save and Send**. In the right pane, click the **Send as PDF** button. The document is attached to the e-mail message. Note that the filename extension is .pdf; when the e-mail process is completed, a PDF formatted version of the file will be attached. Close the message document window without saving any changes.
10. Click the **File** tab, and then click **Save and Send**. In the center pane, click **Publish as Blog Post**, and then, in the right pane, click the **Publish as Blog Post** button. A new document opens with a new Ribbon that shows blog features. If prompted to register a blog account, click Register Later.

11. The document content is formatted and ready to be published on the Web. At this point you would type a blog post title and publish the blog. Close the new document without saving the changes.
12. Leave the Final Board Minutes document open for the next Step-by-Step.

Storing, Accessing, and Sharing Documents

Word also enables you to upload and access documents online so that you can share files with others. You can upload documents to a ***document workspace site***, which is a Web site that provides a central location for storing and sharing files. Documents are stored in a library. Access to the documents can be controlled using encryption, so that users must know the password to gain access to the library or to open folders or files.

VOCABULARY
document workspace site

Microsoft Windows SharePoint Services provides a document workspace site that enables a business to customize document storage and handling. Documents can be stored and updated, information about document status is provided, and employees can access the files remotely, enabling team members to collaborate and work together in real time. You need authorization to publish or access files at a SharePoint site, so introducing and showing SharePoint features is beyond the scope of this lesson.

Microsoft also offers SkyDrive, a free Windows Live service that provides password-protected online storage. You can assign passwords to control who has access to your files. To access SkyDrive, you must have a Windows Live account. The following Step-by-Step will guide you in setting up a personal SkyDrive account.

Step-by-Step 13.13

1. If necessary, open the **Final Board Minutes** file from your solution files.
2. Click the **File** tab, and then click **Save and Send.** In the center pane, click **Save to Web**.
3. If you have a Windows Live ID, click the **Sign-In** button, and then enter your ID (e-mail address) and password and click **OK**. (If you do not have an account, click the link to sign up for Windows Live and follow the directions to create a new account.)
4. If necessary, under Personal Folders, click the **My Documents** folder to select it. Then click the **Save As** button. The Save As dialog box opens. Note that the path where the file will be stored shows a Windows Live network address.
5. You do not need to change the filename, so leave everything as is and click **Save**.
6. Close the Final Board Minutes document. The document has been uploaded to the server.

7. Using your Web browser, go to *http://skydrive.live.com*. If necessary, sign in. Open the My Documents folder, and then click the **Final Board Minutes** document.
8. Click the document icon to view the document in the Word WebApp.
9. If you want full access to the Word features as you edit the document, you can open the document in Word. Above the document window, click the option **Open in Word**. If a prompt appears asking if you trust the source, click **OK**. The document will open in Word on your computer. Close the document and exit Word on your computer.
10. In your browser, click **sign out** in the upper-right corner to sign out of Windows Live. Close your browser.

EXTRA FOR EXPERTS

When you click Download, you can choose to save the file. When you save the file, it is saved in the default Download folder on your computer.

SUMMARY

In this lesson, you learned:

- Tracked changes can appear in up to eight different colors, which helps distinguish changes made by multiple reviewers.
- Reviewers can provide feedback on a document without changing the content by adding comments.
- You can control the markup that shows on the screen or prints in a document.
- Comments can be edited in the markup balloons or in the Reviewing Pane.
- Revisions from multiple documents can be combined into a single document.
- You can accept or reject changes individually in documents, or you can accept or reject some or all changes at the same time.
- To compare documents, you can view them side by side, or you can use the Compare feature, which enables you to show the differences between the two documents using tracked changes in a new document.
- Access to a document can be restricted by assigning a password.
- Before sharing a document, it is good practice to inspect it so that you can control what others see.
- Word offers several options for distributing documents electronically, including e-mail, blogs, and document workspaces.

VOCABULARY REVIEW

Define the following terms:

case-sensitive
comment
digital signature
document workspace site
encryption
markup
metadata
Portable Document Format (PDF)
read-only document
revision bar
XML Paper Specification (XPS)

REVIEW QUESTIONS

TRUE / FALSE

Circle T if the statement is true or F if the statement is false.

T F 1. Deleting the comment text in the Reviewing Pane also removes the comment mark from the document pane.

T F 2. When you attach a digital signature to a document, the document is marked as final.

T F 3. When tracking changes, insertions are always blue with an underline effect and deletions are always red with a strikethrough effect.

T F 4. When showing markup for tracked changes, you can choose to show only the comments in the document, or you can show only the changes for one reviewer.

T F 5. Saving a file as a read-only document is one of the more secure ways to protect a document.

FILL IN THE BLANK

Complete the following sentences by writing the correct word or words in the blanks provided.

1. ________________ is a standard method for encoding data.
2. A(n) ________________ is an attachment to a file or e-mail message that certifies that the information in the file is authentic and safe.
3. The ________________ appears in the left margin and indicates a tracked change related to the paragraph.
4. Data that describes other data is referred to as ________________.
5. A(n) ________________ is a central location for storing and sharing documents.

WRITTEN QUESTIONS

Write a brief answer to the following questions.

1. What are some of the benefits of saving a document in a PDF or XPS format?

2. Describe how to format comments so that they appear only as ScreenTips and not as balloons.

3. Describe how you can create and print a summary of all the tracked changes and comments in a document.

4. What does it mean when a password is referred to as case-sensitive?

5. How can you identify which reviewer made the changes in a document?

 PROJECTS

If you have a SAM 2010 user profile, your instructor may have assigned an autogradable version of the indicated project. If so, log into the SAM 2010 Web site at *www.cengage.com/sam2010* to download the instruction and start files.

PROJECT 13–1

1. Open the **Sales Goal** file from the drive and folder where your Data Files are stored. Save the document as **Revised Sales Goal**, followed by your initials.
2. Toggle on the Track Changes feature. Make note of the current user name and initials and then change the user name to **Reviewer F** and change the initials to **RF**.
3. In the first paragraph, change *$500,000* to **$525,000** and change *$610,000* to **$635,000**. Also in the first paragraph, select the words **worst possible** and apply the italic format.
4. Select the entire first paragraph, and then insert the comment **Confirm these numbers.**.
5. In the second paragraph, delete the second sentence.
6. In the last paragraph, move the last sentence to the beginning of the paragraph. Adjust spacing as necessary.
7. Reset the user name and initials to the settings you noted in Step 2 above.
8. Save the changes and close the document.

 PROJECT 13–2

1. Open the **Will Draft 1** file from the drive and folder where your Data Files are stored. Then open the **Will Draft 2** file from the drive and folder where your Data Files are stored.
2. Compare the two documents, using Will Draft 1 as the original document. Save the new compared document as **Updated Will**, followed by your initials.
3. Review the document revisions:
   a. Accept the revision in the first paragraph.
   b. Reject the revisions in the third paragraph.
   c. In the fourth paragraph, accept all revisions.
   d. Accept the new fifth paragraph.
   e. In the sixth paragraph, reject the change from *bequeath* to *leave* and then accept the final revision in that same paragraph.
4. Toggle off the Track Changes feature. At the end of the document, replace both occurrences of ///// with the current month and year (for example, *April, 2014*).
5. Save the changes to the Updated Will document, and then close the document. Close the Will Draft 1 and Will Draft 2 documents.

PROJECT 13–3

1. Open the **Job Description RA** file from the drive and folder where your Data Files are stored. Then open the **Job Description RB** file from the drive and folder where your Data Files are stored.
2. View the documents side by side with synchronized scrolling.
3. Combine the two documents into a new document, using Job Description RA as the original document. Save the new document as **Final Job Description**, followed by your initials.
4. Reject the change in the footer pane.
5. Accept all the remaining changes in the document.
6. Delete the comment.
7. Save the changes to the Final Job Description document, and then close the document. Close the Job Description RA and Job Description RB documents.

PROJECT 13–4

1. Open the **Consultation Call** file from the drive and folder where your Data Files are stored. Save the document as **Restricted Consultation Call**, followed by your initials.
2. In the DATE cell, insert the current date using the XX/XX/XXXX format.
3. In the TIME cell, insert the current time using the ##:## PM format.
4. Set the editing restrictions for No changes (Read only).
5. Select the row in the document for entering information about the PLAN. Then change the settings to allow all users to freely edit this section of the document.
6. Enforce the protection and enter the password ***YntPYd#134**.
7. Save the changes and close the document. Reopen the document from your solution files. Save the document as **Protected Consultation**, followed by your initials.
8. In the document, under PLAN, type **Scheduled appointment with Dr. Lis for two weeks from today at 10:20 a.m.**.
9. Save the changes to the document. Then encrypt the document using the password **20Ewb100%&**.
10. Save the changes and close the document.

PROJECT 13–5

1. Open the **Challenge** file from the drive and folder where your Data Files are stored.
2. The file is encrypted. Type the password **rrw*F4#67** and click OK.
3. Remove the encryption, and then save the document with the filename **Completed Challenge**, followed by your initials.
4. Position the insertion point at the end of the document. Create a signature line. Use your own name for the signer, and type **IT Manager** for the signer title.
5. Sign the document by typing your name in the signature placeholder. If necessary, select your digital signature to authenticate the signature line.
6. Close the document.

CRITICAL THINKING

ACTIVITY 13–1

Mary manages an insurance office and is responsible for updating the company's office procedures manual. She needs to share the current file for the manual with her workgroup so they can read it, mark revisions, and add comments. Mary's colleagues spend much of the time working outside of the office, and she has a short window of time to get their feedback. What would be the advantages of Mary uploading the file to a SharePoint server?

ACTIVITY 13–2

Mary likes the new Word markup features because she can easily review changes and comments. However, after she combines the changes and comments from all members of the workgroup, she is overwhelmed with the markup. Mary knows how to control the markup so that all the revisions are not shown at once, but she doesn't know where to begin. What suggestions do you have for Mary to complete the task effectively and efficiently?

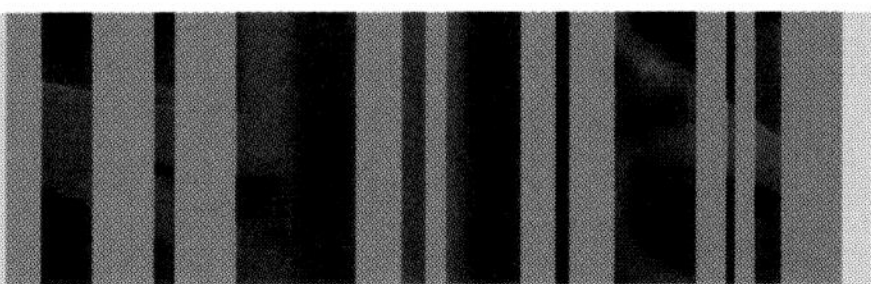

Estimated Time: 2 hours

LESSON 14

Working with Long Documents

■ OBJECTIVES

Upon completion of this lesson, you should be able to:

- Change and organize document views and windows.
- Navigate documents, reorganize content within a document, and search for text and objects.
- Create and modify hyperlinks and bookmarks.
- Create section breaks and format columns.
- Use pagination options, hyphenation, and nonbreaking spaces to control text flow.
- Manage sources, create citations, and create a bibliography.
- Insert footnotes and endnotes.
- Determine the readability level of document content.

■ VOCABULARY

bibliography
bookmark
citation
endnote
footnote
hyphenation
incremental search
nonbreaking hyphen
nonbreaking space
optional hyphen
orphan
pagination
reference marker
section
section break
separator line
widow
works cited page

Working with long documents involves much more than formatting the page numbers. Word provides several features that help you navigate through the pages, search for content, cite sources of information, and control the text flow throughout the pages.

Working with Multiple Documents

When long documents such as reports, studies, and proposals are prepared, the information is often compiled from several different documents. Microsoft Word allows you to open multiple documents and work with all of them at the same time. The number of windows you can open depends on available system memory.

Viewing Documents and Splitting Windows

When multiple documents are open, you have several options for arranging the document windows on your screen. Some of the features are available in Windows and apply to all applications, and some of the features are available only in the Word application.

Step-by-Step 14.1

1. Launch Word. Click the **File** tab, and then click **Open**. Navigate to the drive and folder where your Data Files are stored.
2. To select a range of filenames, click the filename **Apollo 11**, hold down **Shift**, and then click **Apollo 13**. Three filenames are selected. To select another filename in the list, hold down **Ctrl** and click the filename **Moon Missions**. Click **Open**. All four documents open.
3. Point to the Word icon in the taskbar at the bottom of the screen. A thumbnail appears for each open document in the Word application, and the highlighted thumbnail indicates the active document. Move the mouse pointer over each thumbnail to preview the first page of each document. Click the **Apollo 12** thumbnail to make it the active document.
4. Position the mouse pointer over the Word icon in the taskbar, and then position the mouse pointer over the Apollo 13 thumbnail. The title bar in the thumbnail changes and now shows the Close button. Click the **Close** button in the thumbnail to close the document.
5. Right-click a blank area in the taskbar. In the shortcut menu, click **Show windows stacked**. The document windows are stacked on top of each other so that you see each of the documents. If you are running any other applications, those windows will also be stacked. Right-click the taskbar and then click **Show windows side by side**. The three documents are arranged next to each other.

6. Right-click a blank area in the taskbar and then click **Cascade windows**. The windows are arranged in a single stack so that the title bar for each document window is shown.
7. In the Apollo 12 document window, click the **View** tab. In the Window group, click the **Switch Windows** button and then click the filename **Apollo 11**. The Apollo 11 document appears on the top of the stack, and it is now the active document.
8. Click the **View** tab for any one of the document windows. In the Window group, click the **Arrange All** button. Word rearranges the documents on the screen. The three documents are stacked on top of each other; however, the arrangement will vary depending on the number of open documents.
9. Close the Moon Missions and Apollo 12 documents. Maximize the Apollo 11 document window. Scroll down through the document to view the heading *Mission Objective*.
10. If necessary, click the **View** tab. In the Window group, click the **Split** button. The mouse pointer changes and shows a horizontal line that spans the width of the window. Position the mouse pointer above the heading *Mission Objective* and then click. The document window is divided into two panes, as shown in **Figure 14–1**.

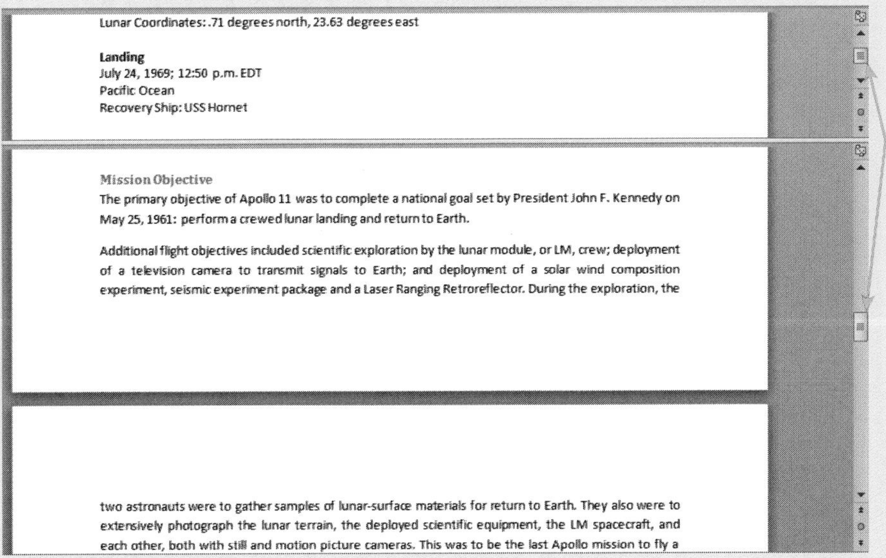

FIGURE 14–1
Document split into two panes

11. Note that each pane has its own vertical scroll bars. Drag the scroll box on the vertical bars in both panes. You will see that both panes contain the same content. Splitting the document window is useful when you are working with a long document and you want to view content in two different parts of the document.

12. To reposition where the document splits, point to the horizontal line that separates the two panes. When the mouse pointer changes to a double-headed arrow, drag the scroll bar up about one inch and drop the horizontal line in a new position.
13. In the Window group, click the **Remove Split** button. The document once again appears in a single pane.
14. Close the document without saving any changes.

Copying and Pasting Content from Multiple Documents

When multiple files are open, you can copy and paste content from one document to another. You can copy up to 24 items from one or more documents to the Office Clipboard. New items are added at the top of the list in the Clipboard pane. When the number exceeds 24, the items at the bottom of the list are removed from the Clipboard. You can paste the items individually or as a group into a document. You can also insert the entire contents of a file into your document without even opening the file.

Step-by-Step 14.2

1. Open the **Apollo 11** and **Mission Highlights** files from the drive and folder where your Data Files are stored. Make the Apollo 11 document the active document, and then save it as **Apollo 11 Revised**, followed by your initials. Also, if necessary, click the **Home** tab and click the **Show/Hide ¶** button to show nonprinting formatting characters.
2. Switch to the Mission Highlights document. In the Clipboard group, click the **Dialog Box Launcher** to open the Clipboard pane. If necessary, click the **Clear All** button to remove all contents from the Clipboard.
3. In the document window, triple-click anywhere in the first paragraph to select the entire paragraph. Copy the selected text to the Clipboard. An item displaying a portion of the new content added to the Clipboard appears at the top of the pane.
4. Scroll to the end of the document and select the last paragraph, beginning *Re-entry procedures.* Copy the selected text to the Clipboard. A new item appears at the top of the Clipboard pane.
5. Scroll to the top of the document so that you can view both the second and the fourth paragraphs. Select the second paragraph. Hold down **Ctrl** and triple-click to select the fourth paragraph. Copy the selected text to the Clipboard. The Clipboard pane now contains three items.

6. Switch to the **Apollo 11 Revised** document. Open the Clipboard pane and, if necessary, show nonprinting formatting characters. In the document, scroll down to the heading *Mission Highlights*. Position the insertion point in front of the first paragraph that begins *Two hours, 44 minutes*. In the Clipboard pane, click the item that begins *Apollo 11 launched* to paste the content into the document.
7. Press **Ctrl+End** to move to the end of the document. Scroll up and position the insertion point in the blank paragraph above the source information.
8. In the Clipboard pane, click the item that begins *Armstrong and Aldrin* to paste the content of that item into the document. Two new paragraphs are inserted in the document. In the Clipboard pane, click the item that begins *Re-entry procedures* to paste the content of that item into the document.
9. In the Clipboard pane, click the **Paste All** button. All the items in the Clipboard pane are inserted in the document. Click the **Undo** button three times to remove all three paste edits. Close the Clipboard pane.
10. Save the changes to the document. Then save the document as **Journeys to the Moon 1**, followed by your initials. Close the Mission Highlights document without saving any changes.
11. Reposition the insertion point at the end of the document, and then press **Enter**. Note that the document currently has five pages. Click the **Insert** tab. In the Text group, click the **Object** button arrow and then click **Text from File**. The Insert File dialog box opens.
12. Navigate to the drive and folder where your Data Files are stored. Select the filename **Apollo 12** and then click **Insert**. Without opening the document, all the content from the Apollo 12 document is inserted in the Journeys to the Moon 1 document at the location of the insertion point. The document now has 10 pages.
13. In the Text group, click the **Object** button arrow and then click **Text from File**. Select the filename **Apollo 13**, hold down **Ctrl** and click **Moon Missions**, and then click **Insert**. All the content from both documents is inserted in the open document. The document now has 18 pages.
14. Save your changes and leave the document open for the next Step-by-Step.

Navigating a Document

The more pages in a document, the more time consuming it is to move around in the document and find content. The Navigation Pane provides features to help you quickly navigate through a document, organize the document content, and find content and objects.

Viewing and Reorganizing the Content

Using the Navigation Pane is similar to viewing a document in Outline view. When you format document headings and subheadings using heading styles, the headings and subheadings appear in the Navigation Pane. Instead of scrolling through the document, you can quickly browse through the headings in the Navigation Pane for a quick overview of the contents, and you can use the Navigation Pane to move to a specific area in the document. Word displays up to nine levels of headings, and the subheadings are indented for easy review. If desired, you can collapse the subheadings so that only the main headings are displayed.

An alternative way to browse document contents is to view thumbnails of all the pages in the document and then click a thumbnail to quickly jump to a specific page.

Step-by-Step 14.3

1. If necessary, open the **Journeys to the Moon 1** file from your solution files. Save the document as **Journeys to the Moon 2**, followed by your initials.
2. Click the **View** tab. In the Show group, enable the **Navigation Pane** option. The Navigation Pane shown in **Figure 14–2** appears, usually at the left side of the screen. You can reposition the pane on your screen by dragging the title bar, and you can also resize the pane by dragging the borders.

FIGURE 14–2
Navigation Pane

3. In the Navigation Pane, right-click the **Apollo 11** heading. In the shortcut menu, point to **Show Heading Levels**, and then click **Show Heading 2** to show only level one and two headings. Right-click the **Apollo 11** heading again and click **Expand All**. The Navigation Pane shows three levels of headings.
4. In the Navigation Pane, click the **Apollo 12** heading. The document window shows the page in the document where the heading appears. Scroll down to page seven and click anywhere below the heading *Mission Highlights*. Notice that the heading is highlighted in the Navigation Pane, indicating your location in the document.
5. In the Navigation Pane, click the **Goals** heading. The insertion point moves to the heading in the document window. Type **The Apollo** and press the **spacebar** to edit the heading. The heading is updated in the Navigation Pane. In the document window, click in front of the heading *Missions*, and then type **The Apollo** and press the **spacebar** to edit that heading.
6. In the Navigation Pane, right-click the **The Apollo Missions** heading. In the shortcut menu, click **Demote**. The heading is changed to a level two heading, and the Heading 2 style is applied to the heading text in the document. Right-click the **The Apollo Missions** heading again, and then click **Promote** to restore the Heading 1 level and style.

7. In the Navigation Pane, under the Apollo 13 heading, right-click the **Mission Highlights** heading. In the shortcut menu, click **New Heading After**. A new level three heading box (the same level as the heading above) appears in the Navigation Pane. Type **Summary**. The new heading appears in the Navigation Pane and in the document, and it is formatted with the Heading 3 style.
8. In the Navigation Pane, right-click the **Summary** heading. In the shortcut menu, click **Promote**. The heading is promoted to a level two. Right-click the **Summary** heading again, and then click **Promote**. The heading is now a level one heading, and the heading in the document window is formatted with the Heading 1 style.
9. In the Navigation Pane, click the **Collapse** button to the left of the Apollo 11 heading. Both of the subheadings below the heading are hidden in the Navigation Pane. Click the **Expand** arrow to the left of the Apollo 11 heading to show all the subheadings.
10. In the Navigation Pane, click and drag the **Introduction** heading to the top of the list of headings. As you drag the heading, a horizontal bar will appear. Drop the heading at the top of the list. Drag and drop the **The Apollo Goals** heading to position it after the Introduction heading. Then drag and drop the **The Apollo Missions** heading to position it after the The Apollo Goals heading.
11. In the Navigation Pane, click the **Introduction** heading. Press **Enter**. Position the insertion point in the new blank paragraph and type **Journeys to the Moon**. Click the **Home** tab, and in the Styles group, apply the **Title** style to the new paragraph.
12. A new yellow bar appears at the top of the Navigation pane. No text appears in the bar because the paragraph is not formatted with a heading style. This blank bar only appears when new content (not formatted as a heading style) is inserted in the first line of a document. Position the mouse pointer over the bar to show the ScreenTip. You can use this bar to navigate to the top of the document.
13. In the Navigation Pane, click the **Browse the pages of your document** button . Thumbnails of each page in the document appear. Click the **thumbnail** for page four. The insertion point moves to page four in the document window. Click the **Browse the headings in your document** button to show the document headings.
14. Save the changes and leave the document open for the next Step-by-Step.

Finding Text and Objects

The Navigation Pane can do more than just help you move around in a document. For example, you may want to look for specific words that appear throughout the document. The Find command can be accessed in the Navigation Pane to quickly identify all occurrences of the search words. By default, Word completes an incremental search. In an ***incremental search***, as you begin typing the string of characters to search for, Word highlights the matches for the character string in the document. As the search text is augmented, the matches in the document change.

VOCABULARY
incremental search

When searching for text, you may want to further define the search. For example, you may want to find matches for whole words only. You can also search for all occurrences of a specific format in the document, such as all text formatted bold and italic. Or, you may be looking for variations of text. You can use a wildcard character, a keyboard character used to represent one or more characters in a search. The character ? searches for a single character; the character * (asterisk) searches for a string of characters. For example, when the search text is *d?n*, matches will include *Dan* and *Don*. When the search text is *dan**, the matches will include *Daniel*, *Danielle*, and *Danny*. When you want to replace occurrences of matched text with new text and/or formats, you can use the Replace command.

Step-by-Step 14.4

1. If necessary, open the **Journeys to the Moon 2** file from your solution files. Save the document as **Journeys to the Moon 3**, followed by your initials. If necessary, show the **Navigation Pane**, and click the **Browse the headings in your document** button.

TIP

If the Navigation Pane is not displayed, you can use the shortcut keys Ctrl+F.

2. In the Navigation Pane, click the **Search Document** text box and type **Armstrong**. When you finish entering the search text, all the matches in the document are highlighted in the document window. The total number of matches is indicated in the Navigation Pane, as shown in **Figure 14–3**. Some of the headings are highlighted in the Navigation Pane to indicate that matches can be found in those sections of the document.

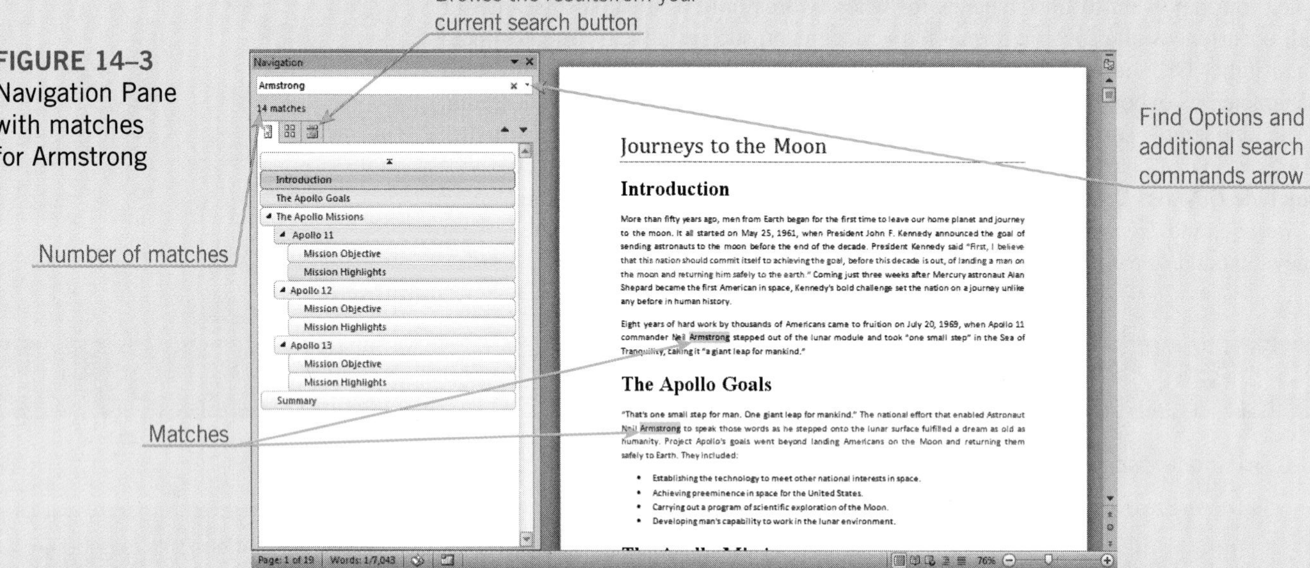

FIGURE 14–3
Navigation Pane with matches for Armstrong

> **TIP**
>
> If you enter the characters slowly, you can watch the process of the incremental search. As you enter each new character, the highlights appear in both the document window and the Navigation Pane.

3. In the Navigation Pane, click the **The Apollo Goals** heading. Then click the **Next Search Result** button. The first occurrence of the search text under the selected heading is highlighted in the document window. Click the **Previous Search Result** button. The previous occurrence of the search text is highlighted.
4. In the Navigation Pane, click the **Browse the pages in your document** button. Only the pages with matches appear in the Navigation Pane.
5. In the Navigation Pane, click the **Browse the results from your current search** button. Items showing some of the document content appear in the pane so you can see the occurrence of the match in the context of the document. Click the item that shows only the name *Neil Armstrong* to go to that location in the document.
6. In the Navigation Pane, on the right side of the Search Document text box, click the **Find Options and additional search commands** arrow. In the menu that opens, you can search for graphics, tables, equations, footnotes/endnotes, and comments. Under Find, click **Graphics**. Click the **Browse the pages in your document** button. Six matches are identified, and the third of those occurrences is selected in the document window.

7. Click the **Find Options and additional search commands** button. Click **Options** to open the Find Options dialog box shown in **Figure 14–4**. These options enable you to further define your search.

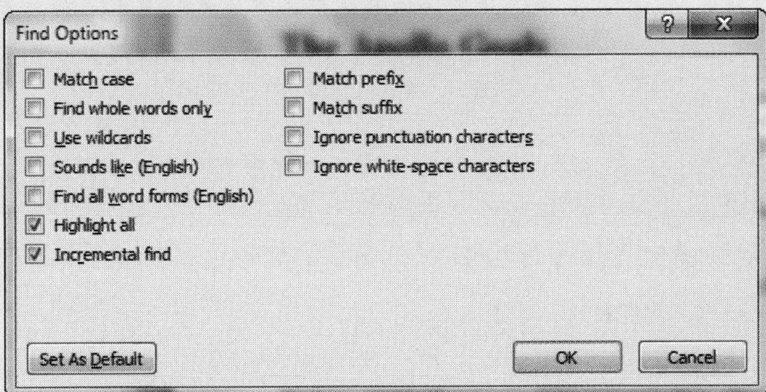

FIGURE 14–4
Find Options dialog box

8. Enable the **Find whole words only** option and click **OK**. In the Navigation Pane, click the **Browse the headings in your document** button. Under the heading *Apollo 11*, click the **Mission Objective** heading. In the Search Document text box, type **crew**. In the document window, the first match in the second paragraph under the heading is highlighted. Notice that the word *crewed* appears in the paragraph above, but it is not highlighted because the search was for whole words only.
9. Click the **Find Options and additional search commands** arrow. Click **Options**, enable the **Use wildcards** option, and then click **OK**. In the Navigation Pane, in the Search text box, type **Aldr*** and press **Enter**. Ten matches for the surname *Aldrin* are highlighted, and all occurrences are in the Apollo 11 section.
10. Click the **Find Options and additional search commands** arrow. Click **Options**, and then disable the option **Use wildcards**. Enable the **Incremental find** option and click **OK**.

11. Click the **Find Options and additional search commands** arrow. Click **Replace** to open the Find and Replace dialog box. In the Find what text box, the previous search text *Aldr** is selected. Type **ALSEP** to enter new search text. Click **More** to show more options, as shown in **Figure 14–5**.

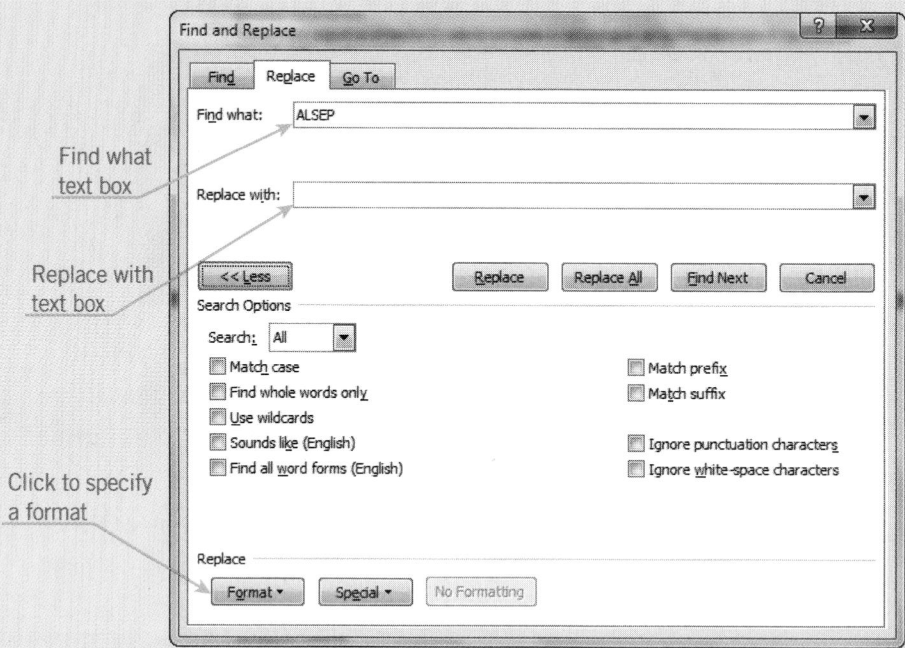

FIGURE 14–5
More options in the Find and Replace dialog box

12. In the lower-left corner of the dialog box, click **Format**, and then click **Font** to open the Find Font dialog box, as shown in **Figure 14–6**. Under Font style, select **Italic** and then click **OK**. The format *Font: Italic* is displayed below the Find what text box.

TIP

As in previous Word versions, you can quickly open the Replace tab in the Find and Replace dialog box by using the shortcut keys Ctrl+H.

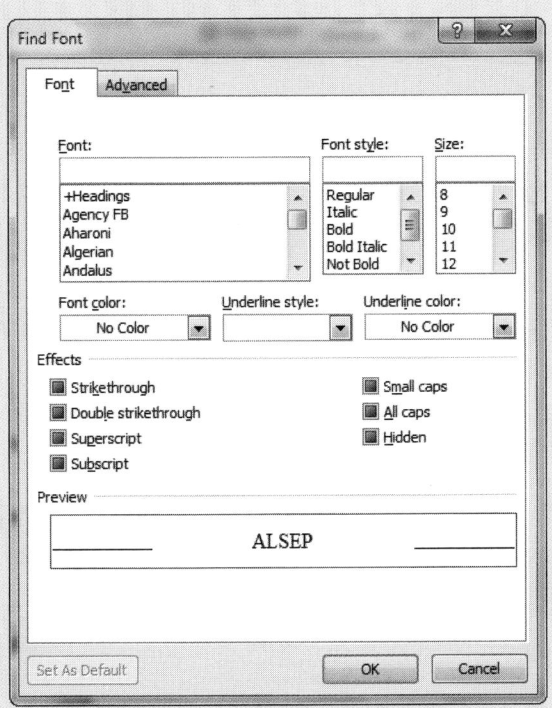

FIGURE 14–6
Find Font dialog box

13. In the Replace with box, type **ALSEP**. Click **Format**, and then click **Font**. Under Font style, click **Regular**, and then click **OK**. The format *Font: Not Bold, Not Italic* is displayed below the Replace with text box. Click **Replace All**. Eight replacements are made. Click **OK**.
14. Close the Find and Replace dialog box. Save the changes and leave the document open for the next Step-by-Step.

Creating and Modifying Hyperlinks

You can create your own navigation tools to help move around within and between your documents. You already know that a hyperlink takes you to a new location. You can use a hyperlink to move quickly to a location in your current document or to another existing document. For example, you can use a hyperlink in Word to jump to a location in another Word document, an Excel worksheet, or a PowerPoint presentation. By default, Word automatically creates a hyperlink when you type a Web or Internet address in a document.

You can select any text or object in a document, then create a hyperlink and specify the document or URL for the link. If desired, you can create ScreenTips for the hyperlinks you create.

Step-by-Step 14.5

1. If necessary, open the **Journeys to the Moon 3** file from your solution files. Save the document as **Journeys to the Moon 4**, followed by your initials. If necessary, show the Navigation Pane with headings displayed. Also, if necessary, show nonprinting formatting characters.
2. In the Navigation Pane, click the **The Apollo Missions** heading. Scroll to the second page to show the three graphics. Select the **Apollo 11** mission patch graphic. Click the **Insert** tab. In the Links group, click the **Hyperlink** button to open the Insert Hyperlink dialog box, as shown in **Figure 14–7**. Your dialog box settings will differ.

FIGURE 14–7
Insert Hyperlink dialog box

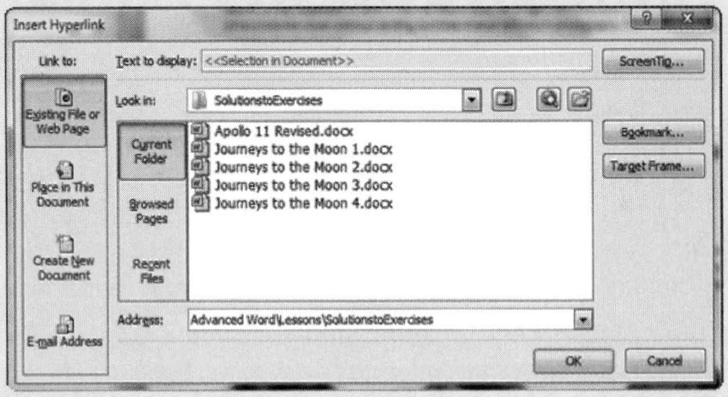

3. Under Link to, the option Existing File or Web Page is already enabled. In the Look in box, navigate to the drive and folder where your Data Files are stored. Select **Apollo 11**.
4. Click **ScreenTip** in the upper-right corner of the dialog box. The Set Hyperlink ScreenTip dialog box opens. Type **Original Apollo 11 document**. Click **OK** to save the ScreenTip, and then click **OK** to complete the hyperlink.
5. Deselect the graphic. Position the mouse pointer over the graphic to display the ScreenTip. Hold down **Ctrl** and click the **Apollo 11** graphic. The Apollo 11 document opens. Close the Apollo 11 document without saving any changes.
6. Position the insertion point in the second blank paragraph below the three graphics. On the Insert tab, in the Links group, click the **Hyperlink** button. Under Link to, the option Existing File or Web Page is already enabled. In the Address text box, type **http://www.nasa.gov**.
7. In the Text to display text box, select any text, if necessary, and then type **Get more information about the Apollo missions.**. Click **ScreenTip**, type **Learn more at NASA.gov/**, and then click **OK** twice to complete the hyperlink. The text in the document is formatted in a different color and underlined to indicate it is a hyperlink.

8. Click anywhere in the hyperlink you just created. In the Links group, click the **Hyperlink** button. Because a hyperlink is already formatted, the Edit Hyperlink dialog box opens.
9. In the Address box, position the insertion point at the end of the existing text and type **missions** to complete the URL. Click **OK** to apply the changes.
10. If you have an Internet connection and your browser is open, hold down **Ctrl** and click anywhere in the hyperlink. If the Web site is still current, the Web page should display in your browser. Close the Web page and switch to the Journeys to the Moon 4 document.
11. On page 2 of the document, right-click the **Apollo XIII** graphic, and in the shortcut menu, click **Hyperlink** to open the Insert Hyperlink dialog box. Under Link to, click the **Place in This Document** option. The document headings appear in the center pane of the dialog box. Click the **Apollo 13** heading.
12. Click **ScreenTip**. Type **Apollo 13 information**, and then click **OK** twice.
13. Deselect the graphic. Hold down **Ctrl** and click the **Apollo XIII** graphic. Page 13 appears in the document window, and the insertion point is positioned in front of the heading *Apollo 13*.
14. Save the changes to the document and leave the document open for the next Step-by-Step.

TIP

If the text is not automatically formatted as a hyperlink, the AutoCorrect option may be turned off. Click the File tab, click Options, and then click Proofing. Click AutoCorrect Options, and then click the AutoFormat As You Type tab. Under Replace as you type, make sure that the Internet and network paths with hyperlinks option is enabled.

Adding a Bookmark

You can also create a navigation tool by inserting a bookmark. A ***bookmark*** is an item or location in a document that you identify and name for future reference so you can jump quickly to a specific location within the same document. For example, you may want to bookmark a word, phrase, or table in a document so you can return to that location without searching for the text. The advantage of using bookmarks over using hyperlinks or the features in the Navigation Pane is that bookmarks do not have to be tied to headings.

VOCABULARY
bookmark

Bookmarks can be placed anywhere within a document. To add a bookmark, you simply identify a location in a document and assign a bookmark name. Bookmark names can be up to 40 characters, must begin with a letter, and can contain numbers. Bookmark names cannot contain blank spaces. To separate words in a bookmark name, use the underscore character. If desired, you can make bookmarks visible in your document, but they will not print. You can edit, cut, copy, move, and paste items that are marked with a bookmark. Unless the content is removed from the document, the bookmark stays with the text.

Step-by-Step 14.6

1. If necessary, open the **Journeys to the Moon 4** file from your solution files. Save the document as **Journeys to the Moon 5**, followed by your initials. If necessary, show the Navigation Pane, with headings displayed.
2. To show bookmarks in the document, click the **File** tab. Click **Options** and then in the Word Options dialog box, click **Advanced**. Scroll down about halfway, and under Show document content, enable the **Show bookmarks** option. Click **OK**.
3. Position the insertion point at the top of the document. In the Navigation Pane, in the Search Document text box, type **explosion**. Click the **Browse the results from your current search** button. In the document window where the first match is highlighted, select **An oxygen tank explosion on board.**
4. If necessary, click the **Insert** tab. In the Links group, click the **Bookmark** button to open the Bookmark dialog box, as shown in **Figure 14–8**. You can drag the dialog box title bar to reposition it on the page.

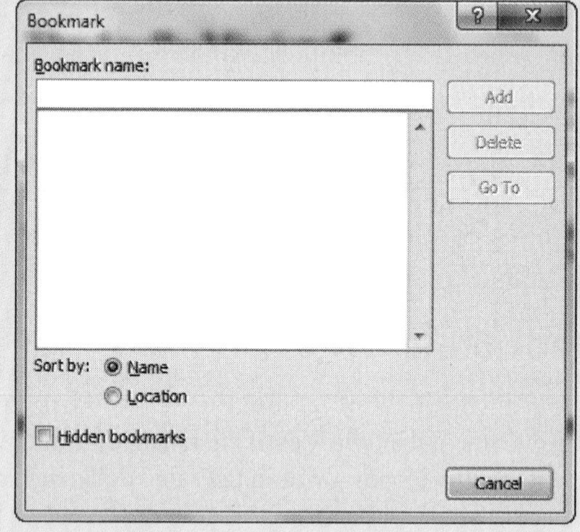

FIGURE 14–8
Bookmark dialog box

5. In the Bookmark name box, type **explosion** and then click **Add**. Deselect the text. Brackets appear before and after the bookmark text. These brackets do not print.
6. In the Navigation Pane, the Browse the results from your current search tab is still displayed, but the matches do not appear. Click the **Next Search Result** button to show the matches again, and then click the item for the last match. In the document window, position the insertion point in front of the paragraph with the highlighted search text. On the Insert tab, in the Links group, click the **Bookmark** button. In the Bookmark name box, type **explosion_cause**. Click **Add**. An I-beam appears to the left of the paragraph. The I-beam will not print.

7. On the Insert tab, in the Links group, click the **Bookmark** button. Under the Bookmark name box, two bookmarks are listed. Click the bookmark name **explosion** and then click **Go To**. The insertion point moves to the first bookmark in the document.
8. In the Bookmark dialog box, in the Bookmark name text box, position the insertion point to the right of the *explosion* text and type **_type**. Click **Add**.
9. Click the **Bookmark** button. Now three bookmarks appear in the list. Click the bookmark name **explosion** and then click **Delete**.
10. Click the bookmark name **explosion_cause** and then click **Go To**. The insertion moves to the paragraph that begins *After an intensive* near the end of the document. Close the dialog box.
11. Click the **File** tab, click **Options**, and then click **Advanced**. Under Show document content, disable the **Show bookmarks** option, and then click **OK**.
12. Even though the bookmarks are no longer visible, they still exist. In the Links group, click the **Bookmark** button, click **explosion_type**, and then click **Go To**. The first bookmarked text is selected. Close the dialog box.
13. On the vertical scroll bar in the lower-right corner of the screen, click the **Select Browse Object** button. Then click the **Go To** button. The Go To tab in the Find and Replace dialog box opens. Under Go to what, click **Bookmark**. In the Enter bookmark name text box, the *exposure_cause* bookmark appears. To the right of the bookmark name, click the **list arrow** to see all bookmarks in the document. Click **Go To** and then close the dialog box.
14. Save the changes and leave the document open for the next Step-by-Step.

TIP

Ctrl+Shift+F5 is a shortcut for Insert Bookmark.

Controlling Text Flow

Monitoring how text flows throughout a multi-page document is important. Word provides several features so you can format text in multiple columns and also control how text flows from one page to the next.

Creating Sections and Formatting Columns

The default setting in a Word document displays all of the text in a single column, approximately six inches wide. Formatting text to display in multiple columns sometimes saves space on a page, and because the width of the line of text is smaller, the text is often easier to read. Word evenly balances the text in the columns, but you can manually control where the text ends in a column by inserting a column break.

VOCABULARY
section
section break

A ***section*** is an area within a document that can have its own separate page formats. When you create a new blank document in Word, the document consists of just one section. When a document has only one section, the page formats, such as page orientation, margins, and headers and footers, apply to the entire document. The page formats are stored in a hidden, nonprinting end-of-file marker. If you want to change the page formats for only a portion of the document, you need to divide the document into multiple sections and then change the settings for the section that contains the content you want to format differently. To divide the document into multiple sections, you insert a ***section break***, which divides the document into sections. The section break is indicated with a formatting mark, and all page formatting settings for the section that precedes the section break are stored in that mark. Therefore, if you delete a section break, the preceding content becomes part of the following section and assumes the formatting of that section.

Step-by-Step 14.7

1. If necessary, open the **Journeys to the Moon 5** file from your solution files. Save the document as **Journeys to the Moon 6**, followed by your initials. If necessary, show the Navigation Pane. Also, if necessary, show nonprinting formatting characters.
2. In the Navigation Pane, click the **Browse the headings in your document** button and then click the **The Apollo Goals** heading. The insertion point should be positioned in front of the heading in the document window.
3. Click the **Page Layout** tab. In the Page Setup group, click the **Breaks** button, and then, under Section Breaks, click **Continuous**. A continuous section break formatting mark appears at the end of the paragraph above the heading, as shown in **Figure 14–9**. If necessary, scroll up to see the section break. Because you selected a continuous break, the text below the section break will continue on the same page.

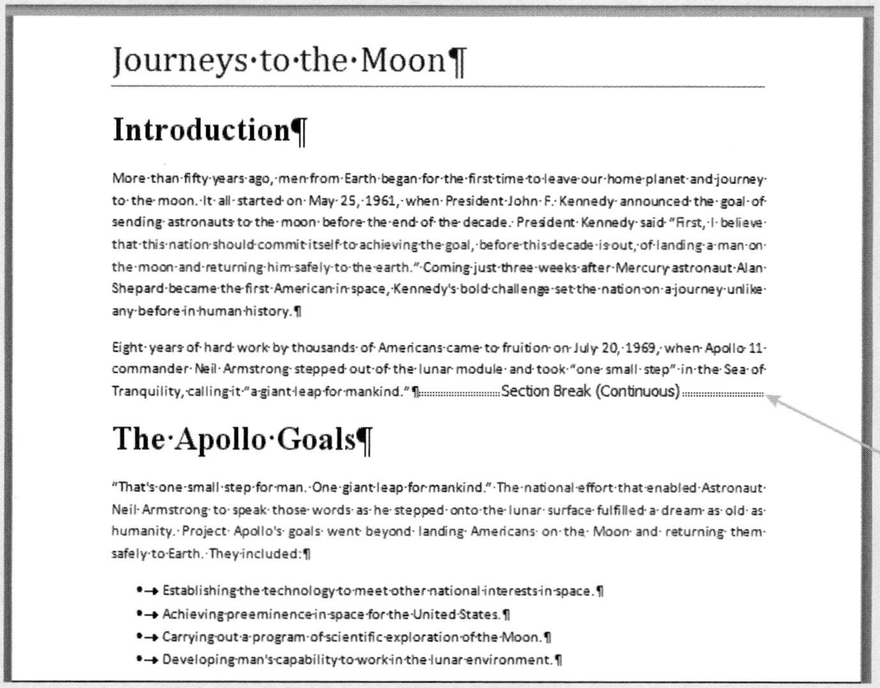

Journeys·to·the·Moon¶

Introduction¶

More·than·fifty·years·ago,·men·from·Earth·began·for·the·first·time·to·leave·our·home·planet·and·journey·to·the·moon.·It·all·started·on·May·25,·1961,·when·President·John·F.·Kennedy·announced·the·goal·of·sending·astronauts·to·the·moon·before·the·end·of·the·decade.·President·Kennedy·said·"First,·I·believe·that·this·nation·should·commit·itself·to·achieving·the·goal,·before·this·decade·is·out,·of·landing·a·man·on·the·moon·and·returning·him·safely·to·the·earth."·Coming·just·three·weeks·after·Mercury·astronaut·Alan·Shepard·became·the·first·American·in·space,·Kennedy's·bold·challenge·set·the·nation·on·a·journey·unlike·any·before·in·human·history.¶

Eight·years·of·hard·work·by·thousands·of·Americans·came·to·fruition·on·July·20,·1969,·when·Apollo·11·commander·Neil·Armstrong·stepped·out·of·the·lunar·module·and·took·"one·small·step"·in·the·Sea·of·Tranquility,·calling·it·"a·giant·leap·for·mankind."¶ Section Break (Continuous)

The·Apollo·Goals¶

"That's·one·small·step·for·man.·One·giant·leap·for·mankind."·The·national·effort·that·enabled·Astronaut·Neil·Armstrong·to·speak·those·words·as·he·stepped·onto·the·lunar·surface·fulfilled·a·dream·as·old·as·humanity.·Project·Apollo's·goals·went·beyond·landing·Americans·on·the·Moon·and·returning·them·safely·to·Earth.·They·included:¶

- Establishing·the·technology·to·meet·other·national·interests·in·space.¶
- Achieving·preeminence·in·space·for·the·United·States.¶
- Carrying·out·a·program·of·scientific·exploration·of·the·Moon.¶
- Developing·man's·capability·to·work·in·the·lunar·environment.¶

Continuous section break formatting mark

FIGURE 14–9
Continuous section break

4. Make sure the insertion point is positioned somewhere below the section break. In the Page Setup group, click the **Margins** button, and then click **Narrow**. The margins for all the text below the section break change are not as wide, and the flow of text changes.
5. To remove the section break, in the document, click the **Section Break (Continuous)** formatting mark and then press **Delete**. The text above the section break is now formatted with the same margin settings as the text that was below the section break. In the Page Setup group, click the **Margins** button, and then click **Normal**.
6. In the Navigation Pane, click the **Apollo 11** heading. In the document window, under the quotation *"The Eagle has landed...,"* select the crew and backup crew member information. Be sure to include both headings and the ending paragraph mark in the selection.
7. On the Page Layout tab, in the Page Setup group, click the **Columns** button, and then click **Two**. Word automatically inserts continuous section breaks above and below the selected content, and the content is arranged in two columns.

8. In the Navigation Pane, click the **Mission Objective** heading for Apollo 11. Select the two paragraphs below the heading, including the ending paragraph mark. Click the **Columns** button, and then click **More Columns** at the bottom of the menu to open the Columns dialog box, shown in **Figure 14–10**.

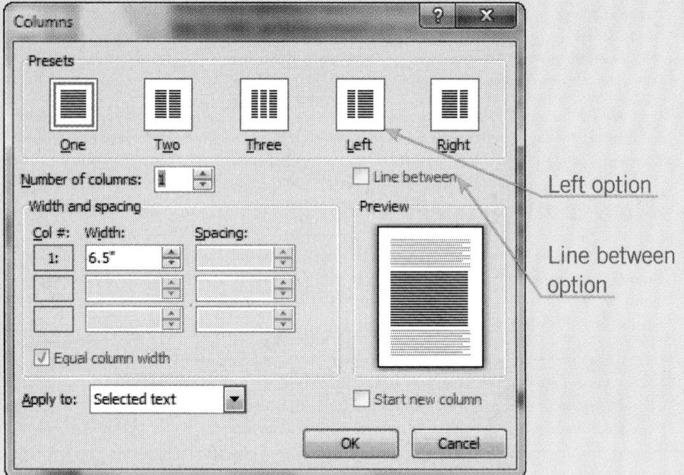

FIGURE 14–10
Columns dialog box

9. Under Presets, enable the **Left** option. In the Number of columns box, change the number to **3** and enable the **Line between** option. A preview of the three-column format appears in the Preview pane in the dialog box, and the column on the left is not as wide as the other two columns. Click **OK**. With the text still selected, click the **Columns** button and click **More Columns**. Change the number of columns to **2** and click **OK**. Word automatically controls the text flow so that the column lengths are balanced.
10. To create a manual column break, position the insertion point in front of the second paragraph in the left column. On the Page Layout tab, in the Page Setup group, click the **Breaks** button and then click **Column**. The text after the insertion point is moved to the top of the next column. Click the **Undo** button.
11. Position the insertion point in front of the first line of text below the heading *Mission Highlights*. Then use the vertical scroll bar (or the wheel on the mouse) to scroll down until you can see the source information for Apollo 11. Hold down **Shift** and click the mouse pointer at the end of the paragraph ending with *...July 24, 1969*. Be sure to include the paragraph marker. All the text between the two clicks is selected.
12. Click the **Columns** button, and then click **More Columns**. Enable the **Left** option, enable the **Line between** option, and then click **OK**.

13. Navigate to the Apollo 12 information. Format the list of crew and backup crew members in two even columns. Format all the content under the headings *Mission Objective* and *Mission Highlights* in two columns, using the Left option and adding a line between the columns. Navigate to the Apollo 13 information and apply the same column formats to the same content areas.

14. Save the document and leave the document open for the next Step-by-Step.

Using Pagination Options

Pagination is the system by which text and objects are manipulated to create the page layout. Just as text automatically wraps to the next line when the content extends beyond the right margin, lines in a paragraph automatically wrap to the next page. When a page fills with text and graphics, Word inserts an automatic page break so that the content will flow to the next page. Sometimes, though, the automatic page break will separate lines of text or entire paragraphs that you want to keep together. Of course, you can control the flow of text by manually inserting page breaks, but if you later edit or rearrange the content, the pagination will change and your manual adjustments may result in a page break in the wrong place. Using Word's pagination options can save you time and ensure that the text flows from one page to the next as desired.

One of Word's pagination options prevents widows and orphans. A ***widow*** is the last line of a multiline paragraph that is split from the other lines in the paragraph and wraps to the next page or column. An ***orphan*** is the first line of a multiline paragraph that is split from the other lines in the paragraph and appears at the bottom of a page or a column. When the Widow/Orphan option is enabled, a single line of text will not be separated from other lines in the same paragraph and appear on a different page. Heading styles commonly include pagination formats to prevent widows and orphans.

Other pagination options enable you to format paragraphs so that they stay together and appear on the same page. For example, when formatting document content with headings, you want to keep the headings attached to the first paragraph that follows the heading so that the heading doesn't appear by itself on a different page. And if the content includes a bulleted list, you probably don't want that list to be split between two pages.

VOCABULARY

pagination

widow

orphan

Step-by-Step 14.8

1. If necessary, open the **Journeys to the Moon 6** file from your solution files. Save the document as **Journeys to the Moon 7**, followed by your initials. If necessary, show the Navigation Pane. Also, if necessary, show nonprinting formatting characters.

2. In the Navigation Pane, click the **Apollo 12** heading. In the document window, note the marker to the left of the heading, as shown in **Figure 14–11**. The marker indicates that a pagination format is applied to the paragraph.

FIGURE 14–11
Marker to indicate pagination format

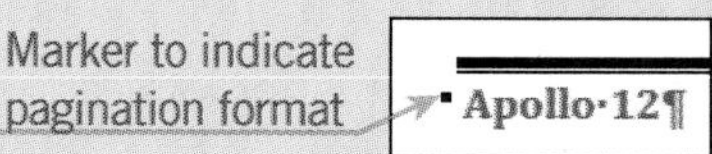

3. Make sure the insertion point is positioned in the heading paragraph. Click the **Home** tab. In the Paragraph group, click the **Dialog Box Launcher**. If necessary, click the **Line and Page Breaks** tab to show the dialog box settings shown in **Figure 14–12**. (You can also access this dialog box from the Page Layout tab, which is described below in Step 10.)

FIGURE 14–12
Paragraph dialog box

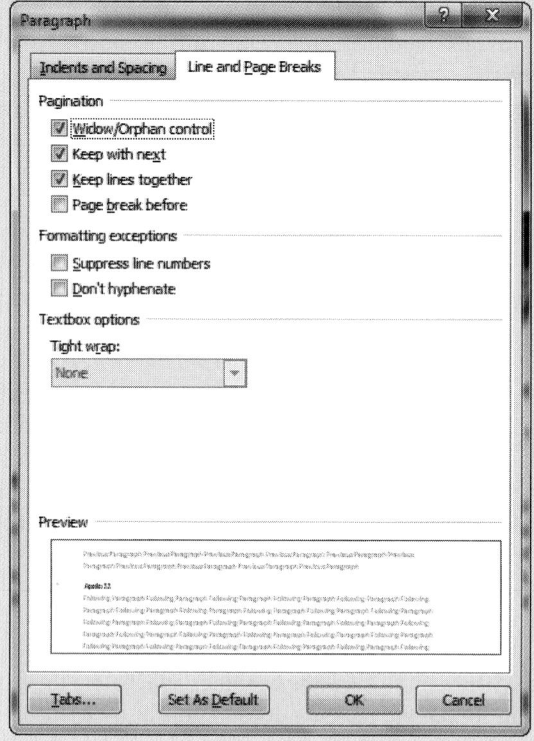

4. Note that under Pagination, the Widow/Orphan control, Keep with next, and Keep lines together options are already enabled. With these options enabled, the heading will not appear on a page by itself without the first line of the first paragraph.
5. Under Pagination, enable the **Page break before** option and click **OK**. The heading and content below the heading move to the next page. This pagination setting will ensure that the heading always begins at the top of a new page.

6. In the document window, triple-click the heading **Apollo 12** to select the entire heading, including the ending paragraph mark. In the Clipboard group, double-click the **Format Painter** button to copy the paragraph formats.
7. In the Navigation Pane, click the **Apollo 13** heading. In the document window, click anywhere in the heading **Apollo 13**. The paragraph formats are updated to include the Page break before format, and the heading and content below the heading move to the next page.
8. In the Navigation Pane, click the **Apollo 11** heading. In the document window, click anywhere in the heading **Apollo 11** to apply the paragraph formats. Even though the heading is positioned at the top of a page, applying the formats will ensure that the formatting will remain consistent. Click the **Format Painter** button (or press **Esc**) to toggle off the feature.
9. In the Navigation Pane, click the heading **The Apollo Goals**. In the document window, select the four paragraphs in the bulleted list. Be sure to include the ending paragraph mark after the fourth bulleted item.
10. Click the **Page Layout** tab, then in the Paragraph group, click the **Dialog Box Launcher**. Enable the **Keep lines together** option. If edits cause changes in the text flow, the four bulleted paragraphs will not be separated. Click **OK**.
11. Scroll down to show the three graphics on your screen. Select the entire sentence above the graphics that begins *Use the following links*. Be sure to include the ending paragraph mark.
12. On the Page Layout tab, in the Paragraph group, click the **Dialog Box Launcher**. Enable the **Keep with next** option, and then click **OK**. The selected paragraph will not be separated from the graphics because the graphics are anchored in the next paragraph.
13. In the Navigation Pane, click the **Mission Highlights** heading for Apollo 12. Depending on how the text flows in your document, this heading may be orphaned from the text that follows because the heading is followed by a section break. The heading style pagination settings are not effective because of the section break. If the heading is orphaned in your document, insert a manual page break by clicking the **Breaks** button in the Page Setup group and then clicking **Page**.
14. Save the changes to the document and leave the document open for the next Step-by-Step.

TIP

When you want to keep two or more paragraphs together using a Keep with next text flow option, do not select the last paragraph of the group (because you do not want to keep it with the next paragraph).

Using Hyphens and Nonbreaking Spaces

VOCABULARY
hyphenation
optional hyphen
nonbreaking hyphen
nonbreaking space

When a word doesn't fit within a line of text, Word automatically wraps the word to the next line. This is especially noticeable when the justified paragraph format is applied. The result usually shows a lot of white space between words in the line where the word would not fit. The ***hyphenation*** setting allows a word at the end of a line to split between syllables, which results in more uniform spacing so that more text will fit in a line.

An ***optional hyphen*** is a special formatting character used to indicate where a word can be divided. When an optional hyphen is inserted in a word, the word will not be divided and the hyphen will not print unless the word is pushed to the end of the line and the entire word will not fit on the line. If that happens, the word will be divided at the optional hyphen, the hyphen will print, and the text following the hyphen will wrap to the next line. A ***nonbreaking hyphen*** is a format used to indicate hyphenated words that should not be split if the hyphen falls at the end of a line. For example, if a person's last name has a hyphen, such as Smith-Conners, you can make sure the surname is not split between two lines. A ***nonbreaking space*** is a format used to indicate words that should not be split between lines, such as dates and measurements.

Step-by-Step 14.9

1. If necessary, open the **Journeys to the Moon 7** file from your solution files. Save the document as **Journeys to the Moon 8**, followed by your initials. If necessary, show the Navigation Pane. Also, if necessary, show nonprinting formatting characters.
2. The document contains several white spaces in the lines of text. Hyphenating the text will help to eliminate the white spaces and also fit more text within a line. Move the insertion point to the beginning of the document. On the Page Layout tab, in the Page Setup group, click the **Hyphenation** button and then click **Manual**.
3. Word proposes the first word to hyphenate: *send-ing*. The hyphen in the word is highlighted in the upper-left corner of the document window. Note that all the characters of the word *send-ing* appear on the same line in the document. The hyphen you see is an optional hyphen, and the word will only be divided with a hyphen if all of the word doesn't fit on the line. Click **Yes**.
4. The next proposed hyphenation is *Pres-i-dent*. In the dialog box, the second hyphen is highlighted. In the upper-left corner of the document window, the hyphen appears after *Presi* and the hyphen is highlighted. Click the **left arrow** key to select the first hyphen in the dialog box. By selecting the first hyphen, you have indicated that you prefer the word to be divided after *Pres* instead of after *Presi*. Click **Yes**. Notice that the optional hyphenation in the document window now displays as *Pres-ident*.

5. Click **Cancel** to close the dialog box, and then click the **Home** tab. In the Paragraph group, click the **Show/Hide ¶** button to hide the nonprinting formatting characters. Depending on where the line of text wraps in the document, the hyphen may no longer appear in the word *President.* The hyphen is optional, and if it is not needed in this text flow, it will not appear.
6. This is a long document and hyphenating manually will take a long time. Click the **Page Layout** tab. In the Page Setup group, click the **Hyphenation** button, and then click **Hyphenation Options** to open the Hyphenation dialog box, as shown in **Figure 14–13**.

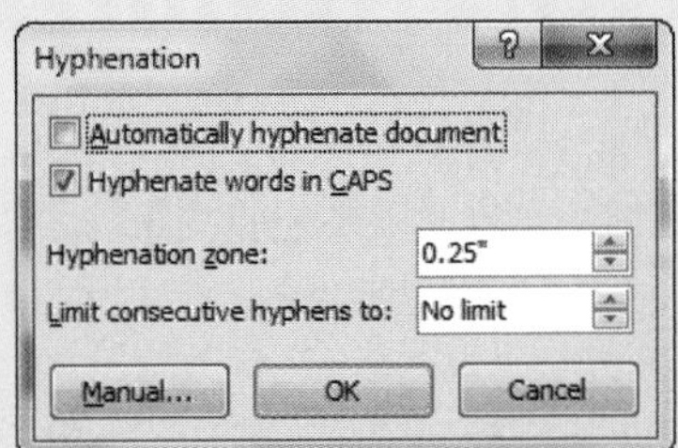

FIGURE 14–13
Hyphenation dialog box

7. Enable the **Automatically hyphenate document** option. Disable the **Hyphenate words in CAPS** option so that acronyms are not hyphenated. Click **OK**. The hyphenation feature is applied to the entire document and the text flow is readjusted. Many of the white spaces are eliminated or reduced.
8. In the Navigation Pane, click the **Apollo 13** heading. Search for *Roger,* and then click in the paragraph with the search result. Depending on the flow of text in your document, *Roger* may be hyphenated and split between lines. If Roger is not divided, and if no other words in the current paragraph are divided at the end of a line, move to the next paragraph that shows a divided word.
9. In the Paragraph group, click the **Dialog Box Launcher**. If necessary, show the Line and Page Breaks tab. Under Formatting exceptions, enable the **Don't hyphenate** option and then click **OK**. The automatic hyphenation is removed from the current paragraph. If needed, you could manually hyphenate the words in this paragraph.

TIP

To remove the hyphenation feature from multiple paragraphs, select the paragraphs before enabling the Don't hyphenate option in the Paragraph dialog box.

10. In the Navigation pane, click the **Mission Highlights** heading for Apollo 13. Click the **Home** tab. In the Paragraph group, click the **Show/Hide ¶** button to show the nonprinting formatting characters.
11. In the first line under the heading, delete the blank space between *5* and *½*. With the insertion point positioned between the 5 and the 1, hold down **Ctrl** and **Shift** and then press the **spacebar**. A nonbreaking space is inserted, and a small circle appears between the numbers *5* and *½*. Those numbers will always appear on the same line.

12. In the fifth line of the same paragraph, you will see *S-11*. Delete the hyphen. With the insertion point positioned between the *S* and *11*, hold down **Ctrl** and **Shift** and press the **hyphen** key. The nonbreaking hyphen will prohibit the *S* and *11* from being divided between lines.
13. Although a nonbreaking hyphen displays larger than a normal hyphen when nonprinting formatting characters are showing, the nonbreaking hyphen prints the same as a normal hyphen. Click the **Show/Hide ¶** button to hide the nonprinting formatting characters. The nonbreaking hyphen appears normal.
14. Save the changes to the document and leave the document open for the next Step-by-Step.

Citing Sources

VOCABULARY
citation

A ***citation*** is a reference in a document that credits the source of information or other content, such as a picture or a chart, or references specific legal cases, statutes, or other authorities in legal documents. Several formal styles can be used for citing sources. Each style has its own set of rules for referencing the sources, and the style used is directed by the objective of the document. For example, the academic field customarily uses the MLA and APA styles. The Chicago style is often used in journalism and publishing. Within the document, citations are referenced either in the line of text or in a footnote or endnote, depending on the style.

Managing Sources

Citing sources in the proper format is a tedious task because there are so many rules regarding the required information and how to format it. Word offers some valuable features to help you manage your sources and make sure you use the correct capitalization, spacing, and indentation. Each time you create a new source, the source information is saved in the Current List, which is saved with the current document. You can also save the source information in a Master List on your computer, which is saved on your computer and stores sources from all your documents. Then as you work in the current document or future documents, you can easily find and access the source information you have already saved.

Step-by-Step 14.10

1. If necessary, open the **Journeys to the Moon 8** file from your solution files. Save the document as **Journeys to the Moon 9**, followed by your initials. Show nonprinting formatting characters.
2. Open the **Apollo Resources** file from the drive and folder where your Data Files are stored. The document provides a list of resources that were used to create the content for the Journeys to the Moon document.

3. In the Apollo Resources document, position the insertion point in front of the first paragraph marker. Click the **References** tab. In the Citations & Bibliography group, click the **Manage Sources** button to open the Source Manager dialog box, as shown in **Figure 14–14**. The Master List in your dialog box will be different.

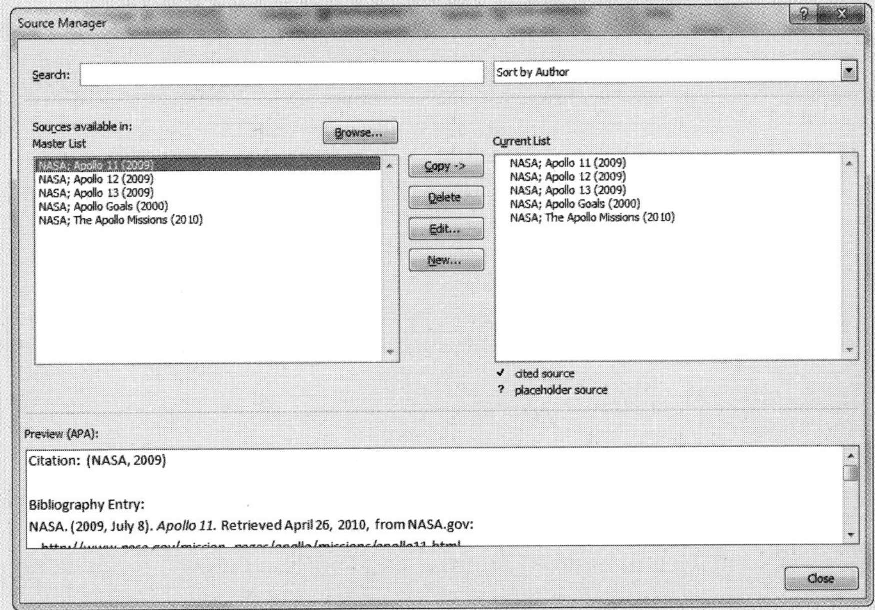

FIGURE 14–14
Source Manager dialog box

4. Select all the sources in the Current List, and then click **Copy**. The copied sources are now stored on your computer and will be available for other documents. Close the dialog box, and then close the Apollo Resources document without saving any changes.
5. In the Journeys to the Moon 9 document, click the **References** tab. In the Citations & Bibliography group, click the **Style** list arrow and then click **APA Fifth Edition**.
6. In the Citations & Bibliography group, click the **Manage Sources** button. In the Master List, select the following sources:

   NASA; Apollo 12 (2009)

   NASA; Apollo 13 (2009)

   NASA; Apollo Goals (2000)

   NASA; The Apollo Missions (2010)
7. Click **Copy** to copy the selected sources to the Current List. The sources will be saved with the current active document.

8. Click **New** to open the Create Source dialog box, as shown in **Figure 14–15**. Your dialog box settings will be different. The form guides you to enter the information you will need to create a citation and bibliography following the APA Fifth Edition style rules.

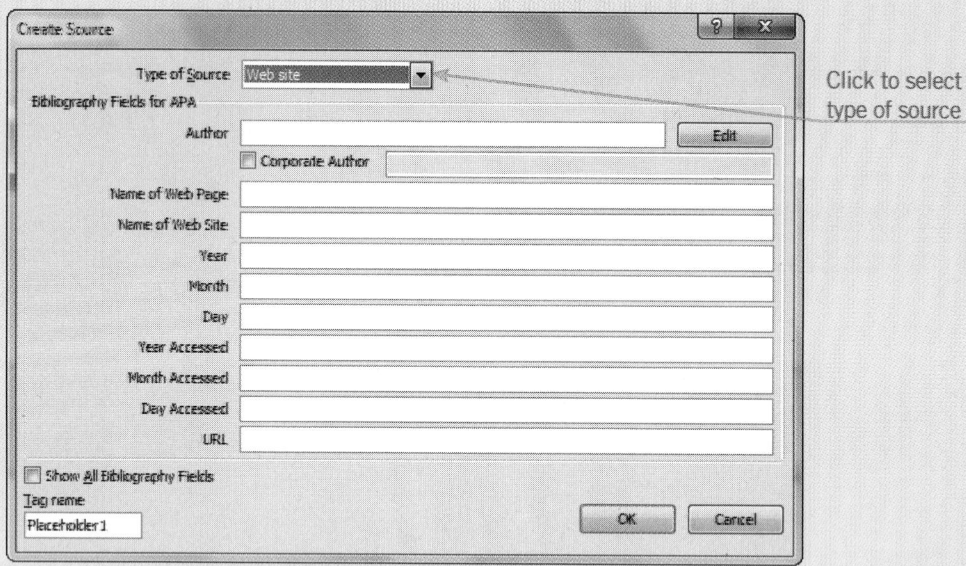

FIGURE 14–15
Create Source dialog box

9. Click the **Type of Source** list arrow and then scroll down, if necessary, and select **Web site**. The form changes to adapt for the information required for the type of source.

10. In the Author text box, type **NASA** and then enable the **Corporate Author** option. Complete the form by entering the following source information.

    Name of Web Page: **The Apollo Program**

    Name of Web Site: **NASA.gov**

    Year: **2009**

    Month: **November**

    Day: **6**

    Year Accessed: **2010**

    Month Accessed: **April**

    Day Accessed: **26**

    URL: **http://www.nasa.gov/mission_pages/apollo/missions/index.html**

11. Proofread the information to make sure it is accurate, and then click **OK**. The new source is added to both the Master List and the Current List.

12. In the Current List, select the source **NASA; Apollo Goals (2000)**. Then click **Edit** to open the Edit Source dialog box. In the URL box, after *www*, change the period to a hyphen. Click **OK**. When prompted to save the changes in both lists, click **Yes**. Close the dialog box.

13. Save the changes and leave the document open for the next Step-by-Step.

TIP

When creating a Web source, you can save it by copying the URL in your browser and then pasting it in the Create Source dialog box.

Creating Citations

When you insert a citation in the body of the document, Word inserts a field and automatically applies a format based on the selected style. At any time you can update the fields, or you can convert the fields to static text.

Step-by-Step 14.11

1. If necessary, open the **Journeys to the Moon 9** file from your solution files. Save the document as **Journeys to the Moon 10**, followed by your initials.
2. If necessary, click the **References** tab. In the Citations & Bibliography group, make sure the selected Style is **APA Fifth Edition**.
3. Navigate to the heading *The Apollo Goals.* Position the insertion point at the end of the paragraph directly above the heading. In the Citations & Bibliography group, click the **Insert Citation** button. The sources from the Current List appear in the menu that opens. Click **NASA The Apollo Missions, (2010)**. The citation reference to NASA is automatically inserted in the document and formatted as a field.
4. Under the heading *The Apollo Goals*, position the insertion point at the end of the last bulleted item. In the Citations & Bibliography group, click the **Insert Citation** button and then click **NASA Apollo Goals, (2000)**. Scroll down to the end of The Apollo Missions information (below the patches) and delete the Source Information section.
5. In the Navigation Pane, click the **Apollo 12** heading. Scroll up to the previous page (page 7) and delete the Source Information section at the bottom of the page.
6. Position the insertion point after the last paragraph on the page and before the section break. Click the **Insert Citation** button, and then click **NASA Apollo 11, (2009)**. The citation *(NASA, 2009)* is inserted in the document.
7. Navigate to the end of the Apollo 12 information and delete the Source Information section. Position the insertion point after the last paragraph on the page (and before the section break) and insert the citation **NASA Apollo 12, (2009)**. If necessary, delete the extra paragraph marker so that there will not be a full blank page before the Apollo 13 information.
8. Navigate to the end of the Apollo 13 information at the end of the document and delete the Source Information section and the heading *Summary.* Insert a citation for **NASA Apollo 13, (2009)** at the end of the last paragraph.

> **TIP**
>
> Placeholder tag names are numbers assigned by default, but you can customize the placeholder tag name with whatever tag you want.

9. Navigate to the top of the document. Under the heading *Introduction*, in the first paragraph, position the insertion point after the quotation mark following the quotation by President Kennedy. Click the **Insert Citation** button and then click **Add New Placeholder**. Word proposes a name, *Placeholder 1*, for the placeholder. Click **OK**.
10. In the Citations & Bibliography group, click the **Manage Sources** button. Notice that check marks appear next to the sources you have already cited in the document. In the Current List, click **Placeholder 1** and then click **Edit**. The Edit Source dialog box opens.
11. Click the **Type of Source** list arrow. Scroll down to the bottom of the list and select **Miscellaneous**. Complete the form by entering the following source information.

    Author: **President John F. Kennedy**

    Title: **Special Message to the Congress on Urgent National Needs**

    Publication Title: **Delivered in person before a joint session of Congress**

    Year: **1961**

    Month: **May**

    Day: **25**

    City: **Washington**

    State/Province: **D.C.**
12. Click **OK**. Click the **Copy** button to save the source in the Master List. Close the dialog box. Notice that the placeholder in the document is updated to show the citation *Kennedy, 1961*.
13. To view the other citations in the document, press **F11** to move to the next field. The next citation is selected. Click the **list arrow** for the field. In the shortcut menu, click **Convert citation to static text**. The citation is no longer formatted in a field and it will not be updated if you edit the source information. Click the **Undo** button.
14. Save the changes and leave the document open for the next Step-by-Step.

> **TIP**
>
> To remove a citation, click the tab on the left side of the field to select the entire field, then click Delete.

Creating a Bibliography

> **VOCABULARY**
> **bibliography**
> **works cited page**

A ***bibliography*** is a list of source materials that are used in the preparation of a work. The bibliography, often referred to as a ***works cited page***, is normally placed at the end of a document. Manually creating a bibliography is a tedious task because you must enter all the source information following a specified format. Fortunately, Word can do all that work automatically, and you can create a bibliography with a couple of clicks. Word generates the bibliography using the information stored in the Current List in the Source Manager. The format for the bibliography is based on the selected style. Placeholder citations do not appear in the bibliography. If you change citations or add and delete sources, you can quickly update the field instead of creating a new bibliography.

Step-by-Step 14.12

1. If necessary, open the **Journeys to the Moon 10** file from your solution files. Save the document as **Journeys to the Moon 11**, followed by your initials.
2. Position the insertion point at the end of the document. Click the **Page Layout** tab, and in the Page Setup group, click the **Breaks** button. Under Section Breaks, click **Next Page**. A new section is added to the document, and the new section begins on the next page.
3. With the insertion point positioned at the top of the new section, click the **References** tab. In the Citations & Bibliography group, click the **Bibliography** button, and then click **Bibliography**. A built-in bibliography appears with an alphabetical list of all the sources in the Current List. Scroll up to review the bibliography.
4. Click to position your insertion point below the bibliography and then press **Enter**. In the Citations & Bibliography group, click the **Bibliography** button again, and then click **Works Cited**.
5. Scroll up to review the *Works Cited* bibliography. Another bibliography appears, but the information is preceded with the title *Works Cited* instead of *Bibliography*. Click the **Undo** button to remove the second bibliography.
6. Click anywhere inside the bibliography content. Note that all the content is contained in a field. The content is already formatted with a hanging indent. If desired, you can edit the formats.
7. Click the **Manage Sources** button, and then click **New**. Click the **Type of Source** list arrow and then click **Book**. Complete the form by entering the following source information.

   Author: **Seamans, Robert C., Jr.**

   Title: **PROJECT APOLLO The Tough Decisions**

   Year: **2005**

   City: **Washington, D.C.**

   Publisher: **National Aeronautics and Space Administration**
8. Click **OK**, and close the Source Manager dialog box.
9. If necessary, click anywhere within the bibliography to select it. Press **F9** to update the fields in the bibliography. The new source is added to the bibliography.
10. Save the changes and leave the document open for the next Step-by-Step.

Creating Footnotes and Endnotes

VOCABULARY

footnote

endnote

reference marker

separator line

Footnotes and endnotes allow you to add information to a document or cite the source of content. A ***footnote*** appears at the bottom of the same page where it is referenced. An ***endnote*** is placed along with other notes at the end of a document. Both types of notes are linked to a reference marker in the text, which is a superscript number or a custom character, such as an asterisk. The ***reference marker*** indicates that a note with a matching number or character is at the bottom of the page or at the end of the document. When you use numbers to reference each note, Word automatically assigns the numbers for you. If you rearrange your text or move, copy, or delete a note, Word will automatically renumber the reference marker in the document and rearrange the order of the notes.

To insert a footnote, position your insertion point in the line of text and click the Insert Footnote button. Word automatically inserts the reference marker and a separator line at the bottom of the page. The ***separator line*** separates the body text from the footnote area. Then you can enter the note text in the footnote area.

After you insert footnotes in a document, you can change them to endnotes and vice versa. If you have a combination of footnotes and endnotes in the same document, you can swap the notes so that the footnotes become endnotes and the endnotes become footnotes.

EXTRA FOR EXPERTS

If you copy text with a footnote/endnote reference, when you paste the text into a PowerPoint slide or an Excel worksheet, the note text will also display.

Step-by-Step 14.13

1. If necessary, open the **Journeys to the Moon 11** file from your solution files. Save the document as **Journeys to the Moon 12**, followed by your initials. If necessary, show the Navigation Pane.
2. In the Navigation Pane, under *Apollo 11*, click the **Mission Highlights** heading. In the document window, under the heading *Mission Highlights*, position the insertion point at the end of the first paragraph.
3. If necessary, click the **References** tab. In the Footnotes group, click the **Insert Footnote** button. The reference marker is inserted in the body of the document, and a separator line and the reference marker appear at the bottom of the page, as shown in **Figure 14–16**.

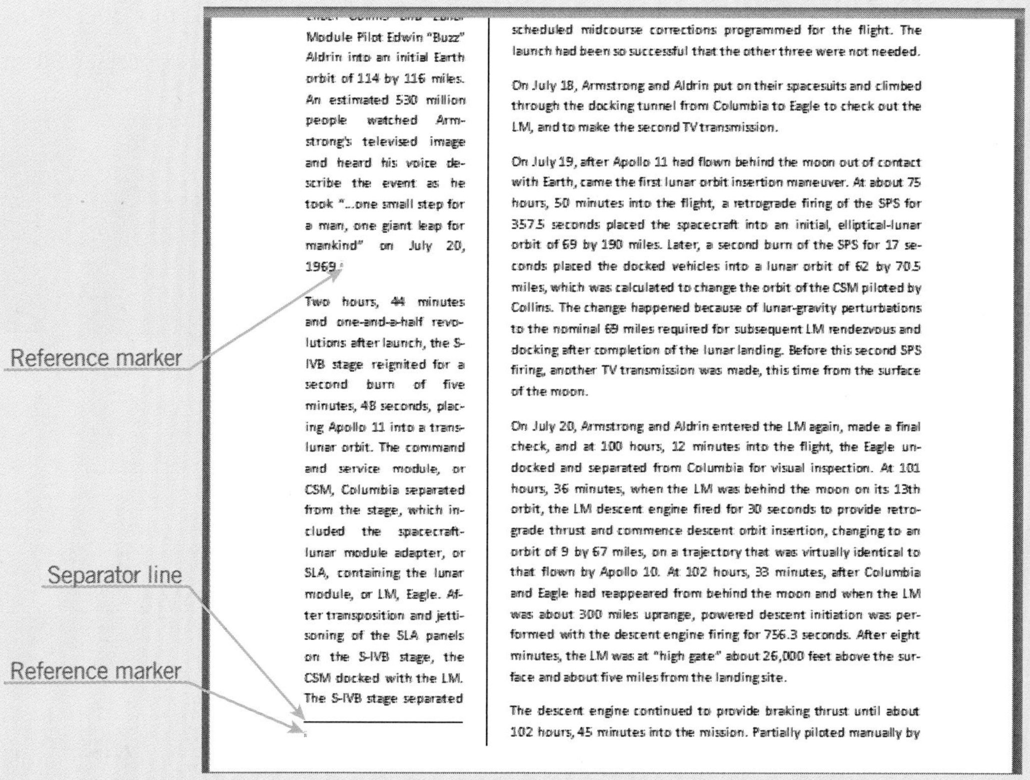

Module Pilot Edwin "Buzz" Aldrin into an initial Earth orbit of 114 by 116 miles. An estimated 530 million people watched Armstrong's televised image and heard his voice describe the event as he took "...one small step for a man, one giant leap for mankind" on July 20, 1969.[1]

Two hours, 44 minutes and one-and-a-half revolutions after launch, the S-IVB stage reignited for a second burn of five minutes, 48 seconds, placing Apollo 11 into a translunar orbit. The command and service module, or CSM, Columbia separated from the stage, which included the spacecraft-lunar module adapter, or SLA, containing the lunar module, or LM, Eagle. After transposition and jettisoning of the SLA panels on the S-IVB stage, the CSM docked with the LM. The S-IVB stage separated

[1]

scheduled midcourse corrections programmed for the flight. The launch had been so successful that the other three were not needed.

On July 18, Armstrong and Aldrin put on their spacesuits and climbed through the docking tunnel from Columbia to Eagle to check out the LM, and to make the second TV transmission.

On July 19, after Apollo 11 had flown behind the moon out of contact with Earth, came the first lunar orbit insertion maneuver. At about 75 hours, 50 minutes into the flight, a retrograde firing of the SPS for 357.5 seconds placed the spacecraft into an initial, elliptical-lunar orbit of 69 by 190 miles. Later, a second burn of the SPS for 17 seconds placed the docked vehicles into a lunar orbit of 62 by 70.5 miles, which was calculated to change the orbit of the CSM piloted by Collins. The change happened because of lunar-gravity perturbations to the nominal 69 miles required for subsequent LM rendezvous and docking after completion of the lunar landing. Before this second SPS firing, another TV transmission was made, this time from the surface of the moon.

On July 20, Armstrong and Aldrin entered the LM again, made a final check, and at 100 hours, 12 minutes into the flight, the Eagle undocked and separated from Columbia for visual inspection. At 101 hours, 36 minutes, when the LM was behind the moon on its 13th orbit, the LM descent engine fired for 30 seconds to provide retrograde thrust and commence descent orbit insertion, changing to an orbit of 9 by 67 miles, on a trajectory that was virtually identical to that flown by Apollo 10. At 102 hours, 33 minutes, after Columbia and Eagle had reappeared from behind the moon and when the LM was about 300 miles uprange, powered descent initiation was performed with the descent engine firing for 756.3 seconds. After eight minutes, the LM was at "high gate" about 26,000 feet above the surface and about five miles from the landing site.

The descent engine continued to provide braking thrust until about 102 hours, 45 minutes into the mission. Partially piloted manually by

Reference marker

Separator line

Reference marker

FIGURE 14–16
Footnote reference markers

4. Type the following text. (Because the footnote appears on the same page at the bottom of the column, some of the paragraph text in the left column will move to the top of the next column.)

   Onboard audio recordings of conversations of the crew members during the Apollo 11 mission are available at the NASA Web site. Go to NASA.gov and search for the keywords *audio recordings Apollo 11*.

5. Position the mouse pointer over the reference marker in the body of the document. The footnote text appears in a ScreenTip, so you don't need to scroll to the bottom of the page to read the note.

6. In the Navigation Pane, click the **The Apollo Missions** heading. Position the insertion point at the end of the first paragraph below the heading. In the Footnotes group, click the **Insert Footnote** button. The reference marker number 1 is inserted. Word automatically changed the other reference marker to number 2 because it appears later in the document.

7. Type the following text.

   The Lunar Sample Laboratory Facility at the Johnson Space Center is the chief repository for materials returned from the moon during the Apollo era.

TIP

Instead of clicking the Insert Footnote button, you can insert a continuously numbered footnote by pressing Alt+Ctrl+F.

8. On the References tab, in the Footnotes group, click the **Dialog Box Launcher** to open the Footnote and Endnote dialog box, as shown in **Figure 14–17**.

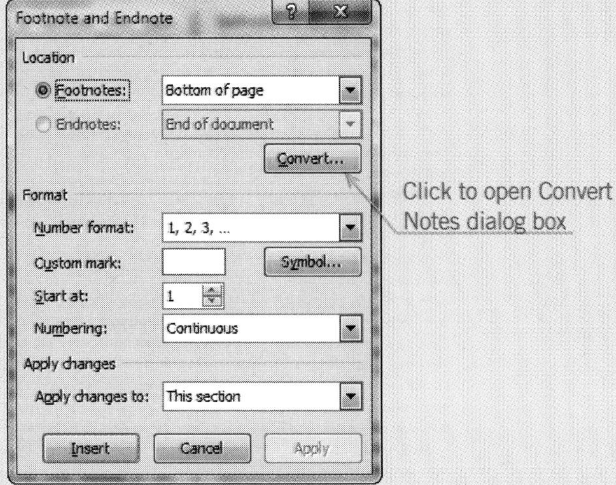

FIGURE 14–17
Footnote and Endnote dialog box

9. Click the **Number format** list arrow and then click **i, ii, iii, ...** Click the **Apply changes to** list arrow and then click **Whole document**. The footnotes appear in different sections, so you want the new format to apply to all the sections in the document. Click **Apply**. The reference markers change to the new number format.
10. Go to page two. Position the insertion point at the end of the second paragraph. On the References tab, in the Footnotes group, click the **Dialog Box Launcher**. Under Format, in the Custom mark text box, type * (asterisk). Click **Insert**. Type **The Apollo program came to an end in December 1972.**.
11. Select the * reference marker in the document and cut the marker to the Clipboard. Scroll up to the top of the document, click to position the insertion point at the end of the first paragraph under the heading *Introduction*, and then paste the reference marker.
12. At the bottom of page one, select the first note (with an asterisk), and then press **Delete**. You can delete the note text, but you cannot delete the reference marker below the separator line. Click **OK** to close the alert box. Scroll back to the top of the page, select the * reference marker, and press **Delete**. The reference marker is removed from the body text, and the note is removed from the bottom of the page.
13. In the Footnotes group, click the **Dialog Box Launcher**. In the Footnote and Endnote dialog box, under Location, click **Convert**. In the Convert Notes dialog box, click **OK**. Close the dialog box and navigate to the end of the document. The notes appear below a separator line. Click the **Undo** button.
14. Save the changes and leave the document open for the next Step-by-Step.

Analyzing Content and Readability

Word offers yet another automated tool that will help you in the preparation of long documents. After you finish checking the spelling and grammar in your document, you can perform an analysis of the content and determine the reading level of the document. The analysis generates statistics including word count, average number of words per sentence, and the average number of characters per word. Word calculates several readability scores based on a rating of the average number of syllables per word and the number of words per sentence.

The readability levels are indicated with three scores: (1) the percentage of passive sentences; (2) the Flesch Reading Ease score; and (3) the Flesch-Kincaid Grade level score. The Flesch Reading Ease score provides a rating based on a 100-point scale; the higher the score, the easier the content is to understand. A good score to aim for is between 60 and 70 in order for most people to easily understand the document. The Flesch-Kincaid Grade Level score is a rating based on a U.S. grade level. For example, a score of 11.0 means that an eleventh grader can understand the document. Scores of at least 7.0 to 8.0 are good for most documents.

Step-by-Step 14.14

1. If necessary, open the **Journeys to the Moon 12** file from your solution files.
2. To quickly check the number of pages and word count, click the **Review** tab. In the Proofing group, click the **Word Count** button. The Word Count dialog box shown in **Figure 14–18** opens and shows the statistics for the number of pages, words, characters, paragraphs, and lines. Your statistics may differ.

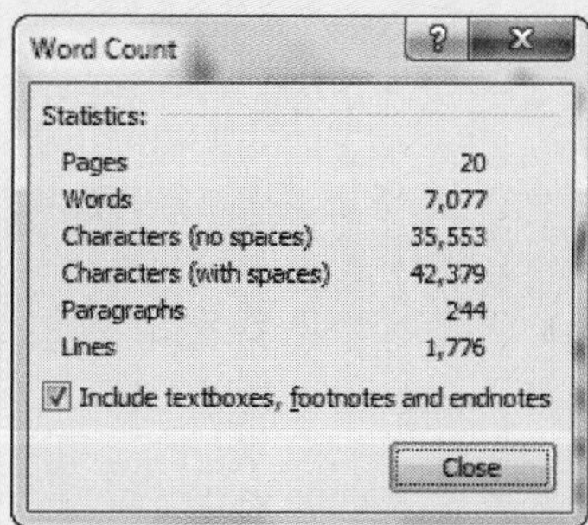

FIGURE 14–18
Word Count dialog box

3. Close the dialog box.
4. Click the **File** tab, and then click **Options**. Click **Proofing**. Under When correcting spelling and grammar in Word, enable the **Show readability statistics** option. Click **OK**.
5. To analyze the readability, move the insertion point to the beginning of the document. In the Proofing group, click the **Spelling & Grammar** button.

TIP

If you have previously completed a spelling and grammar check and ignored suggestions and rules or made corrections, you will see a message indicating that text marked with "Do not check spelling or grammar" was skipped. The skipped text is the text you already changed or ignored in a previous spell check. If you get this prompt, click OK to proceed.

6. You will need to pass through many suggested edits. Ignore all spellings and all rules. When the dialog box opens and confirms that the spelling and grammar check is complete, click **OK**. The Readability Statistics dialog box opens, as shown in **Figure 14–19**. Your statistics may differ.

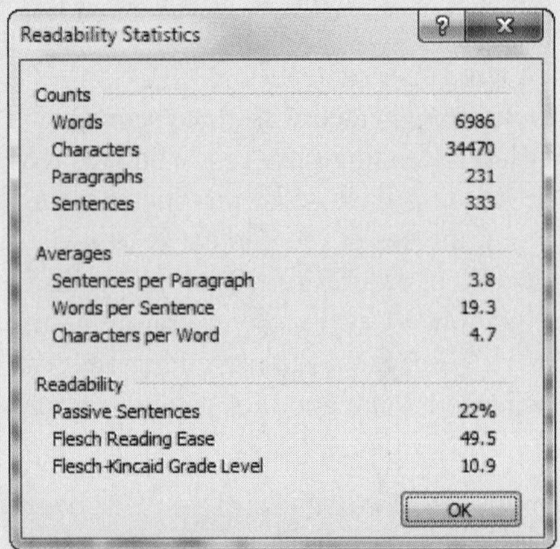

FIGURE 14–19
Readability Statistics dialog box

7. Press **Alt+Print Screen**. A capture of the active window is saved on the Clipboard. Click **OK** to close the dialog box.
8. Open a new blank document and press **Ctrl+V** to paste the Clipboard item in the document.
9. Save the document as **Journeys to the Moon Readability**, followed by your initials. Close the document and close the Journeys to the Moon 12 document without saving.

SUMMARY

In this lesson, you learned:

- You can open and work with several documents at the same time, and there are several ways to arrange multiple document windows to make it easy to switch between documents.
- The Navigation Pane provides several features for browsing documents, reorganizing the document content, and finding text and objects.
- Hyperlinks and bookmarks are features you can add to a document to quickly navigate within a document.
- You can divide a document into sections to apply different page layout formats to portions of the document.
- You can control text flow from one page to the next by applying pagination options.
- You can enable a hyphenation setting so that Word will automatically split long words between syllables when the entire word will not fit at the end of a line of text.
- You can control text flow from one line to the next by creating nonbreaking hyphens and nonbreaking spaces.
- Creating citations and bibliographies is made simple by using the Source Manager.
- You can also create footnotes and endnotes to cite sources, and you can easily convert footnotes to endnotes and vice versa.
- Word provides a feature that analyzes document content and determines the readability level of the document content.

VOCABULARY REVIEW

Define the following terms:

bibliography	incremental search	reference marker
bookmark	nonbreaking hyphen	section
citation	nonbreaking space	section break
endnote	optional hyphen	separator line
footnote	orphan	widow
hyphenation	pagination	works cited page

REVIEW QUESTIONS

TRUE / FALSE

Circle T if the statement is true or F if the statement is false.

T F 1. When you open a new blank document in Word, the document is already formatted with multiple sections.

T F 2. The Find command can be accessed in the Navigation Pane.

T F 3. The academic field customarily uses the MLA and APA styles to format citations and bibliographies.

T F 4. When you have copied 24 items to the Clipboard, you must clear the Clipboard before you can copy more items.

T F 5. Placeholder citations appear in the bibliography along with the other sources cited in the document.

MATCHING

Match the correct term in Column 2 to its description in Column 1.

Column 1	Column 2
______ 1. An area that can have its own separate page formats	A. citation
______ 2. A type of search in which the matches for the search change as the text is augmented	B. incremental
______ 3. The last line of a paragraph split from the other lines in the paragraph	C. bibliography
______ 4. Setting that provides more uniform spacing of a line of text	D. hyphenation
______ 5. Document element automatically generated based on the sources stored in the Current List in the Source Manager	E. orphan
	F. widow
	G. section

WRITTEN QUESTIONS

Write a brief answer to the following questions.

1. What is the advantage of using bookmarks instead of hyperlinks?

2. Describe the difference between the wildcard characters ? and *.

3. Inserting manual page breaks to control text flow is quick and easy, so why would you apply paragraph formats to keep lines of text together?

4. What is the benefit of having the bibliography formatted in a field?

5. Describe why you would insert a placeholder citation in a document.

PROJECTS

If you have a SAM 2010 user profile, your instructor may have assigned an autogradable version of the indicated project. If so, log into the SAM 2010 Web site at *www.cengage.com/sam2010* to download the instruction and start files.

PROJECT 14–1

1. Open the Lease file from the drive and folder where your Data Files are stored. Save the document as **Final Lease**, followed by your initials.
2. Change the paper size to Legal 8.5" × 14". Change the top and bottom margins to 1.0". Change the left margin to 1.5" and change the right margin to 1.0".
3. Position the insertion point in front of the first paragraph under the title LEASE AGREEMENT that begins *This Lease Agreement*. Select the text in the document, except for the title, and apply the Justify alignment format.
4. Automatically hyphenate the document.
5. At the end of the document, format the last paragraph of text, blank paragraphs, and signature lines so that all the lines stay together.
6. Create some bookmarks to help users quickly navigate to information in this contract.
   a. Search for the first occurrence of *landlord*, select the phrase *James R. Kraus, hereinafter known as the Landlord*, create a bookmark, and name the bookmark **landlord**.
   b. Search for the first occurrence of *tenant*, select the phrase *Jennifer Lynn Hamilton, hereinafter known as the Tenant*, create a bookmark, and name the bookmark **tenant**.
   c. Search for the first occurrence of *home*, select the phrase *943 Ashcreek Drive, Centerville, Ohio 45458-3333*, create a bookmark, and name the bookmark **address**.
   d. Search for the first occurrence of *rental rate*, select the phrase *a monthly rental rate of five hundred seventy-five dollars ($575)*, create a bookmark, and name the bookmark **rate**.
   e. Search for the first occurrence of *security deposit*, select the phrase *a Security Deposit of one month's rent, five hundred seventy-five dollars ($575)*, create a bookmark, and name the bookmark **deposit**.
   f. Search for the first occurrence of *late charge*, select the phrase *a late charge of fifteen dollars ($15) for every day past the due date*, create a bookmark, and name the bookmark **late_charge**.
7. Use the bookmark to go to the address in the document. Replace the hyphen in the postal code with a nonbreaking hyphen.
8. Save the changes and close the document.

SAM PROJECT 14–2

1. Open the Family Disaster Plan file from the drive and folder where your Data Files are stored. Save the document as **Family Disaster Plan**, followed by your initials. Then close the document.
2. Open the Returning Home file from the drive and folder where your Data Files are stored. Save the document as **Preparing for Natural Disasters 1**, followed by your initials.
3. Enter the following new text at the top of the document.

   PREPARING FOR NATURAL DISASTERS
   It is important that we improve the nation's ability to prepare for and respond to public health emergencies.
   To prepare for emergencies, you need to be aware of health threats and how to protect yourself and others. The resources below will help you prepare for natural disasters and severe weather.

   Get information about how to create a family disaster plan.
4. Apply the Title style to the first line of text.
5. Move the insertion point to the end of the document. Insert text from the following Data Files: **Extreme Heat**, **Floods**, **Landslides**, and **Tornadoes**.
6. Use the Navigation Pane to reorganize the contents. Move the *Returning Home after a Disaster* heading to the end of the document. Then move the *Extreme Heat* heading so that the Heat section follows the section on Tornadoes.
7. Format the heading *Returning Home after a Disaster* to include a page break before the heading.
8. Position the insertion point in front of the heading *Floods*. Select all the text from this point to the end of the document. With the text selected, apply a two-column format with a line between the columns.
9. Select each of the five level-one headings and apply a one-column format.
10. Automatically hyphenate the document, but do not hyphenate words in CAPS.
11. Insert a page number style of your choice in the lower-right corner of the document.
12. At the beginning of the document, select the sentence *Get information about how to create a family disaster plan.* Create a hyperlink to the file **Family Disaster Plan** in the drive and folder where your solution files are stored. Create a ScreenTip that displays **Family Disaster Plan**.
13. Save the changes and leave the document open for the next Project.

PROJECT 14–3

1. If necessary, open the **Preparing for Natural Disasters** 1 file from your solution files. Save the document as **Preparing for Natural Disasters 2**, followed by your initials.
2. Open the Natural Disasters Sources file from the drive and folder where your Data Files are stored.
3. Copy all the sources in the Current List for the Natural Disasters document to the Master List on your computer. Then close the Natural Disasters document without saving any changes.
4. Copy the following Centers for Disease Control and Prevention sources to Preparing for Natural Disasters 2 document.

   Develop a Family Disaster Plan
   Extreme Heat: A Prevention Guide to Promote Your Personal Health and Safety
   Key Facts About Flood Readiness
   Landslides and Mudslides
   Returning Home After a Disaster
5. Create the following new source for a Web site.
   Author: **Centers for Disease Control and Prevention** (Corporate Author)
   Name of Web Page: **Tornadoes: Being Prepared**
   Name of Web Site: **CDC.gov**
   Year: **2007**
   Month: **October**
   Day: **18**
   Year Accessed: **2010**
   Month Accessed: **April**
   Day Accessed: **26**
   URL: **http://emergency.cdc.gov/disasters/tornadoes/prepared.asp**
6. Edit the source Key Facts About Flood Readiness. The date for the Web page is **2009, March 27**. Update both lists.
7. Navigate to the end of the Floods section. Remove the source information. At the end of the last paragraph, insert a citation for **Key Facts About Flood Readiness**.
8. Navigate to the end of the Landslides section. Remove the source information. At the end of the last paragraph, insert a citation for **Landslides and Mudslides**.
9. Navigate to the end of the Tornadoes section. Remove the source information. At the end of the last paragraph, insert a citation for **Tornadoes: Being Prepared**.
10. Navigate to the end of the Extreme Heat section. Remove the source information. At the end of the last paragraph, insert a citation for **Extreme Heat: A Prevention Guide to Promote Your Personal Health and Safety**.
11. Navigate to the end of the Returning Home after a Disaster section. Remove the source information. At the end of the last paragraph, insert a citation for **Returning Home after a Disaster: Be Healthy and Safe**.
12. Insert a next page section break. Format the new section with a one-column format. Create a bibliography.
13. Save the changes and close the document.

PROJECT 14–4

1. Open the Soil file from the drive and folder where your Data Files are stored. Save the document as **Final Soil**, followed by your initials.
2. Select the heading *Pollution-Eating Bacteria* and apply paragraph formatting to keep the heading with the next line of text.
3. Repeat the paragraph format for the remaining four headings.
4. Select the heading *Soil Washing* and create a bookmark. Name the bookmark **soil_washing**.
5. Position the insertion point at the beginning of the second paragraph that begins *Liquids and solvents....* Insert a bookmark and name the bookmark **cleanup_costs**.
6. Use the Navigation Pane to find matches for PCBs. Insert a numbered footnote after the first occurrence. For the note, type **Polychlorinated biphenyls**.
7. Position the insertion point at the end of the third paragraph that ends *...puts people at risk*. Insert a numbered footnote. For the note, type **Direct contact and airborne migration**.
8. Click anywhere in the document. Find the acronym EPA. Insert a numbered footnote after the acronym. For the note, type **Environmental Protection Agency**.
9. Convert the footnotes to endnotes.
10. Save the changes and close the document.

CRITICAL THINKING

ACTIVITY 14–1

You learned in this lesson that you can change page formats for individual sections in a document. You have already practiced changing section formats for columns. The following is a list of other section formats that you can change. Pick three formats from this list and describe when and why you would change this format for only one section in a document and not the whole document.

- Margins
- Paper size or orientation
- Page borders
- Vertical alignment
- Page numbering
- Line numbering

ACTIVITY 14–2

A document is divided into three sections. The text in the first section in the document is formatted in two columns; the top and bottom margins are set to 1 inch, and the left and right margins are set to .5 inch. The text in the second section in the document is formatted in three columns; the top and bottom margins are set to .5 inch, and the left and right margins are set to 1 inch. The text in the third section in the document is formatted in one column, and the margins are all set to 1 inch. If the two section breaks are deleted, what column format and margin settings will apply?

Estimated Time:
2 hours

LESSON 15

Creating Indexes and Tables of Contents, Figures, and Authorities

■ OBJECTIVES

Upon completion of this lesson, you should be able to:

- Identify index entries and indicate a range of pages for an index entry.
- Create an index entry for a cross-reference.
- Generate and update an index.
- Create a table of contents using heading styles.
- Create a table of contents using fields.
- Update a table of contents.
- Insert captions and create a table of figures.
- Create a table of authorities.

■ VOCABULARY

cross-reference

index

passim

table of authorities

table of contents

table of figures

When presented with a document of ten or more pages, readers usually like to survey the contents. They might be interested in a specific topic discussed in the document, or they might be looking for specific information referenced in the document. Lists of the topics, specific information, tables, and figures can help the reader navigate to specific areas in the document. Word provides several features to help you create these types of lists.

Creating and Updating an Index

VOCABULARY
index
cross-reference

An ***index*** is an alphabetic listing of pertinent words and phrases that reference the page numbers where the related topics appear in the document. The index usually appears at the end of a document. An index is a valuable tool when it includes the right choice of entries. Index entries often include the main ideas and/or subjects of the document, various headings and subheadings, special terms, and acronyms.

The index is usually formatted with multiple levels of entries. The entries in the first level are called main entries. The entries in the second level are called subentries. Depending on the detail of the index, additional levels of subentries can be formatted.

Marking Index Entries Manually

Any word in a document can be marked (identified) as an index entry. You can mark index entries as you create the document, or after you finish writing the document. When you mark an index entry, a field is inserted at the location of the insertion point. The field is formatted as hidden text. To show these fields in the document as you work, the nonprinting formatting characters must be displayed. If you want to mark a range of pages for an index entry that spans multiple pages, you can mark a bookmark for the index entry. Because the bookmark identifies the range of text, the field for the index entry can be inserted anywhere in the document.

If the index entry is often referred to with another name or word, such as *MLA* and *Modern Language Association*, you can format a marked entry with text instead of a page number by creating a cross-reference. A ***cross-reference*** is a reference from one part of a document to related material in another part of the document. In an index, a cross-reference refers the reader to another index entry. Since the cross-reference does not refer to a specific page, you can insert the cross-reference field anywhere in the document. For example, you can insert a cross-reference when the need for one becomes evident as you work in the document, or you can insert all cross-references at the beginning or end of the document.

Step-by-Step 15.1

1. Open the **Apollo Missions 11-17** file from the drive and folder where your Data Files are stored. Save the document as **Apollo Missions 1**, followed by your initials.
2. If necessary, on the Home tab in the Paragraph group, click the **Show/Hide ¶** button to display nonprinting formatting characters. Also, if necessary, show the Navigation Pane.

3. Click the **File** tab, click **Options**, and then click **Display**. Under Always show these formatting marks on the screen, make sure that the Hidden text option is disabled. (If necessary, click the **check box** to remove the check mark.) Click **OK**.
4. Mark a main index entry by selecting text:
   a. In the Navigation Pane, click the **Apollo 11** heading. In the document window, select the words **Apollo 11**. (Do not include the paragraph mark in the selection.)
   b. Click the **References** tab. In the Index group, click the **Mark Entry** button. The Mark Index Entry dialog box opens, as shown in **Figure 15–1**. Notice that the selected text is displayed in the Main entry text box.

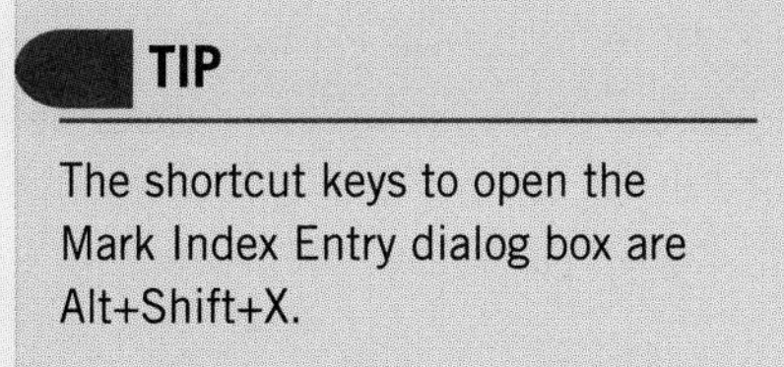

TIP

The shortcut keys to open the Mark Index Entry dialog box are Alt+Shift+X.

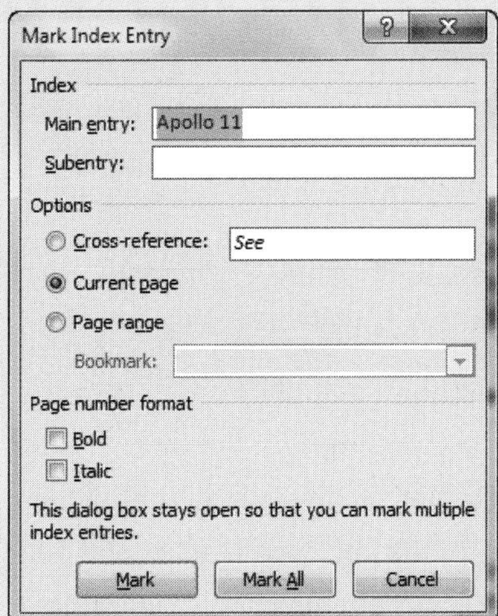

FIGURE 15–1
Mark Index Entry dialog box

   c. Under Page number format, enable the **Bold** and **Italic** options to format page number references in bold and italic in the index.
   d. Click **Mark**. The dialog box stays open, but the index entry field is inserted at the end of the selected text. If necessary, reposition the dialog box on the screen so you can see the field for the index entry, as shown in **Figure 15–2**.

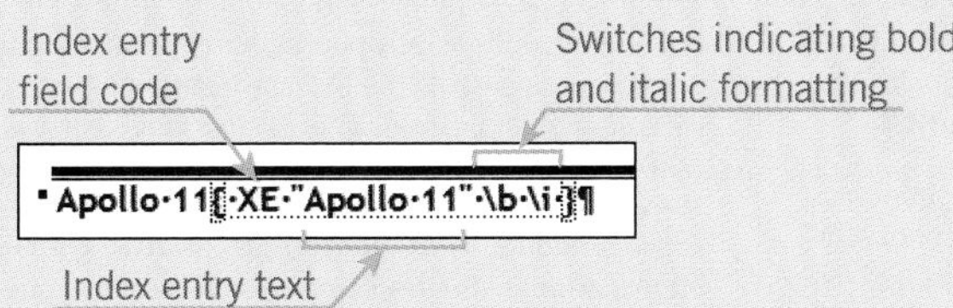

FIGURE 15–2
Index entry field

   e. Note the components in the field. The XE in the field stands for index entry. The index entry text is enclosed in quotation marks. A backslash (\) within the field is a switch that provides additional instructions for formatting the characters bold and italic.

5. Mark a main index entry without selecting text:
   a. In the Navigation Pane, click the **Apollo 12** heading. In the document window, position the insertion point at the end of the heading *Apollo 12*.
   b. Click the **title bar** for the Mark Index Entry dialog box. The current entry in the Main entry text box disappears. Click the **Main entry** text box and type **Apollo 12**. The Bold and Italic options should still be enabled.
   c. Click **Mark**. The index entry field is inserted in the document at the location of the insertion point.
6. Mark additional index entries:
   a. Navigate to the Apollo 13 section, and in the document window, select the **Apollo 13** heading. (Do not include the paragraph mark in the selection.)
   b. Click the **title bar** for the Mark Index Entry dialog box. The selected text appears in the Main entry text box.
   c. Click **Mark**.
   d. Repeat Steps 6a, 6b, and 6c to create index entries for the headings for the Apollo 14–17 sections.
7. Mark a subentry under a main entry:
   a. Navigate to the heading *Mission Objective* for Apollo 11.
   b. Click the **title bar** for the Mark Index Entry dialog box. Click the **Main entry** text box and type then **Apollo 11**.
   c. Position the insertion point in the Subentry text box and type **mission objective**.
   d. Click **Mark**. Note that in the XE field, the main entry text and the subentry text are separated by a colon, as shown in **Figure 15–3**.

FIGURE 15–3
Index entry field inserted into a document

Index entry field

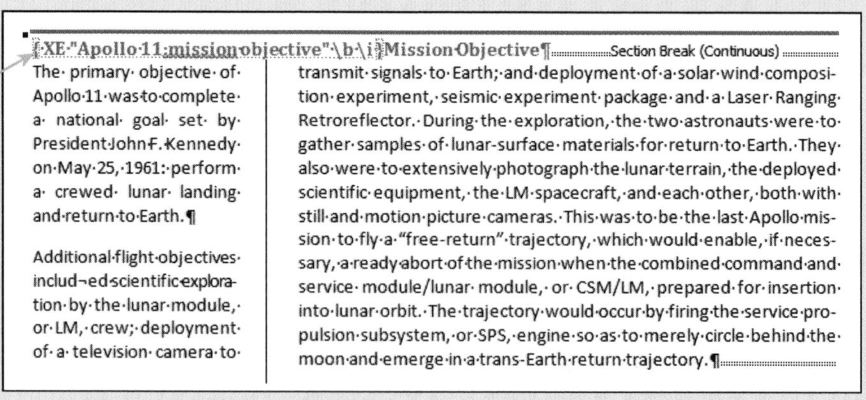

{ XE "Apollo 11:mission objective" \b \i }Mission Objective¶ Section Break (Continuous)

The primary objective of Apollo 11 was to complete a national goal set by President John F. Kennedy on May 25, 1961: perform a crewed lunar landing and return to Earth.¶

Additional flight objectives includ¬ed scientific exploration by the lunar module, or LM, crew; deployment of a television camera to transmit signals to Earth; and deployment of a solar wind composition experiment, seismic experiment package and a Laser Ranging Retroreflector. During the exploration, the two astronauts were to gather samples of lunar-surface materials for return to Earth. They also were to extensively photograph the lunar terrain, the deployed scientific equipment, the LM spacecraft, and each other, both with still and motion picture cameras. This was to be the last Apollo mission to fly a "free-return" trajectory, which would enable, if necessary, a ready abort of the mission when the combined command and service module/lunar module, or CSM/LM, prepared for insertion into lunar orbit. The trajectory would occur by firing the service propulsion subsystem, or SPS, engine so as to merely circle behind the moon and emerge in a trans-Earth return trajectory.¶

8. Repeat Steps 7a–8d to mark an additional subentry for the heading *Mission Highlights* for Apollo 11. Type **Apollo 11** as the main entry, and then type **mission highlights** for the subentry text.

9. Mark a level 3 subentry:
   a. Go to the top of the document and search for the first occurrence of *TV transmission*. It is in the Apollo 11 Mission Highlights section. In the document window, position the insertion point after the matched text.
   b. In the Mark Index Entry dialog box, type the main entry **Apollo 11**.
   c. In the Subentry text box, type **mission highlights:TV transmission**.
   d. Click **Mark**.
10. Mark an additional level 3 index subentry:
    a. Navigate to the heading *Apollo 15*, and then search for *lunar samples*. In the document window, position the insertion point after the match in the Apollo 15 section.
    b. In the Mark Index Entry dialog box, type the main entry **Apollo 15**.
    c. In the Subentry text box, type **mission highlights:lunar samples**.
    d. Click **Mark**.
11. Mark all instances of a specific word or text phrase:
    a. Move the insertion point to the top of the document and search for the first occurrence of *Neil Armstrong*. There are four matches.
    b. In the Search box, edit the search text to show only *Armstrong*. There are 14 matches and they are all in the Apollo 11 section. In the Navigation Pane, click the **Browse the results from your current search** button, and then click the first match.
    c. Click the **title bar** for the Mark Index Entry dialog box, and edit the main entry to show **Armstrong, Neil**.
    d. Click **Mark All**. An XE field is inserted after each of the 14 occurrences of the word *Armstrong*.
12. Create a bookmark to mark a range of pages:
    a. In the Navigation Pane, click the **Browse the headings in your document** button, and then click the **Apollo 17** heading. Select all the content for the Apollo 17 mission, including the heading. (The content spans across three pages.)
    b. Click the **Insert** tab. In the Links group, click the **Bookmark** button. In the Bookmark name box, type **Apollo_17** and then click **Add**.
    c. In the Mark Index Entry dialog box, if necessary, change the main entry to **Apollo 17**. In the subentry box, type **mission details**.
    d. Under Options, enable the **Page range** option.
    e. In the Bookmark text box, click the **list arrow** and select **Apollo _17**.
    f. Click **Mark**.

TIP

Typographical errors can affect the accuracy of your index. Proofread each index entry for which you type the entry text. If you find an error after you click Mark, position the insertion point in the field text in your document and make the necessary correction.

TIP

A bookmark name can be up to 40 characters, and it must begin with a letter. The bookmark name can contain only letters, numbers, and the underscore character; it cannot contain spaces.

13. Create a cross-reference to another index entry:
    a. Position the insertion point at the beginning of the document.
    b. In the Mark Index Entry dialog box, type the main entry **Sea of Tranquility**.
    c. Under Options, enable the **Cross-reference** option. In the Cross-reference text box, after *See*, type **lunar locations**.
    d. Click **Mark**.
14. Close the Mark Index Entry dialog box. Save the changes and then close the document.

AutoMarking Index Entries

To automatically mark entries, you must first create an Index AutoMark file to identify words to be included in the index. When you apply the AutoMark feature, Word automatically inserts codes for all occurrences of the words identified in the AutoMark file. Although AutoMarking is quick and convenient, the downside is that none of the index entries are customized.

Index entries are case sensitive, so you need to pay attention to lowercase and uppercase letters as you create index entries in the Index AutoMark file. For example, when *Crew* is capitalized in the document, it must be shown with initial caps when identifying the text to be marked. You must also make sure the capitalization is correct for main entries and subentries.

Step-by-Step 15.2

1. Open the **Index Entries** file from the drive and folder where your Data Files are stored. Save the document as **AutoMark Index Entries**, followed by your initials.
2. Note that the data in the left column identifies the words or phrases to be marked for the index. The data in the right column shows how the entries should appear in the index. Note that some of the entries include colons to distinguish subentries.
3. Note also that some of the cells at the bottom of the right column are blank. If the cell in the right column is blank, Word will create an entry exactly the same as the text in the left column.
4. Add the following additional entries in the blank cells at the end of the list.

Kennedy	**president:President John F. Kennedy**
Nixon	**president:President Richard M. Nixon**
Crew	**crew**
Backup Crew	**backup crew**

5. By default, the AutoCorrect settings enable the option to capitalize the first letter of sentences, so as you enter index entries, the first word is formatted with initial caps. Make corrections as needed so the capitalization is consistent with that shown in the right column in Step 4. Correct capitalization will avoid creating two main entries for the same word (such as *President* and *president*).
6. Save the changes and close the document.
7. Open the **Apollo Missions 1** document from your solution files and save the document as **Apollo Missions 2**, followed by your initials.
8. Click the **References** tab. In the Index group, click the **Insert Index** button to open the Index dialog box, as shown in **Figure 15–4**.

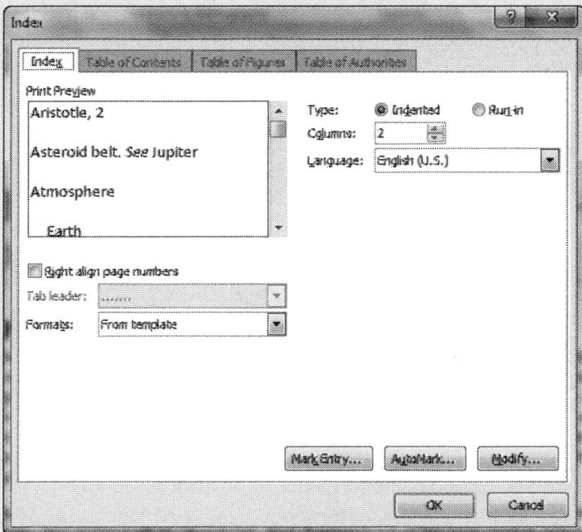

FIGURE 15–4
Index dialog box

9. Click **AutoMark**. Navigate to the drive and folder where your solution files are stored. Select the **AutoMark Index Entries** file and click **Open**.
10. Scroll through the document and you will see many new XE coded fields.
11. Save the changes and leave the document open for the next Step-by-Step.

Generating, Formatting, and Updating an Index

After all index entries have been marked, you can pull them together to create the index. This is often referred to as generating the index. You should make all changes and revisions to your document before you generate the index. If you make changes to the document after the index is created, the page number references in the index may no longer be correct; you will then need to update your index. When you update an index, you will lose any formatting you applied to the index.

Generally, you will format the index on a page by itself at the end of a document. Entries in the index are arranged in alphabetic order with letters inserted as separators to organize the list. Word offers nine built-in styles to help you format the index. An indented index displays all subentries indented below the main entry. To save space, a run-in index can be created, displaying subentries on the same line as the main entries.

The option to show nonprinting formatting characters should be disabled when you generate the index. If nonprinting characters are displayed, the hidden text (such as field codes) will be included in the pagination, which may result in incorrect page numbers in the index.

Step-by-Step 15.3

1. If necessary, open the **Apollo Missions 2** file from your solution files. Save the document as **Apollo Missions 3**, followed by your initials.
2. Position the insertion point at the end of the document, and insert a page break.
3. If necessary, click the **Home** tab. In the Paragraph group, click the **Show/Hide ¶** button to turn off the display of nonprinting formatting characters.
4. Click the **References** tab. In the Index group, click the **Insert Index** button. The Index dialog box opens.
5. Select format settings for the index:
   a. Scroll through the Print Preview pane. Note that the subentries are shown indented.
   b. To the right of Type:, enable the **Run-in** option. Scroll through the Print Preview pane. All the subentries are combined in one paragraph instead of appearing on separate lines. Enable the **Indented** option.
   c. Under the Print Preview pane, click the **Formats** list arrow and click each format to preview the available styles.
   d. In the Formats box, select **Formal**. Note that the Right align page numbers option is now enabled and a tab leader is inserted between the entry and the page number.
   e. Click **OK**. The index is inserted as a field at the position of the insertion point. Note that the page number formats are inconsistent: The AutoMark entries do not include the bold and italic formats.
6. Scroll to the top of the index and position the insertion point in front of the letter *A*. Press the **up arrow** to position the insertion point in the blank paragraph above the index.
7. Type **Index**. Without moving the insertion point, click the **Home** tab, and in the Styles group, click the **Heading 1** style.
8. In the index, note that the name of a backup crew member (Brand) is missing. If necessary, show the Navigation Pane. In the Navigation Pane, click the **Apollo 15** heading.

EXTRA FOR EXPERTS

You can modify the built-in style format *From template* by clicking the Modify button in the Index dialog box.

9. In the document window, in the Backup Crew column, select the name **Brand**. Click the **References** tab. In the Index group, click the **Mark Entry** button. The main entry box will display *Brand.* Edit the main entry to show **Brand, Vance DeVoe**. Enable the **Bold** and **Italic** options, and then click **Mark All**. Close the Mark Index Entry dialog box.
10. Click the **Home** tab. In the Paragraph group, click the **Show/Hide ¶** button to toggle off the display of nonprinting formatting characters.
11. In the Navigation Pane, click the **Index** heading. To update the index, click anywhere inside the index to select the field containing the index. Click the **References** tab, and in the Index group, click the **Update Index** button. The index is updated and now the name *Brand* appears under the letter *B*.
12. Note that when you updated the index, the heading style was removed from the title above the index. Click anywhere in the Index title. Click the **Home** tab. In the Styles group, click the **Heading 1** style.
13. Save the changes and leave the document open for the next Step-by-Step.

TIP

Alternatives to clicking the Update Index button: press F9, or right-click anywhere within the index and select Update Field in the shortcut menu.

Creating and Updating a Table of Contents

A ***table of contents*** shows a sequential order of the contents contained within the document, providing an overview of the topics in a document. In Print Layout view, you can use the table of contents to quickly locate page numbers for specific information. In Web Layout view, the entries in the table of contents are formatted as hyperlinks. When you click a hyperlink, the insertion point moves to that section of the document.

Each entry in the table of contents is formatted on a separate line. The entry name is separated from the page number by a tab character. You can choose from nine built-in styles.

If you plan to include both an index and a table of contents in your final document, you should create the index first so the page numbers for the index can be included in the table of contents.

VOCABULARY
table of contents

Using Heading Styles to Create a Table of Contents

A table of contents can be created based on heading styles already applied within a document. These heading styles may be built-in heading styles supplied by Word or outline-level styles assigned when you create a document in outline format. When Word's heading styles are already applied in the document, Word will recognize the styles and generate the table of contents based on the first three levels of headings.

The option to show nonprinting formatting characters should be disabled when you generate the table of contents. If nonprinting characters are displayed, the hidden text (such as field codes) will be included in the pagination. With hidden text included, page numbers in the table of contents may be inaccurate. If you edit the document after generating the table of contents, be sure to update the table of contents to ensure page numbers and headings are accurate.

Step-by-Step 15.4

1. If necessary, open the **Apollo Missions 3** file from your solution files. Save the document as **Apollo Missions 4**, followed by your initials. If necessary, turn off the display of nonprinting formatting characters. Also, if necessary, show the Navigation Pane.
2. Position the insertion point at the beginning of the document, and insert a page break. Then once again position the insertion point at the top of the document.
3. Click the **References** tab. In the Table of Contents group, click the **Table of Contents** button to open the Table of Contents gallery, as shown in **Figure 15–5**.

FIGURE 15–5
Table of Contents gallery

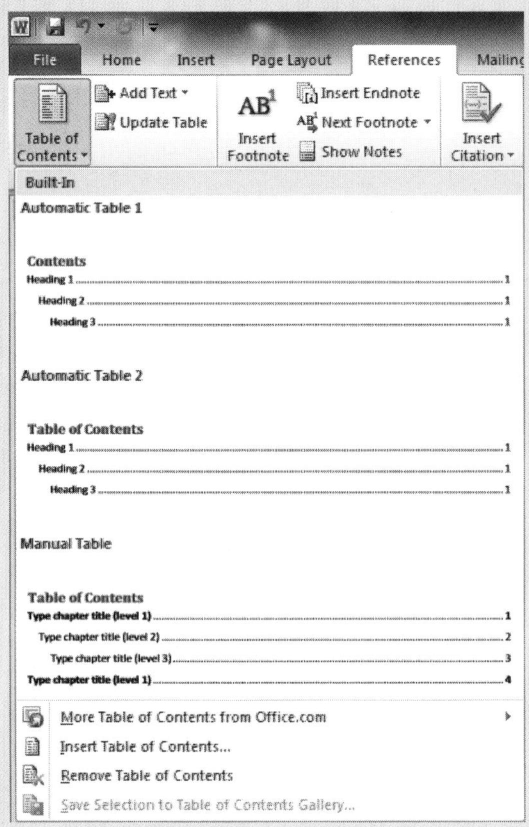

4. At the bottom of the list, click **Insert Table of Contents** to open the Table of Contents dialog box, as shown in **Figure 15–6**. Note that the dialog box provides two preview panes: Print Preview and Web Preview.

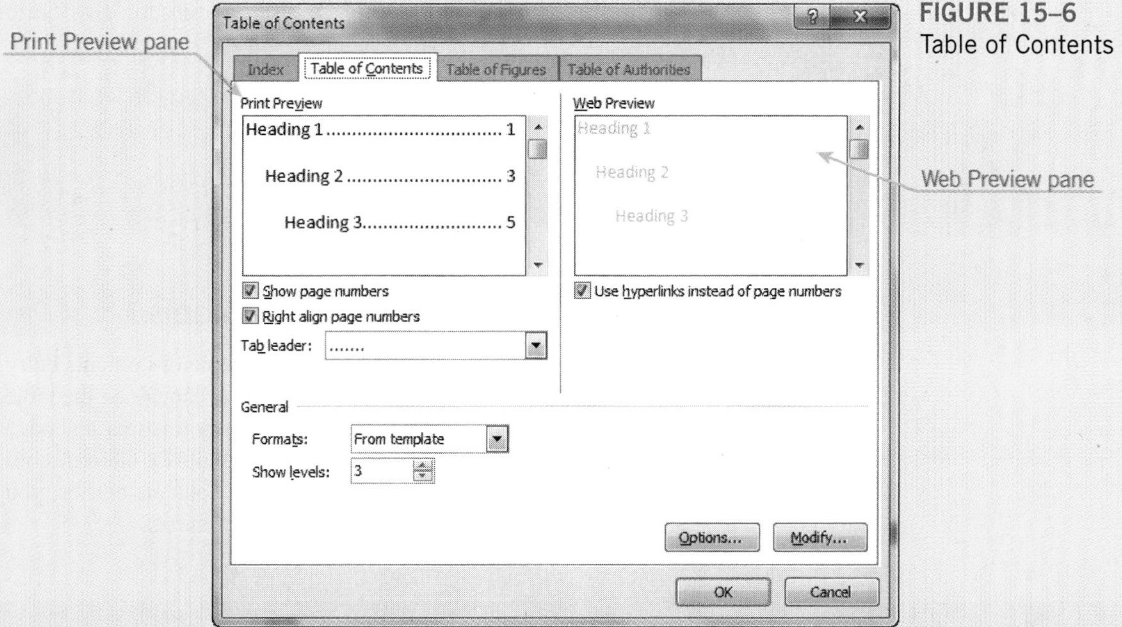

FIGURE 15–6
Table of Contents dialog box

5. Under General, click the **Formats** list arrow and preview some of the styles in both panes. Then select the **Formal** style. Because you chose the Formal style, the Right align page numbers option and the Tab leader options are enabled.
6. The document uses three levels of headings, so no other changes are necessary. Click **OK**. The table of contents is inserted as a field.
7. Position the insertion point at the top of the document, in front of the table of contents. Type **Table of Contents** and press **Enter**. Do not be concerned that the text appears in all caps. Position the insertion point anywhere in the new paragraph. Click the **Home** tab, and then in the Styles group, click the **Heading 1** style.
8. Note in the table of contents that the heading *Apollo 11* appears on page three. In the Navigation Pane, collapse the Apollo 11 heading and then drag the heading and position it in front of the Apollo 15 heading.
9. Navigate back to the top of the document. Notice that the page number for Apollo 11 did not change. Click anywhere in the table of contents field to select it. Click the **References** tab. In the Table of Contents group, click the **Update Table** button. A prompt opens and the Update page numbers only option is enabled. Click **OK**. Note that the page number is changed to 16. Also note that the heading format did not change.
10. Click the **Undo** button to restore the table of contents before the update. Click the **Undo** button again to restore the Apollo 11 heading and the related content back to its previous location in the document.
11. Save the changes to the document.

12. Position the insertion point at the beginning of the document. Switch to Web Layout view. The entries in the table of contents are displayed as hyperlinks. Hold down **Ctrl** and click one of the links to go to that location in the document.
13. Close the document.

Inserting Fields to Create a Table of Contents

If your document does not have obvious headings for every table of contents entry (or if your headings are not formatted with heading styles), you can create the table of contents using fields. The TC field is used to identify the entry (the text and page number) to appear in the table of contents. By default, Word builds a table of contents by styles. When you insert fields to identify the table of contents entries, you must change this default setting before compiling the table of contents.

Step-by-Step 15.5

1. Open the **Financial Review** file from the drive and folder where your Data Files are stored. Save the document as **Revised Financial Review**, followed by your initials.
2. On the Home tab, in the Paragraph group, toggle on the display of non-printing formatting characters so you will see the table of contents field entries as you create them. The entries will be formatted as hidden text.
3. Add a Level 1 table of contents entry in a field:
    a. Position the insertion point at the end of the heading *FINANCIAL PERFORMANCE AND SOLVENCY*. The page number will be referenced to this location.
    b. Click the **Insert** tab. In the Text group, click the **Quick Parts** button and then click **Field** to open the Field dialog box, as shown in **Figure 15–7**.

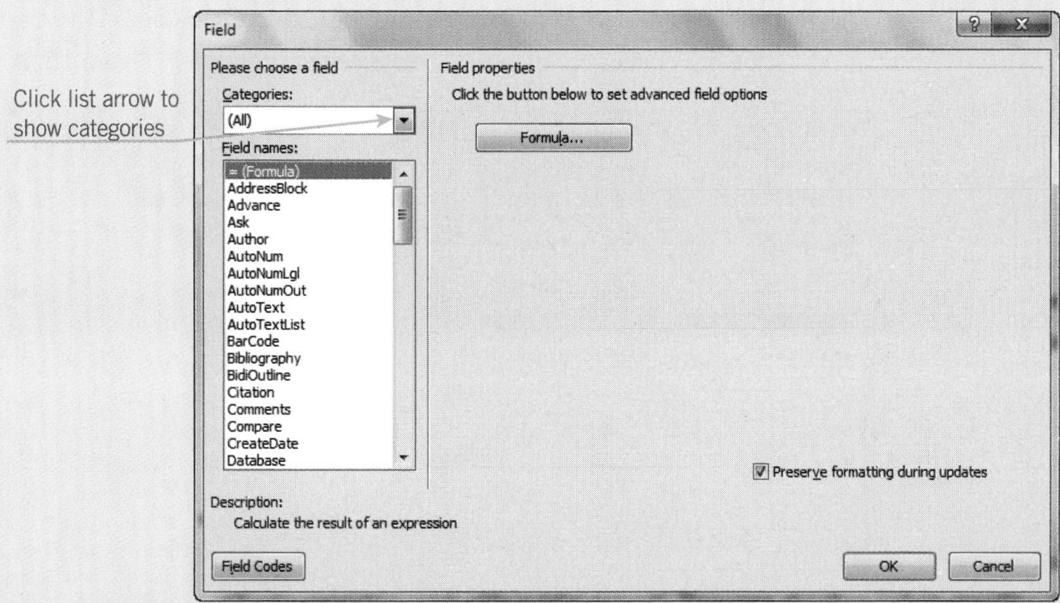

FIGURE 15–7
Field dialog box

c. Click the **Categories** list arrow and then select **Index and Tables**.
d. Under Field names, select **TC** (not TOC).
e. In the center pane, under Field properties, position the insertion point in the Text entry box. Type **FINANCIAL PERFORMANCE AND SOLVENCY**.
f. Click **OK**. A field with the TC code is inserted at the location of the insertion point.

4. Position the insertion point after the heading *ACCOUNTING SYTEMS*. Repeat Steps 3b–3f to create a Level 1 table of contents entry. For the text entry, type **ACCOUNTING SYSTEMS**.
5. Add a Level 2 table of contents entry in a field:
   a. Position the insertion point at the end of the heading *Chart of Accounts*. In the Text group, click the **Quick Parts** button and then click **Field**.
   b. In the Field dialog box, under Field names, select **TC**. In the Text entry box, type **Chart of Accounts**.
   c. Under Field options, enable the **Outline level** option, and then in the text box, type **2**.

d. In the lower-left corner of the dialog box, click **Field Codes**. The dialog box changes to display the field codes as shown in **Figure 15–8**.

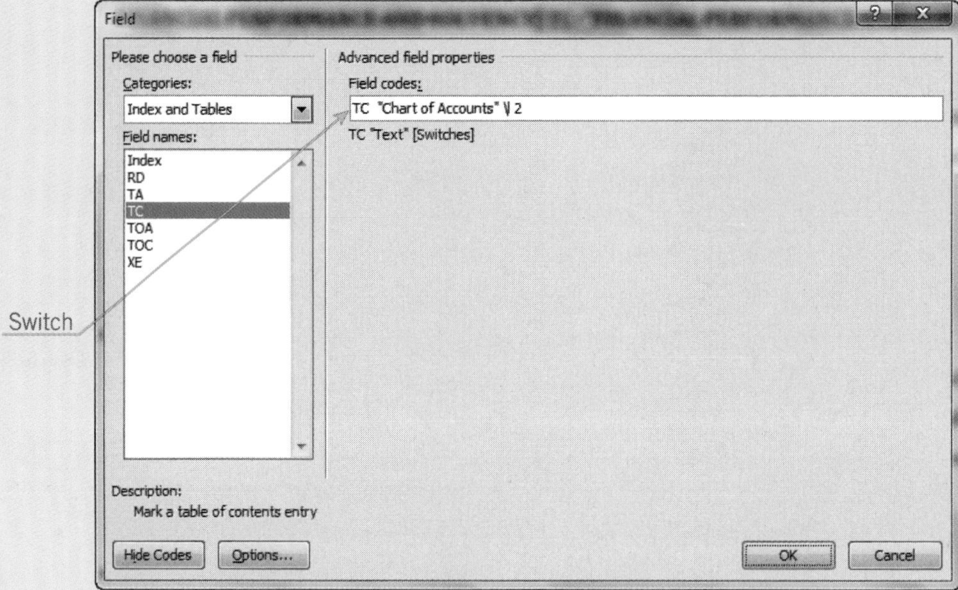

FIGURE 15–8
Field dialog box with field codes displayed

e. The codes that Word uses to identify the table of contents entry are displayed in the Field codes box. Notice that the code includes the switch \l2.

f. Click **Hide codes**. Click **OK**.

6. Position the insertion point at the end of the heading *General Ledger*. Repeat Steps 5a and 5b to create a Level 2 table of contents entry. In the Text entry box, type **General Ledger** and set the Outline level to **2**. Click **OK**.
7. Position the insertion point at the end of the heading *Accounts Payable*. Repeat Steps 5a and 5b to create a level 3 table of contents entry. In the Text entry box, type **Accounts Payable**. Enable the **Outline level** option, and then in the text box, type **3**. Click **OK**.
8. Position the insertion point at the end of the heading *Accounts Receivable*. Repeat Steps 5a and 5b to create a level 3 table of contents entry. In the Text entry box, type **Accounts Receivable**. Enable the **Outline level** option, and in the text box, type **3**. Click **OK**.
9. Scroll through the remaining pages of the document. You will see that fields have already been inserted for the remaining headings. Position the insertion point at the beginning of the document. Insert a page break, and then position the insertion point at the beginning of the document again (in front of the Page Break line).
10. Click the **Home** tab. In the Paragraph group, click the **Show/Hide ¶** button to turn off the display of nonprinting formatting characters.

11. Click the **References** tab. In the Table of Contents group, click the **Table of Contents** button, and then click **Insert Table of Contents**. The Table of Contents dialog box opens. In the dialog box, click **Options** to open the Table of Contents Options dialog box, as shown in **Figure 15–9**.

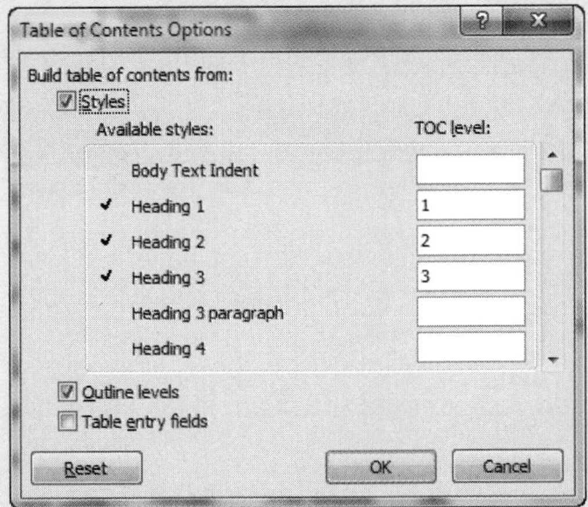

FIGURE 15–9
Table of Contents Options dialog box

12. Enable the **Table entry fields** option. Click **OK** twice to accept the changes and close the dialog boxes. The table of contents is inserted at the location of the insertion point.
13. Position the insertion point at the top of the document, in front of the table of contents field. Type **Table of Contents** and then press **Enter**. Do not be concerned if the text you entered appears in all caps. Position the insertion point anywhere within the new heading. Click the **Home** tab. In the Styles group, click the **Title** style.
14. Save the changes and close the document.

Updating a Table of Contents

If changes are made in the document after the table of contents is created, changes may also be necessary in the table of contents. If the pagination changes, the page references in the table of contents may be incorrect. If headings were edited or deleted, or new headings were added, the list of headings in the table of contents would need to be edited. Updating the table of contents is quick and easy. You simply update the field.

The page on which the table of contents appears should be numbered separately from the rest of the document. Usually, page numbers for front matter, such as a table of contents, are formatted in lowercase Roman numerals. Therefore, when you format page numbers, you need to format the table of contents page(s) in a different section so it will have its own page number formats.

Step-by-Step 15.6

1. Open the **Apollo Missions 4** file from your solution files. Save the document as **Apollo Missions 5**, followed by your initials. Toggle on the display of nonprinting formatting characters.
2. Position the insertion point in front of the Page Break line below the table of contents and press **Delete**. Then click the **Page Layout** tab. In the Page Setup group, click the **Breaks** button. Under Section Breaks, click **Next Page**.
3. Position the insertion point on the first page, anywhere above the section break. Note that the number 1 appears in the footer pane. Click the **Insert** tab. In the Header & Footer group, click the **Footer** button, and then click **Edit Footer**. The Ribbon adapts to show more features.
4. In the Header & Footer group, click the **Page Number** button, and then click **Format Page Numbers** to open the Page Number Format dialog box, as shown in **Figure 15–10**.

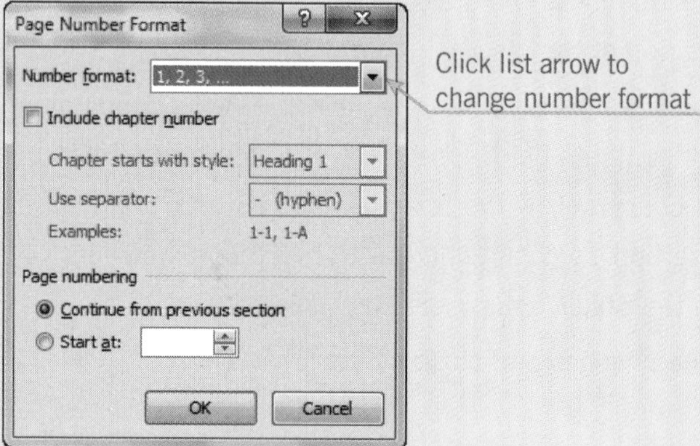

FIGURE 15–10
Page Number Format dialog box

5. Click the **Number format** list arrow and then select **i, ii, iii, ...** Click **OK**. Note that the number style changes in the document window.
6. Scroll down to the second page in the document, and then double-click in the footer pane.
7. In the Header & Footer group, click the **Page Number** button and then click **Format Page Numbers** to open the Page Number Format dialog box. Under Page numbering, enable the **Start at** option. In the text box, make sure the number 1 is displayed. Click **OK**. The number 1 appears at the bottom of the second page in the document.
8. On the Header & Footer Tools Design tab, in the Options group, enable the **Different First Page** option. With this setting enabled, a page number will not print on the first page of this section.
9. Double-click anywhere in the document window to make it active. Turn off the display of nonprinting formatting characters.

10. Navigate to the first page and click anywhere in the table of contents to select it. Click the **References** tab. In the Table of Contents group, click the **Update Table** button. When prompted to update the page numbers or to update the entire table of contents, make sure the Update page numbers only option is enabled and click **OK**. The table of contents is updated and now shows the heading *INTRODUCTION* on page 1.
11. Save the changes and close the document.

Creating a Table of Figures

A table of figures is similar to a table of contents. A ***table of figures*** provides a sequential list of all the figures (such as tables, equations, pictures, charts, graphs, and other illustrations) included in a document. This list can be very useful when a document contains several illustrations.

VOCABULARY
table of figures

Before you create a table of figures, the figures in your document must be formatted with captions. As you have already learned, a caption is a label that identifies a figure, and Word automatically updates the caption numbers as you add captions in the document. However, when you delete or move a caption, you must manually update the captions. The caption is not attached to the figure, so when you copy and paste a figure, make sure you include the caption in the selection.

Inserting an AutoCaption

Word offers three different options for caption labels (Equation, Figure, or Table). You can customize the caption label by changing the label name, choosing where the caption appears, and changing the format of the caption number. Word automatically assigns consecutive numbers to captions. You can enable a setting to automatically add a caption each time you insert an object (such as a table or graphic) in the document.

Step-by-Step 15.7

1. Open the **Calories** files from the drive and folder where your Data Files are stored. You do not need to save the file in your solutions folder.
2. Open the **Nutrition Facts** file from the drive and folder where your Data Files are stored. Save the document as **Revised Nutrition Facts**, followed by your initials.

3. Click the **References** tab. In the Captions group, click the **Insert Caption** button to open the Caption dialog box, as shown in **Figure 15–11**.

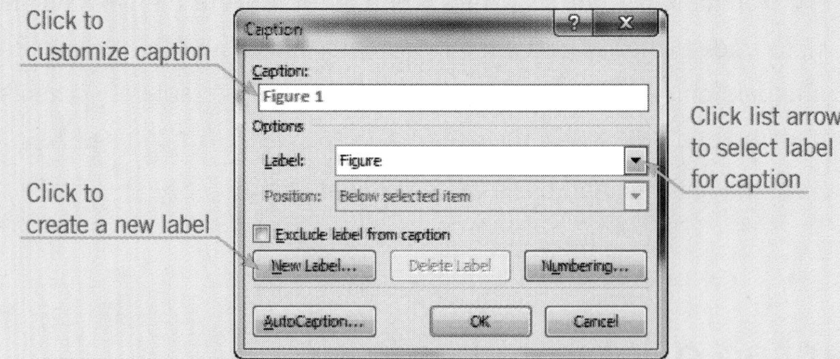

FIGURE 15–11
Caption dialog box

4. Click the **Label** list arrow and then select **Table**. Note that the Caption box shows *Table 1*. Click **Numbering** to open the Caption Numbering box. Click the **Format** list arrow and then select **A,B,C...**. Click **OK**. Note that the Caption box now shows *Table A*.
5. Click **AutoCaption** to open the AutoCaption dialog box. Under Add caption when inserting, scroll down and enable the **Microsoft Word Table** option, as shown in **Figure 15–12**. (Make sure the check mark appears in the box.) Note that captions are not limited to figures and tables. With this setting enabled, Word will automatically add captions to all Word tables as they are inserted, and the setting applies to all Word documents.

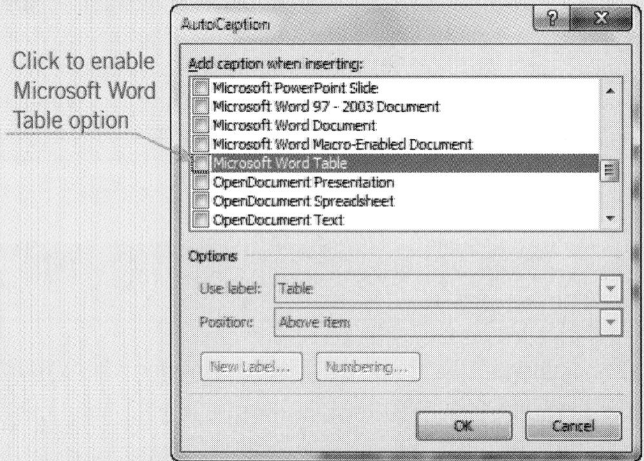

FIGURE 15–12
AutoCaption dialog box

6. Under Options, the Use label box should already show **Table**. If necessary, in the Position box, select **Above item**. Click **OK**.
7. Switch to the **Calories** document and copy the first table (green/vegetables) to the Clipboard. Switch to the **Revised Nutrition Facts** document. Position the insertion point in the blank paragraph after the second paragraph in the body of the document. Paste the table.

8. Note that the caption *Table A* appears above the inserted table. Position the insertion point after the letter *A* in the caption, press the **spacebar**, and then type **Vegetable Calories.**
9. Switch to the **Calories** document. Copy the second table (blue/nuts) to the Clipboard. Switch to the **Revised Nutrition Facts** document, and then paste the table in the blank paragraph at the end of the document.
10. Note that the caption *Table B* appears above the inserted table. Edit the caption by adding **Nut Calories.**
11. Switch to the **Calories** document. Copy the third table (orange/fruits) to the Clipboard. Switch to the **Revised Nutrition Facts** document, and paste the table in the blank paragraph after the third paragraph in the body of the document.
12. Note that the caption *Table B* appears above the inserted table. Scroll down and you will see that the caption for the third table in the document was updated to show the caption *Table C.* Go back to Table B and edit the caption by adding **Fruit Calories.**
13. If necessary, click the **References** tab. In the Captions group, click the **Insert Caption** button and then click **AutoCaption** to open the AutoCaption dialog box. Disable the **Microsoft Word Table** option. Click **OK.**
14. Save the changes to the Revised Nutrition Facts document. Close both documents.

TIP

To copy the table to the Clipboard, point to the upper-left corner of the table and then click the Table Selector icon to select the table. Then click the Copy button (or press Ctrl+C).

Inserting a Customized Caption

If desired, you can create a new label to add to the list of labels for captions. For example, instead of referring to the figure as a table, you may want the caption to show a different label, such as Illustration or Graphic.

Step-by-Step 15.8

1. Open the **Apollo Missions 5** file from your solution files. Save the document as **Apollo Missions 6**, followed by your initials. If necessary, show the Navigation Pane and nonprinting formatting characters.
2. Navigate to the heading *Apollo 12.* Position the insertion point in the blank paragraph below the table of crew members.
3. Click the **References** tab. In the Captions group, click the **Insert Caption** button to open the Caption dialog box.
4. Under Options, click the **Label** list arrow and select **Table**. Click **Numbering**, select **1,2,3**, and then click **OK**.

5. Click the **Caption** text box. The insertion point is positioned to the right of the caption label *Table 1*. Press the **spacebar**, and then type **Apollo 12 Crew Members**. Click **OK**. The caption text is inserted at the insertion point.
6. Navigate to the heading *Apollo 11* and position the insertion point in the blank paragraph below the table of crew members. In the Captions group, click the **Insert Caption** button. In the Caption text box, press the **spacebar** and then type **Apollo 11 Crew Members**. Click **OK**. Note that the caption shows *Table 1*.
7. Navigate to the heading *Apollo 12*. Note that the caption shows *Table 2*. Word automatically adjusted the table number.
8. Navigate to each of the remaining Apollo headings (13–17) and insert a table caption under the crew information using the text *Apollo XX Crew Members* and replacing the *XX* with the appropriate mission number.
9. Navigate to the heading *Apollo 11*. Position the insertion point in the blank paragraph below the graphic of the Apollo 11 patch.
10. In the Captions group, click the **Insert Caption** button. Click **New Label** to open the New Label dialog box. Type **Illustration** and click **OK**. Note that the Caption box now shows *Illustration 1*. Click the **Label** list arrow. The new label *Illustration* appears in the list.
11. Click the **Caption** text box. Press the **spacebar** and type **Apollo 11 Mission Patch**. Click **OK**. Press **Ctrl+E** to center the caption.
12. Navigate to each of the remaining Apollo headings (12–17) and insert and center an illustration caption under the mission patch. Use the text *Apollo XX Mission Patch* and replace the *XX* with the appropriate mission number.
13. Save the changes and leave the document open for the next Step-by-Step.

Inserting a Table of Figures

Creating a table of figures is similar to creating a table of contents. One distinctive difference, though, is that the table of figures is based on captions instead of fields, so if new captions are added to the document, even though the caption numbers are automatically updated, the table of figures cannot be updated. If the document is edited, you must replace the existing table of figures with a new table.

In Print Layout view, you can use the table of figures to quickly locate a specific illustration by identifying the page number where the illustration appears. In Web Layout view, the entries in the table of figures are formatted as hyperlinks, which you can use to quickly navigate to an illustration.

You can create multiple tables of figures in the same document. For example, you can create a table of illustrations and a table of figures. There is no hidden text related to figure captions; therefore, the pagination is not affected. However, if the document includes other hidden text, you need to turn off the display of nonprinting characters before compiling the table of figures.

Step-by-Step 15.9

1. If necessary, open the **Apollo Missions 6** file from your solution files. Save the document as **Apollo Missions 7**, followed by your initials.
2. Position the insertion point at the end of the document. Insert a page break. Type **List of Tables** and press **Enter**. Toggle off the display of non-printing formatting characters.
3. Click the **References** tab. In the Captions group, click the **Insert Table of Figures** button to open the Table of Figures dialog box, as shown in **Figure 15–13**. Notice that the dialog box includes two preview panes: Print Preview and Web Preview.

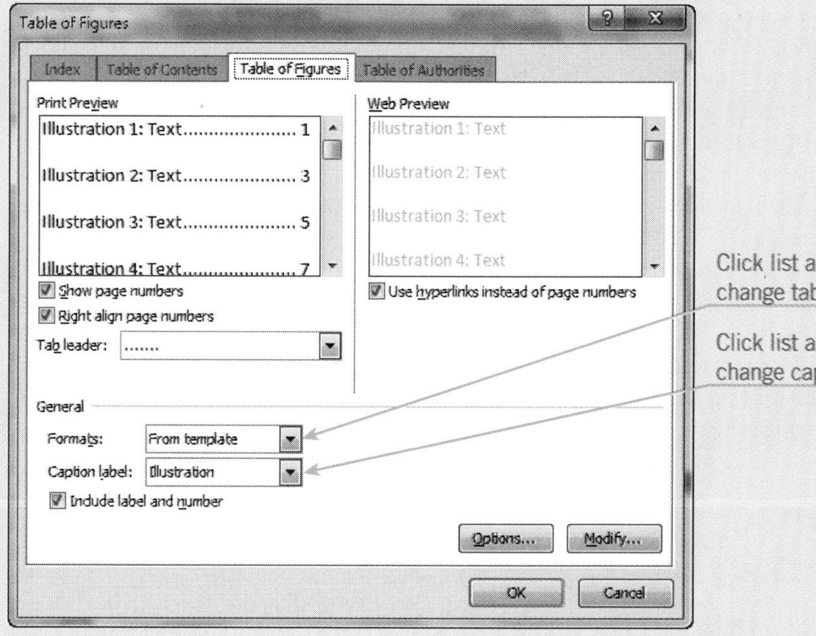

FIGURE 15–13
Table of Figures dialog box

4. Under General, click the **Formats** list arrow and select **Formal**. Click the **Caption label** list arrow and select **Table**. Click **OK**. A list of the seven tables is inserted at the location of the insertion point.
5. Press **Enter** two times. Type **List of Illustrations** and press **Enter**. Click the **Insert Table of Figures** button. In the Formats box, make sure the Formal style is selected. In the Caption label box, select **Illustration**. Click **OK**. A list of the seven illustrations is inserted at the location of the insertion point.

6. Save the changes to the document.
7. Switch to Web Layout view. Hold down **Ctrl** and click one of the links to navigate to a table or illustration. Because the width of the page is expanded in this view, the table caption does not appear below the table.
8. Close the document.

Creating a Table of Authorities

VOCABULARY
table of authorities
passim

A table of authorities is often used in the legal profession. A ***table of authorities*** summarizes the references used in a legal document. The references might be cases, statutes, rules, or other sources. When completed, the table of authorities closely resembles a table of contents. Because of the variety of reference types, when you mark each reference, you can specify a category. Then when the table of authorities is created, the references can be organized by categories.

Before you can create a table of authorities, you must insert fields to mark the citations (references to specific legal cases, statutes, or other legal documents) in the document. You mark citations in much the same way you mark index entries. You can mark an individual reference to a citation, or you can mark all references to a citation at once. As you enter the required fields, you can create both short and long citations. A short citation indicates the text you want Word to search for in the document, such as *Johnston v. IVAC Corp*. A long citation shows the text as it will appear in the table of authorities, such as *Johnston v. IVAC Corp., 885 F.2d 1574, 1577, 12 USPQ2d 1382, 1384 (Fed. Cir. 1989).*

Inserting a table of authorities is similar to inserting a table of figures. The table is inserted at the location of the insertion point. Like tables of figures, you can choose a built-in style. Like indexes and tables of contents, a table of authorities is based on fields, so if the document is edited, the table of authorities can easily be updated.

The word ***passim*** is used to indicate that terms, passages, or page references occur frequently in the work cited. In Word, the default setting *Use passim* formats multiple page references on the same line in a table of authorities. For example, if the same citation appears on pages 2 and 3, the citation will appear only once in the table of authorities with a reference to both page numbers.

Step-by-Step 15.10

1. Open the **Freedman Case** file from the drive and folder where your Data Files are stored. Save the document as **Freedman Case Summary,** followed by your initials. If necessary, show nonprinting formatting characters.
2. In the first paragraph, select **Lanham Act § 43(a), 15 U.S.C. 1125(a) (1982)**. Click the **References** tab. In the Table of Authorities group, click the **Mark Citation** button to open the Mark Citation dialog box, as shown in **Figure 15–14**. Your settings may differ. Note that the text you selected in the document window appears in both the Selected text and the Short citation boxes.

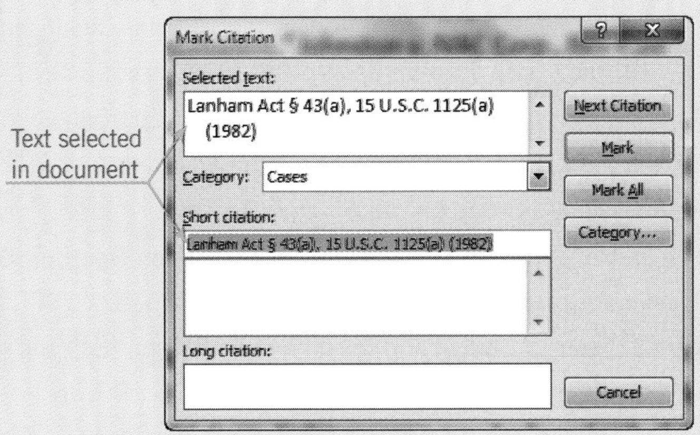

FIGURE 15–14
Mark Citation dialog box

3. In the Category box, select **Statutes**. Click **Mark All**. Note that the selected text now appears in the Long Citation box, and this is how the citation will appear in the table of authorities. A TA field containing the citation text is inserted into the document. Leave the Mark Citation dialog box open. Reposition the dialog box on the screen so you can see the document window.
4. Click in the document window, and in the first paragraph, select **Minnesota Deceptive Trade Practices Act ("MDTPA"), Minn. Stat. § 325D.44**. Then click the **title bar** for the Mark Citation dialog box. *Statutes* is already selected in the Category box. Click **Mark All**.
5. In the second paragraph, select **Johnston v. IVAC Corp., 885 F.2d 1574, 1577, 12 USPQ2d 1382, 1384 (Fed. Cir. 1989)**.
6. In the Mark Citation dialog box, click the **Category** list arrow and then select **Cases**.
7. Click anywhere in the Short Citation box and then use the left arrow key to position the insertion point after the period in the word *Corp.*. Beginning with the comma, delete all characters to the right so that the short citation box displays only *Johnston v. IVAC Corp.* Then click **Mark All**. Word will search for and mark all occurrences of the short citation. Note that the full citation still appears in the Long Citation box, as shown in **Figure 15–15**.

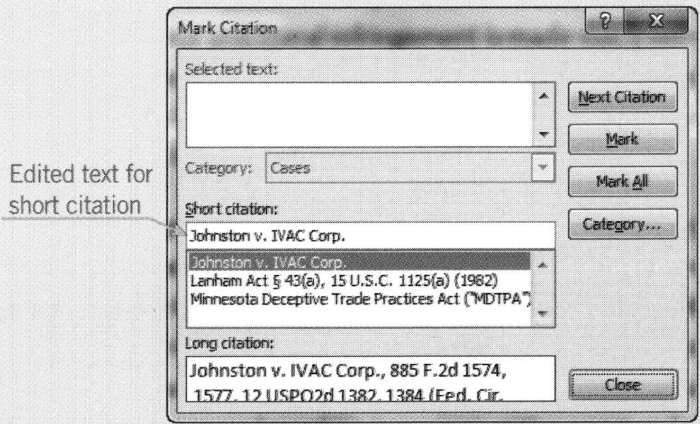

FIGURE 15–15
Mark Citation dialog box with an edited short citation

8. At the end of the second paragraph, select **Becton Dickinson & Co. v. C.R. Bard, Inc., 922 F.2d 792, 795-96 (Fed. Cir. 1990)**. In the Mark Citation dialog box, *Cases* is already selected in the Category box. Edit the Short Citation box to show only *Becton Dickinson & Co. v. C.R. Bard, Inc.*, and then click **Mark All**.
9. At the end of the fourth paragraph, select **Wilson Sporting Goods Co. v. David Geoffrey & Assoc., 904 F. 2d 677, 683, 14 USPQ2d 1942, 1947-48 (Fed. Cir. 1990)** and create a case citation. Edit the short citation to display *Wilson Sporting Goods Co. v. David Geoffrey & Assoc.*. Then click **Mark All**.
10. Close the Mark Citation dialog box. Toggle off the display of nonprinting formatting characters.
11. Position the insertion point at the beginning of the document, and insert a page break. Again, position the insertion point at the beginning of the document. Type **Table of Authorities** and press **Enter**.
12. Click the **References** tab. In the Table of Authorities group, click the **Insert Table of Authorities** button to open the dialog box shown in **Figure 15–16**. Your settings will differ.

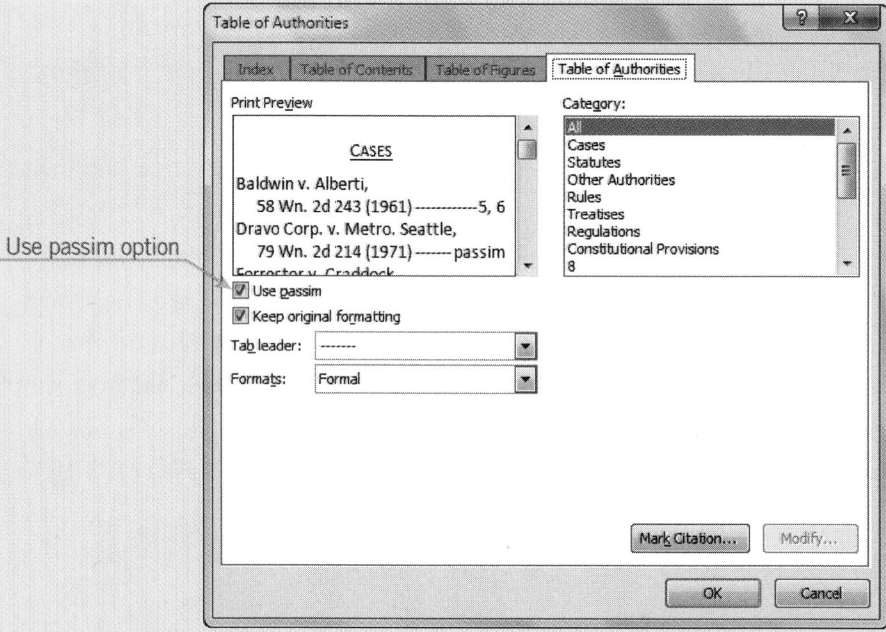

FIGURE 15–16
Table of Authorities dialog box

13. Under Category, make sure that **All** is selected. In the Formats box, select **Formal**. The Use passim option should be enabled. Click **OK**. The table of authorities is inserted at the location of the insertion point. Note that the *Johnston v. IVAC Corp.* case appears only once in the table of authorities and shows two page references.
14. Save the changes and close the document.

SUMMARY

In this lesson, you learned:

- To create an index, you must first mark the index entries.
- Word enables you to format bookmarks and cross-references to create customized index entries.
- If a document is revised, you can quickly update the fields in an index.
- You can use Word's heading styles or outline-level styles to create a table of contents, or you can create a table of contents using fields.
- If edits are made in the document that affect pagination or headings, the table of contents can be easily updated.
- Word's caption feature enables you to label and automatically number figures throughout a document.
- When the figures in a document include captions, you can automatically create a table of figures.
- To create a table of authorities, you must first mark the citations. Marking citations is similar to marking index entries.

VOCABULARY REVIEW

Define the following terms:

cross-reference
index
passim
table of authorities
table of contents
table of figures

REVIEW QUESTIONS

TRUE / FALSE

Circle T if the statement is true or F if the statement is false.

T F 1. If you plan to include both an index and a table of contents in your final document, you should create the table of contents first.

T F 2. To create a table of figures, you must apply captions to the figures.

T F 3. To format the table of contents page numbers differently from the other pages in the document, you need to create a new section for the table of contents.

T F 4. A cross-reference in an index is an entry followed by text instead of a page number.

T F 5. When you delete or move captions in a document, Word automatically updates all the caption numbers in the document.

MULTIPLE CHOICE

Select the best response for the following statements.

1. When you ________________, Word automatically performs an update.

   A. mark an index entry
   B. add a caption
   C. apply a new heading style
   D. insert a citation

2. When marking citations for a table of authorities, the ________________ shows the text as it will appear in the table of authorities.

   A. long citation
   B. short citation
   C. TA field
   D. citation category

3. When creating a(n) ________________, you can specify a category to organize the entries.

   A. index
   B. table of figures
   C. table of contents
   D. table of authorities

4. A(n) ______________ is an alphabetical listing of pertinent words and phrases contained in a document.

   A. index
   B. table of figures
   C. table of authorities
   D. table of contents

5. ______________ are case sensitive.

   A. Citations
   B. Table of contents entries
   C. Captions
   D. Index entries

WRITTEN QUESTIONS

Write a brief answer to the following questions.

1. What are the advantages to creating a table of contents based on the heading styles in a document?

2. Why would you use the run-in option when formatting an index?

3. Why would you show a table of figures in Web Layout view?

4. Why would you create a bookmark for an index entry?

5. When generating a table of figures, should the display of nonprinting formatting characters be on or off, and why?

PROJECTS

If you have a SAM 2010 user profile, your instructor may have assigned an autogradable version of the indicated project. If so, log into the SAM 2010 Web site at *www.cengage.com/sam2010* to download the instruction and start files.

PROJECT 15–1

1. Open the **Foreign Trade** file from the drive and folder where your Data Files are stored. Save the document as **Revised Foreign Trade**, followed by your initials.
2. Create a new label **Chart** for captions.
3. Read the content above the first chart to create an appropriate customized caption, and then, using the Chart label, insert a caption in the blank paragraph below the chart. Center the caption.
4. Using the Chart label, create and insert custom captions below the other two charts. Center the captions.
5. Insert a table of figures on a new page at the end of the document using the Simple format. Add the heading **TABLE OF FIGURES** above the table in bold and centered formatting.
6. Save, print, and close the document.
7. Exit Word. If prompted to save changes to the Normal global template, click No.

SAM PROJECT 15–2

1. Launch Word and open the **Natural Disasters** file from the drive and folder where your Data Files are stored. Save the document as **Revised Natural Disasters 1**, followed by your initials.
2. Mark main index entries for each of the following phrases where they occur in the level 2 headings. Use the same capitalization shown below. Do not format the page numbers for the index entries in bold and italic.

   Floods
   Landslides
   Tornadoes
   Extreme Heat
   Wildfires
3. Navigate to the Prepare a Family Disaster Plan section. Create a subentry index entry for the heading *Create a Plan*. The main entry text should show **Family Disaster Plan**. The subentry text should show **Create a Plan**.
4. Create a second subentry for the Family Disaster Plan section. Select the **Practice Your Plan** heading. The main entry text should show **Family Disaster Plan**. The subentry text should show **Practice Your Plan**.
5. Create a cross-reference in the index. Use **mudslides** for the main entry. Use **landslides** for the cross-reference text.
6. The document already has field entries for three bookmarks. Create an index entry for each of the bookmarks:
   a. Use the main entry **Family Disaster Plan** to create an index for the bookmark **family_disaster_plan**.
   b. Use the main entry **Natural Disasters and Severe Weather** to create an index entry for the bookmark **natural_disasters_severe_weather**.
   c. Use the main entry **Returning Home After a Disaster** to create an index entry for the bookmark **returning_home**.
7. Open the **Disaster Index Entries** file from the drive and folder where your Data Files are stored. Save the document as **Updated Disaster Index Entries**, followed by your initials.
8. Add the following index entries to the list. Be sure to use the capitalization exactly as shown below. When the new entries are completed, save the changes and close the document.

Health Threats	**health threats**
Emergency Supplies	**emergency supplies**
Evacuate	**evacuate**
hazards	**hazards**
Intense Storms and Rainfall	**intense storms and rainfall**
Funnel Cloud	**funnel cloud**
American Red Cross	**American Red Cross**

9. AutoMark the index entries stored in the Updated Disaster Index Entries file.
10. Insert a page break at the end of the document. Type **INDEX** and press Enter. Apply the Heading 1 style to the new heading.
11. Position the insertion point in the blank paragraph after the heading *INDEX*. Toggle off the nonprinting formatting characters, and then generate an indented index using the Modern style.
12. Save the changes and leave the document open for the next project.

PROJECT 15–3

1. If necessary, open the **Revised Natural Disasters 1** file from your solution files. Save the document as **Revised Natural Disasters 2**, followed by your initials. Toggle on the nonprinting formatting characters.
2. Insert a Next Page section break at the beginning of the document. Position the insertion point at the top of the document. Type **Table of Contents** and then press Enter two times.
3. Select the heading and the blank paragraph below the heading. Apply the Normal style, then change the font size to 14 point and apply the bold format. With the text and blank paragraph still selected, use the Line and Paragraph Spacing button to remove the space after the paragraphs.
4. Deselect the text and position the insertion point in the blank paragraph below the new heading. Toggle off nonprinting formatting characters, and then insert a table of contents using the Distinctive style, showing 3 levels. If the table of contents does not fit on one page, click anywhere in the field to select it and then remove the space before the paragraph.
5. Use the Page Number button on the Insert tab to insert a Plain Number 3 style page number at the bottom of the first section in the document, the table of contents page. Then format the page number in the i, ii, iii number format.
6. In the next section of the document that begins with the heading *EMERGENCY PREPAREDNESS*, use the Page Number button to format the page numbers in the second section of the document. Continue to use the Plain Number 3 style, but change the number format to the 1, 2, 3 format. Set the numbers to start at 1. Then format the footer with a different first page setting so that the page number does not appear on the first page in that section.
7. Save the changes and close the document.

PROJECT 15–4

1. Open the **Fohey Case** file from the drive and folder where your Data Files are stored. Save the document as **Fohey Case Summary**, followed by your initials.
2. Locate and mark all occurrences of the following citations in the document. Notice that there are two categories of citations. For the case citations, create a short citation using the italicized text.

   Statute:
   17 U.S.C. § 117(a)(1)

   Cases:
   Universal City Studios, Inc. v. Corley, 273 F.3d 429, 438-39 (2d Cir.2001)
   Aymes v. Bonelli, 47 F.3d 23, 26 (2d Cir. 1995)
3. Insert a page break at the beginning of the document, and then generate a table of authorities on a separate page at the beginning of the document, using the Distinctive style and with the Use passim option enabled.
4. Enter the heading **Table of Authorities** above the table. The heading should be centered with bold and italic formatting.
5. Save and close the document.

CRITICAL THINKING

ACTIVITY 15–1

In this lesson, you used hyperlinks to navigate throughout a document. Do you usually review documents online, or do you prefer to read hard copies of the document? Write a short paragraph explaining your preference for reading documents.

ACTIVITY 15–2

You need to create an index for a five-page document. What do you think would be better—creating the index entries by manually marking them or by AutoMarking the index entries? Write a short paragraph about which feature you would use to create the index entries and explain your reasoning.

Estimated Time: 1.5 hours

LESSON 16

Working with Macros

■ OBJECTIVES

Upon completion of this lesson, you should be able to:

- Create a macro-enabled document.
- Name, store, record, and run a macro.
- Choose a macro security setting.
- Create a document template to store macros.
- Create shortcuts to run macros.
- Edit macros.
- Copy, delete, and rename macro projects.
- Add a digital signature to a macro project.

■ VOCABULARY

code

macro

macro project

VBA (Visual Basic for Applications)

virus

As you work with documents, you most likely perform some repetitive tasks such as creating customized headers and footers or setting page margins and paper sizes. Although Word provides several features to make these tasks easy, you must still perform multiple actions to complete the tasks. In this lesson, you will learn how to turn these multiple actions into a single step.

Understanding Macros

VOCABULARY
macro
code
VBA (Visual Basic for Applications)

A ***macro*** is a group of sequential commands and actions combined as a single command to automatically complete a task. Word provides numerous macros that are ready for you to use. For example, each time you use the building blocks to insert a page number, all the actions to create and format the header or footer are completed automatically. Creating your own macros enables you to automate repetitive tasks, such as inserting the document path and filename in a header or footer pane.

To create a macro, you record a sequence of commands and actions. As you record the macro, the actions are translated into code. ***Code*** is a set of instructions and data for a computer program. The code that Word creates is for ***VBA (Visual Basic for Applications)***, which is a computer programming language and environment designed for use within Office and other Microsoft applications. Developers use VBA to automate processes.

Creating and Storing Macros in a Document

You can store macros in a document or in a template. Storing a macro in a document is quick and convenient, but it does have its limitations. When macros are stored in a document, the macros are only available in that document.

The following scenario helps to explain why you would create a macro for an individual document. You have a Word file that contains contact information for individuals registered to attend a conference. The contact information will later be converted and used in a database. Because commas can cause problems when converting text for the database file, users are asked to avoid using commas when entering the contact information in the Word document. However, the document is frequently updated by multiple users, and sometimes commas are included in the contact information. To save time reviewing the information and repetitively removing commas when necessary, you can create a macro to do this for you.

WARNING

When exiting Word in this lesson, click **Don't Save** when you are prompted to save changes to the global Normal.dotm template.

Creating a Macro-Enabled Document

When you store a macro in a document, the document must be saved in macro-enabled document format, which allows you to run the macro when the document is active. The default format for a Word document has the file extension .docx. The format for a macro-enabled document has the file extension .docm.

Step-by-Step 16.1

1. Open the **Registrations.docx** file from the drive and folder where your Data Files are stored.
2. Click **File** and then click **Save As**. Navigate to the folder where your solution files are stored.

3. In the File name text box, type **Updated Registrations 1**, followed by your initials. Click the **Save as type** box and select **Word Macro-Enabled Document (*.docm)**. Then click **Save**.
4. Click the **File** tab and then click **Options**. In the left pane of the Word Options dialog box, click **Advanced**. Scroll down to the Save section, as shown in **Figure 16–1**.

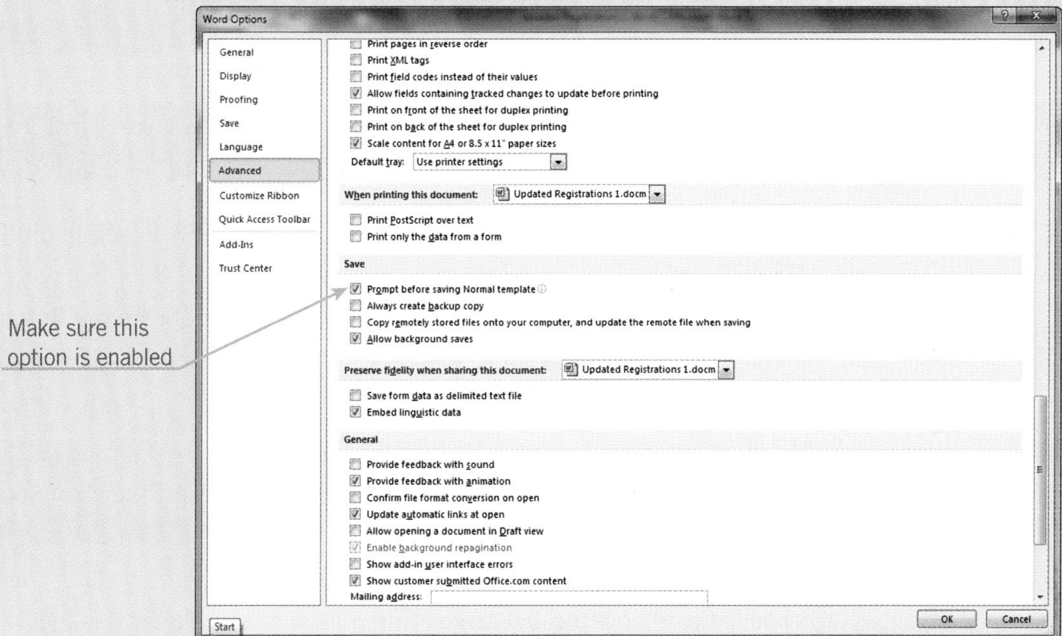

FIGURE 16–1
Advanced options for working with Word

5. If necessary, enable the **Prompt before saving Normal template** option and then click **OK**. Turning on this prompt will prevent you from accidentally saving changes to the Normal template.
6. Leave the document open for the next Step-by-Step.

Naming and Storing a Macro

Before recording the sequence of commands and actions, you must name the macro and assign a location to store it. By default, Word assigns a name to each macro you create, such as *Macro1* and *Macro2*. To help identify the macro, you can create a unique name that describes the task, such as *PersonalFooter* or *table_format*. A macro name must begin with a letter and can contain up to 80 letters and numbers. The name cannot contain spaces or symbols, but you can use the underscore character.

Unless you specify a different location, Word saves macros in the Normal (*.dotm) template. You can save the macro to the normal template, the current document, or a document template.

Recording the Macro Actions

It is important that you plan the actions required to perform the task before you begin recording a macro. You can use the Undo command, but any mistakes and corrections you make as you record will be saved in the macro. You should make every effort to avoid prompts Word might display that require a response from you. For example, if you record an action to close a document, Word may ask you to save the changes to the document. To avoid this prompt, plan to save the document before closing it.

Take your time and concentrate on the steps described in the next Step-by-Step. The recording process does not have a time limit!

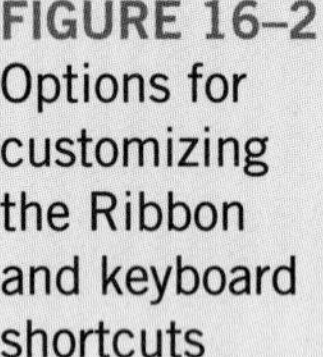

Step-by-Step 16.2

1. If necessary, open the **Updated Registrations 1.docm** file from your solution files.
2. Scroll through the document and identify occurrences of commas in the contact information (for a name, suffix, between the city and state, and before phone extensions). You will create a macro to find and remove these commas.
3. If the Developer tab is displayed on the Ribbon, go to Step 4. If you do not see the Developer tab on the Ribbon, click the **File** tab, click **Options**, and then click **Customize Ribbon**. In the right pane, under Main Tabs, enable the **Developer** option as shown in **Figure 16–2**, and then click **OK**.

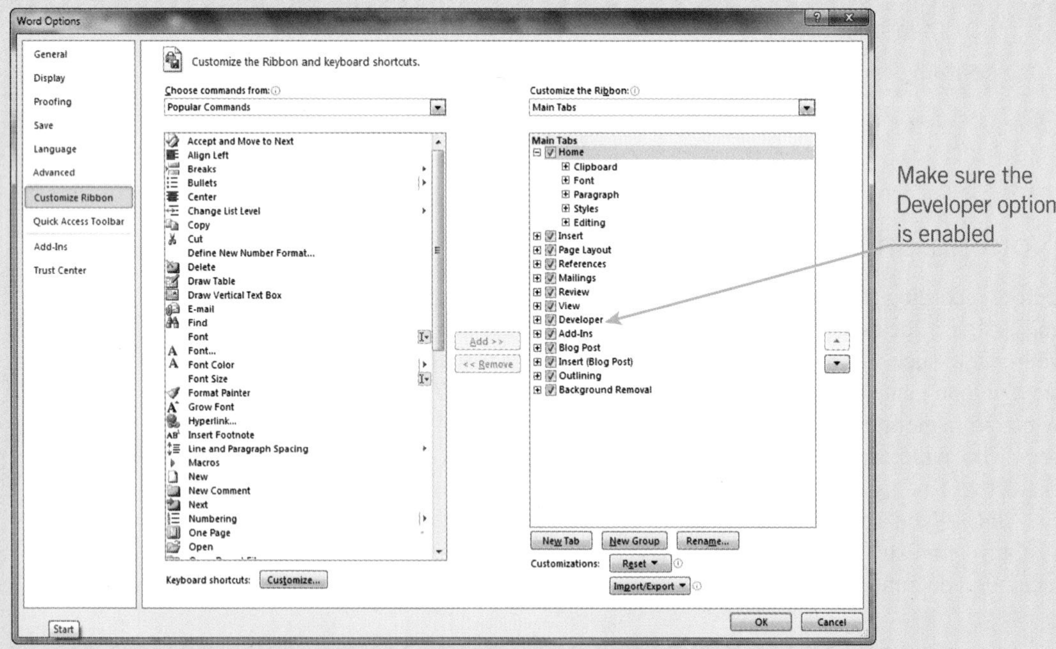

FIGURE 16–2 Options for customizing the Ribbon and keyboard shortcuts

4. Click the **Developer** tab. In the Code group, click the **Record Macro** button to open the Record Macro dialog box, as shown in **Figure 16–3**. Note the Record Macro button in the status bar. You can use this button as an alternative for opening the Record Macro dialog box.

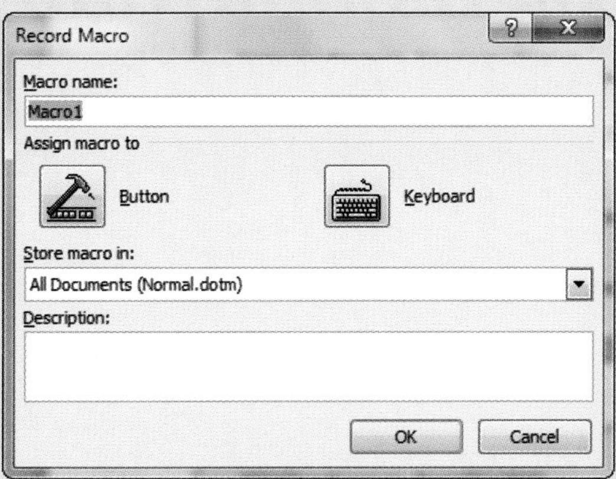

FIGURE 16–3
Record Macro dialog box

5. In the Macro name box, type **NoCommas**.
6. Click the **Store macro in** list arrow, and then select your solution file **Updated Registrations 1.docm (document)**.
7. Under Description, type **Remove commas from contact information.**.
8. Click **OK**. Note that the Stop Recording button appears in the status bar and the mouse pointer changes to a pointer with a cassette tape. On the Developer tab, in the Code group, two new buttons, Stop Recording and Pause Recording, appear. See **Figure 16–4**.

TIP

Remember that from this point on every action is being recorded as part of the macro. Therefore, be sure you understand the instructions before performing each action.

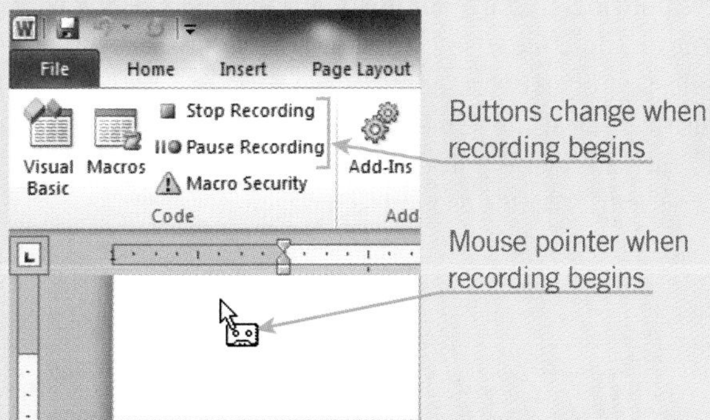

FIGURE 16–4
Code group on the Developer tab during a recording

9. Perform the actions to find and replace all commas:
   a. Press **Ctrl+H** to open the Replace tab in the Find and Replace dialog box.
   b. In the Find what box, type a single comma.
   c. Leave the Replace with box empty.
   d. Click the **More** button. If necessary, under Search Options, change the option in the Search box to **All** to ensure that the macro will always search the entire document.

   e. Click **Replace All**. A prompt appears indicating that eight replacements have been made. Click **OK**.
   f. Close the Find and Replace dialog box.
10. On the Developer tab, in the Code group, click the **Stop Recording** button.
11. Scroll through the document. Note that all commas have been removed from the contact information.
12. Save the changes and leave the document open. If you exit Word and see a prompt to save changes to the global template Normal.dotm, click Don't Save.

Running Macros

VOCABULARY
virus

Sometimes computer viruses are stored in macros. A ***virus*** is a computer program designed to replicate itself, and viruses often cause damage to computer data. Once stored in a macro, the virus can be copied to the Normal.dotm template when the macro is executed. Once copied to the Normal.dotm template, the virus can be attached to all new documents and thereby cause damage to documents and the computer operating system. To counter potential corruption, Word offers several security levels for running macros.

Choosing a Macro Security Setting

When you open a Word template or load an add-in that was already installed with Word, macros within the file are automatically enabled. However, when you run a macro that you or someone else created, you should apply Word's macro security settings. Unless your network administrator enforces a security level, you can change the security level at any time. But before you choose a security level, you must understand the implications for each level. **Table 16–1** describes Word's four options for macro security levels as well as a developer setting.

TABLE 16–1 Macro security settings

MACRO SETTINGS	DESCRIPTION
Disable all macros without notification	All macros are disabled and will not function.
Disable all macros with notification	This is the default setting. A warning is displayed whenever Word encounters a macro from a source that is not on your list of trusted sources, allowing you to choose whether or not to enable the macro.
Disable all macros except digitally signed macros	Only macros that are digitally signed can be executed. If you have already trusted the source, a digitally signed macro will be executed without notification. If you have not trusted the source, you will be notified and you can choose to enable the macro and/or add the publisher as a trusted source. If the macro is not digitally signed, however, the macro is disabled without notification.
Enable all macros (not recommended; potentially dangerous code can run)	All macros run without any notification.
Trust access to the VBA project object model	Created for developers, this setting provides security by limiting access to code that is written for a VBA (Visual Basic for Applications) environment and object model.

You can also choose security settings to automatically enable macros stored in specific folders and documents or from designated publishers.

NET BUSINESS

The first widespread macro virus was Melissa. On March 26, 1999, the macro Melissa traveled to numerous computers through a Microsoft Word document attached to an e-mail message. When the receiver of the e-mail message opened the Word document, the macro was triggered. Melissa then accessed the victim's e-mail address book and sent copies of the e-mail to fifty entries in the address book. The virus spread quickly around the world. Microsoft and anti-virus computer security companies responded quickly, issuing warnings and supplying fixes to counteract the virus and minimize the impact. Despite all efforts, many corporate and government e-mail gateways were overloaded and forced to shut down because of the massive volume of e-mails. Within a week after the virus was exposed, a suspected virus writer was arrested. Melissa raised the awareness that safeguards must be in place when sharing documents. Security settings in current Microsoft Office software versions provide strong protection against macro viruses.

Step-by-Step 16.3

1. If necessary, open the **Updated Registrations 1.docm** file from your solution files.
2. Click the **File** tab and then click **Options**. In the left pane of the Word Options dialog box, click **Trust Center** to open security options. In the right pane, click **Trust Center Settings**. If necessary, click **Macro Settings** to display the options, as shown in **Figure 16–5**.

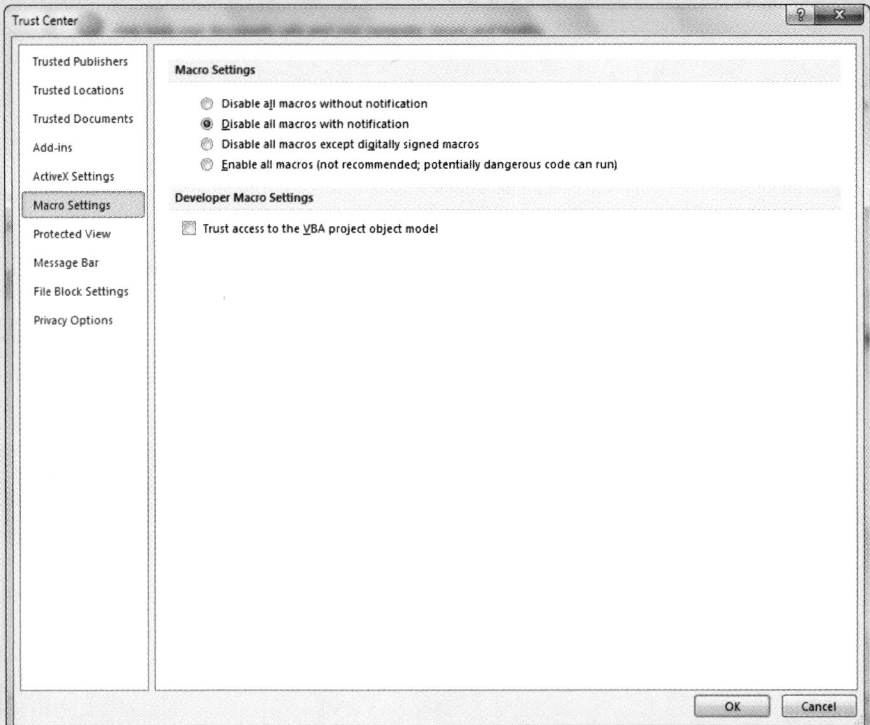

FIGURE 16–5
Trust Center Macro Settings

3. Make a note of the current security setting so you can reset the option to the original setting at the end of the lesson (in Step-by-Step 16.12).
4. If necessary, enable the **Disable all macros with notification** option.
5. In the left pane, click **Trusted Locations** to display the options, as shown in **Figure 16–6**.

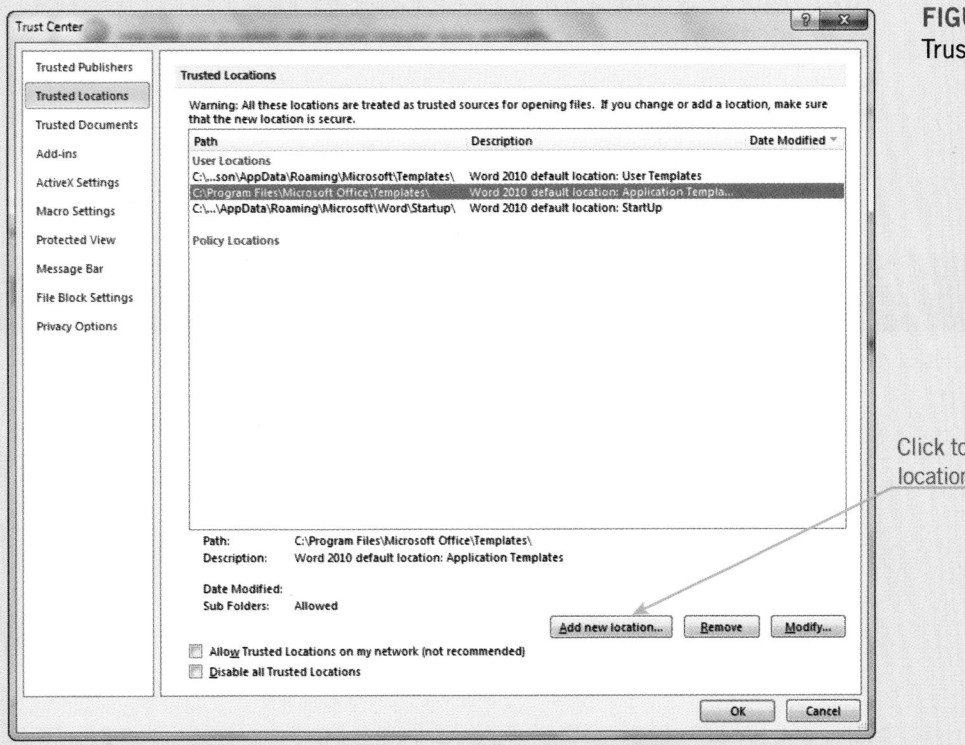

FIGURE 16–6
Trust Center Trusted Locations

6. In the lower-right corner, click **Add new location** to open the Microsoft Office Trusted Location dialog box, as shown in **Figure 16–7**. Your settings will differ.

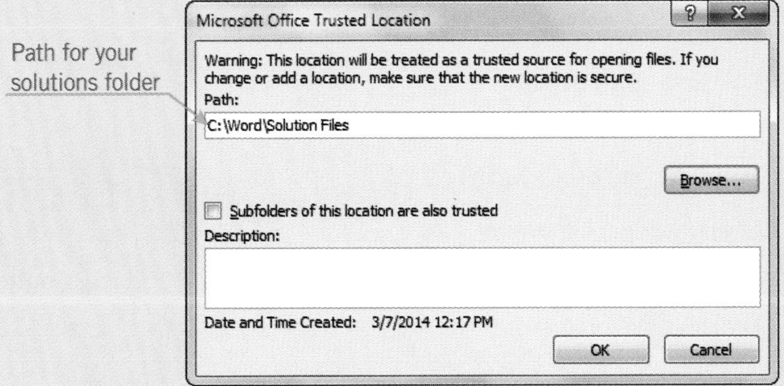

FIGURE 16–7
Microsoft Office Trusted Location dialog box

7. Click **Browse**. Navigate to the folder where you save your solution files. Click **OK** to close the Browse dialog box.
8. The path for your solution files folder should appear in the Path text box. Click **OK** three times to close the dialog boxes.
9. Leave the document open for the next Step-by-Step. If you exit Word and see a prompt to save changes to the global template Normal.dotm, click Don't Save.

WARNING

If you are ending your Word session now, or any time before you complete the remaining Step-by-Steps in this lesson, you must restore all the settings you changed. Go to Step-by-Step 16.12 and complete all seven steps to restore the changed settings.

Running a Macro

You can run your macro by opening the Macros dialog box. (Later in the lesson, you will use shortcuts to run macros.) Before applying the macro, be sure to select the appropriate text or reposition the insertion point. For example, if the macro actions involve inserting a graphic, be sure the insertion point is positioned in the correct location.

Step-by-Step 16.4

1. If necessary, open the **Updated Registrations 1.docm** file from your solution files. Save the document as **Updated Registrations 2**, followed by your initials. Make sure the file is saved with the extension .docm.
2. If you are beginning a new Word session, click the File tab, then click Options. In the left pane, click Trust Center, and then click Trust Center Settings. For Macro Settings, make sure the option Disable all macros with notification is enabled. Make sure your solutions folder is included in the Trusted Locations list.
3. Navigate to page 2. In the first blank form, add the following contact information for a new conference registration. Use the Tab key to navigate through the form. Include the commas so you can later test the macro to remove the commas.

   Maria Sanchez

   TechKnow

   541 East 29th Street

   Oklahoma City, OK 73129

   405-555-3114, ext. 4041

   msanchez@techknow.xyz
4. On the Developer tab, in the Code group, click the **Macros** button to open the Macros dialog box, as shown in **Figure 16–8**.

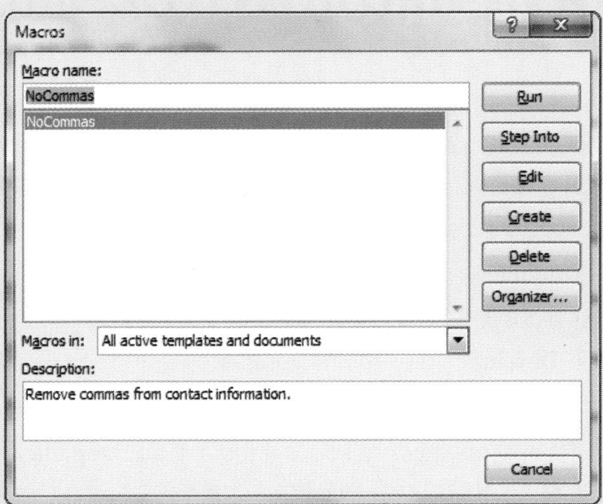

FIGURE 16–8
Macros dialog box

5. Under Macro name, only macros in all active templates and documents appear. If necessary, select **NoCommas**. Then click **Run**.
6. Note that the two commas (after Oklahoma City and before the phone extension) have been removed from the new contact information you just added.
7. Save the changes and close the document.

TIP

If your macro did not run correctly, go back to Step-by-Step 16.2 and repeat Steps 4–10 to re-create the macro using the same name. Answer Yes when prompted to replace the existing macro.

Creating a Document Template to Store Macros

If you want the macros that you create to be available for other documents, you should store the macros in the Normal.dotm template or in a document template. When stored in the Normal.dotm template, the macros are available to all users of the computer for all documents and at any time. When macros are stored in a document template, they are available only when the document template is global or is attached to a document. The advantage to storing macros in a document template is that you can copy the document template, share macros with others, and use the macros on other computers.

You can only attach one template to a document. As you work with a Word document, you may want to access additional macros that are available in other templates. If you make those other templates global, you can access macros available in the global templates as well as those in the attached template. Templates marked as global using the Templates and Add-ins dialog box remain global until you exit Word. When you launch Word again, the templates that were previously global will appear in the list of templates in the Templates and Add-ins dialog box, but they will not be marked as global. To make the templates in this list global again, you must check the box next to the template name.

Because you may share a classroom computer with others, you will store the macros that you create in this lesson in a document template. You already created a personal document template in Lesson 10, but it is not macro-enabled, so you cannot store macros in that template. The new personal document template you create in the next Step-by-Step will be saved in a macro-enabled format.

WARNING

To successfully complete the remaining Step-by-Steps and Projects, you must make sure the template and security settings are set correctly, so read the steps thoroughly and work through them diligently.

Step-by-Step 16.5

1. Open a new blank document. If you are beginning a new Word session, click the File tab, and then click Options. In the left pane, click Trust Center, and then click Trust Center Settings. For Macro Settings, make sure the option Disable all macros with notification is enabled. Click Trusted Locations and make sure your solutions folder is included in the Trusted Locations list. Close all dialog boxes.
2. Click the **Developer** tab. In the Templates group, click the **Document Template** button to open the Templates and Add-ins dialog box.
3. Under Global templates, select and remove all templates listed. When all global templates are removed from the list, click **OK**.
4. Click the **File** tab and then click **Save As** to open the Save As dialog box. Navigate to the folder where your solution files are stored.
5. In the File name box, type **Personal Template 2**, followed by your initials.
6. In the Save as type box, select **Word Macro-Enabled Template (*.dotm)**. Click **Save**. Your personal template contains all the macros provided in the Normal.dotm template, and you can add your own macros to the template.
7. Close the Personal Template 2 document template.
8. Open the **Updated Registrations 2.docm** file from your solution files, and save it as **Updated Registrations 3**, followed by your initials. Make sure the file is saved with the extension .docm.
9. Click the **Developer** tab. In the Templates group, click the **Document Template** button to open the Templates and Add-ins dialog box, as shown in **Figure 16–9**. Your settings may differ.

FIGURE 16–9
Templates and Add-ins dialog box

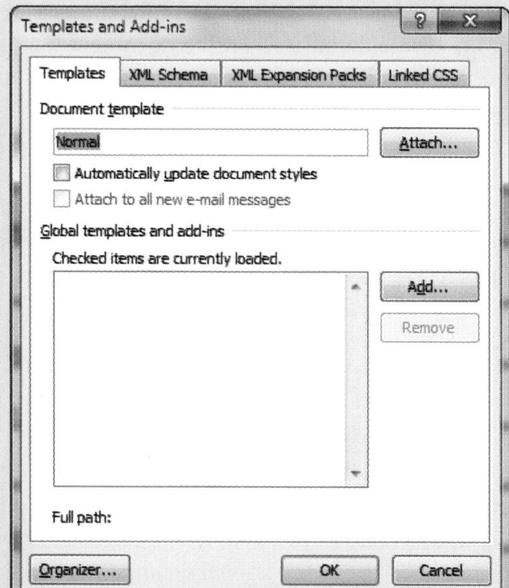

10. Click **Attach** and then navigate to the folder where you save your solution files. Select your **Personal Template 2** document template, and then click **Open**.
11. Under Checked items, click **Add**. Navigate to and select your **Personal Template 2** document template, and then click **OK**. Click **OK** to close the Templates and Add-ins dialog box. Your Personal Template 2 document will be global during this Word session.
12. Save the changes and close the document.

EXTRA FOR EXPERTS

If you don't attach your personal template to a document, you will still have access to the macros if the template is global. The advantage of attaching the template is that you know the macros will be available when you reopen the document in the future.

Creating and Deleting Macro Shortcuts

You have the option to assign a keyboard shortcut or a button to a macro. You cannot assign a shortcut key combination and a button at the same time, but you can create a second shortcut after the macro is recorded, which you will learn how to do in Step-by-Step 16.8. If you no longer use a macro, you can delete the shortcut.

EXTRA FOR EXPERTS

To print a list of the key assignments saved in a document or template, open the document or template. Click the File tab, click Print, and then under Settings, click the first list arrow (usually shows Print All Pages). Under Document Properties, select Key Assignments and then click Print.

Creating a Macro with a Keyboard Shortcut

When you create a keyboard shortcut, you must choose a key combination that is not already assigned to other commands or functions. If the key combination is already assigned to another command or function, Word will display a message indicating that those keys have already been assigned.

Step-by-Step 16.6

1. Open the **Personal Template 2.dotm** document template from your solution files.
2. If you are beginning a new Word session, click the File tab, and then click Options. In the left pane, click Trust Center, and then click Trust Center Settings. For Macro Settings, make sure the option Disable all macros with notification is enabled. Make sure your solutions folder is included in the Trusted Locations list.
3. Click the **Developer** tab. Create a new macro:
    a. In the Code group, click the **Record Macro** button.
    b. In the Macro name text box, type **Path_Filename_Header**.
    c. Click the **Store macro in** list arrow, and then select **Documents Based On Personal Template 2.dotm**.
    d. In the Description text box, type **Insert path and filename in a header.**.

TIP

If an error message appears indicating that the macro could not be created, close the template and save any changes, if prompted. Reopen the template file, and continue.

4. Assign a keyboard shortcut to the macro:
   a. Under Assign macro to, click the **Keyboard** icon. The Customize Keyboard dialog box opens, as shown in **Figure 16–10**.

FIGURE 16–10
Customize Keyboard dialog box

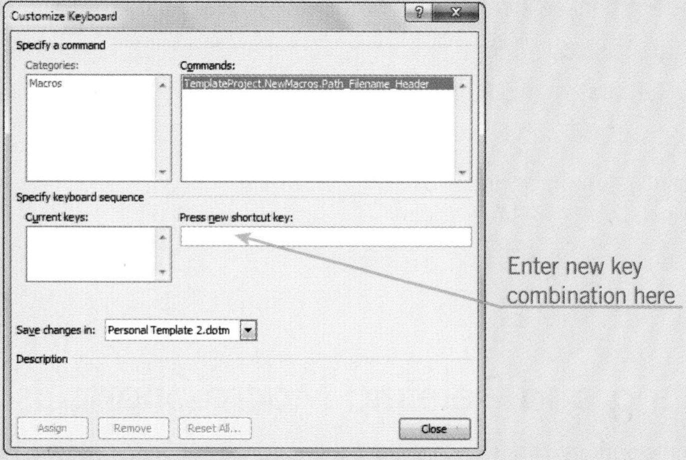

   b. The insertion point is positioned in the Press new shortcut key box. Press and hold the **Alt** key and then press the number **9**. (If Word tells you that the Alt+9 key combination is already assigned, choose another similar combination.)
   c. If necessary, click the **Save changes in** list arrow and then select your Personal Template 2.dotm document template.
   d. Click **Assign** and then click **Close**.
5. Perform the actions to insert the path and filename in a header:
   a. Click the **Insert** tab. In the Header & Footer group, click the **Header** button. At the bottom of the menu, click **Edit Header**. The insertion point moves to the header pane.
   b. On the Header & Footer Tools Design tab, in the Insert group, click the **Quick Parts** button and then click **Field** to open the Field dialog box, as shown in **Figure 16–11**.

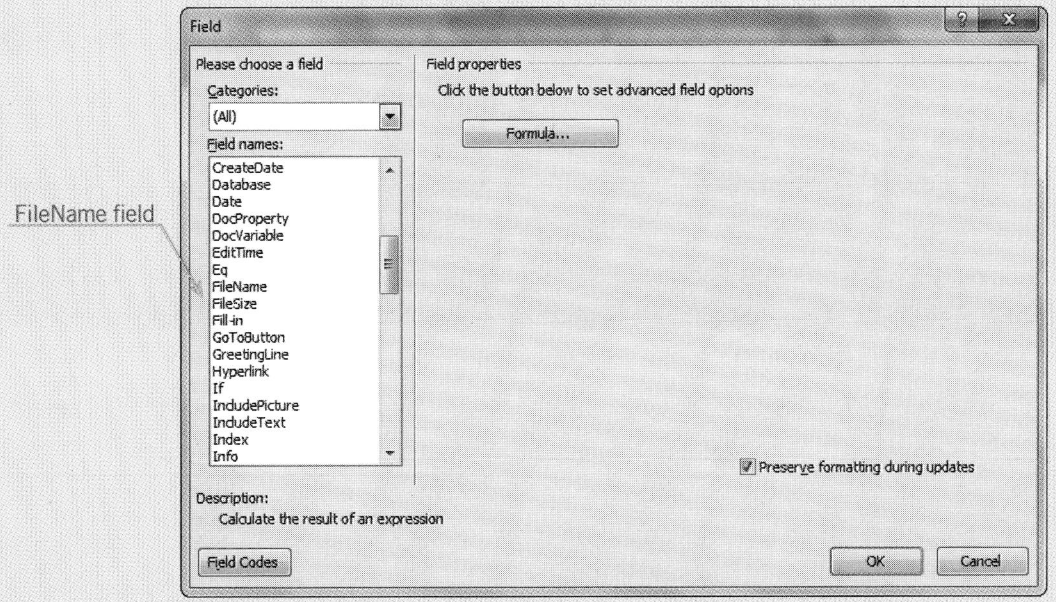

FIGURE 16–11
Field dialog box

c. Under Field names, scroll down and select **FileName**. The dialog box adapts to show more options. In the center pane, under Format, select **Lowercase**. In the pane on the right, under Field options, enable the **Add path to filename** option. Then click **OK**.

d. In the Close group, click the **Close Header and Footer** button.

6. Click the **Developer** tab. In the Code group, click the **Stop Recording** button.
7. Close the document template. When prompted to save changes, click **Save**.
8. Open the **Updated Registrations 3.docm** file from your solution files.
9. Press and hold **Alt** and press **9**. The new header, showing the path and filename, is inserted in the header pane and appears on all three pages of the document.
10. Save the changes and close the document.

Creating a Macro with a Button Shortcut

When you create a button shortcut for a macro, the new button is added to the Quick Access Toolbar.

When recording a macro, you can use the mouse to choose commands and click buttons, but you cannot record mouse movements within the document window. For example, you cannot click the mouse to position an insertion point or drag to select text. Instead, you must use keystrokes to complete these actions. So when planning the steps for the macro you should also consider the keyboard shortcuts you can use to navigate through the document. If you are interrupted during the recording process, you can temporarily stop recording and then resume recording at a later time.

Step-by-Step 16.7

1. Open your **Personal Template 2.dotm** document template from your solution files.
2. If you are beginning a new Word session, click the File tab, and then click Options. In the left pane, click Trust Center, and then click Trust Center Settings. For Macro Settings, make sure the option Disable all macros with notification is enabled. Make sure your solutions folder is included in the Trusted Locations list.
3. Click the **Developer** tab, and in the Templates group, click the **Document Template** button to open the Templates and Add-ins dialog box. Under Global templates and add-ins, Personal Template 2 should be in the list with a check mark. Do one of the following:
    a. If the Personal Template 2 is in the list and checked, close the Templates and Add-ins dialog box and then go to Step 4.
    b. If the Personal Template 2 template is in the list but it is not checked, select the check box to make the template global. Click **OK**. Save and close the document template. Then reopen the document template and confirm that the Personal Template 2 template is global. Close the Templates and Add-ins dialog box and leave the Personal Template 2 document template open.
    c. If the template does not appear in the list, click **Add**, navigate to your solutions folder, select **Personal Template 2**, and click **OK**. Make sure the Personal Template 2 is checked. Click **OK**. Save and close the document template. Reopen the document template and confirm that the Personal Template 2 template is global. Close the Templates and Add-ins dialog box and leave the Personal Template 2 document template open.
4. Create a new macro:
    a. In the Code group, click the **Record Macro** button.
    b. In the Macro name text box, type **LegalFormat**.
    c. Click the **Store macro in** list arrow and select **Documents Based On Personal Template 2.dotm**.
    d. In the Description text box, type **Margin and paper size formats for legal documents.**.
    e. Under Assign macro to, click the **Button** icon to open the Word Options for customizing the Quick Access Toolbar, as shown in **Figure 16–12**. Your settings may differ.

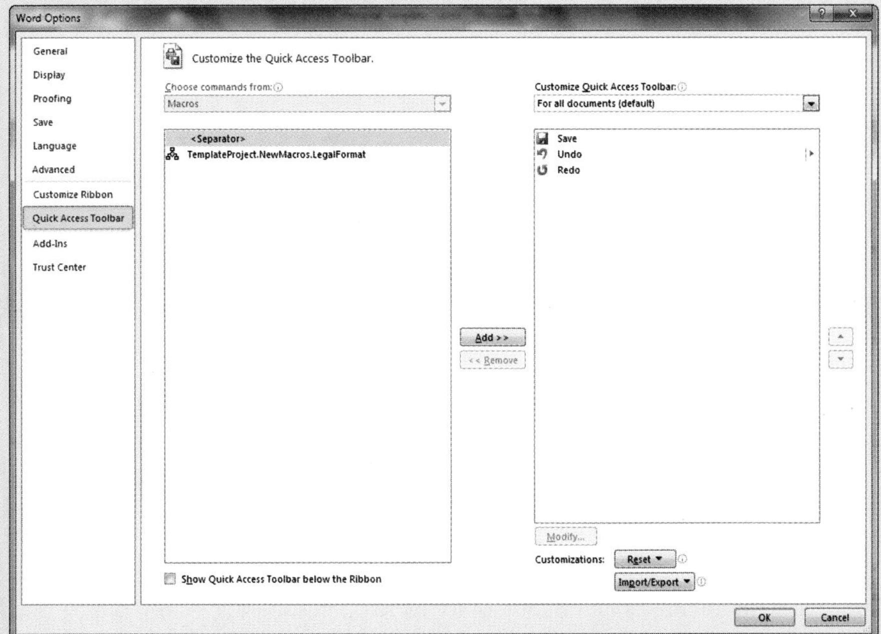

FIGURE 16–12
Options for customizing the Quick Access Toolbar

   f. In the left pane, select the macro name **TemplateProject.NewMacros.LegalFormat**. Click **Add** to add the new button to the Quick Access Toolbar. Click **OK** to close the dialog box.

5. Note that a new button appears on your Quick Access Toolbar. Position the mouse pointer over the button to display the ScreenTip.
6. Record the following steps to format margins and paper size:
   a. Press and hold the **Ctrl** key and then press **Home** to make sure the insertion point is positioned at the top of the document.
   b. Click the **Page Layout** tab. In the Page Setup group, click the **Size** button and then click **Legal 8.5" × 14"**.
   c. In the Page Setup group, click the **Margins** button. At the bottom of the menu, click **Custom Margins** to open the Page Setup dialog box.
   d. On the Margins tab, under Margins, set the margins as follows: top: **2"**; bottom: **1"**; left: **1.5"**; and right: **0.75"**.
   e. Click **OK.**
7. Click the **Developer** tab. In the Code group, click the **Pause Recording** button. At this point you can open new documents, scroll through the active document, or just take a break before continuing to record actions for the macro.
8. In the Code group, click the **Resume Recorder** button to continue recording.

9. Record the following steps to create a section break and change the margin settings in the new section:
   a. Press and hold the **Ctrl** key and then press **G**. Under Enter page number, type **2** and then click **Go To** to move to the top of the second page in the document. (However, the insertion point does not move because there is no second page in this document template.) In the Find and Replace dialog box, click **Close**.
   b. Click the **Page Layout** tab. In the Page Setup group, click the **Breaks** button. Under Section Breaks, click **Continuous**.
   c. Press and hold the **Ctrl** key and then press the **down arrow** to move the insertion point down one paragraph to ensure that you are in the second section of the document. (The insertion point does not move in this document.)
   d. In the Page Setup group, click the **Margins** button. At the bottom of the menu, click **Custom Margins** to open the Page Setup dialog box.
   e. On the Margins tab, under Margins, change the top margin to **1.5"**. The other margin settings should be okay as is: bottom: 1"; left: 1.5"; and right: .75".
   f. At the bottom of the dialog box, under Preview, make sure the Apply to setting shows **This section**. Then click **OK**.
   g. Click the **Developer** tab. In the Code group, click the **Stop Recording** button.
10. Close the document template. When prompted to save the changes, click **Save**.
11. Open the **Investment Club.docx** file from the drive and folder where your Data Files are stored. Save the document as **Investment Club Agreement 1**, followed by your initials. Make sure the file is saved with the extension .docx.
12. On the Quick Access Toolbar, click the **TemplateProject.NewMacros.LegalFormat** button. Because your Personal Template 2 document template is global, the macro is available.
13. Scroll through the document and make sure the margin settings for the first page and all subsequent pages look accurate. The first page should have a top margin of 2" and all remaining pages in the document should have a top margin of 1.5".
14. Save the changes and close the document.

WARNING

If you are ending your Word session now, or any time before you complete the remaining Step-by-Steps in this lesson, you must restore all the settings you changed. Go to Step-by-Step 16.12 and complete all seven steps to restore the changed settings.

Creating and Deleting Shortcuts for Existing Macros

Perhaps when you created a macro you did not create a shortcut, or maybe you created a keyboard shortcut and now you want to create a button for the macro. You can easily create shortcuts for existing macros, and you can customize the button icons.

Step-by-Step 16.8

1. Open your **Personal Template 2.dotm** document template.
2. Click the **File** tab, then click **Options**. In the left pane, click **Quick Access Toolbar**. Under Choose commands from, click the **list arrow** and then click **Macros**. A list of all macros appears.
3. Click the **TemplateProject.NewMacros.Path_Filename_Header** macro, and then click **Add**. A new button appears on the Quick Access Toolbar.
4. At the bottom of the right pane, click **Modify** to open the Modify Button dialog box, as shown in **Figure 16–13**.

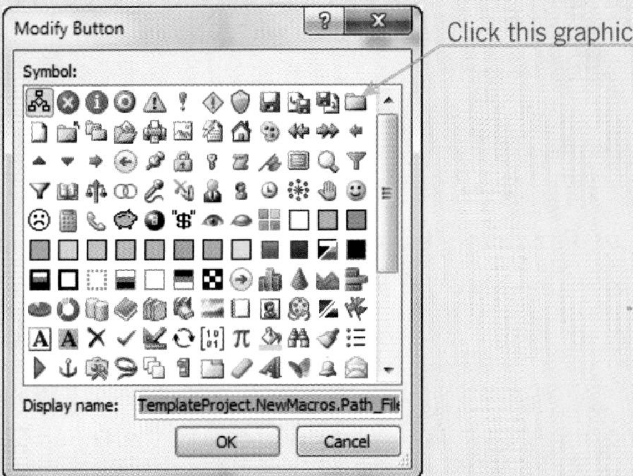

FIGURE 16–13
Modify Button dialog box

5. Click the last button in the first row to select the folder icon for the button, and then click **OK**. Note that the button for the Quick Access Toolbar is updated in the dialog box.
6. In the left pane, click **Customize Ribbon**. Below the center pane, next to Keyboard shortcuts, click **Customize** to open the Customize Keyboard dialog box.

7. Under Categories, scroll to the bottom of the list and select **Macros.** The dialog box options change and the available macros are displayed. Under Macros, select the **Path_Filename_Header** macro to show the dialog box shown in **Figure 16–14**. The keys already assigned appear in the Current keys list. Your settings may differ.

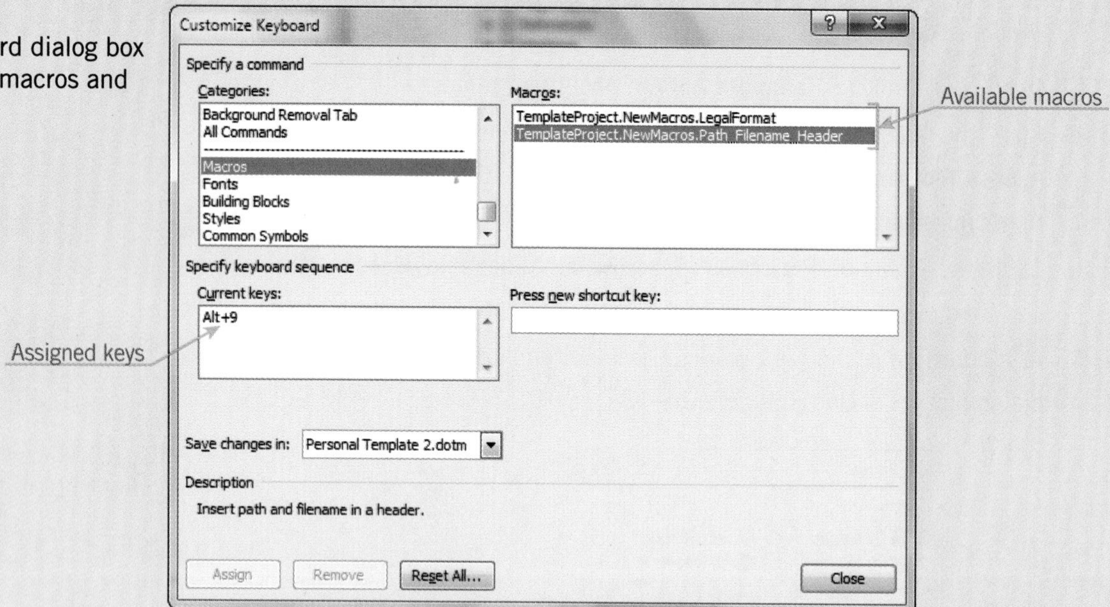

FIGURE 16–14
Customize Keyboard dialog box showing available macros and assigned keys

8. Click in the **Press new shortcut key** box. Press and hold the **Alt** key and then press the number **6**. (If Word tells you that the Alt+6 key combination is already assigned, choose another similar combination.)
9. Make sure the Save changes in setting shows your **Personal Template 2.dotm** document template. Click **Assign** and then click **Close**. Click **OK** to close the Word Options dialog box.
10. Right-click the **TemplateProject.NewMacros.LegalFormat** button on the Quick Access Toolbar, then click **Remove from Quick Access Toolbar**.
11. Click the **File** tab and then click **Options.** In the left pane, click **Customize Ribbon**. At the bottom, next to Keyboard shortcuts, click **Customize** to open the Customize Keyboard dialog box. Under Categories, scroll down and click **Macros**, and then, under Macros, click the **Path_Filename_Header** macro.
12. Under Specify keyboard sequence, in the Current keys box, select **Alt+6.** At the bottom of the dialog box, click **Remove.**
13. Close the dialog box and click **OK** to close the Word Options dialog box.
14. Save the changes and close the document template.

Editing Macros

Generally the easiest way to change a macro is to record it again. When you create a new macro using an existing macro name, Word will prompt you to replace the existing macro with the new recording. However, if the macro is complex and the changes you want to make are minor (such as changing one margin setting or changing the macro name), you should consider editing the macro code. Each instruction you recorded in the macro appears in Visual Basic code.

You can edit the code in the Visual Basic Editor (VBE) window. Even if you're not familiar with VBA code, you will most likely recognize some of the code information and be able to edit some parts of the code. The first line of a macro code begins with the word *Sub*, which is then followed by the name of the macro. If you included a description when you created the macro, the description appears below the Sub line. The last line of the macro code shows *End Sub*.

TIP

You can use the VBA Help feature to learn more about the code information.

Step-by-Step 16.9

1. Open your **Personal Template 2.dotm** document template.
2. If you are beginning a new Word session, click the File tab, click Options, click Trust Center, and then click Trust Center Settings. For Macro Settings, make sure the option Disable all macros with notification is enabled. Make sure your solutions folder is included in the Trusted Locations list.
3. Click the **Developer** tab, and in the Code group, click the **Macros** button to open the Macros dialog box, as shown in **Figure 16–15**. Even though you deleted the new button from the Quick Access Toolbar, the LegalFormat macro is still stored in your personal template.

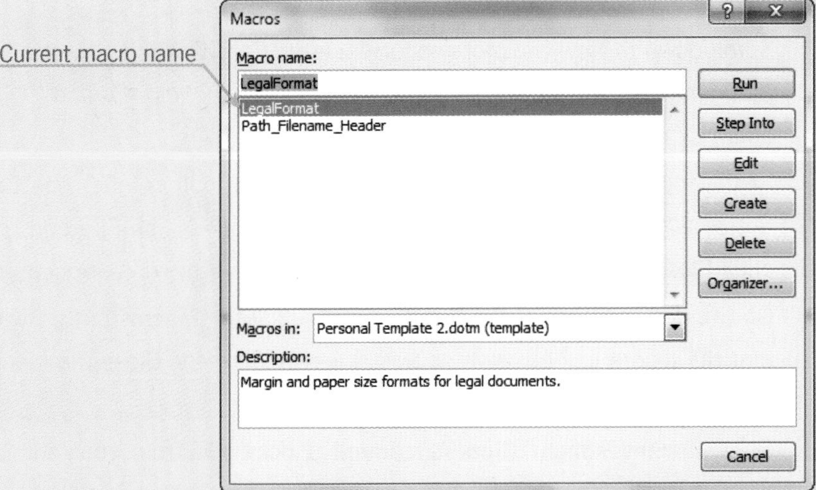

FIGURE 16–15
Macros dialog box

4. Under Macros, if necessary, select **LegalFormat**. Click **Edit**. The VBA window and the Visual Basic Editor (VBE) open, as shown in **Figure 16–16**. The code in your Visual Basic Editor window may be a little different.

FIGURE 16–16
Microsoft Visual Basic Editor in the VBA window

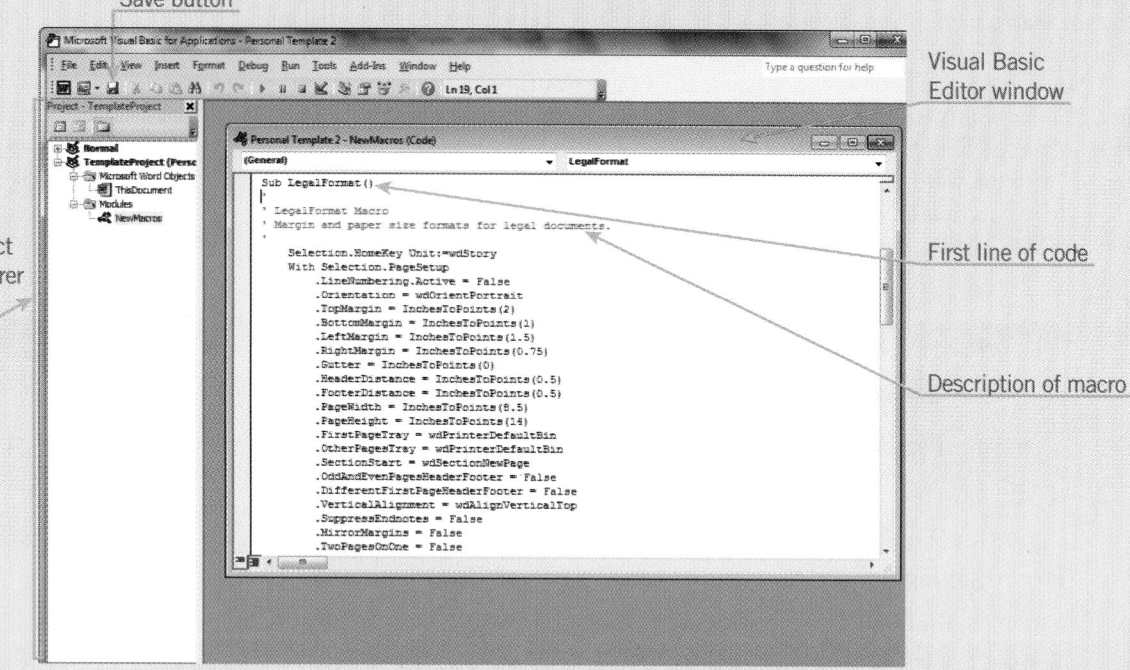

> **TIP**
>
> If an error message appears indicating that the project is unviewable, close the VBA application, close the template file, and then close Word. Relaunch Word, open the template file, open the VBA application again, and then select the template name in the Project Explorer pane.

5. At the top of the Visual Basics Editor window, rename the macro by changing the first line of code. Edit the line so it reads **Sub Legal_Formats ()**.
6. Scroll down to the second occurrence of *End With*. Seven lines below that point, in the line reading *RightMargin = InchesToPoints (0.75)*, change the 0.75 to **1**.
7. Scroll down to view two more occurrences of *End With*. Nine lines below that point, in the line reading *RightMargin = InchesToPoints (0.75)*, change the 0.75 to **1**.
8. At the top of the window, on the VBA standard toolbar, click the **Save** button to save the changes to the macro code. Click **File** and then click **Close and Return to Microsoft Word** to close the VBA application.
9. On the Developer tab, in the Code group, click the **Macros** button. Note that the macro name is now shown as *Legal_Formats*. Close the Macros dialog box, and then close the document template.
10. Open the **Investment Club Agreement 1.docx** file from your solution files. Save the document as **Investment Club Agreement 2**, followed by your initials. Make sure the file is saved with the extension .docx.
11. Click the **Developer** tab. In the Templates group, click the **Document Template** button, click **Attach**, navigate to and select your **Personal Template 2** document template, click **Open**, and then click **OK**.

12. In the Code group, click the **Macros** button. *Legal_Formats* should already be selected. Click **Run**.
13. Scroll through the document to confirm that the right margin on all pages is adjusted to 1".
14. Save the changes and close the document.

Copying, Deleting, and Renaming Macro Projects

When macros are stored in a document or in a template, they are stored as a collection in a ***macro project***. The default name for the macro project is *NewMacros*. You can rename a macro project, which helps you keep your macros organized.

To make the macros available to other documents and other users, you can copy a macro project to the Normal (default) template or to another document template. Options in the Organizer dialog box enable you to copy, delete, and rename only projects. You cannot copy or rename individual macros using the Organizer options. When you no longer want to use a macro, you can open the Macros dialog box and remove the macro from the macro project.

VOCABULARY
macro project

Step-by-Step 16.10

1. Open the **Personal Template 2.dotm** document template from your solution files.
2. Click the **Developer** tab. In the Code group, click the **Macros** button to open the Macros dialog box.
3. Click **Organizer**, and if necessary, click the **Macro Project Items** tab to open the Organizer dialog box, as shown in **Figure 16–17**.

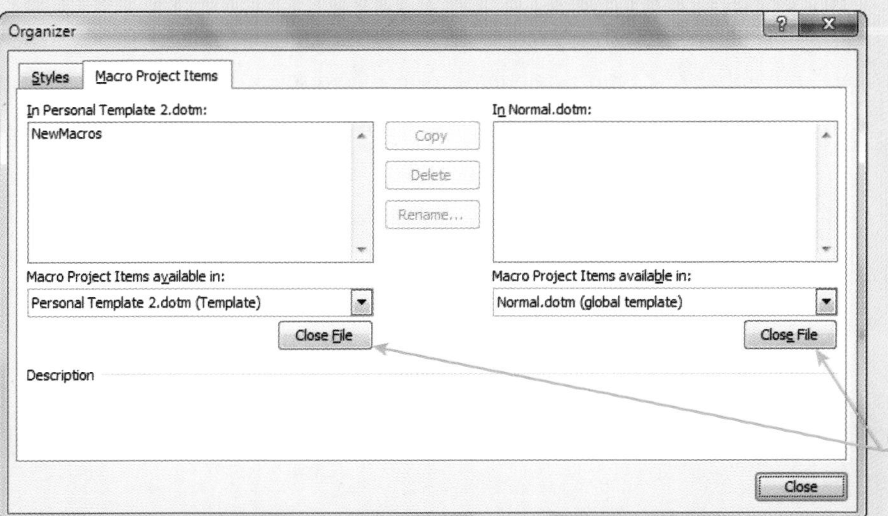

FIGURE 16–17
Organizer dialog box

4. In the left pane, the NewMacros project group in your Personal Template 2 document template appears. Select **NewMacros**.
5. To rename the project group, click **Rename**. In the Rename dialog box, type **Lesson16** and then click **OK**.
6. In the left pane, under Macro Project Items available in, click **Close File**. Then click **Open File** and navigate to the folder where your solution files are stored.
7. In the lower-right corner of the Open dialog box, click the **File type** box and select **All Files (*.*)**. Select **Updated Registrations 3.docm** and then click **Open**. The left pane changes to show the NewMacros project group in the Updated Registrations 3.docm macro-enabled document.
8. In the pane on the right, under Macro Project Items available in, click **Close File**. Then click **Open File** and navigate to the folder where your solution files are stored. Select your **Personal Template 2.dotm** document template and then click **Open**.
9. In the left pane, *NewMacros* should already be selected. Click **Copy**. The NewMacros group is copied to the document template. Close the Organizer dialog box.
10. On the Developer tab, in the Code group, click the **Macros** button. Notice that the NoCommas macro is now available in the document template.
11. Close the Macros dialog box. Save the changes to the document template.
12. Open the **Updated Registrations 3.docm** document from your solution files. Save the document as **Updated Registrations 4**, followed by your initials. Make sure the file is saved with the extension .docm.
13. Click the **Developer** tab. In the Code group, click the **Macros** button. Select the macro **Project.NewMacros.NoCommas** and then click **Delete**. When prompted to confirm deletion of the macro, click **Yes**. The macro is no longer stored in the document, but as you can see, the macro is still stored in the document template as TemplateProject.NewMacros.NoCommas.
14. Close the Macros dialog box. Save the changes and close the document. Close the Personal Template 2 document template, and leave Word open for the next Step-by-Step.

Signing a Macro Project

If you plan to share your macros with others, signing the macro project by adding a digital signature will enable users who run the macro to identify its creator and be assured that the macro has not been altered. Earlier in this lesson, Table 16–1 provided descriptions for several macro security settings. Depending on the security settings, users may not be able to open a document with macros unless the macro project or template is signed.

Signing a macro template or project is similar to signing a Word document. You can use the digital signature you created in Lesson 13. If the valid digital certificate is on your computer, the project is re-signed when you make changes to the macro code. However, if another user edits the code after the project is signed, the digital signature becomes invalid.

Step-by-Step 16.11

1. To view the digital signatures on your computer:
   a. Launch Internet Explorer.
   b. Click the **Tools** button and then click **Internet Options**.
   c. In the Internet Options dialog box, click the **Content** tab. Under Certificates, click **Certificates**. A list of digital signatures available on your computer appears. Check to see if the digital signature you created in Lesson 13 is in the list.
   d. Close both dialog boxes and then close Internet Explorer.
   e. If your personal signature was not in the list, go to Step 2. If your personal signature was in the list, go to Step 3.
2. To create a new digital certificate:
   a. On the taskbar, click the **Start** button, click **All Programs**, click **Microsoft Office**, click **Microsoft Office 2010 Tools**, and then click **Digital Certificate for VBA Projects**.
   b. In the Create Digital Certificate dialog box, in the Your certificate's name box, enter your first and last names.
   c. Click **OK** twice to close the dialog boxes.
3. Attach a digital signature to your document template:
   a. Open the **Personal Template 2** file from your solution files.
   b. Click the **Developer** tab. In the Code group, click the **Visual Basic** button. If you do not see the Project Explorer pane (as shown in Figure 16–16) with the heading *Project – TemplateProject*, click **View** and then click **Project Explorer**.

c. In the Project Explorer pane, select **TemplateProject (Personal Template 2)**. Click **Tools** and then click **Digital Signature** to open the Digital Signature dialog box, as shown in **Figure 16–18**.

FIGURE 16–18
Digital Signature dialog box

d. If your digital signature does not appear under Sign as, click **Choose**. In the Windows Security dialog box, select your certificate and then click **OK**.

e. Your digital signature should now appear below Sign as. Click **OK** to close the Digital Signature box.

f. Click the **Save** button on the toolbar at the top of the application window, then close the VBA application and return to the Word document.

4. Close the Personal Template 2 document template.

Restoring Settings

Even if you don't share your computer with others, it's good practice to review the settings you have customized before ending a Word session. For example, if you don't want the changes to affect future documents, it is easier to restore the original settings before exiting Word. That way you don't need to remember to change the settings when you start a new Word session. In this lesson, you made changes to the security settings and global templates. The following steps will help you restore those settings before you end a Word session.

Step-by-Step 16.12

1. Click the **File** tab and then click **Options**. In the left pane, click **Trust Center**. Click **Trust Center Settings**.
2. Click **Macro Settings**, and if necessary, reset the default setting to the original setting noted in Step-by-Step 16.3, Step 3.
3. Click **Trusted Locations**, and if necessary, remove your solutions folder from the list. Click **OK** twice to close the dialog boxes.

4. If you added new macro buttons to the Quick Access Toolbar, right-click each of the buttons on the toolbar and then select **Remove from Quick Access Toolbar**.
5. Click the **Developer** tab. In the Templates group, click the **Document Template** button to open the Templates and Add-ins dialog box. Under Global templates and add-ins, remove your personal templates from the list.
6. If the Developer tab did not appear in the Ribbon when you began the lesson (see Step-by-Step 16.2, Step 3), click the **File** tab and then click **Options**. In the left pane, click **Customize Ribbon**. In the right pane, under Main Tabs, uncheck the **Developer** tab name to hide the Developer tab, and then click **OK**.
7. Exit Word. If prompted to save changes to the global Normal.dotm template, click **Don't Save**.

SUMMARY

In this lesson you learned:

- You can store a macro in a document or in a template. When stored in a document, macros are only available for that document.
- When you create a macro, you record the sequence of actions necessary to perform a task.
- Word enforces a security level for running macros. Depending on the security level, you may need to enable macros when you open a document.
- To make macros available for other documents, you can store them in the normal template or in a document template.
- To create shortcuts to run a macro, you can assign a shortcut key combination or you can add a new button to the Quick Access Toolbar.
- To run a macro, you can use the Macros dialog box or a keyboard or button shortcut.
- When you want to change a macro, you can re-record it or you can edit it in the Microsoft Visual Basic Editor.
- You can copy macro projects to make them available to other documents and users. When you no longer need a macro, you can delete it from the macro project.
- You can rename macro project groups to help organize your macros.
- When sharing macros with others, you should sign the macro project by adding a digital signature.

VOCABULARY REVIEW

Define the following terms:

code
macro
macro project
VBA (Visual Basic for Applications)
virus

REVIEW QUESTIONS

TRUE / FALSE

Circle T if the statement is true or F if the statement is false.

T F 1. The default format for a Word document is macro-enabled.

T F 2. Word already has numerous macros available.

T F 3. When you delete a macro shortcut, the macro is also deleted.

T F 4. All macro buttons look the same.

T F 5. To rename a macro, you must edit the VBA code.

MULTIPLE CHOICE

Select the best response for the following statements.

1. When recording a macro, ________________.
   A. you can use the mouse to reposition the insertion point
   B. you can use keyboard shortcuts to navigate through the document
   C. you can use the mouse to select text
   D. none of the above
2. When a macro is stored in a document template, ________________.
   A. the macro is available to only the active document
   B. the macro is stored in the normal (default) template
   C. the macro is available to all users and to all documents at any time
   D. the macro is available when the document template is attached to a document or made global
3. When you store a macro in a document, ________________.
   A. a document template must be attached
   B. the macro is available to all users for all documents at any time
   C. the macro must first be listed as a trusted source
   D. the document must be macro-enabled
4. By default, Word stores macros ________________.
   A. in a document template
   B. in the current document
   C. in the Normal (dotm) template
   D. none of the above
5. If you want to choose when to enable the macro, in the macro security settings, you should choose the option to ________________.
   A. disable all macros without notification
   B. disable all macros with notification
   C. disable all macros except digitally signed macros
   D. enable all macros

WRITTEN QUESTIONS

Write a brief answer to the following questions.

1. What are the advantages of storing macros in a document template?

2. Why will Word not accept the macro names *Print 4*, *4Copies*, or *Print4**?

3. When looking at a filename extension, how can you determine if the document is macro-enabled?

4. When you edit a macro, why does the VBA window open?

5. What happens when you create a new macro using an existing macro name?

PROJECTS

If you have a SAM 2010 user profile, your instructor may have assigned an autogradable version of the indicated project. If so, log into the SAM 2010 Web site at *www.cengage.com/sam2010* to download the instruction and start files.

PROJECT 16–1

1. Open the **Resume.docx** file from the drive and folder where your Data Files are stored. Save the document as a macro-enabled document and name the document **Final Resume**, followed by your initials. Make sure the file is saved with the extension .docm.
2. Click the File tab, and then click Options. In the left pane, click Trust Center, and then click Trust Center Settings. For Macro Settings, make sure the option Disable all macros with notification is enabled. Click Trusted Locations and make sure your solutions folder is included in the Trusted Locations list. Close all dialog boxes.
3. Create a new macro:
   a. Name the macro **SaveAs_XPS**.
   b. Store the macro in the current document.
   c. Describe the macro as **Save the document in XPS format**.
   d. Create a keyboard shortcut using the key combination Alt+6. (Make sure the changes are saved to the current document.)
4. Record the actions to save the document in the XPS format, using the same filename and folder where you save your solution files. (When the XPS document opens, close it and then stop recording.)
5. Add a new button for the *SaveAs_XPS* macro to the Quick Access Toolbar. Modify the button icon with a graphic of your choice.
6. Center the content on the page vertically:
   a. Click the Page Layout tab.
   b. In the Page Setup group, click the Dialog Box Launcher.
   c. In the Page Setup dialog box, click the Layout tab.
   d. Under Page, in the Vertical alignment box, select Center.
   e. Click OK. If prompted about the margins set outside the printable area, click Ignore.
7. Save the changes to the document.
8. Run the *SaveAs_XPS* macro to create a new file in the XPS format. The new XPS file is saved with the same name as the previous XPS document. Every time you update the resume, you can run the macro to update the XPS version of the document.
9. Close the XPS document window and close the Final Resume document.
10. Open the folder where you save your solution files. You should see two solution files for this project: the *Final Resume.docm* file and the *Final Resume.xps* file. Close the folder.

SAM PROJECT 16–2

1. Open a new blank document and save it as a new macro-enabled template using the filename **Personal Template 3.dotm**.
2. If you are beginning a new Word session, click the File tab, then click Options. In the left pane, click Trust Center, and then click Trust Center Settings. For Macro Settings, make sure the option Disable all macros with notification is enabled. Make sure your solutions folder is included in the Trusted Locations list.
3. Make the Personal Template 3.dotm document template global. Close the Personal Template 3 document template.
4. Open a new blank document. To create random text, type **=rand(5,5)** and then press Enter.
5. Practice the required actions to format text in two columns with a line between the columns. Use the following tips as a guide:
   a. Open the Columns dialog box. (*Hint*: On the Page Layout tab, click the Columns button, then click More Columns.)
   b. Select the options for two columns with a line between the columns and click OK.
6. Close the document without saving the changes.
7. Open the **Personal Template 3** document template.
8. Create the new macro:
   a. Name the macro **Columns2**.
   b. Store the macro in your Personal Template 3 document template.
   c. Describe the macro as **Format text in columns with a line between the columns.**.
   d. Record the actions.
   e. Stop the recording.
9. Save the changes and then close the document template.
10. Open the **Profile.docx** file from the drive and folder where your Data Files are stored. Save the document as **Revised Profile 1**, followed by your initials. Make sure the file is saved with the extension .docx.
11. Attach your Personal Template 3.dotm document template to the document.
12. Create a keyboard shortcut for the Columns2 macro by applying the key combination Alt+5. Make sure you save the keyboard shortcut in your Personal Template 3.dotm document template.

13. Run the Columns2 macro.
14. Save the changes, and when prompted to save changes to the document template, click Yes. Close the document.

WARNING

If you are ending your Word session now, or any time before you complete the remaining Projects in this lesson, you must restore all the settings you changed. Go to Step-by-Step 16.12 and complete all seven steps to restore the changed settings.

PROJECT 16–3

1. If you are beginning a new Word session, click the File tab, then click Options. In the left pane, click Trust Center, and then click Trust Center Settings. For Macro Settings, make sure the option Disable all macros with notification is enabled. Make sure your solutions folder is included in the Trusted Locations list.
2. Open the **Personal Template 3** file from your solution files. Make the template global.
3. Open the Organizer dialog box. In the left pane, open the **Final Resume.docm** document from your solution files.
4. Rename the NewMacros project **SaveFormat**.
5. In the right pane of the Organizer dialog box, open your **Personal Template 3.dotm** file.
6. Copy the SaveFormat project from the Final Resume.docm file to your Personal Template 3.dotm document template.
7. Close the Organizer dialog box. When prompted to save the changes to the Final Resume.docx document, click Save. Save the changes to the Personal Template 3.dotm document template and leave the document open.
8. Edit the Columns2 macro:
   a. Open the Macros dialog box. Select the Columns2 macro and click Edit.
   b. In the first line of the code, change *Sub Columns2* to *Sub Columns***3**.
   c. Change the Green heading from *Columns2 Macro* to *Columns3 Macro*.
   d. In the line reading *.SetCount NumColumns:=2*, change the number of columns to **3**.
   e. In the line reading *.Width = InchesToPoints (3)*, change the *3* to **1.5**.
9. Save the changes to the VBA code, and then close the VBA window and return to the Word application. Close the document template.
10. Open the **Revised Profile 1.docx** file from your solution files and save the document as **Revised Profile 2**, followed by your initials. Make sure the file is saved with the extension .docx.
11. Open the Macros dialog box and run the Columns3 macro.
12. Save the changes to the Revised Profile 2.docx file and close the file.

WARNING

If you are ending your Word session now, or any time before you complete the remaining Projects in this lesson, you must restore all the settings you changed. Go to Step-by-Step 16.12 and complete all seven steps to restore the changed settings.

PROJECT 16–4

1. Open the **Personal Template 3** file from your solution files.
2. Open a new blank document. Click the Insert tab, click the Screenshot button, and then click Screen Clipping.
3. Wait a moment for the active document to fade away. Drag the mouse pointer over the Quick Access Toolbar to identify the area to capture in the clipping. When you release the mouse button, the active document appears and the clipping is inserted in the document.
4. Save the document with the screenshot as **Quick Access Toolbar Screenshot**, followed by your initials. Make sure the file is saved with the extension .docx. Close the document.
5. Open the VBA application and attach your digital signature to the TemplateProject (Personal Template 3).
6. Save the changes in the VBA application window, and then return to the Word application.
7. Close the document template.
8. Go to Step-by-Step 16.12 and complete all seven steps to restore the settings you changed.

CRITICAL THINKING

ACTIVITY 16–1

Celeste was recording a macro when she was interrupted by a co-worker who needed some information. Celeste temporarily paused the recording to assist her co-worker. When Celeste returned to her document, she couldn't remember the last action before she stopped. What would you have done if you were Celeste?

ACTIVITY 16–2

Celeste always creates both keyboard shortcuts and buttons for all macros stored in the Normal.dotm template on all computers in the office. Five macros have been saved. Is it really necessary to create both types of shortcuts? Do you think this is a good idea? Explain why.

Estimated Time:
1.5 hours

LESSON 17

Customizing Settings

OBJECTIVES

Upon completion of this lesson, you should be able to:

- Add and delete buttons on the Quick Access Toolbar.
- Customize the Ribbon.
- Modify the default document formats.
- Modify the document display settings.
- Change the edit settings.
- Change the save settings.
- Set AutoCorrect exceptions.
- Create a custom dictionary.

VOCABULARY

main tabs

tool tabs

The Word application has numerous commands and settings for displaying, editing, and saving documents. In the previous Word lessons, features have been introduced using the default settings. To improve your productivity as you work with Word, you can customize some of these settings to change how Word displays items and responds to your input.

Customizing the Quick Access Toolbar

The Quick Access Toolbar has been designed to provide quick access to the commands you use most often. You may find that you use commands that do not appear in the default Quick Access Toolbar. To save time accessing these commands, you can add buttons to the toolbar. In the previous lesson, you learned to add buttons to the Quick Access Toolbar to run macros. You can also add buttons for all other Word commands, including commands that don't appear on the Ribbon.

You can add an unlimited number of buttons to the Quick Access Toolbar, but putting too many buttons on it may defeat the purpose. So as you add new buttons, you may need to remove existing buttons. You can remove buttons individually, or you can remove multiple buttons you have added by resetting the toolbar to its default settings. When you reset the toolbar settings, any of the default buttons you removed will be restored on the toolbar.

When you customize the settings in Word, the changes are automatically saved to the application. However, it is easy to restore the default settings.

WARNING

As you work through the activities in this lesson, information will be provided to reset the Word application with the default settings. If you end the Word session before completing this lesson, be sure to restore the default settings before exiting Word.

Step-by-Step 17.1

1. Launch Word. Click the **File** tab, and then click **Options**. In the left pane of the Word Options dialog box, click **Quick Access Toolbar** to open the dialog box shown in **Figure 17–1**. Your settings may differ. A list of popular commands appears in the center pane, and a list of the current buttons on the Quick Access Toolbar appears in the right pane.

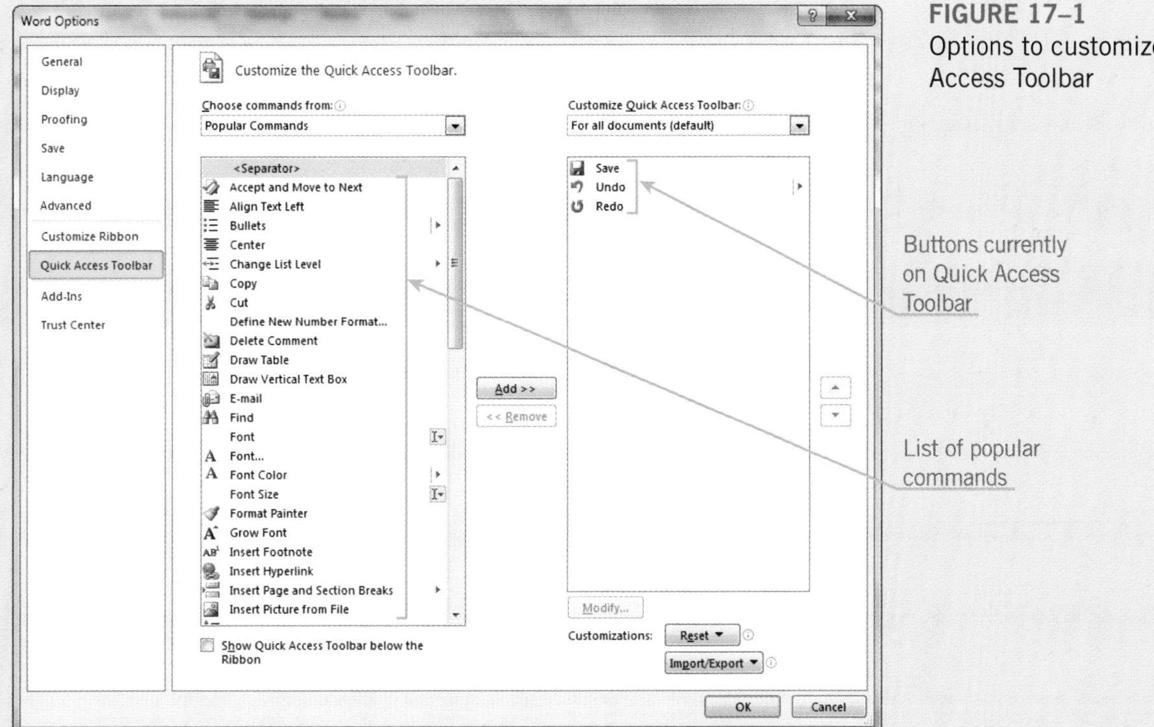

FIGURE 17–1
Options to customize the Quick Access Toolbar

2. Scroll down in the list of popular commands and select **New**. Then click **Add** to add the New button to the toolbar. The New button, with an icon, now appears in the list of Quick Access Toolbar buttons in the right pane.
3. In the center pane, under Choose commands from, click the **list arrow** and then click **All Commands**. The list in the center pane changes. Scroll through the list. As you can see, the list is quite extensive.

4. Under Choose commands from, click the **list arrow** again to show the options for selecting commands, as shown in **Figure 17–2**. This list helps you quickly locate commands by first clicking the tab where the command appears on the Ribbon.

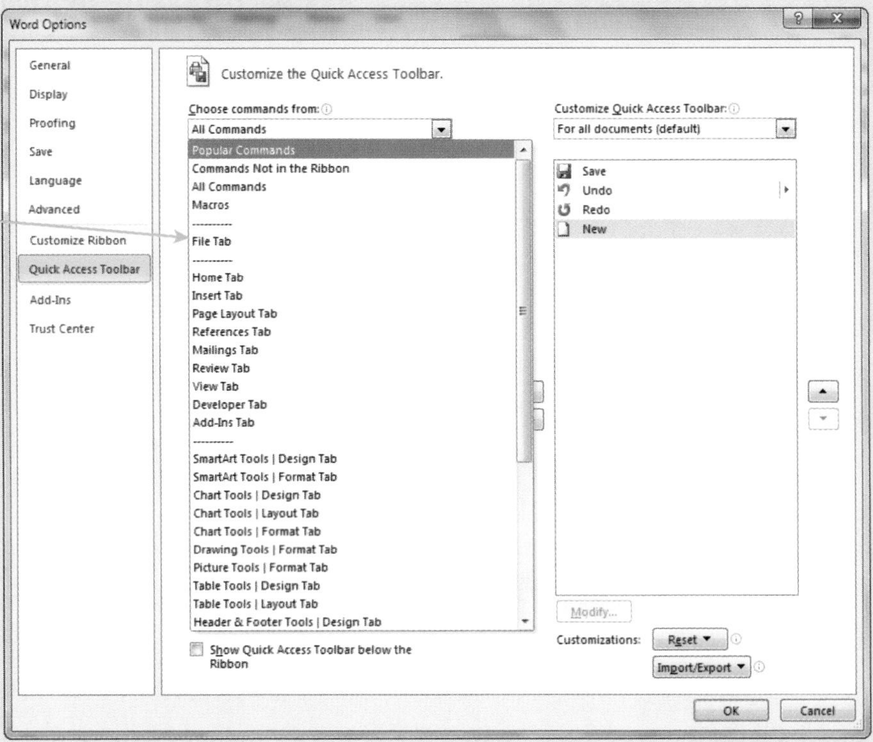

FIGURE 17–2
Options for choosing commands for the Quick Access Toolbar

5. In the list of tabs in the center pane, click **File Tab**. The list now shows all the commands that can be accessed using the File tab on the Ribbon. In the center pane, scroll down and select **Quick Print**. Click **Add**. A new button with an icon is added to the list of buttons for the Quick Access Toolbar.

> **TIP**
>
> The Quick Print command sends the document to the printer without an opportunity to preview it.

6. In the center pane, under Choose commands from, click the **list arrow** and then click **Commands Not in the Ribbon**. To access these commands, you must open dialog boxes or menus. Select **All Caps**, and then click **Add**. Scroll down farther in the list, select **Hanging Indent**, and then click **Add**. In the lower-right corner of the dialog box, click **OK**.

7. Four new buttons appear on the Quick Access Toolbar. Click the **New** button on the Quick Access Toolbar. A new document opens. Type the following sentence.

   When the hanging indent format is applied to a paragraph, the first line of the paragraph is not indented, but all subsequent lines in the paragraph are indented from the left margin.

> **TIP**
>
> If you don't recognize a button icon, you can position the mouse pointer over the button to view the ScreenTip.

8. Press **Enter** two times. Click the **All Caps** button on the Quick Access Toolbar to toggle on the font effect. Type your **first name**. Click the **All Caps** button again to toggle off the font effect, and then press the **spacebar** and type your **last name**.
9. Click anywhere in the first paragraph of text, and then click the **Hanging Indent** button. The hanging indent format is applied to the paragraph.
10. Right-click the **Save** button on the Quick Access Toolbar, and then click **Remove from Quick Access Toolbar**. The button no longer appears on the toolbar.
11. Click the **File** tab, and then click **Options**. In the left pane of the Word Options dialog box, click **Quick Access Toolbar**. In the right pane, in the list of current buttons, select **All Caps**. Then click **Remove**. The button is removed from the list.
12. In the lower-right corner of the dialog box, click **OK**. The All Caps button no longer appears on the Quick Access Toolbar, but the toolbar still contains three buttons that you added.
13. Click the **File** tab, and then click **Options**. In the left pane of the Word Options dialog box, click **Quick Access Toolbar**. In the lower-right corner of the dialog box, click **Reset**, and then click **Reset only Quick Access Toolbar**. When prompted to restore the Quick Access Toolbar to its default contents, click **Yes**, and then click **OK** to close the dialog box. All buttons you added are removed from the Quick Access Toolbar, and the default buttons are restored.
14. Close the document without saving the changes, and leave Word open for the next Step-by-Step.

Customizing the Ribbon

A new feature in Word 2010 enables you to customize the Ribbon. The Ribbon consists of two types of tabs: main tabs and tool tabs. The ***main tabs*** appear on the Ribbon when you launch the application. The ***tool tabs*** are contextual and appear on the Ribbon only when you select objects in a document.

The default Ribbon is loaded with commonly used commands. You may not use all of those commands, and there may be other commands that you frequently use that do not appear on the Ribbon. You can reorganize the Ribbon so that your favorite commands appear together on a single tab.

VOCABULARY

main tabs

tool tabs

Reorganizing Tabs, Groups, and Commands on the Ribbon

You can choose which tabs to display on the Ribbon, and you can rename all the default tabs. You can also rearrange the order of the tabs and/or the groups on the tabs. Reorganizing tabs and groups for the Ribbon is similar to rearranging document headings in Outline view. You can expand and collapse the names, and you can drag and drop the names to reorganize where the tabs and groups appear on the Ribbon. However, you cannot move default commands within a group or from one group to another. You also cannot change the icon assigned to a command button on a default tab or in a default group.

When you customize the Ribbon in Word, the changes are saved in the Word application; no changes will appear in the Ribbon for other applications such as Excel and PowerPoint. You can easily restore the default settings for an individual tab or for the entire Ribbon.

Step-by-Step 17.2

1. Click the **File** tab, and then click **Options**. In the left pane of the Word Options dialog box, click **Customize Ribbon**. The current configuration of the Ribbon appears in the right pane, as shown in **Figure 17–3**. Your settings may differ.

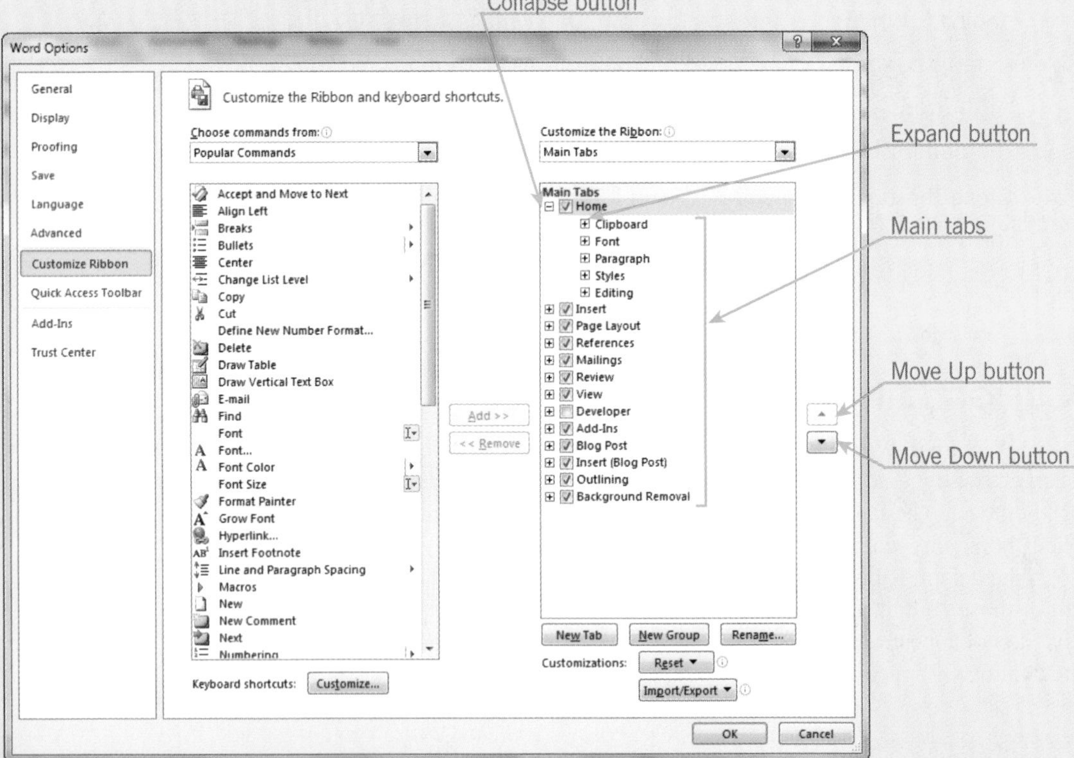

FIGURE 17–3 Options for customizing the Ribbon

2. In the right pane, under Customize the Ribbon, click the **list arrow** and then click **Tool Tabs**. Scroll down to view all the default Tool Tabs that are available. Click the **list arrow** again, and then click **Main Tabs**.

3. In the right pane, under Main Tabs, click the **check box** next to Mailings to disable the tab. (When disabled, the check box is unchecked.)
4. In the right pane, under Main Tabs, select **Page Layout**. In the lower-right corner of the dialog box, click **Rename** to open the Rename dialog box. Type **Document Layout**, and then click **OK**. The tab name is now *Document Layout*.
5. In the right pane, drag and drop the **Review** tab name so it is repositioned just above the Insert tab name. To the left of the Review tab name, click the **Expand** button to show all the groups on the Review tab.
6 In the list of groups on the Review tab, select **Proofing**. Then click the **Move Up** button on the right side of the pane five times to reposition the Proofing group just after the Clipboard group on the Home tab.
7. In the right pane, in the list of groups on the Review tab, select **Chinese Conversion**. Then click **Remove** (between the center and right panes). The group is removed from the tab.
8. In the right pane, in the list of groups on the Review tab, select **Language**. In the lower-right corner of the dialog box, click **Rename** to open the Rename dialog box. Type **Translate**, and then click **OK**. The group name is now *Translate*.
9. To the left of the Review tab name, click the **Collapse** button to hide the list of groups on the tab.
10. In the lower-right corner of the screen, click **OK**. On the Ribbon, note that the Review tab is now positioned to the right of the Home tab, the Home tab now shows the Proofing group to the right of the Clipboard group, the Page Layout tab is now the Document Layout tab, and the Mailings tab is not shown.
11. Click the **File** tab, and then click **Options**. In the left pane, click **Customize Ribbon**. In the right pane, select **Review**.
12. In the lower-right corner of the dialog box, click **Reset** and then click **Reset only selected Ribbon tab**. In the right pane, next to the Review tab name, click the **Expand button** to show the list of groups. Note that the Proofing and Chinese Conversion groups are included in the list, and the name for the Language group was restored. No changes were made to the other tabs.
13. In the lower-right corner of the dialog box, click **Reset** and then click **Reset all customizations**. When prompted to delete all customizations, click **Yes**.
14. Click **OK** to accept the changes and close the Word Options dialog box. The entire Ribbon is restored to the default settings.

TIP

To expand or collapse a tab or group, you can double-click the tab or group name.

EXTRA FOR EXPERTS

The Proofing group also still appears under the Home tab, so you have essentially copied the Proofing group and it now appears on two different tabs in the Ribbon.

Adding and Removing Groups, Commands, and Tabs on the Ribbon

For quicker access to commands that you use frequently, you can customize the Ribbon by adding new commands. You cannot add new commands to default groups. To add new commands to a tab, you must first create a new custom group. You can create new groups on all tabs. When you add new commands to a custom group, you can assign custom icons to the buttons for the commands. If you want to add several new groups and commands, you can add new main tabs and tool tabs to the Ribbon.

You can remove all of the new tabs, groups, and commands that you create. You can also remove default commands and groups from all of Word's default tabs. However, you cannot remove the default tabs that appear on the Ribbon. If you don't want a default tab to appear on the Ribbon, you can hide the tab.

Step-by-Step 17.3

1. Click the **File** tab, and then click **Options**. In the left pane, click **Customize Ribbon**. If necessary, click the **Expand** button next to Home to show all the groups on the Home tab.
2. To create a new group on a default tab, first select the desired tab. In the right pane, select **Home**. In the lower-right corner of the dialog box, click **New Group**. The group name *New Group (Custom)* appears at the end of the list of groups on the Home tab.
3. To rename the new group, make sure the group name you want to change is selected. (*New Group (Custom)* is already selected.) Click **Rename**. In the Rename dialog box, type **My Stuff**, and then click **OK**. The new group name *My Stuff (Custom)* appears in the right pane. The word *(Custom)* will not appear on the Ribbon tab.
4. To add a command to the group, first select the group. (*My Stuff (Custom)* is already selected.) In the left pane, under Choose commands from, click the **list arrow** and then click **Commands Not in the Ribbon**. Scroll down in the list of commands and select **Close All**. Then click **Add**.
5. To change the button icon for the new Close All command, make sure the command is selected. (*Close All* is already selected.) Click **Rename** to open the Rename dialog box, as shown in **Figure 17–4**. At the end of the fourth row of icons, click the **hand** icon and then click **OK**. The new icon replaces the original icon in the right pane.

TIP

The Close All command will close all open documents at the same time. If one or more documents have unsaved changes, Word will prompt you before closing those documents.

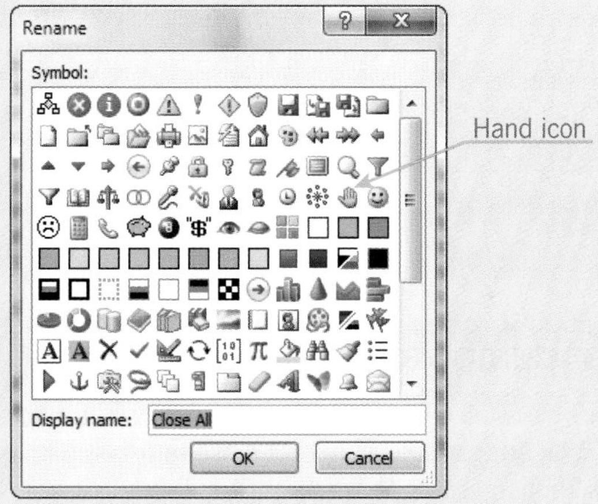

FIGURE 17–4
Rename dialog box with options for icons

6. To create a new tab, select an existing tab. In the right pane, select **View**. In the lower-right corner of the dialog box, click **New Tab**. In the list of tabs in the right pane, *New Tab (Custom)* appears below the selected tab, and *New Group (Custom)* appears below the new tab entry. This new tab will appear to the right of the View tab on the Ribbon.
7. In the right pane, select **New Tab (Custom)**. Then, in the lower-right corner of the dialog box, click **New Group**. The new tab now has two groups. Select **New Tab (Custom)**. Click **Rename** and in the Rename dialog box, type your **first name** and **last name** and then click **OK**.
8. In the list of groups on the new tab, select the first **New Group (Custom)**. Then click **Rename**, type **Favorites**, and click **OK**.
9. The Favorites (Custom) group should still be selected. In the center pane, under Choose commands from, click the **list arrow**, and then click **Popular Commands**. Under Popular Commands, select **Copy** and click **Add**. Then add the **Paste (Paste)** command and the **Cut** command to the new Favorites group.

TIP

Hover the mouse over the command name to show a ScreenTip to distinguish the two Paste commands.

10. In the right pane, use the drag-and-drop method to reposition the commands in the Favorites group so they appear in this sequence: *Cut*, *Copy*, and *Paste*.
11. In the right pane, select **Cut** and then click **Remove**. The command is removed from the group.
12. Click **OK** to close Word Options. The new tab with two groups appears on the Ribbon.
13. Click the **File** tab, and then click **Options**. In the left pane of the Word Options dialog box, click **Customize Ribbon**. In the right pane, select the custom tab with your name and then click **Remove**. Click **OK** to close the Word Options dialog box. The tab and all the groups and commands on the tab are removed. However, the Custom group *My Stuff* still appears on the Home tab.

14. Leave Word open for the next Step-by-Step. If you are ending your Word session, restore the entire Ribbon to the Default settings. (In the Word Options dialog box, click Customize Ribbon, click Reset, and then click Reset all customizations. When prompted to delete all customizations, click Yes.)

Exporting and Importing Customizations

You can share your customized Ribbon and Quick Access Toolbar by exporting the settings to a file. Then other users can import those settings and replace their Ribbon and Quick Access Toolbar settings with the customized settings.

In the next Step-by-Step, you'll export custom Ribbon and Quick Access Toolbar settings to a new file. If you have restored the Ribbon to the default settings, you can still complete the steps.

Step-by-Step 17.4

1. Click the **File** tab, and then click **Options**. In the left pane of the Word Options dialog box, click **Customize Ribbon**.
2. In the lower-right corner of the dialog box, click **Import/Export** and then click **Export all customizations**. The File Save dialog box opens.
3. Navigate to the drive and folder where you save your solution files. In the File name box, change the filename to **Word Customizations**, followed by your initials. Note that Word assigns the document extension *.exportedUI*. Then click **Save**.
4. In the Word Options dialog box, click **Reset** and then click **Reset all customizations**. Click **Yes** to delete the customizations. Then click **OK** to accept the changes and close the Word Options dialog box.
5. Click the **File** tab, and then click **Options**. In the left pane, click **Customize Ribbon**.
6. Click **Import/Export**, and then click **Import customization file**. The File Open dialog box opens.
7. Navigate to the drive and folder where you save your solution files. Select the .exportedUI file you just saved and click **Open**. A prompt appears to confirm changing the settings. Click **Yes** and then click **OK** to close the Word Options dialog box. The Ribbon now shows the customized settings you saved.

8. Click the **File** tab, and then click **Options**. In the left pane, click **Customize Ribbon**. Click **Reset** and then click **Reset all customizations**. Click **Yes** and then click **OK** to accept the changes and close the Word Options dialog box. The custom group *My Stuff* no longer appears on the Home tab.
9. Leave Word open for the next Step-by-Step.

Modifying the Default Document Formats

As you already know, the font style and font size, paragraph line spacing, and document margins are always the same when you open a new blank document. The document formats are determined by the Normal.dotm template. Changing the default settings is easy, and you can save the new settings to the active template so that all new documents based on that template will be formatted with the new settings.

As you learned in Lesson 10, when you attach a template to a document, that template becomes the active template. In the next Step-by-Step, you create and attach a personal template to a document. Then as you change some default settings, the settings will be saved in the personal template and not in the Normal.dotm template. After saving settings to a template file, you can create new documents based on the template and you can share the template with colleagues.

Throughout this lesson, if you are prompted to save changes to the Normal.dotm template, click No.

Step-by-Step 17.5

1. If necessary, open a new blank document. Click the **File** tab, and then click **Save As** to open the Save As dialog box.
2. Navigate to the drive and folder where you save your solution files. In the File name box, type **Personal Template 4**, followed by your initials. In the Save as type box, select **Word Template (*.dotx)**. Click **Save**.

3. On the Home tab, in the Font group, click the **Dialog Box Launcher** to open the Font dialog box. If necessary, click the **Font** tab to display the options shown in **Figure 17–5**.

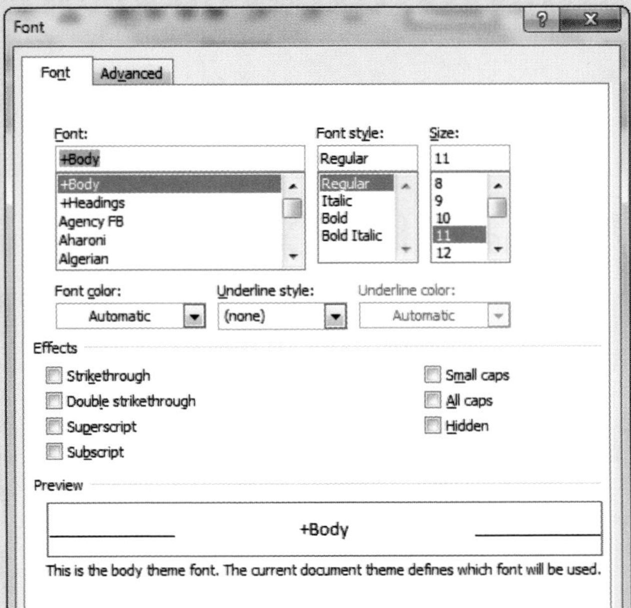

FIGURE 17–5
Font tab in the Font dialog box

4. In the Font text box, type **g** to move down in the list to show all the fonts beginning with the letter *g*. Select **Georgia**. Under Size, select **12** point. Click **Set as Default**. A prompt appears asking you to confirm the changes, as shown in **Figure 17–6**.

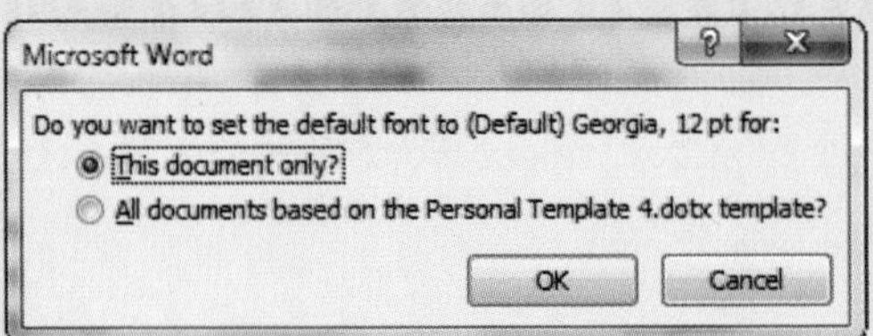

FIGURE 17–6
Prompt to confirm default font change

5. Select the **All documents in Personal Template 4.dotx template?** option, and then click **OK**.

6. In the Paragraph group, click the **Dialog Box Launcher** to open the Paragraph dialog box. Under Spacing, change the After setting to **0 pt.** Under Line spacing, change the setting to **Single**. Your settings should match those shown in **Figure 17–7**.

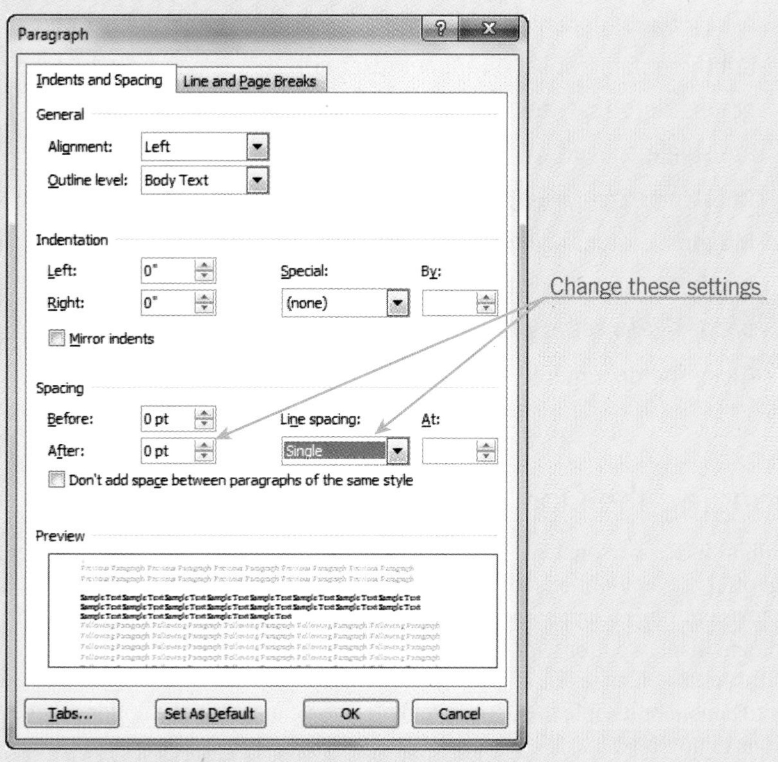

FIGURE 17–7
Paragraph dialog box

7. Click **Set As Default**. A prompt appears to confirm the changes. Select the **All documents in Personal Template 4.dotx template?** option, and then click **OK**.
8. Change the Page Setup settings:
   a. Click the **Page Layout** tab. In the Page Setup group, click the **Margins** button and then click **Custom Margins** to open the Page Setup dialog box.
   b. On the Margins tab, change the top margin to **1.5"**.
   c. In the Page Setup dialog box, click the **Paper** tab. Under Paper size, change the setting to **Legal**.
   d. In the Page Setup dialog box, click the **Layout** tab. Under Headers and footers, enable the **Different first page** option.
   e. Click **Set As Default**. A prompt appears to confirm the changes, which include all three Page Setup settings. Click **Yes**.
9. Save the changes to the document and then close the document.
10. To open a new document based on the document template, click the **File** tab and then click **New**. Under Available Templates, click the **New from existing** icon. The New from Existing Document dialog box opens.
11. If necessary, navigate to the drive and folder where you save your solution files. Select the file **Personal Template 4.dotx**, and then click **Create New**.

12. A new blank document opens. Type **=rand(3,3)** and press **Enter** to create three paragraphs of random text, with three sentences in each paragraph. Note that the font size is Georgia 12 point, and the paragraphs are single-spaced with no extra space between paragraphs.
13. Click the **Page Layout** tab, and then in the Page Setup group, click the **Margins** button. The top margin is set to *1.5"*. Click the document to close the menu. In the Page Setup group, click the **Size** button. The paper size is set at *Legal 8.5 x 14"*. Close the menu.
14. Close the document without saving the changes.

Changing the Document Display Settings

Everyone has a personal preference for how content displays on the screen, and Word offers several options to control the display. If you're not comfortable with the way text and objects appear on your screen, you can modify the settings using the document display options.

Table 17–1 lists several document display options and describes why you would want to enable or disable the options and how you can access the options in the Word Options dialog box.

TABLE 17–1 Document display options

OPTION	PURPOSE	LOCATION IN WORD OPTIONS DIALOG BOX
Show Mini Toolbar on selection	When enabled, a transparent image of the Mini toolbar appears when you select text. If you don't use the Mini toolbar and you find it gets in your way, you can disable this option.	General options, under User Interface options
Show white space between pages in Print Layout view	When you disable this option, in Print Layout view, the white space for the top and bottom margins does not appear. This saves space on your screen as you review the document.	Display options, under Page display options
Show highlighter marks	When disabled, highlighted content appears normal and the highlight color does not appear on the screen or in printed copies. This option is useful when you've marked content with highlights and you want to print the document without the highlights.	Display options, under Page display options
Show document tooltips on hover	When disabled, the ScreenTips that Word provides will not be displayed.	Display options, under Page display options

TABLE 17–1 Document display options (continued)

OPTION	PURPOSE	LOCATION IN WORD OPTIONS DIALOG BOX
Show text wrapped within the document window	When enabled, the flow of text changes to fit the window when the document window is resized. This option only affects the display when the document appears in Draft, Outline, and Web Layout views. In Page Layout view, even when the option is enabled, if the document window is not as wide as the line of text, some of the text does not show.	Advanced options, under Show document content
Show picture placeholders	If the document contains many graphics, you can scroll through the document more quickly by showing placeholders instead of the pictures.	Advanced options, under Show document content
Show text boundaries	When enabled, you won't need to use the rulers to estimate the text area. This option is useful when you are positioning objects on a page.	Advanced options, under Show document content
Use draft font in Draft and Outline views	Depending on the fonts used in the document, this option can make documents easier to read; it does not affect how the document prints.	Advanced options, under Show document content
Show this number of Recent Documents...	You can choose the number of recent documents that appear in the Recent Documents list in Backstage view. The number can be set between 0 and 50.	Advanced options, under Display
Show measurements in units of...	This option affects rulers and settings in dialog boxes. You can choose to show units in inches, centimeters, millimeters, points, and picas.	Advanced options, under Display

In the following Step-by-Step, you will enable and disable some of these options to see the effect on how content is displayed on your screen.

Step-by-Step 17.6

1. Open a new blank document. Type **=rand(14,5)** and press **Enter** to create 14 paragraphs of random text, with five sentences in each paragraph.
2. Position the insertion point at the top of the document. Insert a clip art image of a box. Resize the image so it is approximately 5 inches high by 5 inches wide.
3. Click the **View** tab. In the Zoom group, click the **One Page** button. Scroll to the bottom of the first page so you can view parts of both the first and second pages. Notice the white space at the bottom of the first page and at the top of the second page.

4. Click the **File** tab, and then click **Options**. In the left pane of the Word Options dialog box, click **Display** to display the options shown in **Figure 17–8**. If your settings differ, make a note of the differences, because at the end of the Step-by-Step, you will need to restore all the settings.

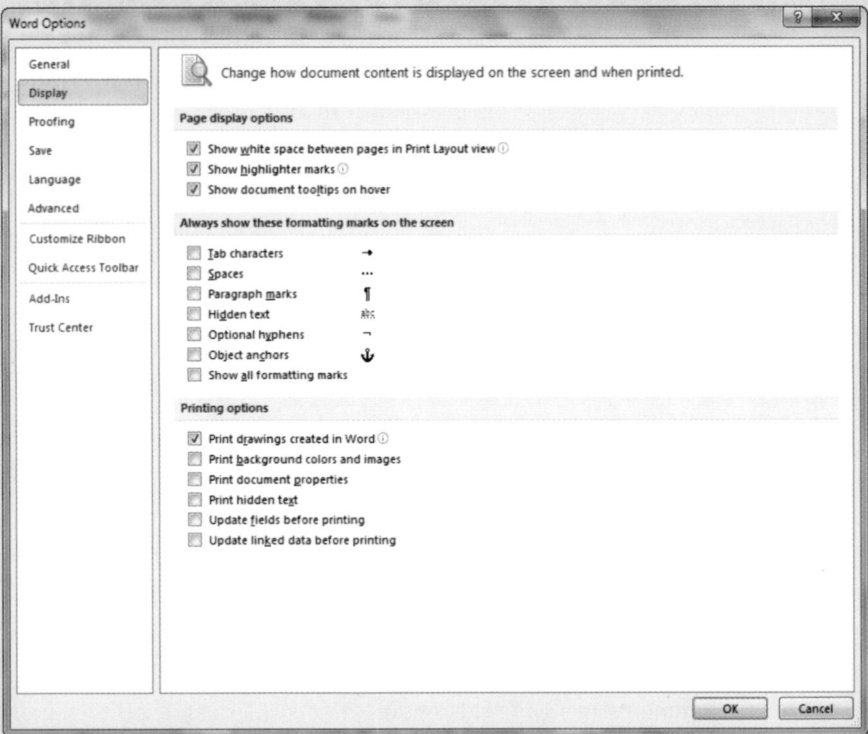

FIGURE 17–8
Options for display settings

5. Under Page display options, disable the option **Show white space between pages in Print Layout view**. Click **OK** to close the Word Options dialog box.
6. If necessary, scroll down to show parts of both the first and second pages. Now the white space for the bottom and top margins no longer appears, and a divider line indicates the break between the two pages.
7. Point to the divider line. The mouse pointer changes to a double-headed arrow, as shown in **Figure 17–9**. Double-click the divider line and the white space appears.

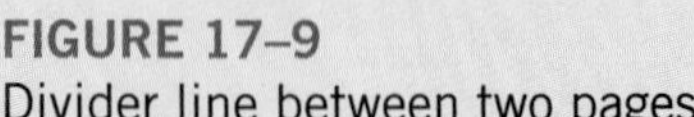
FIGURE 17–9
Divider line between two pages

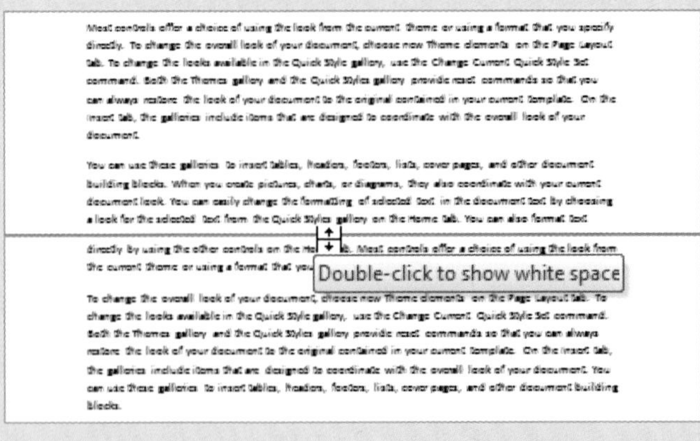

8. Position the mouse pointer in the break between the two pages. When the pointer changes to a double-headed arrow, double-click to hide the white space. Double-click the divider line again to show the white space and restore the default setting.
9. Click the **File** tab, and then click **Options**. In the left pane, click **Advanced**. Scroll down to the middle of the list to display the settings shown in **Figure 17–10**. If your settings differ, make a note of the differences, because at the end of the Step-by-Step, you will need to restore all the settings.

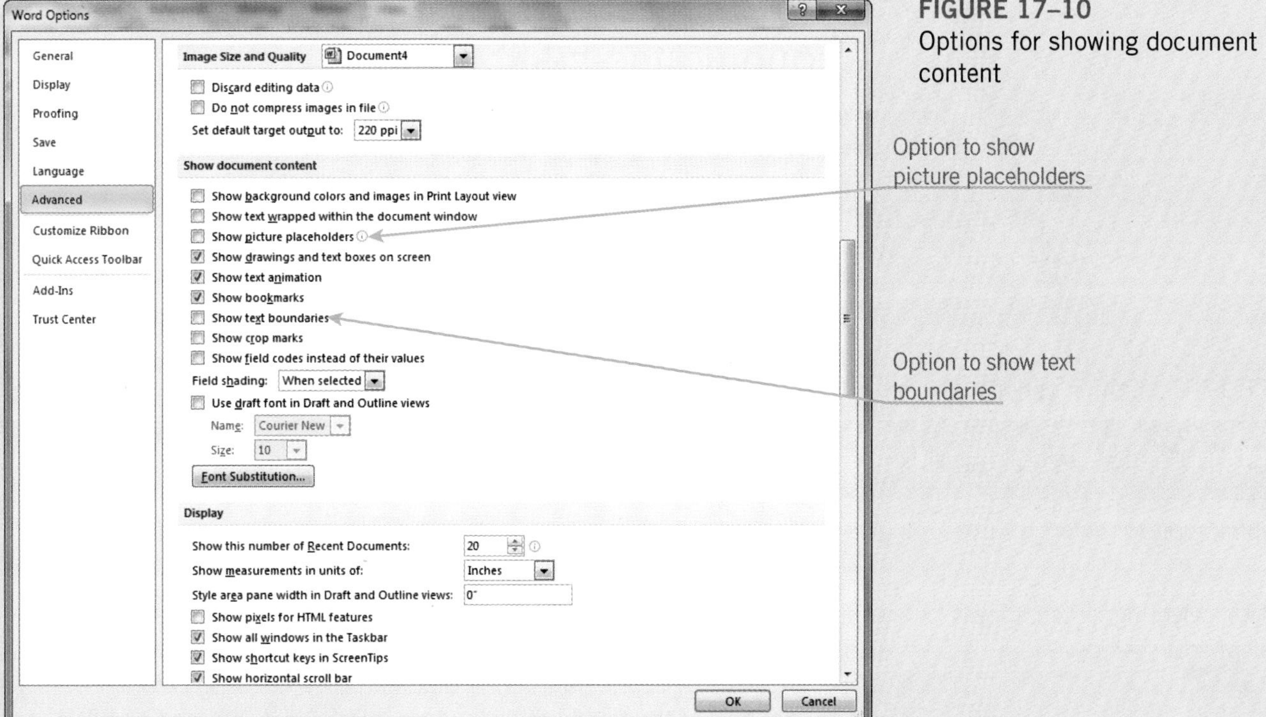

FIGURE 17–10
Options for showing document content

10. Under Show document content, enable the options **Show text boundaries** and **Show picture placeholders**. Click **OK** to close the Word Options dialog box. Notice that the clip art image no longer appears, but a placeholder indicates where the image was inserted. Also, text boundaries now appear. These boundaries will not print.
11. Click the **File** tab, and then click **Options**. In the left pane, click **Advanced**. Scroll down to the middle of the list and, under Show document content, disable the options **Show text boundaries** and **Show picture placeholders**. Compare your settings for Advanced options to those in Figure 17–10 (and any differences you noted) to make sure the settings are the same as when you began working in this Step-by-Step. Make any necessary changes.

12. In the left pane, click **Display**. Compare your settings for Display options to those in Figure 17–8 (and any differences you noted) to make sure the settings are the same as when you began working in this Step-by-Step. Make any necessary changes, and then click **OK** to accept the changes and close the Word Options dialog box.
13. Leave the document open for the next Step-by-Step. (If you are ending your Word session now, you can close the document without saving the changes.)

Changing the Edit Settings

Word provides many default settings to help you edit document content. For example, you can drag and drop content, and you can quickly select text and replace it with different text. You may find that you need to change these settings to fit your needs for editing documents.

Table 17–2 lists several editing options; it describes why you would want to enable or disable the options and how you can access them. To access the editing options, click Advanced in the left pane of the Word Options dialog box.

TABLE 17–2 Editing options

OPTION	PURPOSE
Typing replaces selected text	When this option is disabled, the selected content is not removed and new content is inserted in front of the selected content.
When selecting, automatically select entire word	When enabled, whole words and the blank space after the word are selected when you double-click a word. Also, if you use the mouse to drag across text and you select part of one word and then continue to drag the mouse over part of the text in the next word, all the text in both words is automatically selected.
Allow text to be dragged and dropped	Some users prefer to use cut and paste instead of drag and drop. If you find you often accidentally drag and drop selected text, you can disable this option.
Use smart paragraph selection	If this option is enabled, when you triple-click to select a paragraph, the paragraph mark is included in the selection. The paragraph formatting is stored with the paragraph mark and, therefore, stays with the selected paragraph.
Use smart cursoring	When this option is enabled, the insertion point moves as you scroll through the document. Then, when you press the arrow keys to reposition the insertion point, the insertion point responds on the current page in view instead of its previous position.
Keep track of formatting	This option is useful when you need formatting to be consistent throughout a document. When formats are inconsistent, such as line spacing for paragraphs, Word will identify the paragraph with the inconsistent line spacing with a wavy blue underline.

TABLE 17–2 Editing options (continued)

OPTION	PURPOSE
Mark formatting inconsistencies	To use this option, you must also enable the Keep track of formatting option. When formatting is similar to, but not exactly the same as, other formatting in the document, the content will be underscored with a wavy blue underline.
Show AutoComplete suggestions	When enabled, this option provides ScreenTips that suggest text entries to complete the word or phrase.

In the following Step-by-Step, you will enable and disable various options to see how they affect some of the editing features in Word.

Step-by-Step 17.7

1. If necessary, open a new blank document, type **=rand(14,5)**, and press **Enter** to create 14 paragraphs with five sentences in each paragraph. If necessary, click the **View** tab, and in the Zoom group, click **One Page**.
2. Hold down **Ctrl** and press **Home** to reposition the insertion point at the top of the document.

TECHNOLOGY CAREERS

If you have fast and accurate typing skills and a good eye for detail, there are several data entry and information processing career opportunities for you. ***Word processors and typists*** work with word processing applications to create and edit a variety of documents such as correspondence, reports, forms, and contracts. In addition to typing skills, word processors and typists also need skills in proofreading documents, identifying and correcting spelling, grammar, and punctuation errors, and formatting documents. Data entry keyers enter numbers and information in a form, such as medical records and membership information. Accuracy is emphasized because inaccurate data leads to inaccurate records, and errors result in high business expenses. ***Data entry keyers*** are also often responsible for correcting errors and compiling and sorting data. Technology allows many data entry and information processing workers to work flexible hours, both part- and full-time, and the flexibility to work out of their homes.

3. Click the **File** tab, and then click **Options**. In the left pane of the Word Options dialog box, click **Advanced** to display the options shown in **Figure 17–11**. Make sure the option **Use smart cursoring** is enabled. If your settings differ, make a note of the differences, because at the end of the Step-by-Step, you will need to restore all the settings. Then click **OK** to close the Word Options dialog box.

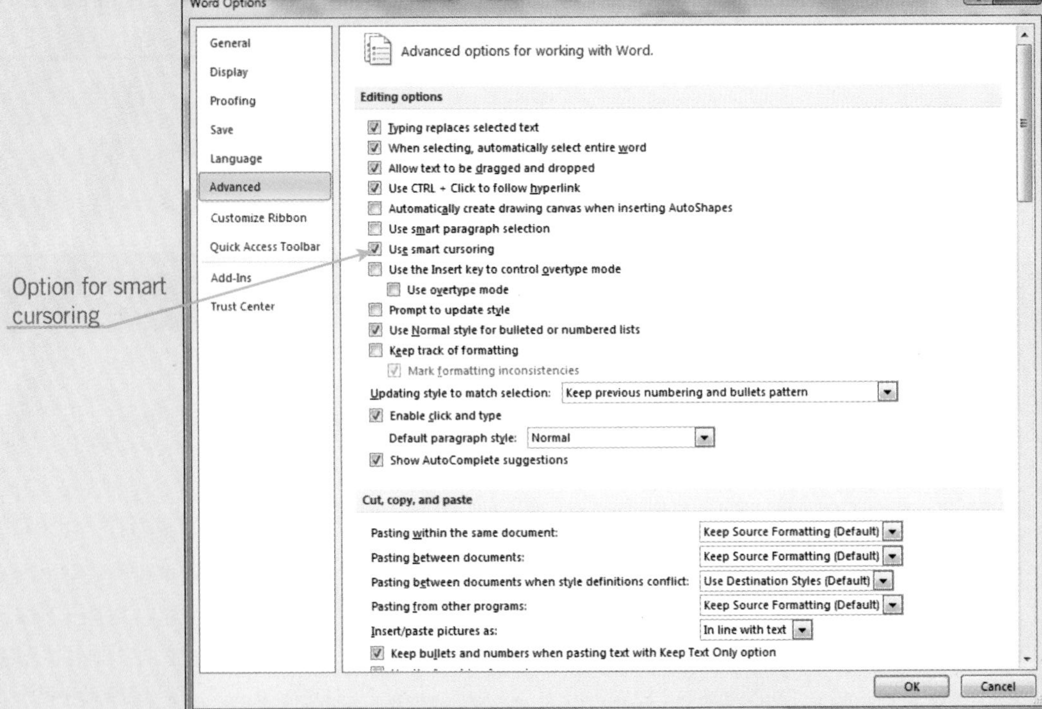

FIGURE 17–11
Options for editing

4. Use the mouse to scroll down in the document to view about half of the content on the second page. Press the **down arrow**. The insertion point is repositioned near the bottom of visible content on the second page. Scroll to the top of the document so you can view the first paragraph. Press the **up arrow**. The insertion point is repositioned at the top of the first page.
5. Click the **File** tab, and then click **Options**. In the left pane, click **Advanced**. Under Editing options, disable the option **Use smart cursoring**. Click **OK** to close the Word Options dialog box.
6. Use the mouse to scroll down in the document to view all the content on the second page. Press the **down arrow**. The view changes to show the first page of the document, and the insertion point is repositioned one line below its original position at the top of the first page. The insertion point did not move when you scrolled through the document using the mouse.

7. Click the **File** tab, and then click **Options**. In the left pane, click **Advanced**. Under Editing options, enable the option **Use smart cursoring**.
8. Under Editing options, enable the options **Keep track of formatting** and **Mark formatting inconsistencies**. Click **OK** to close the Word Options dialog box.
9. Position the insertion point at the end of the document. Then change the font point size from 11 to **12**.
10. Type your name. Because of the inconsistency in the font format, Word marks the new text with a wavy blue line.
11. Click the **File** tab, and then click **Options**. In the left pane, click **Advanced**. Under Editing options, disable the options **Mark formatting inconsistencies** and **Keep track of formatting**. Click **OK** to close the Word Options dialog box.
12. Close the document without saving the changes.
13. Click the **File** tab, and then click **Options**. In the left pane, click **Advanced**. Compare your settings for the Advanced options to those in Figure 17–11 (and any differences you noted) to make sure the settings are the same as when you began working in this Step-by-Step. Make any necessary changes, and then click **OK** to accept the changes and close the Word Options dialog box.
14. Leave Word open for the next Step-by-Step.

Changing the Save Settings

Word's default settings for saving documents include the file format and the drive and folder where files are saved. You can also specify a path to save draft files for offline editing.

Word automatically saves draft versions as you work with a document. The frequency of saving depends on your Word settings. For example, you can set the option to save a draft version every three minutes. When you close the document, the draft versions are deleted. You can also enable an option so that if you accidentally close a document without saving the changes, a draft version will automatically be saved, and then you would be able to access that draft version. Draft versions are useful if you are not tracking changes when you are creating or editing a document. If you've been working on the document for a long time, you can compare the current document with an earlier draft version of that same document to see the changes that you have made.

Table 17–3 lists several save options; it describes why you would want to enable or disable the options and how you can access them.

TABLE 17–3 Save options

OPTION	PURPOSE	LOCATION IN WORD OPTIONS DIALOG BOX
User name and Initials	The information provides the author name in the document properties.	General options, under Personalize your copy of Microsoft Office
Save AutoRecover information	This setting controls how frequently AutoRecover files are saved as you work with a document.	Save options, under Save documents
Default file location	The default file location is the My Documents folder. You can change the setting to save to a different drive and folder. You do not need to save all files in the default file location, but if you don't designate a different path, the file will be saved in the default file location.	Save options, under Save documents
Server drafts location	If you share documents using a document management server, you can designate a location to save server draft files.	Save options, under Offline editing options for document management server files
Embed fonts in the file	You can embed the fonts in the document file so other users can view and use the fonts, even if they don't have the fonts installed on their computers.	Save options, under Preserve fidelity when sharing this document

In the following Step-by-Step, you will explore how to access some of the save options in Word. You will not make any changes in the Word save settings in this Step-by-Step.

Step-by-Step 17.8

1. Open a new blank document.
2. Click the **File** tab, and then click **Options**. In the left pane of the Word Options dialog box, click **Save** to display the options shown in **Figure 17–12**. Your settings may differ.

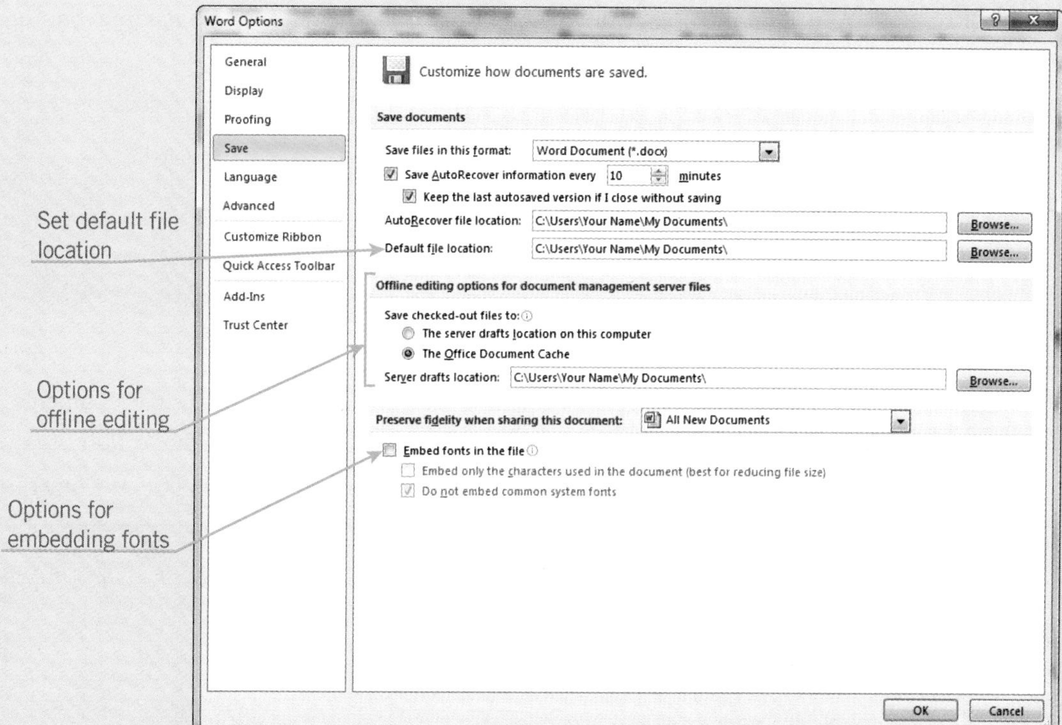

FIGURE 17–12 Options for saving documents

3. Under Save documents, you can change the default document format and the frequency of AutoRecover saving. You can also change the default settings for where the AutoRecover files and all other files are saved. Make a note of the drive and folder for the AutoRecover and Default file locations.
4. Note that under Offline editing options for document management server files, you can change the drive and folder for storing server drafts.
5. Note that under Preserve fidelity when sharing this document, you can choose to embed fonts in the file. By embedding fonts, you can be sure the document will show the fonts you used when you created the file, even if the user doesn't have those fonts installed on their computer.
6. Click **Cancel** to close the Word Options dialog box without making any changes.

7. Click the **File** tab to show the Backstage view. Depending on the AutoRecover settings, if you were working on a saved document, you may see one or more autosaved versions of the open document, as shown in **Figure 17–13**.

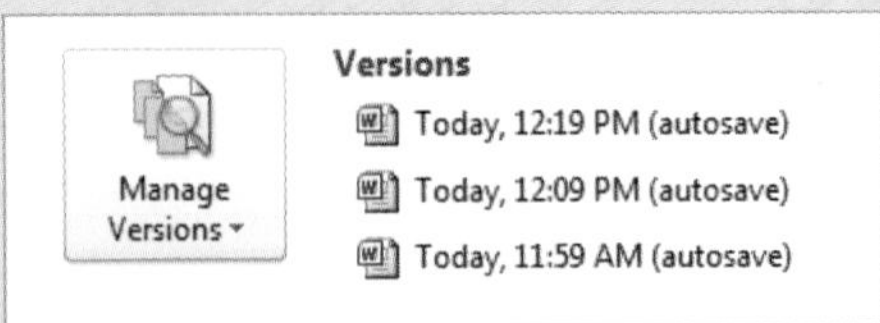

FIGURE 17–13
Autosaved versions in Backstage view

8. Click **Manage Versions**, and then click **Recover Unsaved Documents.** The Open dialog box opens and shows the folder where the AutoRecovery drafts are saved (as noted in Step 3 above). If the save option *Keep the last autosaved version if I close without saving* is enabled, an automatically saved version may appear in the Open dialog box, as shown in the example in **Figure 17–14**.

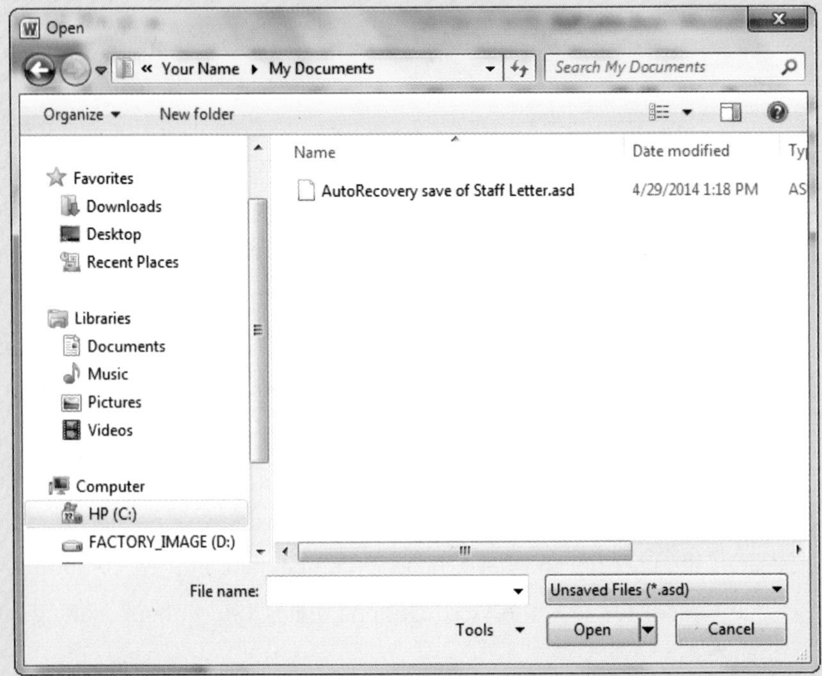

FIGURE 17–14
Open dialog box with example of an AutoRecovery saved document

9. Click **Cancel** to close the dialog bog.
10. Click the **File** tab and leave Word open for the next Step-by-Step.

Customizing the AutoCorrect Feature

You already know that the AutoCorrect feature automatically corrects commonly misspelled words immediately after an error is typed. The default settings in Word provide a long list of AutoCorrect entries. You can customize the list by creating your own AutoCorrect entries. To illustrate, if you frequently type certain words incorrectly, you can add the misspelled words to the AutoCorrect list so Word will always correct your mistake.

You can also use AutoCorrect to quickly insert text you use over and over again. For example, you may frequently enter your full name in documents. You can create an AutoCorrect entry using your initials, and then every time you type your initials followed by a blank space, Word will automatically insert your full name.

Sometimes you frequently use terms and phrases that have unique spellings and/or capitalization, and you don't want Word to correct those spellings. For example, the spellings of personal, company, and product names cannot always be found in a dictionary. To store names that you do not want Word to correct automatically, you can create a list of exceptions for three different categories: (1) words or text after which you do not want Word to capitalize (such as an abbreviation that includes a period); (2) words or text in initial caps; and (3) other corrections that do not fall within the first two categories.

In the next Step-by-Step, you will add a new entry to the AutoCorrect list and you will create two AutoCorrect exceptions. However, because you may be sharing a computer, you will delete the new entry and the two exceptions at the end of the Step-by-Step.

Step-by-Step 17.9

1. If necessary, open a new blank document. Click the **File** tab, and then click **Options**. In the left pane of the Word Options dialog box, click **Proofing**.
2. Under AutoCorrect options, click **AutoCorrect Options**. The AutoCorrect dialog box opens, as shown in **Figure 17–15**. In the scrolling list at the bottom of the window, the text shown in the left column is automatically replaced with the text shown in the right column.

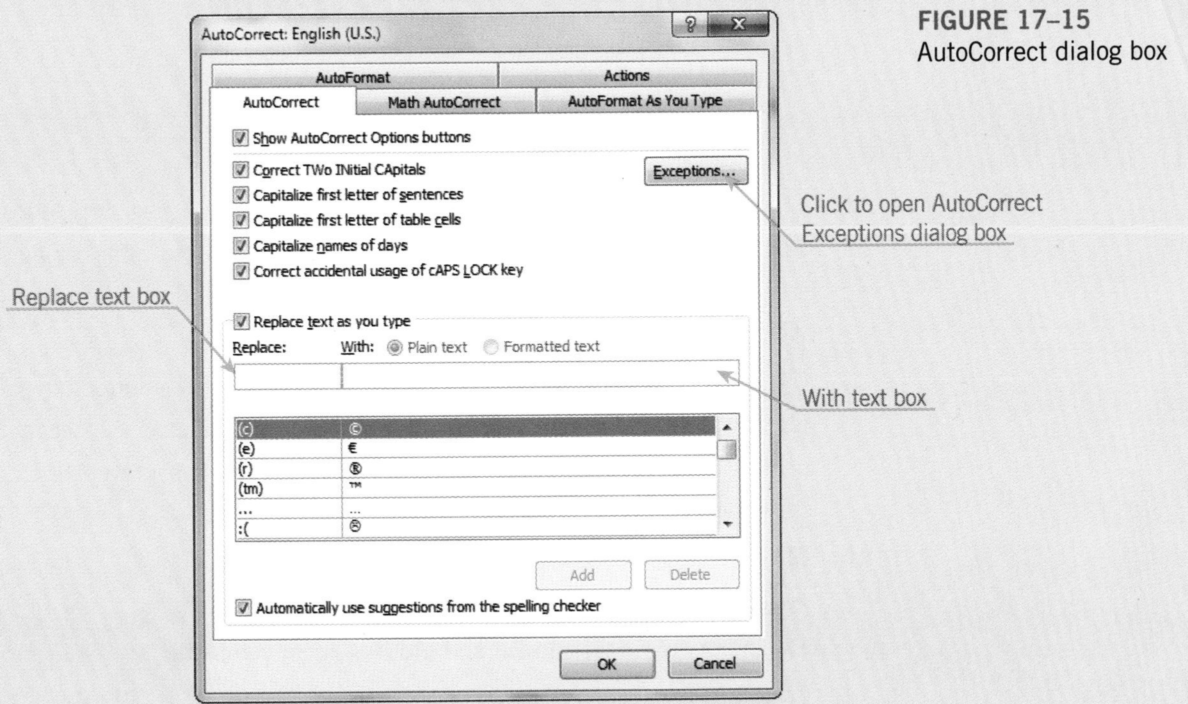

FIGURE 17–15
AutoCorrect dialog box

3. Scroll through the list of frequently misspelled words until you see *agian* in the left column. Note that Word will automatically correct this misspelling to *again*.
4. In the Replace text box, type **wrd**. In the With text box, type **word**. Click **Add**. Click **OK** to close the AutoCorrect dialog box, and then click **OK** to close the Word Options dialog box.
5. Type the following sentence exactly as shown with the misspelled words. Notice as you type that Word automatically corrects the misspelled words.

   Sometimes we misspell the same wrd agian and agian. As soon as you press the spacebar or end the sentence with a period, Word immediately corrects the misspellings.

TIP

You can add words to the AutoCorrect list when using the spelling checker by clicking the AutoCorrect option in the Spelling and Grammar dialog box.

6. Click the **File** tab, and then click **Options**. In the left pane, click **Proofing**, and then click **AutoCorrect Options**.
7. In the AutoCorrect dialog box, click **Exceptions**. The AutoCorrect Exceptions dialog box opens, as shown in **Figure 17–16**. Notice that Word already provides a list of exceptions for first-letter capitalization.

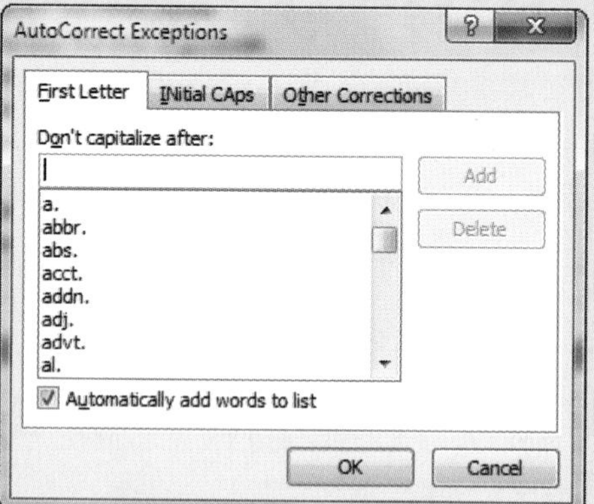

FIGURE 17–16
AutoCorrect Exceptions dialog box

8. In the text box under Don't capitalize after, type **Ltd.**. Then click **Add**. Normally, Word would capitalize the first letter in a word after a blank space following *Ltd.* due to the period, but this exception will prevent Word from capitalizing the next word that follows.
9. Click the **INitial CAps** tab. In the text box under Don't correct, type **EXcel** and then click **Add**. Normally, Word would lowercase the second capital letter in the word *EXcel*, but this exception will prevent Word from making that AutoCorrect change.
10. Click **OK** three times to close the dialog boxes.
11. Press the **spacebar** and then type the following sentence:

    The merger of EXcel and Durand Ltd. is almost complete.
12. Click the **File** tab, click **Options**, click **Proofing**, and then click **AutoCorrect Options**. In the Replace text box, type **wrd**. Word scrolls to that AutoCorrect entry in the list box. With the *wrd* entry selected, click **Delete**.

13. Click **Exceptions**. On the INitial CAps tab, select the entry **EXcel** and click **Delete**. Click the **First Letter** tab, and under Don't capitalize after, type the letter **l** (a lowercase L), select **ltd.**, and then click **Delete**. Click **OK** three times to close the dialog boxes and the Word Options.
14. Close the document without saving the changes.

Creating a Custom Dictionary

When you run a spelling checker, Word compares the text to a list of common words stored in a standard dictionary. When Word flags a possibly misspelled word, you can add the word to the dictionary, but it is not added to the standard dictionary. Instead, the word is added to a new custom dictionary named CUSTOM.DIC. If you frequently use proper names and acronyms that are not in Word's standard dictionary, you will find that adding those words to a custom dictionary is helpful so they aren't flagged as unknown or misspelled words during a spell check. When you add words to a dictionary, the words are added to the custom dictionary designated as the default dictionary.

Every Office 2010 application shares the file CUSTOM.DIC. If you share a computer, multiple individuals are contributing to the word list in the CUSTOM.DIC dictionary, and though it might be useful to have words added to the dictionary list, you don't have complete control of the list. To confirm that a word is in the list, you would need to review the list of words in the dictionary. An alternative solution is to create a separate custom dictionary. For example, you can create a custom dictionary for legal terms, one for medical terms, and another for engineering terms. Then you can add the new dictionary to Word's dictionary list and make it active. During a spell check, Word will check the standard dictionary, the default custom dictionary, and any other custom dictionaries that are active.

Step-by-Step 17.10

1. Open a new blank document. Click the **File** tab, and then click **Options**. In the left pane of the Word Options dialog box, click **Proofing**.
2. Under When correcting spelling in Microsoft Office programs, click **Custom Dictionaries**. The Custom Dictionaries dialog box opens, as shown in **Figure 17–17**. Your settings may differ. The CUSTOM.DIC default dictionary appears under Dictionary List.

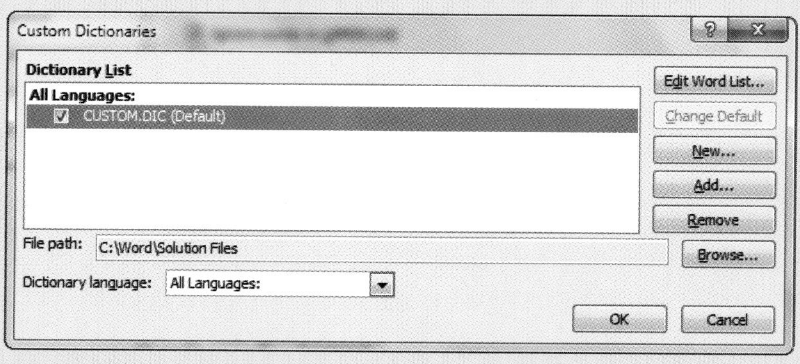

FIGURE 17–17
Custom Dictionaries dialog box

3. In the dialog box, click **New** to open the Create Custom Dictionary dialog box.
4. Navigate to the drive and folder where you save your solution files. In the File name box, type **UltraTech**, followed by your initials. Do not change the file type. Word will add the .dic extension to the filename. Click **Save**.
5. In the Custom Dictionaries dialog box, select the **UltraTech** dictionary. Click **Edit Word List**. A dialog box for the new UltraTech dictionary opens. Currently, the Dictionary list contains no words. In the Word(s) text box, type **UltraTech** and then click **Add**. The new word is added to the Dictionary list.
6. Add two more words to the list:
   a. Click the Word box, type **coextrusion**, and then click **Add**.
   b. Click the Word box, type **coextrusions**, and then click **Add**.
   c. Click **OK**.
7. Now the Dictionary List shows two dictionaries. Both dictionaries have check marks, so they are both active. Select the **UltraTech** dictionary. (Be sure not to uncheck it.) Click **Change Default**. The order of the dictionaries is changed, and the UltraTech dictionary is now the default dictionary.
8. Click **OK** twice to close the dialog boxes.
9. Open the **LLDPE Blends and Coextrusions** file from the drive and folder where your Data Files are stored. Save the document as **Revised LLDPE Blends and Coextrusions**, followed by your initials.
10. If your Proofing settings are set to check spelling as you type, a wavy red line will appear below unknown words. Right-click the first unknown word, **Lepri**. In the shortcut menu, click **Add to Dictionary**. The word is added to the UltraTech dictionary because that is the default dictionary.
11. Click the **Review** tab, and then click the Spelling & Grammar button. When the word *comonomer* is flagged as an unknown spelling, click **Add to Dictionary**. A prompt appears indicating that the spelling and grammar check is complete. If the proofing option to show readability statistics is enabled, the Readability Statistics dialog box opens. Click **OK** to complete the spell check.
12. Save the changes to the document and close the document.
13. Click the **File** tab, click **Options**, and then click **Proofing**. Click **Custom Dictionaries**. Select the dictionary **UltraTech**, and click **Edit Word List**. Note that the words *Lepri* and *comonomer* appear in the Dictionary list. Click **OK**.
14. In the Custom Dictionaries dialog box, in the Dictionary list under All Languages, disable the **UltraTech** dictionary. When prompted to remove the custom dictionary, click **Yes**. The dictionary remains in the list, but it is not active. The CUSTOM.DIC dictionary is now the default dictionary. Click **OK** two times to close the dialog boxes.

If you are prompted to save changes to the Normal.dotm template upon exiting Word, click No.

SUMMARY

In this lesson, you learned:

- You can customize the Quick Access Toolbar by adding and deleting command buttons.
- You can customize the Ribbon by rearranging the order of the tabs and the groups and commands on the tabs.
- You can add new groups and new commands to the default Ribbon tabs, and you can create new custom tabs on the Ribbon.
- To share customized Ribbon and Quick Access Toolbar settings, you can export the settings to a file.
- You can save default settings to a document template so the settings are available for other documents and on other computers without changing the default settings in the Normal.dotm template.
- If you're not comfortable with the way text and objects appear on the screen, you can modify the display settings.
- Word offers several options for editing documents, and you can customize the editing settings to fit your needs.
- The default save settings include the document file format and location. For offline editing, you can also designate a location for saving documents on a document management server.
- You can customize the list of AutoCorrect entries, and you can also create a list of exceptions so Word does not correct the spelling or capitalization for unique terms and phrases.
- If you often type terms that are not in the main dictionary, you can save time using the spelling checker by creating a custom dictionary to store these terms.

VOCABULARY REVIEW

Define the following terms:

main tabs
tool tabs

REVIEW QUESTIONS

TRUE / FALSE

Circle T if the statement is true or F if the statement is false.

T F 1. When restoring Ribbon settings, you can reset an individual tab without making changes to the other tabs.

T F 2. You can choose which tabs to display on the Ribbon.

T F 3. When you customize the settings in Word, the changes are automatically saved to the application.

T F 4. When you customize the Ribbon in Word, the changes will also appear in the Ribbon for other applications such as Excel and PowerPoint.

T F 5. Word automatically checks all custom dictionaries when the spelling checker is run.

MULTIPLE CHOICE

Select the best response for the following statements.

1. When adding buttons to the Quick Access Toolbar, the buttons ______________.
   A. can be for commands that appear on the Ribbon
   B. can be for commands that do not appear on the Ribbon
   C. can be for popular commands
   D. all of the above
2. When reorganizing default commands on the Ribbon, you ______________.
   A. can copy and paste the commands to other groups
   B. can move the commands within a group
   C. can move the commands from one group to another
   D. cannot move the commands within a default group or from one default group to another
3. To add a new command to the Ribbon, you must ______________.
   A. add the command to a default group
   B. make sure the command does not appear somewhere else on the Ribbon
   C. create a custom group and then add the new command to the new group
   D. create a new tab, then create a new custom group, and then add the new command to the new group
4. The AutoCorrect feature automatically corrects ______________.
   A. commonly misspelled words
   B. all misspelled words
   C. only words included in the default dictionary or an active custom dictionary
   D. repetitive errors in a document
5. ______________ appear on the Ribbon only when you select objects in a document.
   A. Main tabs
   B. Default tabs
   C. Tool tabs
   D. Auxiliary tabs

WRITTEN QUESTIONS

Write a brief answer to the following questions.

1. The Ribbon already provides the most commonly used commands. Why would anyone want to customize the Ribbon?

2. How is reorganizing the tabs, groups, and commands on the Ribbon similar to rearranging document headings in Outline view?

3. How does the AutoCorrect feature save you time when entering frequently used text?

4. What is the purpose of the list of exceptions for AutoCorrect?

5. What is the maximum number of buttons you can add to the Quick Access Toolbar?

PROJECTS

If you have a SAM 2010 user profile, your instructor may have assigned an autogradable version of the indicated project. If so, log into the SAM 2010 Web site at *www.cengage.com/sam2010* to download the instruction and start files.

PROJECT 17–1

1. Open a new blank document. Make a note of the buttons that appear on the Quick Access Toolbar.
2. Add three new buttons to the Quick Access Toolbar. Choose commands that are not already on the Ribbon.
3. Remove the Undo button from the Quick Access Toolbar.
4. Open another new blank document. Click the Insert tab, click the Screenshot button, and then click Screen Clipping. Wait a moment for the active document to fade away. Drag the mouse pointer over the Quick Access Toolbar to identify the area to capture in the clipping. When you release the mouse button, the active document appears and the clipping is inserted in the document.
5. Save the document with the screenshot as Toolbar Screenshot, followed by your initials, and then close the document.
6. Restore the Quick Access Toolbar to its original settings by removing the three new buttons and adding the Undo button. (If the Quick Access Toolbar only showed three buttons at the beginning of the Project—Save, Undo, and Redo—you can use the Reset only Quick Access Toolbar option.)

SAM PROJECT 17–2

1. If necessary, open a new blank document.
2. Hide the References tab on the Ribbon.
3. Create a new tab on the Ribbon, and position it between the Review and the View tabs. Name the new tab Popular.
4. Rename the new custom group Editing.
5. Add a second new group to the Popular tab, and name the new group Formatting.
6. In the custom group Editing, add the Cut, Copy, Paste (Paste), and Find commands. In the custom group Formatting, add the commands Bold, Italic, and All Caps. If desired, assign custom icons to the buttons.
7. Move the View tab on the Ribbon so it appears to the right of the Home tab.
8. Close the Word Options dialog box.
9. Click the Popular tab.
10. Open another new blank document. Click the Insert tab, click the Screenshot button arrow, and then click Screen Clipping. Wait a moment for the active document to fade away. Drag the mouse pointer over the Ribbon to identify the area to capture in the clipping. Include all the Ribbon tabs in the capture. When you release the mouse button, the active document appears and the clipping is inserted in the document.
11. Save the document with the screenshot as **Custom Ribbon Screenshot**, followed by your initials. Then close the document.
12. Export the customized settings to a file. Name the file **Custom Ribbon Settings**, followed by your initials.
13. Reset all customizations to the Ribbon, and close the Word Options dialog box.

PROJECT 17–3

1. Create a custom dictionary titled **Members**, followed by your initials. Make sure you save the dictionary where you save your solution files.
2. Add the following names to the new dictionary:

   Cuffman

   Fulcom

   Harison

   Osbun

   Alano

   Irwig

   Ji

   Salvino

   Ogg

   Terrion

   Cimone
3. Make the Members dictionary the default dictionary. Close the Custom Dictionaries and Word Options dialog boxes.
4. Open the file **Member Directory** from the drive and folder where your Data Files are stored. Save the document as **Revised Member Directory**, followed by your initials.
5. Run the spelling checker and add the unknown member names to the dictionary.
6. Save the changes and close the document.
7. Open the Members custom dictionary to confirm that the new names were saved to the correct dictionary.
8. Uncheck the Members dictionary in the list of dictionaries so it is no longer active. Close any open dialog boxes.
9. Exit Word. If prompted to save changes to the Normal.dotm template when exiting Word, click No.

CRITICAL THINKING

ACTIVITY 17–1

Describe the difference between AutoCorrect and AutoComplete.

ACTIVITY 17–2

List three commands that you think should appear on the Quick Access Toolbar, and explain why you would add each command button to the toolbar.

UNIT REVIEW

Advanced Microsoft Word

REVIEW QUESTIONS

MATCHING

Match the correct term in Column 2 to its description in Column 1.

Column 1	Column 2
_____ 1. a ghost image that appears behind the content of a document	**A.** record
_____ 2. a set of predefined formats you can apply to characters, paragraphs, tables, and numbered and bulleted lists	**B.** data source
_____ 3. a collection of variable information to be used in a merge	**C.** template
_____ 4. the last line of a multiline paragraph that is split from the other lines in the paragraph and wraps to the next page or column	**D.** pull quote
_____ 5. a group of related fields, or a single field, treated as a unit in a data source	**E.** watermark
_____ 6. an object that accesses data stored in the source file	**F.** widow
_____ 7. a format developed by Microsoft that preserves the visual appearance and layout of each page and enables fast viewing and printing	**G.** orphan
_____ 8. a group of sequential commands and actions combined as a single command to automatically complete a task	**H.** sidebar
_____ 9. a file that affects the basic structure of a document and contains document settings (such as fonts, line spacing, margins, and page layout)	**I.** XML Paper Specification (XPS)
_____ 10. an excerpted line or phrase used to draw attention in a document	**J.** macro
	K. style
	L. metadata
	M. embedded object
	N. Portable Document Format (PDF)
	O. linked object

MULTIPLE CHOICE

Select the best response for the following statements.

1. You create a hyperlink to ______________.
   - A. navigate to a Web page
   - B. navigate to another location in the same document
   - C. navigate to a location in another document
   - D. all of the above
2. To create a price list or a catalog, you use the ______________ document type in the mail merge process.
   - A. Labels
   - B. Directory
   - C. Catalog
   - D. Letters
3. The numbered labels for table captions are automatically updated when ______________.
   - A. tables are moved within the document
   - B. tables are deleted from the document
   - C. new tables are inserted in the document
   - D. all of the above
4. A summary of tracked changes appears ______________.
   - A. in the markup area
   - B. in the Review Pane and in the markup area
   - C. only in the Review Pane
   - D. in the document properties that appear in Backstage view
5. When sorting content in a table, ______________.
   - A. you can sort a single column without rearranging the data for the remaining columns
   - B. you can sort all the data based on a specified column
   - C. the sort can be based on three criteria in multiple columns
   - D. all of the above
6. A section break controls the formatting for the ______________.
   - A. content that follows the break
   - B. content that precedes the break
   - C. content that follows and precedes the break
   - D. current page
7. A ______________ is a section format.
   - A. page border
   - B. header and footer
   - C. page number
   - D. all of the above
8. If you want to change a macro, you can ______________.
   - A. edit the VBA code
   - B. re-record the macro using the same macro name
   - C. re-record the macro using a new macro name
   - D. A or B

9. Themes define _______________ in a document.
   A. styles
   B. document formats
   C. colors, fonts, and effects
   D. all of the above
10. When you copy and paste data from an Excel worksheet, _______________.
   A. you have access to all of Excel's data formatting and calculation options
   B. the data is converted to a table
   C. the data is linked to the Excel worksheet and will automatically be updated
   D. you cannot edit the data in the Word document

WRITTEN QUESTIONS

Write a brief answer to the following questions.

1. Explain how using the Navigation Pane to reorganize document content is similar to using Outline view to reorganize document content.

2. How can you protect a document from being edited before distributing it within a workgroup?

3. What is the difference between a document template and a global template?

4. What is the difference between linking and embedding an object?

5. If a chart in a Word document is linked to an Excel worksheet, how do you update changes in the chart data?

6. If you plan to create a table of contents and an index, which should you complete first and why?

7. What are the benefits of creating a custom dictionary?

8. Why would you use the filtering process when completing a mail merge process?

9. Name three paragraph formats that control text flow and explain how they control the text flow.

10. Why is it recommended that you attach a digital signature to a macro project?

PROJECTS

PROJECT 1

1. Create a new macro-enabled document template and save the file as **Personal Template 5.dotm**, followed by your initials.
2. Open the **Ski Club** file from the drive and folder where your Data Files are stored. Save the document as **Ski Club Flyer**, followed by your initials.
3. Attach the Personal Template 5 template to the document.
4. Create two sidebars. Cut and paste the *Show Schedule* text and the *Contact Information* text to the sidebars.
5. Create custom styles for the title, subtitle, and headings. Name the styles **Flyer Title**, **Flyer Subtitle**, and **Flyer Heading**, and save the new styles to the Personal Template 5 template.
6. Under the heading *Practices*, after *Outdoor practices are scheduled as follows:*, convert the five lines of text to a table and then AutoFit the table contents.
7. Insert the picture file Pyramid.JPG from the drive and folder where your Data Files are stored. Resize and format the picture as necessary.
8. Create a macro to apply a custom bullet format. Choose a symbol for the bullet, and apply a color format for the symbol. Name the macro **Bullets**, and save the macro in the Personal Template 5 template.
9. Arrange the content on the page and further enhance the document so it can be used as a one-page flyer to recruit new members. For example, add a page border and/or a page color, justify the text alignment, and add a border to the picture.
10. Save the changes to the document and to the document template. Then save the document in the XPS format.
11. Close the XPS document, and then close the Word document and the document template.

PROJECT 2

1. Open the **Kick City** file from the drive and folder where your Data Files are stored. Save the document as **Final Kick City**, followed by your initials.
2. Apply a style to the headings at the top of each page. Modify the style(s) as needed and add paragraph borders if desired. (You can use a variety of formats for the headings; they do not have to be formatted the same.)

3. Apply a theme. Format a page background and modify settings as desired.
4. On the first page, format all the paragraphs between the title and the table in two columns.
5. Justify the alignment of all text in the document, and then automatically hyphenate the entire document.
6. AutoFit the contents in each table. Apply table styles to each of the tables and modify the table style(s) as desired. (You can use a variety of formats for the tables; they do not have to be formatted the same.)
7. Edit the first table by moving the rows for *Girls U10* and *Girls U8* to the bottom of the table. Then center the table horizontally at the bottom of the first page.
8. If necessary, change the page margins and adjust spacing above and below paragraphs so that the first table fits on the first page. If necessary, insert a column break. The second page should begin with the title *Kick City Soccer Day Camps*. If you change margin and paragraph formats, be sure to apply the changes to the entire document.
9. Edit the second table by deleting the first column.
10. Insert an appropriate clip art image to the right of the table on the second page. Resize the image as needed, and add a picture effect.
11. On the second page, in the first paragraph under the heading, insert a footnote after the word *instructors*. Choose a symbol for the reference mark. In the footnote pane, type **All instructors are certified by the United States Soccer Federation.**.
12. Make any other adjustments to enhance the appearance of the document.
13. Save the changes to the document. Then save the document in XPS format.
14. Close the XPS document, and then close the Word document.

PROJECT 3

1. Open the **Home Remedies** file from the drive and folder where your Data Files are stored. Save the document as **Final Home Remedies**, followed by your initials.
2. Mark the following words or groups of words that occur in the paragraphs below the headings. Do not apply the bold and italic formats for the page numbers format.
   a. Under *Minor Ills*, mark **sore throat** and **relax**.
   b. Under *Cure-Alls*, mark **bleeding gums**, **fever blister**, **eyestrain**, and **chicken pox**.
   c. Under *Insect Bites*, mark **mosquito bite**.
3. AutoMark the remaining index entries using the file **Home Remedies Entries**, which is stored in the drive and folder where your Data Files are stored.
4. Insert a page break at the end of the document. Generate the index, using a style of your choice, and then add the heading **Index** above the index. Format the heading for a single column, apply the Heading 1 style, and center the heading.
5. Create a table of contents:
   a. Insert a next page section break at the top of the document.
   b. Generate the table of contents in the new section at the top of the document, using a style of your choice.
   c. Add the heading **Table of Contents** above the table of contents. Apply the Heading 1 style and center the heading.
6. Add page numbers to the document:
   a. In the table of contents section, format the page numbers in the lower-right corner of the document, using a footer style of your choice. Format the page numbers with lowercase roman numerals (i, ii, iii).
   b. In the next section of the document, format a page number in the lower-right corner of the page, starting at number 1. Change the number to the 1, 2, 3 format, and show the page number on the first page.
   c. Update the page numbers in the table of contents.
7. Save the changes and close the document.

PROJECT 4

1. Open the **Pet Travel 1** file from the drive and folder where your Data Files are stored. Save the document as **Final Pet Travel**, followed by your initials.
2. The source information for the document content is provided at the end of the document. Add the source to the master list and the current list in the Source Manager (using the MLA Sixth Edition style settings). Then delete the four lines that reference the source at the end of the document. (*Hint*: The author is a corporate author.)
3. At the end of the last paragraph, insert a citation to reference the source you just added.
4. Position the insertion point at the end of the document and then insert the contents of the *Pet Travel 2* file, which is stored in the drive and folder where your Data Files are stored.
5. The source information for the document content is provided at the end of the document. Add the source to the master list and the current list in the Source Manager (using the MLA Sixth Edition style settings). Then delete the five lines that reference the source at the added content at the end of the document.
6. At the end of the last paragraph in the document, insert a citation to reference the source you just added.
7. Insert a page break at the end of the document, and then create a works cited page on the last page of the document.
8. Add page numbers to the bottom of each page. Choose a page number format and footer style of your choice.
9. Save the changes and close the document.

SIMULATION

Charles Feenstra is the vice president of marketing for a distribution company. The sales figures for the first and second quarters are compiled, and Charles asks you to review a letter he drafted to the company's four regional managers.

JOB 1

1. Open the **Sales Letter** file from the drive and folder where your Data Files are stored. Save the document as **Revised Sales Letter**, followed by your initials.
2. Convert the sales data to a table.
3. Format and sort the table contents:
   a. Center and bold the column headings.
   b. Add another row to the end of the table, and in the cell directly below *Southern*, type **Total**. Apply bold formatting to the *Total* row heading.
   c. Calculate the row and column totals.
   d. AutoFit the columns for contents, and center the table horizontally.
   e. Right-align the numbers in the *Year to Date* column.
   f. Sort the table contents in ascending alphabetic order based on the region names. Do not include the column headings or the *Total* row in the sort.
   g. Remove the table borders so they do not print.
4. Create a new custom dictionary named **Marketing.dic**, followed by your initials, and save the new dictionary with your solution files. Add Feenstra to the custom dictionary.
5. Toggle on the Track Changes feature. (Make sure the user name and initials are yours.) Review the document and make any necessary changes to correct spelling, punctuation, and grammar. Read the document content thoroughly; Word does not flag all the errors.
6. Add at least one comment to the document. If you don't have any revisions that require a comment to explain or justify the edit, then make a comment about the letter. Remember, Mr. Feenstra is a colleague, so be positive!
7. Restrict access to the table data. Use the password **jck0429!**.
8. Remove your custom dictionary from the dictionary list.
9. Save the changes and leave the document open for the next Job.

JOB 2

Mr. Feenstra reviewed your edits and agreed to everything, but he doesn't have experience working with revision marks, so he asks you to finalize the document.

1. If necessary, open the **Revised Sales Letter** file from your solution files. Save the document as **Final Sales Letter**, followed by your initials.
2. Turn off editing restrictions, and accept all the changes in the document.
3. Delete all the comments from the document.
4. If necessary, toggle off the track changes feature.
5. The letter will be printed on company stationery. Insert seven blank lines at the top of the document.
6. Save the document, and then inspect it and remove personal information.
7. Mark the document as final.
8. Leave the document open for the next Job.

JOB 3

Mr. Feenstra asks you to prepare final copies for each of the regional managers. He provides a data source with the names and addresses for company managers.

1. Open the **Managers** file from the drive and folder where your Data Files are stored. Save the document as **Updated Managers 1**, followed by your initials. Close the document.
2. If necessary, open the **Final Sales Letter** file from your solution files. Enable the editing, and then save the document as **Sales Letter Main Document**, followed by your initials.
3. Position the insertion point at the top of the document and press the down arrow six times. Type **June 18,** and then press spacebar and type the current year.
4. Complete the mail merge process for letters:
   a. Use the Sales Letter Main Document file as the main document.
   b. Use the Updated Managers 1 file as the data source.
   c. Include all the records in the merge. Edit Edith Kleiber's record by changing her last name to **Hunter**.
   d. Sort the records in ascending alphabetic order by last name.
   e. Complete the main document by inserting individual fields for the name and address below the date, following the format below.
   <<Title>> <<FirstName>> <<LastName>>
   <<JobTitle>>
   <<Company>>
   <<Address1>>
   <<City>>, <<State>> <<PostalCode>>
   f. Use the GreetingLine field to insert a salution. This is a business letter, so punctuate the greeting line with a colon.
   g. Preview the results and make any necessary changes.
   h. Merge all the records to a new document.
5. Save the new document as **Merged Sales Letter 1**, followed by your initials, and close the merged document. Save changes to the main document and close it. When prompted to save the changes to the *Updated Managers 1* data source file, click Yes.
6. Open a new blank document. Save the document as **Envelopes Main Document**, followed by your initials.

7. Complete the mail merge process for envelopes:
   a. Use the settings for size 10 envelopes.
   b. Use the same recipient list you used in Step 4.
   c. Preprinted envelopes will be used, so you do not need to include a return address. Complete the main document by inserting individual fields for the name and address, following the format below.
      <<Title>> <<FirstName>> <<LastName>>
      <<JobTitle>>
      <<Company>>
      <<Address1>>
      <<City>>, <<State>> <<PostalCode>>
   d. Preview the envelopes and make any necessary changes.
   e. Merge all the records to a new document. Save the new file as **Merged Sales Letter Envelopes 1**, followed by your initials.
8. Close the merged envelopes document. Then save the changes and close the main document.

JOB 4

Mr. Feenstra recently hired three new district managers, and he asks you to create copies of the letter for each of them.

1. Open the **Updated Managers 1** file from your solution files. Save the document as **Updated Managers 2**, followed by your initials.
2. Add the following names and addresses to the table, and then save the changes and close the document.

   Ms. Heidi Baldridge
   District Manager
   Micro Innovations
   233 Maple Avenue
   Trenton, NJ 08618-3401
   Region: **Eastern**

   Mr. Mike Heitkamp
   District Manager
   Micro Innovations
   18 Lownes Lane
   Springfield, PA 19064-5545
   Region: **Eastern**

   Ms. Marjorie Lashley
   District Manager
   Micro Innovations
   16620 SE 27th Street
   Bellevue, WA 98008-8856
   Region: **Western**
3. Open the **Sales Letter Main Document** file from your solution files. When prompted to place data from your database and continue, click Yes.
4. Complete the mail merge process for letters:
   a. Use the Updated Managers 2 file as the data source.
   b. Sort the data source in ascending alphabetic order by last name.
   c. Filter the data source for the job title District Manager.
   d. Preview the results and make any necessary changes.
   e. Merge all the records to a new document and save the new document as **Merged Sales Letter 2**, followed by your initials.
5. Close the merged document. Then close the main document, saving the changes.
6. Open the **Envelopes Main Document** file from your solution files. If prompted to place data from your database and continue, click Yes.

7. Complete the mail merge process for envelopes:
   a. Use the Updated Managers 2 file as the data source.
   b. Filter the data source for district managers.
   c. Preview the results and make any necessary changes.
   d. Merge all the records to a new document. Save the new file as **Merged Sales Letter Envelopes 2**, followed by your initials.
8. Close the merged envelopes document. Then close the main document, saving changes. If prompted to save the changes to the data source, click Yes.

JOB 5

Mr. Feenstra is preparing for a meeting with the regional and district managers. He asks you to create a bar chart using the table data that was included in the sales letter.

1. Open a new blank document.
2. Insert a bar chart, and then enter the table data provided in the Sales Letter Main Document file. Only use the region names and the first and second quarter sales figures. Do not chart the *Year to Date* column or the *Total* row.
3. Above the chart, add the chart title **First and Second Quarter Sales**.
4. Reposition the legend at the lower-right corner of the chart.
5. Change the page layout to landscape orientation, and resize the chart to fill the page.
6. Change the chart type to a column chart. Apply a style that you think best presents the data, and adjust chart elements if necessary.
7. Save the document as **Quarterly Sales Chart**, followed by your initials. Close the document.

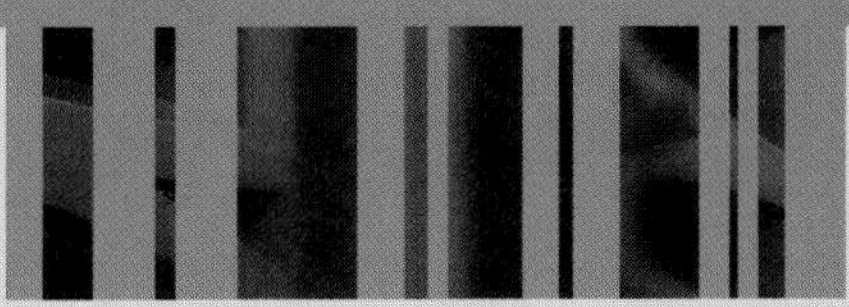

Estimated Time for Unit: 20.5 hours

ADVANCED

MICROSOFT EXCEL UNIT

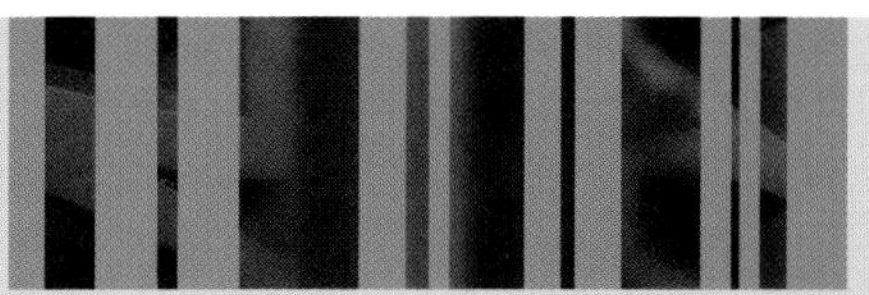

Estimated Time: 2.5 hours

LESSON 9

Applying Advanced Formats to Worksheets

OBJECTIVES

Upon completion of this lesson, you should be able to:

- Create custom number formats.
- Use conditional formatting rules.
- Create conditional formatting formulas.
- Format tables.
- Create custom AutoFilters.
- Apply themes.
- Switch banded rows and columns.
- Add or delete rows and columns in tables.
- Add totals to tables.

VOCABULARY

conditional formatting formulas

custom AutoFilter

banded columns

banded rows

tables

themes

Introduction

Microsoft Excel comes equipped with a number of advanced tools and features that empower you to create professional-looking spreadsheets using advanced formatting techniques, such as tables, themes, and conditional formatting. In this lesson, you will learn how to apply advanced features to data in a worksheet. You will also learn about custom AutoFilters.

Creating Custom Number Formats

Occasionally you may need to apply a number format that is not already predefined in the existing number formats. For example, the date format Year-Month, which would display a date in the format 2014-March, is not one of the formats available in Excel. You can create your own format by selecting the Custom category in the Format Cells dialog box.

Formats are composed of codes. These codes are simply strings of characters that represent the actual data, such as *m* for *month*, *d* for *day*, and *y* for *year*. You can easily create your own codes by assembling these characters in a certain order. **Table 9–1** describes the various character codes you can select.

TABLE 9–1 Format codes

FORMAT CODE	WHAT IT MEANS
0	Placeholder for a digit. A zero will appear if there is not another number available.
#	Placeholder for a digit. Nothing will appear if there is not another number available..
; (semicolon)	Divides the parts of the format code.
$	Puts a dollar sign with the number at the same location it appears in the format code.
%	Puts a percent sign with the number at the same location it appears in the format code.
, (comma)	Puts a comma with the number at the same location it appears in the format code.
. (decimal)	Puts a decimal with the number at the same location it appears in the format code.
M or m	Used for months in dates or for minutes in time.
D or d	Used for days.
Y or y	Used for years.
H or h	Used for hours.
S or s	Used for seconds.
: (colon)	Used to separate hours, minutes, and seconds.

Step-by-Step 9.1

1. Open the **Customer** file from the drive and folder where your Data Files are stored.
2. Save the workbook as **Customer List**, followed by your initials.
3. Select the range **E4:E22**.
4. On the Ribbon, click the **Home** tab. In the Cells group, click the **Format** button, and then click **Format Cells**.
5. If necessary, click the **Number** tab in the Format Cells dialog box.
6. Select **Custom** from the Category list box.
7. Highlight the text in the Type text box, and then type **yyyy-mm**. (Entering *y* four times represents the complete year number—hence, the year will be displayed as 2014. Entering *m* twice represents the month as two digits, such as 02 for February.) Your dialog box should appear similar to **Figure 9–1**.

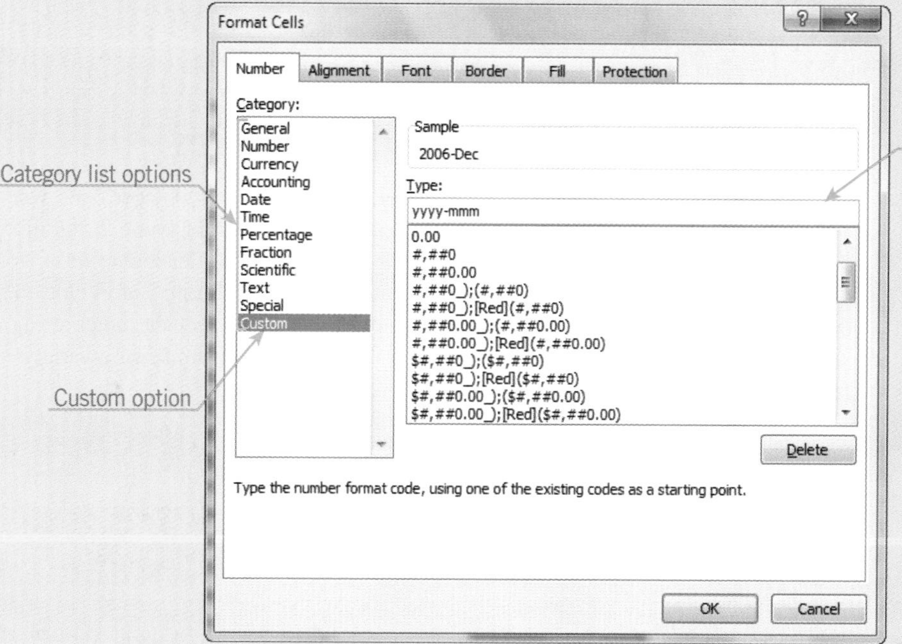

FIGURE 9–1
Custom format in Format Cells dialog box

8. Click **OK** and then look at your dates. Next, you will modify the custom format you just created.
9. Verify that the range E4:E22 is still selected, click the **Format** button, and then click **Format Cells**.
10. Select **Custom** from the Category list box, if necessary, and then click the custom format you just created. Type one more **m** in the Type text box so your final format is yyyy-mmm.

11. Click **OK** and then view the results. Notice that the day of the month is abbreviated with three letters, as shown in **Figure 9–2**.

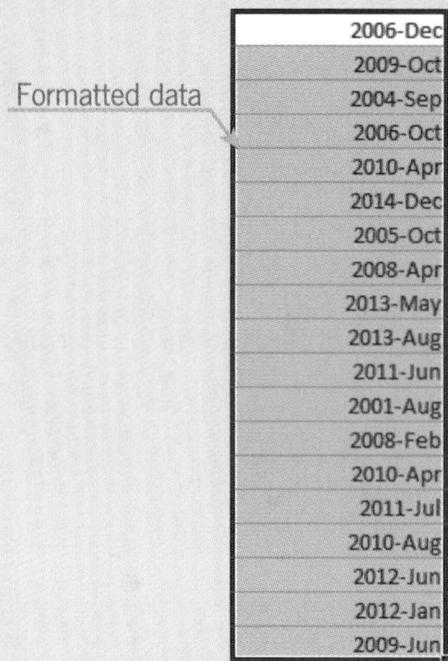

FIGURE 9–2
Custom date format

12. Save, print, and close the workbook.

Using Conditional Formatting Rules

Conditional formatting applies a font, border, or pattern to worksheet cells when certain conditions exist in those cells. For example, you might want to highlight products that are your top sellers. By applying conditional formats and criteria, you can then view the cell formats to see which cells met the condition. Before you start entering the conditional formatting rules, you will need to select the range of data where you want Excel to apply the formats. You can select from a wide variety of formats available in the New Formatting Rule dialog box.

EXTRA FOR EXPERTS

You can remove conditional formatting rules by clicking the Styles group on the Home tab, clicking the Conditional Formatting button arrow, and then clicking Clear Rules.

Step-by-Step 9.2

1. Open the **Employee** file from the drive and folder where your Data Files are stored.
2. Save the workbook as **Employee List** followed by your initials.
3. Select the range **I4:I21**. These cells contain the hourly wage rates for each of the hourly employees.
4. On the Ribbon, click the **Home** tab. In the Styles group, click the **Conditional Formatting** button.
5. Click **New Rule** on the Conditional Formatting menu. The New Formatting Rule dialog box opens, as shown in **Figure 9–3**.

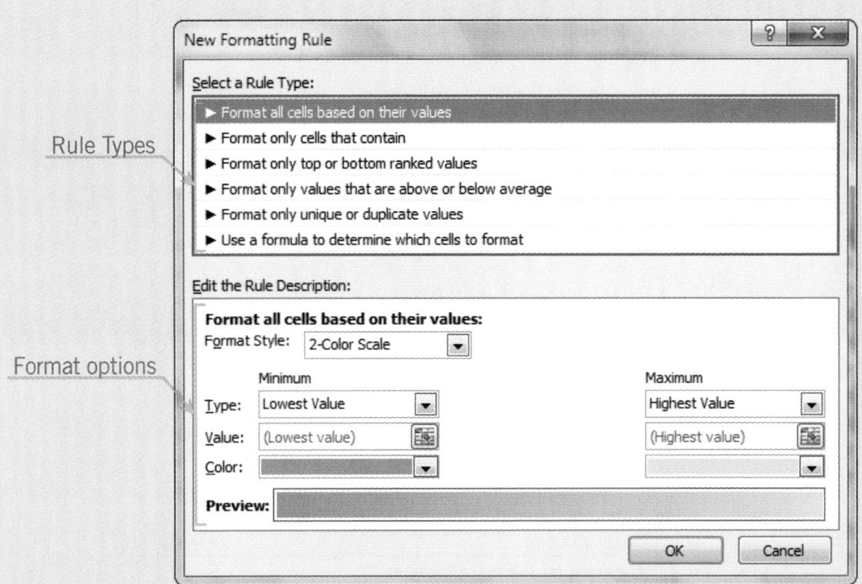

FIGURE 9–3
New Formatting Rule dialog box

6. Click the **Format only values that are above or below average** option.
7. Click the **Format values that are** menu arrow and then select **below**.
8. Click the **Format** button to display the Format Cells dialog box.
9. Click the **Fill** tab to shown the fill colors, and then select the blue color in the middle of the top row.
10. Click **OK** to close the Format Cells dialog box.
11. Click **OK** to close the New Formatting Rule dialog box and display the formatted cells. Check to see if the formats were applied correctly. You will now clear these formats for the next exercise.
12. On the Home tab in the Styles group, click the **Conditional Formatting** button, point to **Clear Rules**, and then click **Clear Rules from Entire Sheet**.
13. Leave the workbook open for the next Step-by-Step.

Creating Conditional Formatting Formulas

The conditional formatting you applied in the previous exercise uses options that are available in the New Formatting Rule dialog box. However, sometimes the option you need is not available. You would then need to create your own conditional format rule based on a formula called a ***conditional formatting formula***. For example, you might want to find all of the values in a selected range that are greater than an amount located in that range. You might have a cell in the selected range with an amount of $500, and you want to find out how many other cells in this range have an amount greater than $500. In addition, if the amount in this cell changes to $600, you want the same conditional formatting to appear without having to enter another formula.

VOCABULARY
conditional formatting formula

EXTRA FOR EXPERTS

You can create a custom format for your conditional format by clicking the Format button in the New Formatting Rule dialog box.

Step-by-Step 9.3

1. Select the range **I4:I21**, which contains the hourly wages.
2. On the Ribbon, click the **Home** tab. In the Styles group, click the **Conditional Formatting** button.
3. Click **New Rule** on the Conditional Formatting menu. The New Formatting Rule dialog box opens.
4. Click the **Use a formula to determine which cells to format** option.
5. Click in the **Format values where this formula is true** text box.
6. Type **=I4<$I$4** in the text box, as shown in **Figure 9–4**.

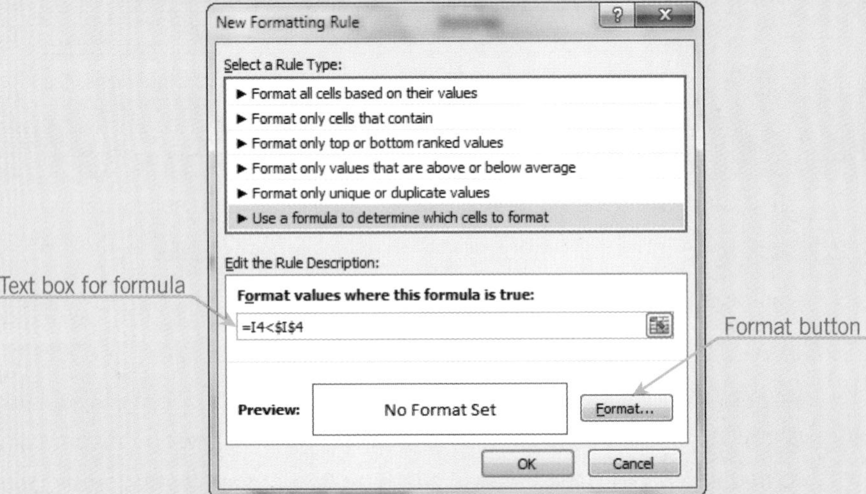

FIGURE 9–4 New Formatting Rule dialog box with formula entered

7. Click the **Format** button to display the Format Cells dialog box.
8. Click the **Fill** tab to show the fill colors, and then click the orange color in the top row.
9. Click **OK** to close the Format Cells dialog box.
10. Click **OK** to close the New Formatting Rule dialog box and display the formatted cells. View the formats based on the condition you entered, as shown in **Figure 9–5.**

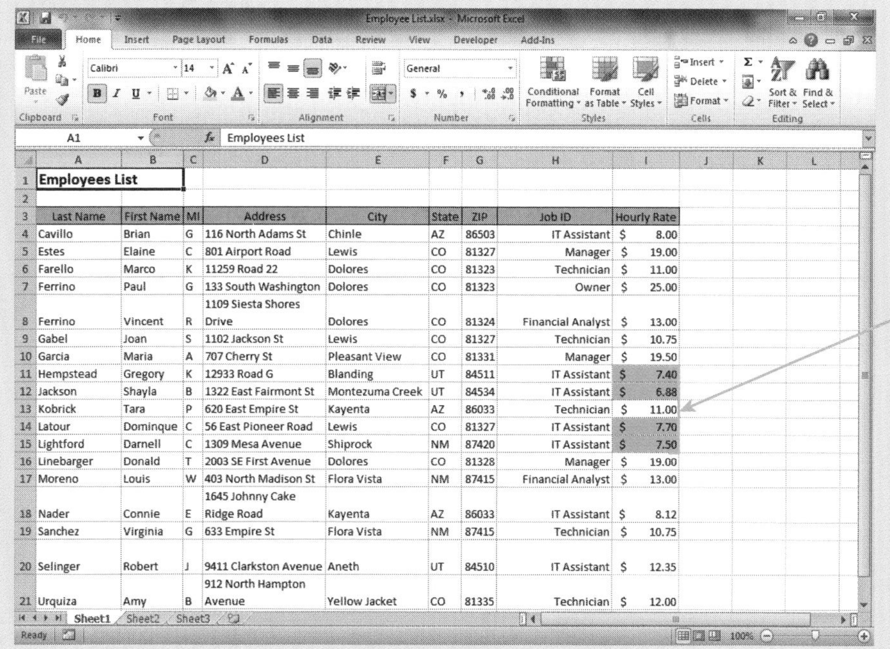

	A	B	C	D	E	F	G	H	I
1	Employees List								
2									
3	Last Name	First Name	MI	Address	City	State	ZIP	Job ID	Hourly Rate
4	Cavillo	Brian	G	116 North Adams St	Chinle	AZ	86503	IT Assistant	$ 8.00
5	Estes	Elaine	C	801 Airport Road	Lewis	CO	81327	Manager	$ 19.00
6	Farello	Marco	K	11259 Road 22	Dolores	CO	81323	Technician	$ 11.00
7	Ferrino	Paul	G	133 South Washington	Dolores	CO	81323	Owner	$ 25.00
8	Ferrino	Vincent	R	1109 Siesta Shores Drive	Dolores	CO	81324	Financial Analyst	$ 13.00
9	Gabel	Joan	S	1102 Jackson St	Lewis	CO	81327	Technician	$ 10.75
10	Garcia	Maria	A	707 Cherry St	Pleasant View	CO	81331	Manager	$ 19.50
11	Hempstead	Gregory	K	12933 Road G	Blanding	UT	84511	IT Assistant	$ 7.40
12	Jackson	Shayla	B	1322 East Fairmont St	Montezuma Creek	UT	84534	IT Assistant	$ 6.88
13	Kobrick	Tara	P	620 East Empire St	Kayenta	AZ	86033	Technician	$ 11.00
14	Latour	Dominque	C	56 East Pioneer Road	Lewis	CO	81327	IT Assistant	$ 7.70
15	Lightford	Darnell	C	1309 Mesa Avenue	Shiprock	NM	87420	IT Assistant	$ 7.50
16	Linebarger	Donald	T	2003 SE First Avenue	Dolores	CO	81328	Manager	$ 19.00
17	Moreno	Louis	W	403 North Madison St	Flora Vista	NM	87415	Financial Analyst	$ 13.00
18	Nader	Connie	E	1645 Johnny Cake Ridge Road	Kayenta	AZ	86033	IT Assistant	$ 8.12
19	Sanchez	Virginia	G	633 Empire St	Flora Vista	NM	87415	Technician	$ 10.75
20	Selinger	Robert	J	9411 Clarkston Avenue	Aneth	UT	84510	IT Assistant	$ 12.35
21	Urquiza	Amy	B	912 North Hampton Avenue	Yellow Jacket	CO	81335	Technician	$ 12.00

Formatted cells met criteria

FIGURE 9–5 Conditional formatting applied

11. Save, print, and close the workbook.

Formatting Tables

After entering data into a worksheet, the design of the worksheet can enhance the appearance of the data. ***Tables*** provide professional presentation features for displaying worksheet data. Formatting tables works best when there are not any existing background colors. You should also be sure that there are no blank columns

VOCABULARY
tables

or rows. Excel offers quite a variety of table formats in the Table Format gallery shown in **Figure 9–6**.

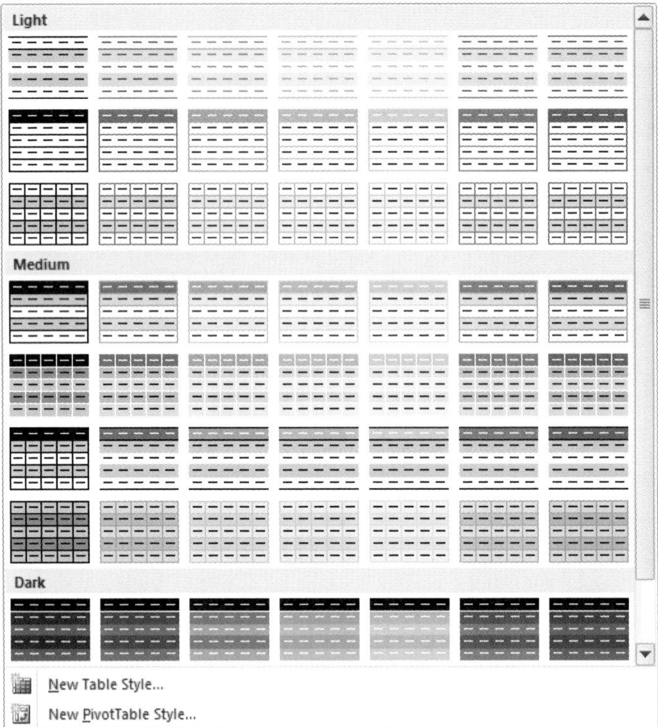

FIGURE 9–6 Table Format gallery

After you select a format for your table, the Table Tools Design tab appears on the Ribbon. AutoFilters are automatically added to the data when you format data as a table.

EXTRA FOR EXPERTS

You can add the AutoFormat button to the Quick Access Toolbar. To add this feature, click the Customize Quick Access Toolbar arrow, click More Commands, click the Choose commands from menu arrow, and then click Commands Not in the Ribbon. Click the AutoFormat option, click the Add button, and then click OK.

EXTRA FOR EXPERTS

If you want to remove AutoFilters from a table, you can select the row with the AutoFilters and then click the Sort & Filter button in the Editing group. Finally, click the Filter option to remove the filters.

Step-by-Step 9.4

1. Open the **Tool** file from the drive and folder where your Data Files are stored.
2. Save the workbook as **Tool Sales** followed by your initials. Notice that the text in the worksheet has very basic formatting. The column headings simply have a bold format applied.
3. Click any cell in the range.
4. On the Home tab in the Styles group, click the **Format as Table** button to display the Table Format gallery.
5. Select the **Table Style Medium 2** option, which is the second table in the first row of the Medium group. The Format As Table dialog box opens with the range =$A$3:$F$15 displayed.

6. Click **OK**. The table formats are displayed as shown in **Figure 9–7**. *Note*: If this range did not appear in the Format as Table dialog box, you could type this range in the Where is the data for your table text box and then click OK.

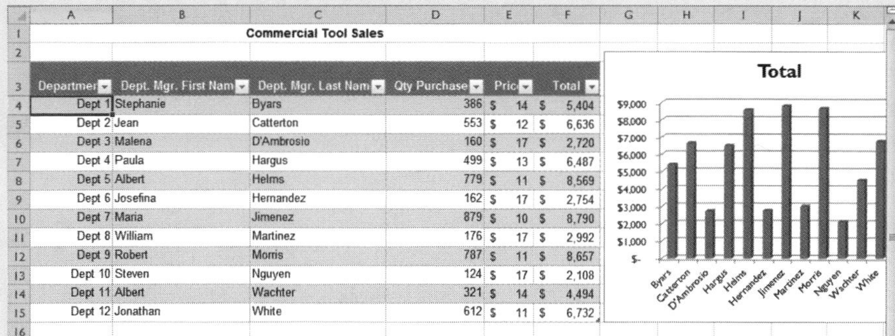

Departmer	Dept. Mgr. First Nam	Dept. Mgr. Last Nam	Qty Purchase	Pric	Total
Dept 1	Stephanie	Byars	386	$ 14	$ 5,404
Dept 2	Jean	Catterton	553	$ 12	$ 6,636
Dept 3	Malena	D'Ambrosio	160	$ 17	$ 2,720
Dept 4	Paula	Hargus	499	$ 13	$ 6,487
Dept 5	Albert	Helms	779	$ 11	$ 8,569
Dept 6	Josefina	Hernandez	162	$ 17	$ 2,754
Dept 7	Maria	Jimenez	879	$ 10	$ 8,790
Dept 8	William	Martinez	176	$ 17	$ 2,992
Dept 9	Robert	Morris	787	$ 11	$ 8,657
Dept 10	Steven	Nguyen	124	$ 17	$ 2,108
Dept 11	Albert	Wachter	321	$ 14	$ 4,494
Dept 12	Jonathan	White	612	$ 11	$ 6,732

FIGURE 9–7
Formatted table

7. Reduce the column widths for columns B and C so that these column headings are displayed in two rows in the same cell. Next, you will add formats to the worksheet title so that it blends better with the table formats.
8. Click **cell A1**, and then, on the Home tab in the Styles group, click the **Cell Styles** button.
9. In the Themed Cell Styles section of the Cell Styles gallery, click **20% Accent1**, which is the first option in this grouping.
10. In the Font group, click the **Bold** button **B** to add bold formatting to the text in cell A1.
11. Save, print, and leave the workbook open for the next Step-by-Step.

EXTRA FOR EXPERTS

To convert a table back to a normal range, but keep the data and table style formatting, click anywhere in the table. Click the Design tab on the Ribbon, then click the Convert to Range option in the Tools group. Click Yes when asked if you want to convert the table to a normal range.

Creating Custom AutoFilters

VOCABULARY
Custom AutoFilter

The ***Custom AutoFilter*** is a feature that lets you display only cells that meet specific criteria. Excel has predefined filters for numbers such as Greater Than, Less Than, Above Average, and Below Average, as shown on the AutoFilter Number list options in **Figure 9–8**.

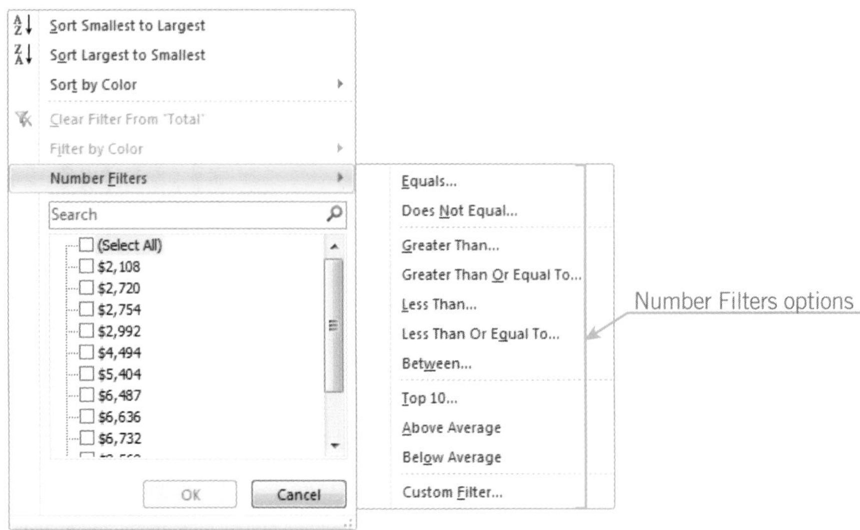

FIGURE 9–8 AutoFilter Number list options

If the filtered data is text, the Text Filter options are Equals, Does Not Equal, Begins With, Ends With, Contains, Does Not Contain, and Custom Filters. Sometimes you may need to filter for number data that is not already defined in the Number Filters menu. For example, you may want to filter a range of data that requires two filters, such as Greater Than and Less Than. In this case, you need to create a custom AutoFilter.

Step-by-Step 9.5

1. Click the **Filter** arrow, located next to the title, for the Total column.
2. Click the **(Select All)** check box. All the columns are now deselected.
3. Point to **Number Filters**, and then click **Custom Filter**. The Custom AutoFilter dialog box opens.
4. In the top row of the Custom AutoFilter dialog box, click the **down arrow** under Total and then select **is greater than**.
5. Click in the text box at the top-right in the Custom AutoFilter dialog box and then type **5000**. You could select an option from the list, but typing the exact number into the text field gives you more control over the filter process.

6. In the second row, click the **down arrow** in the left text box and select **is less than**.
7. Click in the text box to the right of the second row and then type **7000**. Excel will find the totals that are in the range of greater than 5000 and less than 7000. Your dialog box should resemble the one shown in **Figure 9–9**.

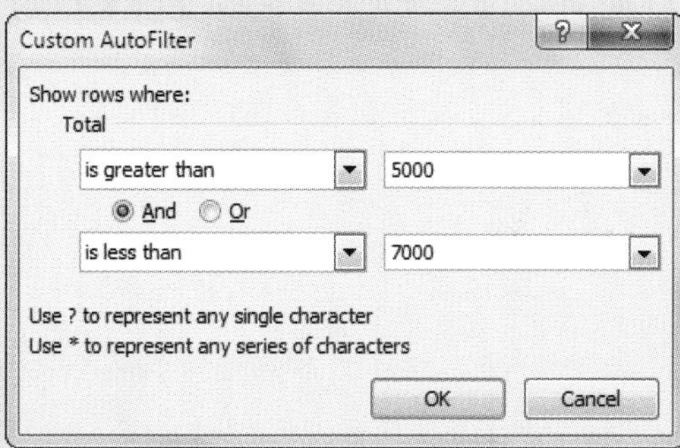

FIGURE 9–9
Custom AutoFilter dialog box

8. Click **OK**. If necessary, increase the size of the chart so that the names appear. The results of the filtering will be displayed, as shown in **Figure 9–10**.

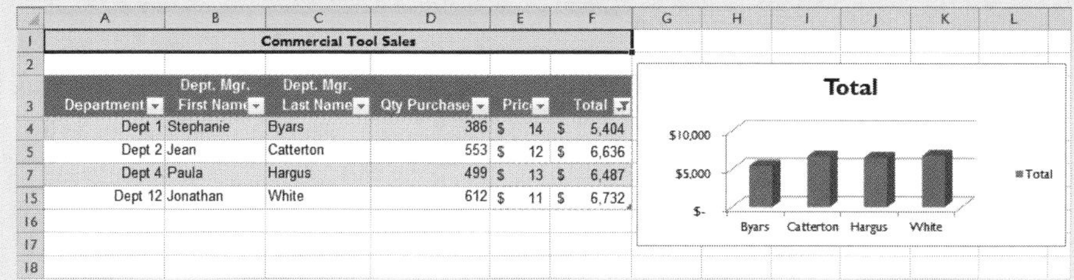

FIGURE 9–10
Results of Custom AutoFilter

9. Save, print, and close the workbook.

Applying Themes

VOCABULARY
themes

Themes are a simple way to make your worksheet appear more professional. With themes, you can have borders, background colors, shading, and graphic effects applied instantly to an entire workbook. Several themes are available with Excel 2010, and each theme has a specific look. The themes that are loaded with Excel 2010 are located in the Theme gallery, as shown in **Figure 9–11**.

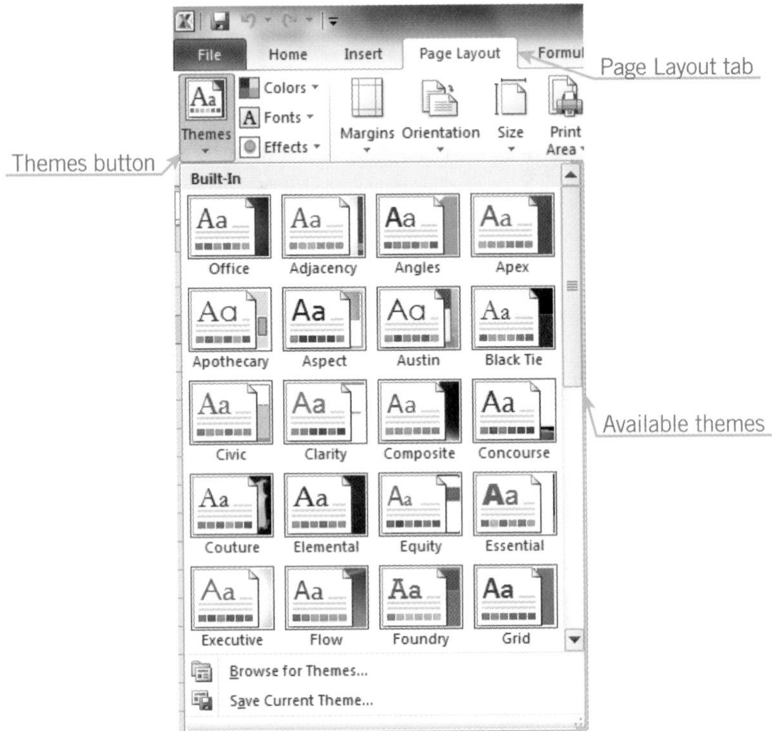

FIGURE 9–11 Theme Gallery

Theme formats apply to your entire workbook with the exception of very few objects, such as an embedded object. So, if you change a theme in one worksheet, all other worksheets will appear with the same theme. In addition, the same themes that you apply in Excel are also available in other Microsoft Office applications, such as Word, PowerPoint, and Access. Before you apply a theme, you need to add some basic formatting to the data, such as a table format, so that Excel knows how to apply the theme to your worksheet.

Step-by-Step 9.6

1. Open the **Themes** file from the drive and folder where your Data Files are stored.
2. Save the workbook as **Applied Themes** followed by your initials.
3. On the Ribbon, click the **Page Layout** tab. In the Themes group, click the **Themes** button. The Theme gallery displays.

4. Move the pointer over the various theme options in the Theme gallery to view the different formats.
5. Click the **Austin** theme to change the formats in your worksheet.
6. Click the **Customer Returns** worksheet tab to view this worksheet. Notice that the Austin theme is also applied to this worksheet.
7. Click the **Themes** button, and then select the **Hardcover** theme. View the new formats in your worksheet.
8. Click **cell A1**. Then, on the Home tab in the Font group, click the **Fill Color** button arrow and then select a fill color that will coordinate with the Hardcover theme.
9. Click the **Customer Purchases** worksheet and then select cell A1, or any cell in the column headings. On the Home tab in the Editing group, click the **Sort & Filter** button arrow, and then click **Filter**. The AutoFilters should now be removed, as shown in **Figure 9–12**.

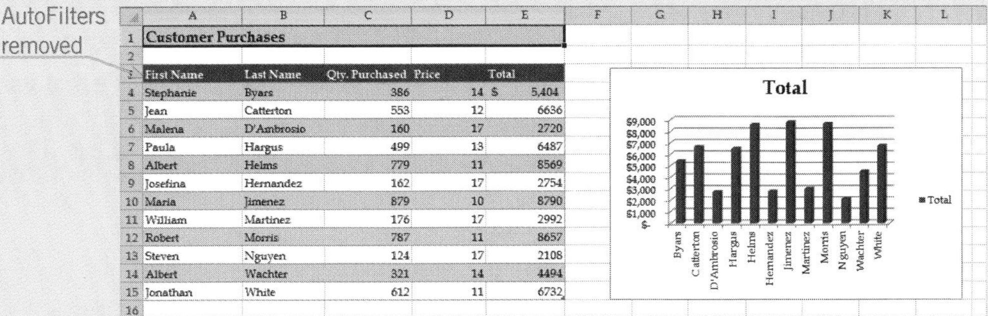

First Name	Last Name	Qty. Purchased	Price	Total
Stephanie	Byars	386	14	$ 5,404
Jean	Catterton	553	12	6636
Malena	D'Ambrosio	160	17	2720
Paula	Hargus	499	13	6487
Albert	Helms	779	11	8569
Josefina	Hernandez	162	17	2754
Maria	Jimenez	879	10	8790
William	Martinez	176	17	2992
Robert	Morris	787	11	8657
Steven	Nguyen	124	17	2108
Albert	Wachter	321	14	4494
Jonathan	White	612	11	6732

FIGURE 9–12
AutoFilters removed from theme

10. Save the workbook and leave it open for the next Step-by-Step.

Switching Banded Rows and Columns

When you create a table, the rows and columns appear with different formats. Typically, one row will have a lighter format, and the adjacent row will have a darker format. This type of formatting is referred to as banding. For example, if you choose a theme that includes the color blue, you would have one row in a white or light blue and the next row in a darker blue. The following row will appear with the lighter row again. These same formats appear in columns. Excel refers to the row format as ***banded rows*** and the column format as ***banded columns***. You have the option to switch between banded rows and banded columns. These options are available on the Table Tools Design tab, which appears after you add table formatting as shown in **Figure 9–13**.

VOCABULARY
banded rows
banded columns

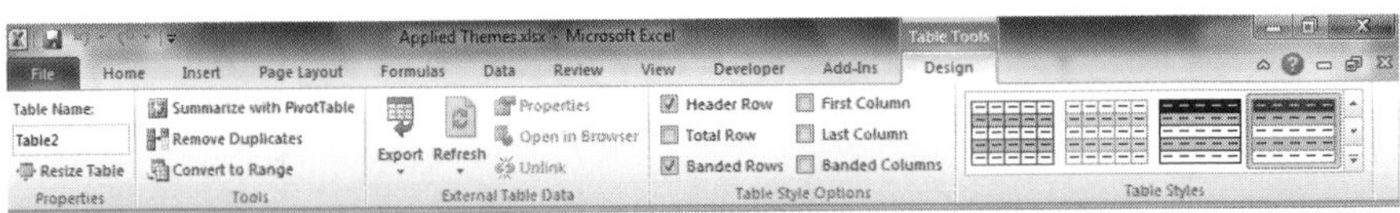

FIGURE 9–13 Table Tools Design tab on Ribbon

Step-by-Step 9.7

1. Save the workbook as **Applied Themes 2**.
2. In the Themes workbook, select any cell within the data.
3. On the Ribbon, click the **Table Tools Design** tab. In the Table Style Options group, notice that the Banded Rows check box is selected and the Banded Columns check box is not selected, as shown in Figure 9–13.
4. Click the **Banded Rows** check box to deselect it. Notice how the heavy shading in alternating rows is removed.
5. Click the **Banded Columns** check box to select it. Your table should now appear with alternating columns shaded, as shown in **Figure 9–14**.

FIGURE 9–14 Banded columns

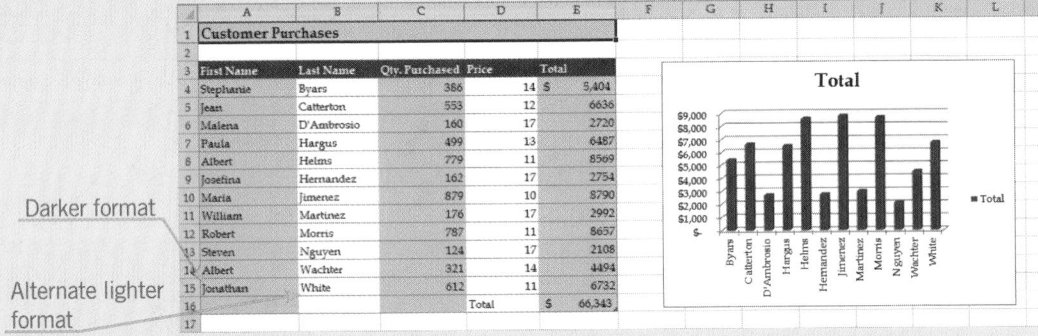

6. Click the **Customer Returns** worksheet tab. Note that while themes are applied to the entire workbook, individual formatting features, such as banded rows and columns, are unique to the worksheet in which they were applied.
7. Save, print, and close the workbook.

Adding or Deleting Rows and Columns in Tables

When you apply banded rows or banded columns to a table, you will want the same formatting to appear if you need to add or delete a column or row. To keep the table formatting intact, it is best to use the commands on the Insert and Delete menus in the Cells group on the Home tab.

After selecting a range within a table where you want a new row or column to appear, click the Insert button arrow in the Cells group on the Home tab and you will see the available menu commands as shown in **Figure 9–15**.

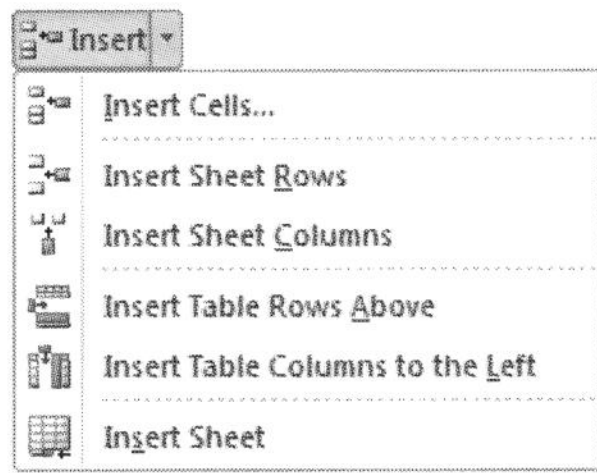

FIGURE 9–15 Insert menu options

Selecting the Insert Table Rows Above command inserts a row in the table above the selected range. Also, notice that you can insert a column to the left of a selected column. These commands are also available when you right-click a selection in the table.

TIP

You can type in any cell next to the column on the right side of the table and the column formats will automatically appear in this column after you press Enter.

TIP

If the last cell in the lower-right corner of a table is selected, you can press Tab to create a new, formatted row.

Step-by-Step 9.8

1. Open the **Team** file from the drive and folder where your Data Files are stored.
2. Save the workbook as **Team List** followed by your initials.
3. Select the range **B9:D9**. You will insert a new row in the table.
4. On the Home tab in the Cells group, click the **Insert** button arrow and then click **Insert Table Row Above**.
5. Click a cell outside the table to view the formatting.
6. Type **23487**, **Basketball**, and **BASK-2** into cells **B9:D9** respectively.
7. Click in **cell E9**, type **Jan-2014**, and then press **Enter**. Notice how Column E is now formatted the same as Column D. Next, you will delete a row.
8. Select range **B12:E12**.
9. On the Home tab in the Cells group, click the **Delete** button and then click **Delete Table Rows**.

Compare your table to **Figure 9–16**.

FIGURE 9–16 Revised table

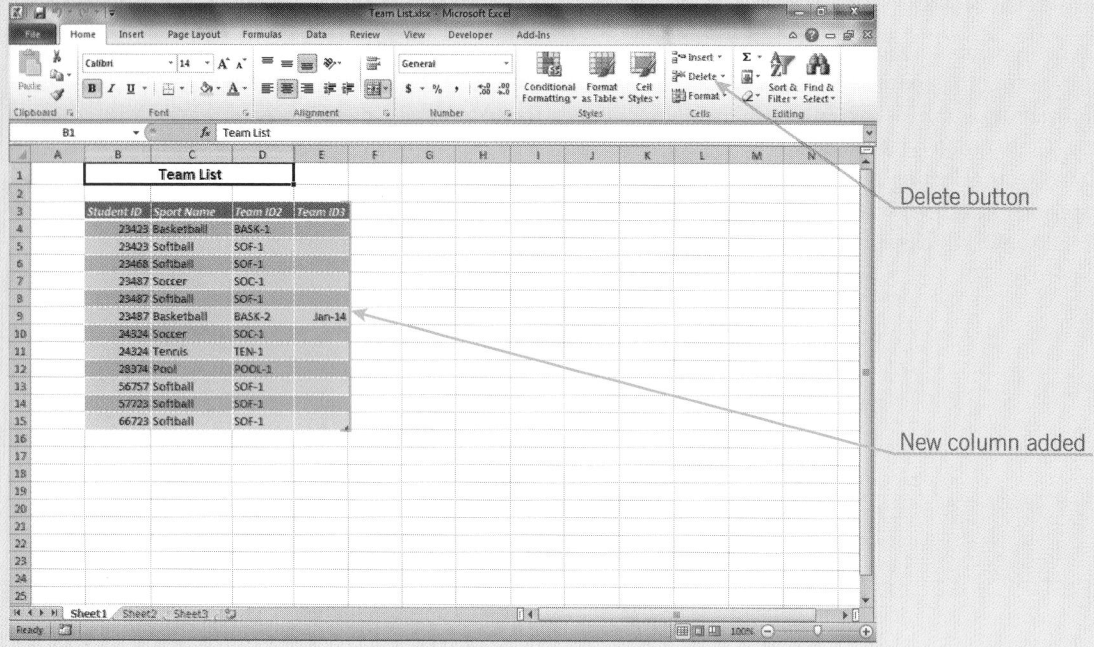

10. Save, print, and close the workbook.

Adding Totals to Tables

After formatting data as a table, you may want to add totals to the rows or columns of data. Excel recognizes data that is formatted as a table and retains the format when you add totals on the bottom row of the table or next to the far-right column. To add totals to rows in a table, you type a new column heading next to the far-right column heading and press Enter. Or, you can type a formula next to the last cell in the top row of data underneath where the column heading would appear. When you press Enter, Excel automatically enters this formula for each of the remaining rows in the table. Excel also gives you the option to add a total row at the bottom of a column in a table by selecting Total Row in the Table Style Options group on the Design tab. Excel will add a total to the bottom of the column at the far-right side of the table. You can also select another function from the Functions list that appears on the new row.

Step-by-Step 9.9

1. Open the **Bakery** file from the drive and folder where your Data Files are stored.
2. Save the workbook as **Bakery Sales** followed by your initials.

3. Click **cell D3**, type **Totals**, and then press **Enter**. Notice how the new Column D is formatted exactly like the rest of the table, as shown in **Figure 9–17**. You will use this column to add totals to the table.

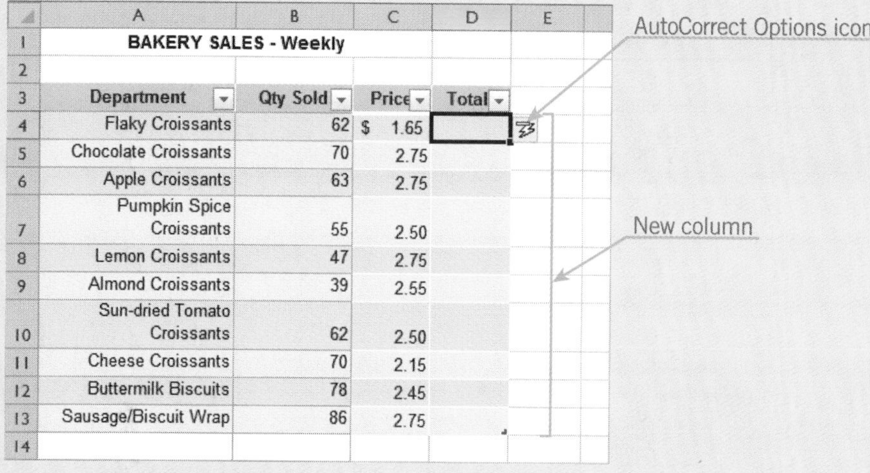

FIGURE 9–17
Table with new column

4. In cell D4, type = (equal sign) to start a formula.
5. Click **B4**.
6. Type * (asterisk) for multiplication.
7. Click **cell C4** and then press **Enter**. Column D now contains column totals throughout the table.
8. On the Ribbon, click the **Design** tab.
9. In the Table Style Options group, click the **Total Row** check box. Excel adds a row with a formula that sums the row totals.
10. Click **cell D14**, click the **down arrow** to display the Function list, and then click **Average**. The total function changes to show the average function for the column. The average sales amount now appears in cell D14.
11. To change the Average function back to the Sum function, click **D14**, click the **down arrow**, and then click **Sum** from the Function list. Next, you will change the text color for the new row so that it is easier to read.
12. Select **A14:D14**.

13. On the Home tab, in the Font group, click the **Font Color** arrow and then click **Black, Text 1, Lighter 5%** located in the bottom row of the Theme colors. The completed table should appear as shown in **Figure 9–18**.

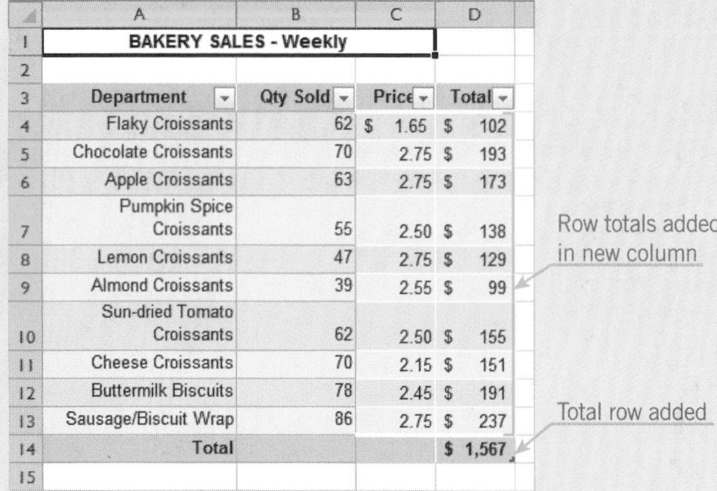

	A	B	C	D
1	BAKERY SALES - Weekly			
2				
3	Department	Qty Sold	Price	Total
4	Flaky Croissants	62	$ 1.65	$ 102
5	Chocolate Croissants	70	2.75	$ 193
6	Apple Croissants	63	2.75	$ 173
7	Pumpkin Spice Croissants	55	2.50	$ 138
8	Lemon Croissants	47	2.75	$ 129
9	Almond Croissants	39	2.55	$ 99
10	Sun-dried Tomato Croissants	62	2.50	$ 155
11	Cheese Croissants	70	2.15	$ 151
12	Buttermilk Biscuits	78	2.45	$ 191
13	Sausage/Biscuit Wrap	86	2.75	$ 237
14	Total			$ 1,567
15				

FIGURE 9–18
Table with totals added

14. Save, print, and close the workbook.

SUMMARY

In this lesson, you learned:

- You can create a custom number format and apply it to data in the worksheet cells.
- Conditional formatting rules enable you to highlight data that meets specific criteria.
- Conditional formatting formulas let you highlight data based on the criteria you enter in the formula.
- Formatting data and text as a table applies various professional formats and filters.
- Custom AutoFilters give you the option to apply specific filters based on criteria entered into the custom AutoFilter dialog box.
- Themes let you apply a formatting scheme throughout the workbook, thereby eliminating the time-consuming task of applying individual formats in each worksheet.
- You can select and change banded rows and banded columns in a table.
- You can add a total row and total column in a table.

VOCABULARY REVIEW

Define the following terms:

conditional formatting formulas
Custom AutoFilter
banded columns
banded rows
tables
themes

REVIEW QUESTIONS

TRUE / FALSE

Circle T if the statement is true or F if the statement is false.

T F 1. You can apply a theme to a worksheet that does not have any formatting.

T F 2. Filters are automatically applied when you format data as a table.

T F 3. You can add a SUM function at the top of a total column in a table, and when you press [Enter], the formula is copied to the remaining cells in the column.

T F 4. The SUM function is the only function available for a total row or column.

T F 5. Both conditional formatting rules and conditional formatting formulas apply formats to cells that meet only one specific criterion.

FILL IN THE BLANK

Complete the following sentences by writing the correct word or words in the blanks provided.

1. The format character ______________ is used for months in a format code.
2. ______________ applies a font, border, or pattern to worksheet cells when certain conditions exist in those cells.
3. After basic formatting is applied to the worksheet data, ______________ let you add borders, background colors, shading, and graphic effects instantly to an entire workbook.
4. The format character ______________ is used for hours in a format code.
5. AutoFilters are automatically added to the data when you format data as a(n) ______________.

WRITTEN QUESTIONS

Write a brief answer to the following questions.

1. What is the difference between the following date codes: *yyyy-mmm-dd* and *mmmm-yyyy*?

2. Explain the process to enter a formula for conditional formatting.

3. How would you add a theme to worksheet data that does not have any formatting?

4. Explain the process for creating a Custom AutoFilter.

5. How would you add a column with totals to a table?

PROJECTS

If you have a SAM 2010 user profile, your instructor may have assigned an autogradable version of the indicated project. If so, log into the SAM 2010 Web site at *www.cengage.com/sam2010* to download the instruction and start files.

PROJECT 9–1

1. Open the **Team – Revised** file from the drive and folder where your Data Files are stored.
2. Save the workbook as **Team Assignments** followed by your initials.
3. Create a custom number format that changes the date formats in column F to Jan-15. Do not add a year to the format since all the team assignments are in 2014.
4. Format the worksheet title, the column headings, and column D with a light gray background color.
5. Save, print, and close the workbook.

SAM PROJECT 9–2

1. Open the **Store Lease Dates** file from the drive and folder where your Data Files are stored.
2. Save the workbook as **Store Lease Dates Information** followed by your initials.
3. Add table formatting of your choice to the data.
4. Create a custom AutoFilter for the Lease Date column that filters the data within the date range 6/15/2014 through 12/31/2014.
5. Format the worksheet title font using the same color and formatting as the table column headings.
6. Save, print, and close the workbook.

PROJECT 9–3

1. Open the **Coach Assignment** file from the drive and folder where your Data Files are stored.
2. Save the workbook as **Coach Assignment Information** followed by your initials.
3. Add table formatting to your worksheet. Select a style that includes background shading in the cells.
4. Remove the filters.
5. Apply a theme to your worksheet.
6. Remove the banded row formatting.
7. Add banded column formatting.
8. Save, print, and close the workbook.

PROJECT 9–4

1. Open the **Home Sales** file from the drive and folder where your Data Files are stored.
2. Save the workbook as **Home Sales – 2014** followed by your initials.
3. Add conditional formatting to the Total column that formats sales greater than 1,500,000.
4. Use a custom format for the conditional formatting that highlights the cell with a yellow cell background (fill) color.
5. Change the conditional formatting to highlight cells with sales over 1,750,000. Use the same yellow fill color.
6. Save, print, and close the workbook.

CRITICAL THINKING

ACTIVITY 9–1

You are the new manager of the New Internet Products Corporation. After reviewing workbooks created by the former manager, you decide to enhance the data contained in the files by applying different formatting features.

1. Open the **Trendy Resort** file from the drive and folder where your Data Files are stored, and then save it as **Trendy Resort Projected Sales** followed by your initials.
2. Format the First Year worksheet using the formatting features you learned about in this lesson. Apply a conditional format to the projected sales data, and use conditional formatting to highlight those projected sales figures that exceed $60,000 for any month and any division. Format the title and subtitle as desired.
3. Save and print the worksheet in landscape orientation so all the data fits on one page, then close the workbook.

ACTIVITY 9–2

1. Open the **Budget** file from the drive and folder where your Data Files are stored, and then save it as **Proposed Budget** followed by your initials.
2. Format the data as a table with a dark text color.
3. Add a column for department totals and a total row.
4. Format the headings with a similar color as the formatted table.
5. Save and print the worksheet in landscape orientation so all the data fits on one page, then close the workbook.

Estimated Time: 2.5 hours

LESSON 10

Using Advanced Chart Features

OBJECTIVES

Upon completion of this lesson, you should be able to:

- Switch rows and columns in charts.
- Add a data table to a chart.
- Add data labels to data markers.
- Create sparklines.
- Design combination charts.
- Construct a gauge chart.
- Create a chart template.
- Apply a chart template.

VOCABULARY

chart floor
chart template
combination chart
data labels
data markers
data point
data series
data table
gauge chart
horizontal gridlines
primary axis
secondary axis
sparklines
vertical gridlines
x-axis
y-axis

Introduction

Charts are a great solution for presenting data in Excel graphically. Charts are simple to make and format. You can quickly change one type of chart to another if you need to show data in a different perspective. Excel has many chart formatting features that you can apply to a chart to make it a professional representation of the data. In this lesson, you will learn how to apply advanced chart features to charts.

Understanding How Charts Are Created

Charts are created from data in a worksheet. This data is typically arranged in columns and rows. **Figure 10–1** shows an example of data that will be used to create a chart. The rows contain data for different types of pizza. The columns show the pizza sales by month.

Columns show monthly pizza sales

Rows show types of pizza

	A	B	C	D	E	F	G
1	***Byar's Pizza Franchise***						
2	***Quarterly Report***						
3							
4		**April**	**May**	**June**			
5	***Cheese***	$ 15,000.00	$ 16,545.00	$ 17,000.00			
6	***Pepperoni***	15,750.00	17,550.00	19,250.00			
7	***Sausage***	9,000.00	10,150.00	11,225.00			
8	***Veggie***	3,450.00	5,555.00	7,000.00			
9	***Anchovy***	1,500.00	1,400.00	1,300.00			
10	**Total**	**$44,700.00**	**$51,200.00**	**$55,775.00**			
11							
12							

FIGURE 10–1 Worksheet with columns and rows of data

The type of chart you choose determines how the data in the rows and columns will appear in the chart. For example, the pizza data in this example was plotted as a Line chart, as shown in **Figure 10–2**. Notice that the types of pizza are placed on the horizontal axis, and the monthly sales are placed on the vertical axis. The horizontal axis is called the ***x-axis***, and the vertical axis is called the ***y-axis***. Each line of data in the chart is a ***data series***.

VOCABULARY

x-axis

y-axis

data series

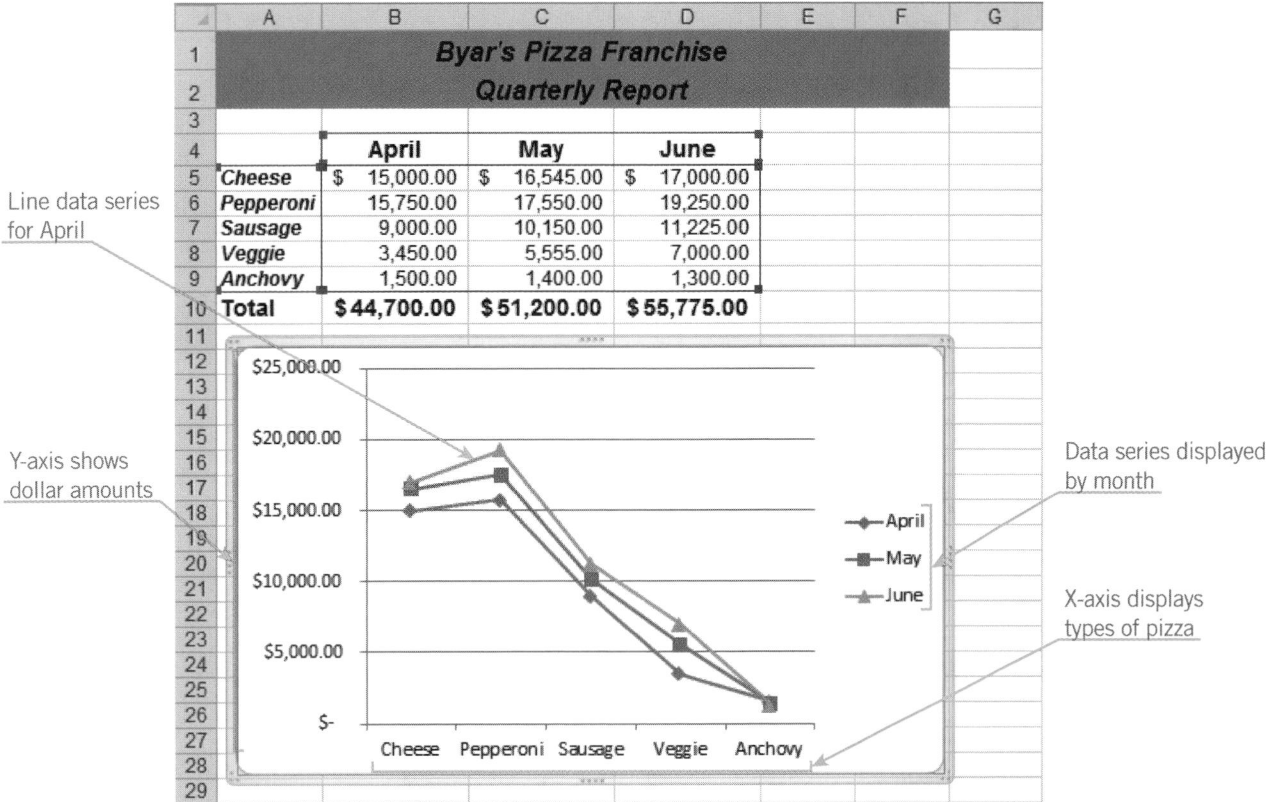

FIGURE 10–2 Line chart created from worksheet data

EXTRA FOR EXPERTS

When creating a chart, do not select the data totals when selecting the data for the chart. Because the totals are typically much larger numbers than the data itself, the chart would not display the data series accurately.

Switching Rows and Columns in Charts

After creating a chart, you may find that you want to switch the order of how chart data is displayed. You can do this using the Switch Row/Column button on the Design tab. In **Figure 10–3**, the pizza data has been switched so that the x-axis displays the months and the data series shows the sales amount for each type of pizza.

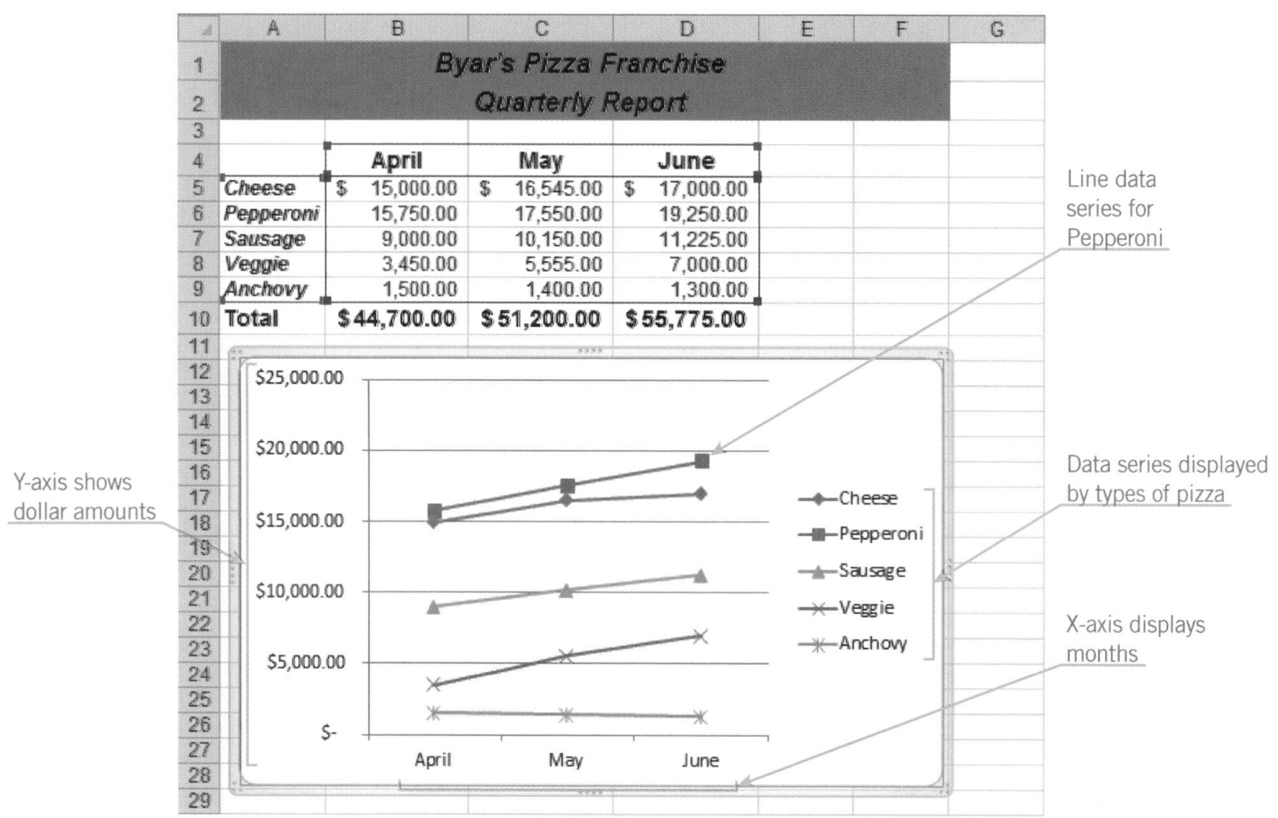

FIGURE 10–3 Chart with rows and columns switched

Step-by-Step 10.1

1. Open the **Byars Pizza** file from the drive and folder where your Data Files are stored.
2. Save the workbook as **Byars Pizza Sales**, followed by your initials. You will use the data in the worksheet to create a chart.
3. Select the range **A4:D9**.
4. On the Ribbon, click the **Insert** tab.
5. In the Charts group, click the **Line** button, and then click the **Line with Markers** button, the first 2-D Line chart in the second row.
6. Move the chart by clicking the Selection box around the chart and dragging it to **A11:F27**, then compare your screen to **Figure 10–4**.

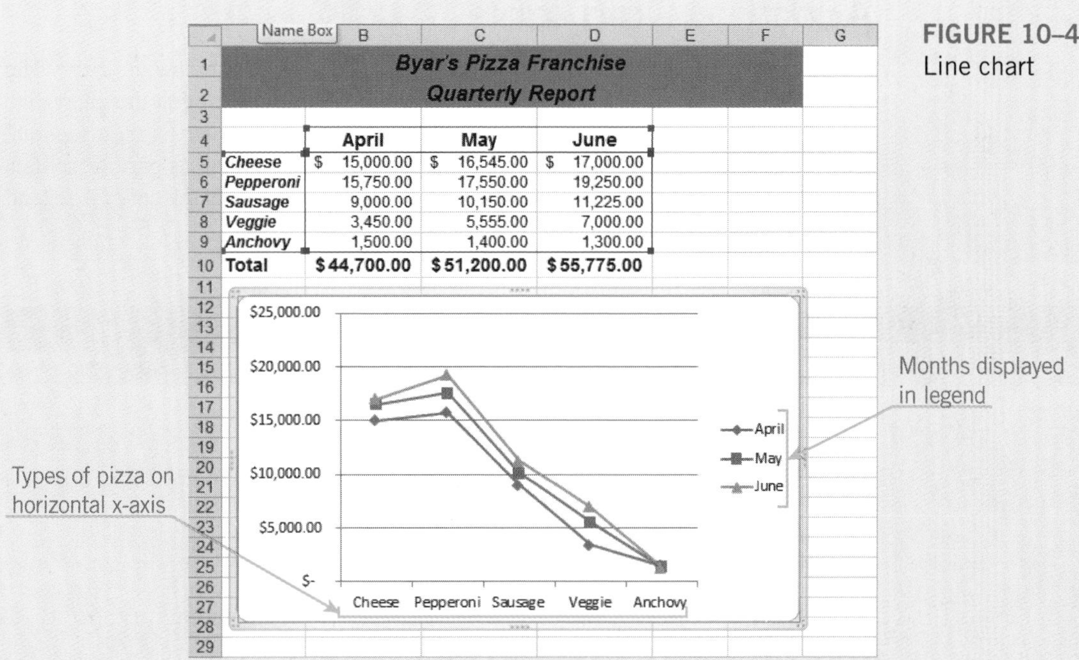

FIGURE 10–4
Line chart

7. On the Ribbon, click the **Design** tab and then in the Data group, click the **Switch Row/Column** button. Notice how the horizontal axis shows the months and the vertical axis shows the sales by pizza type, as shown in **Figure 10–5**.

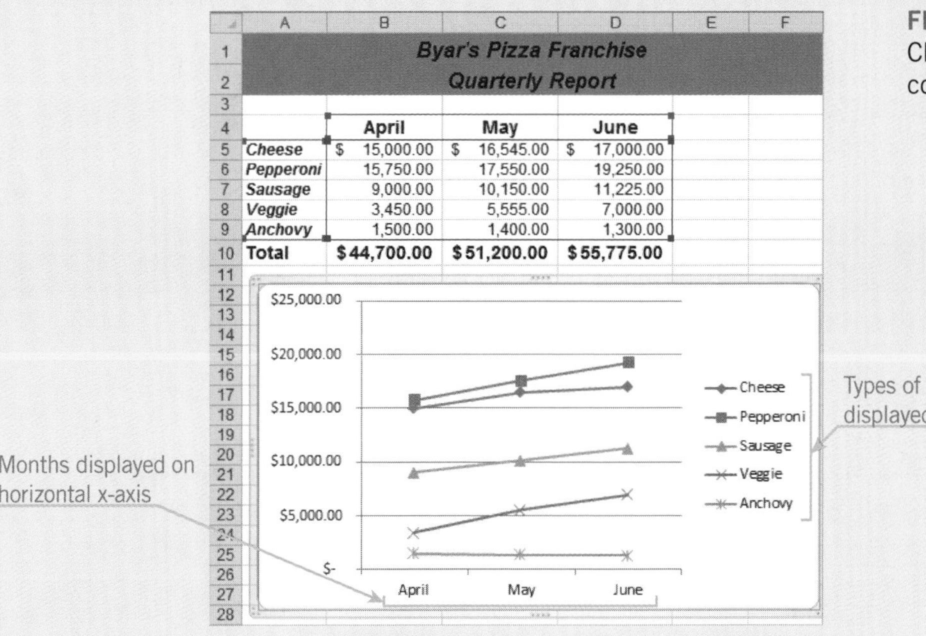

FIGURE 10–5
Chart with rows and columns switched

8. Save the workbook and leave it open for the next Step-by-Step.

Adding a Data Table

VOCABULARY
data table

A ***data table*** displays the data used to create a chart. It appears below the chart. The data table lets you quickly view the worksheet data while looking at the chart data series. The data table feature is especially useful when your chart is on a separate sheet in the workbook. You can choose to have the legend appear as part of the data table rather than having the legend displayed in a separate part of the chart. A legend is a list that shows the colors and symbols used in a chart.

Step-by-Step 10.2

1. Verify that the chart is selected.
2. On the Ribbon, click the **Design** tab, if it is not already selected. You will first move the chart to a new sheet.
3. In the Location group, click the **Move Chart** button.
4. In the Move Chart dialog box, click the **New sheet** option button.
5. In the New sheet text box, type **Sales Chart.**
6. Click **OK**. The chart moves to a new sheet named Sales Chart.
7. On the Layout tab in the Labels group, click **Data Table** and then click **Show Data Table with Legend Keys**. Your chart appears as shown in **Figure 10–6**.

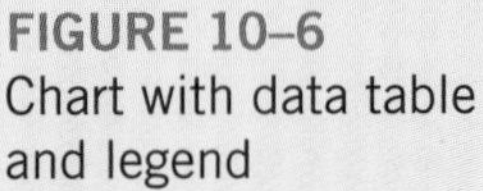

FIGURE 10–6
Chart with data table and legend

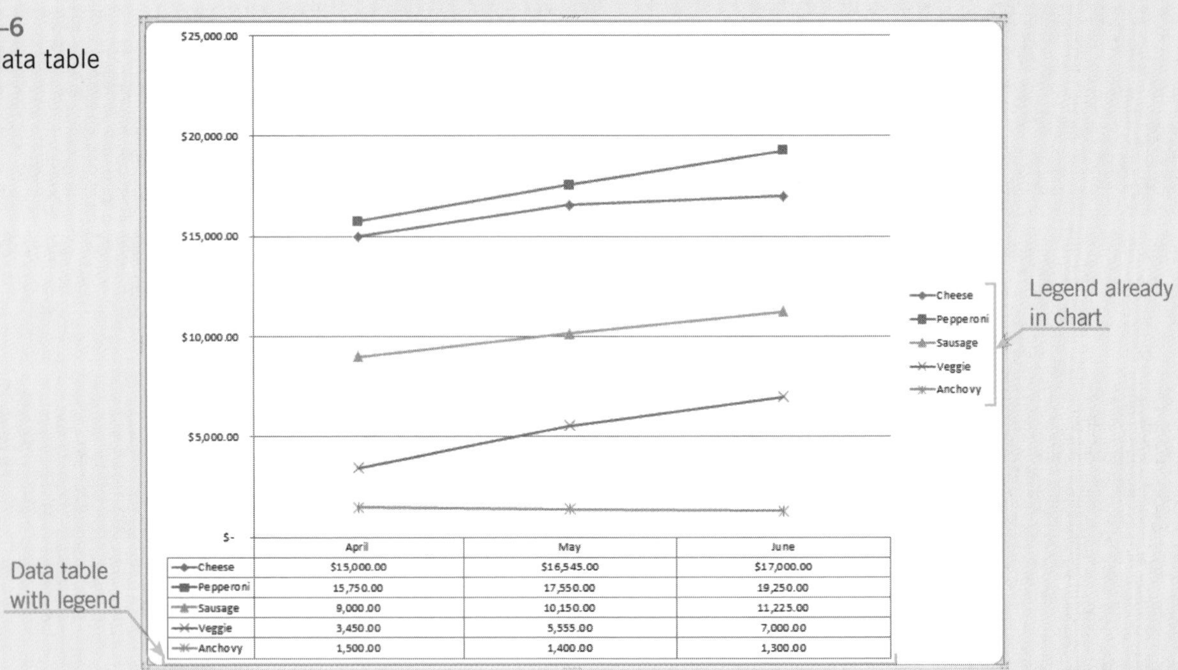

	April	May	June
Cheese	$15,000.00	$16,545.00	$17,000.00
Pepperoni	15,750.00	17,550.00	19,250.00
Sausage	9,000.00	10,150.00	11,225.00
Veggie	3,450.00	5,555.00	7,000.00
Anchovy	1,500.00	1,400.00	1,300.00

8. Click the legend on the right side of the chart and then press **Delete**. Since the data table has a legend, you no longer need the original legend.

9. On the Layout tab in the Labels group, click **Chart Title**, and then click **Above Chart** to add a chart title. The chart title appears above the line chart and is selected. When you start typing the chart title, your text will replace this text and the title you type will be displayed.
10. Type **Byars Pizza Sales** for the chart title, and then press **Enter**. The chart title appears above the chart as shown in **Figure 10–7**.

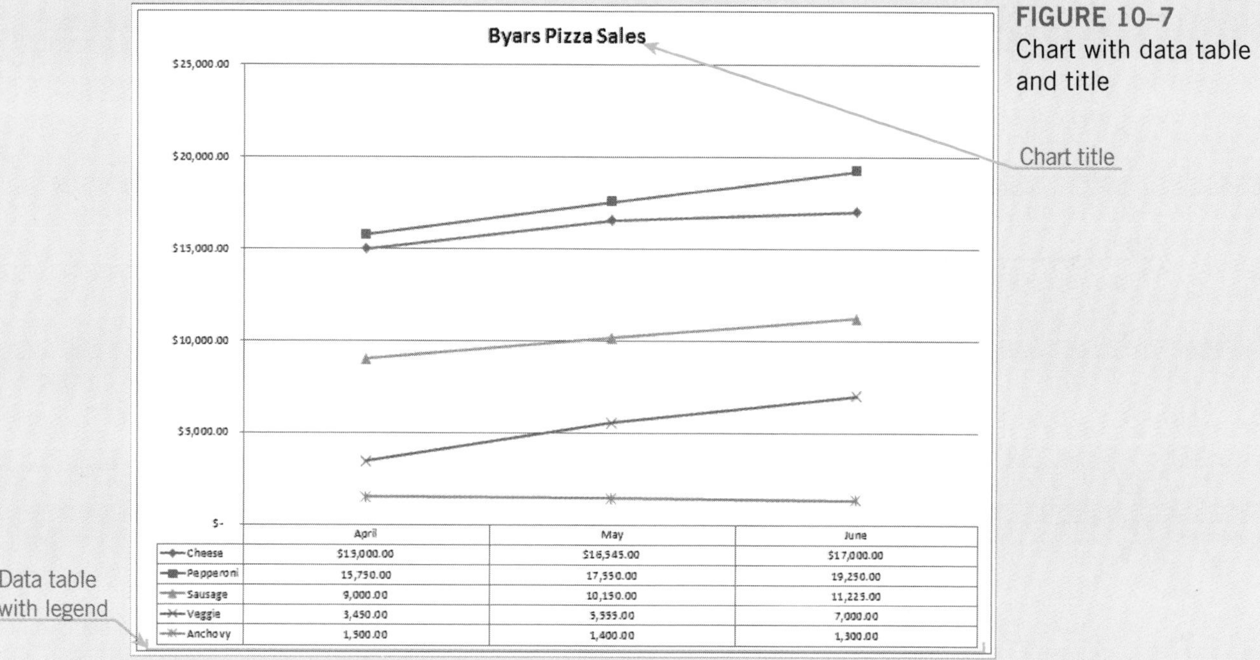

FIGURE 10–7
Chart with data table and title

11. Save the workbook and leave it open for the next Step-by-Step.

Adding Data Labels to Data Series

A ***data label*** can appear as numbers or text next to each data marker in the data series. The ***data markers*** represent where the actual data would be in the chart. For example, you might have a range of data in the worksheet with 500, 1500, and 1000 in the data range. In a line chart, the line would start at 500 and a line segment would be drawn to 1500. Another line segment would be drawn from 1500 to 1000. Each

VOCABULARY

data label

data marker

VOCABULARY
data point

place where the line segments start or stop is a ***data point*** and can be displayed with a data marker. Adding data labels allows you to see the value for each data marker in the chart. An example of a chart with data labels is shown in **Figure 10–8**.

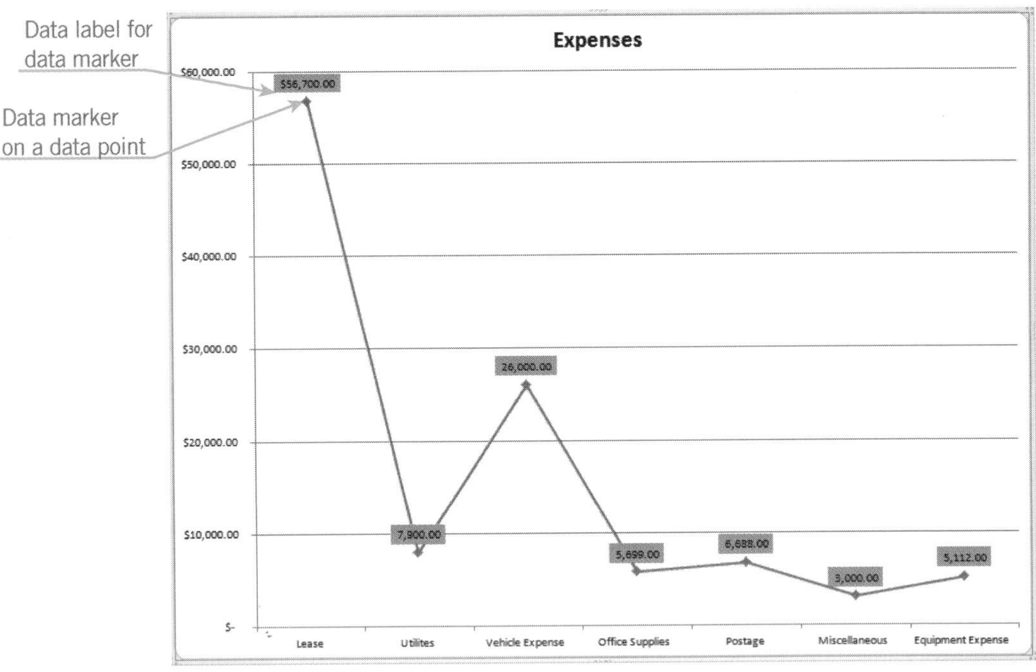

FIGURE 10–8 Chart with data labels

You can place the data labels to the left, right, top, or bottom of the data points. Data label features, such as color and border outlines, can be changed.

Step-by-Step 10.3

1. With the Sales Chart sheet selected, click the **Layout** tab on the Ribbon, if necessary.
2. In the Layout group, click the **Data Labels** button and then click **Above**. The labels display above the line series; however, some of the labels run into the line markers, so you decide to try another option.
3. Click the **Data Labels** button again and then click **Left**. You will now format the labels.
4. Click any one of the data labels that you just added.
5. Click **Data Labels**, and then click **More Data Label Options**.
6. In the Format Data Labels dialog box, click the **Fill** option on the left side, as shown in **Figure 10–9**.

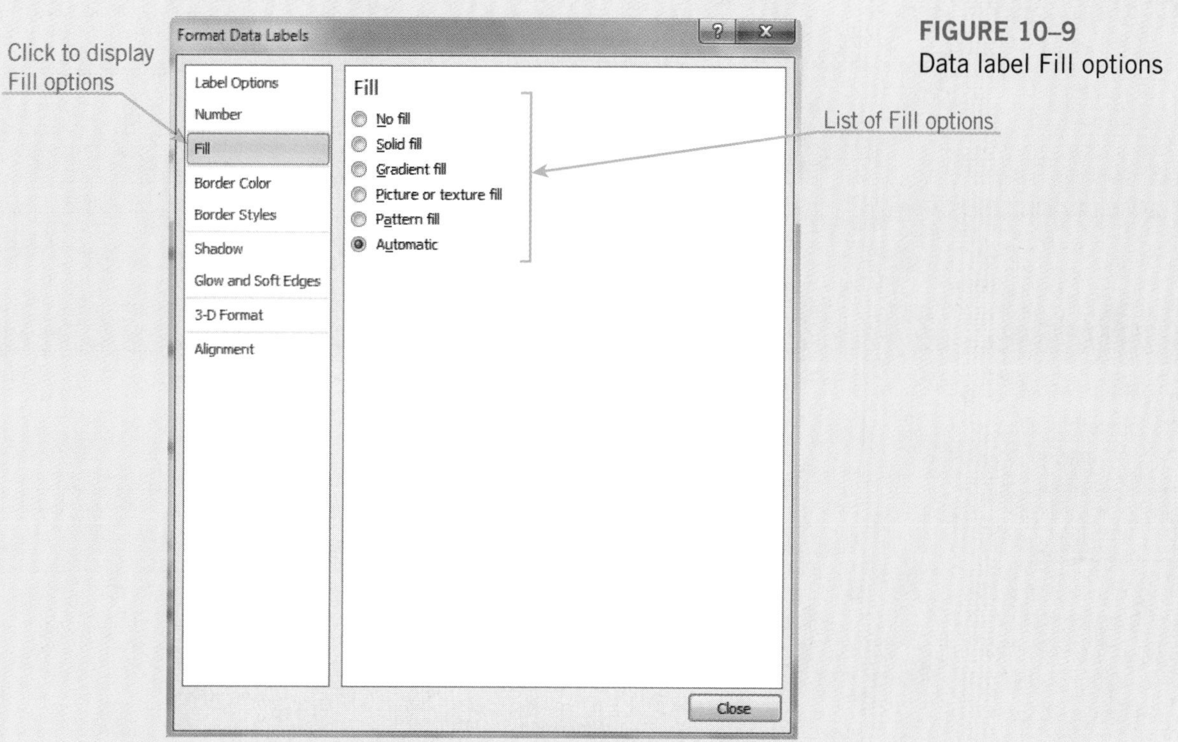

FIGURE 10–9
Data label Fill options

7. Click the **Solid fill** option button on the right side of the dialog box.
8. Click the **Color** arrow and then choose the **Red, Accent 2, Lighter 40%** option.
9. Click **Close**.

10. Repeat Steps 4–9 to apply the same color format to the remaining data labels. Your completed chart should resemble the one shown in **Figure 10–10**.

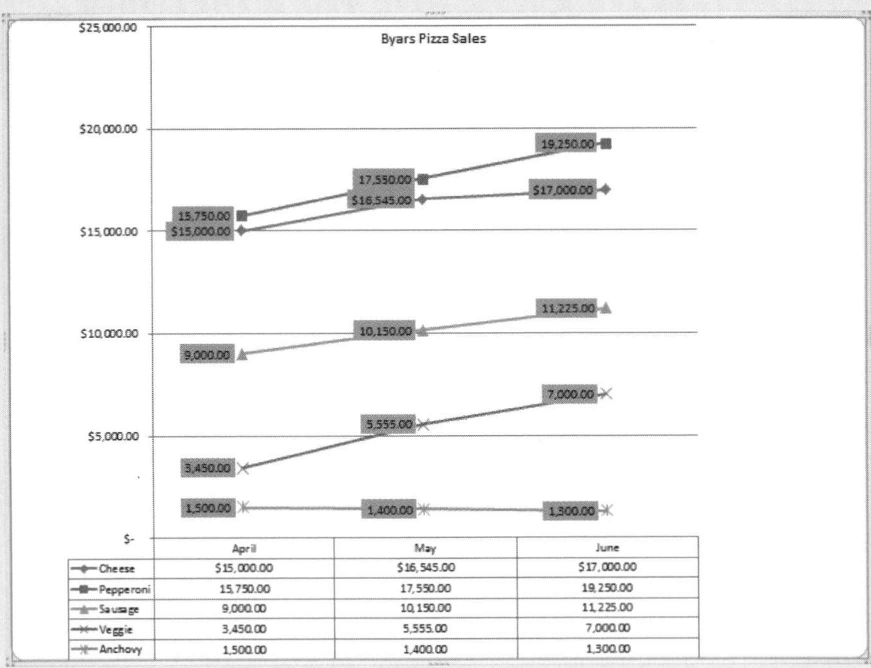

FIGURE 10–10
Completed chart with data labels

EXTRA FOR EXPERTS

You can copy and paste formats from one label to another using the Format Painter feature. Select a label that has the formats you want to copy, then click the Format Painter button in the Clipboard group on the Home tab. Click the Format Painter over the label that you want to apply the formatting to. The text's format changes to the new format. You can double-click the Format Painter button to keep it selected. This is useful when you want to format multiple labels. Click it again to turn it off.

11. Save, print, and close the workbook.

Creating Sparklines

VOCABULARY
sparkline

A new feature introduced in Excel 2010 is the addition of sparklines. A ***sparkline*** is a miniature chart that can be displayed in a single row or column of data. You can also create these small charts for each row or column of data within a worksheet. Sparklines are displayed next to the data they represent. Since sparklines are so compact, you can fit them on several adjacent rows or columns of data. After you create sparklines, you can add data markers. You can have the high, low, first, and last points on a sparkline display with data markers. If you select the Markers feature, all data points on the sparklines will be highlighted. You can format sparklines easily using colors and styles.

Excel has three types of sparklines: Line, Column, and Win/Loss. An example of each is shown in **Figure 10–11**.

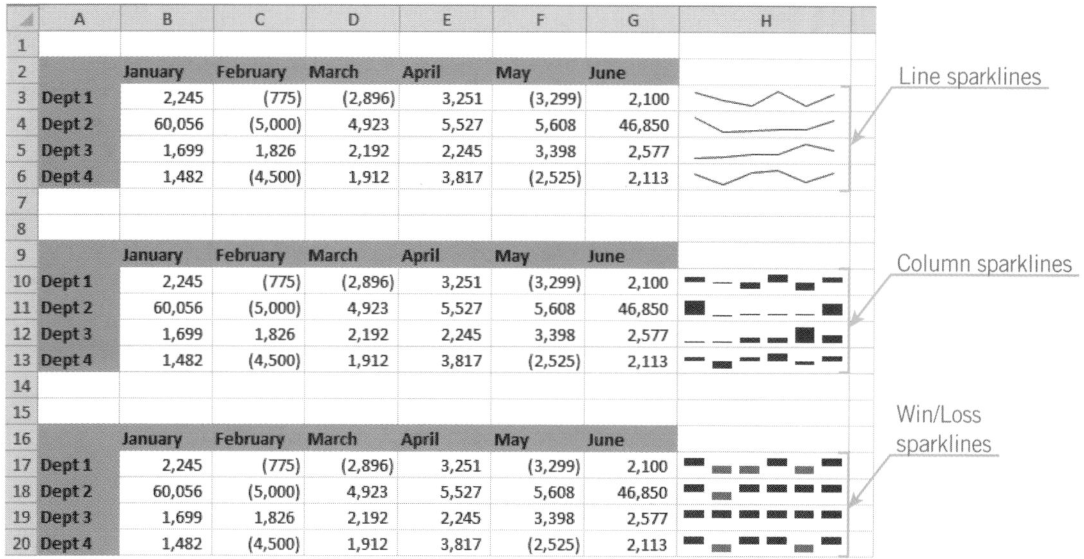

	A	B	C	D	E	F	G	H
1								
2		January	February	March	April	May	June	
3	Dept 1	2,245	(775)	(2,896)	3,251	(3,299)	2,100	
4	Dept 2	60,056	(5,000)	4,923	5,527	5,608	46,850	
5	Dept 3	1,699	1,826	2,192	2,245	3,398	2,577	
6	Dept 4	1,482	(4,500)	1,912	3,817	(2,525)	2,113	
7								
8								
9		January	February	March	April	May	June	
10	Dept 1	2,245	(775)	(2,896)	3,251	(3,299)	2,100	
11	Dept 2	60,056	(5,000)	4,923	5,527	5,608	46,850	
12	Dept 3	1,699	1,826	2,192	2,245	3,398	2,577	
13	Dept 4	1,482	(4,500)	1,912	3,817	(2,525)	2,113	
14								
15								
16		January	February	March	April	May	June	
17	Dept 1	2,245	(775)	(2,896)	3,251	(3,299)	2,100	
18	Dept 2	60,056	(5,000)	4,923	5,527	5,608	46,850	
19	Dept 3	1,699	1,826	2,192	2,245	3,398	2,577	
20	Dept 4	1,482	(4,500)	1,912	3,817	(2,525)	2,113	

FIGURE 10–11 Types of sparklines

Step-by-Step 10.4

1. Open the **College Book** file from the drive and folder where your Data Files are stored.
2. Save the workbook as **College Book Sales**, followed by your initials.
3. Select **B4:G12**.
4. On the Ribbon, click the **Insert** tab and then in the Sparklines group, click **Line**. The Create Sparklines dialog box opens, as shown in **Figure 10–12**. In the Create Sparklines dialog box, you select the cell or range of cells where the sparklines will appear.

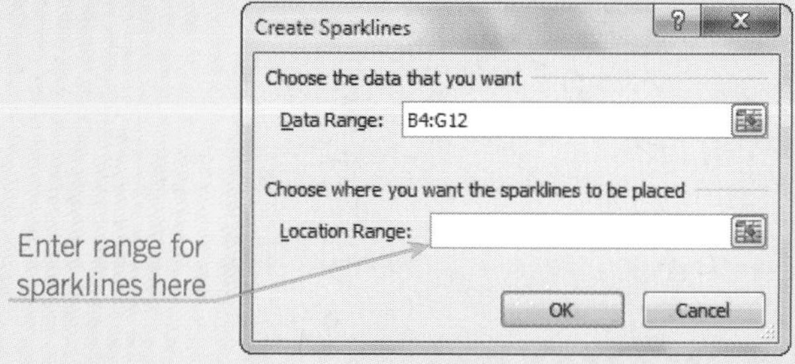

FIGURE 10–12
Create Sparklines dialog box

5. Move the Create Sparklines dialog box out of the way, if necessary, so that you can select the range **H4:H12**. When you release the mouse button, the selected range appears in the Location Range text box.

6. Click **OK**, then compare your worksheet to **Figure 10–13**. Next, you will make Column H wider so that you can see more detail on the sparklines.

FIGURE 10–13
Worksheet with sparklines added

	A	B	C	D	E	F	G	H
1	College Book Sales							
2								
3		January	February	March	April	May	June	
4	Department 01	2,245	775	2,896	3,251	3,299	2,100	
5	Department 02	60,056	4,103	4,923	5,527	5,608	46,850	
6	Department 03	1,699	1,826	2,192	2,245	3,398	2,577	
7	Department 04	1,482	4,500	1,912	3,817	2,525	2,113	
8	Department 05	2,555	2,747	7,200	4,961	5,015	3,204	
9	Department 06	20,900	4,625	5,550	6,450	4,900	4,165	
10	Department 07	2,231	2,398	2,878	4,302	2,200	1,955	
11	Department 08	7,500	1,576	1,891	2,231	1,800	2,542	
12	Department 09	2,114	2,273	2,727	2,900	1,699	2,345	
13								
14								

Sparklines

7. Right-click the **Column H** heading, then click **Column Width** from the shortcut menu. Type **25** in the Column width box and then click **OK**.
8. Select the range **H4:H12** that contains the sparklines.
9. Click the **Design** tab and then, in the Show group, click the **High Point** check box.
10. In the Style group, click the **Marker Color** button arrow, point to **High Point**, and then select **Red** for the data marker color.
11. In the Style group, click the **More** arrow to display the available styles for the sparklines.
12. Position the mouse pointer over Sparkline Style Accent 5, Darker 25% to see the Live Preview of this style in the chart. Then, click to select it. Your completed worksheet should resemble **Figure 10–14**.

TIP

You can also click in a column cell, click Format in the Cells group on the Home tab, and then click Column Width to change the width of a column.

FIGURE 10–14
Sparklines with style and high point markers

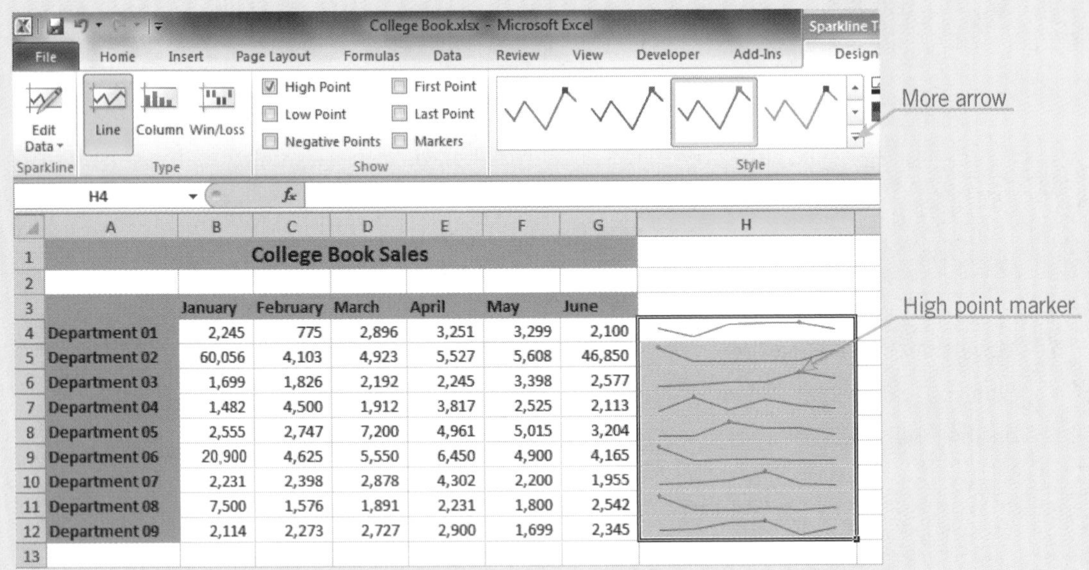

	A	B	C	D	E	F	G	H
1	College Book Sales							
2								
3		January	February	March	April	May	June	
4	Department 01	2,245	775	2,896	3,251	3,299	2,100	
5	Department 02	60,056	4,103	4,923	5,527	5,608	46,850	
6	Department 03	1,699	1,826	2,192	2,245	3,398	2,577	
7	Department 04	1,482	4,500	1,912	3,817	2,525	2,113	
8	Department 05	2,555	2,747	7,200	4,961	5,015	3,204	
9	Department 06	20,900	4,625	5,550	6,450	4,900	4,165	
10	Department 07	2,231	2,398	2,878	4,302	2,200	1,955	
11	Department 08	7,500	1,576	1,891	2,231	1,800	2,542	
12	Department 09	2,114	2,273	2,727	2,900	1,699	2,345	
13								

13. Save, print, and close the workbook.

Creating a Combination Chart

You can create a chart that shows data on two y-axes for the purpose of showing different data. This type of chart is called a ***combination chart***. For example, you may have data that shows rainfall amounts measured in inches over several months. Then, you may want to also show the percentage change between the rainfall amounts. You now have two different types of data series: one expressed in inches and the other as percentages. In Excel, you can create a chart that shows both data series in one chart. The y-axis on the left side of the chart is called the ***primary axis.*** The y-axis on the right side of the chart is called the ***secondary axis.*** **Figure 10–15** shows a combination chart that displays rainfall in inches and the change in rainfall in percentages. The primary axis displays the rainfall in inches, and the secondary axis displays the percentage change in rainfall.

VOCABULARY

combination chart

primary axis

secondary axis

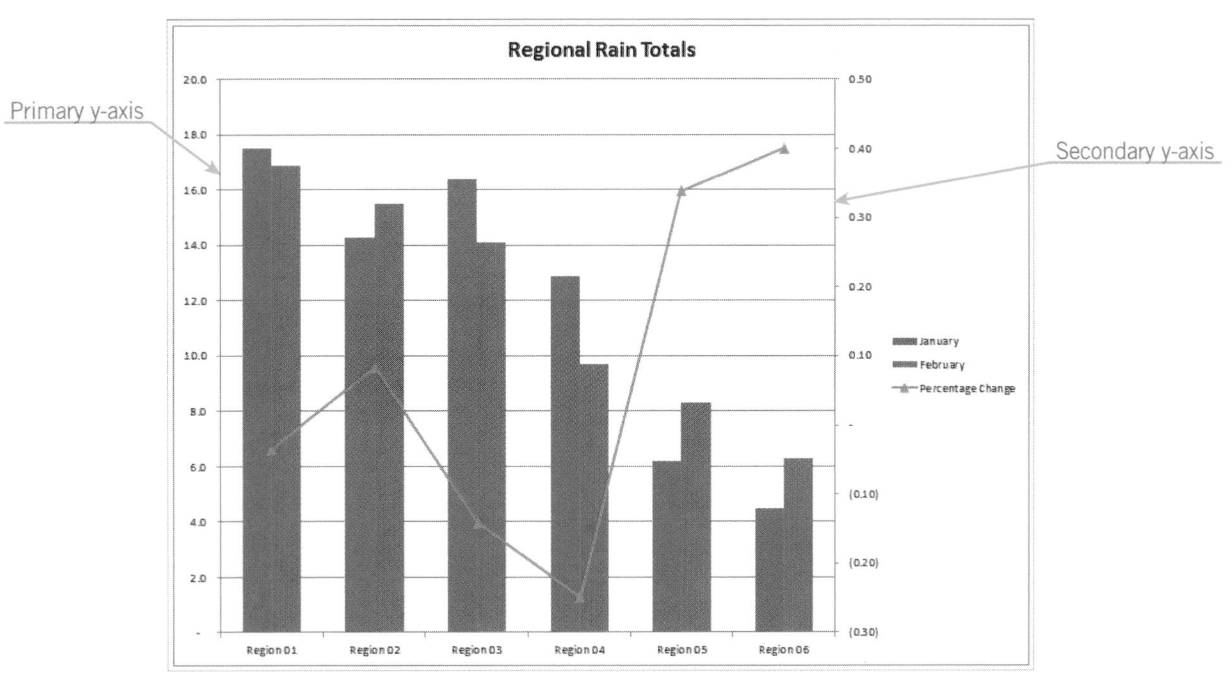

FIGURE 10–15 Combination chart

When making a chart with two y-axes, you will need to use two-dimensional, or 2-D data series. The legend will show the format for each series so that you can identify them in the chart.

Step-by-Step 10.5

1. Open the **Rain Totals** file from the drive and folder where your Data Files are stored.
2. Save the file as **Rain Totals Change** followed by your initials.
3. Select the range **A5:C11**, then press and hold **Ctrl** as you select the nonadjacent range **E5:E11** by dragging from E5 to E11.
4. Press **F11** to create a chart on its own sheet.
5. Double-click the **Chart 1** sheet tab, then type **Rain Chart** to change the chart sheet tab name. The chart is displayed in **Figure 10–16**.

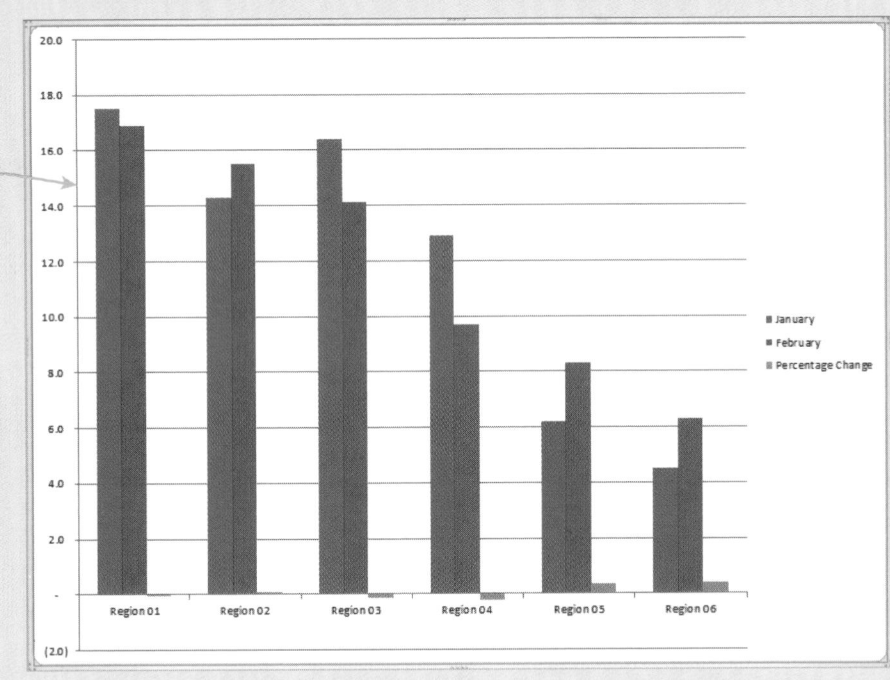

FIGURE 10–16
Rain Totals chart with one y-axis

6. Right-click any data marker for the Percentage Change series, then click **Change Series Chart Type**.
7. In the Change Chart Type dialog box, click the **Line** category on the left, and then click the **Line with Markers** chart type. See **Figure 10–17**.

EXTRA FOR EXPERTS

To instantly create a chart in its own chart sheet, simply select the range of data you want in the chart and press F11. Excel generates a chart with column data series. You can then, if necessary, enhance the chart features.

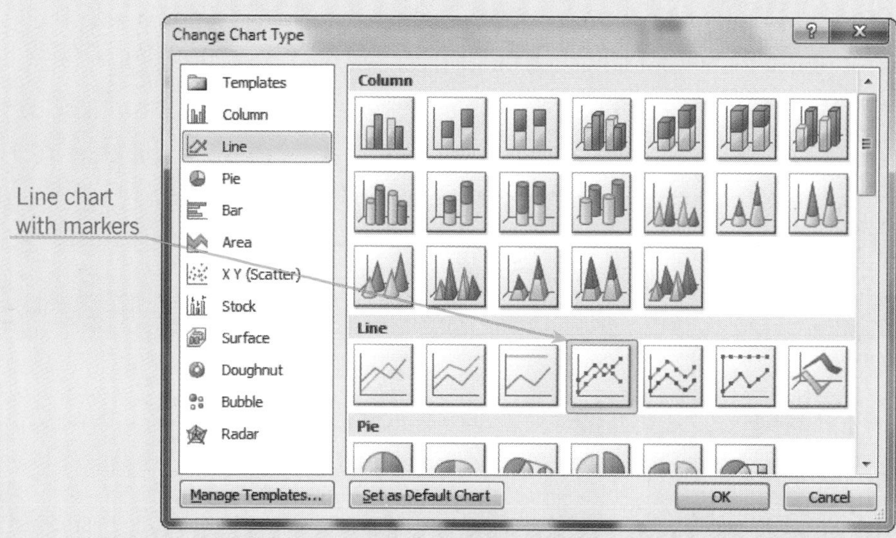

FIGURE 10–17
Change Chart Type dialog box

8. Click **OK** to close the Change Chart Type dialog box. Notice the legend displays the new line series type for Percentage Change.
9. Click any line data series marker to select the entire series.
10. On the Ribbon, click the **Format** tab and then in the Current Selection group, click **Format Selection** to display the Format Data Series dialog box.
11. In the Format Data Series dialog box, verify that the Series Options category is selected on the left, and then click the **Secondary Axis** option button on the right-side. The dialog box should appear as shown in **Figure 10–18**.

FIGURE 10–18
Format Data Series dialog box

12. Click the **Close** button to close the Format Data Series dialog box. Then, click the **Layout** tab, click **Chart Title**, and then click **Above Chart** to add a title to the chart.
13. Type **Regional Rain Totals** for the chart title, then deselect the title. Your completed chart should appear as shown in **Figure 10–19**.

FIGURE 10–19
Completed combination chart

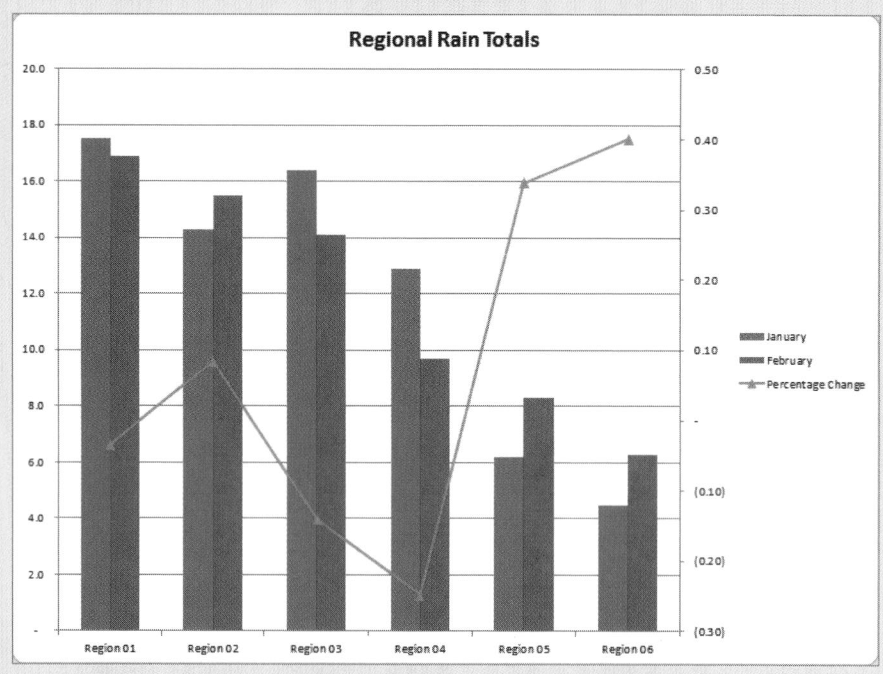

14. Save and close the workbook.

Creating Gauge Charts

VOCABULARY
gauge chart

A ***gauge chart***, or progress chart, shows the amount of progress accomplished toward a goal. For example, you may belong to an organization that promotes walking for better health. The organization might have a goal to collect \$50,000 in donations during a specific period of time. A gauge chart shows how much money has been collected from donations as a percentage of the goal. For example, if \$20,329 has been collected, about 41 percent of the goal is met. You can show this progress in a gauge chart.

The chart in **Figure 10–20** shows that the donation goal is entered into cell B19, and cell B18 shows the total of cells B5:B16. The percentage is calculated by dividing the donation total by the donation goal. In a gauge chart, the chart is based on one cell of data: the percentage shown in cell B21.

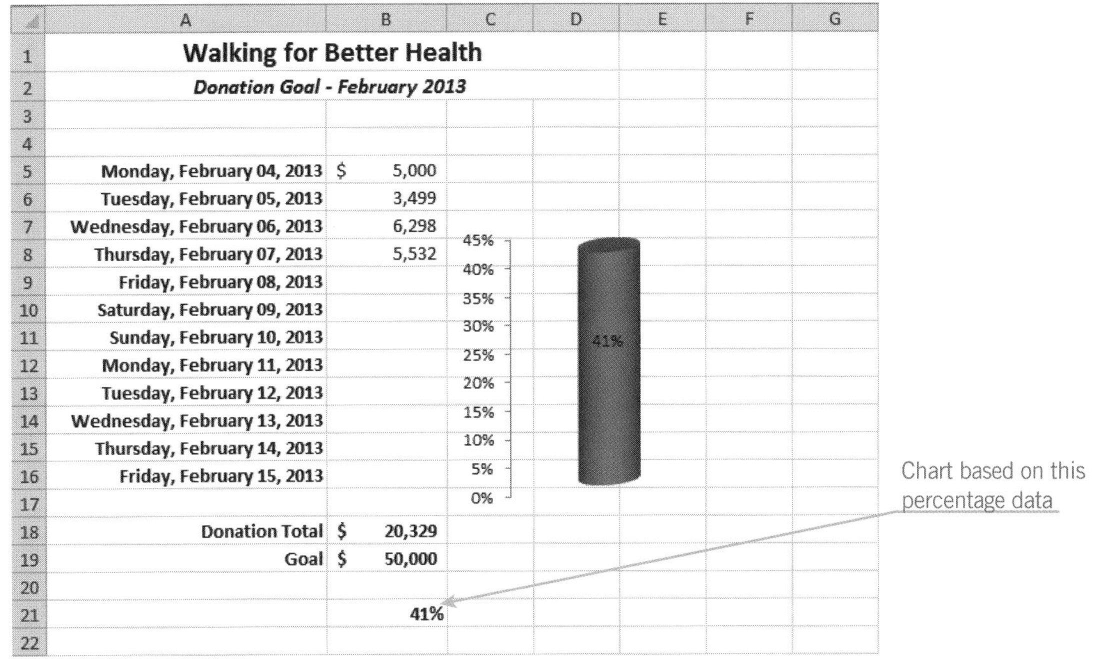

	A	B
1	**Walking for Better Health**	
2	***Donation Goal - February 2013***	
3		
4		
5	Monday, February 04, 2013	$ 5,000
6	Tuesday, February 05, 2013	3,499
7	Wednesday, February 06, 2013	6,298
8	Thursday, February 07, 2013	5,532
9	Friday, February 08, 2013	
10	Saturday, February 09, 2013	
11	Sunday, February 10, 2013	
12	Monday, February 11, 2013	
13	Tuesday, February 12, 2013	
14	Wednesday, February 13, 2013	
15	Thursday, February 14, 2013	
16	Friday, February 15, 2013	
17		
18	Donation Total	$ 20,329
19	Goal	$ 50,000
20		
21		41%
22		

FIGURE 10–20 Gauge chart

As additional amounts are entered in the donation range, the percentage figure shown in cell B21 will increase. In a gauge chart, it is helpful to show this percentage in the chart. Other chart elements, such as the gridlines, legend, and chart floor, can be removed. Chart gridlines are the horizontal and vertical lines within the chart itself and are called ***horizontal gridlines*** and ***vertical gridlines***. The ***chart floor*** is the foundation, or base, of a 3-D chart.

VOCABULARY

horizontal gridlines

vertical gridlnes

chart floor

Step-by-Step 10.6

1. Open the **Donation** file from the drive and folder where your Data Files are stored, and then save the workbook as **Donation Goal**, followed by your initials. You will calculate the percentage of donations received for an animal rescue shelter.
2. Select **cell B21** and then type the formula **=B18/B19** to calculate the percentage of donations received based on the goal. Next, you will create a cylinder chart to display the percentage.
3. Select **cell B21**, and then click the **Insert** tab. In the Charts group, click **Column**, and then click **Clustered Cylinder**.

4. Move and resize the chart to fit within the range **D5:H21**, as shown in **Figure 10–21**. Next you will remove chart elements so that only the cylinder data series is displayed.

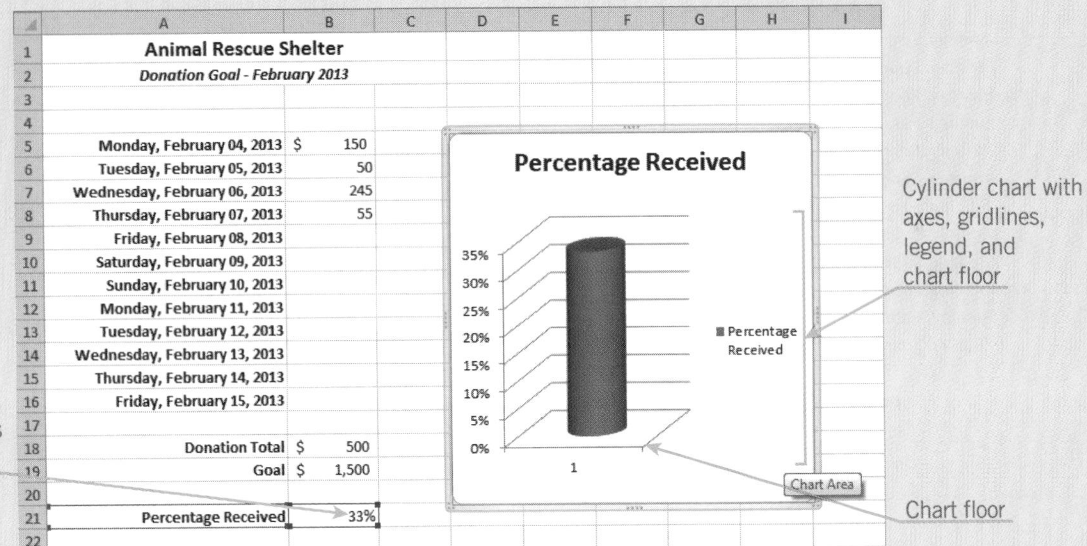

FIGURE 10–21
Gauge chart moved and resized

5. Click the **Layout** tab, then in the Axes group, click **Axes**, point to **Primary Horizontal Axis**, and then click **None** to remove the horizontal chart axis. Click **Axes** again, point to **Primary Vertical Axis**, and then click **None** to remove the vertical chart axis.
6. In the Legends group, click **Legend** and then click **None** to remove the legend.
7. In the Axes group, click **Gridlines**, point to **Primary Horizontal Gridlines**, and then click **None** to remove the horizontal chart gridline. Click **Gridlines** again, point to **Primary Vertical Gridlines**, and then click **None** to remove the vertical gridlines. The chart floor is the final chart feature to be removed.
8. In the Background group, click **Chart Floor**, and then select **None**. The chart floor is removed. Next, you will add the percentage value to the column.
9. In the Labels group, click **Data Labels**, and then click **More Data Label Options**. In the Format Data Labels dialog box, click **Number** on the left and then click **Percentage** in the Category list.
10. Double-click the value in the Decimal places text box, then type **0** (zero) so that there are no decimal places in the percentage. Click **Close** to close the dialog box.
11. Drag the percentage data label to the middle of the cylinder.
12. On the Ribbon, click the **Home** tab. In the Font group, click the **Font Size** buttton arrow, click **16**, and then click the **Bold** button.

13. Select **cell B9**, type **210**, and then press **Enter** to see how the progress increases in the chart. The percentage should now be 47%, as shown in **Figure 10–22**.

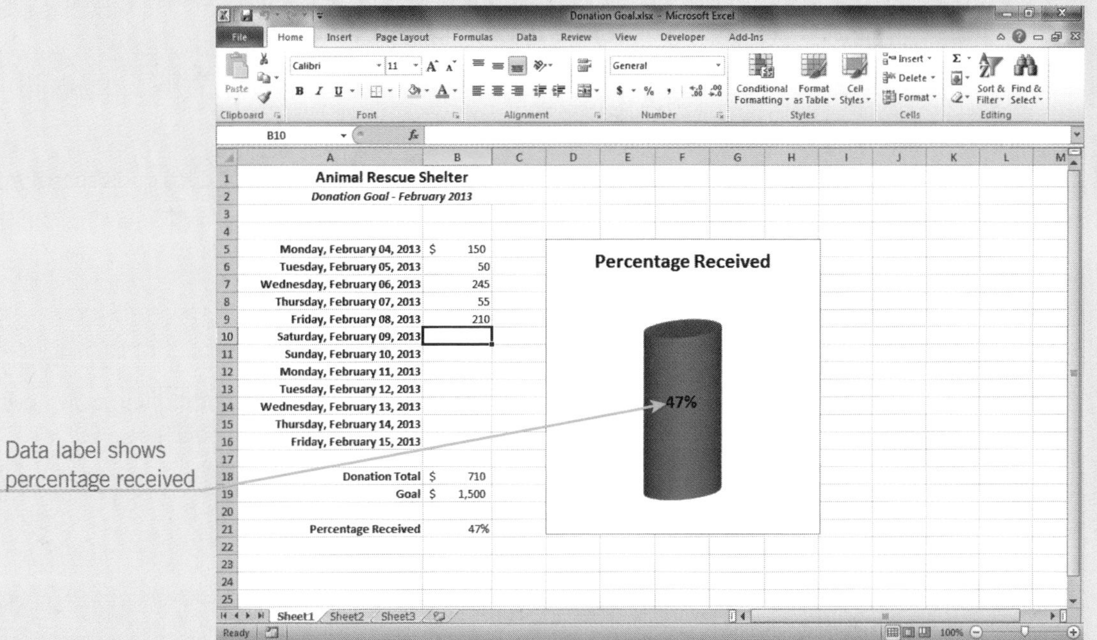

FIGURE 10–22 Gauge chart reflecting change

14. Save, print, and close the workbook.

Creating Chart Templates

Excel has a variety of chart styles and formats that you can apply to a chart. You may find, however, that you tend to make the same changes to charts to fit a specific professional design. If so, you can create a ***chart template*** by creating a chart and adding the formats and settings that are unique to the charts you want to create. You then save the chart as a template. When you create your next chart, you can simply select the chart, apply your chart template, and the features will be instantly applied. Chart templates are saved in the same default location as the preformatted chart templates.

VOCABULARY
chart template

EXTRA FOR EXPERTS

Excel provides templates online at *www.office.microsoft.com*. Once at the site, click the Templates tab.

Step-by-Step 10.7

1. Open the **College Clothing** file from the drive and folder where your Data Files are stored, then save the workbook as **College Clothing Sales**, followed by your initials.
2. Select the range **A5:G16**, and then press **F11** to create a chart in its own sheet.
3. Click the **Design** tab and then, in the Chart Styles group, click the **More** arrow (the bottom arrow in the Chart Styles group) to display the Chart Styles gallery.
4. Select **Style 26**.
5. Click the **Layout** tab, then in the Axes group, click **Axes**, point to **Primary Horizontal Axis**, and then click **More Primary Horizontal Axis Options**. The Format Axis dialog box opens, as shown in **Figure 10–23**.

FIGURE 10–23
Format Axis dialog box

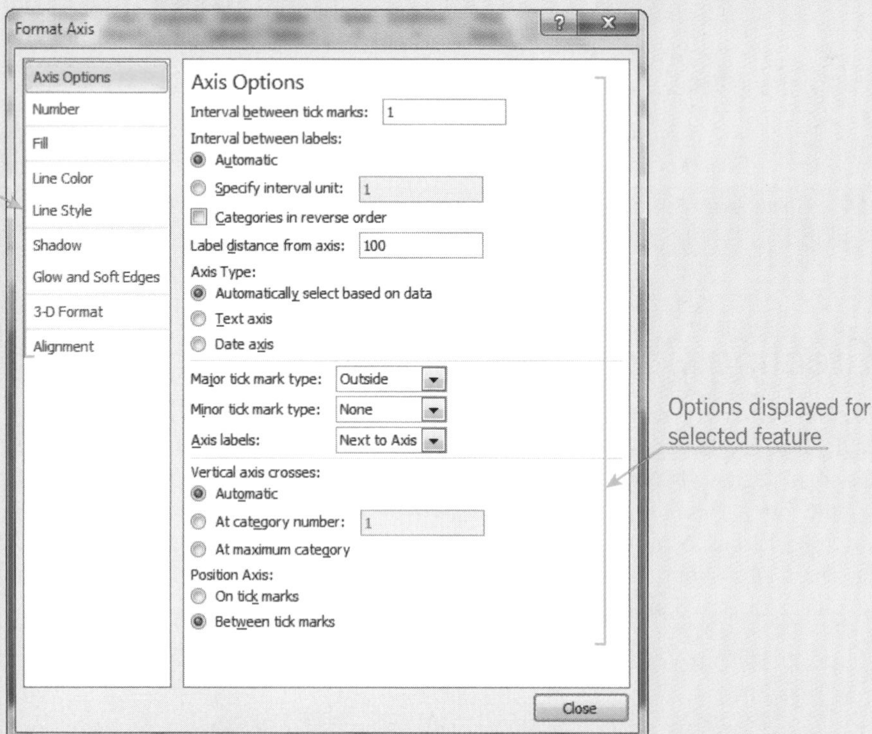

6. In the Format Axis dialog box, click **Alignment** on the left.
7. In the **Custom Angle** text box, type **45** to add a 45° angle to the text, and then click **Close** to close the dialog box.
8. In the Labels group, click **Chart Title**, click **Above Chart**, type **University Sales**, and then press **Enter.**
9. Verify that the chart title is still selected, and then click the **Home** tab. In the Font group, click the **Font Color** arrow button and then click **Dark Blue, Text 2, Lighter 40%.**

10. Click the **Design tab**, and then in the Type group, click **Save As Template** to open the Save Chart Template dialog box, as shown in **Figure 10–24**.

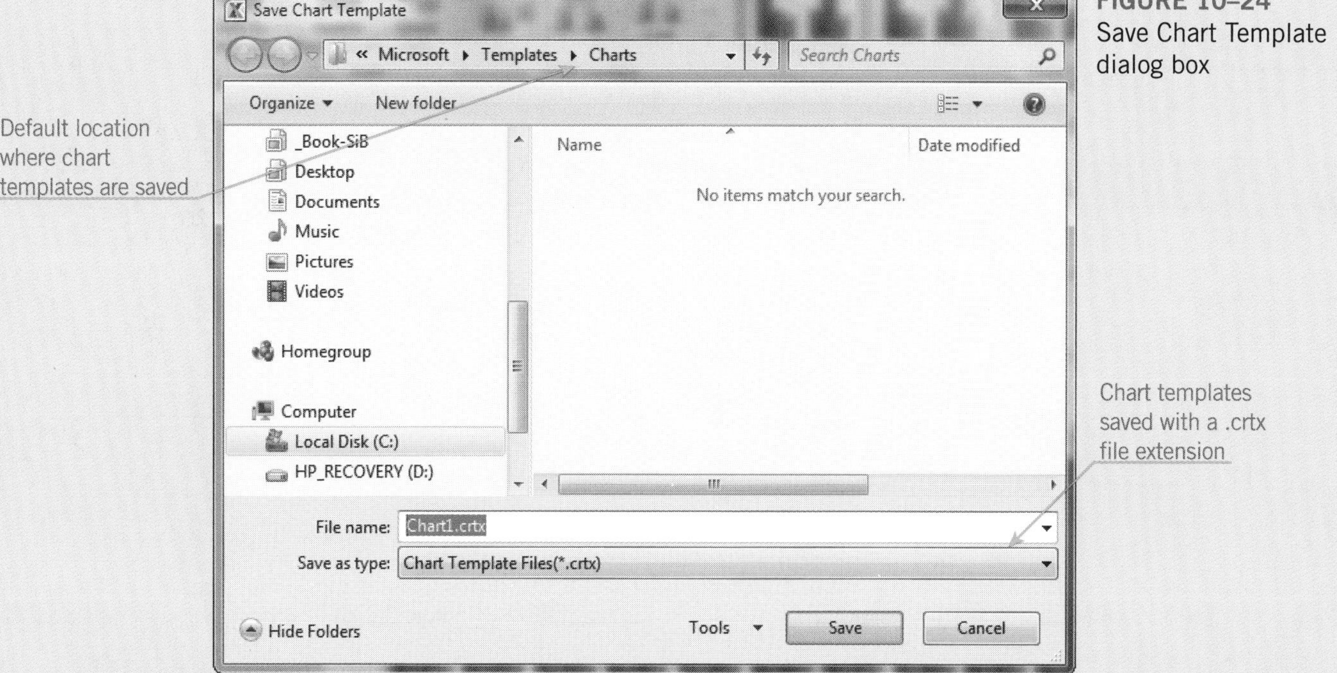

FIGURE 10–24
Save Chart Template dialog box

11. In the File name text box, type **Business Chart Template** followed by your initials.
12. Click **Save**. The chart template is now ready to use.
13. Save and close the workbook.

Applying a Chart Template

After creating a chart template, you can apply it to new charts that you create. Applying a chart template to a chart will save you time because you will not need to change each chart feature individually. The chart template applies all the chart elements in the template at one time.

Step-by-Step 10.8

1. Open the **University Expenses** file from the drive and folder where your Data Files are stored, then save it as **University Expenses Chart** followed by your initials.
2. Select **A5:M10**.

3. On the Ribbon, click the **Insert** tab, then in the Charts group, click the **Charts dialog box** launcher to display the Insert Chart dialog box as shown in **Figure 10–25**.

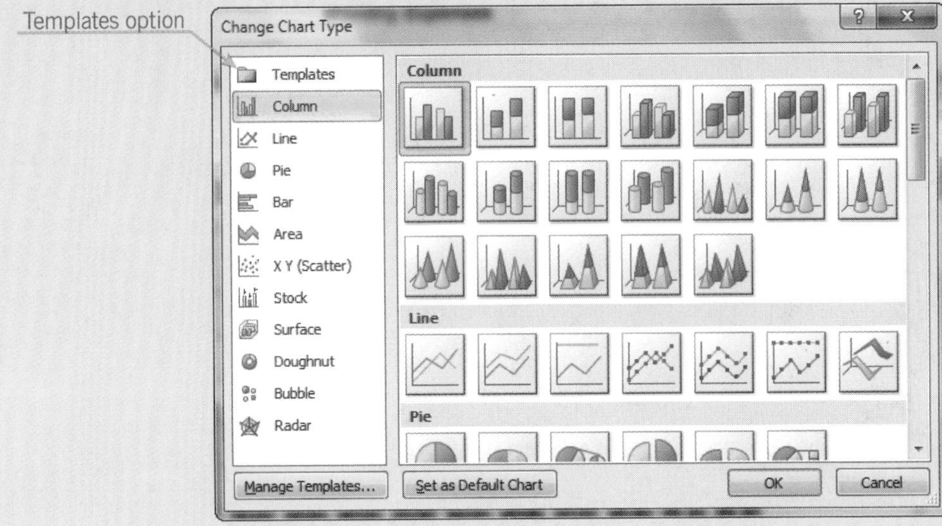

FIGURE 10–25
Insert Chart dialog box

4. Click **Templates** to display the available templates as shown in **Figure 10–26**.

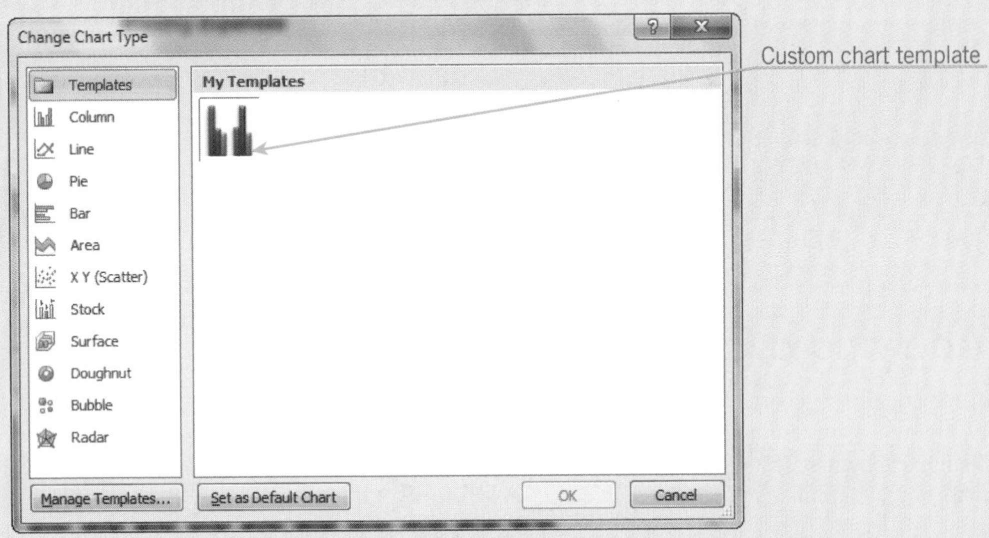

FIGURE 10–26
Insert Chart dialog box with Templates selected

5. Click the chart icon under **My Templates**.
6. Click **OK** to close the Insert Chart dialog box. The Business Chart template is applied to your chart.

7. Move and resize the chart to fit within the range **C13:L34**.
8. Click the chart title, type **Monthly Expenses Chart**, and then click outside the chart title to deselect it. The completed chart should appear as shown in **Figure 10–27**.

FIGURE 10–27
Chart template applied

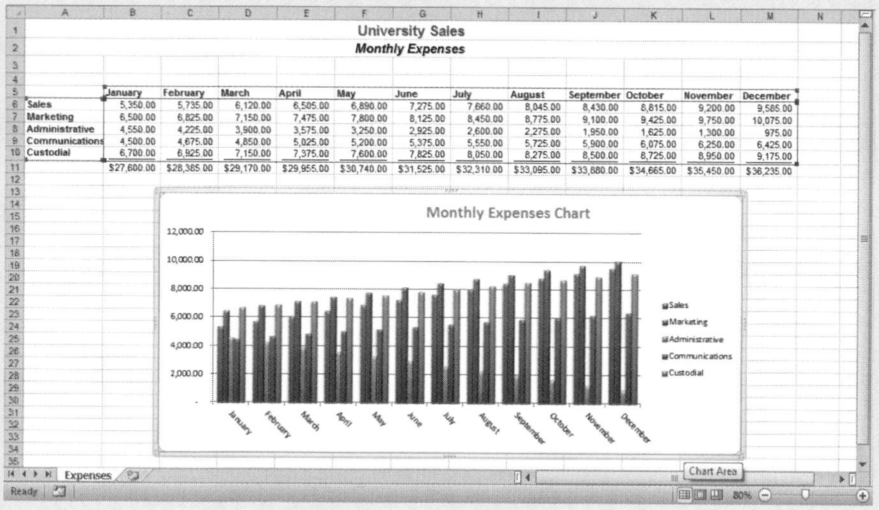

University Sales

Monthly Expenses

	January	February	March	April	May	June	July	August	September	October	November	December
Sales	5,350.00	5,735.00	6,120.00	6,505.00	6,890.00	7,275.00	7,660.00	8,045.00	8,430.00	8,815.00	9,200.00	9,585.00
Marketing	6,500.00	6,825.00	7,150.00	7,475.00	7,800.00	8,125.00	8,450.00	8,775.00	9,100.00	9,425.00	9,750.00	10,075.00
Administrative	4,550.00	4,225.00	3,900.00	3,575.00	3,250.00	2,925.00	2,600.00	2,275.00	1,950.00	1,625.00	1,300.00	975.00
Communications	4,500.00	4,675.00	4,850.00	5,025.00	5,200.00	5,375.00	5,550.00	5,725.00	5,900.00	6,075.00	6,250.00	6,425.00
Custodial	6,700.00	6,925.00	7,150.00	7,375.00	7,600.00	7,825.00	8,050.00	8,275.00	8,500.00	8,725.00	8,950.00	9,175.00
	$27,600.00	$28,385.00	$29,170.00	$29,955.00	$30,740.00	$31,525.00	$32,310.00	$33,095.00	$33,880.00	$34,665.00	$35,450.00	$36,235.00

Monthly Expenses Chart

9. Save, print, and close the workbook.

SUMMARY

In this lesson, you learned:

- You can switch rows and columns of data in a chart.
- A data table that shows the data used to create a chart can be added to the chart.
- Data labels can be added to data markers in a data series.
- A sparkline is a miniature chart that can be displayed in a single row or column of data.
- You can design a combination chart that has two y-axes.
- You can construct gauge charts that show progress towards a goal.
- A chart template can be created for a chart design that will be used repeatedly.
- Chart templates can be applied to charts after they are created.

VOCABULARY REVIEW

Define the following terms:

chart floor
chart template
combination chart
data labels
data markers
data series
data table
gauge chart
horizontal gridlines
primary axis
secondary axis
sparklines
vertical gridlines
x-axis
y-axis

REVIEW QUESTIONS

TRUE / FALSE

Circle T if the statement is true or F if the statement is false.

T F **1.** Data labels display the chart data and are shown below the chart.

T F **2.** Sparklines can display a Line, Column, or Win/Loss chart for each row of data in a worksheet.

T F **3.** Data labels can only be placed to the left or right of the data series.

T F **4.** In a chart with two y-axes, the y-axis on the left is referred to as the primary axis and the y-axis on the right side is called the secondary axis.

T F **5.** A gauge chart shows the amount of progress toward a goal.

FILL IN THE BLANK

Complete the following sentences by writing the correct word or words in the blanks provided.

1. A(n) ________________ shows the data used to create the chart and is shown below the chart.
2. ________________ can appear as numbers or text next to each data marker in the data series.
3. A(n) ________________ is a miniature chart.
4. A(n) ________________ includes specific chart formatting that may be applied to other charts after you create them.
5. The ________________ is considered the foundation of the chart and is located at the base of the chart.

WRITTEN QUESTIONS

Write a brief answer to the following questions.

1. Explain the process to create a chart template.

2. What are the key features of a gauge chart?

3. Explain the process to switch rows and columns of data in a chart.

4. Explain the difference between a data table and a data label.

5. How would you create Line sparklines in a worksheet?

PROJECTS

If you have a SAM 2010 user profile, your instructor may have assigned an autogradable version of the indicated project. If so, log into the SAM 2010 Web site at *www.cengage.com/sam2010* to download the instruction and start files.

PROJECT 10–1

1. Open the **Income** file from the drive and folder where your Data Files are stored. Save the workbook as **Income Statement** followed by your initials.
2. Create a chart in its own worksheet based on the expenses in range A10:B16.
3. Delete the legend.
4. Add the chart title **2013 Expenses** above the chart.
5. Add data labels for the Outside End location.
6. Save, print, and close the workbook.

SAM PROJECT 10–2

1. Open the **Projected Earnings** file from the drive and folder where your Data Files are stored, and then save the file as **Projected Earnings by Department** followed by your initials.
2. Add Line sparklines for each row in column H.
3. Change the sparkline color to red.
4. Add High Point markers to the sparklines.
5. Add Low Point markers to the sparklines.
6. Save and close the workbook.

PROJECT 10–3

1. Open the **Pie Sales** file from the drive and folder where your Data Files are stored, and then save it as **Pie Sales First Quarter 2013** followed by your initials.
2. Create a chart in its own worksheet based on the first quarter pie sales. You will need to select nonadjacent ranges to create the chart.
3. Switch the columns and rows so that the months appear on the x-axis and the sales amounts appear on the y-axis.
4. Add a chart title above the chart with the text **First Quarter 2013 Pie Sales**.
5. Add a data table with a legend key.
6. Delete the legend on the right side of the chart.
7. Save and close the workbook.

CRITICAL THINKING

ACTIVITY 10–1

You are the assistant manager of a college bookstore. You would like to impress the store manager with your Excel skills. She asks you to create charts based on quarterly sales. You ask her what type of formatting she would like to see in the charts, and you then create a chart template including these features.

1. Open the **College** file from the drive and folder where your Data Files are stored, and then save it as **College Bookstore** followed by your initials.
2. Create a column chart in a chart sheet named **First Quarter**. Format the chart with the colors of your choice.
3. Add **First Quarter Sales** as a title for the chart.
4. Add a data table with a legend key to the chart.
5. Add data labels at the outside end of the markers in the data series.
6. Decide whether the legend should be removed.
7. Save the chart features as a template with the name **Quarterly Sales** followed by your initials.
8. Save and print the worksheet in landscape orientation and so all the data fits on one page, then close the workbook.

ACTIVITY 10–2

You are a real estate broker and owner of GMRE Real Estate. You prefer to view your listings graphically in a chart. You use Excel to create your chart.

1. Open the **GMRE Real Estate** file from the drive and folder where your Data Files are stored to create the chart.
2. Save the workbook as **GMRE Real Estate Listings** followed by your initials.
3. Create a column chart using the data in the **Address**, **City**, **State**, and **Sales Price** columns.
4. Add data labels in the center of the data markers.
5. Change the chart sheet name to **Listings Chart**.
6. Save and close the file.

Estimated Time: 2 hours

LESSON 11

Improving Data Accuracy

OBJECTIVES

Upon completion of this lesson, you should be able to:

- Use advanced sorting.
- Add subtotals to worksheet data.
- Create a validation rule.
- Enter data in a validation range.
- Circle invalid data.
- Improve data entry accuracy using drop-down lists.
- Convert text to columns.
- Combine text.
- Use a Watch Window.

VOCABULARY

concatenation
data validation
delimiter
destination range
grand total
subtotal
validation range
validation rule
Watch Window

Introduction

In this lesson, you will learn about several Excel features that enable you to work efficiently and accurately with worksheet data. The Subtotal feature instantly adds a formula that totals the worksheet data to a cell. The Subtotal feature also formats the worksheet in an outline, which lets you automatically display or hide data. This feature will save you time and increase your productivity.

You will also learn how you can use the Data Validation feature to set rules about how data can be entered. Adding data validation to your worksheet cells helps you monitor the accuracy of the data that's being entered. Excel places circles around any invalid data using the Circle Invalid Data feature. You can also create drop-down lists from which you can select data to control the type of data entered in cells.

In addition, you will learn two new data options: one for combining data and another for separating data. With the first option, you learn how to increase accuracy by letting Excel combine data using a process called ***concatenation***. The second option, Convert Text to Columns, separates data for you, rather than you having to retype it yourself.

VOCABULARY
concatenation

Finally, Excel offers a Watch Window feature that enables you to view data from one worksheet while you enter or view data in another worksheet. Using a Watch Window lets you view two sets of data at once for convenience. To use any of these accuracy features, you first need to make sure your data is sorted with precision.

Advanced Sorting

You learned how to sort data in ascending order, A to Z, and descending order, Z to A. This method works well for simple alphabetical and numeric data. For all other types of data, such as dates, you'll find you need more options for sorting data. Excel offers a variety of sorting options, and you can create custom sorting options. You can also sort multiple columns of data at one time.

In this next Step-by-Step, you will first sort text in alphabetical order and then using different sort levels, such as Division. In addition, you will learn how to sort data based on four sort levels.

Step-by-Step 11.1

1. Open the **New Lock** file from the drive and folder where your Data Files are stored.
2. Save the workbook as **New Lock Sales**, followed by your initials.
3. Click in any cell under a column heading, and then click the **Data** tab on the Ribbon.
4. In the Sort & Filter group, click the **Sort** button. The Sort dialog box opens, as shown in **Figure 11–1**. For the first sort level, you will sort the column data for division.

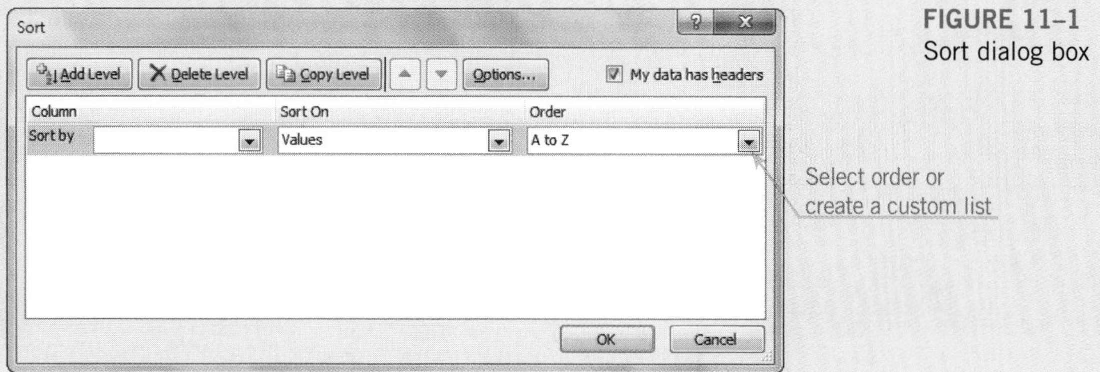

FIGURE 11–1
Sort dialog box

5. In the Sort dialog box, click the **Sort by** arrow, and then click **Division**. A division is an area where a company's regional sales offices are located. You will now sort the column data by month.
6. In the Sort dialog box, click the **Add Level** button. Click the **Then by** arrow, and then click **Month**.
7. Click the **Order** arrow, then click **Custom List** to view the custom list of sort options. The Custom Lists dialog box opens.
8. In the Custom Lists dialog box, click **January, February, March, April**, and then click **OK** to close the dialog box.
9. Click the **Add Level** button, click the **Then by** arrow, and then click **Last Name** to add another level of sorting.
10. Repeat Step 9 to add another level to the Sort dialog box for **First Name**. Your dialog box should appear similar to **Figure 11–2**.

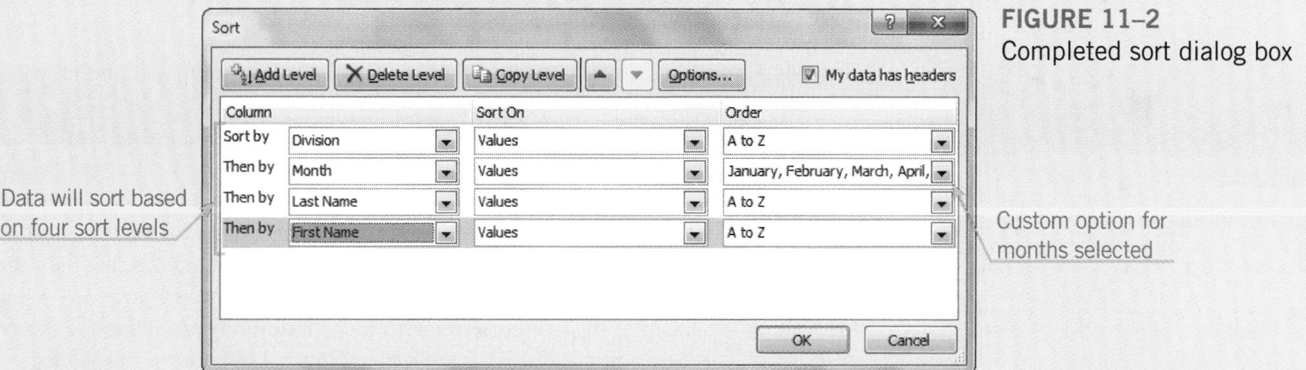

FIGURE 11–2
Completed sort dialog box

11. Click **OK** to sort the data, then view the worksheet data based on the sort options you entered, as shown in **Figure 11–3**.

FIGURE 11–3
Data sorted based on four sort levels

	A	B	C	D	E
1	New Lock Corporation				
2	Employee Sales				
3					
4	Division	Month	Sales	Last Name	First Name
5	East	January	$ 69,306	Baines	Bill
6	East	January	$ 138,639	Clavell	Fugi
7	East	January	$ 49,484	Gebal	Barbara
8	East	January	$ 69,750	Hassell	Sue
9	East	February	$ 72,217	Baines	Bill
10	East	February	$ 144,461	Clavell	Fugi
11	East	February	$ 51,562	Gebal	Barbara
12	East	February	$ 72,680	Hassell	Sue
13	East	March	$ 78,717	Baines	Bill
14	East	March	$ 157,463	Clavell	Fugi
15	East	March	$ 56,202	Gebal	Barbara
16	East	March	$ 79,221	Hassell	Sue
17	North	January	$ 162,457	Crawford	Katie
18	North	January	$ 164,576	Khorjin	Fugi
19	North	February	$ 169,280	Crawford	Katie
20	North	February	$ 171,488	Khorjin	Fugi
21	North	March	$ 184,515	Crawford	Katie
22	North	March	$ 186,922	Khorjin	Fugi
23	South	January	$ 53,208	Dominquez	Gary
24	South	January	$ 39,802	Gonzalez	Lisa
25	South	January	$ 101,222	Hernandez	Sally
26	South	January	$ 193,400	Holder	Howard
27	South	January	$ 179,862	Hussam	Ali
28	South	January	$ 75,001	Welch	JoAnne
29	South	February	$ 55,443	Dominquez	Gary

12. Save, print, and leave the workbook open for the next Step-by-Step.

Adding Subtotals

You can add formulas to a worksheet that instantly calculate totals within the worksheet data using Excel's Subtotal feature.

VOCABULARY
subtotal
grand total

A ***subtotal*** is the total of only specific parts of the data. The ***grand total*** is the total for all the data.

The Subtotal feature is useful when you want to view totals in the worksheet data but you don't want formulas permanently entered into the worksheet at that time. The Subtotal feature quickly calculates subtotals and grand totals, but they can be removed when you're finished viewing or printing the data. **Figures 11–4** and **11–5** show the location of inventory items in a craft store. These items are stored in aisles on the east and west side of the store. Figure 11–4 shows the worksheet before subtotals are calculated, and Figure 11–5 shows the worksheet with subtotals applied. Notice how subtotals appear after each department.

	A	B	C	D	E	F	G
1	Arts & Crafts, Inc.						
2	*Inventory*						
3							
4	**Store Aisle Location**	**Shelf Location**	**Item No.**	**Description**	**Quantity in Stock**	**Cost**	**Total Cost in Inventory**
5	East - 3A	4L	12-223	Paint - Blue	45	$ 0.99	$ 44.55
6	East - 3A	4L	12-295	Paint - White	35	$ 0.99	$ 34.65
7	East - 3A	4L	12-230	Paint - Green	39	$ 0.99	$ 38.61
8	East - 3A	7L	12-305	Paint - Yellow	25	$ 0.99	$ 24.75
9	East - 3A	6L	12-231	Paint - Purple	45	$ 0.99	$ 44.55
10	East - 3A	7L	12-307	Paint - Light Yellow	25	$ 0.99	$ 24.75
11	East - 4A	9R	15-223	Varnish - Clear	26	$ 3.99	$ 103.74
12	East - 4A	9R	15-993	Varnish - Satin	3	$ 3.99	$ 11.97
13	East - 4A	9R	15-152	Varnish - Extra Gloss	15	$ 3.99	$ 59.85
14	East - 4A	10R	15-223	Varnish - Almost Clear	26	$ 3.99	$ 103.74
15	East - 4A	10R	15-998	Varnish - Gold Satin	24	$ 3.99	$ 95.76
16	East - 5A	5L	12-259	Paint - Eggshell	35	$ 0.99	$ 34.65
17	East - 5A	5L	12-237	Paint - Light Green	39	$ 0.99	$ 38.61
18	West - 1B	11R	50-116	16" Wicker Basket	14	$ 1.99	$ 27.86
19	West - 1B	13R	50-120	20" Wicker Basket	21	$ 2.39	$ 50.19
20	West - 1B	12R	50-117	17" Wicker Basket	17	$ 1.99	$ 33.83
21	West - 2B	14R	50-121	21" Wicker Basket	18	$ 2.59	$ 46.62
22							
23							

FIGURE 11–4 Data before subtotals applied

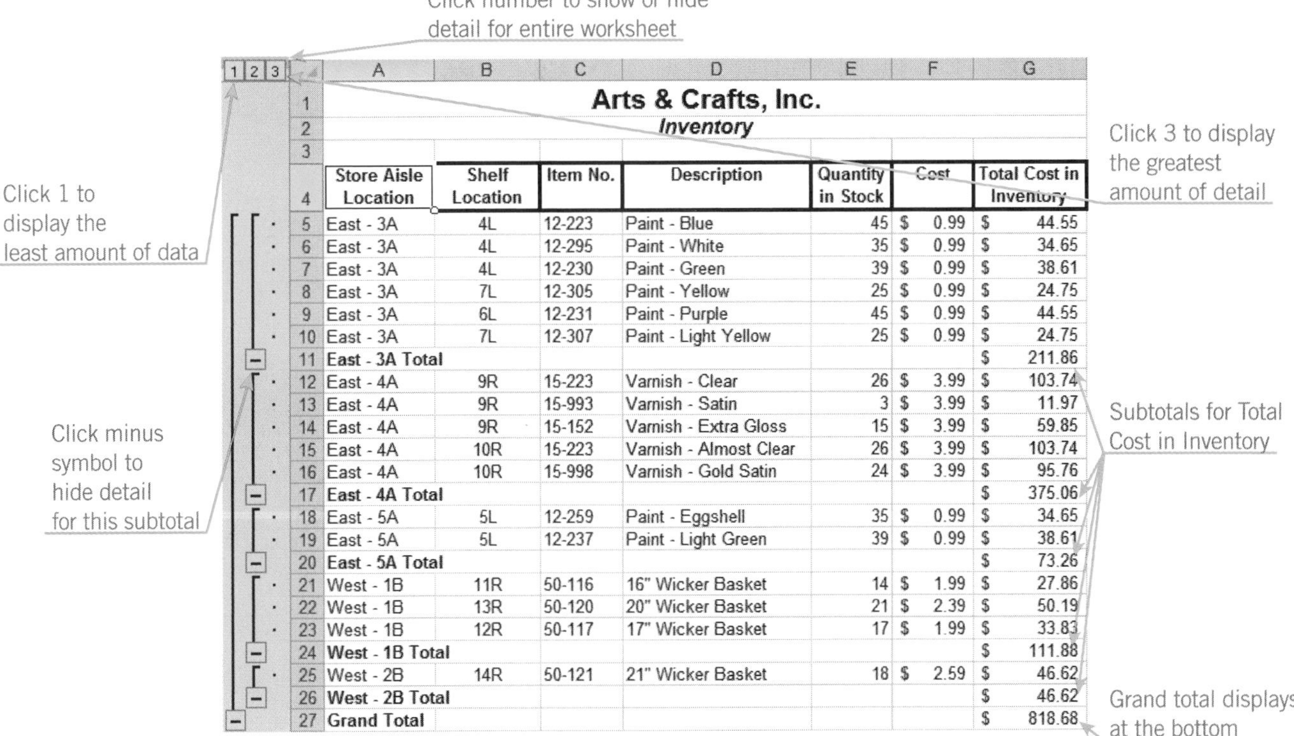

	A	B	C	D	E	F	G
1	Arts & Crafts, Inc.						
2	*Inventory*						
3							
4	**Store Aisle Location**	**Shelf Location**	**Item No.**	**Description**	**Quantity in Stock**	**Cost**	**Total Cost in Inventory**
5	East - 3A	4L	12-223	Paint - Blue	45	$ 0.99	$ 44.55
6	East - 3A	4L	12-295	Paint - White	35	$ 0.99	$ 34.65
7	East - 3A	4L	12-230	Paint - Green	39	$ 0.99	$ 38.61
8	East - 3A	7L	12-305	Paint - Yellow	25	$ 0.99	$ 24.75
9	East - 3A	6L	12-231	Paint - Purple	45	$ 0.99	$ 44.55
10	East - 3A	7L	12-307	Paint - Light Yellow	25	$ 0.99	$ 24.75
11	**East - 3A Total**						$ 211.86
12	East - 4A	9R	15-223	Varnish - Clear	26	$ 3.99	$ 103.74
13	East - 4A	9R	15-993	Varnish - Satin	3	$ 3.99	$ 11.97
14	East - 4A	9R	15-152	Varnish - Extra Gloss	15	$ 3.99	$ 59.85
15	East - 4A	10R	15-223	Varnish - Almost Clear	26	$ 3.99	$ 103.74
16	East - 4A	10R	15-998	Varnish - Gold Satin	24	$ 3.99	$ 95.76
17	**East - 4A Total**						$ 375.06
18	East - 5A	5L	12-259	Paint - Eggshell	35	$ 0.99	$ 34.65
19	East - 5A	5L	12-237	Paint - Light Green	39	$ 0.99	$ 38.61
20	**East - 5A Total**						$ 73.26
21	West - 1B	11R	50-116	16" Wicker Basket	14	$ 1.99	$ 27.86
22	West - 1B	13R	50-120	20" Wicker Basket	21	$ 2.39	$ 50.19
23	West - 1B	12R	50-117	17" Wicker Basket	17	$ 1.99	$ 33.83
24	**West - 1B Total**						$ 111.88
25	West - 2B	14R	50-121	21" Wicker Basket	18	$ 2.59	$ 46.62
26	**West - 2B Total**						$ 46.62
27	**Grand Total**						$ 818.68

FIGURE 11–5 Data after subtotals applied

When you use the Subtotal feature, you will need to decide where you want the subtotals to be placed in the worksheet data. For example, if you have columns of inventory data by store aisle, as in Figure 11–4, you can have inventory subtotals placed after each aisle. Be sure to sort the data first so that the items for the subtotal are grouped together.

When you add subtotals to a worksheet, the worksheet is displayed in an outline format. The outline format makes viewing the subtotals easier. In the outline format, you can click the minus button (–) to collapse or hide the data. You click the plus button (+) to expand or redisplay the data.

Notice in Figure 11–5 that the numbers 1, 2, and 3 also appear in the outline. These numbers let you display as much or as little data as you want for the entire worksheet. Selecting 1 only displays the grand total. Selecting 2 only shows the subtotals with no other data, and selecting 3 displays all the worksheet data.

To add subtotals, you select the Subtotal button to display the available options you can select in the Subtotal dialog box, as shown in **Figure 11–6**.

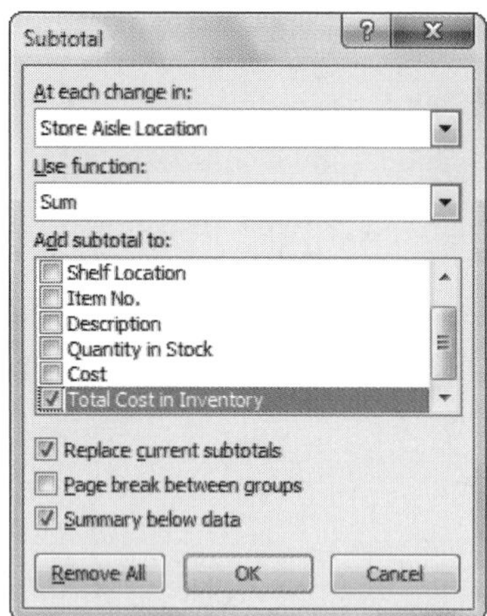

FIGURE 11–6 Subtotal dialog box

The options available in the Subtotal dialog box are described in **Table 11–1**.

TABLE 11–1 Options in the Subtotal dialog box

OPTION	DESCRIPTION
At each change in	This option lets you select the column of data that will determine how data is grouped for subtotaling.
Use function	Selecting this option lets you select the summary calculation to be performed. You may choose Sum, Average, Count, Min, Max, Product, or one of several statistical calculations.
Add subtotal to	This option determines in which column the subtotal will be placed.
Replace current subtotals	When subtotals already exist, using this option replaces existing subtotals.
Page break between groups	Selecting this option creates a page break between each group subtotal.
Summary below data	This option inserts subtotals and a grand total below the detailed data.
Remove All	Selecting this option removes subtotals from data.

Step-by-Step 11.2

1. Click **cell A4** or any cell with a column heading.
2. On the Ribbon, click the **Data** tab, and then in the Outline group, click the **Subtotal** button.
3. Click the **list arrow** below "At each change in", then click **Division** to have subtotals placed after each division. Next, you will select the Sum option to total the data.
4. Click the **Use function** list arrow and then click **Sum**.
5. In the Add subtotal to section, click each marked check box to remove all check marks from the list.
6. In the Add subtotal to section, click the **Sales** check box to add a check mark, and then compare your Subtotal dialog box to **Figure 11–7**.

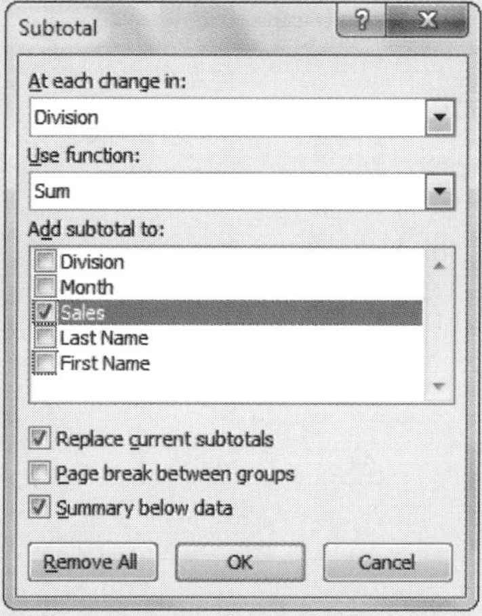

FIGURE 11–7
Completed Subtotal dialog box

7. Click **OK** to close the Subtotal dialog box, and then widen the columns to view the subtotals, if necessary.
8. In the Outline pane on the left side of the workbook data, click **2** so that only the Division subtotals appear, as shown in **Figure 11–8**.

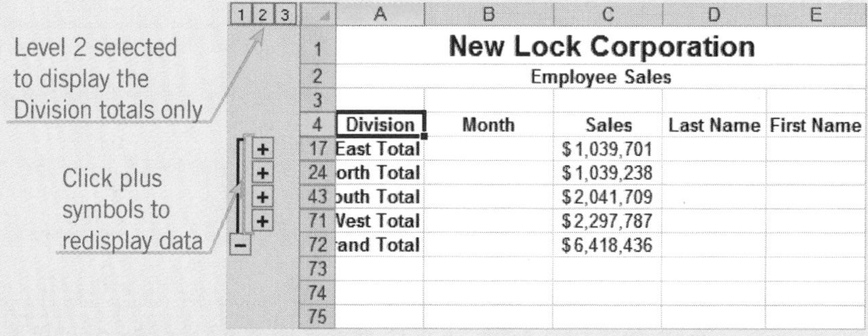

FIGURE 11–8
Data with only Division subtotals displayed

EXTRA FOR EXPERTS

To remove subtotals from the data, click any cell with data. Click the Subtotal button and then click Remove All in the Subtotal dialog box.

9. In the Outline pane, click **1** to display only the grand total.
10. In the Outline pane, click **3** to display all the data with the subtotals.
11. In the Outline pane, click the **minus symbol (–)** next to East Total. Notice how the data for the East division is collapsed, but the data and totals for the other divisions are still displayed.
12. Save, print, and close the workbook.

Creating a Data Validation Rule

VOCABULARY
data validation
validation rule
validation range

When you or someone else will be adding or changing data to the same worksheet, you may want to use the ***Data Validation*** feature to ensure that the data is entered as accurately as possible. Adding a ***validation rule*** allows you to set parameters for worksheet cells where values will be entered. For example, an inventory sheet may contain cells with cost values. If you know that the costs for the products are always within a certain range of values, you can define this range of values in the Settings tab of the Data Validation dialog box. The range of cells that you select to apply the validation rule is called the ***validation range***.

You can also create an input message that displays when a cell in the validation range is selected. When the cell is selected, the input message appears stating how the data should be entered or what values are acceptable. Using the Error Alert tab in the Data Validation dialog box, you can create an error alert that appears when a value you enter does not fall within the range.

Several style options are available for the Error Alert tab in the Data Validation dialog box, as shown in **Figure 11–9**.

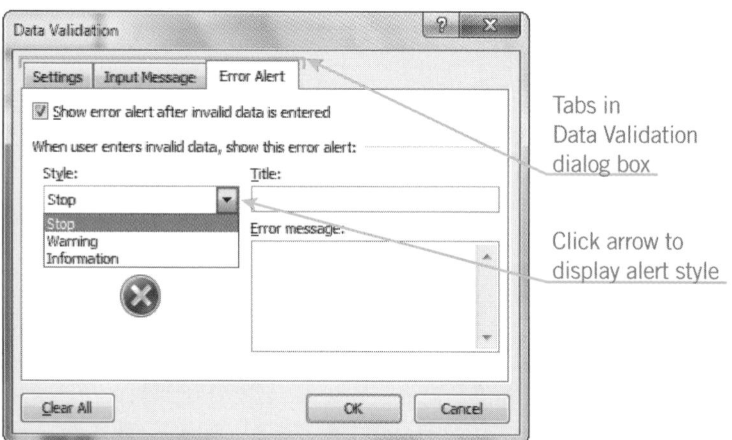

FIGURE 11–9 Data Validation dialog box

The available style options are the Stop style, Warning style, and Information style. If the Stop style is selected in the Error Alert tab, you will not be allowed to enter any value that does not meet the criteria. Choosing the Warning style displays a warning dialog box but allows the data to be entered. The Information style option also allows data to be entered but simply displays an information box with a message that the data entered is invalid.

Step-by-Step 11.3

1. Open the **Fan Fair** file from the drive and folder where your Data Files are stored, and then save the workbook as **Fan Fair Inventory**, followed by your initials. You will now add a validation rule to a range of cells.
2. Select **E6:E21**.
3. On the Ribbon, click the **Data** tab, and then in the Data Tools group, click the **Data Validation** button to open the Data Validation dialog box.
4. In the Data Validation dialog box, click the **Allow** list arrow and then click **Decimal**. Selecting Decimal will allow the user to enter a dollar amount with two decimals.
5. Click the **Data** list arrow and then click **between**, if necessary.
6. Click in the **Minimum** box, and then type **4.00**. 4.00 is the minimum amount that may be entered.
7. Click in the **Maximum** box, and then type **17.00**. 17.00 is the maximum amount that may be entered. The completed Settings tab in the Data Validation dialog box should appear as shown in **Figure 11–10**. You will now enter an input message for the data validation.

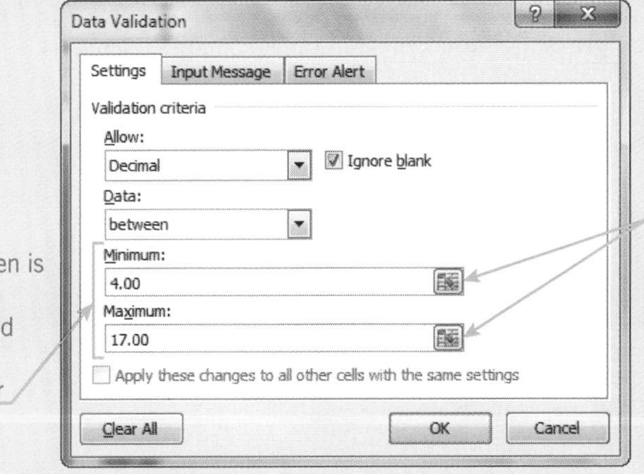

FIGURE 11–10
Completed Settings tab in Data Validation dialog box

8. Click the **Input Message** tab in the Data Validation dialog box, click in the **Title** text box, and then type **Data Entry Requirement**.

TIP

When the exact amounts that you want to enter in the Data Validation dialog box are in the worksheet, you can click the Collapse dialog box button and then select the cell with the amount.

9. Click in the **Input message** text box and then type **Enter an amount between $4.00 and $17.00**. The completed Input Message tab is shown in **Figure 11–11**.

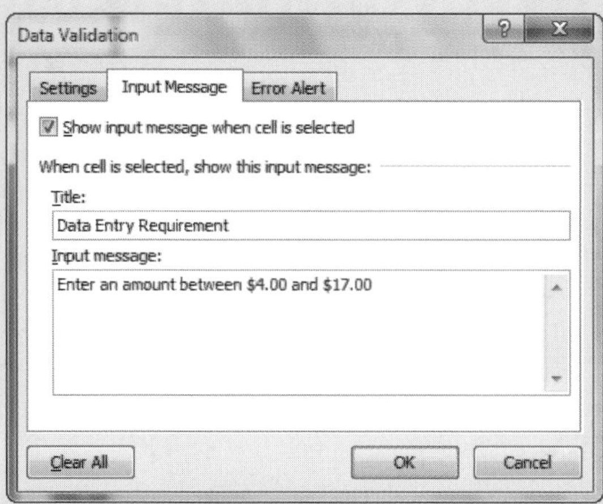

FIGURE 11–11
Completed Input Message tab in Data Validation dialog box

10. Click the **Error Alert** tab. This tab allows you to add an error message if an incorrect amount of data is entered.
11. Click the **Style** list arrow and then click **Warning**.
12. In the Title text box, type **Incorrect Data Entered**.
13. Click in the **Error message** text box and then type **The amount entered must be between $4.00 and $17.00**, as shown in **Figure 11–12**.

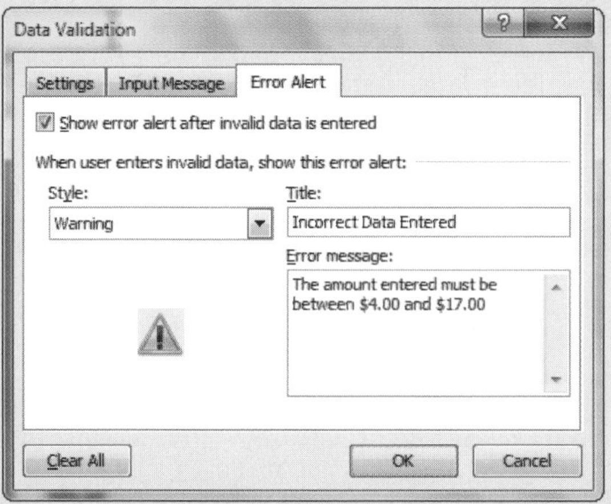

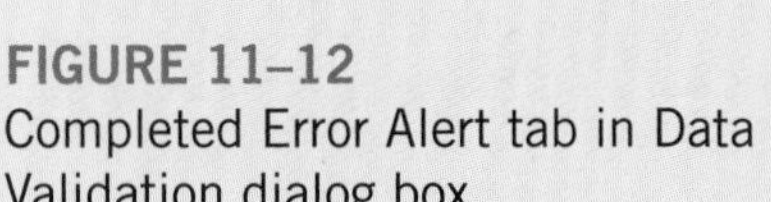
FIGURE 11–12
Completed Error Alert tab in Data Validation dialog box

14. Click **OK** to close the Data Validation dialog box.
15. Save the workbook and leave it open for the next Step-by-Step.

Entering Data into a Validation Range

After you select a range and enter a validation rule for the validation range, the data entered into this range is monitored. If the data is invalid, a message will appear to let you know what is wrong. The error message gives you the option to select No or

Continue. Select No if you do not want to enter the data, and select Continue to enter the data. In this next Step-by-Step, you will enter data in the validation range.

Step-by-Step 11.4

1. Click **cell E6**. Notice the input message that appears when you select the cell, as shown in **Figure 11–13**.

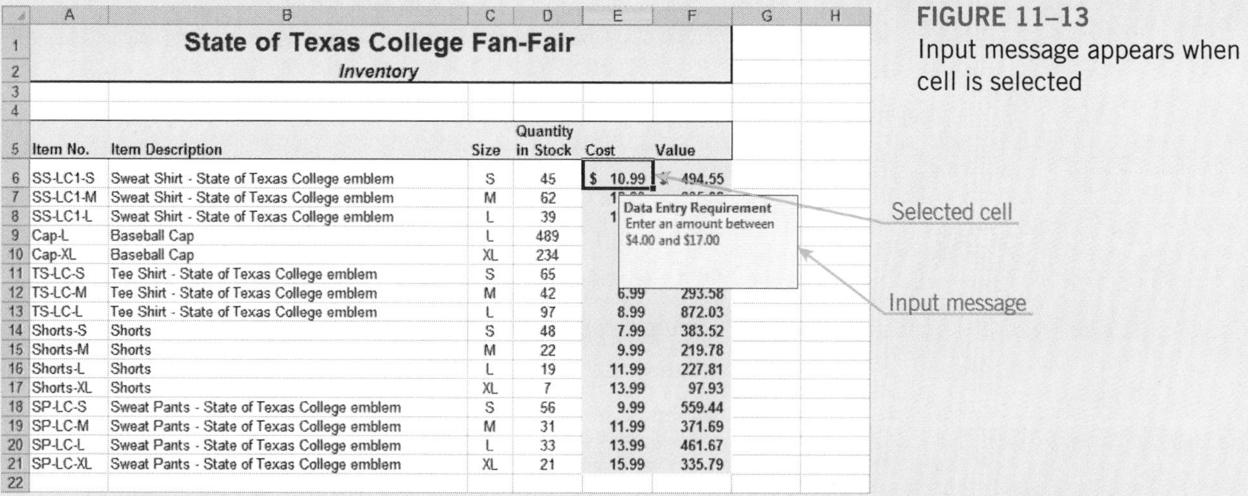

	A	B	C	D	E	F
1		State of Texas College Fan-Fair				
2		Inventory				
5	Item No.	Item Description	Size	Quantity in Stock	Cost	Value
6	SS-LC1-S	Sweat Shirt - State of Texas College emblem	S	45	$ 10.99	$ 494.55
7	SS-LC1-M	Sweat Shirt - State of Texas College emblem	M	62		
8	SS-LC1-L	Sweat Shirt - State of Texas College emblem	L	39		
9	Cap-L	Baseball Cap	L	489		
10	Cap-XL	Baseball Cap	XL	234		
11	TS-LC-S	Tee Shirt - State of Texas College emblem	S	65		
12	TS-LC-M	Tee Shirt - State of Texas College emblem	M	42	6.99	293.58
13	TS-LC-L	Tee Shirt - State of Texas College emblem	L	97	8.99	872.03
14	Shorts-S	Shorts	S	48	7.99	383.52
15	Shorts-M	Shorts	M	22	9.99	219.78
16	Shorts-L	Shorts	L	19	11.99	227.81
17	Shorts-XL	Shorts	XL	7	13.99	97.93
18	SP-LC-S	Sweat Pants - State of Texas College emblem	S	56	9.99	559.44
19	SP-LC-M	Sweat Pants - State of Texas College emblem	M	31	11.99	371.69
20	SP-LC-L	Sweat Pants - State of Texas College emblem	L	33	13.99	461.67
21	SP-LC-XL	Sweat Pants - State of Texas College emblem	XL	21	15.99	335.79

FIGURE 11–13 Input message appears when cell is selected

2. Type **20.00** into cell E6 and then press **Enter**. The error message appears as shown in **Figure 11–14**.

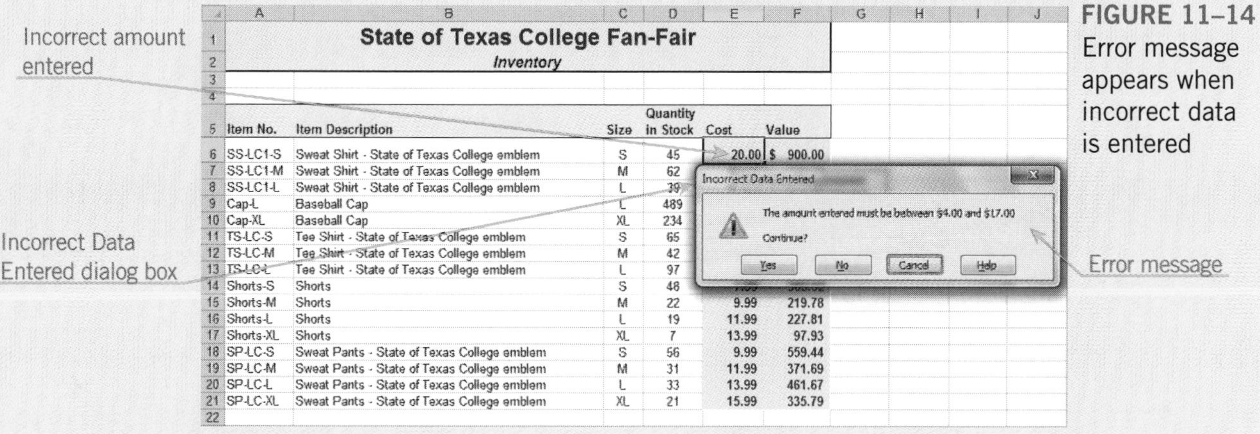

	A	B	C	D	E	F
1		State of Texas College Fan-Fair				
2		Inventory				
5	Item No.	Item Description	Size	Quantity in Stock	Cost	Value
6	SS-LC1-S	Sweat Shirt - State of Texas College emblem	S	45	20.00	$ 900.00
7	SS-LC1-M	Sweat Shirt - State of Texas College emblem	M	62		
8	SS-LC1-L	Sweat Shirt - State of Texas College emblem	L	39		
9	Cap-L	Baseball Cap	L	489		
10	Cap-XL	Baseball Cap	XL	234		
11	TS-LC-S	Tee Shirt - State of Texas College emblem	S	65		
12	TS-LC-M	Tee Shirt - State of Texas College emblem	M	42		
13	TS-LC-L	Tee Shirt - State of Texas College emblem	L	97		
14	Shorts-S	Shorts	S	48		
15	Shorts-M	Shorts	M	22	9.99	219.78
16	Shorts-L	Shorts	L	19	11.99	227.81
17	Shorts-XL	Shorts	XL	7	13.99	97.93
18	SP-LC-S	Sweat Pants - State of Texas College emblem	S	56	9.99	559.44
19	SP-LC-M	Sweat Pants - State of Texas College emblem	M	31	11.99	371.69
20	SP-LC-L	Sweat Pants - State of Texas College emblem	L	33	13.99	461.67
21	SP-LC-XL	Sweat Pants - State of Texas College emblem	XL	21	15.99	335.79

FIGURE 11–14 Error message appears when incorrect data is entered

3. In the Incorrect Data Entered dialog box, click **No,** type **11.99** in cell E6, and then press **Enter**. The amount is now entered into the cell.
4. Save the workbook and leave it open for the next Step-by-Step.

Circling Invalid Data

In addition to using data validation to specifically detail the valid data that should be entered, you can use the Circle Invalid Data feature to have circles drawn around data that does not meet the data validation requirements. The circles act as a visual reminder of which cells contain invalid data.

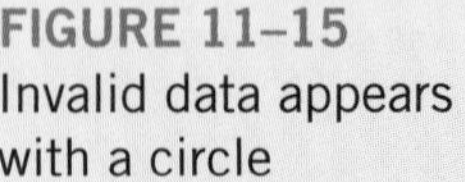

Step-by-Step 11.5

1. Save the workbook as **Fan Fair Inventory – 2**, followed by your initials.
2. Click **cell E7**, type **122.99**, and then press **Enter**.
3. Click **Yes** to continue.
4. Click **cell E18**, type **99.99**, and then press **Enter**.
5. Click **Yes** to continue. Two cells now have data outside the validation range of $4.00 and $17.00.
6. On the Ribbon, click the **Data** tab. In the Data Tools group, click the **Data Validation** button arrow, and then click **Circle Invalid Data**. Red circles appear, around cells E7 and E18, as shown in **Figure 11–15**.

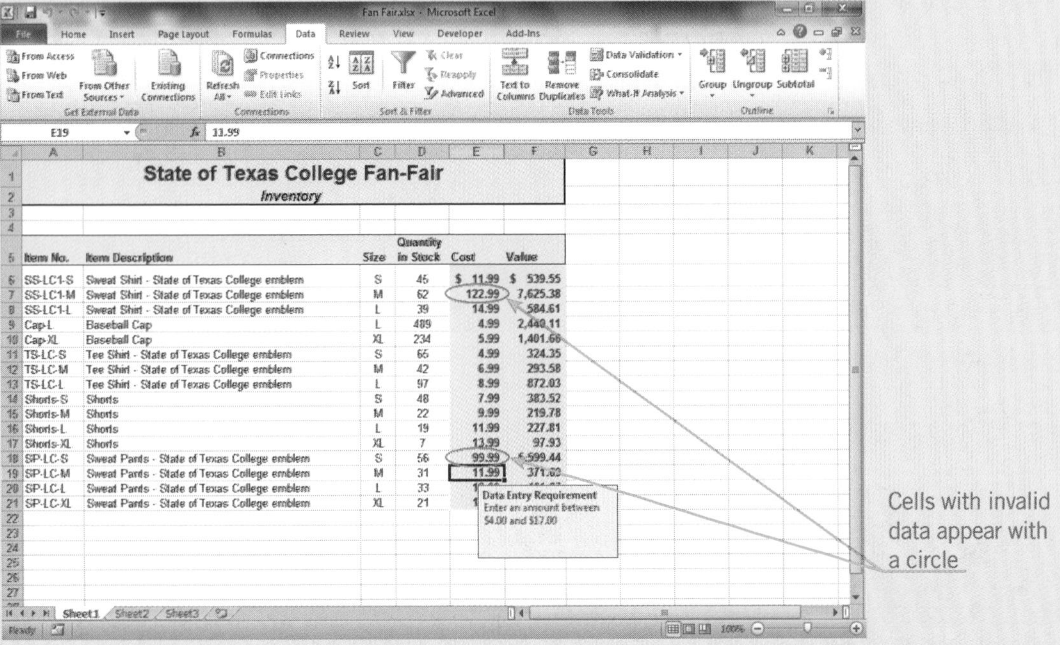

FIGURE 11–15
Invalid data appears with a circle

7. Click in **cell E7**, type **13.99**, and then press **Enter** to correct the first validation error.
8. In cell E18, type **9.99**, and then press **Enter**. Notice that the circles are now gone.
9. Save, print, and close the workbook.

Adding a Drop-Down List for Selections

To further increase data accuracy, you can add drop-down lists that display specific selections from which you can choose. Drop-down lists are very useful when only specific data can be entered into a cell. To create a drop-down list, it is easier if you first create a range of cells that has the selections that should appear in the list. For example, if you have a range of cells in which you only want specific areas (such as north, south, east, or west) to appear, you can create a list with only these selections. This list can be created in another worksheet. Then, you will enter the cell range with the list information in the Data Validation dialog box.

When you select a cell with the data validation, an arrow appears to the right of the cell. You can then click the arrow to display the list.

Step-by-Step 11.6

1. Open the **Arts & Crafts** file from the drive and folder where your Data Files are stored, then save the workbook as **Arts & Crafts Inventory**, followed by your initials. You will now add a drop-down list to a range of cells.
2. Select **A5:A50**. Because you have selected additional cells below the existing data, several more rows of data may be added.
3. On the Ribbon, click the **Data** tab, and then in the Data Tools group, click **Data Validation**.
4. In the Data Validation dialog box, click the **Settings** tab, click the **Allow** list arrow, and then click **List**.
5. Click the **Collapse dialog box** button.
6. Click the **Locations in Store** worksheet tab. The store aisle locations appear, as shown in **Figure 11–16**.

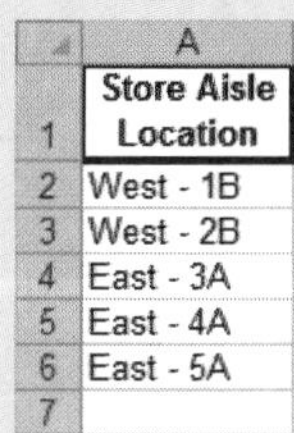

FIGURE 11–16
Store aisle locations

7. Select cells **A2:A6**, as shown in **Figure 11–17**. The data in the five cells will serve as the five choices in the drop-down list.

FIGURE 11–17
Collapsed Data Validation dialog box

8. Click the **Expand dialog box** button to restore the Data Validation dialog box, and then compare your dialog box to **Figure 11–18**.

FIGURE 11–18
Completed Settings tab in the Data Validation dialog box

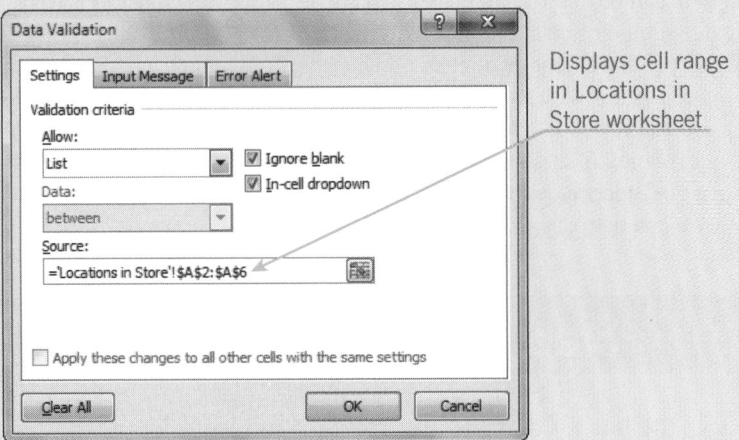

9. In the Data Validation dialog box, click the **Input Message** tab to add an input message.
10. Click in the **Input Message** text box and then type **Click arrow to select value from the list**.
11. Click **OK** to close the Data Validation dialog box.
12. Click in **cell A22**, and then click the list arrow to display the list of store aisle locations, as shown in **Figure 11–19**.

FIGURE 11–19
Store Aisle Location data validation list

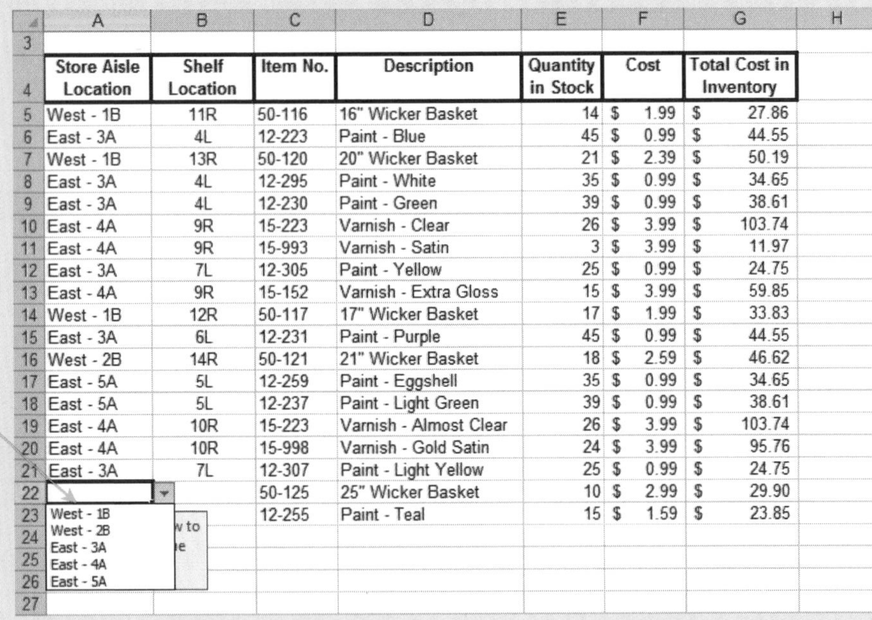

Store Aisle Location	Shelf Location	Item No.	Description	Quantity in Stock	Cost	Total Cost in Inventory
West - 1B	11R	50-116	16" Wicker Basket	14	$ 1.99	$ 27.86
East - 3A	4L	12-223	Paint - Blue	45	$ 0.99	$ 44.55
West - 1B	13R	50-120	20" Wicker Basket	21	$ 2.39	$ 50.19
East - 3A	4L	12-295	Paint - White	35	$ 0.99	$ 34.65
East - 3A	4L	12-230	Paint - Green	39	$ 0.99	$ 38.61
East - 4A	9R	15-223	Varnish - Clear	26	$ 3.99	$ 103.74
East - 4A	9R	15-993	Varnish - Satin	3	$ 3.99	$ 11.97
East - 3A	7L	12-305	Paint - Yellow	25	$ 0.99	$ 24.75
East - 4A	9R	15-152	Varnish - Extra Gloss	15	$ 3.99	$ 59.85
West - 1B	12R	50-117	17" Wicker Basket	17	$ 1.99	$ 33.83
East - 3A	6L	12-231	Paint - Purple	45	$ 0.99	$ 44.55
West - 2B	14R	50-121	21" Wicker Basket	18	$ 2.59	$ 46.62
East - 5A	5L	12-259	Paint - Eggshell	35	$ 0.99	$ 34.65
East - 5A	5L	12-237	Paint - Light Green	39	$ 0.99	$ 38.61
East - 4A	10R	15-223	Varnish - Almost Clear	26	$ 3.99	$ 103.74
East - 4A	10R	15-998	Varnish - Gold Satin	24	$ 3.99	$ 95.76
East - 3A	7L	12-307	Paint - Light Yellow	25	$ 0.99	$ 24.75
		50-125	25" Wicker Basket	10	$ 2.99	$ 29.90
		12-255	Paint - Teal	15	$ 1.59	$ 23.85

13. Click **West – 2B** in the data validation list.
14. Save, print, and close the workbook.

Converting Text to Columns

The Convert Text to Columns feature is a great method for separating data in a worksheet, such as first and last names. By letting Excel separate the data for you, rather than you typing the data yourself, accuracy is significantly improved.

The Convert Text to Columns Wizard provides a step-by-step process to help you choose how to separate your data. You will need to choose whether you want to separate the data based on a delimiter or fixed width. A ***delimiter*** is a character, such as a comma, space, or a tab, used to separate data. Using a delimiter works best if your data has a similar format, such as *firstname lastname*, where a space separates the text. The Fixed Width option lets you mark the exact place where the data will be split, such as after 15 characters. When you apply the Fixed Width option, cells will be split at the exact location you specify, even if that is not where you want all the data to split.

After you define how you want to separate the data, you will need to enter a destination range. The ***destination range*** is the location in the worksheet where the separated data will be placed.

VOCABULARY
delimiter
destination range

Step-by-Step 11.7

1. Open the **Computer Training Students** file from the drive and folder where your Data Files are stored, and then save the workbook as **Computer Training Students List** followed by your initials. You will insert two columns to make room for the students' first names and last names.
2. Drag to select any cells in columns **C** and **D**.
3. On the Ribbon, click the **Home** tab. In the Cells group, click the **Insert Cells** button arrow, and then click **Insert Sheet Columns**. Now that you made room for the names, the first names will appear in Column C and the last names will appear in Column D. Next, you will split the data.
4. Select **B2:B25**.

5. On the Ribbon, click the **Data** tab, and then in the Data Tools group, click the **Text to Columns** button. The Convert Text to Columns Wizard opens, as shown in **Figure 11–20**.

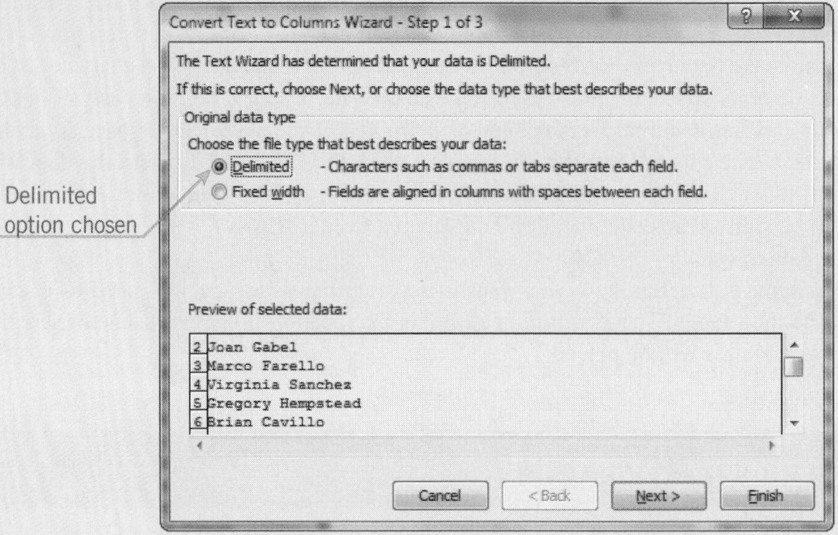

FIGURE 11–20
Convert Text to Columns Wizard – Step 1 of 3

6. Click the **Delimited** option button, if necessary, and then click **Next**.
7. In the Convert Text to Columns – Step 2 of 3 dialog box, click the **Space** check box to indicate that you would like a space to separate the first name and the last name.
8. Verify that the remaining check boxes are not checked, and then compare your screen to **Figure 11–21**.

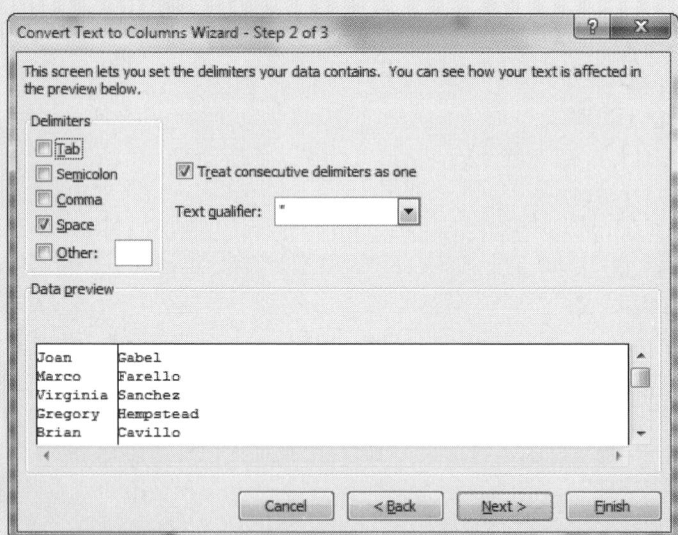

FIGURE 11–21
Convert Text to Columns Wizard – Step 2 of 3

9. Click **Next** to display the Convert Text to Columns – Step 3 of 3 dialog box, and then click the **Text** option button in the Column data format section.
10. Click the **Collapse dialog box button** and then select **C2:D25** to select the range for the last names.

11. Click the **Expand dialog box button** to redisplay the dialog box, and then compare your dialog box to **Figure 11–22**.

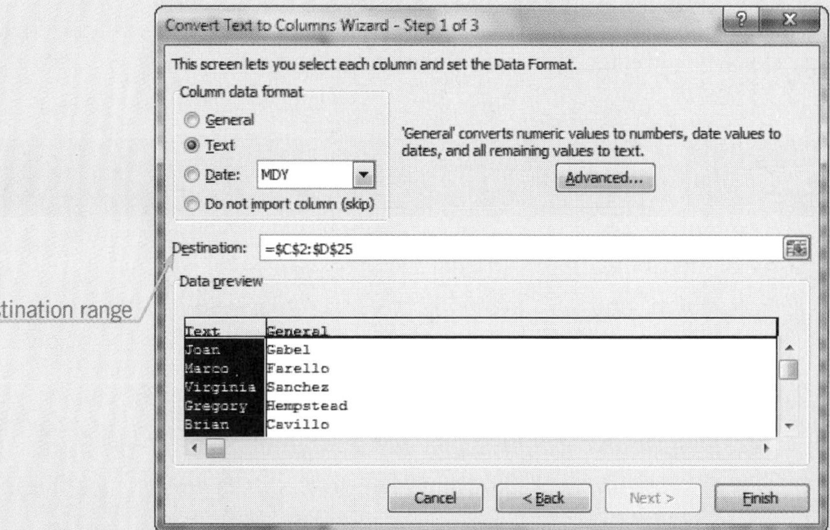

FIGURE 11–22
Convert Text to Columns Wizard – Step 3 of 3

12. Click **Finish**.
13. Click **cell C1**, type **First Name**, press **[Tab]** to select cell D1, and then type **Last Name**.

Your converted data should appear as displayed in **Figure 11–23**.

	A	B	C	D	E	F	G	H
1	Student Number	Student Name	First Name	Last Name	Address	City	State	ZIP
2	1001	Joan Gabel	Joan	Gabel	1102 Jackson Street	Lewis	CO	81327
3	1002	Marco Farello	Marco	Farello	11259 Road 22	Dolores	CO	81323
4	1003	Virginia Sanchez	Virginia	Sanchez	633 Empire Street	Flora Vista	NM	87415
5	1004	Gregory Hempstead	Gregory	Hempstead	12933 Road G	Blanding	UT	84511
6	1005	Brian Cavillo	Brian	Cavillo	116 North Adams Street	Chinle	AZ	86503
7	1006	Cynthia Jones	Cynthia	Jones	755 Cherry Street	Pleasant View	CO	81331
8	1007	Anthony Laporte	Anthony	Laporte	620 East Empire Street	Kayenta	AZ	86033
9	1008	Tara Kobrick	Tara	Kobrick	620 East Empire Street	Kayenta	AZ	86033
10	1009	Darnell Lightford	Darnell	Lightford	1309 Mesa Avenue	Shiprock	NM	87420
11	1010	Louis Moreno	Louis	Moreno	403 North Madison Street	Flora Vista	NM	87415
12	1011	Paul Ferrino	Paul	Ferrino	133 South Washington	Dolores	CO	81323
13	1012	Richard Conlee	Richard	Conlee	307 Memorial Drive	Kirtland	NM	87417
14	1013	Connie Nader	Connie	Nader	1645 Johnny Cake Ridge Road	Kayenta	AZ	86033
15	1014	Robert Selinger	Robert	Selinger	9411 Clarkston Avenue	Aneth	UT	84510
16	1015	Rachel Thompson	Rachel	Thompson	623 South Hampton Way	Farmington	NM	87499
17	1016	Shayla Jackson	Shayla	Jackson	1322 East Fairmont Street	Montezuma Creek	UT	84534
18	1017	Amy Urquiza	Amy	Urquiza	912 North Hampton Avenue	Yellow Jacket	CO	81335
19	1018	Thomas White	Thomas	White	322 South Cripple Creek Avenue	Aneth	UT	84510
20	1019	Dora Langston	Dora	Langston	1155 NE Highland Parkway	Shiprock	NM	87420
21	1020	Dominque Latour	Dominque	Latour	56 East Pioneer Road	Lewis	CO	81327
22	1021	Maria Garcia	Maria	Garcia	707 Cherry Street	Pleasant View	CO	81331
23	1022	Donald Linebarger	Donald	Linebarger	1998 SE First Avenue	Dolores	CO	81328
24	1023	Vincent Ferrino	Vincent	Ferrino	1109 Siesta Shores Drive	Dolores	CO	81324
25	1024	Elaine Estes	Elaine	Estes	801 Airport Road	Lewis	CO	81327

FIGURE 11–23
Converted data

14. Save, print, and close the workbook.

Combining Text

Separating first and last names into separate cells makes it easier to sort the columns with the data by last name and then by first name. However, there may be times when you want the first name and last name combined as one value in a single cell. For example, you may need the first and last name in one cell when merging Excel data to create letters in Microsoft Word.

To join the values of cells together, you use the Concatenate function. The Concatenate function combines the text from two or more cells into one cell.

You can also add other text, such as spaces, into the Concatenate function. For example, you may want to add a space when you are putting first name and last name together in a single cell so that there is a space to separate them. To add text, you include the text, such as a space, between quotation marks. For example, to add a space, you would enter " " into the Concatenate function.

Step-by-Step 11.8

1. Open the **Employees** file from the drive and folder where your Data Files are stored, and save the workbook as **Employees List**, followed by your initials.
2. Click any cell in Column D. You are going to add a new column where the employees' combined first and last names will be placed.
3. On the Ribbon, click the **Home** tab. In the Cells group, click the **Insert Cells** button arrow and then click **Insert Sheet Columns**.
4. Click in **cell D4**. This cell is the first cell in which the combined text will be placed. On the Ribbon, click the **Formulas** tab, and then in the Function Library group, click the **Insert Function** button. The Insert Function dialog box opens, as shown in **Figure 11–24**.

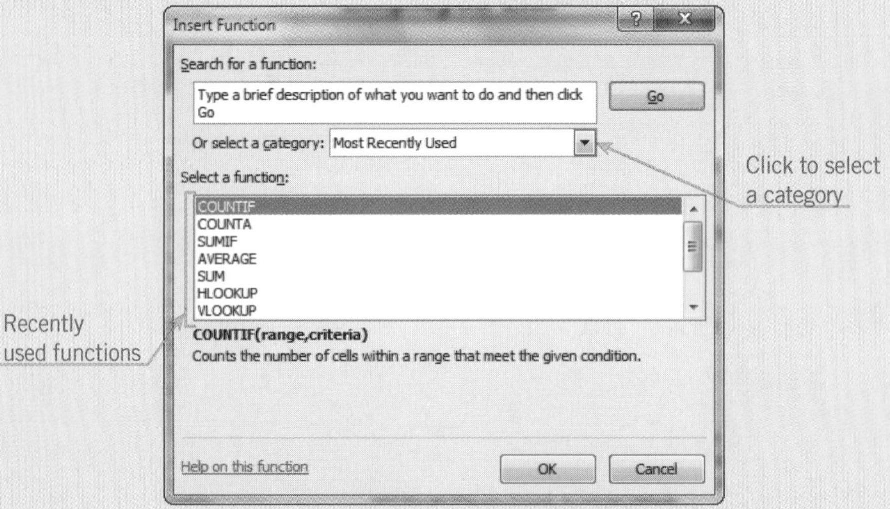

FIGURE 11–24
Insert Function dialog box

5. Click the **Or select a category** list arrow, and then click **Text**.
6. In the Select a function section, click **CONCATENATE**, and then click **OK** to display the Function Arguments dialog box.
7. In the Function Arguments dialog box, type **A4** in the Text1 text box.
8. Click in the **Text2** text box and then type **" "** (quote space quote) to add a space between the first name and middle initial.
9. In the Text3 text box, type **B4**.

10. Click in the Text4 text box and type " " (quote space quote) to add a space between middle initial and last name, then type **C4** in the Text5 text box. The completed dialog box should appear as shown in **Figure 11–25**.

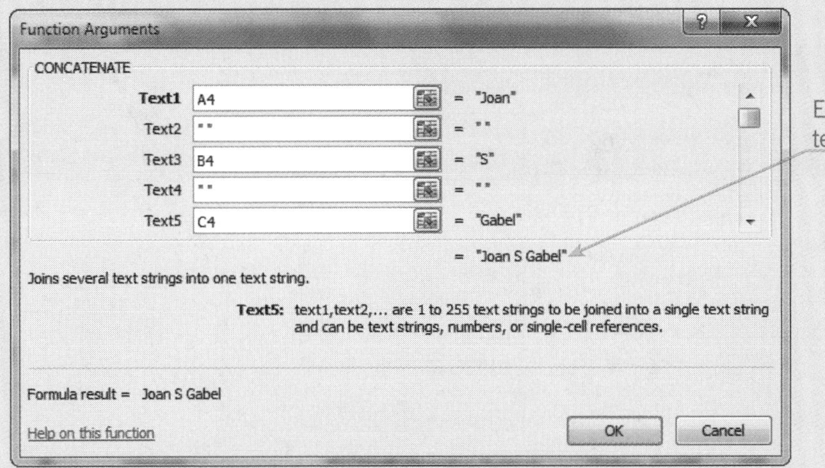

FIGURE 11–25 Completed Function Arguments dialog box

11. Click **OK** to close the Function Arguments dialog box.
12. Click **cell D4**, point to the **Fill handle** in the lower-right corner of cell D4, and then drag the **Fill handle** down to cell D27. Next, you will increase the width of column D to display the complete name.
13. Increase the column width, if necessary. Click in any cell outside of column D so you can view the results. The completed worksheet should appear as shown in **Figure 11–26**.

	A	B	C	D	E	F	G	H
3	First Name	Middle Initial	Last Name		Address	City	State	ZIP
4	Joan	S	Gabel	Joan S Gabel	1102 Jackson Street	Lewis	CO	81327
5	Marco	K	Farello	Marco K Farello	11259 Road 22	Dolores	CO	81323
6	Virginia	G	Sanchez	Virginia G Sanchez	633 Empire Street	Flora Vista	NM	87415
7	Gregory	K	Hempstead	Gregory K Hempstead	12933 Road G	Blanding	UT	84511
8	Brian	G	Cavillo	Brian G Cavillo	116 North Adams Street	Chinle	AZ	86503
9	Cynthia	Z	Jones	Cynthia Z Jones	755 Cherry Street	Pleasant View	CO	81331
10	Anthony	L	Laporte	Anthony L Laporte	620 East Empire Street	Kayenta	AZ	86033
11	Tara	P	Kobrick	Tara P Kobrick	620 East Empire Street	Kayenta	AZ	86033
12	Darnell	C	Lightford	Darnell C Lightford	1309 Mesa Avenue	Shiprock	NM	87420
13	Louis	W	Moreno	Louis W Moreno	403 North Madison Street	Flora Vista	NM	87415
14	Paul	G	Ferrino	Paul G Ferrino	133 South Washington	Dolores	CO	81323
15	Richard	P	Conlee	Richard P Conlee	307 Memorial Drive	Kirtland	NM	87417
16	Connie	E	Nader	Connie E Nader	1645 Johnny Cake Ridge Road	Kayenta	AZ	86033
17	Robert	J	Selinger	Robert J Selinger	9411 Clarkston Avenue	Aneth	UT	84510
18	Rachel	O	Thompson	Rachel O Thompson	623 South Hampton Way	Farmington	NM	87499
19	Shayla	B	Jackson	Shayla B Jackson	1322 East Fairmont Street	Montezuma Creek	UT	84534
20	Amy	B	Urquiza	Amy B Urquiza	912 North Hampton Avenue	Yellow Jacket	CO	81335
21	Thomas	M	White	Thomas M White	322 South Cripple Creek Avenue	Aneth	UT	84510
22	Dora	V	Langston	Dora V Langston	1155 NE Highland Parkway	Shiprock	NM	87420
23	Dominque	C	Latour	Dominque C Latour	56 East Pioneer Road	Lewis	CO	81327
24	Maria	A	Garcia	Maria A Garcia	707 Cherry Street	Pleasant View	CO	81331
25	Donald	T	Linebarger	Donald T Linebarger	1998 SE First Avenue	Dolores	CO	81328
26	Vincent	R	Ferrino	Vincent R Ferrino	1109 Siesta Shores Drive	Dolores	CO	81324
27	Elaine	C	Estes	Elaine C Estes	801 Airport Road	Lewis	CO	81327

Column with concatenated data

FIGURE 11–26 Concatenated data in worksheet

14. Save, print, and close the workbook.

Adding a Watch Window

VOCABULARY
Watch Window

You can add cells of data into a Watch Window if you want to be able to view the data while working in another worksheet. The ***Watch Window*** lets you view the data that you specify, as shown in **Figure 11–27**.

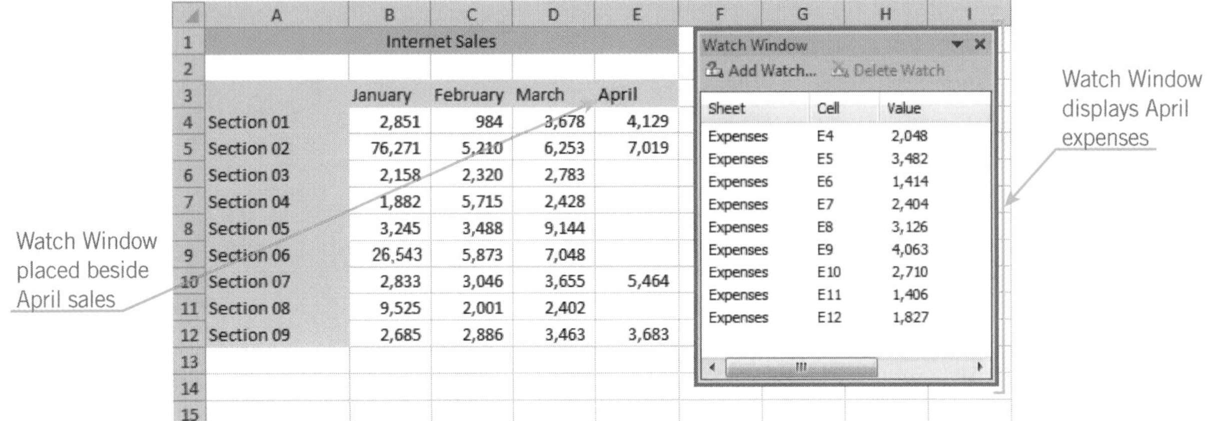

FIGURE 11–27 Worksheet with Watch Window

In this example, the data in the Watch Window is located on a worksheet named Expenses. The Watch Window shows the cell number and the value for the cell. By placing the Watch Window next to sales, you will be able to see when the sales amount is greater than the expenses for each section. And, when sales are greater than expenses, that section should have a profit.

The Watch Window remains visible regardless of which worksheet you are using in the workbook, and it remains open while the workbook is open. When you reopen the Watch Window, it will display the range of data you previously selected.

When the Watch Window first appears, it will include workbook name, worksheet name, cell range name (if any), cell name, value, and formula (if any). In the Watch Window, you can hide the column headings by dragging the right side of the column heading to the left until the column heading is no longer visible.

Step-by-Step 11.9

1. Open the **College Book Sales** file from the drive and folder where your Data Files are stored, then save the workbook as **College Book Sales and Expenses**, followed by your initials.
2. Click the **Expenses** worksheet tab to view the department expenses, as shown in **Figure 11–28**. You will now create a Watch Window for expenses.

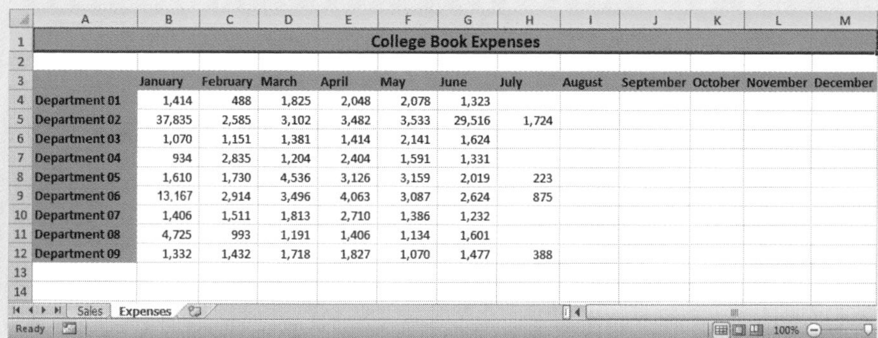

	A	B	C	D	E	F	G	H	I	J	K	L	M
1	College Book Expenses												
2													
3		January	February	March	April	May	June	July	August	September	October	November	December
4	Department 01	1,414	488	1,825	2,048	2,078	1,323						
5	Department 02	37,835	2,585	3,102	3,482	3,533	29,516	1,724					
6	Department 03	1,070	1,151	1,381	1,414	2,141	1,624						
7	Department 04	934	2,835	1,204	2,404	1,591	1,331						
8	Department 05	1,610	1,730	4,536	3,126	3,159	2,019	223					
9	Department 06	13,167	2,914	3,496	4,063	3,087	2,624	875					
10	Department 07	1,406	1,511	1,813	2,710	1,386	1,232						
11	Department 08	4,725	993	1,191	1,406	1,134	1,601						
12	Department 09	1,332	1,432	1,718	1,827	1,070	1,477	388					
13													
14													

FIGURE 11–28
Expenses worksheet

3. On the Ribbon, click the **Formulas** tab, and then in the Formula Auditing group, click the **Watch Window** button. The Watch Window appears, as shown in **Figure 11–29**.

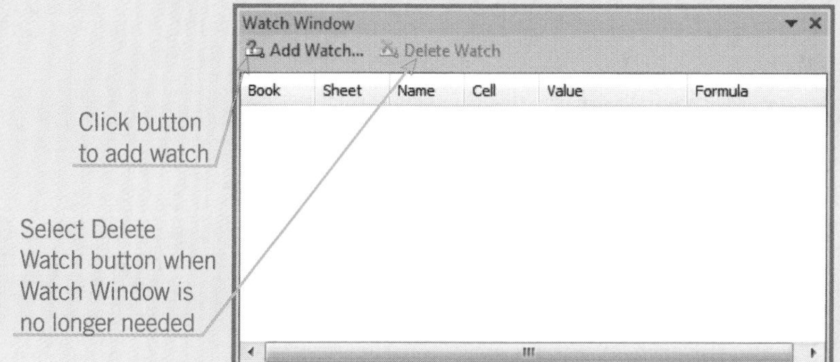

FIGURE 11–29
Watch Window

4. In the Watch Window, click the **Add Watch** button to display the Add Watch dialog box. This dialog box is where you select the cell or cells that you want displayed in the Watch Window.
5. Select the range **H4:H12**. The data in these cells will be visible in the Watch Window. The completed Add Watch dialog box opens, as shown in **Figure 11–30**.

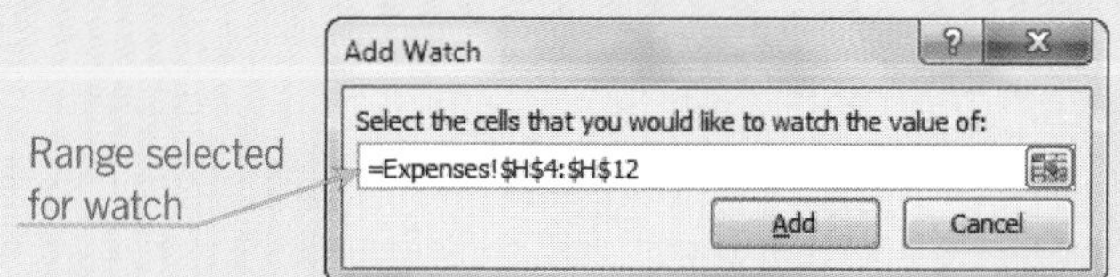

FIGURE 11–30
Add Watch dialog box

6. Click the **Add** button. The Watch Window displays the workbook name, worksheet name, name of cell (if a name was created), and cell name. You will need to increase the size of the Watch Window to view all the values. See **Figure 11–31**.

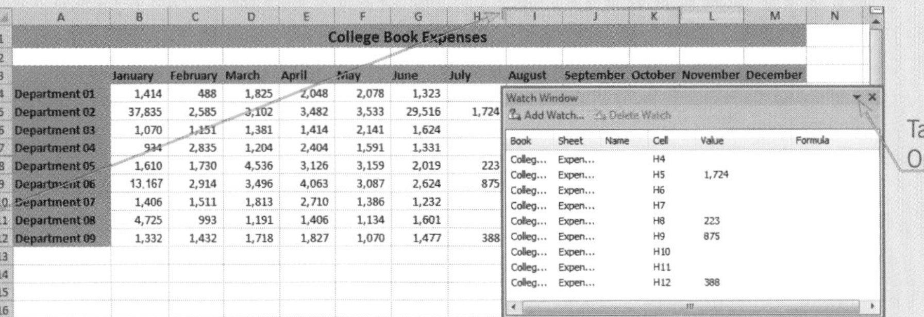

FIGURE 11–31 Watch Window needs to be expanded

Cell amounts not displayed

Task Pane Options arrow

7. Click the **Sales** worksheet tab. Notice that the Watch Window remains open. You will now resize the Watch Window and move it next to Column H. If you were going to enter July sales data, this would allow you to view July expenses as you enter July sales data.
8. On the Watch Window, click the **Task Pane Options** arrow, and then click **Size**. The mouse pointer becomes a double-arrow pointer, as shown in **Figure 11–32**.

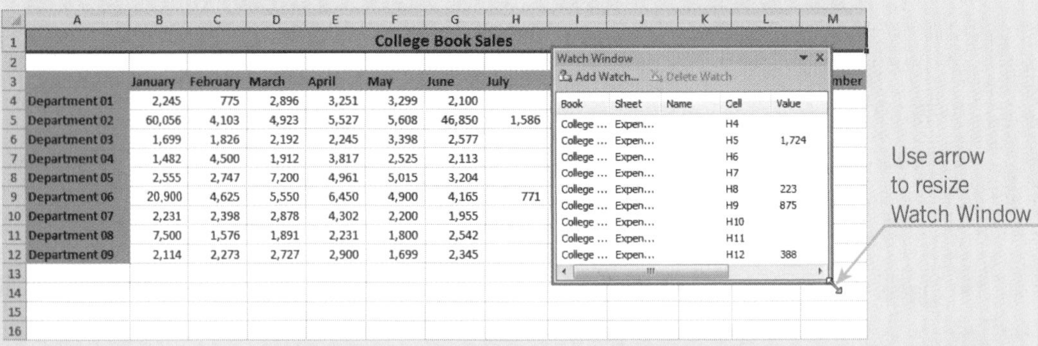

FIGURE 11–32 Resizing the Watch Window

Use arrow to resize Watch Window

9. Drag the **arrow** pointer to resize the window, then click the mouse button when the window is the desired size. You will now decrease the size of the columns so that only the Cell and Value columns appear in the Watch Window.
10. Place your mouse pointer over the right side of the column heading for Book and drag it to the left until it is no longer displayed.
11. Decrease the size of the Sheet, Name, and Formula columns until they are no longer displayed.
12. Drag the window next to column H, as shown in **Figure 11–33**.

EXTRA FOR EXPERTS

If you want to change the cells displayed in the Watch Window, click in the first cell in the window and then Shift + Click on the last cell. Then, click the Delete Watch button. You can then add another range to the Watch Window by selecting the Add Watch button.

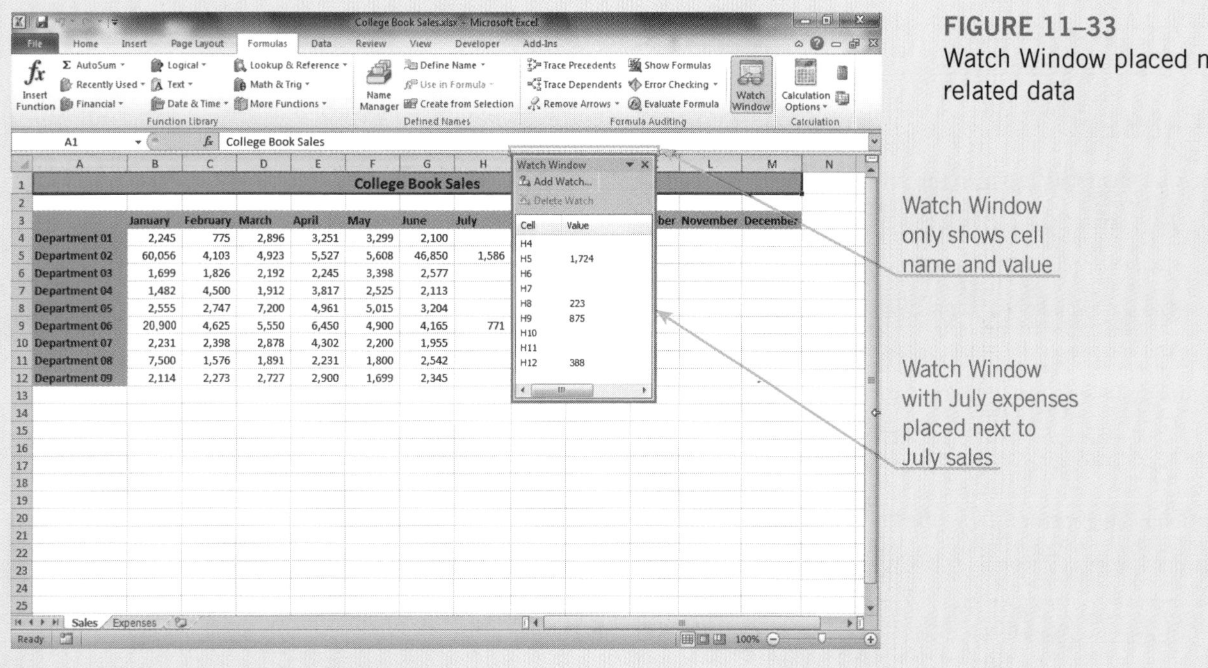

FIGURE 11–33
Watch Window placed next to related data

13. Save and close the workbook.

SUMMARY

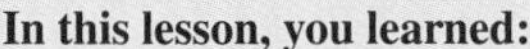

In this lesson, you learned:

- You can use advanced sorting features to organize worksheet data.
- Adding subtotals to worksheet data lets you instantly view totals in the worksheet.
- Adding a validation rule to a range improves accuracy when data is entered.
- When you enter data in a validation range, you can create input and error messages for the range.
- You can choose to have the Data Validation feature place circles around invalid data.
- You can improve data entry accuracy with drop-down lists.
- Rather than retyping data, you can use the Convert Text to Columns feature to separate data from one cell into multiple cells.
- Text from multiple cells can be combined into one cell using the Concatenate feature.
- The Watch Window lets you view data from one worksheet while you work in other worksheets.

VOCABULARY REVIEW

Define the following terms:

concatenation
data validation
delimiter
destination range
grand total
subtotal
validation range
validation rule
Watch Window

REVIEW QUESTIONS

TRUE / FALSE

Circle T if the statement is true or F if the statement is false.

T F **1.** To separate data from one cell into multiple cells, you use the Concatenate function.

T F **2.** If you want to view data from one worksheet while you are working in another one, you could use the Watch Window.

T F **3.** The Data Validation feature offers the ability to create a drop-down list from which you can select data.

T F **4.** You can use the Subtotal feature to quickly add subtotals and a grand total to columns of worksheet data.

T F **5.** The only way to tell if invalid data is entered into a validation range is to look for an error message.

FILL IN THE BLANK

Complete the following sentences by writing the correct word or words in the blanks provided.

1. When a worksheet is in the outline view when using subtotals, the minus symbol lets you ________________ data and the plus symbol lets you ________________ data.
2. The ________________ feature is used to separate data from one cell into multiple cells.
3. To display data from one worksheet while you are entering data into another worksheet, you would use the ________________ feature.
4. The type of message that explains how or what data should be entered when you select a cell is called a(n) ________________ message.
5. On the Error Alert tab in the Data Validation dialog box, if the ________________ style is selected, you will not be allowed to enter a value that does not meet the criteria.

WRITTEN QUESTIONS

Write a brief answer to the following questions.

1. Explain the process for combining text, such as a person's name, from multiple cells into one cell.

2. Explain the three styles that are available on the Error Alert tab in the Data Validation dialog box.

3. Write a brief description of the process to combine a date that is separated into three cells (one for month, one for date, and one for year) into one cell.

4. Describe how you would show more or less detail of a worksheet after adding subtotals to worksheet data.

5. List at least four types of information displayed in the Watch Window.

PROJECTS

If you have a SAM 2010 user profile, your instructor may have assigned an autogradable version of the indicated project. If so, log into the SAM 2010 Web site at *www.cengage.com/sam2010* to download the instruction and start files.

PROJECT 11–1

1. Open the **Pharmacy** file from the drive and folder where your Data Files are stored, and save the workbook as **Pharmacy Refills**, followed by your initials.
2. Sort the data by Prescription Number and then by Refill Date.
3. Add subtotals to the data and use the Count function at each change in Prescription Number. Add the count to the Prescription Number column.
4. Save, print, and close the workbook.

SAM PROJECT 11–2

1. Open the **Pacific Sales** file from the drive and folder where your Data Files are stored and then save the workbook as **Pacific Sales by Employee**, followed by your initials.
2. Use the Concatenate formula to join the first name and last name of the employees together in Column F. Separate the first name and last name with a space.
3. Use the Data Validation feature to add a drop-down list to cells F68:F500 that provides a list of the 21 employees. *Note*: You might want to create a list of the employees on another worksheet, so you can select this range in the Data Validation dialog box.
4. Enter **Employee Name** as the column title in cell F4.
5. Create an input message for the validation range F68:F500 that does not have a title, but does indicate that employees should be selected from the list.
6. Create an error alert for the validation range F68:F500. Use the Stop style option so only employees in the list may be entered into the cells. Add the word **Error** as the title and add the text **You may only enter employees from the provided list** as the error message.
7. Test a cell in the validation range to see if the input message and drop-down list display accurately.
8. Save, print, and close the workbook.

PROJECT 11–3

1. Open the **Local Dept Sales** file from the drive and folder where your Data Files are stored.
2. Save the workbook as **Local Dept Sales and Expenses**, followed by your initials.
3. Add a Watch Window to the Expenses worksheet that displays the June Sales data.
4. Resize the Watch Window to display the amounts.
5. Save and close the workbook.

CRITICAL THINKING

ACTIVITY 11–1

In a new Excel workbook, create a data list of large household items. Include columns for item categories, item names, year purchased, and the estimated value of the item. Format the data as desired. Use the Subtotal feature to show and hide various levels of data. Save the workbook as **Household Inventory**, followed by your initials. An example of household inventory is shown in **Figure 11–34**.

	A	B	C	D
1	*Household Inventory*			
2				
3	R	Name	Year Purchased	Estimated Value
4	Electronics	Computer	2012	$ 3,000
5	Electronics	Printer	2012	$ 1,500
6	Electronics	Television	2014	$ 2,000
7	Electronics	Stereo System	2014	$ 1,500
8	Electronics	Speakers	2014	$ 750
9	**Electronics Total**			$ 8,750
10	Furniture	Living Room Couch	2010	$ 3,000
11	Furniture	Living Room Chairs	2010	$ 2,500
12	Furniture	Bedroom 1 Suite	2012	$ 5,250
13	Furniture	Bedroom 2 Suite	2013	$ 3,500
14	Furniture	Bedroom 3 Suite	2014	$ 2,750
15	Furniture	Armoire	2009	$ 3,000
16	Furniture	Dining Room Table	2009	$ 1,500
17	Furniture	Buffet	2009	$ 2,000
18	**Furniture Total**			$ 23,500
19	Appliances	Stove	2010	$ 1,200
20	Appliances	Double Oven	2010	$ 1,500
21	Appliances	Refrigerator	2010	$ 1,000
22	Appliances	Dishwasher	2010	$ 750
23	Appliances	Freezer	2010	$ 700
24	**Appliances Total**			$ 5,150
25	**Grand Total**			$ 37,400

FIGURE 11–34 Example of household inventory worksheet

ACTIVITY 11–2

Create a workbook with data relevant to your life that requires a Watch Window. Think of two sets of information that would be helpful to see at the same time. For example, you might want to create two schedules of games for two different sports that you play to see if there are any conflicts. Or you might want to create a list of calorie counts for approved diet foods and another worksheet that keeps track of the food you eat daily. Use two worksheets in your workbook and save the workbook as **Watch Window**, followed by your initials.

Estimated Time: 2.5 hours

LESSON 12

Creating PivotTables and PivotCharts

OBJECTIVES

Upon completion of this lesson, you should be able to:

- Create a PivotTable.
- Sort and filter PivotTable data.
- Modify a PivotTable.
- Change value calculations and formats.
- Update data and refresh the PivotTable.
- Create a PivotChart.
- Filter a PivotChart.
- Modify a PivotChart.
- Add a slicer to a PivotTable.

VOCABULARY

child
parent
pivot
PivotChart
PivotTable
slicer

Introduction

Excel offers a unique method for changing the way data can be displayed using the PivotTable feature. A PivotTable lets you rearrange worksheet data so you can analyze it in a variety of ways. You can also create a PivotChart to graphically display the PivotTable. Excel 2010 has a new feature called the slicer. The slicer, which looks like a free-floating note pad, includes column headings that you click to filter data in a PivotTable. The slicer is easy to use, professional in appearance, and prints with the PivotTable.

Creating a PivotTable

VOCABULARY
PivotTable
pivot

A ***PivotTable*** looks like an ordinary table; however, the data in a PivotTable can be rearranged and summarized in different ways so that you can view the data from various perspectives. Your worksheet typically has columns and rows of related data. Sometimes you might want to change the order of this data, so you can look at it differently.

As its name suggests, a PivotTable lets you ***pivot*** or rearrange the data. You can place the PivotTable in the same worksheet as the data used to create the PivotTable, or you can place the PivotTable in its own worksheet. After the PivotTable is created, you can continue to rearrange it.

When you create a PivotTable, you do not need to use all of the data in the worksheet; you can select only the data you want to view. The data that you choose needs to have column headings. Any blank columns or blank rows need to be removed from the worksheet data.

For example, you may have a worksheet with data for students applying for student loans. This data might include columns for Last Name, First Name, Class Level, Major, Grade Point Average, and Student Loan Amount. Using a PivotTable, you could rearrange the data in many different ways. You could quickly reorganize the data by Class Level and Student Loan Amount in an easy-to-read format. You might also want to see the total of all student loans.

To rearrange the data, you drag the column headings into the Report Filter, Column Labels, Row Labels, and Values areas in the PivotTable Field List dialog box. Doing so rearranges the worksheet data into a PivotTable based on your selections, as shown in **Figure 12–1**.

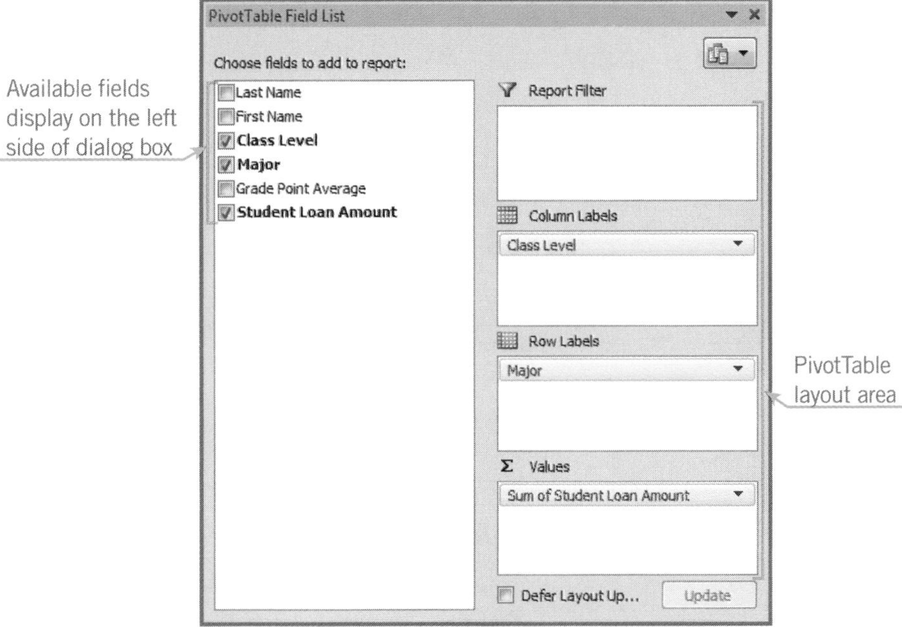

FIGURE 12–1 PivotTable Field List dialog box

Based on this example, the various Class Levels (Freshman, Sophomore, Junior, and Senior) will appear as column headings. The Majors, such as Finance, Education, and History, will display on the rows. The sum of Student Loan Amounts will show as the values.

In this next Step-by-Step, you will create a PivotTable based on student loan information.

Step-by-Step 12.1

1. Open the **Student Loans** file from the drive and folder where your Data Files are stored.
2. Save the workbook as **Student Loans - 2014**, followed by your initials. The worksheet contains student loan data, as shown in **Figure 12–2**. You will use the data to create a PivotTable in a new worksheet.

FIGURE 12–2
Worksheet data for PivotTable

	A	B	C	D	E	F
1	**Madison College**					
2	*Student List*					
3						
4	***Last Name***	***First Name***	***Class Level***	***Major***	***Grade Point Average***	***Student Loan Amount***
5	Aannestad	JoAnne	Junior	History	2.7	$ 2,500
6	Alkier	Sallye	Freshman	Finance	2.6	$ 445
7	Ascot	Ali	Junior	Education	4.0	$ -
8	Bennett	Jack	Junior	Finance	2.6	$ -
9	Buescher	David	Sophomore	Chemistry	3.0	$ 3,244
10	Caldwell	Jack	Senior	Music	3.1	$ 1,450
11	Coats	Grace	Senior	Economics	3.7	$ 200
12	Conlee	Howard	Sophomore	Finance	3.4	$ 2,778
13	Cortez	Lisa	Senior	Economics	3.8	$ 623
14	D'Ambrosio	David	Freshman	Music	3.2	$ 757
15	Estes	Stephanie	Freshman	Biology	3.8	$ 5,138
16	Feraco	Gary	Senior	History	3.0	$ 775
17	Ferrino	Howard	Sophomore	History	3.5	$ -
18	Gabel	Grace	Freshman	Finance	2.3	$ 1,450
19	Garcia	Bryce	Freshman	Business	3.4	$ 11,000
20	Gattis	Lilly	Junior	Economics	3.4	$ 1,490
21	Hargus	Joy	Junior	Finance	2.7	$ 1,358
22	Hernandez	Brian	Senior	Music	3.1	$ 1,850
23	Hernandez	Cynthia	Sophomore	History	3.1	$ 9,000
24	Jackson	Anthony	Senior	Finance	3.7	$ 450
25	Johnson	Darnell	Junior	Biology	2.5	$ 2,569
26	Johnson	Tara	Junior	Finance	2.3	$ 775
27	Kobrick	Louis	Sophomore	Education	3.6	$ -

Students

Ready

Column headings will appear as fields

Worksheet data to be used in PivotTable

3. Select **cell A4** or any cell in the worksheet data, so that Excel knows where the data for the PivotTable is located.
4. On the Ribbon, click the **Insert** tab, and then click the **PivotTable** button in the Tables group. The Create PivotTable dialog box opens.
5. Verify that **A4:F60** appears in the Table/Range text box. Note that you could also change the range if you wanted.
6. Select the **New Worksheet** option button, if necessary, then click **OK**. The PivotTable Field List dialog box appears on the right side of the worksheet and the PivotTable pane is shown on the left, as seen in **Figure 12–3**.

TIP

You can also choose to place the PivotTable in the existing worksheet by clicking the Existing Worksheet option button in the Create PivotTable dialog box.

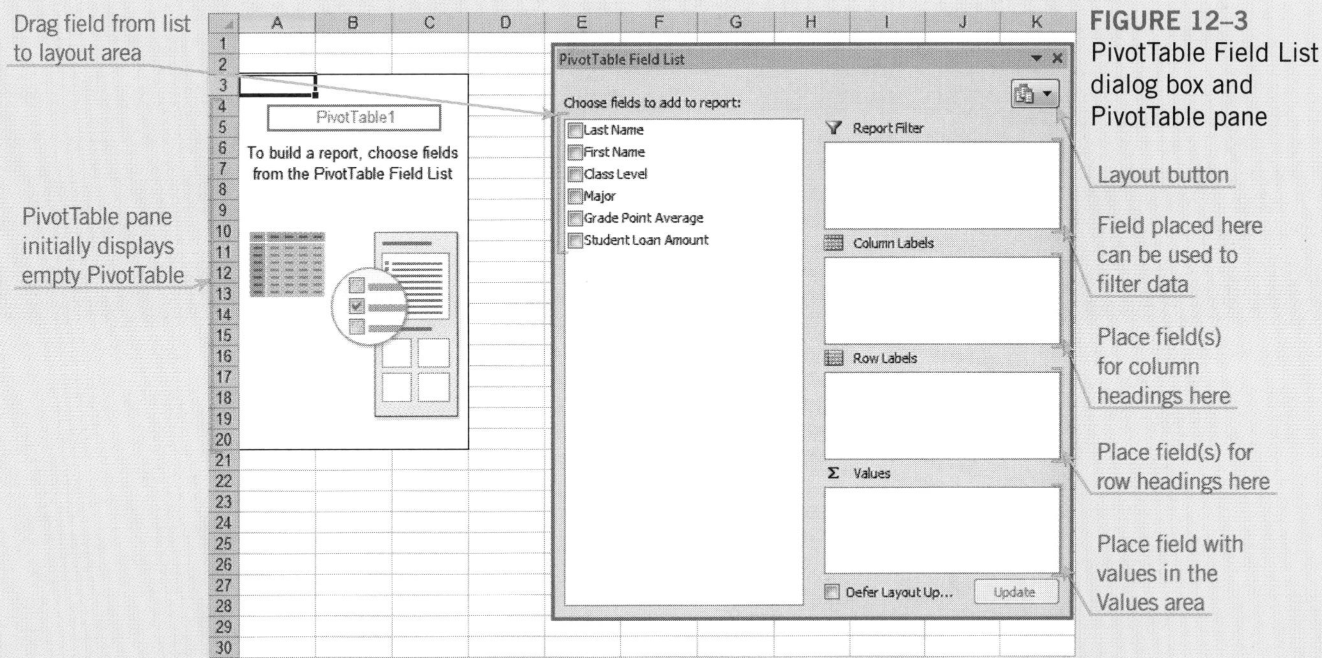

FIGURE 12–3 PivotTable Field List dialog box and PivotTable pane

7. At the upper-right corner of the PivotTable Field List dialog box, click the **Layout button**, then click **Fields Section and Areas Section Side by Side**. There are five possible ways to view the layout of the PivotTable Field List.
8. In the PivotTable Field List dialog box, place the mouse pointer over **Major** and drag it into the **Row Labels** area. Notice how the PivotTable begins to form in the pane to the left as you drag column headings into the PivotTable Field List dialog box. See **Figure 12–4**.

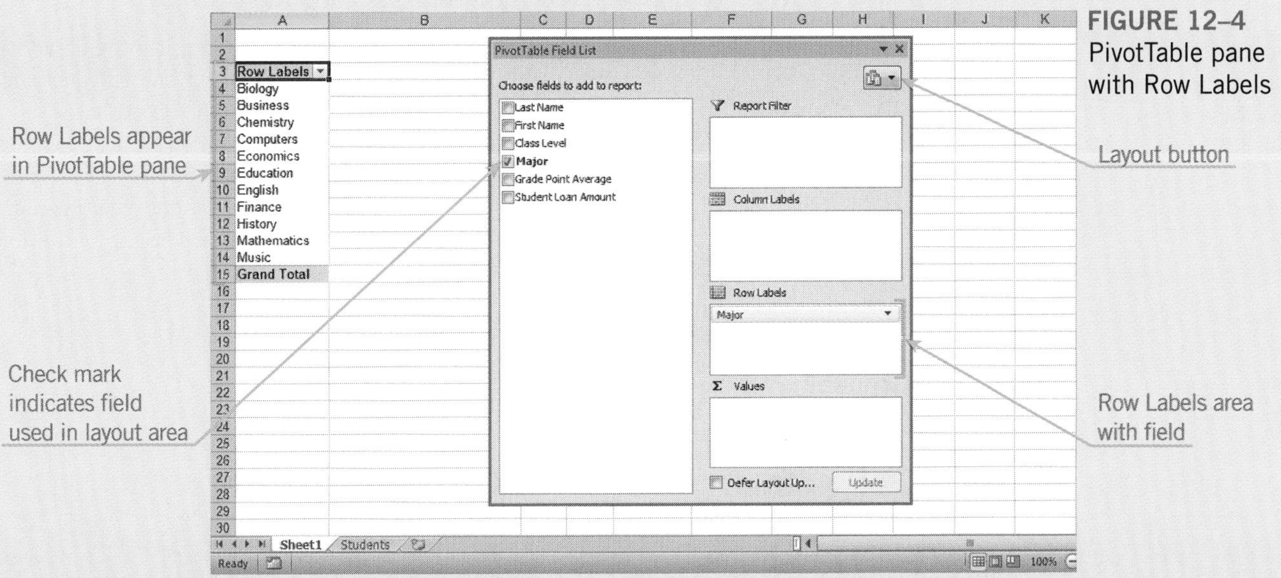

FIGURE 12–4 PivotTable pane with Row Labels

9. Drag **Class Level** to the **Column Labels** area.

10. Drag **Student Loan Amount** to the **Values** area. Your PivotTable Field List dialog box and PivotTable pane should resemble **Figure 12–5**.

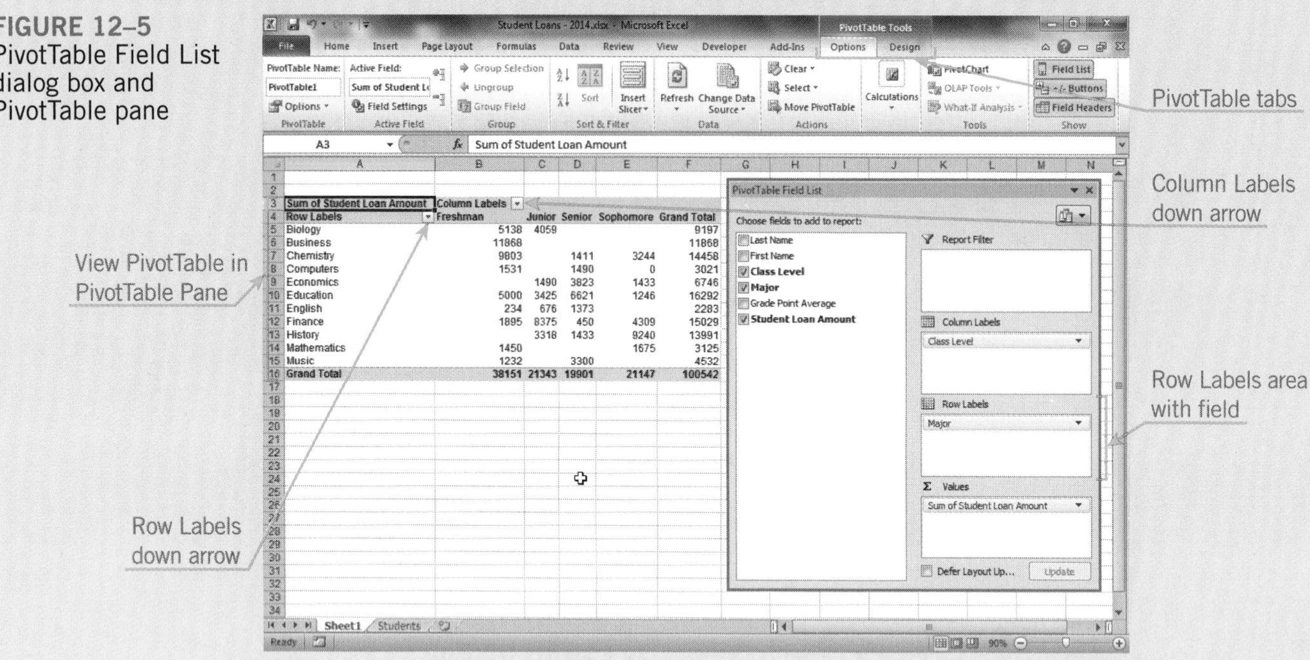

FIGURE 12–5 PivotTable Field List dialog box and PivotTable pane

11. If necessary, click the **Options** tab on the Ribbon, and then click the **Field List** button in the Show group to close the PivotTable Field List.
12. Save the workbook and leave it open for the next Step-by-Step.

Sorting and Filtering PivotTable Data

After you create the PivotTable, you can sort and filter the data to provide additional ways to analyze it. The sort and filter options are displayed when you click the Column Labels down arrow or the Row Labels down arrow on the PivotChart.

You can select a sort option to sort the data in ascending order, from A to Z, or in descending order, from Z to A. Numbers would sort lowest to highest in ascending order and highest to lowest in descending order. When you filter data, the data you want to show is displayed and the rest of the data is hidden. The sort and filter options for Column Labels are shown in **Figure 12–6**.

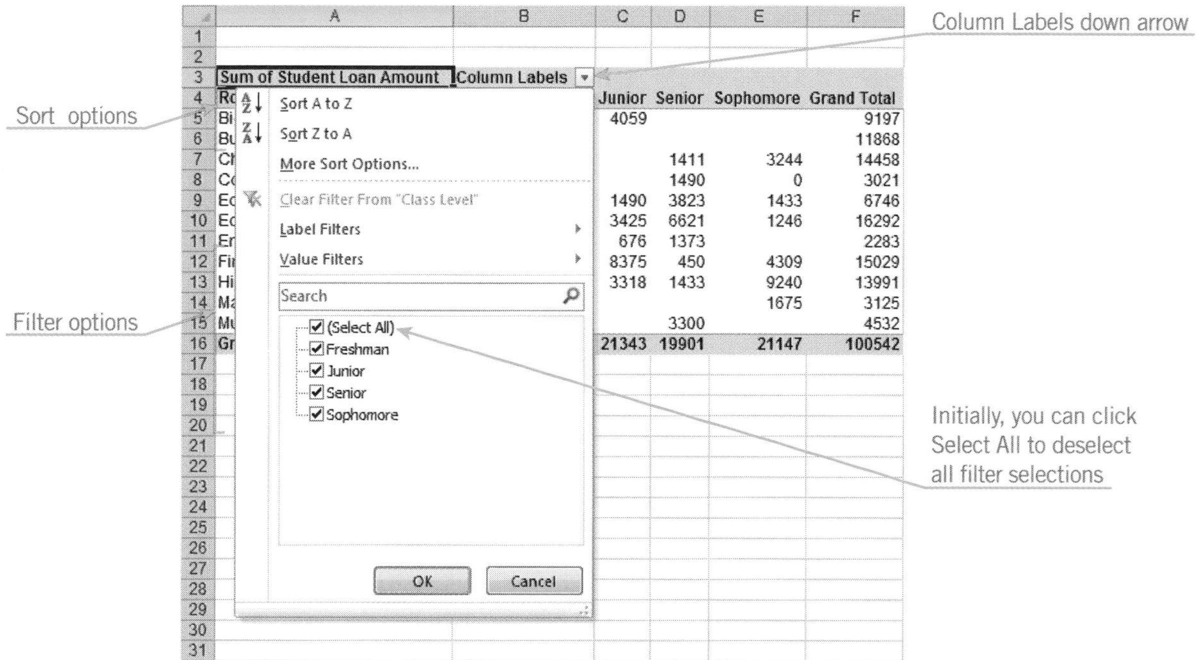

FIGURE 12–6 Sort & Filter Options list

To deselect all of the filter selections, you click Select All. Then, you can click the selection or selections you want to use in the filter.

After you sort or filter the data, a graphic, like a ScreenTip, appears when you place your mouse pointer over the Column Labels and Row Labels down arrows. This graphic lets you know how the data is sorted and filtered. In the next Step-by-Step, you will first filter data and then sort it.

Step-by-Step 12.2

1. In cell B3, click the **down arrow** next to the Column Labels heading.
2. Click the **Select All** check box to remove the check marks from the Class Level check boxes. You are going to filter the data to view only the Junior and Senior class levels.
3. Click the **Junior** and **Senior** check boxes to select them.

4. Click **OK** to view the filtered results, as shown in **Figure 12–7**.

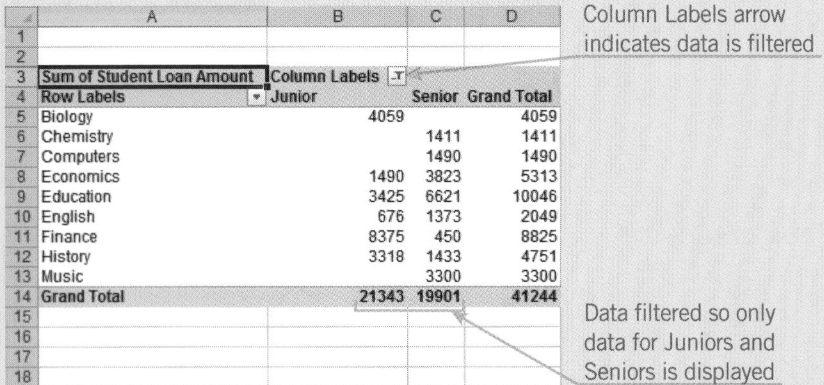

Sum of Student Loan Amount	Column Labels		
Row Labels	Junior	Senior	Grand Total
Biology	4059		4059
Chemistry		1411	1411
Computers		1490	1490
Economics	1490	3823	5313
Education	3425	6621	10046
English	676	1373	2049
Finance	8375	450	8825
History	3318	1433	4751
Music		3300	3300
Grand Total	21343	19901	41244

FIGURE 12–7
Filtered PivotTable

5. In cell A4, click the **Row Labels** down arrow.
6. In the Sort & Filter list, select **Sort Z to A**. You want to view the Majors in a descending order alphabetically.
7. In cell A4, place the mouse pointer over the down arrow and notice that a graphic appears, letting you know that Class Level is filtered and Major is sorted Z to A, as shown in **Figure 12–8**.

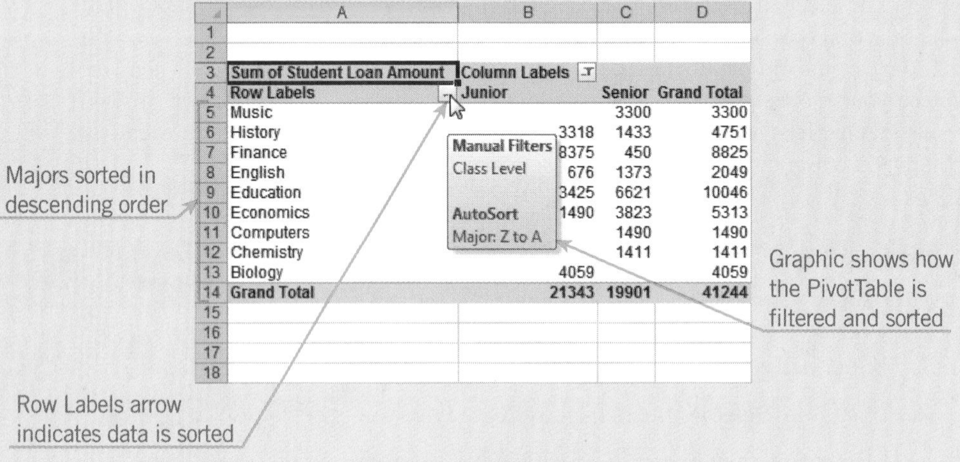

Sum of Student Loan Amount	Column Labels		
Row Labels	Junior	Senior	Grand Total
Music		3300	3300
History	3318	1433	4751
Finance	8375	450	8825
English	676	1373	2049
Education	3425	6621	10046
Economics	1490	3823	5313
Computers		1490	1490
Chemistry		1411	1411
Biology	4059		4059
Grand Total	21343	19901	41244

FIGURE 12–8
Filtered and sorted PivotTable

8. Save the workbook and leave it open for the next Step-by-Step.

Modifying the PivotTable

After you create the PivotTable, you can continue to rearrange the data. To change the location of rows and columns, you simply need to redisplay the PivotTable Field List dialog box and shift the order of the fields. You can also add additional levels of detail. For example, you can add two fields, such as Major and Last Name, to an area of the PivotTable Field List, such as Row Labels. The modified PivotTable will display the student's last name under his or her major.

When you add levels of fields, Outline buttons appear in the PivotTable so that you can show or hide these levels. Clicking the minus symbol hides the data, and clicking the plus sign displays the data.

Step-by-Step 12.3

1. If necessary, click the **Options** tab, and then click the **Field List** button in the Show group to display the PivotTable Field List dialog box.
2. Drag the **Last Name** field so that it is below Major in the Row Labels area. The student's last name is now displayed beneath their major, as shown in **Figure 12–9**.

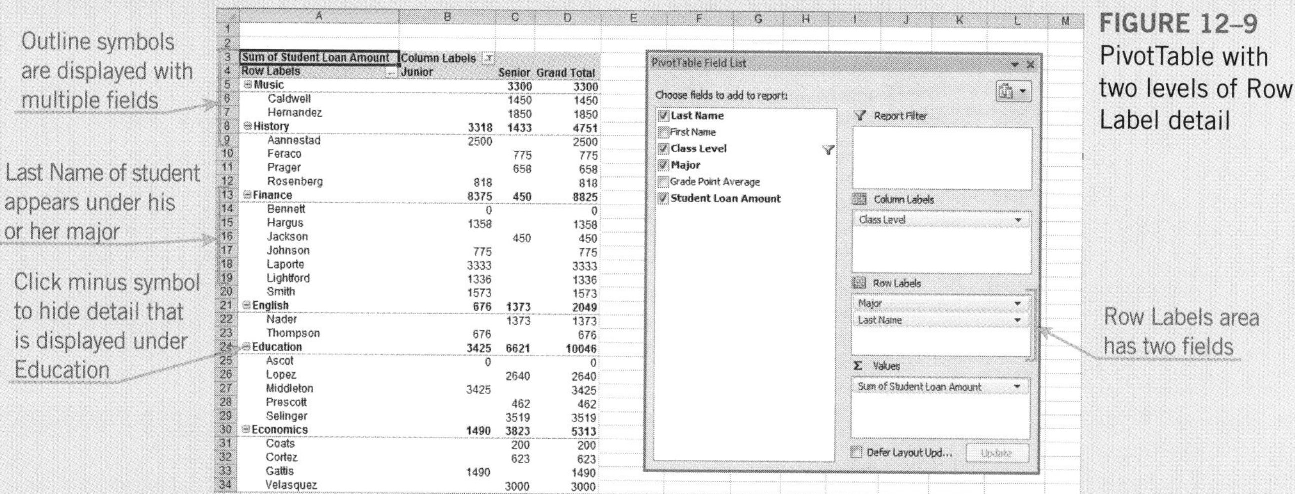

FIGURE 12–9 PivotTable with two levels of Row Label detail

3. Click the **Field List** button in the Show group to close the PivotTable Field List dialog box. You will now change the sort order on Major.
4. In cell A4, click the **Row Labels** down arrow, and then click **Sort A to Z**.

5. Click the **Field Headers** button in the Show group to remove the Row Labels and Column Labels field headers. The modified PivotTable appears as shown in **Figure 12–10**.

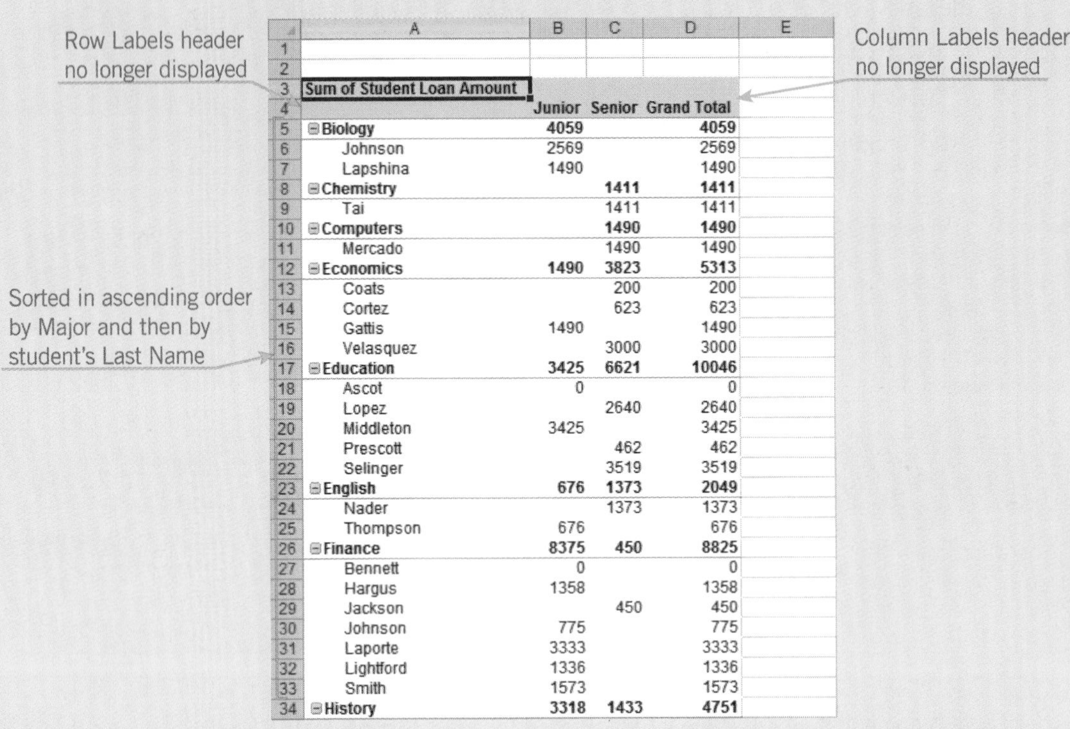

	A	B	C	D	E
1					
2					
3	Sum of Student Loan Amount				
4		Junior	Senior	Grand Total	
5	⊟Biology	4059		4059	
6	Johnson	2569		2569	
7	Lapshina	1490		1490	
8	⊟Chemistry		1411	1411	
9	Tai		1411	1411	
10	⊟Computers		1490	1490	
11	Mercado		1490	1490	
12	⊟Economics	1490	3823	5313	
13	Coats		200	200	
14	Cortez		623	623	
15	Gattis	1490		1490	
16	Velasquez		3000	3000	
17	⊟Education	3425	6621	10046	
18	Ascot	0		0	
19	Lopez		2640	2640	
20	Middleton	3425		3425	
21	Prescott		462	462	
22	Selinger		3519	3519	
23	⊟English	676	1373	2049	
24	Nader		1373	1373	
25	Thompson	676		676	
26	⊟Finance	8375	450	8825	
27	Bennett	0		0	
28	Hargus	1358		1358	
29	Jackson		450	450	
30	Johnson	775		775	
31	Laporte	3333		3333	
32	Lightford	1336		1336	
33	Smith	1573		1573	
34	⊟History	3318	1433	4751	

FIGURE 12–10
Sorted PivotTable without field headers

6. Save the workbook and leave it open for the next Step-by-Step.

Changing Formats and Value Calculation

When you first create a PivotTable, the numbers are brought in, but their formats are not. You may want to change the format of the PivotTable data so the people viewing it will know that the data are dollar amounts, percentages, or just numbers with a comma to separate thousands. For example, if someone looks at the data in a PivotTable and sees 3.79, they will not know if it is $3.79, 3.79%, or just 3.79. Adding formats to the values will help them know what the values represent.

In addition, you may want to calculate the data differently, such as a percentage of the total amount. You can change how the values in a PivotTable are displayed and calculated by choosing the Calculations button in the Calculations group and selecting Show Values As. Then, you choose an option in the Show Values As list, as shown in **Figure 12–11**.

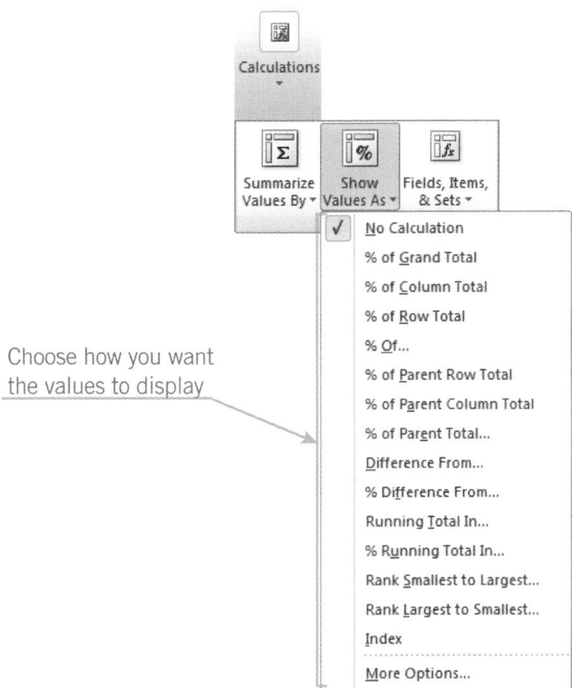

FIGURE 12–11 Show Values As list

You can quickly change the format and calculation by redisplaying the Show Values As list and selecting another option. Or, you can select No Calculation to return the PivotTable format back to how it looked when you first created it.

You can also create your own calculation using any of the options that end with an ellipsis (…). The Parent options refer to data that has more than one level of detail. When there is more than one level, the main row heading is referred to as the ***parent*** and the level of detail below this level is the ***child***.

VOCABULARY
parent
child

Step-by-Step 12.4

1. Select **B5:D42**.
2. Click the **Home** tab and then click the **Comma Style** button in the Number group.
3. To remove the decimal places, click the **Decrease Decimal** button twice.
4. Click any cell in the PivotTable that contains numerical data.
5. Click the **Options** tab, click the **Calculations** button, select the **Show Values As** button arrow in the Calculations group, and then click **% of Grand Total**.

6. Click the **minus symbol** next to Biology to hide the student last name data below the major. Notice that the minus symbol is now a plus symbol, as shown in **Figure 12–12**.

FIGURE 12–12
Values as a percentage of grand total

	A	B	C	D
1				
2				
3	Sum of Student Loan Amount			
4		Junior	Senior	Grand Total
5	⊞Biology	9.84%	0.00%	9.84%
6	⊟Chemistry	0.00%	3.42%	3.42%
7	Tai	0.00%	3.42%	3.42%
8	⊟Computers	0.00%	3.61%	3.61%
9	Mercado	0.00%	3.61%	3.61%
10	⊟Economics	3.61%	9.27%	12.88%
11	Coats	0.00%	0.48%	0.48%
12	Cortez	0.00%	1.51%	1.51%
13	Gattis	3.61%	0.00%	3.61%
14	Velasquez	0.00%	7.27%	7.27%
15	⊟Education	8.30%	16.05%	24.36%
16	Ascot	0.00%	0.00%	0.00%
17	Lopez	0.00%	6.40%	6.40%
18	Middleton	8.30%	0.00%	8.30%
19	Prescott	0.00%	1.12%	1.12%
20	Selinger	0.00%	8.53%	8.53%
21	⊟English	1.64%	3.33%	4.97%
22	Nader	0.00%	3.33%	3.33%
23	Thompson	1.64%	0.00%	1.64%
24	⊟Finance	20.31%	1.09%	21.40%
25	Bennett	0.00%	0.00%	0.00%
26	Hargus	3.29%	0.00%	3.29%
27	Jackson	0.00%	1.09%	1.09%
28	Johnson	1.88%	0.00%	1.88%
29	Laporte	8.08%	0.00%	8.08%
30	Lightford	3.24%	0.00%	3.24%
31	Smith	3.81%	0.00%	3.81%
32	⊟History	8.04%	3.47%	11.52%
33	Aannestad	6.06%	0.00%	6.06%
34	Feraco	0.00%	1.88%	1.88%

Student Loan amount as a percentage of grand total

7. Click the **minus symbols** next to Chemistry, Computers, Economics, Education, English, Finance, History, and Music to hide all of the last names. Your modified PivotTable should appear as shown in **Figure 12–13**.

FIGURE 12–13
All majors with collapsed data

	A	B	C	D
1				
2				
3	Sum of Student Loan Amount			
4		Junior	Senior	Grand Total
5	⊞Biology	9.84%	0.00%	9.84%
6	⊞Chemistry	0.00%	3.42%	3.42%
7	⊞Computers	0.00%	3.61%	3.61%
8	⊞Economics	3.61%	9.27%	12.88%
9	⊞Education	8.30%	16.05%	24.36%
10	⊞English	1.64%	3.33%	4.97%
11	⊞Finance	20.31%	1.09%	21.40%
12	⊞History	8.04%	3.47%	11.52%
13	⊞Music	0.00%	8.00%	8.00%
14	Grand Total	51.75%	48.25%	100.00%
15				

Plus signs appear when data is collapsed

PivotTable only shows Student Loan totals by Major as a percentage of Grand Total

8. Right-click the **worksheet tab** and then select **Rename** from the shortcut menu to rename the worksheet with the PivotTable.
9. Type **PivotTable**, and then press **Enter** to display the new worksheet name.
10. Save the workbook and leave it open for the next Step-by-Step.

Updating Data and Refreshing the PivotTable

The data used to create the PivotTable can be changed; however, the data in the PivotTable will not be updated to reflect this change until you click the Refresh button. Once you click the Refresh button, located in the Data group on the Options tab, the PivotTable data is updated to reflect the changes to the worksheet data.

Step-by-Step 12.5

1. View the percentage in cell C6 of the PivotTable. The current percentage for senior chemistry majors is 3.42%.
2. Click the **Students** worksheet tab to view the worksheet data.
3. Select **cell F52**.
4. Type **14,111** and then press **Enter**.
5. Click the **PivotTable** worksheet tab, and then click any cell in the PivotTable. Notice the percentage in cell C6 is still 3.42%.
6. Click the **Options** tab, and in the Data group, click the **Refresh** button to refresh the PivotTable data. The percentage in cell C6 is now 26.16%, as shown in **Figure 12–14**.

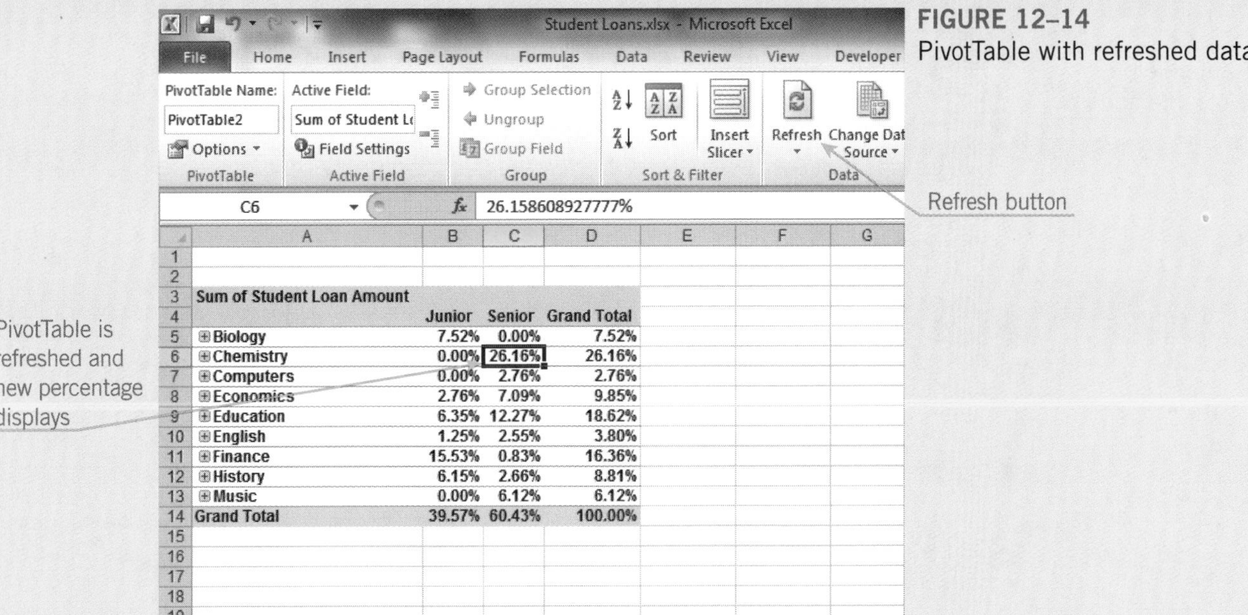

FIGURE 12–14 PivotTable with refreshed data

7. Save and print the PivotTable worksheet, then close the workbook.

Creating a PivotChart

Not only can you rearrange the data in a worksheet by creating PivotTables, you can create a visual representation of this data in a ***PivotChart***. When you create a PivotChart with worksheet data, a PivotTable is created at the same time. If you have already created a PivotTable, you can create a PivotChart based on the PivotTable.

VOCABULARY
PivotChart

The PivotTable and PivotChart are linked. If a change is made to the PivotTable, the associated PivotChart changes as well. If changes are made to the PivotChart, the PivotTable reflects this change too.

Each PivotChart type (with the exception of pie charts) typically has two axes: a horizontal axis and a vertical axis. The horizontal axis usually plots the categories along the bottom of the chart. The vertical axis usually plots values, such as dollar amounts, along the left side of the chart.

Step-by-Step 12.6

1. Open the **Discount Internet** file from the drive and folder where your Data Files are stored.
2. Save the file as **Discount Internet Sales** followed by your initials.
3. Select **cell A4** or any cell in the worksheet data.
4. On the Ribbon, click the **Insert** tab, click the **PivotTable** button arrow in the Tables group, and then click **PivotChart**.
5. If necessary, type or select **A4:E67** in the Table/Range text box. Make sure the New Worksheet option button is selected and then click **OK**. The PivotTable Field List dialog box opens with an empty PivotTable and PivotChart, as shown in **Figure 12–15**.

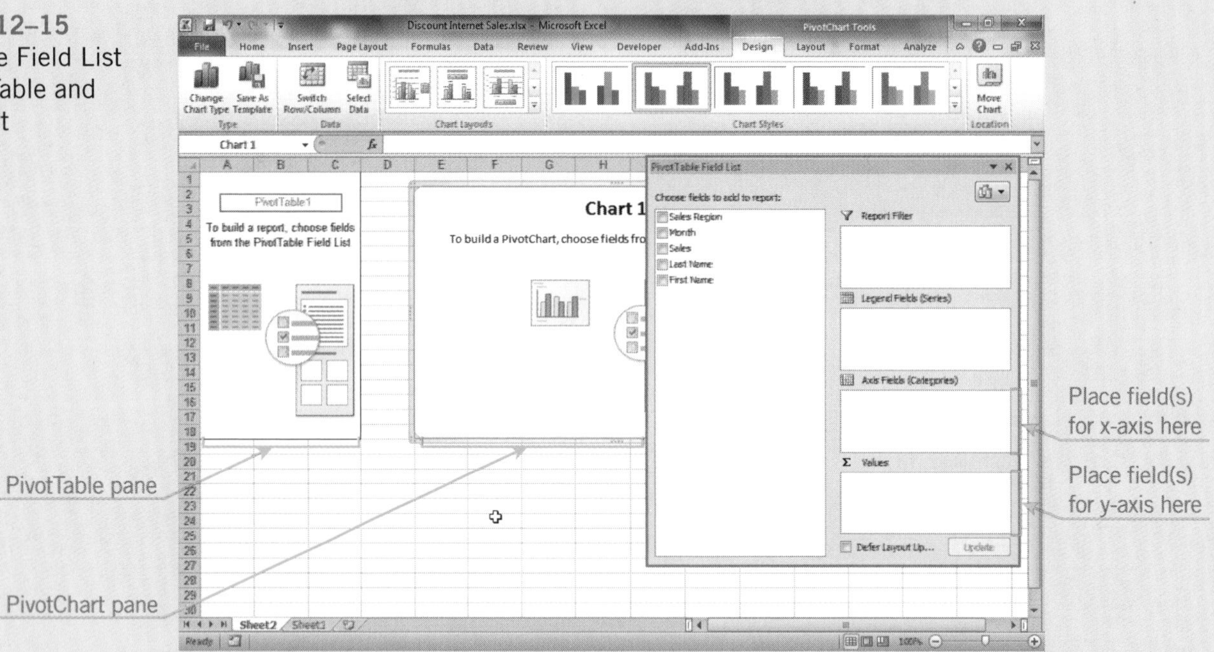

FIGURE 12–15 PivotTable Field List for PivotTable and PivotChart

6. In the PivotTable Field List dialog box, place the mouse pointer over **Sales Region** and drag it into the **Axis Fields** area to have each Sales Region appear on the horizontal axis.
7. Next, drag **Sales** to the **Values** area so that the dollar amount will display in the chart and dollars will show on the vertical axis.

8. Drag **Month** to the **Axis Fields** area below Sales Region to add months along with the sales region on the horizontal axis. The PivotTable Field List dialog box, PivotTable, and PivotChart should appear as shown in **Figure 12–16**.

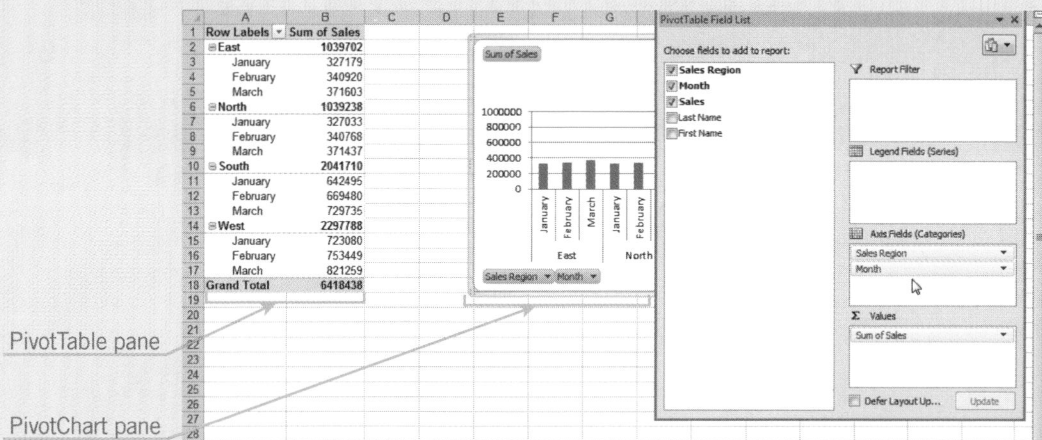

FIGURE 12–16 PivotTable and PivotChart

9. Click the **Analyze** tab and then in the Show/Hide group, click the **Field List** button to close the PivotTable Field List dialog box.
10. Save the workbook and leave it open for the next Step-by-Step.

Filtering the PivotChart

Just as you can filter PivotTable data, you can filter PivotChart data as well. You may want to filter a PivotChart so that less data appears in the chart. For example, your chart may include the twelve months on the horizontal axis, and you may want to view the chart with only one month of data. When you filter the PivotChart, the same filtered data appears in the PivotTable. Chart filters are located in the chart itself. In the next Step-by-Step, you will first reformat the PivotTable data. Then, you will filter the chart.

Step-by-Step 12.7

1. Select **B2:B18** to reformat the values.
2. Click the **Home** tab, and in the Number group, click the **Comma Style** button .

3. With the range still selected, click the **Decrease Decimal** button in the Number group twice to remove the decimals from the numbers. Notice how the data in the chart is also reformatted. See **Figure 12–17**.

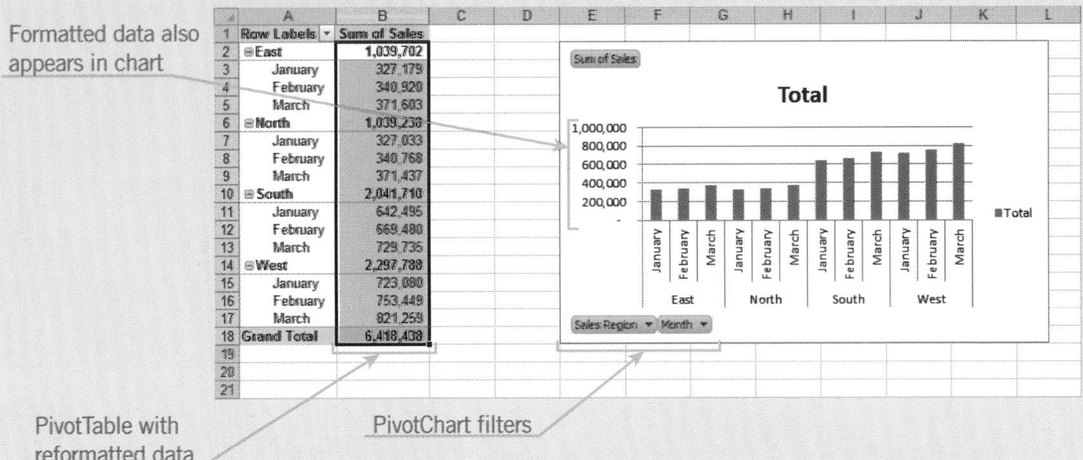

FIGURE 12–17 Reformatted PivotTable and PivotChart

4. Click the **Month** down arrow in the PivotChart to display the sort and filter options.
5. Click the **Select All** check box to remove the filter arrows for months, so that you can filter by a certain month or a couple of months.
6. Click the **January** check box, and then click **OK**. Now only sales for January are displayed in the PivotTable and PivotChart, as shown in **Figure 12–18**.

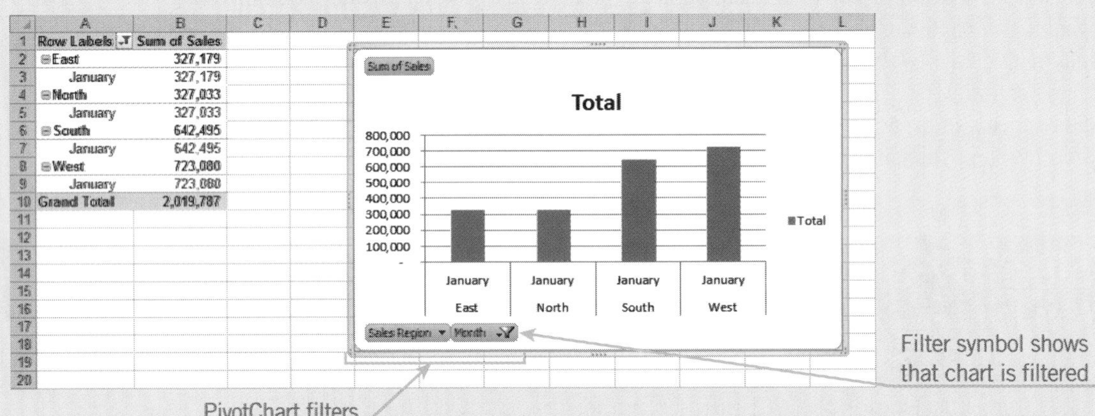

FIGURE 12–18 Filtered PivotChart and PivotTable

7. Click the **Month** down arrow, click the **Select All** check box, and then click **OK** to redisplay the months.
8. To filter by Sales Region so only a specific region or regions are displayed, click the **Sales Region** down arrow. Then click the **Select All** check box to deselect it.
9. Click the **South** check box to select it, and then click **OK**. Your PivotTable and PivotChart should appear as shown in **Figure 12–19**.

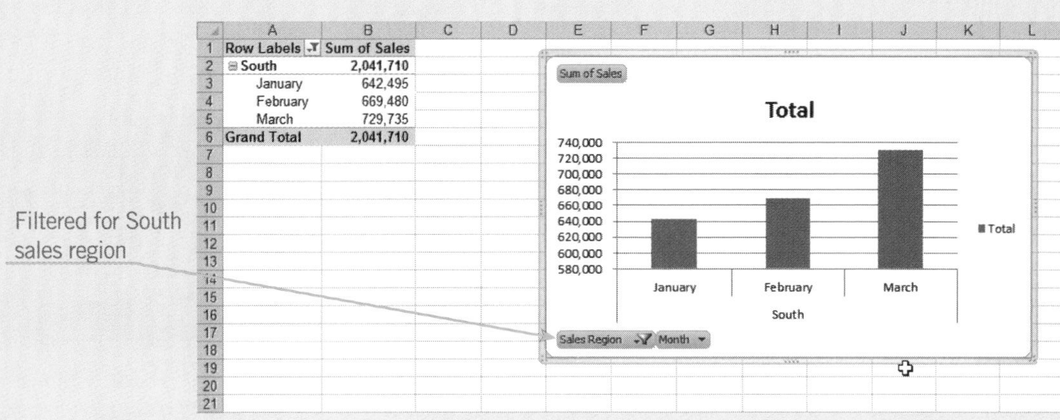

FIGURE EX–19 Completed PivotTable and PivotChart

10. Save the workbook and leave it open for the next Step-by-Step.

Modifying the PivotChart

PivotCharts can be modified just like ordinary Excel charts. For example, you can change the chart type and add chart styles. When the PivotChart is selected, additional tabs appear on the Ribbon. These tabs are designated for making changes to the PivotChart. You will now change the PivotTable chart type and chart style.

Step-by-Step 12.8

1. Click the **PivotChart** to select it.
2. On the Ribbon, click the **Design** tab and then in the Type group, click the **Change Chart Type** button so that you can change the chart type.
3. In the Change Chart Type dialog box, click **Column** on the left, if necessary, and then click the **3-D Clustered Column** chart in the first row. See **Figure 12–20**.

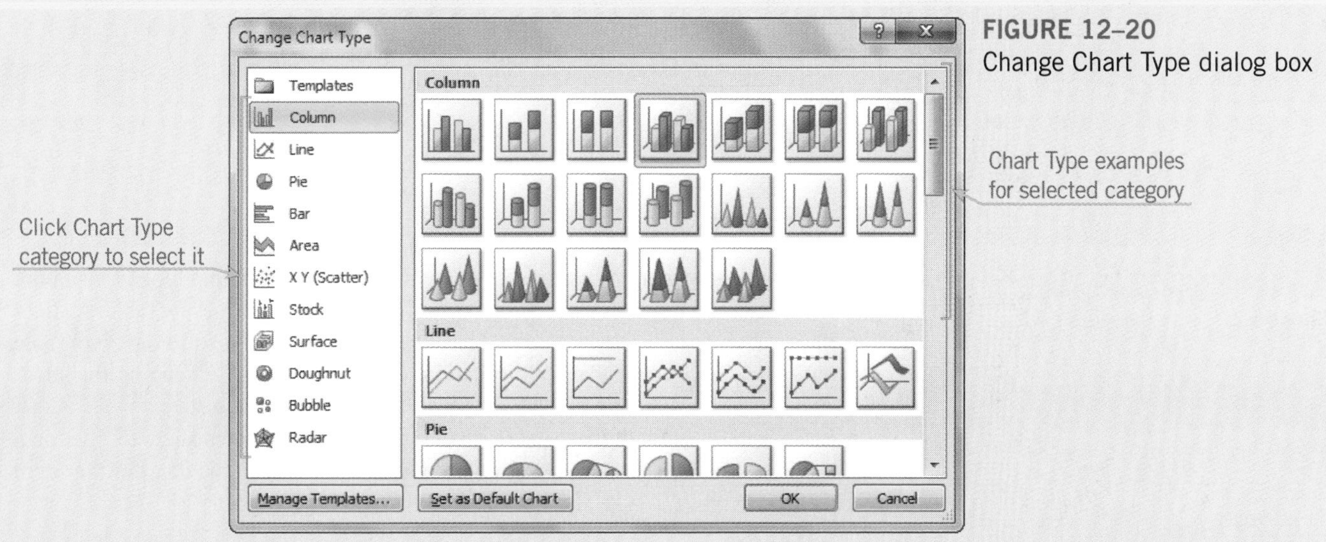

FIGURE 12–20 Change Chart Type dialog box

4. Click **OK** to close the Change Chart Type dialog box.
5. On the Design tab, in the Chart Styles group, click the **More** button arrow to display the Chart Styles, as shown in **Figure 12–21**.

FIGURE 12–21
Chart styles

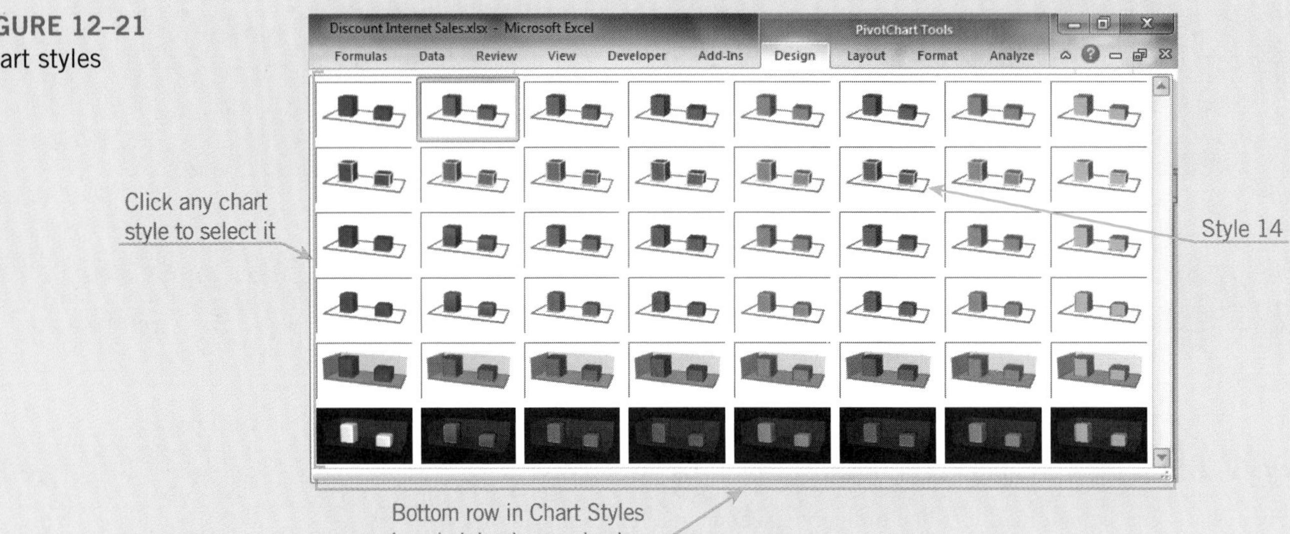

6. Select **Style 14** in the second row of the Chart Style options. Your chart should appear as shown in **Figure 12–22**.

FIGURE 12–22
PivotChart with new style applied

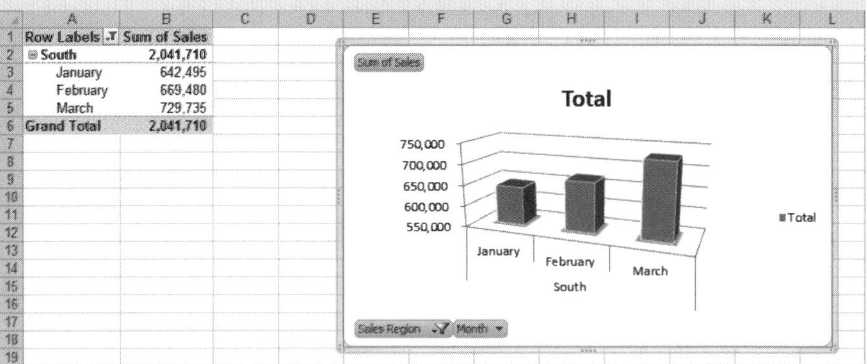

7. Save, print the worksheet with the PivotTable and PivotChart, and then close the workbook.

Using the Slicer

VOCABULARY
slicer

The ***slicer*** is a new feature in Excel 2010. It is a visual control that looks like a note pad. Clicking selections on the slicer lets you filter your data in a PivotTable. A slicer acts like a filter, but it is easier to use. The slicer can be placed next to the PivotTable and remains visible so that selections can be easily accessed. By keeping the slicer displayed, you can hide and display data by clicking items in the slicer.

Each field (column of data) in the PivotTable can have its own slicer to filter data for the column. When an item is highlighted in the slicer, only the data for that item is displayed. In **Figure 12–23**, only December is highlighted, so only December data is displayed in the PivotTable.

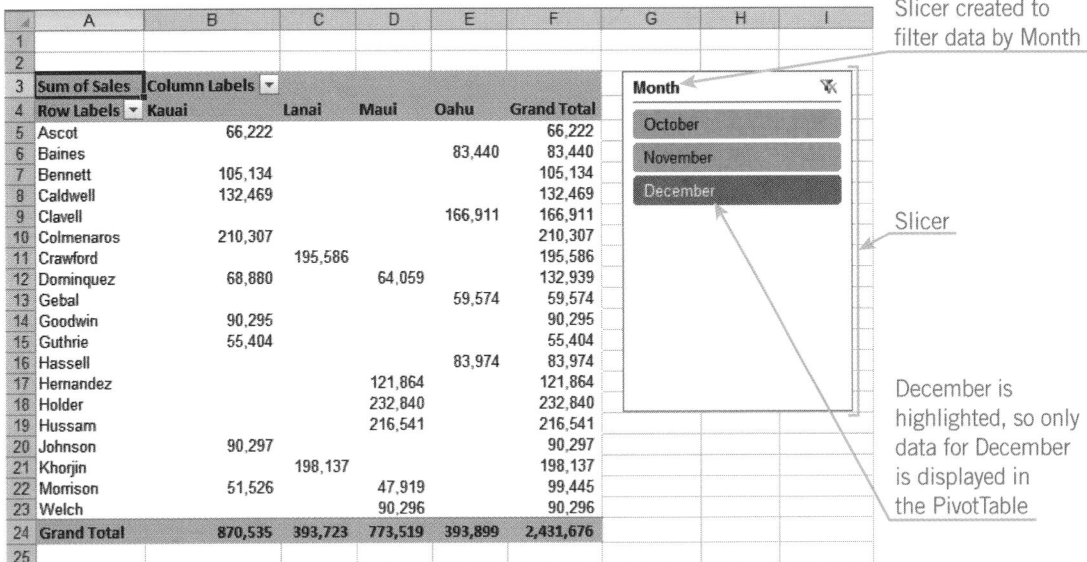

Sum of Sales	Column Labels				
Row Labels	Kauai	Lanai	Maui	Oahu	Grand Total
Ascot	66,222				66,222
Baines				83,440	83,440
Bennett	105,134				105,134
Caldwell	132,469				132,469
Clavell				166,911	166,911
Colmenaros	210,307				210,307
Crawford		195,586			195,586
Dominquez	68,880		64,059		132,939
Gebal				59,574	59,574
Goodwin	90,295				90,295
Guthrie	55,404				55,404
Hassell				83,974	83,974
Hernandez			121,864		121,864
Holder			232,840		232,840
Hussam			216,541		216,541
Johnson	90,297				90,297
Khorjin		198,137			198,137
Morrison	51,526		47,919		99,445
Welch			90,296		90,296
Grand Total	870,535	393,723	773,519	393,899	2,431,676

FIGURE 12–23 Slicer created to filter Month data

When a slicer is first displayed, it appears with a basic design. However, you can choose another style for the slicer on the Options tab. For example you may want the slicer to appear with similar colors as your worksheet The slicer will print when you print the worksheet. If you do not want the slicer to print, you can drag it out of the print range or right-click it and choose Remove from the shortcut menu.

Step-by-Step 12.9

1. Open the **Division Sales** file from the drive and folder where your Data Files are stored.
2. Save the file as **Division Sales for Hawaii** followed by your initials.
3. Click the **PivotTable worksheet** tab to view the PivotTable.
4. Select **cell A3** or any cell in the PivotTable.

5. On the Ribbon, click the **Options** tab and then click **Insert Slicer** in the Sort & Filter group. The Insert Slicers dialog box opens, as shown in **Figure 12–24**.

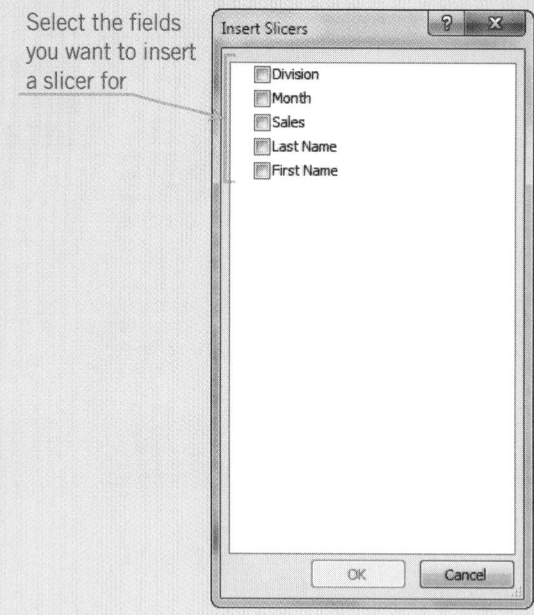

FIGURE 12–24
Insert Slicers dialog box

6. Click the **Month** check box to have a slicer appear for the months in the PivotTable.
7. Click **OK**. Next, you will move the slicer next to the PivotTable.
8. Place your mouse pointer over the Month slicer and drag it to the side of the PivotTable. When the slicer is first displayed, all of the items are selected, as shown in **Figure 12–25**.

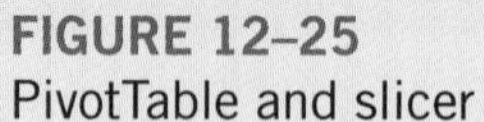

FIGURE 12–25
PivotTable and slicer

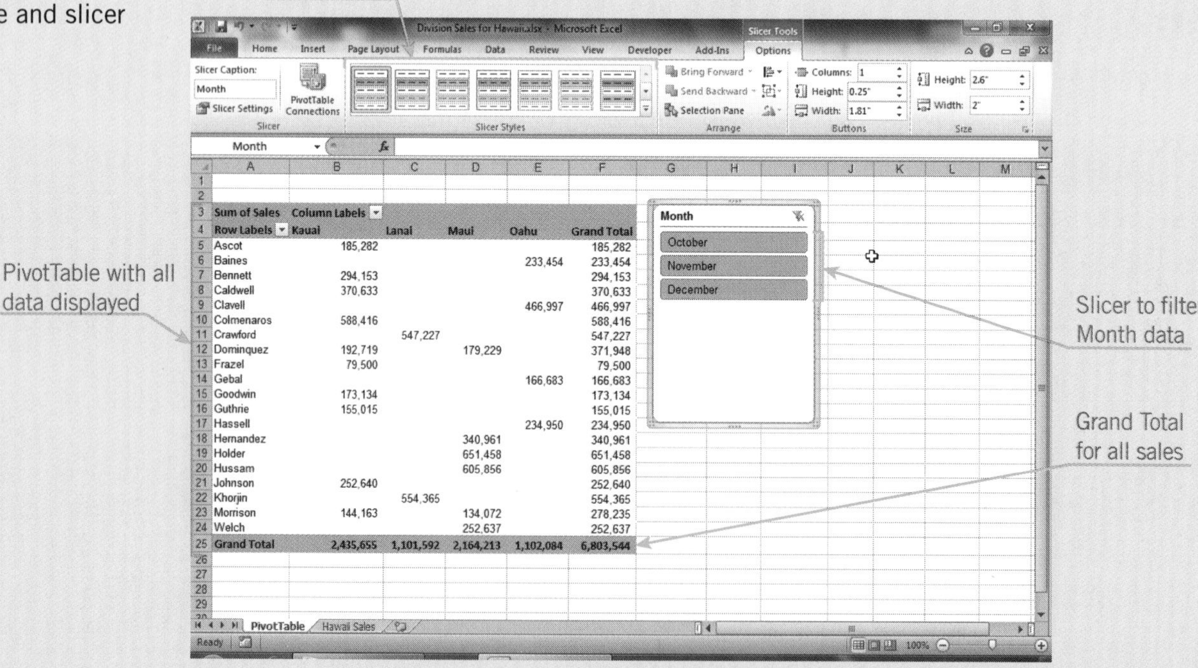

Sum of Sales	Column Labels				
Row Labels	Kauai	Lanai	Maui	Oahu	Grand Total
Ascot	185,282				185,282
Baines				233,454	233,454
Bennett	294,153				294,153
Caldwell	370,633				370,633
Clavell				466,997	466,997
Colmenaros	588,416				588,416
Crawford		547,227			547,227
Dominquez	192,719		179,229		371,948
Frazel	79,500				79,500
Gebal				166,683	166,683
Goodwin	173,134				173,134
Guthrie	155,015				155,015
Hassell				234,950	234,950
Hernandez			340,961		340,961
Holder			651,458		651,458
Hussam			605,856		605,856
Johnson	252,640				252,640
Khorjin		554,365			554,365
Morrison	144,163		134,072		278,235
Welch			252,637		252,637
Grand Total	2,435,655	1,101,592	2,164,213	1,102,084	6,803,544

9. On the Month slicer, click **October**. Only sales for October are displayed in the PivotTable, as shown in **Figure 12–26**.

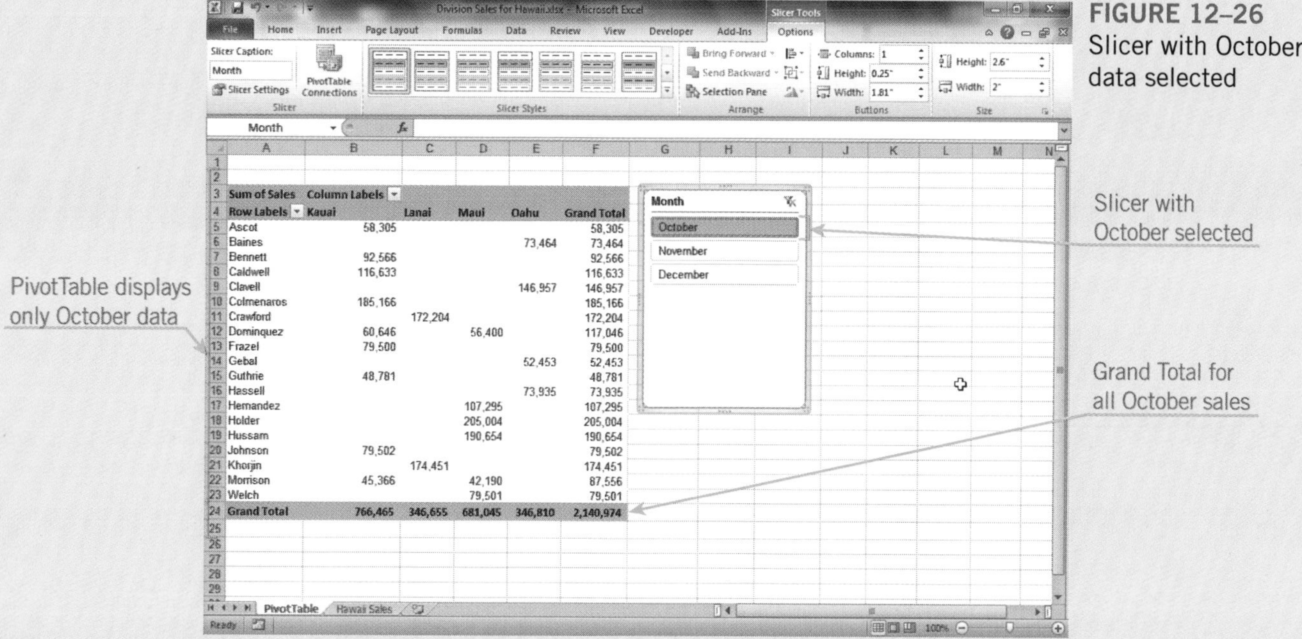

FIGURE 12–26
Slicer with October data selected

10. Press and hold **Shift** and then click **November** on the Month slicer to view sales for both October and November. Now, two months of data are displayed in the PivotTable.

11. Verify that the Month slicer is selected, and then, on the Options tab, click the **More** button in the Slicer Styles group. The Slicer Styles appear as shown in **Figure 12–27**.

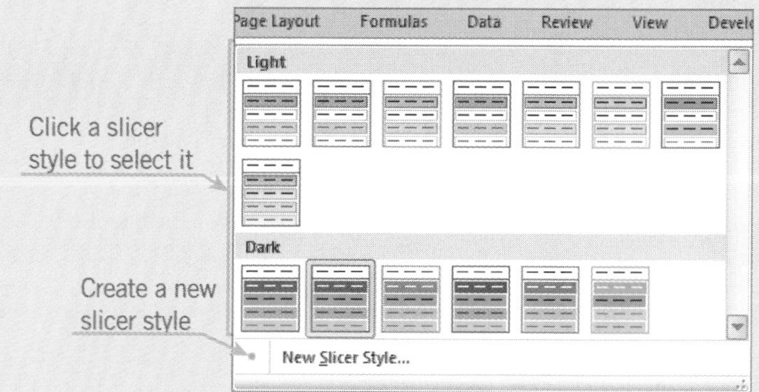

FIGURE 12–27
Slicer styles

12. Select **Slicer Style Dark 2**, as shown in **Figure 12–28**.

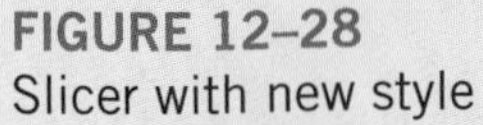

FIGURE 12–28
Slicer with new style

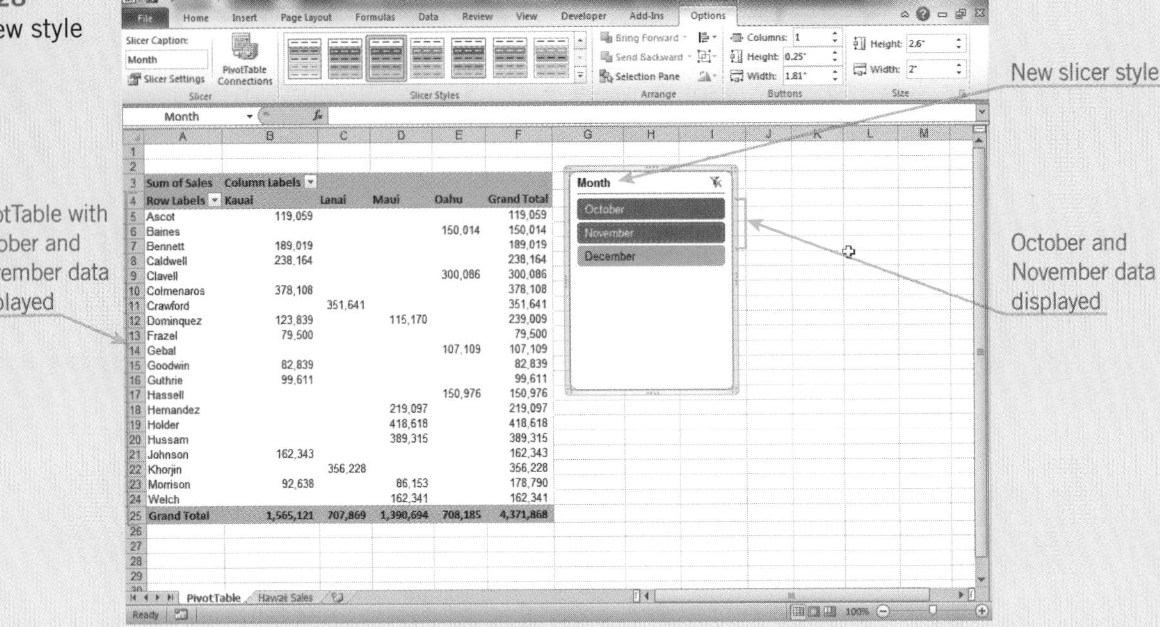

13. Save, print the worksheet with the PivotTable and the slicer, and then close the workbook.

SUMMARY

In this lesson, you learned:

- You can create PivotTables based on worksheet data.
- You can sort and filter PivotTable data.
- After a PivotTable is created, it can be modified.
- You can change formats and value calculations in a PivotTable.
- After you update worksheet data that was used to create a PivotTable, you need to refresh the PivotTable to display the changes.
- PivotCharts can be created with PivotTables.
- PivotCharts can be filtered.
- After a PivotChart is created, it can be modified.
- Adding a slicer to a PivotTable lets you filter data.

VOCABULARY REVIEW

Define the following terms:

child
parent
pivot
PivotChart
PivotTable
slicer

REVIEW QUESTIONS

TRUE / FALSE

Circle T if the statement is true or F if the statement is false.

T F 1. You can place the PivotTable in the same worksheet as the data used to create the PivotTable or on a separate worksheet in the workbook.

T F 2. You can change the layout of a PivotTable after it has been created using the PivotTable Field List.

T F 3. Excel automatically creates a PivotTable when you create a PivotChart.

T F 4. A slicer can be used to filter data in a PivotTable.

T F 5. PivotTables can be filtered, but a PivotChart cannot be filtered.

FILL IN THE BLANK

Complete the following sentences by writing the correct word or words in the blanks provided.

1. If data that was used to create a PivotTable is changed, you update the PivotTable by clicking the ______________ button.
2. Data in a PivotTable can be filtered using the filter buttons in the Field Header cells or by using the ______________.
3. The design of a slicer can be changed by selecting a(n) ______________.
4. To collapse data in a PivotTable that has multiple row headings, you click the ______________.
5. To remove the filter arrows in the Sort & Filter list, you click the ______________ check box.

WRITTEN QUESTIONS

Write a brief answer to the following questions.

1. After a PivotTable has been created, how would you rearrange it to view another perspective of the data?

2. If you make changes to the data that is used to create a PivotTable, how do you update the data in the PivotTable?

3. What is the purpose of a slicer?

4. Explain how you would filter a PivotChart.

5. Explain how you would change the chart style for a PivotChart.

PROJECTS

If you have a SAM 2010 user profile, your instructor may have assigned an autogradable version of the indicated project. If so, log into the SAM 2010 Web site at *www.cengage.com/sam2010* to download the instruction and start files.

PROJECT 12–1

You will create a PivotTable that shows the total sales amounts of products in each of two stock areas.

1. Open the P K Industries file from the drive and folder where your Data Files are stored, and save it as **P K Industries Analysis** followed by your initials.
2. Create a PivotTable with the following setup:

   Column Labels: **Stock Area**

   Row Labels: **Item #**

   Values: **Total Product Value in Inventory**
3. Add a currency format with two decimal places to the product values. (Adjust the column widths if necessary.)
4. Remove the Field Headers.
5. Change the name of the worksheet with the PivotTable to **Stock Area Analysis**.
6. Print the PivotTable. Save and close the workbook.

SAM PROJECT 12–2

You will create a PivotTable that shows grade point averages for students by their last name.

1. Open the Spelling Bee file from the drive and folder where your Data Files are stored, and save it as **Spelling Bee Groups** followed by your initials.
2. Create a PivotTable with the following setup:

   Column Labels: **Competition Group**

   Row Labels: **State**

   Last Name

   First Name

   Values: **Fees Still Due**
3. Add a slicer to filter on **Competition Group**.
4. Select 1 in the slicer so that only data for Competition Group 1 will be displayed in the PivotTable.
5. Change the PivotTable worksheet name to **Competition Groups**.
6. Print the PivotTable with the slicer.
7. Save and close the workbook.

PROJECT 12–3

You will create a PivotTable that shows employee sales by region.

1. Open the Virginia Sales file from the drive and folder where your Data Files are stored, and save it as **Virginia Sales by Region** followed by your initials.
2. Create a PivotTable on a new worksheet with the following setup:

   Column Labels: **Region**

   Row Labels: **Employee**

   Values: **Sales**
3. Close the PivotTable Field List.
4. Print the PivotTable.
5. Save and close the workbook.

CRITICAL THINKING

ACTIVITY 12–1

You are the manager for a production company. You will be giving a presentation to the company owner this afternoon, and you want to create a PivotChart and PivotTable that show the total electricity costs for each of the departments.

1. Open the Electricity file from the drive and folder where your Data Files are stored, and save it as **Electricity Usage** followed by your initials.
2. Create a PivotChart that shows **Departments** on the horizontal axis and **Usage** as the Value.
3. Change the chart type to a three-dimensional column.
4. Format the usage numbers to a comma style with one decimal place.
5. Print the PivotTable and PivotChart.
6. Save and close the workbook.

ACTIVITY 12–2

Using Excel's Help system, find information on how you can turn off the Grand Totals for Rows and Columns in a PivotTable. Write a brief explanation of this procedure.

Estimated Time: 2.5 hours

LESSON 13

Using Powerful Excel Functions

■ OBJECTIVES

Upon completion of this lesson, you should be able to:

- Use the COUNT and COUNTA functions.
- Utilize the COUNTBLANK function to count blank cells.
- Use the Subtotal function with filtered data.
- Create a named range.
- Use a named range in a function.
- Use a SUMIF function.
- Search for data using VLOOKUP.
- Search for data using HLOOKUP.

■ VOCABULARY

condition

criteria

function number

lookup table

Introduction

Excel offers a variety of powerful tools that allow you to increase your productivity by using functions to count, sum, and locate specific information. This lesson discusses a number of these extremely useful functions. First, you will count numerical data in a range using the COUNT function. Counting data is important if you are doing such tasks as a head count of employees or volunteers. Next, you will count cells that have text with the COUNTA function. To count the number of cells without content, you will use the COUNTBLANK function.

Once again, you will use the Subtotal function. But, this time, you will expand its capabilities by counting filtered cells. You'll learn about the SUMIF function that is used to total only cells that meet a certain condition. To save time when you enter functions, you will learn how to name ranges of data.

Finally, you will see the advantage of using LOOKUP functions to find data. LOOKUP functions find data in a lookup table. The VLOOKUP function locates data when it is displayed vertically in the lookup table. The HLOOKUP function finds data when it is displayed horizontally in the lookup table. You will explore each of these features in this lesson.

Using COUNTA versus COUNT

Excel provides two functions for counting cells: one for counting cells with numeric data and another for counting cells with text. To find the total number of cells that have numeric data, you use the COUNT function. To count cells with text, you use the COUNTA function. The COUNTA function can count cells if they contain text or a combination of text and numbers. In the next Step-by-Step, you will use the COUNT function to count the total of numeric values in a column and the COUNTA function to count the number of cells in a column that have text.

Step-by-Step 13.1

1. Open the **Antique Class** file from the drive and folder where your Data Files are stored.
2. Save the workbook as **Antique Class Enrollment**, followed by your initials. You will first use the COUNT function to count the number of cells with numeric data.
3. Click **cell E36**.
4. Type the function **=COUNT(E5:E34)** and then press **Enter**. Excel shows a count of 30. See **Figure 13–1**.

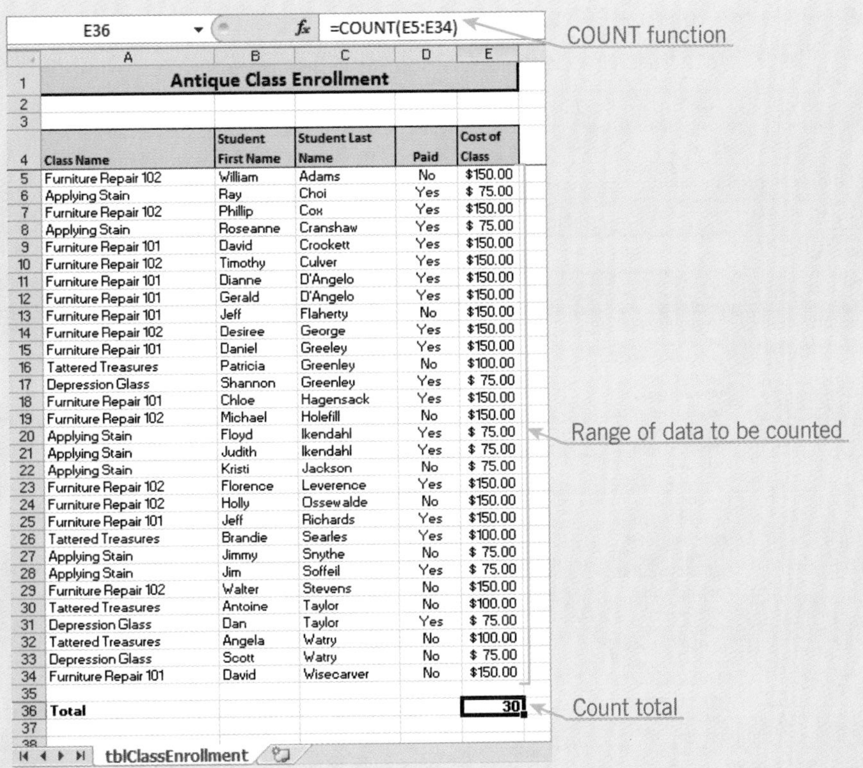

E36 =COUNT(E5:E34)

	A	B	C	D	E
1	Antique Class Enrollment				
2					
3					
4	Class Name	Student First Name	Student Last Name	Paid	Cost of Class
5	Furniture Repair 102	William	Adams	No	$150.00
6	Applying Stain	Ray	Choi	Yes	$ 75.00
7	Furniture Repair 102	Phillip	Cox	Yes	$150.00
8	Applying Stain	Roseanne	Cranshaw	Yes	$ 75.00
9	Furniture Repair 101	David	Crockett	Yes	$150.00
10	Furniture Repair 102	Timothy	Culver	Yes	$150.00
11	Furniture Repair 101	Dianne	D'Angelo	Yes	$150.00
12	Furniture Repair 101	Gerald	D'Angelo	Yes	$150.00
13	Furniture Repair 101	Jeff	Flaherty	No	$150.00
14	Furniture Repair 102	Desiree	George	Yes	$150.00
15	Furniture Repair 101	Daniel	Greeley	Yes	$150.00
16	Tattered Treasures	Patricia	Greenley	No	$100.00
17	Depression Glass	Shannon	Greenley	Yes	$ 75.00
18	Furniture Repair 101	Chloe	Hagensack	Yes	$150.00
19	Furniture Repair 102	Michael	Holefill	No	$150.00
20	Applying Stain	Floyd	Ikendahl	Yes	$ 75.00
21	Applying Stain	Judith	Ikendahl	Yes	$ 75.00
22	Applying Stain	Kristi	Jackson	No	$ 75.00
23	Furniture Repair 102	Florence	Leverence	Yes	$150.00
24	Furniture Repair 102	Holly	Ossewalde	No	$150.00
25	Furniture Repair 101	Jeff	Richards	Yes	$150.00
26	Tattered Treasures	Brandie	Searles	Yes	$100.00
27	Applying Stain	Jimmy	Snythe	No	$ 75.00
28	Applying Stain	Jim	Soffeil	Yes	$ 75.00
29	Furniture Repair 102	Walter	Stevens	No	$150.00
30	Tattered Treasures	Antoine	Taylor	No	$100.00
31	Depression Glass	Dan	Taylor	Yes	$ 75.00
32	Tattered Treasures	Angela	Watry	No	$100.00
33	Depression Glass	Scott	Watry	No	$ 75.00
34	Furniture Repair 101	David	Wisecarver	No	$150.00
35					
36	Total				30
37					

tblClassEnrollment

FIGURE 13–1
COUNT function counts numeric data

5. Click **cell C36.**
6. Type the function **=COUNT(C5:C34)** and press **Enter**. Notice how 0 appears as the result, because cells C5:C36 contain no numeric data. Next, you will use the COUNTA function.
7. Click **cell C36.**

8. Type the function **=COUNTA(C5:C34)** and then press **Enter**. The number 30, which is the count of students in the class and is textual data, appears in the cell, as shown in **Figure 13–2**.

FIGURE 13–2
COUNTA function counts cells with text

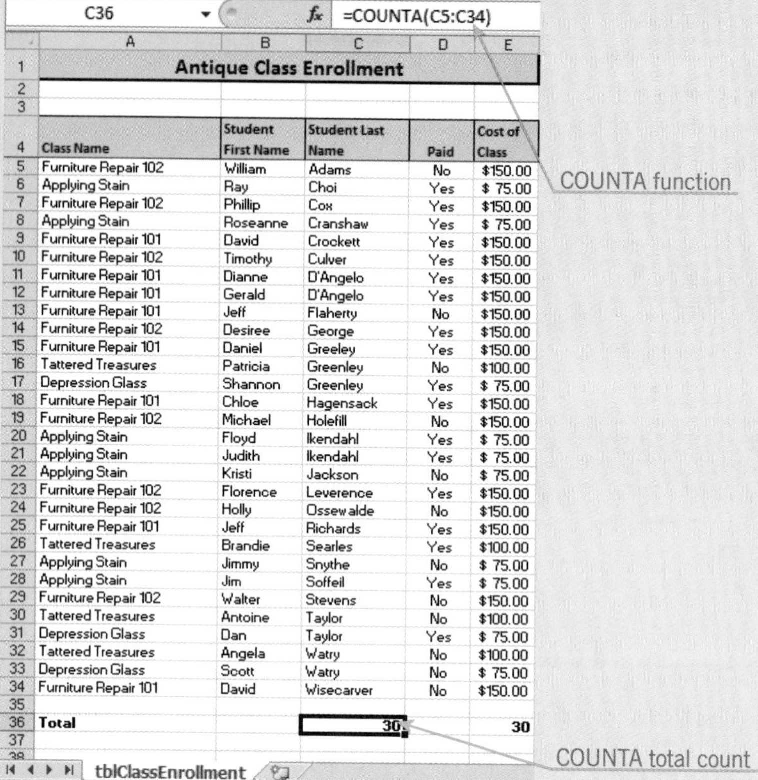

	A	B	C	D	E
1	Antique Class Enrollment				
2					
3					
4	Class Name	Student First Name	Student Last Name	Paid	Cost of Class
5	Furniture Repair 102	William	Adams	No	$150.00
6	Applying Stain	Ray	Choi	Yes	$ 75.00
7	Furniture Repair 102	Phillip	Cox	Yes	$150.00
8	Applying Stain	Roseanne	Cranshaw	Yes	$ 75.00
9	Furniture Repair 101	David	Crockett	Yes	$150.00
10	Furniture Repair 102	Timothy	Culver	Yes	$150.00
11	Furniture Repair 101	Dianne	D'Angelo	Yes	$150.00
12	Furniture Repair 101	Gerald	D'Angelo	Yes	$150.00
13	Furniture Repair 101	Jeff	Flaherty	No	$150.00
14	Furniture Repair 102	Desiree	George	Yes	$150.00
15	Furniture Repair 101	Daniel	Greeley	Yes	$150.00
16	Tattered Treasures	Patricia	Greenley	No	$100.00
17	Depression Glass	Shannon	Greenley	Yes	$ 75.00
18	Furniture Repair 101	Chloe	Hagensack	Yes	$150.00
19	Furniture Repair 102	Michael	Holefill	No	$150.00
20	Applying Stain	Floyd	Ikendahl	Yes	$ 75.00
21	Applying Stain	Judith	Ikendahl	Yes	$ 75.00
22	Applying Stain	Kristi	Jackson	No	$ 75.00
23	Furniture Repair 102	Florence	Leverence	Yes	$150.00
24	Furniture Repair 102	Holly	Ossewalde	No	$150.00
25	Furniture Repair 101	Jeff	Richards	Yes	$150.00
26	Tattered Treasures	Brandie	Searles	Yes	$100.00
27	Applying Stain	Jimmy	Snythe	No	$ 75.00
28	Applying Stain	Jim	Soffeil	Yes	$ 75.00
29	Furniture Repair 102	Walter	Stevens	No	$150.00
30	Tattered Treasures	Antoine	Taylor	No	$100.00
31	Depression Glass	Dan	Taylor	Yes	$ 75.00
32	Tattered Treasures	Angela	Watry	No	$100.00
33	Depression Glass	Scott	Watry	No	$ 75.00
34	Furniture Repair 101	David	Wisecarver	No	$150.00
35					
36	Total		30		30
37					

9. Save, print, and close the workbook.

Using COUNTBLANK

The COUNTBLANK function counts the number of cells that do not have any numbers or text entered in them. You may want to count blank cells to see how many cells do not contain data.

For example, you might have a worksheet that has a list of volunteers for each day of the week. Volunteers enter the number of hours they can work in any given day. On the days that a volunteer will not be working, the cell is left blank. So, if you want to see how many open volunteer slots you have for a certain day, you could use the COUNTBLANK function to count the empty cells. Then, if you see that one of the days has quite a few blanks, you could call other volunteers to see if they might be able to help.

In the next Step-by-Step, the library has a list of 24 volunteers. They need 12 volunteers working per day at the library. If the day of the week has more than 12 blanks, you will need to contact more volunteers to see if they might be able to help.

Step-by-Step 13.2

1. Open the **Library Volunteers** file from the drive and folder where your Data Files are stored.
2. Save the workbook as **Library Volunteers – June 2014**, followed by your initials. The library needs 12 volunteers working per day. You need to find the days that do not have enough volunteers.
3. Click **cell C31**.
4. Type the function **=COUNTBLANK(C6:C29)** and then press **Enter** to view the result. You will now copy the formula to the rest of the cells.
5. Click in **cell C31**. Place your mouse pointer over the fill handle in the lower-right corner of this cell, and then click and drag to cell **I31**. The COUNTBLANK function is now copied to each of these cells. Notice that Tuesday, Wednesday, and Thursday do not have enough volunteers, as shown in **Figure 13–3**.

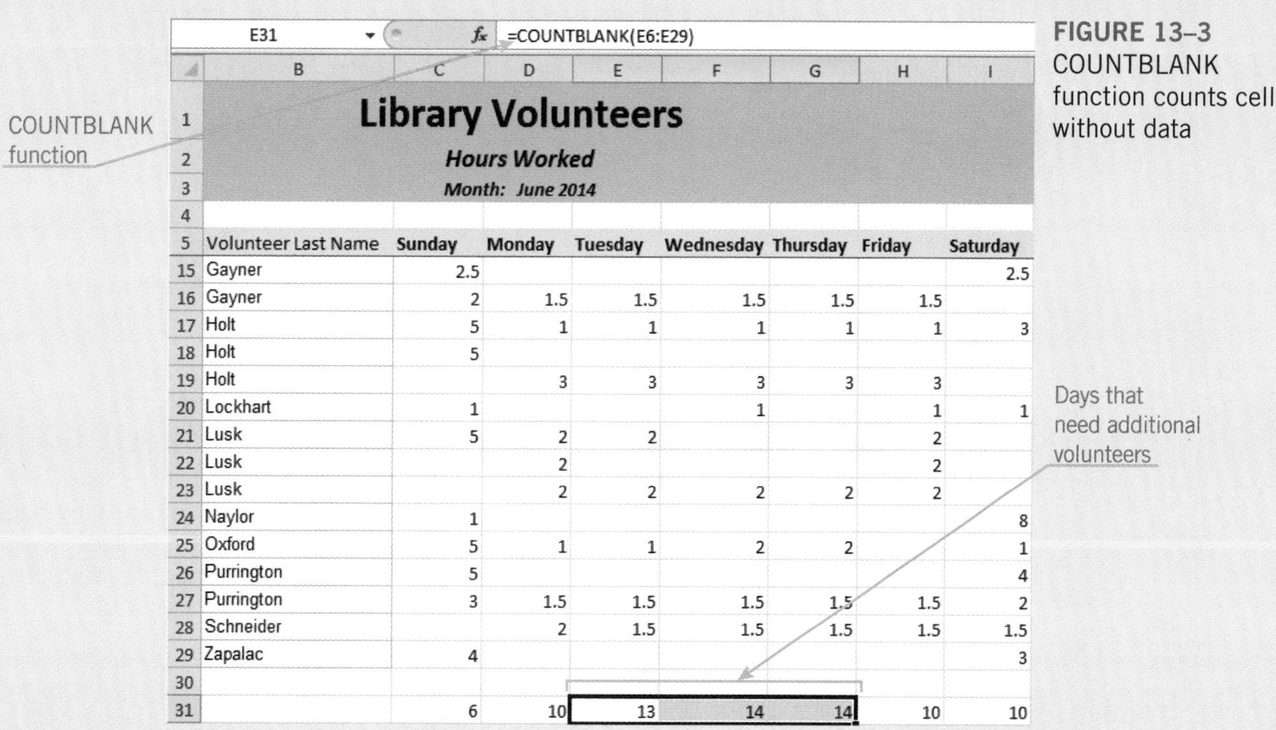

	B	C	D	E	F	G	H	I
1	Library Volunteers							
2	Hours Worked							
3	Month: June 2014							
4								
5	Volunteer Last Name	Sunday	Monday	Tuesday	Wednesday	Thursday	Friday	Saturday
15	Gayner	2.5						2.5
16	Gayner	2	1.5	1.5	1.5	1.5	1.5	
17	Holt	5	1	1	1	1	1	3
18	Holt	5						
19	Holt		3	3	3	3	3	
20	Lockhart	1			1		1	1
21	Lusk	5	2	2			2	
22	Lusk		2				2	
23	Lusk		2	2	2	2	2	
24	Naylor	1						8
25	Oxford	5	1	1	2	2		1
26	Purrington	5						4
27	Purrington	3	1.5	1.5	1.5	1.5	1.5	2
28	Schneider		2	1.5	1.5	1.5	1.5	1.5
29	Zapalac	4						3
30								
31		6	10	13	14	14	10	10

FIGURE 13–3 COUNTBLANK function counts cells without data

6. Save, print, and close the workbook.

Counting Filtered Cells Using the Subtotal Function

The Subtotal function is quite powerful and provides additional summing capabilities. When you used the Subtotal function previously by clicking the Subtotal button on the Data tab, data was summed within the data range to give you subtotals and a grand total.

The Subtotal function can also be used to count, sum, or average filtered data. When you filter data, sometimes you may want to count the number of filtered cells in a column. After the data is filtered, only the cells for the item you filtered will be displayed; the other cells will be hidden. If you use the COUNT function, it will count all cells in the column whether they are hidden or not. Using the Subtotal function lets you count only cells that are displayed.

VOCABULARY
function number

The Subtotal function is =SUBTOTAL (function number, data range). The ***function number*** is a number that represents a calculation. The function number lets you control the calculation that the Subtotal function performs, such as sum, count, or average. A list of commonly used Subtotal function numbers and the calculations they perform is shown in **Table 13–1**.

TABLE 13–1 Commonly used Subtotal function numbers

FUNCTION NUMBER	WHAT IT CALCULATES
1	AVERAGE
2	COUNT
3	COUNTA
4	MAX
5	MIN
9	SUM

Even though the function is Subtotal, the function number tells Excel what to do with the range of data. When you used the Subtotal function previously, Excel used function number 9. This function number is included when you click the Subtotal button, because it calculates the subtotals within the data and gives you a grand total, which is a very useful feature. You will now use the Subtotal function to count filtered data.

Step-by-Step 13.3

1. Open the **Class Enrollment** file from the drive and folder where your Data Files are stored.
2. Save the workbook as **Class Enrollment Totals**, followed by your initials. You will use the data to create a count of the number of students enrolled in classes.

3. Click **cell A4** or any cell under a column heading.
4. On the Ribbon, click the **Data** tab, and then click the **Filter** button in the Sort & Filter group.
5. In cell A4, click the **filter arrow**.
6. Click the **(Select All)** check box. All of the columns are now deselected.
7. Click the **4** check box and then click **OK**. The list of classes is filtered to show only Class Number 4.
8. Select **cell B46**, type the function **=SUBTOTAL(2,B5:B44)**, and then press **Enter**. Notice how all of the cells in column B are counted, showing that nine students are enrolled in Class Number 4. See **Figure 13–4**.

B46 | =SUBTOTAL(2, B5:B44)

	A	B	C	D	E	F
1	Dance Classes Unlimited					
2						
3						
4	Class Numbe	Student Numbe	Paid	Cost of Class		
9	4	9	Yes	$ 35.00		
10	4	10	Yes	$ 35.00		
11	4	15	Yes	$ 35.00		
12	4	16	Yes	$ 35.00		
13	4	18	Yes	$ 35.00		
14	4	25	Yes	$ 35.00		
15	4	29	No	$ 35.00		
16	4	31	No	$ 35.00		
17	4	33	Yes	$ 35.00		
45						
46		9				
47						

SUBTOTAL function

Number of students registered for Class Number 4

FIGURE 13–4
SUBTOTAL function counts displayed cells

9. Save, print, and close the workbook.

Creating Named Ranges

When you use functions, you usually type in a range of cells, such as =SUM(A5:A40). Rather than typing this range, you can give the range a meaningful name and use it in the function. For example, if the range of data, A5:A40, is the data for the month of April, you could name this range April. Then, you could enter this name in the function as =SUM(April). Named ranges are helpful if you need to use a range in several functions. You just need to remember the name of the range rather than the beginning and ending cell names.

If you want to use a name range with two words, you will need to use an underscore (_), rather than a space, to separate the words. Excel does not accept spaces in named ranges. In the next Step-by-Step, you will name two ranges of data.

Step-by-Step 13.4

1. Open the **Student Gymnastics** file from the drive and folder where your Data Files are stored.
2. Save the workbook as **Student Gymnastics - Paid**, followed by your initials.
3. Select the range **B5:B44**.
4. Click in the **Name Box** located to the far left on the formula bar. Notice how the cell name in the Name Box becomes highlighted.
5. Type **Paid**, press **Enter**, and then compare your screen to **Figure 13–5**.

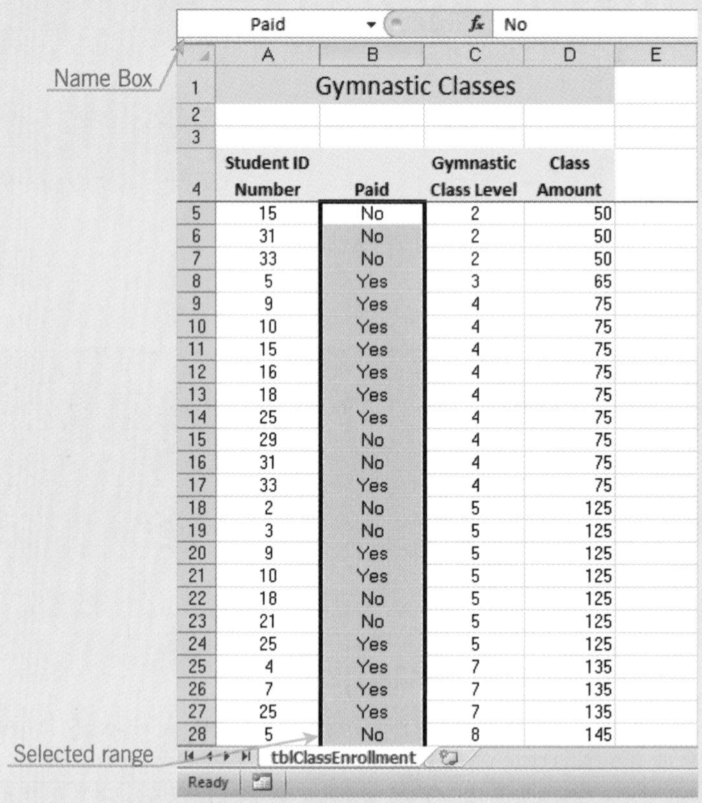

	A	B	C	D	E
1	Gymnastic Classes				
2					
3					
4	Student ID Number	Paid	Gymnastic Class Level	Class Amount	
5	15	No	2	50	
6	31	No	2	50	
7	33	No	2	50	
8	5	Yes	3	65	
9	9	Yes	4	75	
10	10	Yes	4	75	
11	15	Yes	4	75	
12	16	Yes	4	75	
13	18	Yes	4	75	
14	25	Yes	4	75	
15	29	No	4	75	
16	31	No	4	75	
17	33	Yes	4	75	
18	2	No	5	125	
19	3	No	5	125	
20	9	Yes	5	125	
21	10	Yes	5	125	
22	18	No	5	125	
23	21	No	5	125	
24	25	Yes	5	125	
25	4	Yes	7	135	
26	7	Yes	7	135	
27	25	Yes	7	135	
28	5	No	8	145	

FIGURE 13–5
Name Box with name entered

6. Select the range **D5:D44**.
7. Click in the **Name Box** and then type **Amount**.
8. Press **Enter**.
9. Save the workbook and leave it open for the next Step-by-Step.

Using a Named Range in a Function

After you name a range, Excel remembers that name. You select a named range by clicking the Name Box down arrow and then selecting the named range that you want to include in a function. The named range then becomes highlighted in the worksheet. Using named ranges in functions is convenient because you can enter the range name instead of the cell names. If you update the range, such as by adding new cells to it, the results of the formula that use the range will be updated as well. As you are typing the range name into the formula, a border appears around the cells to help you confirm whether you are entering the correct range name.

Step-by-Step 13.5

1. Click **cell D46**.
2. Type **=SUM(Amount)**. This function will total the data in the Amount column.
3. Press **Enter**. The result, $4,910, is the total of the class amounts.
4. Add an accounting number format without decimal places to cell D46. Your screen should appear as shown in **Figure 13–6**.

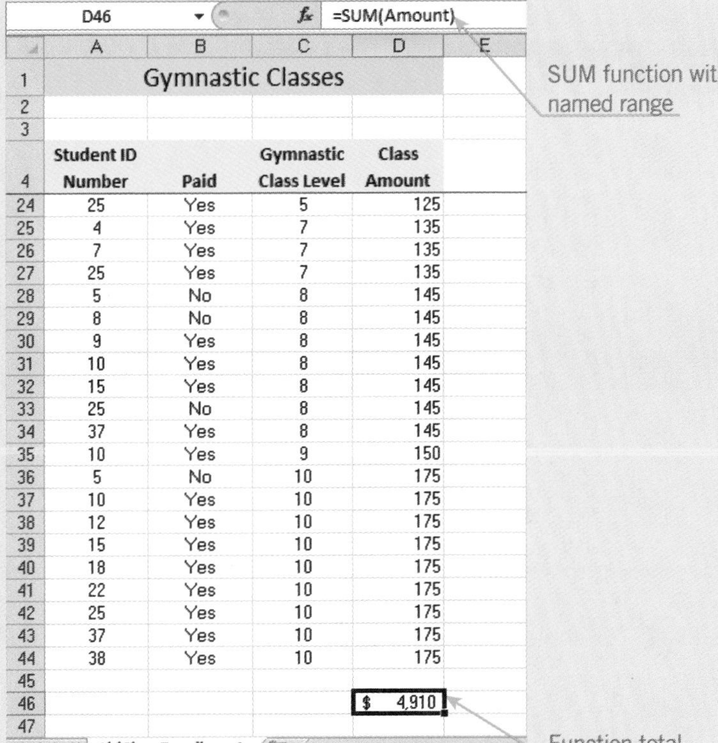

	A	B	C	D
1	Gymnastic Classes			
2				
3				
4	Student ID Number	Paid	Gymnastic Class Level	Class Amount
24	25	Yes	5	125
25	4	Yes	7	135
26	7	Yes	7	135
27	25	Yes	7	135
28	5	No	8	145
29	8	No	8	145
30	9	Yes	8	145
31	10	Yes	8	145
32	15	Yes	8	145
33	25	No	8	145
34	37	Yes	8	145
35	10	Yes	9	150
36	5	No	10	175
37	10	Yes	10	175
38	12	Yes	10	175
39	15	Yes	10	175
40	18	Yes	10	175
41	22	Yes	10	175
42	25	Yes	10	175
43	37	Yes	10	175
44	38	Yes	10	175
45				
46				$ 4,910
47				

FIGURE 13–6
Function with named range

5. Save the workbook and leave it open for the next Step-by-Step.

Using the SUMIF Function

You have previously used the SUM function to get the total amount for data in a range of cells. The SUM function quickly calculates the total when you click the SUM button on the Home tab. The SUMIF function is another form of the SUM function. The SUMIF function will only total data that meets a certain condition. In other words, data will be included in the total if the condition is true.

VOCABULARY
condition
criteria

A ***condition*** is a requirement that needs to be met. ***Criteria*** are the conditions you are searching for in a data range. For example, you might have a list of students who signed up for gymnastics classes. If they paid for the class, a Yes is entered in the cell next to their student ID number. If they did not pay, the word No is shown. The conditions for this example are either yes or no; either they have paid or not. So when you enter criteria into the function, you select one of these conditions. Excel will then search the data range for cells that match the criteria.

The SUMIF function is =SUMIF(range,criteria,sum_range). Range refers to the cells of data that you want Excel to use when it searches for the criteria. Criteria are the information that Excel will look for in the range. If data in the range matches the criteria, Excel will then look to the sum_range. The data in the sum_range that is located in the same row as data in the range will be included in the total.

An example of a SUMIF function is shown in **Figure 13–7**.

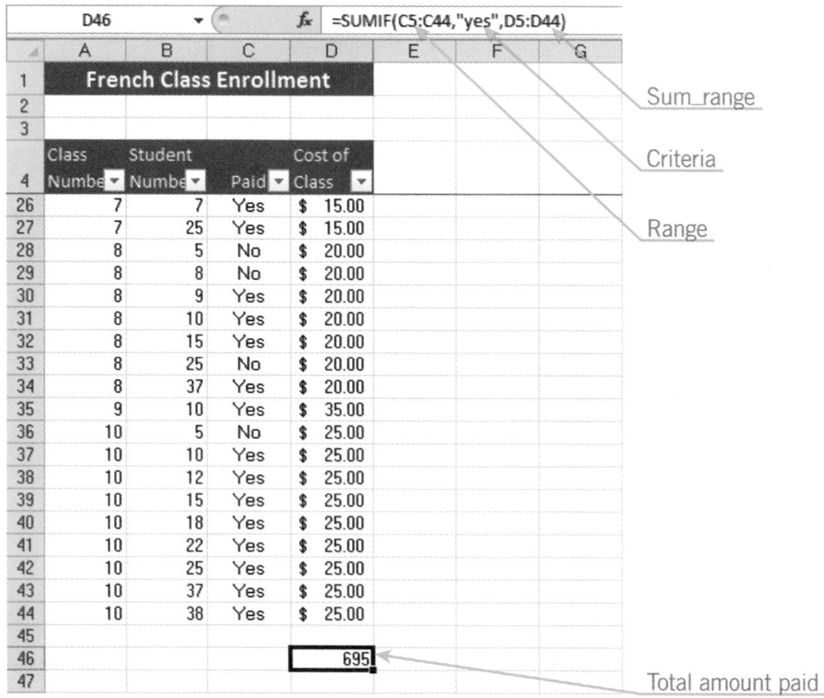
D46 =SUMIF(C5:C44,"yes",D5:D44)

	A	B	C	D
1	French Class Enrollment			
2				
3				
4	Class Number	Student Number	Paid	Cost of Class
26	7	7	Yes	$ 15.00
27	7	25	Yes	$ 15.00
28	8	5	No	$ 20.00
29	8	8	No	$ 20.00
30	8	9	Yes	$ 20.00
31	8	10	Yes	$ 20.00
32	8	15	Yes	$ 20.00
33	8	25	No	$ 20.00
34	8	37	Yes	$ 20.00
35	9	10	Yes	$ 35.00
36	10	5	No	$ 25.00
37	10	10	Yes	$ 25.00
38	10	12	Yes	$ 25.00
39	10	15	Yes	$ 25.00
40	10	18	Yes	$ 25.00
41	10	22	Yes	$ 25.00
42	10	25	Yes	$ 25.00
43	10	37	Yes	$ 25.00
44	10	38	Yes	$ 25.00
45				
46				695
47				

FIGURE 13–7 Example of SUMIF Function

In this next Step-by-Step, you will calculate the total amount students have paid for their classes. Only the amounts actually paid by students, indicated by a "yes" next to their name, will be included in the sum. Since the criteria for the function are text, you will need to use quote marks, as in "yes". You can also use named ranges in the SUMIF function.

Step-by-Step 13.6

1. Click **cell D48**.
2. Type the function **=SUMIF(Paid,"yes",Amount)**. Notice how borders appear around the named ranges as you type them into the formula.
3. Press **Enter**. You see that $3,500 has been collected from students who have paid for their classes.
4. Add an accounting number format without decimal places to **cell D48**. See **Figure 13-8**. Next, you will add text in column A to show the difference between the two totals.

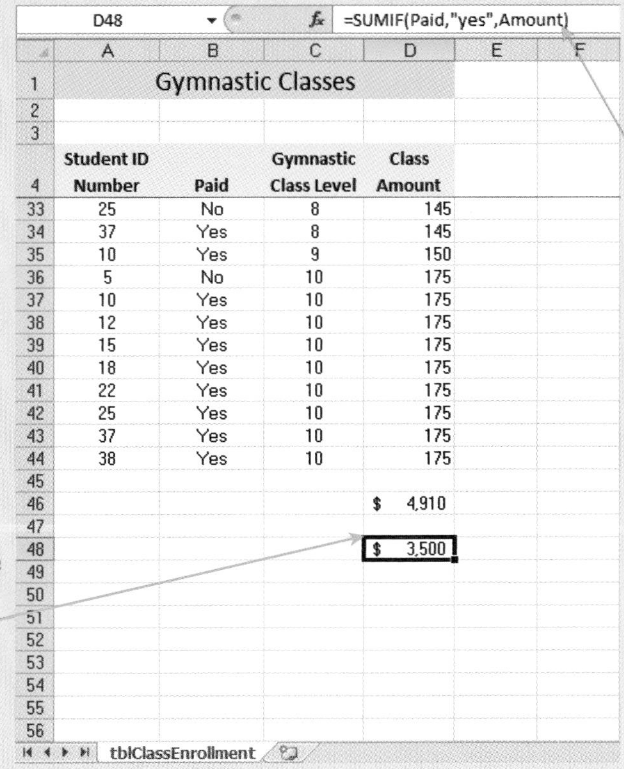

D48 =SUMIF(Paid,"yes",Amount)

	A	B	C	D	E	F
1	Gymnastic Classes					
2						
3						
4	Student ID Number	Paid	Gymnastic Class Level	Class Amount		
33	25	No	8	145		
34	37	Yes	8	145		
35	10	Yes	9	150		
36	5	No	10	175		
37	10	Yes	10	175		
38	12	Yes	10	175		
39	15	Yes	10	175		
40	18	Yes	10	175		
41	22	Yes	10	175		
42	25	Yes	10	175		
43	37	Yes	10	175		
44	38	Yes	10	175		
45						
46				$ 4,910		
47						
48				$ 3,500		
49						
50						
51						
52						
53						
54						
55						
56						

tblClassEnrollment

FIGURE 13–8 SUMIF function using named ranges

SUMIF function with named range

Borders appear around the named ranges as you type them in the formula

5. Select **cell A46**, then type **Total Class Amount**.
6. Select **cell A48**, then type **Total Paid**.

7. Select **cells A46** and **A48**, then select the **Home** tab and in the Alignment group, click the **Align Text Left** button. Click in **cell A49** and view the results. Compare your screen to **Figure 13–9**.

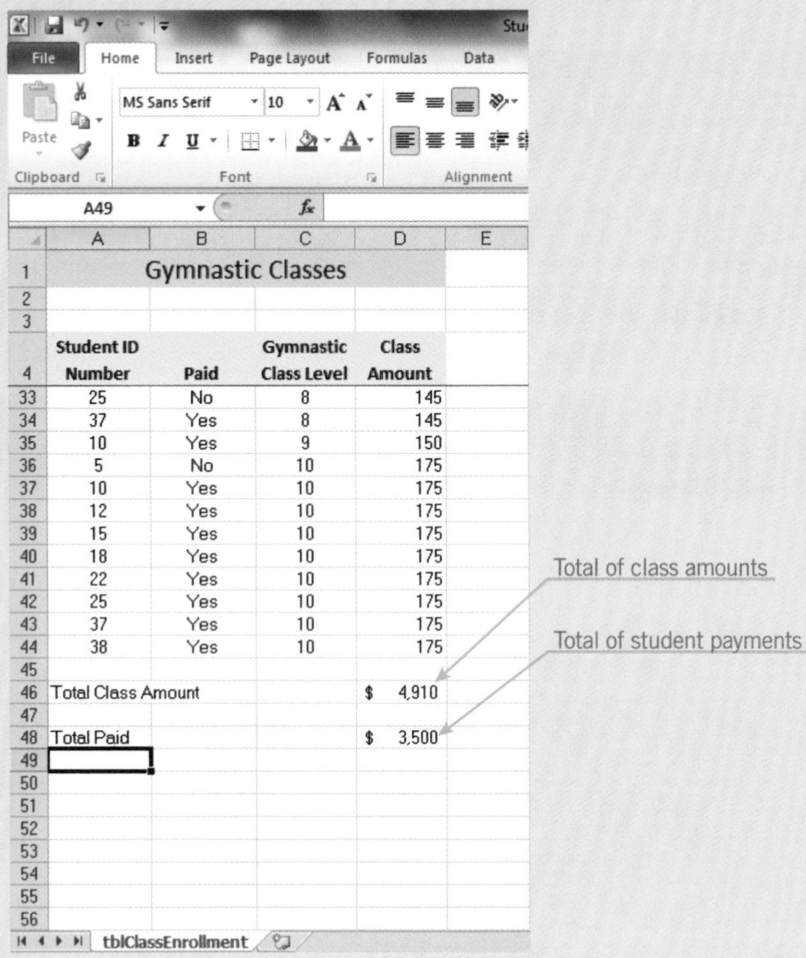

	A	B	C	D
1	Gymnastic Classes			
4	Student ID Number	Paid	Gymnastic Class Level	Class Amount
33	25	No	8	145
34	37	Yes	8	145
35	10	Yes	9	150
36	5	No	10	175
37	10	Yes	10	175
38	12	Yes	10	175
39	15	Yes	10	175
40	18	Yes	10	175
41	22	Yes	10	175
42	25	Yes	10	175
43	37	Yes	10	175
44	38	Yes	10	175
46	Total Class Amount			$ 4,910
48	Total Paid			$ 3,500

FIGURE 13–9
SUMIF function results

8. Save, print, and close the workbook.

Creating a VLOOKUP Function

VOCABULARY
lookup table

LOOKUP functions allow you to find data that already exists rather than looking for the data yourself. This feature is very useful when you need to make a decision based on a range of data. For example, suppose you had several levels of Spanish classes and each level had a different cost. Rather than trying to figure out the cost of the class, you can let Excel look up and determine the cost for you. The range of data with the class costs is called the lookup table. A ***lookup table*** is the range of data you create in either a vertical or horizontal format, which Excel will use to match against the criteria. In this case, a lookup table with a vertical format is used for the class level. When the class level is located in the lookup table, this amount is entered into the cell for the cost of that class.

You use the VLOOKUP function when the range of data, or lookup table, is listed vertically in columns. When you use the VLOOKUP function, you will need to enter information into the Function Arguments dialog box. You will enter the Lookup_value, the Table_array, and the Col_index_num. The Lookup_value is the value that Excel will look for in the first column of the lookup table. Table_array is the range of cells for the lookup table. The final information Excel needs for the function is the column number from the table. The column number is the column in the lookup table that has the data you want to bring from the table into the cell with the function. An example of a LOOKUP function is shown in **Figure 13–10**.

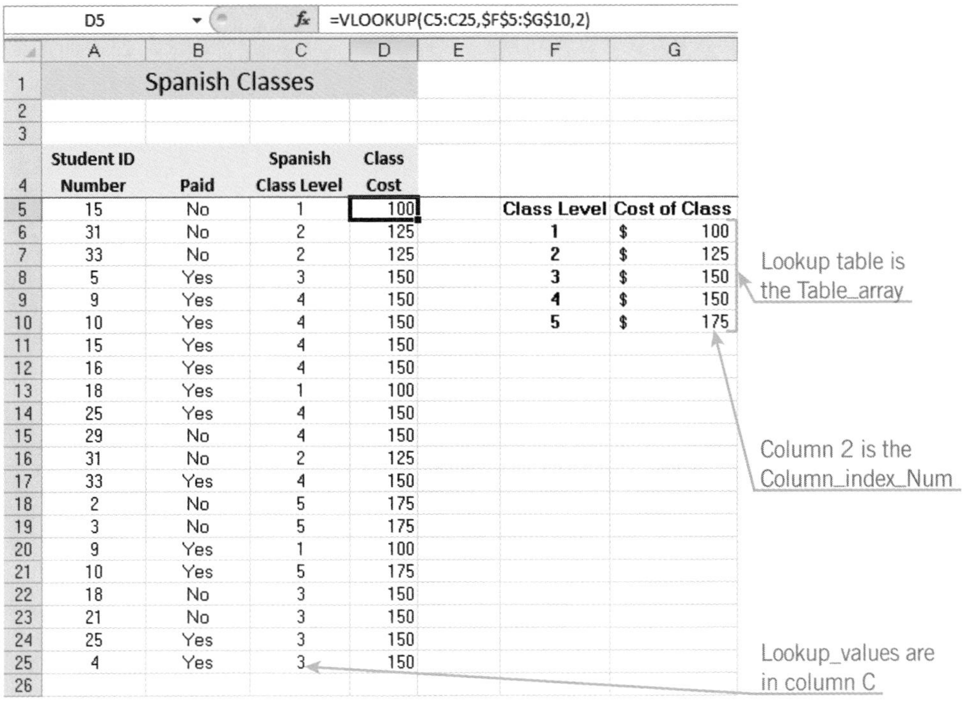

D5 =VLOOKUP(C5:C25,$F$5:$G$10,2)

	A	B	C	D	E	F	G
1		Spanish Classes					
2							
3							
4	Student ID Number	Paid	Spanish Class Level	Class Cost			
5	15	No	1	100		Class Level	Cost of Class
6	31	No	2	125		1	$ 100
7	33	No	2	125		2	$ 125
8	5	Yes	3	150		3	$ 150
9	9	Yes	4	150		4	$ 150
10	10	Yes	4	150		5	$ 175
11	15	Yes	4	150			
12	16	Yes	4	150			
13	18	Yes	1	100			
14	25	Yes	4	150			
15	29	No	4	150			
16	31	No	2	125			
17	33	Yes	4	150			
18	2	No	5	175			
19	3	No	5	175			
20	9	Yes	1	100			
21	10	Yes	5	175			
22	18	No	3	150			
23	21	No	3	150			
24	25	Yes	3	150			
25	4	Yes	3	150			
26							

Lookup table is the Table_array

Column 2 is the Column_index_Num

Lookup_values are in column C

FIGURE 13–10 Example of VLOOKUP function

In Figure 13–10, the cost of the Spanish classes needed to be entered in column D, the Class Cost column. The VLOOKUP function matched the Class Level in column C to the table with class costs in cells F6:G10. The correct class cost was then placed into the cells in column D.

Step-by-Step 13.7

1. Open the **PCI Sales** file from the drive and folder where your Data Files are stored. Save the workbook as **PCI Sales Bonuses**, followed by your initials. Next, you will name the ranges to be used in the VLOOKUP function.
2. Select the range **E6:E11**, click in the **Name Box**, type **Total_Sales**, and then press **Enter**.
3. Select the range **H6:I12**, click in the **Name Box**, type **Bonus_Table**, and then press **Enter**.

4. Select **cell F6**.
5. Click the **Formulas** tab, and then click the **Lookup & Reference** arrow button in the Function Library group. The Lookup & Reference list is displayed, as shown in **Figure 13–11**.

FIGURE 13–11
Lookup & Reference list

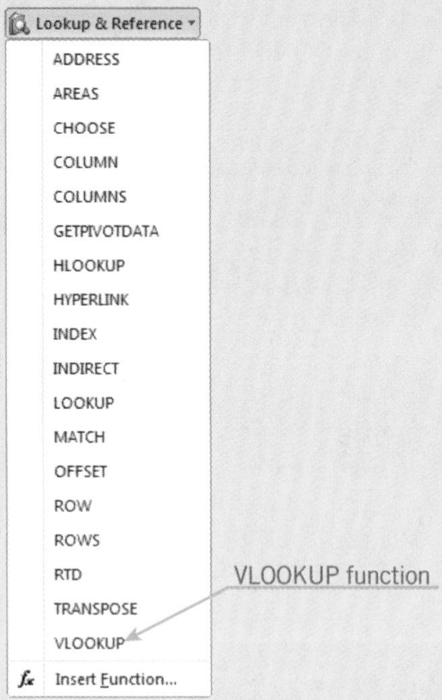

6. Click **VLOOKUP** from the list. The Function Arguments dialog box for VLOOKUP opens, as shown in **Figure 13–12**.

FIGURE 13–12
Function arguments for VLOOKUP dialog box

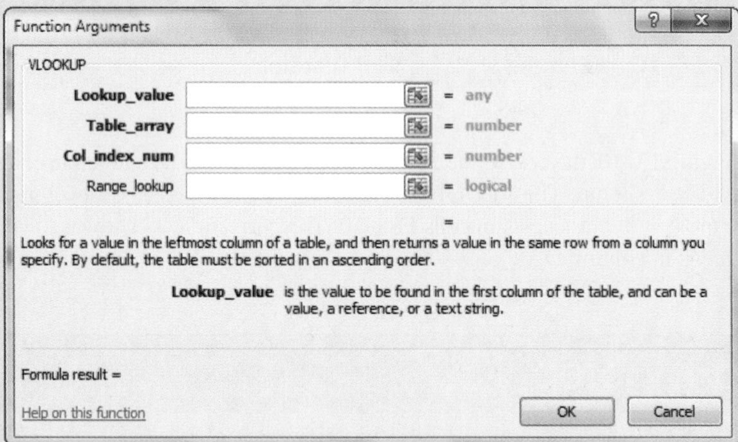

7. Click in the **Lookup_value** text box, and then type **Total_Sales** to find the sales amount for each salesperson. You will now enter the range for the bonus table.
8. Click in the **Table_array** text box and then type **Bonus_Table**.

9. Click in the **Col_index_num** text box, and then type **2** to indicate which column in the bonus table should be searched for the bonus amount. The bonus column, which is the second column in the bonus table, contains the data to be entered into cell F6. The completed dialog box should appear as shown in **Figure 13–13**.

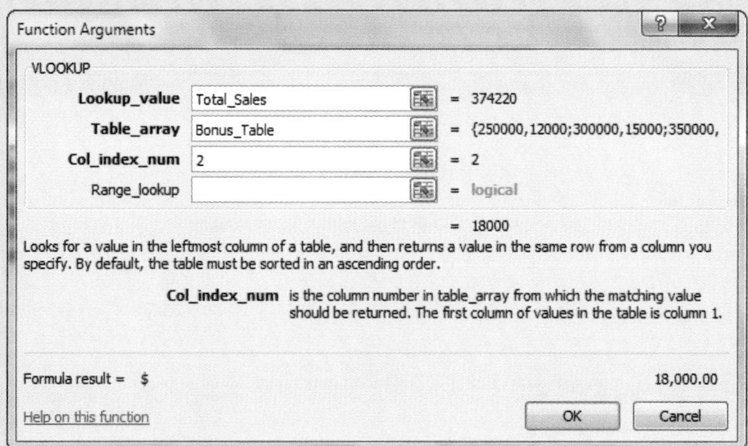

FIGURE 13–13
Completed Function Arguments for VLOOKUP dialog box

10. Click **OK**.

11. To copy the formula in cell F6 to cells F7:F11, place your mouse pointer over the **fill handle** in the lower-right corner of cell F6, and then click and drag to cell **F11**. Your completed worksheet should appear as shown in **Figure 13–14**.

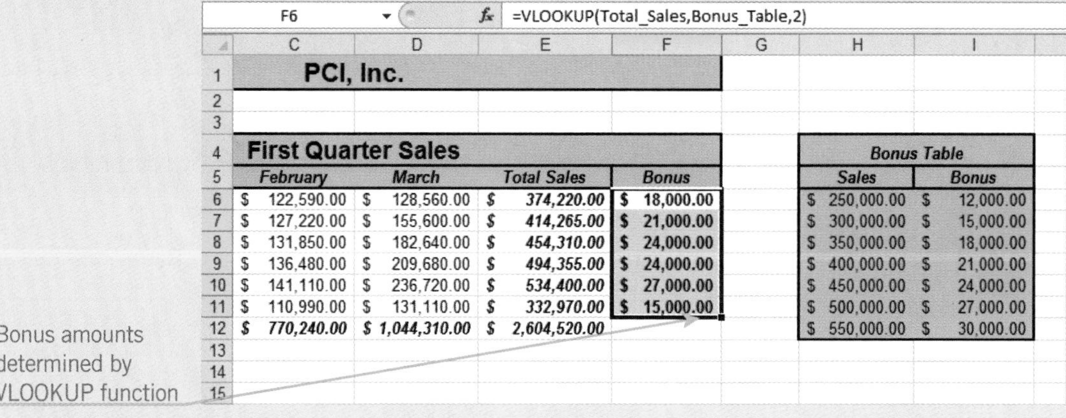
F6 =VLOOKUP(Total_Sales,Bonus_Table,2)

	C	D	E	F	G	H	I
1	PCI, Inc.						
2							
3							
4	First Quarter Sales					Bonus Table	
5	February	March	Total Sales	Bonus		Sales	Bonus
6	$ 122,590.00	$ 128,560.00	$ 374,220.00	$ 18,000.00		$ 250,000.00	$ 12,000.00
7	$ 127,220.00	$ 155,600.00	$ 414,265.00	$ 21,000.00		$ 300,000.00	$ 15,000.00
8	$ 131,850.00	$ 182,640.00	$ 454,310.00	$ 24,000.00		$ 350,000.00	$ 18,000.00
9	$ 136,480.00	$ 209,680.00	$ 494,355.00	$ 24,000.00		$ 400,000.00	$ 21,000.00
10	$ 141,110.00	$ 236,720.00	$ 534,400.00	$ 27,000.00		$ 450,000.00	$ 24,000.00
11	$ 110,990.00	$ 131,110.00	$ 332,970.00	$ 15,000.00		$ 500,000.00	$ 27,000.00
12	$ 770,240.00	$ 1,044,310.00	$ 2,604,520.00			$ 550,000.00	$ 30,000.00
13							
14							
15							

Bonus amounts determined by VLOOKUP function

FIGURE 13–14
Worksheet with VLOOKUP results

12. Print the worksheet. Save and close the workbook.

Using the HLOOKUP Function

You learned that a VLOOKUP function looks in the lookup table when the table is arranged vertically in columns. Use the HLOOKUP function when the data in the lookup table is listed horizontally in rows.

When you use the HLOOKUP function, you will need to enter the Lookup_value, Table_array, and the Row_index_num information into the Function Argument dialog box. For the Lookup_value, you will need to specify what to look for in the lookup table. Table_array is the range of cells for the lookup table. You will also need the row number from the table that has the data you want returned to the cell with the HLOOKUP function. An example of an HLOOKUP function is shown in **Figure 13–15**.

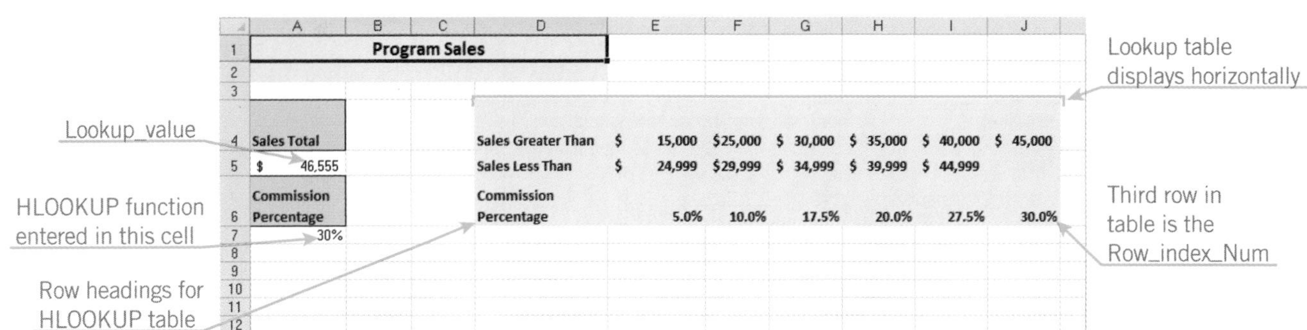

FIGURE 13–15 Example of HLOOKUP function

In this figure, the salespersons receive a commission based on their total amount of sales. The commission is shown as a percentage. For example, if the salesperson made $25,500 in sales, he or she would get a 10 percent commission, or $2,550. The commission percentage appears in cell A7. The HLOOKUP function matches the sales amount in cell A5 to the sales and commission lookup table located in cells E4:J6. Notice how the table is displayed horizontally.

Step-by-Step 13.8

1. Open the Booth file from the drive and folder where your Data Files are stored. Save the workbook as **Booth Sales**, followed by your initials.
2. Click **cell A7**.
3. Click the **Formulas** tab, and then click the **Lookup & Reference** button arrow in the Function Library group.
4. Click **HLOOKUP** from the list. The Function Arguments dialog box for HLOOKUP opens.
5. Click in the **Lookup_value** text box, and then type **A5** to find the commission percentage. You will now enter the range for the bonus table.
6. Click in the **Table_array** text box and then type **$E$4:$J$6**.
7. Click in the **Row_index_num** text box and then type **3**. Row 3 is the commission percentage row, which is the third row in the table. The completed dialog box should appear as shown in **Figure 13–16**.

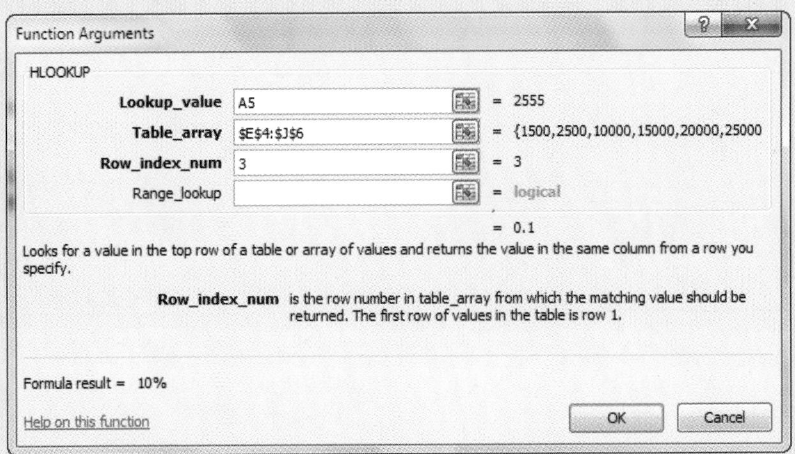

FIGURE 13–16
Function Arguments for HLOOKUP dialog box

8. Click **OK**.
9. Click **cell A5**.
10. Type **2555** and then press **Enter**. A 10% commission percentage appears in cell A7. See **Figure 13–17**.

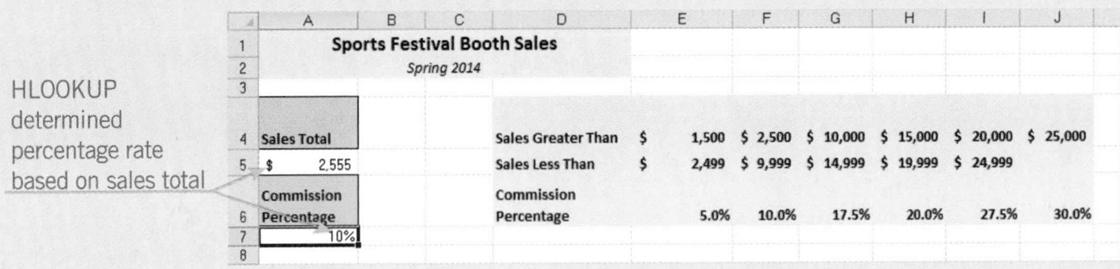

FIGURE 13–17
Worksheet with HLOOKUP results

11. Save, print, and close the workbook.

SUMMARY

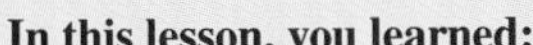

In this lesson, you learned:

- The COUNT function counts cells with numeric data and the COUNTA function counts cells with text or a combination of text and numbers.
- You can use COUNTBLANK to count cells without any data.
- The SUBTOTAL function can be used to count filtered data.
- You can name a range of data.
- A named range can be used in a function.
- The SUMIF function totals data that meet a certain condition.
- You can use the VLOOKUP function to find data that is displayed vertically in a lookup table.
- You can use the HLOOKUP function to find data that is displayed horizontally in a lookup table.

VOCABULARY

Define the following terms:

condition
criteria
function number
lookup table

REVIEW QUESTIONS

TRUE / FALSE

Circle T if the statement is true or F if the statement is false.

T F 1. VLOOKUP locates data in a range that displays data vertically.

T F 2. The COUNTA function is used to count data in a filtered list.

T F 3. The SUMIF function totals all cells in a range.

T F 4. Named ranges cannot be used in functions.

T F 5. The Subtotal function is used to count blank cells.

FILL IN THE BLANK

1. A(n)________________ is a requirement that needs to be met.
2. The ________________ function is used to count filtered data.
3. The ________________ function will calculate only cells that meet a certain requirement.
4. To count blank cells, you would use the ________________ function.
5. If you have a lookup table that is displayed vertically, you would use the ________________ function.

WRITTEN QUESTIONS

Write a brief answer to the following questions.

1. What is the difference between the VLOOKUP function and the HLOOKUP function?

2. Explain the difference between the COUNT and COUNTA functions.

3. Explain what the 1, 2, 3, and 9 function numbers calculate when used with the Subtotal function.

4. Explain how you would count cells that do not have any data, such as text or numbers.

5. If you use a range of cells frequently, explain what you could do to make entering this range into a function easier to remember.

PROJECTS

If you have a SAM 2010 user profile, your instructor may have assigned an autogradable version of the indicated project. If so, log into the SAM 2010 Web site at *www.cengage.com/sam2010* to download the instruction and start files.

PROJECT 13–1

1. Open the **Spanish Class** file from the drive and folder where your Data Files are stored. Save the workbook as **Spanish Class Costs**, followed by your initials.
2. Add a VLOOKUP function to cell D5 that looks at the Spanish Class Level in column C, compares it to the table data in cells F6:G10, and returns the appropriate cost to cell D5.
3. Copy the formula to the remaining cells in column D.
4. Save, print, and close the workbook.

SAM PROJECT 13–2

1. Open the **Chinese Class** file from the drive and folder where your Data Files are stored. Save the workbook as **Chinese Class Enrollment**, followed by your initials.
2. Add AutoFilters to the columns.
3. Filter the Class Number column for class 5.
4. In cell A46, use the Subtotal function to count the number of students in class 5.
5. Save, print, and close the workbook.

PROJECT 13–3

1. Open the **Bonus** file from the drive and folder where your Data Files are stored. Save the workbook as **Bonus for Sports**, followed by your initials.
2. Create a HLOOKUP formula in cell **A7** that will look at the amount of sales entered into cell A5, compare it to the HLOOKUP table, and enter the correct percentage in cell A7.
3. Select cell **A5** and type **67,500**.
4. View the percentage result in cell A7.
5. Save, print, and close the workbook.

CRITICAL THINKING

ACTIVITY 13–1

Your boss at Houston Eastern/Central Oil asks you to create a LOOKUP function in the company's sales report indicating the commission percentage based on program manager sales. Open the **Sales** file from the drive and folder where your Data Files are stored, and then save the workbook as **Sales Commissions** followed by your initials. The data file includes the company sales commission report. You decide to create an HLOOKUP function that will calculate the sales commission percentage based on the amount of sales that are entered into cell A5. By adding this function, your boss can quickly let the program managers know their commission rate. You test the HLOOKUP to see if the correct commission percentage is returned for the sales total of $46,555.

ACTIVITY 13–2

As the new manager of the local library, you discover that the previous manager used the CHOOSE function instead of a LOOKUP function. You decide to research the CHOOSE function to see if it would work better for looking up values vertically. Create a document explaining the result of your research and save it as a Word document with the file name **CHOOSE Function**, followed by your initials.

Estimated Time: 2.5 hours

LESSON 14

Creating and Using Macros

OBJECTIVES

Upon completion of this lesson, you should be able to:

- Understand macros.
- Review macro security settings.
- Record a macro.
- Save a macro as a macro-enabled workbook.
- Run a macro.
- Edit a macro.
- Create a button.
- Align and format a button.
- Open a macro-enabled workbook.

VOCABULARY

button

code

macro

virus

Introduction

VOCABULARY
macro
code
virus

A ***macro*** automates a common, repetitive task you perform in Excel, thereby saving valuable time. In this lesson, you will learn how to create macros. You will then run the macro, which means to have the macro perform the automated task. You will also learn how to make changes to a macro and how to add a macro to a button that can be clicked to run the macro.

Understanding Macros

A macro simply records a series of steps that you do frequently, such as formatting text. For example, you may want to format all worksheet titles using the same font, size, color, and alignment. Continuously repeating these steps can be time consuming. Macros can simplify repetitive tasks. When you create a macro, Excel records the selections you make on the Ribbon as well as the keystrokes you use. Visual Basic for Applications (or VBA) is the program used to create macros. VBA is a programming language that is embedded into applications such as Excel.

When a macro is being recorded, all of the selections you make are translated into code. ***Code*** is simply the macro actions formatted in easy-to-read sentences, just like text in a book.

Before you record a macro, it is important to review and understand macro security settings.

Reviewing Macro Security Settings

Macros are susceptible to a virus attack. A ***virus*** is a computer program that is designed to reproduce by copying itself and attaching to other programs in a computer. Viruses can cause extreme damage to data on your computer. If a virus attaches itself to a macro, it can cause damage when you run the macro. To help protect your data from the corruption caused by a virus hidden in a macro, you can set one of four macro security levels in Excel: *Disable all macros without notification*, *Disable all macros with notification*, *Disable all macros except digitally signed macros*, and *Enable all macros.* The Disable all macros with notification option is the default setting unless you choose another. **Table 14–1** explains each setting in detail.

TABLE 14–1 Macro security level options

MACRO SECURITY LEVEL OPTIONS	DESCRIPTION
Disable all macros without notification	Disables harmful content, but does not notify you.
Disable all macros with notification	Harmful content will be disabled and a notification appears on the Message Bar, just below the Ribbon, letting you know that the macro is disabled unless you click the Enable Content button on the Message Bar.
Disable all macros except digitally signed macros	Only macros that are digitally signed and come from a trusted source will be executed.
Enable all macros	Allows all macros to run and does not offer any protection.

As a best practice, you should set the security level in Excel to Disable all macros with notification or Disable all macros except digitally signed macros. In the next Step-by-Step, you will view the macro settings currently set for Excel.

Step-by-Step 14.1

1. Start Excel, click the File tab on the Ribbon, then click the Options button. The Excel Options dialog box opens, as shown in **Figure 14–1**. You choose macro security level settings in the Trust Center section of the Excel Options dialog box.

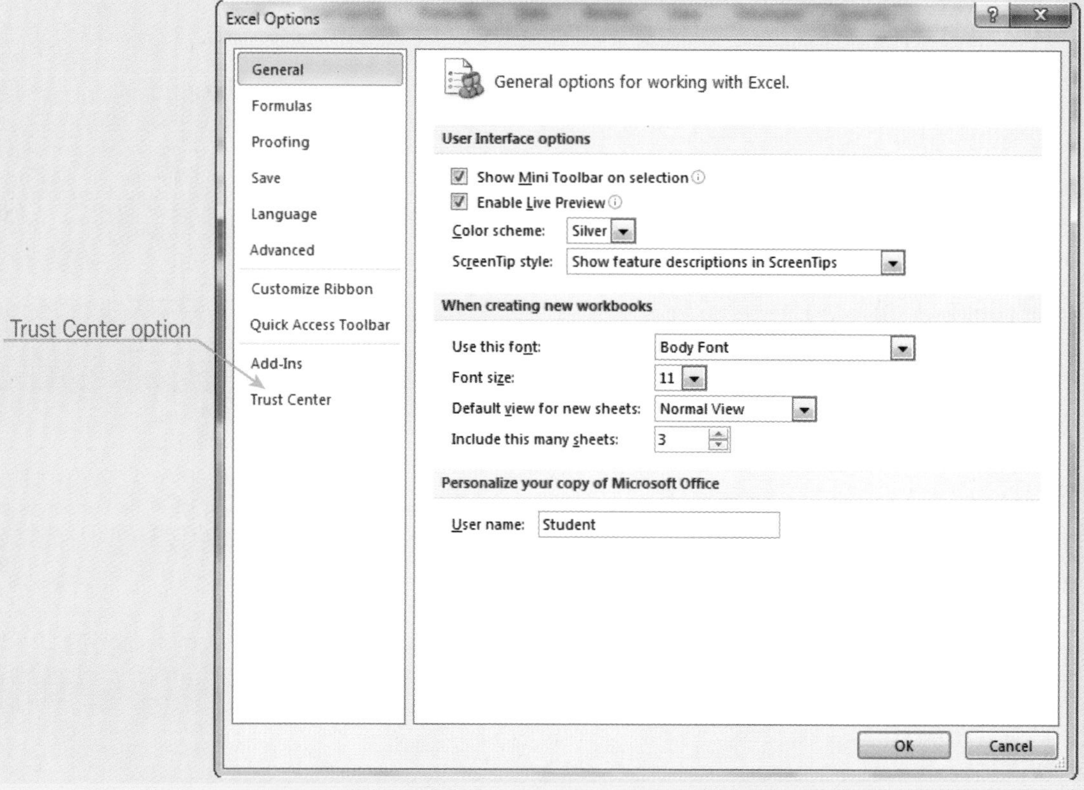

FIGURE 14–1
Excel Options dialog box

2. In the Excel Options dialog box, click **Trust Center** on the left and then click the **Trust Center Settings** button on the right.

3. Click **Macro Settings** on the left to display the macro settings, as shown in **Figure 14–2**. Notice that the default setting is on. Now that you have viewed the settings, you will close the dialog boxes.

FIGURE 14–2
Trust Center dialog box

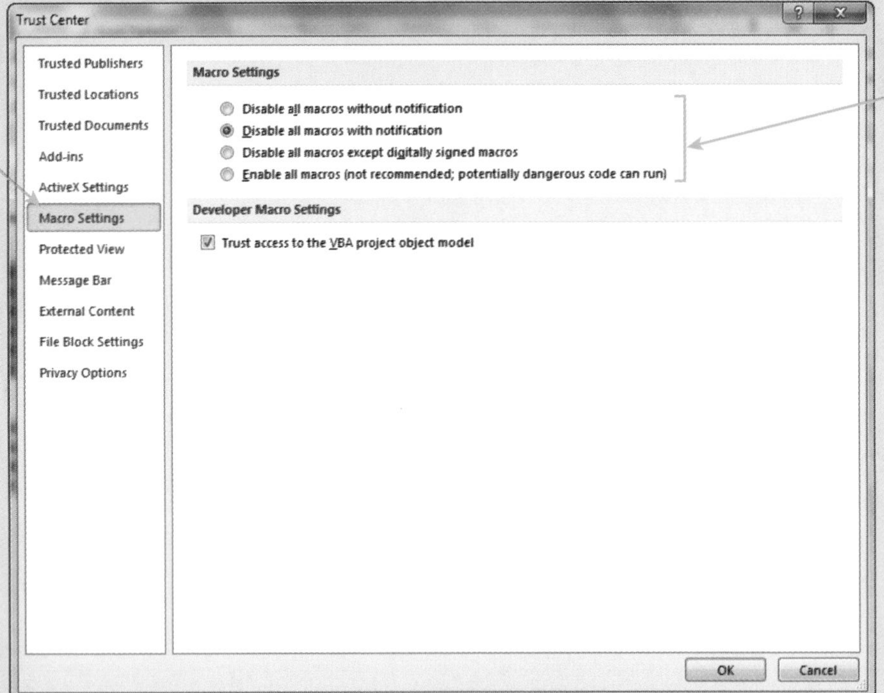

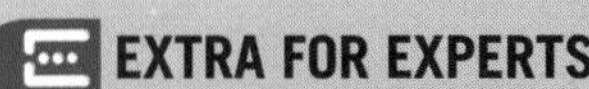

EXTRA FOR EXPERTS

Macro settings can also be viewed by clicking the Developer tab on the Ribbon, then clicking the Macro Security button in the Code group.

4. In the Trust Center dialog box, click **OK**.
5. In the Excel Options dialog box, click **OK**.

Recording a Macro

To begin recording a macro, you click the Record Macro button in the Code group on the Developer tab. Once you choose options in the Record Macro dialog box and close it, the macro records every task you do in Excel. The options in the Record Macro dialog box are described in **Table 14–2**.

TABLE 14–2 Record Macro dialog box options

RECORD MACRO OPTIONS	DESCRIPTION
Macro name	Enter an easily identifiable name for the macro. The first character of the macro name must be a letter. Other characters can be letters, numbers, or an underscore. Since spaces cannot be used in the name, an underscore can be used to separate words.
Shortcut key	Assign a key or keys that will be used in combination with the Ctrl key to run a macro. This setting is optional. Try to avoid using letters already assigned to shortcut keys, such as Ctrl+C, which is used to copy data.
Store macro in	From the drop-down list, you can select to store the macro in This Workbook so it is available when the current workbook is opened. You can also choose to store the macro in the Personal Macro Workbook, which makes it available any time you use Excel. Or, you can store the macro in a new workbook.
Description	Create a brief description of the macro to use for future reference. Entering a description is optional.

In the next Step-by-Step, you will record a macro that applies formats to worksheet data.

Step-by-Step 14.2

1. Open the **School Budget** file from the drive and folder where your Data Files are stored. Click the **First Semester** worksheet tab, if necessary.
2. On the Ribbon, click the **Developer** tab and then click the **Record Macro** button in the Code group. The Record Macro dialog box opens, as shown in **Figure 14–3**.

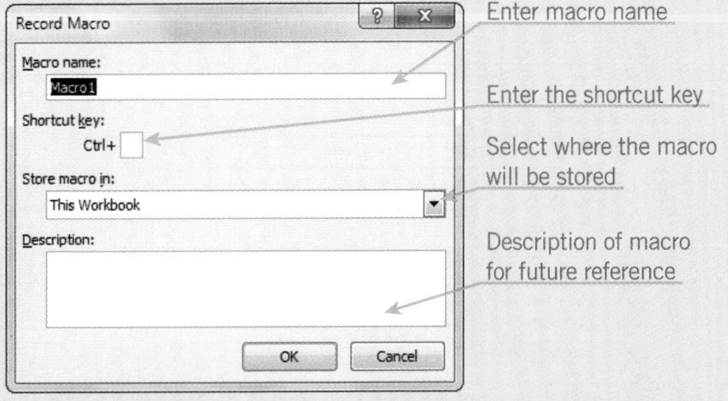

FIGURE 14–3 Record Macro dialog box

3. In the Record Macro dialog box, type **Formats** in the Macro name text box.
4. Click in the **Shortcut key** text box, press and hold the **Shift** key, and then press **F**. The shortcut key for the Formats macro will be Ctrl+Shift+F.

5. Click in the **Description** text box and then type **Adds text format and cell background colors**. The completed dialog box should appear as shown in **Figure 14–4**.

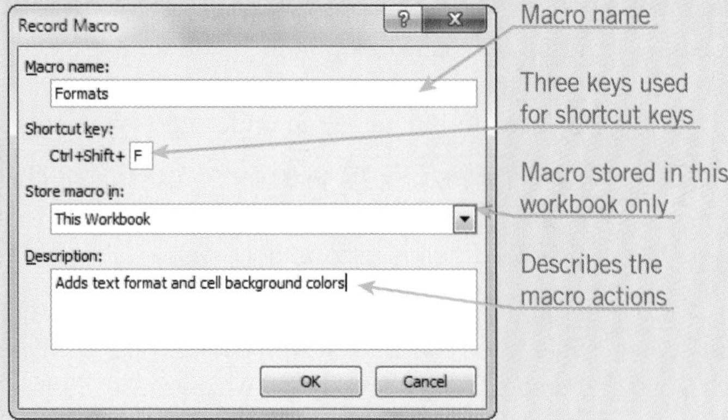

FIGURE 14–4
Completed Record Macro dialog box

EXTRA FOR EXPERTS

If the Developer tab is not displayed on the Ribbon, you can add it. To add the Developer tab to the Ribbon, select the File tab and then click Options. In the Excel Options dialog box, select Customize Ribbon. Check for the presence of an unchecked Developer tab in the Customize the Ribbon column. If the Developer tab is in this column, click to select it. Then, click OK. You are now able to select the Developer tab.

If the Developer tab is not in the Customize the Ribbon column, check to see if the Developer tab is in the list of tabs on the right side of the dialog box. Then, click the Choose commands from arrow and click All Tabs. Under the Main Tabs list heading, click Developer. To move the Developer tab to the right side of the dialog box with the other tabs, click the Add button. Finally, click OK to close the Excel Options dialog box.

6. Click **OK** to close the Record Macro dialog box. Notice that the Record Macro button changed to the Stop Recording button on the Developer tab in the Code group because Excel is now recording everything you do.
7. Select the range **A4:A9**.
8. Click the **Home** tab, and then click the **Bold** button **B** in the Font group.
9. Click the **Fill Color** button arrow, and then choose **Red, Accent 2, Lighter 40%**.
10. Select the range **A12:A15**.
11. Click the **Bold** button **B** in the Font group, click the **Fill Color** button arrow, and then choose **Yellow**.
12. Select the range **B4:B15**.
13. In the Number group, click the **Comma Style** button **,**. The Comma Style format will add decimal places and a comma to separate thousands.
14. Click the **Developer** tab, and then click the **Stop Recording** button in the Code group. The worksheet shows the formatting options you chose. See **Figure 14–5**. Leave the workbook open for the next Step-by-Step.

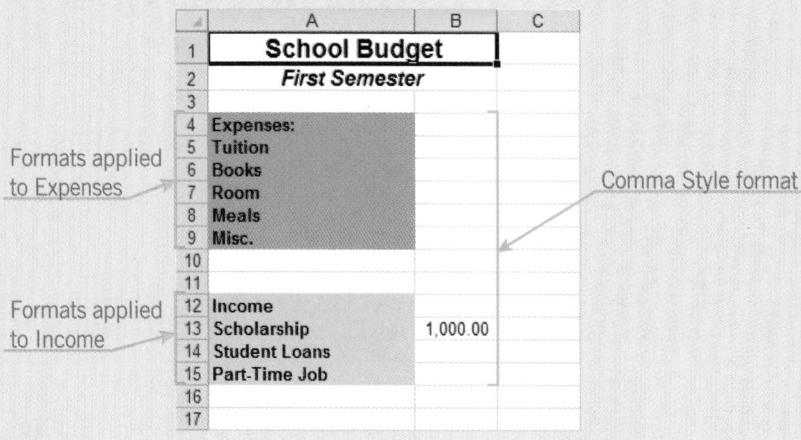

FIGURE 14–5
First Semester worksheet with formats applied

Saving a Workbook as a Macro-Enabled Workbook

A workbook that is saved in Excel is saved in the default format with the file extension .xlsx. If you want to save a workbook that has a macro, you will need to save it with the .xlsm file extension in the Save dialog box. The file extension .xlsm is used for a macro-enabled workbook. A macro-enabled workbook lets you save the macro in the workbook and then run the macro. You can also save an ordinary Excel workbook as a macro-enabled workbook using the Save As command.

In the next Step-by-Step, you will save the workbook as a macro-enabled workbook.

EXTRA FOR EXPERTS

You can also start and stop recording of a macro by clicking the Macro button located in the status bar next to Ready. When you click this Macro button, the Record Macro dialog box opens. When you are finished recording the macro, you click the Macro button again to stop recording.

Step-by-Step 14.3

1. In the School Budget workbook, click the **File** tab and click **Save As**.
2. In the Save As dialog box, click after the ***t*** in School Budget in the File name text box, press the **Spacebar**, and then type **First Year** followed by your initials. The file name should be School Budget First Year.
3. Click the **Save as type** list arrow to display the available file types, as shown in **Figure 14–6**.

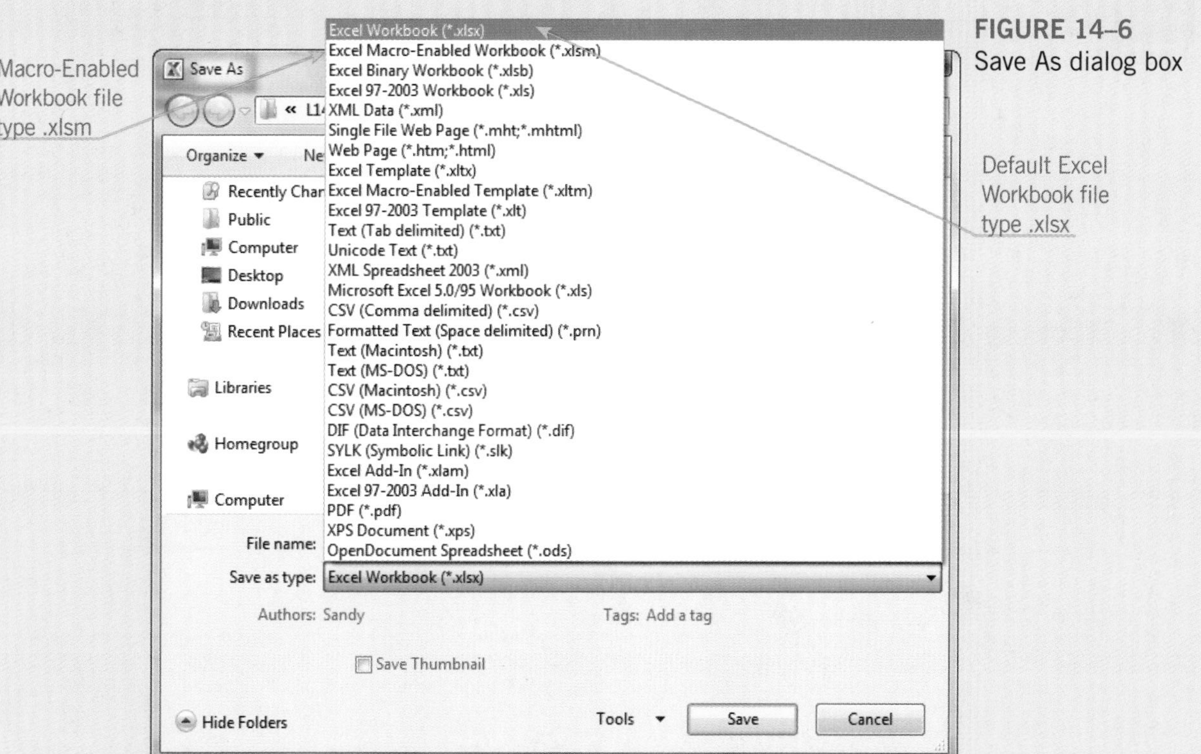

FIGURE 14–6
Save As dialog box

4. Click **Excel Macro-Enabled Workbook (*.xlsm)**.
5. Click **Save** to close the Save As dialog box.

6. Leave the workbook open for the next Step-by-Step. In the next Step-by-Step, you will run the macro to apply the same formatting to the other worksheets.

Running a Macro

After a macro is created, it is ready to use. Excel provides different ways to run a macro. You can use a shortcut key combination if you created one in the Record Macro dialog box. Or, on the Developer tab in the Code group, you can select the Macros button. When you select the Macros button, the Macro dialog box appears. You then click the macro you want and click the Run button. You will now run the Formats macro to apply the same formatting used in the First Semester worksheet to the remaining worksheets in the workbook.

Step-by-Step 14.4

1. Click the **Second Semester** worksheet tab to display the data as it currently appears as shown in **Figure 14–7**.

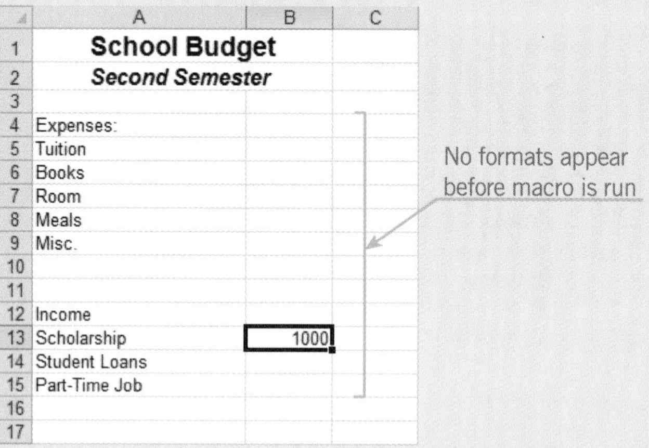

FIGURE 14–7
Second Semester worksheet

2. Press **Ctrl+Shift+F**. The formats you recorded in the macro are applied to the Second Semester worksheet, as shown in **Figure 14–8**.

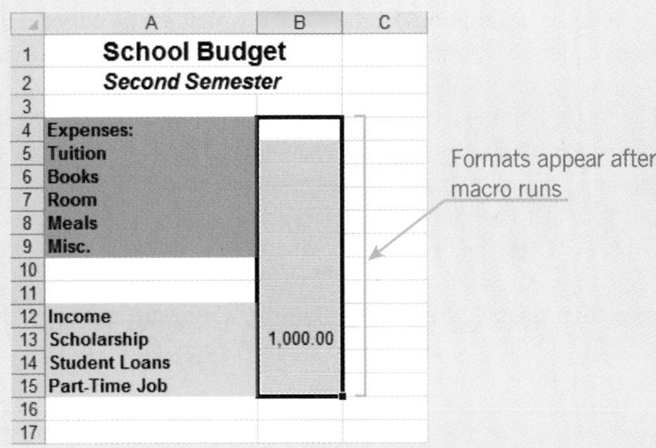

FIGURE 14–8 Second Semester worksheet with formats applied

3. Click the **Third Semester** worksheet tab.
4. On the Ribbon, click the **Developer** tab, and then click the **Macros** button in the Code group.
5. Make sure the Formats macro is selected and then click **Run**.
6. Click the **Fourth Semester** worksheet tab.
7. Press **Ctrl+Shift+F**. All four worksheets now have the same formatting.
8. Save the workbook and leave it open for the next Step-by-Step.

EXTRA FOR EXPERTS

You can assign a combination of keys, such as Ctrl+Q or Ctrl+Shift+F to the macro. Then, when you are ready to run the macro, press the key combination assigned to the macro and Excel will execute the recorded tasks.

Editing a Macro

After you run a macro, you may want to make changes to it. Macros are easy to edit, once you become familiar with working with the code in VBA. To edit a macro, you need to make changes to the code. Modifying code is similar to modifying text in a Microsoft Word document. You can type text into the code and use the Delete, Backspace, and Enter keys as well as the Copy and Paste commands. An example of the code used in a macro is shown in **Figure 14–9**.

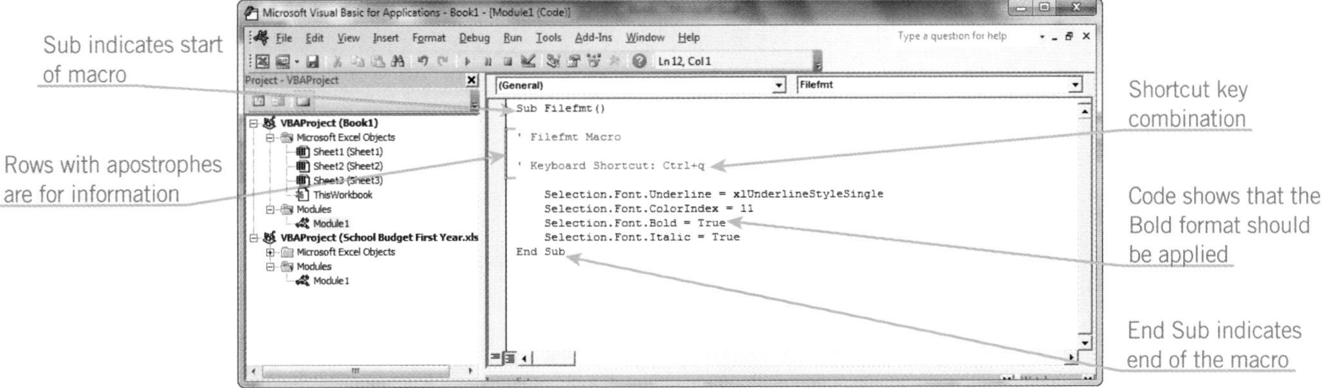

FIGURE 14–9 Example of a macro in VBA code

The code word *Sub* appears at the top of the macro, indicating the start of the macro. Under Sub, the descriptions of the macro, which are preceded with an apostrophe to differentiate them from the actual macro, are listed. In this case, the code shows the name of the macro and the shortcut key combination, Ctrl+Q, used to run the macro. The tasks that make up the macro are listed next. The next rows of code show the formats used. You use True or False to describe if the format is turned on or off. For example, the row Selection.Font.Bold = True means that the macro will apply the bold format to a selected cell. If you do not want the bold format, you would delete the word True and type False. Finally, the code *End Sub* signals the end of the macro.

When you edit a macro, you will need to run the macro again for the changes to be applied in the workbook. In the next Step-by-Step, you will edit the Formats macro by adding the Italic format to the text.

Step-by-Step 14.5

1. In the Code group, click the **Macros** button. The Formats macro is displayed in the Macro dialog box, as shown in **Figure 14–10**.

FIGURE 14–10
Macro dialog box

2. Verify that the Formats macro is highlighted, then click the **Edit** button. The Microsoft Visual Basic for Applications window opens, as shown in **Figure 14–11**. You will add the Italic format to the macro.

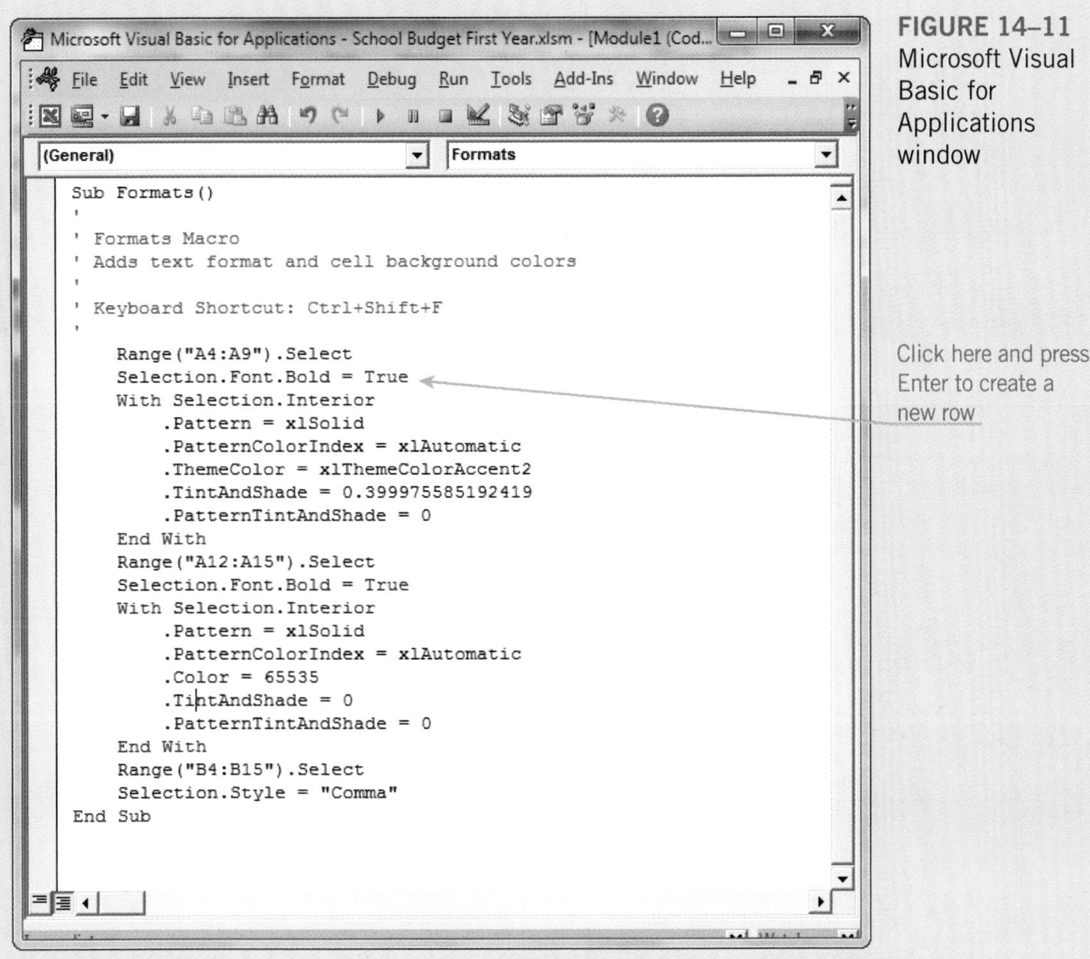

FIGURE 14–11 Microsoft Visual Basic for Applications window

3. Click at the end of the first line: **Selection.Font.Bold=True**, then press **Enter** to make room for a new row of code.

4. Type **Selection.Font.Italic=True**, then compare your new macro code to **Figure 14–12**.

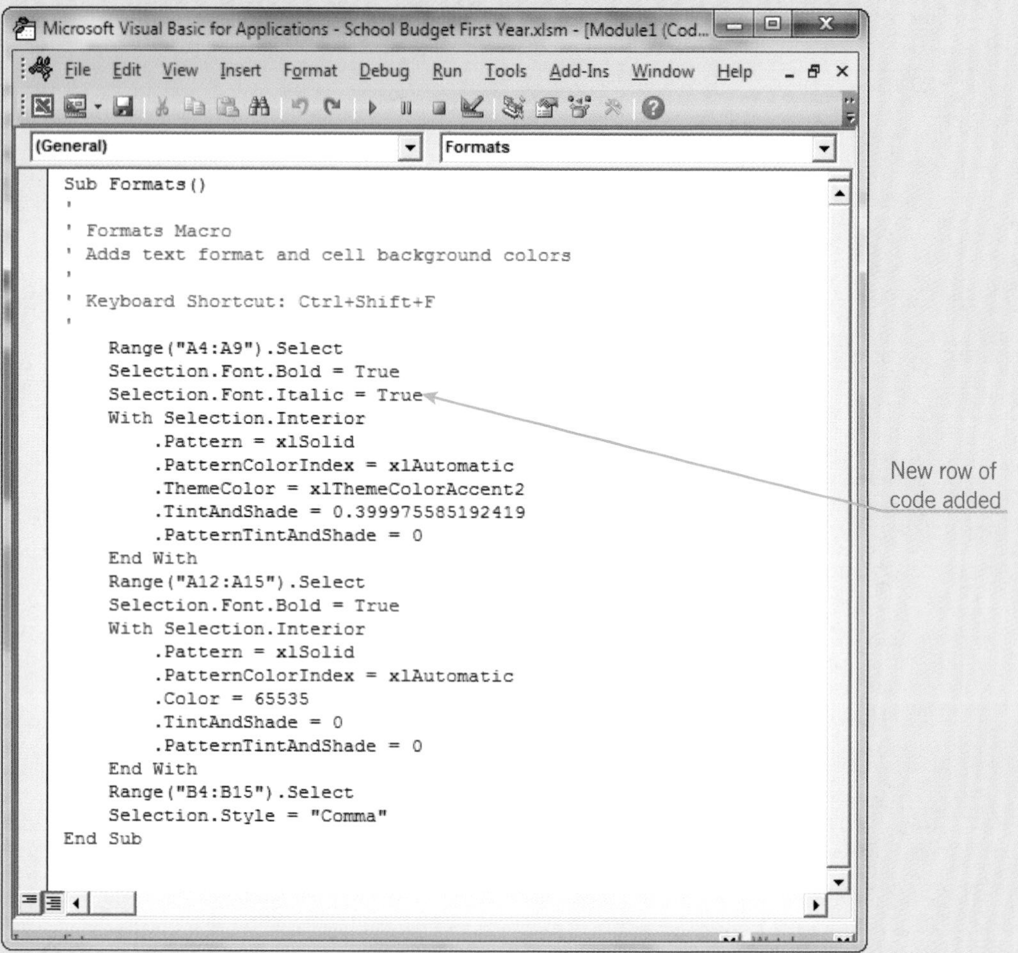

FIGURE 14–12 Making edits to the Formats macro

5. In the Microsoft Visual Basic for Applications window, click the **Save** button on the toolbar.
6. Click the **View Microsoft Excel** button on the toolbar to return to the Excel worksheet.
7. Click the **Fourth Semester** worksheet.
8. Press **Ctrl+Shift+F**, then compare your screen to **Figure 14–13**. The Formats macro is applied to the text and includes the updated Italic format.

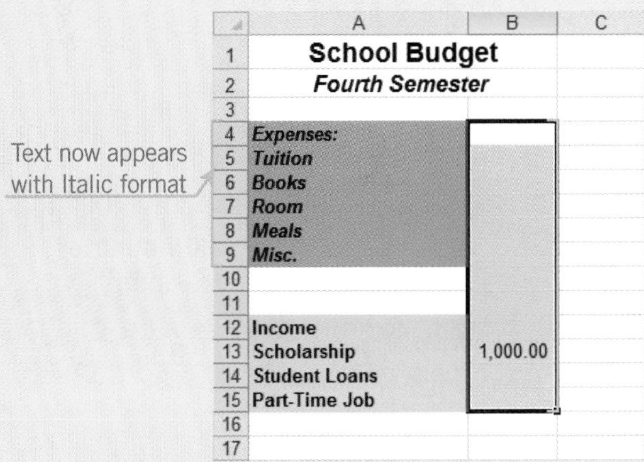

FIGURE 14–13
Fourth Semester worksheet with new formats

9. Apply the Formats macro to the **First Semester**, **Second Semester**, and **Third Semester** worksheets.
10. Save and close the workbook.
11. Close the Microsoft Visual Basic for Applications window by clicking the Close button in the upper-right corner of the window.

Creating a Button

Excel has many types of Form Controls that allow you to create items that would go on a form, such as a check box, scroll bar, and button. A ***button*** is called a control because it controls the actions that are assigned to it. When you create a button, you are asked to assign a macro to it. When you click the button, the macro will run.

VOCABULARY
button

You create a button by first choosing the Button form control and then drawing the button where you want it to appear in the worksheet. When you release the mouse button, the Assign Macro dialog box opens, prompting you to select the macro you want assigned to the button. You will draw two buttons in the worksheet and assign macros to them.

Step-by-Step 14.6

1. Open the **Pet Store** file from the drive and folder where your Data Files are stored. Save the workbook as a macro-enabled workbook with the file name **Pet Store Inventory**, followed by your initials.
2. On the Ribbon, click the **Developer** tab, if necessary. In the Controls group, click the **Insert** arrow button to display the available controls.
3. Click the **Button (Form Control)**, which is the first control in the top row.

4. Using **Figure 14–14** as a guide, hold the left mouse button down and then drag to create a button in cells A1:A3, which is the approximate size as the one shown. Release the mouse button. The Assign Macro dialog box opens, as shown in **Figure 14–15**.

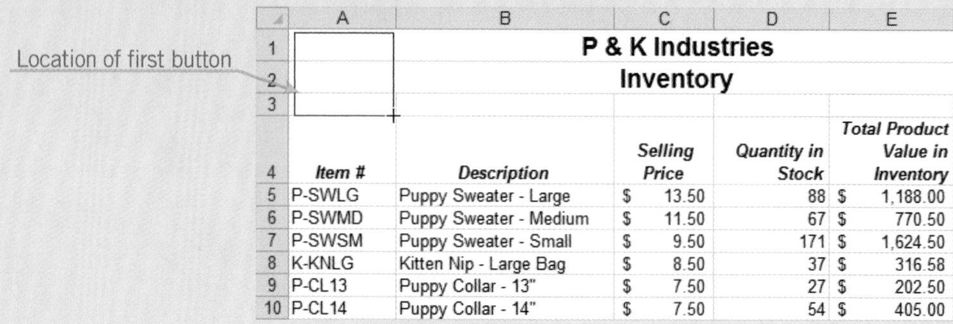

	A	B	C	D	E
1		P & K Industries			
2		Inventory			
3					
4	Item #	Description	Selling Price	Quantity in Stock	Total Product Value in Inventory
5	P-SWLG	Puppy Sweater - Large	$ 13.50	88	$ 1,188.00
6	P-SWMD	Puppy Sweater - Medium	$ 11.50	67	$ 770.50
7	P-SWSM	Puppy Sweater - Small	$ 9.50	171	$ 1,624.50
8	K-KNLG	Kitten Nip - Large Bag	$ 8.50	37	$ 316.58
9	P-CL13	Puppy Collar - 13"	$ 7.50	27	$ 202.50
10	P-CL14	Puppy Collar - 14"	$ 7.50	54	$ 405.00

FIGURE 14–14
Approximate size of button

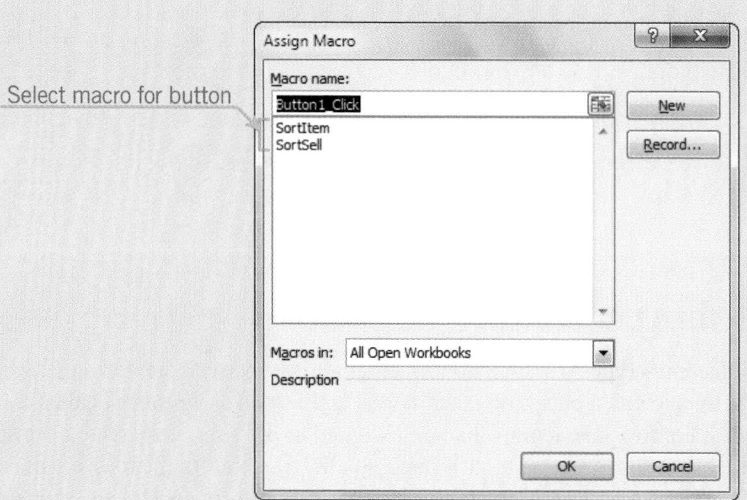

FIGURE 14–15
Assign Macro dialog box

5. Click **SortItem**, and then click **OK**. The button appears, as shown in **Figure 14–16**. Next, you will change the name of the button to a more meaningful name. To edit button text, you must right-click the button and choose Edit Text.

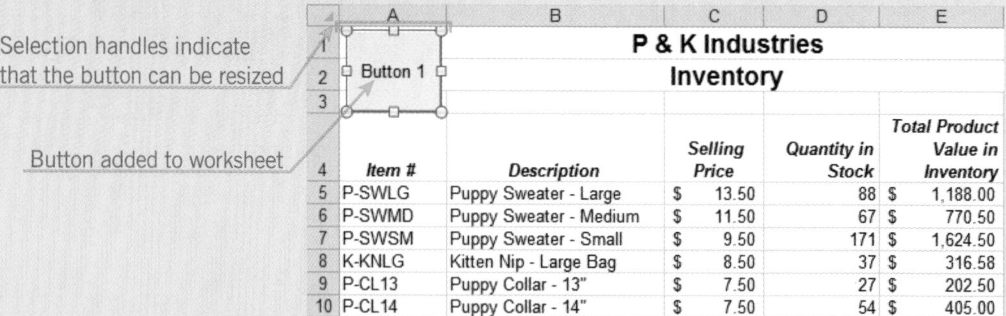

	A	B	C	D	E
1		P & K Industries			
2	Button 1	Inventory			
3					
4	Item #	Description	Selling Price	Quantity in Stock	Total Product Value in Inventory
5	P-SWLG	Puppy Sweater - Large	$ 13.50	88	$ 1,188.00
6	P-SWMD	Puppy Sweater - Medium	$ 11.50	67	$ 770.50
7	P-SWSM	Puppy Sweater - Small	$ 9.50	171	$ 1,624.50
8	K-KNLG	Kitten Nip - Large Bag	$ 8.50	37	$ 316.58
9	P-CL13	Puppy Collar - 13"	$ 7.50	27	$ 202.50
10	P-CL14	Puppy Collar - 14"	$ 7.50	54	$ 405.00

FIGURE 14–16
Worksheet with button

6. With the mouse pointer over the button, right-click the **button**, and then select **Edit Text** from the shortcut menu.

7. Highlight the existing text, press **Delete**, and then type **Sort by Item#**.
8. Click outside the button to view the results, and then test the button by clicking it. The worksheet data should be sorted by Item #. Next, you will create another button for the SortSell macro.
9. In the Controls group, click the **Insert** button and then click the **Button (Form Control)**. Draw another button of the same size to the right of the Sort by Item# button.
10. Click **SortSell** in the Assign Macro dialog box, and then click **OK**.
11. Right-click the new button and then click **Edit Text**.
12. Highlight the existing text, press **Delete**, and then type **Sort by Selling Price**.
13. Click outside the button to view the results. Compare your buttons to **Figure 14–17**. In the next Step-by-Step, you will align and resize the buttons.

Two buttons added

Sort by Item # | Sort by Selling Price

P & K Industries
Inventory

	A	B	C	D	E	F
4	*Item #*	*Description*	*Selling Price*	*Quantity in Stock*	*Total Product Value in Inventory*	
5	K-CL04	Kitten Collar - 4"	$ 5.50	45	$ 247.50	
6	K-CL05	Kitten Collar - 5"	$ 5.50	86	$ 473.00	
7	K-CL06	Kitten Collar - 6"	$ 5.50	554	$ 3,047.00	
8	K-CL07	Kitten Collar - 7"	$ 5.50	252	$ 1,386.00	
9	K-CL08	Kitten Collar - 8"	$ 6.50	66	$ 429.00	
10	K-CL09	Kitten Collar - 9"	$ 6.50	123	$ 799.50	
11	K-CL10	Kitten Collar - 10"	$ 6.50	504	$ 3,276.00	
12	K-CL11	Kitten Collar - 11"	$ 6.50	279	$ 1,813.50	
13	K-KNLG	Kitten Nip - Large Bag	$ 8.50	37	$ 316.58	
14	K-KNSM	Kitten Nip - Small Bag	$ 6.00	387	$ 2,322.00	
15	K-TOYB	Kitten Toy - Bird	$ 2.10	382	$ 802.20	
16	K-TOYM	Kitten Toy - Mouse	$ 2.10	28	$ 57.98	
17	K-TOYS	Kitten Toy - Snake	$ 2.10	111	$ 233.10	
18	P-CL05	Puppy Collar - 5"	$ 5.50	100	$ 550.00	
19	P-CL06	Puppy Collar - 6"	$ 5.50	23	$ 125.37	
20	P-CL07	Puppy Collar - 7"	$ 5.50	419	$ 2,304.50	
21	P-CL08	Puppy Collar - 8"	$ 5.50	90	$ 495.00	
22	P-CL09	Puppy Collar - 9"	$ 6.50	156	$ 1,014.00	
23	P-CL10	Puppy Collar - 10"	$ 6.50	600	$ 3,900.00	
24	P-CL11	Puppy Collar - 11"	$ 6.50	456	$ 2,964.00	
25	P-CL12	Puppy Collar - 12"	$ 6.50	117	$ 760.50	
26	P-CL13	Puppy Collar - 13"	$ 7.50	27	$ 202.50	
27	P-CL14	Puppy Collar - 14"	$ 7.50	54	$ 405.00	

Inventory | Sheet2 | Sheet3

Ready

FIGURE 14–17 Worksheet with both buttons added

14. Click the buttons one at a time to test the macros, save the workbook, and leave it open for the next Step-by-Step.

Aligning and Formatting Buttons

When you create several buttons in one workbook, aligning them can be difficult. Fortunately, Excel gives you an easy way to align and resize buttons. Since buttons have macros associated with them, you cannot click a button to select it without running the macro assigned to it.

To select a button with an assigned macro, you right-click the button. A shortcut menu appears. If you do not want any of the selections from the shortcut menu, click outside the menu to remove it from view. To select another button, press and hold Shift, and then right-click the other button. With more than one button selected, the Format tab appears on the Ribbon. The Format tab has options that let you make changes to the buttons, such as aligning buttons by their tops, bottoms, left sides, right sides, or centers.

You can also right-click a button and choose Format Control from the shortcut menu. The Format Control dialog box opens so you can make changes to the text format. When more than one object is selected, Format Object displays on the shortcut menu instead of Format Control. In the next Step-by-Step, you will align and change the text format for the buttons.

Step-by-Step 14.7

1. Place your mouse pointer over either button, then right-click to select it.
2. Place your mouse pointer over the other button, press and hold **Shift**, and then right-click the other button to select both buttons.
3. Click the **Format** tab and then click the **Align** button arrow in the Arrange group. The alignment options appear, as shown in **Figure 14–18**.

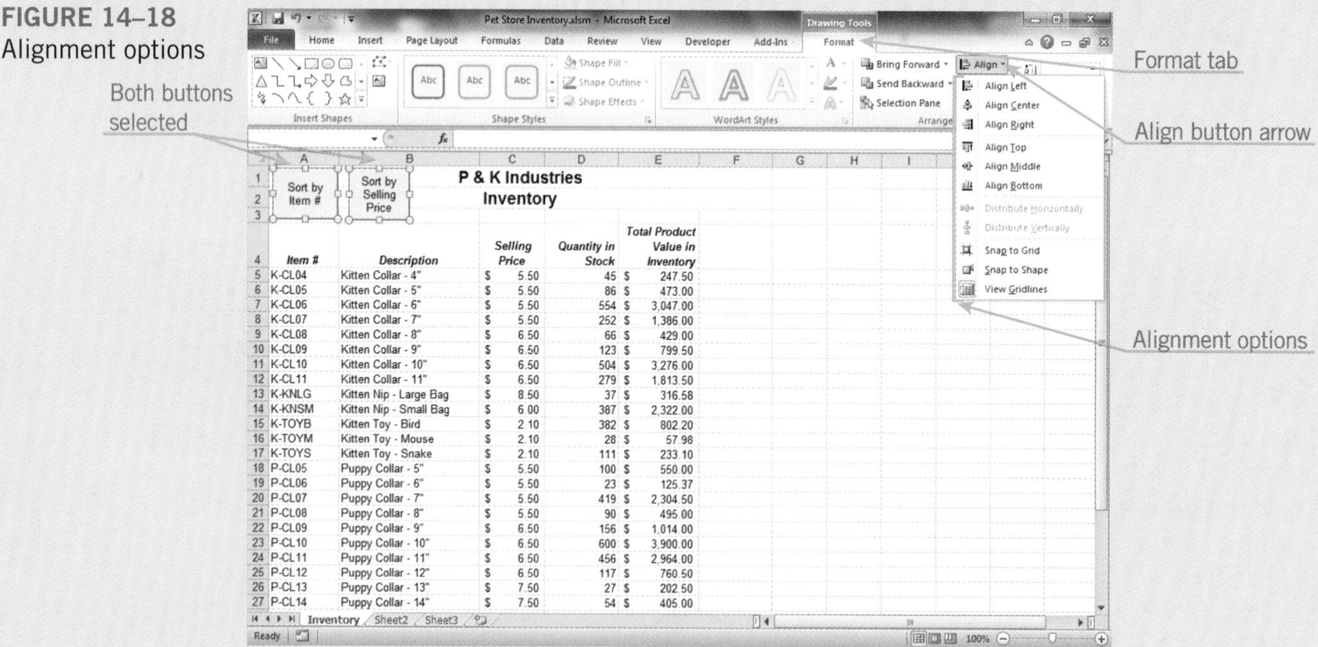

FIGURE 14–18
Alignment options

4. Click **Align Top** to align the buttons by their top edges. The tops of the buttons are the same distance from the top of the worksheet.

5. With both buttons still selected, right-click a button and then click **Format Object** from the shortcut menu. The Format Control dialog box opens, as shown in **Figure 14–19**.

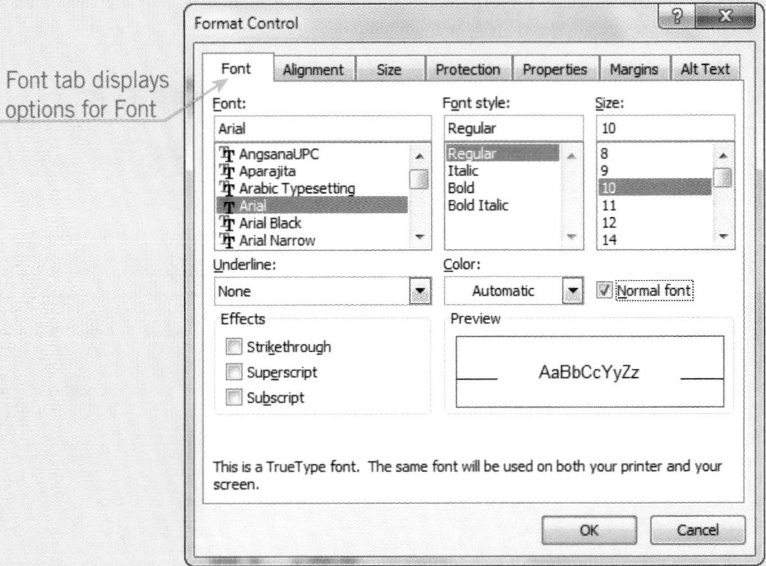

FIGURE 14–19
Format Control dialog box

6. In the Font Style list, click **Bold**.
7. Click the **Color** arrow, then click **Blue** located in the second row.
8. Click **OK** to close the Format Control dialog box. Your buttons appear with bold blue text. Compare your screen to **Figure 14–20**.

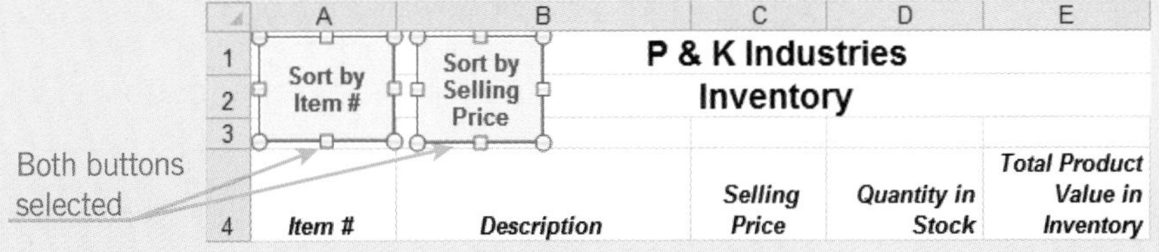

FIGURE 14–20
Aligned and formatted buttons

9. Click outside the buttons to deselect them.
10. Save and close the workbook.

Opening a Macro-Enabled Workbook

When you open a workbook with macros, a security warning appears on the Message Bar. The message lets you know that the macros have been disabled. This warning is displayed whenever the Disable all macros with notification option is chosen in the Macro Settings section of the Trust Center. To enable the macros, click the Enable Content button on the Message Bar. In the next Step-by-Step, you will open a macro-enabled workbook, enable the workbook macros, and run the macro that adds total functions to the data.

Step-by-Step 14.8

1. Open **Month End** from the drive and folder where your Data Files are stored. The security warning appears on the Message Bar, as shown in **Figure 14–21**.

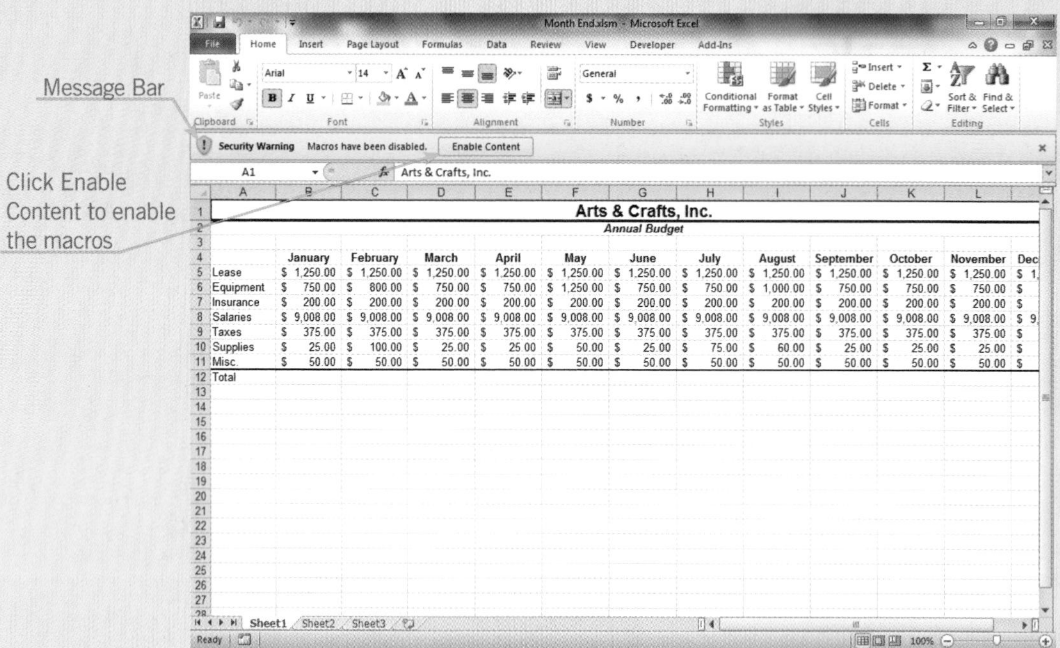

FIGURE 14–21 Message Bar with security warning

2. Save the workbook as **Month End Budget**, followed by your initials.
3. Click the **Enable Content** button.
4. Click the **Developer** tab, and then click the **Macros** button in the Code group.
5. Verify that the **Totals** macro is selected, and then click the **Run** button.
6. Click in **cell A1** to view the results of the Total function applied to each of the columns, as shown in **Figure 14–22**.

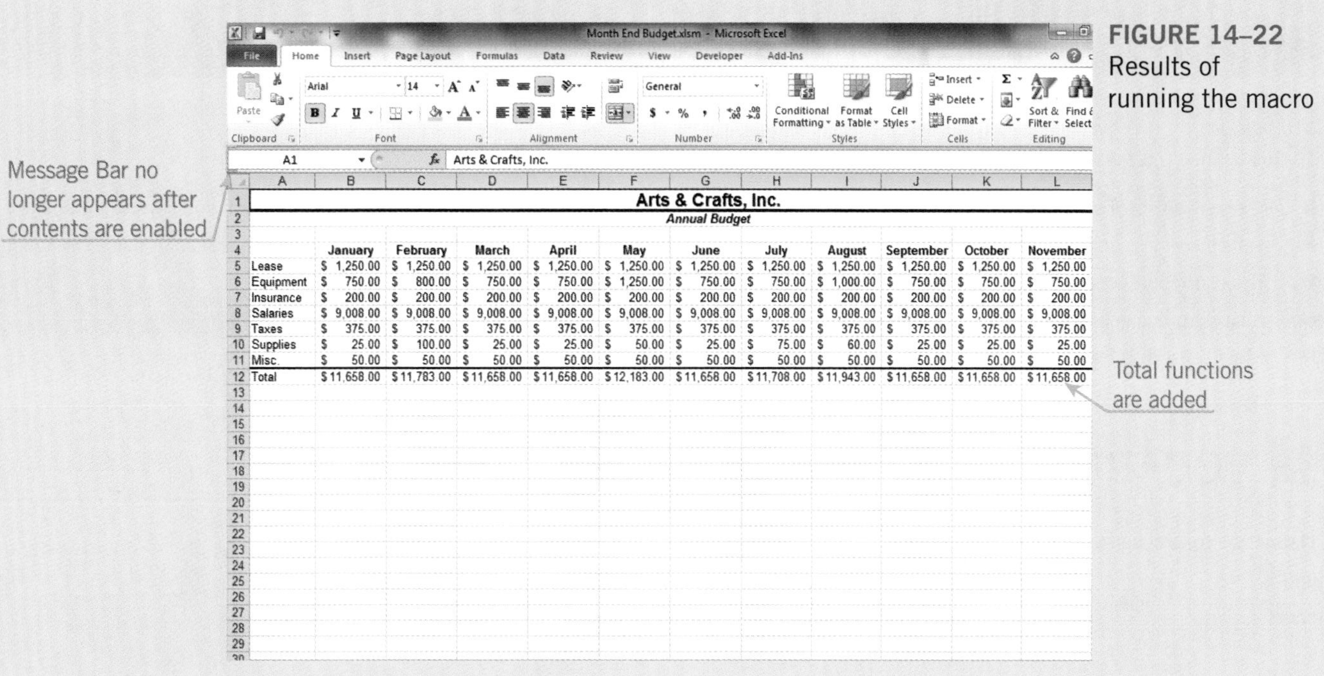

	January	February	March	April	May	June	July	August	September	October	November
Lease	$ 1,250.00	$ 1,250.00	$ 1,250.00	$ 1,250.00	$ 1,250.00	$ 1,250.00	$ 1,250.00	$ 1,250.00	$ 1,250.00	$ 1,250.00	$ 1,250.00
Equipment	$ 750.00	$ 800.00	$ 750.00	$ 750.00	$ 1,250.00	$ 750.00	$ 750.00	$ 1,000.00	$ 750.00	$ 750.00	$ 750.00
Insurance	$ 200.00	$ 200.00	$ 200.00	$ 200.00	$ 200.00	$ 200.00	$ 200.00	$ 200.00	$ 200.00	$ 200.00	$ 200.00
Salaries	$ 9,008.00	$ 9,008.00	$ 9,008.00	$ 9,008.00	$ 9,008.00	$ 9,008.00	$ 9,008.00	$ 9,008.00	$ 9,008.00	$ 9,008.00	$ 9,008.00
Taxes	$ 375.00	$ 375.00	$ 375.00	$ 375.00	$ 375.00	$ 375.00	$ 375.00	$ 375.00	$ 375.00	$ 375.00	$ 375.00
Supplies	$ 25.00	$ 100.00	$ 25.00	$ 25.00	$ 50.00	$ 25.00	$ 75.00	$ 60.00	$ 25.00	$ 25.00	$ 25.00
Misc.	$ 50.00	$ 50.00	$ 50.00	$ 50.00	$ 50.00	$ 50.00	$ 50.00	$ 50.00	$ 50.00	$ 50.00	$ 50.00
Total	$11,658.00	$11,783.00	$11,658.00	$11,658.00	$12,183.00	$11,658.00	$11,708.00	$11,943.00	$11,658.00	$11,658.00	$11,658.00

FIGURE 14–22 Results of running the macro

7. Save and close the workbook.

SUMMARY

In this lesson, you learned:

- Macros can automate frequently used tasks.
- You can review and change macro security settings.
- You can record a macro.
- A workbook can be saved as a macro-enabled workbook.
- After a macro is created, you can run the macro.
- If changes need to be made to a macro, you can edit the macro.
- Buttons are a type of form control that have a macro assigned to them.
- Buttons can be aligned and formatted.
- When you open a macro-enabled workbook, you can enable the workbook contents and run any macros in the workbook.

VOCABULARY REVIEW

Define the following terms:

button
code
macro
virus

REVIEW QUESTIONS

TRUE / FALSE

Circle T if the statement is true or F if the statement is false.

T F 1. Macros can automate frequently used tasks.

T F 2. To run a macro, you can only use the shortcut keys assigned to the macro.

T F 3. When you create a macro, Excel translates the macro into Visual Basic for Applications code.

T F 4. Once you run a macro, it cannot be edited.

T F 5. When you open a macro-enabled workbook, you click Enable Content so the macros will work.

FILL IN THE BLANK

1. The programming language that is embedded into Excel for macros is called ______________.
2. To save a workbook with a macro, you save it in the ______________ file format.
3. Since clicking a button runs a macro, to change the text formats on a button, you need to ______________ the button to select it.
4. If you want to stop recording a macro, you can select the Stop Recording button on the Developer tab or the Stop Recording button on the ______________.
5. A(n) ______________ is called a control because it controls the actions that are assigned to it.

WRITTEN QUESTIONS

Write a brief answer to the following questions.

1. What is a macro?

2. Explain how you would edit a macro.

3. Explain how to create a button.

4. How do you edit text that appears on the button?

5. How do you return to your worksheet from the Microsoft Visual Basic for Applications window?

PROJECTS

If you have a SAM 2010 user profile, your instructor may have assigned an autogradable version of the indicated project. If so, log into the SAM 2010 Web site at *www.cengage.com/sam2010* to download the instruction and start files.

PROJECT 14–1

1. Open the **Arts and Crafts** file from the drive and folder where your Data Files are stored.
2. Save the workbook as a macro-enabled workbook with the file name **Arts and Crafts Expenses**, followed by your initials.
3. Create a macro that inserts a blank column to the left of whichever cell is selected when the macro is run. Name the macro **Insert_Column** and assign a shortcut key of your choice.
4. Run the macro to be certain it works.
5. Print the worksheet.
6. Save and close the workbook.

SAM PROJECT 14–2

1. Open the **College Budget** file from the drive and folder where your Data Files are stored.
2. Save the workbook as a macro-enabled workbook with the file name **College Budget – Annual**, followed by your initials.
3. In the First Year worksheet, record a macro named **Blue_Format** without using shortcut keys. The macro should include the following formats:
   - Aqua, Accent 5, Lighter 40% cell background to cells **B4:G4**
   - Aqua, Accent 5, Lighter 60% cell background to cells **A5:A11**
   - Aqua, Accent 5, Lighter 40% cell background to cells **B12:G12**
4. Click the Second Year worksheet tab.
5. Create a button in cells D1:D2 and assign the Blue_Format macro to the button.
6. Click the button to apply the formats to the Second Year worksheet. Edit the button text to read **Add formats** using a bold font.
7. Save and print the workbook.
8. Close the workbook.

PROJECT 14–3

1. Open the **College Book** workbook from the drive and folder where your Data Files are stored.
2. Select Enable Contents.
3. Save the workbook in its macro-enabled workbook file type, and save the file as **College Book Sales**, followed by your initials.
4. Edit the **File_format** macro to include bold format to cells **A4:A12**.
5. Run the macro.
6. Print the worksheet.
7. Save and close the workbook.

CRITICAL THINKING

ACTIVITY 14–1

You are preparing an Excel worksheet for your company's year-end close. Open the **Project Sales** workbook from the drive and folder where your Data Files are stored and save it as a macro-enabled workbook with the file name **Project Sales Totals**, followed by your initials. Create a macro that totals each month's expenses and places them in row 18. Print the worksheet when you are done. Save and close the workbook.

ACTIVITY 14–2

Think of a macro you could write in Excel that could be applied to a document for your personal use. For example, think of your weekly schedule at your job, earnings, salary increases, or savings plans. Write the purpose of your macro and what it would accomplish for you.

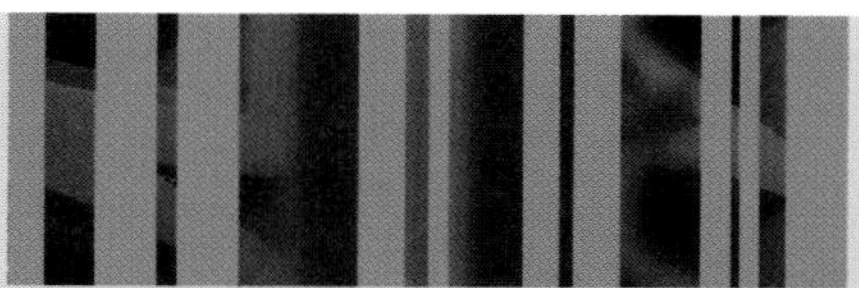

Estimated Time: 2.5 hours

LESSON 15

Working with Auditing and Analysis Tools

OBJECTIVES

Upon completion of this lesson, you should be able to:

- Use the Trace Precedents feature.
- Use the Trace Dependents feature.
- Use the Trace Error feature.
- Check for errors in functions.
- Perform a what-if analysis using the Goal Seek feature.
- Create a scenario.
- View the scenario summary.
- Consolidate data.
- Create a one-way data table.

VOCABULARY

audit

consolidating

dependent

precedent

Scenario Manager

tracer arrow

Introduction

Excel offers a number of tools that give you the ability to check for accuracy in formulas, solve problems with formulas, and analyze existing data. Using the auditing features such as Trace Precedents, Trace Dependents, and Trace Error, you can check for potential problems in cells that are used in a formula. The Trace Precedents feature finds the cells that are used in the function. The Trace Dependents feature looks for formulas that use data in a selected cell. The Trace Error feature locates cells that are used in the formula to assist in identifying the source of the error. To locate errors with formulas or functions, you can use the Error Checking tool.

You use the Goal Seek feature when you need to know the value required to arrive at a specific goal. The Scenario Manager is useful when you want to find out the result of a scenario based on changing data in several cells. Finally, you can use the Data Table feature when you want to project the results of a function in several cells, not just the one cell containing the function.

Using Trace Precedents

VOCABULARY
audit
precedent
tracer arrow

When you ***audit*** something, you are checking it for accuracy. When you look at a function in Excel to see if it is correct, you are doing an audit of that function. Excel's auditing feature, Trace Precedents, finds the cells that are used in the function. ***Precedents*** refer to cells that supply the values used in a function.

The Trace Precedents feature is useful if you want to confirm that the cells you intended to use in the function are in fact used by the function or if the result of a function does not look correct. Using this feature can help you locate the source of a problem.

For example, if you click a cell that has a SUM function and then click the Trace Precedents button, the cells that are used in this function are surrounded by a border. An arrow called a ***tracer arrow*** is drawn to the cell with the SUM function, as shown in **Figure 15–1**.

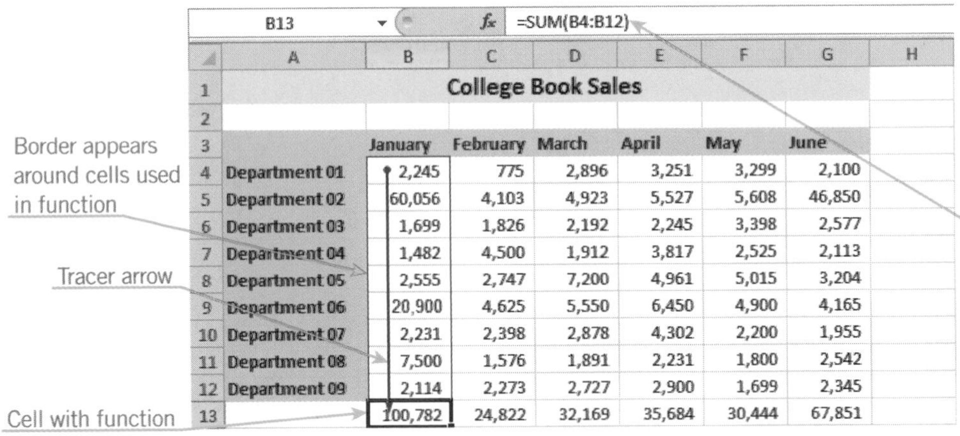

B13 =SUM(B4:B12)

	A	B	C	D	E	F	G	H
1	College Book Sales							
2								
3		January	February	March	April	May	June	
4	Department 01	2,245	775	2,896	3,251	3,299	2,100	
5	Department 02	60,056	4,103	4,923	5,527	5,608	46,850	
6	Department 03	1,699	1,826	2,192	2,245	3,398	2,577	
7	Department 04	1,482	4,500	1,912	3,817	2,525	2,113	
8	Department 05	2,555	2,747	7,200	4,961	5,015	3,204	
9	Department 06	20,900	4,625	5,550	6,450	4,900	4,165	
10	Department 07	2,231	2,398	2,878	4,302	2,200	1,955	
11	Department 08	7,500	1,576	1,891	2,231	1,800	2,542	
12	Department 09	2,114	2,273	2,727	2,900	1,699	2,345	
13		100,782	24,822	32,169	35,684	30,444	67,851	

FIGURE 15–1 Example of trace precedents

If the precedent cells are in a range of cells in the same row or column, a border is placed around them. When you print the worksheet, the tracer arrows in your worksheet will print as well. However, when you save the file, the tracer arrows are removed.

Step-by-Step 15.1

1. Open the **Grades** file from the drive and folder where your Data Files are stored.
2. Save the workbook as **History Grades**, followed by your initials. The workbook includes test grades for a history test.
3. Click **cell E19**. This cell has the function that averages the test scores. You want to check the function for accuracy.
4. Click the **Formulas** tab, then click the **Trace Precedents** button in the Formula Auditing group. The range of cells used in the function has a border. A tracer arrow displays from cell B6 and points to cell E19, as shown in **Figure 15–2**.

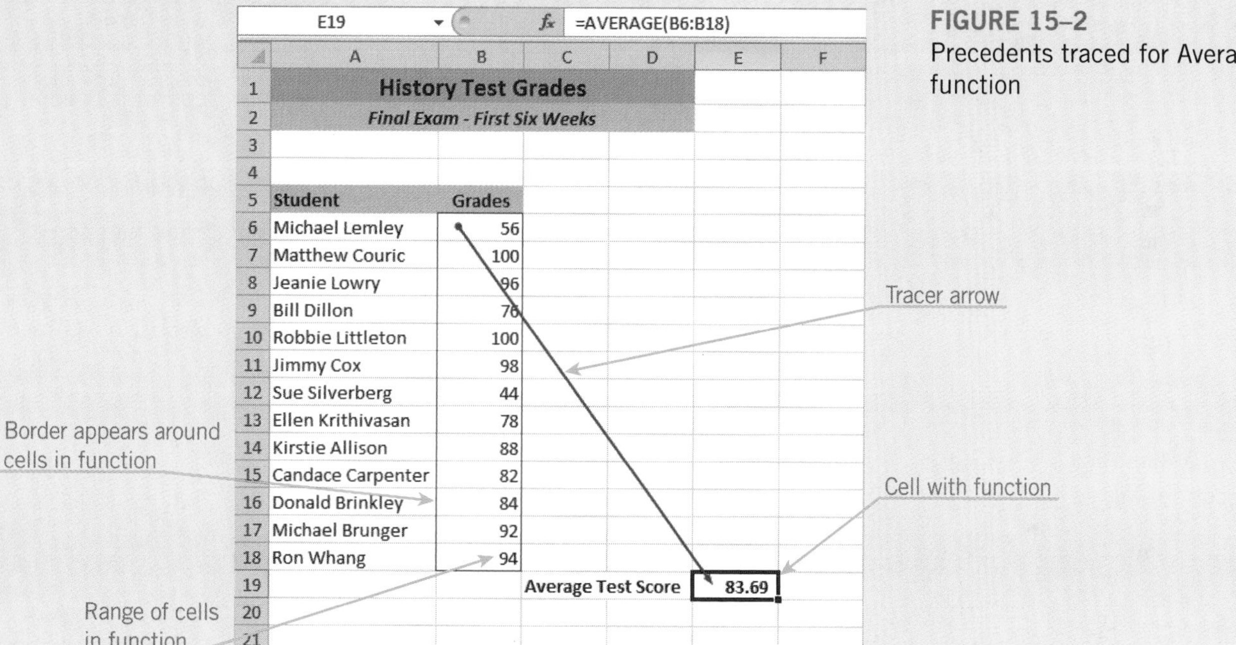

FIGURE 15–2
Precedents traced for Average function

5. Print the worksheet.
6. In the Formula Auditing group, click the **down arrow** next to the Remove Arrows button and select **Remove Precedent Arrows** from the list.
7. Save the workbook and leave it open for the next Step-by-Step.

EXTRA FOR EXPERTS

Remember, a formula is typed in by the user and can be simple, such as =B5 + B6. Functions are shown next to parentheses and require arguments, such as =SUM(B5:B6).

Using Trace Dependents

VOCABULARY
dependent

The Trace Dependents feature works by locating formulas and/or functions that depend on the value in a selected cell. For example, if you select a cell containing data and then click the Trace Dependents button, a tracer arrow is drawn from the selected cell, called the ***dependent***, pointing to the cell with the function. In other words, the function depends on the data in the selected cell to calculate the answer. You may find that several functions depend on the data in the selected cell and, in that case, you will have several tracer arrows drawn from that cell to the various functions.

After you click the Trace Dependents or Trace Precedents buttons, you can remove the tracer arrows by clicking the Remove Arrows button in the Formula Auditing group. The Remove Arrows button gives you the option to remove the Trace Dependents tracer arrows, the Trace Precedents tracer arrows, or all the tracer arrows. In the next Step-by-Step, you will add Trace Dependents tracer arrows and then remove them.

Step-by-Step 15.2

1. Click **cell B7.** You could select any cell with data to see if it is used in a function.
2. In the Formula Auditing group, click the **Trace Dependents** button. The Trace Dependents tracer arrow points to cell E19 with the function.
3. Click **cell B15**.
4. Click the **Trace Dependents** button. Both cells B7 and B15 have tracer arrows that point to the cell with the function, as shown in **Figure 15–3**.

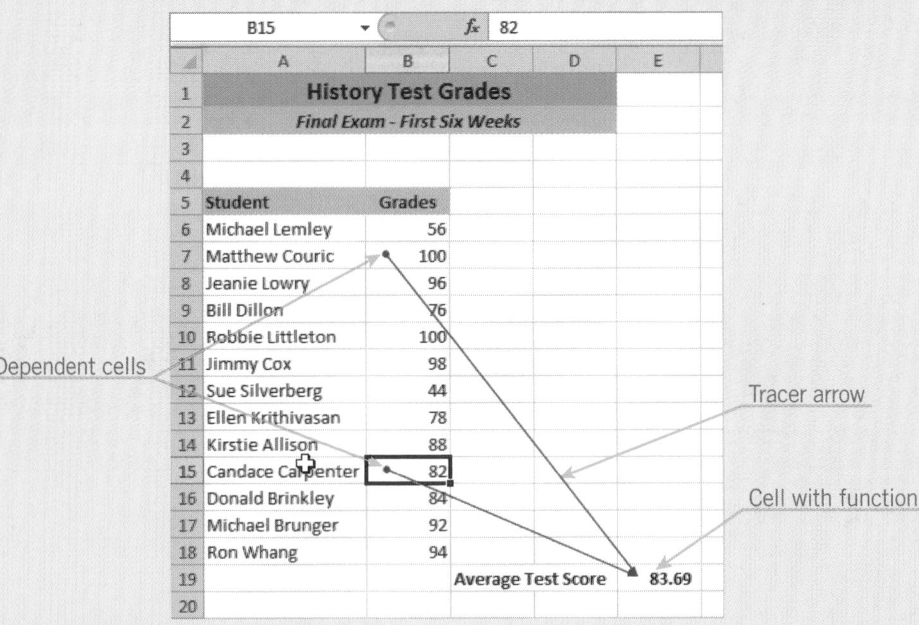

FIGURE 15–3
Average function depends on cells with tracer arrows

5. Print the worksheet.
6. Save and close the workbook.

Using Trace Error

Sometimes when you are entering formulas or functions, you may notice that an error displays instead of the result of the formula or function. For example, if you enter an Average function in a cell but #DIV/0! appears instead, the calculation includes an error. The #DIV/0! error indicates that either the function is dividing by a zero or that cells used in the function have missing data. To locate the source of the error, you click the cell with the error and then click the Trace Error command. Once the error is traced, you can make changes to the data to correct the error.

In addition, Excel displays an information icon next to the cell with the error status. When you click the icon, a list containing the error and options for resolving the error appears. The error found using Trace Error is highlighted in the list. Divide by Zero Error is an example of a possible error. Seeing the error helps you fix the error in the cell. If you want more assistance, you can select Help on this Error from the list to access the Help feature in Excel. In the next Step-by-Step, you will trace errors found when an Average function was copied.

Step-by-Step 15.3

1. Open the **Book Sales** file from the drive and folder where your Data Files are stored.
2. Save the workbook as **Yearly Book Sales**, followed by your initials.
3. Click **cell G14**. This cell contains an error. Next you will use the Trace Error feature to find the problem.
4. In the Formula Auditing group, click the **Error Checking** button arrow, and then click **Trace Error**. The cells used in the formula are surrounded by a border, and a tracer arrow points from these cells to the function in cell G14, as shown in **Figure 15–4**. Notice the information icon that appears next to the function.

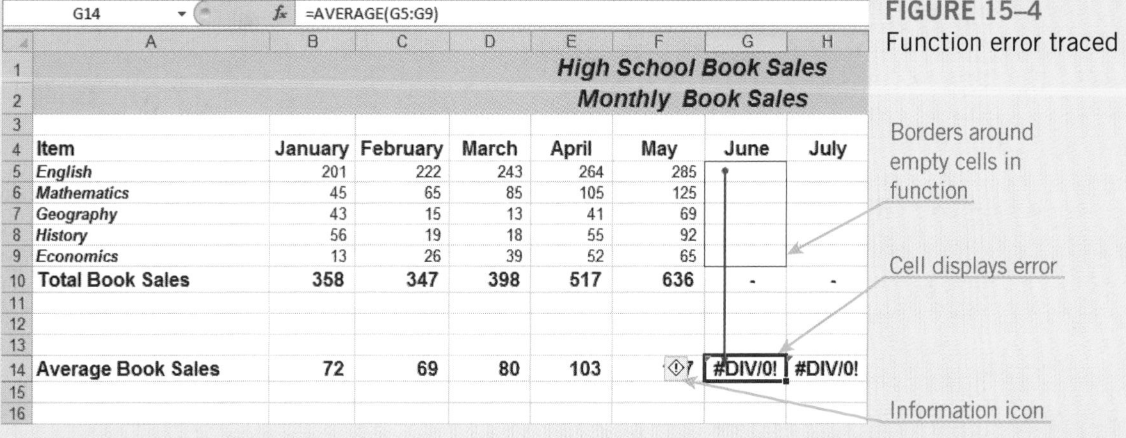

FIGURE 15–4 Function error traced

5. Click the **information icon** arrow to display the information list, as shown in **Figure 15–5**. The Divide by Zero Error is highlighted, providing information about the error. Next, you will trace the error for adjacent cells that also show an error.

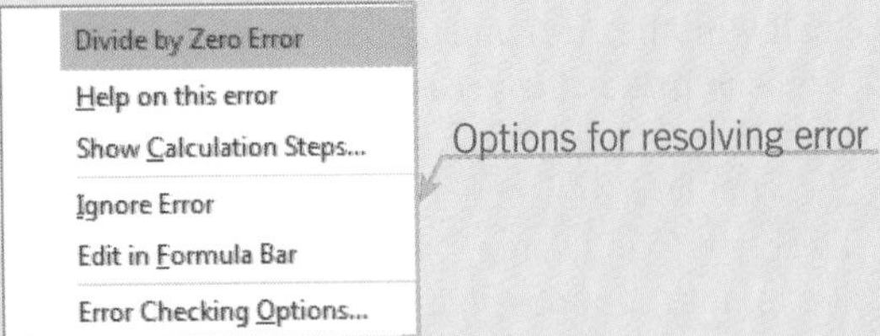

FIGURE 15–5 Information list

6. Select **cell H14**.
7. Click the **Error Checking** arrow button, and then click **Trace Error**. The cells used in this function are surrounded by a border. You realize that this error occurs not because the Average function is averaging zeros, which would not result in an error. Instead, you see that Columns G and H contain no data. You will now enter zeros in the cells that are used by the function.
8. Select **cell G5**, type **0**, and then press **Enter**.
9. Type **0** in cells **G6:G9** and then save the workbook to remove the tracer arrows.
10. Type **0** in cells **H5:H9**. Compare your completed worksheet to **Figure 15–6**.

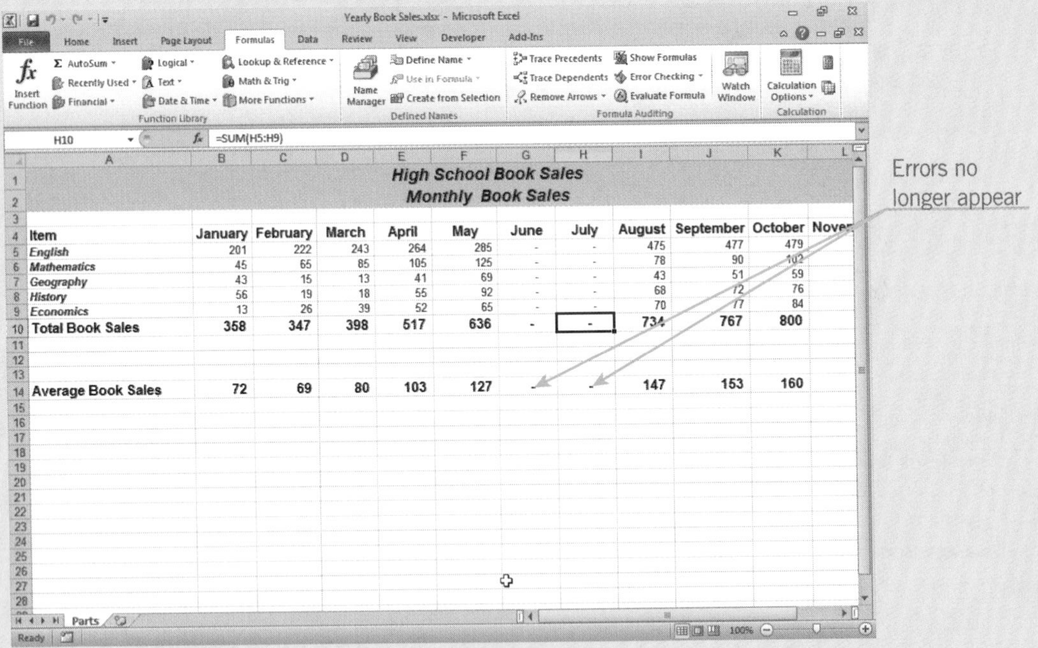

FIGURE 15–6 Corrected worksheet

11. Save and close the workbook.

Checking for Errors

The Trace Error feature is helpful when you are just tracing one cell for an error. The Error Checking feature is a better choice when your worksheet has lots of data and you want Excel to check all of the formulas and functions in the worksheet for potential problems. When an error is located, the Error Checking dialog box gives you information about the error. In this dialog box, you can choose to show the calculation steps to help identify where the problem occurs. If no errors are found, a dialog box lets you know that the error check for the worksheet is complete.

Step-by-Step 15.4

1. Open the **Auto Parts** file from the drive and folder where your Data Files are stored.
2. Save the workbook as **Auto Parts Sales**, followed by your initials.
3. Click the **Formulas** tab, then in the Formula Auditing group, click the **Error Checking** button arrow, and then click **Error Checking**. The Error Checking dialog box opens, letting you know that an error occurred with the AVERAGE function in cell N14. You may need to move the dialog box out of the way so that you can see the function with the border in cell N14. See **Figure 15–7**.

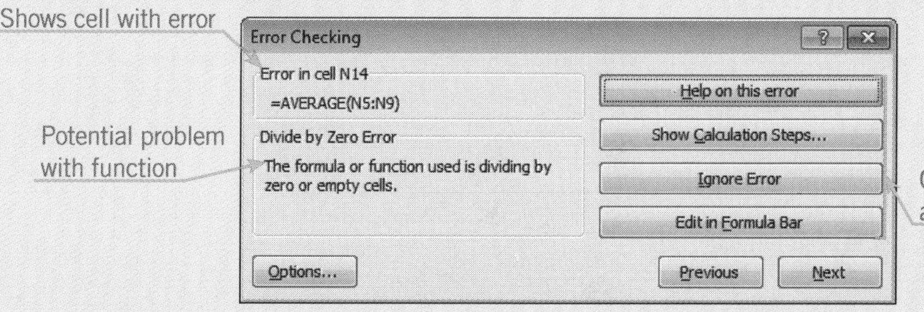

FIGURE 15–7
Error Checking dialog box

4. In the Error Checking dialog box, click the **Show Calculation Steps** button to open the Evaluate Formula dialog box. In the Evaluate Formula dialog box, the function is displayed in the Evaluation box, as shown in **Figure 15–8**. You decide to continue to evaluate the function to see more information about the error.

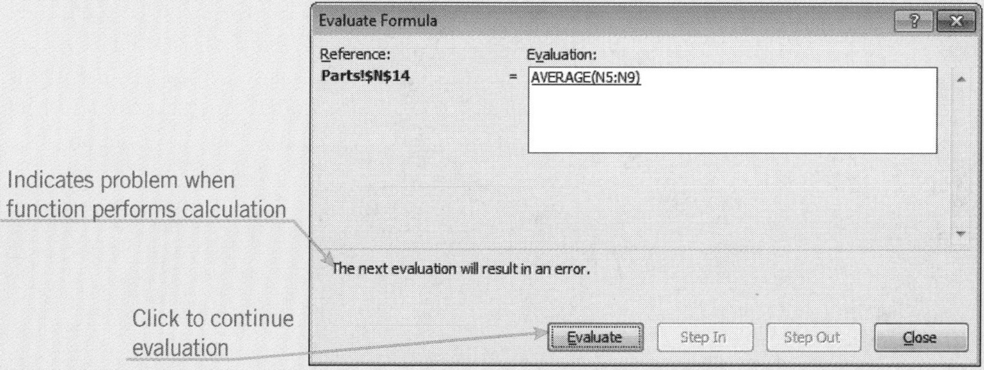

FIGURE 15–8
Evaluate Formula dialog box

5. Click the **Evaluate** button. The Evaluation box now shows the results of the function when calculated. See **Figure 15–9**.

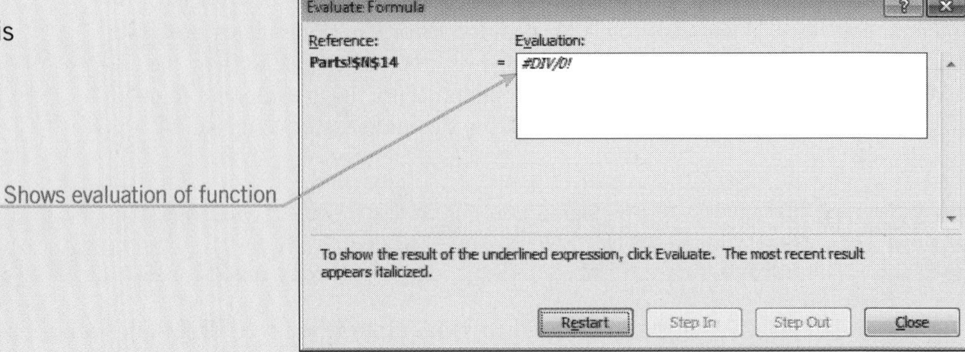

FIGURE 15–9
Evaluation box when function is evaluated

6. Close the Evaluate Formula dialog box.
7. Click the **Next** button to see if the worksheet contains any additional errors. A message box appears letting you know that no additional errors were found and the error check is complete. See **Figure 15–10**.

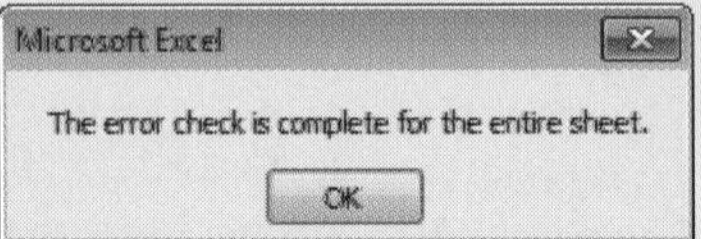

FIGURE 15–10
Message box

8. Click **OK** to close the message box.
9. Select **cell N14**, if necessary, and then press **Delete** to delete the formula that should not be in this cell.
10. Save and close the workbook.

Performing a What-if Analysis Using the Goal Seek Feature

Functions and formulas usually perform mathematical calculations using known values. Sometimes, however, you may know the result (the goal), but you don't necessarily know the values needed to arrive at the goal. For example, you may want to save $15,000 for your first year of college that starts five years from now. You need to know how much to save each month in order to meet this goal. The **Goal Seek** feature finds the unknown value you need in order to accomplish your goal.

The Goal Seek feature is referred to as a "what-if" analysis tool. In other words, "What if I want to save $15,000 in five years, how much do I need to save each month?" When you use Goal Seek, you will be asked for some information in the Goal Seek dialog box, shown in **Figure 15–11**.

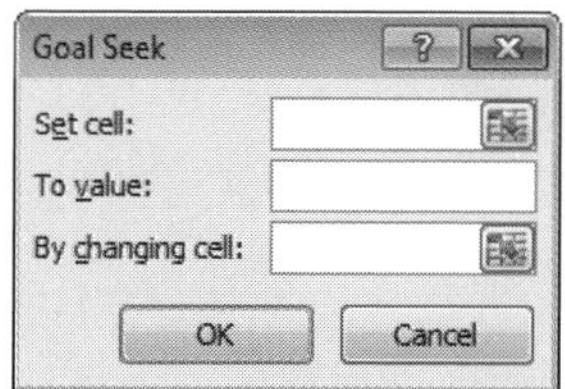

FIGURE 15–11 Goal Seek dialog box

In the Set cell text box, you enter the cell containing the function that Excel uses to find the answer. Next, enter the desired goal in the To value text box. In the By changing cell text box, you enter the cell where you want the answer displayed.

Step-by-Step 15.5

1. On the Ribbon, click the **File** tab, click **New**, and then double-click **Blank workbook**. You will use a new workbook for this Step-by-Step. Save the workbook as **College Fund Goal**, followed by your initials.
2. Click **cell C5**. Because this is a blank worksheet, you can select any cell in which to enter the formula. You will enter a formula that finds out how much money you need to save each month for five years in order to save $15,000.
3. Type **=A5*12*5** and then press **Enter**. This formula takes the unknown monthly savings amount in cell A5 and multiplies it by 12 payments per year for 5 years. Cell A5 is chosen at random; you could choose another cell to accomplish the same goal.
4. Select **cell C5**, and then click the **Data** tab.
5. In the Data Tools group, click the **What-If Analysis** arrow button, and then click **Goal Seek**. You should see cell C5 in the Set cell text box, as shown in **Figure 15–12**.

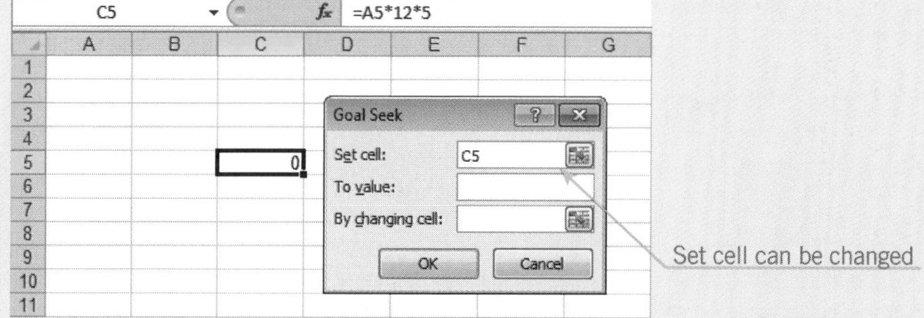

FIGURE 15–12
The Goal Seek dialog box

6. Click in the **To value** text box, then type **15000**. This is the goal value, the amount of money you wish to save. Notice that you do not need to enter the comma, but it is okay if you do.

7. Click in the **By changing cell** text box, and then type **A5**. This cell will show the goal seek solution. The completed dialog box should appear as shown in **Figure 15–13**.

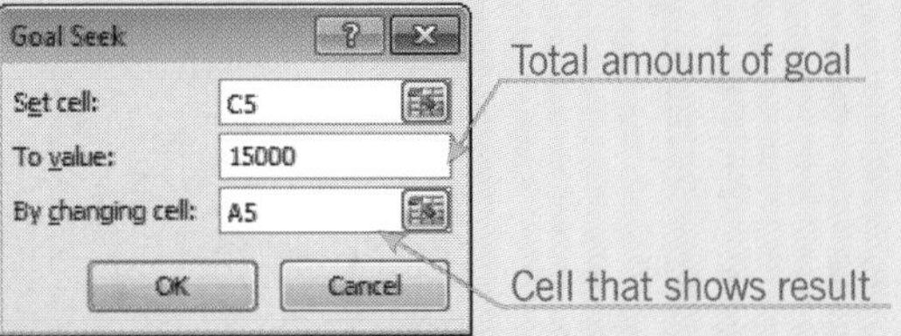

FIGURE 15–13
Completed Goal Seek dialog box

8. Click **OK**. The Goal Seek Status dialog box opens to let you know that it has found a solution, as shown in **Figure 15–14**.

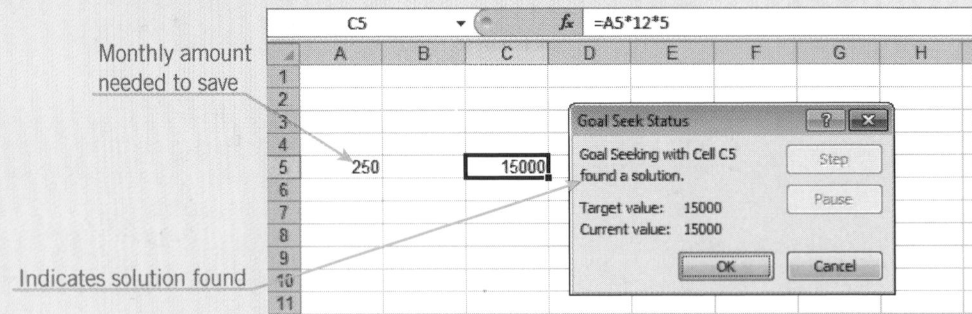

FIGURE 15–14
Goal Seek Status dialog box

9. Click **OK** to close the Goal Seek Status dialog box. Next you will use Goal Seek to find out how much money needs to be saved each month if you need $17,500 for the first year of college.
10. Click the **What-If Analysis** arrow button, and then click **Goal Seek**.
11. Verify that cell C5 is still displayed in the Set cell text box, click in the **To value** text box, and then type **17500**.
12. Press **Tab** to move to the By changing cell text box, and then type **A5**. Click **OK**, then compare your screen to **Figure 15–15**.

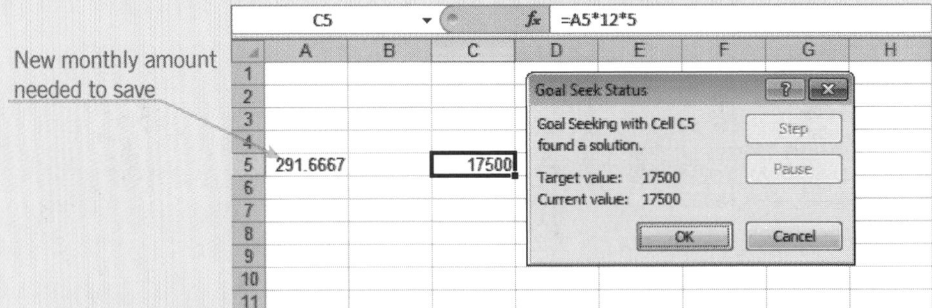

FIGURE 15–15
Completed Goal Seek Status dialog box with new value

13. Click **OK** to close the Goal Seek Status dialog box, and then click in **cell A5**.
14. Click the **Home** tab, and then click the **Accounting Number Format** button $ in the Number group to apply the currency format with two decimal places.
15. Save and close the workbook.

Creating Scenarios

Another type of "what-if" analysis is the Scenario feature. When you use Goal Seek, it focuses on changing one cell of data. By comparison, the ***Scenario Manager*** performs a "what-if" analysis that lets you change several cells of data.

Scenarios are sometimes used to view various changes in expenses. For example, some of your expenses may increase while others may decrease. You can create a scenario based on expenses increasing and another scenario based on expenses decreasing. Using scenarios to view these changes lets you see how much more or how much less money you or your company will make in the future. When you create scenarios, you need to give the scenario a name, such as Best Case for the decrease in expenses or Worst Case for the increase in expenses. In addition, you may want to create a scenario with the original data so you can refer back to it.

VOCABULARY
Scenario Manager

Step-by-Step 15.6

1. Open the **Blooming Yards** file from the drive and folder where your Data Files are stored, and then save the workbook as **Blooming Yards Income and Expenses**, followed by your initials.
2. Click the **Data** tab. In the Data Tools group, click the **What-If Analysis** button arrow, and then click **Scenario Manager**. The Scenario Manager dialog box opens, as shown in **Figure 15–16**. Notice that it does not show any scenarios yet. You will now add one.

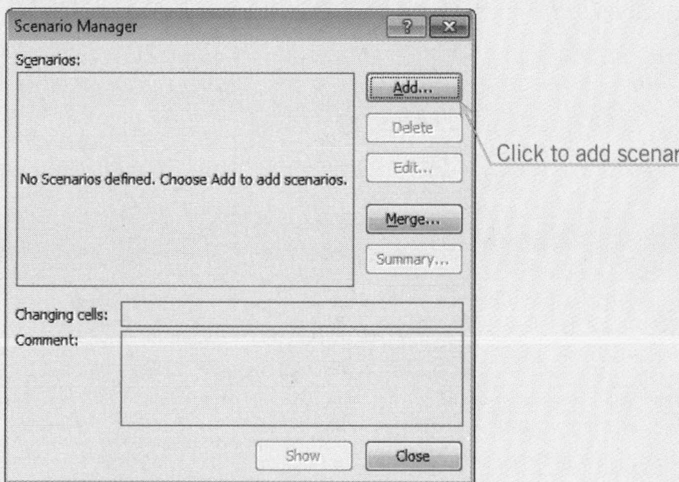

FIGURE 15–16
Scenario Manager dialog box

3. Click the **Add** button to display the Add Scenario dialog box, as shown in **Figure 15–17**. Notice that you can select the Prevent changes check box in the Add Scenario dialog box to avoid unwanted changes to the scenarios, such as someone opening the workbook and editing the scenarios.

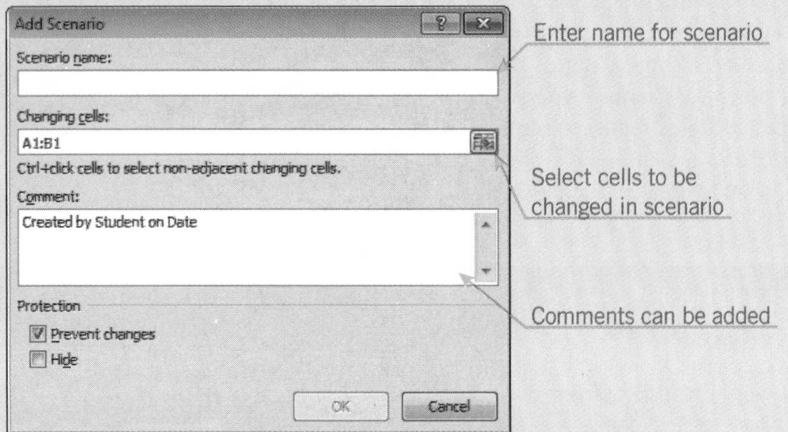

FIGURE 15–17
Add Scenario dialog box

4. In the Scenario name text box, type **Current Expenses**.
5. Press **Tab** to move to the Changing cells text box, then type **B10:B17**. You select this range of cells because they are the actual expenses related to planting trees and flowers.
6. Click **OK**. The values you entered in the Changing cells text box appear in the Scenario Values dialog box, as displayed in **Figure 15–18**. Values in the other cells in the range are displayed as well.

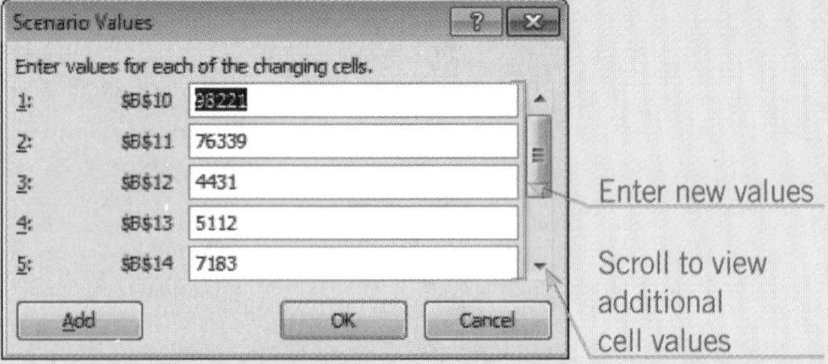

FIGURE 15–18
Scenario Values dialog box

7. Click **OK**. The current expenses are saved, and the Scenario Manager dialog box opens.
8. Click **Add**.
9. In the Scenario name text box, type **Best Case Scenario**, then click **OK**.
10. In the text box next to $B$10 type **85000**, press **Tab** to move to the text box next to $B$11, and then type **70000**. This scenario will show us what would happen if the Flowers expense went down to $85,000 and the Fruit/Vegetables expense decreased to $70,000.
11. Click **OK** to close the Scenarios Values dialog box. The Best Case Scenario is completed.

12. Click **Add**. In the Scenario name text box, type **Worst Case Scenario**, and then click **OK**.
13. In the text box next to $B$10 type **105000**, press **Tab** to move to the next text box, type **85000**, and then click **OK** to close the Scenario Values dialog box. This scenario will show what would happen if expenses increased. The Scenario Manager dialog box should appear as shown in **Figure 15–19**.

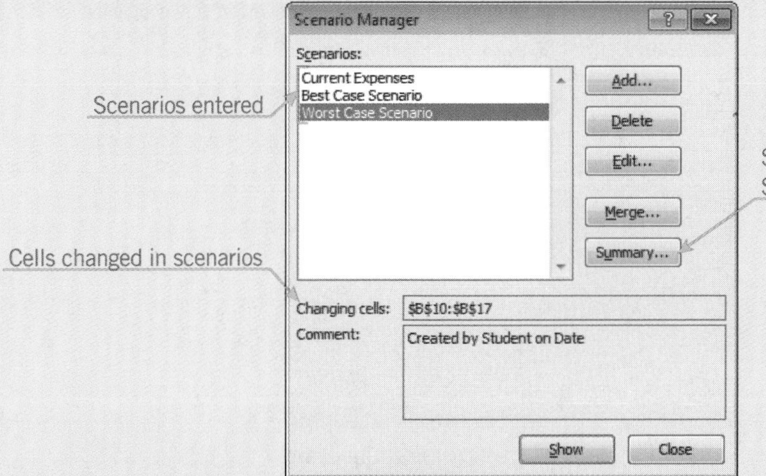

FIGURE 15–19
Scenario Manager dialog box with scenarios

14. Leave the workbook open for the next Step-by-Step.

Viewing the Scenario Summary

After you've created scenarios, the Scenario Manager lets you view them in a formatted report on a separate worksheet. Excel automatically names the new worksheet *Scenario Summary* and applies formatting to the data. Each time you request a scenario summary, Excel creates a new worksheet that includes the data currently in the worksheet.

Step-by-Step 15.7

1. In the Scenario Manager dialog box, click the **Summary** button. The Scenario Summary dialog box opens, as shown in **Figure 15–20**.

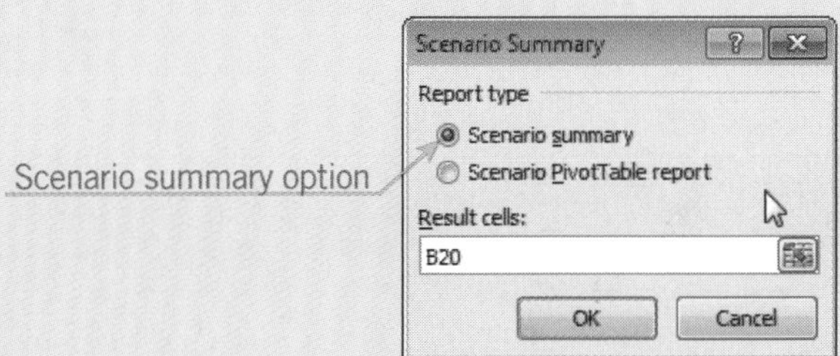

FIGURE 15–20
Scenario Summary dialog box

2. With the Scenario summary option button selected, click **OK** to display the Scenario Summary. Compare your screen to **Figure 15–21**. Next, you will change some of the current values.

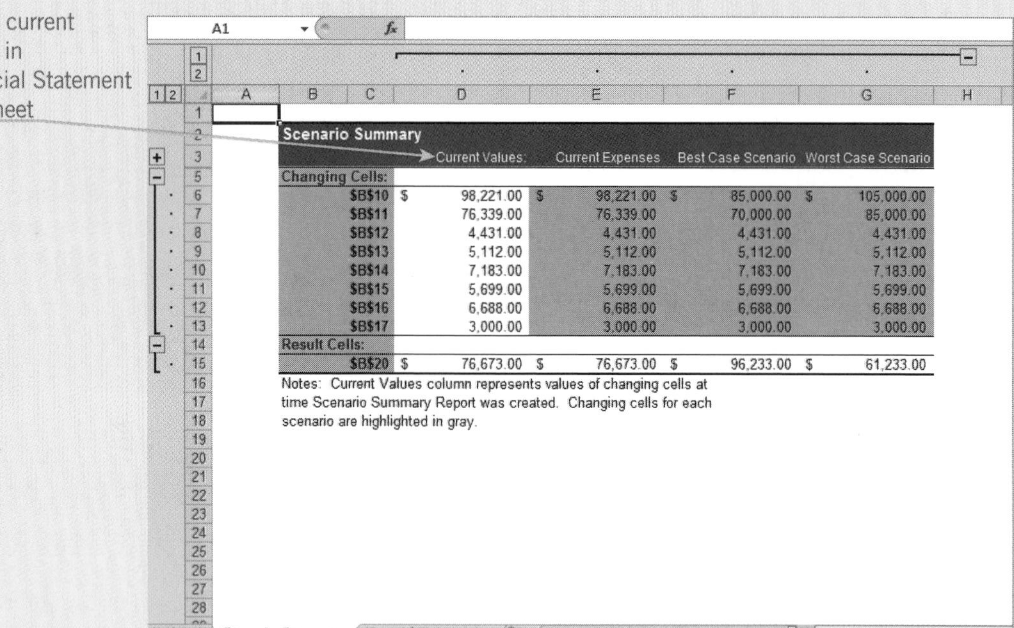

Scenario Summary					
		Current Values:	Current Expenses	Best Case Scenario	Worst Case Scenario
Changing Cells:					
	$B$10	$ 98,221.00	$ 98,221.00	$ 85,000.00	$ 105,000.00
	$B$11	76,339.00	76,339.00	70,000.00	85,000.00
	$B$12	4,431.00	4,431.00	4,431.00	4,431.00
	$B$13	5,112.00	5,112.00	5,112.00	5,112.00
	$B$14	7,183.00	7,183.00	7,183.00	7,183.00
	$B$15	5,699.00	5,699.00	5,699.00	5,699.00
	$B$16	6,688.00	6,688.00	6,688.00	6,688.00
	$B$17	3,000.00	3,000.00	3,000.00	3,000.00
Result Cells:					
	$B$20	$ 76,673.00	$ 76,673.00	$ 96,233.00	$ 61,233.00

Notes: Current Values column represents values of changing cells at time Scenario Summary Report was created. Changing cells for each scenario are highlighted in gray.

FIGURE 15–21
Scenario Summary worksheet

3. Click the **Financial Statement** worksheet tab. You will now change data in the worksheet and then create a new scenario summary.
4. Select **cell B17** and then type **500**.
5. Select **cell B14**, type **5345**, and then press **Enter**.
6. On the Data tab in the Data Tools group, click the **What-If Analysis** button arrow, and then click **Scenario Manager**.
7. Click the **Summary** button.
8. Click **OK**. The new Scenario Summary worksheet appears as shown in **Figure 15–22**. Notice that the data you revised in the worksheet is shown in this scenario summary.

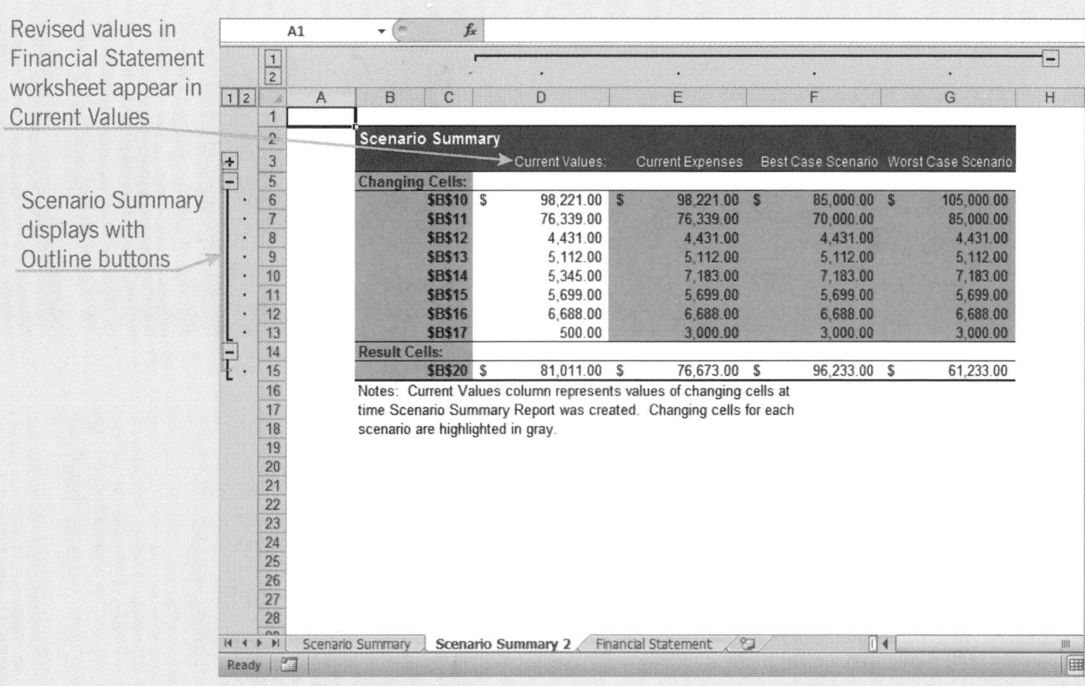

	Current Values:	Current Expenses	Best Case Scenario	Worst Case Scenario
Changing Cells:				
$B$10	$ 98,221.00	$ 98,221.00	$ 85,000.00	$ 105,000.00
$B$11	76,339.00	76,339.00	70,000.00	85,000.00
$B$12	4,431.00	4,431.00	4,431.00	4,431.00
$B$13	5,112.00	5,112.00	5,112.00	5,112.00
$B$14	5,345.00	7,183.00	7,183.00	7,183.00
$B$15	5,699.00	5,699.00	5,699.00	5,699.00
$B$16	6,688.00	6,688.00	6,688.00	6,688.00
$B$17	500.00	3,000.00	3,000.00	3,000.00
Result Cells:				
$B$20	$ 81,011.00	$ 76,673.00	$ 96,233.00	$ 61,233.00

Notes: Current Values column represents values of changing cells at time Scenario Summary Report was created. Changing cells for each scenario are highlighted in gray.

FIGURE 15–22 New Scenario Summary worksheet

9. Save, print, and close the workbook.

Consolidating Data

To consolidate means to combine or unite. In Excel, ***consolidating*** involves bringing data from several worksheets together into one worksheet. You can choose various functions to use when consolidating, such as Sum, Average, or Count, just to name a few. You can consolidate data from several worksheets in the same workbook or between several workbooks.

VOCABULARY
consolidating

The Consolidate feature is very flexible. The data that you consolidate does not need to be in the exact location in each of the worksheets. In the Consolidate dialog box, you can select the cells you want to consolidate, or, if you named the ranges, you can enter the range names.

You also choose the function you want to use, such as SUM, to consolidate data. In the next Step-by-Step, you will consolidate data from three worksheets into one worksheet so that you can see the totals.

Step-by-Step 15.8

1. Open the **Coastal Sales** file from the drive and folder where your Data Files are stored, and then save the workbook as **Coastal Sales – First Quarter**, followed by your initials. The workbook has four worksheets: First Quarter Sales, January, February, and March. You will add the data from the monthly worksheets into the First Quarter Sales worksheet. In each of the monthly worksheets, the range C5:C25 has been named using the month name.

2. Click the **First Quarter Sales** worksheet tab, then select **B5:B25**.
3. Click the **Data** tab, and then click the **Consolidate** button in the Data Tools group. The Consolidate dialog box opens, as shown in **Figure 15–23**.

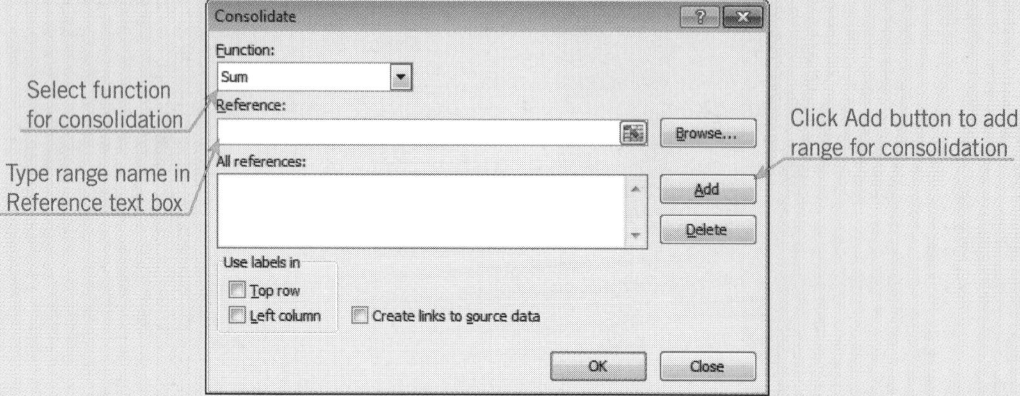

FIGURE 15–23
Consolidate dialog box

4. In the Reference text box, type **January**, and then click the **Add** button.
5. In the Reference text box, type **February**, and then click the **Add** button.
6. In the Reference text box, type **March**, click the **Add** button, and then compare your screen to **Figure 15–24**.

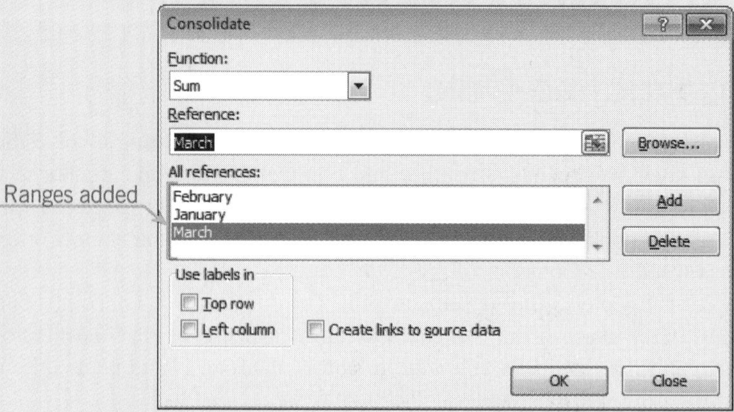

FIGURE 15–24
Completed Consolidate dialog box

7. Click **OK** to close the Consolidate dialog box, then view the consolidated totals in the First Quarter Sales worksheet shown in **Figure 15–25**.

	A	B	C	D	E
1		**Coastal Sales**			
2		**Quarterly Sales by Employee**			
3					
4	**Division**	**Sales**	**Last Name**	**First Name**	**Employee Name**
5	West	$ 174,794	Jones	David	David Jones
6	East	$ 220,240	Barbaros	Jeremiah	Jeremiah Barbaros
7	West	$ 277,503	Bennett	Tai	Tai Bennett
8	West	$ 349,653	Caldwell	Sue	Sue Caldwell
9	East	$ 440,563	Clavell	Fugi	Fugi Clavell
10	West	$ 555,110	Colmenaros	Gary	Gary Colmenaros
11	North	$ 516,252	Crawford	Katie	Katie Crawford
12	West	$ 181,810	Dominquez	David	David Dominquez
13	South	$ 169,084	Dominquez	Gary	Gary Dominquez
14	East	$ 157,248	Gebal	Barbara	Barbara Gebal
15	West	$ 146,240	Giraddelli	Lilly	Lilly Giraddelli
16	West	$ 136,004	Gonzalez	Kate	Kate Gonzalez
17	South	$ 126,483	Gonzalez	Lisa	Lisa Gonzalez
18	West	$ 238,334	Frazel	Sallye	Sallye Frazel
19	East	$ 221,650	Lazares	Sue	Sue Lazares
20	South	$ 321,661	Hernandez	Sally	Sally Hernandez
21	South	$ 238,337	Welch	JoAnne	JoAnne Welch
22	South	$ 614,583	Holder	Howard	Howard Holder
23	South	$ 571,562	Hussam	Ali	Ali Hussam
24	West	$ 238,340	Johnson	Jerome	Jerome Johnson
25	North	$ 522,986	Khorjin	Fugi	Fugi Khorjin
26					
27					
28					
29					

First Quarter Sales / January / February / March

Ready

Total of data from other worksheets now in First Quarter Sales worksheet

FIGURE 15–25
Consolidated data in First Quarter Sales worksheet

8. Save, print, and close the workbook.

EXTRA FOR EXPERTS

If you are consolidating data from multiple workbooks, you can select the Create links to source data check box in the Consolidate dialog box. This option automatically updates combined data. Whenever data changes in one workbook, the combined data is updated.

Creating a One-Way Data Table

A one-way data table uses one function to change cells that use this function. For example, you may have a PMT function that finds the monthly payment of a car loan. To find the payment amount, you need certain information, such as the amount owed on the car, the interest rate, and the number of months for the loan. You can then use the PMT function to find out how much the loan payment will be each month.

You may want to find out how much the monthly payment would be if you reduced the number of months used to pay for the car. Your monthly payment would increase, but the interest you would save might be worth it, if you can afford the new monthly payment amount. Using a data table, you can instantly calculate the new monthly payment. An example of a one-way data table is shown in **Figure 15–26**.

D5 =PMT(B7/12,B6,-B8)

	A	B	C	D	E
1	Car Loan				
2	*Find Payoff Information*				
3		Current Values	Alternative Number of Months	Payment Amount	
4					
5				$ 105.06	
6	Number of Months	60	48	$ 127.91	
7	Interest Rate	5.5%	36	$ 166.08	
8	Car Loan Balance	$5,500.00	24	$ 242.53	
9					
10					

Cell with PMT formula

New monthly payment amounts

Cells with various numbers of months

FIGURE 15–26 Example of a one-way data table

Notice that the payment function is in cell D5. The payment function works by using the number of months in cell B6, the interest rate in cell B7, and the car loan balance in cell B8 to calculate the monthly payment shown in cell D5. To change the number of months, you would enter this data into the cells next to the original values. In this example, you enter the new months in cells C6:C8. Notice that the function needs to be placed one column over and one row up from the new data. All of the cells with data that will be used in the data table need to be filled with a color. Excel only recognizes cells with color fills as part of the data table

Step-by-Step 15.9

1. Open the **Credit Card** file from the drive and folder where your Data Files are stored.
2. Save the workbook as **Credit Card Payoff**, followed by your initials.
3. Click **cell D5** and view the payment function. Notice that the function uses the number of months in cell B6. You will now enter the additional number of months to pay off the credit card.
4. Select **cell C6**, type **48**, and then press **Enter**.
5. Type **36** in cell C7, and then press **Enter**.
6. Type **24** in cell C8, and then press **Enter**. You will now add a fill color to the range that you want to use in the data table.
7. Select **C5:D8**.
8. Click the **Home** tab, click the **Fill Color** button arrow in the Font group, and then click **Dark Blue, Text 2, Lighter 80%**, (the fourth color in the second row). Your worksheet should resemble **Figure 15–27**.

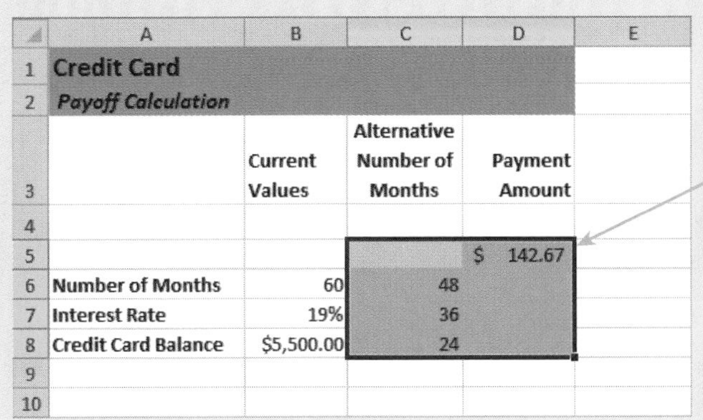

FIGURE 15–27
Worksheet formatted for data table

	A	B	C	D	E
1	Credit Card				
2	Payoff Calculation				
3		Current Values	Alternative Number of Months	Payment Amount	
4					
5				$ 142.67	
6	Number of Months	60	48		
7	Interest Rate	19%	36		
8	Credit Card Balance	$5,500.00	24		
9					
10					

9. Click the **Data** tab, click the **What-If Analysis button** in the Data Tools group, and then click **Data Table**. The Data Table dialog box opens, as shown in **Figure 15–28**.

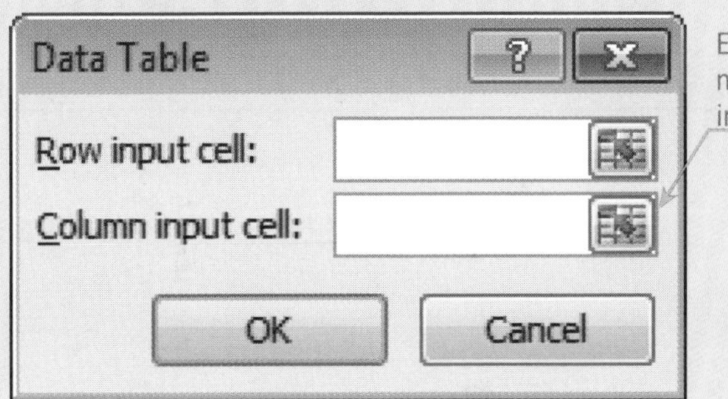

FIGURE 15–28
Data Table dialog box

10. Click in the **Column input cell** text box, and then type **B6**.
11. Click **OK** to close the Data Table dialog box. See **Figure 15–29**.

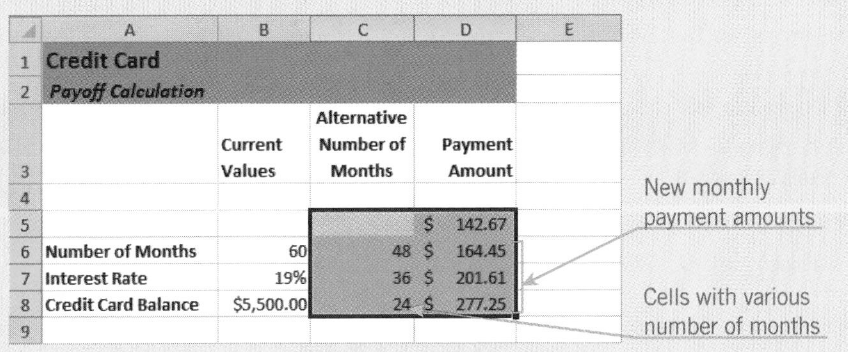

FIGURE 15–29
Worksheet with data table results

	A	B	C	D	E
1	Credit Card				
2	Payoff Calculation				
3		Current Values	Alternative Number of Months	Payment Amount	
4					
5				$ 142.67	
6	Number of Months	60	48	$ 164.45	
7	Interest Rate	19%	36	$ 201.61	
8	Credit Card Balance	$5,500.00	24	$ 277.25	
9					

12. Click cell **C8**, type **12**, and then press **Enter**. Notice the payment amount in D8 changes to $506.86.
13. Save, print, and close the workbook.

SUMMARY

In this lesson, you learned:

- The Trace Precedents feature finds the cells that are used in the function.
- The Trace Error feature locates cells that are used in a formula to assist in identifying the source of an error.
- The Trace Dependents button works by locating formulas or functions that depend on the value in a selected cell.
- If a cell containing a formula has an error, the Trace Error feature displays the cells used in the formula.
- You can check for errors throughout an entire worksheet, using the Error Checking feature.
- The Goal Seek feature can perform a "what-if" analysis based on a single function.
- The Scenario Manager performs a "what-if" analysis and lets you view the results based on changing several cells of data.
- You can view scenarios in the scenario summary.
- Data from multiple worksheets can be totaled using the Consolidate feature.
- A one-way data table shows various results for a function within a range of cells.

VOCABULARY REVIEW

Define the following terms:

audit	dependent	Scenario Manager
consolidating	precedent	tracer arrow

REVIEW QUESTIONS

TRUE / FALSE

Circle T if the statement is true or F if the statement is false.

T F **1.** Consolidating data involves combining values from several worksheets together and showing the total of these values in another worksheet.

T F **2.** You can only create one scenario for a set of values.

T F **3.** If you select a cell with data and click the Trace Dependents button, Excel will draw an arrow from the selected cell pointing to the cell with the function that references that cell.

T F **4.** To check all formulas and functions in a workbook, you use the Error Checking option.

T F **5.** Goal Seek helps you find a value to meet a goal.

FILL IN THE BLANK

1. If you want to use a "what-if" analysis tool to find a value for a single cell of data, you use the ________________ feature.
2. To do a "what-if" analysis that focuses on changing several cells of data, you would use the ________________ feature.
3. To locate the source of an error in a function, you could click in the cell with the function and then click the ________________ tool.
4. If you want to check for problems in all the formulas and functions in a workbook, you use the ________________ feature.
5. A(n) ________________ uses one function to produce results in several cells.

WRITTEN QUESTIONS

Write a brief answer to the following questions.

1. What is the difference between Trace Error and Error Checking?

2. What is the purpose of Goal Seek?

3. What can the Scenario Manager feature show you?

4. Explain the difference between consolidating data in one workbook versus consolidating data using several workbooks.

5. Explain the term audit.

PROJECTS

If you have a SAM 2010 user profile, your instructor may have assigned an autogradable version of the indicated project. If so, log into the SAM 2010 Web site at *www.cengage.com/sam2010* to download the instruction and start files.

PROJECT 15–1

1 Open the **Supplies** file from the drive and folder where your Data Files are stored.
2. Save the workbook as **Office Supplies**, followed by your initials.
3. Search all the formulas and functions for potential errors.
4. If errors are found, correct them.
5. Save and close the workbook.

PROJECT 15–2

1. Open the **International Sales** file from the drive and folder where your Data Files are stored.
2. Save the workbook as **International Sales Financials**, followed by your initials.
3. Create a scenario showing the current values.
4. Create a scenario that shows the values of the current expenses. For the changing cells, type the range **B10:B16**.
5. Create another scenario named **Increased Lease and Utilities Expense**. Enter the following expenses into the scenario:

   B10 (Lease): 75000

   B11 (Utilities): 9000
6. Create another scenario named **Decreased Lease and Utilities Expense**. Enter the following expenses into the scenario:

   B10 (Lease): 45000

   B11 (Utilities): 7000
7. Click the Summary button and create a scenario summary.
8. Save and close the workbook.

PROJECT 15–3

1. Click the File tab, click New, and then double-click Blank workbook. Save the workbook as **Down Payment Goal**, followed by your initials.
2. Select cell C5.
3. Type **=A5*12*10** and then press Enter. This formula takes the unknown monthly savings amount in cell A5 and multiplies it by 12 payments per year for 10 years.
4. Select cell C5, and on the Data tab, in the Data Tools group, click the What-If Analysis button, and then click Goal Seek.
5. Click in the To value text box, then type **25000**. This is the goal value.
6. Click in the By changing cell box, then type **A5**. This cell will show the Goal Seek solution.
7. Click OK.
8. Add the Accounting Number Format to cells A5 and C5.
9. Save and close the workbook.

CRITICAL THINKING

ACTIVITY 15–1

1. Open the **Trees and Landscaping** file from the drive and folder where your Data Files are stored.
2. Save the workbook as **Trees and Landscaping Financials**, followed by your initials.
3. Create a scenario named **Increased Sales** that increases the income for Trees Planted.
4. Create another scenario that shows a decrease in income in Trees Planted, then assign an appropriate name to the scenario.
5. Create a scenario summary that shows the current values, the increased income, and the decreased income.
6. Save and close the workbook.

ACTIVITY 15–2

1. Think of a data table you could create in Excel that could be applied to a document you use for personal use. For example, you may want to pay off your student loans or you may want to refinance your loans at a lower interest rate. Create the data table in Excel and save it as **Payoff**, followed by your initials.

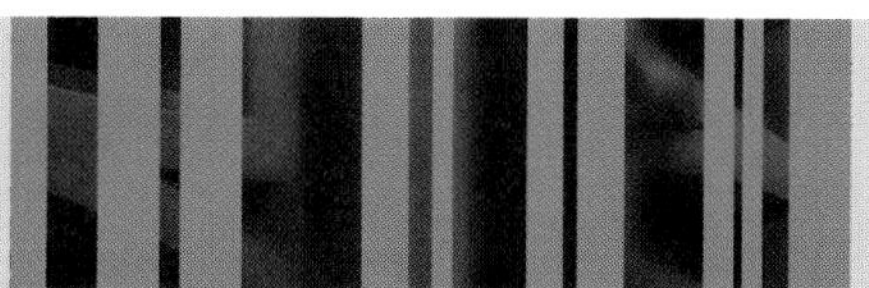

Estimated Time: 2 hours

LESSON 16

Protecting, Tracking, and Sharing Workbooks

OBJECTIVES

Upon completion of this lesson, you should be able to:

- Add password protection to a worksheet.
- Remove password protection from a worksheet.
- Add password protection to a workbook.
- Remove password protection from a workbook.
- Enable the Track Changes feature.
- Change a workbook with tracked changes.
- Accept or reject tracked changes.
- Disable the Track Changes feature.
- Create a shared workbook.
- Modify a shared workbook.

VOCABULARY

case sensitive

decrypt

disable

enable

encrypt

password

shared workbook

Introduction

To protect your Excel data from unwanted changes, you can add password protection to worksheets and workbooks. Adding password protection to the entire workbook prevents anyone who does not know the password from opening or viewing the file. If you add password protection to individual worksheets, only the people who know the password can make changes to them.

If you want to keep track of the changes made in a workbook, you can enable the Track Changes feature. Then, when a change is made, Excel will record the date and time of the change, the person who made the change, the previous entry in the cell, and the changed entry in the cell. As you review the changes, you can accept or reject each change.

Shared workbooks allow you to work in the same workbook with other users at the same time. The Track Changes feature is also available with shared workbooks.

Adding Password Protection to a Worksheet

When you have a worksheet that several people have access to, you run the risk of unwanted changes, whether a user makes them intentionally or accidentally. To prevent changes to a worksheet, you can protect it with a password.

VOCABULARY
password
case sensitive

A ***password*** refers to a sequence of characters, known only by you, that is required for access to the file. Passwords are ***case sensitive***. In other words, if a password contains capital letters, you will need to enter the password using the same capital letters. In this next Step-by-Step, you will password-protect a worksheet.

Step-by-Step 16.1

1. Open the **State College** file from the drive and folder where your Data Files are stored.
2. Save the workbook as **State College Inventory**, followed by your initials.
3. On the Ribbon, click the **Review** tab, and then click the **Protect Sheet** button in the Changes group. The Protect Sheet dialog box opens, as shown in **Figure 16–1**.

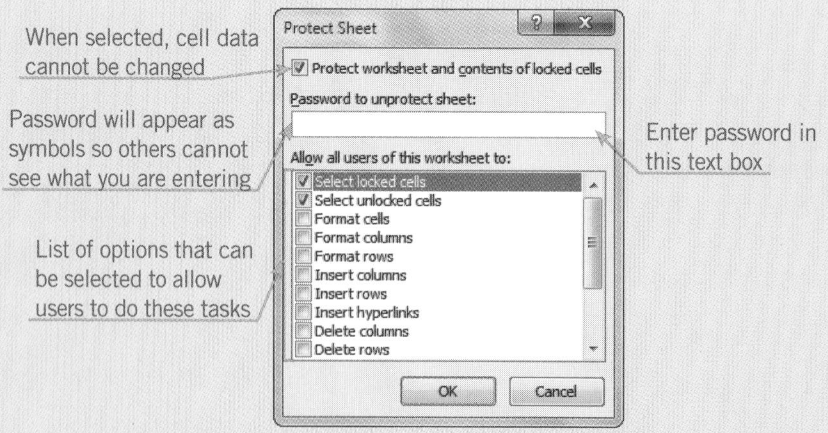

FIGURE 16–1
Protect Sheet dialog box

4. In the Password to unprotect sheet text box, type **Cat**.

5. Click **OK** to close the Protect Sheet dialog box. You are prompted to confirm your password by typing it again in the Confirm Password dialog box, as shown in **Figure 16–2**.

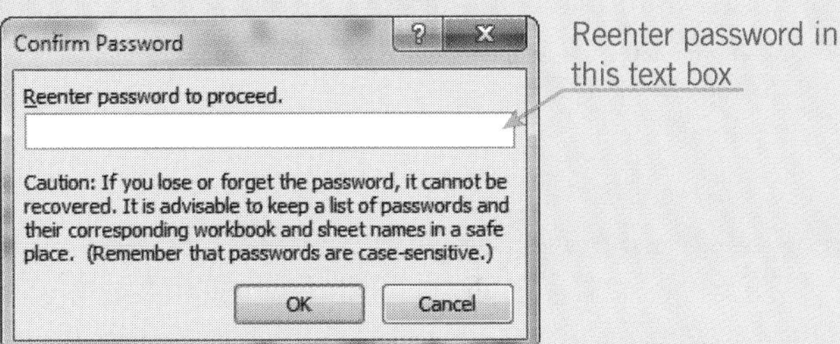

FIGURE 16–2
Confirming password

6. In the Reenter password to proceed text box, type **Cat**.
7. Click **OK** to close the Confirm Password dialog box. On the Review tab, notice that the Unprotect Sheet button is available since protection is applied to the worksheet.
8. Select **cell D10**, type **3**. Notice that a message box appears letting you know that the cell you are trying to change is protected. See **Figure 16–3**.

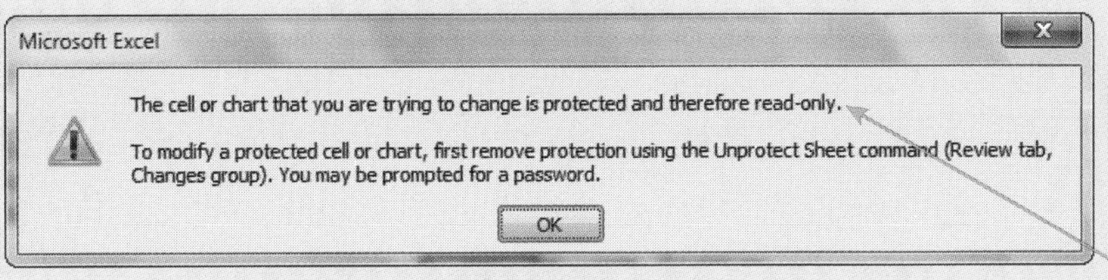

FIGURE 16–3
Protection warning message box

9. Click **OK** to close the message box, and then select the **Home** tab. Notice how most of the buttons are not available, indicating that changes cannot be made to the worksheet.
10. Right-click **cell A5**, and then select **Clear Contents** from the shortcut menu. The message box appears.
11. Click **OK** to close the message box.
12. Click the **Insert Worksheet** button next to the Inventory worksheet.
13. In the new worksheet, select **cell A5**, type **500**, and then press **Enter**. A message box does not appear since this worksheet is not protected.
14. Save the workbook and leave it open for the next Step-by-Step.

Removing Password Protection from a Worksheet

When a worksheet is password protected, changes cannot be made to it. If you need to change data or other information on the worksheet, you will need to remove the password protection. When you are finished making the changes, you can add the password protection to the worksheet again. Next, you will remove password protection from the worksheet.

Step-by-Step 16.2

1. Click the **Inventory** worksheet tab.
2. Click the **Review** tab, and then click the **Unprotect Worksheet** button in the Changes group. The Unprotect Sheet dialog box is shown in **Figure 16–4**.

FIGURE 16–4 Unprotect Sheet dialog box

Unprotect Sheet

Password:

OK Cancel

Enter password in this text box

3. In the Password text box, type **Cat** and then click **OK**.
4. Select **cell D10**, type **350**, and then press **Enter**. The worksheet is unprotected so you are able to make changes to it. Compare your worksheet to **Figure 16–5**.

FIGURE 16–5 Unprotected worksheet with change

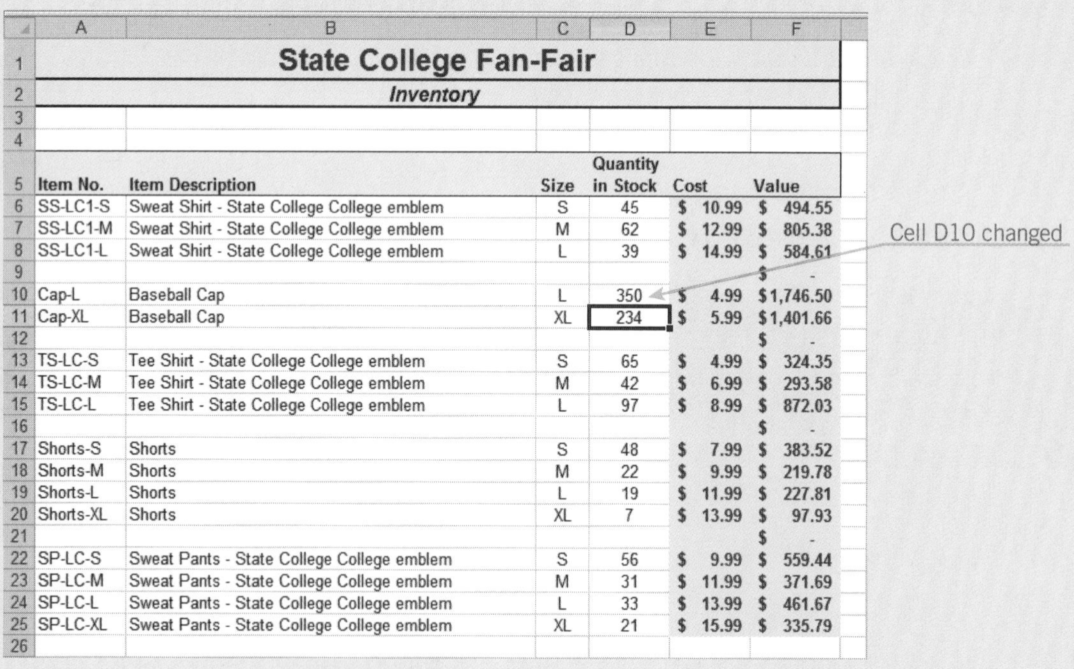

State College Fan-Fair

Inventory

	A	B	C	D	E	F
5	Item No.	Item Description	Size	Quantity in Stock	Cost	Value
6	SS-LC1-S	Sweat Shirt - State College College emblem	S	45	$ 10.99	$ 494.55
7	SS-LC1-M	Sweat Shirt - State College College emblem	M	62	$ 12.99	$ 805.38
8	SS-LC1-L	Sweat Shirt - State College College emblem	L	39	$ 14.99	$ 584.61
9						$ -
10	Cap-L	Baseball Cap	L	350	$ 4.99	$1,746.50
11	Cap-XL	Baseball Cap	XL	234	$ 5.99	$1,401.66
12						$ -
13	TS-LC-S	Tee Shirt - State College College emblem	S	65	$ 4.99	$ 324.35
14	TS-LC-M	Tee Shirt - State College College emblem	M	42	$ 6.99	$ 293.58
15	TS-LC-L	Tee Shirt - State College College emblem	L	97	$ 8.99	$ 872.03
16						$ -
17	Shorts-S	Shorts	S	48	$ 7.99	$ 383.52
18	Shorts-M	Shorts	M	22	$ 9.99	$ 219.78
19	Shorts-L	Shorts	L	19	$ 11.99	$ 227.81
20	Shorts-XL	Shorts	XL	7	$ 13.99	$ 97.93
21						$ -
22	SP-LC-S	Sweat Pants - State College College emblem	S	56	$ 9.99	$ 559.44
23	SP-LC-M	Sweat Pants - State College College emblem	M	31	$ 11.99	$ 371.69
24	SP-LC-L	Sweat Pants - State College College emblem	L	33	$ 13.99	$ 461.67
25	SP-LC-XL	Sweat Pants - State College College emblem	XL	21	$ 15.99	$ 335.79
26						

Cell D10 changed

5. Save and close the workbook.

Adding Password Protection to a Workbook

To prevent a workbook from being opened by an unauthorized person, you can password-protect a workbook. If someone tries to open a password-protected workbook, he or she will be first prompted to enter the password in a dialog box. If the password is not entered correctly, the workbook will not open. Passwords for a workbook are case sensitive; they must be entered exactly as when they were created.

When you password-protect a workbook, you are encrypting the file. ***Encrypting*** means that the information in the file is scrambled. Therefore, if an unauthorized person tries to pry into the file, they will only see unreadable text and symbols. You may have seen news reports in which unauthorized individuals use their computer knowledge to gain unauthorized access to a person's file. Using passwords will help prevent this from happening.

VOCABULARY
encrypting

To make sure you have access to a protected file in case you lose the password, you should create an unprotected backup of the file and store it in another location.

Step-by-Step 16.3

1. Open the **Employee** file from the drive and folder where your Data Files are stored.
2. Save the workbook as **Employee List**, followed by your initials.
3. Click the **File** tab and then click **Info**, if necessary. The Protect Workbook button is located in the Info section of the File window, as shown in **Figure 16–6**.

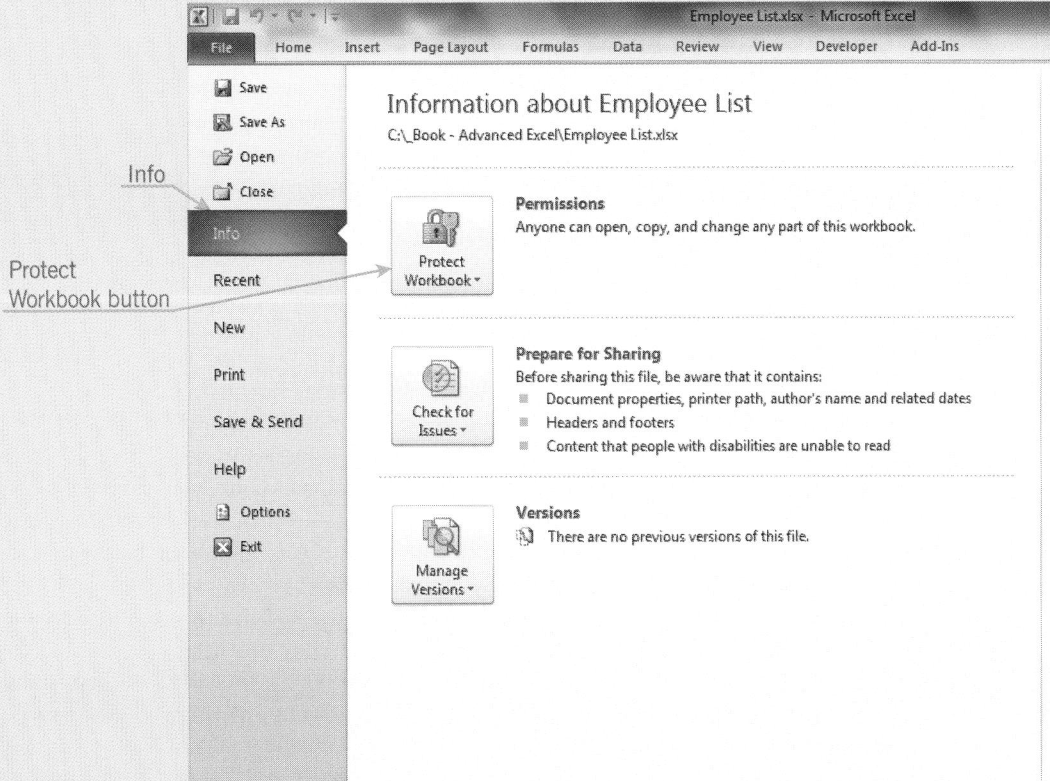

FIGURE 16–6
Info section of the File window

4. Click the **Protect Workbook** button to display the workbook protection options, as shown in **Figure 16–7**.

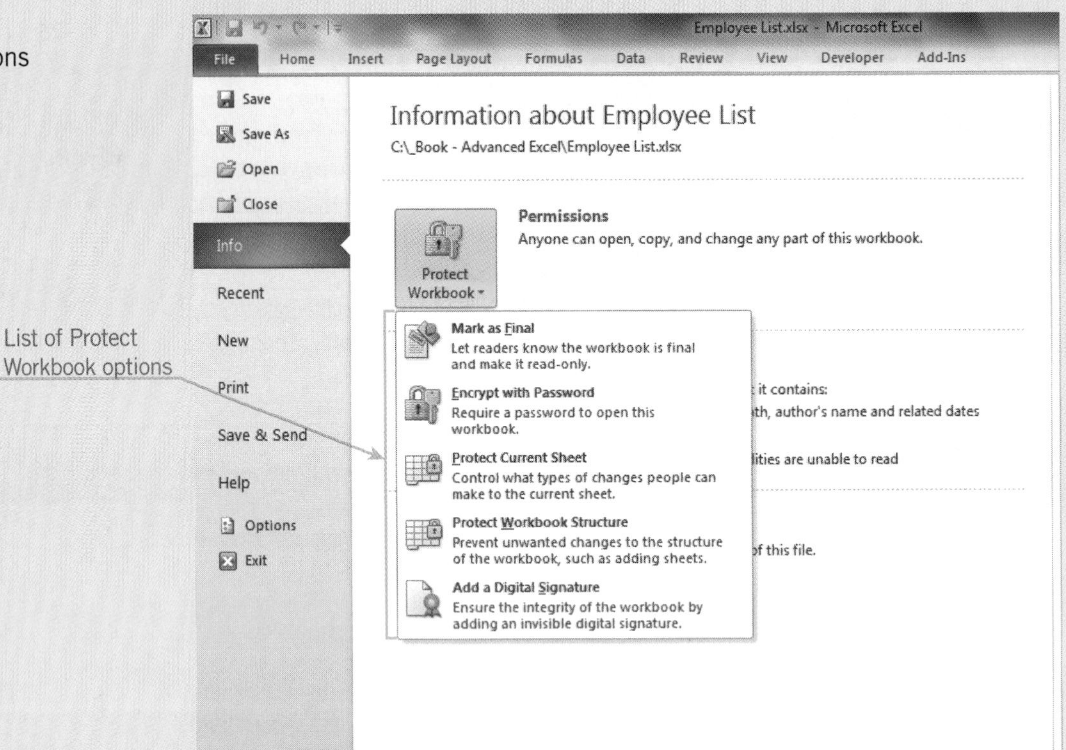

FIGURE 16–7
Protect Workbook options

5. Click the **Encrypt with Password** option to display the Encrypt Document dialog box.
6. In the Password text box, type **Cat** and then press **Enter**.
7. In the Confirm Password dialog box, type **Cat** in the Reenter password text box, and then press **Enter**. The workbook is now password protected.
8. Save and close the workbook.

Removing Password Protection from a Workbook

VOCABULARY
decrypting

If you need to let others access a password-protected workbook, you can remove the password protection without giving out the password. When you remove the password protection, you are ***decrypting*** the workbook, or removing the encryption. If you want to be sure that the original file is not changed, you can create a copy of the workbook and remove the password from the copied file. Then, you still have the original password-protected workbook.

In this next Step-by-Step, you will open the password-protected workbook and save the file with another filename so you still have a copy of the workbook with a password. Then, you will remove the password from the new file.

Step-by-Step 16.4

1. Open the **Employee List** file and notice that the Password dialog box opens, as shown in **Figure 16–8**.

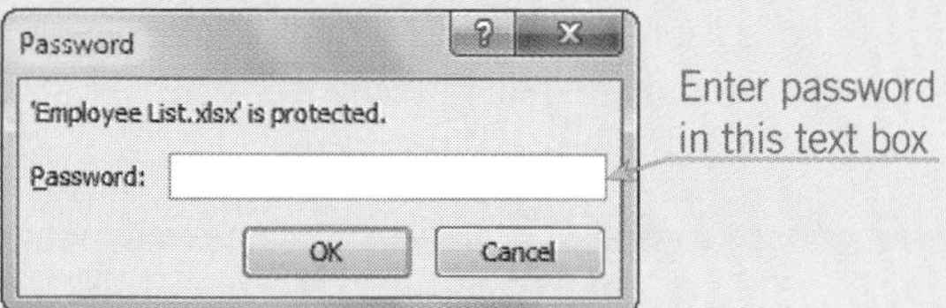

FIGURE 16–8
Password dialog box

2. In the Password text box, type **Cat** and then click **OK**.
3. Save the workbook as **Employee List – Revised**, followed by your initials.
4. Click the **File** tab and then select **Info**, if necessary. Notice that a message appears under Permissions showing that a password is required to open this workbook.
5. Click the **Protect Workbook** button, and then click **Encrypt with Password**. The Encrypt Document dialog box opens, as shown in **Figure 16–9**. The encrypted password is shown in the Password text box.

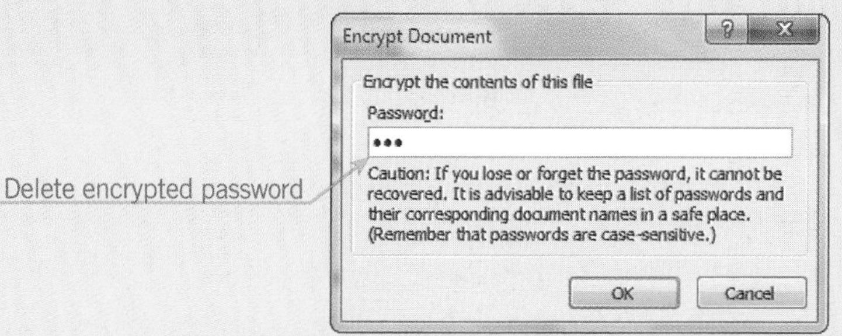

FIGURE 16–9
Encrypt Document dialog box

6. Highlight the password in the Password text box, and then press [**Delete**].
7. Click **OK** to close the Encrypt Document dialog box.
8. On the File tab, click **Save**.
9. Close the workbook.
10. Open the **Employee List – Revised** workbook. Notice that you are not asked for a password.
11. Save and close the workbook.

EXTRA FOR EXPERTS

If you do not want any more changes made to a workbook, you can mark it as final. When you mark a workbook as final, the workbook opens as a read-only file. To mark a workbook as final, click the File tab, click Info, click the Protect Workbook button, and then click Mark as Final.

Enabling the Track Changes Feature

The Track Changes feature shows changes made to an Excel worksheet. When Track Changes is enabled, cells that have been changed appear with a border. Also, Excel identifies the name of the person who made the change and the date of the change. The border will appear around the changed cells until the file is closed. When the file is reopened, the border does not appear, but Excel still keeps a history of the changes. If the Track Changes feature is enabled, it makes the workbook a shared file. When a file is shared, several people can make changes to the workbook at the same time.

VOCABULARY
enable

The advantage of tracking changes is that you can go back and review the changes in the workbook. And, as you review the changes, you can accept or reject each change. You ***enable*** the Track Changes feature by clicking the Track changes while editing check box in the Highlight Changes dialog box. In the dialog box, you can choose *When* (when should changes be tracked), *Who* (whose changes should be tracked), and *Where* (which range of cells should be tracked) options. You can also choose whether you want the changes to be highlighted on the screen or listed on a new sheet.

Step-by-Step 16.5

1. Open the **Water Usage** file from the drive and folder where your Data Files are stored, and then save the workbook as **Water Usage by Department**, followed by your initials.
2. On the Ribbon, click the **Review** tab.
3. In the **Changes** group, click the **Track Changes** button arrow, and then click **Highlight Changes.**

The Highlight Changes dialog box opens, as shown in **Figure 16–10**.

FIGURE 16–10
Highlight Changes dialog box

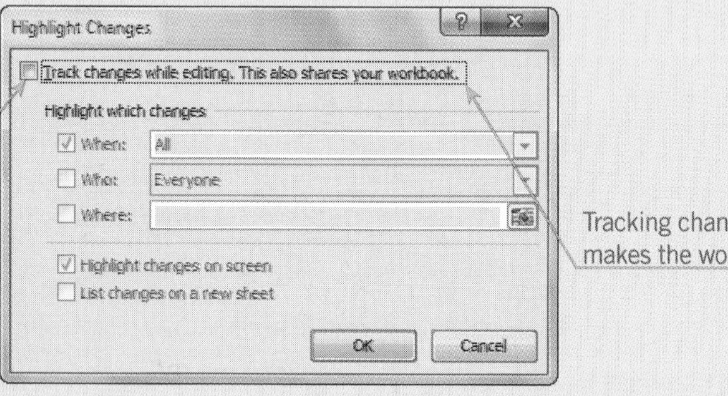

4. In the Highlight Changes dialog box, click the **Track changes while editing** check box to select it. Notice that the workbook will be shared when you select this option.
5. If necessary, click the **arrow** to the right of the When text box, and then click **All**, as shown in **Figure 16–11**. All changes made to the workbook will be tracked.

FIGURE 16–11
Options for when to highlight changes

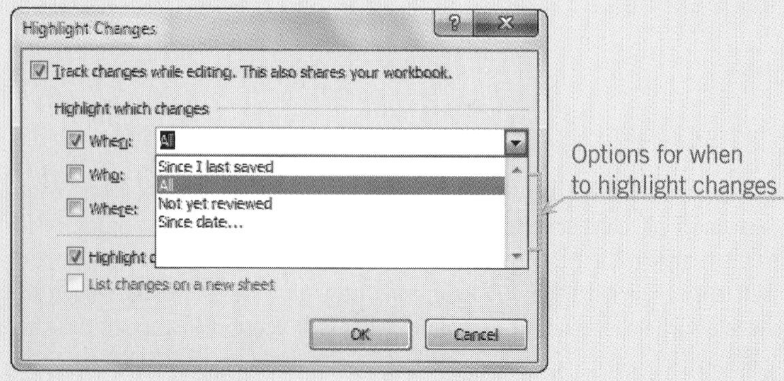

6. Click the **Who** check box, then verify that the option is set to Everyone.
7. Click the **Where** check box.
8. Click the **Collapse dialog box** button next to the Where text box.
9. Select the range **C5:C49**.
10. Click the **Expand dialog box** button to return to the Highlight Changes dialog box.
11. Click the **Highlight changes on screen** check box, if necessary, and then compare your dialog box to **Figure 16–12**. Selecting this option will display a triangle in the upper-left corner and a border around each cell that has been changed.

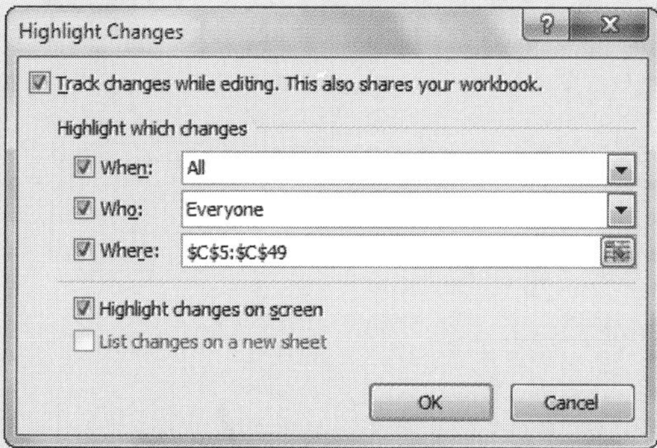

FIGURE 16–12
Completed Highlight Changes dialog box

12. Click **OK** to close the Highlight Changes dialog box.
13. You may receive a message that this action will now save the workbook and asking if you want to continue. Click **OK**. Notice that the word Shared appears on the Excel title bar after the filename.
14. Save the workbook and leave it open for the next Step-by-Step.

Making Changes in a Workbook with Tracked Changes

When you see a cell with a border around it, you know that a change has been made. If you place your mouse pointer over the highlighted cell, a callout will appear showing the date, time, original cell data, changed data for the cell, and the name of the person who made the change. Excel does not track changes to worksheet names and formats applied to cells or data. For this next Step-by-Step, you will change data in two cells in the worksheet with the Track Changes feature enabled.

Step-by-Step 16.6

1. Select **cell C5**.
2. Type **654.3**, and then press **Enter**.

3. In cell C6, type **595.9** and then press **Enter**.
4. Select **C10**, type **640.0**, and then press **Enter**. Compare your screen to **Figure 16–13**.

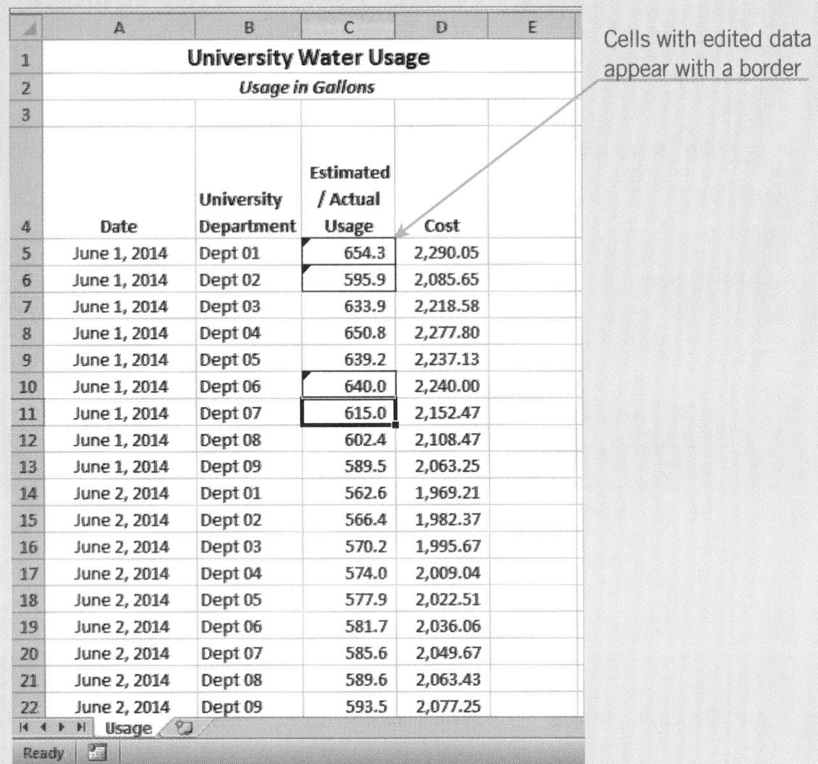

	A	B	C	D	E
1	University Water Usage				
2	*Usage in Gallons*				
3					
4	Date	University Department	Estimated / Actual Usage	Cost	
5	June 1, 2014	Dept 01	654.3	2,290.05	
6	June 1, 2014	Dept 02	595.9	2,085.65	
7	June 1, 2014	Dept 03	633.9	2,218.58	
8	June 1, 2014	Dept 04	650.8	2,277.80	
9	June 1, 2014	Dept 05	639.2	2,237.13	
10	June 1, 2014	Dept 06	640.0	2,240.00	
11	June 1, 2014	Dept 07	615.0	2,152.47	
12	June 1, 2014	Dept 08	602.4	2,108.47	
13	June 1, 2014	Dept 09	589.5	2,063.25	
14	June 2, 2014	Dept 01	562.6	1,969.21	
15	June 2, 2014	Dept 02	566.4	1,982.37	
16	June 2, 2014	Dept 03	570.2	1,995.67	
17	June 2, 2014	Dept 04	574.0	2,009.04	
18	June 2, 2014	Dept 05	577.9	2,022.51	
19	June 2, 2014	Dept 06	581.7	2,036.06	
20	June 2, 2014	Dept 07	585.6	2,049.67	
21	June 2, 2014	Dept 08	589.6	2,063.43	
22	June 2, 2014	Dept 09	593.5	2,077.25	

Usage

Ready

FIGURE 16–13
Worksheet with tracked changes

5. Save and close the workbook. You will reopen the workbook in the next step to see how the file opens and remembers the history of tracked changes.

Accepting or Rejecting Tracked Changes

As you review changes made to cells, you can accept or reject the changes. The Accept or Reject Changes dialog box will show the name of the person who made the change, the date and time of the change, the cell name, the original data in the cell, and the changed data. You can accept or reject each change one at a time or you can accept or reject all changes at once. In this next Step-by-Step, you will accept and reject changes.

Step-by-Step 16.7

1. Reopen the **Water Usage by Department** file.
2. Click the **Review** tab, on the Review tab, click the **Track Changes** arrow button, and then click **Accept/Reject Changes** in the Changes group. The Select Changes to Accept or Reject dialog box opens, as shown in **Figure 16–14**.

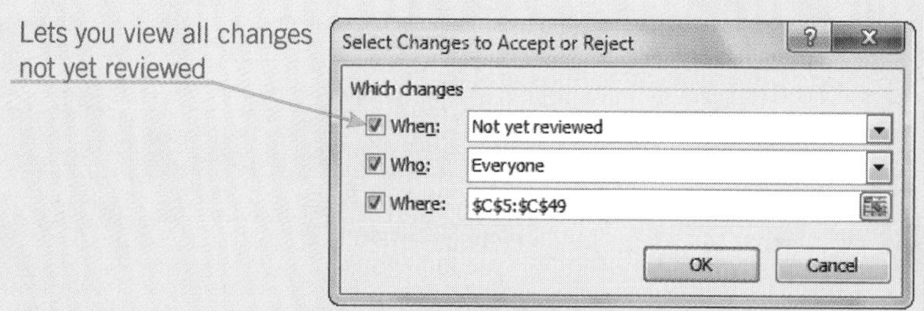

FIGURE 16–14 Select Changes to Accept or Reject dialog box

3. Verify that *Not yet reviewed* is located in the When text box, and then click **OK**. The Accept or Reject Changes dialog box opens, as shown in **Figure 16–15**. The first change that appears is the change to cell C5.

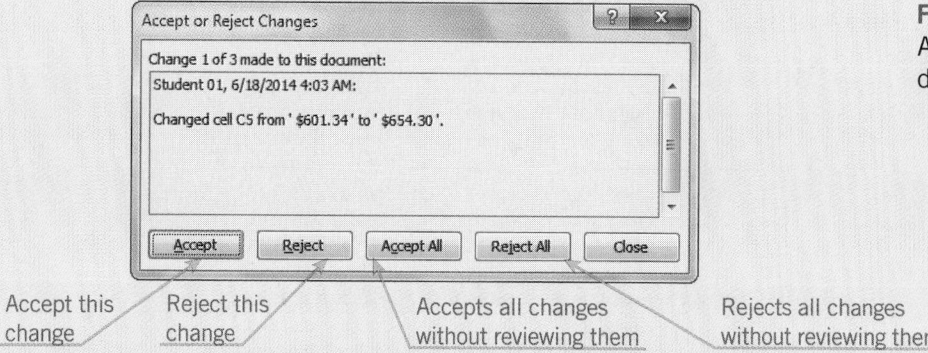

FIGURE 16–15 Accept or Reject Changes dialog box

4. Click the **Accept** button to accept the first change. The dialog box now shows the change made to cell C6.
5. Click the **Accept** button to accept the second change. The dialog box now shows the change made to cell C10. You realize that you do not need the change in cell C10.

6. Click the **Reject** button. The Accept or Reject Changes dialog box closes. Compare your screen to **Figure 16–16**.

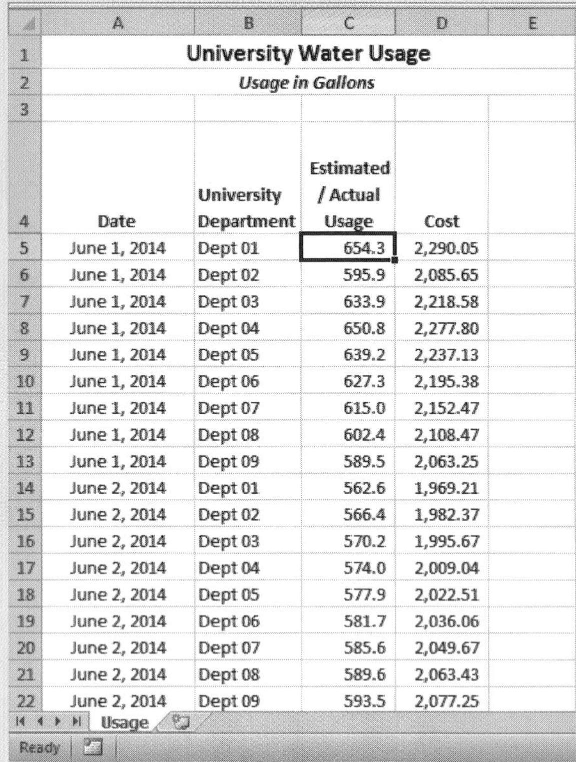

	A	B	C	D	E
1	University Water Usage				
2	Usage in Gallons				
3					
4	Date	University Department	Estimated / Actual Usage	Cost	
5	June 1, 2014	Dept 01	654.3	2,290.05	
6	June 1, 2014	Dept 02	595.9	2,085.65	
7	June 1, 2014	Dept 03	633.9	2,218.58	
8	June 1, 2014	Dept 04	650.8	2,277.80	
9	June 1, 2014	Dept 05	639.2	2,237.13	
10	June 1, 2014	Dept 06	627.3	2,195.38	
11	June 1, 2014	Dept 07	615.0	2,152.47	
12	June 1, 2014	Dept 08	602.4	2,108.47	
13	June 1, 2014	Dept 09	589.5	2,063.25	
14	June 2, 2014	Dept 01	562.6	1,969.21	
15	June 2, 2014	Dept 02	566.4	1,982.37	
16	June 2, 2014	Dept 03	570.2	1,995.67	
17	June 2, 2014	Dept 04	574.0	2,009.04	
18	June 2, 2014	Dept 05	577.9	2,022.51	
19	June 2, 2014	Dept 06	581.7	2,036.06	
20	June 2, 2014	Dept 07	585.6	2,049.67	
21	June 2, 2014	Dept 08	589.6	2,063.43	
22	June 2, 2014	Dept 09	593.5	2,077.25	

FIGURE 16–16
Worksheet after reviewing changes

7. Save the workbook and leave it open for the next Step-by-Step.

Disabling the Track Changes Feature

VOCABULARY
disable

If you decide that you no longer need to track changes in the workbook, you can disable the Track Changes feature. When you ***disable*** Track Changes, the workbook will no longer be shared. Before you disable the Track Changes feature, you should make sure all the changes are reviewed, accepted, or rejected since all change history will be removed when you disable this feature. You will now disable the Track Changes feature from the workbook.

Step-by-Step 16.8

1. In the Changes group, click the **Track Changes** button arrow, and then click **Highlight Changes**.
2. In the Highlight Changes dialog box, click the **Track changes while editing** check box to deselect it.

3. Click **OK** to close the Highlight Changes dialog box. A message box appears letting you know selecting this option will remove the workbook from shared use, as shown in **Figure 16–17**.

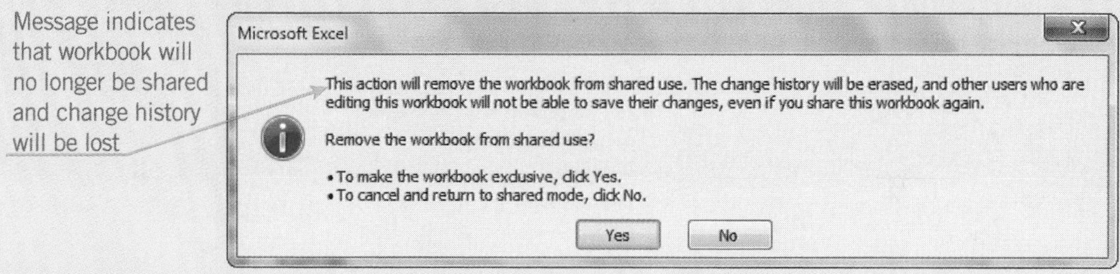

FIGURE 16–17 Message about removing workbook from shared use

4. Click **Yes**. Notice that the word Shared is no longer in the Excel title bar.
5. Save and close the workbook.

Creating a Shared Workbook

The Share Workbook feature allows several people to work in a workbook simultaneously. For example, an airline company may have several employees that need to view a workbook containing reservation rate information. Allowing multiple employees to view and make changes to a workbook at one time helps to maximize efficiency and productivity.

With a ***shared workbook***, changes made by multiple users are tracked. You can then choose to accept or reject these changes. If a conflict occurs from different people making changes to the same cell, Excel provides a prompt that enables you to resolve the conflict by choosing which change you want to keep. You enable the Share Workbook feature using the Share Workbook dialog box.

VOCABULARY
shared workbook

The Advanced tab in the Share Workbook dialog box, shown in **Figure 16–18**, gives you several options for managing workbook changes. These options are described in **Table 16–1**.

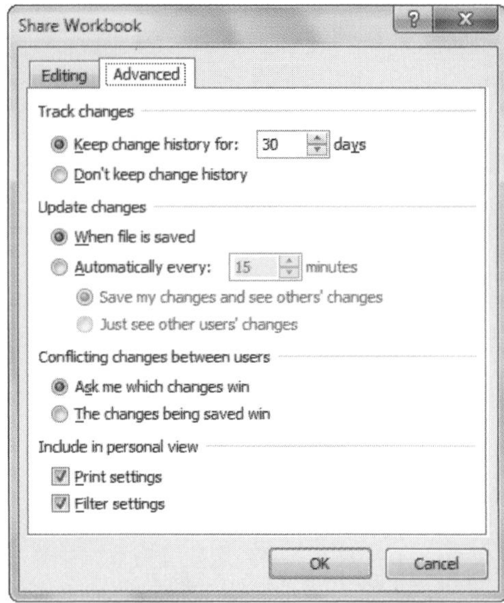

FIGURE 16–18 Advanced tab settings in the Share Workbook dialog box

TABLE 16–1 Advanced options in the Share Workbook dialog box

OPTION	DESCRIPTION
Track changes	You can choose to keep a history of changes made to the shared file or select the option so no history of changes will be kept.
Update changes	Allows you to update changes automatically when the file is saved or based on the minutes you enter, such as update changes every 15 minutes.
Conflicting changes between users	The Ask me which changes win option displays the Resolve Conflict dialog box so that you may see which changes caused a conflict. You can then decide which changes to keep. The second option automatically keeps the changes made within the file being saved.
Include in personal view	Allows you to keep your personal print options, such as page breaks, as well as any filter settings.

In the next Step-by-Step, you will enable a workbook to be shared.

Step-by-Step 16.9

1. Open the **Airline Rates** file from the drive and folder where your Data Files are stored.
2. Save the workbook as **Airline Rates Shared**, followed by your initials.
3. Click the **Review** tab, and then click the **Share Workbook** button in the Changes group. The Share Workbook dialog box opens, as shown in **Figure 16–19**.

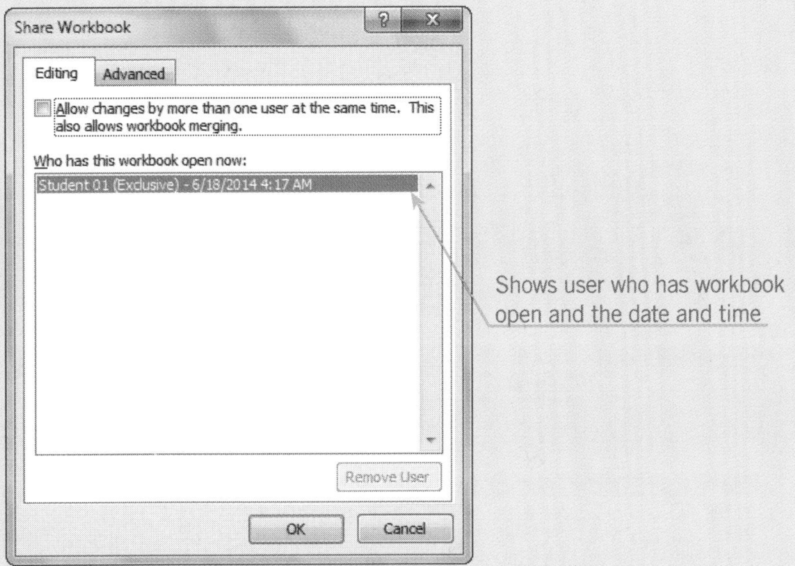

FIGURE 16–19
Share Workbook dialog box

4. Click the **Allow changes by more than one user at the same time** check box to select it.
5. Click the **Advanced** tab.
6. In the Update changes section, click the **Automatically every 15 minutes** option button to select it.
7. Click **OK** to close the Share Workbook dialog box. A message box appears letting you know that the workbook will now be saved.
8. Click **OK** to save the workbook and close the message box.
9. Leave the workbook open for the next Step-by-Step.

Modifying a Shared Workbook

When you make changes to a shared workbook, Excel keeps track of the changes. However, the changes are not marked with a border as they are when the Track Changes feature is used.

For this next Step-by-Step, you will edit data in the workbook. You will save and close the workbook, and then reopen the workbook. By saving, closing, and reopening the shared workbook, you will be pretending to be another user opening and making changes to the workbook. After making changes, you will save the workbook and then go through the process of reviewing, accepting, and rejecting changes.

Step-by-Step 16.10

1. Click **cell C10**.
2. Type **300**, and then press the **Tab** key to move to cell D10.
3. Type **600**, and then press **Enter**.
4. With **cell C11** selected, type **80**, and then press **Enter**.
5. Save and close the workbook.
6. Reopen the **Airline Rates Shared** workbook.
7. Select **cell D11**, type **145**, and then press **Enter**.
8. Save the workbook, and then compare your worksheet to **Figure 16–20**.

FIGURE 16–20
Shared workbook with changes

	A	B	C	D	E
1	Stay in the Air Airlines				
2	Rate Table				
3					
4					
5	Flight From	Flight To	One-Way Fare	Round-Trip Fare	
6	Seattle	Dallas	$ 172.00	$ 215.00	
7	Dallas	New Orleans	$ 79.00	$ 120.00	
8	New Orleans	Atlanta	$ 112.00	$ 200.00	
9	Atlanta	Houston	$ 213.00	$ 400.00	
10	Houston	San Francisco	$ 300.00	$ 600.00	
11	San Francisco	Los Angeles	$ 80.00	$ 145.00	
12	Los Angeles	Chicago	$ 220.00	$ 220.00	
13	Chicago	New York	$ 215.00	$ 360.00	
14	New York	Chicago	$ 172.00	$ 299.00	
15	Dallas	Sacramento	$ 225.00	$ 425.00	
16	San Francisco	Sacramento	$ 75.00	$ 150.00	
17	Dallas	Houston	$ 75.00	$ 150.00	
18	Phoenix	Los Angeles	$ 175.00	$ 330.00	
19	New York	Phoenix	$ 335.00	$ 575.00	
20	Seattle	Chicago	$ 240.00	$ 385.00	
21	Chicago	Los Angeles	$ 225.00	$ 395.00	
22	Kansas City	Houston	$ 118.00	$ 212.00	
23	Salt Lake City	New York	$ 198.00	$ 375.00	
24	Augusta	Philadelphia	$ 98.00	$ 176.00	
25	Miami	Dallas	$ 196.00	$ 355.00	
26	Los Angeles	New York	$ 300.00	$ 575.00	
27					

9. On the Review tab in the Changes group, click the **Track Changes** button arrow and then click **Accept/Reject Changes**.
10. Make sure the **When** check box is selected with the **Not yet reviewed option** selected, and then click **OK** to start reviewing the changes. The Accept or Reject Changes dialog box shows the first cell where a change was made, including the date and time the change was made as well as the amount in the cell before the change was made. See **Figure 16–21**.

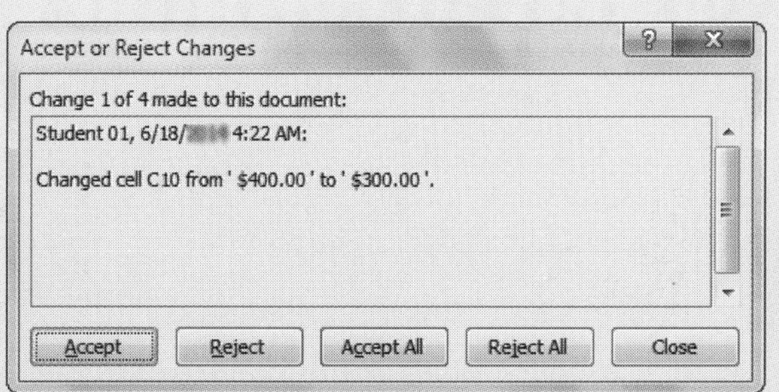

FIGURE 16–21
Accept or Reject Changes dialog box

11. Click **Accept** to accept the change.
12. Click **Accept** to accept the next change.
13. Click **Reject** twice to reject the changes in cells C11 and D11, then compare your screen to **Figure 16–22**.

	A	B	C	D	E
1	**Stay in the Air Airlines**				
2	***Rate Table***				
3					
4					
5	Flight From	Flight To	One-Way Fare	Round-Trip Fare	
6	Seattle	Dallas	$ 172.00	$ 215.00	
7	Dallas	New Orleans	$ 79.00	$ 120.00	
8	New Orleans	Atlanta	$ 112.00	$ 200.00	
9	Atlanta	Houston	$ 213.00	$ 400.00	
10	Houston	San Francisco	$ 300.00	$ 600.00	
11	San Francisco	Los Angeles	$ 79.00	$ 113.00	
12	Los Angeles	Chicago	$ 220.00	$ 220.00	
13	Chicago	New York	$ 215.00	$ 360.00	
14	New York	Chicago	$ 172.00	$ 299.00	
15	Dallas	Sacramento	$ 225.00	$ 425.00	
16	San Francisco	Sacramento	$ 75.00	$ 150.00	
17	Dallas	Houston	$ 75.00	$ 150.00	
18	Phoenix	Los Angeles	$ 175.00	$ 330.00	
19	New York	Phoenix	$ 335.00	$ 575.00	
20	Seattle	Chicago	$ 240.00	$ 385.00	
21	Chicago	Los Angeles	$ 225.00	$ 395.00	
22	Kansas City	Houston	$ 118.00	$ 212.00	
23	Salt Lake City	New York	$ 198.00	$ 375.00	
24	Augusta	Philadelphia	$ 98.00	$ 176.00	
25	Miami	Dallas	$ 196.00	$ 355.00	
26	Los Angeles	New York	$ 300.00	$ 575.00	
27					
28					

FIGURE 16–22
Worksheet with shared changes completed

14. Save and close the workbook.

SUMMARY

In this lesson, you learned:

- You can add password protection to a worksheet to prevent unwanted changes.
- When password protection is no longer needed, you can remove it from a worksheet.
- You can add password protection to an entire workbook.
- A password can be removed from the workbook.
- You can track changes in a workbook by enabling the Track Changes feature.
- The Track Changes feature keeps a history of the changes made.
- You can accept or reject tracked changes.
- If you no longer need to track changes, you can disable the Track Changes feature.
- Several users can use the same workbook at the same time with the Share Workbook feature enabled.
- You can make changes to a shared workbook.

VOCABULARY

Define the following terms:

case sensitive
decrypt
disable
enable
encrypt
password
shared workbook

REVIEW QUESTIONS

TRUE / FALSE

Circle T if the statement is true or F if the statement is false.

T F **1.** When a worksheet is password protected, the worksheet cannot be viewed.

T F **2.** After password protection is added to a workbook, it cannot be removed.

T F **3.** If the Track Changes feature is enabled, a border appears around cells that are changed.

T F **4.** You can accept or reject tracked changes.

T F **5.** If several users need to view and make changes to a workbook at the same time, you can enable the Share Workbook feature.

FILL IN THE BLANK

Complete the following sentences by writing the correct word or words in the blanks provided.

1. A(n) ________________ is a sequence of characters, known only to you, that is required for access to a file if it is protected.
2. Passwords are ________________, which means that if a password is CAT, it cannot be entered as "cat" or "Cat".
3. When you password-protect a workbook, you are ________________ the workbook data so that if an unauthorized person tries to pry into the file, they will see only unintelligible symbols.
4. If a workbook is shared, you will see the word ________________ appear in the Excel title bar.
5. When the Track Changes feature is enabled, a(n) ________________ appears around a cell when a change is made to it.

WRITTEN QUESTIONS

Write a brief answer to the following questions.

1. Explain the features of a workbook with the Track Changes features enabled.

2. Explain the benefits of creating a shared workbook.

3. Explain what is meant by the term case sensitive.

4. Explain how you would remove password protection from a workbook.

5. Explain why you might want to reject a change when using Track Changes.

PROJECTS

If you have a SAM 2010 user profile, your instructor may have assigned an autogradable version of the indicated project. If so, log into the SAM 2010 Web site at *www.cengage.com/sam2010* to download the instruction and start files.

PROJECT 16–1

1. Open the **Cost and Sales** file from the drive and folder where your Data Files are stored.
2. Save the workbook as **Cost and Sales Prices**, followed by your initials.
3. Add password protection to the Inventory worksheet using the password **Dog5**.
4. Click any cell in the worksheet and try to make a change. You should see a message box letting you know that the worksheet is protected.
5. Click OK to close the message box.
6. Save and close the workbook.

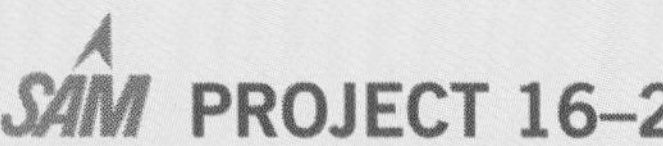

PROJECT 16–2

1. Open the **Best Diamonds** file from the drive and folder where your Data Files are stored.
2. Save the workbook as **Best Diamonds List**, followed by your initials.
3. Enable the Track Changes features using All for When and Everyone for Who.
4. Click OK to save the workbook.
5. Click cell B9, type **3300**, and then press Enter.
6. Click cell B16, type **7350**, and then press Enter.
7. Click the Track Changes button, and then click Accept/Reject Changes. If necessary, click OK to save the workbook.
8. Reject the change in cell B9.
9. Accept the change in B16.
10. Save and close the workbook.

PROJECT 16–3

1. Open the **New York College** file from the drive and folder where your Data Files are stored.
2. Save the workbook as **New York College Sports**, followed by your initials.
3. Add password protection to the workbook with the password **Kitten**.
4. Save and close the workbook.
5. Open the **New York College Sports** workbook.
6. Enter the password so you can view the file.
7. Click cell D6, type **50**, and then press Enter.
8. Save and close the workbook.

CRITICAL THINKING

ACTIVITY 16–1

Hobby Store is a company owned by two brothers. As the company's accountant, you make changes to the product costs and quantities on a regular basis. Both brothers want to review your changes. You decide to open the **Hobby Store** file and use the Track Changes feature. You've just received the price changes as shown below.

CELL	CHANGE
F8	1.99
E22	40

Turn on the Track Changes feature and then make these changes. When you are done, print the worksheet. Save the workbook as **Hobby Store Inventory**, followed by your initials.

ACTIVITY 16–2

You want to create a shared workbook for people on your office project team. Using Excel's Help system, explain if it is possible to create a shared workbook on a computer network.

Estimated Time: 1.5 hours

LESSON 17

Importing and Exporting Data

OBJECTIVES

Upon completion of this lesson, you should be able to:

- Import data from Microsoft Access.
- Import a text file.
- Use the Document Inspector.
- Save a file as a PDF document.
- Export a file to SkyDrive.
- Use signature lines.

VOCABULARY

delimited
export
fixed width
import
signature line
SkyDrive

Introduction

VOCABULARY
import
export

Excel offers the ability to import and export data. ***Importing*** refers to bringing data from other programs, such as Access or Word, into an Excel workbook. ***Exporting*** refers to taking Excel data from a workbook and sending it to another program or to the Web. Before you export data, you may want to save the file as a PDF (Portable Document File). When the workbook is saved as a PDF, it can be viewed without having to install Excel to open it.

In Excel, you can hide comments and columns or rows of data, which allows you to present specific information to different audiences. Before you send a workbook to other individuals or export it to the Web, you can use the Document Inspector to find any hidden information and then choose whether to remove it from the workbook.

To share a workbook with others on the Web, you can export the file to the Web. Microsoft provides 25GB of free space on the Web for each individual who creates a SkyDrive account. In this lesson, you will also learn about signature lines. Signature lines provide security for a file. They inform users that the file format is final and cannot be changed, and that a signature is required on the signature line.

Importing Data from Microsoft Access

Microsoft Access is a database program included in some versions of Microsoft Office. Access is used to store large amounts of data and provides for easy viewing and printing of data. If you use Access, you may want to bring the data from Access into Excel so that you can add formulas and analyze the data. Excel works well with Access data and provides an easy method for importing data from an Access database into an Excel workbook. The next Step-by-Step takes you through the process of importing Access data into Excel.

Step-by-Step 17.1

1. Start Excel, and then create a new workbook.
2. On the Ribbon, click the **Data** tab, and then click the **From Access** button in the Get External Data group. The Select Data Source dialog box opens, as shown in **Figure 17–1**.

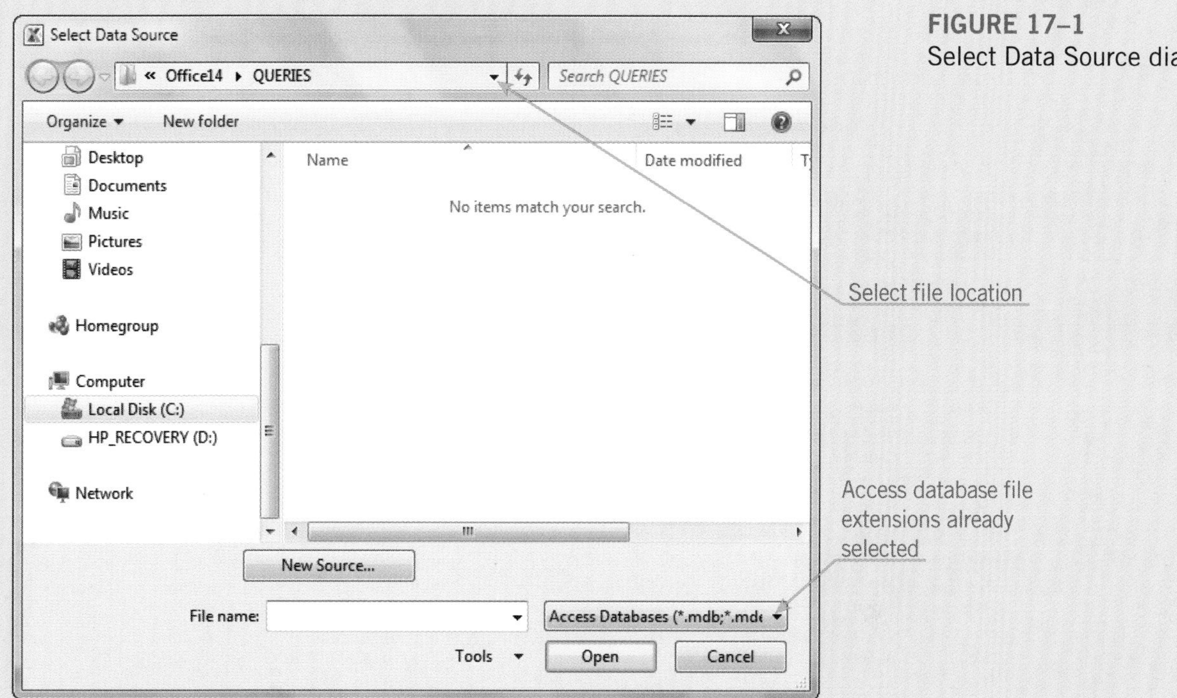

FIGURE 17–1
Select Data Source dialog box

3. Navigate to the drive and folder where you store your Data Files, click **Customer.accdb**, and then click **Open**. The Import Data dialog box opens, as shown in **Figure 17–2**. The Import Data dialog box offers options for viewing the imported data.

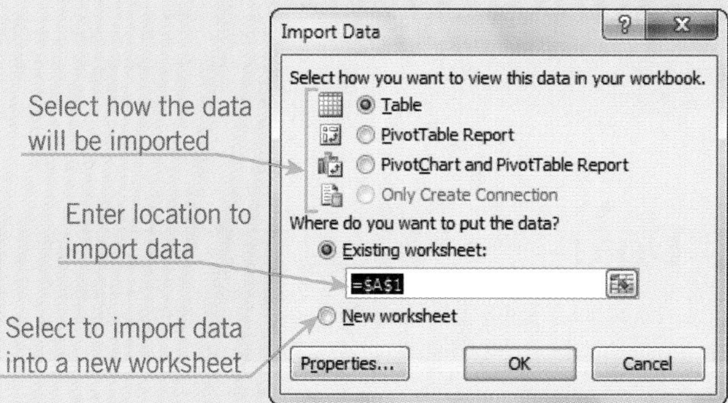

FIGURE 17–2
Import Data dialog box

4. Accept the default option (Table) and then click **OK** to import the data. The data appears in the worksheet in the form of a table with AutoFilters. See **Figure 17–3**.

FIGURE 17–3 Imported Access data

Data imported as a table

AutoFilters added to imported data

	A	B	C	D	E	F	G	H
1	CustID	CustFirst	CustLast	Phone	DOB	Gender	Balance	PlanID
2	1	Ted	Sabus	(970) 644-1214	12/11/1954	M	0	4983
3	2	Tabitha	Sabus	9706441214	10/14/1956	F	0	4983
4	3	Shannon	Sabus	9706442100	9/10/1990	F	0	4983
5	4	Steven	Nguyen	4351224545	10/12/1976	M	30	498-1112-A
6	5	Rose	Baaz	5054778989	4/12/1970	F	0	OP-87-A087
7	6	Geoffrey	Baaz	5054778989	12/31/2001	M	0	OP-87-A087
8	7	Albert	Cardenas	9285515547	10/14/1965	M	0	498-1112-A
9	8	Sonia	Cardenas	9285515547	4/12/1968	F	0	498-1112-A
10	9	Daniel	Cardenas	9285515547	5/12/2002	M	0	498-1112-A
11	10	Jonathan	Cardenas	9285515547	8/22/2004	M	0	498-1112-A
12	11	Paula	Hargus	5057441889	6/11/1970	F	24	OP-87-A087
13	12	Steven	Hargus	5057441889	8/14/2000	M	0	OP-87-A087
14	13	Christina	Hargus	5057441889	2/14/1998	F	0	OP-87-A087
15	14	Malena	D'Ambrosio	4354441233	4/15/1980	F	0	2B8973AC
16	15	Gina	Mercado	9705143212	6/17/1979	F	12	4983
17	16	William	Gabel	9702234156	7/4/1980	M	0	4983
18	17	Maria	Gabel	9702234157	8/12/1980	F	0	4983
19	18	Anders	Aannestad	5054996541	9/11/1974	M	35	498-1112-A
20	19	Dusty	Alkier	4356931212	4/5/1940	M	0	A089
21	20	Kevin	Wachter	4354778989	6/22/1972	M	40	A089
22	21	Cesar	Lopez	9706312222	1/14/1977	M	0	4983
23	22	Josefina	Hernandez	5054986478	6/30/1978	F	0	OP-87-A087
24	23	Jennifer	Ramsey	9288883545	11/21/1980	F	0	498-1112-A
25	24	Kimberley	Schultz	9286472477	1/16/1969	F	0	498-1112-A

Sheet1 Sheet2 Sheet3

Ready

5. Save the workbook as **Access Import**, followed by your initials.
6. Close the workbook.

Importing Text Data

VOCABULARY
delimited
fixed width

You can import text into an Excel worksheet. In Excel, you can change the fonts, formats, and analyze the imported data. Text formats that can be imported into Excel include .txt, .csv, or .prn.

When you import text, the Text Import Wizard opens and walks you through steps to import the data. In the first step of the Text Import Wizard, you need to identify the type of data in the imported file as delimited or fixed width. ***Delimited*** data is separated by a tab, semicolon, comma, or space. ***Fixed width*** data is separated at the same place in each cell, such as after 15 characters. If you select the Delimited option, you need to select which character will be used to separate the columns in Step 2. In the final step of the Text Import Wizard, you select the format for the imported data. Selecting General will convert the number values to a number format, date values to dates, and the remaining text data will be brought in as text. You can also choose to import everything as text, or if all the data are dates, you can select the Date format option. In this next Step-by-Step, you will import text that is in a .txt file format and then make changes to the data after it is imported.

Step-by-Step 17.2

1. Start Excel, and then create a new workbook.
2. Click the **Data** tab, and then click the **From Text** button in the Get External Data group. The Import Text File dialog box opens, as shown in **Figure 17–4**.

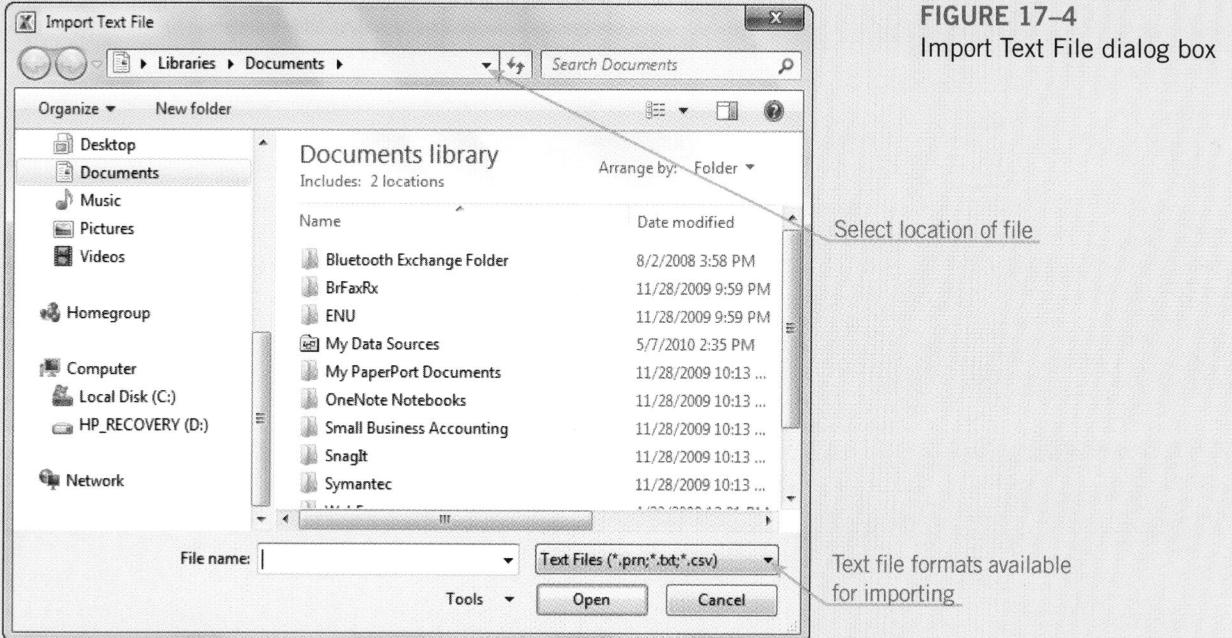

FIGURE 17–4
Import Text File dialog box

3. Navigate to the drive and folder where you store your Data Files, click **Pacific Sales.txt**, and then click **Import**. The Text Import Wizard – Step 1 of 3 dialog box opens, as shown in **Figure 17–5**. The wizard recognizes the imported data as delimited.

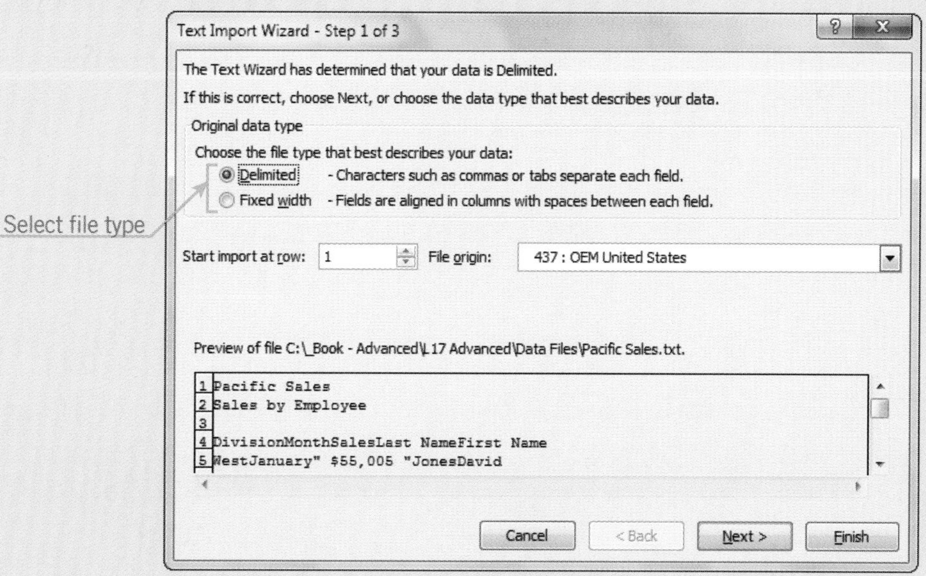

FIGURE 17–5
Text Import Wizard – Step 1 of 3

4. Leave the Delimited option button selected and then click **Next**. The Text Import Wizard – Step 2 of 3 dialog box appears, as shown in **Figure 17–6**. The wizard recognizes that the data is separated by tabs.

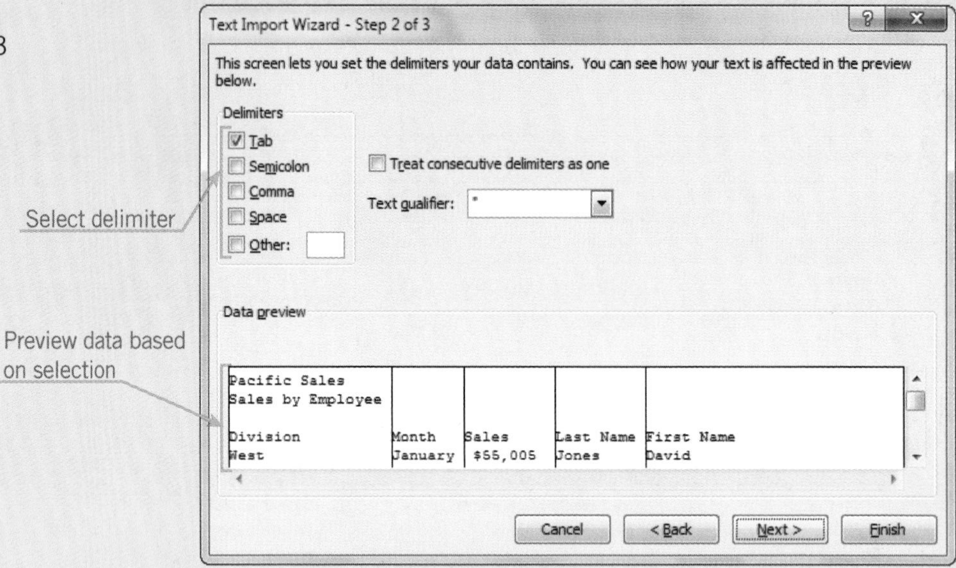

FIGURE 17–6
Text Import Wizard – Step 2 of 3

5. Leave the Tab check box selected and then click **Next**. The Text Import Wizard – Step 3 of 3 dialog box opens, as shown in **Figure 17–7**.

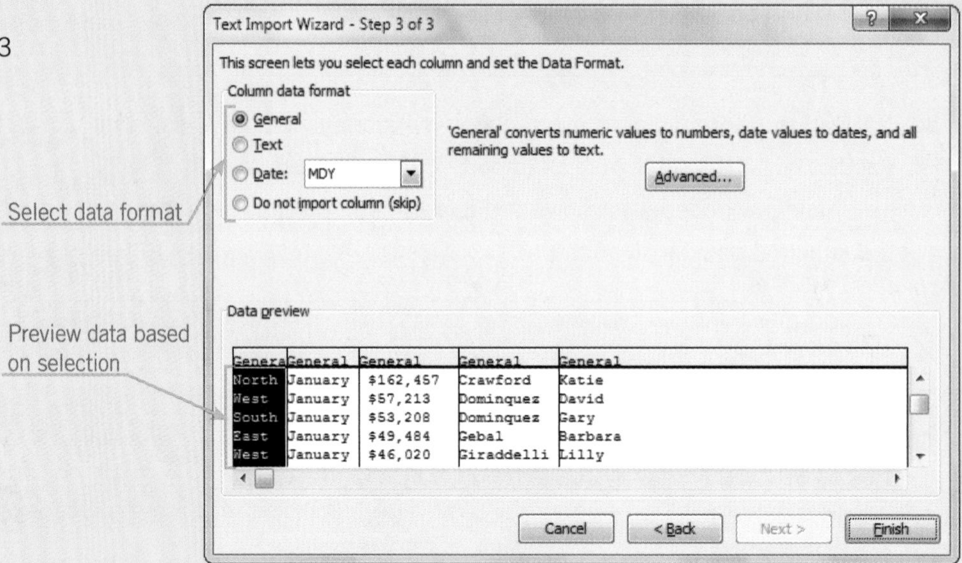

FIGURE 17–7
Text Import Wizard – Step 3 of 3

6. In the Text Import Wizard – Step 3 of 3 dialog box, click the **General** option button, if necessary, and then click **Finish**. The Import Data dialog box opens. You can choose to import the data into the cell you specify in the existing worksheet or in a new worksheet.
7. In the Import Data dialog box, click **OK**.
8. Select **C5:C67**.

9. Click the **Home** tab, and in the Number group, click the **Accounting Number Format** button.
10. Save the workbook as **Text Import** followed by your initials, and then close the file.

Using the Document Inspector

Before you export a workbook, you may want to use the Document Inspector to locate possible hidden and personal information. The Document Inspector then gives you the option to delete this information. Hidden data occurs for many reasons and is typical of workbooks that are shared among several people. Hidden data may be in comments, rows, columns, or even entire worksheets. Personal information could be the author's name or title. It might also include company information that you may not want others to see, such as the company name or manager's name. The Document Inspector first offers a checklist of items it will inspect, and then offers you the ability to delete those items from the workbook. For the next Step-by-Step, you will inspect a workbook yourself and then use the Document Inspector to find hidden data and delete this information.

Step-by-Step 17.3

1. Open the **Students** file from the drive and folder where your Data Files are stored.
2. Save the workbook as **Computer Students**, followed by your initials. You will look for comments and hidden information and then use the Document Inspector to create a checklist of items to inspect.
3. Select **cell H8**. Notice that cell H8 has a triangle in the upper-right corner indicating that this cell has a comment.
4. Click the **Review** tab and then click the **Show/Hide Comment** button. The comment will remain visible as you select another cell.
5. To look for hidden worksheets, right-click the **Students** worksheet tab and then click **Unhide** from the shortcut menu. Notice that a worksheet named College Bound Students is hidden, as shown in **Figure 17–8**.

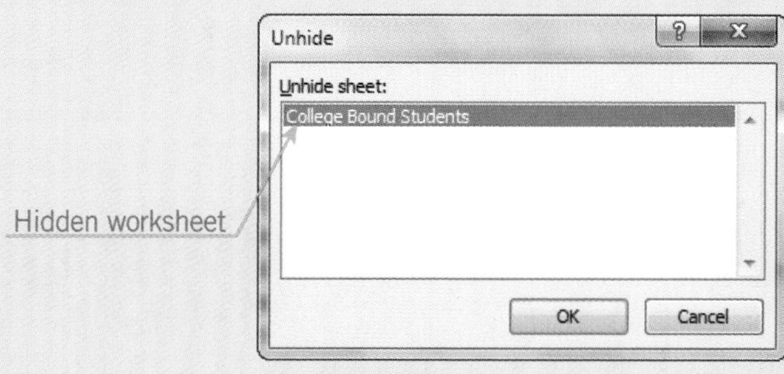

FIGURE 17–8
Unhide dialog box

6. Click **Cancel** to close the Unhide dialog box and keep the College Bound Students worksheet hidden.
7. Click the **File** tab and then click **Print** to view a print preview of the worksheet. Excel automatically adds a page header with the worksheet name and page footer with the page number, as shown in **Figure 17–9**. Information in page headers and footers is another item searched by the Document Inspector.

FIGURE 17–9
Print preview shows header and footer

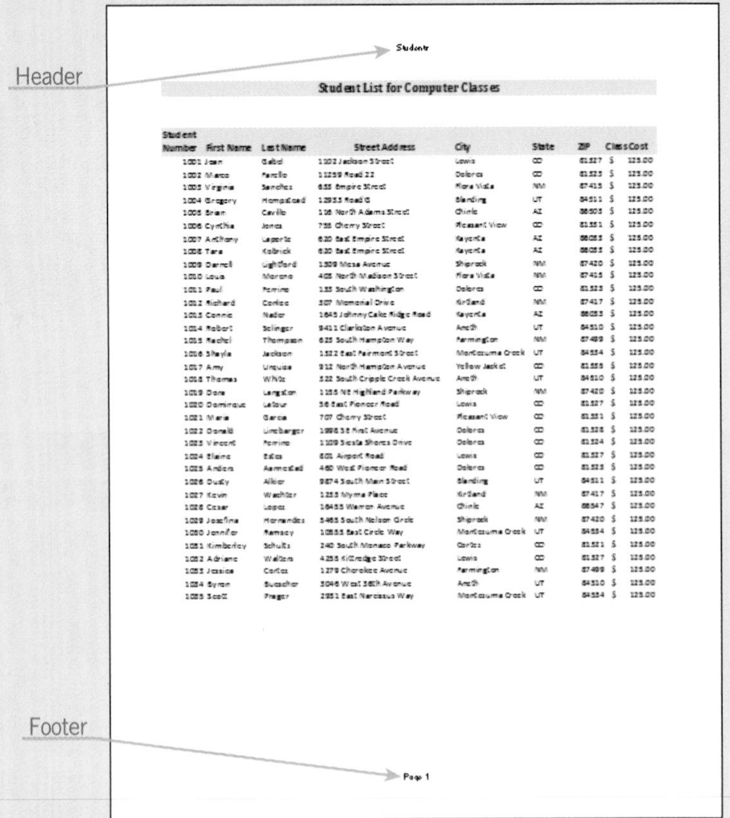

8. On the File tab, click **Info**.
9. Click the **Check for Issues** button. The Check for Issues options display as shown in **Figure 17–10**.

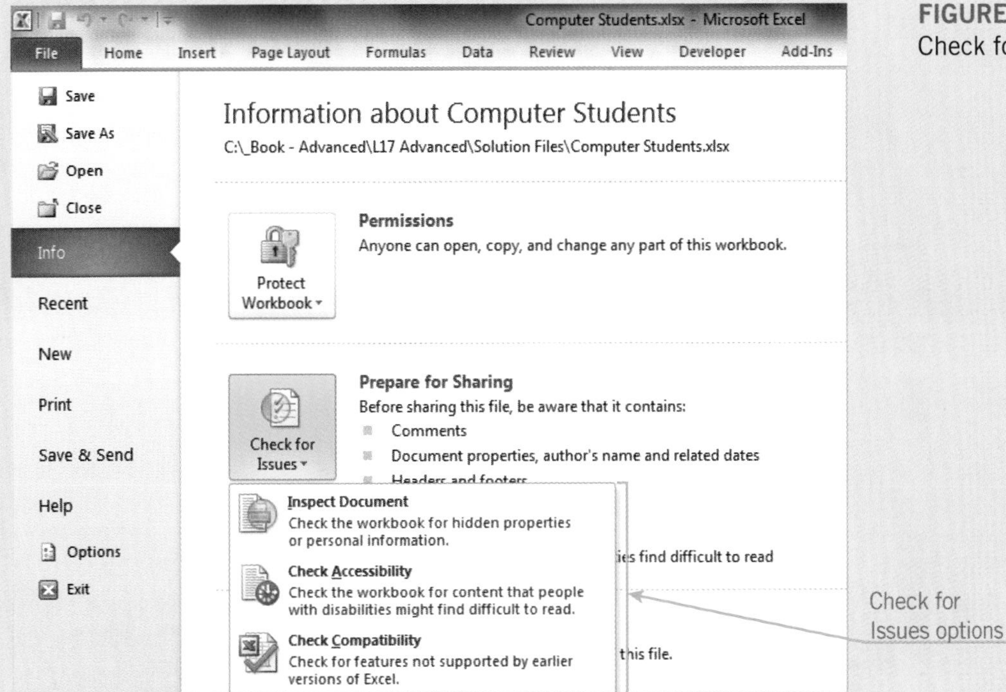

FIGURE 17–10
Check for Issues options

10. Click **Inspect Document**. You may be prompted to save the file before the Document Inspector dialog box opens. The Document Inspector dialog box opens, as shown in **Figure 17–11**. In this dialog box, you can add and remove check marks in order to define what you would like to search for with the Document Inspector.

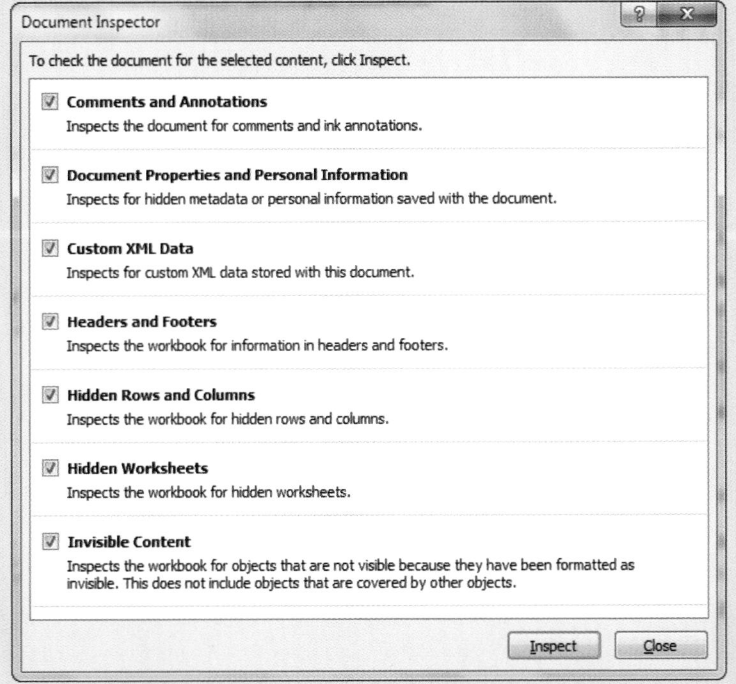

FIGURE 17–11
Document Inspector dialog box

11. Leave all the options selected and then click the **Inspect** button. The Document Inspector returns the search results in a new window, as shown in **Figure 17–12**. In the following steps, you will remove each of these items from the workbook.

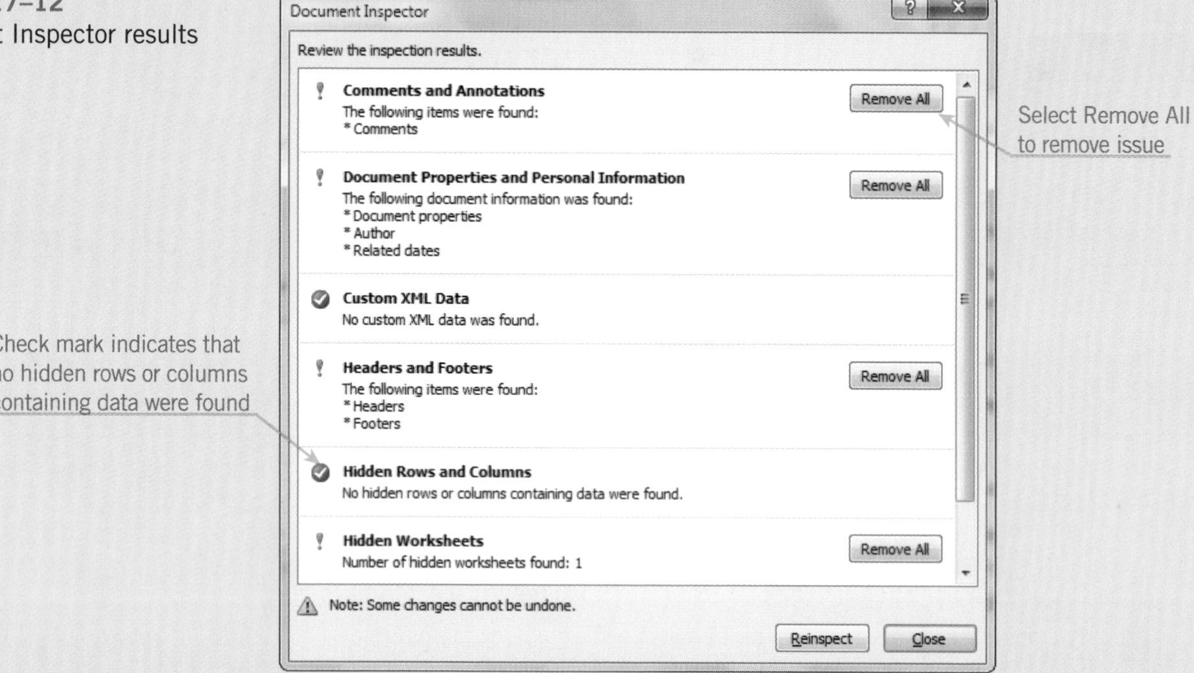

FIGURE 17–12
Document Inspector results

12. Click the **Remove All** button next to **Comments and Annotations**. All comments and annotations are removed from the workbook.

13. Click the **Remove All** button next to **Document Properties and Personal Information** and then again for **Headers and Footers**. The Document Inspector dialog box updates automatically.

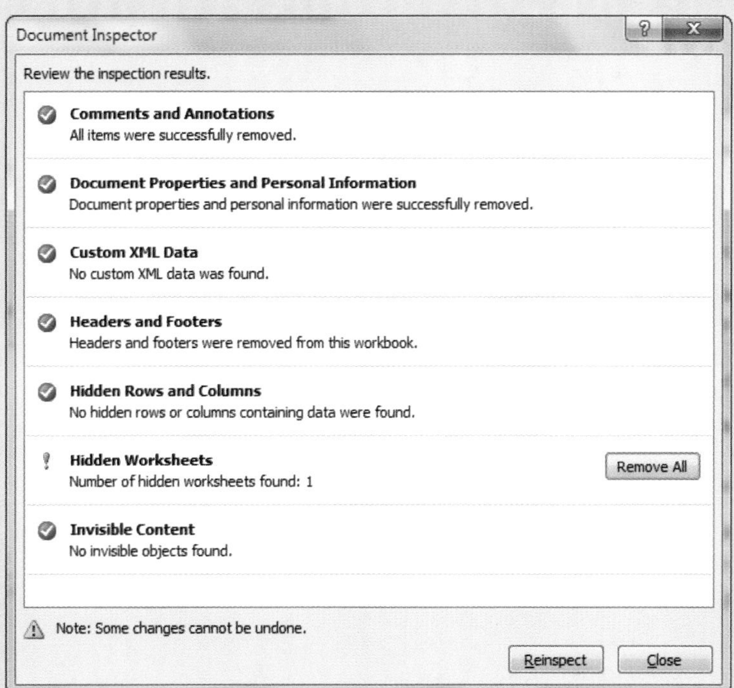

FIGURE 17–13
Document Inspector after removing issues

14. Click **Close** to close the Document Inspector dialog box, click the **Home** tab, and then verify that the comment in cell H8 is removed.
15. Save your work and leave the workbook open for the next Step-by-Step.

Saving a File as a PDF or an XPS Document

PDF stands for portable document format. When a worksheet is saved as a PDF, it can be viewed without the reader needing to install Excel. All of the fonts, formats, and images used in Excel are preserved in the PDF. If the worksheet or workbook is saved in PDF format, it can be e-mailed or uploaded to a Web site. The XPS format was developed by Microsoft and is similar to PDF. XPS also retains the exact look of the Excel document and protects it from being changed. The main difference between the PDF and the XPS is that the PDF is accessible to more people because it is available on most platforms. PDF files can be viewed in Adobe Acrobat or Adobe Reader. If you do not have Adobe Reader on your computer, you can download it at no cost from the Adobe Web site. The XPS format can only be read on some platforms. To save an Excel workbook as a PDF or as an XPS, you click the File tab, click Save & Send, and then click the Create PDF/XPS Document button. In the next Step-by-Step, you will save a file as a PDF and then view the file in Adobe Reader.

Step-by-Step 17.4

1. Click the **File** tab and then click **Save & Send**. The Save & Send options are displayed, as shown in **Figure 17–14**.

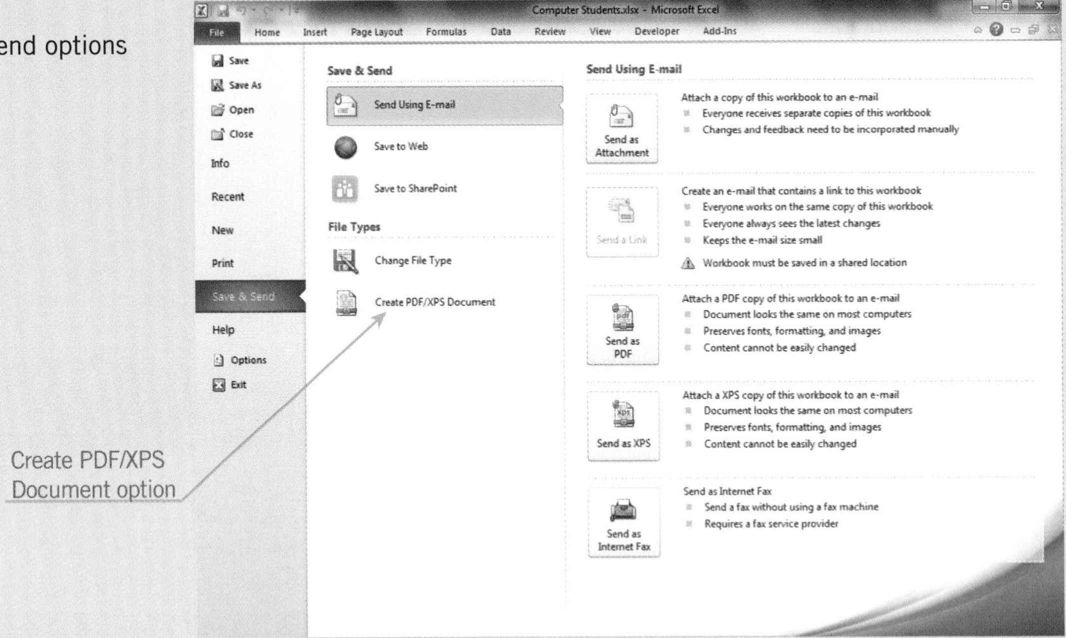

FIGURE 17–14
File tab with Save & Send options

2. Click the **Create PDF/XPS Document** option, then click the **Create PDF/ XPS button**.
3. The Publish as PDF or XPS dialog box opens, as shown in **Figure 17–15**.

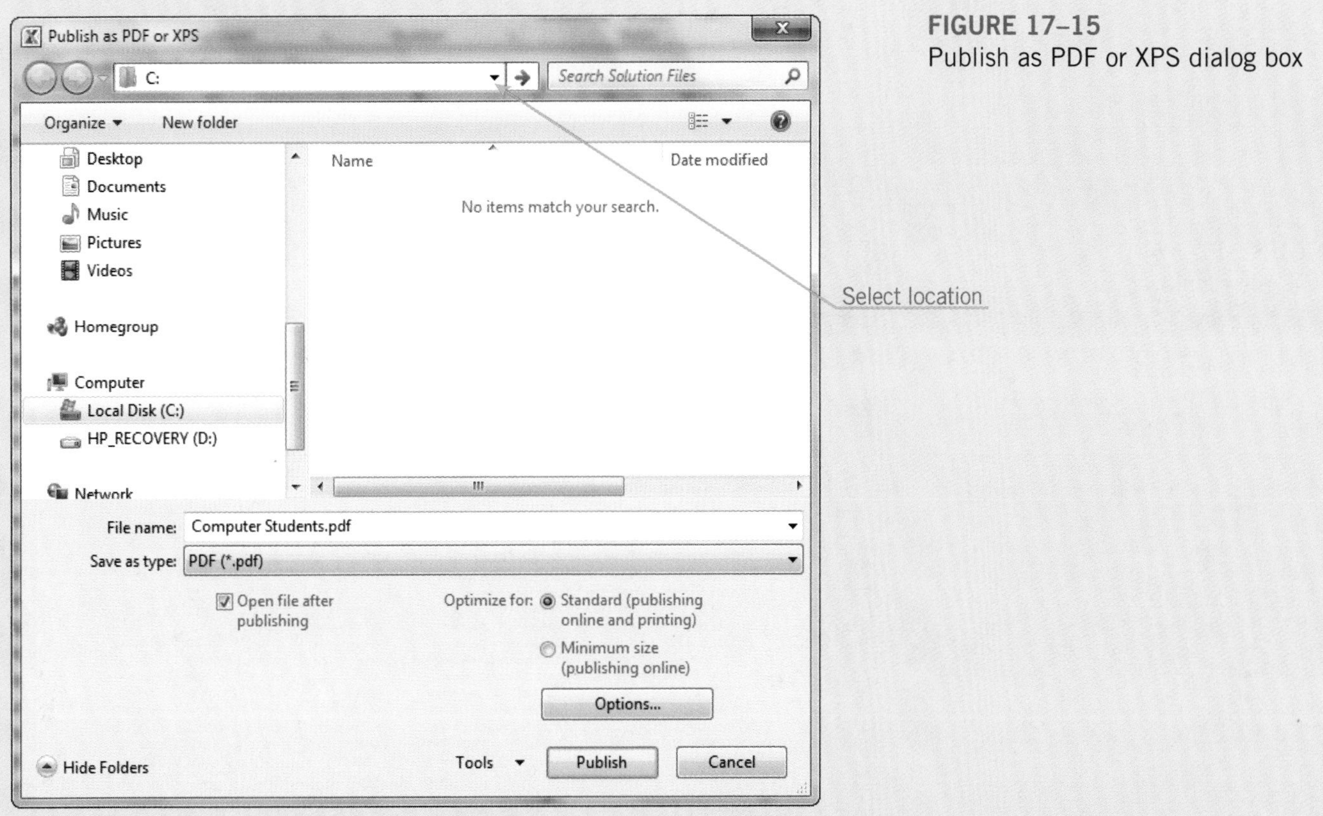

FIGURE 17–15
Publish as PDF or XPS dialog box

4. Verify that the **Open file after publishing** check box is selected (located under Save as type), and then click the **Publish** button. The PDF file opens in Adobe Reader, as shown in **Figure 17–16**. Notice that the file does not display comments, headers, or footers because you removed them using the Document Inspector.

Student List for Computer Classes

Student Number	First Name	Last Name	Street Address	City	State	ZIP	Class Cost
1001	Joan	Gabel	1102 Jackson Street	Lewis	CO	81327	$ 125.00
1002	Marco	Farello	11259 Road 22	Dolores	CO	81323	$ 125.00
1003	Virginia	Sanchez	633 Empire Street	Flora Vista	NM	87415	$ 125.00
1004	Gregory	Hempstead	12933 Road G	Blanding	UT	84511	$ 125.00
1005	Brian	Cavillo	116 North Adams Street	Chinle	AZ	86503	$ 125.00
1006	Cynthia	Jones	755 Cherry Street	Pleasant View	CO	81331	$ 125.00
1007	Anthony	Laporte	620 East Empire Street	Kayenta	AZ	86033	$ 125.00
1008	Tara	Kobrick	620 East Empire Street	Kayenta	AZ	86033	$ 125.00
1009	Darnell	Lightford	1309 Mesa Avenue	Shiprock	NM	87420	$ 125.00
1010	Louis	Moreno	403 North Madison Street	Flora Vista	NM	87415	$ 125.00
1011	Paul	Ferrino	133 South Washington	Dolores	CO	81323	$ 125.00
1012	Richard	Conlee	307 Memorial Drive	Kirtland	NM	87417	$ 125.00
1013	Connie	Nader	1645 Johnny Cake Ridge Road	Kayenta	AZ	86033	$ 125.00
1014	Robert	Selinger	9411 Clarkston Avenue	Aneth	UT	84510	$ 125.00
1015	Rachel	Thompson	623 South Hampton Way	Farmington	NM	87499	$ 125.00
1016	Shayla	Jackson	1322 East Fairmont Street	Montezuma Creek	UT	84534	$ 125.00
1017	Amy	Urquiza	912 North Hampton Avenue	Yellow Jacket	CO	81335	$ 125.00
1018	Thomas	White	322 South Cripple Creek Avenue	Aneth	UT	84510	$ 125.00
1019	Dora	Langston	1155 NE Highland Parkway	Shiprock	NM	87420	$ 125.00
1020	Dominque	Latour	56 East Pioneer Road	Lewis	CO	81327	$ 125.00
1021	Maria	Garcia	707 Cherry Street	Pleasant View	CO	81331	$ 125.00
1022	Donald	Linebarger	1998 SE First Avenue	Dolores	CO	81328	$ 125.00
1023	Vincent	Ferrino	1109 Siesta Shores Drive	Dolores	CO	81324	$ 125.00
1024	Elaine	Estes	801 Airport Road	Lewis	CO	81327	$ 125.00

FIGURE 17–16
PDF file displayed

5. Click **File** on the Adobe Reader menu bar, and then click **Exit** to close the file.

6. Save the workbook and leave it open for the next Step-by-Step.

Exporting a File to SkyDrive

VOCABULARY
SkyDrive

If you need to share your files so that other individuals can view them, you might want to consider placing the files on the Web. Microsoft offers 25 GB of online Web storage for free using the ***SkyDrive*** program. SkyDrive allows you to access and share files online with friends, family members, or co-workers. To access SkyDrive, you must have a Windows Live account.

After you export or upload a file to your SkyDrive account, the file can then be shared and accessed. The file can be downloaded by others from SkyDrive and edited. When the file is downloaded, it opens in Protected View, but it can be edited by clicking the Enable Editing button. If you are concerned about protecting the workbook from being viewed by unauthorized individuals, you can add password protection to the workbook in Excel. In this next Step-by-Step, you will create a SkyDrive account, upload a file to SkyDrive, and then download the file from SkyDrive to your computer.

Step-by-Step 17.5

1. Click the **File** tab, and then click **Save & Send**. In the center pane, click **Save to Web**. Your screen should look similar to **Figure 17–17**.

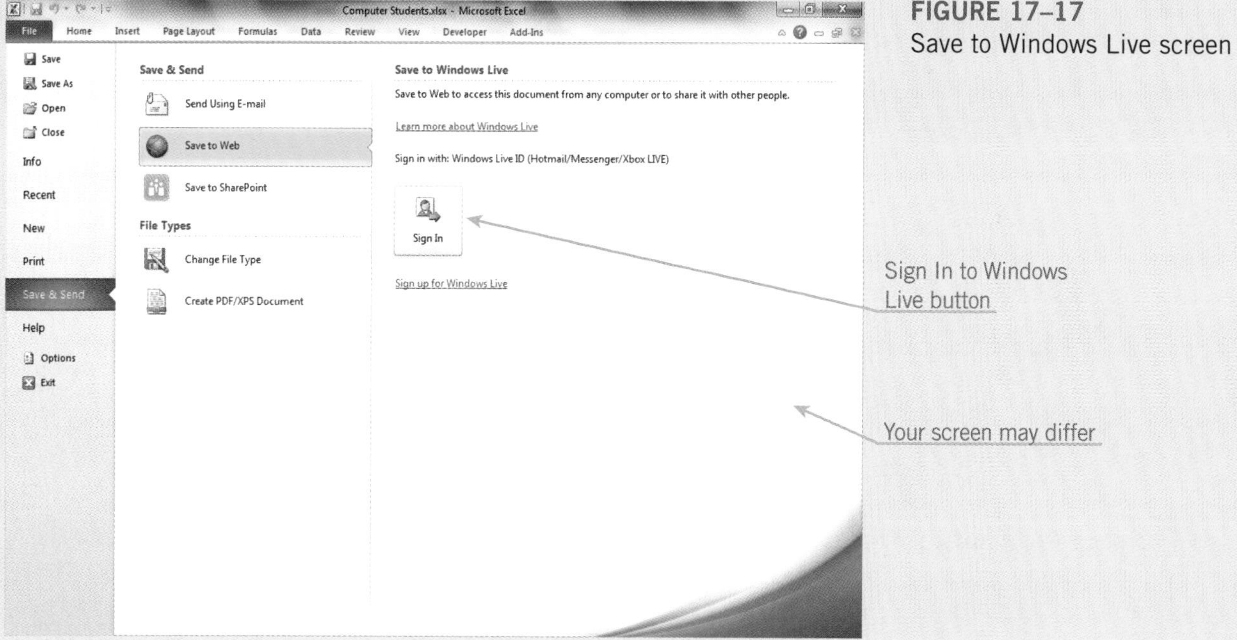

FIGURE 17–17
Save to Windows Live screen

2. If you have a Windows Live ID, click the **Sign In** button, enter your ID and password, and then click **OK**. If you do not have an account, click the **Sign up for Windows Live** link and follow the instructions to create a new account. After you access Windows Live, your screen should appear similar to **Figure 17–18**.

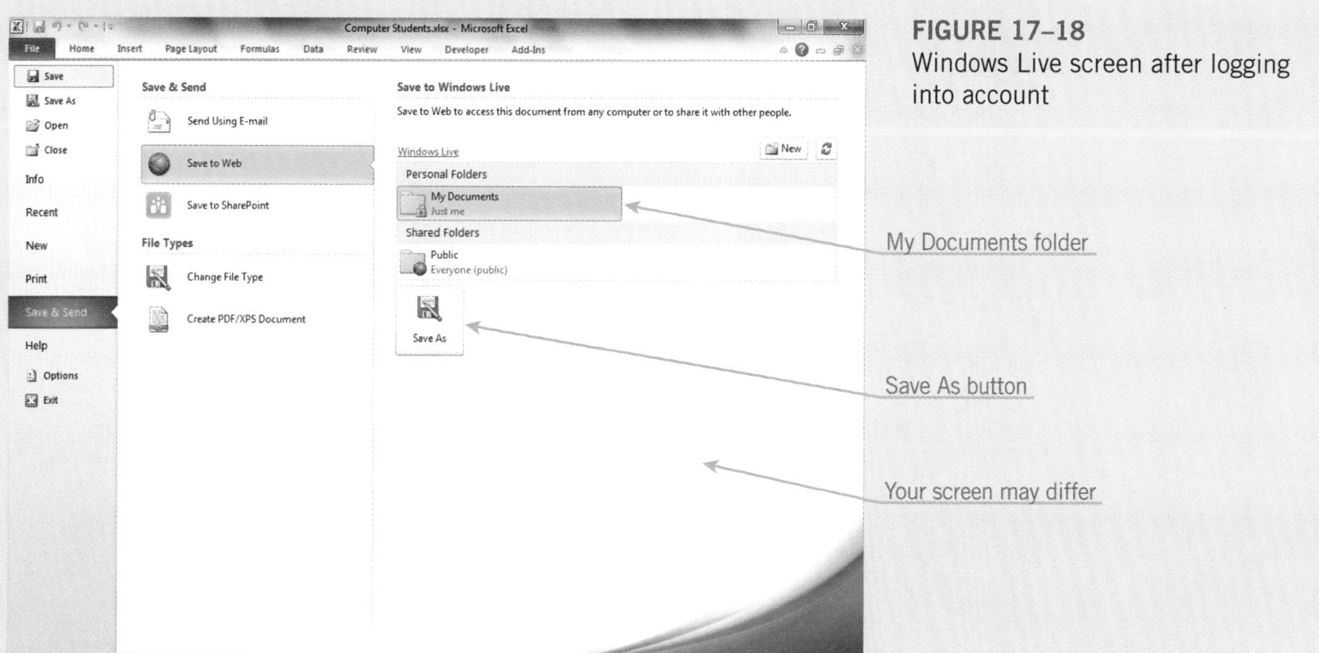

FIGURE 17–18
Windows Live screen after logging into account

3. Click the **My Documents** folder to select it, and then click the **Save As** button. The Save As dialog box opens, as shown in **Figure 17–19**.

FIGURE 17–19
Save As dialog box

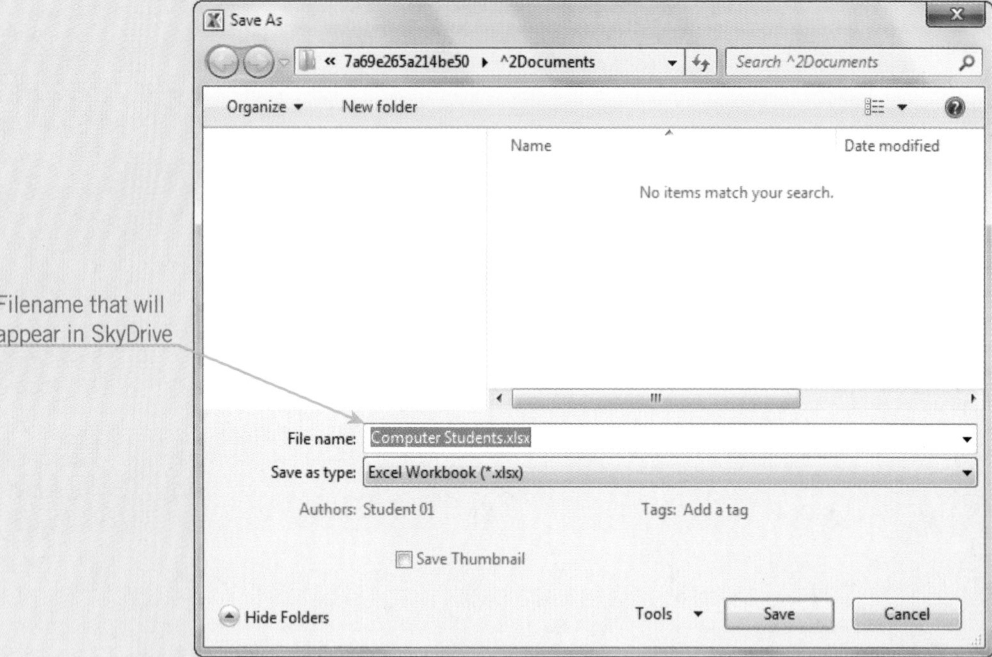

4. Leave the filename as it appears and then click **Save**. The workbook is now available on SkyDrive.
5. Close the workbook. You will now go to the SkyDrive Web site and locate the file.
6. Using your browser, go to **skydrive.live.com**. You should still be signed in.
7. Click the **My Documents** folder and then click the **Computer Students** workbook.
8. If necessary, click the **View** link located above the workbook. Your workbook should appear similar to **Figure 17–20**.

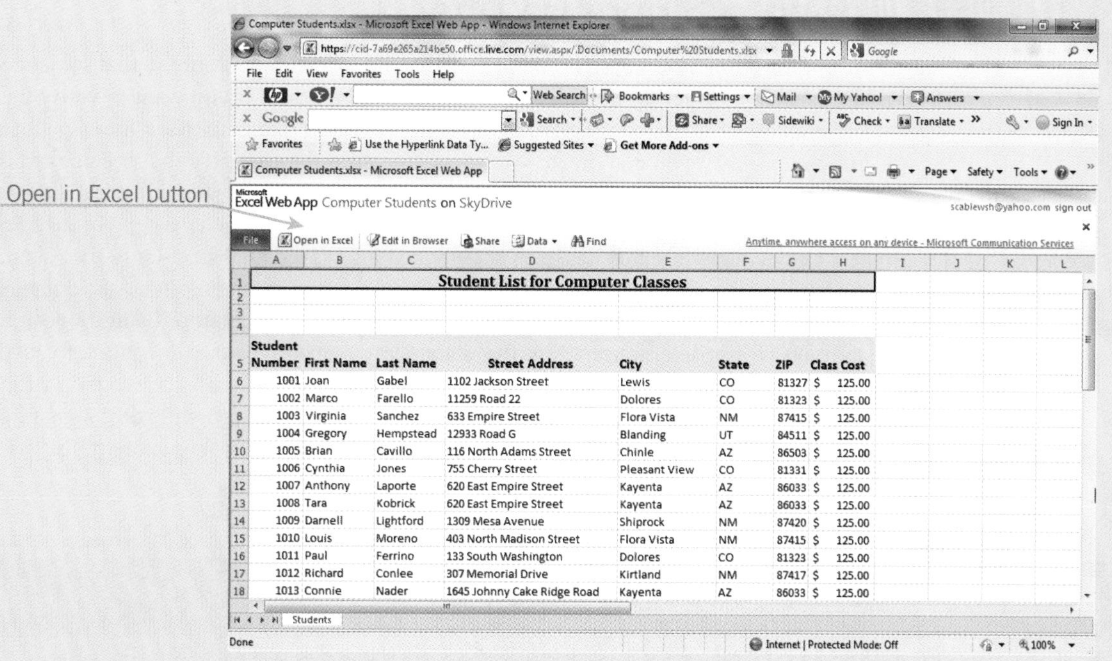

FIGURE 17–20 Viewing workbook in SkyDrive

9. Click the **Open in Excel** button. A message appears indicating that some files may be harmful to your computer.
10. Click **OK** to close the message box.
11. If necessary, enter your Windows Live ID and password, and then click **OK**. The workbook is now open in Excel as a read-only file. See **Figure 17–21**.

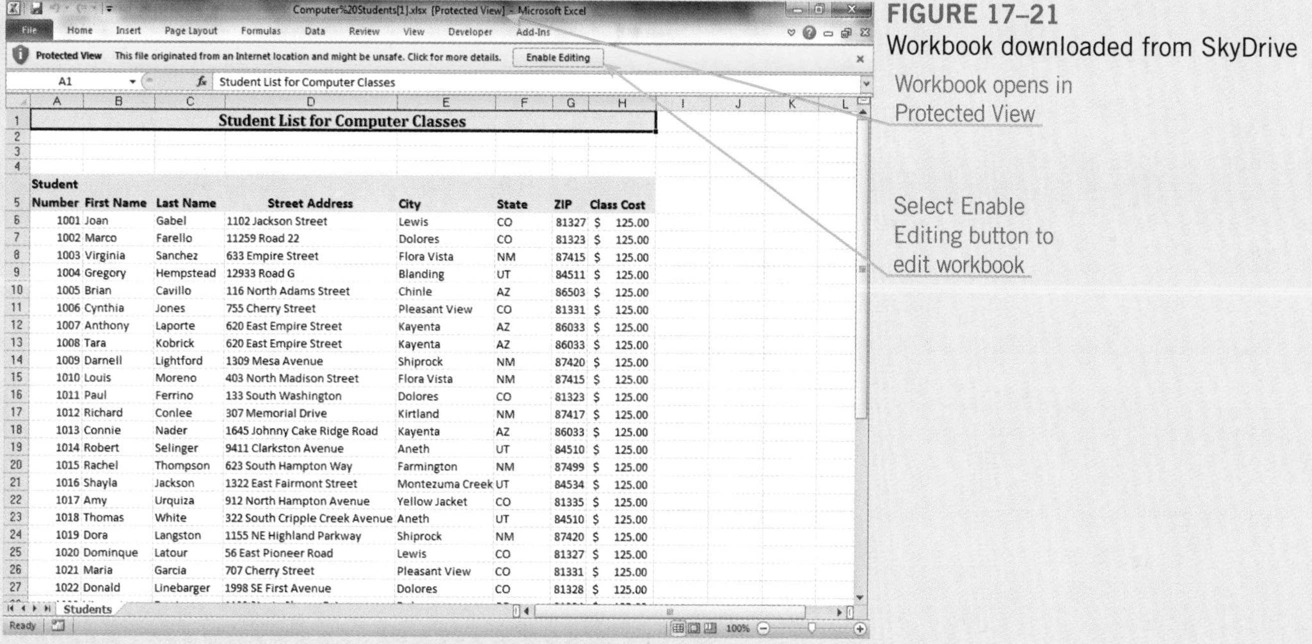

FIGURE 17–21 Workbook downloaded from SkyDrive

12. Close all open workbooks and then close the browser window.

Using a Signature Line

VOCABULARY
signature line

A ***signature line*** is a security feature that you add to a workbook file so that someone else can sign, or verify, the information. This can be useful if you want to verify the authenticity of a file coming from someone else. You can even have the signature line dated. Also, you can create your own signature file to verify that it came from you. The signature file can be created using the Signature Services from the Office Marketplace at a small cost, or you can create a graphic file, such as a .jpg or .tif file.

Once a signature line has been added, the file is saved as a Read-Only file. Then, the person who has an authorized signature can sign the signature line. Any changes made to the workbook after it is signed will result in the signature being removed, and you will not be able to sign the document again. Likewise, if you try to save the workbook with a different name, the signature line will show the words *Invalid signature* above the signature line. In this next Step-by-Step, you will add a signature line to a workbook file. Then, you will open the file and add the signature of the person verifying the workbook data.

Step-by-Step 17.6

1. Open the **Income** file from the drive and folder where your Data Files are stored and then save the workbook as **Income Statement**, followed by your initials.
2. Select **cell A25** and then click the **Insert** tab.
3. In the Text group, click the **Signature Line** button. A message box displays a disclaimer that Microsoft is not legally responsible for warranty of digital signatures.
4. Click **OK**. The Signature Setup dialog box opens, as shown in **Figure 17–22**.

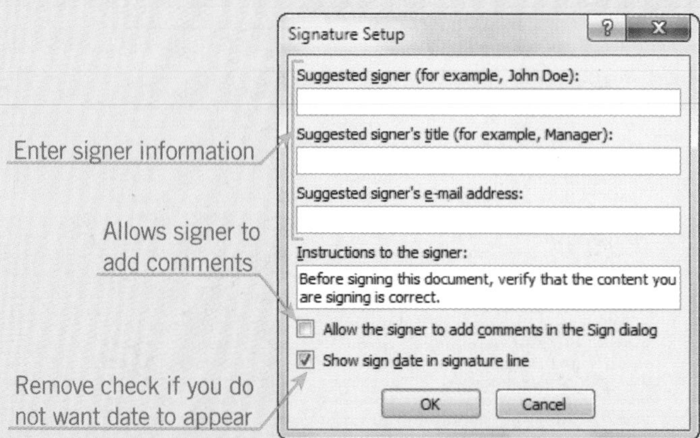

FIGURE 17–22
Signature Setup dialog box

5. In the **Suggested signer** text box, type **Angelina Tarrant**.
6. Click in the **Suggested signer's title** text box, type **Manager**, and then click the **Allow the signer to add comments in the Sign dialog** check box.
7. Click in the **Instructions to the signer** box, type **Verify the income and expenses are correct**, and then click the **Show sign date in signature line** check box to deselect it. Compare your screen to **Figure 17–23**.

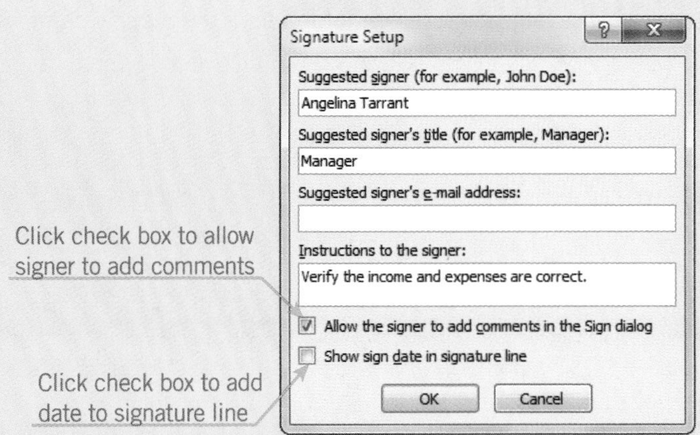

FIGURE 17–23 Completed Signature Setup dialog box

8. Click **OK**. The signature line appears in the worksheet.
9. Save the **Income Statement** file, then save the workbook again as **Income Statement for Verification**, followed by your initials.
10. Close the workbook and then reopen the workbook. Notice the yellow information bar above the formula bar, as shown in **Figure 17–24**.

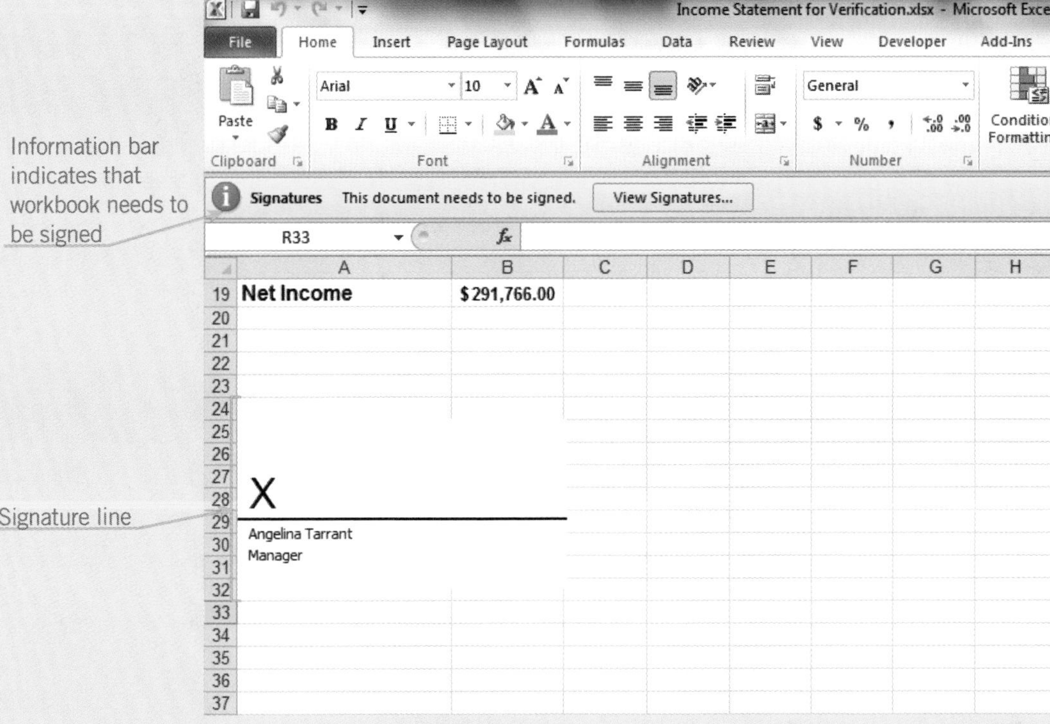

FIGURE 17–24 Worksheet with information bar

11. Right-click the **signature placeholder** and then click **Sign**. Click **OK** to accept the disclaimer. The Sign dialog box opens, as shown in **Figure 17–25**.

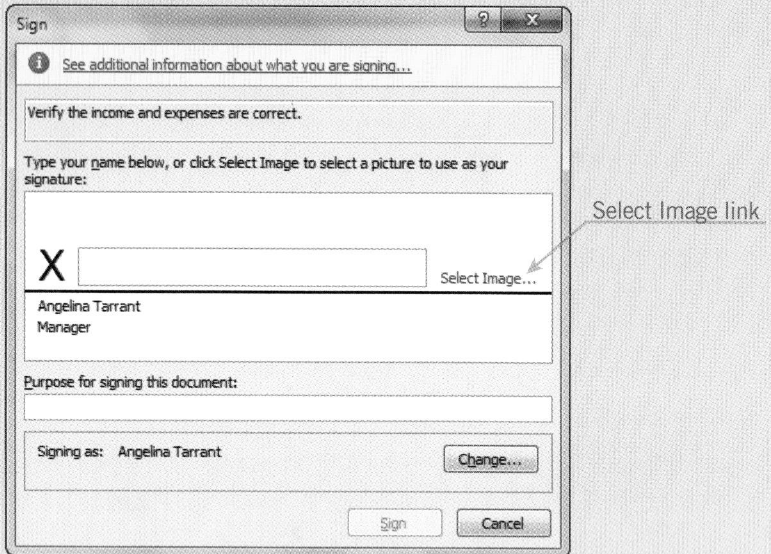

FIGURE 17–25
Sign dialog box

12. Click the **Select Image** link, navigate to your Data Files folder, select the **Angelina Tarrant signature.tif file**, and then click **Select**.
13. Click in the **Purpose for signing the document** text box, and then type **Income and Expenses are correct**. The signature appears in the Sign dialog box, as shown in **Figure 17–26**.

FIGURE 17–26
Sign dialog box with signature

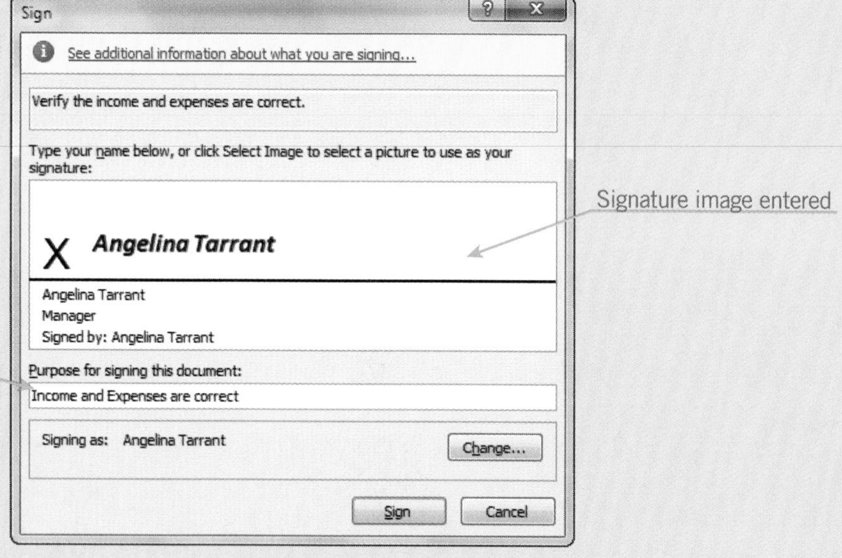

14. Click the **Sign** button. The Signature Confirmation message box appears.
15. Click **OK**. The information bar shows that the workbook is marked as complete. See **Figure 17–27**.

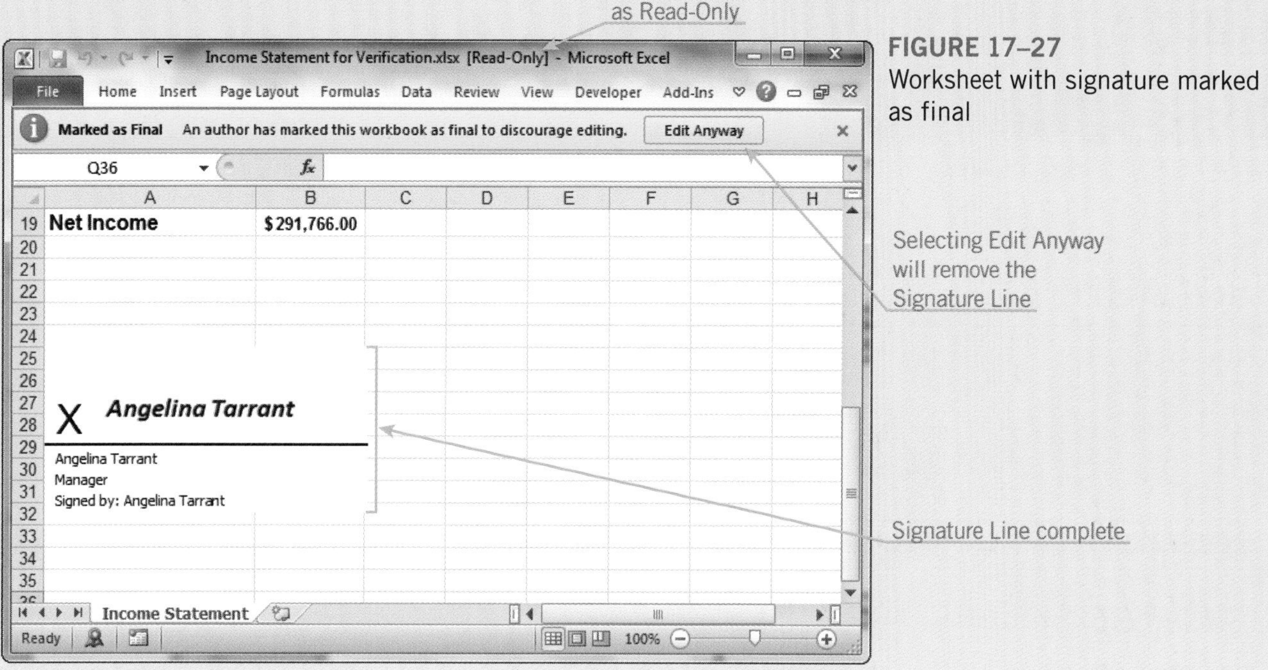

FIGURE 17–27
Worksheet with signature marked as final

16. Close the workbook.

SUMMARY

In this lesson, you learned:

- Data from Microsoft Access can be imported into Excel.
- Text files in the .txt, .csv, and .prn formats can be imported in Excel.
- The Document Inspector locates hidden or sensitive information and lets you keep or remove the data.
- Saving a workbook as a PDF puts the file in a format that can be sent via e-mail, and the document can be viewed without the viewer needing to install Excel.
- An Excel workbook can be exported to SkyDrive.
- Using signature lines adds security to a file so the file cannot be changed without the signature being removed.

VOCABULARY

Define the following terms:

delimited	fixed width	signature line
export	import	SkyDrive

REVIEW QUESTIONS

TRUE / FALSE

Circle T if the statement is true or F if the statement is false.

T F **1.** Workbooks with a signature line can be saved with another filename without removing the signature line.

T F **2.** An Excel workbook can be exported to the Web.

T F **3.** Importing data refers to bringing data from another program into Excel.

T F **4.** Saving an Excel workbook in a PDF file format allows others to view the file without needing to install Excel.

T F **5.** Text data cannot be imported into an Excel workbook.

FILL IN THE BLANK

1. Microsoft provides 25GB of free Web space if you create an account in a program called ______________.
2. When you send a workbook to another program or to the Web, you are said to be ______________ the file.
3. You can use the ______________ ______________ to locate hidden comments, rows, and columns.
4. To bring data from another program into Excel, you need to ______________ the data.
5. If you try to save a workbook that has a signature line with another filename, the signature line will be ______________.

WRITTEN QUESTIONS

Write a brief answer to the following questions.

1. Explain the difference between importing and exporting data.

2. Explain the process for exporting a workbook to SkyDrive.

3. Explain the purpose of the Document Inspector.

4. What is the benefit of saving an Excel workbook as a PDF document?

5. Explain how to import a text file into an Excel workbook.

PROJECTS

If you have a SAM 2010 user profile, your instructor may have assigned an autogradable version of the indicated project. If so, log into the SAM 2010 Web site at *www.cengage.com/sam2010* to download the instruction and start files.

PROJECT 17–1

1. Start a new Excel workbook.
2. Import **Doctors.accdb** from the drive and folder where your Data Files are stored.
3. Save the workbook as **Doctors Import**.
4. Use the ClinicID AutoFilter to filter for ClinicID 8.
5. Save and close the workbook.

SAM PROJECT 17–2

1. Open the **Regional Managers** file from the drive and folder where your Data Files are stored.
2. Save the workbook as **Regional Managers Weekly Sales**, followed by your initials. You will now look for hidden information using the Document Inspector.
3. Remove the document properties and personal information.
4. Remove the headers and footers.
5. Remove the hidden worksheets. Leave the rows and columns hidden.
6. Save and close the workbook.

PROJECT 17–3

1. Open the **Household** file from the drive and folder where your Data Files are stored.
2. Create a PDF file from the workbook with the filename **Household Addresses**.
3. Close the workbook.
4. Open the PDF file.
5. Print the PDF file.
6. Close the PDF file.

CRITICAL THINKING

ACTIVITY 17–1

1. Locate the text file **Arts and Crafts** in the drive and folder where your Data Files are stored, and then import the file into a new workbook. Save the workbook as **A&C Imported File**, followed by your initials.
2. Examine the data and think of at least one formula that you could add to the workbook.
3. Add any formats that you think will enhance the appearance of the worksheet.
4. Print the sheet and then close the workbook.

ACTIVITY 17–2

1. You have imported a text file into Excel that contains the names, ID numbers, and salaries of all employees at your company. You know that you would like the imported data to change if any modifications are made to it in the original file. Use Excel's Help system to find information on updating or refreshing imported data. Explain how you would proceed.

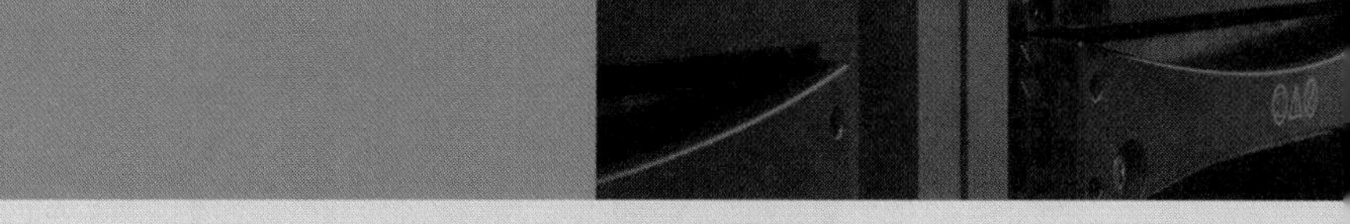

UNIT REVIEW

Advanced Microsoft Excel

REVIEW QUESTIONS

TRUE / FALSE

Circle T if the statement is true or F if the statement is false.

T F 1. Themes enable you to apply borders, background colors, shading, and graphic effects instantly to an entire workbook.

T F 2. When you format data as a table, AutoFilters are automatically added to the data.

T F 3. Protection may be added to worksheets, or to an entire workbook.

T F 4. If you use the Subtotals feature to place subtotals within worksheet data, they cannot be removed.

T F 5. An Excel workbook may be shared and accessed with external users by uploading the file to SkyDrive.

T F 6. A sparkline is a miniature chart that is displayed on its own sheet in a workbook.

T F 7. To improve data accuracy when entering repetitive data, you can create a drop-down list with the data from which to select.

T F 8. A VLOOKUP function finds data in the lookup table when a table is arranged horizontally in columns.

T F 9. Creating a macro is a way to automate some of the common, repetitive tasks you perform in Excel, thereby saving valuable time.

T F 10. If #DIV/0! appears in a cell instead of the results of a formula, you need to delete the formula since it cannot be repaired.

FILL IN THE BLANK

Complete the following sentences by writing the correct word or words in the blanks provided.

1. ____________ applies a font, border, or pattern to worksheet cells when certain conditions exist in those cells.
2. Adding a(n) ____________ below a chart lets you view the worksheet data while looking at the chart data series.
3. To join the values of cells together, you use the ____________ function.
4. The data in a(n) ____________ can be rearranged and summarized in different ways so that you can view the data from various perspectives.
5. The ____________ function counts the number of cells that do not have any numbers or text entered in them.
6. The file extension used for a macro-enabled workbook is ____________.
7. You can use the ____________ feature when your worksheet has lots of data and you want Excel to check all of the formulas and functions in the worksheet for potential problems.
8. To prevent a workbook from being opened by an unauthorized person, you can add a(n) ____________ to the workbook.
9. ____________ refers to bringing data from other programs, such as Access, into an Excel workbook.
10. Before you export a workbook, you may want to use the ____________ to locate possible hidden information in the workbook.

MULTIPLE CHOICE

Select the best response for each of the following statements.

1. In a custom number format that has month, day, and year, you use a ____________ to represent the month.
   A. d
   B. y
   C. m
   D. 0
2. The horizontal axis at the bottom of a chart is the ____________.
   A. X-axis
   B. Y-axis
   C. Z-axis
   D. U-axis
3. A ____________ can appear as numbers or text next to each data marker in the data series.
   A. data point
   B. data list
   C. data axis
   D. data label

4. The ______________ feature is a great method for separating data in a worksheet, such as first and last names.

   A. Concatenate

   B. Text Table

   C. Convert Text to Columns

   D. Data Marker

5. A ______________ is a visual control that looks like a notepad; clicking selections on it lets you filter data in a PivotTable.

   A. sparkline

   B. slicer

   C. Pivot Note

   D. chart

6. A ______________ lets you add a signature to a workbook and marks the workbook as final.

   A. signature line

   B. password

   C. PivotChart

   D. Data Note

7. The ______________ function can count cells if they contain text or numbers.

   A. COUNT

   B. SUBTOTAL

   C. COUNTA

   D. SUM

8. The ______________ function will only total data that meets a certain condition.

   A. Concatenate

   B. COUNTA

   C. COUNTA

   D. SUMIF

9. The ______________ function locates data when it is displayed vertically in the lookup table.

   A. VLOOKUP

   B. HLOOKUP

   C. PivotTable

   D. Filter

10. If several people need to work on a workbook at the same time, you can create a ______________ workbook.

    A. shared

    B. PivotChart

    C. themed

    D. table-style

PROJECTS

PROJECT 1

The annual sales for each employee at New Western are recorded in a workbook. You decide to add a PivotTable and PivotChart to the workbook so that you can view the data in different ways.

1. Open the **New Western** file from the drive and folder where your Data Files are stored.
2. Save the workbook as **New Western Sales** followed by your initials.
3. Create a PivotTable and Pivot Chart in a new worksheet with the following information:

   Axis Fields: **Division**

   Last Name

   Values: **Sales**
4. Decrease the font size on the X-axis until all of the names are displayed.
5. Format the Total column with the Comma Style and no decimal places.
6. Change the worksheet name for the PivotTable and PivotChart to **Sales Table**.
7. Filter the PivotChart so that only the Northwest division is displayed.
8. Save, print, and close the workbook.

PROJECT 2

The expenses for your three years of law school are recorded in a workbook. You want to create a macro that will add formats to each worksheet in the workbook.

1. Open the **Law School** file from the drive and folder where your Data Files are stored.
2. Save the workbook as a macro-enabled workbook with the filename **Law School Budget** followed by your initials.
3. Create a macro named **Formats** with the shortcut key **Ctrl + F** to add formats to the worksheets as follows:
   a. The worksheet title should be **Bold**, **Font Size - 16**, and **Dark Blue, Text 2, Darker 25%**.
   b. The worksheet subtitle should be **Bold**, **Font Size - 12**, **Italic**, **Dark Blue, Text 2, Lighter 40%**.
   c. The ranges **A6:A12** and **B5:L5** should have **Dark Blue, Text 2, Darker 25%** font.
   d. Add totals to the bottom of the month columns.

4. Use the macro to add the formats to each worksheet in the workbook.
5. Save, print, and close the workbook.

PROJECT 3

The Imports file is an income statement. You will create a scenario for store lease, store utilities, and shipping expense variances.

1. Open the **Imports** file from the drive and folder where your Data Files are stored.
2. Save the workbook as **Imports Unlimited** followed by your initials.
3. Create a scenario named **Current Expenses** using the expenses currently in the Income Statement worksheet.
4. Create a scenario named **Increased Expenses**. Enter the following expenses into the scenario:

   Cell **B10** (Store Lease): **83500**

   Cell **B11** (Store Utilities): **26000**

   Cell **B12** (Shipping Expenses): **8500**
5. Create a scenario named **Decreased Expenses**. Enter the following expenses into the scenario:

   Cell **B10** (Store Lease): **45000**

   Cell **B11** (Store Utilities): **20000**

   Cell **B12** (Shipping Expenses): **6000**
6. Print the **Scenario Summary** worksheet.
7. Save and then close the workbook.

PROJECT 4

1. Open the **Corporate** file from the drive and folder where your Data Files are stored.
2. Save the workbook as **Corporate Tees** followed by your initials.
3. Enter a formula in cell **D19** that will calculate the total of the order based on the quantity of tee shirts purchased multiplied by the price.
4. Enable the Track Changes feature to highlight all changes.
5. Enter the following information into the worksheet:

   Cell **B8**: **235**

   Cell **B10**: **Susan Williams**

   Cell **B11**: **630 North Shore Blvd.**

   Cell **B19**: **5**

6. Enter the following information into the worksheet:

   Cell **B8**: **236**

   Cell **B10**: **Juan Lopez**

   Cell **B11**: **444 Southlake**

   Cell **B19**: **2**

7. Open the Select Changes to Accept or Reject dialog box, and then review and accept the changes.
8. Print the worksheet.
9. Save and close the workbook.

CRITICAL THINKING

JOB 1

You are figuring out how much money to save each month for family trips. The monthly amount that needs to be saved will help you determine which trips best fit your budget. You decide to use Goal Seek to find the monthly savings amount for each trip.

1. Open the **Trip Planning** file from the drive and folder where your Data Files are stored.
2. Save the workbook as **Trip Planning Estimates** followed by your initials.
3. You think that the trip to Disneyland will take two years of savings, the trip to Alaska will take four years of savings, and the trip to Costa Rica will take five years of savings. Enter formulas in cells **C4**, **C6**, and **C8** that can be used with Goal Seek to find the monthly payment amount. (*Hint:* You would enter a formula in C4 such as =B4*2*12.)
4. Use Goal Seek to find the monthly payment amount for the trip to Disneyland if it costs $4,000.
5. Use Goal Seek to find the monthly payment amount for the trip to Alaska if it costs $5,000.
6. Use Goal Seek to find the monthly payment amount for the trip to Costa Rica if it costs $7,500.
7. Print the worksheet and save the workbook.
8. Close the workbook.

JOB 2

You are the Inventory Supervisor for a college bookstore. To ensure that your assistants enter correct information into the inventory workbook, you decide to add data validation to the workbook. You will also add drop-down lists to the Item # and Description columns to save time and increase accuracy.

1. Open the **Discount Inventory** file from the drive and folder where your Data Files are stored.
2. Save the workbook as **Discount Interior Inventory** followed by your initials.
3. Add data validation for both the Item # column and the Description column starting in row 65 through row 100. (*Hint*: You should have 17 items for each drop-down list.)
4. To test the drop-down lists, select cell B65, then select W-SWMD.
5. Select cell C65, then select Wallpaper Border – Small.
6. Save and print the Inventory worksheet.
7. Close the workbook.

Estimated Time for Unit: 17.5 hours

ADVANCED

MICROSOFT ACCESS UNIT

Estimated Time: 1.5 hours

LESSON 7

Enhancing Table Design

OBJECTIVES

Upon completion of this lesson, you should be able to:

- Create an input mask.
- Enter data in an input mask field.
- Set validation rules.
- Enter data into a field with a validation rule.
- Set a lookup property.
- Select field values from a list.
- Use the Lookup Wizard to set lookup properties.
- Select data from a list with multiple columns.
- Create a calculated field in a table.

VOCABULARY

Expression Builder
expression
input mask
list box
operator
placeholder
validation rule

Introduction

Microsoft Access is a powerful database application that lets you store, organize, and manipulate vast amounts of data. You should already be familiar with the primary objects that comprise a database: tables, forms, and reports. In these advanced lessons, you'll learn more about each of these objects plus other features that help you manage and control your database records.

In this lesson, you will learn about the various enhancements you can add to tables, such as an input mask. An input mask is a pattern created for a data type, such as (XXX) XXX-XXXX for a telephone number, so that it is entered correctly into a field with the parentheses and the dash. You will also learn about applying validation rules to data so that a message box appears if the data is entered incorrectly. You will then learn how to add lookup properties to a table so that you can select the values you need for a field from a list. You will set lookup values using the Lookup Wizard to display two columns of data in a list, and finally, you will create a calculated field in a table for the purpose of showing actual calculations between fields in the table.

Creating an Input Mask

VOCABULARY
input mask
placeholder

An ***input mask*** is a pattern for common types of data entered in a field. Access includes several input mask formats, such as phone numbers, Social Security numbers, and ZIP codes.

For example, if you need to enter phone numbers using the format (XXX) XXX-XXXX, typing the parentheses and the dash each time you enter a phone number might get tiresome. Instead, you can apply the Phone Number input mask; then all you need to type are the numbers. The input mask inserts the parentheses and hyphen in the correct positions for you.

To create an input mask, you must be in Design view. Select the field for which you want to create the input mask, and then click in the Input Mask text box in the Field Properties pane. After you create the input mask, Access will ask if you want to save the values with the symbols, such as the parentheses and a dash in a phone number. If your computer has plenty of disk space, it should be okay to save the values with the symbols.

You may also select the placeholder for your input mask field. A ***placeholder*** appears in a field before the value is entered. The default placeholder is the underscore. The placeholder simply identifies that an input mask is assigned to the field in the table. In the next Step-by-Step, you will add an input mask to the Phone and Cell Phone fields in an Access table.

EXTRA FOR EXPERTS

To save a database with a different name and in another location, you first open the database, then click the File tab and select Save Database As. Select the location where you want to save the file, and then in the File name text box, type the name for the database before clicking the Save button.

Step-by-Step 7.1

1. Open the **Student Teams** file from the drive and folder where your Data Files are stored. Save the database as **Student Teams Database,** followed by your initials.
2. In the Navigation pane, double-click **tblStudent** to open the table. Notice that the Phone and Cell Phone fields include telephone numbers.

3. On the Home tab, click the **View** button arrow in the Views group and then click **Design View**. The table is displayed in Design view, as shown in **Figure 7–1**.

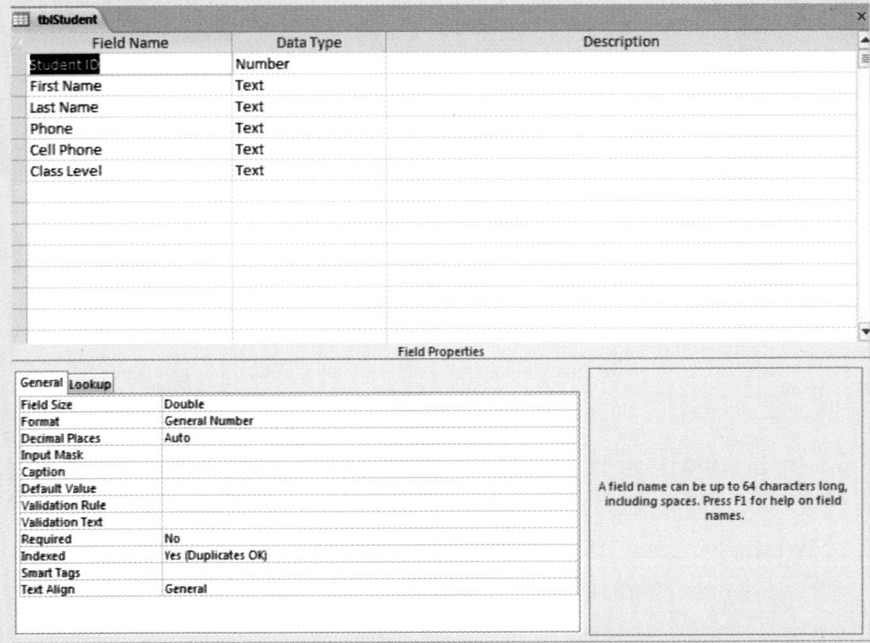

FIGURE 7–1
tblStudent in Design view

4. Click in the **Phone** field name, and then click in the **Input Mask** field in the Field Properties pane, as shown in **Figure 7–2**. Notice that the Build button appears to the right side of the Input Mask field.

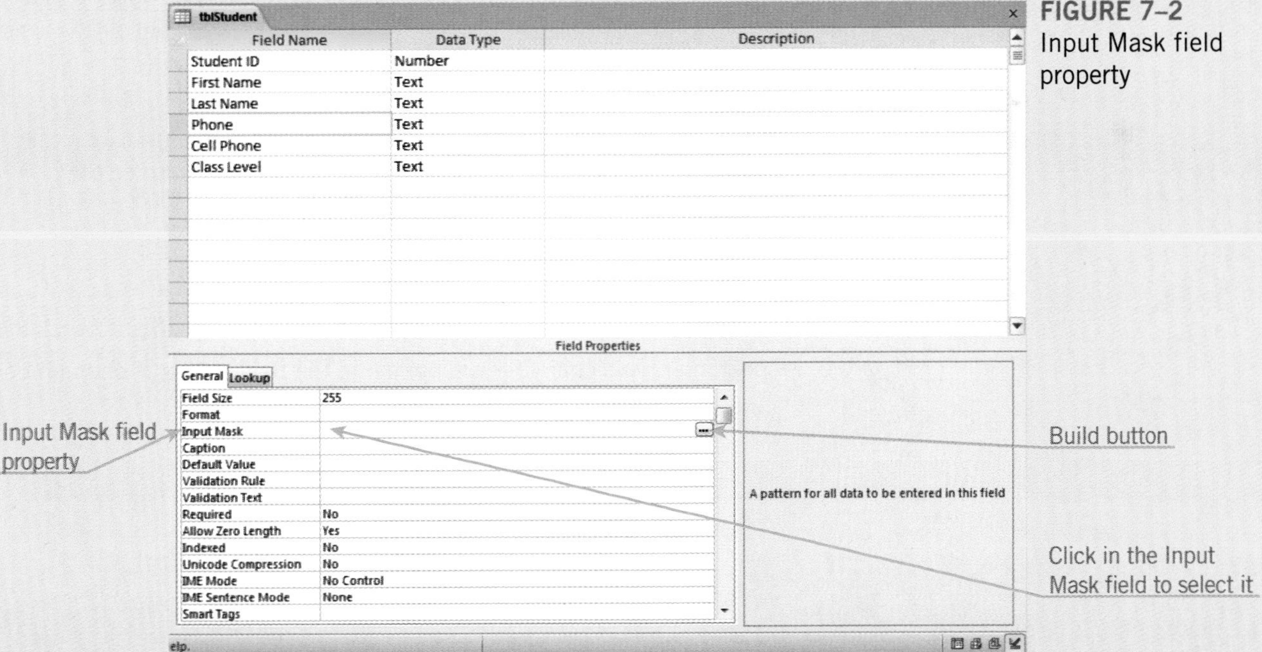

FIGURE 7–2
Input Mask field property

5. Click the **Build** button. The Input Mask Wizard dialog box opens, as shown in **Figure 7–3**.

FIGURE 7–3
Input Mask Wizard dialog box

6. In the Input Mask Wizard dialog box, verify that **Phone Number** is selected, and then click the **Next** button to display the next Input Mask Wizard window. The second window of the Input Mask Wizard dialog box shows options for adding placeholders, as shown in **Figure 7–4**.

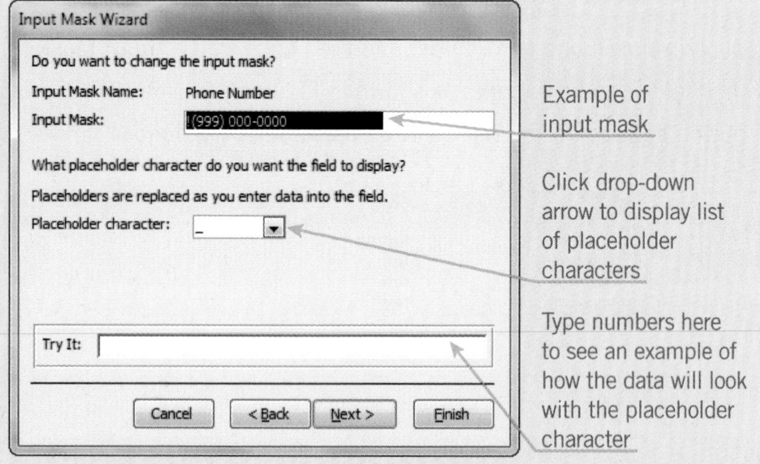

FIGURE 7–4
Input Mask Wizard dialog box with placeholder options

7. Click the **Placeholder character** drop-down arrow, and then select the **#** character. This character will appear in the field until a phone number is entered.

8. Click in the **Try It** text box to the left of the first #, and then type **5551234567**. A sample of how the telephone number will look when data is entered into the field is shown in **Figure 7–5**.

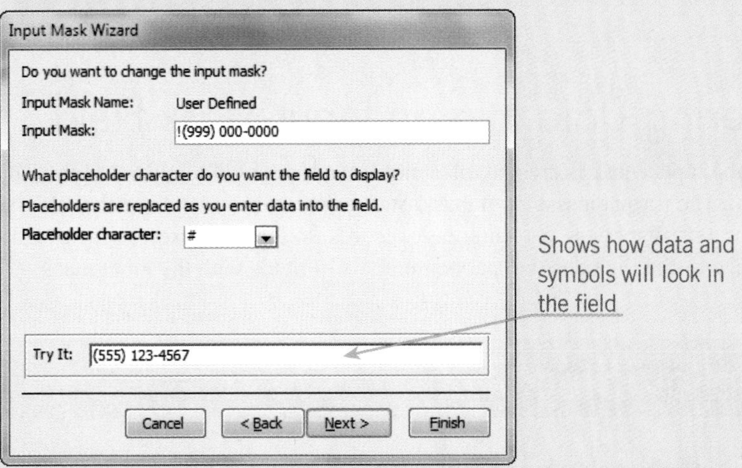

FIGURE 7–5
Input Mask Wizard dialog box with telephone number sample

9. Click **Next** to go to the next window of the Input Mask Wizard. The next window lets you select whether or not you want to store the symbols with the telephone numbers.
10. Click the **With the symbols in the mask, like this** option button to select it, and then click **Next**. The parentheses and dashes will be stored with the telephone numbers. The final Input Mask Wizard window appears, stating that you have completed all the information needed for the input mask. See **Figure 7–6**.

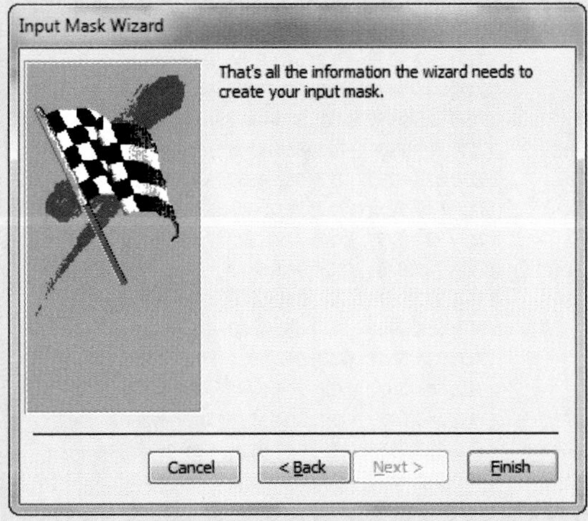

FIGURE 7–6
Final Input Mask Wizard dialog box window

11. Click **Finish** to close the Input Mask Wizard dialog box, then click the **Save** button on the Quick Access toolbar to save the changes to the table.
12. Repeat Steps 4 through 11 to create an Input Mask Wizard for the **Cell Phone** field.

13. Click the **Save** button to save changes to the table.
14. In the Views group, click the **View** button arrow and then click **Datasheet View**. Leave the database and table open for the next Step-by-Step.

Entering Data Into an Input Mask Field

After the input mask is created, placeholders appear in the fields until the values are entered. The format in the input mask, such as parentheses and a dash for a telephone number, will display as you enter new records. In this next exercise, you will enter a new record that includes two phone numbers in fields with the input mask.

Step-by-Step 7.2

1. On the Home tab, click the **New** button in the Records group.
2. In the Student ID field, type **67690** and then press **Tab**.
3. In the First Name field, type **John** and then press **Tab**.
4. In the Last Name field, type **Hernandez** and then press **Tab**.
5. In the Phone field, type **7175559876** and then press **Tab**. Notice that the telephone number symbols appeared automatically.
6. In the Cell Phone field, type **7175552466** and then press **Tab**. Compare your screen to **Figure 7–7**.

FIGURE 7–7
Data entered into fields with input masks

tblStudent

Student ID	First Name	Last Name	Phone	Cell Phone	Class Level
23423	Michael	Lemley	(717) 897-9879	(717) 579-8544	Freshman
23468	Matthew	Couric	(717) 987-9834	(717) 543-2100	Sophmore
23480	Kathy	Reid	(717) 325-4997	(717) 579-8310	Junior
23483	Corey	Graham	(717) 789-7987	(717) 654-8791	Junior
23487	Tai	Zejecka	(717) 879-8797	(717) 653-4687	Sophmore
23648	Mary	Moldrem	(717) 548-7214	(717) 351-2000	Senior
23749	Jeanie	Lowry	(717) 987-9797	(717) 8791-222	Freshman
24324	Bill	Melendez	(717) 787-9787	(717) 249-5312	Freshman
28349	Robbie	Littleton	(717) 987-8979	(717) 247-6555	Senior
28374	Todd	Verde	(717) 554-8765	(717) 645-7987	Sophmore
34248	David	Miller	(717) 234-5612	(717) 542-1032	Junior
34872	Jimmy	White	(717) 531-5671	(717) 246-8798	Junior
56346	Sue	Silverberg	(717) 543-2012	(717) 802-1546	Sophmore
56757	Terry	Kennsington	(717) 635-3154	(717) 864-0123	Senior
57723	Sharon	Stevens	(717) 315-4651	(717) 267-4955	Freshman
66723	Judith	Gonzalez	(717) 213-5795	(717) 798-4321	Freshman
67237	Steven	Ellis	(717) 213-5791	(717) 549-8800	Senior
67634	Alice	Grittner	(717) 354-9873	(717) 246-7841	Senior
67678	Kirstie	Allison	(717) 810-4657	(717) 249-2465	Junior
67686	Candace	Mendosa	(717) 214-6327	(717) 549-8713	Senior
67690	John	Hernandez	(717) 555-9876	(717) 555-2466	Freshman
*					

Input mask places the symbols in the data when it is entered

7. In the Class Level field, type **Freshman** and then press **Enter**.
8. Save your work, close the table, and then close the database.

Set Validation Rules

You can increase accuracy and efficiency of data entry by setting validation rules. ***Validation rules*** are rules that need to be met before the data can be entered. For example, in a company, if the highest hourly wage paid to employees is $50 per hour, you can enter an expression in the validation rule that the dollar amount entered needs to be equal to or less than 50.

The validation rule is entered as an expression in the Expression Builder. The ***Expression Builder*** is where you type, or build, the expression. An ***expression*** is an arithmetic formula that performs a calculation. Using the above example, you would enter the expression <=50. **Table 7–1** shows examples of expressions.

VOCABULARY
validation rules
Expression Builder
expression

TABLE 7–1 Examples of Expressions

EXPRESSION	WHAT IT MEANS
>=900	Data entered needs to be greater than or equal to 900.
[Retail Price]>[Cost]	The value in the Retail Price field needs to be greater than the value in the Cost field. Notice that field name needs to be placed in square brackets.
>#6/30/2014#	Date entered needs to be after June 30, 2014. Notice that the date needs to be between two pound signs.

When you set a validation rule for a field, you have the option to create a message that displays the validation rule to the person entering the data. The message appears when data entered into the field does not meet the validation rule. Using the hourly wage example, if a dollar amount greater than 50 is entered in the field, the message might be something like "Hourly rates cannot exceed $50." In the next exercise, the manager at Pacific Sales requires that all sales personnel make at least $40,000 in sales every month. You will enter a validation rule that displays a message if the sales amount is less than $40,000.

Step-by-Step 7.3

1. Open the **Pacific Sales** file from the drive and folder where your Data Files are stored. Save the database as **Pacific Sales Database**, followed by your initials.
2. In the Navigation pane, double-click **Sales Data** to open the table. Review the sales amounts.
3. On the Home tab, click the **View** button arrow, and then click **Design View**.
4. Click in the **Sales** field.

5. Click in the **Validation Rule** field in the Field Properties pane, and then compare your screen to **Figure 7–8**.

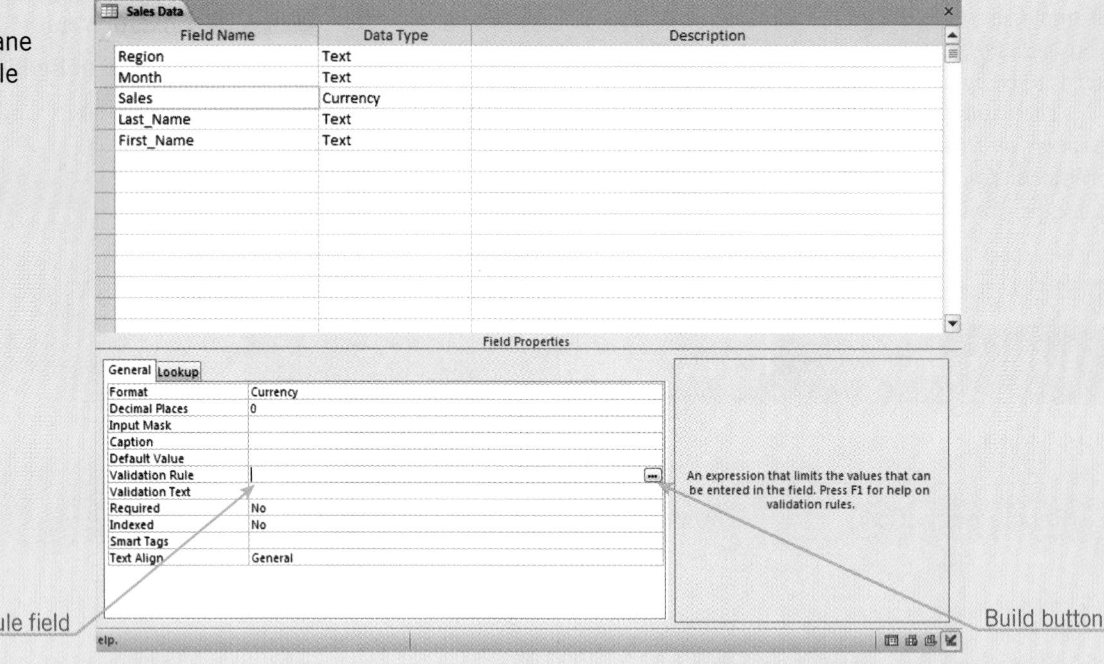

FIGURE 7–8
Field Properties pane with Validation Rule field selected

6. Click the **Build** button located on the right side of the Validation Rule field.
7. In the Expression Builder text box, type **>=40000**. See **Figure 7–9**.

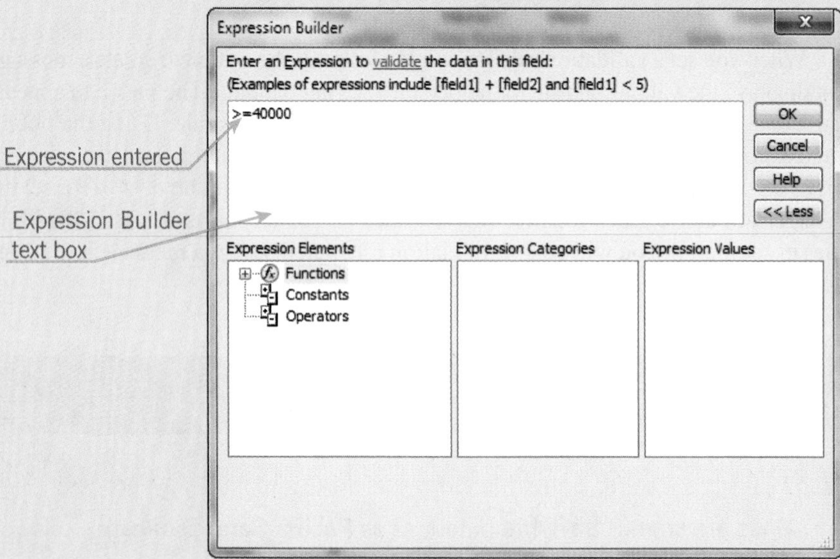

FIGURE 7–9
Expression Builder dialog box

8. Click **OK**. Next, you will enter the text that appears in the message box when the data entered does not meet the rule.

9. Click in the **Validation Text** field in the Field Properties pane, and then type **Sales need to be at least $40,000**, as shown in **Figure 7–10**.

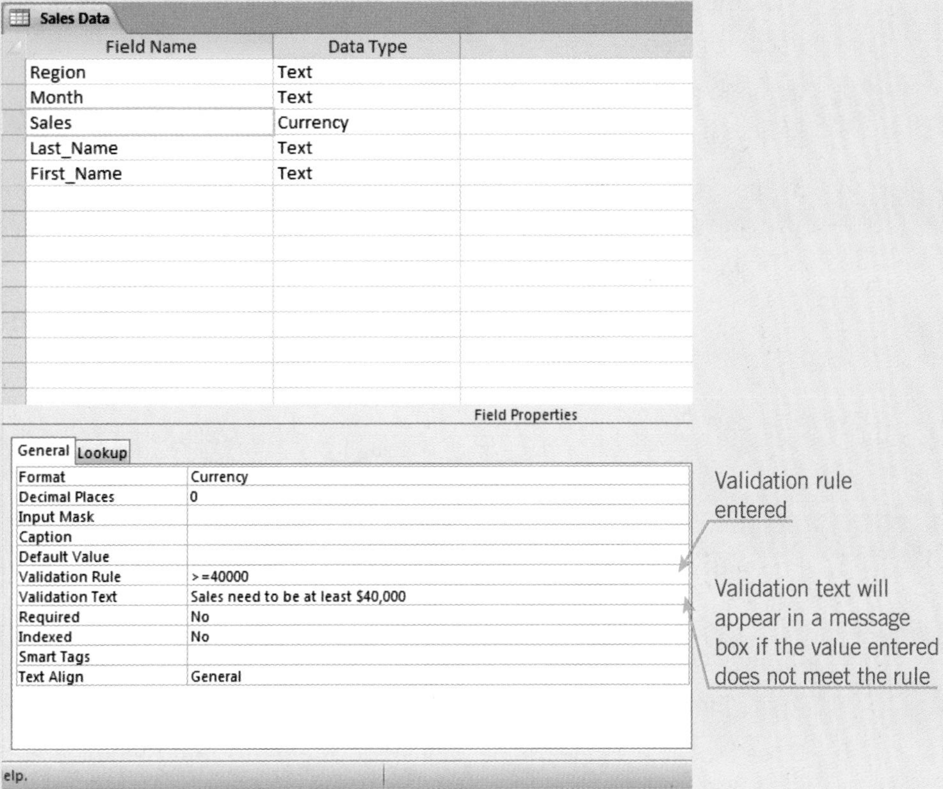

FIGURE 7–10
Validation rule and message

10. On the Quick Access toolbar, click the **Save** button. A message box may appear indicating that Data integrity rules have been changed and existing data will be tested for the new rule.
11. Click **Yes**, if necessary.
12. In the Views group, click the **View** button arrow and then click **Datasheet View**. Keep the file open for the next Step-by-Step.

Add Data Into a Field with a Validation Rule

When a validation rule is created, data entered into the field must meet the rule requirements. In the next exercise, you will enter a record with a field that has a validation rule. You will first enter the data incorrectly to see the message, and then you will reenter the data correctly.

Step-by-Step 7.4

1. Click the **Home** tab, if necessary, and then click the **New** button in the Records group.
2. In the Region field, type **West** and then press **Tab**.
3. In the Month field, type **April** and then press **Tab**.
4. In the Sales field, type **39450** and then press **Tab**. A message box appears, as shown in **Figure 7–11**. You realize that you entered data that does not pass the rule.

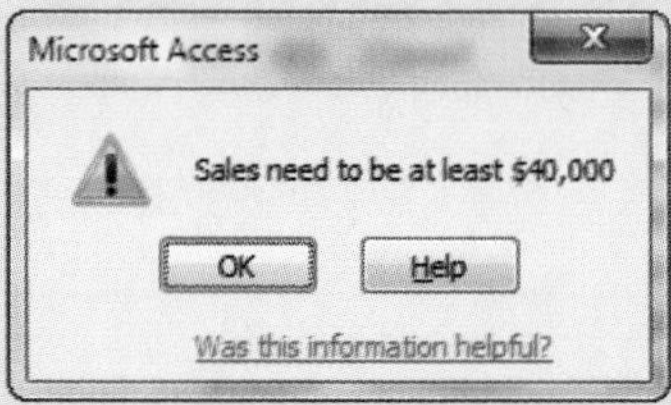

FIGURE 7–11
Message box displays validation rule

5. Press **Backspace** until 39450 is deleted, type **49450**, and then press **Tab**.
6. In the Last Name field, type **Johnson** and then press **Tab**.
7. In the First Name field, type **Jerome** and then press **Enter**.
8. Close the table and leave the database open for the next Step-by-Step.

Setting a Lookup Property

A lookup property offers a list of values that you can select. The list of values can be from another field or in a query. You can also create your own list of lookup values. When the field or list of values appears, you simply select the value you want entered into the selected field. Setting lookup properties can help prevent data entry errors.

You can set lookup properties in the Lookup tab in the Field Properties pane, or you can use the Lookup Wizard to take you step by step through the process. You can select whether you want the lookup property to be in the form of a text box, list box, or combo box. A text box is used when you want to enter data. A ***list box*** lets you select more than one value, and a combo box lets you enter a value or select a value from a list. In the following exercise, you will setup lookup properties in the Lookup tab of the Field Properties pane.

VOCABULARY
list box

Step-by-Step 7.5

1. In the Navigation pane, double-click **Region** to open the Region table. Notice that this table contains the four sales regions.
2. Close the table.
3. Right-click the **Sales Data** table, and then select **Design View** from the shortcut menu.
4. Click the **Region** field, and then click the **Lookup** tab in the Field Properties pane. See **Figure 7–12**.

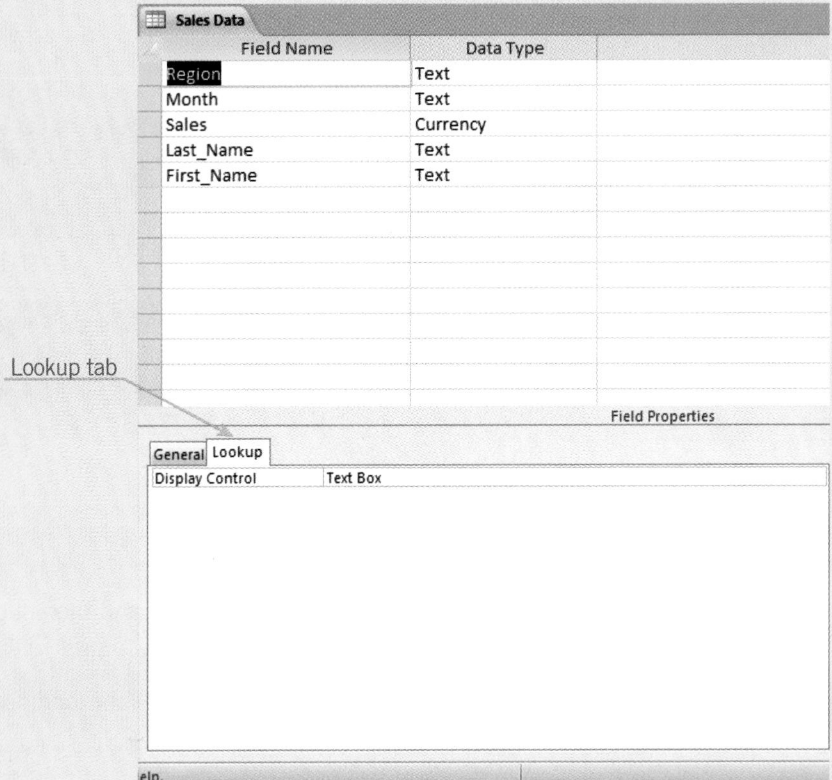

FIGURE 7–12
Lookup tab in the Field Properties pane

5. Click the **Display Control** drop-down arrow, and then click **List Box**. Several settings for List Box appear in the Field Properties pane, as shown in **Figure 7–13**. These settings help you define how the list should function. The Table/Query option is already selected as the Row Source Type. Since you will be creating the list from a field in a table, this option is correct. Next, you will enter Region table as the Row Source.

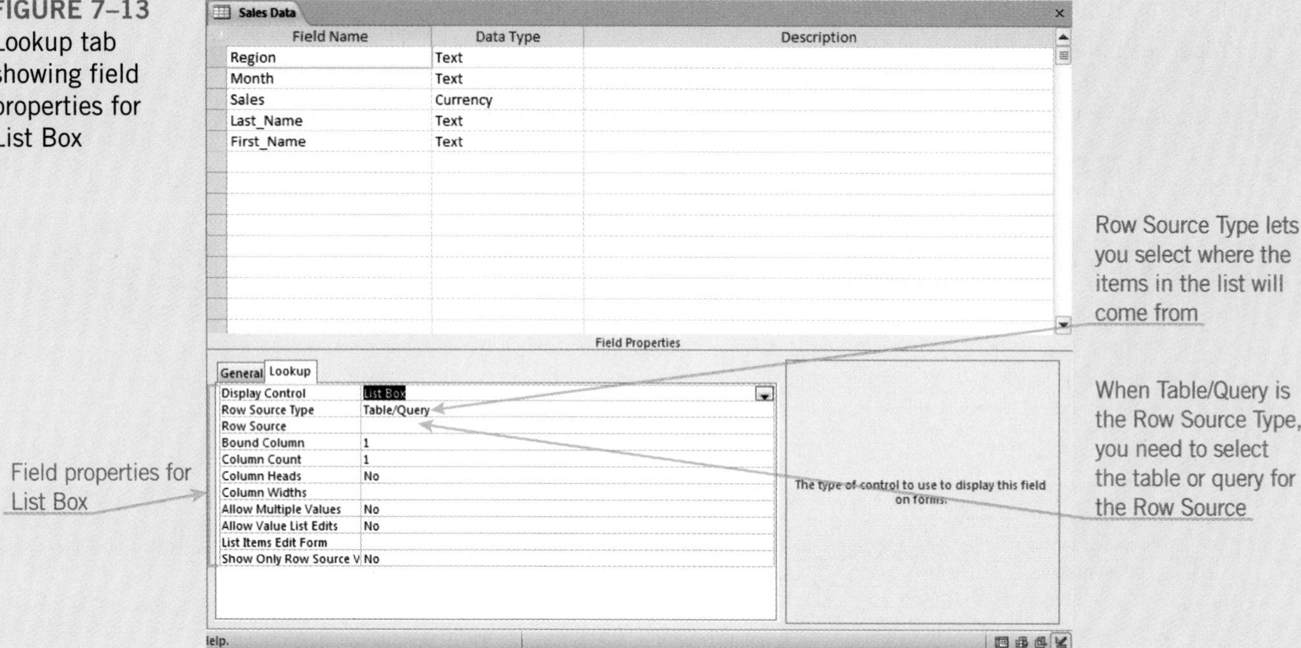

FIGURE 7–13 Lookup tab showing field properties for List Box

6. Click in the **Row Source** field, click the **drop-down arrow**, and then click **Region**. The List Box will now display data from the Region table.
7. Click the **Region** field in the Field Name column, and then compare your screen to **Figure 7–14**.

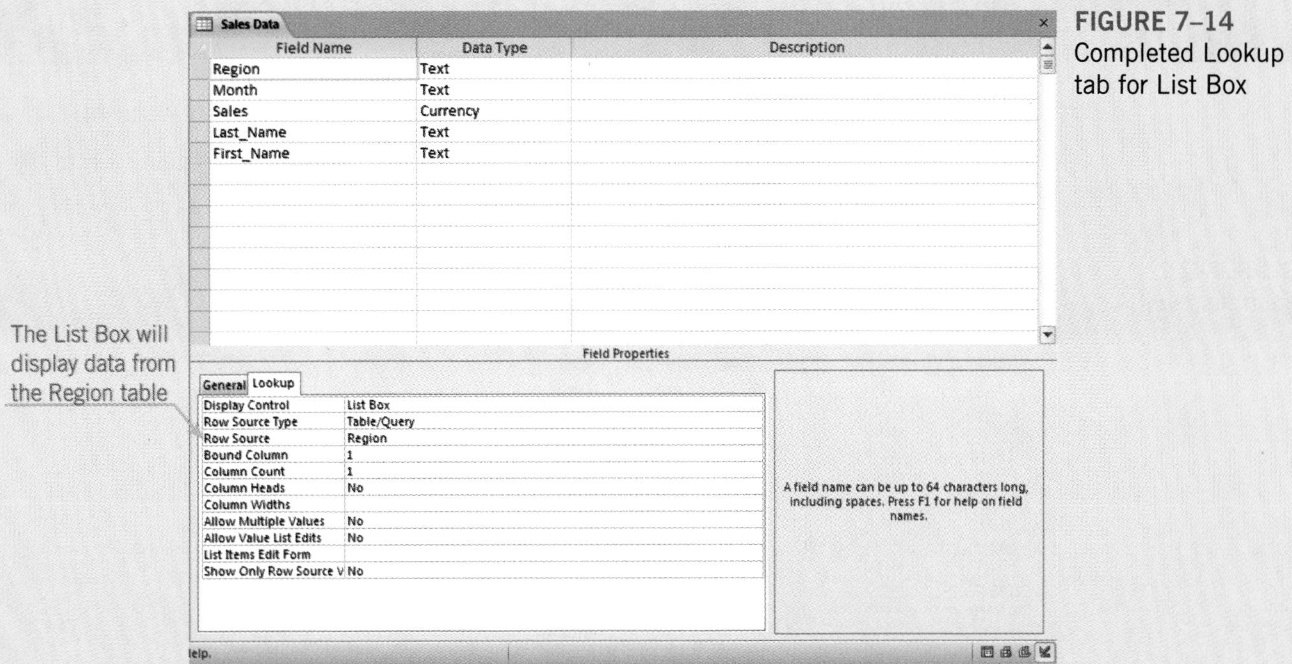

FIGURE 7–14 Completed Lookup tab for List Box

8. Click the **Save** button on the Quick Access toolbar.
9. In the Views group, click the **View** button arrow and then click **Datasheet View**.
10. Leave the table open for the next Step-by-Step.

Selecting Field Values From a List

After you set the lookup properties for a field, a drop-down arrow will appear in the field when it is selected. You click the drop-down arrow to display the list. Then, you choose the value that you want entered into the field from the list. In the following exercise, you will enter data into a field from the list.

Step-by-Step 7.6

1. In the Records group, click the **New** button to start a new record.
2. In the new record, click the **drop-down arrow** in the **Region** field to display the list for regions, as shown in **Figure 7–15**.

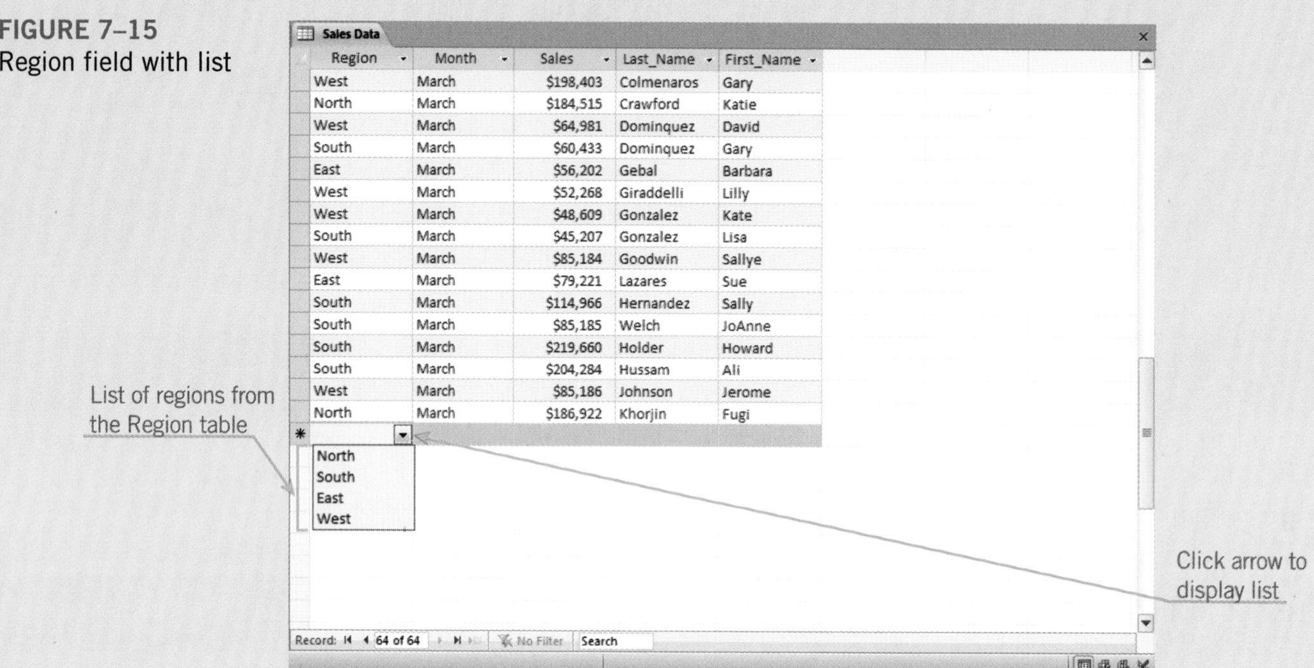

FIGURE 7–15
Region field with list

3. Click **East** and then press **Tab**.
4. In the Month field, type **April** and then press **Tab**.
5. In the Sales field, type **53982** and then press **Tab**.
6. In the Last Name field, type **Gebal** and then press **Tab**.
7. In the First Name field, type **Barbara** and then press **Enter**.
8. Save your work, close the table, and then close the database.

Using the Lookup Wizard to Set Lookup Properties

When you create lookup properties in the Lookup pane, your selections are limited, such as selecting the entire table. However, you may find that you need to create lookup properties with additional options. For example, you may have a field that has product numbers, such as **PK-SWSM**. Just looking at the product number, you may not recognize the product. But if you have the product description displayed in the column next to the product number, you will be able to identify the product, such as **PK-SWSM Puppy Sweater – Small**. To have more than one field appear in the list, you need to create lookup properties using the Lookup Wizard.

In the next exercise, you will set lookup properties with two descriptions using the Lookup Wizard.

Step-by-Step 7.7

1. Open the **P & K Industry** file from the drive and folder where your Data Files are stored. Save the database as **P & K Industry Database**, followed by your initials.
2. Double-click the **Products** table to view the data, look at the Item Number and Description fields, and then close the table.
3. Double-click the **Sales Order** table to view the data. Notice how the Item Number and Description fields are in this table as well.
4. In the Views group, click the **View** button arrow and then click **Design View**.
5. Click in the field next to **Item Number** in the Data Type column.
6. Click the **Data Type** drop-down arrow, and then select **Lookup Wizard** from the Data Type menu. The first dialog box for the Lookup Wizard opens, as shown in **Figure 7–16**.

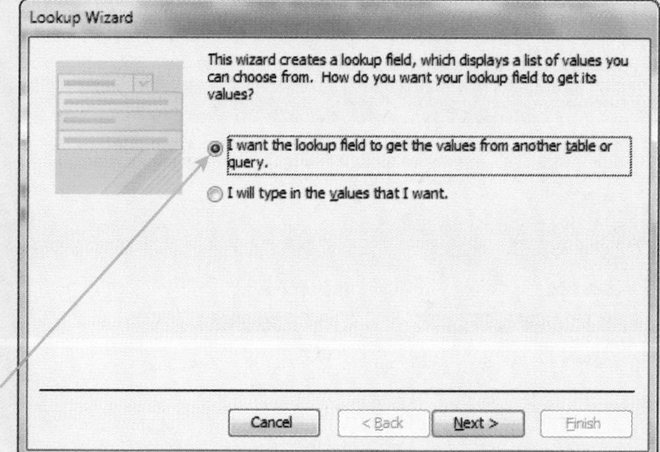

FIGURE 7–16
First window in the Lookup Wizard dialog box

7. Verify that the **I want the lookup field to get the values from another table or query** option button is selected, then click **Next**. The second window of the Lookup Wizard dialog box appears, as shown in **Figure 7–17**. The Products table should be selected.

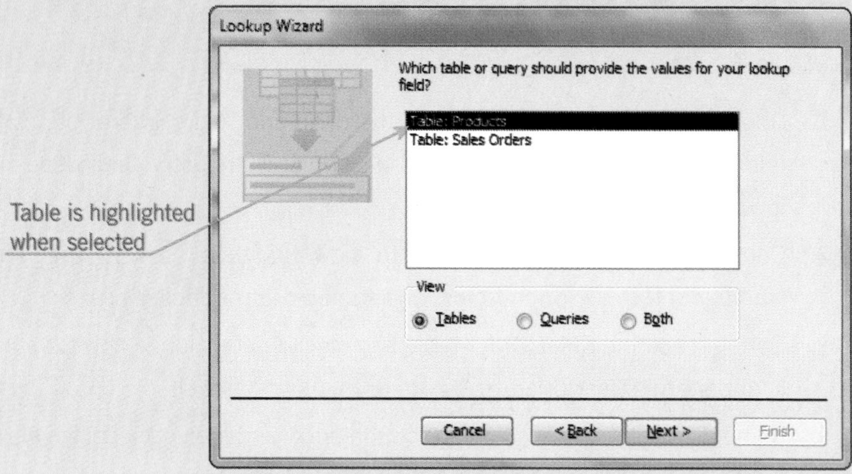

FIGURE 7–17
Second window in the Lookup Wizard dialog box

8. Click **Next** to select the fields you want in the lookup field.
9. Verify that the **Item Number** field is selected, and click the **Select single field** button to move this field from the Available Fields area to the Selected Fields area. The Select single field button is the single arrow button in the dialog box, as shown in **Figure 7–18**.

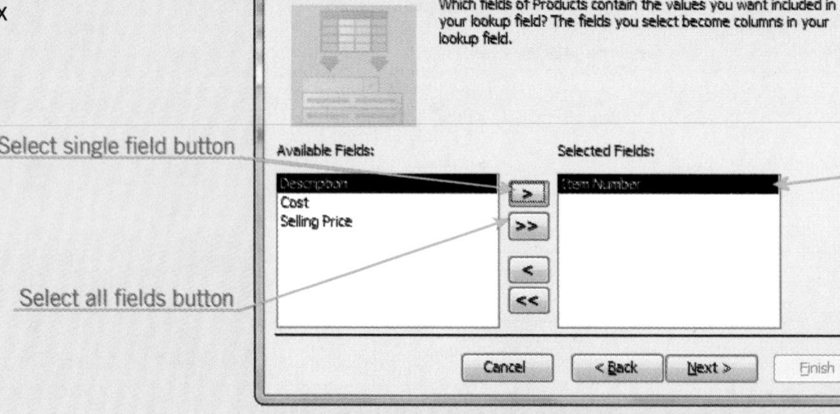

FIGURE 7–18
Third window in the Lookup Wizard dialog box

10. Verify that the **Description** field is selected, click the **Select single field** button, then click **Next** to view the fourth window of the Lookup Wizard dialog box.
11. Click the **down arrow** to the left of Ascending, select **Item Number** to sort the data by this field, and then click **Next**. The fifth window of the Lookup Wizard dialog box is displayed, as shown in **Figure 7–19**.

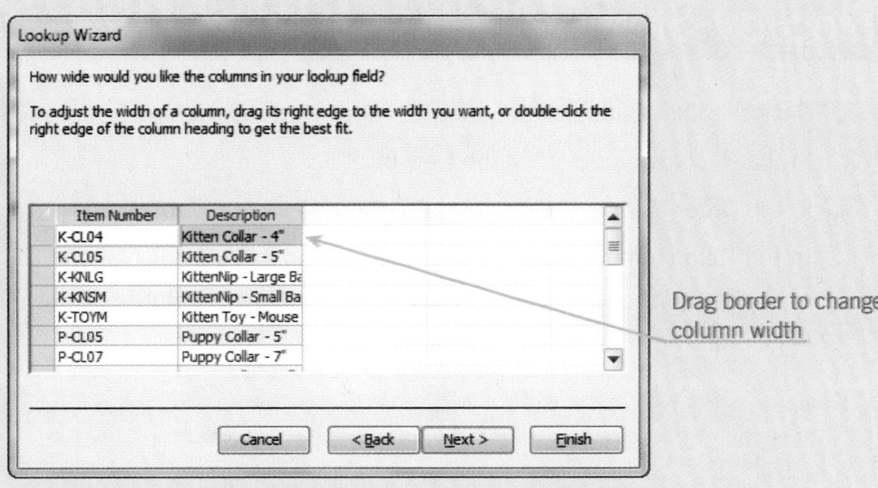

FIGURE 7–19
Fifth window in the Lookup Wizard dialog box

12. Place the mouse pointer over the right border of the **Item Number** heading, then drag to the left to decrease the size of this field to display all of the description. Place your mouse pointer over the left border of the **Description** heading, and then drag to the right to increase the size of this field. In the next window, you will select the field that contains the value you want stored in the table.
13. Click **Next**. You want to store the Item Number in the Item Number field, so you leave this option selected.
14. Click **Next**, and then type **Item Number** in the *What label would you like for your lookup field?* text box. When you enter data, Item Number will appear at the top of the list.
15. Click **Finish**. A message box appears letting you know that the table needs to be saved so the relationship between the Item Number fields in the Sales Orders table and the Products table can be created. When these tables are related, you can select an item from the Products table and it will be entered into the Sales Products table.
16. Click **Yes** and remain in this screen for the next Step-by-Step.

Selecting Data From a List with Multiple Columns

Using the Lookup Wizard to set lookup properties allows you to have more than one column of data appear in the list. Having more than one column of data helps you identify the correct value to select. Even though two columns are displayed in the list, data from only one field is entered into the field when you select an item. For the following exercise, you will enter a record and in the field with the lookup properties, you will display the list with multiple columns before you make a selection.

Step-by-Step 7.8

1. Click the **View** button arrow, and then click **Datasheet View**.
2. In the Records group, click the **New** button.
3. In the **Order Number** field, type **1061** and then press **Tab**.
4. In the **Item Number** field, click the **drop-down arrow** to display the list of options as shown in **Figure 7–20**. Notice that even with the changes in column width, you still cannot view all of the information.

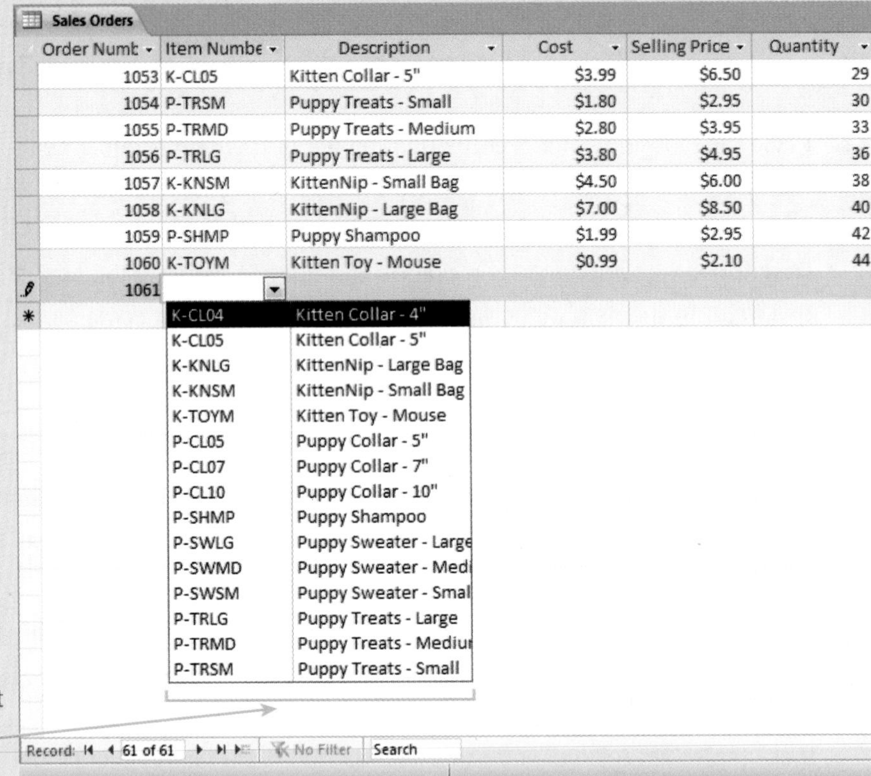

FIGURE 7–20
List with multiple columns

5. Click **P-SWSM Puppy Sweater - Small**, and then press **Tab**.
6. In the Description field, type **Puppy Sweater - Small** and then press **Tab**.
7. In the Cost field, type **6.65** and then press **Tab**.
8. In the Selling Price field, type **9.50** and then press **Tab**.
9. In the Quantity field, type **15**, and then press **Enter**.
10. Close the table and leave the database open for the next Step-by-Step.

Creating a Calculated Field in a Table

Access 2010 has a new feature that allows you to create a calculated field in a table. If you have two fields in a table, such as Quantity and Selling Price, you can multiply the values in these two fields and show the result in the calculated field in the table. And, if an amount in either of these fields changes, the result in the calculated field will show the new result.

Using a calculated field saves you time by printing reports directly from the table rather than needing to create a query to perform the calculation and then display a report from the query.

You create the calculated field using the Expression Builder. The Expression Builder displays the fields from the table. You will then select fields that you want to be calculated. In addition, you will choose the operators that you want to use. ***Operators*** are the mathematical characters—such as plus (+), minus (–), multiplication (*), and division (/)—that determine the type of calculation in the expression. In the next exercise, you will create a calculated field in the Sales Orders table.

VOCABULARY
operators

Step-by-Step 7.9

1. Right-click the **Sales Orders** table, and then click **Design View** from the shortcut menu.
2. Click in the field under Quantity in the Field Name column, and then type **Order Total**.
3. Press **Tab**, and then click the **Data Type** drop-down arrow to display a list of the data types, as shown in **Figure 7–21**.

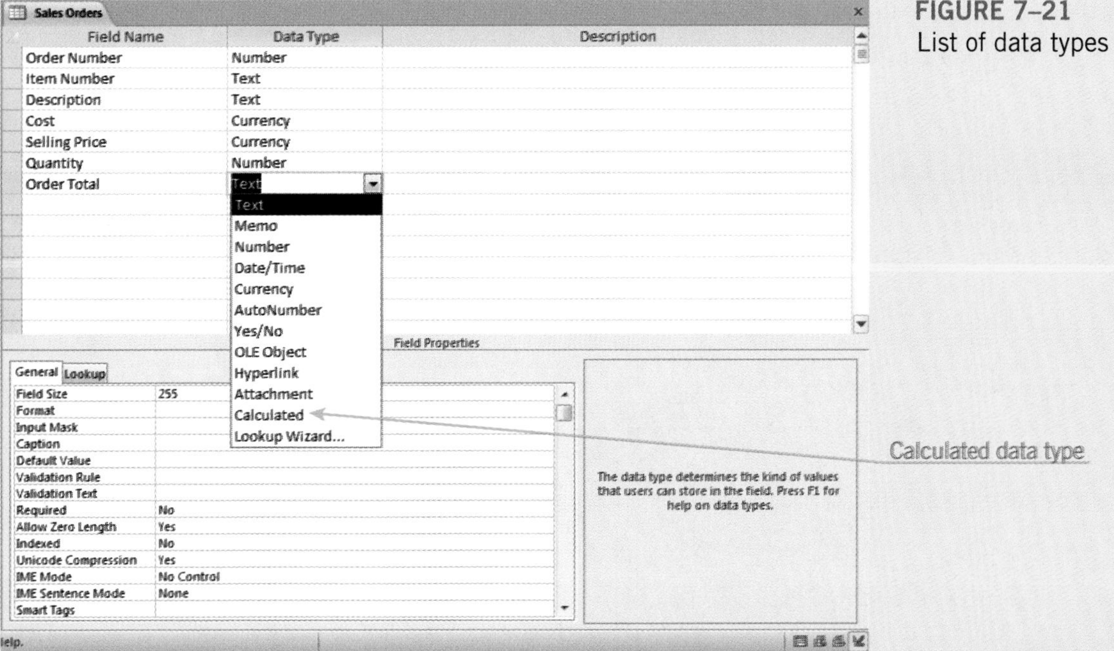

FIGURE 7–21
List of data types

4. Click **Calculated**. The Expression Builder dialog box opens, as shown in **Figure 7–22**.

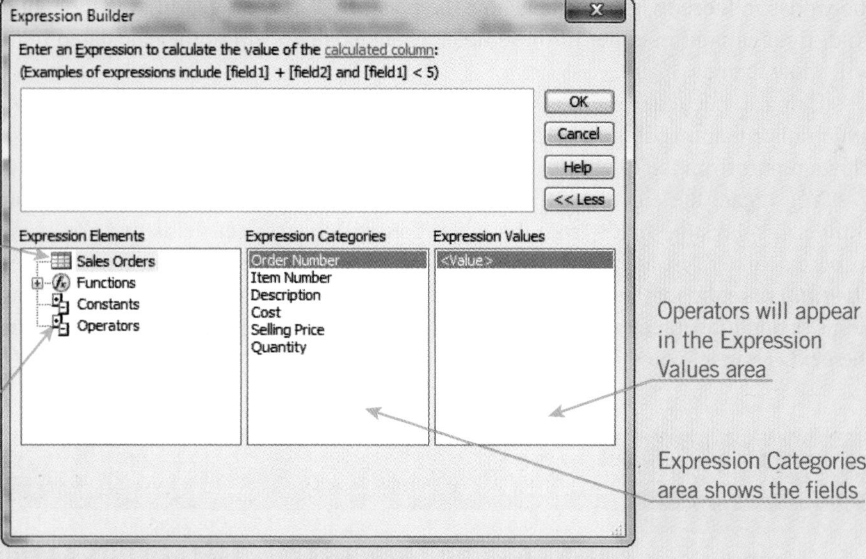

FIGURE 7–22
Expression Builder dialog box for Calculated field

5. In the Expression Categories section, double-click **Quantity** to move it up to the top expression box.
6. In the Expression Elements section, click **Operators** to display the operators in the Expression Values area.
7. Double-click * in the Expression Values area. An asterisk is the symbol for multiplication.
8. Click **Sales Orders** in the Expression Elements area to redisplay the table fields in the Expression Categories area.
9. In the Expression Categories area, double-click **Selling Price** to move it into the top expression box. Compare your screen to **Figure 7–23**.

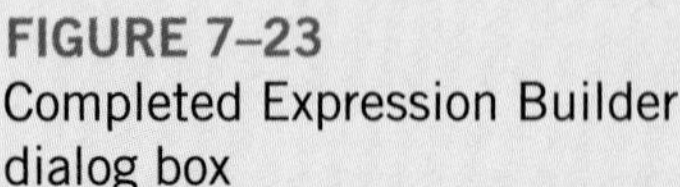

FIGURE 7–23
Completed Expression Builder dialog box

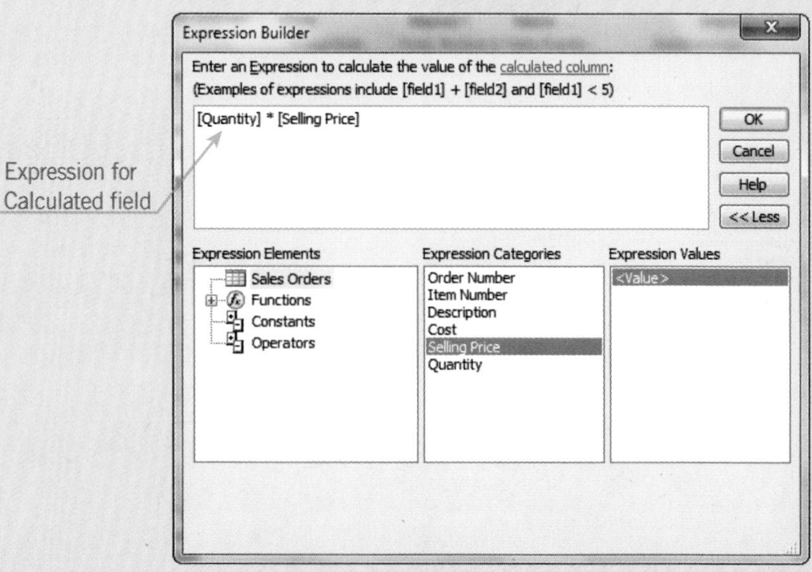

10. Click **OK** to close the Expression Builder dialog box.
11. Click the **Save** button on the Quick Access toolbar.
12. In the Views group, click the **Datasheet View** button. Review the results of the calculated field. See **Figure 7–24**. Notice how the Order Total field displays the Quantity multiplied by the Selling Price.

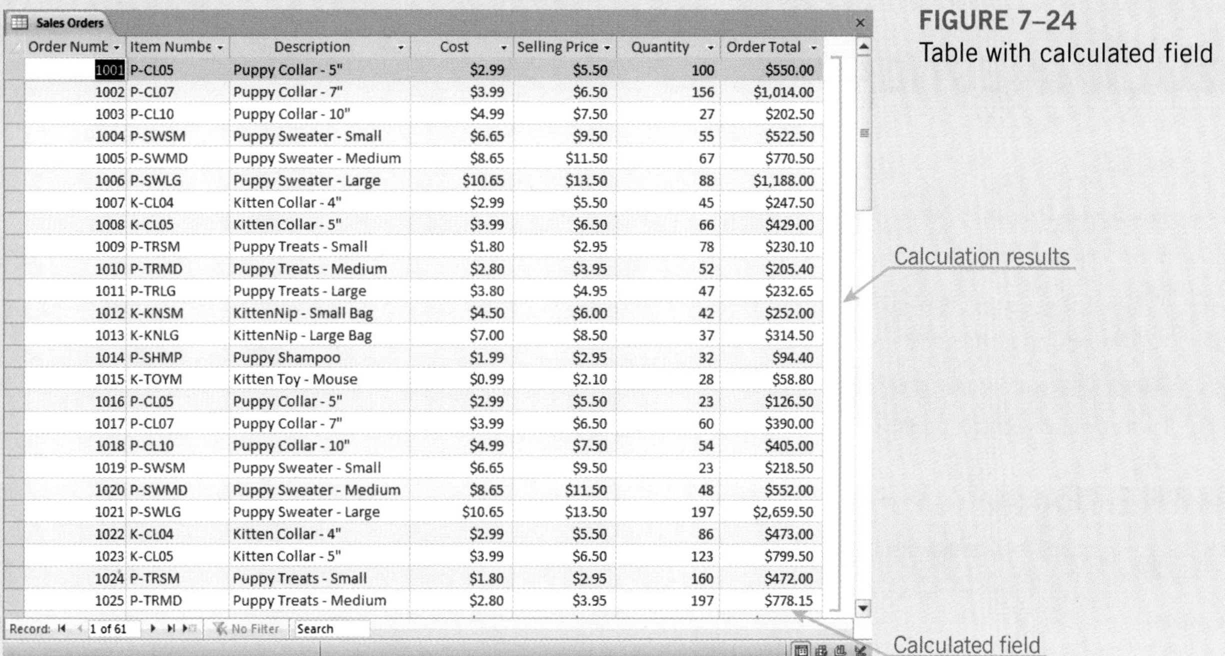

Sales Orders

Order Numb	Item Numbe	Description	Cost	Selling Price	Quantity	Order Total
1001	P-CL05	Puppy Collar - 5"	$2.99	$5.50	100	$550.00
1002	P-CL07	Puppy Collar - 7"	$3.99	$6.50	156	$1,014.00
1003	P-CL10	Puppy Collar - 10"	$4.99	$7.50	27	$202.50
1004	P-SWSM	Puppy Sweater - Small	$6.65	$9.50	55	$522.50
1005	P-SWMD	Puppy Sweater - Medium	$8.65	$11.50	67	$770.50
1006	P-SWLG	Puppy Sweater - Large	$10.65	$13.50	88	$1,188.00
1007	K-CL04	Kitten Collar - 4"	$2.99	$5.50	45	$247.50
1008	K-CL05	Kitten Collar - 5"	$3.99	$6.50	66	$429.00
1009	P-TRSM	Puppy Treats - Small	$1.80	$2.95	78	$230.10
1010	P-TRMD	Puppy Treats - Medium	$2.80	$3.95	52	$205.40
1011	P-TRLG	Puppy Treats - Large	$3.80	$4.95	47	$232.65
1012	K-KNSM	KittenNip - Small Bag	$4.50	$6.00	42	$252.00
1013	K-KNLG	KittenNip - Large Bag	$7.00	$8.50	37	$314.50
1014	P-SHMP	Puppy Shampoo	$1.99	$2.95	32	$94.40
1015	K-TOYM	Kitten Toy - Mouse	$0.99	$2.10	28	$58.80
1016	P-CL05	Puppy Collar - 5"	$2.99	$5.50	23	$126.50
1017	P-CL07	Puppy Collar - 7"	$3.99	$6.50	60	$390.00
1018	P-CL10	Puppy Collar - 10"	$4.99	$7.50	54	$405.00
1019	P-SWSM	Puppy Sweater - Small	$6.65	$9.50	23	$218.50
1020	P-SWMD	Puppy Sweater - Medium	$8.65	$11.50	48	$552.00
1021	P-SWLG	Puppy Sweater - Large	$10.65	$13.50	197	$2,659.50
1022	K-CL04	Kitten Collar - 4"	$2.99	$5.50	86	$473.00
1023	K-CL05	Kitten Collar - 5"	$3.99	$6.50	123	$799.50
1024	P-TRSM	Puppy Treats - Small	$1.80	$2.95	160	$472.00
1025	P-TRMD	Puppy Treats - Medium	$2.80	$3.95	197	$778.15

Record: 1 of 61 No Filter Search

FIGURE 7–24
Table with calculated field

13. Close the table and then close the database.

SUMMARY

In this lesson, you learned:

- An input mask improves the accuracy of the data entered, such as automatically adding symbols like parentheses and a dash in a telephone number field.
- After an input mask is created for a field, just the values need to be typed into the field, not the symbols.
- Validation rules prevent inaccurate data from being entered into a field.
- Setting a lookup property in the Lookup tab in the Field Properties pane creates a list from which values can be selected.
- After lookup properties are set up for a field, you simply need to click a value from a list to select it.
- Using the Lookup Wizard to set lookup properties allows you to have more than one column of information in the list.
- A calculated field can be added to a table to perform calculations on fields in the table.

 VOCABULARY REVIEW

Define the following terms:

Expression Builder
expression
input mask
list box
operator
placeholder
validation rule

REVIEW QUESTIONS

TRUE / FALSE

Circle T if the statement is true or F if the statement is false.

T F 1. If the expression >=900 is entered as a validation rule, the data entered into the field needs to be greater than or equal to 900.

T F 2. In Access, you can create a calculated field in a table.

T F 3. Validation rules are rules that need to be passed before the data can be entered in a field.

T F 4. Setting lookup properties can help prevent data entry errors.

T F 5. The default placeholder for input masks is the underscore.

FILL IN THE BLANK

1. A(n) ______________ is an arithmetic formula that performs a calculation.
2. A(n) ______________ improves the accuracy of the data entered, such as automatically adding symbols like dashes in a Social Security number field.
3. A(n) ______________ is a pattern for certain types of data entered in a field.
4. After you set up the lookup properties for a field, a(n) ______________ will appear in the field when it is selected.
5. You can add ______________ properties to a field to display data from another table in a list from which you can make a selection.

WRITTEN QUESTIONS

Write a brief answer to the following questions.

1. Explain how the expression [Retail Price]>[Cost] would be used in a validation rule.

2. Explain the benefit of using the Lookup Wizard versus entering lookup properties in the Lookup pane.

3. When a person enters data that does not pass a validation rule, what can you do that will help them understand the problem with their data?

4. Give an example of placeholders for an input mask in a field for zip codes.

5. Explain the purpose of a calculated field in a table.

PROJECTS

If you have a SAM 2010 user profile, your instructor may have assigned an autogradable version of the indicated project. If so, log into the SAM 2010 Web site at *www.cengage.com/sam2010* to download the instruction and start files.

PROJECT 7–1

1. Open the **Division Sales** file from the drive and folder where your Data Files are stored. Save the database as **Division Sales Database**, followed by your initials.
2. Create a lookup property for the Division field in the Sales Data table that creates a list box using the Divisions table. The list created from the Divisions table should only have one field or column displayed.
3. After you create the lookup property, switch to Datasheet view.
4. Enter the following record:

   Division: **Division 3**

   Month: **April**

   Sales: **55190**

   Last_Name: **Welch**

   First_Name: **JoAnne**
5. Close the table and then close the database.

SAM PROJECT 7–2

1. Open the **Internet Sales** file from the drive and folder where your Data Files are stored. Save the database as **Internet Sales Database**, followed by your initials.
2. Create an input mask for the Social Security field.
3. Use the **#** symbol as the placeholder in the input mask, and store the symbols with the data.
4. View the changes in Datasheet view.
5. Enter the following record into the table:

   First Name: **Emily**

   Last Name: **Manz**

   SSN: **555220987**

   Address: **1612 East Loop**

   City: **Cortez**

   State: **CO**

   ZIP: **81321**
6. Close the table and then close the database.

PROJECT 7–3

1. Open the **Pet Sales** file from the drive and folder where your Data Files are stored. Save the database as **Pet Sales Database**, followed by your initials.
2. Create a calculated field in the table with the field name **Order_Total.**
3. The calculated field will need to multiply Selling Price by Quantity.
4. Save the table.
5. Switch to Datasheet view to review the results.
6. Close the table and then close the database.

CRITICAL THINKING

ACTIVITY 7–1

As the new division manager, you want to enhance the table design in the company's sales database. Open the **Sales** database from the drive and folder where your Data Files are stored, and then save it as **Sales Database**, followed by your initials. Create a calculated field that shows the price difference between the Selling Price field and the Cost field. Name the field **Markup**. View the table results in Datasheet view. Close the database.

ACTIVITY 7–2

Think of a Lookup field you could use in a database table for your personal use. For example, think of a table that includes a weekly sports schedule. The table might include weeks identified as Week 1, Week 2, Week 3, and so on. Or, you might also have a table that has all the names of the coaches.

Estimated Time:
2.0 hours

LESSON 8

Using Advanced Queries

OBJECTIVES

Upon completion of this lesson, you should be able to:

- Create a parameter query.
- Run a parameter query.
- Prepare a table for action queries.
- Use an append query.
- Change data with an update query.
- Use wildcards in a query.
- Use parameters and wildcards in a query.
- Create a crosstab query.

VOCABULARY

action query

append

criterion

parameter

wildcard character

Introduction

Queries are operations that let you locate specific information in tables. You use a query to ask Access a question. When you run the query, the answer is displayed. In this lesson, you will explore parameter queries, which ask you to enter search data each time you run the query. You will also learn how to prepare a table for action queries. Action queries, such as an append query or an update query, make changes to the records in a table. An append query adds records from one table and puts them in another table. An update query actually changes records in a table based on the information you enter. Finally, you'll discover the advantages of crosstab queries, which rearrange the data in a table or query into another format.

Creating a Parameter Query

VOCABULARY
parameter
criterion

Parameter queries increase efficiency by providing a single query that you may use many times with a different criterion each time the query runs. ***Parameter*** means to vary. ***Criterion*** refers to the specific information you are searching for. For example, in a large table of customers, you might need to search for an individual customer. Rather than creating a query for each customer, you can create a parameter query, which allows you to enter a new criterion each time you run the query. And, when tables are related, which means they have a common field, you can display information from more than one table.

To create a parameter query, you enter a "prompt" in the Criteria cell of the desired field. This prompt appears above the text box where you type the search criterion and lets you know the type of information you need to enter. When you save the query, you add *qry-* before the query name to easily recognize it as a query in a list. For example, if you have a table and a query with the same name, you can easily spot the query because it will have the *qry-* before the name.

Step-by-Step 8.1

1. Open the **Book Sales** file from the drive and folder where your Data Files are stored. Save the database as **Book Sales Database**, followed by your initials. You will now create a parameter query to look up an employee by their Employee ID number.
2. Click the **Create** tab, and then click the **Query Design** button in the Queries group to display the Query Design window.
3. In the Show Table dialog box, click **Sales Department** to select it, if necessary, and then click **Add**. The Sales Department table is now added to the Query Design window.
4. Click the **Sales Orders** table, and then click **Add**.
5. Click the **Close** button to close the Show Table dialog box. If you want to increase the size of the tables in Query Design window to see all of the fields, place the mouse pointer over the bottom of the table field list and drag down until you see the entire list of fields. Compare your screen to **Figure 8–1**.

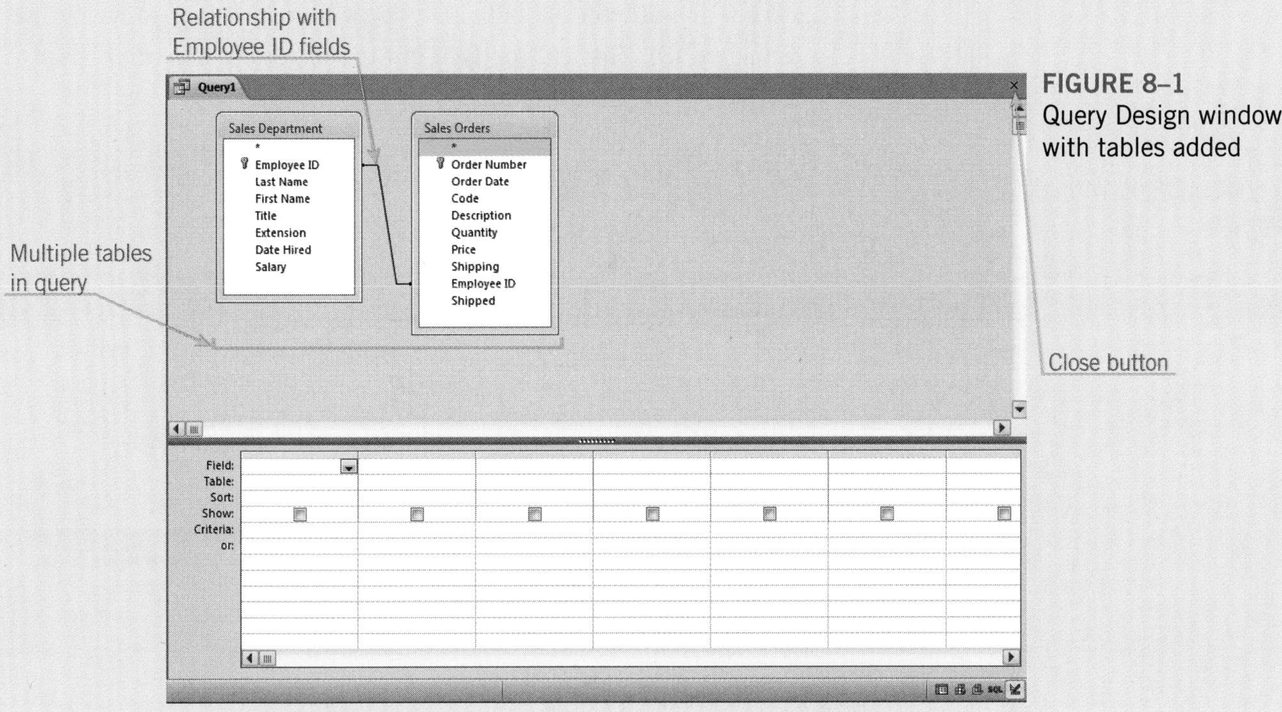

FIGURE 8–1
Query Design window with tables added

6. In the Sales Department table, double-click the following fields to add them to the design grid in the order shown: **Employee ID**, **First Name**, and **Last Name**.
7. In the Sales Orders table, double-click the following fields to add them to the design grid in the order shown: **Order Number** and **Description**. Next, you will create a calculated field.
8. Right-click the empty field to the right of the Description field in the design grid to display the shortcut menu, and then click **Zoom**. See **Figure 8–2**.

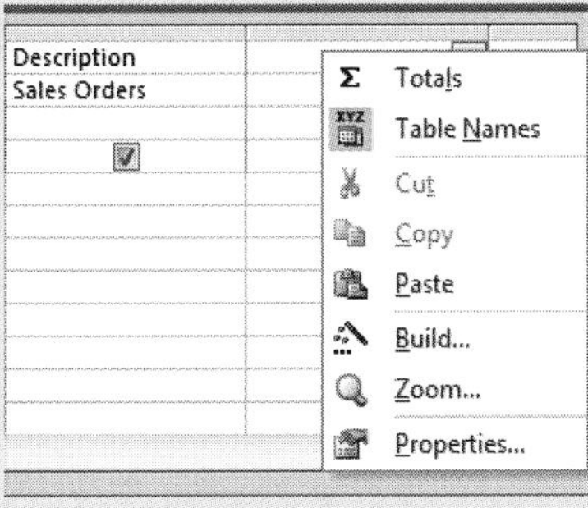

FIGURE 8–2
Shortcut menu

9. Type **Order Total:[Quantity]*[Price]** in the Zoom dialog box. The text before the colon is what will appear at the top of column, and the information after the colon is the expression.
10. Click **OK** to close the Zoom dialog box. Next, you will enter the parameter, which will appear in the message box as a prompt.

11. Click in the **Criteria** cell in the Employee ID field, and then type **[Enter Employee ID]**. The text you type in the square brackets will appear as the title for the parameter dialog box. See **Figure 8–3**.

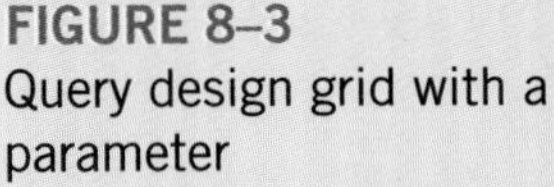

FIGURE 8–3
Query design grid with a parameter

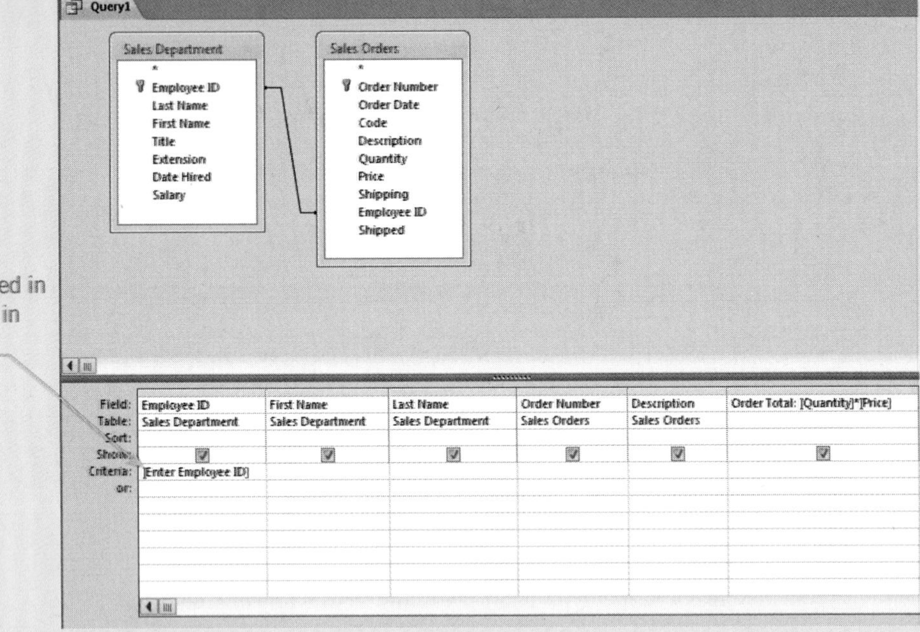

12. Save the query as **qry-Employee Sales**. Leave the query open for the next Step-by-Step.

Running a Parameter Query

After you create a parameter query, you will need to run the query so that it displays the message box where you enter the criterion. Each time you run the query, you can type a different criterion in the text box. Being able to run a query to provide the same or different criterion each time you run it saves time because a new query does not have to be created for each new search criterion.

You run a query by clicking the Run button on the Design tab, clicking the View button in the Results group, or double-clicking the query in the Navigation pane.

Step-by-Step 8.2

1. On the Ribbon, click the **Query Tools Design** tab and then click the **Run** button in the Results group. The Enter Parameter Value dialog box opens, as shown in **Figure 8–4**.

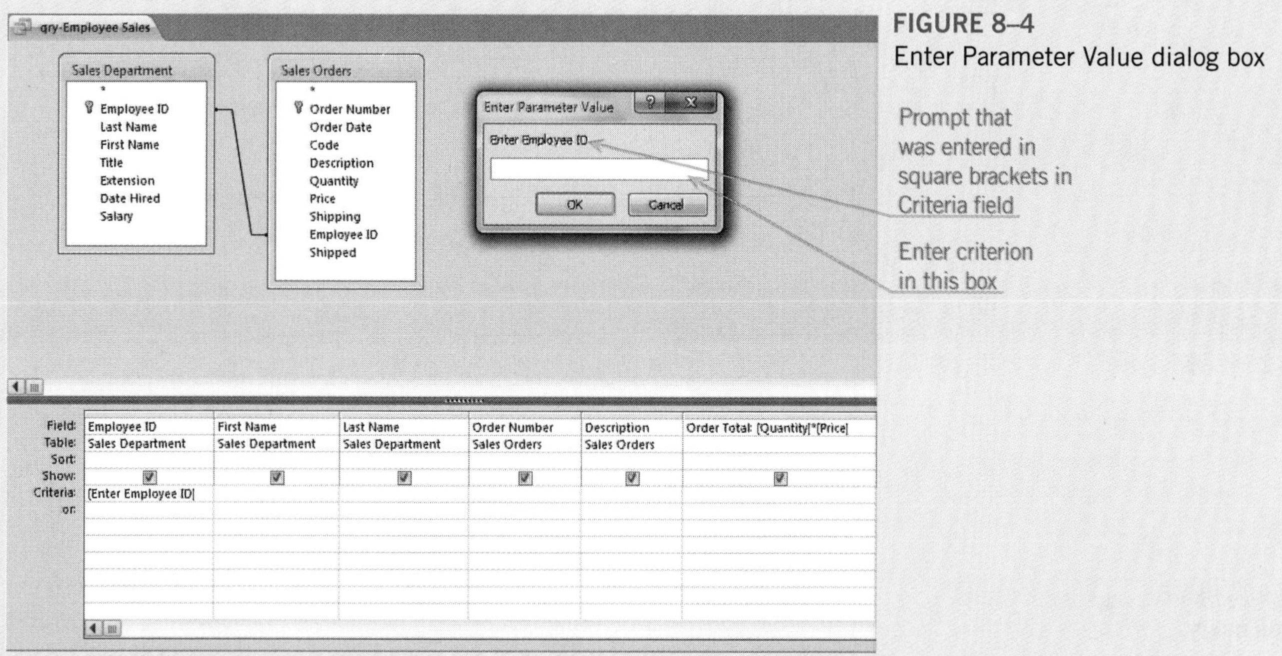

FIGURE 8–4
Enter Parameter Value dialog box

2. Type **N175** to display the sales results for John Carroll, and then click **OK**. See **Figure 8–5**.

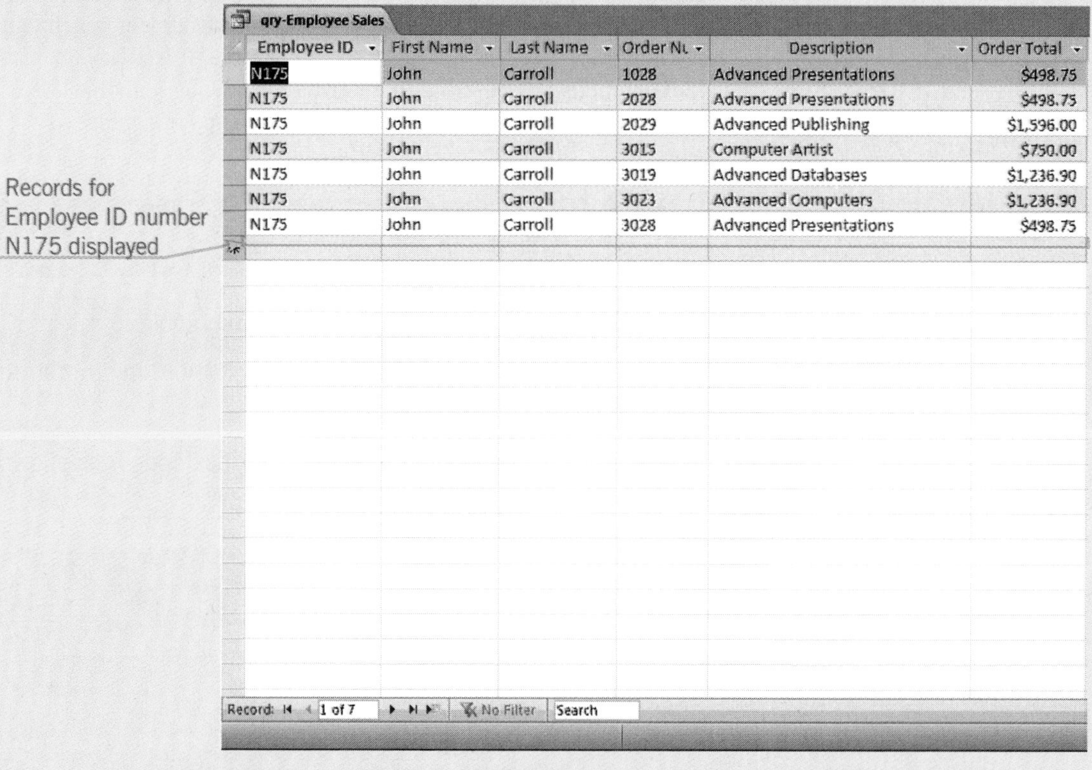

Employee ID	First Name	Last Name	Order Nu	Description	Order Total
N175	John	Carroll	1028	Advanced Presentations	$498.75
N175	John	Carroll	2028	Advanced Presentations	$498.75
N175	John	Carroll	2029	Advanced Publishing	$1,596.00
N175	John	Carroll	3015	Computer Artist	$750.00
N175	John	Carroll	3019	Advanced Databases	$1,236.90
N175	John	Carroll	3023	Advanced Computers	$1,236.90
N175	John	Carroll	3028	Advanced Presentations	$498.75

FIGURE 8–5
Datasheet for query with parameter

3. On the Ribbon, click the **Home** tab and then click the **View** button in the Views group to return to the Query Design window.

4. On the Ribbon, click the **Query Tools Design** tab and then click the **Run** button in the Results group.

5. Type **N550** and then press **Enter** to display the sales results for Kelly Gordon.
6. Close the query by clicking the **Close** button in the upper-right corner of the query window. Next, you will run the query.
7. In the Navigation pane, double-click the **qry-Employee Sales** query. The Enter Parameter Value dialog box opens.
8. Type **N440** and then press **Enter** to display the sales results for Karen Lopez.
9. Close the query. Leave the database open for the next exercise.

Preparing a Table for Action Queries

VOCABULARY
action query

An ***action query*** makes changes to the records in a table. For example, you can use an update action query to instantly update all the employee salaries in a table by five percent. Since the records in the table are changed as soon as you run the query, you cannot undo the changes. To protect the data in the table, it is best to make a copy of the table before you run the query. Then, if the query does not work as you expected, you have the copy of the table with the correct data to continue working.

Before you run an action query, you will want to compare the fields in the tables. Records may not be added correctly if the fields in the two tables do not match. For example, one table may have one less field than the other table. It is always best to check the data types and fields in both tables before you run the query. In this lesson, you will check the data types in both tables and then make a copy of a table.

Step-by-Step 8.3

1. In the Navigation pane, click once on the **Sales Orders** table to select it.
2. On the Ribbon, click the **Home** tab, and then click the **Copy** button in the Clipboard group.
3. Click the **Paste** button. The Paste Table As dialog box opens, as shown in **Figure 8–6**.

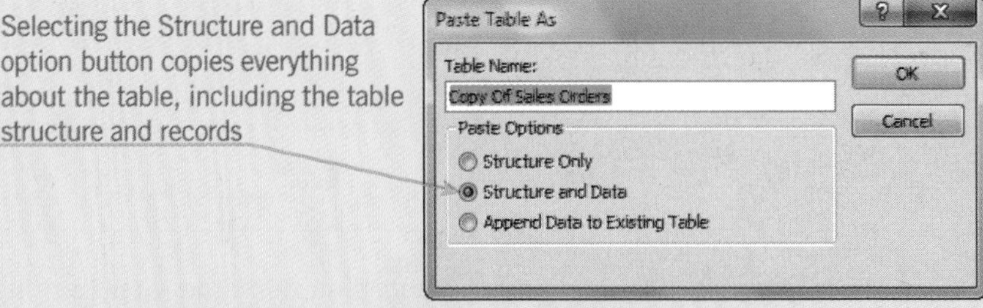

FIGURE 8–6
Paste Table As dialog box

4. In the Paste Table As dialog box, verify that the **Structure and Data** option button is selected, and then click **OK**. The copied table will now serve as a backup of the table in case an error occurs in an action query.

5. Open the **Sales Orders** table and the **April Sales** table in Design View, as shown in **Figure 8–7**.

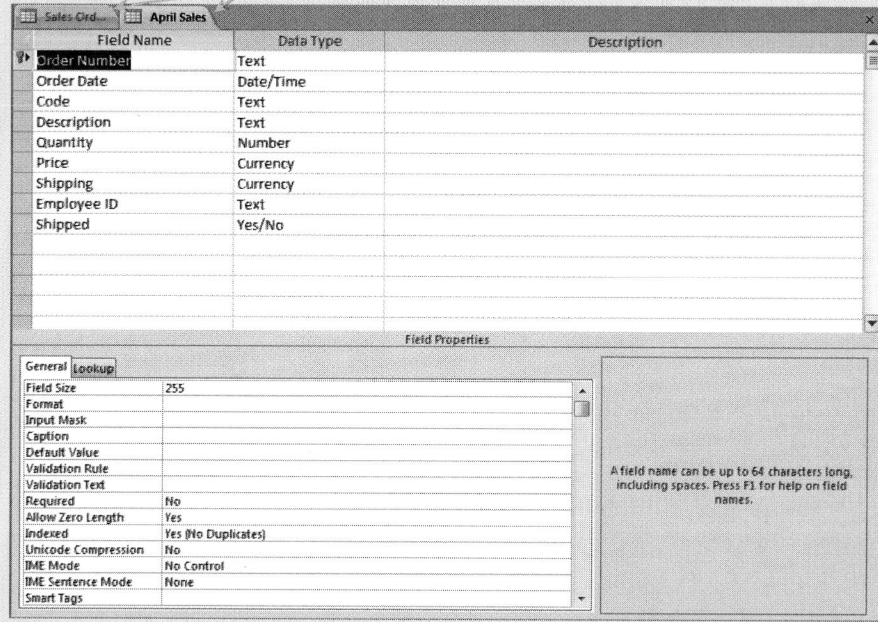

FIGURE 8–7
Opened tables in Design view

6. Click the **Sales Orders** tab and the **April Sales** tab to review the data types in each table. Each table does have the same data types for the fields.
7. Close the Sales Orders and April Sales tables.

Using an Append Query

An append query moves data from one table to another table. The word ***append*** means to add. When you use an append query, you add the table that has the records you want added to another table. Then, you need to add the fields to the query design

VOCABULARY
append

grid for the fields that will contain the data to be appended to another table. To add all of the fields at one time, you can double-click the table name title to select all of the fields. The fields will be highlighted and selected, as shown in **Figure 8–8**.

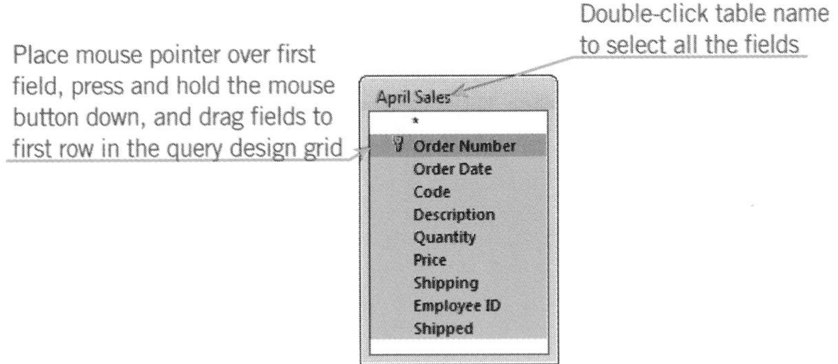

FIGURE 8–8 Table with all fields selected

Then, you place the mouse pointer over the first field in the highlighted fields, press and hold down the mouse button, and drag them to the first row in the query design grid.

When you click the Append button, you will need to select the table where the records will be added. A new row will appear in the query design grid, as shown in **Figure 8–9**.

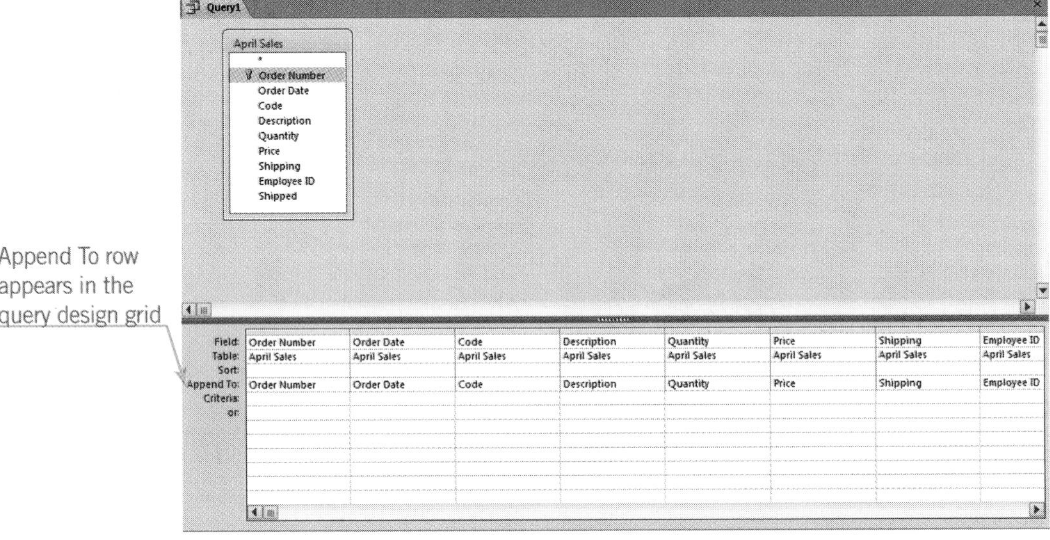

FIGURE 8–9 Append query window

When you run the query, the records are instantly added. At this point, you should not save the query because doing so may cause the query to accidentally run again. The records would then be added for a second time. Next, you will use an append query.

Step-by-Step 8.4

1. On the Ribbon, click the **Create** tab and then click the **Query Design** button in the Queries group.
2. Double-click **April Sales** in the Show Table dialog box to place it in the Query Design window, and then click the **Close** button to close the Show Table dialog box.
3. Double-click the **April Sales** title in the Table Field List title bar. Place your mouse pointer over the first field in the list of selected fields, then press and hold the left mouse button down and drag the fields to the first row in the query grid.
4. If necessary, click the **Query Tools Design** tab and then click the **Append** button in the Query Type group. The Append dialog box opens, as shown in **Figure 8–10**.

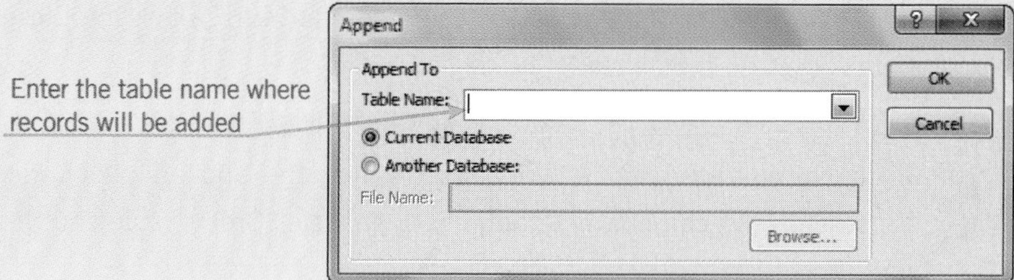

FIGURE 8–10 Append dialog box

5. In the Append dialog box, click the **Table Name** drop-down arrow and then click **Sales Orders** from the list. Click **OK** and then compare your screen to **Figure 8–11**.

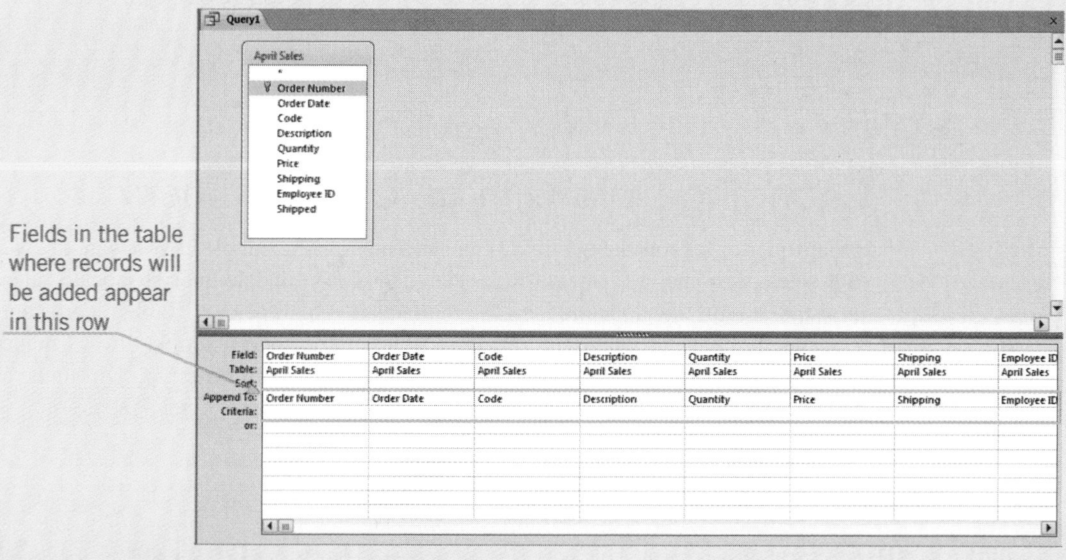

FIGURE 8–11 Query Design window for append query

6. On the Query Tools Design tab, click the **Run** button in the Results group. A message box appears stating that you are about to append thirty rows of data, as shown in **Figure 8–12**.

FIGURE 8–12
Append message box

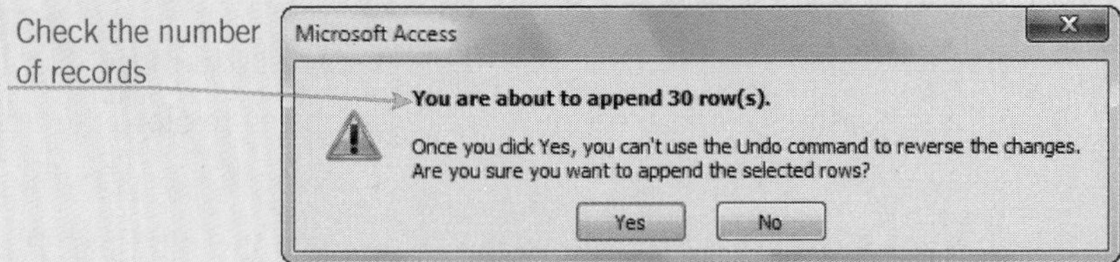

7. Click **Yes**. Note that if you were to click the Run button again, all of the records in the April Sales table would be added to the Sales Orders table for a second time. To prevent this action from accidentally happening, you will first check to see if the records were added to the Sales Orders table and then close the query without saving it.
8. In the Navigation pane, double-click the **Sales Orders** table to open it. Scroll down in the table to review the orders for April. Click the **Close** button to close the Sales Orders table.
9. Click the **Close 'Query1'** button to close the query.
10. Click **No** so the query is not saved. Since the append query was successful, you can now delete the Copy Of Sales Orders table and the April Sales table.
11. In the Navigation pane, right-click **Copy Of Sales Orders** table, click **Delete** from the shortcut menu, and then click **Yes** to confirm the deletion.
12. Delete the **April Sales** table. Leave the database open for the next exercise.

Changing Data with an Update Query

Update queries let you change field values in a table. For example, if you want to give your sales personnel a 6 percent raise, you can use an update query to locate sales personnel within the table and increase their salaries by 6 percent. Table records are permanently changed when you run the update query, so you should always make a copy of the table before running the query. In this next exercise, you will make a copy of the Sales Department table and then give the sales personnel a raise.

Step-by-Step 8.5

1. Click once on the **Sales Department** table to select it. On the Home tab, click the **Copy** button and then click the **Paste** button. Verify that the **Structure and Data option button** is selected in the Paste Table As dialog box, and then click **OK**.
2. Double-click the **Sales Department** table to open it. Notice that the salary for Sally Loyal is $54,800. Also notice that there are nine Sales Reps. Keep this amount in mind so you can check the results of the updated data. Click the **Close 'Sales Department'** button to close the table.
3. On the Ribbon, click the **Create** tab and then click the **Query Design** button in the Queries group.
4. Double-click the **Sales Department** table in the Show Table dialog box to place it in the Query Design window, and then close the Show Table dialog box.
5. Double-click the **Title** field and the **Salary** field to move them to the query design grid.
6. Click the **Query Tools Design** tab, and then click the **Update** button in the Query Type group.
7. Click in the **Criteria** field in the Title field, and then type **Sales Rep**.

8. Click in the **Update To** field under Salary, and then type **[Salary]*1.03**. This calculation will give the sales representatives a 3 percent raise. Compare your screen to **Figure 8–13**.

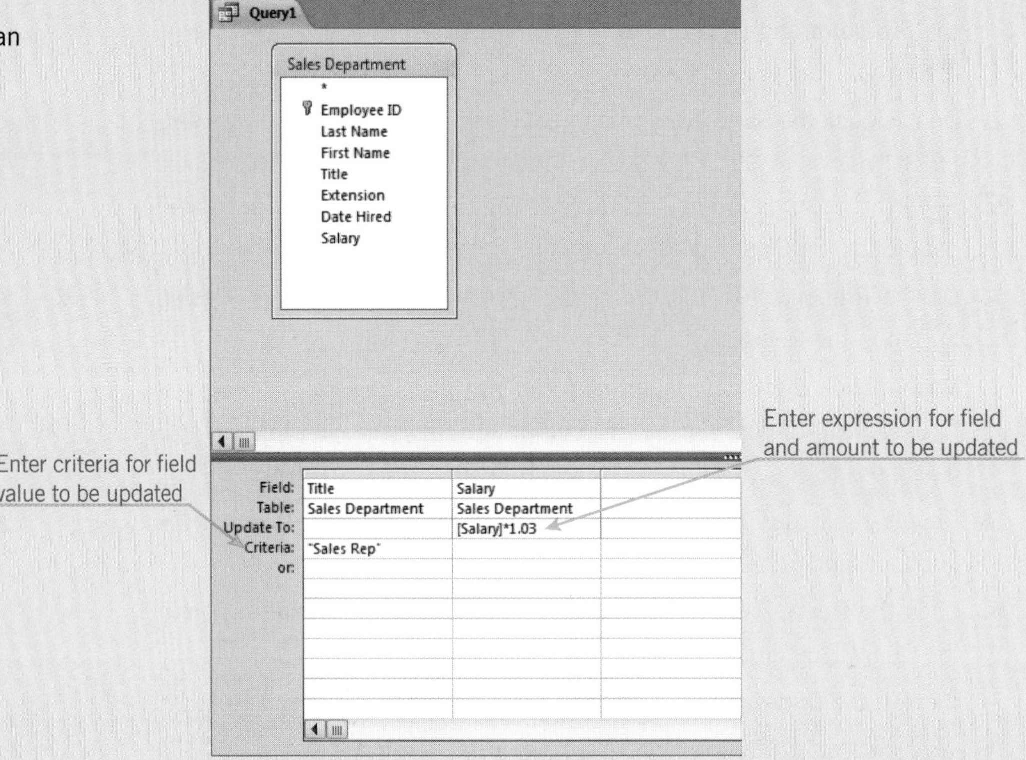

FIGURE 8–13
Query Design window for an update query

9. Click the **Run** button in the Results group, and then click **Yes** in the message box that follows.
10. In the Navigation pane, double-click the **Sales Department** table to open it. Notice that the salary for Sally Loyal is $56,444. Her salary shows the 3 percent increase ($54,800 * 1.03 = $56,444).
11. Click the **Close 'Sales Department'** button to close the Sales Department table. Now that you have checked to see that the update query was successful, you will close the query without saving it.
12. Click the **Close 'Query1'** button to close the query. Click **No** to close the query without saving the changes.
13. Since the query successfully updated salaries for the Sales Reps, you can delete the copy you made. Right-click the **Copy of Sales Department** table, click **Delete** from the shortcut menu, and then select **Yes** in the message box.

Using Wildcards in a Query

VOCABULARY
wildcard character

A ***wildcard character*** is a character, such as an asterisk, that you can use to represent incomplete or unknown information. For example, you may know that a person's last name begins with Del, but you do not know how to spell the rest of it. In a query, you can search for the person by typing del*. The asterisk is the wildcard character. The wildcard character lets Access know that it should look for any last name that starts with Del. The query result may show people with last names of Delagarza, Delaware, or Del Gado. In other words, any person's last name that starts with Del will be displayed, regardless of what comes after Del.

You can use a wildcard character with letters or numbers in any order. For example, if you type *del*, Access will find last names such as Adelgo, Delagarza, Del Gado, and Begedel. Access looks at what is between the asterisks and returns an answer. In other words, it will not matter what comes before or after the del; any last name with del will be displayed. In this next exercise, you will use wildcards to look for various book titles.

Step-by-Step 8.6

1. On the Ribbon, click the **Create** tab and then click the **Query Design** button in the Queries group.
2. Double-click **Sales Orders** in the Show Table dialog box to add the table to the Query Design window, and then close the Show Table dialog box.
3. Double-click the **Order Number**, **Order Date**, **Description**, **Quantity**, and **Price** fields to add them to the query design grid. Next, you will use wildcards to see how many database books were ordered.
4. Click in the **Criteria** field under the Description column.

5. Type ***database*** and then press **Enter**. Notice that Access automatically adds the word Like and quote marks around the criteria. Compare your screen to **Figure 8–14**.

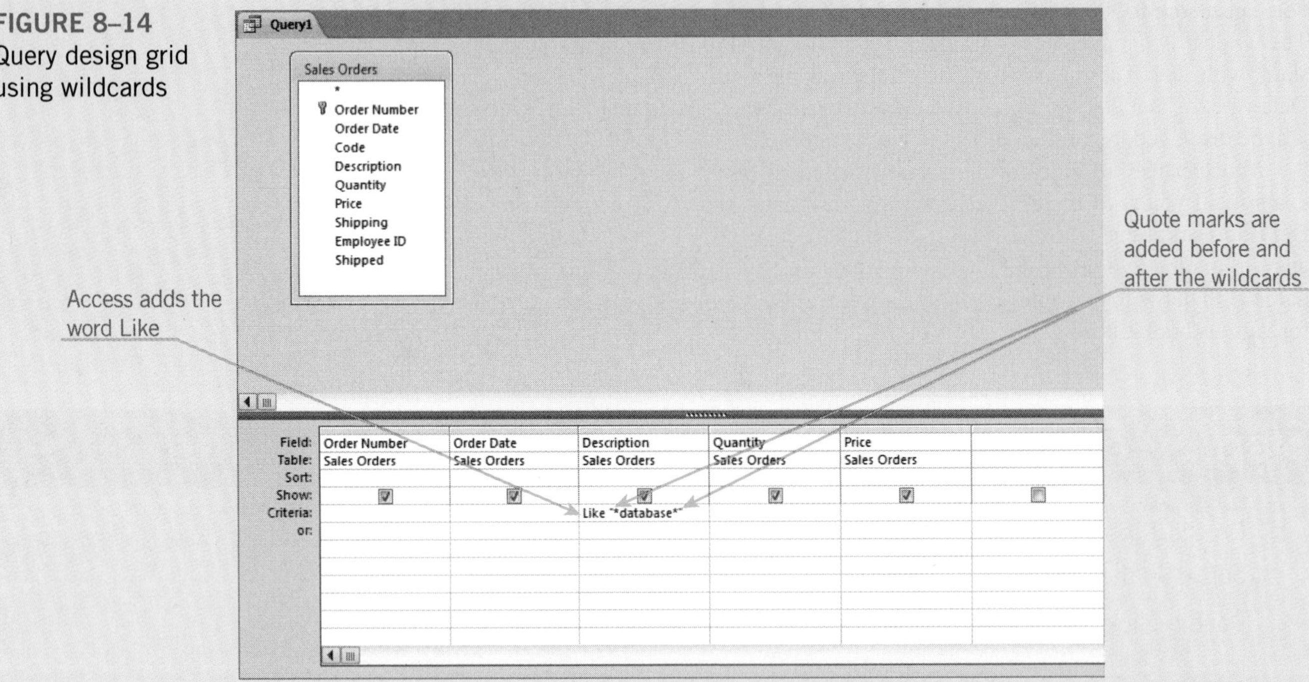

FIGURE 8–14
Query design grid using wildcards

6. Click the **Run** button to view the results as shown in **Figure 8–15**.

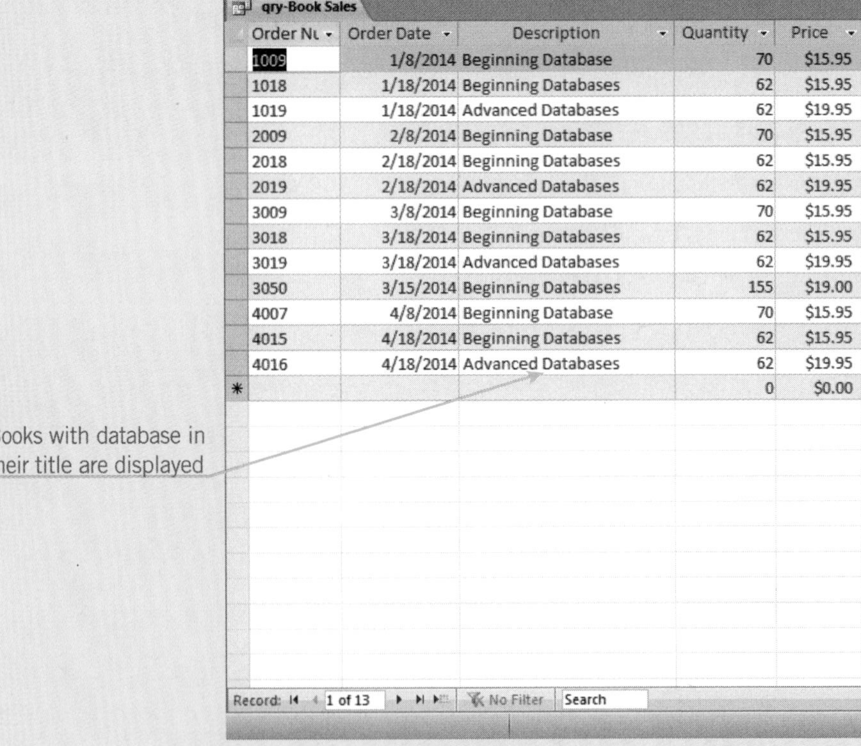

Order Nu	Order Date	Description	Quantity	Price
1009	1/8/2014	Beginning Database	70	$15.95
1018	1/18/2014	Beginning Databases	62	$15.95
1019	1/18/2014	Advanced Databases	62	$19.95
2009	2/8/2014	Beginning Database	70	$15.95
2018	2/18/2014	Beginning Databases	62	$15.95
2019	2/18/2014	Advanced Databases	62	$19.95
3009	3/8/2014	Beginning Database	70	$15.95
3018	3/18/2014	Beginning Databases	62	$15.95
3019	3/18/2014	Advanced Databases	62	$19.95
3050	3/15/2014	Beginning Databases	155	$19.00
4007	4/8/2014	Beginning Database	70	$15.95
4015	4/18/2014	Beginning Databases	62	$15.95
4016	4/18/2014	Advanced Databases	62	$19.95
*			0	$0.00

FIGURE 8–15
Query datasheet with wildcard results

7. Click the **View** button in the Views group to return to the Query Design window. Clicking the View button will toggle you between the two windows.
8. Click the **Save** button on the Quick Access toolbar, and then type **qry-Book Sales** in the Query Name text box in the Save As dialog box.
9. Click **OK**. Remain in Query Design window for the next Step-by-Step.

Using Parameters and Wildcards in a Query

You learned that using parameters in a query displays a message box where you can type different search criteria each time you run the query. In addition, you discovered that wildcards can be used instead of exact text or numbers when looking for data. For added flexibility, Access allows you to use parameters and wildcards in the same query. Using both parameters and wildcards allows you to enter only the criterion that you are sure of in the provided message box. In this next exercise, you will use a parameter and wildcards in the same Criteria field.

Step-by-Step 8.7

1. Click in the **Criteria** field under the Description column, and then press **Delete** or **Backspace** to delete the criteria.

2. In the Criteria cell, type **Like "*" & [Enter search text] & "*"**. Entering a parameter with wildcards lets you enter a word or a few letters of your search term. In this example, you are looking for any books that contain "publish" in their title. Notice that you cannot see the entire Description field, as shown in **Figure 8–16**. In the next step, you will increase the width of this field.

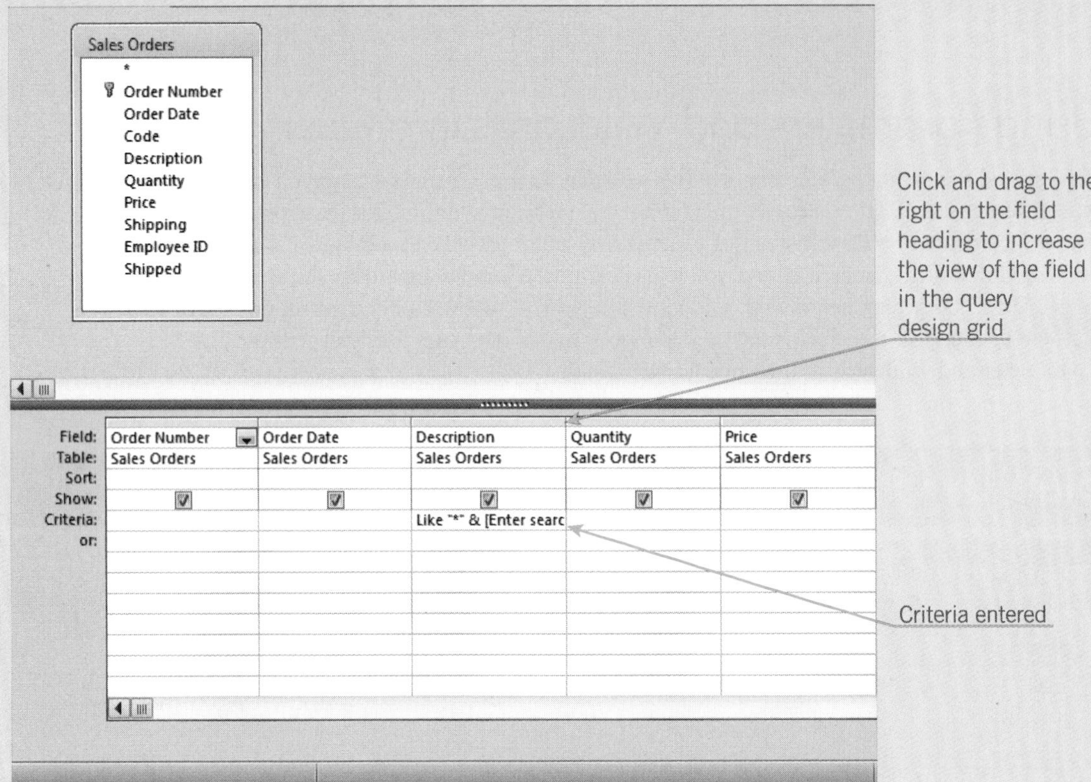

FIGURE 8–16
Query with criteria entered

3. Place the mouse pointer on the right side of the bar above the Description field name, and drag to the right to increase the width of the field in the query design grid so you can see all of the criteria. See **Figure 8–17**.

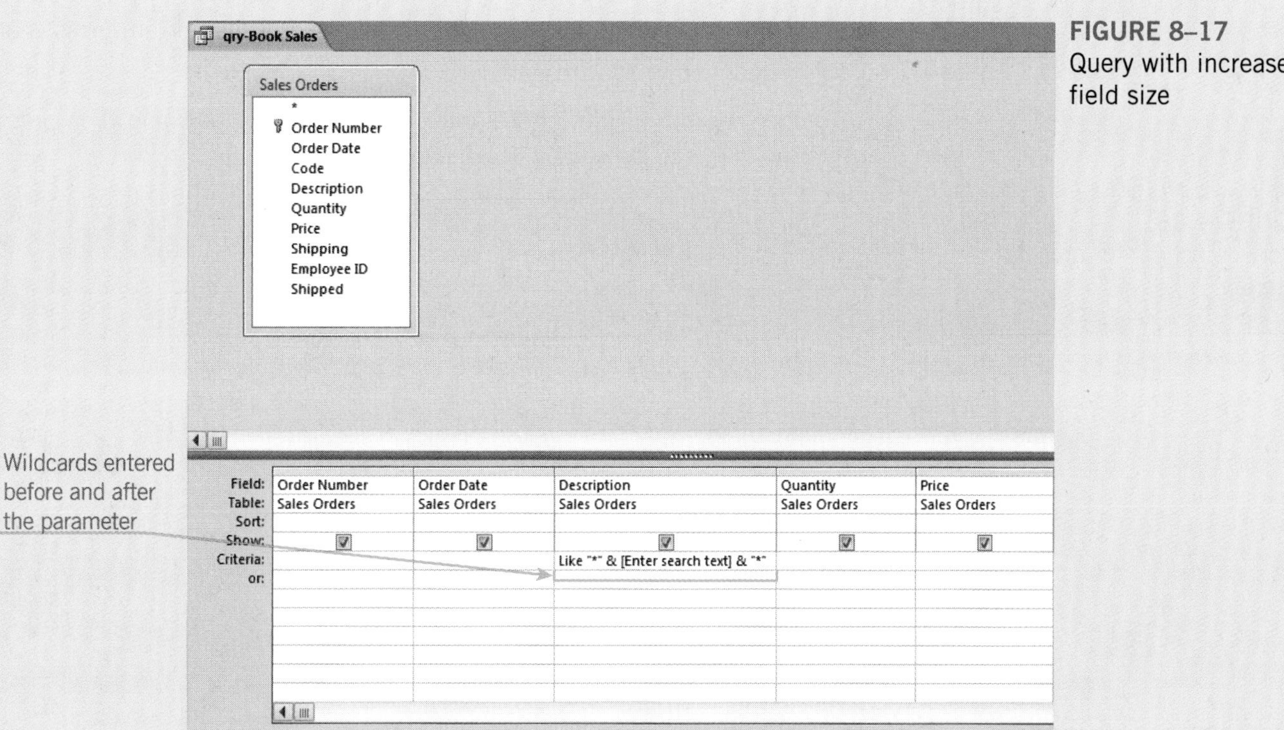

FIGURE 8–17 Query with increased field size

4. Click the **Save** button.
5. Click the **Run** button. The Enter Parameter Value dialog box opens.
6. In the Enter Parameter Value dialog box, type **publish**, and then click **OK**. The Query datasheet shows the results for all books that contain "publish" in their title. See **Figure 8–18**.

qry-Book Sales

Order Nu	Order Date	Description	Quantity	Price
1010	1/12/2014	Beginning Publishing	80	$15.95
1011	1/12/2014	Advanced Publishing	80	$19.95
1012	1/12/2014	Desktop Publishing for Beginners	115	$19.95
1020	1/21/2014	Beginning Publishing	55	$15.95
1021	1/21/2014	Advanced Publishing	55	$19.95
1025	1/28/2014	Desktop Publishing for Beginners	95	$19.95
2010	2/12/2014	Beginning Publishing	80	$15.95
2011	2/12/2014	Advanced Publishing	80	$19.95
2012	2/12/2014	Desktop Publishing for Beginners	215	$19.95
2020	2/21/2014	Beginning Publishing	55	$15.95
2021	2/21/2014	Advanced Publishing	55	$19.95
2025	2/28/2014	Desktop Publishing for Beginners	95	$19.95
2029	2/12/2014	Advanced Publishing	80	$19.95
2030	2/12/2014	Desktop Publishing for Beginners	215	$19.95
3010	3/12/2014	Beginning Publishing	80	$15.95
3011	3/12/2014	Advanced Publishing	80	$19.95
3012	3/12/2014	Desktop Publishing for Beginners	315	$19.95
3020	3/21/2014	Beginning Publishing	55	$15.95
3021	3/21/2014	Advanced Publishing	55	$19.95
3025	3/28/2014	Desktop Publishing for Beginners	95	$19.95
3029	3/12/2014	Advanced Publishing	80	$19.95
3030	3/12/2014	Desktop Publishing for Beginners	215	$19.95
3051	3/15/2014	Beginnina Publishing	193	$15.95
4008	4/14/2014	Beginning Publishing	80	$15.95
4009	4/14/2014	Advanced Publishing	80	$19.95

Record: 1 of 31 No Filter Search

Books with publish in their title are displayed

FIGURE 8–18 Query datasheet for publish criteria

7. Click the **View** button to return to the Query Design window.

8. Click the **Run** button. You want to find book sales for all books that include the word "presentations".
9. Type **present** in the Enter Parameter Value dialog box, and then press **Enter**. Compare your screen to **Figure 8–19**.

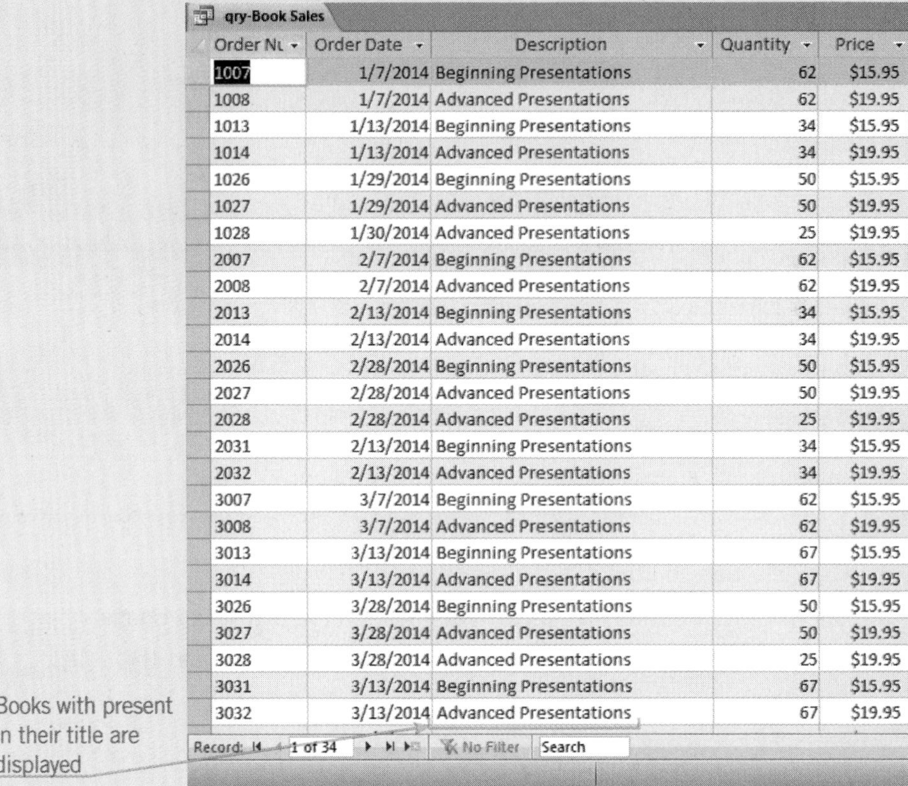
qry-Book Sales

Order Nu	Order Date	Description	Quantity	Price
1007	1/7/2014	Beginning Presentations	62	$15.95
1008	1/7/2014	Advanced Presentations	62	$19.95
1013	1/13/2014	Beginning Presentations	34	$15.95
1014	1/13/2014	Advanced Presentations	34	$19.95
1026	1/29/2014	Beginning Presentations	50	$15.95
1027	1/29/2014	Advanced Presentations	50	$19.95
1028	1/30/2014	Advanced Presentations	25	$19.95
2007	2/7/2014	Beginning Presentations	62	$15.95
2008	2/7/2014	Advanced Presentations	62	$19.95
2013	2/13/2014	Beginning Presentations	34	$15.95
2014	2/13/2014	Advanced Presentations	34	$19.95
2026	2/28/2014	Beginning Presentations	50	$15.95
2027	2/28/2014	Advanced Presentations	50	$19.95
2028	2/28/2014	Advanced Presentations	25	$19.95
2031	2/13/2014	Beginning Presentations	34	$15.95
2032	2/13/2014	Advanced Presentations	34	$19.95
3007	3/7/2014	Beginning Presentations	62	$15.95
3008	3/7/2014	Advanced Presentations	62	$19.95
3013	3/13/2014	Beginning Presentations	67	$15.95
3014	3/13/2014	Advanced Presentations	67	$19.95
3026	3/28/2014	Beginning Presentations	50	$15.95
3027	3/28/2014	Advanced Presentations	50	$19.95
3028	3/28/2014	Advanced Presentations	25	$19.95
3031	3/13/2014	Beginning Presentations	67	$15.95
3032	3/13/2014	Advanced Presentations	67	$19.95

Record: 1 of 34 No Filter Search

FIGURE 8–19
Query datasheet for present criteria

10. Click the **Close 'qry-Book Sales'** button to close the query.
11. Close the database.

Creating a Crosstab Query

A crosstab query rearranges data in a table or query so that it appears in another format. Typically records in a table appear in rows, and the columns display the information for the field. Crosstab queries let you arrange the information you want to place in the rows and columns. Crosstab queries also calculate a Sum, Avg, Count, or other type of calculation that you choose for numerical data. The completed crosstab query displays the data in a spreadsheet-like format.

Step-by-Step 8.8

1. Open the **Healthcare Training** file from the drive and folder where your Data Files are stored. Save the database as **Healthcare Training Database**, followed by your initials.
2. On the Ribbon, click the **Create** tab and then click the **Query Wizard** button in the Queries group. The New Query dialog box opens, as shown in **Figure 8–20**.

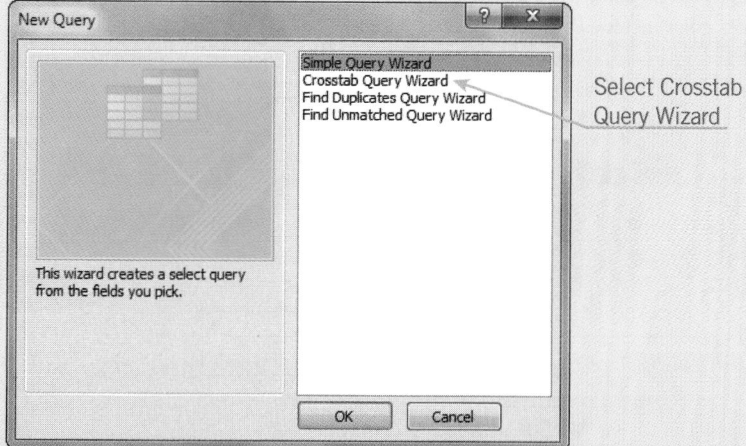

FIGURE 8–20
New Query dialog box

3. Double-click **Crosstab Query Wizard** in the New Query dialog box. The first window of the Crosstab Query Wizard opens. See **Figure 8–21**.

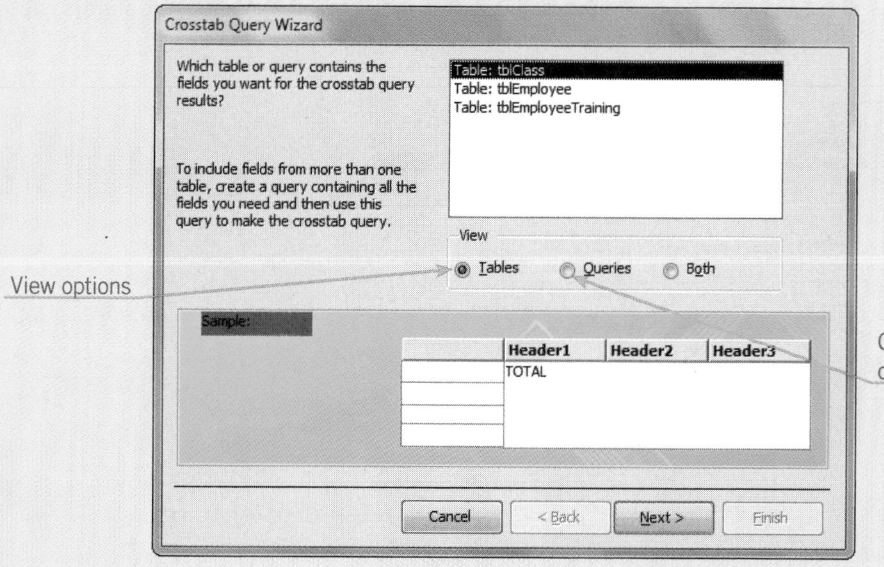

FIGURE 8–21
First Crosstab Query Wizard dialog box

4. Click the **Queries** option button in the View section of the dialog box.
5. Verify that **qry-TrainingCostAndDate** is selected, and then click the **Next** button. Next, you will click the field you want for the row headings.

6. Click **Description** for the row headings so that you can see the description for each class. Then, click the **Select Single Field** button. Compare your screen to **Figure 8–22**.

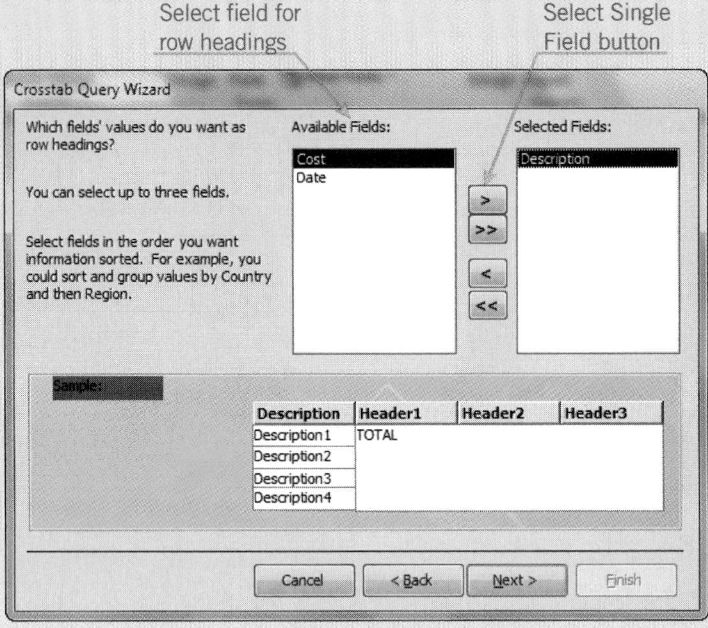

FIGURE 8–22
Description field selected for row headings

7. Click **Next**. You will now select the field for the column headings.
8. Click **Date**, and then click **Next.** You will be asked how you want the date to be displayed, such as by year, quarter, or month.
9. Click **Year** as the interval for the grouping for the Date column. See **Figure 8–23**.

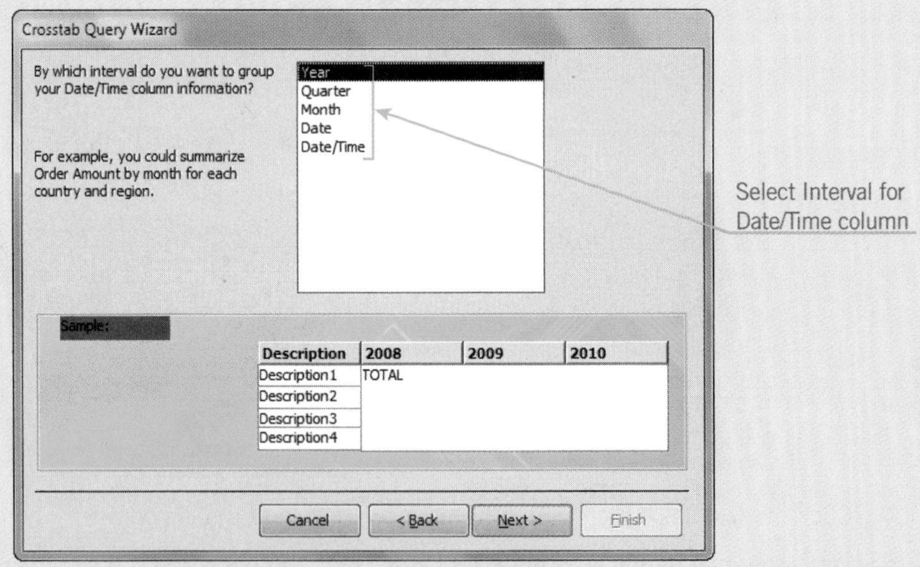

FIGURE 8–23
Year selected as grouping for Date

10. Click **Next**.
11. Click **Sum** in the Functions area to view the total cost for the classes. See **Figure 8–24**.

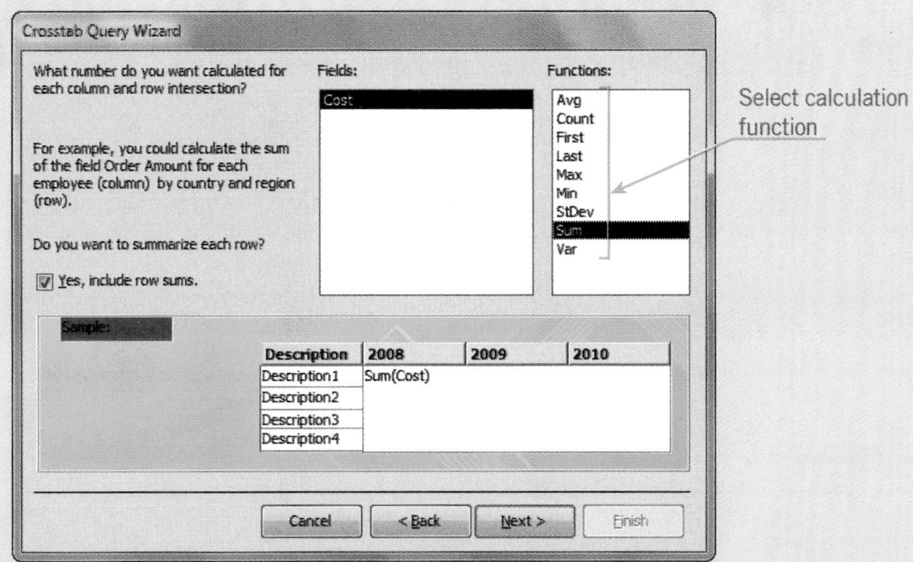

FIGURE 8–24
Sum selected to view total costs

12. Click **Next**.
13. Delete the existing text in the text box below "What do you want to name your query?", type **qry-ClassCostAnalysis**, and then click **Finish**. The Crosstab query datasheet appears, as shown in **Figure 8–25**. Notice that the icon that appears before the crosstab query is different than for a select query.

qry-ClassCostAnalysis

Description	Total Of Cos	2011	2012	2013	2014
Adult CPR Recertification	$100.00	$40.00	$30.00	$20.00	$10.00
Child/Infant CPR	$15.00				$15.00
Child/Infant CPR Recertification	$50.00	$20.00		$20.00	$10.00
First Aid	$15.00	$15.00			
Nutritional Supplements	$25.00		$25.00		
Yoga	$50.00		$50.00		

Record: 1 of 6 No Filter Search

FIGURE 8–25
Results of crosstab query

14. Click the **Close** button to close qry-ClassCostAnalysis. Then click the **Close** button on the Access title bar to close the database and exit Access.

SUMMARY

In this lesson, you learned:

- Parameter queries display a dialog box for you to enter information each time you run the query.
- It is best to make a copy of a table before you run an action query.
- An append query can add records from one table to another table.
- Using an update query lets you quickly change records in a table.
- Using wildcards in queries allows for the flexibility of not knowing a complete phrase or spelling.
- Using both parameters and wildcards allows you to enter only the criteria that you are sure of in the provided message box.
- A crosstab query places data in a spreadsheet-like format.

VOCABULARY REVIEW

Define the following terms:

action query
append
criterion
parameter
wildcard character

REVIEW QUESTIONS

TRUE / FALSE

Circle T if the statement is true or F if the statement is false.

T F 1. If you want to add records from one table to another table, you use a parameter query.

T F 2. A wildcard, such as an asterisk, can be used in searches when you do not know the exact spelling of a person's last name.

T F 3. It is safe to run an action query that makes changes to records in a table without first making a copy of the table.

T F 4. Append queries increase efficiency by providing a single query that you may use many times with various criteria each time the query runs.

T F 5. Parameters and wildcards cannot be used in the same query on the same Criteria row.

FILL IN THE BLANK

1. A(n) ________________ query rearranges data in a table or a query so that it appears in another format.
2. A(n) ________________ query can instantly update several records in a table at one time.
3. ________________ means to vary.
4. ________________ is the data you are searching for.
5. If you are not certain of the exact spelling of a person's last name, you could use a(n) ________________ in the query.

WRITTEN QUESTIONS

Write a brief answer to the following questions.

1. Explain what you should do with a table before you run an action query that makes changes to the table.

2. Explain the difference between an update query and an append query.

3. Explain the process for creating a crosstab query.

4. Give examples of when you could use an action query. Use different examples than those used in this lesson.

5. Explain the word and characters that are added in a Criteria cell when you use a wildcard.

PROJECTS

If you have a SAM 2010 user profile, your instructor may have assigned an autogradable version of the indicated project. If so, log into the SAM 2010 Web site at *www.cengage.com/sam2010* to download the instruction and start files.

PROJECT 8–1

1. Open the **Pet Supplies** file from the drive and folder where your Data Files are stored. Save the database as **Pet Supplies Database**, followed by your initials.
2. Create an update query that finds the records in the Inventory table whose *Product ID* field begins with **4**. Update the *Reorder Point* field to **10**. (*Hint*: Use the criteria of 4* in the *Product ID* field.)
3. Save the query as **Qry-Product 400 Reorder Change**. Close the query.
4. Open the Inventory table and view the changes. Sort the Inventory table by the *Product ID* field. Print the table.
5. Close the query and then close the database file.

SAM PROJECT 8–2

1. Open the **Atlantic Sales** file from the drive and folder where your Data Files are stored. Save the database as **Atlantic Sales Database**, followed by your initials.
2. Create a parameter query for the Sales Data table. In the Design window, add the Region, Month, Sales, Last_Name, and First_Name fields to the query grid. Since each field in the table will be included in the query, think of a quick way to put each field in the query grid.
3. Enter a prompt in the Region field that will prompt the user to enter a region.
4. Sort the query in ascending order by the Last Name field, and then add another sort in ascending order to the First Name field.
5. Save the query as **Qry-Sales by Region**.
6. Run the parameter query using West as the criterion. Adjust the column widths if necessary. Print the query results.
7. Run the query using the North and the East parameters. Print the results of each query.
8. Close the query and the database file.

PROJECT 8–3

1. Open the **Teams** file from the drive and folder where your Data Files are stored. Save the database as **Teams Database**, followed by your initials.
2. Create a parameter query with wildcards that search tblStudent for students' last names in the Last Name field. The query should be able to search for a student's last name based on the first letter of the student's last name. The query should also display all of the fields from the table.
3. Save the query as **Qry-Student Search**.
4. Run the query and search for any student's last name that begins with Lo.
5. Print the results of the query.
6. Close the query and the database file.

CRITICAL THINKING

ACTIVITY 8–1

Open the **Regional Sales** file from the drive and folder where your Data Files are stored, and then save the database as **Regional Sales Database** followed by your initials.

You are a new database administrator for a company in Massachusetts. When you review the Access database, you realize that the sales for January and February are in a table named Sales Data. However, the person entering the sales data created a new table for the March sales. You decide to correct this data by adding the records from the March Sales table into the Sales Data table.

ACTIVITY 8–2

As a professor at Collinsborough Community College, you're going to give a presentation to your Access class on the various types of action queries. Write a brief summary of the types of action queries discussed in this lesson and give an example of when you would use each query.

Estimated Time: 2.5 hours

LESSON 9

Using Advanced Form Features

OBJECTIVES

Upon completion of this lesson, you should be able to:

- Understand the importance of consistent form design.
- Apply a theme to a form.
- Add a logo.
- Create command buttons.
- Add a new field to an existing form.
- Create a combo box.
- Size and align a control.
- Use a combo box in a new record.
- Add a calculated control.
- Change tab order.

VOCABULARY

calculated control
combo box
command button
live preview
logo
tab order
theme

Introduction

In this lesson, you will learn the importance of using a consistent design for all the forms in a database. A consistent design can be created with the use of themes. Themes add borders and colors to forms. You will also learn how to add command buttons to forms. A command button can be clicked to move within a form or to open another form. Then, you will add a new field to an existing form. A combo box that displays a list of options will also be created in the form. You will then add a calculated control that calculates the total of fields in a form. And, finally, you will change the order of how you move between the fields in a form, called the tab order.

Understanding the Importance of Consistent Form Design

Most people use forms to enter and retrieve data. If all the forms in your database share the same design, users will have an easier time using the forms. When designing forms, you will want to decide what color scheme, fonts, and general layout to use. Because users expect to find similar features in the same location on each form, consistency in design will simplify the data entry. Visually appealing forms make working in the database more enjoyable and efficient.

When designing forms, pay close attention to key features, such as titles, field organization, form layout, and error prevention. The form title should clearly identify the purpose of the form, such as *Customer Order Form*. Fields should be arranged in a meaningful order, such as First Name, Last Name, Street Address, City, State, and ZIP. The form layout should have a professional appearance and minimal graphics, so that the focus remains on the data. You can also reduce the chance of errors if you add features that let the user select information from a list rather than typing the data into a field. After you decide on a design for the form, you may want to write down the features in a check list so that you can look at the list each time you create a form. By using a list, you can ensure that the forms share the same design.

Applying a Theme to a Form

VOCABULARY

themes

live preview

Themes are preset designs that include borders, background colors, shading, and graphic effects. Themes can be applied to an entire form to give it an attractive and professional appearance. Several themes are available with Access 2010, and each theme has a specific look. If you apply a theme to a form in a database, it is automatically applied to all forms in the database. If you make a change to a theme, such as changing the theme colors, all of the forms in the database will be updated with the new appearance. Using themes is a quick way to design forms and ensures consistency among them.

Themes are available in the Themes gallery on the Ribbon. If you move your mouse pointer over a theme in the Themes gallery, it is temporarily applied to the form so that you can see how your form would look with that theme applied. This feature is called ***live preview***. In this next exercise, you will apply a theme to one form and then open another form in the database to see that the theme is applied to both forms.

Step-by-Step 9.1

1. Open the **Internet Sales** file from the drive and folder where your Data Files are stored. Save the database as **Internet Sales Database**, followed by your initials.
2. Open the **Employees** form and the **Regional Sales** form to view the formatting. Then, close both forms by clicking the **Close** button ☒ located in the upper-right corner of the form.
3. Right-click the **Employees** form, then click **Design View** from the shortcut menu to open it in Design view. The form will appear as shown in **Figure 9–1**. Next, you will look at the Themes gallery.

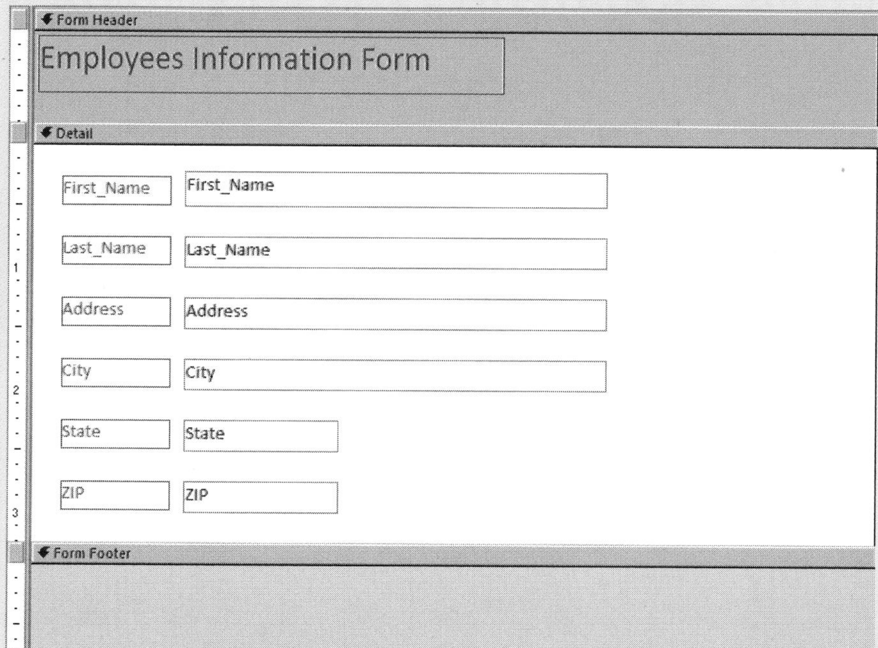

FIGURE 9–1
Employees form in Design view

4. On the Ribbon, click the **Design** tab and then click the **Themes** button in the Themes group. The Themes gallery opens, as shown in **Figure 9–2**.

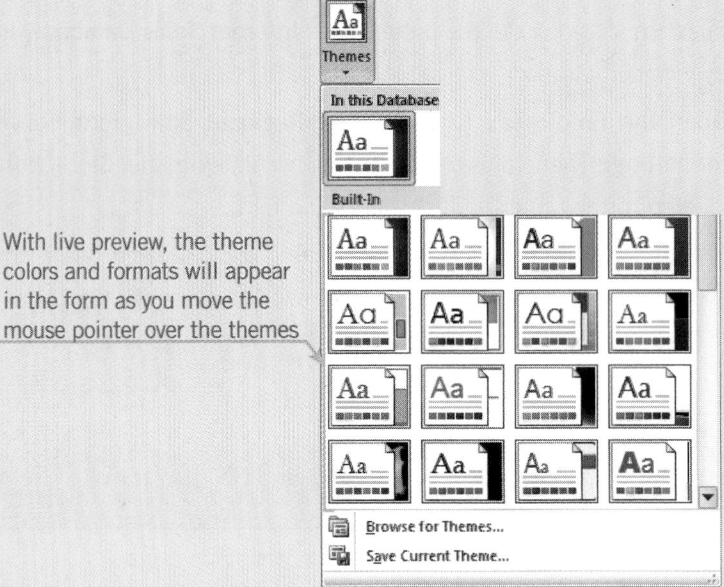

FIGURE 9–2
Themes gallery

5. Move your mouse pointer over the themes. The live preview feature shows you how the form will appear with the various themes applied.
6. Scroll down in the Themes gallery, and then click **Solstice**. The themes are listed alphabetically in the gallery. Notice the background color applied to the heading.
7. Click the **Save** button on the Quick Access toolbar to save the change made to the form.

8. Open the **Regional Sales** form and notice that the Solstice theme is also applied to this form. See **Figure 9–3**.

Solstice theme colors display in the Form Header and in the Detail section

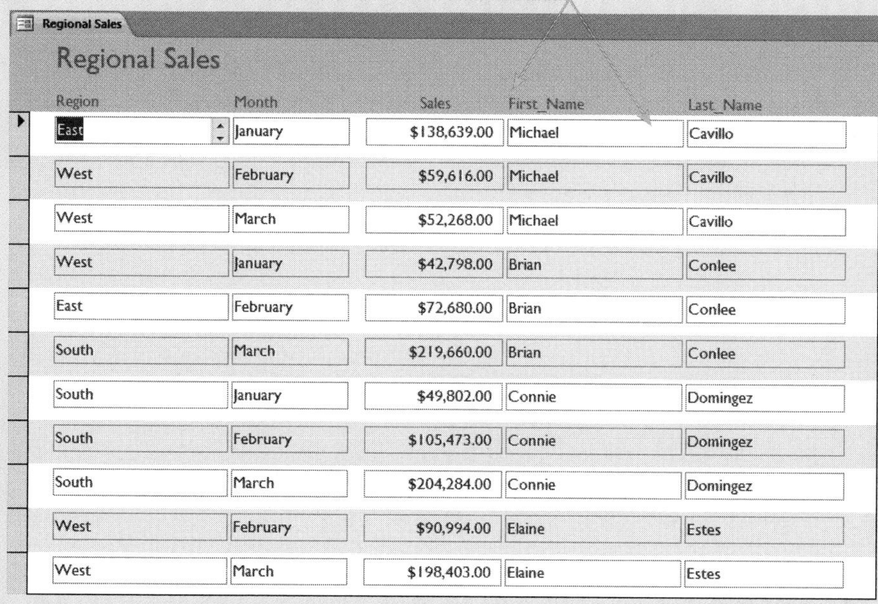

Regional Sales

Region	Month	Sales	First_Name	Last_Name
East	January	$138,639.00	Michael	Cavillo
West	February	$59,616.00	Michael	Cavillo
West	March	$52,268.00	Michael	Cavillo
West	January	$42,798.00	Brian	Conlee
East	February	$72,680.00	Brian	Conlee
South	March	$219,660.00	Brian	Conlee
South	January	$49,802.00	Connie	Domingez
South	February	$105,473.00	Connie	Domingez
South	March	$204,284.00	Connie	Domingez
West	February	$90,994.00	Elaine	Estes
West	March	$198,403.00	Elaine	Estes

FIGURE 9–3
Regional Sales form in Design view

9. Close both forms and leave the database open for the next Step-by-Step.

Adding a Logo

Another way you can add consistency to forms is to add a logo. A ***logo*** is a graphic or picture that can be placed in a form. A logo usually represents a company name or identity. Placing the logo in the same area in each form gives them a consistent look that helps users feel comfortable using the form. In this next exercise, you will add a logo to each form. You will then modify the logo by changing its properties using the Property Sheet pane. The Property Sheet pane displays all of the properties for a selected object.

VOCABULARY
logo

Step-by-Step 9.2

1. Open the **Regional Sales** form in Design view.
2. Click anywhere in the Form Header section. You will now add a logo to the Form Header.

3. On the Design tab, click the **Logo** button in the Header / Footer group. The Insert Picture dialog box opens, as shown in **Figure 9–4**.

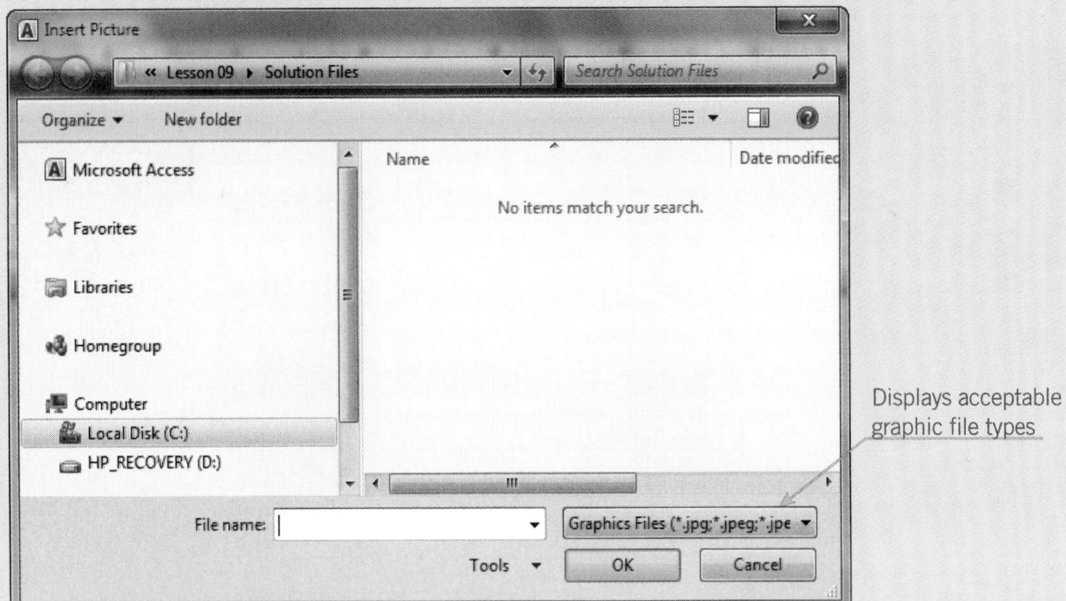

FIGURE 9–4
Insert Picture dialog box

4. Navigate to the drive and folder where your Data Files are stored. Click the **Internet Sales Logo** file, and then click **OK**. The logo is automatically placed in the upper-left corner of the Form Header and remains selected, as shown in **Figure 9–5**. A dashed border appears next to the logo to prevent its size from being changed. In the next step, you will remove this border so you can resize the logo.

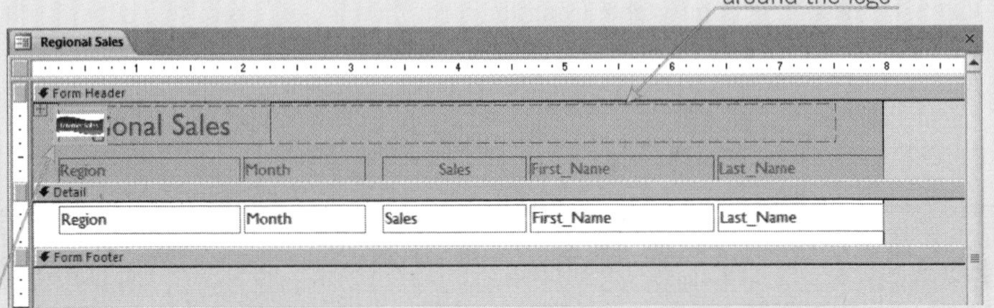

FIGURE 9–5
Logo placed in Form Header

5. Click the **dashed border** to select it and then press the **Delete** key to delete the border.
6. Click the **logo** to select it. Place the mouse pointer over the logo and when you see the pointer change to a four-headed arrow, press and hold the mouse button, then drag it to the right of the Regional Sales title, as shown in **Figure 9–6**. Next, you will resize the graphic.

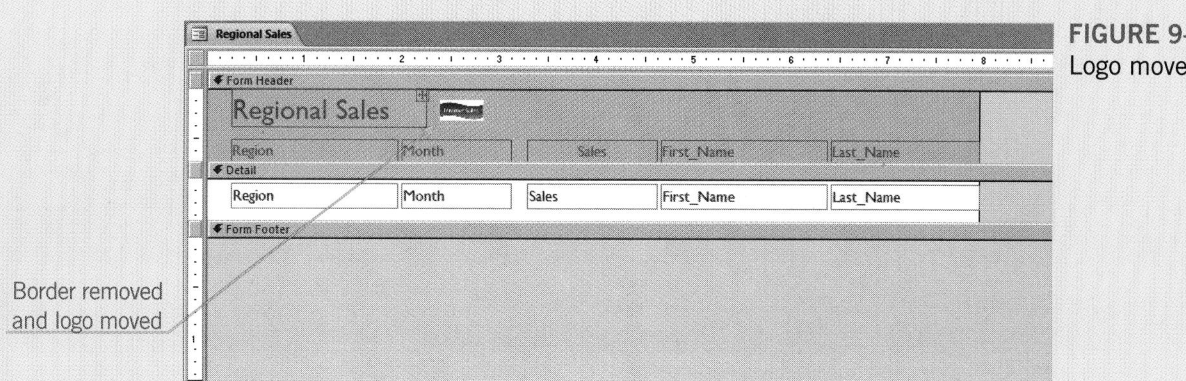

FIGURE 9–6
Logo moved

7. Place the mouse pointer over the lower-right corner of the logo and then when the mouse pointer becomes a double-sided diagonal arrow, click and drag down and to the right to increase the size of the logo so that it resembles **Figure 9–7**. You will now change the alignment of the logo so that it will be on the right side of the label in the Report Header.

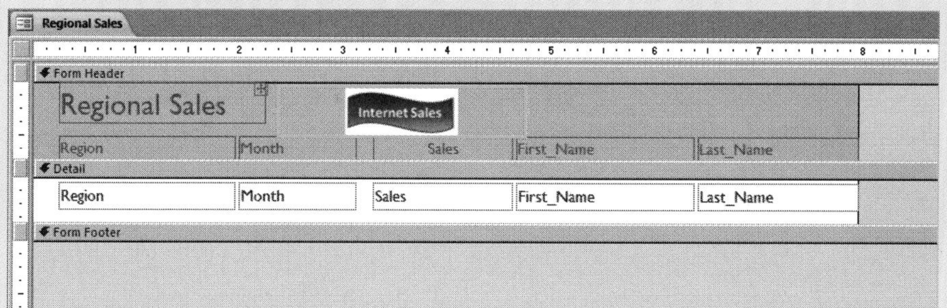

FIGURE 9–7
Logo resized

8. Click the **Property Sheet** button in the Tools group. The Property Sheet pane appears on the right side of the window.
9. If necessary, on the Property Sheet pane, click the **Format** tab, click the **Picture Alignment** property, click the **drop-down arrow** on the right to display the picture alignment options as shown in **Figure 9–8**, and then click **Top Left**.

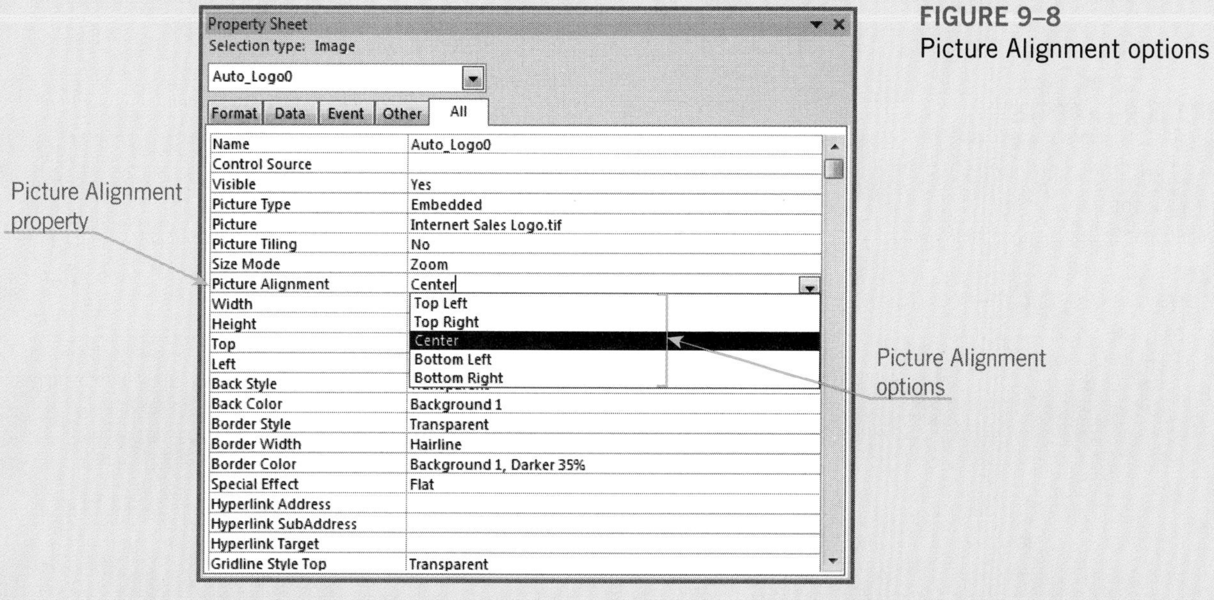

FIGURE 9–8
Picture Alignment options

10. Click the **Property Sheet** button to close the Property Sheet pane, then click the **View** button in the Views group to display the form in Form view. See **Figure 9–9**.

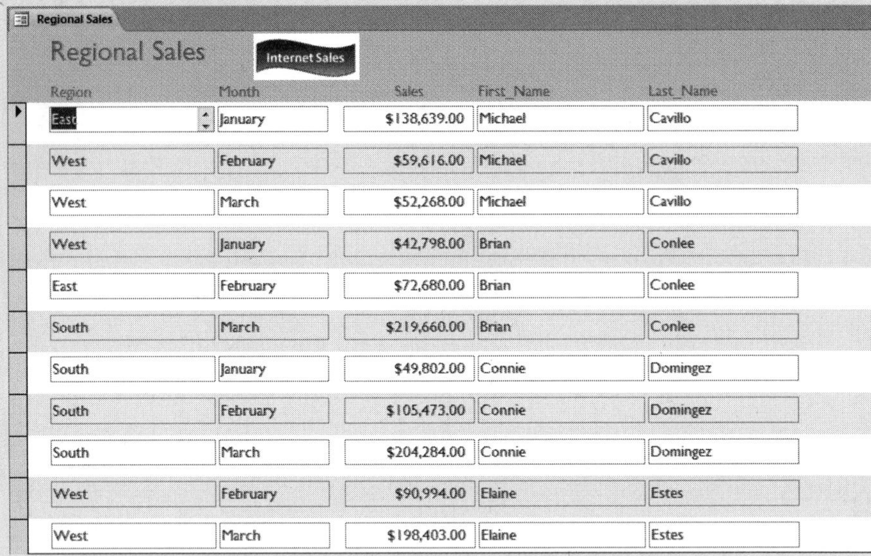

FIGURE 9–9
Regional Sales form with logo

11. Click the **Save** button and then close the form. For design consistency, you will now add the same logo to the Employees form.

12. Open the Employees form in Design view. Add the Internet Sales logo to the form header, then compare your screen to **Figure 9–10**.

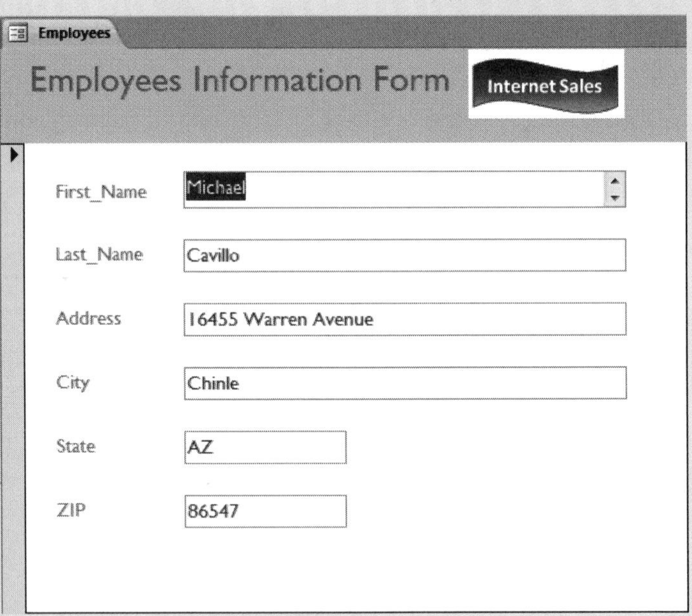

FIGURE 9–10
Employees form with logo

EXTRA FOR EXPERTS

You may see gridlines and dots appear on your form in Design view. If you want to hide the dots and gridlines, right-click in the section where they are, and then click Grid from the shortcut menu. Repeat the same step to show dots and gridlines.

13. Click the **Save** button. Leave the Employees form open for the next Step-by-Step.

Creating Command Buttons

One way to make forms easier to use is to include command buttons. A ***command button*** is a button that users can click to perform common tasks, such as moving to the next record in a form or adding a record. These buttons are known as record navigation and record operation command buttons. Record navigation refers to moving within the records in a form, such as going to the next record or to the previous record. Record operation options let you add a command button with a task, such as adding a new record. Both record navigation and record operation work with the records within a form. Even though Access offers its own navigation buttons in the document window, command buttons make navigating easier.

To create a command button, you choose the appropriate button on the Ribbon and then drag the mouse pointer that appears into the shape of a button. Command buttons can be made from text or graphics to indicate the purpose of the button. In this next exercise, you will create a command button using the Command Button Wizard, and you will create three command buttons in the Detail section of the form.

VOCABULARY
command button

Step-by-Step 9.3

1. If necessary, switch to Design view. You are going to add a command button to the right side of the form.
2. Place the mouse pointer over the right border in the Detail section and then drag to the right until you are at the **7.5 inch mark** on the ruler, as shown in **Figure 9–11**. This will make room for the command button.

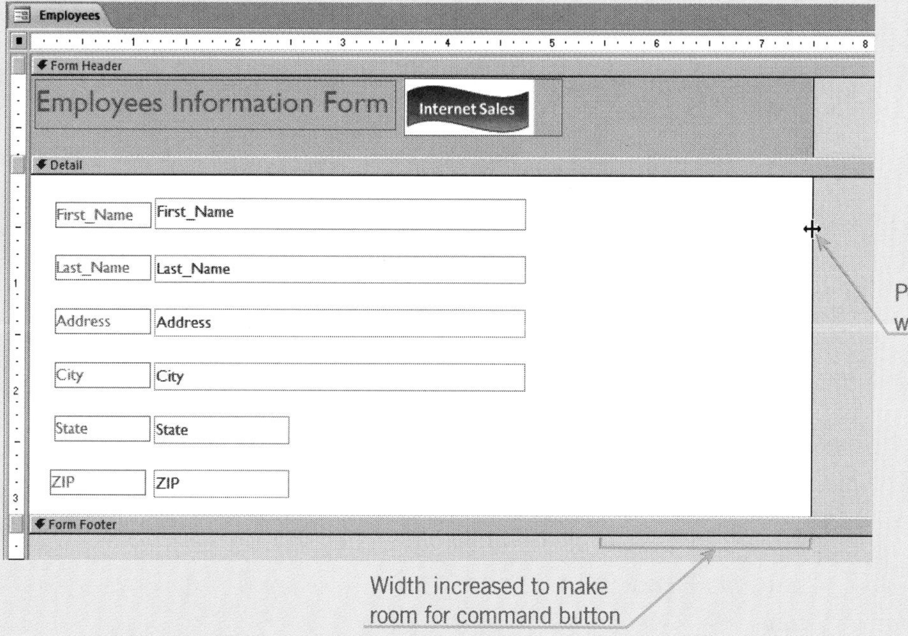

FIGURE 9–11 Increasing the width of the Employees form

3. Click the **Button** button in the Controls group. Place your mouse pointer in the right side of the Detail section and then drag out the shape of a button. The Command Button Wizard dialog box opens, as shown in **Figure 9–12**. Notice that Record Navigation is selected in the Categories box.

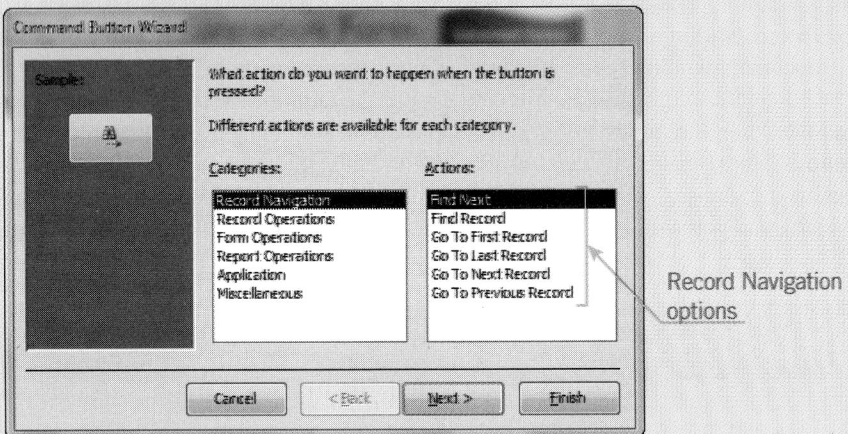

FIGURE 9–12
Command Button Wizard dialog box

4. Click the **Go To Next Record** action and then click **Next**. The next window of the Command Button Wizard dialog box appears, as shown in **Figure 9–13**. Next, you will choose to have text to appear on the button and enter the button text.

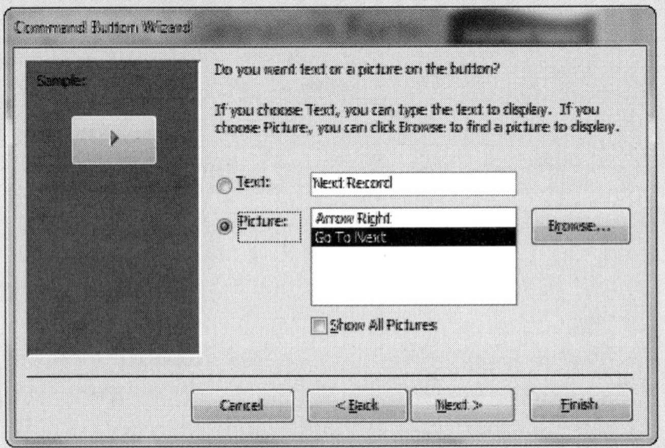

FIGURE 9–13
Next window of the Command Button Wizard dialog box

5. Click the **Text** option button, click in the text box before the words Next Record text, type **Go to**, and then press **[Spacebar]**. Compare your screen to **Figure 9–14**.

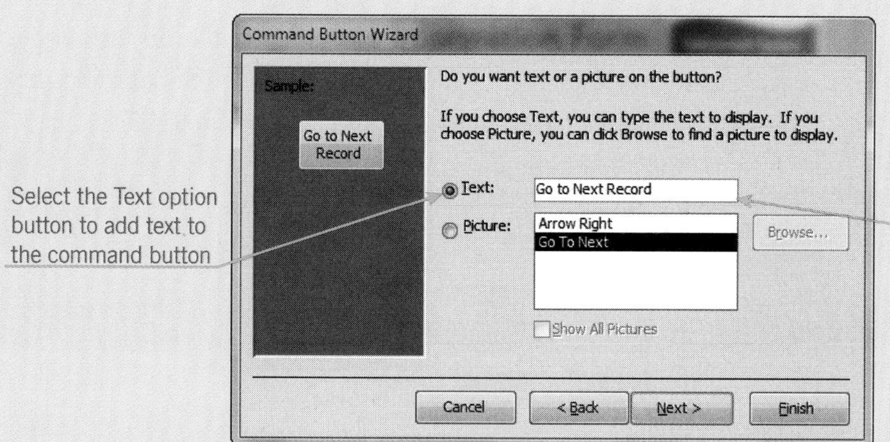

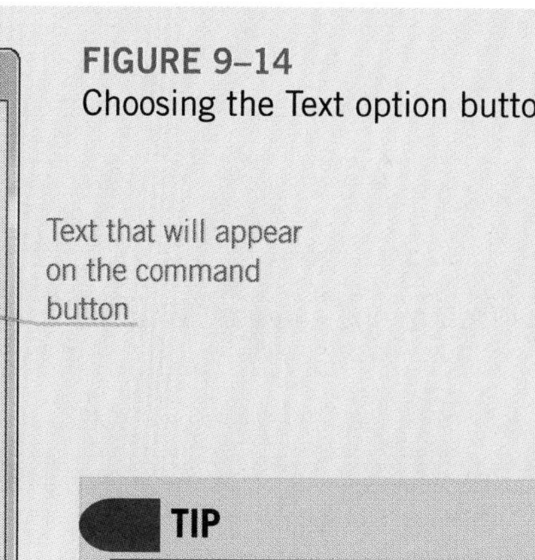

FIGURE 9–14
Choosing the Text option button

6. Click **Next**, accept the default name in the text box, and then click **Finish**. The completed command button appears on the form, as shown in **Figure 9–15**.

TIP

Access automatically assigns a generic name followed by the next consecutive number, which can then be changed to a more descriptive name.

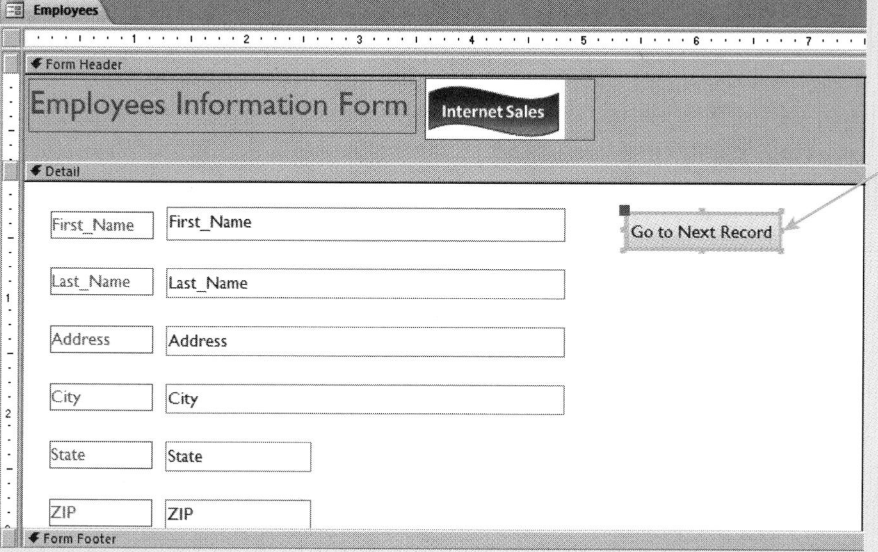

FIGURE 9–15
Form with command button

7. Using the Command Button Wizard, create a command button that moves to the previous record using the text **Go to Previous Record** on the button. Next, you will add a command button that uses record operations.

8. Click the **Button** button, draw a button under the Go to Previous Record button, and then click **Record Operations** in the Categories box of the Command Button Wizard dialog box. See **Figure 9–16**.

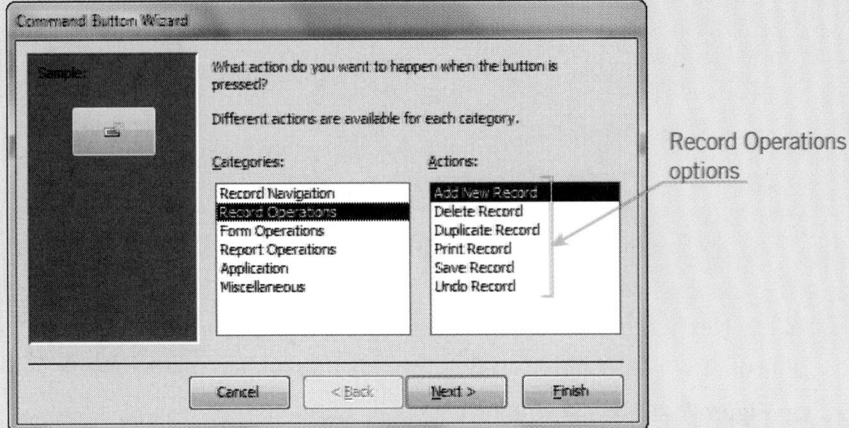

FIGURE 9–16
Record Operations category

9. Click **Next**, click between the words *Add* and *Record* in the text box, and then type **New**, as in "*Add New Record*".
10. Click **Next**, and then click **Finish**. Your form should appear similar to **Figure 9–17**. In the next step, you will select all of the buttons in order to resize and align them.

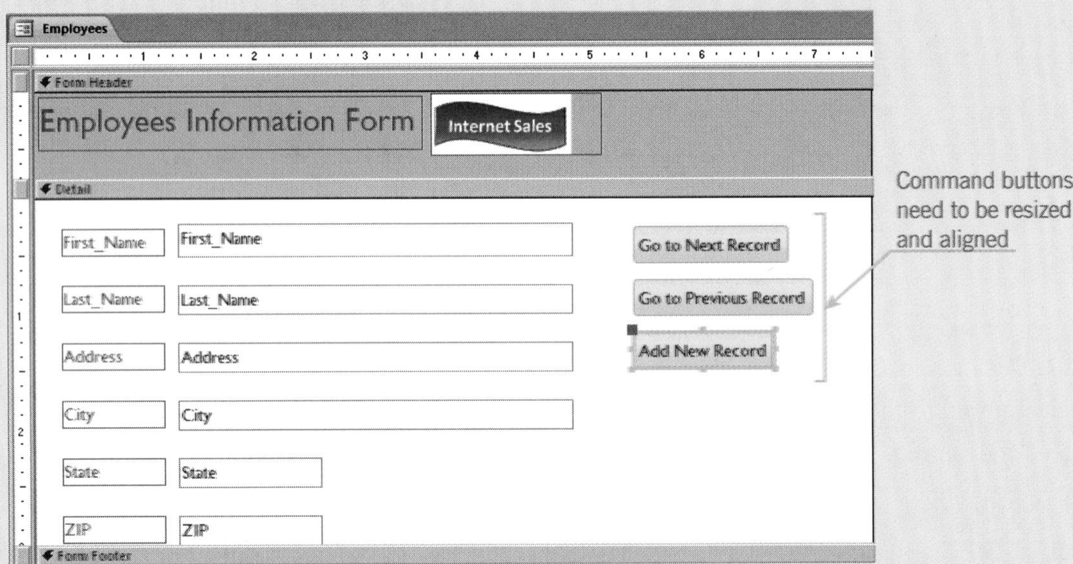

FIGURE 9–17
Form with command buttons

11. Verify that the **Add New Record** button is still selected, press and hold the **Shift** key, click the **Go to Next Record** button, and then click the **Go to Previous Record** button so that all three buttons are selected. *Note*: You can also draw a selection marquee around all three command buttons to select them.

12. On the Ribbon, click the **Arrange** tab, click the **Size/Space** button in the Sizing & Ordering group, and then click **To Widest** to increase the size of the buttons to the size of the widest button. You will now evenly distribute the space between the buttons.
13. Click the **Size/Space** button in the Sizing & Ordering group, and then click **Equal Vertical**.
14. Click the **Align** button, and then click **Left** to align the left side of each button. Click outside the buttons to deselect them. See **Figure 9–18**.

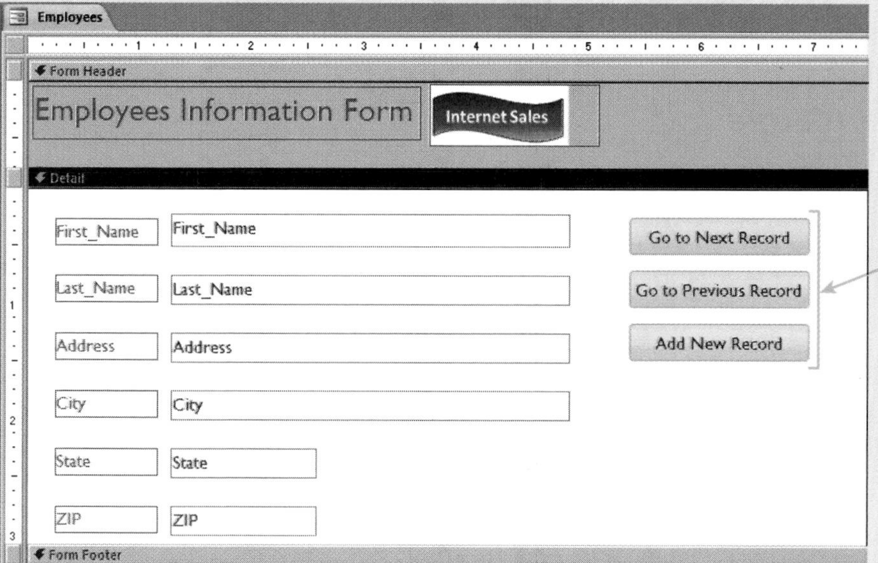

FIGURE 9–18
Command buttons aligned and resized

15. Switch to Form view and then click each of the command buttons to verify that they are working correctly. Save and close the form, and leave the database open for the next Step-by-Step.

Adding a New Field to an Existing Form

After you create a form, you may find that additional fields need to be added to the form. For example, you may have created a form that displays sales information with the name of an employee that made the sale. Now, you decide that you want to add the employee identification number field to the form to make it easier to locate records for that employee.

Since the form is already created, the fields are in alignment and have equal spacing between them. When you add a new field, you will need to align the new field with the other fields. A form field has two parts: the label and the text box. The label typically appears on the left side of the field and identifies the information in the field. The text box displays the actual information from the table. In this next exercise, you will add a field to an existing form and then align the field.

Step-by-Step 9.4

1. Open the **Regional Sales** form in Design view. Increase the form width by dragging the right edge of the form to the right about one inch.
2. On the Design tab, click the **Add Existing Fields** button in the Tools group to display the Field List pane, as shown in **Figure 9–19**. Then, click the **Show all tables** link at the top of the Field List pane.

FIGURE 9–19
Field List pane

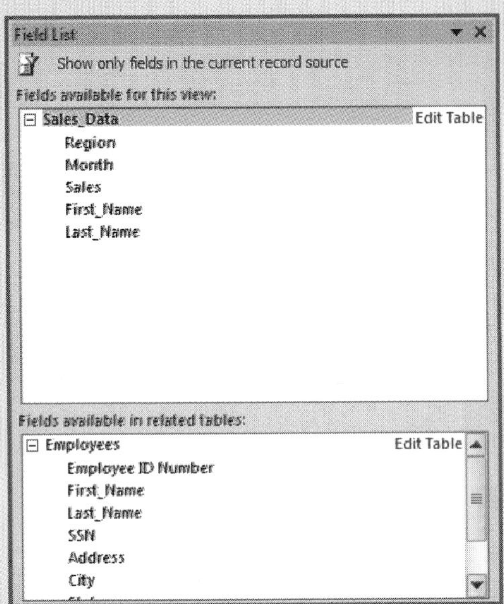

3. Click the **plus sign** next to Employees, right-click the **Employee ID Number** field to display the shortcut menu, as shown in **Figure 9–20**, and then click **Add Field to View**.

FIGURE 9–20
Field List shortcut menu

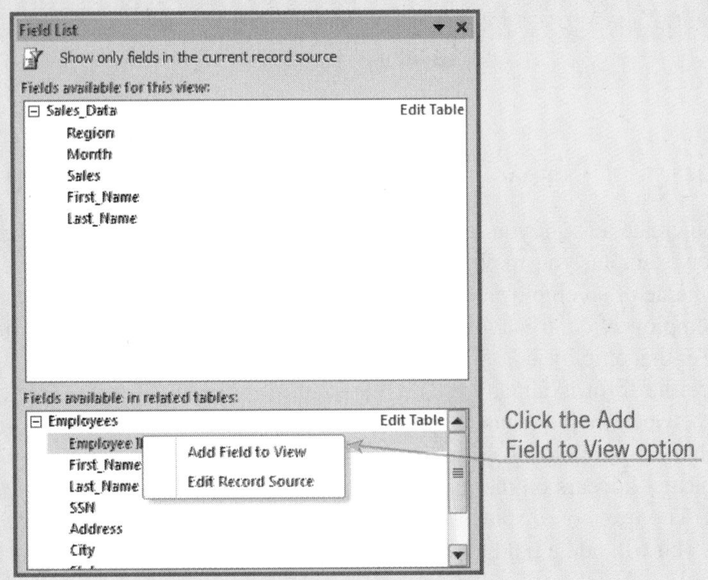

4. Click the **Add Existing Fields** button in the Tools group to close the Field List pane. Notice that the new field is located at the bottom of the Detail section as shown in **Figure 9–21**. In this next step, you will move the field.

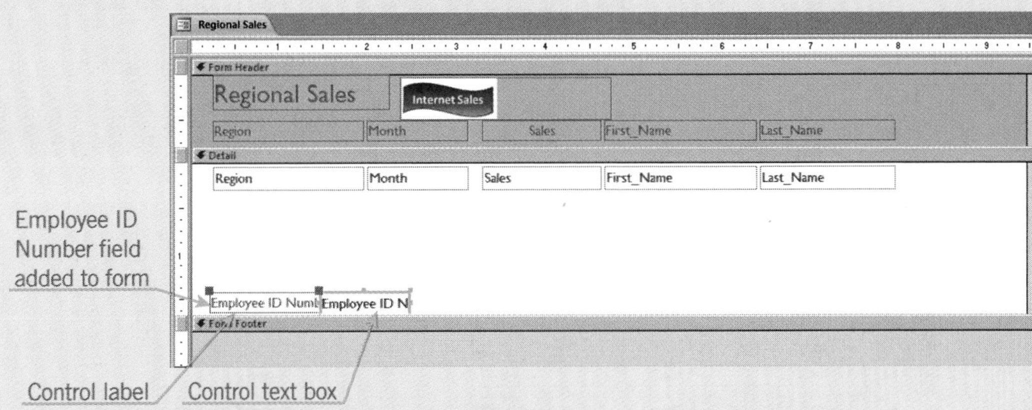

FIGURE 9–21 Form with new field in Design view

5. Select the **Employee ID Number** text box and drag it to the right side of the form next to Last_Name.
6. Right-click the **Employee ID Number** field label and click **Cut**. Click in the Form Header section, right-click, and then select **Paste**. Drag the **Employee ID Number** field label to the right of the Last_Name label.
7. Click the **View** button arrow in the Views group, and then click **Form View**. Notice that the field is not in alignment with the other fields, as shown in **Figure 9–22**. Next, you will align the field.

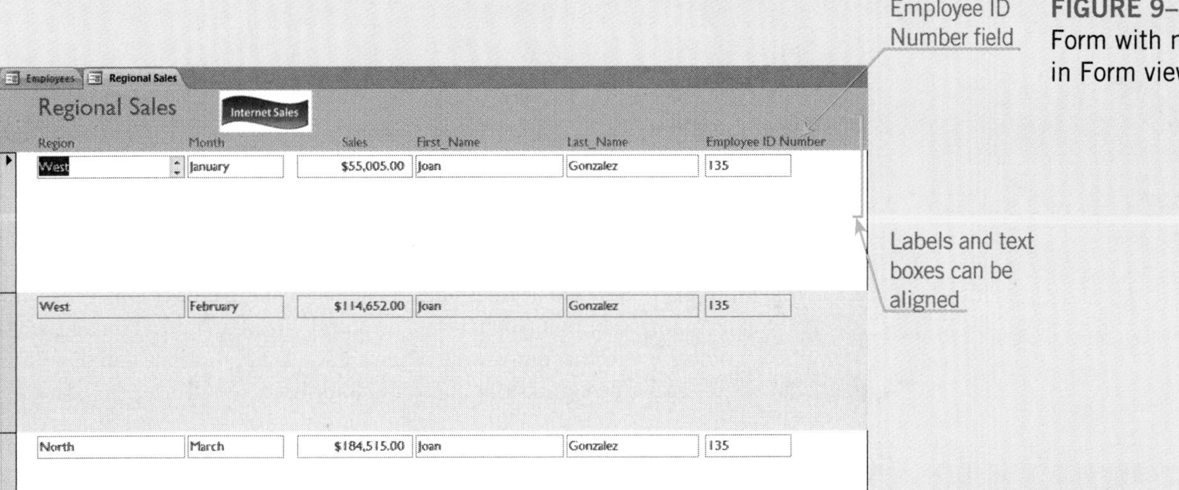

FIGURE 9–22 Form with new field in Form view

8. Click the **View** button arrow in the Views group, then click **Design View**.
9. Click outside the field to deselect it. You will now align the fields.
10. Click the label on the right side and increase the width by dragging the right selection handle to the right. You will now select each of the field labels to align them.

11. Select each of the field labels, click the **Arrange** tab, click the **Align** button, and then click **Bottom**.
12. Click the **Employee ID Number** text box, and then select each of the text boxes for the fields.
13. Click the **Align** button and click **Top**. To decrease the size of the Detail section, click at the top of the Form Footer section bar and drag it upward until only the fields are displayed, and then switch to the Form view. Your form should appear similar to **Figure 9–23**.

FIGURE 9–23
Form view displays new field

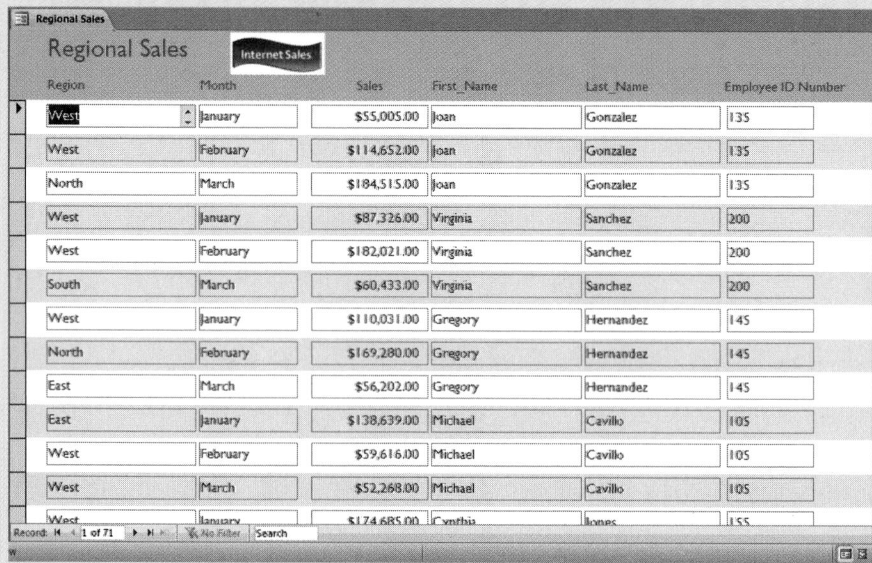

14. Save and close the form, then close the database.

Creating a Combo Box

VOCABULARY
combo box

A ***combo box*** displays a list of values and lets you select one from the list. This feature adds efficiency to the data entry process. Rather than typing information in a field, you simply select the value you want from a list. Selecting the value rather than typing it in the field helps decrease the chance of making typographical errors.

As with a command button, you can use a control wizard to add a combo box to a form. Like other wizards, a control wizard asks a series of questions and then uses your answers to create the combo box control in a form.

Step-by-Step 9.5

1. Open the **Pets Unlimited** file from the drive and folder where your Data Files are stored. Save the database as **Pets Unlimited Database**, followed by your initials.

2. Open the **Purchases** form in Design view to view the form. Notice that the form just has Product ID, Price, and Quantity fields, but not the Product Description field. See **Figure 9–24**. You will add a combo box for the Product Description field to the form.

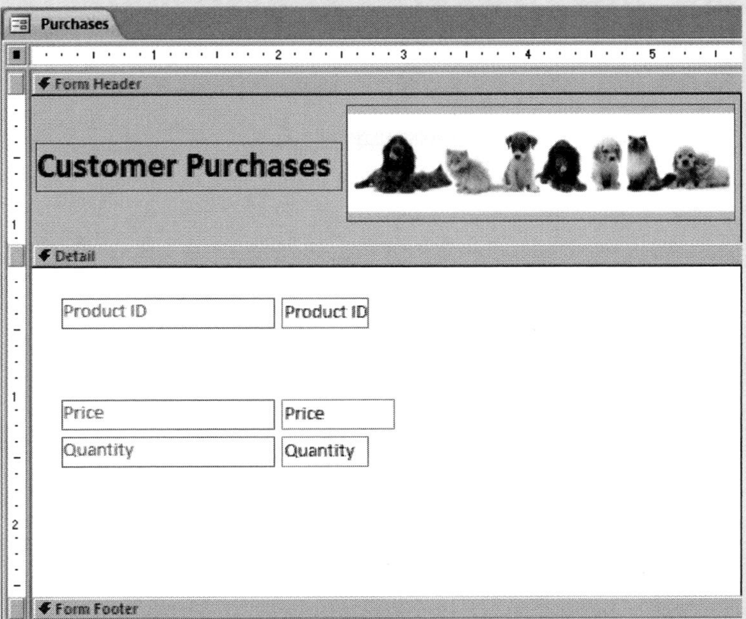

FIGURE 9–24
Purchases form

3. Click the **Combo Box** button in the Controls group, then place your mouse pointer under the Product ID text box and click. The Combo Box Wizard dialog box opens, as shown in **Figure 9–25**.

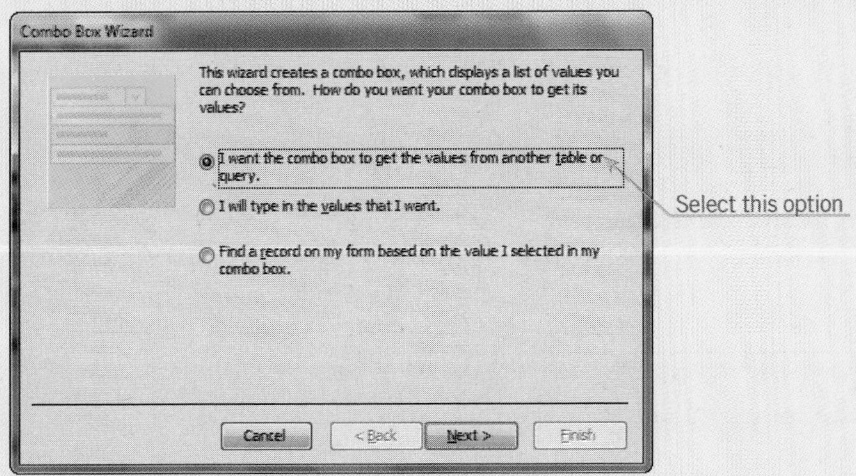

FIGURE 9–25
Combo Box Wizard dialog box

4. Verify that the **I want the combo box to get the values from another table or query** option button is selected, and then click **Next**. In the next window, click **Table: Inventory** as shown in **Figure 9–26**. Click **Next**. You will now select the field from the table that you want for the combo box.

FIGURE 9–26
Select table option

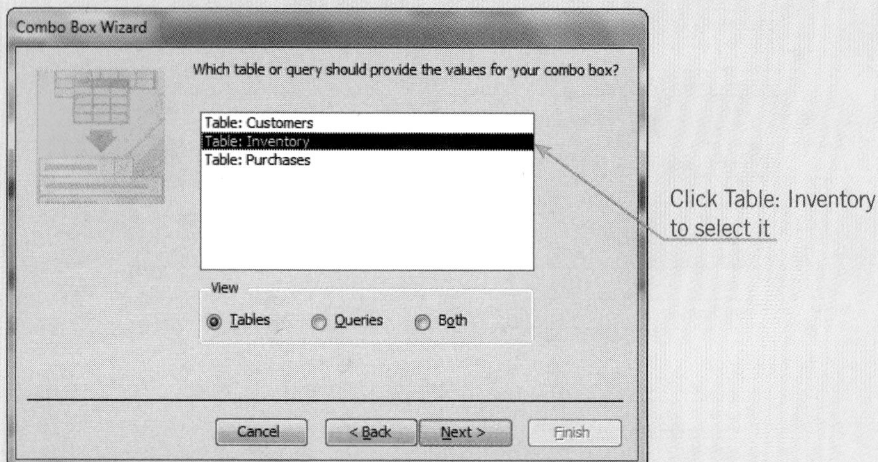

5. Click the **Product Description** and then click the **Select Single Field** button to move the field to the Selected Fields box on the right, as shown in **Figure 9–27**. This field will store the data selected from the combo box list. Click **Next**. You will select the sort order for the field in the next step.

FIGURE 9–27
Select field for combo box

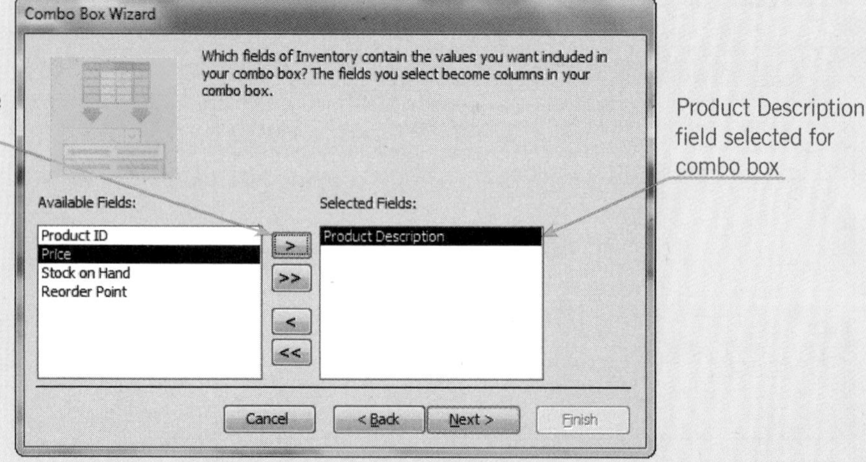

6. Click the first drop-down arrow, click **Product Description** to display it in ascending alphabetical order, and then click **Next**. You will now increase the size of the column so that all of the text in the field is displayed.

EXTRA FOR EXPERTS

To change from ascending order to descending order in any of the Wizard dialog boxes, you click the Ascending button. Then, the word Descending appears on the button.

7. Place your mouse pointer over the right edge of the **Product Description** column heading and drag to the right to increase the size of the column, as shown in **Figure 9–28**. Click **Next**.

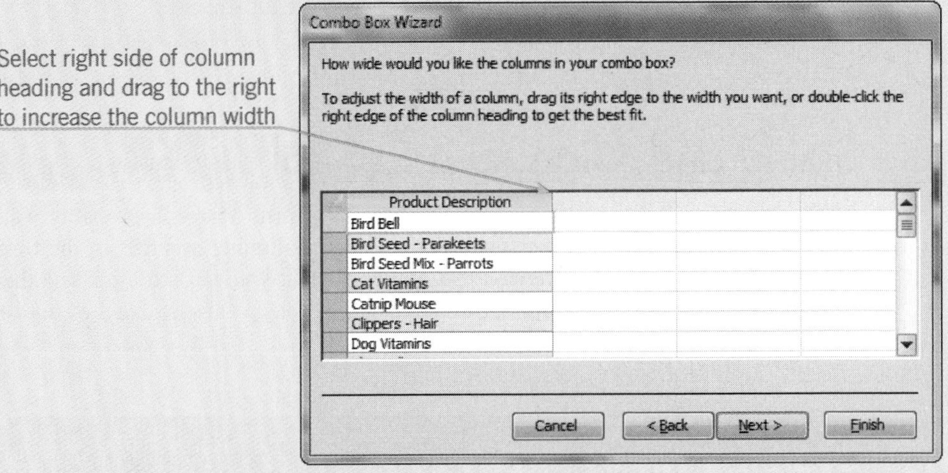

FIGURE 9–28
Column heading adjustment

8. Verify that the **Remember the value for later use** option button is selected, and then click **Next**. Product Description is shown as the column label.
9. Click **Finish**. The completed combo box appears in the form. Compare your screen to **Figure 9–29**. You will now add a control source to the combo box so that it will display the product descriptions.

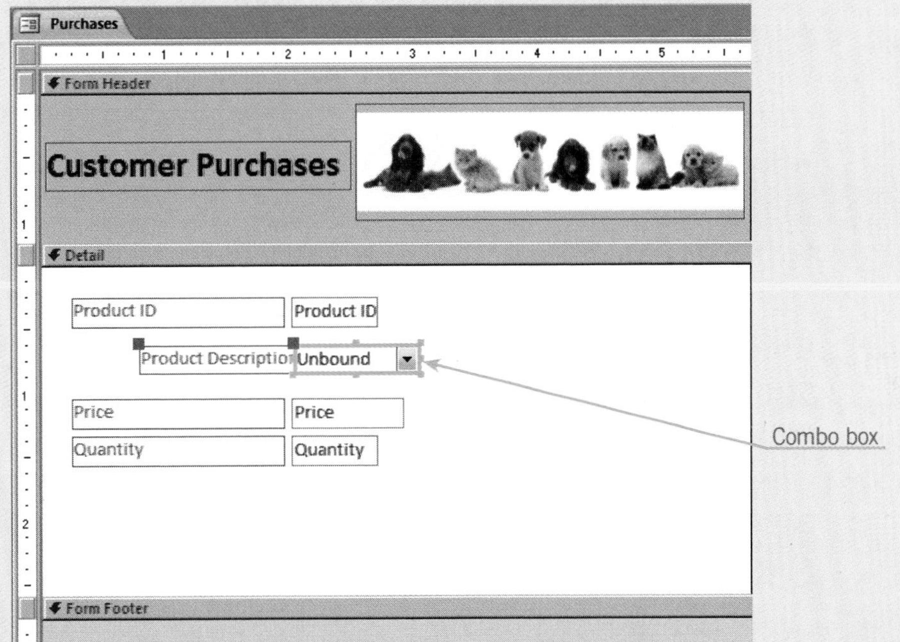

FIGURE 9–29
Combo Box placed in form

10. With the combo box selected, click the **Property Sheet** button in the Tools group.

11. If necessary, click the All tab and in **Control Source**, click the drop-down arrow, and then click **Product Description**.
12. Click the **Property Sheet** button to close the Property Sheet pane.
13. Save the form and keep it open for the next Step-by-Step.

Sizing and Aligning a Control

After you add a control, such as a combo box, to a form, you will probably want to align it with the fields in the form. Access makes aligning controls in the form a simple process. You select the controls and fields that you want to align and then choose the desired alignment options on the Ribbon. You can also resize the controls so that they look consistent with the fields.

Step-by-Step 9.6

1. Drag the **Product Description** label to the left so it is aligned approximately with the other field labels. You will now change the font color.
2. Press and hold the **Shift** key, and then click on each of the other field labels.
3. Click the **Home** tab, click the **Font Color** button arrow in the Text Formatting group, click **Black, Text 1**, and then click the **Bold** button **B**. Next, you will arrange the labels so that they are equally spaced.
4. With the field labels selected, click the **Arrange** tab, click the **Size/Space** button in the Sizing & Ordering group, and then click **Equal Vertical**. You will now align the labels to the left.
5. Click the **Align** button in the Sizing & Ordering group, and then click **Left** to align the field labels left. Next, the text boxes need to be aligned.
6. Click the **Product ID** field text box and then while pressing and holding the **Shift** key, click each of the field text boxes.
7. Click the **Align** button in the Sizing & Ordering group, and then click **Left** to align the field labels left.
8. Click the **Arrange** tab, click the **Size/Space** button in the Sizing & Ordering group, and then click **Equal Vertical**. Compare your screen to **Figure 9–30**.

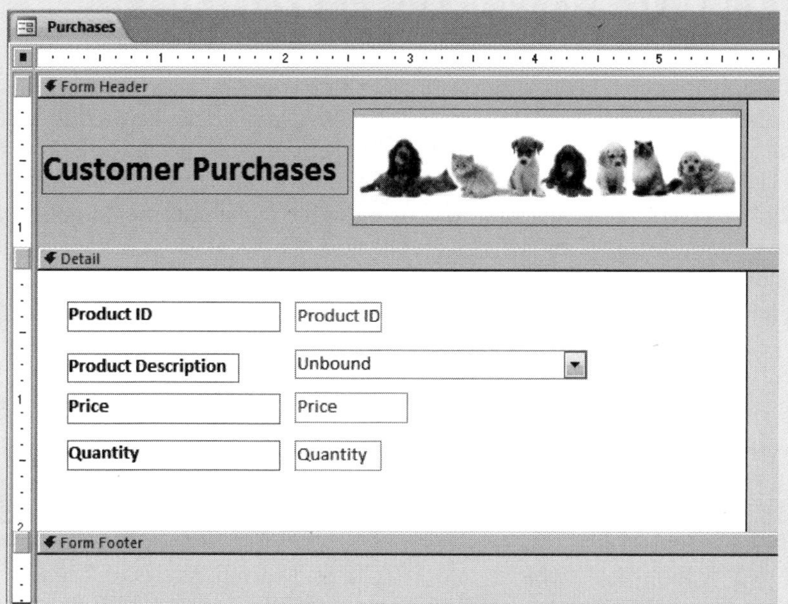

FIGURE 9–30
Completed form with combo box

9. Click the **Design** tab, and then click the **View** button in the Views group. You can now see how the form appears after the changes.
10. Save the form and leave it open for the next Step-by-Step.

Using the Combo Box in a New Record

A combo box makes it easy to add information into a new record. Normally, you type data into a field. However, with a combo box, you simply click the combo box arrow and select an option from the list. By selecting an option from the combo box list and not typing lengthy text, you increase the accuracy of the information.

Step-by-Step 9.7

1. Click the **Home** tab on the Ribbon.
2. Click the **New** button in the Records group, click in the **Product ID field**, and then type **486**.
3. Click the **Product Description** arrow to display the product descriptions, and then click **Flea Collar – Cats**.
4. Press **Tab**. Notice that when you pressed Tab, you were not moved to the Price field. You will correct this order of movement later. If necessary, you may need to move back to the field with Product ID number 486. Click in the Price field, and then type **3.21**.
5. Press **Enter** to move to the **Quantity** field, type **50**, and then press **Enter**.
6. Save the form and leave the database open for the next Step-by-Step.

Adding a Calculated Control

VOCABULARY
calculated control

You can add a control that contains a calculation to a form. This calculation can be addition, subtraction, multiplication, division or one of the many other calculations available in the Expression Builder. A ***calculated control*** can be used to perform calculations on the values in other fields. For example, you may have an order form that has a quantity field and a price field. Adding a calculated control, you could multiply the value in the quantity field by the value in the price field to display the order total. If the values in the fields are changed, the calculated control recalculates and displays the new values.

Just like adding a new field to an existing form, you will need to align this control. In this next exercise, you will add a calculated control that displays an order total.

Step-by-Step 9.8

1. Verify that the Purchases form is open and switch to in Design view, click the **Design** tab, and then click the **Text Box** button in the Controls group.
2. Click under the Quantity field, as shown in **Figure 9–31**.

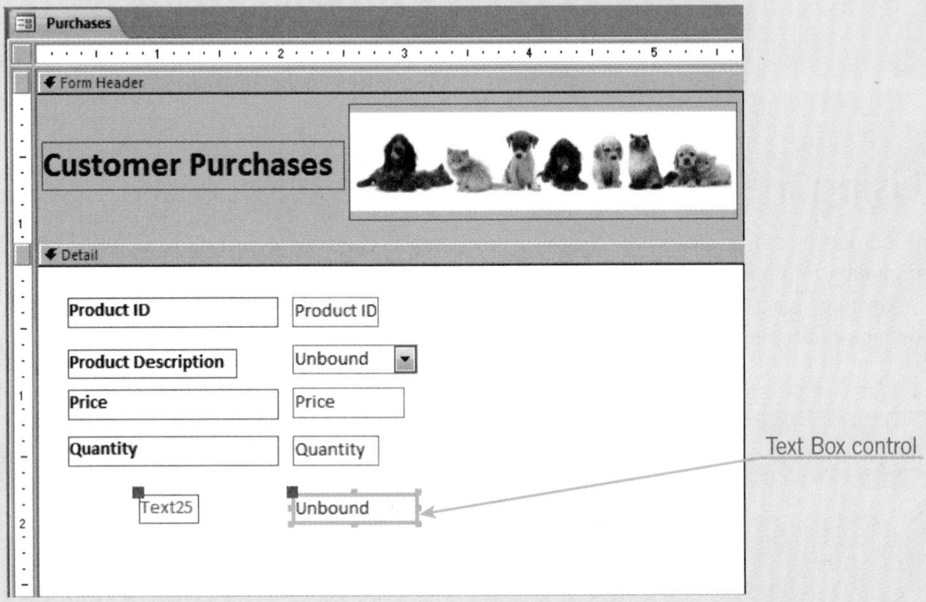

FIGURE 9–31
Form with Text Box control

3. With the text box selected, click the **Design** tab and then click the **Property Sheet** button in the Tools group. You will now open the Expression Builder to enter the calculation.
4. On the Property Sheet pane, click the **Control Source** property and then click the **Build** button. The Expression Builder dialog box opens.
5. To start the calculation, type = (equal sign) in the expression box. Next, you will add a field to the calculation.

6. In the Expression Elements area on the left side, double-click **Pets Unlimited Database**, click the plus sign next to **Forms**, click the plus sign next to **Loaded Forms**, and then click **Purchases**. You should now see the fields and labels for the Purchases form displayed in the Expression Categories area.
7. Double-click the **Price** field to place it in the Expression box at the top.
8. Type *. The asterisk option is used for multiplication.
9. In the Expression Categories area, double-click the **Quantity** field. See **Figure 9–32**.

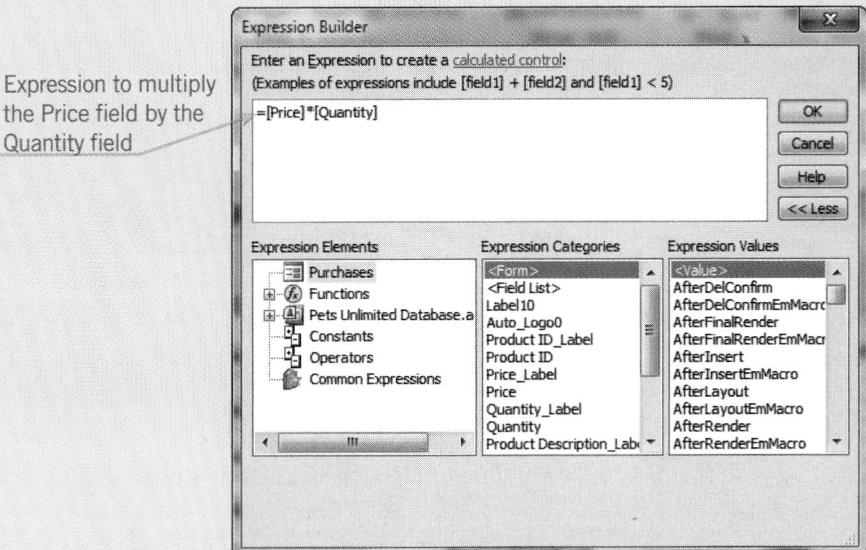

FIGURE 9–32
Completed Expression Builder dialog box

10. Click **OK**. In the Property Sheet pane, click in the Format box, click the arrow on the right to display the formats, and then click **Currency**.
11. Align and distribute the labels and text boxes using the Size/Space button options and the Align button options.

12. Click once on the field label for the calculated control and then click again. Your insertion point appears in the label. Delete the existing text and then type **Total**.

13. Add bold formatting to the **Total** label, and change the font color to Black, Text 1. Compare your screen to **Figure 9–33**.

FIGURE 9–33
Calculated control in the form

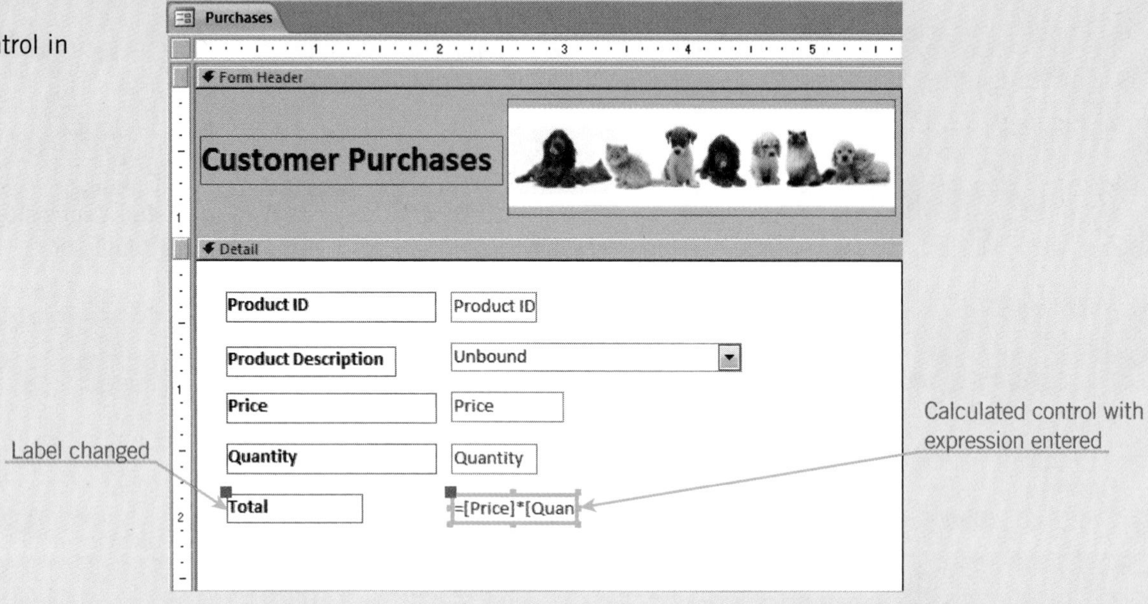

14. Save the form and leave it open for the next Step-by-Step.

Changing Tab Order

VOCABULARY
tab order

Tab order is the order of movement in a record when you press the Tab key. Pressing the Tab key moves you from one field to another in a form. The tab order in a form should flow logically, such as from the top of the form to the bottom. However, if you add a new field or calculated control to a form, the tab order within the record changes. For example, if you add a new field between two existing fields, Access recognizes the new field and places it as the last tab stop in the form rather than between the fields where it was placed. In this case, you would be entering data into fields at the bottom of the record and then moving back to the top of the form to enter data into a new field. This movement would break the logical order of entering data into the form.

The tab order can be changed in Design view by selecting the Tab Order button in the Tools group of the Design tab. Then you simply click the Auto Order button and the tab order is instantly reordered based on how the fields are located in the form. In this next exercise, you will change the tab order in a form.

Step-by-Step 9.9

1. Switch to Design view, if necessary.
2. Click the **Design** tab, and then click the **Tab Order** button in the Tools group. The Tab Order dialog box opens, as shown in **Figure 9–34**.

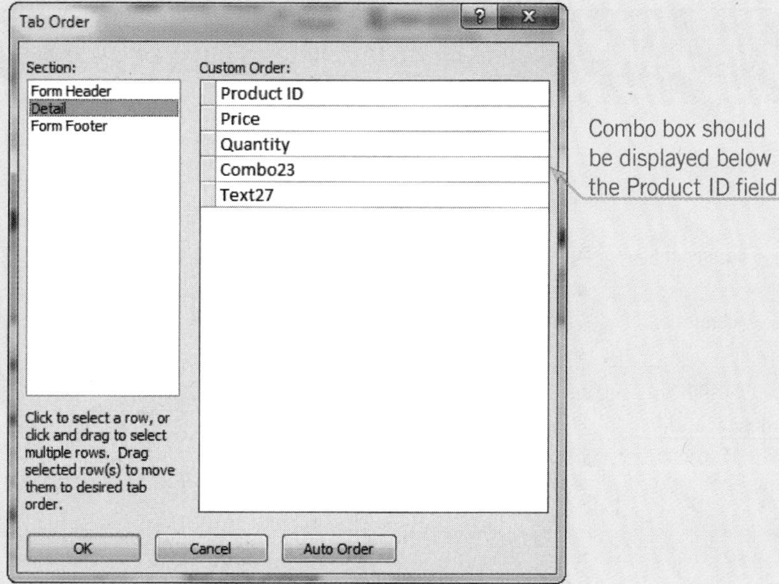

FIGURE 9–34
Tab Order dialog box

3. Click the **Auto Order** button. The tabs are now arranged as they are in the form, as shown in **Figure 9–35**.

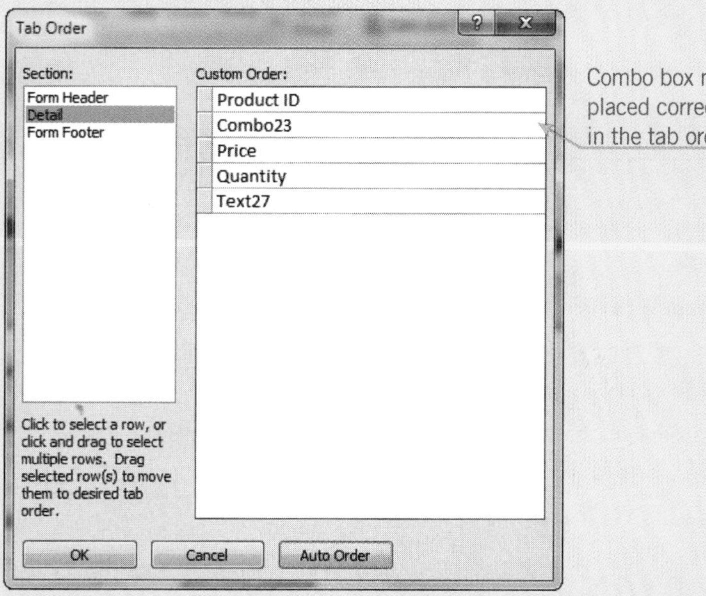

FIGURE 9–35
Tab Order rearranged

4. Click **OK**.
5. Save your work.
6. Click the **View** button to switch to Form view.

7. Press **Tab** to move through each of the fields. You can now move in the order of the fields.
8. Close the form and then close the database.

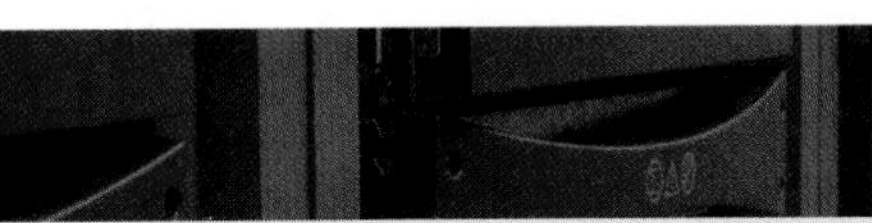

SUMMARY

In this lesson, you learned:

- It is important for every form in a database to have consistent formatting.
- Applying a theme to a form in the database makes changing the form's appearance quick and uniform.
- A logo can be added to a form to enhance design consistency.
- Command buttons can be added to forms for record navigation, such as moving to the next record, and for record operations, such as adding a new form.
- A new field can be added to an existing form.
- A combo box displays a list of values for a field.
- You can size and align controls easily.
- Adding a new record that has a combo box makes data entry easier and more efficient.
- A calculated control can be added to perform calculations on fields in a form.
- The tab order is how you move from one field to another in a form.

VOCABULARY REVIEW

calculated control
combo box
command button
live preview
logo
tab order
theme

REVIEW QUESTIONS

TRUE / FALSE

Circle T if the statement is true or F if the statement is false.

T F 1. A new field cannot be added to a form that already has fields aligned in the form.

T F 2. A command button displays a list of values from which you can make selections.

T F 3. The tab order in a form can be changed.

T F 4. A calculated control can be added to a form that multiplies the values in one field by the values in another field.

T F 5. A logo can be placed in each form in a database in the same position, such as the Form Header, for design consistency.

FILL IN THE BLANK

1. A(n) ______________ can be added to a form to perform a calculation.
2. A(n) ______________ displays a list of values for a field.
3. To make the process of moving to the next record in a form or adding a new record easier, you can add ______________ .
4. For format and design consistency, you can add a(n) ______________ to a form.
5. If you add a new field between two existing fields, you will probably need to change the ______________ so the navigation between records is logical.

WRITTEN QUESTIONS

Write a brief answer to the following questions.

1. Describe the importance of design consistency between all the forms in a database.
2. Explain the difference between a combo box and a command button.
3. Explain how themes make changing formats in forms easier and help to maintain consistency between the forms.
4. Describe how you would add a calculated control to a form.
5. Explain all the steps necessary for adding a new field into an existing form.

PROJECTS

If you have a SAM 2010 user profile, your instructor may have assigned an autogradable version of the indicated project. If so, log into the SAM 2010 Web site at *www.cengage.com/sam2010* to download the instruction and start files.

PROJECT 9–1

1. Open the **Coastal Sales** file from the drive and folder where your Data Files are stored. Save the database as **Coastal Sales Database**, followed by your initials.
2. Apply the Hardcover theme to the Sales Data form.
3. Move the Last Name field to the bottom of the form, and then move the First Name field above the Last Name field.
4. Realign the labels and text boxes.
5. Add equal vertical spacing between the fields.
6. Change the tab order for the fields.
7. Save and close the database.

SAM PROJECT 9–2

1. Open the **Animal Supply Industry** file from the drive and folder where your Data Files are stored. Save the database as **Animal Supply Industry Database**, followed by your initials.
2. Add two command buttons to the **Orders Form**: one to go to the next record and another to add a new record. (*Hint*: You will need to increase the width of the form.)
3. Align and size the command buttons.
4. Add a calculated control under the quantity field that multiplies the Selling Price values by the values in the Quantity field. Use currency formatting for the calculated control.
5. Change the calculated control label to Order Total.
6. Adjust the alignment, spacing, and formatting of the calculated control as necessary to match the other labels and text boxes in the form.
7. View the form in Form view and test the command buttons.
8. Save and close the database.

PROJECT 9–3

1. Open the **Book Sales** file from the drive and folder where your Data Files are stored. Save the database as **Book Sales Database**, followed by your initials.
2. In the Book Orders form, add the Shipping field to the form below the Price field.
3. Realign and adjust the spacing for the fields.
4. Use Auto Order in the Tab Order dialog box to change the tab order.
5. Save and close the database.

CRITICAL THINKING

ACTIVITY 9–1

You are the new database administrator for the Healthcare Training Company. Open the **Healthcare Training** file from the drive and folder where your Data Files are stored and save the database as **Healthcare Training Database**, followed by your initials. Upon inspection of the Employee Information Form, you notice that the fields are not in a logical order. You decide to change the order of the fields to present a more logical flow. You then adjust the alignment and the tab order. When complete, save the form and close the database.

ACTIVITY 9–2

A database is a great way to track an extracurricular activity. Think of a form you can create for a sport that you play or for a school club, such as chess team or student government. You will need to think of the fields you want in the form and how to align them. Think of the formats, fonts, graphics, and colors that you want to use for the form in the database. Apply a theme to the form and then view it in Design view. Feel free to create additional forms for your database, if necessary. Make any necessary adjustments to the form(s) or layout. Save the database as **My Form** and then close Access.

Estimated Time: 2.0 hours

LESSON 10

Adding Advanced Features to Reports

OBJECTIVES

Upon completion of this lesson, you should be able to:

- Create a report from a parameter query.
- Add formatting and a theme to a report.
- Change a control property.
- Add a calculated control to a report.
- Add conditional formatting to a control.
- Add a subreport to a report.
- Create a summary report.
- Add a chart to a report.

VOCABULARY

calculated control

chart

conditional formatting

subreport

Introduction

In this lesson, you will learn to take creating reports to an advanced level. First, you will create a report based on a parameter query, which will require that you enter parameter data before the report will be displayed. Then, you will add a theme to a report, which applies the theme formats to each report in the database. You will change the properties of a report control as well as add a calculated control to a report. In addition, you will add a subreport to an existing report. Finally, you will create a report with summary information and then add a chart to the report.

Creating a Report from a Parameter Query

Basing a report on a parameter query is useful if you need to run multiple reports that display similar information. For example, you may want to see a report for all of your customers who live in Texas. You may also want to see another report for all of your customers who live in California. If you create a report from a parameter query, you could enter Texas as the parameter value for the first report and California as the parameter value for the second report. By using a report based on a parameter query, you do not need to create several reports; you just need to create one report.

As you know, a parameter query displays a message box for you to enter parameter data each time you run the query. When a report is based on a parameter query, each time you open the report, the message box appears. You need to enter data before the report will be displayed. When you enter the parameter data, the report appears showing the information based on the parameter value.

You can also add grouping options to the report. For example, if you want to group your customers by region, such as the North, South, East, and West, you can add a grouping named Region. Then, when you enter a parameter, the report will display with the data grouped by region. In this next exercise, you will create a report based on a parameter query and add grouping to the report.

Step-by-Step 10.1

1. Open the **Computer Sales** file from the drive and folder where your Data Files are stored. Save the database as **Computer Sales Database**, followed by your initials. Next you will open a query in Design view.
2. In the Navigation pane, right-click **qry-Monthly Sales** and then click **Design View** to view the query, as shown in **Figure 10–1**. Notice the Month field contains a parameter that will ask for the month for sale when the query runs.

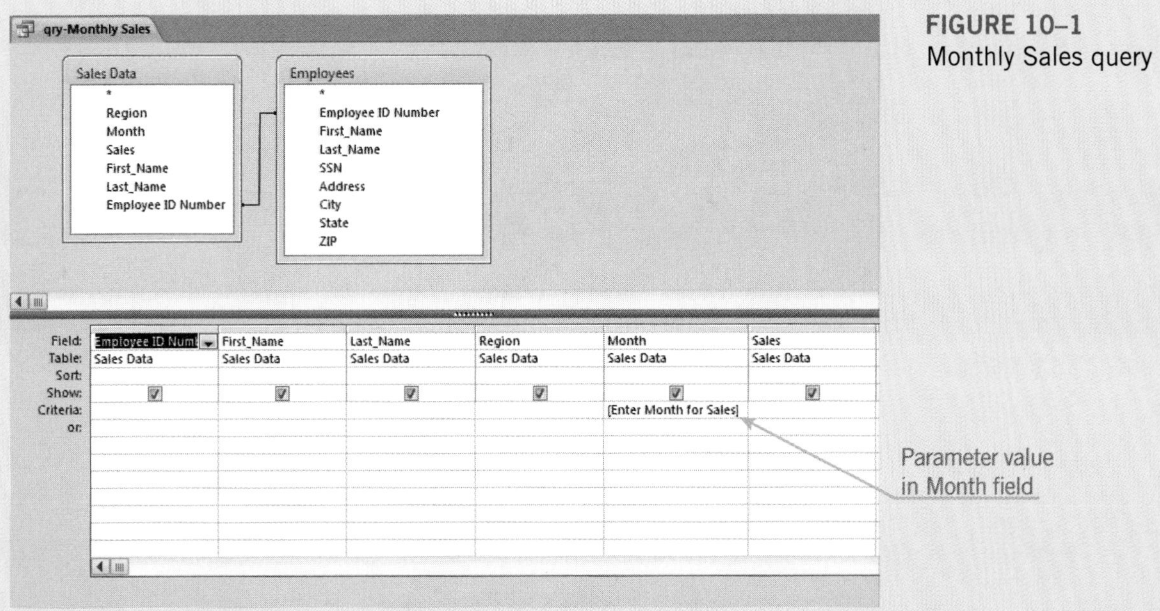

FIGURE 10–1
Monthly Sales query

3. Click the **Close** button to close the query.
4. Verify that qry-Monthly Sales is highlighted in the Navigation pane, click the **Create** tab on the Ribbon, and then click the **Report Wizard** button in the Reports group. The Report Wizard will take you through the steps of creating a report.
5. Double-click the following fields in the order they appear to add them to the Selected Fields list box: **First_Name**, **Last_Name**, **Region**, **Month**, and **Sales**, as shown in **Figure 10–2**.

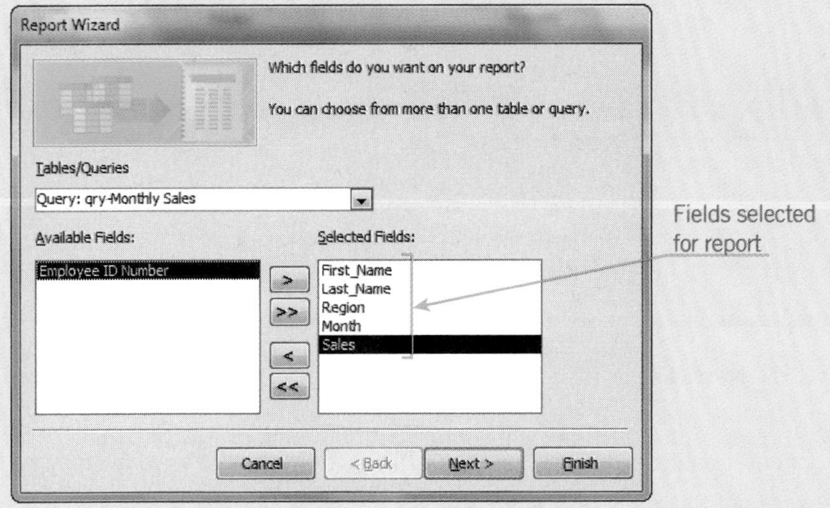

FIGURE 10–2
Report Wizard dialog box

6. Click **Next**, then double-click the **Region** field to add a grouping level. Compare your screen to **Figure 10–3**.

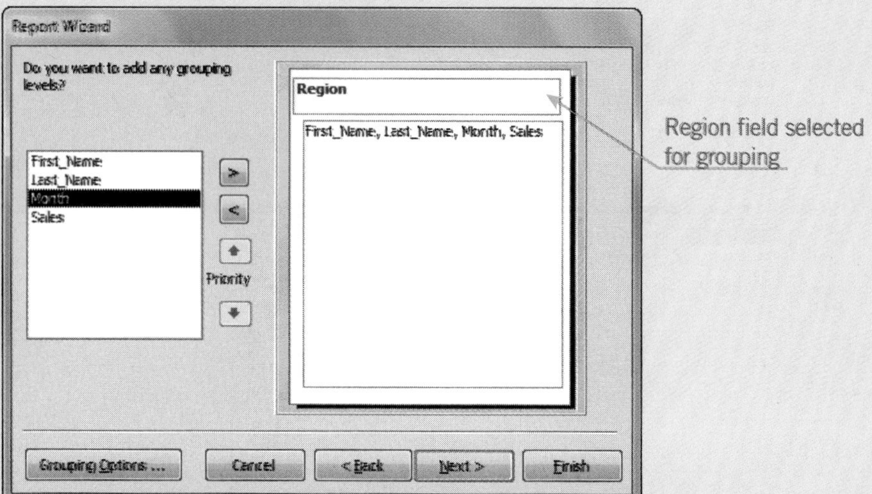

FIGURE 10–3
Report grouping

7. Click **Next**, click the **drop-down arrow** in the first sort box, and then click **Month**.
8. Select **Last_Name** for the next sort box and **First Name** for the third sort box, as shown in **Figure 10–4**.

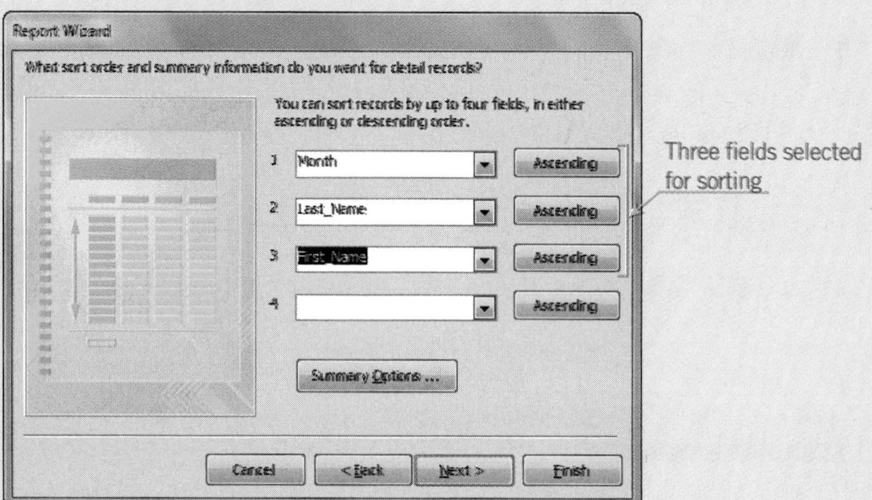

FIGURE 10–4
Fields selected for sorting

9. Click **Next**. Verify that the **Stepped** option button is selected in the Layout section and that the **Portrait** option button is selected in the Orientation section, and then click **Next**. The wizard asks you what title you would like for your report.
10. Click in the text box, delete the existing text, type **Monthly Sales Report**, and then click **Finish**.
11. The Enter Parameter Value dialog box opens, as shown in **Figure 10–5**.

FIGURE 10–5
Enter Parameter Value dialog box

12. Type **March** and then click **OK**. The report with March sales is displayed, as shown in **Figure 10–6**. Notice that the sales amounts need to be assigned a currency format. You will add this format after you apply themes. To view more of the report, click the **Close Shutter Bar** button on the Navigation pane.

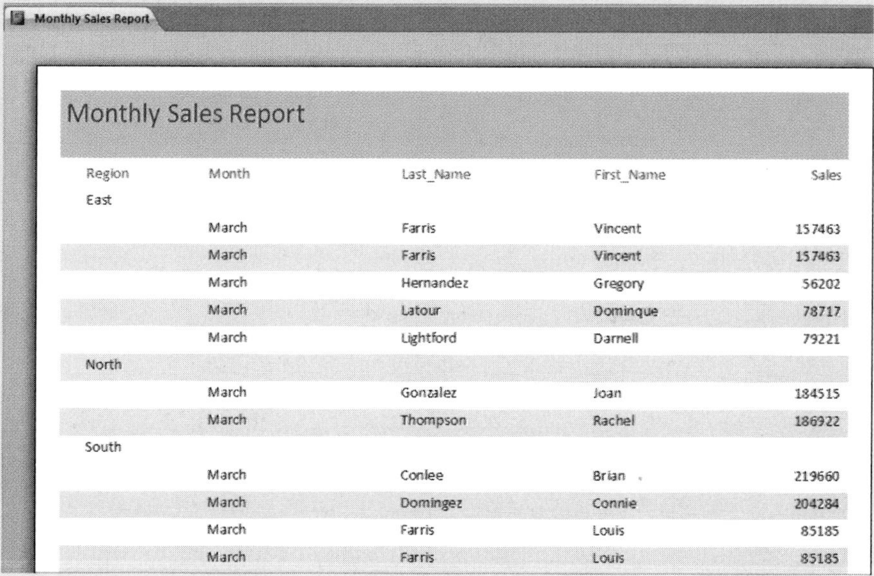

Monthly Sales Report

Region	Month	Last_Name	First_Name	Sales
East				
	March	Farris	Vincent	157463
	March	Farris	Vincent	157463
	March	Hernandez	Gregory	56202
	March	Latour	Dominque	78717
	March	Lightford	Darnell	79221
North				
	March	Gonzalez	Joan	184515
	March	Thompson	Rachel	186922
South				
	March	Conlee	Brian	219660
	March	Domingez	Connie	204284
	March	Farris	Louis	85185
	March	Farris	Louis	85185

FIGURE 10–6
Monthly Sales Report

13. Save the report.
14. Click the **Close Print Preview** button in the Close Preview group at the far right side of the Print Preview tab. Clicking Close Print Preview takes you into Design view. Next you will add some basic formatting and a theme to the report.

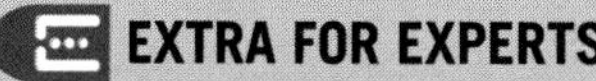

EXTRA FOR EXPERTS

To reopen the Navigation pane, you can click the Open Shutter Bar button.

Adding Formatting and a Theme to a Report

Themes let you add borders, background colors, shading, and graphic effects to an entire report at one time. If you change the theme, all the reports in the database with themes are changed at the same time. Before you add a theme to a report, you might want to add some basic formatting, such as bolding text. By adding basic formatting to a report before you apply a theme, the theme formats are enhanced. For example, if you add bold formats to the fonts in the report, when the theme is applied, the theme color for the fonts will be in a bolder, or darker, font color.

When you select controls in a report, you click to select the control. To select several controls, you press and hold Shift and then click on each control you want to select. By selecting multiple controls, you have the ability to apply formats to several controls at one time. You will now apply formats and a theme to a report.

Step-by-Step 10.2

1. Place the mouse pointer in the **vertical** ruler on the left side of the report to the left of the labels in the Page Header to display the selector arrow, as shown in **Figure 10–7**. Then, click to select all of the Page Header labels.

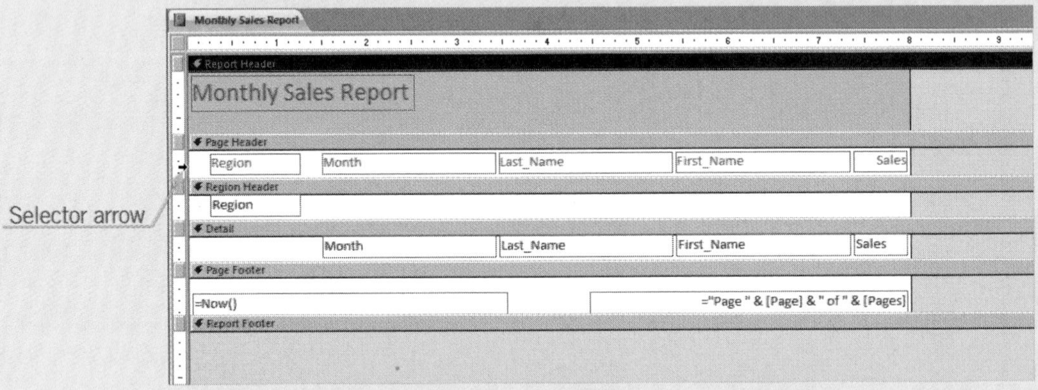

FIGURE 10–7
Selector arrow in ruler

Selector arrow

2. On the Ribbon, click the **Home** tab and then click the **Bold** button **B** in the Text Formatting group.
3. Click the **Font Color** button arrow and then click **Red, Accent 2** in the top row of the Theme Colors group.
4. Click in the **vertical** ruler to the left of the Report Header label, press and hold the **Shift** key, and then click in the ruler to the left of the Region Header label and the Detail labels.
5. Click the **Home** tab, click the **Bold** button **B** in the Text Formatting group, click the **Font Color** button arrow, and then click **Red, Accent 2**.
6. Deselect all, and then click the **Report Header** label to select it.
7. Drag the **right middle selection handle** to the right to resize the Report Header label so that your screen resembles **Figure 10–8**.

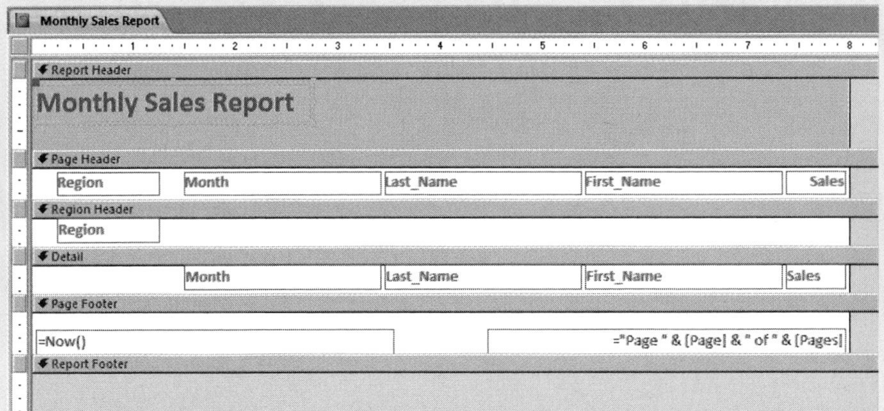

FIGURE 10–8
Labels formatted and resized

8. Click the **report selector** in the upper-left corner of the report where the horizontal and vertical rulers intersect. When the report selector is selected, it appears with a dark square. You have selected the entire report in order to apply a theme.
9. Click the **Design** tab, and then click the **Themes** button arrow in the Themes group to display the Themes gallery, as shown in **Figure 10–9**. Notice how the report formats change as you move the mouse pointer over the themes.

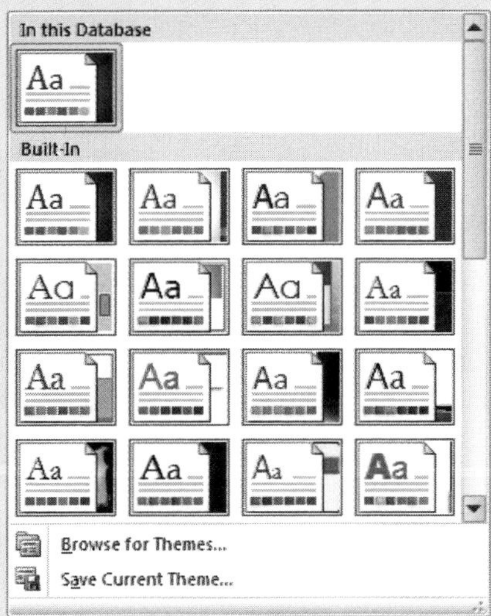

FIGURE 10–9
Themes gallery

10. Click the **Verve** theme to apply the theme to the report and then, if necessary, increase the size of the Report Header label.

11. Save the report, click the **View** button arrow, and then click **Report View.** In the Enter Parameter Value dialog box, type **March**, click **OK**, and then compare your screen to **Figure 10–10**.

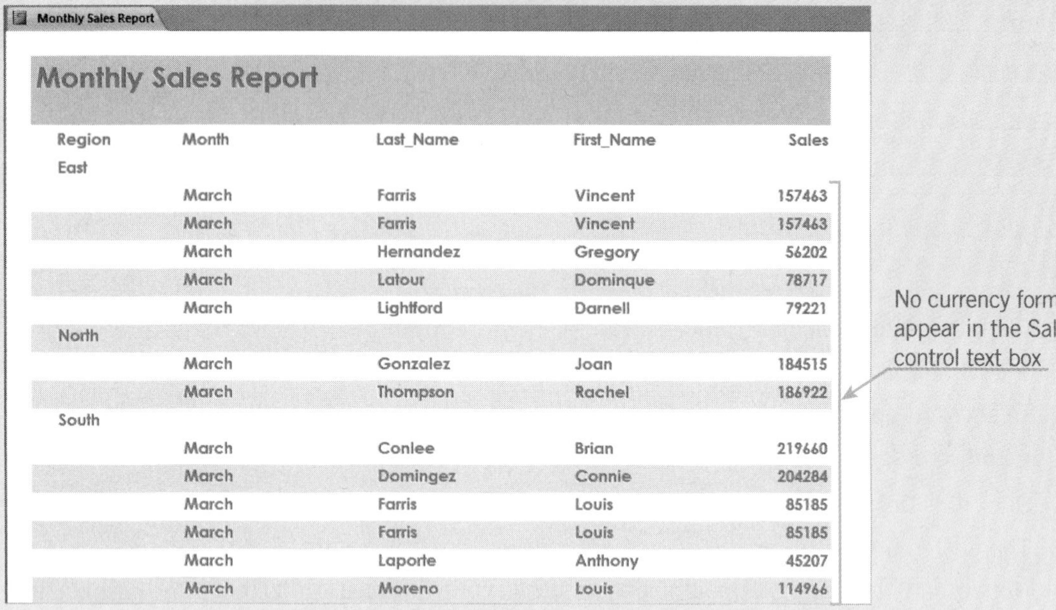

FIGURE 10–10
Report with Verve theme applied

Monthly Sales Report

Monthly Sales Report

Region	Month	Last_Name	First_Name	Sales
East				
	March	Farris	Vincent	157463
	March	Farris	Vincent	157463
	March	Hernandez	Gregory	56202
	March	Latour	Dominque	78717
	March	Lightford	Darnell	79221
North				
	March	Gonzalez	Joan	184515
	March	Thompson	Rachel	186922
South				
	March	Conlee	Brian	219660
	March	Domingez	Connie	204284
	March	Farris	Louis	85185
	March	Farris	Louis	85185
	March	Laporte	Anthony	45207
	March	Moreno	Louis	114966

No currency formats appear in the Sales control text box

12. Switch back to Design view. Leave the report open for the next Step-by-Step.

Changing a Control Property

The controls in a report have multiple properties that can be changed once they are added to the report. For example, if you include a control that shows sales data, the data will appear as a number in the report. However, you might want the data to appear with a currency format. The currency format places the dollar sign and commas in the control. You can also have the data display decimal places. By changing the properties of a control, the data will make more sense to the people who look at the report. For example, the sales amount of 1156789 does not make as much sense as seeing the data displayed as $1,156,789.

A control has two parts, the label and the text box. The label typically appears either above or to the left of the text box and describes what is in the field. The text box displays the actual data from the table. When you change control formats, you will typically be changing the text box when the data is displayed. In this next exercise, you will change the properties for a control.

Step-by-Step 10.3

1. Click the **Sales** text box in the Detail section, and then click the **Property Sheet** button to open the Property Sheet pane

2. On the Property Sheet pane, click the **All** tab if necessary, as shown in **Figure 10–11**. Notice that no formats appear in the Format box.

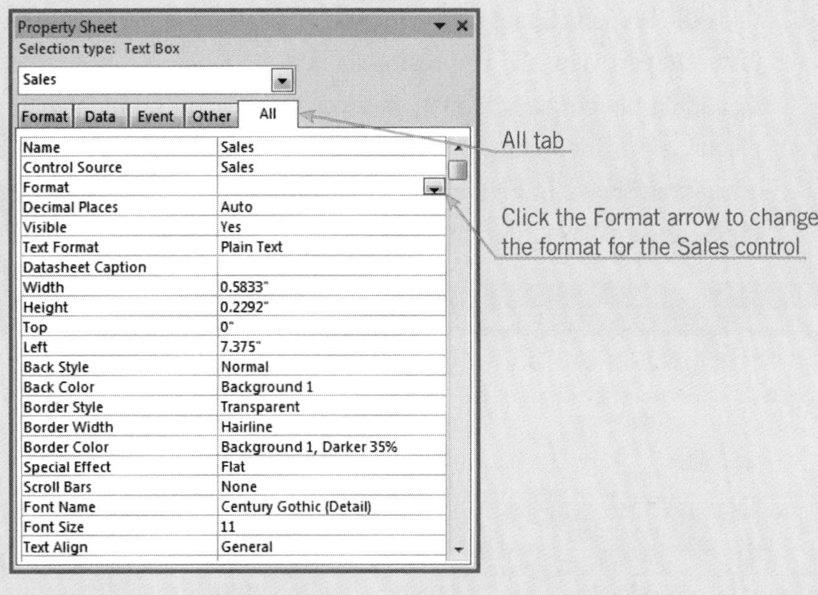

FIGURE 10–11
Property Sheet pane for Sales text box

3. Click in the **Format** field, and then click the **drop-down arrow** to display the format options, as shown in **Figure 10–12**.

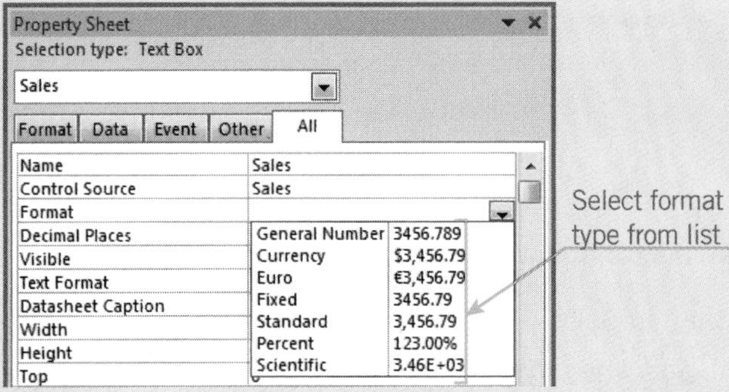

FIGURE 10–12
Format options

4. Click the **Currency** option to add a dollar sign, commas, and decimal places to the control.

5. Click the **Property Sheet** button to close the Property Sheet pane. Switch to the Report view and use **March** as the parameter value. Notice that by adding the currency format, your control may not be wide enough to display all of the numbers and format; instead, number signs (#) may appear, as shown in **Figure 10–13**. You will now increase the width of the Sales text box in Layout view.

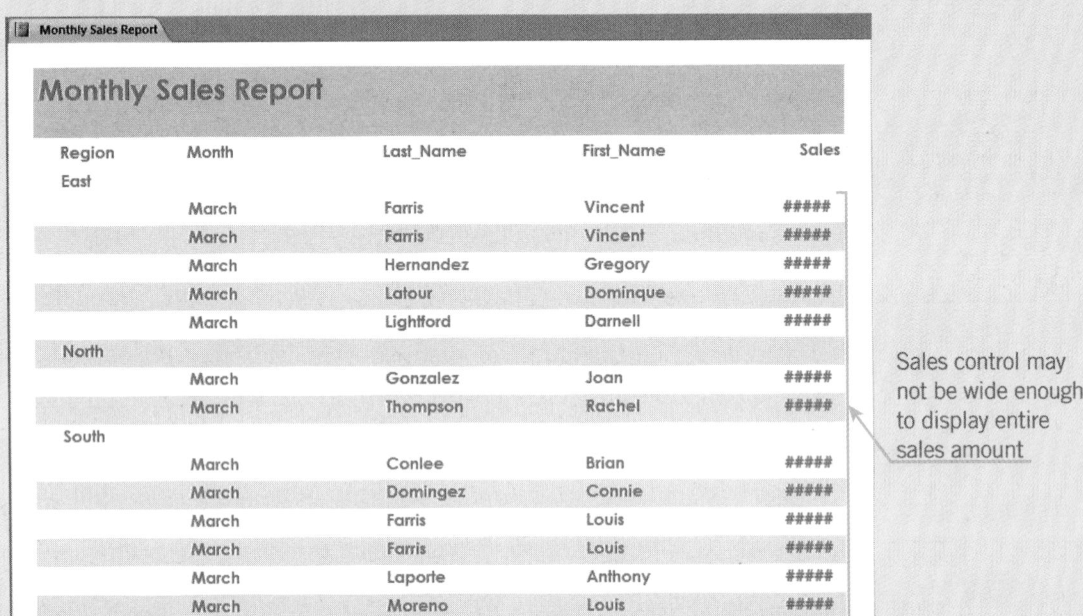

FIGURE 10–13
Sales text box needs to be wider

EXTRA FOR EXPERTS

To move a control in Design view, you can select the control, press and hold the Ctrl key, and then press the arrow keys to move the control right, left, up, or down.

6. Click the **View** button arrow, and then click **Layout View**.
7. Click the top **Sales** text box, place the pointer over the left side of the control, and when the pointer turns into a double-headed arrow, drag to the left to increase the size of the control until the numbers and their formatting appear, as shown in **Figure 10–14**.

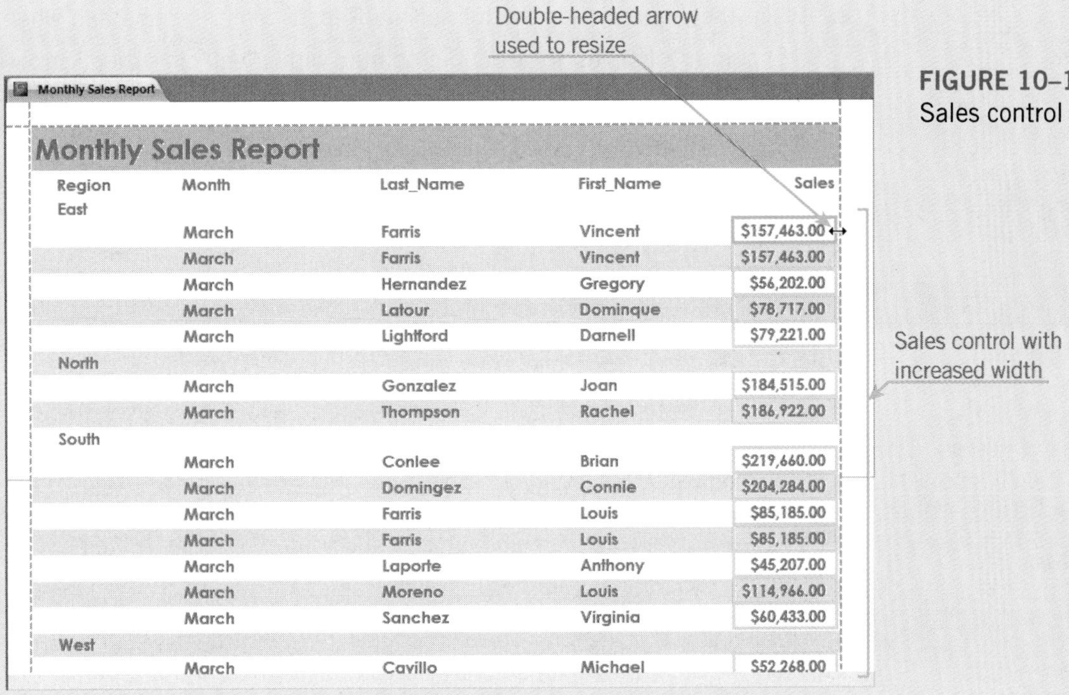

Double-headed arrow used to resize

Region	Month	Last_Name	First_Name	Sales
East				
	March	Farris	Vincent	$157,463.00
	March	Farris	Vincent	$157,463.00
	March	Hernandez	Gregory	$56,202.00
	March	Latour	Dominque	$78,717.00
	March	Lightford	Darnell	$79,221.00
North				
	March	Gonzalez	Joan	$184,515.00
	March	Thompson	Rachel	$186,922.00
South				
	March	Conlee	Brian	$219,660.00
	March	Domingez	Connie	$204,284.00
	March	Farris	Louis	$85,185.00
	March	Farris	Louis	$85,185.00
	March	Laporte	Anthony	$45,207.00
	March	Moreno	Louis	$114,966.00
	March	Sanchez	Virginia	$60,433.00
West				
	March	Cavillo	Michael	$52,268.00

Monthly Sales Report

Sales control with increased width

FIGURE 10–14
Sales control with increased width

8. Save the report and leave it open for the next Step-by-Step.

Adding a Calculated Control to a Report

After you create a report, you might want to add a control that will calculate some of the data in the report. For example, you might have data in a report that shows monthly sales for each employee. However, you would also like to show the total sales for the month. A ***calculated control*** lets you use functions to add a calculation to a report.

By adding a calculated control in the report footer, the total of the sales will be displayed at the end of the report. After you add the control, you can format it. In this next exercise, you will add a calculated control that adds all of the sales data in the report.

VOCABULARY
calculated control

Step-by-Step 10.4

1. Switch to **Design** view. Since you want the calculated control in the Report Footer, you will increase the size of the footer.

2. Place the pointer at the bottom of the Report Footer section and when the pointer changes to a double-pointer with a set of vertical arrowheads, drag the section down to the ½ inch mark on the vertical ruler, as shown in **Figure 10–15**.

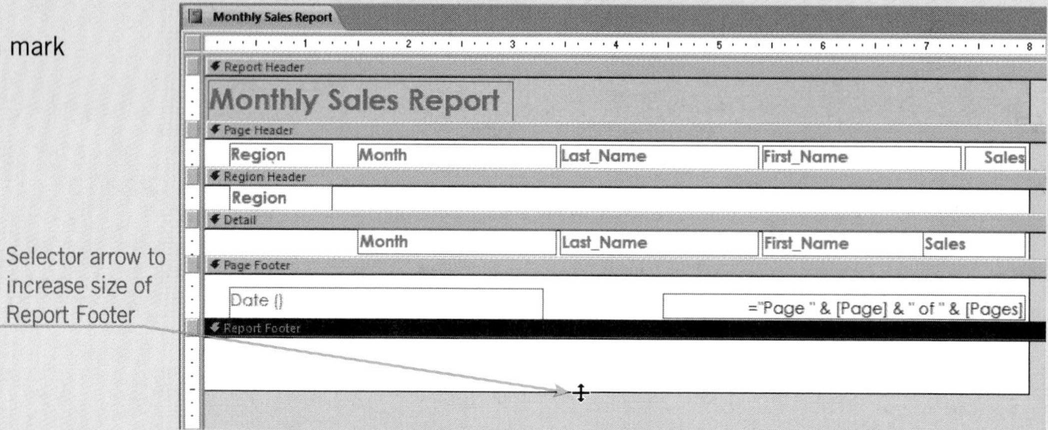

FIGURE 10–15
Report Footer at ½ inch mark

3. On the Design tab, click the **Text Box** button in the Controls group then, in the Report Footer section, click below the Sales text box, as shown in **Figure 10–16**.

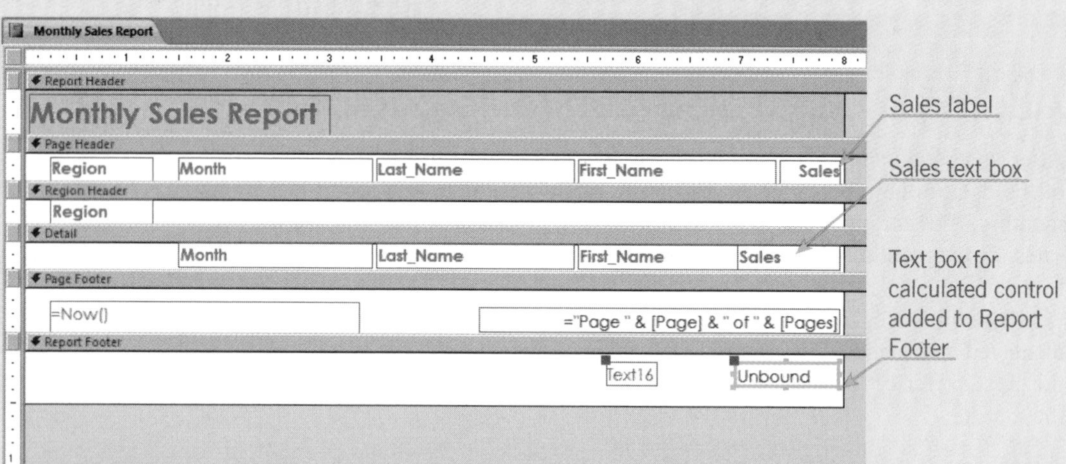

FIGURE 10–16
Report Footer with Text Box control

TIP

If you need to move the control, press and hold the Ctrl key and then press the arrow keys to move it.

4. Click the **Property Sheet** button to display the Property Sheet pane, click the **Control Source** field, and then click the **Build** button on the right side to display the Expression Builder dialog box, as shown in **Figure 10–17**. You will now create the expression that will show the total amount for the Sales control.

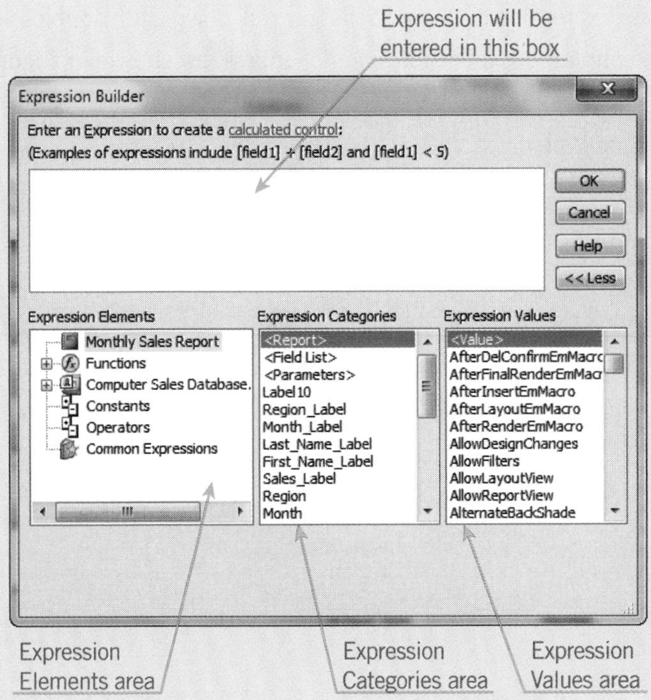

FIGURE 10–17
Expression Builder dialog box

5. Click **Operators** in the Expression Elements list, and then double-click the **Equal** sign (=) in the Expression Values list.
6. Click the **plus sign** to the left of Functions in the Expression Elements list, and then click **Built-In Functions**. Scroll down in the Expression Values list and double-click **Sum**. You will need to replace <<expression>> with the Sales text box value.
7. In the Expression box, click **<<expression>>** to highlight it. The Sales text box needs to be selected and added to the expression.
8. In the Expression Elements list, click **Monthly Sales Report** located above the Functions option.

9. In the Expression Categories list, scroll down and double-click **Sales**. The completed expression should appear as shown in **Figure 10–18**. You will now add the currency format to the calculated control.

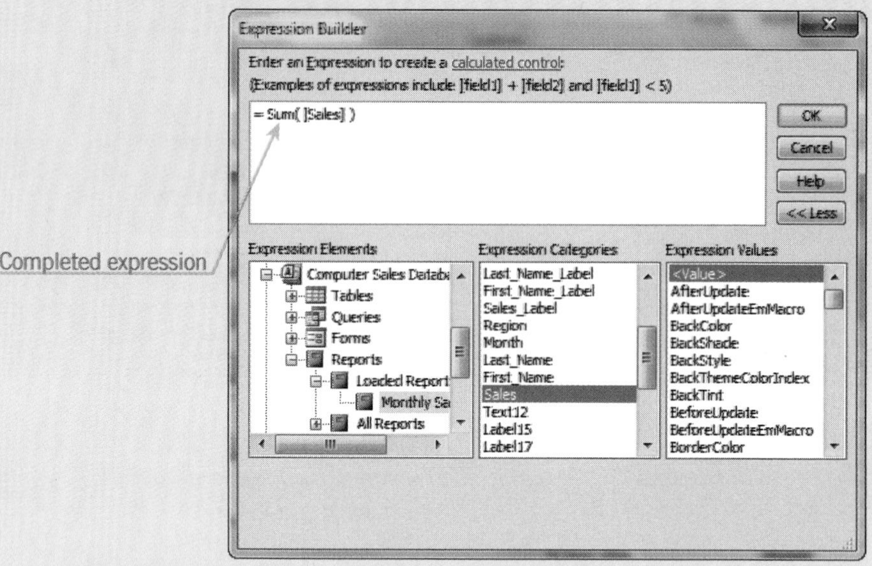

FIGURE 10–18
Completed Expression Builder dialog box

EXTRA FOR EXPERTS

Using the Format Painter button, you can apply formats to more than one object, such as several labels. First, click the field that has the formats you want to apply, then double-click the Format Painter button in the Clipboard group on the Home tab. Double-clicking the tool keeps it active until you click it again to turn it off. Then click each item where you want to apply the format. Click the Format Painter tool again to turn off the feature.

10. Click **OK** to close the Expression Builder dialog box. On the Property Sheet pane, click in the **Format** field, click the **drop-down** arrow, and then click **Currency**.

11. Click the **Property Sheet** button to close the Property Sheet pane, and then replace the text in the label for the text box with **Total**, as shown in **Figure 10–19**.

You will now apply formatting to the text box and label.

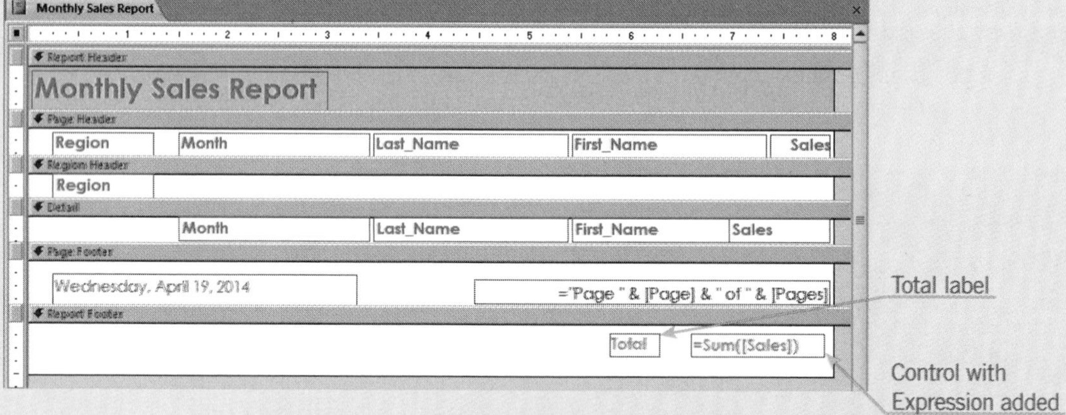

FIGURE 10–19
Control with Expression added

12. Click any label in the Detail section to select it, click the **Home** tab, double-click the **Format Painter** button in the Clipboard group, and then click the **label** and **text box** in the Report Footer. Click the **Format Painter** button again to turn this feature off.

13. Switch to **Layout** view, type **March** for the parameter value, and then view the results. Increase the size of the calculated control text box so that all the numbers and symbols appear, as shown in **Figure 10–20**.

Monthly Sales Report

	March	Conlee	Brian	$219,660.00
	March	Dominguez	Connie	$204,284.00
	March	Farris	Louis	$85,185.00
	March	Farris	Louis	$85,185.00
	March	Laporte	Anthony	$45,207.00
	March	Moreno	Louis	$114,966.00
	March	Sanchez	Virginia	$60,433.00
West				
	March	Cavillo	Michael	$52,268.00
	March	Estes	Elaine	$198,403.00
	March	Farris	Marco	$64,981.00
	March	Farris	Marco	$64,981.00
	March	Garcia	Maria	$99,183.00
	March	Jones	Cynthia	$48,609.00
	March	Kobrick	Tara	$85,184.00
	March	Langston	Dora	$62,474.00
	March	Linebarger	Donald	$124,971.00
	March	Selinger	Robert	$85,186.00
			Total	$2,601,663.00

Wednesday, April 19, 2014 — Page 1 of 1

ut View

FIGURE 10–20
Report in Layout view

Calculated control displays total sales for the report

14. Save the report and leave it open for the next Step-by-Step.

Adding Conditional Formatting to a Control

Conditional formatting allows you to add formatting features to the data based on criteria you specify. In other words, the appearance of the data will differ from one record to another depending on whether the value in the control meets criteria that you specify. You can use conditional formatting to have a different background color, font style, or text color appear in a control so that its values are emphasized when they meet a certain condition. If the value of the control no longer meets the condition, the default formatting for the control will be applied. You can specify up to three conditions for a field. In this next exercise, you will have formatting applied to a control if its value is less than $75,000.

VOCABULARY
conditional formatting

Step-by-Step 10.5

1. Switch to **Design** view.
2. In the Detail section, click the **Sales** text box.

3. On the Ribbon, click the **Format** tab and then click the **Conditional Formatting** button in the Control Formatting group. The Conditional Formatting Rules Manager dialog box opens, as shown in **Figure 10–21**.

FIGURE 10–21
Conditional Formatting Rules Manager dialog box

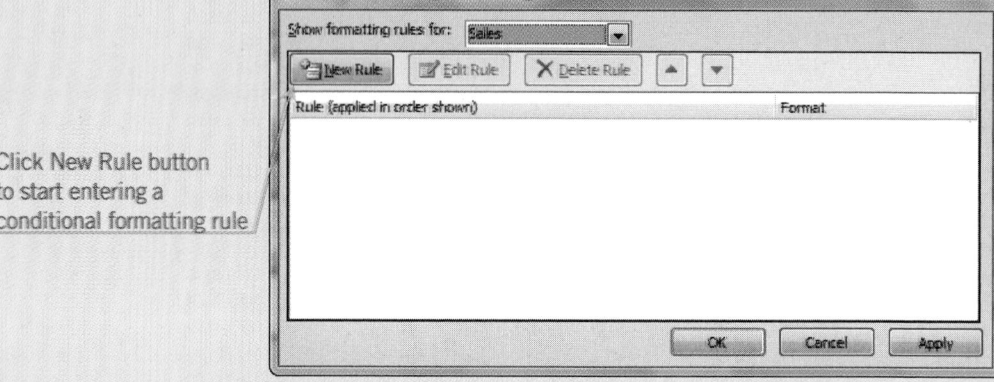

4. Click the **New Rule** button. The New Formatting Rule dialog box opens, as shown in **Figure 10–22**.

FIGURE 10–22
New Formatting Rule dialog box

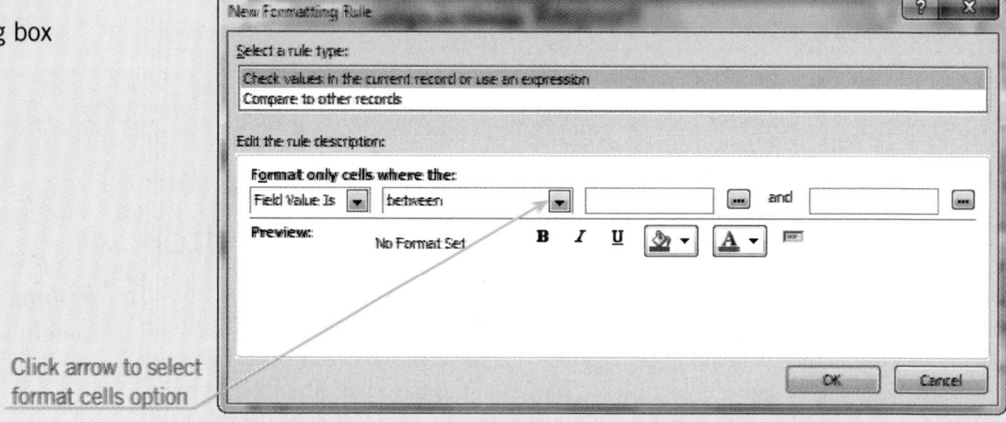

5. Click the **drop-down arrow** next to *between* to display the possible options for the rule description, as shown in **Figure 10–23**, and then click **less than**.

FIGURE 10–23
Options for the rule description

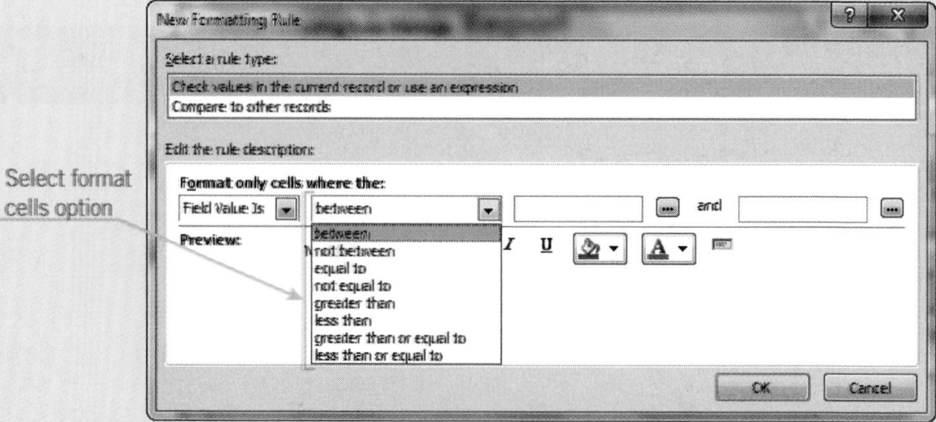

6. Click in the text box to the right and then type **75000**. Entering this amount will select any amount less than $75,000. Next you will add the formatting to the condition so that it will appear in a dark blue when the condition is met.
7. In the Edit Formatting Rule dialog box, click the **Bold** button **B**, click the **Font Color** button arrow, and then click **Dark Blue** (the fourth color in the top row). The completed Edit Formatting Rule dialog box is shown in **Figure 10–24**.

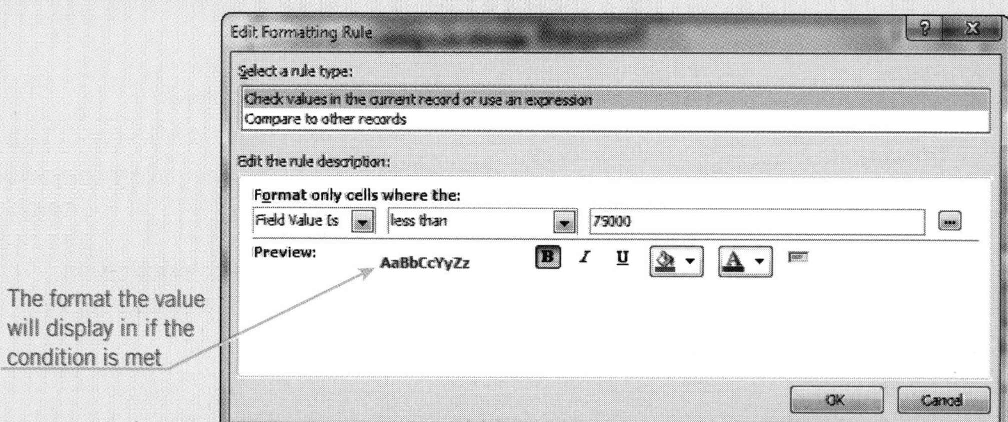

FIGURE 10–24 Completed conditional formatting rule

8. Click **OK** to close the Edit Formatting Rule dialog box, click **Apply**, and then click **OK** to close the Conditional Formatting Rules Manager dialog box.
9. Click the **Home** tab, click the **View** button arrow, and then click **Report View**. Display the results for March. Notice that the amounts less than $75,000 appear in a bold dark blue format. See **Figure 10–25**.

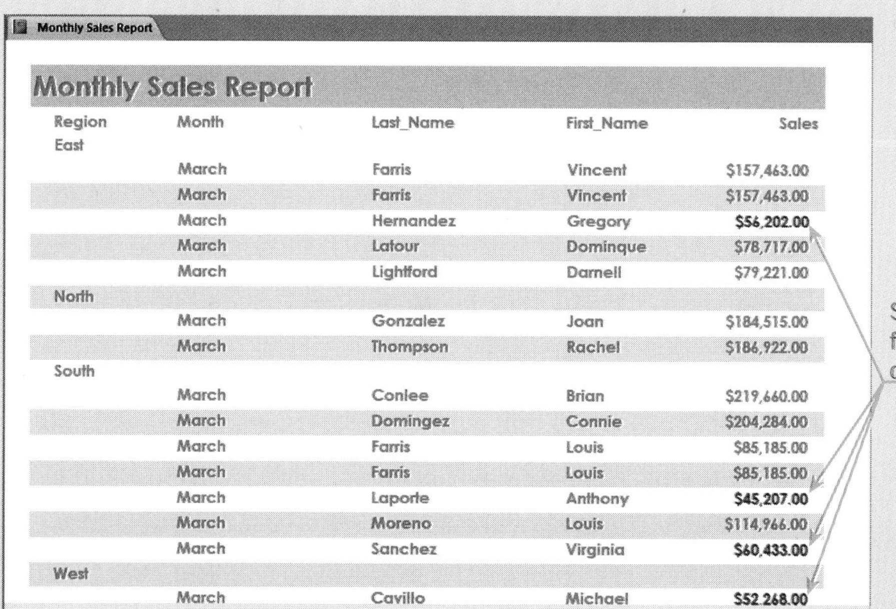

FIGURE 10–25 Report in Layout view

10. Save and close the report.

Adding a Subreport to a Report

VOCABULARY
subreport

After you create a report, you may want to display additional information located in another table in the report as well. ***Subreports*** are reports you create and then embed in another report. The easiest way to add a subreport to a report is with SubReport Wizard. The wizard takes you step by step through the process of adding a subreport. As you work through the wizard, you will be asked to define a link between the two reports. The link needs to be a common field between the two tables. In this next exercise, you will add a subreport to an existing report.

Step-by-Step 10.6

1. On the Navigation pane, right-click **qry-Employee Sales,** and then select **Design View** to view the query. Notice that a parameter is located in the Employee ID Number field that will prompt you to enter an Employee ID Number. Close the query.
2. Right-click **Employee Sales Report** and then select **Design View**. You will now add a subreport that displays employee contact information.
3. Place the pointer over the bottom of the Report Footer section and drag down to 1½" on the vertical ruler. See **Figure 10–26**.

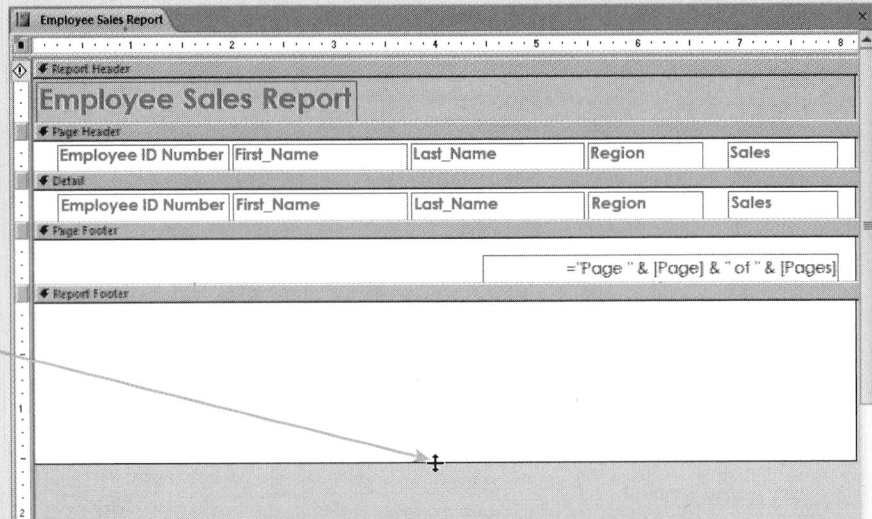

FIGURE 10–26
Report Footer extended for subreport

4. In the Controls group, click the **More** button, then click the **Subform/ Subreport** button.
5. Draw an outline under the controls in the Report Footer section that extends the width of the Report Footer section and is about 1" in depth. See **Figure 10–27**. When you release the mouse button, the SubReport Wizard dialog box opens, as shown in **Figure 10–28**.

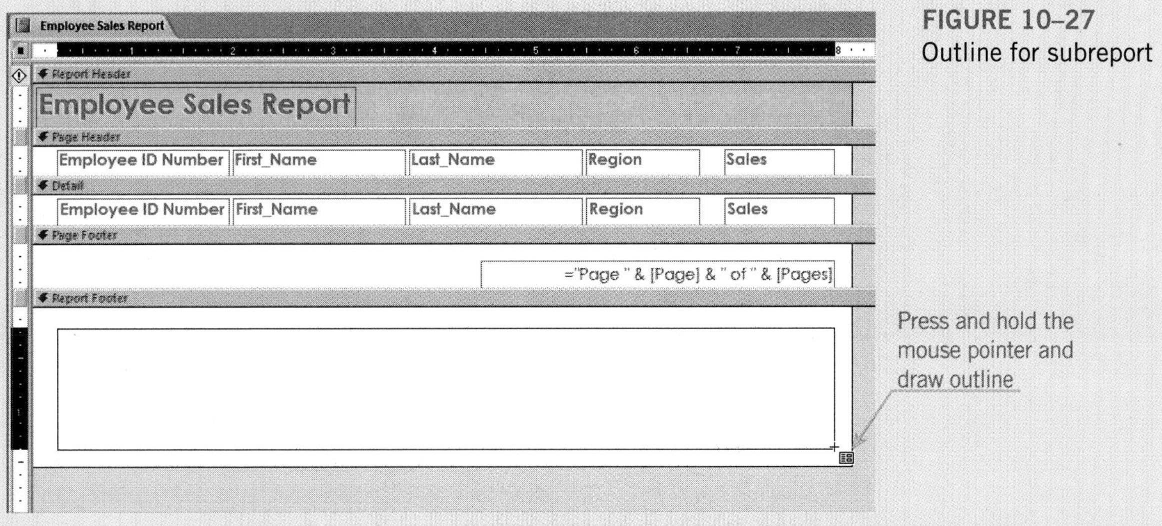

FIGURE 10–27
Outline for subreport

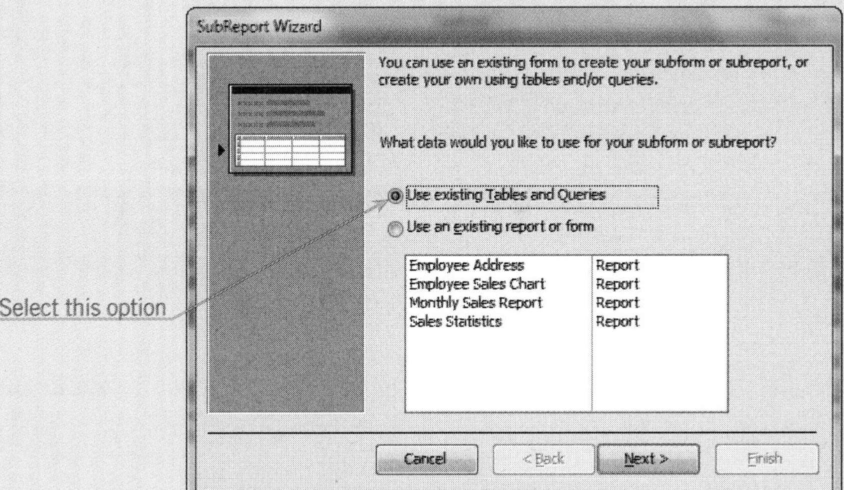

FIGURE 10–28
SubReport Wizard dialog box

6. Verify that the **Use existing Tables and Queries** option button is selected, and then click **Next**.

7. Verify that **Table:Employees** is chosen as the table to choose fields from and then double-click **Employee ID Number**, **Address**, **City**, **State**, and **ZIP** to place these fields in the Selected Fields box. Click **Next**. See **Figure 10–29**. Access recognized the link between the report and subreport as the Employee ID Number field, which is the correct link.

FIGURE 10–29
Define link in SubReport Wizard

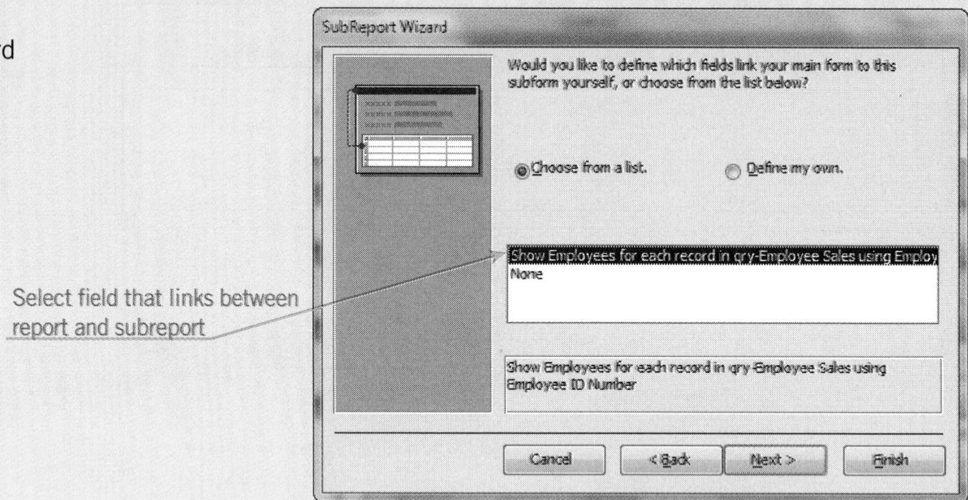

8. Click **Next**.
9. In the name box, type **Employee Address** for the name of the subreport, and then click **Finish**.
10. On the Home tab, click the **View** button arrow and then select **Layout View**. Type **145** in the Enter Parameter Value dialog box, and then click **OK**. Compare your screen to **Figure 10–30**.

FIGURE 10–30
Report and subreport in Layout view

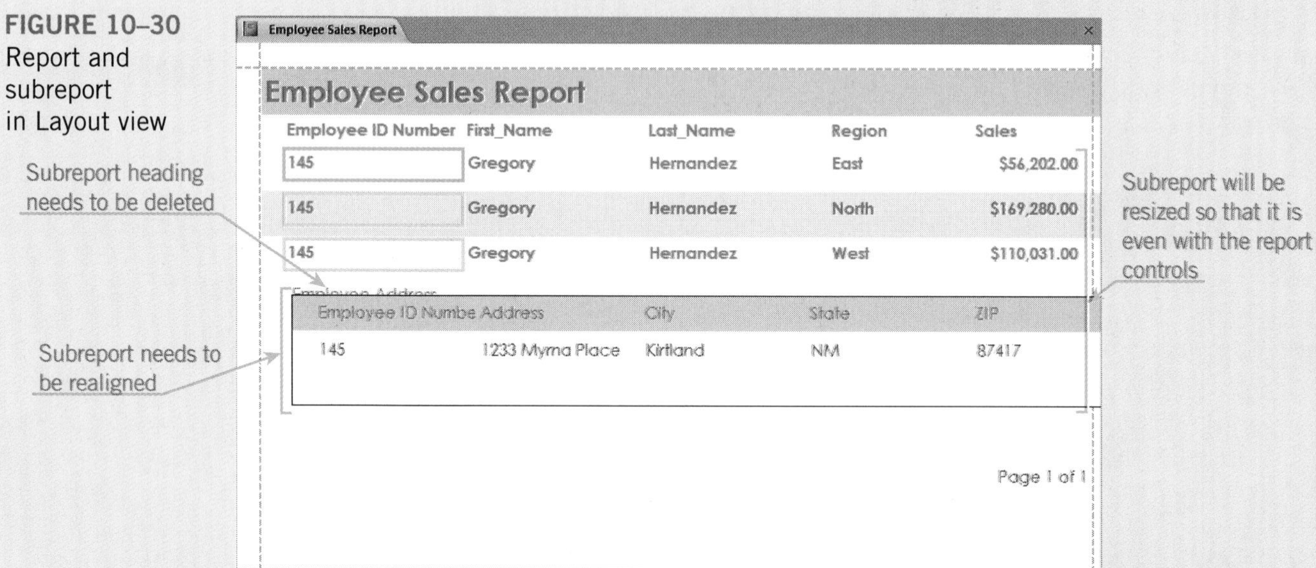

11. Click the **subreport heading**, and then press **Delete** since you do not need it.

12. Place the pointer over the right edge of the subreport and drag left, or right, until it is aligned with the right edge of the Sales control, as shown in **Figure 10–31**.

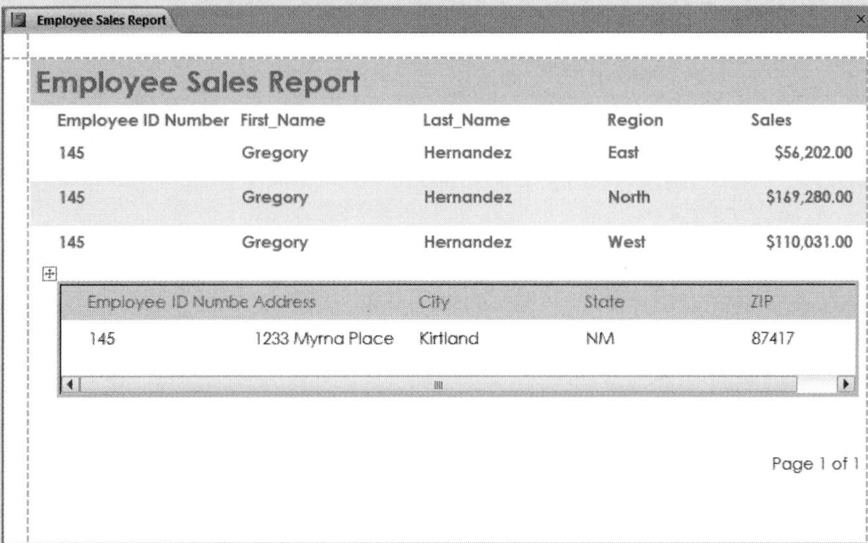

FIGURE 10–31
Subreport realigned

13. Save and close the report. Notice that Employee Address appears as a report in the Navigation pane. Both reports and subreports are displayed in the Reports group.

Creating a Summary Report

If you know ahead of time that you want to have calculations in a report, you can select them as you create the report using the Report Wizard. You can select the Sum, Avg, Min, and Max functions to display in the report. By adding these functions to a report, you might see trends in the data that you may not have seen if these functions were not in the report. For example, you may have sales data that is grouped by regions, such as East and West. Then, you can look at the sales in these regions and the sales person who made the maximum, or highest, sales. You will then see who the top sales people are in your organization.

When you create a summary report, you select the summary options in the Summary Options dialog box. You are given the choices of Sum, Avg, Min, and Max. You can select one, several, or all of the functions. In the next exercise, you will create a summary report for the sales in each region.

Step-by-Step 10.7

1. Click the **Sales Data** table in the Navigation pane to select it, click the **Create** tab, and then click **Report Wizard** in the Reports group.
2. Double-click **Region** and **Sales** to move these fields over to the Selected Fields box, and then click **Next.**

3. Verify that **Region** is selected, click the **Single Field** arrow button to create a grouping level, and then click **Next**. Notice the Summary Options button in this dialog box, as shown in **Figure 10–32**.

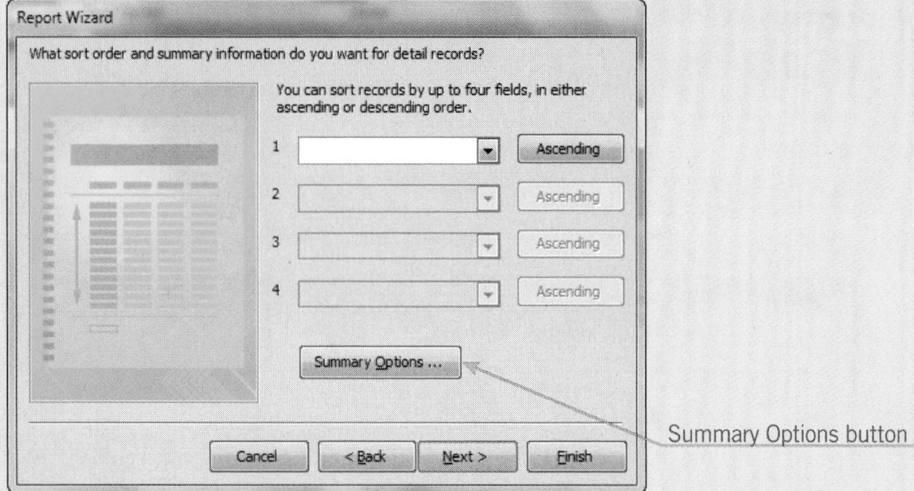

FIGURE 10–32
Report Wizard dialog box with Summary Options button

4. Click the **Summary Options** button to display the Summary Options dialog box, as shown in **Figure 10–33**.

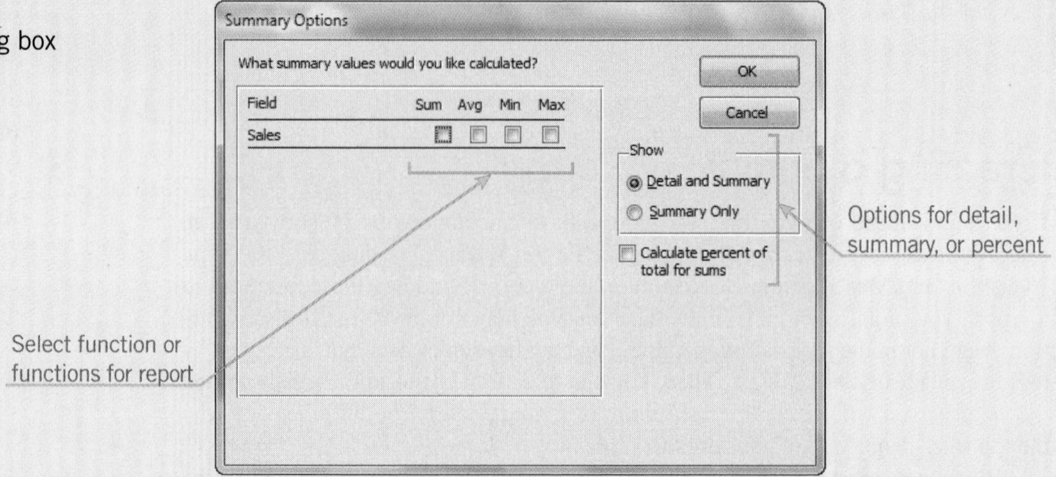

FIGURE 10–33
Summary Options dialog box

5. Click the **Sum**, **Avg**, **Min**, and **Max** check boxes.
6. In the Show section, click the **Summary Only** option button, and then click **OK**.
7. Click **Next,** verify that the **Stepped** option button is selected, and then click **Next**.
8. Type **Sales Statistics** as the name of the report, and then click **Finish**. A preview of the report opens. Notice that you will need to adjust the width of the Sum, Avg, Min, and Max controls.

9. Click the **Close Print Preview** button in the Close Preview group on the Ribbon, click the **View** button arrow, select **Design View**, and then compare your screen to **Figure 10–34**. Next, you will delete the summary heading in the Region Footer section.

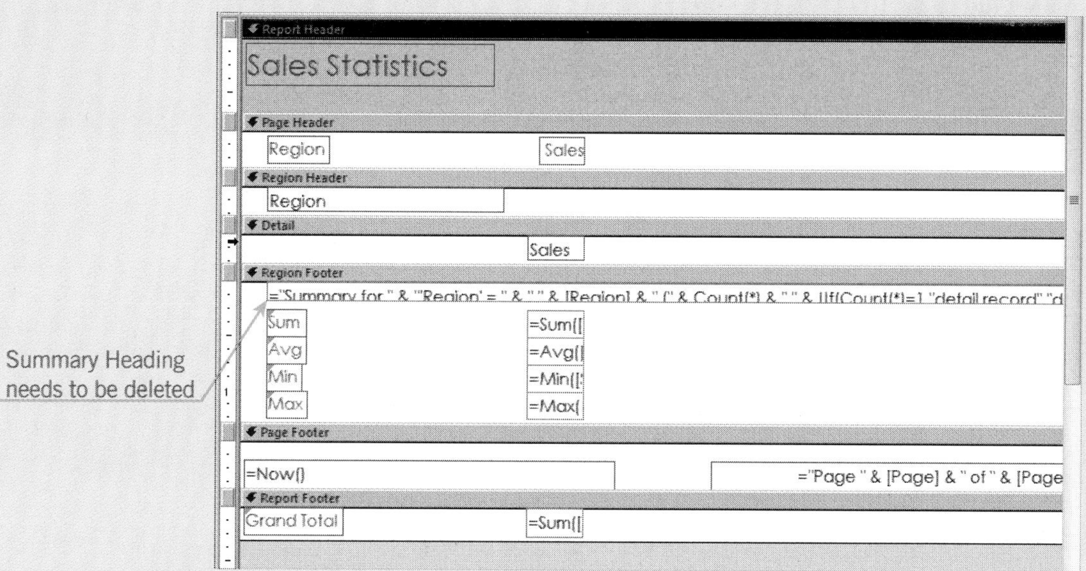

FIGURE 10–34 Sales Statistics report

10. In the Region Footer section, click the **Summary** heading and press **Delete**. You will now resize the text boxes.
11. Switch to the **Layout** view. To select the four function text boxes, choose any region, press and hold the **Shift** key, and click each of the text boxes. Then, place the pointer over the right side of one of the selected text boxes and drag to the right to increase the width of each text box. Next, you will add currency formatting to the text boxes.
12. With the function text boxes selected, click the **Format** tab and then click the **Apply Currency Format** button in the Number group. Switch to Design view. Select the =Sum([Sales]) text box in the Report Footer and then click the **Apply Currency Format** button.
13. Press and hold the **Ctrl** key, click in the vertical margin next to all of the objects, click the **Format** tab, and then click the **Bold** button **B**. Click the **Font Color** button arrow, click **Pink, Accent 2**, click the **Design** tab, click the **Themes** button arrow, and then click **Verve**.

14. Switch to Layout view and resize the Sales controls again, if necessary. Then switch to **Report** view, compare your screen to **Figure 10–35**, then save and close the report.

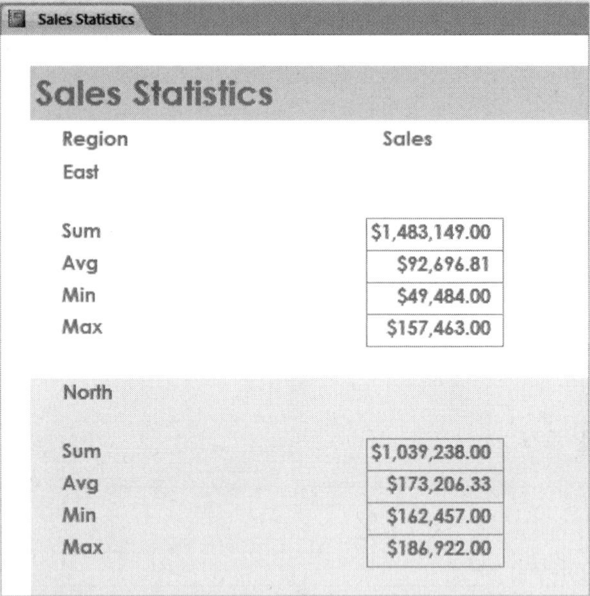

FIGURE 10–35
Final Sales Statistics report

Adding a Chart to a Report

VOCABULARY
chart

A ***chart*** is a graphical display of data. Charts are a great solution for presenting data in Access graphically. Charts are simple to make and format. Access offers formatting features that you can apply to a chart to make it a professional representation of the data. In this lesson, you will learn how to add a chart to a report.

Step-by-Step 10.8

1. Open the **Employee Sales Chart** report in Design view.
2. Select and delete all of the controls in the Page Footer. Then, place the pointer at the top of the Report Footer section and drag up until the Page Footer section heading is against the Report Footer section heading.

   To make room for the chart, you will increase the size of the Report Footer.
3. Place the pointer over the bottom of the Report Footer and drag down to the 4" mark on the vertical ruler.
4. Click the **More** button in the Controls group, and then click the **Chart** button.
5. Draw an outline about the same size as the Report Footer section. The Chart Wizard dialog box opens.

6. Click the **Queries** option button and then click **Queries: qry-Employee Sales**, as shown in **Figure 10–36**.

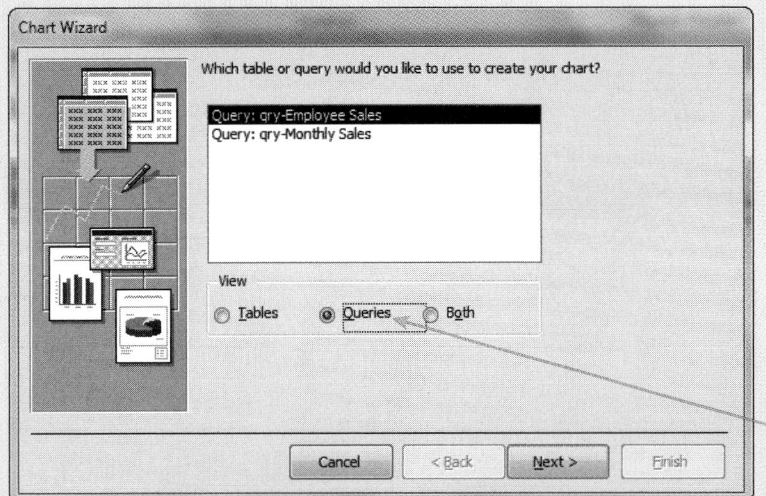

FIGURE 10–36
Chart Wizard dialog box

7. Click **Next**, then double-click the **Employee ID Number** field and then the **Sales** field to move them to the Fields for Chart area.
8. Click **Next**, then click the **3-D Column Chart**, as shown in **Figure 10–37**.

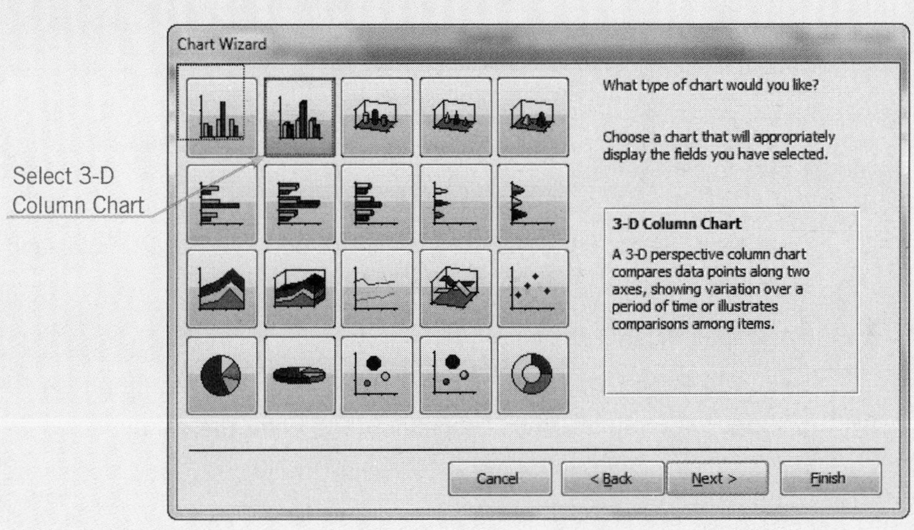

FIGURE 10–37
Select chart type

9. Click **Next** and preview the chart, as shown in **Figure 10–38**. Next, you will change SumOfSales in the chart to Sales.

FIGURE 10–38
Preview Chart

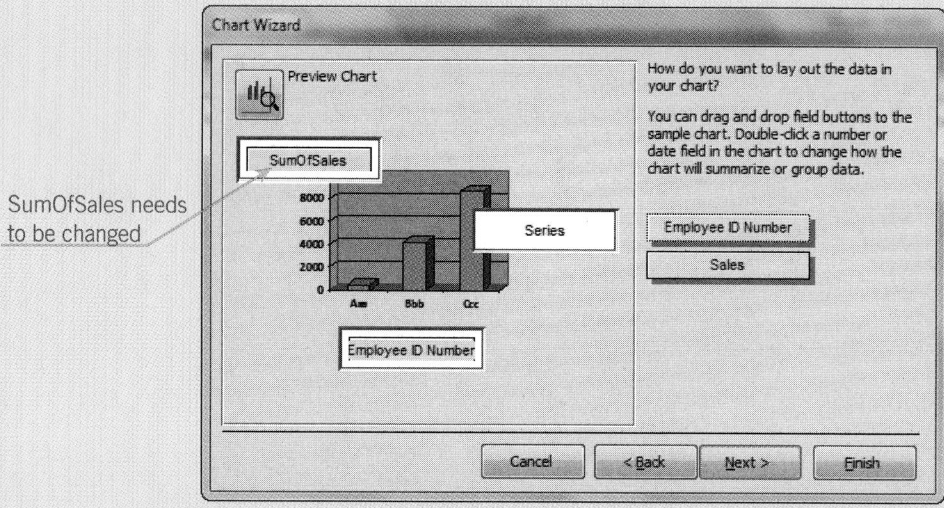

10. Double-click **SumOfSales** to display the Summarize dialog box. See **Figure 10–39**. Click **None** and then click **OK**.

FIGURE 10–39
Summarize dialog box

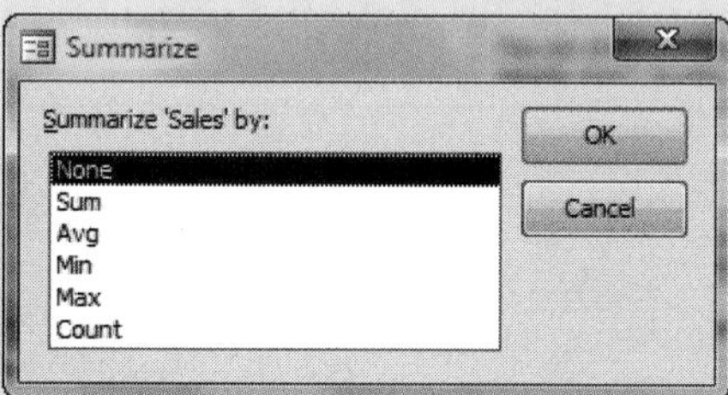

11. Click **Next**. Select **Employee ID Number** for both the Report Fields and the Chart Fields, and then click **Next**.
12. Type **Sales Data** for the chart title, and then click **Finish**.
13. Switch to Report view and view the report and chart for Employee ID number 145. You will then be prompted to enter the parameter again for the chart. After you enter 145 again, the chart should appear as shown in **Figure 10–40**.

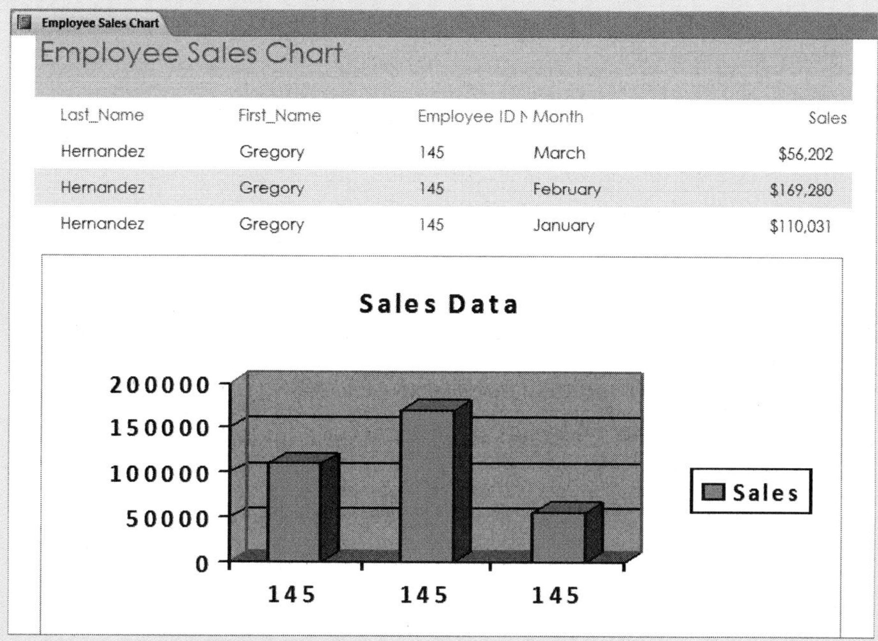

FIGURE 10–40
Report with chart

14. Save the report, and then close the database.

SUMMARY

In this lesson, you learned:

- When you create a report from a parameter query, you will be prompted for data each time you open the report.
- Adding a theme to a report adds text formats, borders, and shading to the report.
- Control properties can be easily changed so that data displayed in the control is properly formatted.
- If you want to total all the data in a report, you can add a calculated control to a report.
- Adding conditional formatting to a control displays the data in a different format if a certain condition is met.
- A report can be added to an existing report using the subreport feature.
- Creating a summary report lets you create reports that can find Sum, Avg, Min, and Max values for the data.
- Adding a chart to a report lets you display the data graphically.

VOCABULARY REVIEW

calculated control
chart
conditional formatting
subreport

REVIEW QUESTIONS

TRUE / FALSE

Circle T if the statement is true or F if the statement is false.

T F 1. Charts can only be added to the Detail section of the report.

T F 2. Conditional formatting will display the control data in a different format if certain criteria are met.

T F 3. A calculated control lets you apply calculations to the data in the report and display the results in the control.

T F 4. Adding a theme to a report applies text colors and shading to the report based on the theme you select.

T F 5. When creating a summary report, you can only choose two functions.

FILL IN THE BLANK

1. A(n) ________________ can be added to a report to perform a calculation using data in the report.
2. To display specific data in a report, such as for a certain region, you can base the report on a(n) ________________.
3. A report that is added to an existing report is called a(n) ________________.
4. If you want sales data greater than $80,000 to appear in a unique format, you can add ________________ to the control.
5. To add a graphical display of the data to a report, you can add a(n) ________________.

WRITTEN QUESTIONS

Write a brief answer to the following questions.

1. Describe the benefits of conditional formatting and give an example.

2. Explain how to add a chart to a report.

3. Explain the benefits of adding a subreport to a report.

4. Describe the steps necessary to change the property of a control from a number format to a currency format with two decimal places.

5. Explain the benefits of a summary report.

PROJECTS

If you have a SAM 2010 user profile, your instructor may have assigned an autogradable version of the indicated project. If so, log into the SAM 2010 Web site at *www.cengage.com/sam2010* to download the instruction and start files.

PROJECT 10–1

1. Open the **Pacific Sales** file from the drive and folder where your Data Files are stored. Save the database as **Pacific Sales Database**, followed by your initials.
2. In the Sales Data Report, resize the controls so that all of the sales data is displayed.
3. Add a calculated control to the report footer that shows a grand total for all the sales in the report. Be sure to align and size the calculated control in the report. (*Hint*: You might need to use the alignment buttons in the Sizing & Ordering group on the Arrange tab.)
4. Change the text in the label to **Grand Total**.
5. Change the control property for the calculated control to Currency with no decimal places.
6. Save the report.
7. Close the database.

PROJECT 10–3

1. Open the **Pet Supplies** file from the drive and folder where your Data Files are stored. Save the database as **Pet Supplies Database**, followed by your initials.
2. Create a report based on the parameter query qry-Customer Sales. Include all of the fields in the query in the report.
3. Sort by Production Description and then by Quantity.
4. Use the Tabular layout.
5. Use Sales by Customer ID for the title.
6. Run the report for Customer ID Number 5. Notice that you need to change the alignment of the Customer ID control so that the data is displayed under the label. Also notice that you need to increase the size of the Product Description label and text box.
7. Realign and resize the Customer ID and the Product Description controls.
8. Save the report.
9. Run the report again for Customer ID Number 5 to be certain the alignment and sizing are correct.
10. Print the report.
11. Close the report and then close the database.

SAM PROJECT 10–2

1. Open the **Regional Sales** file from the drive and folder where your Data Files are stored. Save the database as **Regional Sales Database**, followed by your initials.
2. Open the Sales Data Report in Design view. Then, add a conditional formatting rule to the Sales control that displays sales amounts greater than or equal to $150,000 in a Dark Red, bold font.
3. View the report in Report view to be certain the conditional formatting is working correctly.
4. Save the report.
5. Print the report.
6 Close the database.

CRITICAL THINKING

ACTIVITY 10–1

You are the new database administrator for the Book Sales company. Open the **Book Sales** database and then save it as **Book Sales Database**, followed by your initials. Create a professional report named **High Volume Sales Orders** that will display the Sales Orders. To help management make decisions on sales, the report should display sales figures in another format when the total is greater than $2,000. When complete, save the report, print the report, and close the database.

ACTIVITY 10–2

Think of how you could use conditional formatting in a report that displays sporting events. The report consists of dates, teams, and scores. Write down your thoughts and how you would present this report to a coach.

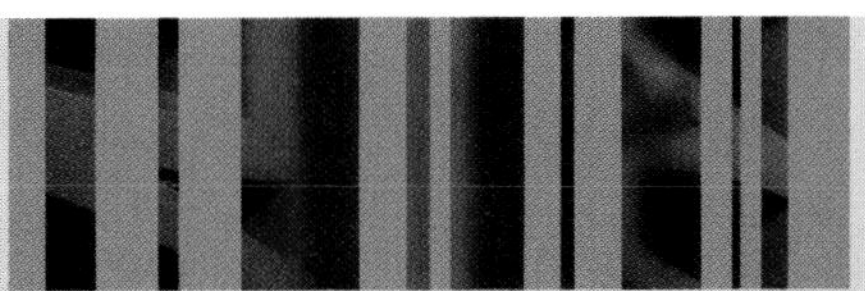

Estimated Time: 2.5 hours

LESSON 11

Creating and Running Macros

OBJECTIVES

Upon completion of this lesson, you should be able to:

- Review macro security settings.
- Record a macro.
- Run a macro.
- Edit a macro.
- Create a macro to open and print reports.
- Run a macro with multiple actions.
- Create an embedded macro.
- View and run an embedded macro.

VOCABULARY

argument
code
comment
embedded macro
filter
macro
run
virus

Introduction

A macro automates common, repetitive tasks you perform in Access, thereby saving valuable time. In this lesson, you will learn about macros and potential viruses. Then, you will learn how to create and run macros. To run a macro means to have it perform a programmed, automated task. You will also learn how to make changes to a macro and how to add a macro to a button that can be clicked to run the macro.

Understanding Macros

VOCABULARY
macro
code
virus

A ***macro*** is a series of actions that you want Access to perform. Macros automate repetitive tasks, such as opening forms, printing reports, and running queries. Rather than doing a set of instructions repeatedly to perform the same task, you can save time and ensure accuracy by creating a macro that performs those actions for you.

When you create a macro, Excel records the selections you make using buttons and commands on the Ribbon as well as the keystrokes you use. Visual Basic for Applications (or VBA) is the program used to create macros. VBA is a programming language that is embedded into applications such as Excel.

When a macro is being recorded, all of the selections you make are translated into code. ***Code*** is simply the macro actions formatted in easy-to-read sentences, just like text in a book. Before you record a macro, it is important to review and understand macro security settings.

Reviewing Macro Security Settings

Macros are susceptible to virus attacks. A ***virus*** is a computer program that is designed to reproduce itself by attaching to other programs in a computer. Viruses can cause extreme damage to data on your computer. If a virus attaches itself to a macro, it can cause damage when you run the macro. To help protect your data from the corruption caused by a virus hidden in a macro, you can set one of four macro security levels in Access: *Disable all macros without notification*, *Disable all macros with notification*, *Disable all macros except digitally signed macros*, and *Enable all macros*. The Disable all macros with notification option is the default setting unless you choose another. **Table 11–1** explains each setting in detail.

TABLE 11–1 Macro security level options

MACRO SECURITY LEVEL OPTIONS	DESCRIPTION
Disable all macros without notification	Disables harmful content, but does not notify you.
Disable all macros with notification	Harmful content will be disabled and a notification appears on the Message Bar, just below the Ribbon, letting you know that the macro is disabled unless you click the Enable Content button on the Message Bar.
Disable all macros except digitally signed macros	Only macros that are digitally signed and come from a trusted source will be executed.
Enable all macros	Allows all macros to run and does not offer any protection.

As a best practice, you should set the security level in Access to Disable all macros with notification or Disable all macros except digitally signed macros. In the next Step-by-Step, you will view the macro settings currently set for Access.

Step-by-Step 11.1

1. Open the **Supplies for Happy Pets** file from the drive and folder where your Data Files are stored. Save the database as **Supplies for Happy Pets Database**, followed by your initials.
2. Click the **File** tab on the Ribbon, then click the **Options** button. The Access Options dialog box opens, as shown in **Figure 11–1**. You choose macro security level settings in the Trust Center section of the Access Options dialog box.

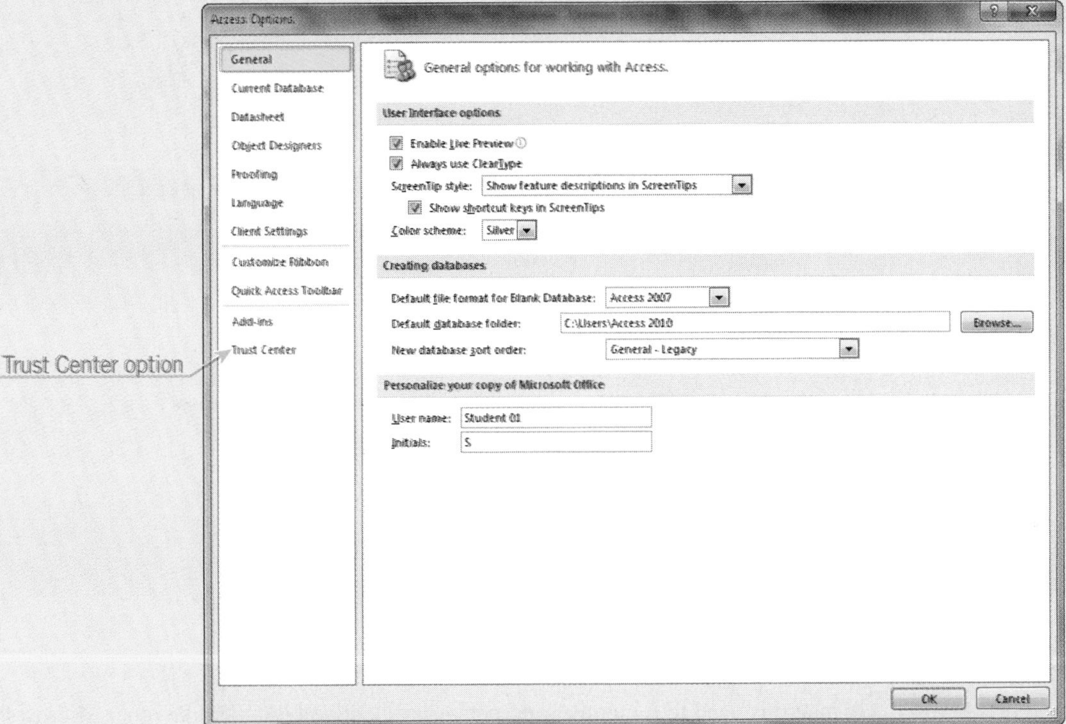

FIGURE 11–1
Access Options dialog box

3. In the Access Options dialog box, click **Trust Center** on the left and then click the **Trust Center Settings** button on the right.

4. Click **Macro Settings** on the left to display the macro settings, as shown in **Figure 11–2**. Notice that the default setting is selected. If your screen does not match Figure 11–2, select the Disable all macros with notification option. Now that you have viewed the settings, you will close the dialog boxes.

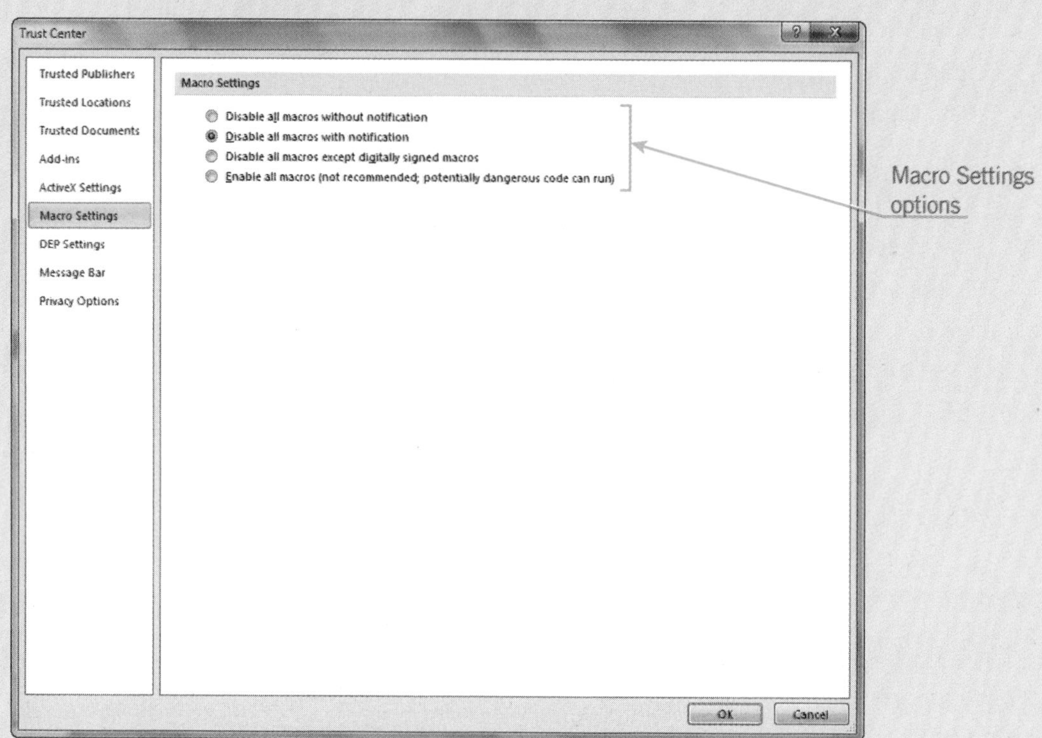

FIGURE 11–2
Trust Center dialog box

5. In the Trust Center dialog box, click **OK**.
6. In the Access Options dialog box, click **OK**.

EXTRA FOR EXPERTS

Macro settings can also be viewed by clicking the Developer tab on the Ribbon, then clicking the Macro Security button in the Code group.

Creating a Macro

A macro is used to remember and perform repetitive tasks. Unlike other Microsoft Office products, such as Microsoft Excel and Microsoft Word, which typically create macros by recording keystrokes as you work, you create an Access macro in the Macro window. To create a macro, you open the Macro window by clicking the Create tab and then clicking the Macro button in the Macros & Code group. In the Macro window, you select actions. Actions perform tasks, such as opening a form. You can select an action using one of several methods. First, you can click the Add New Action arrow in the Macro window, and then scroll through the list until you see the action you want and click on the option. You can also type the action name in the Search box in the Action Catalog to find the action. Another option is to click the plus sign in front of a folder in the Action Catalog to display the actions stored in the folder. The Macro window is shown in **Figure 11–3**.

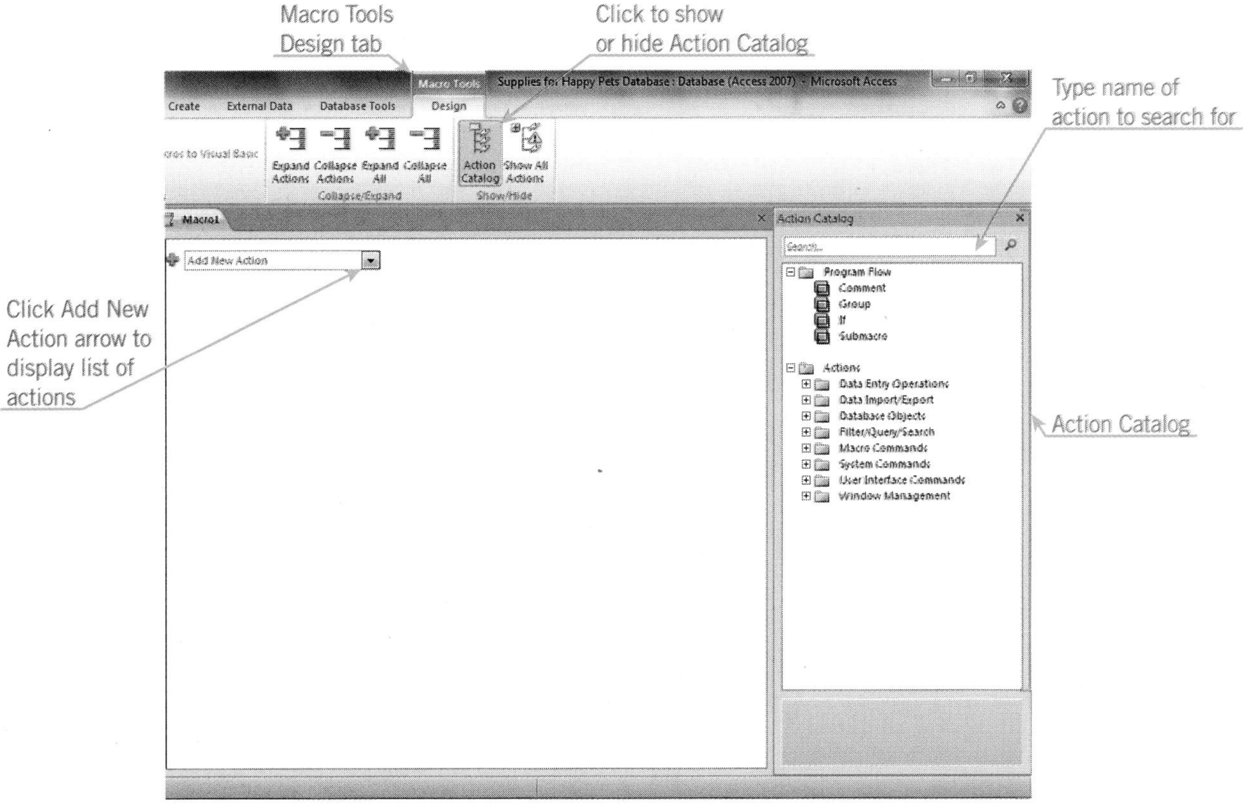

FIGURE 11–3 Macro window for creating macros

After you select an action, Access displays the argument(s) below the action. ***Arguments*** are the additional information that Access needs based on the chosen action. An example of a completed macro is shown in **Figure 11–4**.

VOCABULARY
arguments

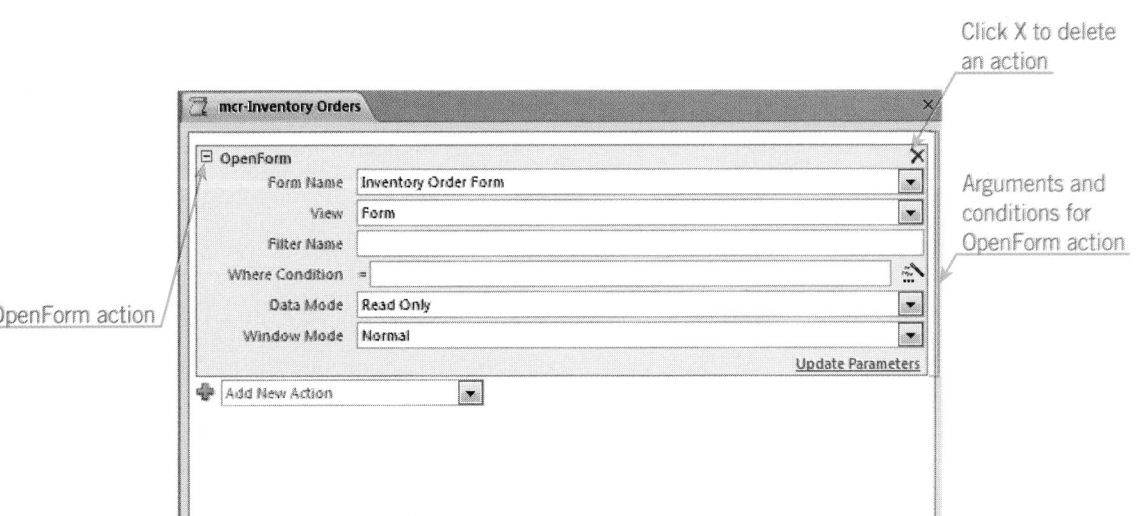

FIGURE 11–4 Macro window with completed macro

While the process for creating macros might sound difficult, it is very easy. In the next Step-by-Step, you will create a macro that opens a form in Read Only view.

Step-by-Step 11.2

1. In the Navigation pane, locate the **Inventory Order Form** and open it to view the contents, as shown in **Figure 11–5**, then, close the form. You will create a macro that opens a form.

Inventory Order Form

Inventory Order Form

Product ID	Product Description	Price	Stock on Hand
150	Wonder Diet - Dogs	$11.92	560
162	Nail Trimmer - Small	$11.03	205
230	Wonder Diet - Cats	$6.26	256
245	Flea Shampoo	$5.62	658
301	Clippers - Hair	$25.37	56
318	Silkie Shampoo	$7.86	632
323	Linatone for Coats	$17.56	248
326	Dog Vitamins	$15.63	77
340	Nail Trimmer - Large	$17.66	963
347	Rawhide Bone - Small	$3.90	145
349	Bird Bell	$15.24	65
358	Lory Nectar - Small	$5.00	25
415	Bird Seed - Parakeets	$8.74	36
417	Cat Vitamins	$14.90	79
486	Flea Collar - Cats	$3.21	130
532	Groomer Brush	$17.24	985

Record: 1 of 27 No Filter Search

FIGURE 11–5
Inventory Order Form

2. Click the **Create** tab, and then click the **Macro** button in the Macros & Code group. The Macro window opens. You will now select an action for the macro.
3. Click the **Add New Action** arrow, scroll through the list, and then click **OpenForm**. See **Figure 11–6**. Next, you will select the arguments for this macro.

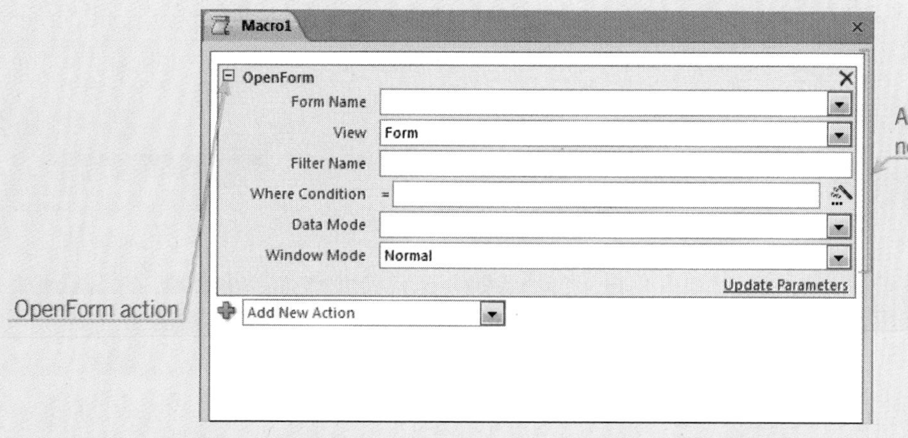

FIGURE 11–6
Macro window with OpenForm action

4. Click the **Form Name** arrow, and then click **Inventory Order Form**. You will now change the data mode for this form to Read Only so that no changes can be made to the form when it is opened.
5. Click the **Data Mode** arrow, and then click **Read Only**. Compare your screen to **Figure 11–7**.

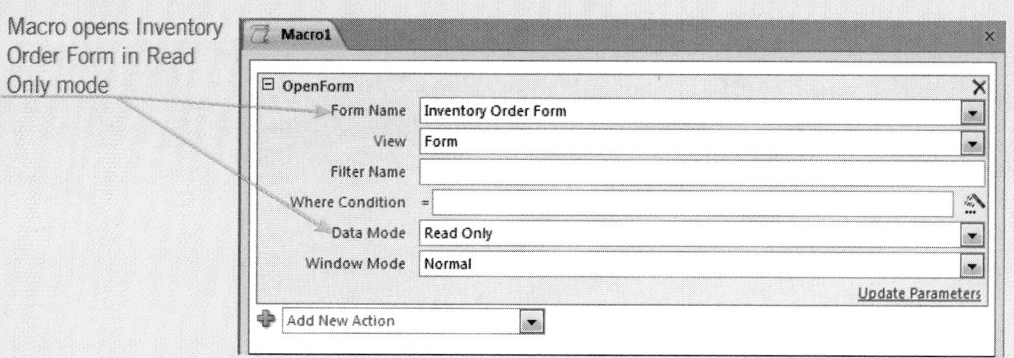

FIGURE 11–7
Macro window with action and arguments

6. Click the **Save** button on the Quick Access toolbar. The Save As dialog box opens, as shown in **Figure 11–8**. Access names each macro consecutively, so your macro number may differ from the figure.

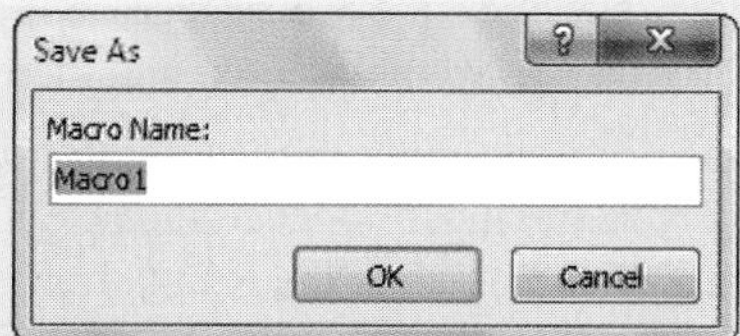

FIGURE 11–8
Save As dialog box for macros

7. Type **mcr-Inventory Orders** in the Macro Name text box, and then click **OK**.

8. Close the macro by clicking the **Close** button in the upper-right corner of the Macro window. A new object group, Macros, appears in the Navigation pane, as shown in **Figure 11–9**.

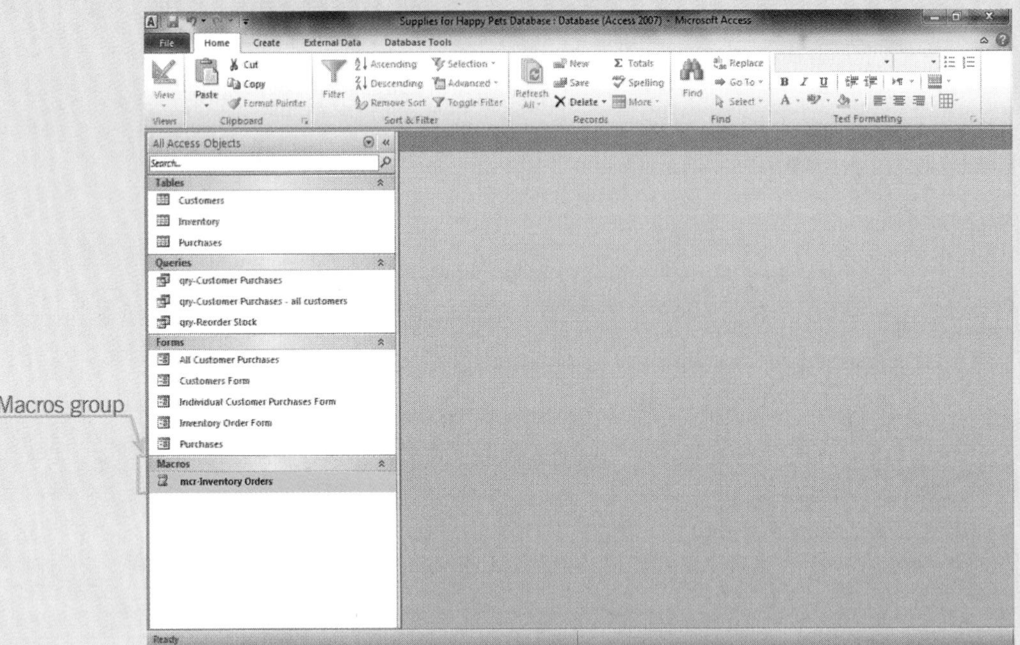

FIGURE 11–9
Navigation pane with Macros group

9. Leave the database open for the next Step-by-Step.

Running a Macro

VOCABULARY
run

After you create and save a macro, you need to ***run*** the macro in order to have it perform the recorded steps. You can run the macro in three ways:

- In the Navigation pane, right-click the macro name, and then click Run on the shortcut menu.
- On the Database Tools tab, click the Run Macro button in the Macro group, select the macro in the Run Macro dialog box, and then click the OK button.
- On the Macro Tools Design tab, click the Run button in the Tools group. This tab appears when you have the macro opened in Design view. The macro that is currently open will run when you click the Run button.

When you run a macro, Access performs the actions listed in the Macro window one after the other. You will now use the three methods mentioned to run the macro that will open the Inventory Order Form in Read Only view.

Step-by-Step 11.3

1. Click the **Database Tools** tab, and then click the **Run Macro** button in the Macro group. The Run Macro dialog box opens, as shown in **Figure 11–10**. Notice that an arrow appears next to the Macro Name text box. The arrow provides a list of all the macros in the database.

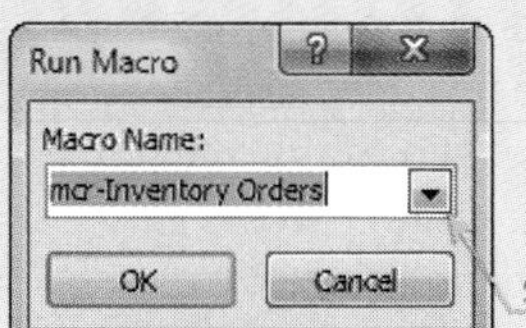

If there is more than one macro in the database, click arrow and select macro from list

FIGURE 11–10
Run Macro dialog box

2. Verify that mcr-Inventory Orders appears in the Macro Name text box, and then click **OK** to run the macro. The Inventory Order Form opens.
3. Click in any text box, such as the Stock on Hand text box, and try to make changes. Notice that changes cannot be made to the form since the form was opened in Read Only mode.
4. Close the form. You will now run the macro by right-clicking the macro in the Navigation pane.
5. In the Macros object group in the Navigation pane, right-click **mcr-Inventory Orders**. The shortcut menu appears, as shown in **Figure 11–11**.

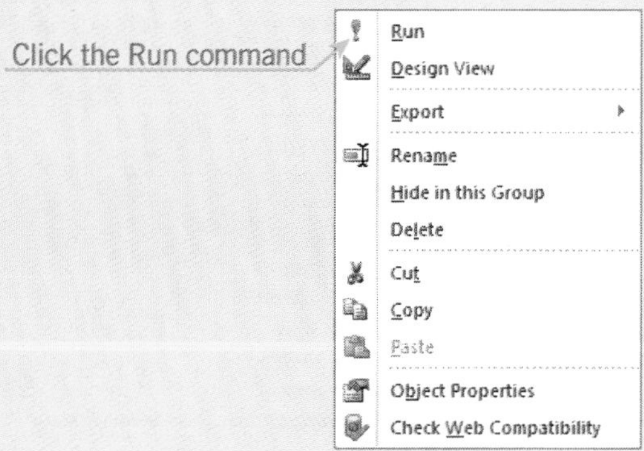

FIGURE 11–11
Shortcut menu for macros

6. Click **Run**. Try to make changes to the data displayed in the form.
7. Close the form.
8. Right-click **mcr-Inventory Orders** in the Navigation pane, and then click **Design View** on the shortcut menu. The Design tab becomes active on the Ribbon.
9. Click the **Run** button in the Tools group.
10. Close the form, but keep the database open for the next Step-by-Step. You will now learn how to edit a macro.

Editing a Macro

VOCABULARY
comment
filter

To edit a macro, you work in the Macro window as you did when you created the macro. When you edit a macro, you can add comments, add new actions, and add additional arguments to an existing action. Because macros often need to be changed, it is a good idea to include a comment for each macro action. A ***comment*** is explanatory text that you can add to a macro that does not affect the way the macro is executed. By adding comments, you can explain the purpose of each action, which is helpful when you are reviewing or editing the macro. Comments appear in green in the macro window, making them easy to identify.

Additional arguments, such as filters, can be added to an action. A ***filter*** displays only certain records based on certain criteria. The filter in a macro is typically based on a query in the database. For example, you may have a query that has criteria entered on a "Stock on Hand field" of less than or equal to 50 (<=50). By adding the filter, the report will only display data for fields with Stock on Hand less than or equal to 50. You will now edit the macro by adding a comment and a filter based on a query.

Step-by-Step 11.4

1. Right-click the **qry-Reorder Stock** query, and then click **Design View** to view the query. Notice that the criteria in the Stock on Hand field is less than or equal to 50, as shown in **Figure 11–12**. Then, close the query.

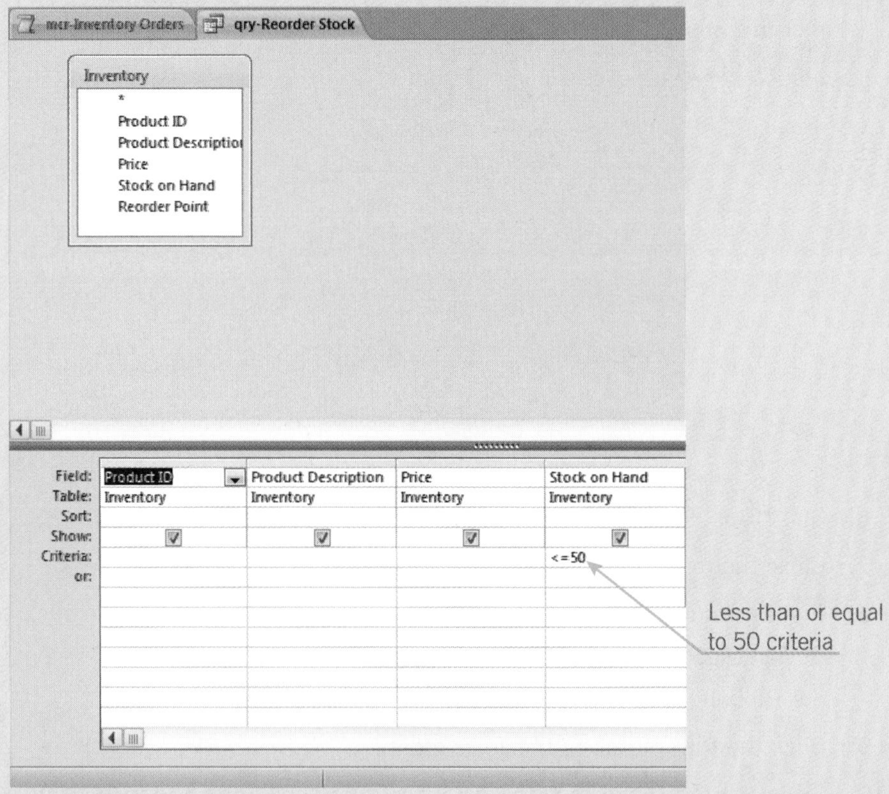

FIGURE 11–12
qry-Reorder Stock in Design view

2. Click the **Design** tab, and then, if necessary, click the **Action Catalog** button in the Show/Hide group to hide the Action Catalog. By hiding the Action Catalog, you have more room to view the macro.

3. Click anywhere in the OpenForm action. Then, click in the **Filter Name** field.
4. Type **qry-Reorder Stock**, as shown in **Figure 11–13**. Next, you will add a comment.

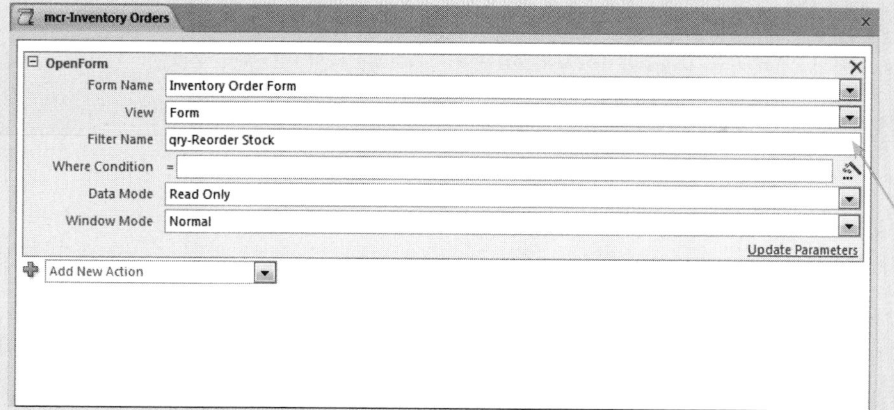

FIGURE 11–13
Macro with filter added

5. Click the **Add New Action** arrow, and then click **Comment**. The Comment box becomes available, as shown in **Figure 11–14**.

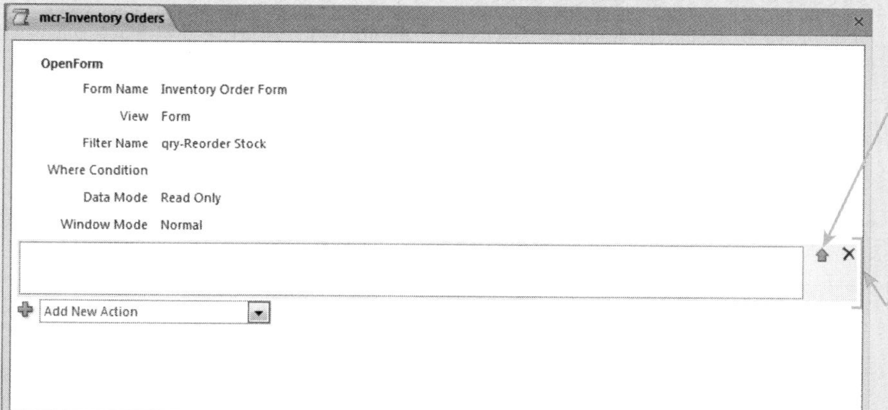

FIGURE 11–14
Macro window with Comment box

6. In the Comment box, type **Opens the Inventory Order Form in Read-Only mode when Stock on Hand is equal to or less than 50.** Next, you will move the comment above the action and arguments.

7. Click the **Move Up** button located to the right of the Comment box, and then click outside the Comment box so you can view the comment in the Macro window. Notice that the comment is displayed in green, as shown in **Figure 11–15**.

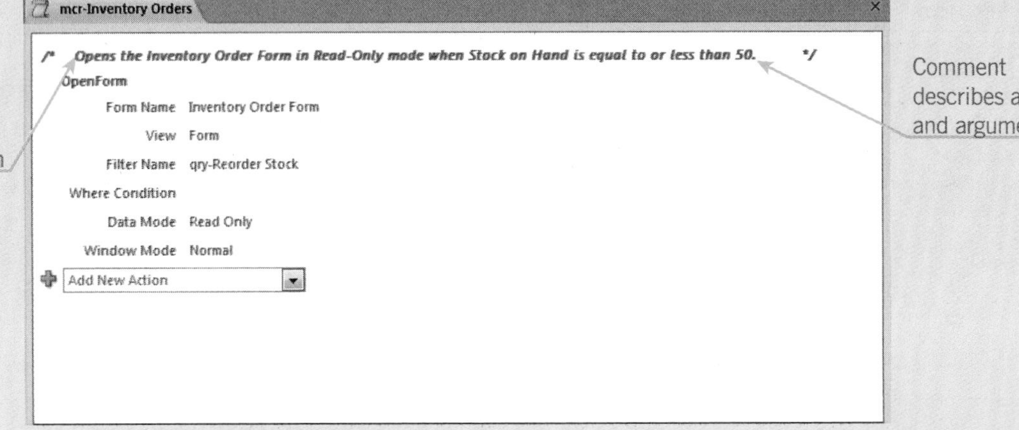

FIGURE 11–15 Comment shown above action

8. Save the macro.
9. Click the **Design** tab, and then click **Run** in the Tools group. The Inventory Order Form is displayed, as shown in **Figure 11–16**.

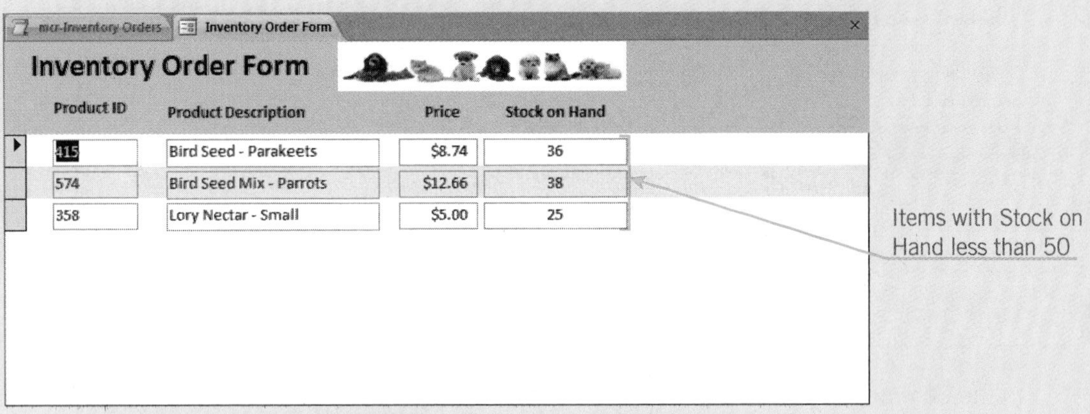

FIGURE 11–16 Form opens when macro runs

10. Close the Inventory Order Form and the Macro window. Keep this database active for the next Step-by-Step.

Creating a Macro to Open and Print Reports

When you record a macro, you can include multiple actions in it. The actions should be entered in a logical order. For example, if you want to print a form, you will probably want to select an action that first opens the report and then select the action to print the form. And, if you did not want the form to remain open after it is printed, you would include another action to close the form. Then, you could enter these actions again to open, print, and close another form.

Creating a macro for these tasks would be helpful if you needed to review the same forms every month. The macro would perform all of these tasks very quickly to save you time. In this next exercise, you will create a macro that opens, prints, and closes multiple forms.

Step-by-Step 11.5

1. Click the **Create** tab, and then click the **Macro** button in the Macros & Code group. You will first add a comment.
2. Click the **Add New Action** arrow, and then click **Comment**. Type **Open, print, and close the All Customer Purchases form.** Next, you will select an action and arguments for the action.
3. Click the **Add New Action** arrow, and then click **OpenForm**.
4. Click the **Form Name** arrow, and then click **All Customer Purchases**. Next, you will select the action to print the form.
5. Click the **Add New Action** arrow, and then click **PrintObject**. You will now select the action to close the form.
6. Click the **Add New Action** arrow, click **CloseWindow**, click the **Object Type** arrow, and then click **Form**.
7. Click the **Object Name** arrow, and then click **All Customer Purchases Form**. Compare your screen to **Figure 11–17**.

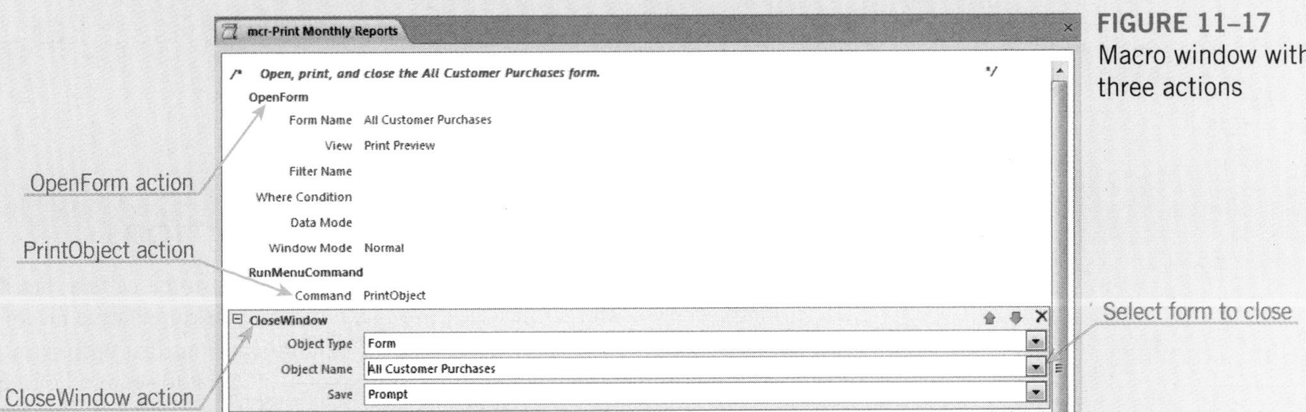

FIGURE 11–17 Macro window with three actions

8. Click the **Add New Action** arrow, and then click **Comment**.
9. Type **Open, print, and close the Inventory Order Form.** Next, you will select an action and arguments.
10. Click the **Add New Action** arrow, and then click **OpenForm**.
11. Click the **Form Name** arrow, and then click **Inventory Order Form**. Next, you will select the action to print the form.
12. Click the **Add New Action** arrow, and then click **PrintObject**. You will now select the action to close the form.

13. Click the **Add New Action** arrow, click **CloseWindow**, click the **Object Type** arrow, click **Form**, click the **Object Name** arrow, and then click **Inventory Order Form**. Compare your screen to **Figure 11–18**.

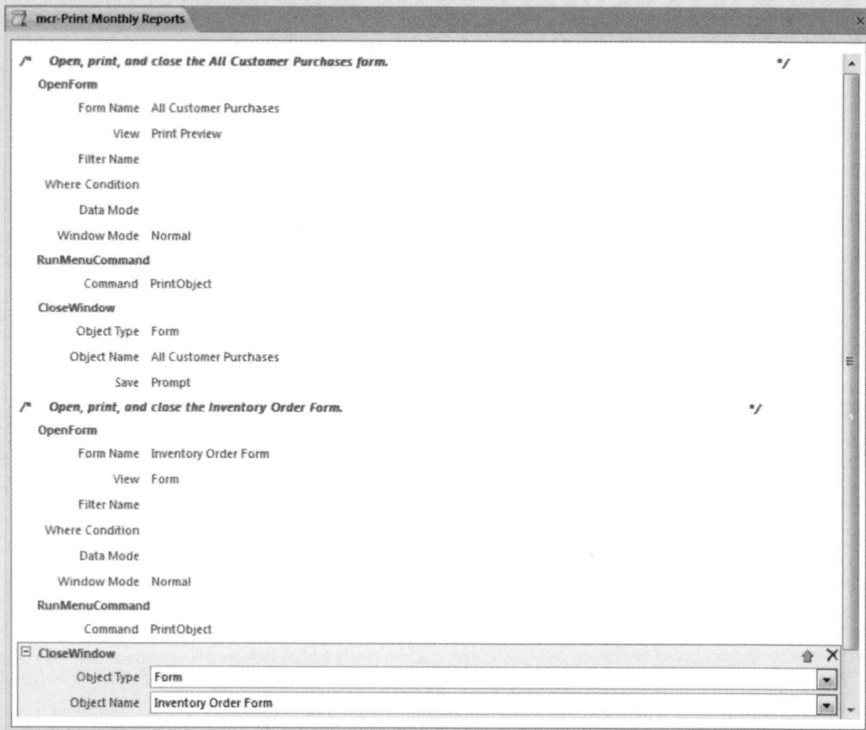

FIGURE 11–18
Macro window with six actions

14. Save the macro as **mcr-Print Monthly Reports**. Keep this screen active for the next Step-by-Step.

Running a Macro with Multiple Actions

It is always a good idea to run a macro after you complete it to be certain that it performs the tasks you chose. Then, if there is a problem, you can edit the macro. For example, you may have created a macro with multiple actions that open, print, and close several forms. Running the macro would double-check to see if all of the forms are closed after the macro runs. In this next exercise, you will run a macro with multiple actions.

Step-by-Step 11.6

1. Click the **Design** tab.
2. Click the **Run** button in the Tools group. You may need to click **OK** each time the Print dialog box opens.
3. Close the Macro window.
4. Keep this screen active for the next Step-by-Step.

Creating an Embedded Macro

VOCABULARY
embedded macro

An ***embedded macro*** is a macro that performs an action within an object, such as a macro that opens a form when you are already viewing another form. An embedded macro can be part of another object, such as a command button. You can create the macro in the Macro window and then attach it to the object. Or, you can create the object and have the macro embedded as you work through a wizard. For example, you may have a form that contains data for customer purchases. However, this form does not contain any information about the customer other than the customer number. As you look through the form with purchases, you may decide that you need to call a customer to ask a question about a purchase. This information is contained in another form that has the customer's name, address, and telephone number. You decide to create a command button that will open the customer form while you are viewing the purchases form. This type of command button, that performs a macro action, would have an embedded macro. In other words, the macro action that the command button performs by opening another form is embedded in the command button.

Embedded macros have events that run the macro, such as On Click. This event indicates that when you click on the object, the macro will run. **Table 11–2** shows several popular form events.

TABLE 11–2 Form events

EVENT NAME	ACTION THAT TRIGGERS THE EVENT
On Load	When the form loads
On Unload	When the form is closed
On Click	When the user clicks the left mouse button on any control on the form
On Dbl Click	When the user double-clicks the left mouse button on any control on the form
Before Update	Before changed data is updated
On Delete	When the user begins to delete a record, but before the record is deleted

As you create a command button in an existing form with form operations, Access will add an event that is applicable to the object. For example, you click a command button to open another form. Therefore, the embedded macro is attached to the On Click command. In this next exercise, you will create an embedded macro using the Command Button Wizard.

Step-by-Step 11.7

1. Open the **Customers Form** in Form view. Notice that this form has the company's name, address, and telephone number, as shown in **Figure 11–19**. Close the form.

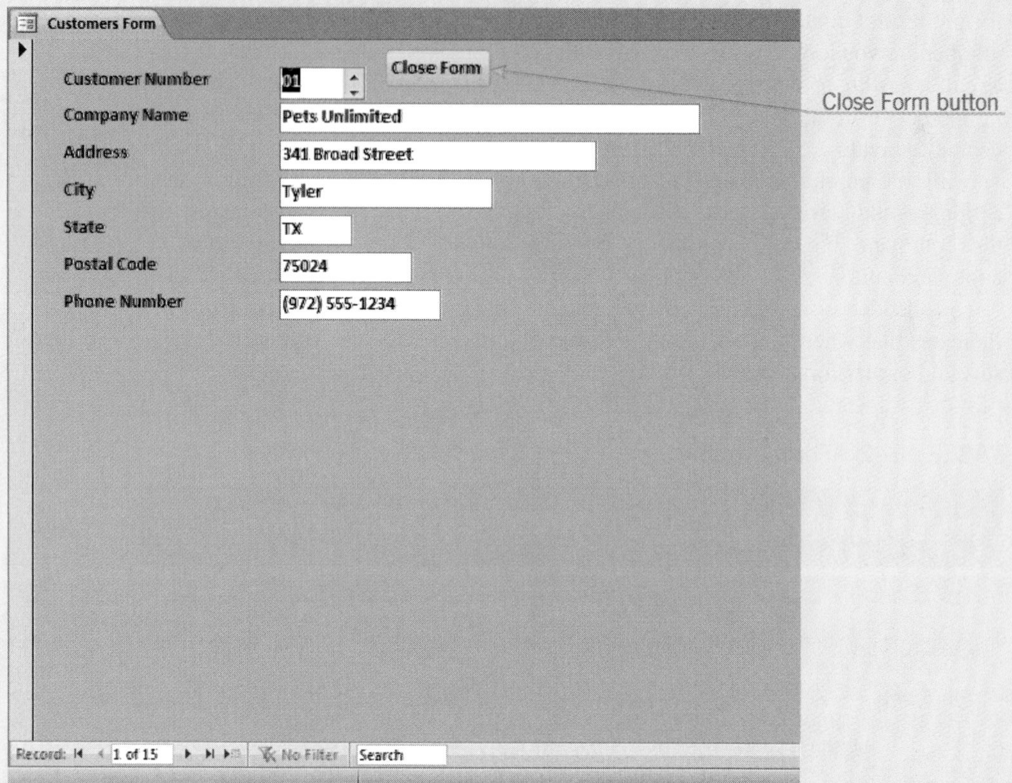

FIGURE 11–19
Customers Form

2. Open the **Individual Customer Purchases Form**, type **05** in the Enter Parameter Value dialog box, and then press **Enter**. You will now add the embedded macro to the Individual Customer Purchases Form.
3. Click the **Home** tab, click the **View** button arrow, and then click **Design View** in the Views group.
4. Click the **Design** tab, and then click the **Button** button in the Controls group.
5. In the Form Header section, draw a rectangle about 1" wide by ½" tall, as shown in **Figure 11–20**. The Command Button Wizard dialog box opens.

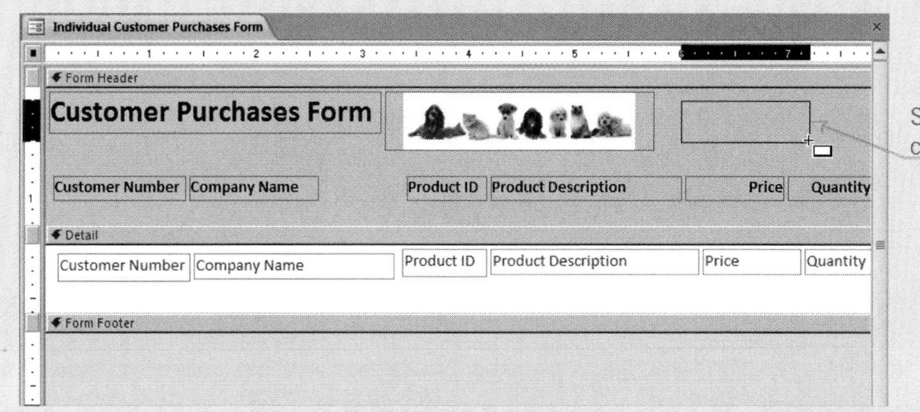

FIGURE 11–20
Button drawn in Form Header

6. In the Command Button Wizard dialog box, click **Form Operations** to view the actions associated with form operations.
7. Click **Open Form**, as shown in **Figure 11–21**. Next, you will select the form you want to open.

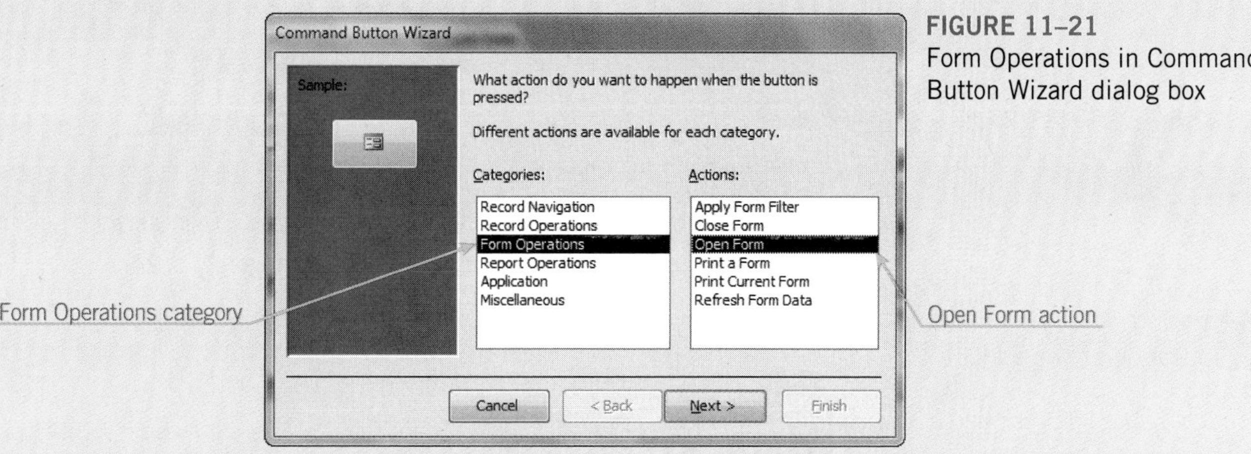

FIGURE 11–21
Form Operations in Command Button Wizard dialog box

8. Click **Next**, and then click **Customers Form**. You will now select the option to display only specific information from the form selected.
9. Click **Next**, and then click **Open the form and find specific data to display**, as shown in **Figure 11–22**.

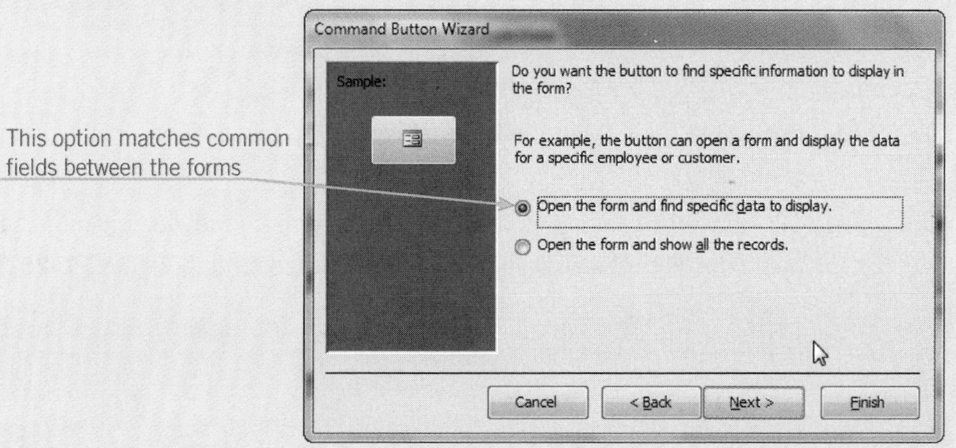

FIGURE 11–22
Choosing what data the button will display in the form

10. Click **Next**. You will now link the field from the Individual Customer Purchases Form with the field in the Customers Form.

11. Click the **Customer Number** field in the Individual Customer area, and then click **Customer Number** in the Customers Form area. Then, click the **double-headed arrow** in the middle of the dialog box. See **Figure 11–23**. You will now enter the text you want to appear on the button.

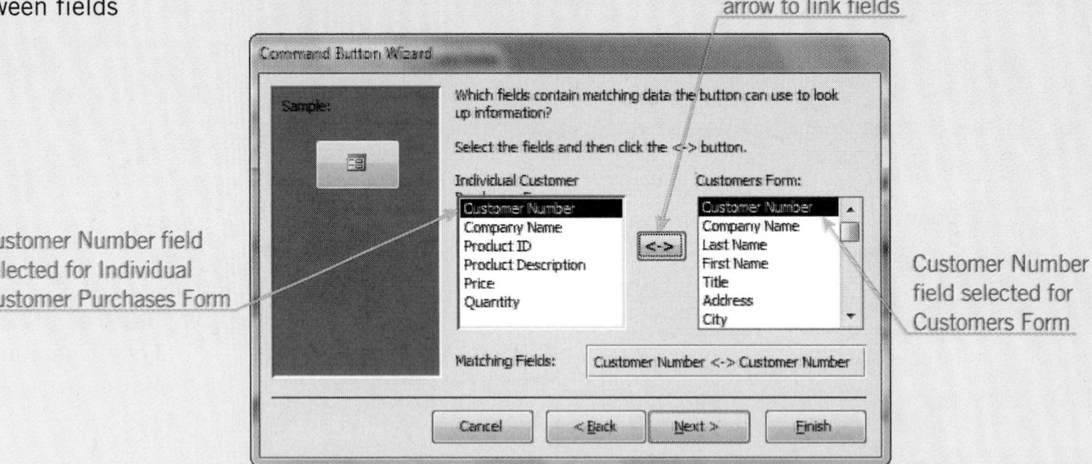

FIGURE 11–23
Completed link between fields

12. Click **Next**, and then click the **Text** option button. Click in the text box and type **Open Customers Form**, as shown in **Figure 11–24**.

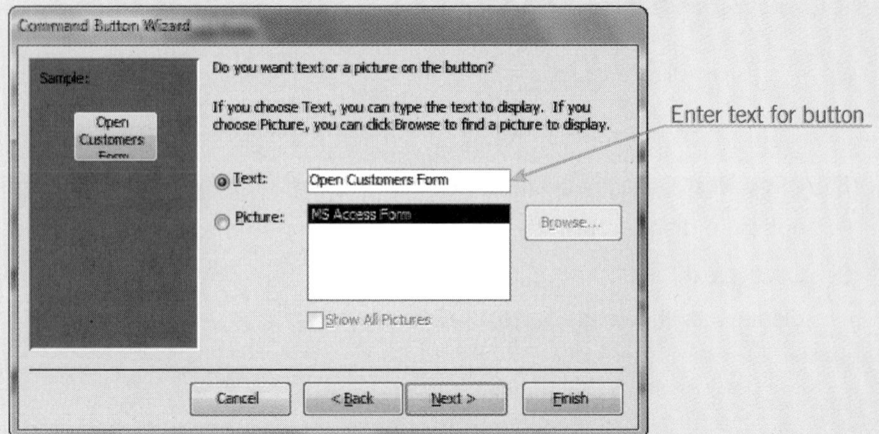

FIGURE 11–24
Text to appear on button added

13. Click **Next**. Type **Open Customers Form** in the text box for a meaningful name, and then click **Finish**.

14. Click the **Home** tab, click the **View** button arrow in the Views group, and then click **Form View**. Compare your completed form to **Figure 11–25**.

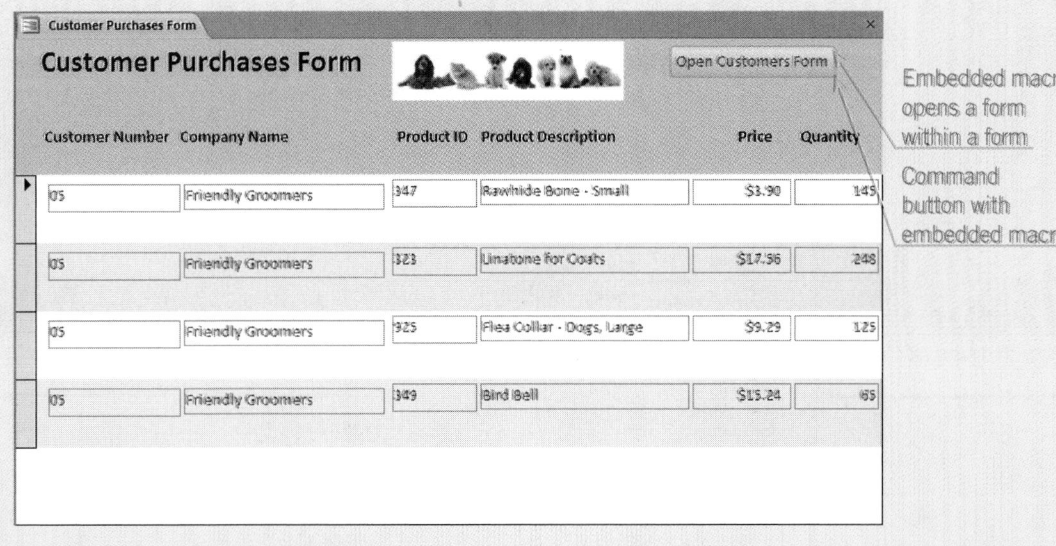

FIGURE 11–25
Completed form

15. Save the form. Keep this screen active for the next Step-by-Step.

Viewing and Running the Embedded Macro

When you create a command button with an embedded macro, you can view the event and the embedded macro using the Property Sheet. The Event tab in the Property Sheet displays a list of events, and any embedded macros will be listed next to the events that have them.

To run the macro, you simply click on the command button. In this next exercise, you will view the Property Sheet and the embedded macro. Then, you will run the macro.

Step-by-Step 11.8

1. Click the **Home** tab, click the **View** button arrow in the Views group, and then click **Design View**.
2. Click on the **command button** you created in the Form Header to select it.
3. Click the **Design** tab, and then click the **Property Sheet** button in the Tools group to display the Property Sheet pane.

4. Click the **Event** tab in the Property Sheet pane. The On Click event shows the embedded macro, as shown in **Figure 11–26**. Next, you will display the embedded macro.

FIGURE 11–26
Property Sheet for command button

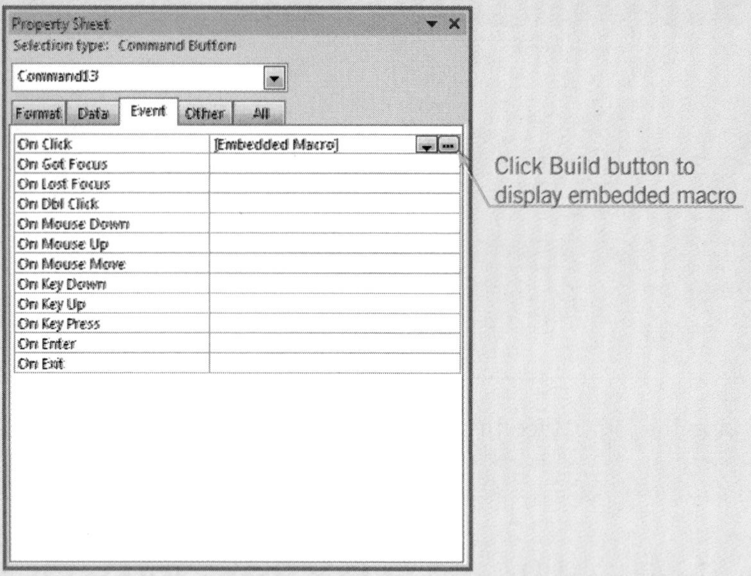

5. Click the **Build** button. The embedded macro displays as shown in **Figure 11–27**.

FIGURE 11–27
Embedded macro

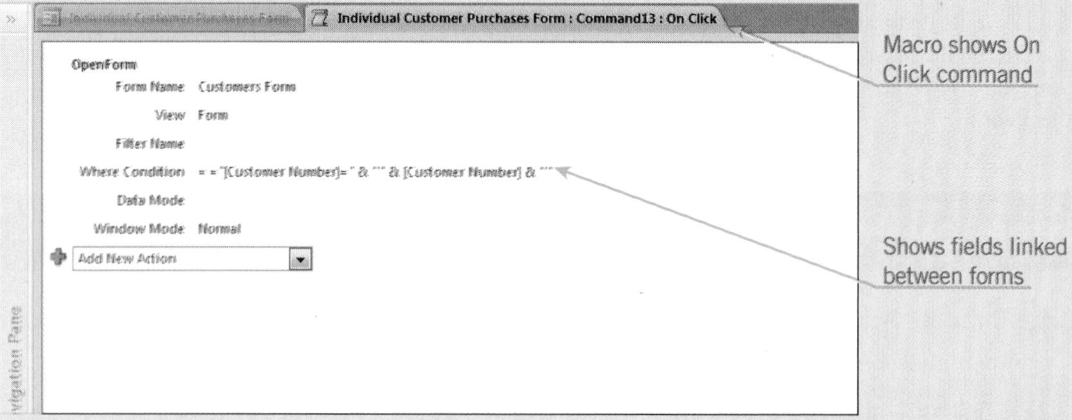

6. Click the **Close** button on the Macro window to close it.
7. Click the **Property Sheet** button to close the Property Sheet pane.
8. Close the **Individual Customer Purchases Form**. Next, you will open the Individual Customer Purchases Form so you can test the command button.
9. Double-click **Individual Customer Purchases Form** in the Navigation pane to open the form. The Enter Parameter Value dialog box opens.
10. Type **05** for the parameter value, and then press **Enter**. The form opens with Customer Number 05 displayed.
11. Click the **Open Customers Form** command button to display this information for Customer Number 05. See **Figure 11–28**.

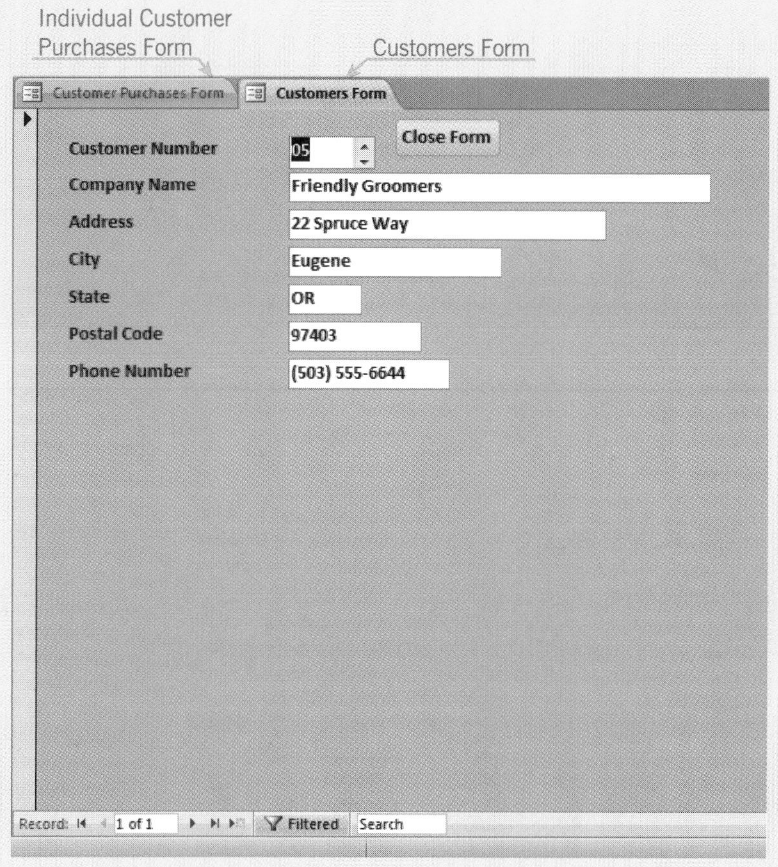

FIGURE 11–28
Customers Form opened from command button

12. Click the **Close Form** command button to close the Customers Form.
13. Close the Individual Customer Purchases Form.
14. Close the database.

SUMMARY

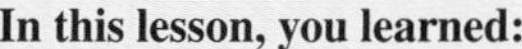

In this lesson, you learned:

- You can view and change macro security settings.
- Recording a macro can save you time for repetitive tasks.
- Running a macro performs the tasks that were recorded.
- Macros can be edited after they are created.
- You can create a macro that opens and prints multiple reports.
- When you run a macro with multiple actions, the actions are performed based on their order in the macro.
- An embedded macro is a macro that can be part of a command button in a form.
- When you view an embedded macro, it appears in the macro window, and you can run the macro by clicking the command button.

VOCABULARY REVIEW

argument
code
comment
embedded macro
filter
macro
run
virus

REVIEW QUESTIONS

TRUE / FALSE

Circle T if the statement is true or F if the statement is false.

T F 1. Macros are not susceptible to virus attacks.

T F 2. A macro is used to remember and perform repetitive tasks.

T F 3. There is only one method to run a macro.

T F 4. After a macro is created, it can be edited.

T F 5. Macros can have more than one action.

FILL IN THE BLANK

1. A(n) ________________ is a macro that performs an action within an object, such as opening a form when you are already viewing a form.
2. The macro security level option that allows all macros to run and does not offer any protection is the ________________ option.
3. ________________ is (are) the additional information that Access needs to perform a task based on the chosen action.
4. A(n) ________________ is explanatory text that you can add to a macro but does not affect the operation of the macro.
5. The On Click event will run a macro when the object is ________________.

WRITTEN QUESTIONS

Write a brief answer to the following questions.

1. What does the *Enable all macros* security level option do?

2. Explain the difference between actions and arguments.

3. Write a brief description of the three different ways you can run a macro.

4. Explain how you can add a filter to a macro.

5. Write a brief description on how you would add a comment to a macro.

PROJECTS

If you have a SAM 2010 user profile, your instructor may have assigned an autogradable version of the indicated project. If so, log into the SAM 2010 Web site at *www.cengage.com/sam2010* to download the instruction and start files.

PROJECT 11–1

1. Open the **Internet Sales** file from the drive and folder where your Data Files are stored. Save the database as **Internet Sales Database**, followed by your initials.
2. Create a macro that opens the Employees form in Read Only data mode.
3. Save the macro as **mcr-View Employees Form**.
4. Close the macro.
5. Run the macro, and then try to make changes to the Employees form.
6. Close the form.
7. Close the database.

PROJECT 11–2

1. Open the **Regional Sales** file from the drive and folder where your Data Files are stored. Save the database as **Regional Sales Database**, followed by your initials.
2. Create a macro that opens the Sales Information form, prints the form, and then closes the form.
3. Add the comment **Opens, prints, and closes the Sales Information Form** to the macro.
4. Move the comment to the top of the macro window.
5. Save the macro as **mcr-Print Regional Data**.
6. Close the macro window.
7. Run the macro for the **East** region.
8. Close the database.

PROJECT 11–3

1. Open the **Book Sales** file from the drive and folder where your Data Files are stored. Save the database as **Book Sales Database**, followed by your initials.
2. Create an embedded macro in the Book Orders form that opens the Sales Department Form.
3. Use the Employee ID field as the field that links the two forms in the macro.
4. Save the Book Orders form.
5. View the Book Orders form in Form View, and then click on the macro button to test it.
6. Close the Sales Department Form.
7. Close the Book Orders form.

CRITICAL THINKING

ACTIVITY 11–1

You are the new database administrator for the Computer Sales Company. You have viewed the **Computer Sales** database. Since you frequently need to print both the Employees form and the Regional Sales form, you decide to create a macro that opens, prints, and closes both the Employees and the Regional Sales forms. Save the database as **Computer Sales Database** followed by your initials.

ACTIVITY 11–2

Think of a database that you could use for school, work, or around your home. Describe a macro that you would create in the database and what task you would have it perform.

Estimated Time:
2.5 hours

LESSON 12

Automating Database Processes

OBJECTIVES

Upon completion of this lesson, you should be able to:

- Create a splash screen.
- Create an AutoExec macro.
- Test an AutoExec macro.
- Create a navigation form.
- Create a second navigation form.
- Design the main navigation form.
- Change startup options.
- Bypass startup options.

VOCABULARY

AutoExec macro
hierarchical
navigation form
splash screen
startup options

Introduction

As you add queries, forms, and reports to your database, you will need to manage access to these objects to make the database easy to use without jeopardizing the security of the data. This lesson begins by teaching you how to create a splash screen that appears when the database is opened. The splash screen instantly familiarizes users with how the database will look. An AutoExec macro is used to display the splash screen. In this lesson, you will also use navigation forms to design and implement user-friendly menus so that users can work with only those parts of the database they need. In addition, you will learn how to restrict the Ribbon tabs and the Navigation pane so that users cannot change or modify the design of your database.

Creating a Splash Screen

VOCABULARY
splash screen

A ***splash screen*** is a form that appears when you open a database that welcomes the user to the database. A splash screen can contain information such as a company's name and the same themes used in the database. You can further personalize the splash screen by adding the company logo and a label with text, such as *Welcome to the Database*, at the top of the form. Next, you will create a splash screen using a background color and an image for the Online Sales Database.

Step-by-Step 12.1

1. Open the **Online Sales** file from the drive and folder where your Data Files are stored. Save the database as **Online Sales Database**, followed by your initials.
2. On the Ribbon, click the **Create** tab and then click **Blank Form** in the Forms group.
3. Click the **Design** tab, and then click the **Add Existing Fields** button in the Tools group to close the Field List pane on the right.
4. Click the **Form1 form area**, and then click the **Format** tab on the Ribbon.
5. Click the **Background Color** button arrow, and then click **Dark Purple, Accent 4, Lighter 60%** in the Font group.
6. Click the **Background Image** button arrow, and then click **Browse.**
7. Navigate to the drive and folder where your Data Files are stored, click **Online Sales Logo.tif**, and then click **OK**.

TIP

You may need to select All Files from the drop-down menu to the right of File name in the Insert Picture dialog box. Compare your screen to **Figure 12–1**.

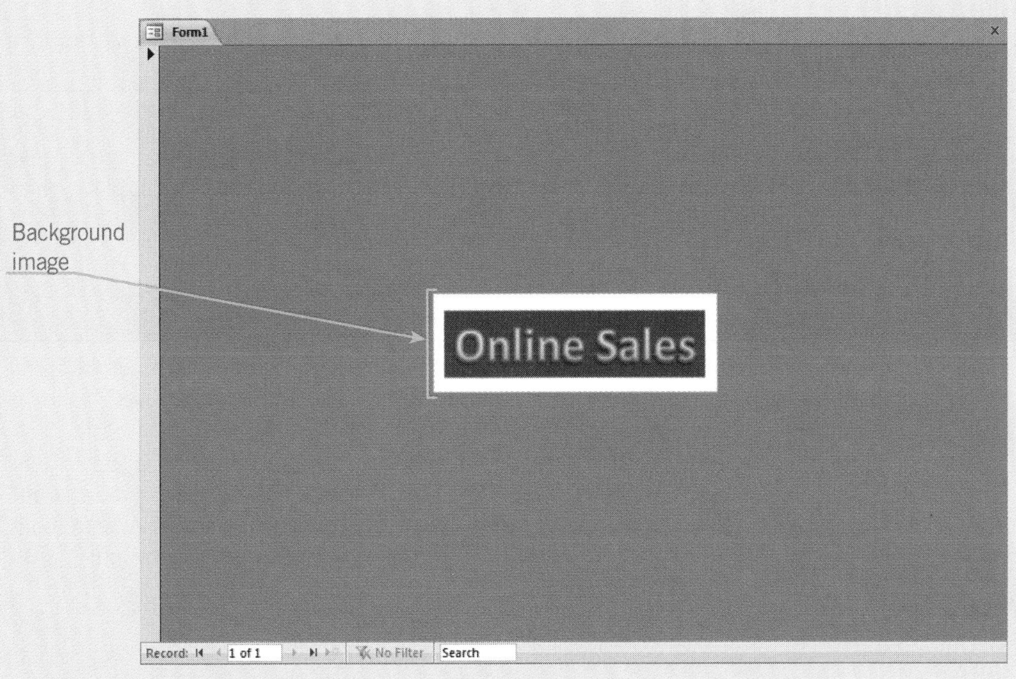

FIGURE 12–1
Splash screen with background image

8. Click the **Design** tab, click the **View** button arrow, and then click **Layout View**.
9. Click the **Label** button in the Controls group, and then click in the upper-left corner of the form.
10. Type **Welcome to the Online Sales Database**, and then press **Enter**.
11. Click the **Format** tab, click the **Font Size** button arrow, and then click **16**.
12. Click the **Bold** button **B** in the Font group, click the **Font Color** button arrow **A**, and then click **Black, Text 1** in the Theme Colors section.
13. Resize the label until it is approximately the same size as shown in **Figure 12–2**. All of the text should be on one line.

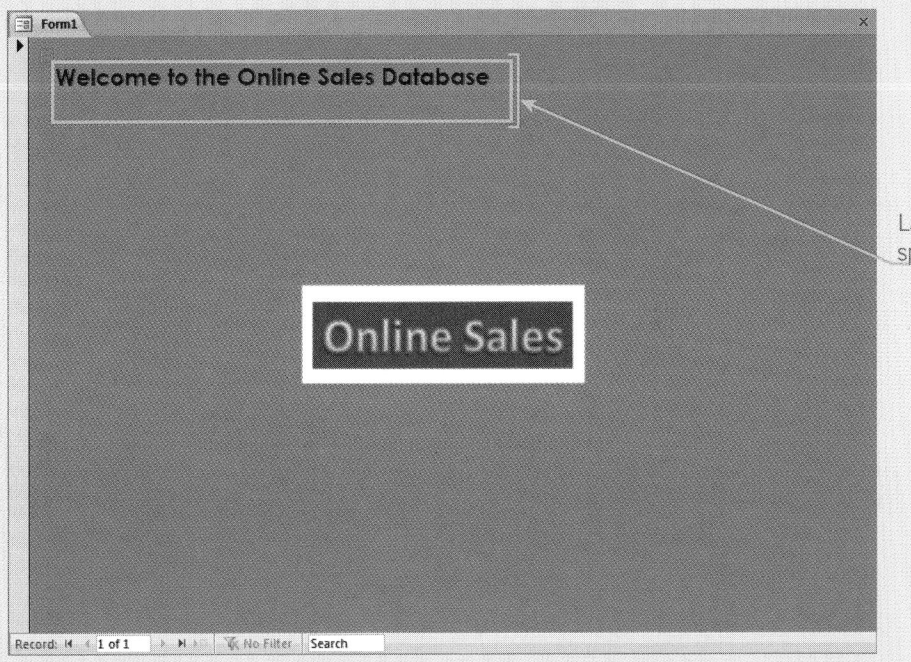

FIGURE 12–2
Splash screen with label

14. Click the **Save** button on the Quick Access toolbar, and then save the form as **Splash Screen**. Close the form, but remain in this database for the next Step-by-Step.

Creating an AutoExec Macro

VOCABULARY
AutoExec macro

An ***AutoExec macro*** allows you to have one or more actions automatically execute when the database is opened. For example, you may want to display a certain form, such as a splash screen, when a user opens the database. An AutoExec macro is perfect for that task. You can only have one AutoExec macro per database file.

To create an AutoExec macro, you use the Macro window to select actions you want Access to perform when the database is opened, and then you save the macro using the name AutoExec. Whenever a user opens a database, Access looks for an AutoExec macro; if one is present, the macro runs before any other tasks are performed. In this next exercise, you will create an AutoExec macro using the OpenForm action, with the Splash Screen form as the argument.

Step-by-Step 12.2

1. Click the **Create** tab, and then click the **Macro** button in the Macros & Code group. Next you will add the OpenForm action so you can open a form when the macro runs.
2. In the Macro1 window, click the **Add New Action** drop-down arrow and then click **OpenForm**. Next you will select the form name.
3. Click the **Form Name** drop-down arrow, and then click **Splash Screen**. See **Figure 12–3**.

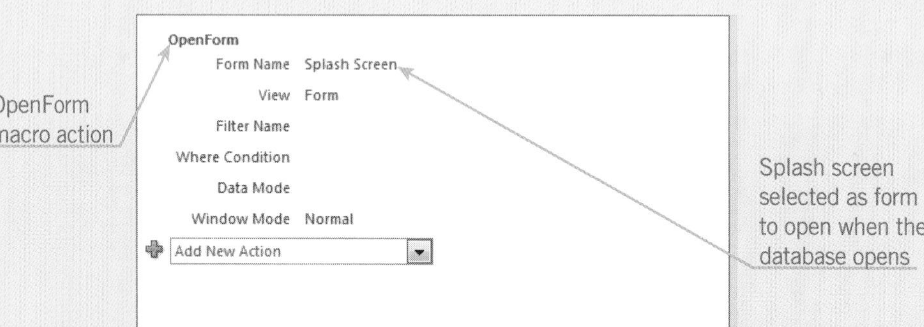

FIGURE 12–3
AutoExec macro

4. Click the **Save** button on the Quick Access toolbar.
5. Type **AutoExec** for the macro name, and then click **OK**.
6. Close the Macro window.

Testing an AutoExec Macro

After you create an AutoExec macro, you should test it to be certain that the macro performs the actions that you want. To run an AutoExec macro, you need to close the database and then reopen the database to run the macro. In this next exercise, you will close and reopen the database to see the splash screen appear.

Step-by-Step 12.3

1. Click the **File** tab, and then click **Close Database**.
2. Open the **Online Sales Database**. The splash screen should appear.
3. Click the **Close Form** button on the splash screen.
4. Remain in this database for the next Step-by-Step.

Creating a Navigation Form

A ***navigation form*** is a special kind of form that has both a main form control and subform controls automatically built in. The use of navigation forms in a database is similar to navigating a Web site. Well-designed Web sites typically have top-level navigation commands and lower-level commands.

VOCABULARY
navigation form

VOCABULARY
hierarchical

Navigation forms in a database typically appear in a hierarchical format to help users select various database objects easily. ***Hierarchical*** refers to the different levels of automation. Forms in the lower level of the hierarchy are produced first. For example, a lower-level navigation form lets you select which report you want to view. Then, you create the navigation form that will be used as the main menu. A main menu form has tabs that let you select the lower-level forms. See **Figures 12–4 and 12–5**.

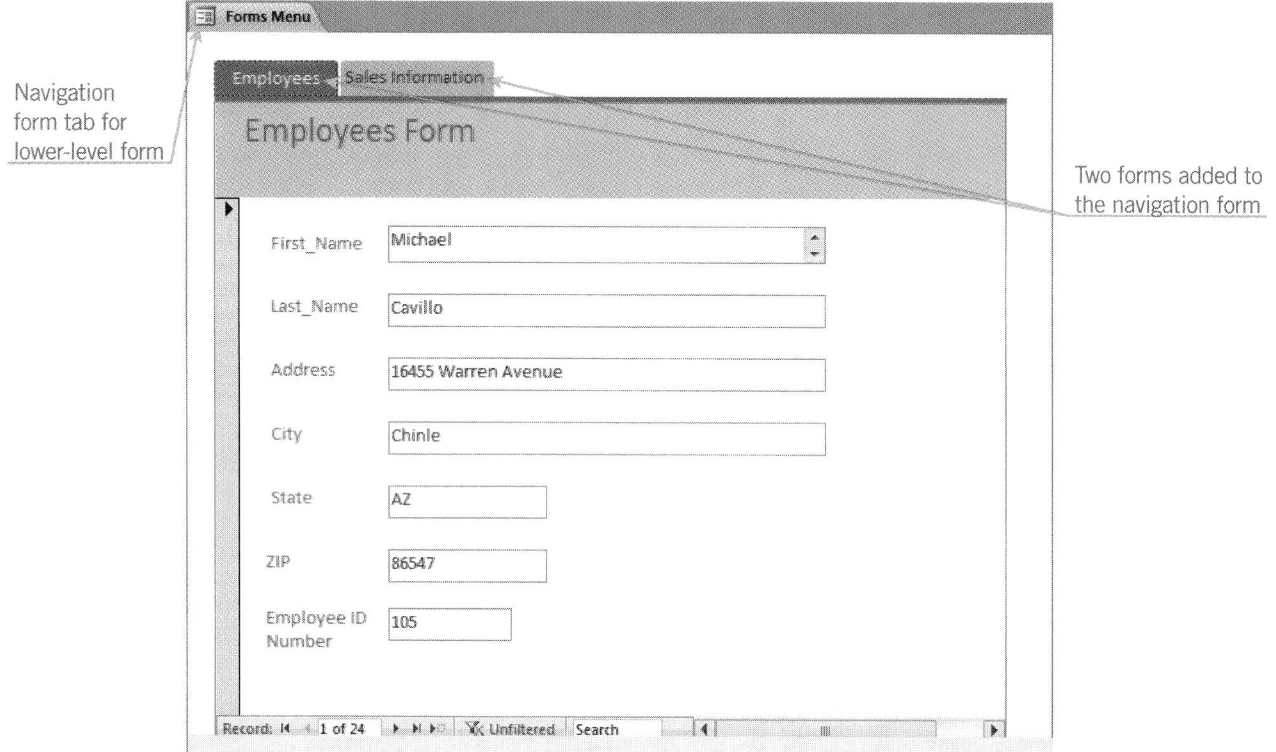

FIGURE 12–4 Lower-level navigation form

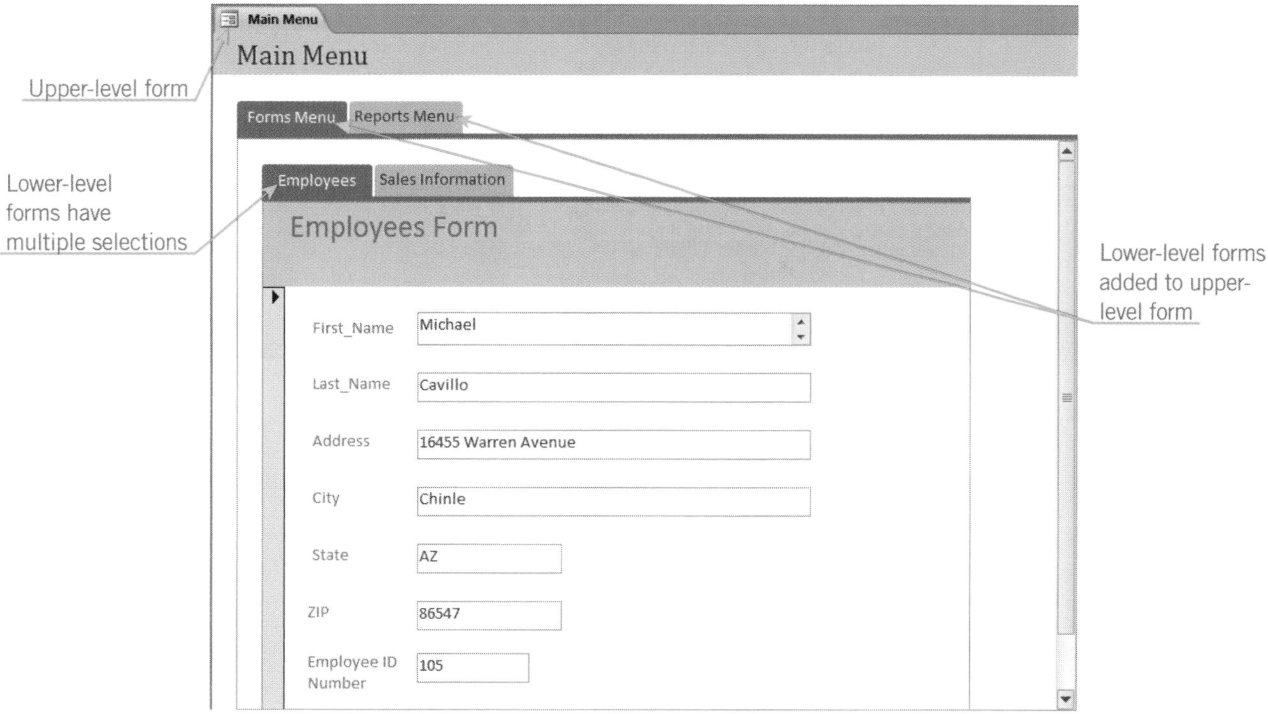

FIGURE 12–5 Upper-level navigation form with lower-level forms added

A navigation form can display tabs for forms, reports, and queries and acts as a main menu for the database. Selecting the tabs on this main menu navigation form lets you instantly view these objects. To add an object, such as a report, to the navigation form, you drag the object directly from the Navigation pane onto the form. A new tab is added to the navigation form; and, selecting this tab lets you view the report in the subform control. The report is still available in the Navigation pane, but you will also have access to it in the navigation form.

Before you begin designing navigation forms, you should decide on the type of layout style you want to use. **Figure 12–6** shows the various types of navigation forms in Access. The icons next to each layout style show you how the tabs will be arranged.

EXTRA FOR EXPERTS

In previous versions of Access, you might have used a Switchboard for the purpose of creating menus in a hierarchical format. With Microsoft Office Access 2010, navigation forms provide this same functionality.

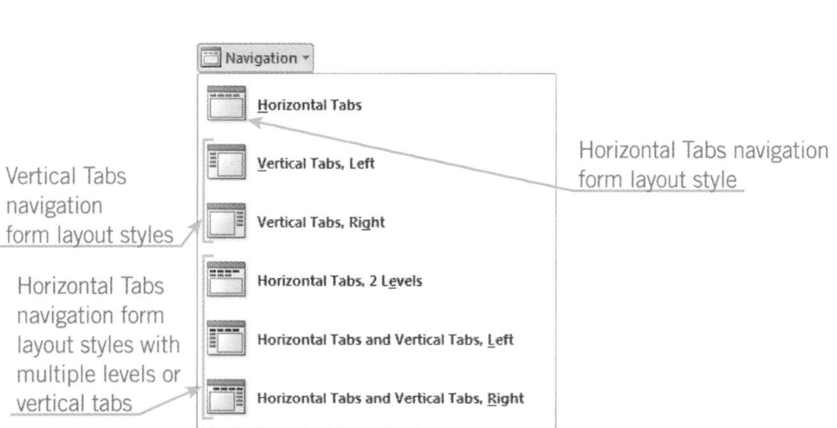

FIGURE 12–6 Types of navigation form layout styles

Once you decide on the navigation form layout style, you should use this same style throughout the database so users do not need to familiarize themselves with a new layout when they select another navigation form. In this next exercise, you will create a Forms Menu, since it is at the lower level of the hierarchy.

Step-by-Step 12.4

1. On the Ribbon, click the **Create** tab, click the **Navigation** button arrow in the Forms group, and then click **Horizontal Tabs**.
2. Close the **Close** button on the Field List pane to close it. The Horizontal Tabs navigation form opens, as shown in **Figure 12–7**. Next, you will add a form to the navigation form.

FIGURE 12–7 Navigation form with horizontal tabs

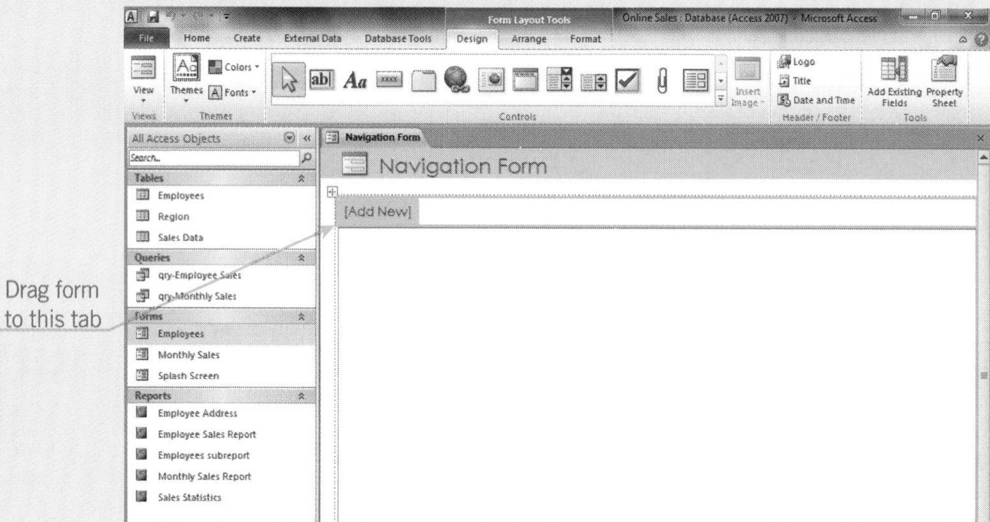

3. In the Navigation pane, drag the **Employees** form in the Forms group on top of the **Add New** tab, as shown in **Figure 12–8**. Release the mouse button. The Employees form appears as a subform in the navigation form but remains available in the Navigation pane. See **Figure 12–9**.

FIGURE 12–8 Form icon appears as you drag object

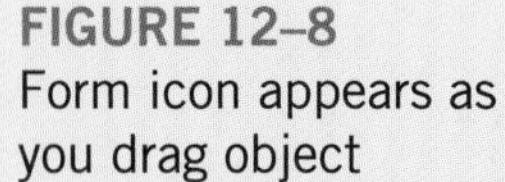

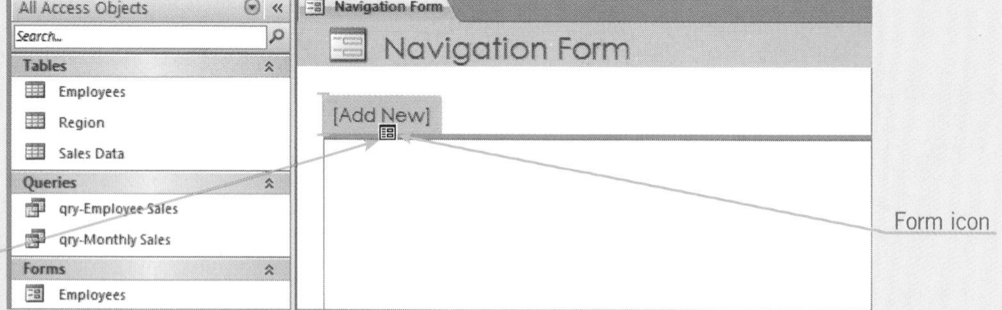

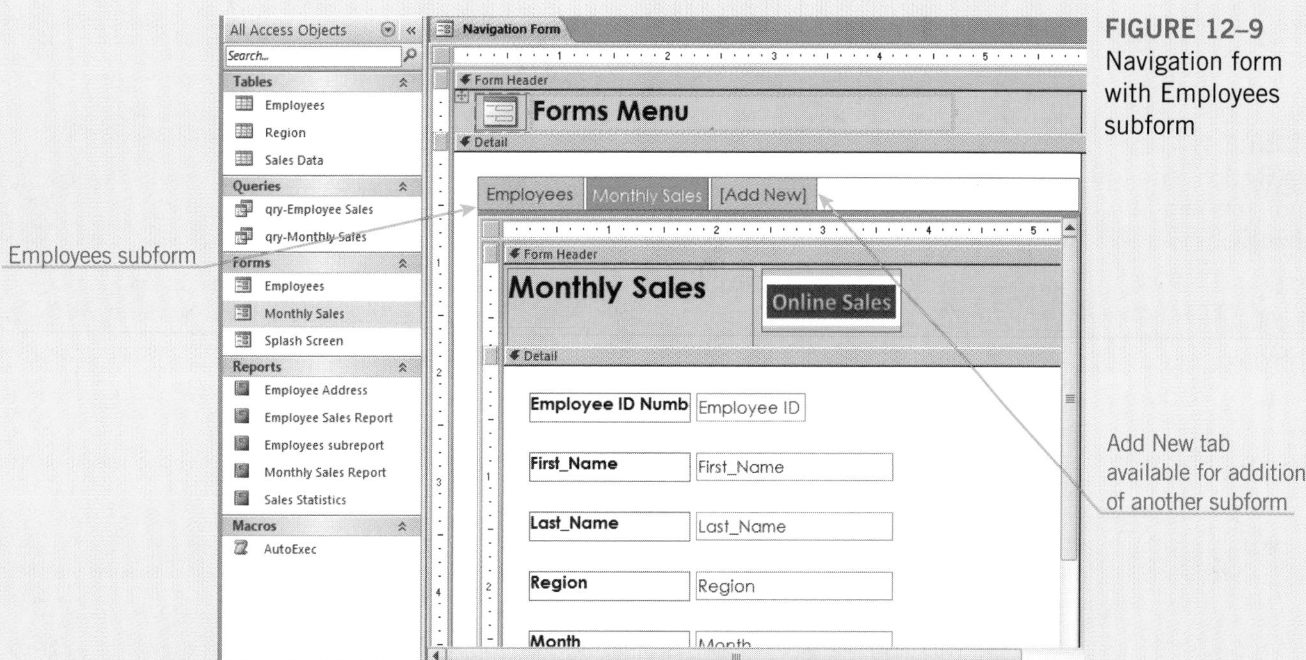

FIGURE 12–9 Navigation form with Employees subform

4. Drag the **Monthly Sales** form in the Navigation pane to the **Add New** tab. The Monthly Sales form is added as a subform.
5. On the Design tab, click the **View** button arrow in the Views group and then click **Design View**.
6. Click in the title in the Form Header where it says Navigation Form, and then type **Forms Menu**.
7. Click outside the label, and then click on the label again to select it. Next, you will change the font for the label.

8. Click the **Format** tab, click the **Bold** button **B** in the Font group, click the **Font Color** button arrow, and then click **Black, Text 1**. See **Figure 12–10**.

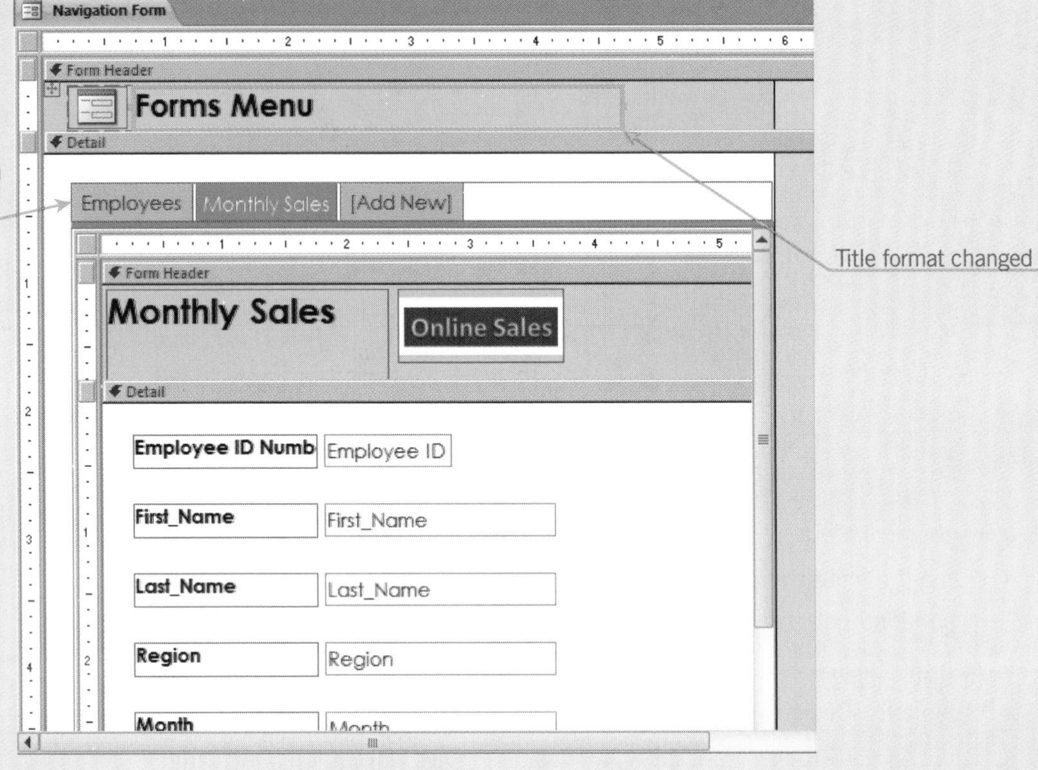

FIGURE 12–10
Navigation form with subforms and title change

9. Click the **Design** tab, click the **View** button arrow, and then click **Form View**. Click each form tab to display the subforms. Notice that when a form is selected, such as Monthly Sales, the tab appears in a darker color. Also notice that in Form view, the Add New tab is not available. See **Figure 12–11**.

TIP

You can change the title in Layout view.

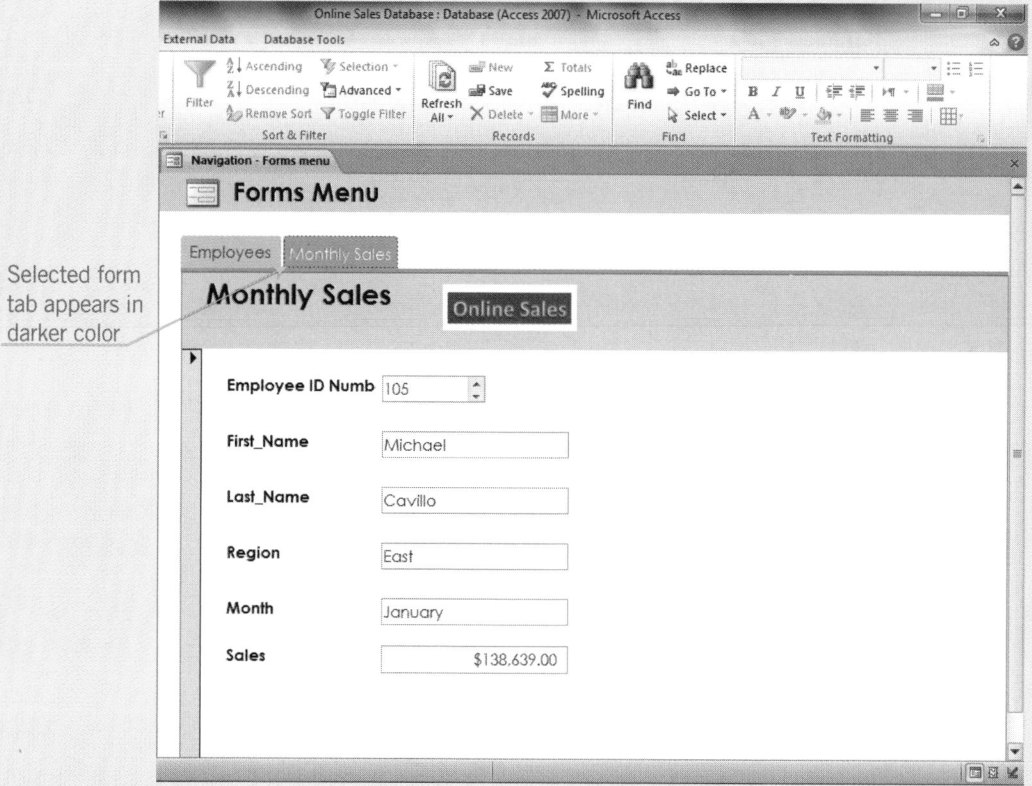

FIGURE 12–11 Forms Menu with Monthly Sales tab selected

10. Save the form as **Navigation Form – Forms Menu**, and then close the form.
11. Keep the database open for the next Step-by-Step.

Creating a Second Navigation Form

You will need to create more than one navigation form. At least two lower-level forms will need to be placed on an upper-level navigation form so that you have more than one selection on the upper-level form. The second navigation form will be at the same lower level as the previous navigation form you created. In this exercise, since you have completed the Forms Menu, you will now create a navigation form for the Reports Menu.

Step-by-Step 12.5

1. Click the **Create** tab, click the **Navigation** button arrow, and then click **Horizontal Tabs** in the Forms group. You will now add subreports to the navigation form.
2. Close the Field List pane, and then drag the **Employee Sales Report** in the Reports group in the Navigation pane to the **Add New** tab. Next, you will add the Monthly Sales Report to the navigation form.

3. Drag the **Monthly Sales Report** to the **Add New** tab. Next, you will add a third report to the navigation form.
4. Drag **Sales Statistics** to the **Add New** tab.
5. Click in the **navigation form** title until the insertion point appears, select the text, and then change the title to **Reports Menu**.
6. Click outside the label, and then click on the label again to select it. Click the **Format** tab, and then click the **Bold** button **B**. Click the **Font Color** button arrow A, and then click **Black, Text 1**. See **Figure 12–12**.

FIGURE 12–12 Navigation form for reports

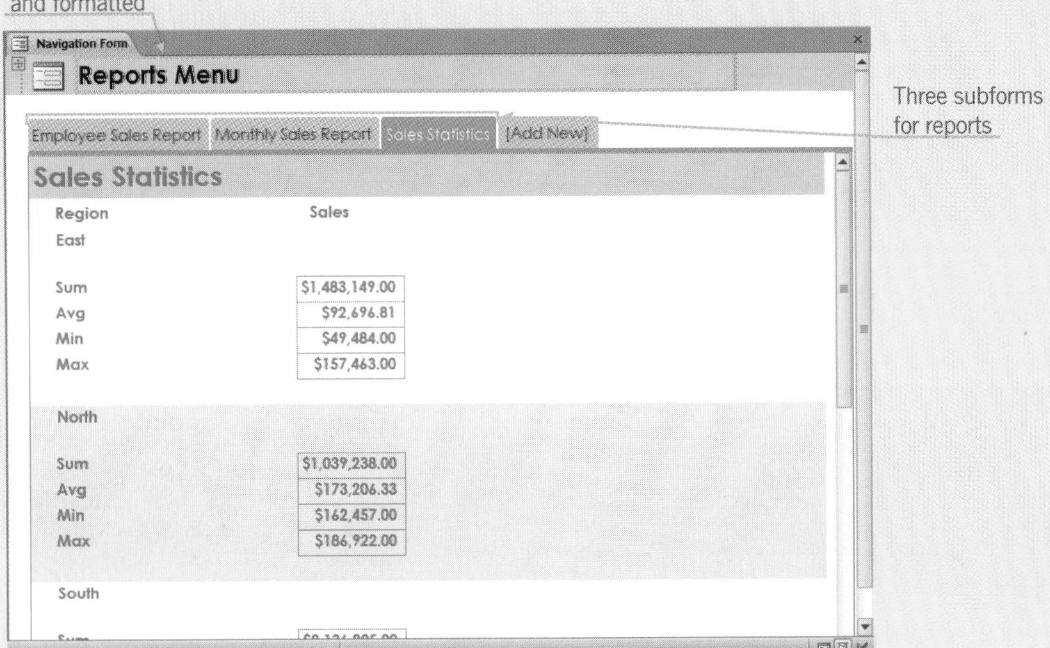

7. Save the form as **Navigation Form – Reports Menu**, and then close the form.
8. Keep the database open for the next Step-by-Step.

Designing the Main Navigation Form

The main navigation form is the upper-level form. It serves as the main menu, letting you select the lower-level navigation forms in the main form. The main navigation form is created last using the other navigation forms that already exist. In this next exercise, you will use the same layout, Horizontal Tabs, and bring the Forms Menu and Reports Menu into this form. Then, you will change their tab names to *Forms Menu* and *Reports Menu*.

Step-by-Step 12.6

1. Click the **Create** tab, click the **Navigation** button arrow in the Forms group, and then click **Horizontal Tabs**. You will now add the Navigation Form – Forms Menu to the navigation form.
2. Drag **Navigation Form – Forms Menu** in the Forms group in the Navigation pane to the **Add New** tab. Next, you will add the Reports menu to the navigation form.
3. Drag the **Navigation Form – Reports Menu** to the **Add New** tab.
4. Click the **Navigation Form** title and change the title to **Main Menu**. Add the Bold format and the Font Color **Black, Text 1** to the title.
5. Save the form as **Navigation Form – Main Menu**. See **Figure 12–13**.

FIGURE 12–13
Main Menu form in Layout view

6. Switch to Design view, and then click **Navigation Form – Forms Menu** to view it, as shown in **Figure 12–14**. Next, you will change the Navigation Form – Forms Menu tab title.

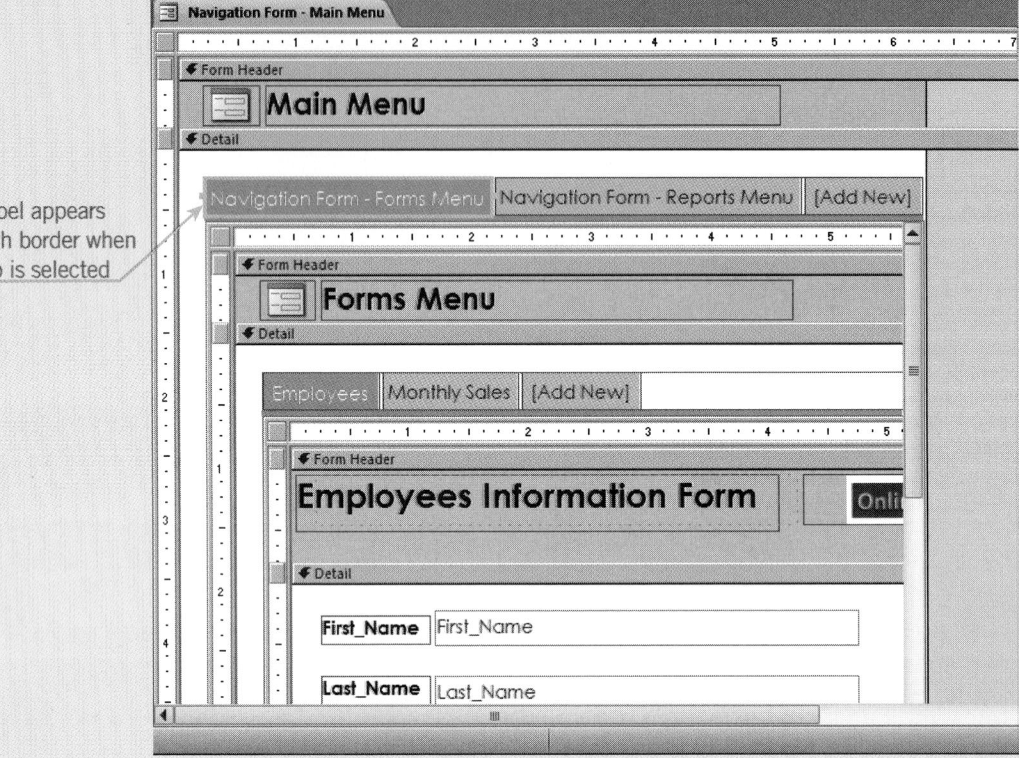

FIGURE 12–14 Selected label on tab title

7. Click in the **Navigation Form – Forms Menu** tab title and then change the title to **Forms Menu**.
8. Verify that the text is still selected, and then apply the bold format and the Black, Text 1 color to the text. You no longer need the title Forms Menu in the Form Header because it is repetitive.
9. Click the **Forms Menu** title in the Form Header section of Navigation Form – Forms Menu, press **Delete**, and then delete the form object in the Form Header section.
10. Place your mouse pointer over the top of the Detail section bar and drag it up until the Detail section bar is directly below the Form Header, as shown in **Figure 12–15**.

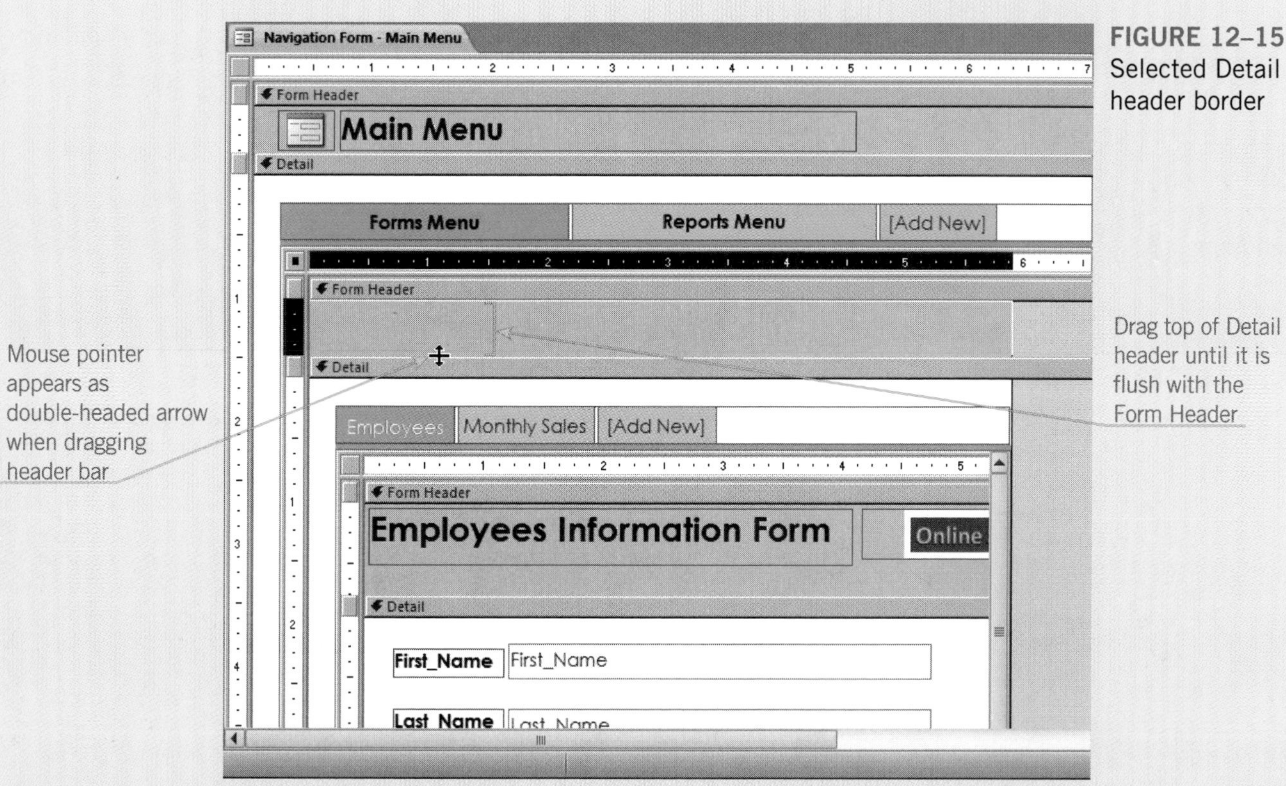

FIGURE 12–15 Selected Detail header border

11. Repeat steps 7 through 10 for the Navigation Form – Reports Menu, changing the title to Reports Menu, then compare your screen to **Figure 12–16**.

FIGURE 12–16 Revised Reports Menu tab

12. Place the mouse pointer over the right edge of the form border and drag to the **8"** mark on the horizontal ruler, as shown in **Figure 12–17**, to make additional room for the report.

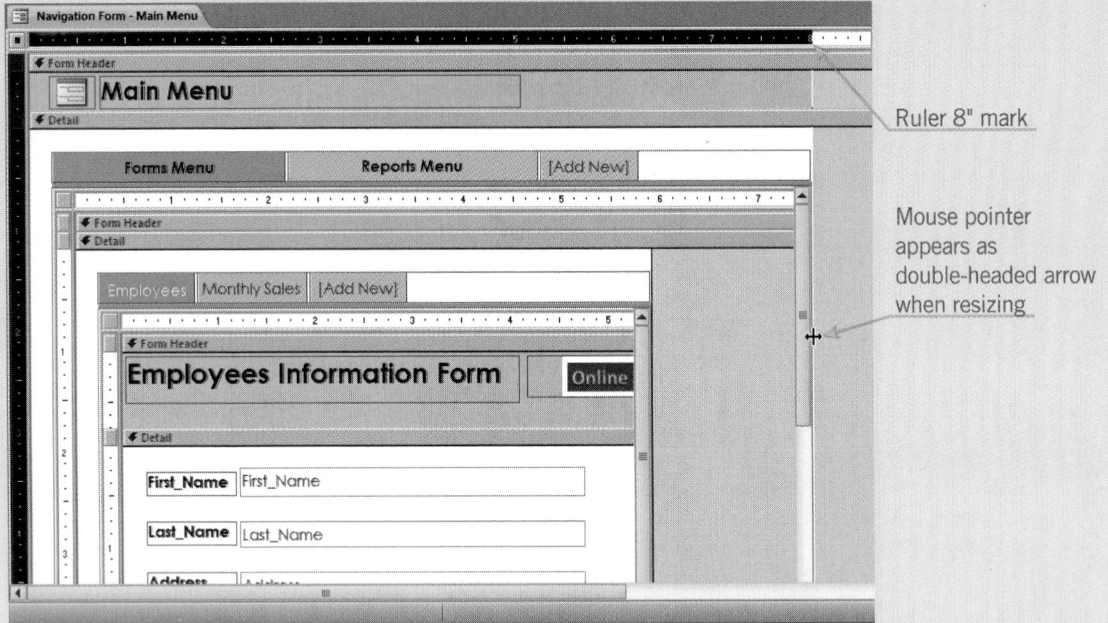

FIGURE 12–17 Resizing Main Menu form

13. Save and close the form.

14 Keep the database open for the next Step-by-Step.

Changing Startup Options

VOCABULARY
startup options

Startup options are options that Access performs when the database is opened. You can specify which startup options are in place. For example, you can choose startup options that hide the Navigation pane and the Ribbon or open a form. If you choose a startup option that opens a form, such as a main menu, it will appear automatically or after the splash screen is closed. Adding startup options can secure the database by hiding selected tabs on the Ribbon and restricting access to menu commands. These actions allow only authorized users, such as the database manager, to work with tables and other objects in Design view. These startup options are located in the Access Options dialog box.

Step-by-Step 12.7

1. Click the **File** tab, and then click **Options** to open the Access Options dialog box.
2. Click **Current Database** in the left pane and view the options available for the current database, as shown in **Figure 12–18**.

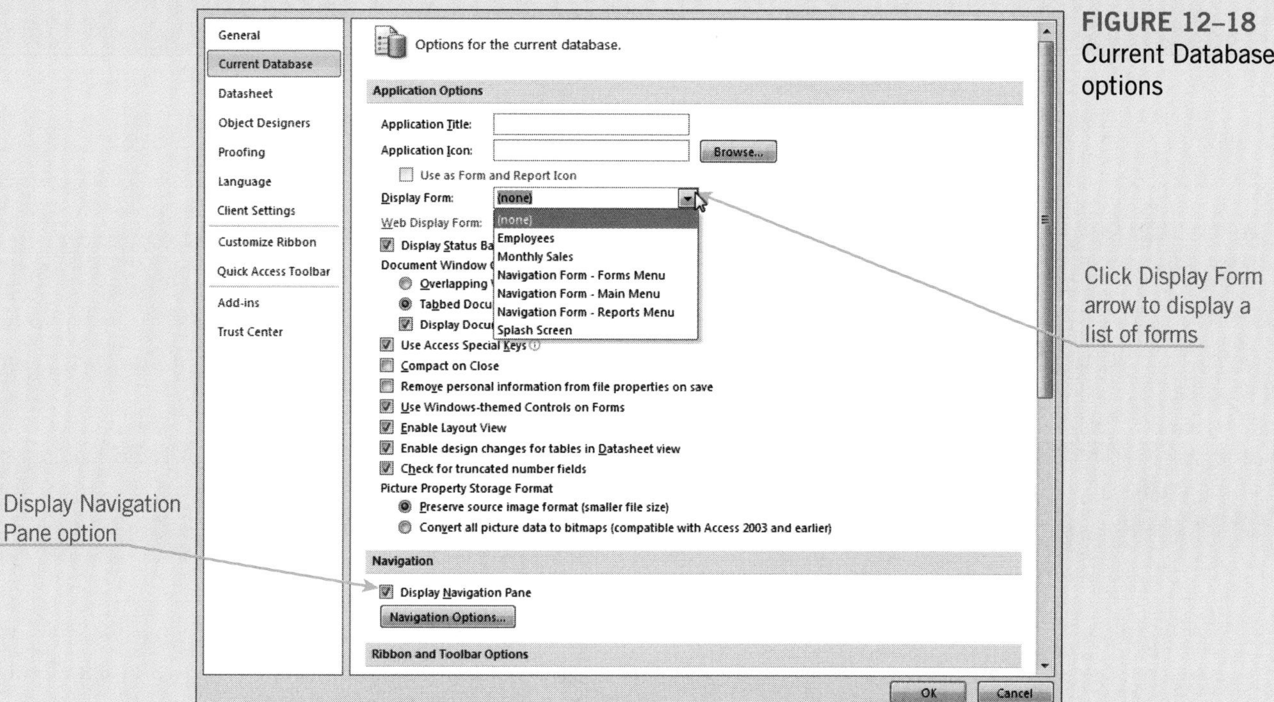

FIGURE 12–18 Current Database options

3. Click the **Display Form** drop-down arrow to view a list of forms that can be selected to appear first after the splash screen closes.
4. Click **Navigation Form – Main Menu** to select it. This form will be the first one to appear after the splash screen closes. Next, you will opt to remove the Navigation Pane from view when the database opens.
5. Click the **Display Navigation pane** check box to deselect it. Next, you will deselect the Allow Full Menus feature so that most of the Ribbon is not displayed.

6. Scroll down in the Current Database options and click the **Allow Full Menus** check box to deselect it, then compare your screen to **Figure 12–19**.

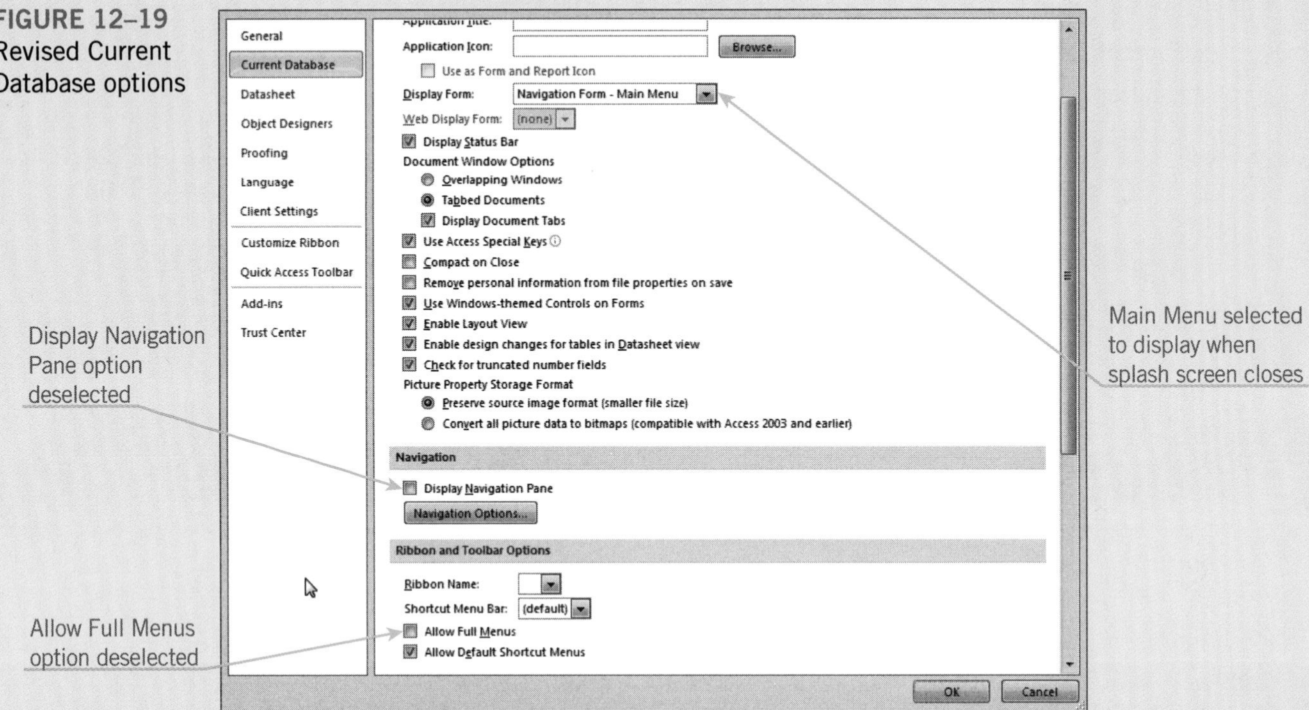

FIGURE 12–19 Revised Current Database options

7. Click **OK** to save the changes. A message box appears stating that the current database needs to be closed before the options can take effect.
8. Click **OK**.
9. Close the **Online Sales Database** file, and then open it to view the startup options.

As shown in **Figure 12–20**, the Navigation form and only the Home and File tabs appear with limited options.

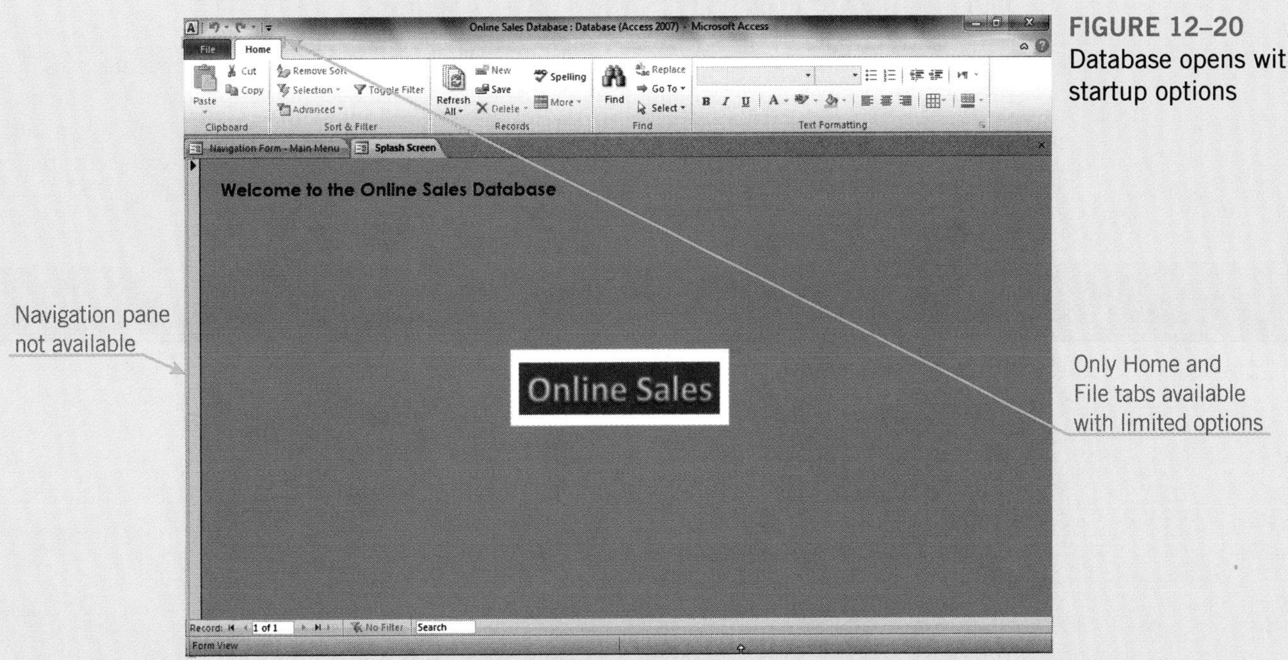

FIGURE 12–20 Database opens with startup options

10. Click the **Close** button on the splash screen. The Main Menu form appears, as shown in **Figure 12–21**.

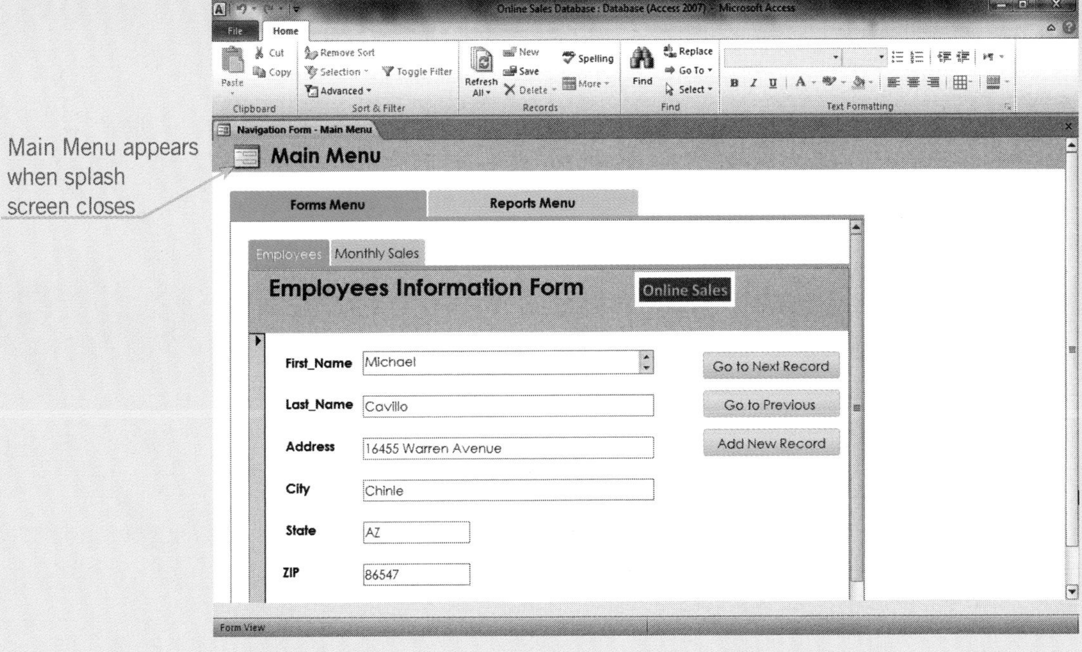

FIGURE 12–21 Main Menu appears as a result of startup options

11. Close the database file.

Bypassing Startup Options

After you set startup options, they are in effect until the next time someone opens the database. If you want to bypass the Current Database options that you set, you can press and hold the Shift key when you open the database. The database opens without the specified startup options, and changes can be made to the database objects. In the next exercise, you will open the database and bypass the startup options.

Step-by-Step 12.8

1. Press and hold the **Shift** key, and then open the **Online Sales Database** file.
2. Release the **Shift** key.
3. Click the **Microsoft Access** button on the taskbar. The database window opens without the startup options, so you can make changes. See **Figure 12–22**.

FIGURE 12–22 Database opens without new startup options

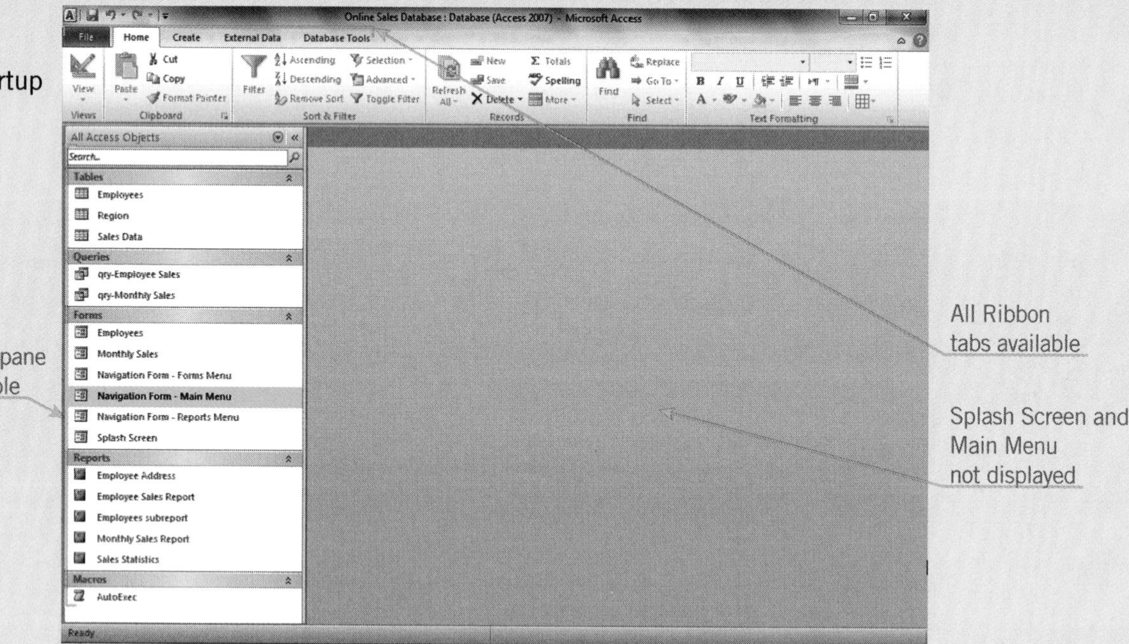

4. Close the database file.

SUMMARY

In this lesson, you learned:

- You can create a splash screen that welcomes users to the database.
- An AutoExec macro runs when the database opens and before any other macros are run.
- After you create an AutoExec macro, you should test the macro to see if it works correctly.
- Navigation forms have both form and subform features automatically built in.
- The main navigation form acts like a main menu.
- The startup options available with Access can be changed to provide additional database security.
- You can bypass startup options when opening a database.

VOCABULARY REVIEW

Define the following terms:

AutoExec macro
hierarchical
navigation form
splash screen
startup options

REVIEW QUESTIONS

TRUE / FALSE

Circle T if the statement is true or F if the statement is false.

T F 1. To open a splash screen when the database opens, you can create an AutoExec macro that has the OpenForm option.

T F 2. The AutoExec macro can only include an action to open a report.

T F 3. To bypass startup options, you press and hold the Shift key when you open the database.

T F 4. A navigation form has the subform feature automatically built in.

T F 5. To add a subform to a navigation form, you drag the form object from the Navigation pane to the Add New tab.

FILL IN THE BLANK

1. To open a database without startup options, you press and hold the ________________ key when you open the database.
2. You can only have one ________________ macro within a single database.
3. When adding a form object into a navigation form, you drag the form object from the ________________ into the navigation form.
4. A macro that runs automatically when you open the database is called the ________________ macro.
5. To hide all tabs except for the File tab and the Home tab, you deselect the ________________ check box in the Access Options dialog box.

WRITTEN QUESTIONS

Write a brief answer to the following questions.

1. What is an AutoExec macro?

2. How do you change startup options?

3. Why is it important for a splash screen to have the same format as the other forms and reports in a database?

4. Describe how you can bypass startup options.

PROJECTS

If you have a SAM 2010 user profile, your instructor may have assigned an autogradable version of the indicated project. If so, log into the SAM 2010 Web site at *www.cengage.com/sam2010* to download the instruction and start files.

PROJECT 12–1

1. Open the **Region Sales** file from the drive and folder where your Data Files are stored. Save the database as **Region Sales Database**, followed by your initials.
2. Create a navigation form that has the Employees and Sales Information forms.
3. Save the navigation form as **Forms Menu** and then close the form.
4. Create a navigation form that has the **Report** for **Employee Numbers and Sales Data by Month** reports.
5. Save the navigation form as **Reports Menu** and then close the form.
6. Create the main navigation form and then bring the Forms Menu and the Reports Menu into this form.
7. Save the form as **Main Menu**.
8. In Design view, delete the label in the Forms Header section of the Forms Menu and then decrease the size of the Form Header.
9. Delete the label in the Reports Menu Form Header section and then decrease the size of the Form Header section.
10. Change the title of the navigation form to **Main Menu**.
11. Save the form.
12. Switch to Form view to view the completed Main Menu.
13. Close the form and close the database.

SAM PROJECT 12–2

1. Open the **Book Sales** file from the drive and folder where your Data Files are stored. Save the database as **Book Sales Database**, followed by your initials.
2. Create a form with a splash screen and add the Book Sales Logo file, which is located in the drive and folder with your Data Files. Add the logo to the Detail section. (*Hint*: You will need to cut it from the Form Header section and paste it into the Detail section.)
3. Add a label with the text **Welcome to the Book Sales Worldwide Database**. (*Hint*: You will need to click the Design tab and in the Controls group, click Label. Then, type the text.)
4. Change the font size to 18 and change the font color to Black, Text 1.
5. Save the form as **Splash Screen**.
6. Create an AutoExec macro that opens the splash screen in a Read-Only Data Mode when the database is opened. Save the macro as AutoExec. Close the Macro window.
7. Close the database.
8. Reopen the database to test the AutoExec macro.
9. Close the database.

PROJECT 12–3

1. Open the **Pets** file from the drive and folder where your Data Files are stored. Save the database as **Pets Database**, followed by your initials.
2. Change the startup options so that the Navigation Main Menu form opens when the database is opened.
3. Change the startup options so that Full Menus are not allowed and the Navigation pane is not available.
4. Close the database.
5. Reopen the database to test the startup options.
6. Close the database.

CRITICAL THINKING

ACTIVITY 12–1

As the new database administrator for the Coastal Sales Corporation, you decide to automate the Coastal Sales database to make it easier to use and to prevent unwanted changes. You first open the **Coastal Sales** file and save it as **Coastal Sales Database**. Then, you create an AutoExec macro that opens the splash screen form. You change the startup options so that the Navigation Main Menu appears after the splash screen form is closed. You also set the startup options to hide the Navigation pane and all but the File and Home tabs on the Ribbon when the database opens.

ACTIVITY 12–2

Think of how you could use the navigation forms in Access to automate a database that contains sports information. For example, the database would probably have the names and contact information of team members, games and practice schedules, and coach information. Write down how you would design the hierarchy of navigation forms to present this information.

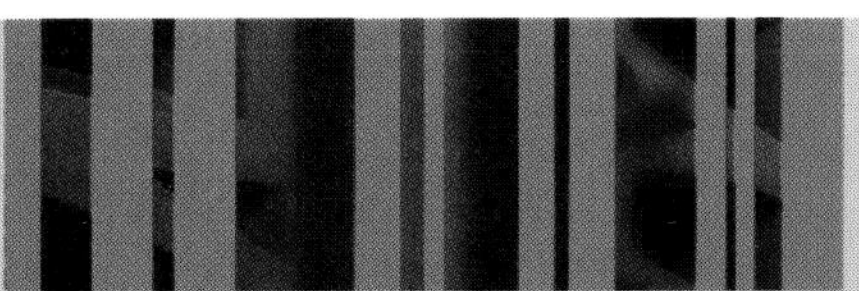

Estimated Time:
2.5 hours

LESSON 13

Programming in Access

■ OBJECTIVES

Upon completion of this lesson, you should be able to:

- Create a new function.
- Test a new function.
- Add a control with defined names to a form.
- Create an If procedure.
- View the procedure results.
- Add an Else statement to a procedure.
- Test a revised procedure.

■ VOCABULARY

code
comment
function
procedure
public
syntax

Introduction

Lesson 13 introduces you to Visual Basic for Applications (VBA) and describes how to use VBA to enhance database processing for users. VBA is the programming language for Microsoft Office programs, including Access. VBA has a set of common features for all Microsoft Office programs. In this lesson, you will learn how to define a new function using VBA. After you define the function, you will test the function to be sure that it is working correctly and then add a Text Box control to a form. Finally, you will write a procedure that uses the function you defined and discover that you can change a procedure after it is created to enhance the actions it performs.

Creating a New Function

VOCABULARY

function

code

syntax

variable name

comment

public

A ***function*** is an action that can be defined in VBA code where you use statements to describe the action you want the function to perform. ***Code*** refers to the ***syntax***, or wording, that is used in VBA. Access already has built-in functions, such as Average, Min, and Max, to calculate an average and to determine minimum and maximum values. If you want to use a function that is not built-in, you will need to define a new function. Defining a new function simply refers to writing VBA code so that the function will perform a certain action.

For example, you might want a function that calculates the number of years between two dates. The function will have two date values referenced using two variables with identifiable variable names. A ***variable name*** is simply a symbolic name that you assign to a value. Creating variable names that make functions easy to understand can help make your database more user-friendly. For example, the variable names in the date function in the above example could be FirstDate and SecondDate.

You will also need to assign a data type to the variables. In the example calculating years, you would assign a date data type to the variables. To identify these variables as date data types, you would use the syntax (FirstDate As Date, SecondDate As Date). When you actually use the function, you will type in date values for these variables.

You can also add a statement that does not perform an action, but helps the person looking at the code identify the purpose of the code. This statement is called a ***comment***. To add a comment, you begin by typing an apostrophe (') before the sentence. Comments appear in green.

If you want the function to be available in various procedures that you may write in the database, you should define the function in a module. Defining a function in a module makes it accessible throughout the database, or ***public***. In this next exercise, you will create a function that will be used to determine the number of years between two dates. You will use the function name YearDiff.

Step-by-Step 13.1

1. Open the **New Sales** file from the drive and folder where your Data Files are stored. Save the database as **New Sales Database**, followed by your initials. You may need to click **Enable Content**.
2. Click the **Create** tab, and then click **Module** in the Macros & Code group. The Visual Basic window appears, as shown in **Figure 13–1**.

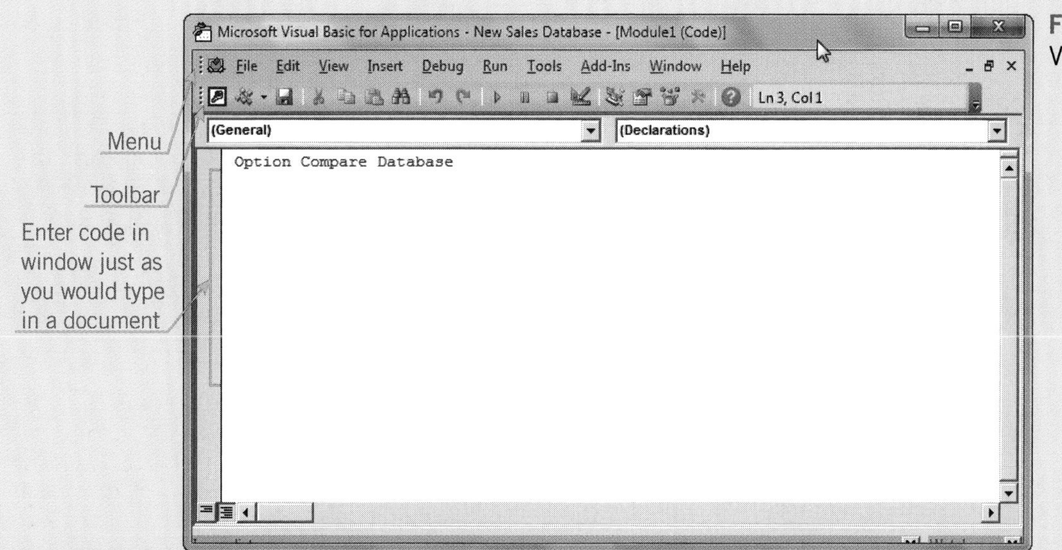

FIGURE 13–1
Visual Basic window

3. In the Visual Basic window, click the **Insert** menu and then click **Procedure**.
4. In the Name box, type **YearDiff**.
5. In the Type section, click the **Function** option button, then verify that the **Public** option button is selected in the Scope section, as shown in **Figure 13–2**.

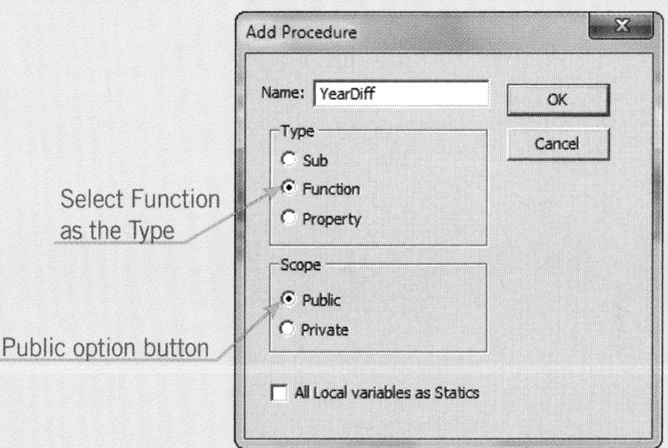

FIGURE 13–2
Add Procedure dialog box

6. Click **OK** to close the Add Procedure dialog box. The new function is added to the VBA window.

7. Click between the parentheses following YearDiff, and then type **FirstDate As Date, SecondDate As Date**, as shown in **Figure 13–3**.

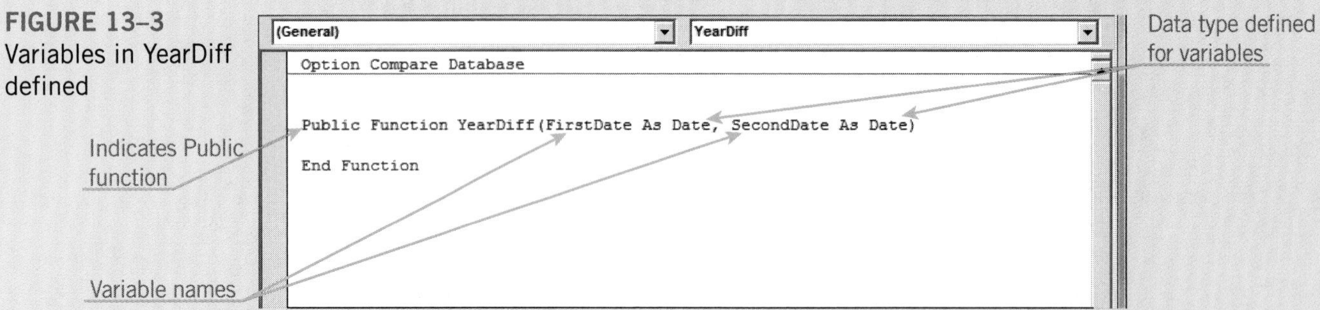

FIGURE 13–3
Variables in YearDiff defined

8. Click outside the close parenthesis, and then press **Enter**. You will now add another line with a comment.
9. Press **Tab**, type **'Determine the number of years between two dates**, and then press **Enter**. The text becomes a comment indicated by the green font. Next, you will indent the line of code before you type it to make it easier to see in the window.
10. Press **Tab** to indent this line, and then type **YearDiff=DateDiff("yyyy", FirstDate,SecondDate)**. Notice that text appears as you type to assist you in creating the function, as shown in **Figure 13–4**.

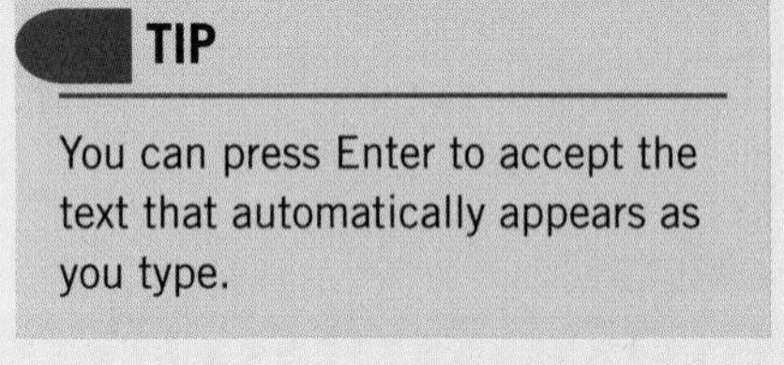

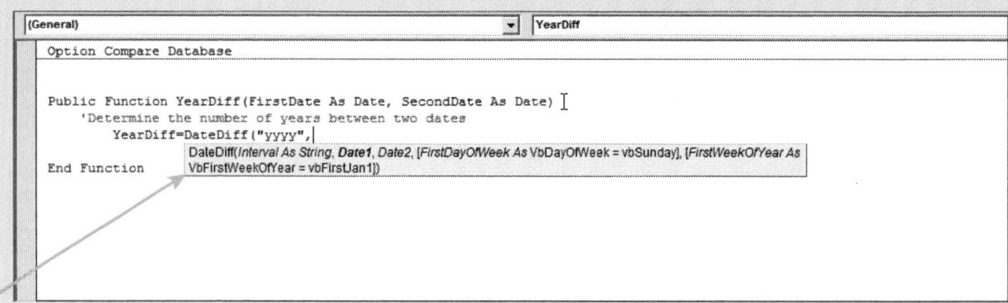

FIGURE 13–4
Help text appears in VBA window

11. Click after the End Function, and then compare your completed YearDiff function to the one shown in **Figure 13–5**.

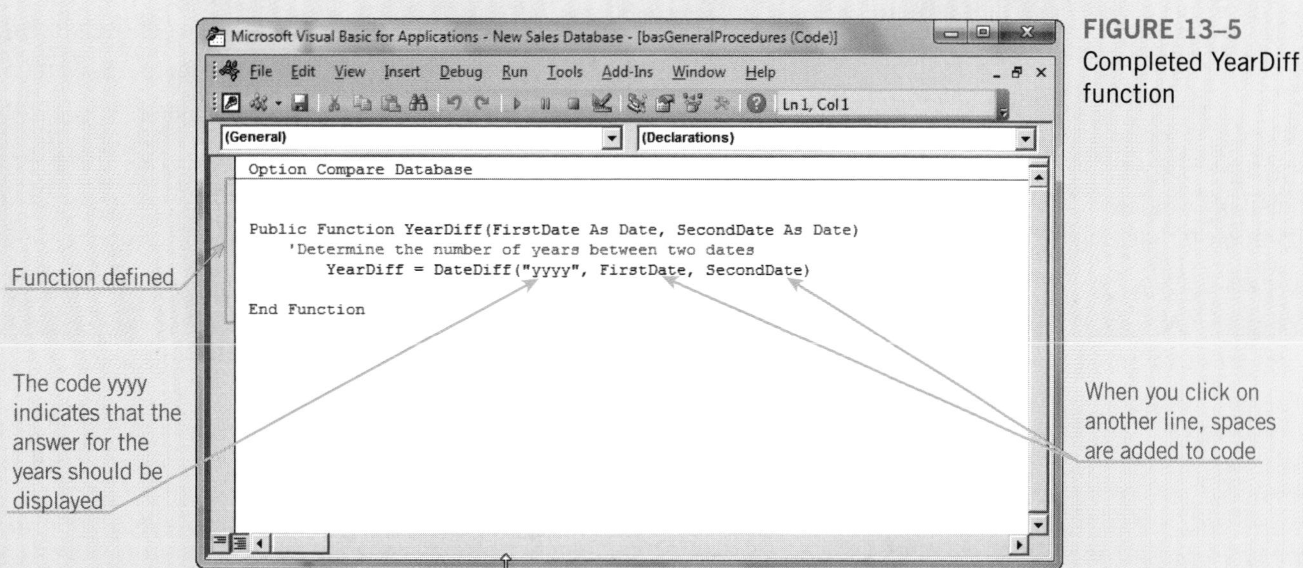

FIGURE 13–5 Completed YearDiff function

12. Click the **Save** button on the toolbar of the Visual Basic window.
13. Type **basGeneralProcedures** in the Module Name text box and then click **OK**.
14. Remain in this database for the next Step-by-Step.

Testing a New Function

After creating a new function, it is smart to check it to make sure the code is correct. The function could contain errors even though the statements have the correct syntax. Even the simplest functions can contain errors, such as spelling errors or logic errors. Logic errors occur when the procedure produces incorrect results. When you enter the dates in the Immediate window, you place a pound sign (#) before and after the date to define when the date starts and ends. To test a function, you use the Immediate window. The Immediate window will return the results of the function based on the values you enter. In order to test the function, you type a question mark (?) before the function name and the variables. In the next exercise, you will test the YearDiff function.

Step-by-Step 13.2

1. In the Visual Basic window, click the **View** menu and then click **Immediate Window**. If you do not see the Immediate window, you may need to increase the size of the window.

2. If necessary, place the mouse pointer over the bottom bar of the window until you see the double-headed arrow, as shown in **Figure 13–6**, then drag the border up until you can see the Immediate window.

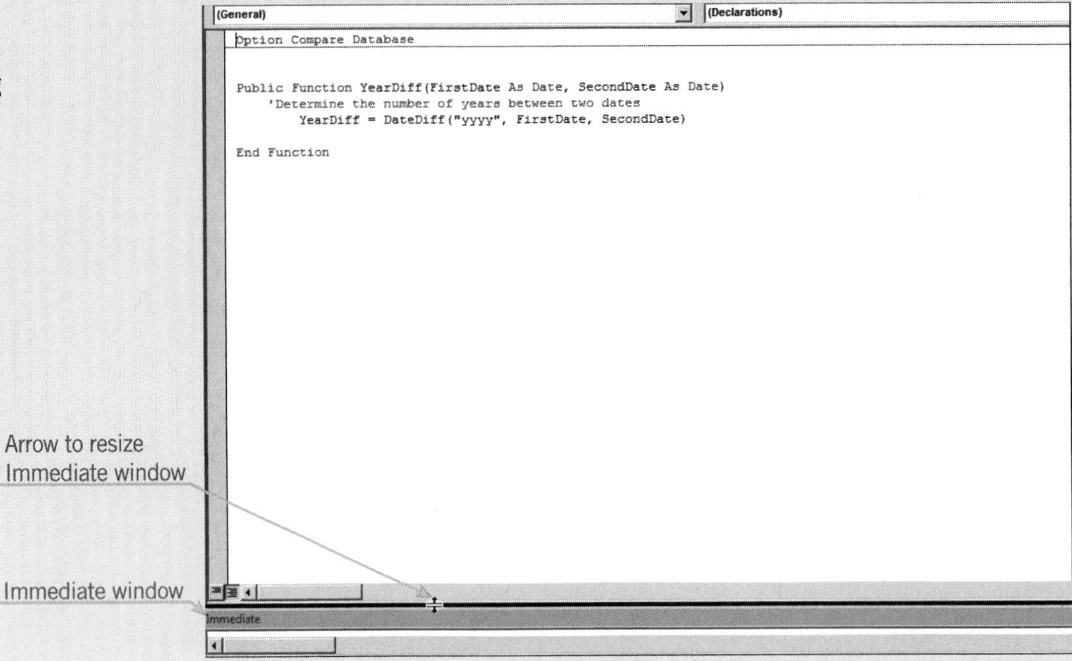

FIGURE 13–6
Immediate window with arrow for resizing

3. Click in the Immediate window, and then type **?YearDiff(#3/15/2006#, #11/25/2013#)**. Notice as you start typing that text appears in the window to help you with the syntax.
4. Press **Enter**. As shown in **Figure 13–7**, the answer, 7, appears in the Immediate window.

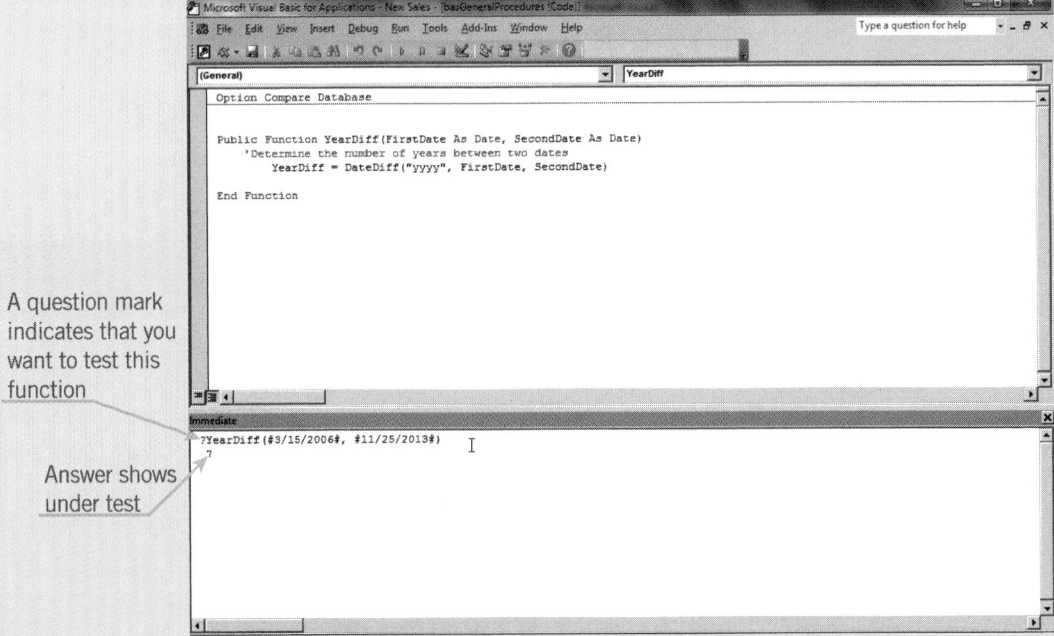

FIGURE 13–7
Answer appears in Immediate window

5. Close the Immediate window by clicking the **Close** button in the upper-right corner of the Immediate window.
6. Click the **File** menu, and then click **Close and Return to Microsoft Access**. The Modules group appears in the Navigation pane with the name of the new module, as shown in **Figure 13–8**.

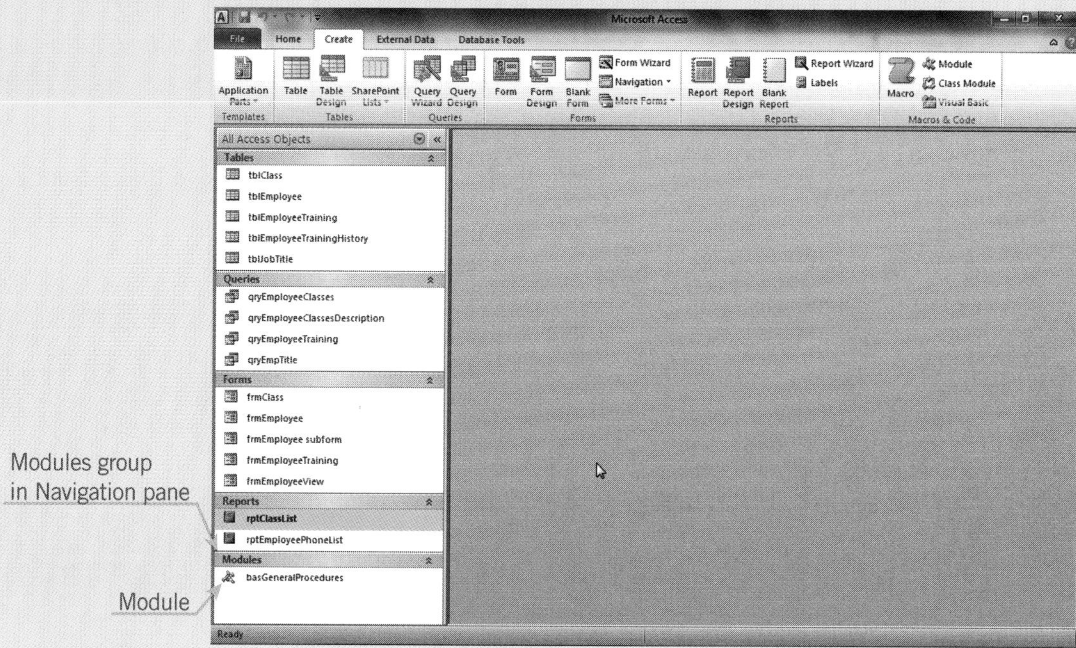

FIGURE 13–8 Module name appears in Modules group

Adding a Control with Defined Names to a Form

You can add controls to a form that display the results of a calculation. If you are going to use a control in a procedure, you first add the control to the form. Then you assign specific names to the parts of the control in the Property Sheet. For example, a Text Box control has two parts: a label part and an unbound part. The label identifies what will appear in the unbound part of the control. The unbound part of the Text Box remains unbound until a field with actual data is assigned to this control. Then, this part of the Text Box is considered bound; in other words, it is bound by the data.

You add names to the parts of the control so that you can use these names in the procedure. It is easier to read and identify the purpose of the function if it has recognizable control names. In the next exercise, you will learn how to assign descriptive names to the label and the unbound part of a Text Box control. The Text Box control that you create will be used in a procedure that you will create later in this lesson.

Step-by-Step 13.3

1. Double-click **frmEmployee** in the Forms section of the Navigation pane.
2. On the Ribbon, click the **Home** tab, click the **View** button arrow in the Views group, and then click **Design View**. You will add a Text Box control below the Date of Birth field.
3. Click the **Design** tab, if necessary, and then click the **Text Box** button in the Controls group.
4. Click in the area below DOB in the Date of Birth field to add a Text Box control, as shown in **Figure 13–9**. If you click too far to the left under this field, the two parts of the control will overlap.

FIGURE 13–9
Text Box control added

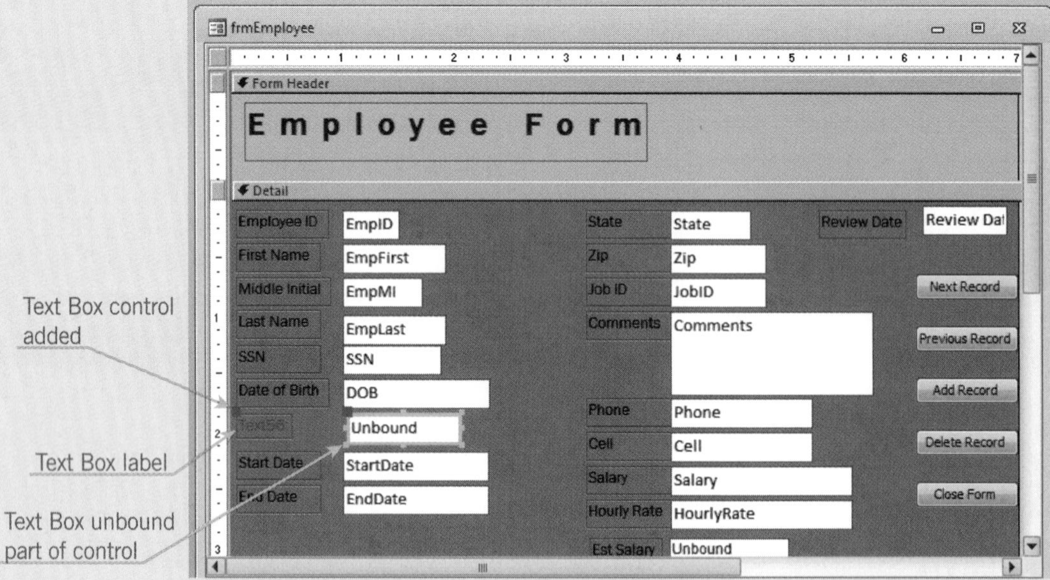

5. Click the **Text Box label** on the left side of the Text Box control, and then click the **Property Sheet** button in the Tools group.
6. In the Property Sheet pane, click the **All** tab, click in the **Name** box, and then type **Age_Label**, replacing the existing text.
7. Click the **Caption** field, and then type **Age**. See **Figure 13–10**. The caption will appear in the title bar in Form view.

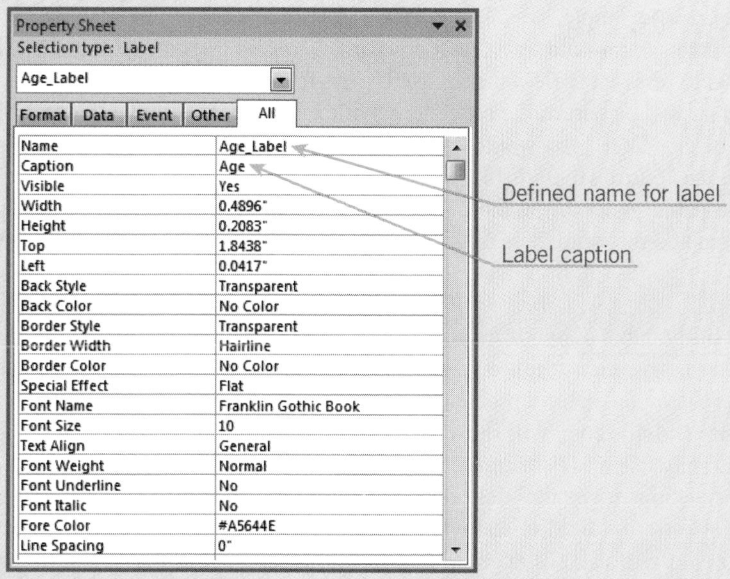

FIGURE 13–10
Property Sheet pane for Text Box label

8. If necessary, drag the Property Sheet pane out of the way so that you can see the entire form. Click the **Unbound** object on the right side of the Text Box control.
9. On the Property Sheet pane, click in the **Name** box, then type **Age** to replace the existing text. This name will be used when you create the procedure.
10. Close the **Design** tab and then click the **Property Sheet** button.
11. Click the **Text Box label**, and then click the **Format** tab on the Ribbon.
12. Click the **Font Color** button arrow, and then click **Black, Text 1** in the Font group.
13. Save the form and remain in this screen for the next Step-by-Step.

EXTRA FOR EXPERTS

After you create a Text Box control in a form, you can press and hold down the Ctrl key and then use the arrow keys to move the text box to a desired location.

Creating an If Procedure

A ***procedure*** is a group of statements written in VBA code that can include several functions. Each function can perform one action or multiple actions. Typically, unless a statement is a comment, it performs an action.

Procedures include code that indicates where the procedure begins and additional code that tells where the procedure ends. The *If* procedure begins with the code word **If** and ends with the code words **End If**. Several statements appear between If and End If.

VOCABULARY
procedure

VBA requires the use of specific syntax so that the procedure performs actions correctly. For example, to calculate the difference between a date in a form and today's date, you would use the code word *Date* for the current date. You would also need to review the field names used in the form because they will be used in the syntax that will be part of the procedure. For example, if the field name in a form for date of birth is DOB, you would use *DOB* as the syntax in the procedure. If you want to make the control label visible in the procedure, you need to add the syntax *Visible* after the name given to the label. After the syntax Visible, you will need to add an equal sign and the word *True* or *False* so that the label will appear or not appear. For example, if you wanted to make the age label used in the last Step-by-Step visible, you would type *Age_Label.Visible=True*. Notice that you use a period to indicate the end of the label name. If this procedure will be used in only one form, it will be entered as a private procedure versus a public procedure that can be used in several objects. When you create a procedure within a form, Access recognizes it as a private procedure and this code will show when you start creating the procedure.

You may use an If statement to check a form field to see if the field is empty. When checking to see if a field does not have a value, you use the *IsNull* syntax. IsNull looks in the field to see whether the field is null (empty). In the next Step-by-Step, you will use a procedure that looks for employees that are still employed and calculates the length of time they have been with the company. You will use the YearDiff function and the Text Box control names you assigned in the previous Step-by-Step.

Step-by-Step 13.4

1. In the upper-left corner of the Form window, click the **Form Selector** to select the form. Notice that when the form is selected, the Form Selector box appears with a dark square. See **Figure 13–11**. You select the Form Selector so that Access knows you will be working within this form. Also notice the right side of the Date of Birth field is identified as DOB.

FIGURE 13–11
Form Selector selected

2. Click the **Property Sheet** button, and then click the **Event** tab in the Property Sheet pane.
3. Click the **Build** button next to the **On Current** event. The Choose Builder dialog box opens, as shown in **Figure 13–12**.

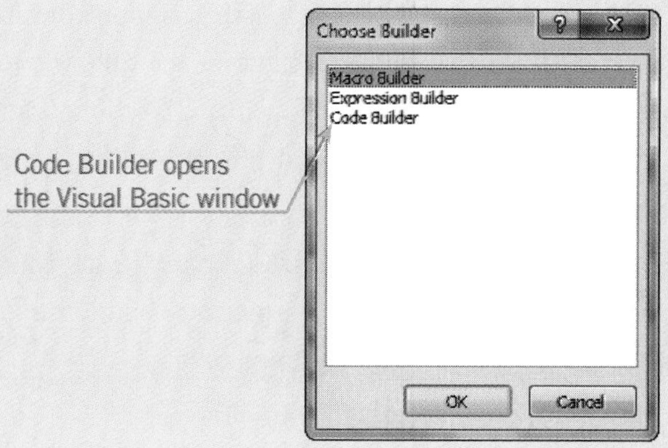

FIGURE 13–12
Choose Builder dialog box

4. Click **Code Builder** and then click **OK**. The Visual Basic window opens, as shown in **Figure 13–13**. Next you will type a comment that explains the procedure. The insertion point should be between the Private Sub and End Sub commands.

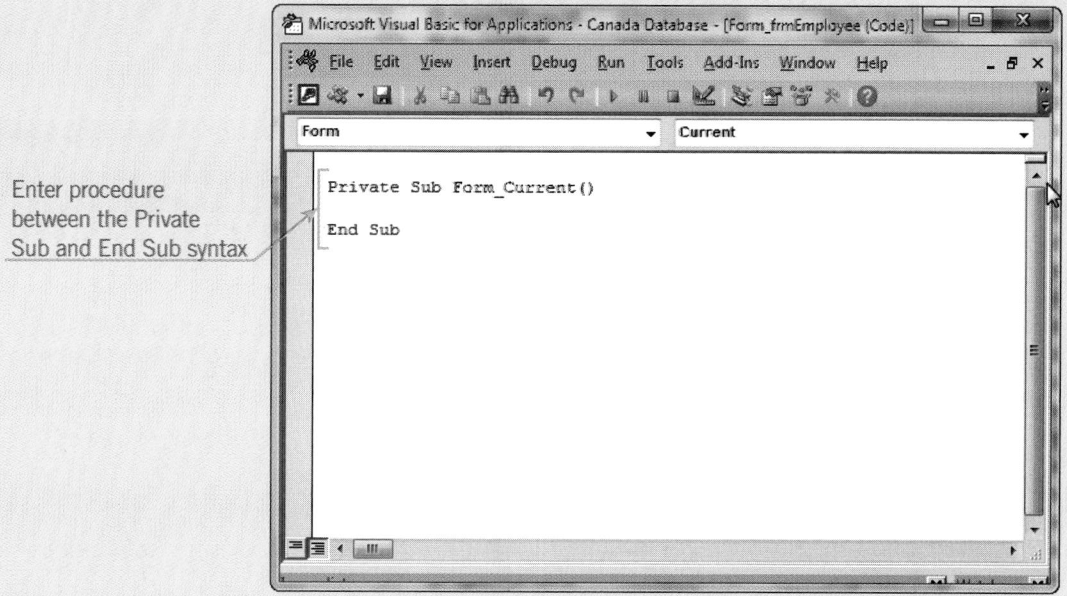

FIGURE 13–13
Visual Basic window

5. Type **'For current employees, display the age of the employee.**
6. Press **Enter** to move to the next line. The comment appears in green. Next, you will type code that looks at the EndDate field; if it is not empty, then the person is still employed with the company. Then, you will review the DOB field and if it is not null, the procedure can continue and calculate the employee's age.
7. Press **Tab** to indent the next statement and then type the following:

   If IsNull (EndDate) And Not IsNull (DOB) Then.

   In the next step, you will add code that calculates the difference between today's date and the employee's date of birth to determine their age.

8. Press **Enter** to start a new line, press **Tab** to indent the line, and then type **Age = YearDiff (DOB, Date)**. Note that each time you move to a new line, spaces are automatically added within the syntax. Indenting each line helps make it clear that the next line is a subset of what occurred in the previous line of code.
9. Press **Enter** and then type **Age_Label.Visible = True**. This line of code will make the Age label visible if the person is still employed with the company and if their DOB field contains data.
10. Press **Enter** and then type **Age.Visible = True**.
11. Press **Enter**, and then press the **Backspace** key to move the next line so that it is even with the If statement.
12. Type **End If**. Compare your screen to **Figure 13–14**.

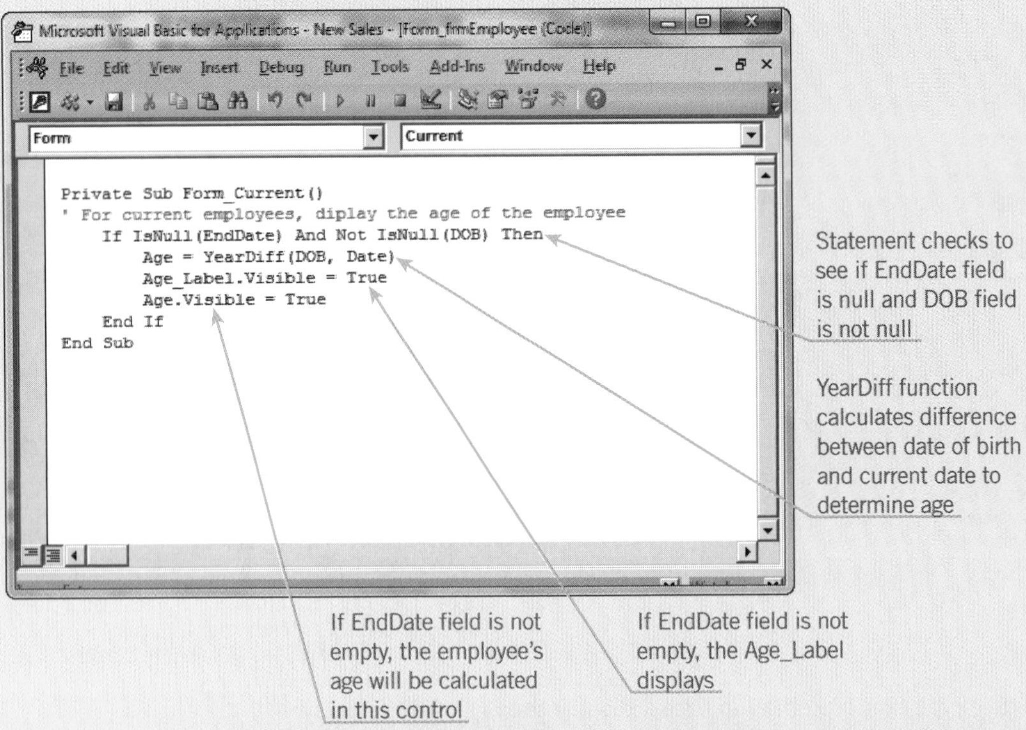

FIGURE 13–14
Visual Basic window with procedure

13. Click the **Save** button on the Visual Basic toolbar. You are saving the function as a part of this form.
14. Close the Visual Basic window. Remain in this screen for the next Step-by-Step.

Viewing the Procedure Results

After creating a procedure, you will need to view the results to be certain that the procedure is doing what you expect. If the procedure is working correctly, the results of the procedure will show accurate results. If the procedure returns incorrect results, the syntax may not be entered correctly or may include a misspelled word. In this next exercise, you will view the Age text box to see if the function is calculating the correct results.

Step-by-Step 13.5

1. Close the Property Sheet pane.
2. Click the **Design** tab, click the **View** button arrow, and then click **Form View**. Notice that the age field appears but an age is not displayed because the employee is no longer employed. You can determine if an employee is no longer employed based on the End Date.
3. Click the **Next Record** button on the right side of the form. The second record appears for a current employee and displays their age, as shown in **Figure 13–15**. Note, the age shown on your screen may differ depending on the current date that you are viewing the form.

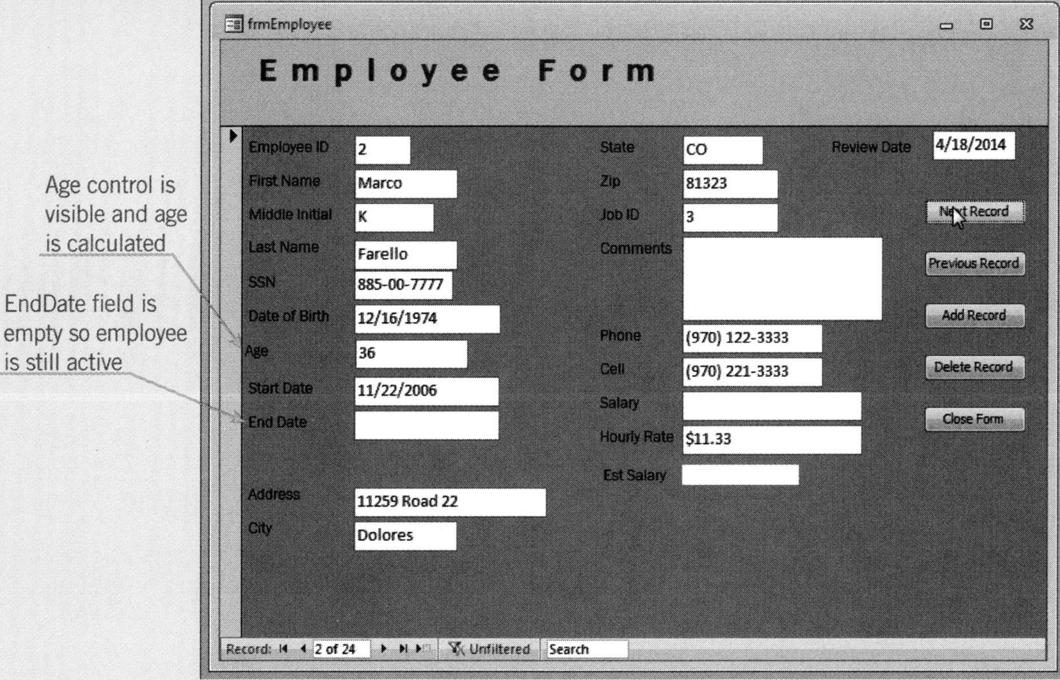

FIGURE 13–15 Record shows age of employee

4. Remain in this screen for the next Step-by-Step.

Adding an Else Statement to the Procedure

In an *If* procedure, you may have the procedure look at a field and check to see if it contains a value. If it does contain a value, the procedure continues; if it doesn't, the procedure ends. However, you may want the procedure to perform a specific action if the field does contain a value and another action if it doesn't contain a value. By placing an *Else* statement in the code, the procedure will perform one action or else it will perform another action. In this next exercise, you will add an *Else* statement to the *If* procedure you created previously. The procedure will determine if the End Date field is empty and, if so, calculate the person's age. Or, if a value is found in the End Date field, the statements after *Else* will run and the Age field will not display.

Step-by-Step 13.6

1. Click the **View** button arrow, and then click **Design View**.
2. Verify that the Form Selector is still selected and then, in the Tools group, click the **Property Sheet** button. If necessary, click the **Event** tab to view this tab. See **Figure 13–16**.

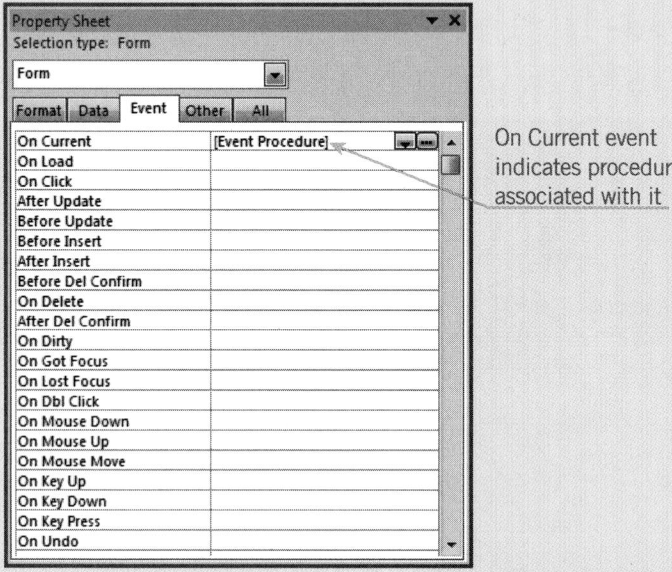

FIGURE 13–16
Event tab indicates procedure in the On Current event

3. Click the **Build** button next to the On Current box to display the Visual Basic for Applications window.
4. Click at the end of the Age.Visible = True line, and then press **Enter** to add another line to the function.
5. Press **Backspace** to line up the row with the If and End If functions.
6. Type **Else** and then press **Enter**.
7. Press **Tab** to indent this line, and then type **Age_Label.Visible=False**.
8. Press **Enter** to move to the next line.
9. Type **Age.Visible=False**. Compare your screen to **Figure 13–17**.

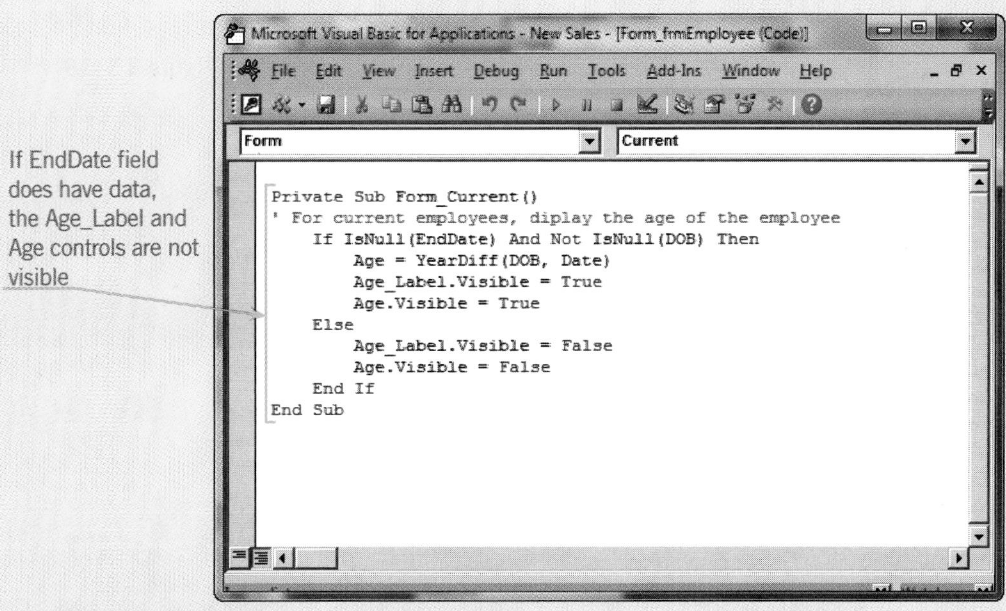

FIGURE 13–17
Revised procedure with Else statement

10. Click the **Save** button on the toolbar in the Visual Basic window.
11. Click the **File** menu, and then click **Close and Return to Microsoft Access**. Close the Property Sheet pane, if necessary.
12. Remain in this screen for the next Step-by-Step.

Testing a Revised Procedure

Even though you tested the function previously, since the procedure has changed, you will need to check it again. You will review the results for several records to be sure that the procedure is working correctly as you move through the records.

Step-by-Step 13.7

1. Click the **View** button arrow, and then click **Form View**.

2. Check to see that the Age field is not displayed on the first record because an end date appears for the employee. See **Figure 13–18**.

FIGURE EX 13–18
Record does not display Text Box for age

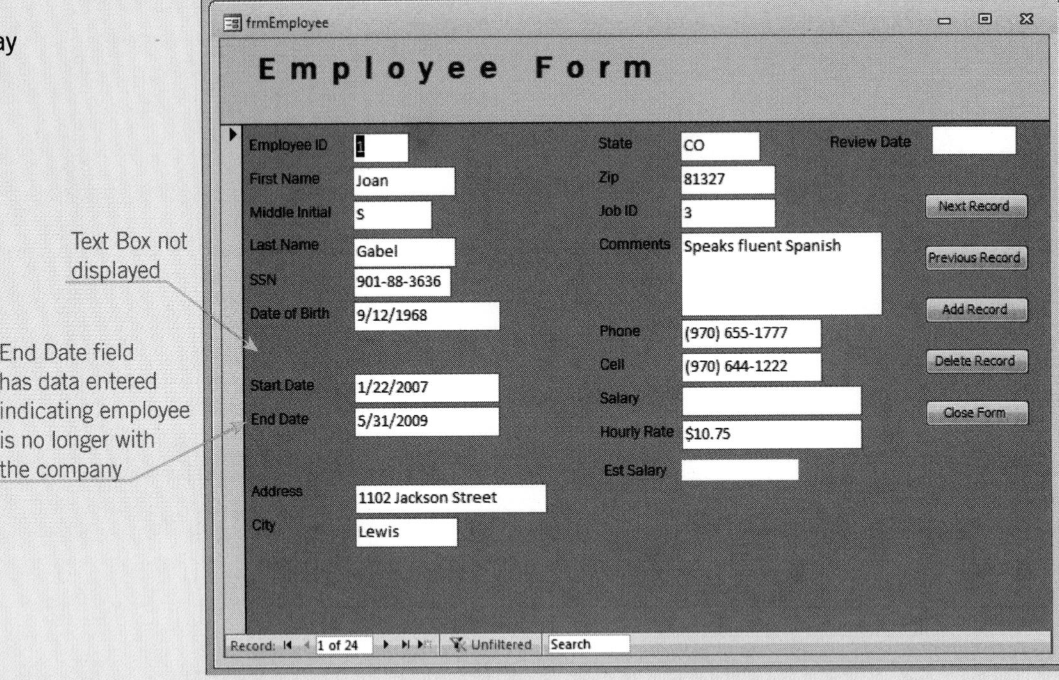

3. Click the **Next Record** button. The age for this current employee is displayed.
4. Save the form by clicking the **Save** button on the Quick Access toolbar.
5. Close the form.
6. Close the database.

SUMMARY

In this lesson, you learned:

- If the function you want to use is not a built-in function, you will need to create a new function.
- After creating a new function, you will need to test the function to see if it produces the correct results.
- You can add a control with defined names to a form.
- An If procedure starts with the *If* syntax and ends with the *End If* syntax.
- You should review the results of an If procedure to be certain that it is working correctly.
- You can add an Else statement to an If procedure.
- A revised procedure will need to be tested.

VOCABULARY REVIEW

Define the following terms:

code	function	public
comment	procedure	syntax

REVIEW QUESTIONS

TRUE / FALSE

Circle T if the statement is true or F if the statement is false.

T F 1. After a procedure is created and tested, it cannot be changed.

T F 2. VBA is an abbreviation for Visual Basic for Applications.

T F 3. A function is an action that can be defined in VBA code where you use statements to describe the action you want the function to perform.

T F 4. Code refers to the syntax, or wording, that is used in VBA.

T F 5. An If procedure begins with an *If* code word and ends with the code words *End If*.

FILL IN THE BLANK

1. If you want a function to be available in more than one procedure, you should define it as a(n) ______________ function.
2. In order to test the function, you need to type a(n) ______________ before the function name and the variables.
3. A(n) ______________ is a symbolic name that you assign to a value.
4. To add a comment, you begin by typing a(n) ______________ before the sentence.
5. Defining a function in a module makes the function accessible throughout the database, also referred to as making the function ______________.

WRITTEN QUESTIONS

Write a brief answer to the following questions.

1. Explain how you would add a comment to a procedure.

2. Describe how a function can be tested.

3. If you want to make a label with the defined name *age* not visible, what code could you use for this action?

4. Explain why a procedure may return incorrect results.

5. Describe what occurs in a procedure if you add the Else statement.

PROJECTS

If you have a SAM 2010 user profile, your instructor may have assigned an autogradable version of the indicated project. If so, log into the SAM 2010 Web site at *www.cengage.com/sam2010* to download the instruction and start files.

PROJECT 13–1

1. Open the **Epic Internet Sales** file from the drive and folder where your Data Files are stored. Save the database as **Epic Internet Sales Database**, followed by your initials.
2. Define a function named **YearDiff** that calculates the difference between two dates. Define the function as public.
3. Add the comment **Determine the number of years between two dates** to the function.
4. For the date variables, use the variable names **FirstDate** and **SecondDate**.
5. Assign the Date data type to both variables.
6. Save the module as **basGeneralProcedures**.
7. Test the function in the Immediate window to see if it is working correctly.
8. Close the database.

SAM PROJECT 13–2

1. Open the **End of Year Sales** file from the drive and folder where your Data Files are stored. Save the database as **End of Year Sales Database**, followed by your initials.
2. Open **basGeneralProcedures** and view the defined function. Notice the YearDiff function is already defined.
3. Close basGeneralProcedures.
4. Open **frmEmployee** in Design view.
5. View the Property Sheet for the Age: field label and Text Box control.
6. Click the Form Selector button.
7. Add an If procedure to the On Current event that uses the YearDiff function to calculate the employee's age by using their date of birth and the current date. (*Hint*: Use the Date variable for the current date.)
8. In the If procedure, make the label and the Text Box control visible when the age is calculated.
9. View the results. (Remember to view several records to be sure the age is calculating correctly.)
10. Save and close the form.
11. Close the database.

PROJECT 13–3

1. Open the **National Events** file from the drive and folder where your Data Files are stored. Save the database as **National Events**, followed by your initials.
2. Open **frmEmployee** in Design view, select the Form Selector, and then click the Property Sheet button.
3. If necessary, click the Event tab to view this tab.
4. Click the Build button next to the On Current box to display the Visual Basic for Applications window.
5. Click at the end of the Age.Visible = True line, and then press Enter to add another line to the function.
6. Add an Else statement, and then add statements to make the Age_Label and Age control not visible if there is data in the EndDate field.
7. Click the Save button on the toolbar in the Visual Basic window, click the File menu, and then click Close and Return to Microsoft Access.
8. Test the new procedure to see if it is working correctly.
9. Close the database

CRITICAL THINKING

ACTIVITY 13–1

Open the **Wholesale International Sales** file and then save it as **Wholesale International Sales Database**. Imagine you are the new database administrator for the Wholesale International Sales Corporation. You decide to automate the Wholesale International Sales database to calculate the difference between dates in the frmEmployee form. You view the basGeneralProcedures procedure and notice that the YearDiff function is defined, but it is not used in the database. You decide to add a Text Box control to frmEmployee that will show the difference in dates between the employee's Start Date and End Date. This control would only need to be displayed for former employees, so you create a procedure that only has the field display when then EndDate field includes data. You use LOE as the code for length of employment when you define the label name and the control name. You decide to review several records to be sure the procedure is working correctly.

ACTIVITY 13–2

Imagine a database that has a form that shows the start date and end date for three sports seasons. Think of how you could add a function and a procedure to calculate the length of a sports season for football, basketball, and baseball. Write down your thoughts and how you would present this report to a coach.

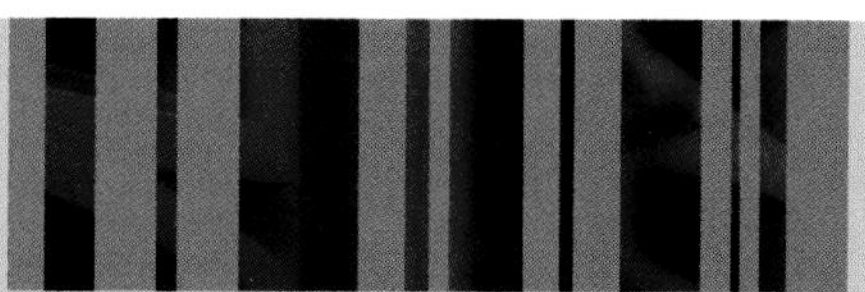

Estimated Time: 2.0 hours

LESSON 14

Creating Database Security and Documentation

■ OBJECTIVES

Upon completion of this lesson, you should be able to:

- Open a database in the Open Exclusive mode.
- Encrypt a database with a password.
- Open an encrypted database.
- Remove encryption from a database.
- Make a backup copy of a database.
- Create database documentation.

■ VOCABULARY

backup

Database Documenter

encryption

Open Exclusive mode

password

Introduction

Microsoft Access offers several security and documentation features to protect a database from losing important information that can be caused by power failures or individuals who maliciously or accidentally delete database objects. To avoid losing database information, you can open a database in the Open Exclusive mode. In this mode, you are the only person who can access the database. You can also add a password to a database in Open Exclusive mode, which encrypts, or scrambles, the data. Encrypting a database places the data in an unintelligible format so it cannot be viewed or understood unless it is opened with the correct password. If necessary, you can also remove the password and encryption to allow easier access to the data. Creating a backup copy of a database is another method for protecting important data. In this lesson, you will also learn about the Database Documenter feature, which is used to create a report that documents each selected object in the database.

Opening a Database in the Open Exclusive Mode

You can open an Access database using several methods, including Open mode, Open Read-Only mode, Open Exclusive Read-Only mode, and Open Exclusive mode. Typically when you open a database, you use the Open mode, which allows several users to open and use the database at the same time. Using the Open Read-Only mode allows multiple users to open a database, but they cannot add or change records and they cannot create new objects. The Open Exclusive Read-Only mode opens the database so that all users except for the current user are locked out; however, the current user can only view the data in the database.

VOCABULARY
Open Exclusive mode

In the ***Open Exclusive mode***, only the person who opened the database can use and make changes to it; all other users are locked out from opening and using the database. This option is typically used when you want to encrypt a database with a password. In this next exercise, you will first open the data file and save it with a new name, then you will close Access. When you start Access again, you will open a database in Open Exclusive mode.

Step-by-Step 14.1

1. Open the **Employee Sales** file from the drive and folder where your Data Files are stored. Save the database as **Employee Sales Database**, followed by your initials.
2. Exit Access.
3. Start Access. The File tab is displayed in the window.
4. Click **Open**.
5. Locate the folder where your Data Files are stored.
6. In the Open dialog box, click **Employee Sales Database** once and then click the **drop-down arrow** next to the Open button. See **Figure 14–1**.

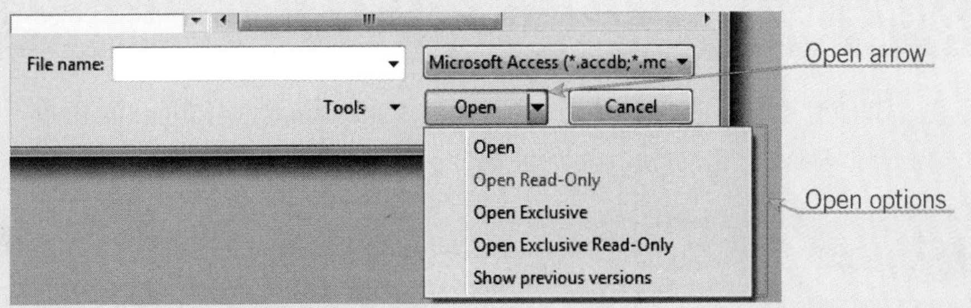

FIGURE 14–1
Open options in the Open dialog box

7. Click the **Open Exclusive** option. The database opens in the Exclusive mode.
8. Remain in this database for the next Step-by-Step.

Encrypting with a Password

If your database has sensitive information, such as Social Security numbers or salary information, you might decide to protect it from unauthorized use. Access 2010 combines two tools for database security: database passwords and encryption. A ***password*** is a collection of characters that a user types to gain access to a file. When a database is password protected, users cannot open the database unless they provide the correct password. When you ***encrypt*** a database with a password, data within the database is made unreadable. This combined safety feature provides stronger protection than previous versions of Access. You can only encrypt a database with a password if the database is opened in the Open Exclusive mode.

VOCABULARY
password
encrypt

In Access, row level locking is turned on by default. Row level locking means that when you change values in a record in an encrypted database, only the changed record will be encrypted, not the entire database. Therefore, when you encrypt a database with row level locking turned off, you will see a message that states a *block cipher is incompatible with row level locking and so row level locking will be ignored.* This message ensures that the entire database will be encrypted. In this next exercise, you will encrypt the database with a password.

Step-by-Step 14.2

1. Click the **File** tab and, if necessary, click the **Info** tab. Notice the Encrypt with Password option is available, as shown in **Figure 14–2**.

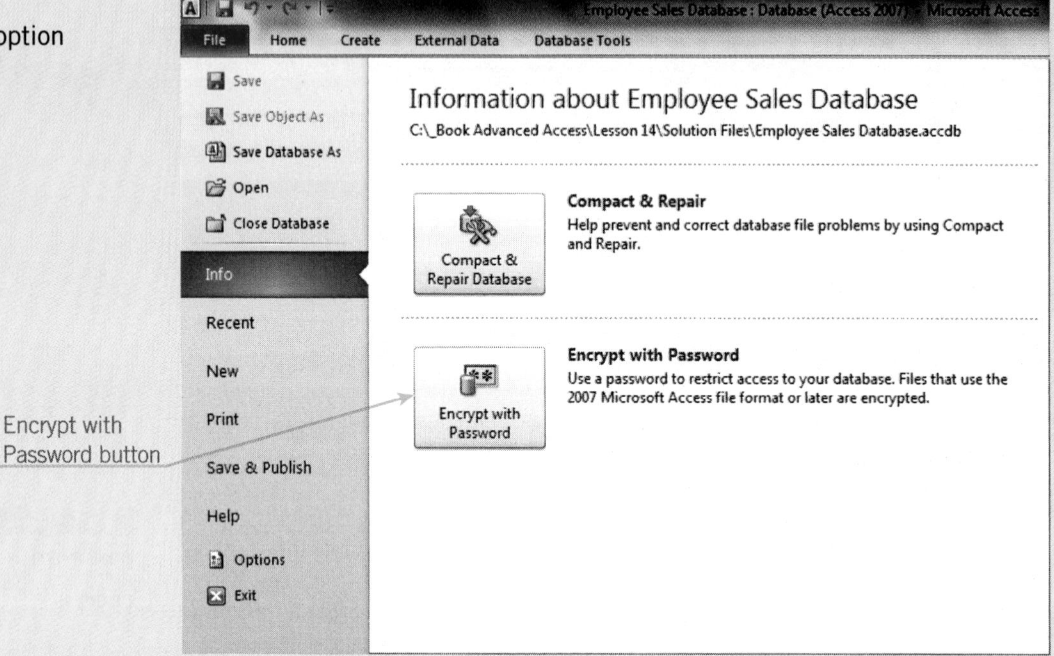

FIGURE 14–2
Encrypt with Password option

2. Click the **Encrypt with Password** button. The Set Database Password dialog box opens, as shown in **Figure 14–3**. Note, if the database is not opened in the Exclusive mode, you would receive an error message at this time.

FIGURE 14–3
Set Database Password dialog box

3. In the **Password** text box, type **CatCat**.
4. Press **Tab** to move to the **Verify** text box, and then type **CatCat** again.
5. Click **OK**. A message appears showing that row level locking will be ignored, as shown in **Figure 14–4**.

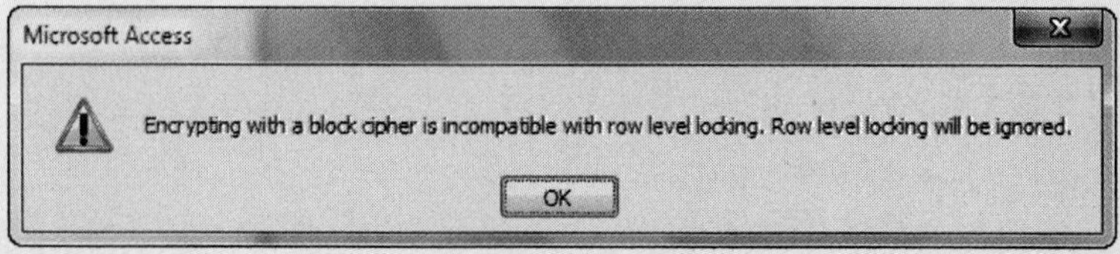

FIGURE 14–4
Message about row level locking

6. Click **OK** to close the message box. Next, you will save the database with another name so you can still have a copy of the encrypted database.
7. Save the database as **Employee Sales Database 2**.
8. In the Password Required text box, type **CatCat** and then press **Enter**.
9. Click **Enable Content** in the Message bar.
10. Close the database.

Opening an Encrypted Database

When opening an encrypted database, you will be asked for a password. After you enter the password, the database should open so that you can view and make changes to the database objects. Until the correct password is entered, no objects in the database can be viewed. In this next exercise, you will open an encrypted database.

Step-by-Step 14.3

1. Open the **Employee Sales Database 2**. The Password Required dialog box opens, as shown in **Figure 14–5**.

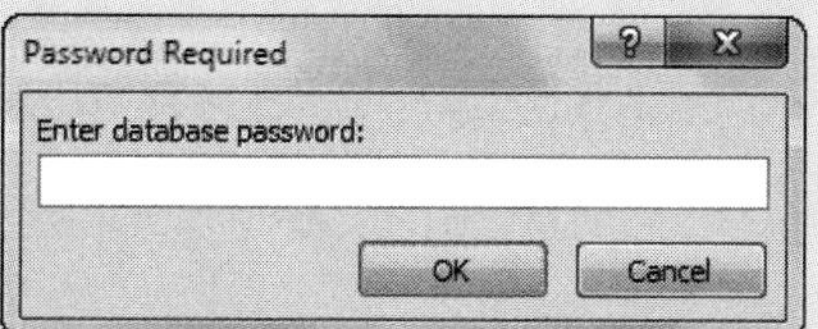

FIGURE 14–5
Password Required dialog box

2. Type **CatCat**.
3. Click **OK**.
4. Open the **Employees** table and view the data.
5. Close the table.
6. Close the database and remain in this screen for the next Step-by-Step.

Removing Encryption from a Database

To remove the password and encryption from a database, you first need to open the database in the Open Exclusive mode. After you enter the password to open the database, you can then remove the encryption using the Remove Encryption button. In this next exercise, you will save the database with a new name so you still have a password-protected and encrypted version of the database.

Step-by-Step 14.4

1. If necessary, click the **File** tab and click **Open**.
2. Navigate to the **Employee Sales Database 2** file.
3. Click the **Open** button arrow, and then click **Open Exclusive**.
4. Type **CatCat** in the Password Required dialog box.
5. Click **OK**.
6. Click the **File** tab. The Decrypt Database option is displayed. See **Figure 14–6**.

FIGURE 14–6
File tab with Decrypt Database option

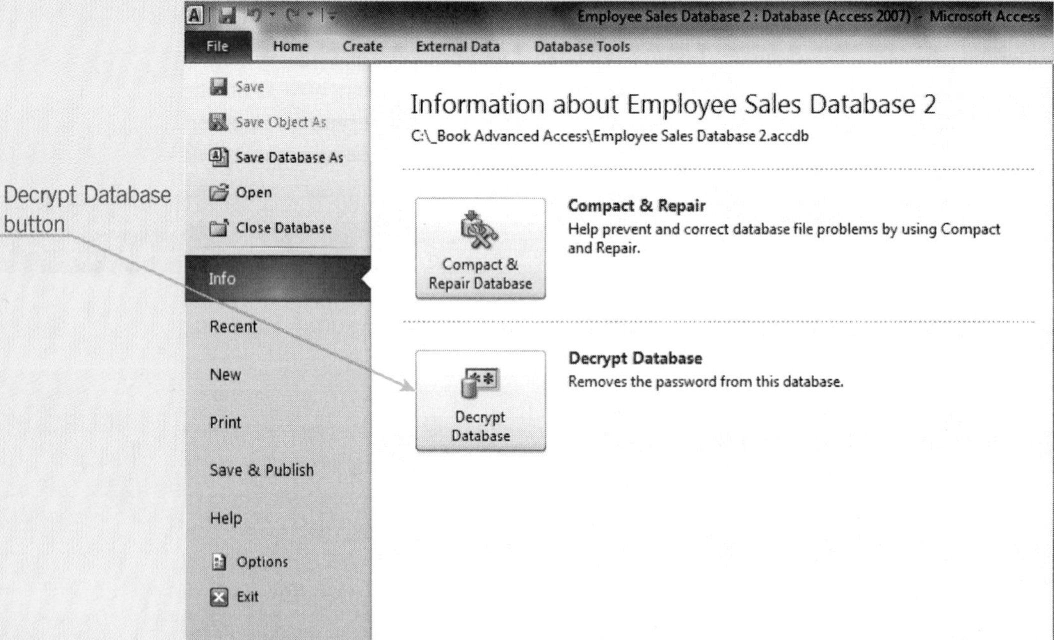

7. Click the **Decrypt Database** button. The Unset Database Password dialog box opens, as shown in **Figure 14–7**.

FIGURE 14–7
Unset Database Password dialog box

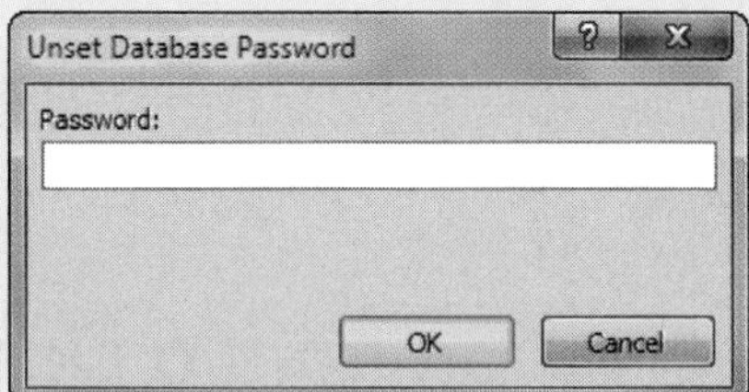

8. Type **CatCat** and then click **OK**.
9. Click the **File** tab. Notice that the Encrypt with Password option is displayed, indicating that the password and encryption are removed.
10. Leave the database open for the next Step-by-Step.

Making a Backup Copy of a Database

It is a good idea to regularly make a backup copy of your database. A ***backup*** is a duplicate copy of your database created by using the Back Up Database option when you save the file. By creating a backup, the database can be restored in the event of a loss resulting from a power failure, a hard disk crash, or malicious or accidental deletion of database objects. A good rule of thumb is to schedule a database backup on a regular basis. For example, you could schedule a backup at the end of each day or at the end of each week. The Back Up Database command uses the same filename and the date that the file was backed up. In this next exercise, you will make a backup copy of a database.

VOCABULARY
backup

Step-by-Step 14.5

1. In the Employee Sales Database, click the **File** tab.
2. Click the **Save & Publish** option. Notice the Back Up Database option, as shown in **Figure 14–8**.

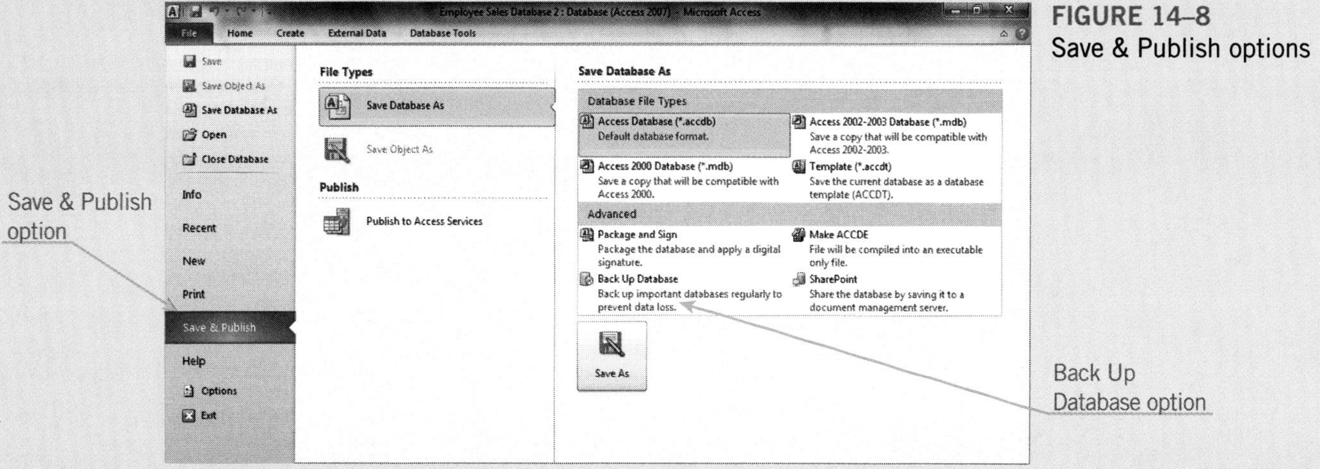

FIGURE 14–8
Save & Publish options

3. Click the **Back Up Database** option. Selecting this option alerts Access that when you click Save As, you want to create a backup of the database.
4. Click the **Save As** button. The Save As dialog box opens, as shown in **Figure 14–9**.

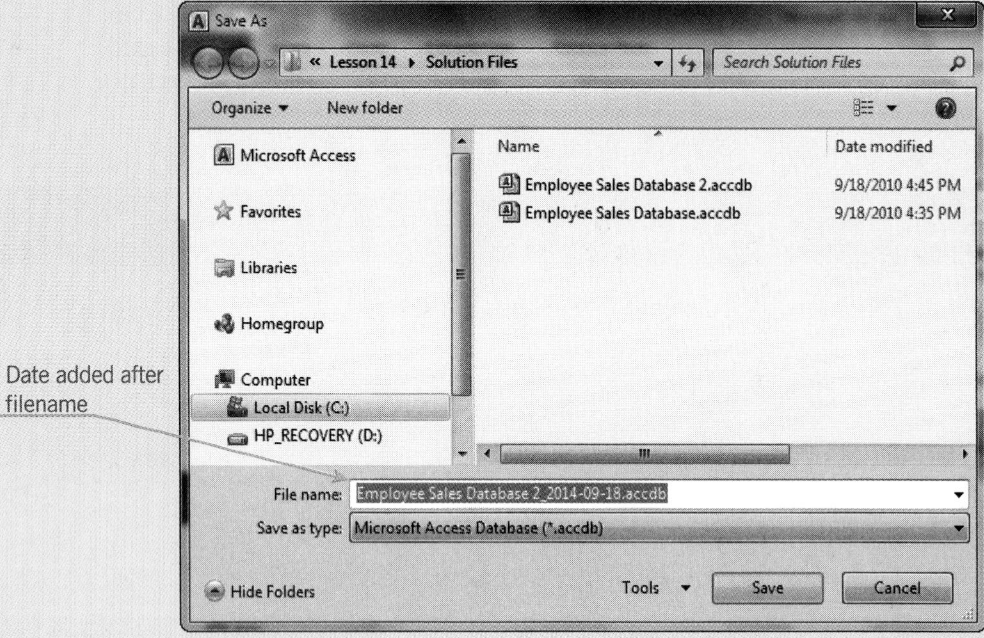

FIGURE 14–9
Save As dialog box

5. Click the **Save** button. Review the Access title bar and notice that Employee Sales Database 2 still appears as the filename.
6. Close the database.
7. In Windows Explorer, navigate to the drive and folder where you saved the backup file, and then view the results. See **Figure 14–10**.

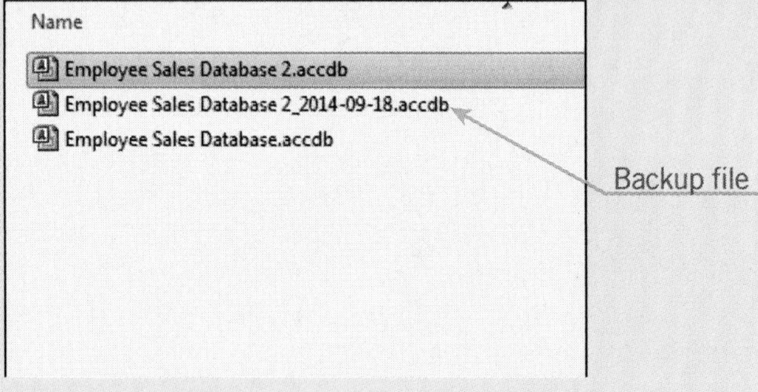

FIGURE 14–10
File list with backup file

8. Close Windows Explorer and return to the Access window.

Documenting the Database Design

Another safety feature for your database is to document the database design in case the file gets damaged or corrupted. The database design refers to the objects in the database, such as tables, queries, forms, reports, macros, and the relationship between these objects. Documenting this design is a good idea so you have it for future reference. In Access, the ***Database Documenter*** produces a report of selected objects or every object in a database. You can document the properties of these objects and the relationships of objects that you select. Then, if a database file gets damaged or corrupted, you should be able to look at the documentation and fix the database or re-create it. In this next exercise, you will create a report that shows information for all the objects in a database.

VOCABULARY
Database Documenter

Step-by-Step 14.6

1. Open the **Happy Pets** file from the drive and folder where your Data Files are stored. Save the database as **Happy Pets Database**, followed by your initials.
2. Click the **Enable Content** button.
3. Click the **Database Tools** tab.
4. In the Analyze group, click the **Database Documenter** button to open the Documenter dialog box, as shown in **Figure 14–11**.

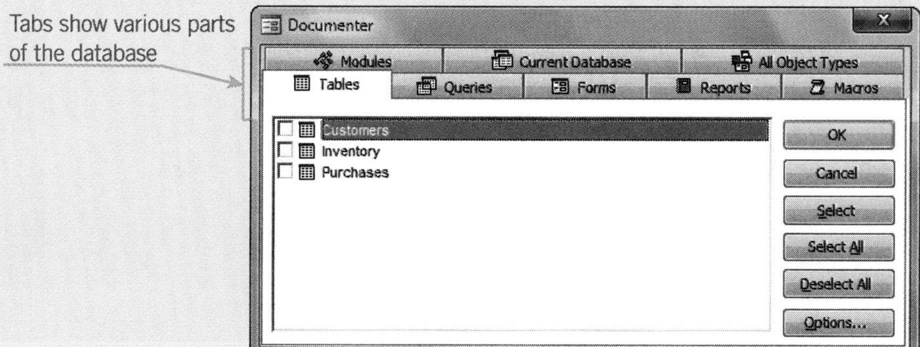

FIGURE 14–11
Documenter dialog box

5. Click the **All Object Types** tab to see all of the objects in the database. To select all of these objects, you can click each check box or click the Select All button.

6. Click the **Select All** button. Compare your screen to **Figure 14–12**.

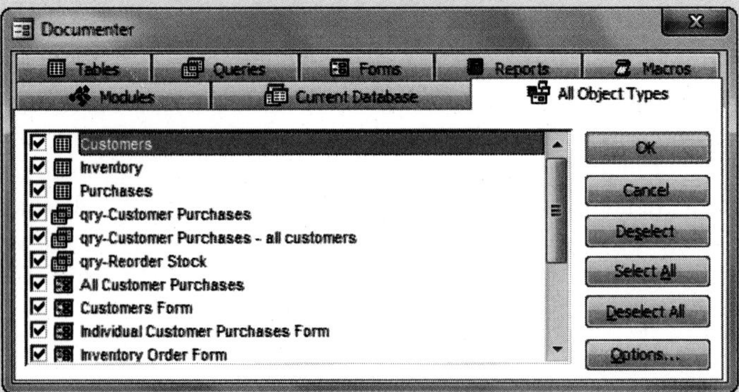

FIGURE 14–12
All Object Types selected

7. Click **OK**. The Object Definition report is displayed. See **Figure 14–13**. To keep a copy of this report, you will save it as a PDF file.

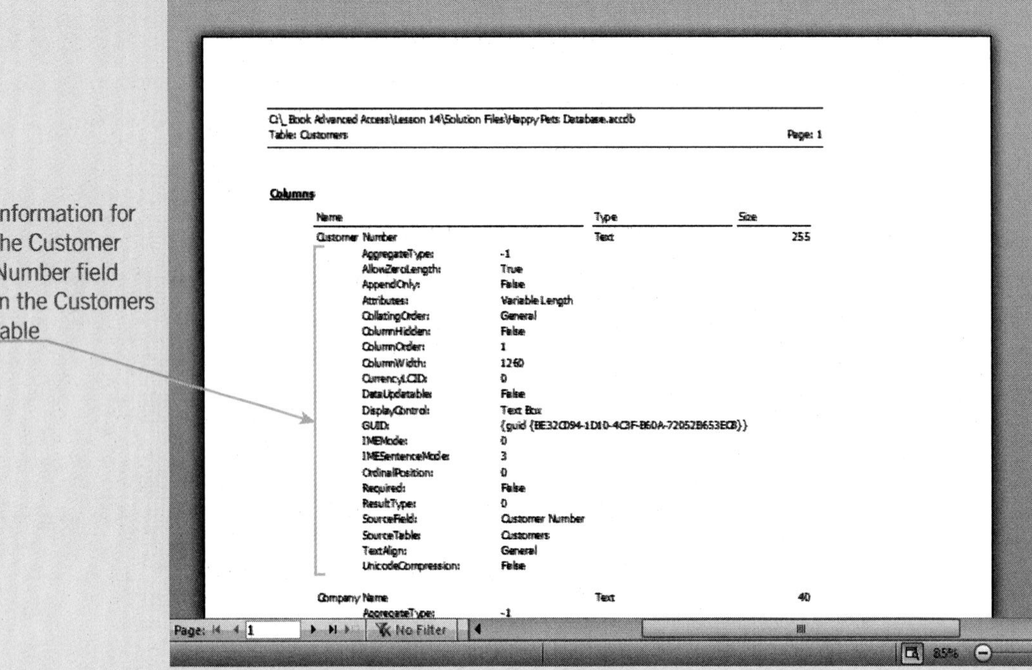

FIGURE 14–13
Object Definition report

8. In the Data group, click the **PDF or XPS** button.
9. Leave the filename as doc_rptObjects.pdf, and then navigate to the drive and folder where your Data Files are stored. Click **Publish**. It will take a minute while the report is converted to a PDF file since there are over 100 pages in this document. The Publish dialog box shows the progress as you wait.
10. Click the **Close** button in the Export – PDF dialog box.
11. In Access, click the **Close Print Preview** button.
12. Close the database.

SUMMARY

In this lesson, you learned:

- When you open a database in the Open Exclusive mode, you are the only individual who can view or make changes to the file.
- Encrypting a database with a password allows only individuals who know the password to open the file.
- Opening an encrypted database requires entering a password.
- The database password and encryption can be removed.
- A backup is a duplicate copy of your database created by using the Back Up Database option when you save the file.
- Documenting the design of a database provides information that can be reviewed if an unwanted change occurs.

VOCABULARY REVIEW

Define the following terms:

backup
Database Documenter
encryption
Open Exclusive mode
password

REVIEW QUESTIONS

TRUE / FALSE

Circle T if the statement is true or F if the statement is false.

T F 1. You can open an encrypted database without a password, but you cannot read the data.

T F 2. The password and database encryption can be removed.

T F 3. A good rule of thumb is to schedule a database backup on a regular basis.

T F 4. Power failures or individuals who maliciously or accidentally delete database objects can cause losses of data in a database.

T F 5. The Open Exclusive Read-Only mode opens the database so that all users except for the current user are locked out and the current user can only view the data in the database.

FILL IN THE BLANK

1. In Access, the ______________ produces a report of selected objects or every object in a database.
2. To add a password and encrypt a database, you need to open the database in ______________ mode.
3. Until a(n) ______________ is entered correctly, no objects in the database can be viewed.
4. To make a copy of a database, you would create a(n) ______________ of the database.
5. A(n) ______________ is a collection of characters that a user types to gain access to a file.

WRITTEN QUESTIONS

Write a brief answer to the following questions.

1. Explain the difference between Open Exclusive Read-Only mode and Open Exclusive mode.

2. Describe what you would do if you only wanted to document the queries in a database.

3. Describe how data loss in a database could occur.

4. Explain the purpose of a backup.

5. Explain the difference between a password and encryption.

PROJECTS

If you have a SAM 2010 user profile, your instructor may have assigned an autogradable version of the indicated project. If so, log into the SAM 2010 Web site at *www.cengage.com/sam2010* to download the instruction and start files.

PROJECT 14–1

1. Open the **Book Sales** file from the drive and folder where your Data Files are stored. Save the database as **Book Sales Database**, followed by your initials.
2. Create a backup of the database.
3. Make sure the date on which you created the backup is in the filename.
4. Close the database.

SAM PROJECT 14–2

1. Open the **Coach Files** file from the drive and folder where your Data Files are stored. Save the database as **Coach Files Database**, followed by your initials.
2. Close the **Coach Files Database** file.
3. Open the **Coach Files Database** in Open Exclusive mode.
4. Encrypt the database with the password **DogDog**.
5. Close the Coach Files Database.
6. Reopen the **Coach Files Database** to test the encryption.
7. Close the database.

PROJECT 14–3

1. Open the **Student Teams** file from the drive and folder where your Data Files are stored. Save the database as **Student Teams Database**, followed by your initials.
2. Use the Database Documenter to document the database.
3. Document all object types.
4. Create a PDF file of the documentation.
5. Name the PDF file **doc_rptObjects – Student Teams.pdf**.
6. Close the database.

CRITICAL THINKING

ACTIVITY 14–1

Open the **Coastal Sales** file from the drive and folder where your Data Files are stored, and then save it as **Coastal Sales Database**. As the new manager for the Coastal Sales Corporation, you decide that the database could use some additional security since it contains customer names, addresses, and sales information. Encrypt the database with the password **CSD2014**. After closing the database, open it to test if you are required to enter a password, then close the database.

ACTIVITY 14–2

Outline the positive aspects and negative aspects of password protecting a database file.

UNIT REVIEW

Advanced Microsoft Access

REVIEW QUESTIONS

TRUE / FALSE

Circle T if the statement is true or F if the statement is false.

T F 1. An input mask is a pattern for common types of data entered in a field.

T F 2. A parameter query allows you to enter a new criterion each time you run the query.

T F 3. It is safe to run an action query without first creating a copy of the table where the actions will be applied.

T F 4. The tab order in a form cannot be changed.

T F 5. Conditional formatting will apply different formats to the control data if certain criteria are met.

T F 6. Macros are susceptible to virus attacks.

T F 7. The AutoExec macro can include an action that opens a form, such as a splash screen.

T F 8. VBA is an abbreviation for Virtual Basic for Applications.

T F 9. A database password and encryption cannot be removed.

T F 10. A wildcard, such as an asterisk, can be used in a query to search for data if you do not know the exact spelling of a person's last name.

FILL IN THE BLANK

Complete the following sentences by writing the correct word or words in the blanks provided.

1. A(n) ________________ query can instantly update several records in a query at one time.
2. To simplify the process of moving from one record to another in a form or adding a new record to a form, you can add ________________.
3. A report that is added to another report is called a(n) ________________.
4. A(n) ________________________ is explanatory text that you can add to a macro, but it does not affect the operation of the macro.
5. To open a database without the startup options, you simply press and hold the ________________ key when you open the database.
6. If you want a function to be available in more than one procedure, you would define the function as a(n) ________________ function.
7. To add a password and encrypt a database, you need to open the database in ________________ mode.

8. A(n) ______________ improves the accuracy of the data entered by automatically adding symbols, such as dashes in a social security number.
9. For format and design consistency, you can add a(n) ______________ to a form.
10. If you want sales data over $150,000 to appear in a unique format, you can add ______________ to the control.

MULTIPLE CHOICE

Select the best response for each of the following statements.

1. The specific information you are searching for in a query is called a ______________.
   A. parameter
   B. criterion
   C. prompt
   D. text
2. If you want to change the way a user moves from field to field in a form record, you change the ______________.
   A. tab order
   B. combo box
   C. query control
   D. format
3. To include a graphical display in a report, you can add a(n) ______________.
   A. calculated control
   B. subform
   C. graph
   D. comment
4. Additional information required to perform a task based on the chosen action in a macro are referred to as ______________.
   A. AutoExec
   B. comment
   C. security level
   D. arguments
5. After you set the lookup properties for a field, a(n) ______________ will appear in the field when it is selected.
   A. arrow
   B. expression
   C. parameter
   D. text control
6. A(n) ______________ can be added to a report to perform calculations using data in the report.
   A. subreport
   B. password
   C. calculated control
   D. input mask

7. You can only have one ______________ within a dabase.

   A. AutoExec macro

   B. function

   C. navigation form

   D. startup

8. An *If* procedure begins with an *If* code word and ends with the code words ______________.

   A. *End*

   B. *End If*

   C. *Sum*

   D. *If Then*

9. The ______________ mode opens the database so that all users except the current user are locked out and a password and encryption can be added to the database.

   A. Open Exclusive

   B. Open Only

   C. Open Exclusive Read-Only

   D. Open

10. The default placeholder for an input mask is the ______________.

    A. asterisk

    B. comma

    C. question mark

    D. underscore

PROJECTS

PROJECT 1

To identify the number of employees at the New Book Sales Corporation, you view the records in the Sales Department table. You decide to add a parameter query where you can enter a title for a group of employees and have all employees in that group displayed in the query results.

1. Open the **New Book Sales** file from the drive and folder where your Data Files are stored. Save the database as **New Book Sales Database**, followed by your initials.
2. Create a parameter query for the Sales Department table. In the Design window, add the Employee ID, Last Name, First Name, and Title fields to the query grid. Since each field in the table will be included in the query, think of a quick way to put each field in the query grid.
3. Enter a prompt in the **Title** field that will prompt the user to enter a title for a group of employees.
4. Sort the query in ascending order by the Last Name field, and then add another sort in ascending order to the First Name field.
5. Save the query as **Qry-Employees by Title**.
6. Run the parameter query using Sales Rep as the criterion. Adjust the column widths if necessary. Print the query results.
7. Run the query using the Sales Assistant and the Sales Manager parameters. Print the results of each query.
8. Close the query and the database file.

PROJECT 2

You have a form that displays purchases made for individual customers. You want to add an embedded macro in the form that will open a second form to display the customer information.

1. Open the **Pet Supplies** file from the drive and folder where your Data Files are stored. Save the database as **Pet Supplies Database**, followed by your initials.
2. Create an embedded macro in the Individual Customer Purchases Form that opens the Customers Form.
3. Use the Customer number field as the field that links the two forms in the macro.
4. Save the Individual Customer Purchases Form.
5. View the Individual Customer Purchases Form in Form View for customer number 10, and then click on the macro button to test it.
6. Close the Customers Form.
7. Close the Individual Customer Purchases Form.
8. Close the database.

PROJECT 3

The Winter Sales file contains information about employee sales. You will create conditional formatting in the Employee Sales Data Report so that employees with sales greater than $125,000 are easy to locate.

1. Open the **Winter Sales** file from the drive and folder where your Data Files are stored.
2. Save the database as **Winter Sales Database** followed by your initials.
3. Open the Employee Sales Data Report to view the data.
4. Switch to Design View.
5. Add a conditional formatting rule to the Sales control that displays sales amounts greater than or equal to $125,000 in a red, bold font.
6. View the report in Report View to be certain the conditional formatting is working correctly.
7. Save the report.
8. Print the report.
9. Close the database.

PROJECT 4

The West Coast Sales file is password protected with the password UnitR. You will open the database and remove the password and encryption. Then, you will use the Database Documenter feature to document the database.

1. Open the **West Coast Sales** file in the appropriate mode so that you can remove the password and encryption.
2. Decrypt the database.
3. Save the database as **West Coast Sales Database**, followed by your initials.
4. Use the Database Documenter to document the database.
5. Document all object types.
6. Document the Properties and Relationships.
7. Create a PDF file of the documentation.
8. Name the PDF file **doc_rptObjects – West Coast Sales.pdf**.
9. Close the database.
10. Open the West Coast Sales Database and check to see that the password is removed.
11. Close the database.

CRITICAL THINKING

JOB 1

As the database administrator for the New Generation Internet Corporation, you want to add automation features to the database. You first decide to create a function that will calculate the difference between two dates. Since you will use the function in several objects throughout the database, you will save it as a public function in a module named basNewProcedures.

1. Open the **New Generation** file from the drive and folder where your Data Files are stored. Save the database as **New Generation Database**, followed by your initials.
2. Define a function named **YearDiff** that calculates the difference between two dates. This function will need to be defined as a public function.
3. Add a comment to the function that explains the purpose of the function.
4. For the date variables, use the variable names **FirstDate** and **SecondDate**.
5. Assign the **Date** data type to both variables.
6. Save the module.
7. Test the function in the Immediate window using the dates 3/15/2006 and 1/15/2014 to see if it is working correctly.
8. Close the module and the database.

JOB 2

As the new database administrator for the Revelation Sales Corporation, you decide to automate the Coastal Sales database to make it easier to use and to prevent unwanted changes. You first open the **Revelation Sales** file and save it as **Revelation Sales Database**. You then create a navigation form for the Main Menu that will include the Navigation – Forms Menu and the Navigation – Reports Menu. Change the tab titles to read Forms Menu and Reports Menu. Change the title of the Main Menu navigation form to read Main Menu, and save the form as Navigation – Main Menu. Then, you change the startup options so that the Navigation – Main Menu form appears when the database is opened. You also set the startup options to hide the Navigation pane and all but the File and Home tabs on the Ribbon when the database opens. Close the database, and then reopen it to be certain that all the features are working correctly. Close the database.

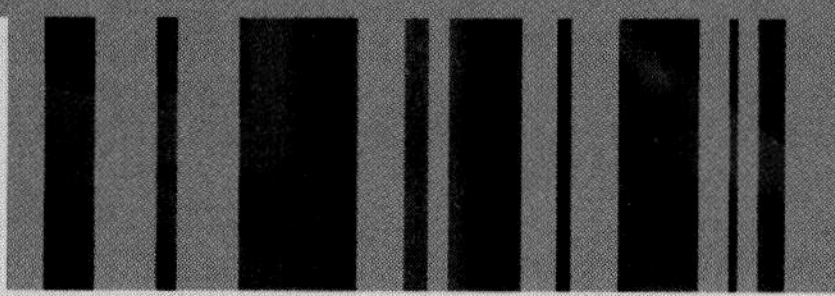

Estimated Time for Unit: 9.5 hours

ADVANCED

MICROSOFT POWERPOINT UNIT

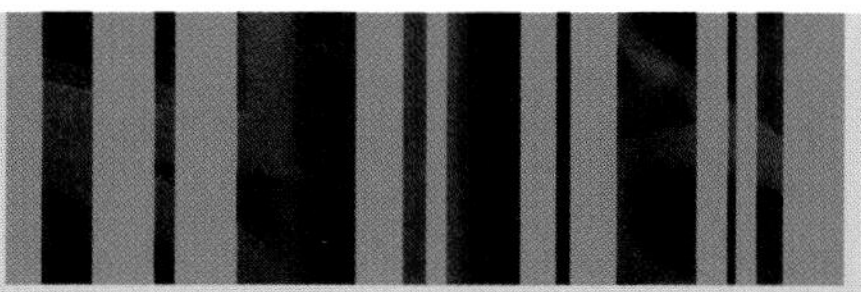

Estimated Time:
1 hour

LESSON 5

Editing and Formatting Slide Content

■ OBJECTIVES

Upon completion of this lesson, you should be able to:

- Customize the AutoCorrect list.
- Create a custom dictionary.
- Insert symbols and adjust character height.
- Number paragraphs and customize bullets.
- Format items for progressive disclosure.
- Create an interactive text box.
- Modify SmartArt graphics.
- Organize slide content and create a summary slide.

■ VOCABULARY

hot spot

image map

progressive disclosure

summary slide

Your first impression of a PowerPoint slide is probably the graphical elements, such as colors, background pattern, and layout. However, text is also an important element, and the text formatting can help you create a very impressive presentation. In this lesson, you will learn how to edit and manipulate text on slides.

Editing and Proofing the Text

Words can be very powerful when the right ones are used effectively. Correct spelling is also important because when your audience notices a misspelled word, you quickly lose credibility. Even when we know how to correctly spell a word, we sometimes type it incorrectly. PowerPoint offers several features to help you proof the text you add to slides. The proofing tools not only check spelling and grammar, but they also check capitalization and formats.

Customizing the AutoCorrect List

PowerPoint's AutoCorrect feature will automatically correct commonly misspelled words, without prompting you, so you may not even realize the correction was made. To ensure you don't misspell words that you commonly use, you can add the words to the AutoCorrect list. You can also customize the AutoCorrect list to include terms and phrases with unique spelling and/or capitalization that you don't want PowerPoint to automatically correct.

In the next Step-by-Step, you will add a new entry to the AutoCorrect list and create an AutoCorrect exception. However, because you may be sharing a computer, you will delete the new entry and the exception at the end of the Step-by-Step.

Step-by-Step 5.1

1. Launch PowerPoint. Open the **Coasting** file from the drive and folder where your Data Files are stored. Save the presentation as **Revised Coasting 1**, followed by your initials.
2. Click the **File** tab, and then click **Options**. In the left pane of the PowerPoint Options dialog box, click **Proofing**.
3. Under AutoCorrect options, click **AutoCorrect Options**. The AutoCorrect dialog box opens, as shown in **Figure 5–1**. (If necessary, click the AutoCorrect tab.) Text shown in the left column (Replace) is automatically replaced with the text shown in the right column (With).

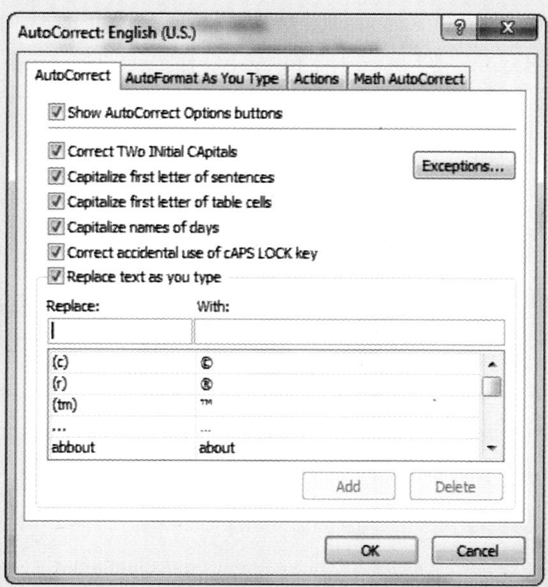

FIGURE 5–1
AutoCorrect dialog box

4. Scroll through the list of frequently misspelled words until you see *acheive*. Note that PowerPoint will automatically correct this misspelling and change the word to *achieve*.
5. In the Replace text box, type **aep**. In the With text box, type **Aventura EXtreme PlayLand**. Click **Add**.
6. In the AutoCorrect dialog box, click **Exceptions** to open the AutoCorrect Exceptions dialog box, as shown in **Figure 5–2**. Click the **INitial CAps** tab. Your dialog box may include a list of exceptions.

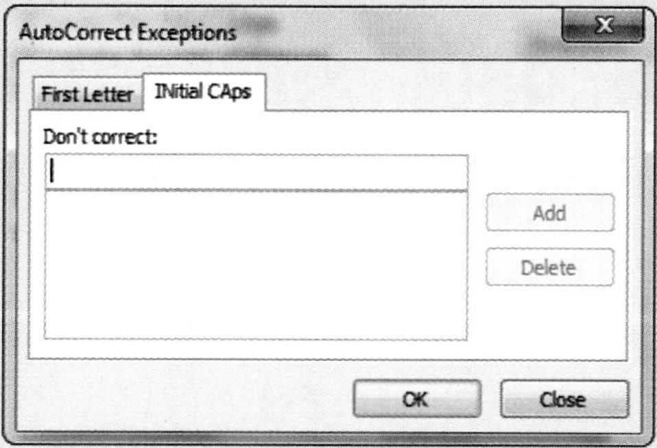

FIGURE 5–2
AutoCorrect Exceptions dialog box

7. In the Don't correct text box, type **EXtreme** and then click **Add**. Normally, PowerPoint would automatically change the second capital letter in the word EXtreme to lowercase, but this exception will prevent PowerPoint from making that AutoCorrect change.
8. Add the following words to the list: **EXperience**, **EXciting**, and **EXhilarating**. Click **OK** three times to close the dialog boxes.
9. On slide 1, click the **Click to add subtitle** placeholder. Type **aep** and then press the **spacebar**. When you press the spacebar, the text you typed is automatically altered to show the park name *Aventura EXtreme PlayLand.*

10. On slide 2, change *Experience* in the title to **EXperience**. In the Click to add text placeholder, type the following three bulleted items:

    EXtreme

    EXciting

    EXhilarating

11. Click the **File** tab, and then click **Options**. In the left pane of the PowerPoint Options dialog box, click **Proofing** and then click **AutoCorrect Options**. In the Replace text box, type **aep**. The entry in the list is selected. Click **Delete**.
12. Click **Exceptions**, and then click the **INitial CAps** tab. Select each of the four entries (EXciting, EXhilarating, EXperience, and EXtreme) and click **Delete**.
13. Click **OK** three times to close the dialog boxes and the PowerPoint options.
14. Save the changes and leave the presentation open for the next Step-by-Step.

Creating a Custom Dictionary

If you frequently use proper names and acronyms that are not in Word's standard dictionary, you will find that adding those words to a custom dictionary is helpful so they aren't flagged as unknown or misspelled words during a spell check. Creating a custom dictionary in PowerPoint is the same as creating a custom dictionary in other Office applications. When you add words to a dictionary, the new words are saved in the dictionary designated as the default dictionary.

Step-by-Step 5.2

1. If necessary, open the **Revised Coasting 1** file from your solution files. Save the presentation as **Revised Coasting 2**, followed by your initials.
2. Go to slide 2. If your Proofing settings are set to check spelling as you type, a wavy red line appears below the unknown words, such as those beginning with *EX*.
3. Click the **File** tab, and then click **Options**. In the left pane of the PowerPoint Options dialog box, click **Proofing**. Under When correcting spelling in Microsoft Office programs, click **Custom Dictionaries** to open the Custom Dictionaries dialog box, as shown in **Figure 5–3**. Your list of available dictionaries may differ. The CUSTOM.DIC default dictionary appears in the Dictionary List.

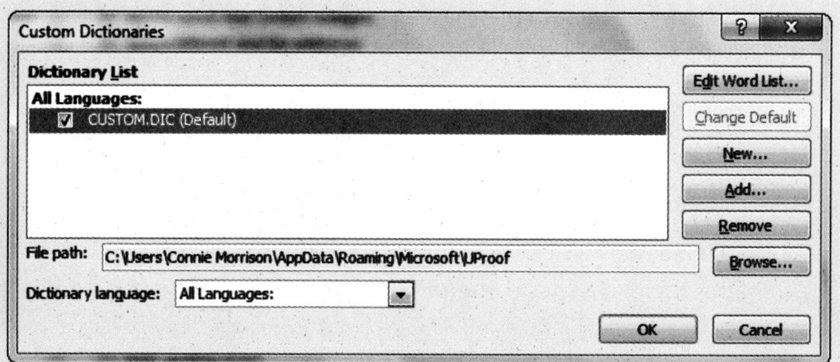

FIGURE 5–3
Custom Dictionaries dialog box

4. In the dialog box, click **New** to open the Create Custom Dictionary dialog box. Navigate to the drive and folder where you save your solution files. In the File name box, type **AEP**, followed by your initials. Do not change the file type. Word will add the .dic extension to the filename. Click **Save**. Now there are two dictionaries in the Dictionary List; the check marks indicate that both dictionaries are active.
5. In the Custom Dictionaries dialog box, select the AEP dictionary if necessary. Click **Edit Word List**. A dialog box for the new AEP dictionary opens. Currently, the Dictionary List contains no words. In the Word(s) text box, type **EXtreme**, click **Add**, and then click **OK**. The new word is added to the Dictionary List.
6. In the Custom Dictionaries dialog box, the AEP dictionary should still be selected. (Be sure not to uncheck it.) Click **Change Default**. In the Dictionary List, the order of the dictionaries is rearranged, and the AEP dictionary is now the default dictionary. When you save a word to the dictionary during a spell check, the word will be saved in the AEP dictionary.
7. Click **OK** twice to close the dialog boxes. Check slides 1 and 2 and note that the wavy red line no longer appears under the word EXtreme.
8. In slide 2, right-click the word **EXperience**. In the shortcut menu, click **Add to Dictionary**. The word is added to the AEP dictionary because that is the default dictionary.
9. Using the same right-click method, add the words *EXciting* and *EXhilarating* to the default dictionary. There are no more red wavy lines on slide 2.
10. Go to slide 1. Add the word *PlayLand* to the dictionary.
11. Click the **Review** tab. In the Proofing group, click the **Spelling** button to start the spell checker. The word *clickety* is flagged as an unknown spelling. Click **Add**. A prompt appears indicating that the spelling check is complete. Click **OK** to close the prompt. Note that the red wavy line no longer displays below the word *clickety*.

12. Click the **File** tab, and then click **Options**. In the left pane of the PowerPoint Options dialog box, click **Proofing**. Click **Custom Dictionaries**. The AEP dictionary is already selected. Click **Edit Word List**. Note that the custom dictionary now lists six words. Click **OK** to close the AEP.dic dialog box.
13. In the Custom Dictionaries dialog box, select **CUSTOM.DIC**, and then click **Change Default**. Click the **AEP** dictionary, and then click **Remove**. Close the dialog box, and then click **OK** again to close the PowerPoint Options dialog box.
14. Save the changes and leave the presentation open for the next Step-by-Step.

Improving the Readability of Slide Content

Using symbols and characters instead of words can help to explain the content in a presentation and also make the text easier to read. Adjusting the height of the font characters can also improve readability. To further clarify the content, you can number lists to indicate a sequence or a ranking of content.

Inserting Symbols and Adjusting Character Height

Sometimes you can improve the readability of the slide content and also reduce the number of words on a slide by inserting special characters and symbols. For example, you can you can use the symbol ≥ instead of *greater than or equal to*. You are not limited to the symbols shown for the current font (called *normal text* in the dialog box). Fonts such as Webdings and Wingdings supply many different types of symbols, shapes, arrows, and numbers.

The Repeat button on the Quick Access Toolbar is useful when inserting the same symbol in different locations throughout the presentation. If you frequently use the Quick Access Toolbar, you can reposition it below the Ribbon for ease of use.

Depending on the font style, the height of numbers and letters may be significantly different. You can easily adjust the character height to make the text easier to read. When you apply the Equalize Character Height option, the selected characters are expanded to fill the height of the line of text. The newly formatted text often appears taller than the surrounding characters, making this format useful when formatting the height of numbers or whole words.

Step-by-Step 5.3

1. If necessary, open the **Revised Coasting 2** file from your solution files. Save the presentation as **Revised Coasting 3**, followed by your initials.
2. On the right side of the Quick Access Toolbar, click the **Customize Quick Access Toolbar** button. At the bottom of the menu, click **Show Below the Ribbon**.
3. Go to slide 8. In the second bulleted item, select the words **of greater than or equal to**. Click the **Insert** tab. In the Symbols group, click the

Symbol button to open the Symbol dialog box, as shown in **Figure 5–4**. Your settings will be different.

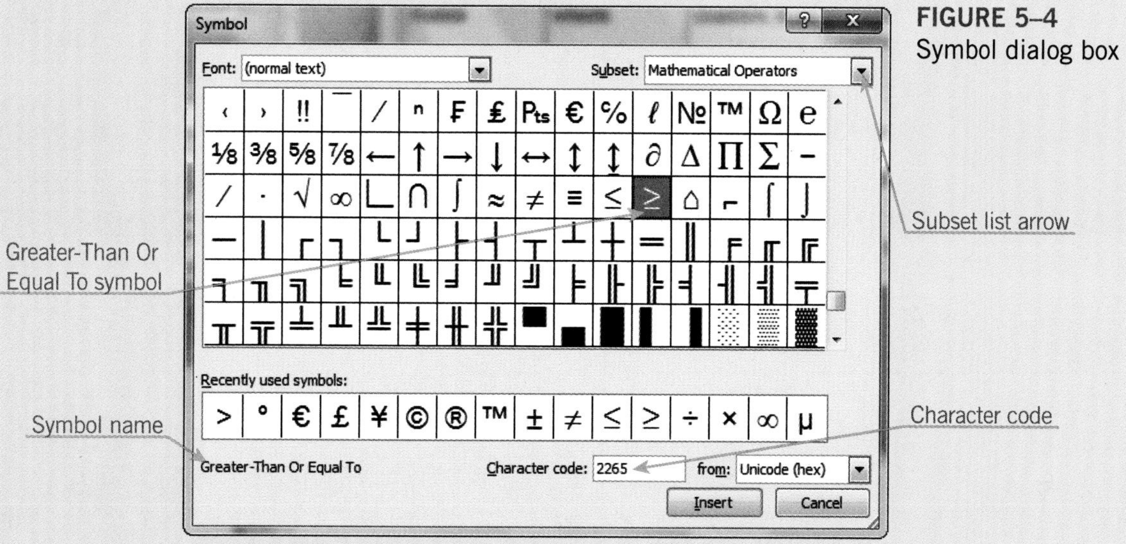

FIGURE 5–4 Symbol dialog box

4. Click the **Subset** list arrow, scroll down and select **Mathematical Operators**, and then click the **Greater-Than Or Equal To** symbol. The name of the symbol displays in the lower-left corner of the dialog box.
5. Click **Insert** and then close the dialog box. The symbol replaces the selected text.
6. Go to slide 5. Position the insertion point in front of the word *Pro.* Click the **Symbol** button to reopen the Symbol dialog box.
7. Click the **Font** list arrow, scroll down to the bottom of the list, and then select **Wingdings**. Find and select a **thumbs-up** symbol. Click **Insert** and then close the dialog box.
8. Go to slide 4. Position the insertion point in front of the word *Pro.* Click the **Repeat** button on the Quick Access Toolbar to insert the thumbs-up symbol.
9. Position the insertion point in front of the word *Con.* Click the **Symbol** button. The Symbol dialog box opens, displaying the Wingdings symbols. Find and select a **thumbs-down** symbol. Click **Insert** and then close the dialog box. Go to slide 5. Position the insertion point in front of the word *Con* and repeat the edit.
10. Go to slide 8. In the first bulleted item, select the number **1**. Click the **Home** tab, and then in the Font group, click the **Dialog Box Launcher** to open the Font dialog box.
11. Under Effects, enable the **Equalize Character Height** option and then click **OK**. The height of the selected text is adjusted to a size comparable to the surrounding text.

12. In the second bulleted item, select the **Greater-Than Or Equal To** symbol and the number **3**. Then click the **Repeat** button on the Quick Access Toolbar. Select the number **5** in the second bulleted item, and click the **Repeat** button again. You cannot include the decimal in the selection because it would then be the same height as the numbers.
13. With the number 5 still selected, double-click the **Format Painter** button in the Clipboard group. Then click the word **scary** in the second bulleted item to apply the font format. Drag the mouse pointer across each of the numbers in the third bulleted item to copy the format and equalize the height for each of those characters. Press **Esc** to toggle off the Format Painter feature.
14. On the Quick Access Toolbar, click the **Customize Quick Access Toolbar** button. At the bottom of the menu, click **Show Above the Ribbon**. Save the changes and leave the presentation open for the next Step-by-Step.

Formatting Bulleted and Numbered Lists

Many of the slide layouts help you organize text data into bulleted lists. To "jazz up" the bulleted list, you can customize the bullets using a symbol. If a list of items indicates a specific sequence or a ranking, you can replace the bullets with numbers. When applying the numbering format, the items are automatically numbered. If you edit the list and add, delete, or rearrange the order of the items, the numbers are automatically updated. If you want to continue the numbered list on a successive slide, you can specify a starting number.

Step-by-Step 5.4

1. If necessary, open the **Revised Coasting 3** file from your solution files. Save the presentation as **Revised Coasting 4**, followed by your initials.
2. Go to slide 11. Select all the items in the bulleted list. If necessary, click the Home tab. In the Paragraph group, click the **Numbering** button. The paragraphs are formatted with numbers 1, 2, 3, and 4.
3. Go to slide 12 and select all the items in the bulleted list. Click the **Numbering** button arrow. At the bottom of the menu, click **Bullets and Numbering** to open the Numbered tab in the Bullets and Numbering dialog box, as shown in **Figure 5–5**. Your settings will differ.

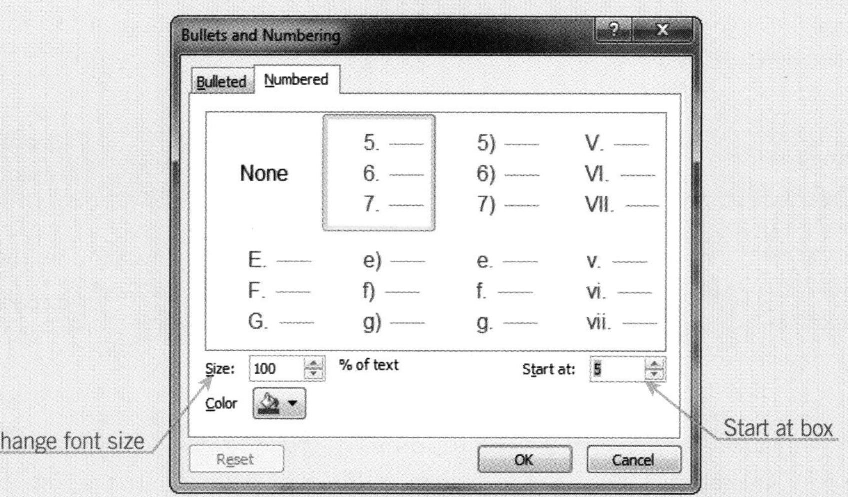

FIGURE 5–5
Numbered tab in the Bullets and Numbering dialog box

4. Select the **1., 2., 3.** number format. Change the setting in the Start at box to **5**. Your settings should match those in Figure 5–5. Note that you can change the font size for the number as a percentage of text. Click **OK**.
5. With the numbered list still selected, click the **Numbering** button arrow, click **Bullets and Numbering**, and then click the **Bulleted** tab. Click **Customize** to open the Symbol dialog box.
6. Click the **Font** list arrow, scroll down, and select **Wingdings**. Then select a symbol showing a check mark inside a box. Click **OK**. The new bullet option is added to the Bulleted tab. Click **OK** again. The bullets are updated to show the new symbol.
7. Go to slide 11. Select the numbered list, and then click the **Repeat** button on the Quick Access Toolbar.
8. Deselect the bulleted list.
9. Save the changes and leave the presentation open for the next Step-by-Step.

Formatting Progressive Disclosure

When delivering a presentation, you can format the titles, subtitles, bulleted and numbered lists, and graphics for progressive disclosure. ***Progressive disclosure*** is a technique that reveals slide content in increments. By using progressive disclosure, the objects will appear one at a time, as opposed to all the objects appearing at the same time, allowing the audience to focus on a single item. To format slide content for progressive disclosure, you apply customized animations. PowerPoint provides numerous animations for entrance, emphasis, exit, and motion path effects. Commonly used and recently used effects appear in the Animation group on the Animations tab. To view all the effects available, click the More button in the Animation group and then select one of the More Effects commands at the bottom of the menu. When formatting animations, you can control the direction from which objects enter or exit the slide and you can also adjust settings to reveal text in specified increments, such as one word at a time, one paragraph at a time, or all paragraphs at once.

VOCABULARY
progressive disclosure

In the next Step-by-Step you will customize the animation for text, but keep in mind that you can also create custom animations for objects such as clip art, charts, and SmartArt graphics.

Step-by-Step 5.5

1. If necessary, open the **Revised Coasting 4** file from your solution files. Save the presentation as **Revised Coasting 5**, followed by your initials.
2. If necessary, go to slide 11. Click anywhere within the bulleted list to select the placeholder. (Do not select all the text in the bulleted list.)
3. Click the **Animations** tab. In the Advanced Animation group, click the **Add Animation** button. At the bottom of the submenu, click **More Entrance Effects**. Under Basic, click the **Peek In** entrance effect. A live preview appears in the Slide pane. Click **OK**. Note that in the Slide pane, each of the items in the bulleted list is assigned a number indicating the sequence of the animated objects.
4. On the Animations tab, in the Advanced Animation group, click the **Animation Pane** button. In the Animation Pane, click the **list arrow** to the right of the #1 animation object *Content Place*. The submenu for the animation object opens, as shown in **Figure 5–6**. Note that the option *Start On Click* is already selected.

FIGURE 5–6
Animation Pane

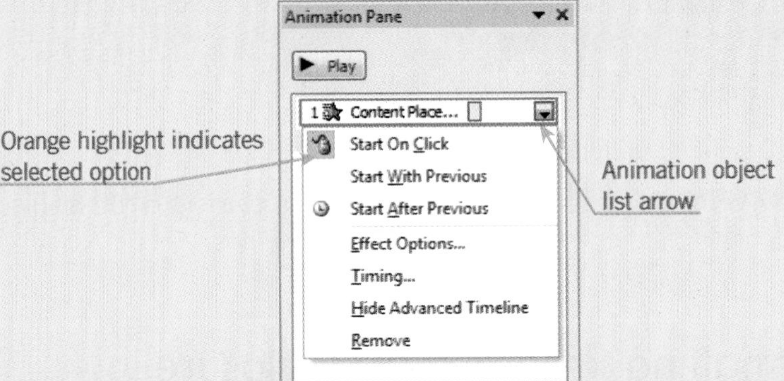

5. In the submenu, click Effect Options. The Peek In dialog box opens, as shown in **Figure 5–7**. Your settings will differ.

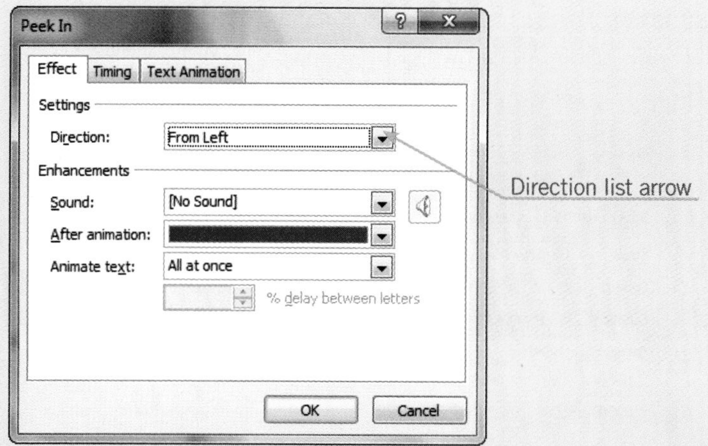

FIGURE 5–7
Effect tab in the Peek In dialog box

6. Under Settings, click the **Direction** list arrow and then click **From Right**. Click the **Text Animation** tab. Click the **Group text** list arrow and then click **All Paragraphs At Once**. Click **OK**. The animation previews on the slide.
7. In the Animation Pane, click the **list arrow** to the right of the #1 animation object **Content Place** and then click **Effect Options**. Click the **Text Animation** tab. Click the **Group text** list arrow and then click **By 1st Level Paragraphs**. Click the **Effect** tab. Under Settings, click the **Direction** list arrow and then click **From Left**. Click the **After animation** list arrow, and then select the **dark red** color in the color grid. When your settings match those shown in Figure 5–7, click **OK**.
8. In the Slide pane, click anywhere within the bulleted list placeholder. (Do not select all the text in the bulleted list.) In the Advanced Animation group, double-click the **Animation Painter** button.
9. Go to slide 12 and click anywhere within the bulleted list to copy the animation formats. Then go to slide 10 and click anywhere within the bulleted list. Click the **Animation Painter** button to toggle off the feature. Note that all the items in the second level paragraphs of the bulleted list are assigned the number 2 in the animation sequence, which means all the items will appear at the same time.
10. In the Animation Pane, click the **Expand** button to show all the animation objects. In the Slide pane, select all the second level bulleted paragraphs. Note that the items are also selected in the

EXTRA FOR EXPERTS

When customizing animations, you can also use the setting to hide the object following the animation. In the Animation Pane, select the object list arrow, click Effect Options, and then click the After animation list arrow. Click Hide After Animation, and then click OK.

EXTRA FOR EXPERTS

To change the order of the animated objects, drag and drop the objects in the Animation Pane.

Animation Pane. In the Animation Pane, click the **list arrow** for the last item. Then click **Timing** to open the Peek In dialog box, as shown in **Figure 5–8**. Your settings will be different.

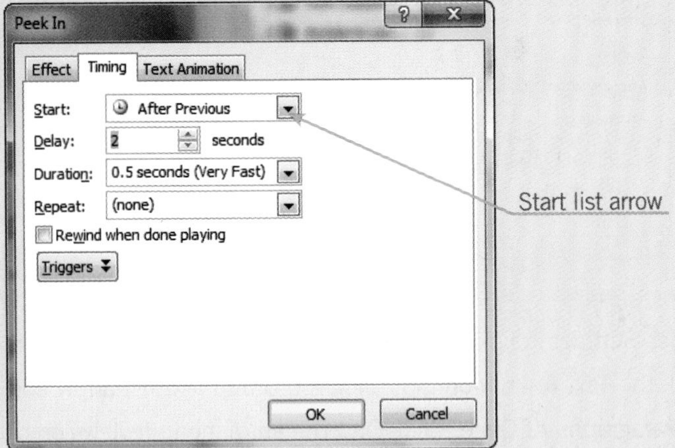

FIGURE 5–8
Timing tab in the Peek In dialog box

11. Click the **Start** list arrow, and then click **After Previous**. Change the Delay setting to **2**. When your settings match those in Figure 5–8, click **OK** and then close the Animation Pane.
12. Click the **Slide Show** tab. In the Start Slide Show group, click the **From Current Slide** button. Click to advance to the first two bulleted items on the slide. Then wait patiently as the second level paragraph bulleted items automatically appear.
13. Click to advance to the next slide and continue to click through the progressive disclosure for all the bulleted items on the last two slides.
14. Press **Esc** to return to Normal view. Save the changes and leave the presentation open for the next Step-by-Step.

Adding Interactive Features to the Slide Content

Adding an interactive feature can help to make a slide show more interesting and a presentation more practical. For example, you can add content to the slides while delivering the presentation, and you can create links to other slides and documents to provide access to additional information.

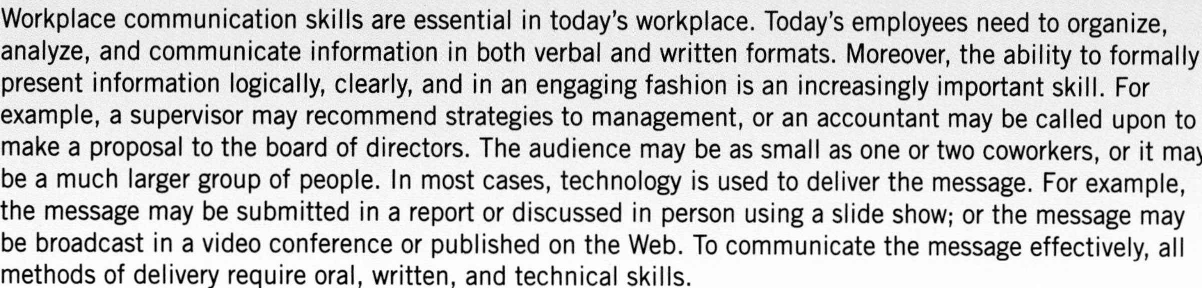

TECHNOLOGY CAREERS

Workplace communication skills are essential in today's workplace. Today's employees need to organize, analyze, and communicate information in both verbal and written formats. Moreover, the ability to formally present information logically, clearly, and in an engaging fashion is an increasingly important skill. For example, a supervisor may recommend strategies to management, or an accountant may be called upon to make a proposal to the board of directors. The audience may be as small as one or two coworkers, or it may be a much larger group of people. In most cases, technology is used to deliver the message. For example, the message may be submitted in a report or discussed in person using a slide show; or the message may be broadcast in a video conference or published on the Web. To communicate the message effectively, all methods of delivery require oral, written, and technical skills.

Adding ActiveX Controls to the Slide

The ActiveX controls on the Developer tab enable you to create interactive objects on a slide. For example, you can insert a text box, adjust the text box size as needed, and access the Properties pane to apply additional formats to the text box such as the font style or size. Then, as you deliver the presentation in Slide Show view, you can type text in the box to update the content on the slide. For example, during a presentation, you ask the audience about their preferences for wooden or steel roller coasters, and then you tally the responses and type the numbers on the slide. When you use this interactive feature, the new content is automatically saved with the presentation.

Step-by-Step 5.6

1. If necessary, open the **Revised Coasting 5** file from your solution files. Save the presentation as **Revised Coasting 6**, followed by your initials.
2. If the Developer tab already appears on the Ribbon, go to Step 3. If the Developer tab does not appear on the Ribbon, click **File** and then click **Options**. In the left pane of the PowerPoint Options dialog box, click **Customize Ribbon**. In the pane on the right, enable the **Developer** option and then click **OK**.
3. Go to slide 6. Click the **Developer** tab. In the Controls group, click the **Text Box (ActiveX Control)** button. The mouse pointer changes to a cross-hair +.
4. In the Click to add text placeholder on the left, under *Wooden*, drag the mouse pointer to create a text box approximately 1 inch high and 1 inch wide. (*Hint*: Show the Ruler.) Center the new text box under the word *Wooden*.

5. Right-click the **text box**, and then click **Properties**. The Properties pane, similar to the one shown in **Figure 5–9**, opens.

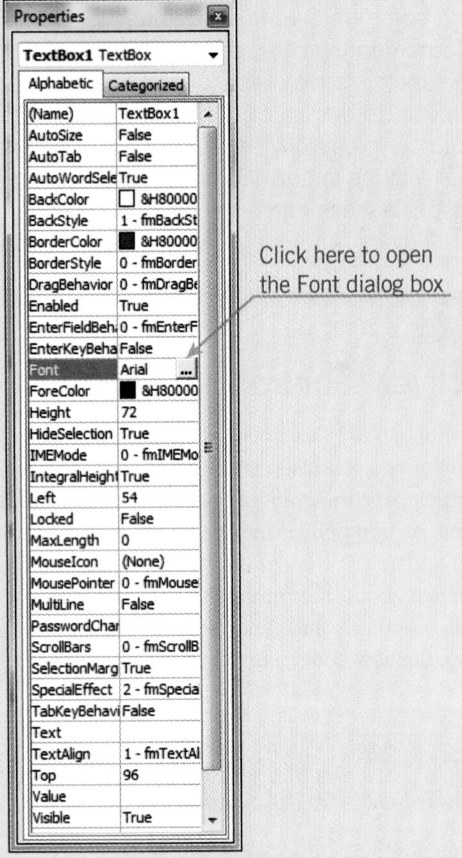

FIGURE 5–9
TextBox1 Properties pane

6. In the left column, click **Font**, and then click the **ellipsis** button (...) in the right column to open the Font dialog box. Change the font size to **36** and then click **OK**. Close the Properties pane.
7. Copy and paste the text box, then reposition the second text box so it is centered under the word *Steel* in the Click to add text placeholder on the right. (*Hint*: Drag and drop the text box, or use the arrow keys.)
8. Save the changes to the presentation.
9. Switch to Slide Show view, showing the current slide. Click the **text box** under *Wooden* and type the number **15**. Click the **text box** under *Steel* and type the number **36**.
10. Press **Esc** to switch to Normal view. Note that the numbers still appear in the interactive boxes.
11. Save the changes and leave the presentation open for the next Step-by-Step.

Modifying SmartArt Graphics

You can easily reorder and resize the shapes in a SmartArt graphic. To work with the shapes individually, you can convert a SmartArt graphic to shapes. For example, you can reposition one or more of the shapes without affecting the other shapes. However, there is no command available for converting the shapes back to a SmartArt graphic.

An ***image map*** a graphic that contains multiple hyperlinks on various parts of the image without dividing the graphic into separate objects. Typically, image maps are used for hyperlinks on Web pages, but you can also create them for PowerPoint slide graphics such as charts and SmartArt graphics.

In the next Step-by-Step, you will format a transparent (invisible) shape on top of a SmartArt shape to identify a ***hot spot***, which is a hyperlink created for a part of the image map. You can have multiple hot spots on a graphic, each mapped to a target. By adding ScreenTips, you can make the user aware of the hot spots.

VOCABULARY
image map
hot spot

Step-by-Step 5.7

1. If necessary, open the **Revised Coasting 6** file from your solution files. Save the presentation as **Revised Coasting 7**, followed by your initials.
2. Launch Word, and then navigate to the drive and folder where your Data Files are stored and open the **Terms.docx** document. Save the document as **Coaster Terms**, followed by your initials, and then close the document. Exit Word.
3. In PowerPoint, go to slide 9. Right-click anywhere within the bulleted list placeholder, point to **Convert to SmartArt**, and then click **More SmartArt Graphics**. In the left pane, click **Cycle**. In the center pane, click the **Nondirectional Cycle** option, as shown in **Figure 5–10**. Click **OK**.

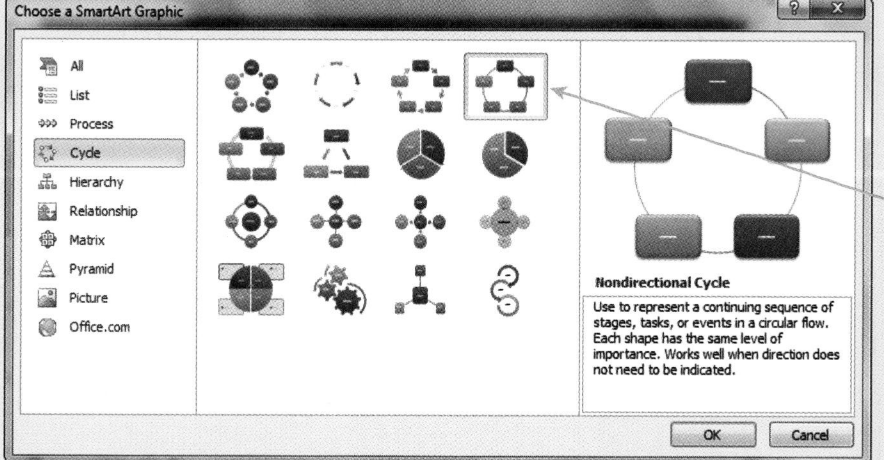

FIGURE 5–10
Cycle category in the Choose a SmartArt Graphic dialog box

4. Maximize the SmartArt graphic by dragging the borders so that the object fills the lower portion of the slide. Then resize and reorder the SmartArt graphic objects:
   a. Click the SmartArt graphic object containing the text *corkscrew* to select it. Press and hold **Ctrl** and select each of the other rounded rectangle objects in the circle. Make sure the selection handles appear around each of the rounded rectangles.
   b. Click the **SmartArt Tools Format tab**. In the Shapes group, click the **Larger** button three times to increase the size of the rounded rectangles. Then click the **Smaller** button once to reduce the size of the rounded rectangles. Deselect the rounded rectangles.
   c. Select the **corkscrew** SmartArt graphic object. Click the **SmartArt Tools Design tab**. In the Create Graphic group, click the **Move Down** button. The *corkscrew* object exchanges positions with the *inverted* object. Click the **Move Up** button to restore the original positions.
   d. The **corkscrew** SmartArt graphic object should be selected. Drag it to the center of the circle. Note that as you move the rounded rectangle, the lines on both sides of the rounded rectangle move with it. Click the **Undo** button on the Quick Access Toolbar to restore the original position of the corkscrew object.
5. Click in a blank area of the SmartArt graphic to select it and to deselect the corkscrew object. Click the **SmartArt Tools Design tab**. In the Reset group, click the **Convert** button and then click **Convert to Shapes**. The shapes look very similar and are arranged the same.
6. Select the **corkscrew** shape and drag the shape to the center of the circle. The connecting lines do not move. Click **Undo** on the Quick Access Toolbar twice to undo moving the shape and to undo converting the SmartArt graphic to shapes.
7. Click the **Insert** tab. In the Illustrations group, click the **Shapes** button. Under Rectangles, click the **Rounded Rectangle** shape. The mouse pointer changes to a cross-hair. Click and drag the mouse pointer over the G-force rounded rectangle in the SmartArt graphic to create a new rectangle shape. Drag the corner shape handles to resize the new rectangle shape as needed so it fits within the G-force SmartArt graphic object, as shown in **Figure 5–11**.

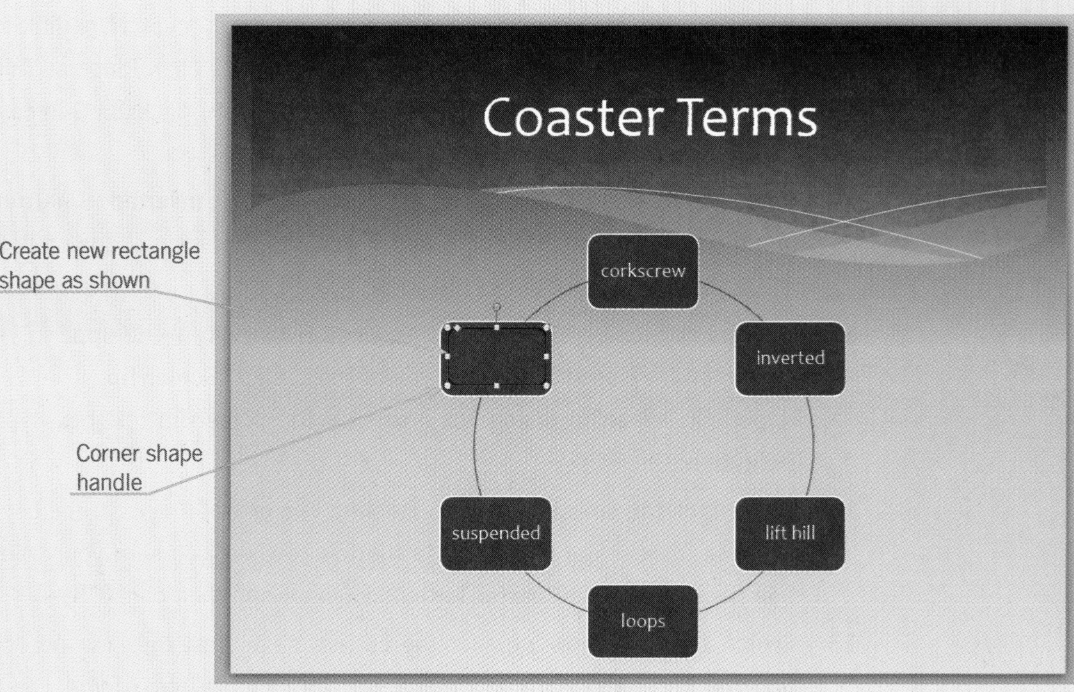

FIGURE 5–11 New shape positioned over the G-force SmartArt graphic object

8. Right-click the new **rounded rectangle** shape and then click **Format Shape** to open the Format Shape dialog box, as shown in **Figure 5–12**. Your settings will differ. Format the shape:
   a. Drag the **Transparency** slider to the right to change the transparency setting to **100%**.
   b. In the left pane, click **Line Color**. In the right pane, click the **No line** option.
   c. Click **Close**. The new shape is still selected, and the text in the G-force SmartArt graphic object is again visible.

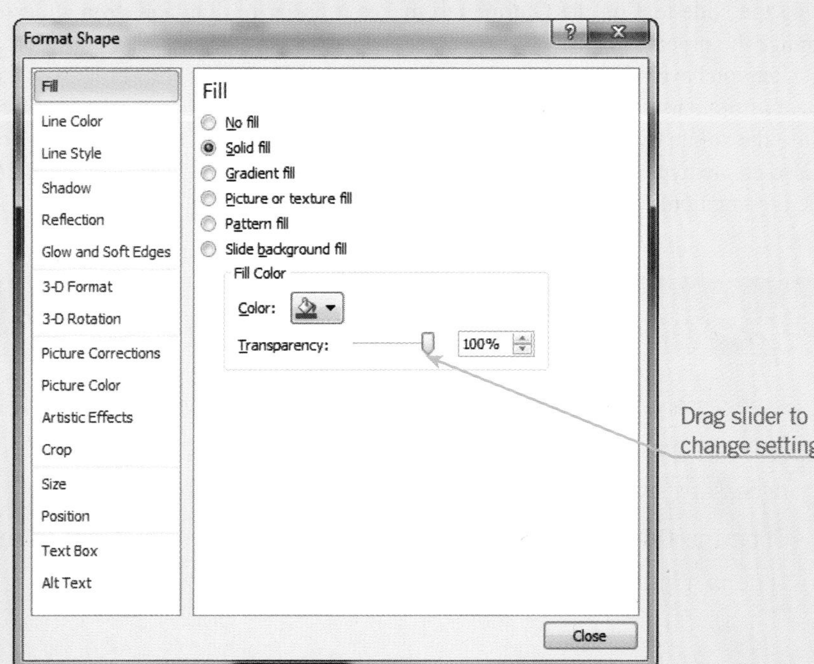

FIGURE 5–12 Format Shape dialog box

9. Right-click the **transparent rectangle** shape, and then click **Hyperlink** to open the Insert Hyperlink dialog box. Under Link to, click **Place in This Document**. Under Select a place in this document:, click **8. G-forces**. Click **OK** to close the dialog box.
10. Create a rounded rectangle shape to cover the **inverted** SmartArt graphic object. Repeat steps 6 and 7 to format the new shape so it is 100% transparent, with no line color.
11. Right-click the new shape, and then click **Hyperlink**. In the upper-right corner of the Insert Hyperlink dialog box, click **ScreenTip**. The Set Hyperlink ScreenTip dialog box opens. In the ScreenTip text box, type **Definition**. Click **OK**.
12. Under Link to:, select the option **Existing File or Web Page**. In the center pane, if necessary, navigate to the folder where you save your solution files. Select the **Coaster Terms** document and then click **OK**.
13. Switch to Slide Show view for the current slide. Test the hot spot for *inverted*. Close the Word document. Test the hot spot for *G-force*. Press **Esc** to switch to Normal view.
14. Save the changes and leave the presentation open for the next Step-by-Step.

Organizing the Presentation Content

Working with a presentation outline is similar to working with an outline in Word. The Outline tab enables you to organize slides and edit the slide text. On the Outline tab, you can add new slides to a presentation, and you can also add new text to a slide. However, you cannot add or edit graphics. Although it is not necessary, collapsing the slide text on the Outline tab makes it easier to drag and drop slides to rearrange the order.

After you have completed the slide content and confirmed the slide order, you can prepare a summary slide. A ***summary slide*** reviews the topics in a presentation. You can use the summary slide as an introduction to or a review of the presentation. You can also create hyperlinks and use the summary slide to help navigate to other slides in the presentation.

VOCABULARY
summary slide

Step-by-Step 5.8

1. If necessary, open the **Revised Coasting 7** file from your solution files. Save the presentation as **Revised Coasting 8**, followed by your initials. If necessary, switch to Normal view.
2. Click the **Outline** tab. All slides appear on the Outline tab, and each slide is numbered. The text for each slide is also displayed.

3. On the Outline tab, edit the text on slide 7 so that each word begins with a capital letter. Note that as you make the change on the Outline tab, the edit is also applied to the text in the Slide pane.
4. On the Outline tab, right-click anywhere in the slide 12 text. In the shortcut menu, click **Collapse**. The bulleted text for the slide is hidden, but the title is still visible on the Outline tab.
5. Click the **slide 6** slide icon to select the slide. Click the **Repeat** button on the Quick Access Toolbar to collapse the slide text.
6. With the insertion point positioned anywhere on the Outline tab, press **Ctrl+A** to select all the slides. Right-click the **selection** and then click **Collapse**. Click anywhere outside the list to deselect the slides.
7. Click the **slide 6** slide icon, and then drag the slide to the position between slides 3 and 4. The slide numbers are adjusted for the new order.
8. Right-click in the slide 9 text. In the shortcut menu, click **Move Up**. Press the **F4** key to repeat the edit and move the slide up one more position.
9. Click the **slide 2** slide icon to select it. Press and hold **Ctrl**, and then click the **slide icons** for slides 7, 8, 9, 10, and 11. Then copy the selection to the Clipboard.
10. On the Outline tab, right-click in the slide 12 text and then click **New Slide**. In the Slide pane, click the **Click to add title** placeholder and type **Summary**. Then click the **Click to add text** placeholder and paste the copied slides from the Clipboard. If necessary, reposition the placeholder so that all the text fits on the slide.
11. Select all the text in the first bulleted item, and then right-click the selection. In the shortcut menu, click **Hyperlink**. If necessary, select Place in This Document. Under Select a place in this document, select **2. The Ultimate EXperience**. Then click **OK**.
12. Create hyperlinks to the corresponding slides for all other items in the bulleted list.
13. Switch to Slide Show view and test the hyperlinks. (*Hint*: Press **End** after testing each link to return to the summary slide.) Press **Esc** to switch to Normal view.
14. Save the changes and close the presentation.

SUMMARY

In this lesson, you learned:

- To ensure that commonly used words are spelled correctly, you can customize the AutoCorrect list and add words to a custom dictionary.
- Special characters can help to make your text more accurate and easier to read.
- You can automatically number paragraphs in a placeholder.
- You can use symbols to customize bullets.
- Animation features enable you to format progressive disclosure to control both when and how slide content appears.
- To make a presentation more engaging, you can add ActiveX controls to the slide content to make the presentation interactive.
- You can easily reorder and resize the shapes in a SmartArt graphic, and to work with the shapes individually, you can convert a SmartArt graphic to shapes.
- You can divide an image into sections and create links for additional information using other types of resources, such as other slides in your presentation or other files on your computer or server.
- The Outline tab enables you to reorganize slides and edit slide text.
- You can create a summary slide from the titles of slides in a presentation.

VOCABULARY REVIEW

Define the following terms:

hot spot
image map
progressive disclosure
summary slide

REVIEW QUESTIONS

TRUE / FALSE

Circle T if the statement is true or F if the statement is false.

T F 1. When you open the Symbols dialog box, the available symbols are limited to the current font style.

T F 2. You can copy animation formats from one object to another and from one slide to another.

T F 3. Both graphics and text appear on the Outline tab.

T F 4. You can only create custom animations for text.

T F 5. To rearrange the order of slides on the Outline tab, you must first collapse the text on the slides you want to move.

MULTIPLE CHOICE

Select the best response for the following statements.

1. Using symbols in slide content ________________.
   - A. can help to clarify the message
   - B. can reduce the number of words
   - C. can make the text easier to read
   - D. all of the above
2. If you frequently use a word or acronym with a unique spelling and you want to save time typing the term or phrase in a document, you should ________________.
   - A. add the term or phrase to a custom dictionary
   - B. add the term or phrase to the standard dictionary
   - C. add the term or phrase to the AutoCorrect list
   - D. any of the above
3. When you add a word to the dictionary during a spell check, the word is saved in ________________.
   - A. the standard dictionary
   - B. the default dictionary
   - C. the document template
   - D. none of the above
4. On the Outline tab, you can ________________.
   - A. change the order of slides
   - B. edit text formats
   - C. add graphics
   - D. all of the above
5. Hyperlinks are used to ________________.
   - A. link to a Web page
   - B. move to a place in the same document
   - C. open a document in another Office application
   - D. all of the above

WRITTEN QUESTIONS

Write a brief answer to the following questions.

1. Describe how to control the font style and size in an interactive text box.

2. Explain how to quickly adjust the size of numbers, symbols, and text characters so the height is comparable to surrounding text.

3. What are the benefits of creating and using a custom dictionary?

4. What is the purpose of progressive disclosure?

5. Describe how to create a summary slide.

PROJECTS

If you have a SAM 2010 user profile, your instructor may have assigned an autogradable version of the indicated project. If so, log into the SAM 2010 Web site at *www.cengage.com/sam2010* to download the instruction and start files.

PROJECT 5–1

1. Open the **Lightning** file from the drive and folder where your Data Files are stored. Save the presentation as **Revised Lightning**, followed by your initials.
2. Scroll through the slides to become familiar with the content.
3. Go to slide 3. Convert the bulleted list to a numbered list, applying the **1., 2., 3.** format.
4. Format all the bulleted items in slides 2, 4, 5, and 6 for progressive disclosure. Apply the **Fade** entrance effect. Set the trigger for the animation to **Start On Click**. Apply an effect option so that when you advance to the next animation, the previous item changes to a dark blue-gray color.
5. Go to slide 3 and create an ActiveX text box approximately 1-¼ inch wide by ½ inch tall. Position the interactive text box over the line at the beginning of item #1. Format the text box font size as **24** point.
6. Create three more interactive text boxes, and position the text boxes over the lines in items # 2, 3, and 4. (*Hint*: You can copy and paste the text boxes.)
7. Move slide 3 to the end of the presentation.
8. Save the changes.
9. Switch to Slide Show view, showing the current slide. Enter the following numbers in the interactive text boxes:

Item #1	**2000**
Item #2	**100**
Item #3	**40,000**
Item #4	**80,000**

10. Switch to Normal view. Then save the changes and close the presentation.

SAM PROJECT 5–2

1. Open the **Employee Manual** file from the drive and folder where your Data Files are stored. Save the presentation as **Revised Employee Manual**, followed by your initials.
2. Scroll through the slides in Normal view to review the information in the manual. Note that the company name *ExperTech* is not a known word in the standard dictionary.
3. Create a custom dictionary. Name the dictionary **ET**, followed by your initials, and be sure to save the dictionary in the folder where you save your solution files. Add the word *ExperTech* to the dictionary. Set the new *ET* dictionary as the default dictionary.
4. Add a new entry to the AutoCorrect list so that *Expertech* is automatically replaced with *ExperTech*.
5. Go to slide 2. In the second bulleted item, position the insertion point after *client base* and type **at Expertech**, then press the **spacebar**. The capitalization of the word should automatically be corrected.
6. Equalize the character height for all the numbers throughout all the slides. (*Hint*: You can use the Repeat button or Format Painter.)
7. Go to slide 1. The company name *ExperTech* is a registered trademark. Insert the registered symbol (®) after the company name (and before ", Inc."). (*Hint*: Look in the Normal text font, Latin-1 Supplement subset.) Also add the registered symbol to the company name on slide 15.
8. In the text box on the yellow graphic on slide 1, position the insertion point below the word *Revised:* and type the current date using the XX/XX/XXXX format.
9. Go to slide 6. Replace the bullets with a custom symbol. Search through the Wingdings font symbols and apply a clock symbol. Increase the size of the symbol as needed.
10. Move slides 8–12 to the end of the presentation so they are positioned just before the last slide.
11. Insert a Title and Content slide at the end of the presentation to create a summary slide. Change the title of the summary slide to **Contents**, and use slides 2, 3, 4, 8, 9, and 10 for the bulleted list. Move the new summary slide so it is the second slide in the presentation. Then create hyperlinks to the corresponding slides for each item in the summary slide.
12. Run a spell check. Add the words *ExperTech's*, *Tashia*, and *Weingartner* to the dictionary.
13. Change the settings so the CUSTOM.dic is the default dictionary. Remove the ET dictionary from the list. Also, delete the entry *Expertech* from the AutoCorrect list.
14. Save the changes. Run the slide show and test the hyperlinks. Make any necessary changes, save the changes, and close the presentation.

PROJECT 5–3

1. In Word, open the **1950 Paint.docx** file from the drive and folder where your Data Files are stored. Save the document as **Before 1950**, followed by your initials. Close the file.
2. Open the **RRP.docx** file from the drive and folder where your Data Files are stored. Save the document as **RRP Rule**, followed by your initials. Close the file and close Word.
3. In PowerPoint, open the **Lead Poisoning.pptx** file from the drive and folder where your Data Files are stored. Save the presentation as **Final Lead Poisoning**, followed by your initials. Scroll through the slides to become familiar with the content.
4. Go to slide 10. Add some symbols to make the blood lead levels easier to read and understand:
   a. Replace the letter *u* with the micro sign symbol, the small Greek letter *mu* (**µ**). (*Hint*: Look in Normal text font, Basic Latin subset.) Repeat the edit to replace the second occurrence of the letter *u* with the micro sign symbol.
   b. Replace the words *Less than* with the Less-Than Sign symbol (<).
   c. The numbers *10* and *19* are a range. Number ranges are usually indicated using en dashes (–). Insert the En Dash symbol (–) and delete the blank space between the two sets of numbers. (*Hint*: Look in the Normal text font, General Punctuation subset.)
5. Add a new entry to the AutoCorrect list to replace *ug* with **µg/dL**.
6. Add the following two items at the end of the bulleted list on slide 10. Copy and paste the En Dash symbol to indicate the ranges.

   20–44 ug/dL moderate lead poisoning

   45–69 ug/dL severe lead poisoning
7. Go to slide 6. Create a hot spot for the *Built before 1950* section of the pie chart. When you format the transparency for the shape, you will also need to remove the line color. Link the hot spot to the *Before 1950* Word document. Add a ScreenTip to display *Paint before 1950*.
8. Create a second hot spot for the *Built before 1978* section of the pie chart. Link the hot spot to the *RRP Rule* Word document. Add a ScreenTip to display *EPA rule*.
9. Run the slide show and test the hyperlinks. Make any necessary corrections.
10. Delete the *ug* entry from the AutoCorrect list.
11. Save the changes and close the presentation.

CRITICAL THINKING

ACTIVITY 5–1

In this lesson, you learned how to rearrange slides and edit text on the Outline tab. Now that you are familiar with the Outline tab features, do you think you will first create an outline and then add graphic and other elements to the slides, or do you think you will create the slides first and then rearrange them as needed? Explain the reasons for your preference.

ACTIVITY 5–2

You created a presentation containing a number of hyperlinks to documents on your intranet. During a cleanup operation, you moved some of the documents to new folders. Now your hyperlinks don't work. What happened and how can you fix the problem?

Use the PowerPoint Help screens to identify the cause of the problem and how to resolve it. Write a brief summary of your findings.

Estimated Time: 2 hours

LESSON 6

Working with Tables and Charts

OBJECTIVES

Upon completion of this lesson, you should be able to:

- Change the table structure.
- Use the drawing tools to modify a table and create a new table.
- Apply a custom table style.
- Use multiple slides to build a table.
- Choose the correct chart type and identify data to be represented in a chart.
- Link to data in an Excel chart.
- Animate chart data.
- Modify and animate an organization chart.

VOCABULARY

axis
axis title
data label
data series
embedded object
legend
linked object
plot area

Tables and charts are useful for presenting a large collection of text or numbers in a meaningful way. This lesson explores features for customizing table and chart formats.

Working with Tables

Table structures and formats are rarely perfect the first time around. It often takes some adjustment to make a table look good on a slide. You can use design and layout tools on the Table Tools tab to modify the table's structure and format.

Changing the Table Structure

If the table contents need to be rearranged, you can drag and drop the data to a new location in the table. However, if you drag and drop data into a cell that already contains data, the data in the destination cell will be replaced with the data you are moving. Therefore, if you want to retain all of the data in a table, you need to add new columns and rows and then drag and drop the data to an empty cell.

To combine the content of two or more cells into a single cell, you can merge the cells by using the Table Eraser tool to remove the cell boundaries. To create a new border within a cell, you can split the cell. You can also create a diagonal border, which enables you to insert two different kinds of information into one table cell.

Remember that slides use large font sizes for ease of reading. Text and numbers you enter in a table should also appear in a large font size. To fit the text and numbers within a cell, you can adjust the font size or the column width. To change column width and row height, you can use the AutoFit command, the Distribute Rows command, or the Distribute Columns command. You can also manually set the spacing, or you simply drag a row or column boundary line to a new position.

Step-by-Step 6.1

1. Open the **Coaster History** file from the drive and folder where your Data Files are stored. Save the presentation as **Revised Coaster History 1**, followed by your initials.
2. Go to slide 2. In the last row of the table, select **6 mph**, and then drag and drop the selected text to the empty cell to the right in the *1800s* column.
3. Position the insertion point anywhere in the *Drop* row. Click the **Table Tools Layout** tab. In the Rows & Columns group, click the **Insert Above** button. Select all the cells in the *Speed* row, and then drag and drop the content in the first cell in the new blank row. Right-click anywhere in the last row, which is now blank, and click **Delete Rows**.
4. Select all the cells in the last three rows of the table. Click the **Table Tools Layout** tab. In the Cell Size group, click the **Distribute Rows** button. The height of the selected rows is distributed equally.
5. Click anywhere in the table to deselect the last three rows. Position the mouse pointer over the right border of the *1800s* column. When the mouse pointer changes to a double-headed arrow, as shown in **Figure 6–1**, double-click to AutoFit the column width to the content.

TIP

If the content does not fit in the destination row, undo the edit and repeat the step. As you drop the selected content, make sure the insertion point is positioned in the first cell of the new row.

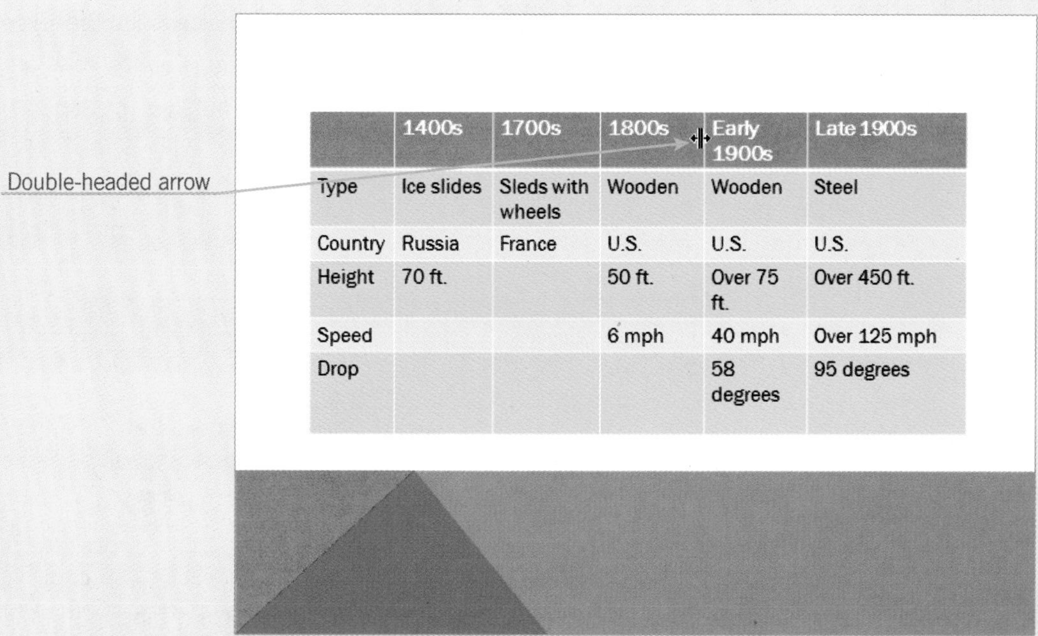

	1400s	1700s	1800s	Early 1900s	Late 1900s
Type	Ice slides	Sleds with wheels	Wooden	Wooden	Steel
Country	Russia	France	U.S.	U.S.	U.S.
Height	70 ft.		50 ft.	Over 75 ft.	Over 450 ft.
Speed			6 mph	40 mph	Over 125 mph
Drop				58 degrees	95 degrees

FIGURE 6–1
AutoFit cell boundary

6. Repeat Step 5 to AutoFit the column width for the *Early 1900s* and *Late 1900s* columns.
7. If necessary, click anywhere in the table to select it. On the Table Tools Design tab, in the Draw Borders group, click the **Table Eraser** button. The mouse pointer changes to an eraser. Click the border between the *Type* and *Country* cells, as shown in **Figure 6–2**. The boundary is removed and the two cells are merged.

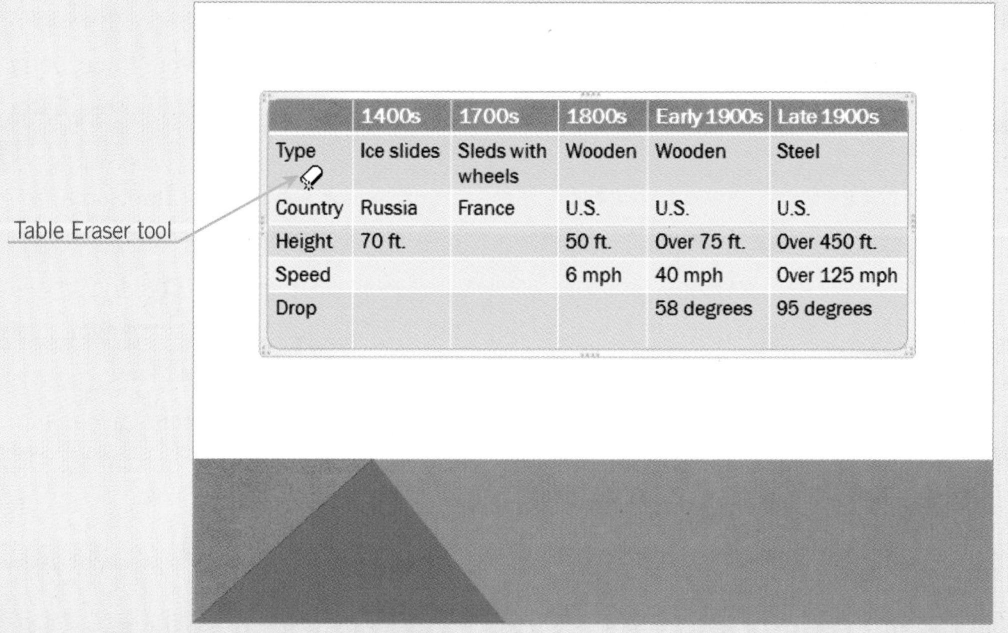

	1400s	1700s	1800s	Early 1900s	Late 1900s
Type	Ice slides	Sleds with wheels	Wooden	Wooden	Steel
Country	Russia	France	U.S.	U.S.	U.S.
Height	70 ft.		50 ft.	Over 75 ft.	Over 450 ft.
Speed			6 mph	40 mph	Over 125 mph
Drop				58 degrees	95 degrees

FIGURE 6–2
Erase cell boundary

8. Click the remaining cell boundaries below all the cells in the *Type* row. When you are done, all the cells in the *Type* and *Country* rows are merged, as shown in **Figure 6–3**. Click anywhere outside the table to toggle off the Table Eraser tool.

FIGURE 6–3
Merged cells in the Type and Country rows

	1400s	1700s	1800s	Early 1900s	Late 1900s
Type Country	Ice slides Russia	Sleds with wheels France	Wooden U.S.	Wooden U.S.	Steel U.S.
Height	70 ft.		50 ft.	Over 75 ft.	Over 450 ft.
Speed			6 mph	40 mph	Over 125 mph
Drop				58 degrees	95 degrees

9. Click the **Type Country** cell. Click the **Table Tools Layout** tab, and in the Merge Group, click the **Split Cells** button. In the Split Cells dialog box, change the Columns setting to **1** and change the Rows setting to **2**. Click **OK**. The cell is split, but all the text appears in the top cell. Click **Undo**.
10. Click the **Type Country** cell. Click the **Table Tools Design** tab, and in the Table Styles group, click the **Borders** button arrow. At the bottom of the drop-down menu, click **Diagonal Up Border**. A diagonal border is added to the active cell. Select the remaining cells in the *Type/Country* row. Click the **Diagonal Up Border** button to apply the diagonal border.
11. In the *Type Country* cell, position the insertion point in front of the word *Country* and press **Enter** twice. Add additional space before the country names in the remaining cells in the first row. You need to press Enter only once before the word *France*.
12. Right-click the table, and then click **Select Table**. Click the **Home** tab. In the Font group, change the font size to **15** point.
13. In the *Type/Country* cell, click anywhere in the word *Country*. In the Paragraph group, click the **Align Text Right** button. Repeat to right-align the country information in the remaining cells in the second row.
14. Select the last three rows of cells. Click the **Table Tools Layout** tab, and in the Alignment group, click the **Center Vertically** button. The selected content is centered vertically within each cell.
15. Save the changes and leave the presentation open for the next Step-by-Step.

Creating a Table Using the Draw Table Tool

The Draw Table tool gives you considerable flexibility in creating a table. If, for example, some rows of the table need to be a different height or some rows need to contain more columns than others, the Draw Table tool may be the best tool because you won't have to spend time splitting and merging cells individually. The Draw Table tool also enables you to size cells precisely within the table, and you can show gridlines to help you align the cell borders.

You can rotate the text within a table cell so that it appears vertical or stacked. When the text is rotated, the spacing between characters changes. To adjust this, you can use the Kerning option in the Font dialog box.

TIP

Choosing the line styles and weights before drawing a table can save formatting time later.

Step-by-Step 6.2

1. If necessary, open the **Revised Coaster History 1** presentation from your solution files. Save the presentation as **Revised Coaster History 2**, followed by your initials. If necessary, click the View tab and show the Ruler.
2. Go to slide 2. If necessary, click the Home tab. In the Slides group, click the **New Slide** button arrow, and then click **Blank**.
3. Click the **Insert** tab. In the Tables group, click the **Table** button, and then click **Draw Table**. The mouse pointer will change to show a pencil.
4. In the white area of the slide, draw a box approximately 8 inches wide by 4½ inches high. (Use the rulers to estimate the box size.) The Table Tools contextual tabs will display on the Ribbon.
5. Click the **Table Tools Layout** tab. In the Arrange group, click the **Align** button, and then click **View Gridlines**. Make adjustments to the size of the table as needed.
6. On the Table Tools Design tab, in the Draw Borders group, click the **Draw Table** button.

TIP

The Draw Table tool stays active until you click the Draw Table button to toggle it off, or once you begin typing text. As soon as you begin typing text, the tool is automatically toggled off.

TIP

You can also show or hide gridlines by clicking the View tab and then enabling or disabling the Gridlines option in the Show group.

7. Use the Draw Table tool to create the cell boundaries shown in **Figure 6–4**. The approximate cell widths and heights are indicated in the figure, and you can show the Ruler and then use the gridlines as a guide. To adjust the cell, you can drag the boundary lines or you can format the cell sizes manually using the settings in the Cell Size group. In the Arrange group, click the **Align** button and then click **View Gridlines** to toggle off the feature.

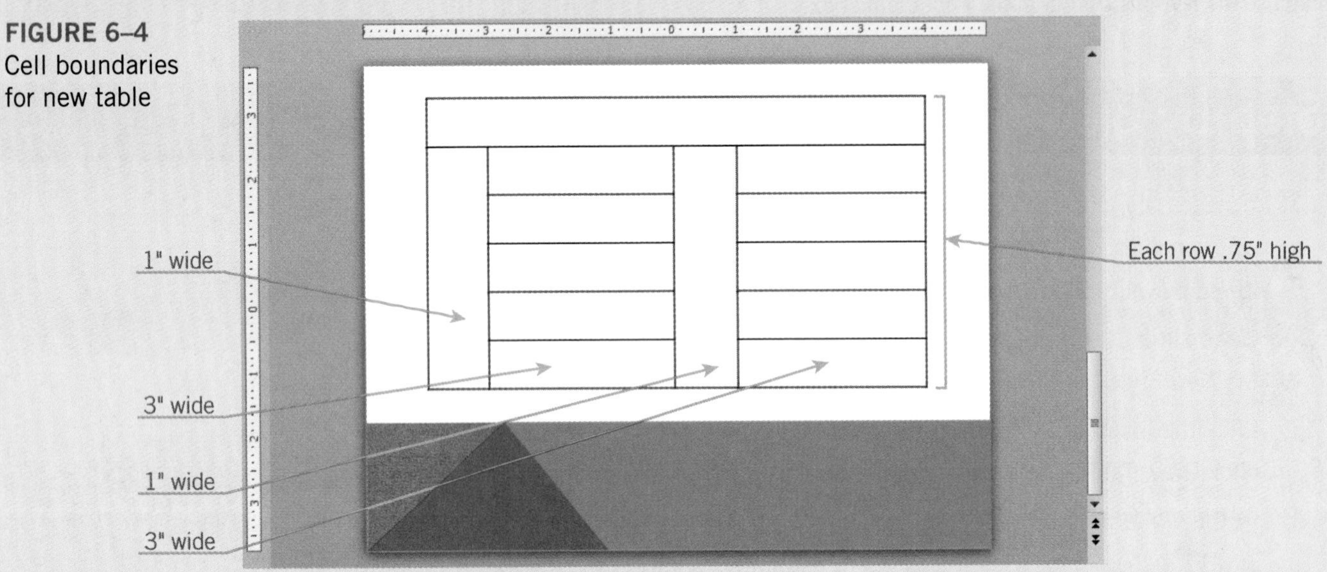

FIGURE 6–4
Cell boundaries for new table

8. Type the table content shown in **Figure 6–5**.

FIGURE 6–5
Table content

Among the Favorites			
Track Layout	Corkscrew	Train Type	Floorless
	Dueling		Inverted
	Figure 8		Launched
	Twister		Stand-up
	Vertical drop		Suspended

9. Click anywhere in the *Track Layout* cell. Click the **Table Tools Layout** tab, and in the Alignment group, click the **Text Direction** button. Click **Stacked**. Repeat the formatting for the *Train Type* cell.

10. Select all the text in the *Track Layout* cell. Click the **Home** tab. In the Font group, click the **Dialog Box Launcher**. In the Font dialog box, click the **Character Spacing** tab. Click the **Spacing** list arrow, and then select **Condensed**. In the By text box, select the text and then type **6**. When your settings match those shown in **Figure 6–6**, click **OK**.

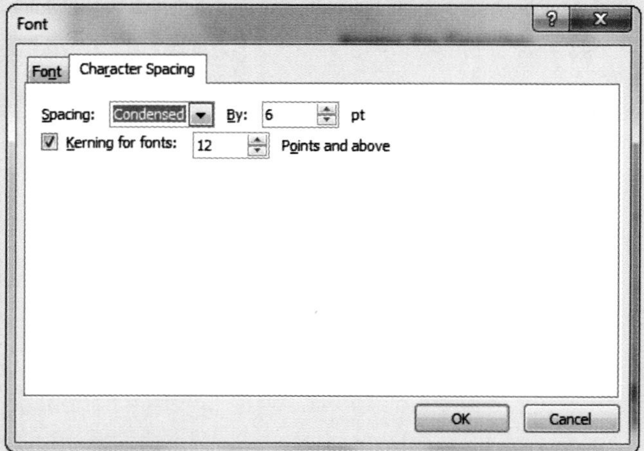

FIGURE 6–6
Character Spacing tab in the Font dialog box

11. Click anywhere in the first row (*Among the Favorites*). Click the **Table Tools Layout** tab. In the Alignment group, click the **Center** button.
12. Select the entire table. In the Alignment group, click the **Center Vertically** button.
13. Click the **Table Tools Design** tab. In the Table Styles group, click the **More** button. Under Best Match for Document, click the third option in the first row, the **Themed Style 1 – Accent 2** table style. If necessary, drag a table corner to position the table in the center of the white area on the slide.
14. Save the changes and leave the presentation open for the next Step-by-Step.

Applying a Custom Table Style

When you create a new table in PowerPoint, a style is applied to the table. A table style provides formats for shading, borders, and effects. The colors used in the style are based on the theme colors of the presentation. You can change the style by applying a different style, or you can modify the existing style by changing some of the formats, such as the shading or border colors. To apply a custom style, you must first remove any existing style. Then you can apply new shading, border, and effect formats. However, you will not be able to save the custom style settings for use in another presentation.

Step-by-Step 6.3

1. If necessary, open the **Revised Coaster History 2** presentation from your solution files. Save the presentation as **Revised Coaster History 3**, followed by your initials. If necessary, go to slide 2.
2. Click anywhere inside the table to display the Table Tools contextual tabs. If necessary, click the Table Tools Design tab. In the Table Styles group, click the **More** button. At the bottom of the menu, click **Clear Table**. All the shading and border colors are removed, including the diagonal borders in the first row.
3. Select all the cells in the second row (*Type/Country*). In the Table Styles group, click the **Borders** button arrow, and then click **Diagonal Up Border**.
4. Right-click the table, and then click **Select Table**. In the Table Styles group, click the **Shading** button arrow. At the bottom of the menu, point to **Table Background**. Under Theme Colors, in the third row, select the **Turquoise, Accent 3, Lighter 60%** color. The color is added to all the table cells.
5. Select all the cells in the first row. Click the **Shading** button arrow. Under Theme Colors, in the first row, select the **Orange, Accent 2** color.
6. All the cells in the first row should still be selected. In the Table Styles group, click the **Effects** button arrow and then point to **Cell Bevel**. Under Bevel, select the last option, the **Art Deco** effect.
7. All the cells in the first row should still be selected. Click the **Home** tab. In the Font group, click the **Font Color** button arrow, and then select the **White, Background 1** font color.
8. Format the first column for consistency with the header row.
9. In the *Type/Country* cell, click the word **Country**. In the Paragraph group, click the **Align Text Right** button.
10. Select all the cells in the first row. In the Paragraph group, click the **Center** button.
11. Click anywhere in the *Type/Country* cell. To change the diagonal border format:
    a. Click the **Table Tools Design** tab.
    b. In the Draw Borders group, click the **Pen Style** list arrow and then select the last option in the drop-down menu.
    c. Click the **Pen Weight** list arrow 1 pt, and then select **1 ½ pt**.
    d. Click the **Pen Color** button, and then select the **White, Background 1** color.
    e. Click the diagonal border in the Type/Country cell to apply the style.

12. Click the **Pen Color** button, and then select the **Orange, Accent 2** color. Then click each of the remaining diagonal borders in the Type/Country row.
13. Click anywhere outside the table to toggle off the Pen tool. Click anywhere within the table to make the table active. In the Table Styles group, click the **Effects** button arrow and then point to **Shadow**. Under Outer, click the last option, the **Offset Diagonal Top Left** effect. Click anywhere outside the table to see the effect.
14. Save the changes and leave the presentation open for the next Step-by-Step.

Using Multiple Slides to Build a Table in a Presentation

Showing all the information in a table all at once can be overwhelming for your audience. You can introduce parts of a table in segments, emphasizing each point individually, and building the table as you progress through the slides. For example, if the table has six columns of information, you can introduce one column at a time on six separate slides.

The Duplicate Slides command enables you to quickly copy and paste one or more selected slides. In the previous Step-by-Steps, you formatted the table about roller coaster history. In the next Step-by-Step, you will duplicate a slide of the *Coaster History* table and create multiple copies of the slide. Then, in reverse order, you will deconstruct the table on each slide, which will allow you to build the table point-by-point when you advance through the slides in Slide Show view.

Step-by-Step 6.4

1. If necessary, open the **Revised Coaster History 3** presentation from your solution files. Save the presentation as **Revised Coaster History 4**, followed by your initials.
2. If necessary, switch to Normal view. On the Slides tab, click the **slide 3** thumbnail. In the Slide pane, select the table.
3. Click the **Table Tools Layout** tab. In the Arrange group, click the **Align** button, and then click **Align Center**. You may not see much change because the table is already centered between the left and right borders. Click the **Align** button again, and then click **Align Middle**. The table is aligned vertically between the top and bottom borders of the slide (not the white area on the slide).
4. Go to slide 2. If necessary, click the Home tab. In the Slides group, click the **New Slide** button arrow, and then click **Duplicate Selected Slides**. A copy of the selected slide is inserted above the active slide (slide 2). On the Quick Access Toolbar, click the **Repeat** button three times to create three more copies of the slide.

5. Go to slide 5. Right-click anywhere in the *Late 1900s* column, and then click **Delete Columns.**
6. Go to slide 4. Select the **Early 1900s** and **Late 1900s** columns. Right-click the selection, and then click **Delete Columns**.
7. Click anywhere outside the table to deselect it, then right-click anywhere in the *Drop* row. Select **Delete Rows**.
8. Go to slide 3. Select and delete the **1800s**, **Early 1900s**, and **Late 1900s** columns. Also select and delete the **Drop** and **Speed** rows.
9. Go to slide 2. Select and delete the **1700s**, **1800s**, **Early 1900s**, and **Late 1900s** columns. Also delete the **Speed** and **Drop** rows.
10. Go to slide 6. Select the table. Click the **Animations** tab. In the Animation group, click the **More** button. At the bottom of the menu, click **More Exit Effects**. Scroll down to the Exciting category and then click the **Pinwheel** exit effect. Click **OK**.
11. Go to Slide 7. Select the table. In the Animation group, click the **More** button. At the bottom of the menu click **More Motion Paths**. Scroll down to the Special category and then click the **Loop de Loop** motion path. Click **OK**. In the Preview group, click the **Preview** button.
12. Select the table. In the Animation group, click the **Custom Path** effect. The mouse pointer changes to a cross-hair. Beginning in the lower-left corner of the slide, drag the mouse pointer to the right and up and down (the path of a roller coaster). When you reach the right side of the slide, drag the pointer back to the center of the slide and then double-click to end the path. The motion path will preview and a line will appear on the slide showing the custom motion path.
13. Go to slide 1, then switch to Slide Show view. Advance through the slides to watch the table progressively develop throughout the presentation and to view the exit and motion path animations.
14. Switch to Normal view. Save the changes and close the presentation.

Working with Charts

A chart provides a graphic representation of data. The first step in creating a chart is to choose a chart type that presents the data in the clearest way possible. To understand the differences in chart types, you must first understand the elements in a chart. **Figure 6–7** identifies the chart elements. **Table 6–1** provides definitions for several of the chart elements.

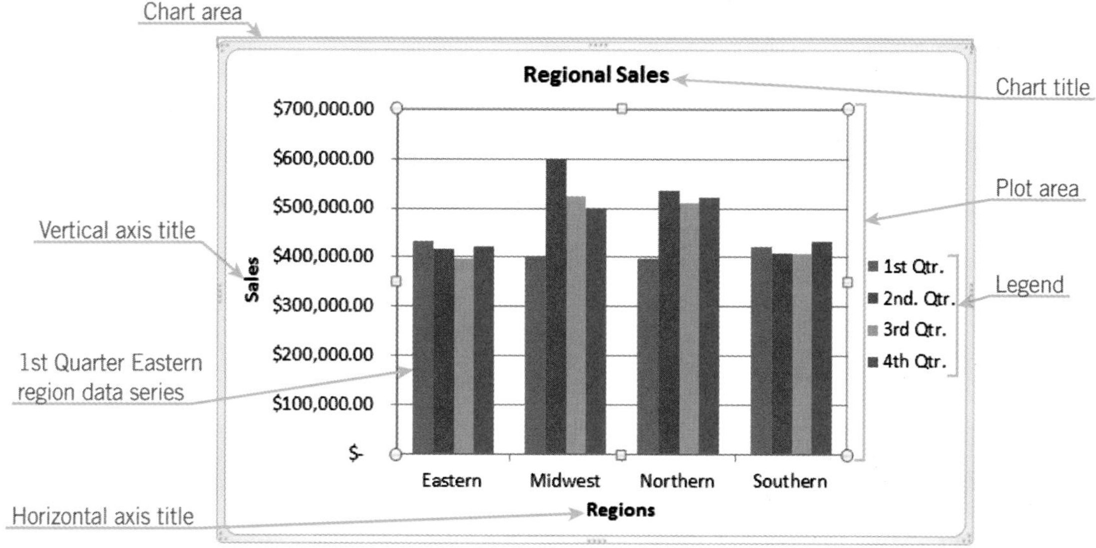

FIGURE 6–7 Chart elements

TABLE 6–1 Definitions of chart elements

CHART ELEMENT	DEFINITION
axis	A line bordering the chart plot area used as a frame of reference for measurement. The y-axis is the vertical axis and usually contains data. The x-axis is the horizontal axis and usually contains categories.
axis title	A label that clarifies what is being measured, such as dollars, number of units, or time spans.
data label	Text or numbers that provide additional information about a value in the data series.
data series	Related data points that are plotted in a chart; each data series in a chart has a unique color or pattern.
legend	A list that identifies the data series indicated by the colors or patterns used in the chart.
plot area	A rectangular border that encloses the two axes and the data series. Depending on the chart formats, the plot area may also include category names, data labels, and axes titles.

VOCABULARY

axis

axis title

data label

data series

legend

plot area

Choosing the Right Chart Type

Charts help to summarize, clarify, and highlight data. An attractive chart can get attention, but it is only useful when the data and values are represented correctly. PowerPoint offers many different types of charts, from the familiar line and pie charts to specialized types such as bubble and radar charts.

PowerPoint also provides several different slide layouts and color schemes for each chart type. The slide layouts include background settings, which can be altered to further enhance the appearance. You can also apply quick styles and borders.

The chart type you choose will depend on the data you want to represent. **Table 6–2** describes the chart types available in PowerPoint.

TABLE 6–2 Chart types

CHART TYPE	DESCRIPTION
Column	Each column in the chart shows the value of one item of data. Effective in making comparisons among individual items or showing changes over a period of time. *Sample use*: Compare company sales by regions.
Line	Each line in the chart shows the changes in the value of one item of data. Effective for showing trends over time. *Sample use*: Show the change in temperatures over a period of time.
Pie	Each portion, or slice, of the pie shows the value of one item and how it relates to a whole unit; the portions total 100 percent. Effective for showing how parts relate to a whole; shows only one data series at a time, such as one column of data. *Sample use*: Show marketing expenses as a percentage of the entire company budget.
Bar	Each bar in the chart shows the value of one item of data. Useful when you want to make comparisons among individual items. *Sample use*: Compare the progress of sales reps achieving sales goals.
Area	Illustrates the magnitude of change over time, displaying the sum of plotted values. Effective for emphasizing trends in total values over time.
X Y (Scatter)	Data points are plotted using two value axes, and are displayed in uneven intervals or clusters. Effective for showing trends in numeric data, especially when there are a large number of data points. *Sample use*: Show scientific data from experiments. If desired, you can draw a "best fit" line where the data points are close together, indicating a stronger correlation.
Stock	Illustrates fluctuation of stocks (or other data) over a period of time; data must be carefully structured to match specific type of chart. *Sample use*: Show the high, low, and close figures for a stock.
Surface	A 3-D surface uses colors and patterns to indicate areas that are in the same value range. Effective in finding combinations between two sets of data.
Doughnut	Illustrates parts as they relate to a whole, like a pie chart, but can be used for more than one data series.
Bubble	Displays sets of values, represented by bubbles. The relative size of each bubble represents another data set. Effective for representing three sets of data.
Radar	A line connects a value axis from the center for each category to all values in the same series. Effective in comparing the collected values of several data series.

Step-by-Step 6.5

1. Open the **Deer Creek Inn** presentation from the drive and folder where your Data Files are stored. Save the presentation as **Updated Deer Creek Inn 1**, followed by your initials.
2. Go to slide 2. Note that a column chart shows a data series representing revenues from lodge rooms, lodge suites, and cabins. The chart makes it easy to compare revenues for the Winter, Spring, Summer, and Fall seasons. Click in the blank area above the legend to select the chart.
3. Click the **Chart Tools Design** tab, and in the Type group, click the **Change Chart Type** button. The Change Chart Type dialog box opens, as shown in **Figure 6–8**.

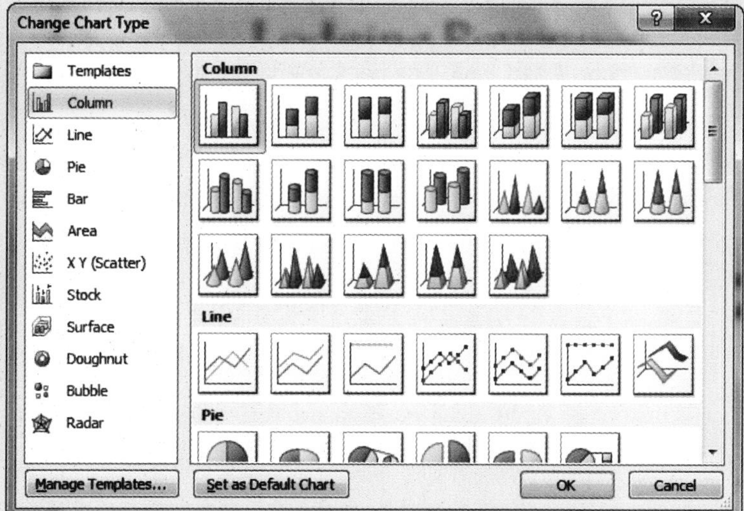

FIGURE 6–8
Change Chart Type dialog box

4. In the right pane of the Change Chart Type dialog box, in the second row under Column, click the second option, the **Stacked Cylinder** chart subtype. Click **OK**. The revenues for all three types of lodging are combined in a single column for each season, and each column reflects total revenue. The vertical axis adjusts to reflect the change as well.
5. Click the **Change Chart Type** button. In the right pane of the dialog box, in the second row under Column, click the third option, the **100% Stacked Cylinder** chart subtype. Click **OK**. Each column in the chart now shows the percentage of revenue generated from each type of lodging for each season. The vertical axis changes again to show percentages.
6. Click the **Change Chart Type** button. In the right pane of the dialog box, in the second row under Column, click the fourth option, the **3-D Cylinder** chart subtype. Click **OK**. Each type of lodging is represented by a separate column for each season.

TIP

A 100% Stacked Cylinder column chart combines the comparison features of a column chart with the proportional features of a pie chart because each cylinder shows the relationship of items to the whole.

7. Click the **Change Chart Type** button. In the left pane of the dialog box, click **Line**. In the right pane, under Line, click the first option, the **Line** chart subtype. Click **OK**. The lines overlap in the chart, and it's not as easy to compare the values for the seasons.
8. Click the **Change Chart Type** button. In the left pane of the dialog box, click **Column**. In the right pane, in the second row under Column, click the first option, the **Clustered Cylinder** chart subtype. Click **OK**.
9. In the Chart Layouts group, click the **More** button. Ten layout options are available. Click the **Layout 10** chart layout.
10. In the Chart Styles group, click the **More** button. Numerous color options are available. In the fifth row, click the second option, the **Style 34** chart style.
11. Click the **Chart Tools Layout** tab. In the Background group, click the **Chart Wall** button and then click **None**. A background shading on the left and back walls of the chart is removed. Click the **Chart Wall** button again and then click **Show Chart Wall**. The background effect is reapplied.
12. In the Background group, click the **Chart Floor** button, and then click **None**. The background shading at the bottom of the chart is removed. Click the **Chart Floor** button again and then click **Show Chart Floor**. The background effect is reapplied.
13. In the Background group, click the **3-D Rotation** button to open the Format Chart Area dialog box. Under Rotation, change the Y setting to **0**, as shown in **Figure 6–9**. Note the change in the chart rotation. Restore the Y setting to **15**. In the left pane, click **Position**. Note that you can alter settings to position the chart precisely. Click **Close**.

FIGURE 6–9
Format Chart Area dialog box

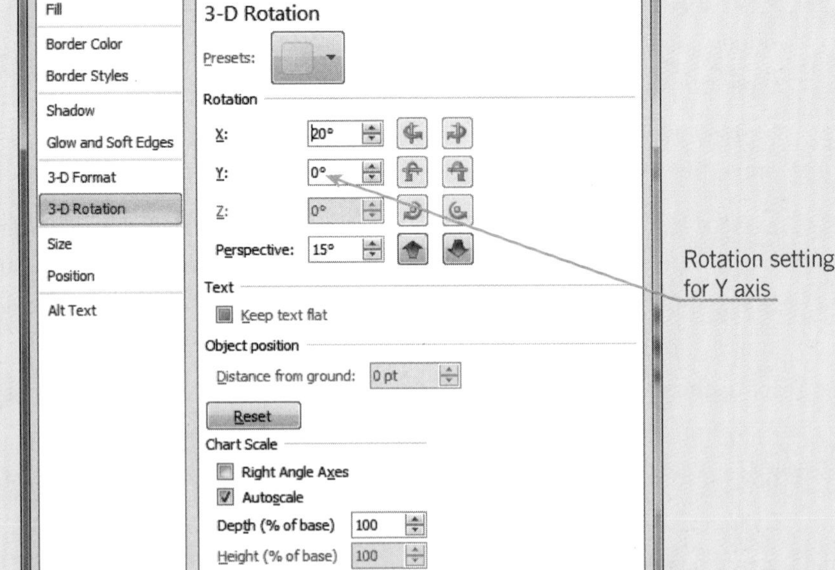

14. Save the changes and leave the presentation open for the next Step-by-Step.

Identifying the Data to be Represented in a Chart

Often the Excel worksheet contains much more data than you want to represent in the chart. You can specify the data that you want to include in the chart. You can also change the direction in which PowerPoint plots data.

TIP

If you do not have Excel installed on your computer, when you create a new chart on a slide, a second window with a datasheet will open.

Step-by-Step 6.6

1. If necessary, open the **Updated Deer Creek Inn 1** presentation from your solution files. Save the presentation as **Updated Deer Creek Inn 2**, followed by your initials.
2. On the Slides tab, right-click the **slide 2** thumbnail, and then click **Duplicate Slide**. On the new slide 3, click in a blank area of the chart to select it. Click the **Chart Tools Design** tab. In the Type group, click the **Change Chart Type** button.
3. In the left pane of the Change Chart Type dialog box, click **Pie**. In the right pane, under Pie, click the second option, the **Pie in 3-D** chart subtype. Click **OK**. Roll over the chart to display the ScreenTips identifying the data series for each slice. Notice that the chart shows data only for one of the data series, *Lodge rooms*. That's because a pie chart represents only one data series.
4. In the Data group, click the **Select Data** button. The Select Data Source dialog box and an Excel worksheet open. Under Legend Entries (Series), click **Cabins**. Your dialog box should match the one shown in **Figure 6–10**. The chart data range is cells A1 through E4.

EXTRA FOR EXPERTS

To use pie charts to compare data, you can insert more than one pie chart on a slide.

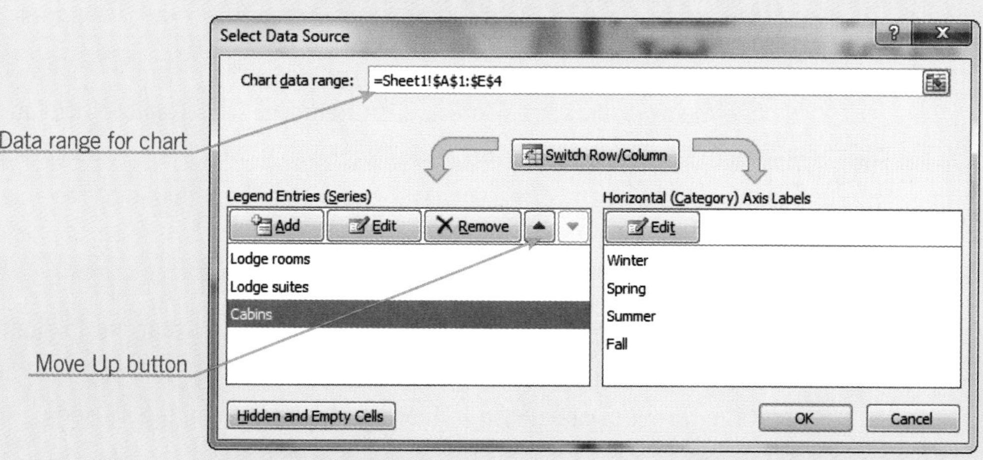

FIGURE 6–10
Select Data Source dialog box

5. Click the **Move Up** button twice to move the *Cabins* data series to the top of the list. A note appears below the Chart data range indicating that the data range is too complex to be displayed. Because of the chart type, not all of the data will appear in the chart.
6. Click **OK**. The chart changes and now represents the values for the revenues for Cabins. Close the worksheet.
7. On the Slides tab, copy slide 2 and paste the copied slide between slides 1 and 2. In the Slide pane on the new slide 2, click in a blank area of the chart to select it. Click the **Chart Tools Design** tab. In the Data group, click the **Select Data** button. The Select Data Source dialog box and an Excel worksheet open.
8. If necessary, reposition the dialog box so you can see the worksheet. The marquee surrounding the cells in the worksheet also indicates the chart data range. Only rows 1 through 4 are included in the chart data range.
9. Drag the mouse pointer across all the data in the worksheet to change the selection. The data range will change in the Chart data range box. The Chart data range box now shows *=Table1[#All]*.
10. Under Legend Entries (Series), the list of data series changes, as shown in **Figure 6–11**.

FIGURE 6–11
New legend entries in Select Source dialog box

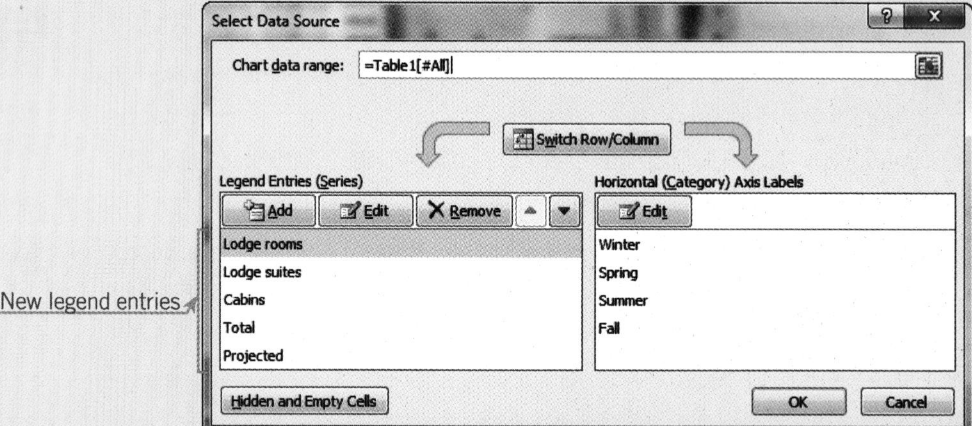

11. In the Select Data Source dialog box, under Legend Entries (Series), *Lodge rooms* is already selected. Click **Remove**. Click **Remove** two more times to remove *Lodge suites* and *Cabins*. Only two data series will now appear in the chart. Click **OK**. The chart compares the Total revenues with the Projected revenues.
12. Switch to the PowerPoint presentation. In the Data group, click the **Switch Row/Column** button. The data is rearranged so that the Total and Projected revenues are represented in the horizontal axis of the chart and the revenues are shown in four columns based on the seasons.

13. Click the **Switch Row/Column** button again to return to the original arrangement of data.
14. Save the changes. Exit Excel. Leave the presentation open for the next Step-by-Step.

Customizing a Data Chart

You can customize a chart by modifying the chart elements. For example, you can add a title to the chart and each axis, position the legend, and choose data labels. The chart elements consist of graphics and text boxes. Just as you select other objects on slides, you can click an element within the chart area to select it. Then you can rearrange the elements in the chart area or use the sizing handles to resize them, and you can show gridlines to help you place the chart elements.

Pie charts give you some unique opportunities for displaying information. You can apply a style from the gallery to create an exploded slice on a pie chart to make it more obvious, or you can manually create the exploded slice by dragging a slice away from the pie chart. Also, 3-D effects enable you to present certain types of data effectively and make your charts more compelling.

EXTRA FOR EXPERTS

If you plan to use a customized chart in the future, you can save the chart as a template. After finalizing the chart, click the Chart Tools Design tab. In the Type group, click the Save As Template button. Enter a filename. The document is saved with the file extension *.crtx*.

Step-by-Step 6.7

1. If necessary, open the **Updated Deer Creek Inn 2** presentation from your solution files. Save the presentation as **Updated Deer Creek Inn 3**, followed by your initials.
2. Go to slide 2. Select the chart, and, if necessary, click the Chart Tools Design tab. In the Type group, click the **Change Chart Type** button. In the left pane of the Change Chart Type dialog box, click **Bar**. In the right pane, under Bar, select the first option, the **Clustered Bar** chart subtype, and then click **OK**.
3. Click the **Chart Tools Layout** tab. In the Labels group, click the **Chart Title** button. Then click **Above Chart** and type **Projected Revenue**.
4. Click the **Axis Titles** button, point to **Primary Vertical Axis Title**, and then click **Rotated Title**. Type **Seasons**.
5. Click the **Axis Titles** button, point to **Primary Vertical Axis Title**, and then click **More Primary Vertical Axis Title Options**. In the right pane, enable the option **Solid fill**. Click the **Color** button, and then click the **Olive Green, Accent 3** theme color. In the left pane, click **Border Color**. In the right pane, enable the option **Solid line**. Click the **Color** button, and then click the **Olive Green, Accent 3** theme color. Click **Close**.
6. Click the **Data Labels** button, and then click **Inside End**. The data values are added to the bars in the chart. Click the horizontal axis values below the chart. When the text box is selected, press **Delete**.

7. Go to slide 4. Select the chart. Click the **Chart Tools Layout** tab. In the Labels group, click the **Legend** button, and then click **Show Legend at Left**. Click to select the **legend** chart object. Click the **Home** tab. In the Font group, change the font size to **24** point.
8. Click the **Chart Tools Format tab**. In the Arrange group, click the **Align** button, and then click **Grid Settings**. In the Grid and Guides dialog box, under Guide settings, click to enable the **Display drawing guides on screen** option, then click **OK**. Click the **legend** chart object to select it, and then using the drawing guides as a guide, align the top of the legend chart object with the horizontal drawing guide.
9. Click the **Chart Tools Layout** tab. In the Labels group, click the **Data Labels** button, and then click **More Data Label Options** to open the Format Data Labels dialog box. See **Figure 6–12**.

FIGURE 6–12
Format Data Labels dalog box

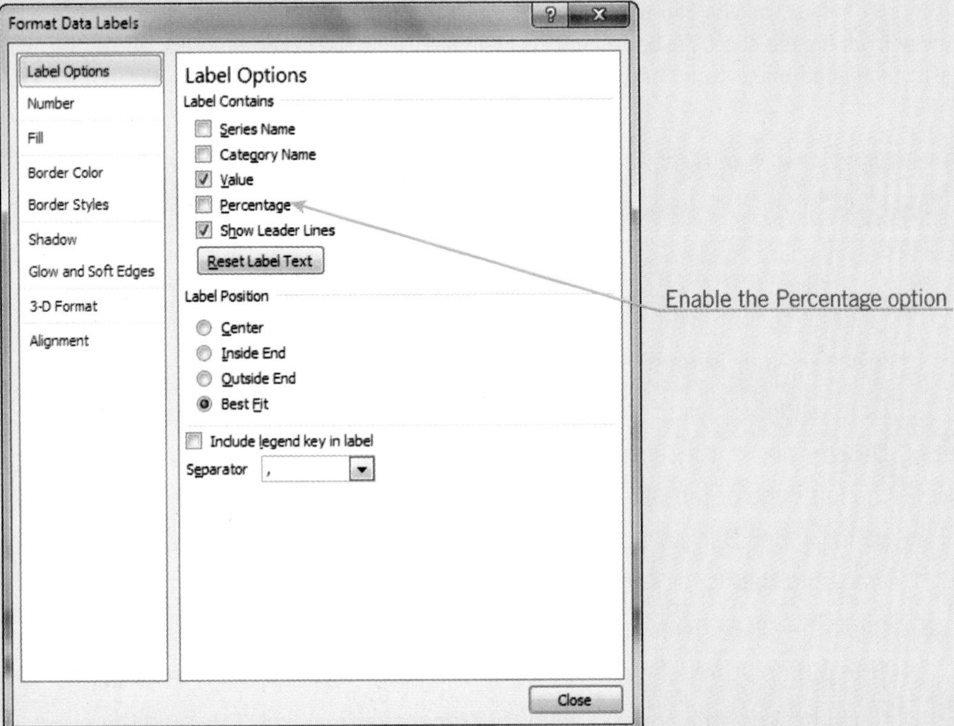

10. In the right pane of the Format Data Labels dialog box, under Label Contains, enable the **Percentage** option. The Value option and the Show Leader Lines option should already be enabled. Click **Close**. The values and the percentages appear in the portions of the pie chart. When the data cannot fit within the portion, a leader line connects the data information.
11. Click the **Data Labels** button, and then click **More Data Label Options**. Disable the **Value** option. Click **Close**.
12. All four percentages should be selected. Right-click one of the percentages to show the Mini toolbar. Change the font size to **24** point. Click the **Chart Title** button, and then click **Centered Overlay Title**. Type **Cabin Revenues**. Select the new text and change the font size to **32** point.

13. Click the **Summer** data series (slice) of the pie chart. Drag it down slightly to pull it away from the rest of the chart, as shown in **Figure 6–13**. (*Hint*: If the other portions separate from the chart, you can drag them back to the center to reconnect them.)

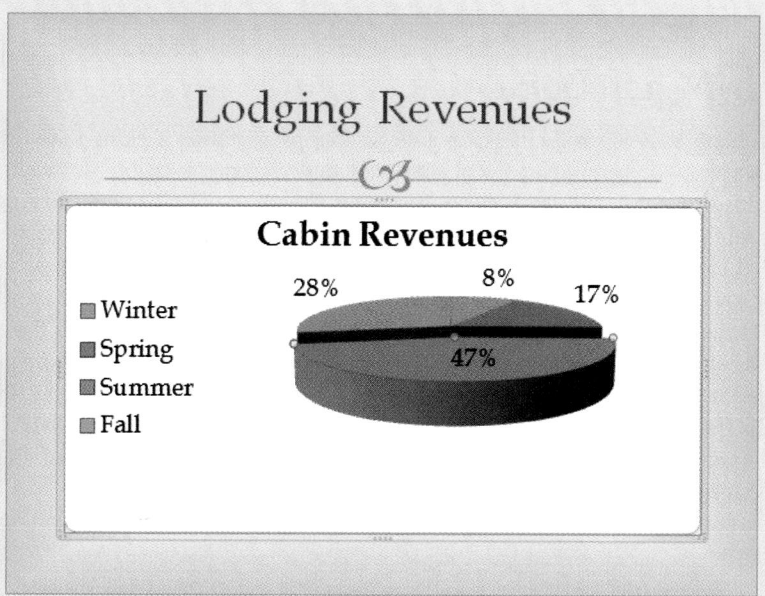

FIGURE 6–13
Exploded slice in pie chart

14. Right-click the pie chart, and then click **3-D Rotation**. The Format Chart Area dialog box opens. In the right pane, under Rotation, change the Y setting to **40**. When your dialog box matches **Figure 6–14**, click **Close**.

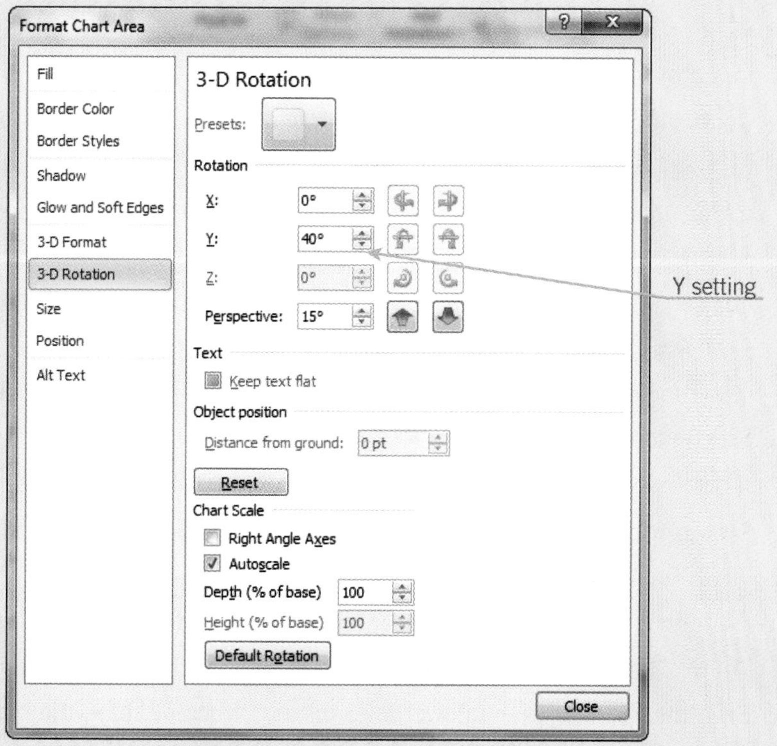

FIGURE 6–14
Format Chart Area dialog box

15. Click the **Chart Tools Format** tab. In the Arrange group, click the **Align** button and then click **Grid Settings**. Under Guide settings, click to disable the **Display drawing guides on screen** option, then click **OK**. Save the changes and leave the presentation open for the next Step-by-Step.

Linking Chart Data

VOCABULARY
embedded object
linked object

If the chart data you would like to include in your presentation is going to be updated in the future, you can import Excel chart data into your presentation file as either an embedded object or a linked object. You may already be familiar with linking and embedding from other units. An ***embedded object*** becomes part of the destination file and can be edited in the destination file. A ***linked object*** is inserted as a static object and accesses data stored in the source file, so you cannot update the linked data in the destination file. You edit linked data by editing the data in the Excel worksheet. When linked data is modified in the source file, the data is automatically updated on the slide when both files are open or when you reopen the destination file. To create linked or embedded objects, you can use the Paste options, which also enable you to use the destination theme (the theme applied to the current slide) or source formatting (the formatting applied to the chart in the source file).

To complete the following Step-by-Step, you must have Excel installed on your computer.

Step-by-Step 6.8

1. If necessary, open the **Updated Deer Creek Inn 3** presentation from your solution files. Save the presentation as **Updated Deer Creek Inn 4**, followed by your initials.
2. Go to slide 5.
3. In Excel, navigate to and open the **Next Year.xlsx** file from the drive and folder where your Data Files are stored. Save the worksheet as **The Year Ahead**, followed by your initials.
4. Click anywhere within the chart to select it. Copy the chart to the Clipboard.
5. Switch to the PowerPoint presentation. Right-click under the heading *The Year Ahead*. In the shortcut menu, under Paste Options, click the **Use Destination Theme & Link Data** button.
6. If necessary, position the chart below the horizontal line under the slide title.
7. Switch to the Excel worksheet. Click cell **B4** and change the value to **75,000**. Click cell **B5** and change the value to **45,000**.
8. Switch to the PowerPoint presentation. Note that the values for the Winter projected revenues are updated.
9. Save the changes to the PowerPoint presentation and leave the presentation open for the next Step-by-Step.
10. Save the changes to the Excel worksheet. Close the file and exit Excel.

Animating Chart Data

You can apply animation effects to create progressive disclosure and control when the chart objects appear. PowerPoint offers several effect options to animate the chart elements. For example, you can animate the chart to appear as one object, to appear by series or category, or to appear by elements in a series or elements in a category. By revealing parts of the chart individually, you can help your audience focus on specific data represented in the chart.

You can also create hyperlinks for an object in a chart. For example, you can create a link to a Web site or to another slide in the presentation.

Step-by-Step 6.9

1. If necessary, open the **Updated Deer Creek Inn 4** presentation from your solution files. Save the presentation as **Updated Deer Creek Inn 5**, followed by your initials.
2. Go to slide 2. Select the chart. Click the **Animations** tab. In the Animation group, click the **Appear** button.
3. In the Advanced Animation group, click the **Animation Pane** button. In the Animation Pane, click the **Content Placeholder** list arrow. In the drop-down menu, click **Effect Options**. The Appear dialog box opens. Click the **Chart Animation** tab.
4. Click the **Group chart** list arrow, and then click **By Element in Category**.
5. Disable the option **Start animation by drawing the chart background**. When the settings in your dialog box match those in **Figure 6–15**, click **OK**.

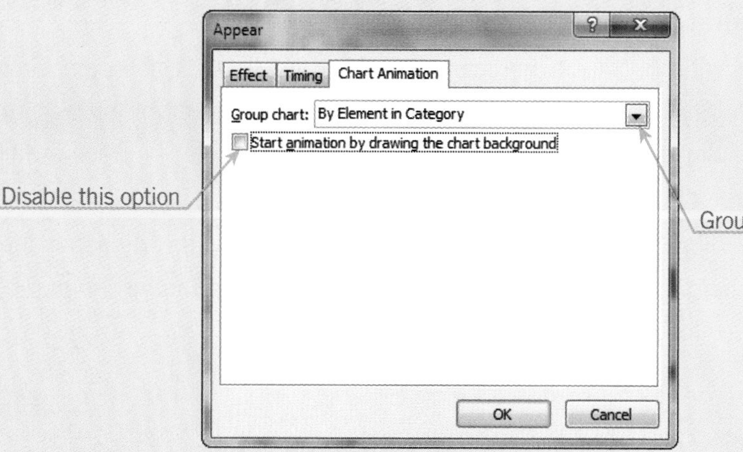

FIGURE 6–15
Appear dialog box with custom settings

6. Click the **Slide Show** tab. In the Start Slide Show group, click the **From Current Slide** button. Click to progressively disclose the elements in each category (season) in the chart. When the chart is fully displayed, press **Esc** to return to Normal view.
7. Go to slide 3. Select the chart. Click the **Animations** tab. In the Animation group, click the **More** button. Under Entrance, click the **Float In** option.

8. In the Animation group, click the **Effect Options** button. The Float Up option is already selected. Under Sequence, click **By Category**.
9. Go to slide 4. Select the chart. In the Animation group, click the **More** button. At the bottom of the menu, click **More Entrance Effects**. The Change Entrance Effect dialog box opens.
10. Under Subtle, click **Expand**, as shown in **Figure 6–16**. Click **OK**.

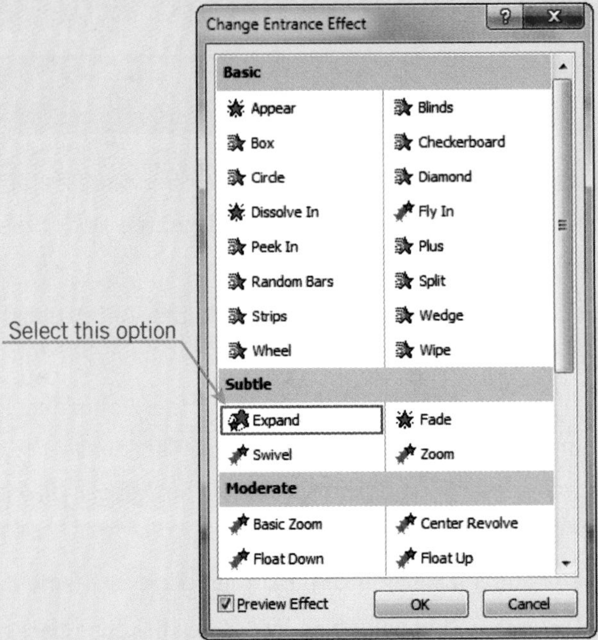

FIGURE 6–16
Change Entrance Effect dialog box with custom animation selected

11. In the Animation group, click the **Effect Options** button, and then click **By Category**.
12. Go to slide 5. Select the chart. Click the **Insert** tab, and in the Links group, click the **Hyperlink** button. In the Insert Hyperlink dialog box, under Link, click **Place in This Document**. Under Select a place in this document, click **2. Lodging Revenues**. Click **OK**.
13. Go to slide 3, and switch to Slide Show view. Review the animations for the charts on slides 3 and 4. Test the hyperlink on the last slide, and then switch back to Normal view.
14. Save the changes and close the presentation.

Modifying an Organization Chart

Organization charts are most commonly used to show the structure of personnel in a company. Over time, employees get promoted and/or the structure of the organization changes. It is easy to add and delete text boxes in an organization chart, but you need to be careful because it can affect the hierarchy of the related text boxes. For example, when you delete a text box, a subordinate text box is automatically moved up in the hierarchy. To promote and demote objects in the hierarchy, you can also use the Promote and Demote buttons on the SmartArt Tools Design tab.

To further enhance the presentation of the organization chart, you can animate the SmartArt graphic and format the elements so that they appear in segments.

After finalizing the organization chart, you can convert the SmartArt graphic to text and the content can be presented in a bulleted list on the slide. You can also copy the text to the Clipboard and use the text in other documents.

Step-by-Step 6.10

1. Open the **Organization** presentation from the drive and folder where your Data Files are stored. Save the presentation as **Revised Organization 1**, followed by your initials.
2. Note that the Engineering Manager reports to the Co-Director on the right. Select the **Co-Director** text box on the right. Be sure to select the white text box and not the blue background box. Then press **Delete**. The Engineering Manager is promoted to the Co-Director level and the Engineering Staff is also promoted to a higher level. On the Quick Access Toolbar, click the **Undo** button.
3. The Co-Director text box should still be selected. Click the **SmartArt Tools Design** tab. In the Create Graphic group, click the **Demote** button. The Co-Director text box is moved down a level.
4. The Co-Director text box is still selected. Press **Delete**. The position is removed without changing the hierarchy. Edit the text in the Co-Director text box at the top of the chart so the title reads **Director**.
5. Click the **Advertising Manager** text box. In the Create Graphic group, click the **Add Shape** button arrow, and then click **Add Shape Below**. In the new text box, type **E-Marketing Manager**.
6. The E-Marketing Manager text box should still be selected. In the Create Graphic group, click the **Promote** button. The text box is moved to the next level above.
7. On the SmartArt Tools Design tab, in the SmartArt Styles group, click the **More** button. Under 3-D, select the second option, the **Inset** SmartArt style.
8. To emphasize the two new staff positions, format the boxes and text with a different color. Select the **Director** text box. Press and hold **Shift** and then click the **E-Marketing Manager** text box. Click the **SmartArt Tools Format** tab. In the Shape Styles group, click the **Shape Fill** button arrow. Under Theme Colors, click the **Red, Accent 2** color.

TIP

You can also promote and demote the organization chart objects by selecting and moving the object text in the Text pane.

9. Click in a blank area to select the whole chart. Click the **Animations** tab. In the Animation group, click the **More** button. At the bottom of the menu, click **More Entrance Effects**. Under Subtle, click **Zoom**, and then click **OK**.

TIP

You can also access the Effect Options by clicking the Effect Options button in the Animation group.

10. If necessary, in the Advanced Animation group, click the Animation Pane button. In the Animation Pane, click the **SmartArt Placeholder** list arrow. Click **Effect Options**, and then click the **SmartArt Animation** tab.
11. Click the **Group graphic** list arrow, and then click **By branch one by one**. Click **OK**.
12. Switch to Slide Show view and review the animations in the organization chart. Switch back to Normal view.

TIP

For a quick preview of the animations, click Play in the Animation Pane.

13. Save the changes. Then save the presentation as **Revised Organization 2**, followed by your initials.
14. If necessary, select the SmartArt object. Click the **SmartArt Tools Design** tab. In the Reset group, click the **Convert** button, and then click **Convert to Text**.
15. Save the changes and close the presentation.

SUMMARY

In this lesson, you learned:

- After creating a table on a slide, you can easily rearrange the content. You can also adjust the font size, AutoFit the columns, and distribute the rows and columns for equal spacing.
- The Draw Table tools are useful for creating or modifying a table, especially for merging and splitting cells.
- PowerPoint provides several features for modifying table styles.
- It is important to choose the correct chart type so that the data and values are represented correctly and for maximum effect.
- You can introduce parts of a table in segments, emphasizing each point individually, and building the table as you progress through the slides.
- You can specify the data that is represented in a chart.
- You can modify the chart elements to clarify the information represented in the chart.
- A linked object must be edited in the source application. The edits will appear in the linked object automatically if the destination document is already open, or the updates will appear when the destination document is reopened.
- You can animate chart objects for progressive disclosure.
- PowerPoint offers many features to help you modify the structure of an organization chart as well as change the chart formats.

VOCABULARY REVIEW

Define the following terms:

axis
axis title
data label
data series
embedded object
legend
linked object
plot area

REVIEW QUESTIONS

TRUE / FALSE

Circle T if the statement is true or F if the statement is false.

T F 1. A table style provides formats for shading, borders, and effects.

T F 2. Column and bar charts are useful in making comparisons among individual items.

T F 3. New columns and rows are automatically added to a table when you drag and drop table data to cells that already have content.

T F 4. A pie chart can show up to three data series, such as three rows of data.

T F 5. You can rotate the text within a table cell so that it appears vertical or stacked.

MULTIPLE CHOICE

Select the best response for the following statements.

1. A ______________ chart is useful in showing trends over time.
   A. column
   B. bar
   C. line
   D. scatter
2. To adjust the column width and row height, you can ______________.
   A. drag the cell boundaries
   B. use the AutoFit command
   C. use the Distribute Rows and Distribute Columns commands
   D. all of the above
3. The Table Eraser tool can be used to ______________.
   A. split cells
   B. merge cells
   C. remove cell content
   D. all of the above
4. To adjust the spacing between characters, ______________.
   A. use the Kerning option
   B. distribute the columns evenly
   C. drag the cell boundaries
   D. change the text alignment
5. If the chart data you would like to include in your presentation is going to be updated in the future, you should consider ______________.
   A. embedding the data in the presentation file
   B. creating an embedded object
   C. linking to the data in the destination file
   D. linking to the data in the source file

MATCHING

Match the correct term in Column 2 to its description in Column 1.

Column 1		Column 2
______	1. encloses the two axes and the data series	A. axis
______	2. text or numbers that provide additional information about a value in the data series	B. data label
______	3. a list that identifies the data series indicated by colors or patterns	C. data series
______	4. a line bordering the chart plot area used as a frame of reference for measurement	D. legend
______	5. related data points that are plotted in a chart	E. plot area

PROJECTS

If you have a SAM 2010 user profile, your instructor may have assigned an autogradable version of the indicated project. If so, log into the SAM 2010 Web site at *www.cengage.com/sam2010* to download the instruction and start files.

PROJECT 6–1

1. Open the **Financial Review** file from the drive and folder where your Data Files are stored. Save the presentation as **Updated Financial Review**, followed by your initials.
2. Go to slide 5. In Excel, open the **Expenses.xlsx** file from the drive and folder where your Data Files are stored. Save the spreadsheet as **Q1 Expenses**, followed by your initials.
3. Copy the chart in the Expenses worksheet. Switch to the presentation and with the **Use Destination Theme & Embed Workbook** paste option, paste the chart on slide 5.
4. Change the chart data range so that the Total is not included in the chart. Apply a chart layout and/or style.
5. Add the chart title **Departmental Travel Expenses**. Move the legend as desired. Add the vertical axis title **Dollars**. Change the font size and attributes of the labels as desired. Resize the chart to fill the slide.
6. Animate the parts of the chart to appear by category, triggered by a click. Apply an appropriate entrance effect for the chart type.
7. Copy slide 5 and paste the copied slide at the end of the presentation.
8. In the new slide 6, change the chart to a 3-D pie chart. Change the chart data range so that the chart shows only the Total data. (*Hint*: Press Ctrl and drag to select the first column and the Total column.) Switch the row/column. Apply a chart layout and/or style if desired.
9. Apply 3-D rotation effects and drag the Airfare portion of the chart from the rest of the chart to explode that slice of the pie.
10. Change the slide title to **Q1 Departmental Travel Expenses**.
11. Add labels to show only percentages in the portions of the pie chart. Resize the chart if necessary so the labels fit within portions of the pie chart.
12. When you copied the chart, the animation effects remained with the new chart. Change the entrance for the animation using an entrance effect appropriate for the chart type.
13. Switch to Slide Show view and test the animations. Make any necessary corrections.
14. Save the changes, close Excel, and close the presentation.

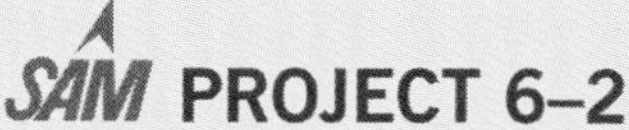

PROJECT 6–2

1. Open the **Wetlands** file from the drive and folder where your Data Files are stored. Save the presentation as **Revised Wetlands**, followed by your initials.
2. Scroll through the slides to become familiar with the content.
3. Go to slide 4. Modify the table as necessary to fit all the information on the slide without overcrowding.
4. Move the content in the last row so that it appears in the first row below the headings.
5. Go to slide 10. Use the Draw Borders tools to create the table shown in **Figure 6–17**. Apply formatting as necessary.

Native Mammals		
Monotremes	**Marsupials**	**Placental Mammals**
Platypus	Planigales Kangaroos Koalas Wombats	Rodents (rats) Bats
Introduced Mammals		
Cows, foxes, goats, foxes, and sheep		

FIGURE 6–17 Table content for Step 5

6. Go to slide 12. Apply a new column chart style. Insert the vertical axis label **In 1,000s of Acres**. If desired, reposition the legend and format the fonts for the legend and the axis title.
7. Copy slide 12 and paste the new slide immediately after slide 12. On the new slide 13, change the chart type to a pie chart. Then select the data for the pie chart to show the 1780 loss. (*Hint*: Select chart data range B1:D2.) Switch the row/column.
8. Add percentage labels and a chart title, **Wetland Loss in 1780**, to make the data clear.
9. Go to slide 14. In Excel, open the **Loss Rate.xlsx** file from the drive and folder where your Data Files are stored. Save the worksheet as **Rate of Loss**, followed by your initials.
10. Copy the chart in the Rate of Loss worksheet. Switch to the presentation and paste the chart as a link, using destination formatting, on slide 14. Close Excel.
11. Add the vertical axis title: **Land Loss in Sq Mi/Yr.**. Resize the chart as needed to fill the slide area. Format and size the axis labels, axis title, and legend for legibility and to fit the theme.
12. Add animations to the charts on slides 12, 13, and 14.
13. Review the chart animations in Slide Show view, then switch back to Normal view.
14. Save the changes and close the presentation.

PROJECT 6–3

1. Open the **Byron Chart** file from the drive and folder where your Data Files are stored. Save the presentation as **Revised Byron Chart**, followed by your initials.
2. Move the *City Attorney* text box so the box is the same level as the *City Manager* and *City Clerk* text boxes.
3. Add a new text box after the *Accounting* text box, with the label **Finance**.
4. Add a new text box below the *Building Inspection* text box, with the label **Planning**. Promote the new text box so it is the same level as the *Building Inspection* text box.
5. Move the *Wastewater Treatment* text box so that it appears one level down from the *Water Utility* text box.
6. Animate the objects in the chart with the **Zoom** entrance effect. Group the objects so that they appear by branch, one by one.
7. Switch to Slide Show view and review the animations.
8. Save the changes and close the presentation.

CRITICAL THINKING

ACTIVITY 6–1

You work for a company whose stock is traded on a local exchange. Your boss has asked you to prepare a chart showing the performance of stock investments over the past month. What kind of information do you need to gather to create such a chart? What kind of chart would you use for this task? Create some hypothetical data and create the necessary chart on a PowerPoint slide.

ACTIVITY 6–2

Typically, an organization chart shows the structure of a company by identifying the various levels of management and job positions. The information does not have to show job titles and people within an organization. Think about other types of information that can be provided in an organization chart. Describe at least one type of information (other than a company's structure) that can effectively be presented in an organization chart.

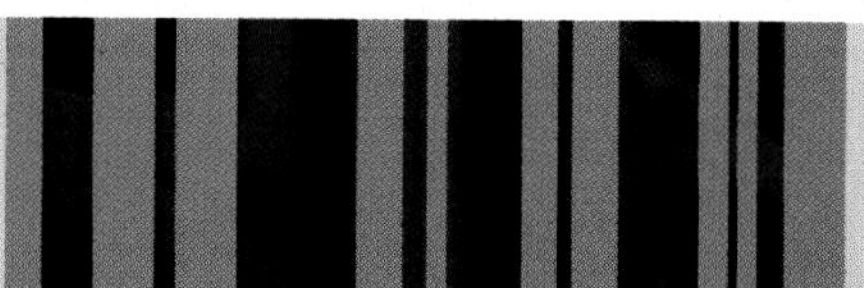

Estimated Time: 2 hours

LESSON 7

Working with Visual and Sound Objects

■ OBJECTIVES

Upon completion of this lesson, you should be able to:

- Crop, resize, reposition, and change graphics.
- Recolor graphics and shapes.
- Insert animated clip art.
- Modify pictures and digital images.
- Convert objects to SmartArt graphics.
- Create a photo album.
- Save a presentation as a video.
- Insert video and sound clips and record a narration.

■ VOCABULARY

aspect ratio
bitmap
bits
crop
nudging
outcrop
pixels
raster graphics
scaling
streaming video
vector graphics

Using visuals and sounds in a presentation helps the audience focus on and comprehend the points in a presentation, making a presentation even more effective. Just as text, tables, and charts are inserted on slides as objects, so are visuals and sounds. All objects can be animated, arranged, and formatted to further enhance the appearance and effectiveness of the slide content.

Working with Graphics

You can access graphics such as digital pictures or clip art from a number of sources, including the Clip Art task pane, the Internet, servers, CD-ROMs, digital cameras, and phones.

After inserting a picture or clip art, you might find that the graphic you choose isn't quite right for the slide. Perhaps the image isn't the right size or you need only part of it, or the colors don't go well with the current design theme. Fortunately, you can modify clip art and pictures so that they complement the presentation and effectively illustrate relevant points in the presentation.

Cropping Graphics

VOCABULARY

crop

outcrop

aspect ratio

If you want to display only a portion of a graphic on a slide, you can ***crop*** the graphic to trim one or more edges of the graphic. To crop, you drag a border to the center of the graphic. Even though a portion of the graphic is hidden, the graphic remains unchanged and you can restore a cropped graphic to its original size by dragging the border away from the center or by using the Reset Picture command. To add blank space around the graphic, you can ***outcrop*** a graphic by dragging a border away from the center of the graphic.

You can crop a graphic to fit or fill a specific shape, or you can crop it to a common picture ***aspect ratio***, which is the ratio between the width and height. The ratio is calculated by dividing the width of the graphic by its height.

Step-by-Step 7.1

1. Open the **Happy Tails** file from the drive and folder where your Data Files are stored. Save the presentation as **Revised Happy Tails 1**, followed by your initials. Scroll through the slides to become familiar with the content.
2. Go to slide 2. In the content placeholder, click the **Clip Art** icon to open the Clip Art task pane.
3. In the Search for text box on the Clip Art task pane, type **dog.** Click the **Results should be** list arrow. Enable the option **Illustrations** and disable all the other options. When your options match those shown in **Figure 7–1**, click the **list arrow** again to collapse the list.

TIP

If there is no content placeholder on the slide, you can access the Clip Art command in the Images group on the Insert tab.

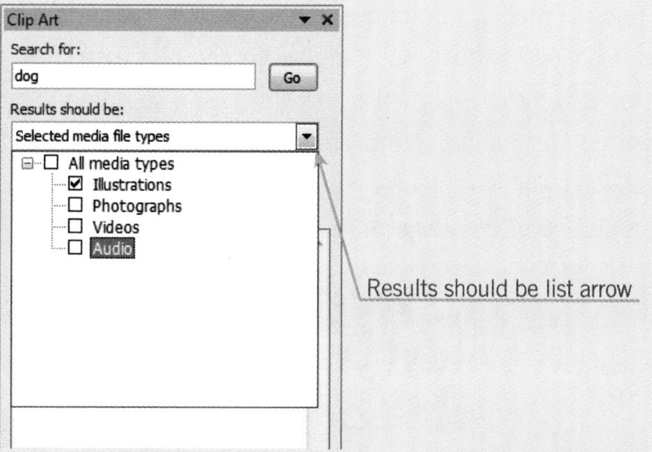

FIGURE 7–1
Media file type options for a clip art search

4. If necessary, enable the Include Office.com content option in the Clip Art task pane, as shown in **Figure 7–2**. Click **Go**. (If you have a current Internet connection, PowerPoint automatically searches for clip art at the Microsoft Office Clip Art and Media Library Web site.)

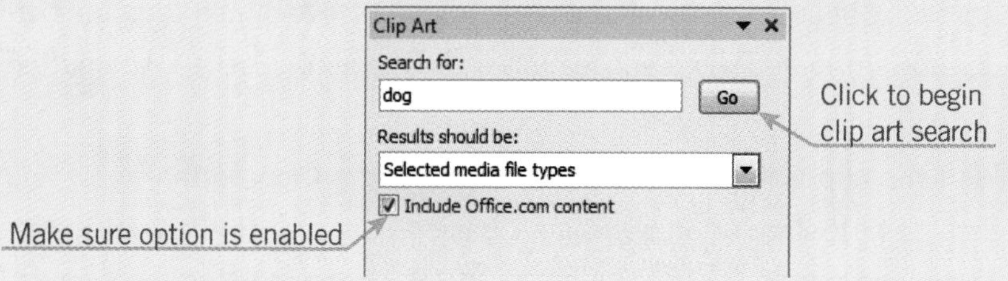

FIGURE 7–2
Options for clip art search

5. Scroll through the search results in the Clip Art task pane and select an illustration of a dog, such as the one shown in **Figure 7–3**. When you select the clip art thumbnail in the Clip Art task pane, the clip art object is inserted in the center of the content placeholder on the slide. Close the Clip Art task pane.

FIGURE 7–3
Sample clip art illustration of a dog

6. With the clip art object selected on the slide, the Picture Tools Format tab appears. In the Size group, click the **Crop** button. The sizing handles surrounding the image on the slide change to thick black lines, as shown in **Figure 7–4**.

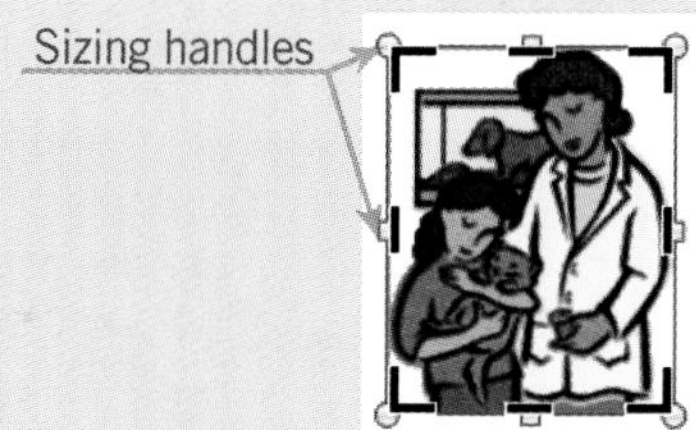

FIGURE 7–4
Sizing handles with cropping feature enabled

7. Position the mouse pointer over the lower-right corner until you see the pointer change to the shape of the corner. Then drag the border upward to remove a portion of the image. As you drag the border, the mouse pointer changes to a cross-hair. When you release the mouse button, you will see the new cropped border as well as the original border. A portion of the image is removed, as shown in **Figure 7–5**.

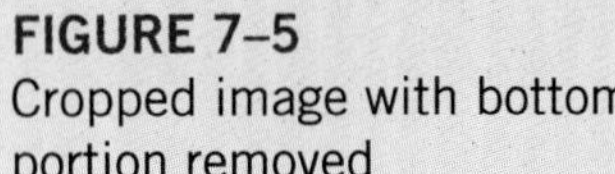

FIGURE 7–5
Cropped image with bottom portion removed

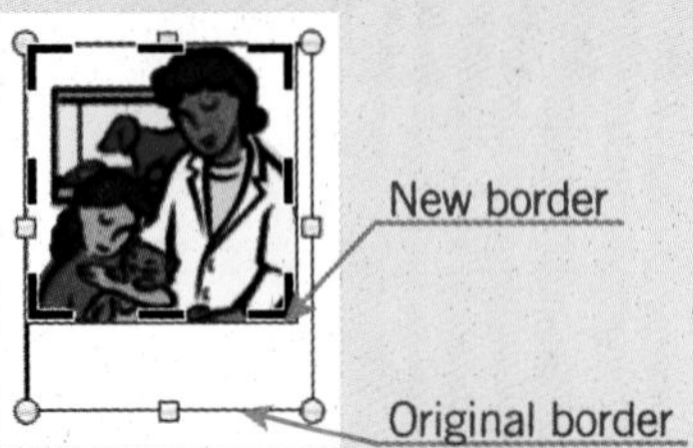

8. In the Adjust group, click the **Reset Picture** button arrow and then click **Reset Picture & Size** to restore the graphic to its original size.
9. With the cropping feature still enabled, position the mouse pointer on the sizing handle in the middle of the top border and then drag the border upward to add more space above the image. Click the **Undo** button on the Quick Access Toolbar.
10. With the clip art object still selected, click the **Crop** button arrow and then point to **Crop to Shape**. Under Basic Shapes, click the **Oval** shape. The image is trimmed to fit within the selected shape. However, depending on the clip art you chose, you may not notice a change. Experiment with cropping to other shapes.
11. Click the **Undo** button arrow and undo all Change Shape edits.
12. In the Size group, note the graphic dimensions for height and width. With the clip art object still selected:
    a. Click the **Crop** button arrow, and then point to **Aspect Ratio**. Under Square, click **1:1**. When you change aspect ratio, the image height and width dimensions change.
    b. With the clip art object still selected, click the **Crop** button arrow and then click **Fit**. The image is adjusted to fit within the new dimensions. However, depending on the clip art you chose, you may not see a change.
13. Use your new understanding of the tools to experiment with various aspect ratio settings, fitting and filling, and new shapes to find a format that works with your clip art. Use the Reset Picture & Size command to start over. When you are satisfied with the results, click the **Crop** button to toggle off the cropping feature.
14. Save the changes and leave the presentation open for the next Step-by-Step.

EXTRA FOR EXPERTS

To crop or outcrop two sides equally at the same time, press and hold CTRL as you drag one of the center cropping handles. The opposite side will also be cropped. To crop or outcrop all four sides equally at the same time, press and hold CTRL as you drag a corner cropping handle.

Resizing, Repositioning, and Changing Graphics

You have several options for resizing a graphic such as a clip art illustration or a picture. The simplest way is to drag one of the selection handles in the direction you want to resize. When resized this way, the graphic does not necessarily maintain its original proportions. You can distort the graphic using this method—which you might want to do to make a particular point. You can enable a setting so that when you adjust the graphic size using a corner sizing handle, the aspect ratio of the graphic is maintained. Sizing a graphic to exact proportions is referred to as ***scaling***. You can enter a specific height or width for the graphic, or you can specify a percentage reduction or enlargement for the graphic.

To reposition an object on a slide, you can drag the object to a new location. To achieve a more precise location for the graphic, you can nudge the object. ***Nudging*** is moving an object vertically or horizontally in small increments. With the object selected, you press one of the arrow keys to move the object. To move in even smaller increments, hold down the Ctrl key as you press the arrow keys.

If you are not satisfied with a picture that was inserted from a file, you can easily replace the picture using the Change Picture button.

VOCABULARY
scaling
nudging

Step-by-Step 7.2

1. If necessary, open the **Revised Happy Tails 1** file from your solution files. Save the presentation as **Revised Happy Tails 2**, followed by your initials.
2. If necessary, go to slide 2 and select the clip art object. Position the mouse pointer over the upper-right corner handle. When the pointer changes to a diagonal double-arrow, drag the corner handle upward and to the right to enlarge the graphic. Then drag the upper-left corner downward and to the right to reduce the graphic size. When you drag a corner handle, the image is resized proportionally.
3. Position the mouse pointer over the middle handle on the top border and drag the border down. Notice that as you drag the border, the height of the picture changes but the width remains the same. The image is no longer proportional. Click the **Undo** button.

4. In the Size group, click the **Dialog Box Launcher** to open the Format Picture dialog box, as shown in **Figure 7–6**. Your settings will differ, depending on the clip art you chose and how you resized the image.

FIGURE 7–6
Format Picture dialog box

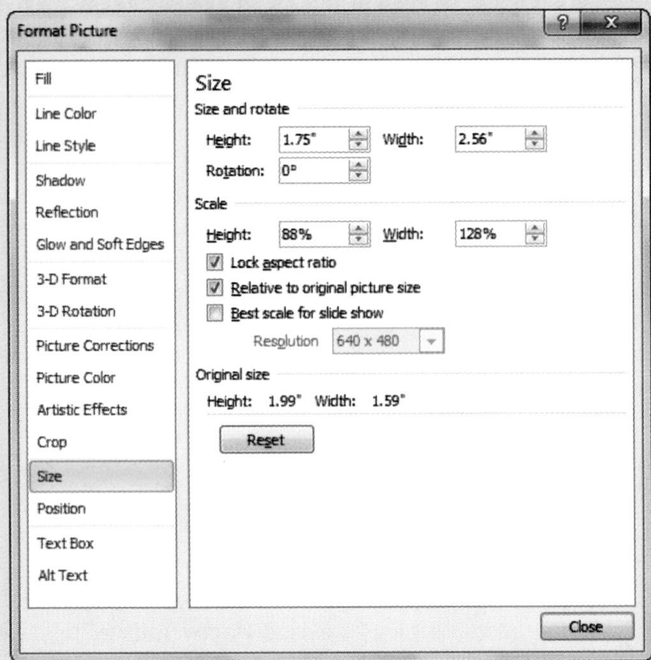

5. Under Scale, make sure the option Lock aspect ratio is enabled. Under Size and rotate, increase the height settings a few increments. Note that as you change the height setting, the width setting automatically adjusts to keep the original proportion of the image. Click **Close**.
6. In the Adjust group, click the **Reset Picture** button arrow and then click **Reset Picture & Size**.
7. Right-click the **clip art** object, and then click **Size and Position** to open the Format Picture dialog box.
8. Disable the option **Lock aspect ratio**. Under Scale, change the Height setting to **75%**. The height size and scale settings both change, but the width settings do not change. Then enable the option **Lock aspect ratio**. Under Original Size, click **Reset**. Close the dialog box. No changes are made to the clip art. Center the clip art object.
9. Go to slide 3. In the placeholder on the right, click the **Insert Picture from File** icon. The Insert Picture dialog box opens. Navigate to the drive and folder where your Data Files are stored. Select the **Taffy.jpg** file, and then click **Insert**.
10. The picture is inserted on the slide. The picture object is selected and the Picture Tools Format tab appears. In the Size group, change the Shape Height to **3"**, as shown in **Figure 7–7**. Because the aspect ratio is locked, the width will automatically adjust.

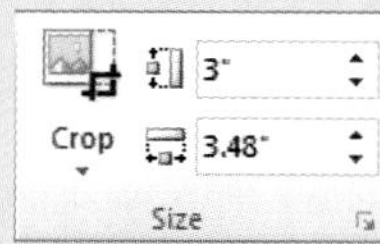

FIGURE 7–7
Size group on the Picture Tools Format tab

11. Drag the picture object upward to align it with the top border of the placeholder on the left. With the picture object still selected, press the **right arrow** key a few times to nudge the object. Then press and hold **Ctrl** and press the **right arrow** key a few times. The image moves in smaller increments.
12. In the placeholder on the left, click the **Insert Picture from File** icon. If necessary, navigate to the drive and folder where your Data Files are stored. Select the **Charlie.jpg** file, and then click **Insert**. You realize you inserted the wrong picture. The Ribbon already displays the Picture Tools Format tab. In the Adjust group, click the **Change Picture** button. Select the **Cuddles.jpg** file, and then click **Insert**. The Charlie picture is replaced with the Cuddles picture.
13. The Cuddles picture is wider than the Taffy picture. Resize and reposition the picture:
    a. Crop the left and right edges of the picture so that the image is approximately 3.6" wide.
    b. With the image selected, in the Size group, click the **Dialog Box Launcher**. Disable the **Lock aspect ratio** option, and then click **Close**.
    c. In the Size group, change the dimensions so that the height is **3"** and the width is **3.48"** (the exact dimensions of the Taffy picture).
    d. Click the **Crop** button to toggle off the cropping feature.
    e. Reposition the cat and dog images side by side on the slide.
14. Save the changes and leave the presentation open for the next Step-by-Step.

EXTRA FOR EXPERTS

To crop or outcrop a graphic to exact dimensions, click the Format Picture Tools tab, and then click the Size group Dialog Box Launcher. In the Format Picture dialog box, click Crop in the left pane, and then enter exact dimensions.

Recoloring Graphics and Shapes

You are not limited to the original colors of a clip art or picture. You can customize a graphic by changing the image colors to match the other colors in the current design theme. You can choose from a large palette of colors or even create your own custom color scheme.

When you add shapes to a slide, you can customize the shape formats with fills, outlines, and effects. After applying custom formats, you can set the shape formatting as the default, so that the next time you insert a shape in the presentation, all of the custom formats will be applied to the new shape. The settings for a default shape are only saved with the current presentation.

Step-by-Step 7.3

1. If necessary, open the **Revised Happy Tails 2** file from your solution files. Save the presentation as **Revised Happy Tails 3**, followed by your initials.
2. Click the **Design** tab. In the Themes group, click the **More** button and then select the **Technic** theme. (*Hint*: The themes are arranged in alphabetical order, and Technic is a built-in theme.)
3. If necessary, go to slide 3. Select the **Taffy (dog) picture** object. Click the **Picture Tools Format** tab. In the Adjust group, click the **Color** button to show the color options, as shown in **Figure 7–8**. (When the image has a background color, such as the Taffy picture, you see more options.)

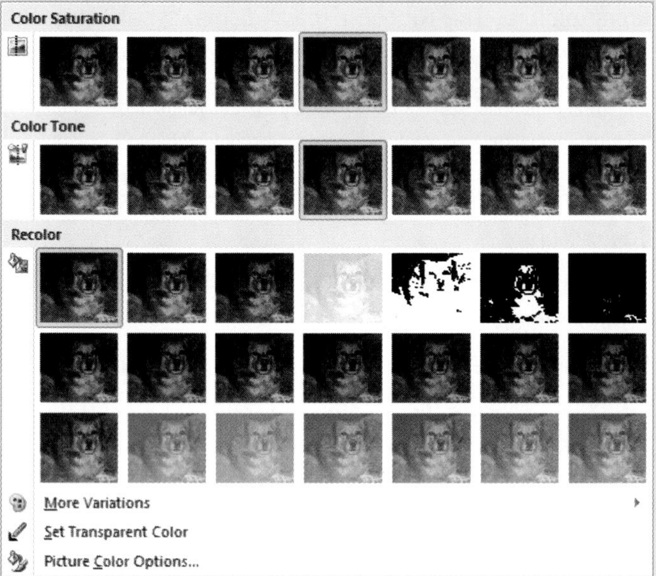

FIGURE 7–8
Color options for picture

4. Under Recolor, hover the mouse pointer over the options to preview the different colors. The colors offered for recoloring are consistent with those in the current color scheme.
5. Point to the menu option **More Variations** to show the color palette. Move the mouse pointer over the colors to preview some of the theme colors. (You'll be able to see part of the picture behind the palette.) Select any color in the palette to change the image color.
6. In the Adjust group, click the **Reset Picture** button to restore the original picture colors.
7. Go to slide 4. Click the **Clip Art** icon in the placeholder on the right. In the Clip Art task pane, search for another illustration of a dog. Choose an image that shows a background color, such as the image shown in **Figure 7–9**. Close the Clip Art task pane.

FIGURE 7–9
Clip art illustration with background color

8. With the clip art object selected on the slide, in the Adjust group, click the **Color** button. At the bottom of the menu, click **Set Transparent Color**. The mouse pointer changes to a pen. Click anywhere in the color background. The background is no longer visible. (If the image has more than one background color, only one of the colors will become transparent.)
9. In the placeholder on the left, click the **Clip Art** icon. Search for and insert an illustration of a cat. Remove the color background, if necessary. Close the Clip Art task pane.
10. Adjust the height of both images so that the images are about the same size. Because of the image backgrounds, the heights may differ. Position the images side by side in the center of the slide. Recolor the images applying the **Aqua, Accent color 1 Dark** color.
11. Go to slide 3. Click the **Insert** tab. In the Illustrations group, click **Shapes**, and then under Callouts, click the **Cloud Callout** shape. Insert a callout shape in the upper-right corner of the slide (connected to the top of the dog's head), and then, in the callout shape, type **Woof!**.
12. Click the **Drawing Tools Format** tab. In the Shape Styles group, click the **Shape Fill** button arrow, point to **Texture**, and then click the **Woven mat** texture. Click the **Shape Outline** button arrow. Under Theme Colors, click the **White, Text 1** theme color. Click the **Shape Outline** button arrow again, point to **Weight**, and then click **2¼ pt**.
13. Right-click the callout shape and in the shortcut menu, click **Set as Default Shape**. Click the **Insert** tab and then click the **Shapes** button. Under Basic Shapes, select the **Heart** shape. Draw a heart shape below the Cuddles (cat) picture. The default formats are applied to the new shape. Type **Meow!**.
14. Save the changes and leave the presentation open for the next Step-by-Step.

TIP

Text fonts and shape effects are also saved with the default shape settings.

Inserting Animated Clip Art

You can also add animated clip art to a slide. One of the media type options in the Clip Art gallery is videos. The clip art videos are GIF (Graphics Interchange Format) files. GIF is a file format that supports animation. The animated GIF files can be inserted using the same process as inserting clip art illustrations.

TIP

You can easily insert clip art of any type (graphics or animated GIFs) that is stored on an accessible disk or server (rather than in the Clip Organizer). To insert clip art stored as a file, click the Insert tab. In the Images group, click the Insert Picture from File button, then navigate to the drive and folder where the file is stored, select the filename, and click Insert.

Once an animated clip art video has been inserted, you can resize it and position it on the slide, but you cannot edit the image as you would other clip art. To modify an animated image, you need to use a program designed especially for creating animated images. Animated clip art images play during a presentation, but unless you apply an animation effect, they do not play in Normal view.

As you apply animations to objects, the animations are numbered in sequence. You can rearrange the order of the animations in the Animation Pane. When you change the order, the animation numbers are automatically updated to reflect the new sequence. You can also add sound effects to slide transitions and animations to "make noise" as the objects and slides appear, such as an applause or the sound of a camera click.

Step-by-Step 7.4

1. If necessary, open the **Revised Happy Tails 3** file from your solution files. Save the presentation as **Revised Happy Tails 4**, followed by your initials.
2. Go to slide 5. Click the **Insert** tab. In the Images group, click the **Clip Art** button to open the Clip Art task pane.
3. In the Search for text box, type **clock**. Click the **Results should be** list arrow and enable the option **Videos**. Disable all other media file type options and click the **list arrow** to close the menu. Make sure the Include Office.com content option is enabled.
4. Click **Go**. When the search results are displayed, scroll through them and select a thumbnail similar to the one shown in **Figure 7–10**. The small icon in the lower-right corner indicates that the clip art image is animated.

FIGURE 7–10
Clip art video with animation icon

5. Note that the animation for the image does not preview in the task pane or in Normal view. Click the **Slide Show** button in the status bar to view the animation. Note that the animation plays automatically.
6. Press **Esc** to switch to Normal view. If you are not satisfied with your selection, delete the object and select another thumbnail from the Clip Art task pane. When you are satisfied with the animated image you have inserted on the slide, close the Clip Art task pane.
7. Resize the image so that it is approximately 2.5" high (or an appropriate height for your chosen image). Reposition the clip art object to the right of the bulleted list.

8. The clip art object should still be selected. Click the **Animations** tab. In the Animation group, click the **More** button. Under Entrance, click the **Fade** entrance effect. The animation previews, and the number *6* appears to the left of the clip art object on the slide.
9. Select the clip art object. In the Advanced Animation group, click the **Animation Pane** button. The Animation Pane opens and the new animation appears at the end of the list (#6), labeled Picture, followed by a number. If necessary, click the Expand button to show all animated objects.
10. In the Animation Pane, drag the new Picture animation and position it between animations 1 and 2, as shown in **Figure 7–11**.

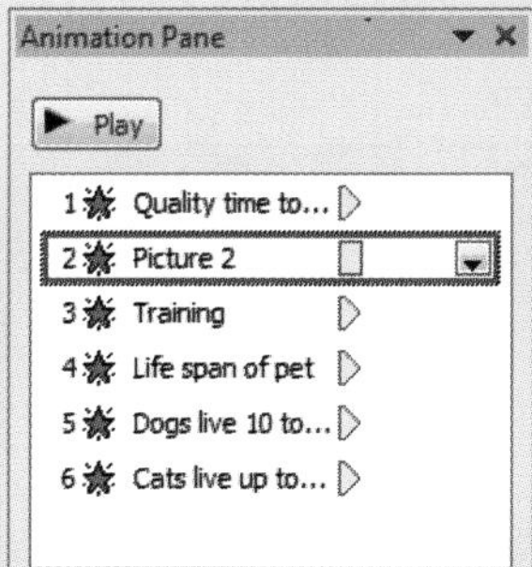

FIGURE 7–11
Animated objects for slide 5 after reorganization

11. Click the **list arrow** for the new Picture animation, and then click **Start With Previous.**
12. Click the **list arrow** for the new Picture animation again, and then click **Effect Options**. Under Enhancements, click the **Sound** list arrow. Scroll down and click **Chime**. Click the **Audio** button to the right of the Sound text box to show the Volume setting. Do not make any changes. Click **OK**. A preview of the audio sound plays.
13. At the top of the Animation Pane, click **Play** to preview the animations. The preview is usually quick. Click the **Slide Show** button and preview the content on the slide, clicking through the animations. When the last bulleted item is displayed (*Cats live up to 20 years*), press **Esc** to return to Normal view.
14. Close the Animation Pane. Save the changes and leave the presentation open for the next Step-by-Step.

Understanding Graphics File Formats

Graphics files can be saved in many different formats. A ***raster graphics*** image, which is also referred to as a ***bitmap***, consists of rows of tiny colored dots called ***pixels*** (short for picture elements) or ***bits*** that compose the image on a computer screen. Raster graphics open quickly, but when you enlarge a raster graphic, the dots are spread over the area and the image can lose definition. A ***vector graphics*** image consists of lines, curves, and shapes. Vector graphics take more time to open, but when you increase and decrease the image size the clarity of the image will not change. Vector graphic formats are typically used when creating documents to be sent to a printer.

VOCABULARY
raster graphics
bitmap
pixels
bits
vector graphics

EXTRA FOR EXPERTS

Another alternative to reduce the file size is to link the picture files to the presentation so they are not saved with the presentation. The photo files must be stored on the same computer when running the presentation. To link the file, click the Insert tab and then click the Picture button. Navigate to the drive and folder where the file is stored. Click the Insert list arrow and then click Link to File.

The size of a picture file in kilobytes (or even megabytes) depends on the file format. JPEG images, for example, tend to be smaller files than TIFF images. The graphic size is also affected by the resolution. The resolution is determined by the number of pixels. The resolution size is frequently referred to as dpi (dots per inch) or ppi (pixels per inch). The higher the number of pixels, the higher the resolution.

Table 7–1 provides information about several graphics file formats that are compatible with PowerPoint.

TABLE 7–1 Graphics file formats

FILE FORMAT	FILE EXTENSION	DESCRIPTION
Bitmap (BMP)	.bmp	This raster graphic format can display millions of colors and is commonly used because it is compatible with several programs. The image quality is retained through numerous saves.
Graphics Interchange Format (GIF)	.gif	This raster graphic format supports animation and transparent background, and it is compatible with almost all Web browsers. Because it is limited to supporting 256 colors, it is good for illustrations, line drawings, and black and white images. Quality of the image is not lost when the file is decompressed, and the image quality is retained through numerous saves.
Joint Photographic Experts Group (JPEG)	.jpg	This raster graphic format can be used for high-quality photos and complex graphics containing millions of colors. It can compress photos into very compact files, so it is commonly used on Web pages and it is useful when sending images via e-mail.
Portable Network Graphics (PNG)	.png	This raster graphic format can display millions of colors, and it is commonly used on Web pages. The format does support transparent background, but unlike GIF, it does not support animation. Quality of the image is not lost when the file is decompressed, and the image quality is retained through numerous saves.
Tag Image File Format (TIFF)	.tif	This raster graphic format can display millions of colors, allows any resolution, and is compatible with many programs. Because it can produce very high-quality images, it is often used in publishing. The file sizes are typically larger than GIF or JPEG formats. This format is best for storing bitmapped images on personal computers. The image quality is retained through numerous saves.
Windows Metafile (WMF)	.wmf	This vector graphic format was designed to be portable between Office applications such as Word, PowerPoint, and Publisher. The format is compatible with both 16- and 32-bit Windows operating systems.
Enhanced Metafile (EMF)	.emf	This vector graphic format is a newer 32-bit version of the Windows Metafile format. The newer version supports more drawing features.

Modifying Pictures and Digital Images

You can use options on the Picture Tools Format tab to adjust the way the picture looks. PowerPoint provides several commands for removing the background, changing the picture colors, adding artistic effects, and formatting borders. The Soften options enable you to remove unwanted marks on a picture, and the Sharpen options enable you to enhance the picture details. The Contrast controls enable you to clarify elements by adjusting the darkest and lightest areas of a picture, and the Brightness controls enable you to adjust the relative lightness of the picture.

Step-by-Step 7.5

1. Open the **Revised Happy Tails 4** file from your solution files. Save the presentation as **Revised Happy Tails 5**, followed by your initials.
2. Go to slide 6. Click the **Insert** tab. In the Images group, click the **Insert Picture from File** button to open the Insert Picture dialog box. Navigate to the drive and folder where your Data Files are stored. Select the file **Kylie.jpg**, and then click **Insert**. The picture is inserted in the slide and most likely covers the entire slide.
3. On the Picture Tools Format tab, in the Size group, change the height to **4"**. Then reposition the picture object in the lower-right corner of the slide.
4. With the picture object still selected, in the Adjust group, click the **Remove Background** button. The picture background changes to a violet color, and the Background Removal tab appears. In the Close group, click the **Keep Changes** button.
5. In the Adjust group, click the **Corrections** button to display the picture corrections options shown in **Figure 7–12**.

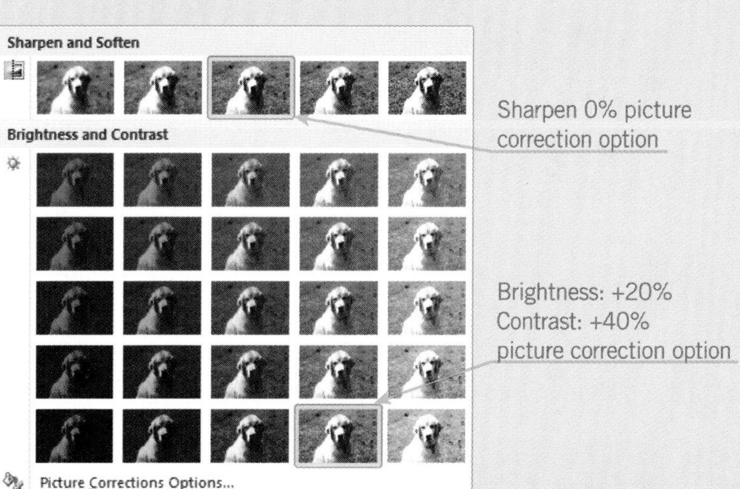

FIGURE 7–12
Corrections options

6. Under Sharpen and Soften, position the mouse pointer over the first option to preview the **Soften: 50%** effect. Then, position the mouse pointer over the last option in the same row, **Sharpen 50%**, to preview the effect. (The Sharpen 0% option should still be enabled.)

7. If necessary, click the Corrections button to display the picture correction options. Under Brightness and Contrast, click the **Brightness: +20% Contrast: +40%** picture correction option, the fourth option in the last row. (See Figure 7-12.)
8. With the picture object still selected, in the Adjust group, click the **Artistic Effects** button to display the options shown in **Figure 7–13**.

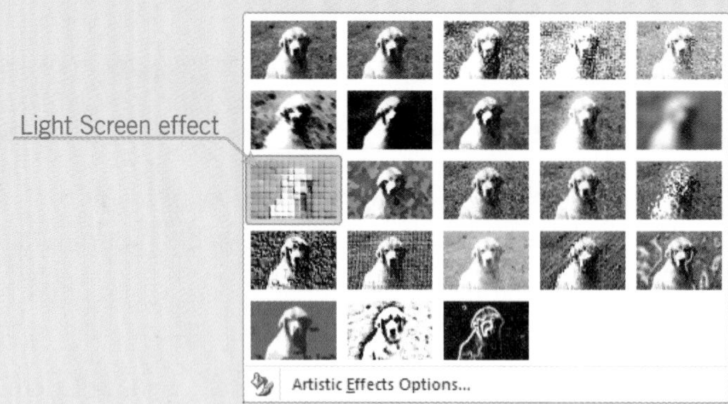

FIGURE 7–13
Artistic effects options

9. Position the mouse pointer over several of the options to preview the various effects. Click the **Light Screen** effect, as shown in Figure 7–13.
10. With the picture object still selected, click the **Artistic Effects** button again. At the bottom of the menu, click **Artistic Effects Options**. The Format Picture dialog box opens. If necessary, reposition the dialog box on the screen so you can see the picture. The same artistic effects options are available, but here you can tweak the settings by changing the transparency and the grid size. Experiment with the settings.
11. In the Format Picture dialog box, click the **Artistic Effect** button, choose a different effect, and then experiment with the settings. When you are satisfied with the artistic effects, close the dialog box.
12. With the picture object still selected, in the Adjust group, click the **Color** button. Under Recolor, click the **Aqua, Accent color 1 Dark** recolor option.
13. Go to slide 3. Select the picture on the left and then click the **Picture Tools Format** tab. In the Picture Styles group, click the **Picture Border** button arrow. Under Theme Colors, click the **Aqua, Accent 1** theme color. Then click the **Picture Border** button arrow again. Point to **Weight** and then click **3 pt**.
14. With the picture still selected, click the **Home** tab. In the Clipboard group, click the **Format Painter** button. Click anywhere inside the photo on the right to copy the border format.
15. Save the changes and leave the presentation open for the next Step-by-Step.

Converting Objects to a SmartArt Graphic

Once clip art images are added to a slide, you can convert the graphics to be included in a SmartArt object; and then of course, you can animate the objects in the SmartArt diagram. You can also convert shapes and WordArt objects to a SmartArt object.

Step-by-Step 7.6

1. If necessary, open the **Revised Happy Tails 5** file from your solution files. Save the presentation as **Revised Happy Tails 6**, followed by your initials.
2. Go to slide 4. Select the cat clip art object, press and hold **Ctrl**, and then select the dog clip art object. Both images should be selected, and the Picture Tools Format tab is displayed.
3. Click the **Picture Tools Format** tab. In the Picture Styles group, click the **Picture Layout** button to display the layout options, as shown in **Figure 7–14**.

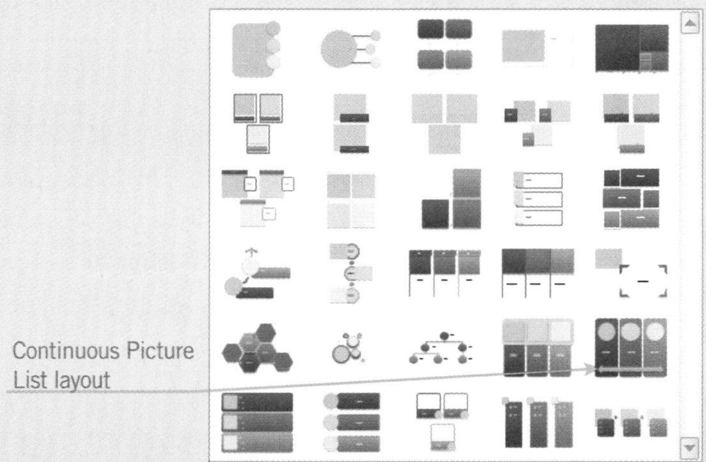

FIGURE 7–14 Picture Layout options

4. Click the **Continuous Picture List** layout, as shown in Figure 7–14. The SmartArt graphic is inserted on the slide, and the clip art images are positioned in the picture placeholders within the SmartArt graphic. In the first text placeholder, type **$650**. In the second text placeholder, type **$1,000**.
5. Select the SmartArt object. The SmartArt Tools Design tab is displayed. In the Layouts group, click the **More** button. Click the **Vertical Picture Accent List** layout. Resize the SmartArt diagram so it is approximately 4" high, and center the graphic below the last line of text.
6. Go to slide 7. In the placeholder, click the **Insert SmartArt Graphic** icon to open the Choose a SmartArt Graphic dialog box. In the left

pane, click **Picture** to display the SmartArt graphic picture options, as shown in **Figure 7–15**.

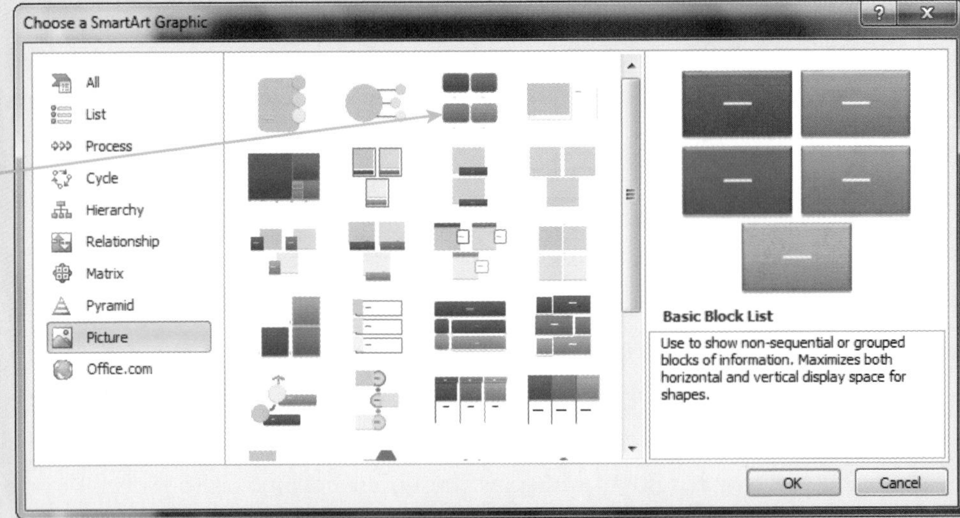

FIGURE 7–15 Choose a SmartArt Graphic dialog box

7. Click the **Picture Caption List** SmartArt graphic, and then click **OK**. Drag the center handle on the right border for the SmartArt graphic inward to reduce the width so the four objects are arranged in two rows, with two objects in each row. Reposition the graphic in the center of the slide.
8. Click the icon in the first object of the diagram. The Insert Picture dialog box opens. If necessary, navigate to the drive and folder where your Data Files are stored. Select the picture file **Blue.jpg** and click **Insert**. The picture is automatically resized and inserted in the picture placeholder. Click the **Text** placeholder below the picture, and type **Blue**.
9. Click the icon in the second object in the first row. Insert the picture file **Taffy.jpg**. Click the icon in the first object in the second row and insert the picture file **Charlie.jpg**. Insert the picture file **Cuddles.jpg** in the last object. Type the names in the caption placeholders below each picture.
10. With the SmartArt graphic selected, click the **Animations** tab. In the Animation group, click the **More** button. Under Entrance, click the **Split** entrance effect.
11. In the Animation group, click the **Effect Options** button and then, under Direction, click **Vertical Out**. A preview of the revised animation plays.
12. Click the **Effect Options** button again, and then, under Sequence, click **One by One**. A preview of the revised animation plays.
13. Go to slide 1. Click the **Slide Show** button in the status bar and review the presentation slides. When you have reviewed the animations on all slides, press **Esc** to return to Normal view.
14. Save the changes and close the presentation.

Creating a Photo Album

The Photo Album feature creates a new presentation for a group of pictures. After you identify the pictures to be included in the photo album, the pictures are arranged on individual slides. You can choose the number of pictures to show on each slide. Photo album templates with preformatted slide borders and picture placeholders are also available at Office.com, or you can create your own template using special effects including themes, transitions, colorful backgrounds, and specific layouts. You can easily rearrange the order of the slides, add captions to the pictures on the slides, format all pictures in black and white, and add frames around the pictures. To provide information about the photos, you can insert text boxes between slides.

You can enhance the appearance of the photos by adjusting the brightness and contrast. You can also recolor the photos and apply artistic effects. If necessary, you can rotate a photo to change from landscape orientation to portrait orientation.

TIP

PowerPoint provides several sample photo album templates that provide a variety of slide layouts for positioning photos. To access the sample templates, click the File tab, and then click New. Under Available Templates and Themes, click the Sample templates icon.

Step-by-Step 7.7

1. If necessary, open a new blank presentation. Click the **Insert** tab. In the Images group, click the **New Photo Album** button. The Photo Album dialog box opens, as shown in **Figure 7–16**.

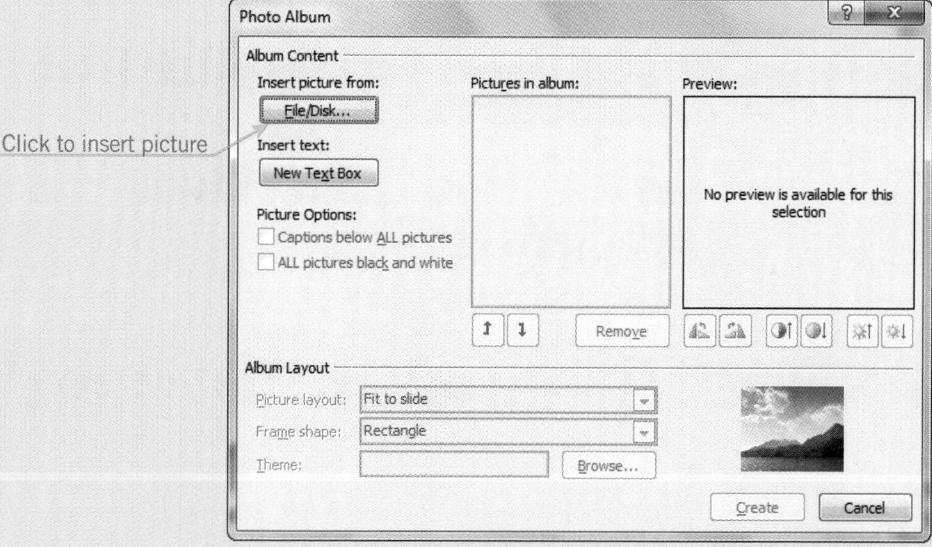

FIGURE 7–16 Photo Album dialog box

2. Under Insert picture from, click **File/Disk**. The Insert New Pictures dialog box opens. If necessary, navigate to the drive and folder where your Data Files are stored. Select the following filenames: (*Hint*: Click the first filename, press and hold **Ctrl**, and then click the remaining filenames.)

   A perfect catch!.jpg

   Focus.jpg

   Let's play!.jpg

   Nap time.jpg

   Run fast.jpg

3. When the five files are selected, click **Insert**.

4. Select options to format the album:
   a. Under Album Layout, click the **Picture layout** list arrow and then click **1 picture**. A preview is displayed at the right.
   b. Under Picture Options, enable the option **Captions below ALL pictures**. The picture filename will appear in the caption.
   c. Enable the option **ALL pictures black and white**. The Preview pane adapts to show the new format. Disable the option to restore the photos to the original colors.
   d. Click the **Frame shape** list arrow, and then click **Rounded Rectangle**. A preview is displayed at the right. Click the **Frame shape** list arrow again, and then click **Simple Frame, White**.
   e. Next to the Theme box, click **Browse** to open the Choose Theme dialog box. The themes saved on your computer are listed. Scroll down and select **Pushpin.thmx**, and then click **Select**.
   f. When your settings match those shown in **Figure 7–17**, click **Create**.

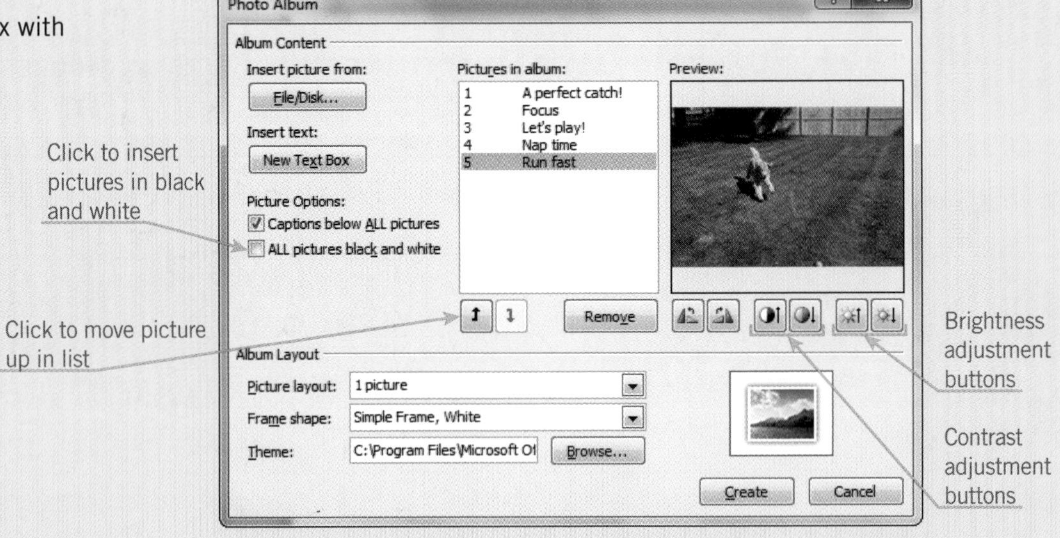

FIGURE 7–17
Photo Album dialog box with new settings

5. Save the presentation as **Pet Photo Album**, followed by your initials.
6. On slide 1, select the text in the title placeholder and type **Love me....** Then press **Enter** and type **Love my dog**. If necessary, edit the name under the title to show your name.
7. Go to slide 2. Note that because of the theme graphic (the pushpin background), the captions do not fit well on all of the slides. To edit the album formats, click the **Insert** tab. In the Images group, click the **New Photo Album** button arrow and then click **Edit Photo Album**. The Edit Photo Album dialog box opens.
8. Make the following changes:
   a. Under Album Layout, click **Browse**, scroll down and select **Hardcover.thmx**, then click **Select**.

b. Under Insert picture from, click **File/Disk**. Select the picture file **Kylie.jpg**, and then click **Insert**. Under Pictures in album, the new picture is selected at the bottom of the list.

c. Under the Preview pane, click the **Rotate Right** button. The photo rotates to a portrait layout in the Preview pane. Click the **Rotate Left** button to return the photo to the default landscape orientation.

d. Under the Preview pane, click each of the **Contrast** buttons as shown in Figure 7–17. The adjustments appear in the Preview pane. Also under the Preview pane, click each of the **Brightness** buttons, as shown in Figure 7–17, and observe the adjustments in the Preview pane.

e. Under the Pictures in album list, click the **Up** arrow five times to move the *Kylie* picture to the top of the list. Use the up and down arrow buttons to rearrange the list in the following order:

Kylie
Let's play!
Focus
A perfect catch!
Run fast
Nap time

f. Under Pictures in album, select the fifth picture, **Run fast**. Under Insert text, click **New Text Box**. The list now shows seven items (six photos and a text box).

9. Click **Update**. Go to slide 7. Select the text in the placeholder and type **After a long day of retrieving the ball....**

10. Go to slide 2. Select the picture on the slide. Click the **Picture Tools Format** tab. In the Picture Styles group, click the **More** button. In the third row, click the **Snip Diagonal Corner, White** picture style.

11. With the picture selected, in the Picture Styles group, click the **Picture Effects** button and then point to **Shadow**. Under Outer, in the second row, click **Offset Center**.

12. Select the caption text **Kylie** and change the font size to **40 point**. Note that the shadow effect is also applied to the caption text. Drag the caption text box down to position it a little lower below the picture.

TIP

You can also add new photos to the album by inserting new slides and then inserting the pictures on the new slides.

TIP

If you are unable to change the font size, right-click the text box and click Format Shape. In the left pane, click Text Box, and under Autofit, select the Do not Autofit option.

13. Select the picture. Click the **Picture Tools Format** tab. In the Adjust group, click the **Compress Pictures** button. The Compress Pictures dialog box opens, as shown in **Figure 7–18**. Under Compression options, disable the option **Apply only to this picture**. Note that you can also choose to delete the cropped area of the picture. Under Target output, you can select options for Print, Screen (good for Web pages), and E-mail. Leave the target settings as is and click **OK**.

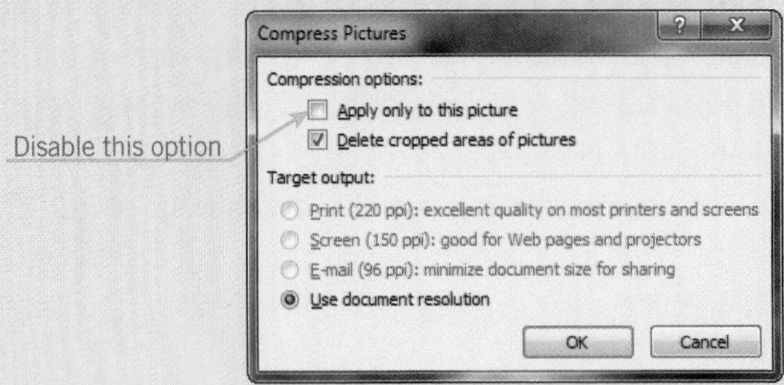

FIGURE 7–18
Compress Pictures dialog box

14. Save the changes and leave the presentation open for the next Step-by-Step.

Saving a Presentation as a Video

You can turn a photo album presentation into a video, or you can apply settings so that the presentation is self-running. Then you can share photos with others by publishing the photo album on the Web, saving it to a DVD, or attaching it to an e-mail. And, of course, you can also print the slides. If you add a lot of high-resolution pictures to a presentation, the file size will grow and the photos may take longer to open in the presentation. If you need to e-mail the presentation file, the file size may be too big. To reduce the file size, you can compress one or all of the pictures.

Once created, you can save the photo album (or any presentation file) as a video in a .wmv format. You can then burn the file to a DVD so you can play the video in a DVD player or play it in the default media player installed on a computer.

Step-by-Step 7.8

1. If necessary, open the **Pet Photo Album** file from your solution files.
2. Go to slide 1. Click the **Transitions** tab. In the Transition to This Slide group, click the **More** button. Under Exciting, click the **Flip** transition. A preview of the transition plays.
3. In the Timing group, note the Advance Slide setting is set for On Mouse Click. Click the **Apply To All** button. It does not appear that any changes are made to the existing slide or to any other slides, but the transition is now applied to all the slides.

4. Click the **File** tab and then click **Save & Send**. In the center pane, under File Types, click **Create a Video** to display the Save & Send options, as shown in **Figure 7–19**.

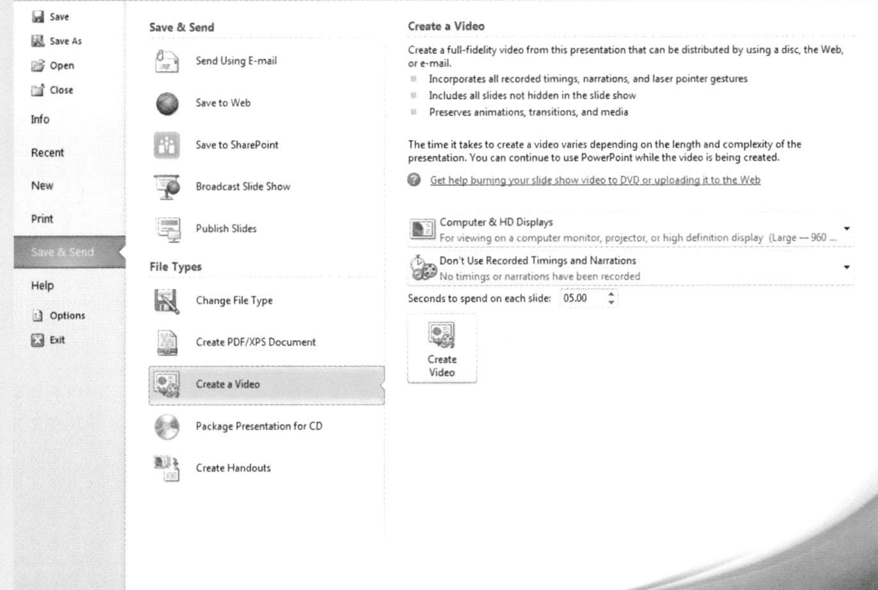

FIGURE 7–19
Save & Send options in Backstage view

5. In the right pane, click the **Computer & HD Displays** button to display additional video format options, as shown in **Figure 7–20**.

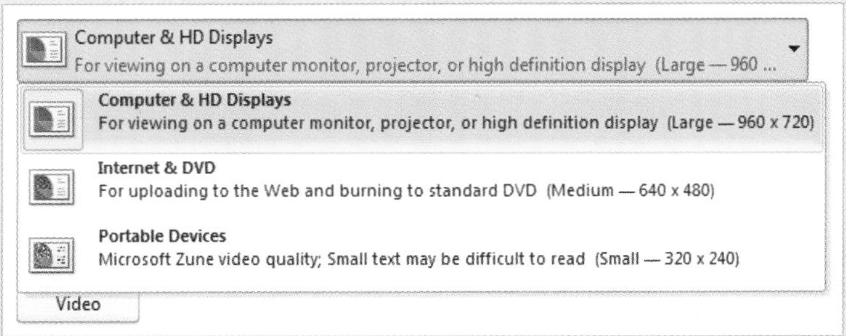

FIGURE 7–20
Video format options

6. Click **Portable Devices.**
7. Note that if timings or narrations had been recorded on the slides, you could choose to exclude them from the video.
8. Change the Seconds to spend on each slide setting to **04.00**.
9. Click the **Create Video** button. The Save As dialog box opens. Navigate to the drive and folder where your solution files are saved. The file type is already set for Windows Media Video (*.wmv), and you do not need to change the filename.
10. Click **Save** and wait for the saving process to complete. It may take a few minutes. The progress status will display in the status bar. When the file conversion is complete, the status message closes.

11. Click the **Start** button, click **Computer**, and then navigate to the drive and folder where your solution files are stored. Locate and then double-click the **Pet Photo Album.wmv** filename. The file will open in the default media player.
12. If necessary, click the **Play/Pause** button and enjoy the video! Note that the transitions occur automatically.
13. When the video stops playing, close the video and the media player window.
14. Close the presentation file without saving the changes.

Working with Video and Sound Clips

Video and sound clips can add an extra dimension to a presentation. Most slides are rather static, so you can make an audience really sit up and take notice by adding a sound object or including a video clip.

Inserting and Editing a Video Clip

When you insert a video file on a slide, the inserted clip resembles a picture and you can resize, move, recolor, and adjust contrast to the video object just as you would a picture. You can also apply a style to the video object on the slide.

You can also format the video to play automatically, and you can choose to show or hide the media controls. When the media controls are visible, you can pause or stop the video, move back or move forward, and adjust the volume.

You can recolor and correct video clips the same as clip art and photos. Select the video clip, and then click the Video Tools Format tab. In the Adjust group, click the Color button.

VOCABULARY
streaming video

PowerPoint supports several video formats. ***Streaming video*** is media sent in a continuous flow of data that can be played from an online source without waiting to download the file. If you have a fast Internet connection, you can stream live video to your computer.

ETHICS IN TECHNOLOGY

You can find pictures and other multimedia objects on the Internet, and computers make it easy to copy or download those files. Often people think that information published on the Internet is in the public domain and free, but that is not always the case. Someone owns the rights to those pictures and media files, and intellectual property law ensures that the owner of the content is entitled to copyright protection. Before you download or copy something from the Internet, consider how you will use the content. For example, you can copy or download any clip art image in the Microsoft Office Clip Art and Media Library without permission and free of charge when you use the images in your own work. However, there are restrictions that prohibit you using the images in a product that you sell. If you are not sure about how you can use the content, check with the owner.

Table 7–2 provides information about the video file formats that are compatible with PowerPoint.

TABLE 7–2 Video file formats

FILE FORMAT	FILE EXTENSION	DESCRIPTION
Advanced Systems Format (ASF)	.asf	This format can be used to stream audio and video content, images, and script commands over a network.
Audio Video Interleave (AVI)	.avi	This is a common format because audio and video content is compressed.
Moving Picture Experts Group (MPEG)	.mpg or .mpeg	This format is often used for creating downloadable movies. It is a common format for videos published on the Internet.
Windows Media Video (WMV)	.wmv	This format is used for both streaming and downloading from the Internet. The format compresses audio and video and requires minimal storage space. To play the format on a non-Windows computer, an extra application must be installed.

PowerPoint offers playback features for videos. After you insert the video on a slide, you can trim the video clip to include only the content relevant to the presentation. Trimming the video clip not only saves time when showing the presentation, but it also reduces the file size. You can choose to zoom to a full-screen view of the video, loop the video so it continues to replay, rewind the video when finished, hide the object when it's not playing, and set the video volume.

When saving a presentation that includes an embedded video, you can reduce the file size and also improve playback performance by compressing the media files. PowerPoint provides three options: Presentation Quality, Internet Quality, and Low Quality. Choosing the right option is important, because the compression might affect the media quality.

EXTRA FOR EXPERTS

Video clips can be quite large and consequently take up a lot of storage space. To reduce the presentation file size, you can create links instead of embedding the videos. When a video is linked in a presentation, the video file must be stored on the same computer when you show the presentation. For best results, save the video clips in the same folder as the presentation file.

Step-by-Step 7.9

1. Open the **Revised Happy Tails 6** file from your solution files. Save the presentation as **Revised Happy Tails 7**, followed by your initials.
2. Go to slide 2. Select the clip art object, and then press **Delete**. In the placeholder, click the **Insert Media Clip** icon. The Insert Video dialog box opens. Navigate to the drive and folder where your Data Files are stored. Select the video file **Frisbee fun.wmv**, and then click **Insert**. An image of the video is inserted on the slide.
3. The media controls appear in the bar below the video object. Click the **Play/Pause** button to preview the video.

4. Click the **Video Tools Playback** tab. In the Editing group, click the **Trim Video** button to open the Trim Video dialog box, as shown in **Figure 7–21**. Your dialog box will differ.

FIGURE 7–21
Trim Video dialog box

5. Drag the **Start bar** to the right to advance to approximately 1½ seconds into the video clip. The time displays above the bar and in the Start Time box below the bar. (You can also trim the end time.) When your dialog box settings are similar to those shown in Figure 7–21, click **OK**.
6. The video object should still be selected. In the Editing group, under Fade Duration, change the Fade In setting to **2.00**. Change the Fade Out setting to **1.00**.
7. Go to slide 1. Click the **Slide Show** tab. In the Set Up group, make sure the Show Media Controls option is enabled. Click the **Slide Show** button in the status bar. Click once to advance to slide 2. Note that the video clip appears, but the video will not start until you position the mouse pointer over the image to show the media controls and then click the Play button. Press **Esc** to return to Normal view.
8. Select the video object. Click the **Video Tools Playback** tab. In the Video Options group, click the **Start** list arrow and then click **Automatically**. Enable the **Hide While Not Playing** option.
9. Click the **Animations** tab. In the Timing group, note that the Start box is empty because the video will start automatically. Change the Delay setting to **2.00**. There will be a 2-second delay before the video begins to play.

10. Go to slide 1. Click the **Slide Show** button in the status bar. Then click to advance to slide 2. Wait, and the video clip will start playing automatically. When the video ends, the clip will disappear. Press **Esc** to switch to Normal view.
11. To add special effects and formats, select the video object. Click the **Video Tools Format** tab and do the following:
    a. In the Video Styles group, click the **More** button. Under Intense, in the third row, click the **Metal Rounded Rectangle** video style.
    b. In the Video Styles group, click the **Video Effects** button and then point to **3-D Rotation**. Under Perspective, select **Perspective Right**.
    c. In the Adjust group, click the **Color** button and select a color option. Click the **Color** button again and then click **Video Color Options**. In the Format Video dialog box, click **Reset** to restore the video to its original color. Click **Close**.
    d. In the Size group, change the height setting to **6**. Reposition the video object in the center of the slide, on top of the title placeholder.
    e. The video object should still be selected. In the Arrange group, click the **Send Backward** button. Then select the title placeholder and position it at the top of the video object and inside the video object border.
12. Select the video object again, and then click the **Video Tools Playback** tab. In the Video Options group, click the **Volume** button, and then click **Mute**. In the Preview group, click the **Play** button to preview the video, which now plays without any sound.
13. Click the **File** tab and then click the **Compress Media** button. In the submenu, click **Internet Quality**. The Compress Media dialog box will open and show the file status. When the compression process is complete, close the Compress Media dialog box.
14. Save the changes and leave the presentation open for the next Step-by-Step.

Inserting a Sound Object

Sound objects can add interesting effects to slides, and adding a sound object is as easy as adding clip art or a picture. If you have downloaded sounds from Microsoft's Online Clip Art and Media Web site, they will appear in the Clip Art task pane. If you have an audio file that you can access on a disk or server, use the Insert Audio command on the Ribbon to locate and insert the sound.

Table 7–3 provides information about the audio file formats that are compatible with PowerPoint.

TABLE 7–3 Audio file formats

FILE FORMAT	FILE EXTENSION	DESCRIPTION
Audio Interchange File Format (AIFF)	.aiff	This high-quality format is commonly used to burn audio CDs. Files are not compressed and, therefore, can be large. The files are commonly used on Macintosh systems.
Audio File Format (AU)	.au	The format is typically used to create sound files for UNIX computers or the Web.
Musical Instrument Digital Interface (MIDI)	.mid or .midi	This is a standard format for interchanging musical information between musical instruments, synthesizers, and computers.
MPEG Audio Layer 3 (MP3)	.mp3	This compressed format is commonly used to store music files and audiobooks on computers and portable devices.
Waveform Audio File Format (WAV)	.wav	This format saves sounds as waveforms (an image that represents an audio signal or recording) and is commonly used on Windows-based computers.

A sound file is inserted on the current slide as an icon. You can test a sound without running the presentation by double-clicking the audio icon in Normal view. You can choose to play the sound automatically or when triggered by a click. If you choose to play the sound automatically, you can arrange the objects so that the audio icon is not visible.

Step-by-Step 7.10

1. Open the **Revised Happy Tails 7** file from your solution files. Save the presentation as **Revised Happy Tails 8**, followed by your initials.
2. Go to slide 4. Select the SmartArt graphic object. Click the **Animations** tab. In the Advanced Animation group, click the **Add Animation** button and then click the **Appear** entrance effect. In the Animation group, click the **Effect Options** button and then click **One by One**.
3. Click the **Insert** tab. In the Media group, click the **Insert Audio** button arrow and then click **Clip Art Audio**. In the Clip Art task pane, click the **Results should be** list arrow. If necessary, enable the **Audio** option and disable all other options. Click the **list arrow** to close the menu. If necessary, enable the option Include Office.com content.
4. In the Search for text box, type **cat** and then click **Go**. Scroll through the list of results and select a meow sound. The audio clip object, a sound icon, is inserted on the slide.

EXTRA FOR EXPERTS

If you search for clip art at the Office.com Web site (instead of using the Clip Art task pane), you can search by category. Also, if you find a particular style that you like, you can search for similar images. Hover the mouse pointer over the image and then click See Similar Images.

5. To preview the sound, click the **Play/Pause** button in the bar below the sound icon on the slide. If you are not satisfied with the audio clip, delete the object and select a different clip in the Clip Art task pane.
6. With the sound icon selected on the slide, click the **Animations** tab. In the Advanced Animation group, click the **Animation Pane** button. In addition to the audio clip, there are four items in the list because each of the two objects consists of two parts: the clip art image and the text box with the dollar amount. If necessary, click the Expand button to view the full list.
7. In the Animation Pane, click the **list arrow** for the meow audio clip object and then click **Start After Previous**.
8. In the Timing group, click the **Move Earlier** button three times to reposition the audio clip object in the task pane so it appears just above *2 Content Placeholder*. A number 1 is displayed next to the sound icon on the slide. The audio clip will play after the cat clip art appears on the slide. Drag the audio clip and position it to the left of the cat image.
9. In the Clip Art task pane, change the Search for text to **dog**. Click **Go**. Review the results and select an audio clip for a barking sound. Close the Clip Art task pane.
10. In the Animation Pane, click the **list arrow** for the barking audio clip object, and then click **Start After Previous**. Drag the audio clip object up one level, just above the Trigger line. The number 2 appears next to the sound icon on the slide, and the audio clip will play after the dog clip art appears.

11. In the Animation Pane, click the **list arrow** for the barking audio clip object, and then click **Effect Options** to open the Play Audio dialog box, as shown in **Figure 7–22**. If the audio clip is quite long, you can shorten the clip by setting a start time in the From time box. To play the audio clip over multiple slides, under Stop playing, you can enable the After option and set the number of slides. Close the dialog box, and then close the Animation Pane.

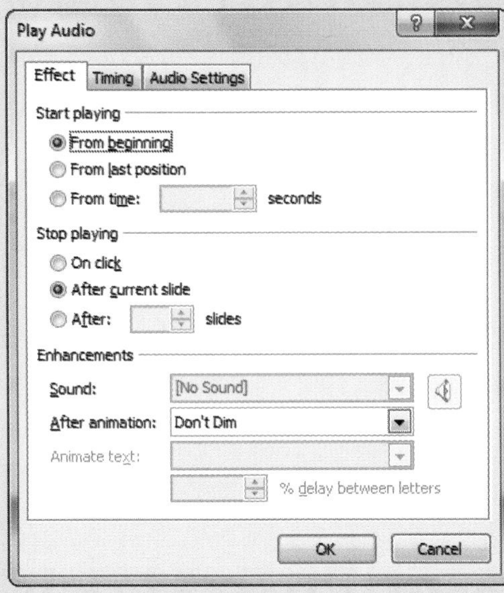

FIGURE 7–22
Effect tab in the Play Audio dialog box

12. In the slide window, drag the sound icons to the right side of the slide border, as shown in **Figure 7–23**. The audio clips will still be saved with the slide, but they will not appear on the slide when you show the presentation.

FIGURE 7–23
Sound icons repositioned on side of slide

13. Click the **Slide Show** button in the status bar. Click to show the cat clip art. The meow audio clip will play immediately after the image appears. Click a second time to show the dog clip art. The barking audio clip will play immediately after the image appears.
14. Press **Esc** to switch to Normal view. Save the changes and leave the presentation open for the next Step-by-Step.

Recording a Narration

You can also record your own sound or narration. Voice narrations are effective for Web-based presentations. To record an audio clip, you must have a sound card and a microphone. The audio clip is recorded and inserted on the current slide as a sound icon. To complete the next Step-by-Step, your computer must have a sound card, a microphone, and speakers.

Step-by-Step 7.11

1. Open the **Revised Happy Tails 8** file from your solution files. Save the presentation as **Revised Happy Tails 9**, followed by your initials.
2. Go to slide 6. Delete the slide title *Also consider....*
3. Click the **Insert** tab. In the Media group, click the **Insert Audio** button arrow and then click **Record Audio** to open the Record Sound dialog box, as shown in **Figure 7–24**.

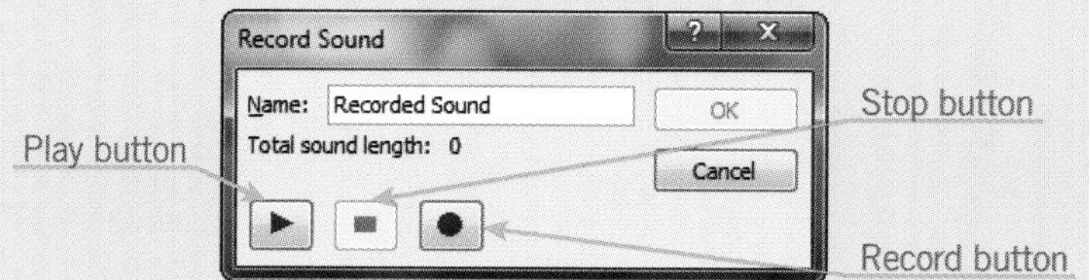

FIGURE 7–24
Record Sound dialog box

4. Select the text in the Name box, and then type **Also consider**.
5. Click the **Record** button. Say the following: **Before adopting a pet, there are some things you should also consider.** Then click the **Stop** button.
6. Click the **Play** button to listen to the recording. If you want to re-record the narration, click Cancel and then repeat Steps 3–5. When you are satisfied with the recording, click **OK**. A sound icon appears on the slide.
7. Click the **Animations** tab. In the Advanced Animation group, click the **Animation Pane** button. In the Animation Pane, reposition the **Also consider** audio clip object so that it is at the beginning of the list.

8. In the Animation Pane, click the **Also consider** list arrow. Click **Timing** to open the Timing tab in the Play Audio dialog box. Click the **Start** list arrow, and then click **After Previous** to set the audio clip to play automatically. Change the Delay setting to **1.5**, and then click **OK**. Close the Animation Pane.
9. Drag the sound icon to the right side of the slide.
10. Go to slide 8. In the last line of text, replace *Your Name* with your own name. Then click anywhere within the bulleted list to select the placeholder.
11. In the Advanced Animation group, click the **Add Animation** button and then at the bottom of the menu click **More Entrance Effects**. Scroll down to the bottom of the menu. Under Exciting, click **Credits** and then click **OK**.
12. In the Timing group, click the **Start** list arrow and then click **With Previous**.
13. Go to slide 1. Click the **Slide Show** button in the status bar and review the presentation.
14. Save the changes and close the presentation.

SUMMARY

In this lesson, you learned:

- You can easily modify graphics by resizing and repositioning them on the slide so they fit the slide design.
- You are not limited to the original colors of a graphic. You can customize a graphic by changing its colors to match the other colors in the current theme.
- One of the media type options in the Clip Art gallery is video, which consists of animated clip art images.
- Graphics files can be saved in many different formats, and the format affects both the resolution quality of the graphic and the file size.
- Graphics on a slide can be converted into a SmartArt object, and the objects in the diagram can then be animated.
- The Photo Album feature makes it quick and easy to put together a presentation of photos.
- Presentations can be saved as videos so that they can be viewed on a DVD player.
- Sound and video clips provide other multimedia interest to a slide show. You can apply animation settings to play the sound and video clips automatically or you can control when they play.
- Video clips can add an extra dimension to a presentation, and after inserting a video clip on a slide, you can trim the clip as needed.
- Sound objects can also add interesting effects to slides. In addition to using audio clips, you can add sounds or narrations that you record.

VOCABULARY REVIEW

Define the following terms:

aspect ratio
bitmap
bits
crop
nudging
outcrop
pixels
raster graphics
scaling
streaming video
vector graphics

REVIEW QUESTIONS

TRUE / FALSE

Circle T if the statement is true or F if the statement is false.

T F 1. You can use the Crop tool to add white space to a graphic.

T F 2. When recoloring graphics, you are limited to the theme colors.

T F 3. You can convert a presentation file to a video file format.

T F 4. You can edit animated clip art images as you would edit any other clip art images.

T F 5. You can apply formats to a video clip on a slide just as you would apply formats to photos.

FILL IN THE BLANK

Complete the following sentences by writing the correct word or words in the blanks provided.

1. ________________ is moving an object vertically or horizontally in small increments.
2. Sizing a graphic so that its proportions are precise is referred to as ________________.
3. The ________________ is the ratio between the image width and image height.
4. The tiny dots that compose a bitmap image are referred to as ________________.
5. Raster graphics are often referred to as ________________.

WRITTEN QUESTIONS

Write a brief answer to the following questions.

1. What is streaming video?

2. Why would you outcrop a graphic?

3. Compare raster and vector graphics and note the advantages and disadvantages of each file format type.

4. What file type(s) would you recommend for publishing pictures on the Internet and why?

5. When you insert photos and video clips on a slide, how do you know what file types you are working with?

PROJECTS

If you have a SAM 2010 user profile, your instructor may have assigned an autogradable version of the indicated project. If so, log into the SAM 2010 Web site at *www.cengage.com/sam2010* to download the instruction and start files.

PROJECT 7–1

1. Open the **Dynamic Park** file from the drive and folder where your Data Files are stored. Save the presentation as **Revised Dynamic Park**, followed by your initials.
2. Apply a design theme to all the slides in the presentation.
3. Go to slide 2. Search for and insert an appropriate illustration or picture to emphasize environmental protection, conserving energy, and promoting healthy lives.
4. Go to slide 3. Search for and insert appropriate graphics to illustrate one or more of the bulleted items on the slide.
5. If necessary, crop the images or change the aspect ratio so that they fit within the content on the slides.
6. Go to slide 4. Insert two graphics to help the audience quickly recognize those who say yes and those who say no. Then select the two images and convert them to a SmartArt graphic that shows pictures and text.
7. In the text placeholders, type **53%** for those who support the proposal and **41%** for those who do not support the proposal. If necessary, resize the SmartArt graphic.
8. Recolor the images, and remove or make the backgrounds transparent if that helps to enhance the slide content.
9. Search for and insert an animated clip and/or an audio clip that complements the content on one of the slides. Animate the objects to appear at the right time.
10. Save the changes. Review the slides in Slide Show view.
11. Save the presentation as a video in your solutions folder. Then close the presentation.

SAM PROJECT 7–2

1. Open the **Motocross.pptx** file from the drive and folder where your Data Files are stored. Save the presentation as **Final Motocross**, followed by your initials.
2. Apply a design to all the slides in the presentation.
3. Go to slide 2. Insert the picture file **MX Start.jpg**. Go to slide 3 and insert the picture file **MX Jump.jpg**.
4. Go to slide 4 and insert the video file **Motocross.wmv**. Format the video to play automatically.
5. Go to slide 5. Insert the picture file **MX Finish.jpg**. Remove the background from the picture. Then insert a clip art image of a checkered flag. Modify the flag as needed (format the background color as transparent or recolor the clip art image) so that it fits with the design and theme.
6. If necessary, crop and/or resize the images on slide 5. Apply animations to both of the images.
7. Apply a picture style to the photos on slides 2 and 3, and also apply a style to the video clip on slide 4. If necessary, adjust the picture and video sizes on slides 2, 3, and 4.
8. Add an audio clip for applause (clapping or cheering) on slide 5. Format the audio clip to play automatically, and hide the sound icon so it does not appear on the slide.
9. Record an audio clip narration for the last slide. For example, you can say "Way to go!" Hide the audio icon on the side of the slide, and format the audio clip to play with the previous, with a slight delay.
10. Add any additional effects that will enhance the presentation.
11. Preview the slides in Slide Show view, then make any necessary changes.
12. Save the changes and then close the presentation.

PROJECT 7–3

1. Create a photo album. Select the following files from your Data Files folder.

    Bright horizon.jpg

    Pink horizon.jpg

    Sunset fog.jpg

    Sunset high waves.jpg

    Sunset silhouette.jpg

    Sunset trees.jpg

    Sunset waves.jpg

    Yellow sunset.jpg

2. Save the presentation as **Hawaiian Sunsets**, followed by your initials.
3. Edit the album formatting as desired. Add an appropriate title, apply a theme, add frames to the pictures, and include picture captions.
4. Edit the captions as needed by changing the font size and repositioning as needed.
5. Format one or more pictures using artistic effects, and adjust the contrast and brightness as needed.
6. Add transitions to the slides, and if desired, advance the slides automatically by setting a time to advance after each slide.
7. If desired, rearrange the sequence of the pictures.
8. Add audio clips to some of the slides. For example, audio clips for nature and ocean waves are available in the Clip Art task pane. Hide the audio icons on the side of the slide, and format the audio clips to play automatically for one or more slides.
9. Save the changes to the presentation. Review the slides in Slide Show view, and make any necessary changes.
10. Save the changes and then close the presentation.

PROJECT 7–4

1. Open the **Service.pptx** file from the drive and folder where your Data Files are stored. Save the presentation as **Revised Service**, followed by your initials.
2. Edit the WordArt on slide 1 to change the title to **Service Quality Feedback**.
3. Convert the WordArt object to a SmartArt object. (***Hint:*** Right-click on the WordArt object, then click **Convert to SmartArt** on the shortcut menu.) Apply the **Target List** SmartArt style.
4. Go to slide 2. Select the bulleted list and convert the text to a SmartArt object. Apply the **Target List** SmartArt style.
5. Go to slide 3. Insert a **Smiley Face** shape (under Basic Shapes) on the right side of the slide, approximately 2½ inches high. Drag the diamond handle on the mouth upward to change the shape to a frowning face.
6. Change the shape fill color to **Yellow**. Change the shape outline color to **Indigo**, **Text 2**, and change the outline weight to **2¼ pt**. Even though this shape does not contain text, you can apply a font color for text by right-clicking or using the buttons on the Home tab. Change the font color to **Indigo**, **Text 2**.
7. Set the shape as the default shape.
8. Go to slide 4. Insert a **Smiley Face** shape, approximately 2½ inches high, on the right side of the slide.
9. Go to slide 5. Insert a **Smiley Face** shape, approximately 2½ inches high, on the right side of the slide.
10. Go to slide 6. Insert a **5-Point Star** shape (under Stars and Banners), approximately 3 inches high, on the right side of the slide. With the shape still selected, type **92%**. Select the new text and change the font size to **28**.
11. Save the changes and then close the presentation

CRITICAL THINKING

ACTIVITY 7–1

When you completed the projects for this lesson, you had the liberty to add special effects to enhance the presentation. With a partner, review your solution files for Projects 7-1, 7-2, and 7-3. Explain to your partner why you chose the design themes, graphics, slide transitions, and sound effects for each presentation. Ask your partner to provide constructive feedback regarding whether or not he or she thinks your choices were effective. Summarize your partner's comments.

ACTIVITY 7–2

You are working with a colleague to prepare a presentation that will be used at a trade show and also published online. Your colleague e-mails you a picture that she says is perfect for the presentation, but she doesn't provide the source of the picture. What questions should you ask your colleague, and what steps should you take, before you use the file? Write a brief report that answers these questions.

Estimated Time: 1.5 hours

LESSON 8

Customizing Slides

OBJECTIVES

Upon completion of this lesson, you should be able to:

- Customize a color scheme and the slide background.
- Customize text and text box shapes.
- Customize slide masters.
- Create a new layout master.
- Insert a new slide master.
- Create a new design template.
- Create a custom show with an agenda slide.
- Use sections to organize slides.

VOCABULARY

agenda slide

color scheme

gradient fill

Using design templates makes formatting slides quick and easy, but as you create presentations, you might find that none of the design templates is exactly right for the slides you want to create. Perhaps you don't like one color in the template—or you like all the colors, but the font is not appropriate. PowerPoint offers many ways to customize slide designs and layouts.

Modifying an Existing Design Template

If you like the look of a particular PowerPoint design template, you can start with that template, add to it, and modify the formats until you are happy with the results. You can apply a new color scheme, create a new slide background, remove graphic elements from a design, change text box shapes, and modify the fonts and the alignment of the text within a text box.

Customizing the Color Scheme

VOCABULARY
color scheme

Each built-in PowerPoint theme has associated color schemes that are accessible in the Theme Colors gallery. A ***color scheme*** is a set of 12 coordinated colors. Two light colors and two dark colors are used for text and background. Six of the colors are used to apply accents to charts, tables, and other objects. One color is used for hyperlinks, and one color is used for followed hyperlinks. You can modify the color scheme, and if desired, you can save the modified color scheme in the Theme Colors gallery for future use.

Step-by-Step 8.1

You will create a custom color scheme and save it in the Theme Colors gallery. Because you may share your computer with others, you will remove the custom theme from the gallery after you create it.

1. Open the **National Parks** file from the drive and folder where your Data Files are stored. Save the presentation as **National Parks Draft 1**, followed by your initials.
2. Scroll through the slides to preview the content. You do not need to review every slide; the presentation has 63 slides. Slides 4 through 62 provide information about the individual U.S. national parks. The intent is to provide a photo for each national park, but for now only the slide for the first park, Acadia, includes a photo.
3. Go to slide 3. To view the color schemes that are available, click the **Design** tab. In the Themes group, click the **Colors** button. The available theme color schemes are displayed, as shown in **Figure 8–1**. Custom color schemes may be listed at the top of your gallery.

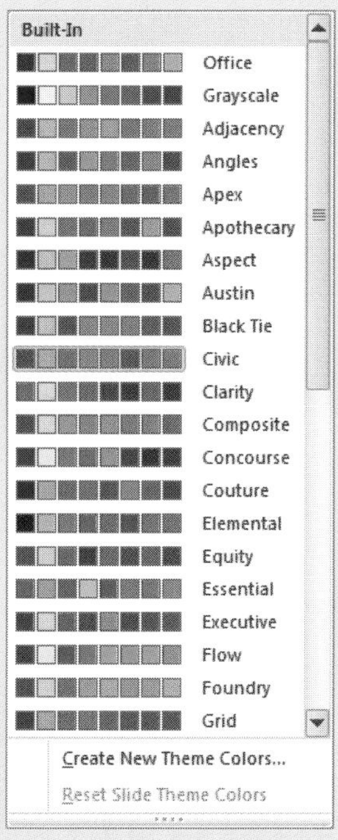

FIGURE 8–1
Theme Colors gallery

4. Position the mouse pointer over several of the color schemes. As you point to each color scheme, a live preview of the color combinations will appear in the Slide pane. Live previews show the changes in text colors, objects, and background colors.
5. Click the **Couture** theme color scheme. The new color scheme is applied to all the slides.
6. In the Themes group, click the **Colors** button. At the bottom of the gallery, click **Create New Theme Colors**. The Create New Theme Colors dialog box opens, as shown in **Figure 8–2**. Note that the dialog box provides two samples of text, objects, and charts in the Sample pane.

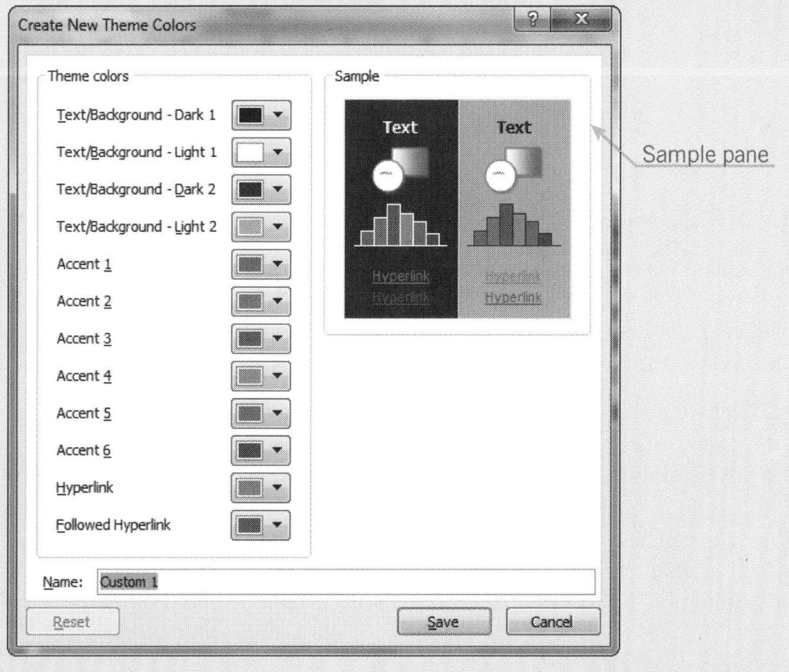

FIGURE 8–2
Create New Theme Colors dialog box

7. To explore the color scheme options:
   a. In the left pane, under Theme colors, click the **Text/Background – Dark 1** list arrow.
   b. Normally you would select a theme color, but to help distinguish the color scheme options, under Standard colors, click the **Dark Red** standard color. The text in the Sample pane reflects the change.
   c. In the left pane, under Theme colors, click the **Accent 1** list arrow. Under Standard Colors, click the **Yellow** standard color. The changes appear in the objects and the charts in both samples.
   d. In the left pane, under Theme colors, click the **Hyperlink** list arrow, and then under Standard Colors, click the **Light Blue** standard color. The hyperlink text changes in both samples.
   e. In the left pane, under Theme colors, click the **Followed Hyperlink** list arrow. At the bottom of the color palette, click **More Colors**. In the Colors dialog box, click the **Standard** tab, and then select a green color. Click **OK**. The followed hyperlink text changes in both samples.
8. At the bottom of the Create New Theme Colors dialog box, in the Name text box, change the color scheme name to **MyTheme**, followed by your initials. (You cannot enter blank spaces.) Then click **Save**.
9. In the Themes group, click the **Colors** button. The new color scheme appears under the heading Custom at the top of the gallery. Right-click the **MyTheme** color scheme, and then click **Delete**. When prompted to delete the theme colors, click **Yes**.
10. Even though you deleted the custom theme, the custom color formats remain. Click the **Colors** button, and then click the **Office** theme color scheme.
11. Save the changes and leave the presentation open for the next Step-by-Step.

Customizing the Slide Background

Depending upon the design template, the background might be a plain color, a shaded color, a texture, or a pattern. The background in a design template might also include graphic elements such as horizontal lines, curves, and objects. If you do not want the graphics to appear on your slides, you can hide the graphics from the background.

VOCABULARY
gradient fill

You can change the slide background to a new fill color from your current color scheme, to any other color on the standard palette, or to a custom color. To add interest to a relatively simple background, you can change the background to a ***gradient fill,*** which is composed of two or more colors that gradually blend from one color to another. You can also use a picture (clip art or photo) to fill the background. Although solid and gradient fill colors are commonly used for backgrounds, sometimes the color is not enough. To add a different emphasis to the slide background, you can apply a texture or pattern background. To tailor the background to your content, you can apply different backgrounds to each slide in a presentation.

Making changes to a background may create the need to modify other objects on the slide. For example, a texture background might make it difficult to read the text, or the text color may not be visible on a color background. So, you may need to change a font color and change the font size or apply the bold format so that the text is easy to read.

Step-by-Step 8.2

1. If necessary, open the **National Parks Draft 1** file from your solution files. Save the presentation as **National Parks Draft 2**, followed by your initials.
2. Go to slide 1. If necessary, click the **Design** tab. In the Background group, enable the **Hide Background Graphics** option. The graphics are removed from the current slide.
3. In the Background group, click the **Background Styles** button. The Background Styles gallery opens, as shown in **Figure 8–3**. The styles are based on the color scheme.

FIGURE 8–3
Background Styles gallery

4. Click **Format Background** to open the Format Background dialog box, as shown in **Figure 8–4**. Currently, the design shows a solid fill. If necessary, drag the dialog box to the right so you can see a portion of the Slides tab and some of the Slide pane.

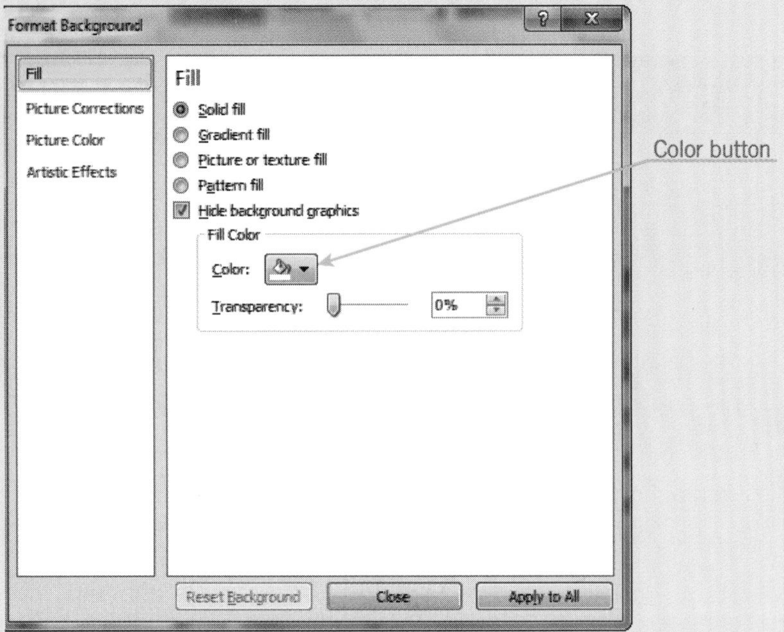

FIGURE 8–4
Format Background dialog box

5. Under Fill Color, click the **Color** button to display the color palette. Under Theme Colors, in the top row, click the **Olive Green, Accent 3** theme color.
6. Enable the **Pattern fill** option. Thumbnails for numerous patterns are displayed in the dialog box. Explore the pattern options:
   a. Click a few of the patterns. Each pattern changes the background in the Slide pane.
   b. Click the **Foreground Color** button, and then select a new theme color. The slide background changes.
   c. Click the **Background Color** button, and then select a new theme color.
   d. At the bottom of the dialog box, click **Reset Background.**
7. Enable the **Gradient fill** option. The dialog box options change, as shown in **Figure 8–5**. Your dialog box will differ because of previously applied gradient formats.

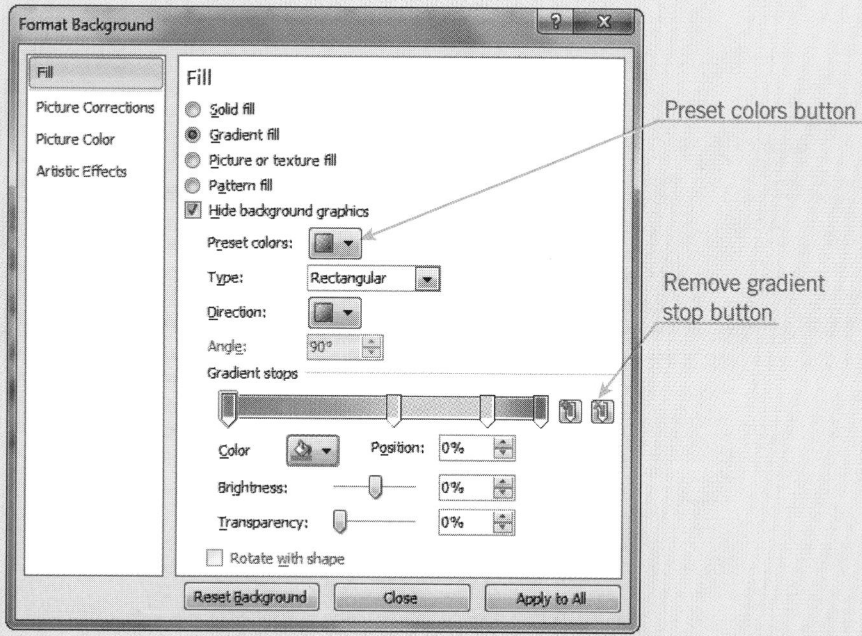

FIGURE 8–5
Gradient fill options

8. Explore the gradient fill options:
   a. Click the **Preset colors** button. A gallery of 24 options opens. In the second row, click the **Fog** preset option.
   b. Click the **Type** list arrow, and then click **Rectangular**.
   c. Click the **Direction** button, and then click the second option **From Bottom Left Corner**.
   d. Click the **Color** button. Under Theme Colors, in the first row, click the **Olive Green, Accent 3** theme color.
   e. The bar shows four Gradient stop options. Drag the second stop from the left back and forth on the bar to see the effect it has on the gradient fill. With the second gradient stop selected, click the **Remove gradient stop** button.
9. Note that the Hide background graphics option is enabled. Click **Apply to All**.

10. Enable the **Picture or texture fill** option. The slide background changes to a Papyrus background. Click the **Texture** button to open the Texture Styles gallery, as shown in **Figure 8–6**. Click the **Texture** button again to close the gallery.

FIGURE 8–6
Texture Styles gallery

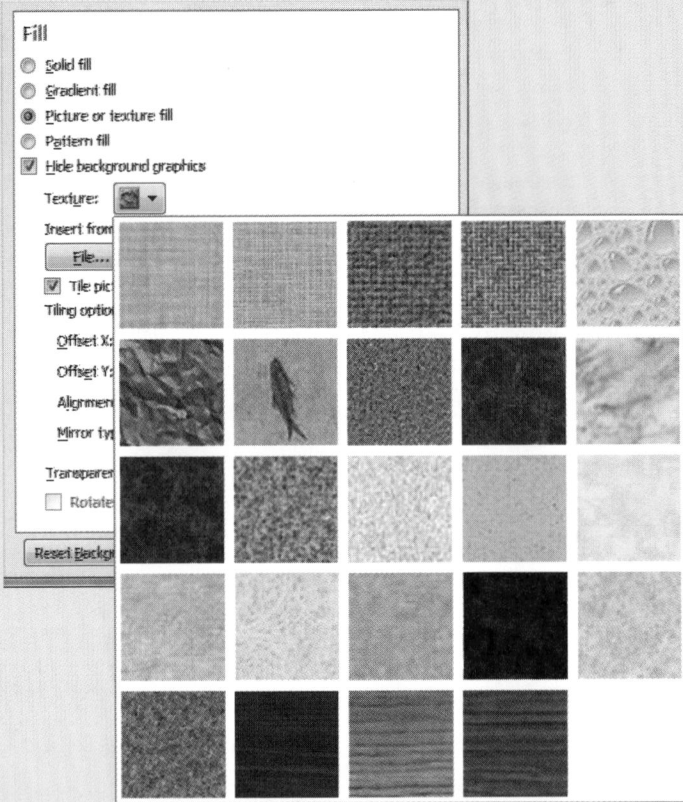

11. Under Insert from, click **File**. Navigate to the drive and folder where your Data Files are stored. Select the filename **Grand Canyon.jpg**, and then click **Insert**. The picture is inserted as the slide background.
12. At the bottom of the dialog box, change the Transparency setting to **15%**. Close the dialog box.
13. Scroll through the first five or six slides to preview the backgrounds and font colors. Adjustments are needed and will be made in the next Step-by-Step.
14. Save the changes and leave the presentation open for the next Step-by-Step.

Customizing Text

There are several ways to add text to a slide. You can add text to placeholders, create a WordArt object, and enter text in shapes. Callout shapes include an embedded text box, but you can, of course, use the Text Box button to create a custom size text box and then format the text box as desired, and even change its shape. Text boxes are especially useful when you want to position several blocks of text on a slide, or when you want to show some text on the slide in a different orientation from the other text. Like all other objects and shapes, you can change the fill color, background, and outline for the text box. And, you can enhance the text within the text box.

In the next Step-by-Step, you will explore options for formatting the text box and the text within the shape. You will explore options to apply text effects, set the text alignment, create columns, set internal margins, and adjust the flow of text within a text box using manual settings or the Autofit setting. To save your formatting changes, you can set the current text box formatting as the default for new text boxes.

All of the formats you apply to a text box shape and the text within the text box are also available for text placeholders, Word Art objects, and other shapes.

Step-by-Step 8.3

1. If necessary, open the **National Parks Draft 2** file from your solution files. Save the presentation as **National Parks Draft 3**, followed by your initials.
2. Go to slide 1, and select all the text in the Title placeholder. Right-click the selected text, and then at the bottom of the shortcut menu, click **Format Text Effects** to open the dialog box shown in **Figure 8–7**.

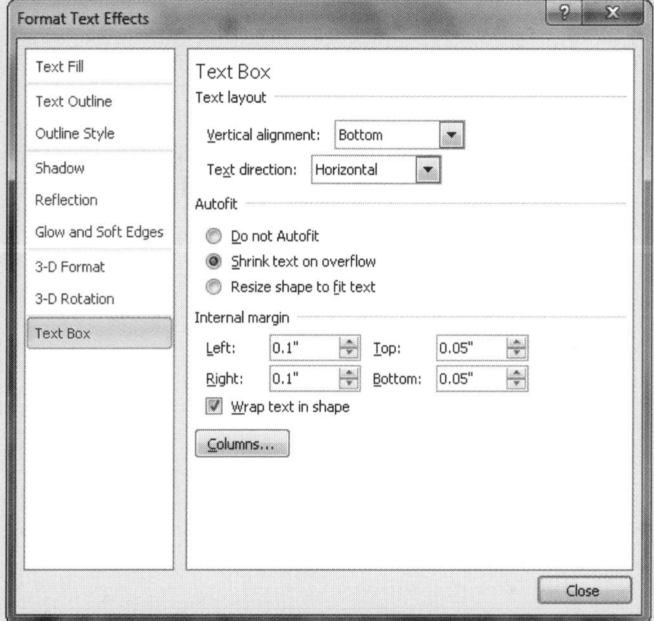

FIGURE 8–7
Format Text Effects dialog box

3. Format the selected text:
   a. In the left pane, click **Text Fill**. New options appear in the right pane. In the right pane, under Fill Color, click the **Color** button. Under Theme Colors, click the **White, Background 1** theme color.

   b. In the left pane, click **Shadow**. New options appear in the right pane. In the right pane, click the **Color** button. Under Theme Colors, click the **Black, Text 1** theme color.
   c. Click **Close** to close the dialog box.
   d. Deselect the text on slide 1. The title is now much easier to read.

4. If necessary, click the **Home** tab. In the Slides group, click the **New Slide** button arrow, and then click the **Blank** layout. If necessary, show the Ruler. Click the **Insert** tab. In the Text group, click the **Text Box** button. The mouse pointer changes to a Text Box Pointer ↓. Click in the Slide pane approximately 1 inch from the upper-left corner, then drag the mouse down and to the right to create a text box approximately 6 inches wide. Note that regardless of how tall you draw the text box, when you release the mouse button, the vertical height of the text box size is automatically adjusted.
5. Type the text below. Note that the text wraps in the text box and the height of the text box automatically adjusts to show the text.

   If you enjoy the outdoors, national parks are great destinations for vacations. While enjoying the scenery, you can also learn about American history.
6. Right-click the text and then click **Format Text Effects**. In the left pane, Text Box is selected, and the Text Box options appear in the right pane. Under Internal margin, note that the option to wrap text in the shape is also enabled. Under Autofit, enable the option **Shrink text on overflow**. Click **Close**.
7. Position the insertion point after the period in the last sentence in the text box, press **spacebar**, and then type **If you're looking for adventure,**. Note that as you enter the new text, the font size shrinks so that the text fits within the current text box size.
8. Drag the lower-right **corner** handle toward the center of the text box size to make the text box smaller. The font size shrinks even more. Drag the lower-right **corner** handle down and to the right to increase the text box size to approximately 6 inches wide by 3 inches high. The font size increases, but even though there is space in the text box, the font does not exceed 18 point, which is the original font size.
9. Right-click the text and then click **Format Text Effects**. Under Autofit, enable the option **Do not Autofit**. Click **Close**.
10. Drag the lower-right **corner** handle inward so the text box is about half of the original size. Note that the font size does not change, and when the text box becomes too small to contain all the text, the text overflows the text box. Even though all of the text does not fit within the text box, all of the text will still appear on the slide.

11. The text box should be selected. Click the **Drawing Tools Format** tab. In the Size group, change the shape height setting to **2.5"**. Change the shape width setting to **7"**.
12. Right-click the text and then click **Format Text Effects**. If necessary, move the dialog box to the right so you can see some of the text box in the Slide pane. Change the text box settings:
    a. Under Text layout, click the **Vertical alignment** list arrow and then click **Middle Centered**. You will see the text move down in the text box.
    b. Under Autofit, enable the option **Resize shape to fit text**. The text box size changes, and there is no longer space at the bottom of the text box.
    c. Under Internal margin, change all four settings to **0.2"**. As you change the settings, you will see the adjustments in the text box.
    d. Under Internal margin, click **Columns**. In the Columns dialog box, change the Number setting to **2** and change the Spacing setting to **0.5"**. Click **OK**.
    e. Close the Format Text Effects dialog box.
13. Position the insertion point after the last character in the text box, press **spacebar**, and then type **you'll find endless opportunities for hiking, biking, whitewater rafting, kayaking, camping, wildlife watching, fishing, rock climbing, and horseback riding.** As you enter the new text, the size of the text box will adapt.
14. Save the changes and leave the presentation open for the next Step-by-Step.

Customizing Text Box Shapes

Just as you can customize backgrounds for slides, you can customize the backgrounds for text boxes. Formatting text boxes is the same as formatting shapes. In the next Step-by-Step, you will explore options for formatting the text box shape.

Step-by-Step 8.4

1. If necessary, open the **National Parks Draft 3** file from your solution files. Save the presentation as **National Parks Draft 4**, followed by your initials.

2. If necessary, go to slide 2. Right-click the text box and then click **Format Shape** to open the dialog box shown in **Figure 8–8**.

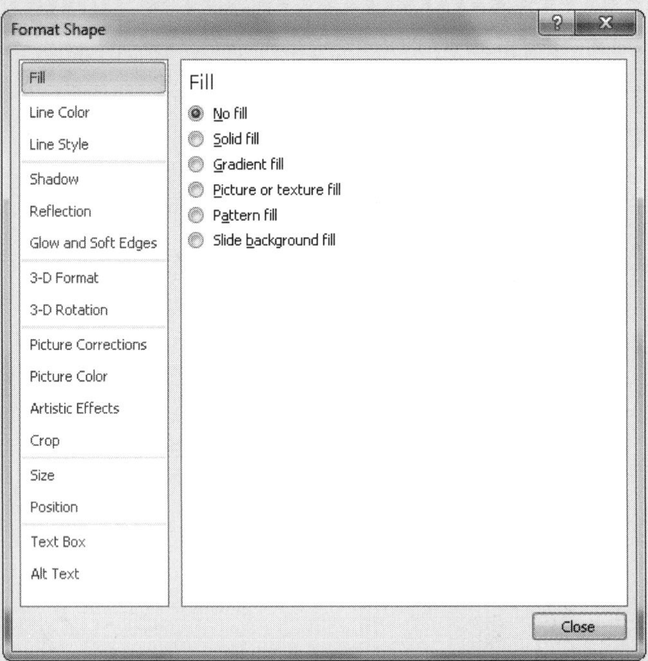

FIGURE 8–8
Format Shape dialog box

3. Format the text box background and border:
   a. In the left pane, Fill is already selected. In the right pane, under Fill, click the **Solid fill** option. Under Fill Color, click the **Color** button. Under Theme Colors, click the **Orange, Accent 6** theme color.
   b. In the left pane, click **Line Color**. In the right pane, click the **Solid line** option. Click the **Color** button. Under Theme Colors, click the **Dark Blue, Text 2** theme color.
   c. In the left pane, click **3-D Format**. In the right pane, under Bevel, click the **Top** button. Under Bevel, click the first option in the second row, **Angle**.
   d. In the left pane, click **Glow and Soft Edges**. In the right pane, click the **Presets** button. Under Glow Variations, click the last option, **Orange, 18 pt glow, Accent color 6**.
   e. Click **Close**.
4. Set the text box formatting as the default for new text boxes:
   a. The text box should be selected. If necessary, click the text box border to select the text box. (If a broken line appears around the text box, the text box is not selected.)
   b. Right-click the selected text box and then click **Set as Default Text Box**.

- c. Deselect the text box. Click the **Insert** tab. In the Text group, click the **Text Box** button. Draw a text box at the bottom of the slide and type your first and last names.
- d. Click outside the text box to see the formatting on the new text box.
- e. On the Quick Access Toolbar, click the **Undo** button arrow and then click **Insert Text Box** to remove the new text box.

5. Go to slide 3. Click anywhere in the Title placeholder to select it. Format the shape with a picture fill:
   - a. Right-click the placeholder and then click **Format Shape**.
   - b. Under Fill, enable the **Picture or texture fill** option.
   - c. Under Insert from, click **File**. Navigate to the drive and folder where your Data Files are stored. Click the filename **Grand Canyon** and then click **Insert**.
   - d. Click **Close**.
6. Format the text effects:
   - a. Right-click the title **FACTS** and then click **Format Text Effects**.
   - b. In the left pane, click **Text Fill**. In the right pane, under Fill color, click the **Color** button. Under Theme Colors, click the **White, Background 1** theme color.
   - c. In the left pane, click **Shadow**. In the right pane, click the **Color** button. Under Theme Colors, click the **Black, Text 1** theme color.
   - d. Click **Close**.
7. Change the shape and the shape size:
   - a. The placeholder should still be selected. Click the **Drawing Tools Format** tab.
   - b. In the Insert Shapes group, click the **Edit Shape** button, and then point to **Change Shape**. Under Rectangles, click the fifth option, **Snip Diagonal Corner Rectangle**.
   - c. On the Drawing Tools Format tab, in the Size group, change the shape height to **3.5"** and the shape width to **1.8"**. Do not be concerned that the shape overlaps other objects on the slide.
8. Format the alignment of the text in the text box:
   - a. Right-click the placeholder and then click **Format Text Effects**.
   - b. In the right pane, under Text layout, click the **Text direction** list arrow and then click **Stacked**.
   - c. Under Internal margin, change the Left and Right settings to **0.4"**.
   - d. Disable the option to **Wrap text in shape**.
   - e. Click **Close**.

9. On the Drawing Tools Format tab, in the Arrange group, click the **Align** button. Click **Align Right**. Click the **Align** button again, and then click **Align Top**.
10. Save the changes and leave the presentation open for the next Step-by-Step.

Working with Multiple Slide Objects

When positioning multiple objects on a slide, you can layer the objects. The Selection Pane is useful when working with layered objects on a slide. In the Selection Pane, you can select, rename, reorder, and group objects.

Sometimes when objects are layered, an object may not be visible because it is positioned behind other objects. The Selection Pane will help you identify all the objects on the slide. You can also choose to hide one or more objects on the slide so you can focus on other objects. When an object is hidden on the slide, the object does not appear on the slide in Slide Show view.

Step-by-Step 8.5

1. If necessary, open the **National Parks Draft 4** file from your solution files. Save the presentation as **National Parks Draft 5**, followed by your initials.
2. If necessary, go to Slide 3. In the Slide pane, select the **Facts** text box. Click the **Drawing Tools Format** tab. In the Arrange group, click the **Selection Pane** button. The Selection Pane shown in **Figure 8–9** displays to the right of the Slide pane. Your Selection Pane may differ.

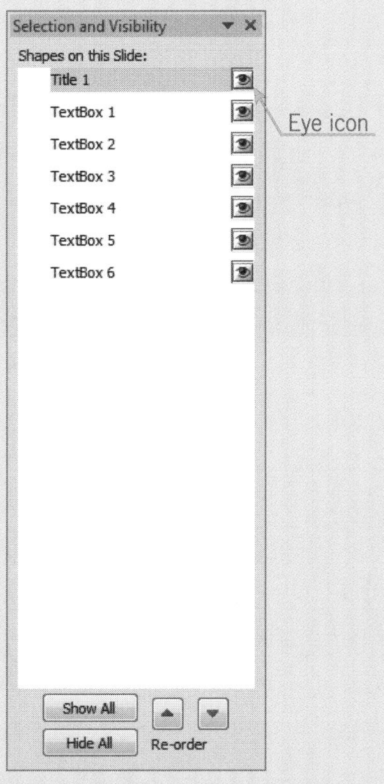

FIGURE 8–9
Selection Pane

3. Note that the Title 1 item (the Facts text box) is selected in the Selection Pane. In the Selection Pane, click the **Eye** icon to the right of Title 1. The icon is now blank, indicating that the object is hidden. Click the blank icon again to make the Title placeholder visible again.
4. In the Selection Pane, click the **TextBox 1** item in the list. The text box object *84,000,000 acres of land* is selected in the Slide pane. In the Selection Pane, click the selected **TextBox 1** object a second time. The insertion point is now positioned in the text box for the list item. Delete the existing text and then type **Acres**.
5. Rename the other *TextBox* items in the Selection Pane list.
   a. Click the **TextBox 2** item in the list. Click a second time and then replace the text with **Oceans**.
   b. Rename the **TextBox 3** item in the list **Landmarks.**
   c. Rename the **TextBox 4** item in the list **Structures**.
   d. Rename the **TextBox 5** item in the list **Heritage**.
   e. Rename the **TextBox 6** item in the list **Parks**.
6. Click the **Eye** icons to hide the objects **Acres**, **Landmarks**, and **Heritage**. Then at the bottom of the Selection Pane, click **Show All**.
7. In the Selection Pane, click the **Title 1** item. Press and hold **Ctrl**, and click each of the other items in the list. All the objects are selected in the Slide pane. Press and hold **Ctrl** and then click the **Title 1** item to deselect it. All but one of the objects are selected.

8. On the Home tab, in the Drawing group, click the **Arrange** button. Under Position Objects, point to **Align**. In the submenu, click **Align Left**.
9. Click the **Arrange** button again. Point to **Align**, and then click **Distribute Vertically**.
10. Click the **Arrange** button again. Point to **Align**, and then click **Align Middle**. The selected objects are now all layered, and only two of the objects are visible in the Slide pane. However, the Selection Pane confirms that there are still seven objects on the slide. None of the objects are hidden, but because they are layered, you cannot see all of them.
11. Click anywhere in the Slide pane to deselect the objects. In the Selection Pane, select the **Oceans** item. At the bottom of the Selection Pane, click the **Send Backward** button. The order changes in the Selection Pane list and in the Slide pane. Click the **Send Backward** button three more times to move the object to the end of the list.
12. In the Selection Pane, select the **Parks** item and then click the **Bring Forward** button four times to move it up the list. Use the Send Backward and Bring Forward buttons to reorder the text box items as follows:

    Parks

    Landmarks

    Heritage

    Structures

    Acres

    Oceans
13. Switch to Slide Show view. Click only once to trigger the animations for the layered objects on the slide. Entrance and exit animations have already been applied. Changing the layered order does not affect the animation order, so the objects will still appear on the slide in the same sequence.
14. When the animations stop and the Oceans object appears, switch to Normal view. Close the Selection Pane.
15. Save the changes and leave the presentation open for the next Step-by-Step.

Customizing the Slide Master and Layout Masters

The slide master is useful when you work with a presentation with a large number of slides because it controls the formatting for all the slides in the presentation. The formats stored in the slide master include themes (color schemes, fonts, and effects) and backgrounds. The slide master also controls placeholders, and it can contain graphics that are part of the design template.

Each slide master has several associated layout masters that define formats for the slide layouts available for the presentation. Each of the layout masters contains the same theme as the associated slide master. When you edit a layout master, the changes apply only to slides formatted with that specific layout. For example, if you change the font for bulleted text on the Title and Content layout master, it will affect only the bulleted items on slides using the Title and Content layout. However, when you edit the slide master, the changes affect all the layout masters. If you change the font for bulleted text on the slide master, all the bulleted items throughout the entire presentation will show the new font.

The slide master and the layout masters contain placeholders for the slide layouts, such as title, subtitle, and content placeholders. You can remove the placeholders or add new placeholders. You can also insert custom graphics or text boxes on slide masters so that the information appears throughout the presentation. This is a good way to add a company logo or name to every slide in a presentation.

The masters include placeholders specifically designed for headers and footers, slide numbers, and dates. You can resize and reposition placeholders, and you can change the text formats. To customize the text for headers and footers on slide masters and layout masters, you must use the Header & Footer button to open the Header and Footer dialog box. You can have the header or footer appear on just one of the slide layouts, on just the title slide, or on all slides in the presentation.

You can also format transitions on slide masters and layout masters, and while working in Slide Master view, you can modify the transition effects and apply sounds.

Step-by-Step 8.6

1. If necessary, open the **National Parks Draft 5** file from your solution files. Save the presentation as **National Parks Draft 6**, followed by your initials.

2. Click the **View** tab. In the Master Views group, click the **Slide Master View** button. Thumbnails for the slide master and each of the layout masters associated with the presentation are displayed in the slide thumbnail pane, as shown in **Figure 8–10**.

FIGURE 8–10
Slide thumbnails pane

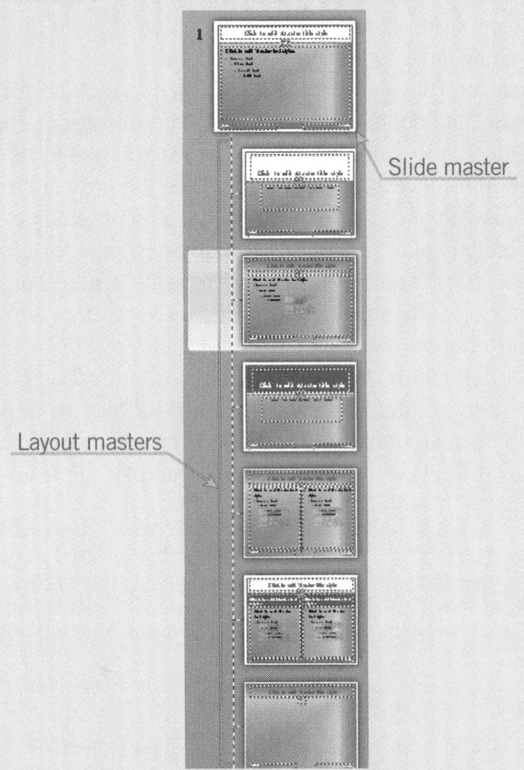

3. The first thumbnail is the slide master. Position the mouse pointer over the thumbnail to show the ScreenTip *1_Civic Slide Master: used by slides(s) 1-64*, which references the design theme (Civic) and the slides to which the formats are applied (slides 1–64).
4. Point to the second thumbnail. This is the layout master for the Title Slide layout, and as the ScreenTip indicates, the layout is currently used for only one slide. Move the mouse pointer over some of the remaining thumbnails. You'll see that some of the layout masters are not used in this presentation.
5. In the slide thumbnail pane, click the **Slide Master** thumbnail at the top. In the Edit pane on the right, click anywhere within the first bulleted item (*Click to edit Master text styles*). Click the **Home** tab. In the Paragraph group, click the **Bullets** button arrow, and then at the bottom of the menu, click **Bullets and Numbering** to open the Bullets and Numbering dialog box. In the lower-left corner of the dialog box, click the **Color** button, and then select the **Dark Blue, Text 2** theme color. Click **OK**. All first-level bullets throughout the presentation will appear in the darker blue color.

6. Click the **Insert** tab. In the Text group, click the **Header & Footer** button to open the Header and Footer dialog box, as shown in **Figure 8-11**. Enable the **Date and time** option. The Update automatically option should be enabled. Enable the **Footer** option, and in the text box type your first and last names. Enable the option **Don't show on title slide**. Click **Apply**. Note that the dates will differ.

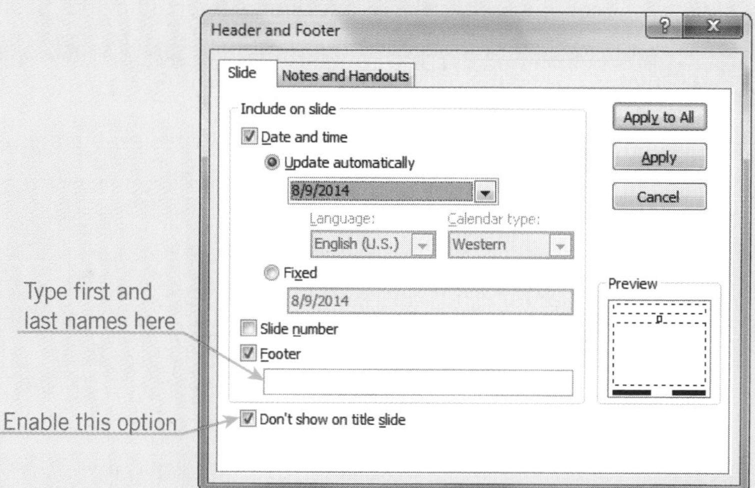

FIGURE 8–11
Header and Footer dialog box

7. In the Edit pane, select the text in the footer text box (in the lower-left corner). Use the Mini toolbar to change the font color to **Dark Blue, Text 2**. Select the date and time field in the date and time footer box and change the font color to **Dark Blue, Text 2**.
8. In the slide thumbnail pane, click the third layout master: the **Section Header layout** thumbnail. Click anywhere within the **Click to edit Master title style** text to select the Title placeholder. Click the **Home** tab, and in the Font group, click the **Increase Font Size** button twice to change the font size to 48 point. Click the **Font Color** button arrow, and then select the **Dark Blue, Text 2** theme color. The changes will only appear on slides formatted with the Section Header layout.
9. At the top of the slide thumbnail pane, click the **Slide Master** thumbnail. Select all five levels of the bulleted list. Click the **Animations** tab. In the Advanced Animation group, click the **Add Animation** button. Under Entrance, click the **Fade** entrance effect.
10. In the Timing group, click the **Start** list arrow and then click **On Click**. In the Animation group, click the **Effect Options** button and make sure the By Paragraph option is selected. Click anywhere to close the menu. All bulleted lists throughout the presentation will be animated, so you won't need to apply the animation format each time you create a bulleted list. A symbol is added to the left of the slide master to indicate animations.

11. In the slide thumbnail pane, click the **Title and Content layout** thumbnail (the second layout master). Click the **Transitions** tab. In the Transition to This Slide group, click the **More** button. Under Subtle, click the **Reveal** transition. The transition will be applied to all slides formatted using the Title and Content layout format.
12. In the Transition to This Slide group, click the **Effect Options** button and then click **Smoothly From Left**. In the Timing group, click the **Sound** list arrow and then click **Camera**. In the Timing group, change Duration setting to **3.00**.
13. Click the **Slide Show** button in the status bar and review the animations and slide transitions for the first four slides. Press **Esc** to switch to Slide Master view. Click the **Slide Master** tab. In the Close group, click the **Close Master View** button.
14. Save the changes and leave the presentation open for the next Step-by-Step.

Creating a New Layout Master

If you have content that is not well-suited to the current slide layouts, you can add a new layout master and create a custom slide layout. To create the new slide layout, you simply insert a new layout master and then insert placeholders on it. The placeholders that you insert are automatically formatted based on the slide master formats. If desired, however, you can customize the placeholder formats for the new layout master, and then the customized formats will apply to all slides using that layout.

After creating the new layout master, you can apply the new layout to new slides as well as to existing slides.

Step-by-Step 8.7

1. If necessary, open the **National Parks Draft 6** file from your solution files. Save the presentation as **National Parks Draft 7**, followed by your initials.
2. Click the **View** tab. In the Master Views group, click the **Slide Master View** button to open the slide thumbnail pane.
3. In the slide thumbnail pane, select the **Two Content layout** thumbnail (the fourth layout master).
4. On the Slide Master tab, in the Edit Master group, click the **Insert Layout** button. A new layout master thumbnail is inserted in the slide thumbnail pane, following the selected thumbnail.

5. Position the mouse pointer over the new layout master thumbnail. The name *Custom Layout Layout* has already been applied. In the Edit Master group, click the **Rename** button. In the Layout name text box, select the existing text, type **Custom Text and Picture**, and then click **Rename**.
6. In the Master Layout group, click the **Insert Placeholder** button arrow and then click **Text**. The mouse pointer changes to a cross-hair +.
7. Drag the mouse pointer to create a placeholder on the left side of the slide. Use the rulers to create a placeholder approximately 5 inches wide and 3 inches high. (*Hint*: You can also click the Drawing Tools Format tab, and set the dimensions in the Size group.) Position the text box below the title placeholder and near the left border of the slide.
8. In the Master Layout group, click the **Insert Placeholder** button arrow and then click **Picture**. Create a placeholder approximately 6 inches wide and 4 inches high. Position the new placeholder so that it aligns with the lower-right corner of the slide. The picture placeholder will overlap the text and date placeholders.
9. In the Close group, click the **Close Master View** button.
10. Go to slide 1. On the Home tab, in the Slides group, click the **New Slide** button arrow. Note that the new layout option appears in the menu. Click the **Custom Text and Picture** thumbnail. A new slide with the new layout formats is added to the presentation. Click **Undo** to remove the new slide from the presentation.
11. On the Slides tab, select the **slide 5** thumbnail. Press and hold down **Ctrl** and **Shift**, and then press **End**. The range of slides 5:64 is selected.
12. With the range of slides selected, in the Slides group, click the **Layout** button and then click the **Custom Text and Picture** thumbnail. The layouts for all the selected slides are now converted to the new slide layout.
13. Go to slide 64. In the Slides group, click the **Layout** button and then click the **Section Header** layout.
14. Save the changes and leave the presentation open for the next Step-by-Step.

EXTRA FOR EXPERTS

To save time, you can base the new layout master on an existing layout master. Right-click the existing layout master thumbnail, and then click Duplicate Layout. The layout master is copied, and a new thumbnail appears in the slide thumbnail pane. Modify the new layout master and rename it.

Inserting a New Slide Master

Each theme has its own set of unique slide layouts. For more complexity and flexibility, you can add additional slide masters. This enables you to access more design templates with more backgrounds, colors, and effects.

Step-by-Step 8.8

1. If necessary, open the **National Parks Draft 7** file from your solution files. Save the presentation as **National Parks Draft 8**, followed by your initials.
2. Click the **View** tab. In the Master Views group, click the **Slide Master View** button to open the slide thumbnail pane.
3. In the Edit Master group, click the **Insert Slide Master** button. A new slide master thumbnail with the number 2 is inserted in the slide thumbnail pane, along with 11 layout masters. Scroll up in the pane. Note that the #1 slide master and the associated 11 layout masters still appear at the top of the list.
4. Position the mouse pointer over the #2 slide master and layout masters thumbnails to see that the formats are not applied to any slides.
5. The #2 slide master should still be selected. In the Background group, click the **Background Styles** button. In the second row of the Background Styles gallery, click the **Style 7** background style.
6. In the Edit Theme group, click the **Themes** button. Scroll down through the Built-In themes and click the **Trek** theme. Note that a new slide master thumbnail with the number 3 appears below the #2 slide master and layout masters.
7. With the #3 slide master thumbnail selected, in the Edit Master group, click the **Rename** button. In the Layout name box, select the existing text, type **My Custom Design** followed by your initials, and then click **Rename**.
8. Position the mouse pointer over the #3 slide master and layout masters thumbnails. Note that the new formats and designs have not been applied to slides in the presentation.
9. In the Edit window, select the text in the Title placeholder. Right-click the selected text, and then use the Mini toolbar to change the font style to **Comic Sans MS** and the font size to **32** point.
10. In the Edit Master group, click the **Preserve** button. A pushpin icon appears to the left of the #3 slide master thumbnail. Even though the master is not being used at this time, the master will be stored with the presentation.
11. Scroll up in the slide thumbnail pane and right-click the **#2 Custom Design Slide Master** thumbnail. Click **Delete Master**. The slide master is removed from the slide thumbnail pane, and the #3 Slide Master is now assigned the number 2.
12. In the Close group, click the **Close Master View** button.

13. If necessary, click the **Home** tab. In the Slides group, click the **New Slide** button arrow. Note that there are two sets of layouts for slides. Click outside the menu to close the menu without selecting a layout.
14. Save the changes and leave the presentation open for the next Step-by-Step.

Customizing the Handout and Note Masters

The handout master controls how the slide thumbnails are arranged for handouts. PowerPoint provides seven different layout options for handouts, so there are seven different handout masters. On each handout master, you can add custom information to the header and footer placeholders.

To control items you want to appear on the notes pages, you use the notes master. You can change the page setup and define the paper size; you can also change the orientation for the slides and notes page. You can also resize the placeholders for the slides and the notes, and you can add custom information to the header and footer placeholders.

Instead of printing handouts directly from PowerPoint, you can create handouts and send them to a Word document. Then you can use Word to format the content and add new content. The slide content is pasted into the Word document. You can choose to paste the content using a link so that when the slides in the presentation change, the handout is automatically updated.

Step-by-Step 8.9

1. If necessary, open the **National Parks Draft 8** file from your solution files. Save the presentation as **National Parks Draft 9**, followed by your initials.
2. Click the **View** tab. In the Master Views group, click the **Handout Master View** button. A layout with six slides appears. In the Page Setup group, click the **Slides Per Page** button. Note that there are seven layout options. Click **6 Slides**.
3. Click the **Insert** tab, and in the Text group, click the **Header & Footer** button. On the Notes and Handouts tab, enable the **Header** option, and in the text box, type **National Parks**. Enable the **Footer** option, and in the text box, type your first and last names. Click **Apply to All**.
4. Click the **Handout Master** tab. Click the **header** placeholder on the left side of the handout window to select the placeholder. Click the **Home** tab. Change the font size to **14 point** and the font color to the **Dark Blue, Text 2** theme color. Select the **footer** placeholder on the left side and apply the same font formats.
5. Click the **Handout Master** tab. In the Close group, click the **Close Master View** button.

6. Click the **File** tab, and then click **Print**. Under Settings, click the **Full Page Slides** button to show the options, as shown in **Figure 8–12**.

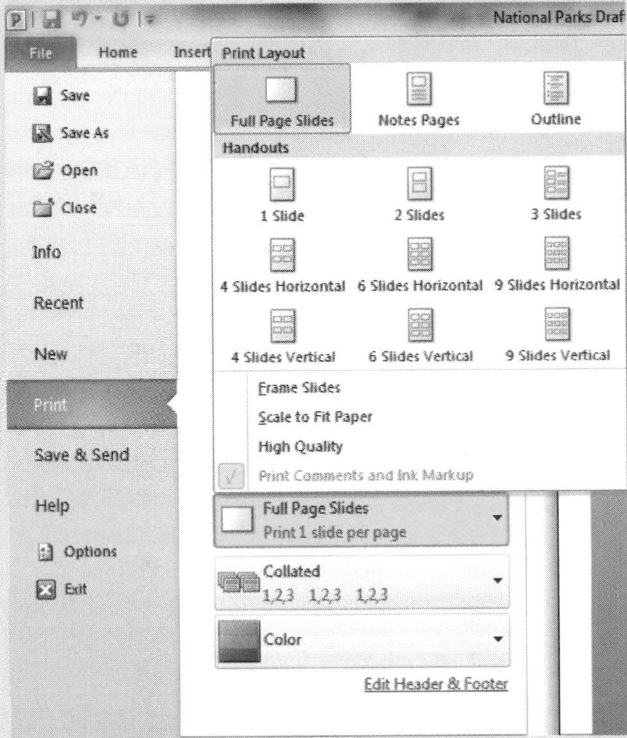

FIGURE 8–12
Print options

7. Under Handouts, select the **4 Slides Horizontal** layout. Note in the preview pane that the information is displayed in the header and footer panes. In the left pane, click **Save & Send**. In the center pane, click **Create Handouts**, and then in the right pane, click the **Create Handouts** button to open the dialog box shown in **Figure 8–13**.

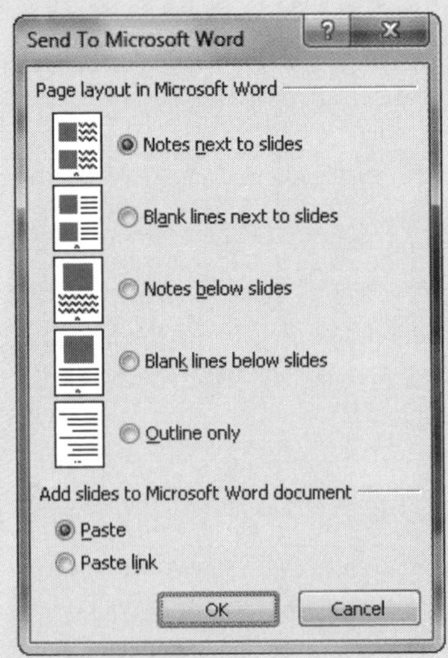

FIGURE 8–13
Send to Microsoft Word dialog box

8. Enable the option **Blank lines next to slides**. Also enable the **Paste link** option, and then click **OK**. Switch to the Word document. Wait patiently for the process to complete, and then save the Word document as **National Parks Handout**, followed by your initials. Exit Word.
9. Click the **View** tab. In the Master Views group, click the **View Notes Master** button.
10. Click the **Insert** tab. In the Text group, click the **Header & Footer** button to open the Header and Footer dialog box. Note that because you already formatted the header and footer for the handout master, the information is already available. Click **Apply to All**.
11. Select the **header** placeholder on the left side. Click the **Home** tab. Change the font size to **14** point and the font color to the **Dark Blue, Text 2** theme color. Select the text in the footer placeholder on the left side and apply the same font formats.
12. Click the **Notes Master** tab. In the Close group, click the **Close Master View** button.
13. Click the **File** tab, and then click **Print**. Under Settings, click the **4 Slides Horizontal** button. Under Print Layout, click **Notes Pages**. Note that the page number appears in the lower-right corner. Click the **Home** tab.
14. Save the changes and leave the presentation open for the next Step-by-Step.

Creating a New Design Template

Using a custom design template is a good way to lend a uniform appearance to presentations generated for specific purposes or by particular presenters. A business, for example, might want to standardize all the presentations created for its use. You've done a lot of work to customize the design for the National Parks presentation. Changes you made to the masters apply only to the current presentation. To save the revisions for future use, you can save the revised design template using a new template name.

You can save your template with your own files or you can let PowerPoint place it in the Templates folder where you can easily choose it for other presentations. If you save the template somewhere other than the Templates folder, you can still apply its formats to a new slide show.

In the next Step-by-Step, you will select and delete multiple slides simultaneously. You can select multiple slides in the Slide pane in Normal view or in Slide Sorter view.

Step-by-Step 8.10

1. If necessary, open the **National Parks Draft 9** file from your solution files.
2. On the Slides tab, click the **slide 1** thumbnail. Press and hold **Ctrl**, and then select the **slide 3** and **slide 4** thumbnails.
3. Click the **slide 1** thumbnail. Press and hold **Shift** and then click the **slide 6** thumbnail. Then press **Ctrl+A** to select all the slides. Press **Delete**.
4. Click the **File** tab, and then click **Save As** to open the Save As dialog box. In the File name box, type **Custom Template**, followed by your initials. In the Save as type box, click the **list arrow** and then click **PowerPoint Template (*.potx)**. The Templates folder should appear in the path at the top of the dialog box. Click **Save**.
5. Click the **File** tab, and then click **Save As**. Navigate to the drive and folder where your solution files are stored. Then click **Save**. The template is now also saved to your solutions folder. Close the template file.
6. Click the **File** tab, and then click **New**. Under Available Templates and Themes, click the **My templates** icon. The New Presentation dialog box opens, showing the personal templates available, as shown in **Figure 8–14**.

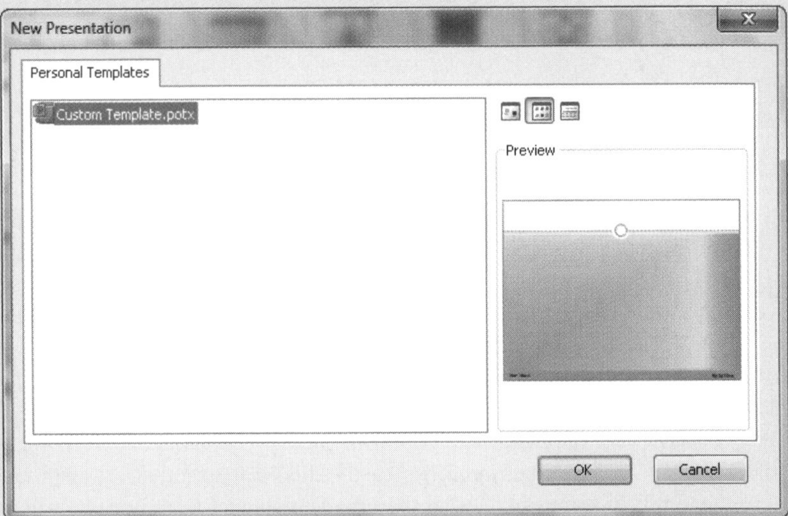

FIGURE 8–14
New Presentation dialog box with Personal Templates tab

7. If necessary, select **Custom Template** and then click **OK**. A new presentation is opened.
8. In the Slides group, click the **New Slide** button arrow. Note that all the layout options are available, including the Custom Text and Picture layout. Click outside the menu to close the menu without inserting a new slide.

9. Click the **View** tab. In the Master Views group, click the **Slide Master View** button. Note that the #1 slide master includes the animation formats. Scroll down through the slide thumbnail pane, and you'll see the #2 slide master and layout masters. In the Close group, click the **Close Master View** button.
10. Click the **File** tab, and then click **New**. Under Available Templates and Themes, click the **My templates** icon. In the New Presentation dialog box, on the Personal Templates tab, right-click **Custom Template**, and then click **Delete**. When prompted to move the file to the Recycle Bin, click **Yes**.
11. Click **Cancel** to close the dialog box. Click the **Home** tab to close Backstage view.
12. Close the new presentation without saving any changes.

Creating a Custom Show with an Agenda Slide

A custom show is actually a presentation within a presentation. To create a custom show, you identify a group of related slides within a presentation. Creating custom shows gives you flexibility when a presentation contains a large number of slides because you can group related topics in the presentation and focus on the slides that are appropriate for a particular audience. For example, the National Parks presentation contains 59 slides providing information about national parks across the United States. If you're presenting to an audience in Utah, you can create a custom show and include only the slides for the parks in Utah. Once you have identified the slides for the custom show, you can reorder them within the custom show.

You are not limited to one show; you can create multiple custom shows from the same presentation. At any time, you can edit, remove, and even make a copy of a custom show.

Once you have created custom shows, you can create an ***agenda slide*** that provides an outline of topics for the presentation. Agenda slides are especially useful for presentations with custom shows. You can identify the topics on the agenda slide and create a hyperlink for each topic so you can easily navigate to different sections of the presentation. You can also apply a format so that you will automatically return to the agenda slide after the last slide in the custom show appears.

VOCABULARY
agenda slide

Step-by-Step 8.11

1. Open the **National Parks Draft 9** file from your solution files. Save the presentation as **National Parks Draft 10**, followed by your initials.

2. Click the **Slide Show** tab. In the Start Slide Show group, click the **Custom Slide Show** button, and then click **Custom Shows**. The Custom Shows dialog box opens. Click **New** to open the Define Custom Show dialog box, as shown in **Figure 8–15**.

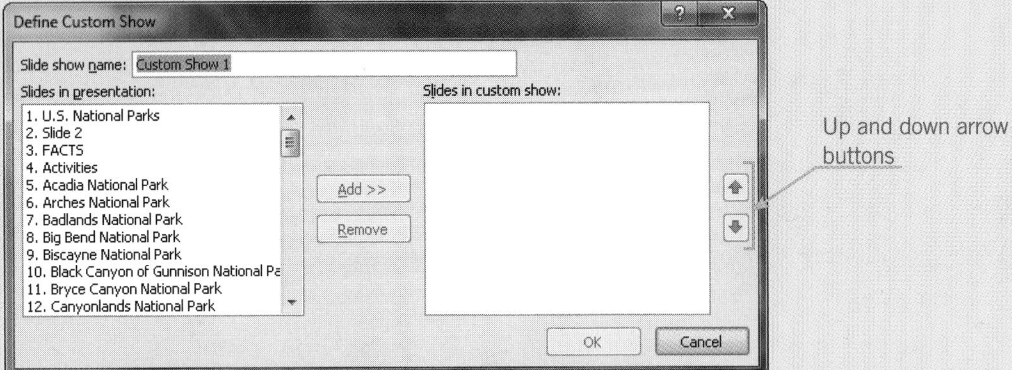

FIGURE 8–15 Define Custom Show dialog box

3. In the Slide show name text box, type **Utah National Parks**. Under Slides in presentation, click **6. Arches National Park**. Press and hold **Ctrl** and click the following slides:

   11. Bryce Canyon National Park

   12. Canyonlands National Park

   13. Capitol Reef National Park

   63. Zion National Park

4. Click **Add>>**. The selected slides are copied to the pane on the right.
5. Under Slides in custom show, select **2. Bryce Canyon National Park**, and then click the **up arrow** button. Then select **3. Canyonlands National Park** and then click the **down arrow** button to move the slide down in the list. Return the list to alphabetical order, and then click **OK**.
6. In the Custom Shows dialog box, click the **New** button and create a new custom show named **California National Parks**. Add the following slides to the new custom show, and then click **OK**.

   15. Channel Islands National Park

   19. Death Valley National Park

   36. Joshua Tree National Park

   39. Kings Canyon National Park

   42. Lassen Volcanic National Park

   50. Redwood National Park

   53. Sequoia National Park

   62. Yosemite National Park

7. Click **New** and create a third custom show named **Alaska National Parks**. Add the following slides to the new custom show and click **OK**, then close the Custom Shows dialog box.

   20. Denali National Park

   23. Gates of the Arctic National Park

   24. Glacier Bay National Preserve

   37. Katmai National Park

   38. Kenai Fjords National Park

   40. Kobuk Valley National Park

   41. Lake Clark National Park

   60. Wrangell-Saint Elias National Park

8. Go to slide 4. To create an agenda slide, click the **Home** tab. In the Slides group, click the **New Slide** button arrow and then click the **Blank** layout from the #1 layout masters. Click the **Insert** tab. In the Illustrations group, click the **Insert SmartArt Graphic** button. Under List, in the second row, click the **Vertical Box List** SmartArt graphic, and then click **OK**.
9. In the first placeholder, type **Alaska**. In the second placeholder, type **California**. And in the third placeholder, type **Utah**.
10. Select and then right-click the text in the **Alaska** SmartArt object, and then click **Hyperlink**. In the Insert Hyperlink dialog box, under Link to, click **Place in This Document**. Under Select a place in this document, scroll down to Custom Shows and click **Alaska National Parks**. Enable the **Show and return** option. When your dialog box matches the one shown in **Figure 8–16**, click **OK**.

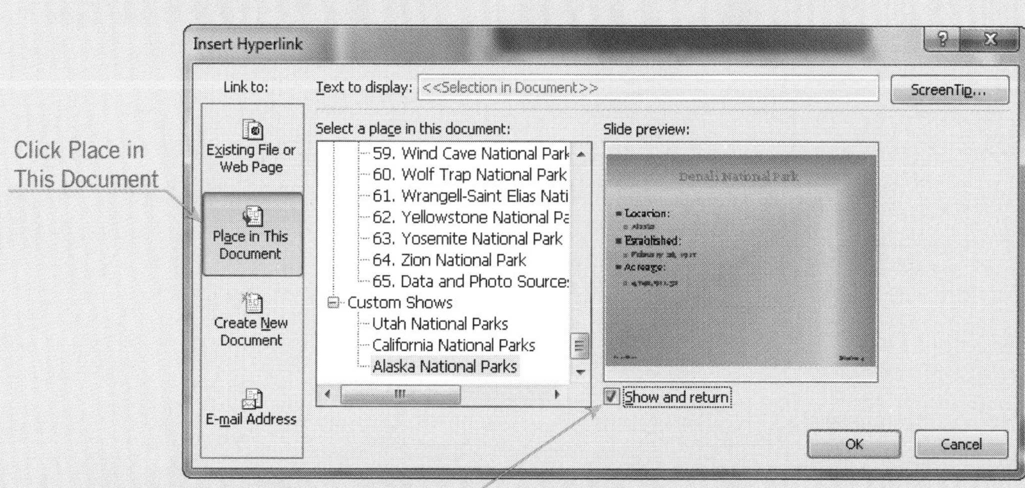

FIGURE 8–16 Insert Hyperlink dialog box

11. Create similar hyperlinks to the remaining two custom shows. Be sure to enable the **Show and return** option.

12. Click the **Design** tab. In the Themes group, click the **Colors** button. At the bottom of the menu, click **Create New Theme Colors**. Under Theme colors, click the **Hyperlink** list arrow and change the color setting to the **White, Text 1** theme color. Click **Save**. The hyperlinked text is now visible on the SmartArt objects.
13. Save the changes. Click the **Slide Show** button on the status bar. Click the last hyperlink, **Utah**, and preview the slides in the custom show. When you advance through all the slides in the Utah National Parks custom show, PowerPoint will return to slide 5. If time permits, preview the slides in the other two custom shows. When you click at the end of each custom show, you will return to the agenda slide.
14. Switch to Normal view. Save the changes and leave the presentation open for the next Step-By-Step.

TIP

To start a custom show, click the Slide Show tab. In the Start Slide Show group, click Custom Slide Show and then click Custom Shows. In the Custom shows list, select a show and then click Show.

Using Sections to Organize Slides

When a presentation has numerous slides, like the National Parks presentation, navigating through the slides can be tedious. To organize the slides, you can separate slides in a presentation into different sections. After creating the sections, you can view them in both Slide Sorter view and Normal view. You can collapse one or more sections, which will enable you to focus on a specific section of slides in the presentation. The sections are also useful if you share presentations with others because you can direct them to a specific section.

Step-by-Step 8.12

1. If necessary, open the **National Parks Draft 10** file from your solution files. Save the presentation as **National Parks Draft 11**, followed by your initials.
2. Go to slide 6 and, in the status bar, click the **Slide Sorter view** button. If necessary, click the **Home** tab. In the Slides group, click the **Section** button and then click **Add Section**. A section bar is inserted before the selected slide, as shown in **Figure 8–17**.

FIGURE 8–17
New section added in Slide Sorter view

3. In the Slides group, click the **Section** button and then click **Rename Section**. The Rename Section dialog box opens. In the Section name text box, type **Parks A-C** and then click **Rename**.
4. Scroll down and click the **slide 20** thumbnail. In the Slides group, click the **Section** button and then click **Add Section**. Right-click the new section bar and click **Rename Section**. In the Section name text box, type **Parks D-G** and then click **Rename**.

5. Switch to Normal view. On the Slides tab, scroll down and click the **slide 33** thumbnail. If necessary, click the **Home** tab. In the Slides group, click the **Section** button and then click **Add Section**. A new section bar appears in the Slides tab, as shown in **Figure 8–18**.

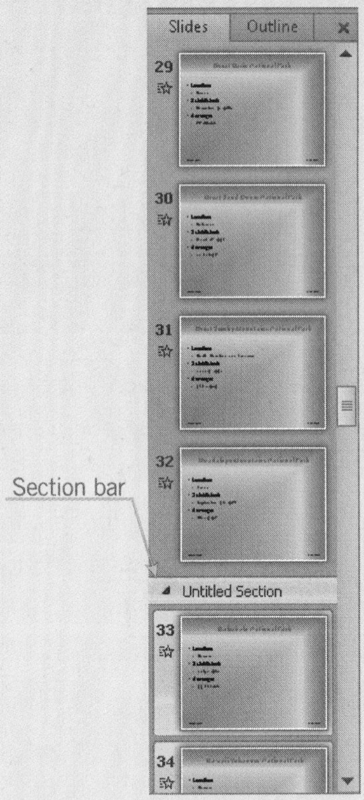

FIGURE 8–18
New section added in Normal view

6. In the Slides tab, right-click the section bar and then click **Rename Section**. In the Section name text box, type **Parks H-N** and then click **Rename**.
7. In the Slides tab, click the **slide 49** thumbnail, create a new section, and name the section **Parks O-Z**. Double-click the **Parks O-Z** section bar. The section is collapsed and the slides are hidden. The section bar shows that there are 17 slides in the section.
8. Scroll up and double-click the **Parks A-C** section bar. Then double-click the **Parks D-G** section bar.
9. Scroll to the top of the Slides tab. Right-click the **Default Section** section bar and rename the section **Introduction**. Then, collapse the slides in the section.
10. In the Slides tab, drag the Parks D-G section bar to move the section above the Parks A-C section.
11. Switch to Slide Sorter view. Click the **Parks H-N** section bar to select all the slides in that section. Then double-click the **Parks H-N** section bar to collapse the slides. All the sections should now be collapsed.

12. Right-click the **Parks D-G** section bar, and then click **Move Section Down** to reposition the section so that it follows the Parks A-C section.
13. Right-click any one of the section bars, and then click **Expand All**. All the sections are expanded. Right-click any one of the section bars, and then click **Collapse All**. Then, expand the **Introduction** section.
14. Save the changes and close the presentation.

SUMMARY

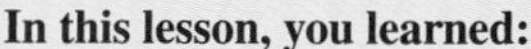

In this lesson, you learned:

- Changing the color scheme is a quick way to give slides a fresh new look. To fine-tune the look of a presentation, you can change individual colors in the color scheme and you can save the custom scheme in the Theme Colors gallery.
- You have many options for changing the background of a slide. You can change the color, create a gradient of one or more colors, add a texture, or use a pattern. You can also use graphics to create backgrounds.
- There are several features available for modifying the appearance and flow of text within a text box. You can also add backgrounds, outlines, and special effects to text boxes.
- Slide masters and layout masters control the placement of text and other items on a slide, as well as color, font, style, and size of text. When you modify a slide master, the new formats are applied to all slides based on the master.
- Masters also provide placeholders specifically designed for headers and footers, slide numbers, and dates. To customize your presentation, resize and reposition these placeholders and/or change the text formats.
- You can add additional layout masters to a presentation, and you can customize the layout and placeholder formats on the layout master.
- More than one slide master can be added to a presentation, giving you access to a wider range of design templates.
- After modifying the slide designs and layouts, you can save the customized settings as a new design template and make the template available for future use.
- Custom shows are like presentations within presentations. Gathering slides into a custom show allows you to control groups of slides during a presentation.
- Slides can be organized in sections, making it easier to navigate the slides—especially when a presentation consists of a large number of slides.

VOCABULARY REVIEW

Define the following terms:

agenda slide

color scheme

gradient fill

REVIEW QUESTIONS

TRUE / FALSE

Circle T if the statement is true or F if the statement is false.

T F 1. A presentation is limited to 11 layout masters.

T F 2. You can use pictures and clip art to create a slide background.

T F 3. If you change the alignment of a title on a layout master, you will see the same change in all titles on all slides in the presentation.

T F 4. When you edit the slide master, the changes affect all the layout masters.

T F 5. If you choose to hide design graphics on a slide, the graphics are automatically removed from all slides in the presentation.

FILL IN THE BLANK

Complete the following sentences by writing the correct word or words in the blanks provided.

1. A(n) ________________ is a set of coordinated colors.
2. A(n) ________________ provides an outline of topics for the presentation.
3. A(n) ________________ is composed of two or more colors that gradually blend from one color to another.
4. The ________________ controls the formatting for all the slides in the presentation.
5. When saving a design template, you use the ________________ file extension.

WRITTEN QUESTIONS

Write a brief answer to the following questions.

1. What types of formats are stored in a slide master?

2. After customizing slide designs and layouts, how can you save the changes so you can apply the same design and formats in future projects?

3. What are the advantages of creating multiple slide masters for a presentation?

4. What are the benefits of creating custom shows?

5. Why does a color scheme provide two different color settings for hyperlinks?

PROJECTS

PROJECT 8–1

1. Open the **Time Management** file from the drive and folder where your Data Files are stored. Save the presentation as **Final Time Management**, followed by your initials.
2. On slide 1, replace *Your Name* with your first and last names.
3. Create three custom shows:
   a. Name the first custom show **Step 1** and include slides 7–10.
   b. Name the second custom show **Step 2** and include slides 11–13.
   c. Name the third custom show **Step 3** and include slides 14–16.
4. Go to slide 6. Format the text in each SmartArt object to link to the related custom shows. Choose the setting to return to slide 6 once you have advanced through the custom show slides.
5. Apply a new color scheme and/or modify the color scheme as needed. For example, make sure the color scheme is appropriate for the presentation content, and make sure the hyperlink colors work in the SmartArt object on slide 6.
6. Go to slide 18. Hide the background graphics. Then format the slide background using clip art.
7. If necessary, adjust the font formats so you can easily read the text on the slide.
8. If time permits, add clip art to the slides to enhance the presentation.
9. Preview the presentation in Slide Show view.
10. Save the changes and close the presentation.

PROJECT 8–2

1. Open the **Building Renovation** file from the drive and folder where your Data Files are stored. Save the presentation as **Final Building Renovation**, followed by your initials.
2. Format the slide background using clip art of a blueprint (or another appropriate image). Apply the background to all slides in the presentation. If necessary, adjust the image transparency.
3. Depending on the background image, you may want to modify the theme colors.
4. Modify the slide master:
   a. Change the master title style font to **Arial Rounded MT Bold**.
   b. Change the font size to **40 point**.
   c. If necessary, change the font color to complement the background image.
   d. Insert the footer text **Twilight Enterprises** on all pages. Change the footer font size to **16 point**, and change the font color to fit with the color scheme you selected.
5. Modify the Title and Content layout master:
   a. If necessary, change the font color and size for the bulleted text so that you can easily read it with the slide background image.
   b. Apply a different bullet style for the first-level bullet.
   c. Animate the bulleted lists with an entrance effect, starting On Click.
   d. Apply a slide transition.
6. Insert and format a new layout master.
   a. Name the new layout master **Custom Credits**.
   b. Remove the title and footer placeholders.
   c. Insert a text placeholder that fills most of the slide.
   d. Remove the bullets formats in the placeholder.
   e. Select the text placeholder and apply the entrance effect **Credits**. Format the animation to start **With Previous**.
7. Format a header and footer for the handout and notes masters. The header should show *Building Renovation* and the footer should show *Twilight Enterprises.*
8. In Normal view, create a new slide at the end of the presentation based on the new Custom Credits layout. In the placeholder, type the following, and then add your name at the bottom of the list.

   Thanks to:

   Angela Forest

   Joshua Winton

   Kong Zo Chang

9. Preview the slides in Slide Show view. Make any necessary corrections or apply additional formats to enhance the slides.
10. Preview the handouts and notes pages in Backstage view to make sure the headers and footers appear. Save the changes to the presentation.
11. Delete all the slides in the presentation, and then save the presentation as a template with your solution files. Name the new template file **Building Renovation Design**, followed by your initials.
12. Close the presentation template.

PROJECT 8–3

1. Click the File tab, and then click New. Under Available Templates and Themes, click the Sample templates icon. Select the Five Rules thumbnail, and then click the Create button.
2. Save the new document as **Organized Five Rules**, followed by your initials.
3. Scroll through the slides to become familiar with the content. Note that there are 56 slides in the presentation. You may not have time now to review the entire presentation thoroughly, but when you do, preview all the slides in Slide Show view. There's a lot to learn from the content, and you'll view some very effective uses of animations, transitions, and audio clips.
4. Switch to Slide Sorter view. Create sections to organize the slides. Name each section so you can easily identify the slide content. Note that you may need to fully review the slide content to determine the section breaks.
5. Collapse all of the sections except the first section.
6. Save the changes and close the presentation.

CRITICAL THINKING

ACTIVITY 8–1

In a Word document, write a brief paragraph to compare working with sections in a PowerPoint presentation to working in Outline view in a Word document.

ACTIVITY 8–2

In this lesson, you worked with the handout master and the notes master. You may have noticed that in these views the Ribbon provided commands for themes, colors, and backgrounds. Do you think you would ever use these features to format handouts and notes pages? Write a brief paragraph, and explain the reason for your response.

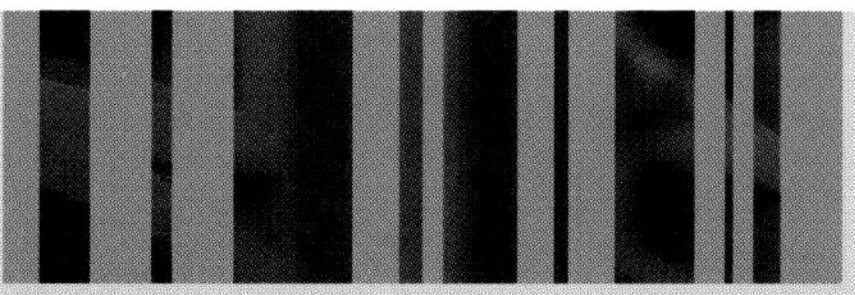

Estimated time:
1.5 hours

LESSON 9

Importing and Exporting Information

■ OBJECTIVES

Upon completion of this lesson, you should be able to:

- Reuse slides from another presentation.
- Copy and paste slides to Word documents.
- Create slides from a Word outline.
- Import a table from a Word document.
- Export slide information to a Word outline.
- Embed worksheet data and link an Excel chart in a slide.
- Copy data from an Access table.
- Save a slide as a graphic file.

■ VOCABULARY

export

import

integration

slide library

This lesson introduces you to techniques for exchanging information between PowerPoint presentations and between PowerPoint and other Office applications, including Word, Excel, and Access.

Reusing Slides from Another Presentation

Suppose you are creating a presentation and realize that you already prepared some slides for the topic in another presentation. Do you have to re-create the slides? No way! You can easily copy and paste selected content onto a new slide, or you can copy and reuse entire slides.

To copy and paste slides from one presentation to another, both presentations must be open. If the presentation containing the slides you want to copy is large and you want to pick and choose among the slides, the Reuse Slides command is probably a better choice. You can scroll through the entire presentation and select individual slides you want to reuse, or you can insert all of the slides at once. Reusing slides has the additional advantage that you do not have to open the presentation file containing the slides you want to import.

When you use either method to copy slides from one presentation to another, the design template for the current (or destination) presentation is applied to the copied slides by default. However, you can choose to keep the formatting from the original (or source) presentation of the copied slides.

VOCABULARY
slide library

You can also reuse files from a ***slide library***, which is a special type of library used to store presentation slides. Those who have access to a slide library can publish slides to the library as well as use slides that are stored in the library. When you reuse slides from a slide library, you can choose to receive notification when changes are made to the slide stored in the slide library. To access slides in a slide library, you must have a connection to a server running Microsoft Office SharePoint Server 2007 or Microsoft SharePoint Server 2010, which is beyond the scope of this lesson.

Step-by-Step 9.1

1. Open the **Community Service** file from the drive and folder where your Data Files are stored. Save the presentation as **Revised Community Service 1**, followed by your initials. Scroll through the slides to get familiar with the content.
2. Open the **Blood Drive** file from the drive and folder where your Data Files are stored. Go to slide 1. In the Slide pane, select all the text (including the Register symbol) in the placeholder in the lower-right corner of the slide. In the Clipboard group, click the **Copy** button.
3. Switch to the Revised Community Service 1 presentation. On slide 1, click anywhere within the Subtitle placeholder. In the Clipboard group, click the **Paste** button.
4. Switch to the Blood Drive presentation. On the Slides tab, select the **slide 2** thumbnail and then click the **Copy** button. Close the Blood Drive presentation file without saving any changes.

5. In the Revised Community Service 1 presentation, on the Slides tab, select the **slide 4** thumbnail. In the Clipboard group, click the **Paste** button. The slide from the Blood Drive presentation is inserted after slide 4, with the formatting of the Revised Community Service 1 presentation.
6. In the Slides group, click the **New Slide** button arrow, and then at the bottom of the menu, click **Reuse Slides**. The Reuse Slides pane, similar to the one shown in **Figure 9–1**, opens on the right side of the document window. Your pane will differ.

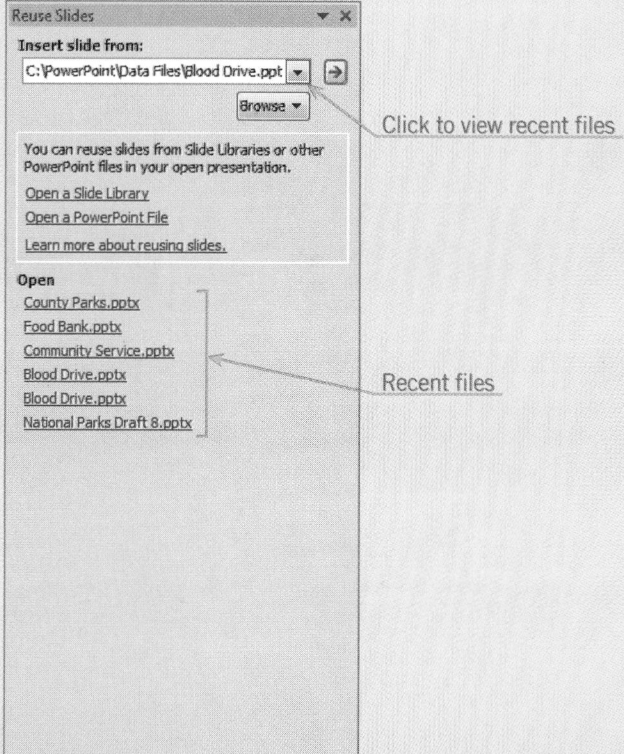

FIGURE 9–1
Reuse Slides pane

7. In the Reuse Slides pane, under Insert slide from, click the **list arrow**. Recently accessed files appear in the list. Click the **list arrow** again to hide the list.
8. In the Reuse Slides pane, click **Browse** and then click **Browse Slide Library**. The Select a Slide Library dialog box opens. If your computer is connected to a server running SharePoint, you can browse to access the slide library here. Click **Cancel** to close the dialog box.

9. In the Reuse Slides pane, click **Browse** and then click **Browse File**. Navigate to the drive and folder where your Data Files are stored. Select the filename **Blood Drive** and then click **Open**. On the Slides tab, click the **slide 5** thumbnail. Thumbnails for the slides in the Blood Drive presentation appear in the Reuse Slides pane, as shown in **Figure 9–2**. If you are accessing slides from a slide library in SharePoint, the Reuse Slides pane will look very similar.

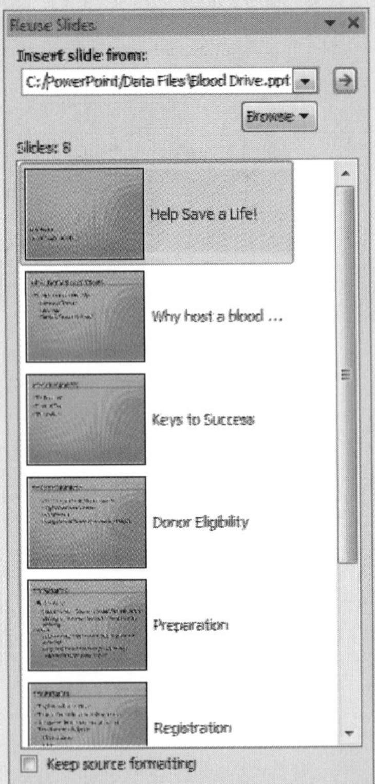

FIGURE 9–2 Thumbnails for the Blood Drive slides

10. In the Reuse Slides pane on the right, position the mouse pointer over the **Keys to Success** (slide 3) thumbnail to view a large image of the thumbnail, as shown in **Figure 9–3**. The slide title appears at the bottom of the slide.

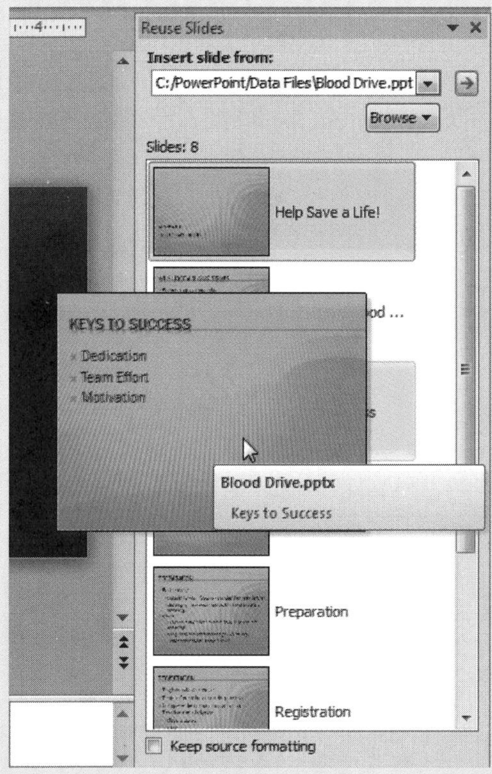

FIGURE 9–3
Enlarged preview of the Keys to Success (slide 3) thumbnail

11. Click to select the enlarged **Keys to Success** (slide 3) thumbnail. In the Slide Thumbnail pane on the left, you will see that the slide has been inserted into the Revised Community Service presentation after slide 5. Also note that the new slide is formatted with the same design as the other slides in the presentation, and the slide title appears at the top of the slide.

12. Switch to Slide Sorter view. Position the insertion point between slide 7 and slide 8, scrolling down if necessary. In the Reuse Slides pane, click **Browse** and then click **Browse File**. Select the filename **Food Bank**, and then click **Open**. Thumbnails of the presentation file appear in the Reuse Slides pane.

13. In the Reuse Slides pane, click the **Organize a Food Drive** (slide 2) thumbnail. Then click the **Volunteer at the Food Bank** (slide 3) thumbnail. Then click the **Donate Professional Services** (slide 5) thumbnail.

14. In the upper-right corner of the Reuse Slides pane, click the **Close** button. Save the changes and leave the presentation open for the next Step-by-Step.

TIP

To maintain the original design of the reused slides, at the bottom of the Reuse Slides pane, enable the Keep source formatting option.

TIP

To reuse all slides in a presentation, right-click any one of the thumbnails and then click Insert All Slides.

Sharing Information among Applications

VOCABULARY
import
export
integration

If information already exists in another Office application, such as Word, Excel, or Access, you do not need to type and format the information again in PowerPoint. Instead, you can import or export the information. When you ***import*** content, you bring it into one application from another compatible application. When you ***export*** content, you send it from one application to another.

Sharing the information among the applications is often referred to as ***integration***. Integrating applications not only saves time, but it also ensures consistency in data because when you retype information, you risk making errors. To share the information, you can copy and paste content, link data from one application to another, embed content as an object, or convert the content to a different file format.

When you link data to a slide, you can edit the data only in its source application. For example, if a slide contains a link to data in an Excel worksheet, you must return to the worksheet in Excel to edit the data. Changes you make in the Excel worksheet then appear in the linked object on a slide. A linked object is stored in the source file (in this example, the Excel worksheet), but it is not stored in the destination file (in this example, the PowerPoint presentation). A linked object on a PowerPoint slide is actually a picture of the object in the source application. Linking is not permanent—you can easily break a link if you no longer want the linked object to update in the destination document. When a link is broken, the object remains in the destination document as a picture and you can still resize and move it on the slide, but you cannot edit the data.

When you embed an object on a slide, you can edit the data in PowerPoint using commands from the source application. For example, if a slide contains an embedded Excel worksheet, you double-click the embedded worksheet to edit the data. Excel's commands will be displayed, and you can make the edits without leaving PowerPoint. An embedded object is stored in the destination file (in this example, the presentation).

You might wonder when you should use each of these four integration options. **Table 9–1** describes when you would use each method.

TABLE 9–1 Integration options

OPTION	WHEN TO USE
Copy and Paste (default setting)	Useful when the imported information does not need to be updated. Most information can be copied and pasted, and there are usually format options available when pasting copied information.
Link	Useful when you want to keep the data current. The object is not stored in the destination file, so linking is an advantage if file space for the destination file is limited.
Embed	Useful when you want the imported information to be stored in the destination file and you want to be able to edit the source data in the destination application. Because the embedded object is stored in the destination file, the destination file size might be quite large.
Convert	Useful when the shared information must be stored in a specific format to be recognized in the destination application.

Copying and Pasting Content between Slides and Word Documents

PowerPoint offers features that enable you to easily create slides from existing content in Word documents. Text, tables, and charts created in Word can be imported into a PowerPoint presentation, and information contained on PowerPoint slides can be exported to a Word document.

Not only do slides provide information, but they are also usually quite decorative. You can add both information and pizzazz to documents created in other Office applications by copying PowerPoint slides and pasting them into Word documents. When you paste a copied slide into Word, the slide is inserted as a picture. Like any other graphic object, you can move, resize, and control how text wraps around the picture. You can also use the picture tools to format the picture. You can choose to paste the picture as a linked object so that when changes are made in the presentation file, the linked picture in the Word document is also updated.

Step-by-Step 9.2

1. If necessary, open the **Revised Community Service 1.pptx** file. Save the presentation as **Revised Community Service 2**, followed by your initials.
2. Launch Word. Open the **Long-Term Care.docx** file from the drive and folder where your Data Files are stored. Save the document as **Revised Long-Term Care**, followed by your initials.
3. Switch to the PowerPoint window. If necessary, switch to Normal view. On the Slides tab, scroll up and select the **slide 1** thumbnail. In the Clipboard group, click the **Copy** button.
4. Switch to the Word window. At the top of the document, position the insertion point after the last character in the title.
5. In the Clipboard group, click the **Paste** button arrow and then click **Paste Special**. The Paste Special dialog box opens, as shown in **Figure 9–4**. Note that the default setting will paste the copied slide as a picture in PNG format.

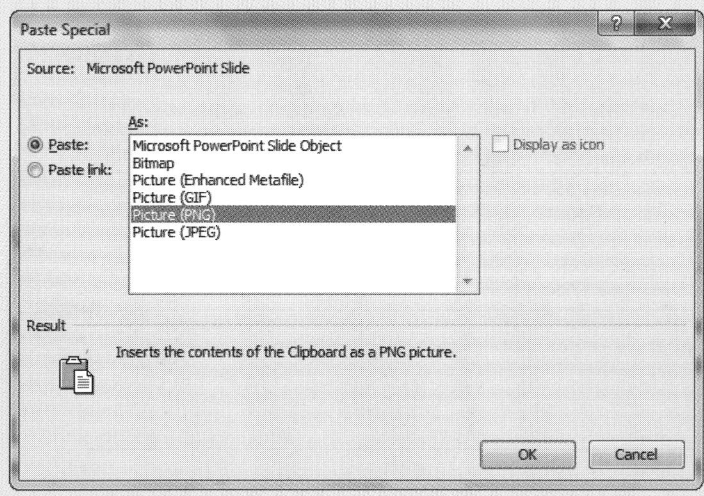

FIGURE 9–4
Paste Special dialog box

6. In the dialog box, enable the **Paste link** option. The list of options changes, and the Microsoft PowerPoint Slide Object is automatically selected. Note that Result information at the bottom of the dialog box indicates that the contents will be inserted as a picture with a shortcut link to the source file. Click **OK**. The picture is inserted in the document.
7. Right-click the **picture**, and then in the shortcut menu, click **Format Object**. In the Format Object dialog box, click the **Size** tab. Under Height, change the Absolute setting to **1"**. Under Width, click the **Absolute** text box. The width is automatically adjusted to 1.34".
8. In the Format Object dialog box, click the **Layout** tab. Under Wrapping style, click the **Square** option and then click **OK**. The picture is resized and repositioned on the page.
9. Use the mouse to drag and reposition the slide object to the right of the title and just above the blue line below the title. Right-click the **picture**, and then click **Format Object**. Click the **Layout** tab and, under Wrapping style, click the **Behind text** option and then click **OK**. The blue underline below the title is now visible across the entire width of the page.
10. Switch to the PowerPoint window. On slide 1, position the insertion point in front of the text *Strategic Solutions, Inc.®*. Press **Enter**, and then position the insertion point in the new blank line. Type **Community Service Projects**.
11. Switch to the Word document. Right-click the **slide** object, and then click **Update Link**. The picture now shows the new text.
12. Right-click the **slide** object, and then in the shortcut menu, point to **Linked Slide Object**. In the submenu, click **Links** to open the Links dialog box, as shown in **Figure 9–5**. Click **Break Link**. When prompted to break the selected link, click **Yes**. The picture of the object remains unchanged, but any changes made in the source file will no longer affect the object on the slide.

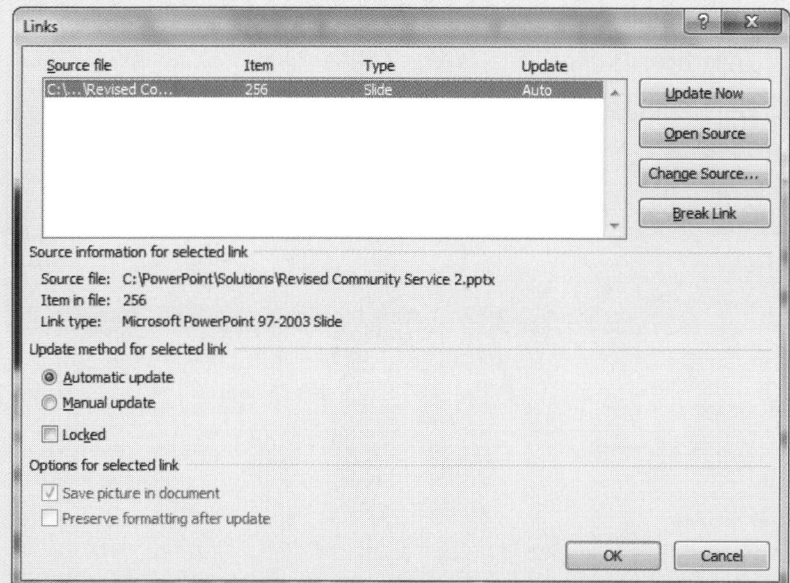

FIGURE 9–5
Links dialog box

13. Save the changes to the Word document and close the file. Leave the Word application open.
14. Switch to the PowerPoint window. Save the changes to the presentation and leave the presentation open for the next Step-by-Step.

Creating Slides from a Word Outline

One of the easiest ways to import information into PowerPoint is to create slides from an outline created in a Word document. You don't need to retype the information from the outline onto the slides or even open the Word document. PowerPoint imports all the content formatted with heading styles to create titles and bulleted lists at various levels. If heading styles are not applied in the Word document, an individual slide is created for each paragraph in the document.

PowerPoint creates only Title and Text layout slides, so if you are importing the information into a new blank presentation file, you might need to create a Title slide at the beginning of the presentation.

Step-by-Step 9.3

1. If necessary, open the **Revised Community Service 2.pptx** file. Save the presentation as **Revised Community Service 3**, followed by your initials.
2. Switch to Slide Sorter view. Scroll down to the end of the slides and position the insertion point to the right of slide 12.

3. In the Slides group, click the **New Slide** button arrow and then click **Slides from Outline**. The Insert Outline dialog box opens, as shown in **Figure 9–6**. Your dialog box will differ.

FIGURE 9–6
Insert Outline dialog box

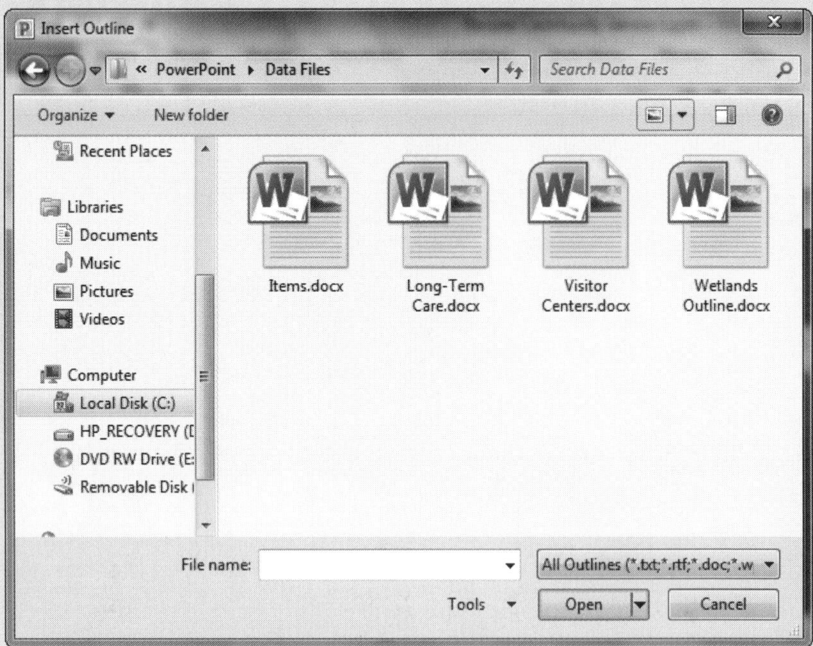

4. Navigate to the drive and folder where your Data Files are stored. Select the filename **Long-Term Care.docx**, and then click **Insert**. Five new slides are created and inserted at the end of the presentation, with the same design applied. Note that each new slide is formatted with the Title and Text layout.
5. Double-click the **slide 13** thumbnail to show the slide in Normal view. Select the slide title and use the Mini toolbar to change the font color to white.
6. On the Slides tab, click the **slide 16** thumbnail. If necessary, select and reposition the placeholder on the slide so that all of the content appears on the slide.
7. Save the changes and leave the presentation open for the next Step-by-Step.

Importing a Table from Word

Although PowerPoint offers features for creating and formatting a table on a slide, if the table already exists in a Word document, importing the table from Word will save you time. To import table data, you select the data and copy it to the Clipboard. In PowerPoint, you can choose from several Paste Special options to paste the copied data. **Table 9–2** describes the benefits of each Paste Special option.

When you copy a table onto a PowerPoint slide, the table content is embedded in the slide and you can then use the PowerPoint table commands to format the table and rearrange the table contents.

TABLE 9–2 Paste Special options

OPTION	BENEFITS
Use Destination Styles	The table formats in the presentation theme are applied to the imported table.
Keep Source Formatting	The table formats applied in the Word document are applied to the imported table.
Embed	The table is embedded with the source formatting. You can use the PowerPoint table commands to edit the table data and modify the table styles.
Picture	The table is inserted as a picture. You can resize and reposition the picture, but you cannot edit the table data or modify the table styles.
Keep Text Only	All formatting is removed, and only the table text is imported on the slide. You can edit and format the text as desired.

Step-by-Step 9.4

1. If necessary, open the **Revised Community Service 3.pptx** file. Save the presentation as **Revised Community Service 4**, followed by your initials.
2. If necessary, launch Word. Open the **Items.docx** file from the drive and folder where your Data Files are stored. Save the document as **Updated Items**, followed by your initials.
3. Select the entire table, and then copy the table to the Clipboard.
4. Switch to the PowerPoint window. If necessary, switch to Normal view. Go to slide 8. Select and then delete the content placeholder with the bulleted items.
5. Right-click the Slide pane. Note that in the shortcut menu, under Paste Options, there are five buttons. See **Figure 9–7**. Position the mouse pointer over each button to show a ScreenTip and a live preview of the pasted contents on the slide.

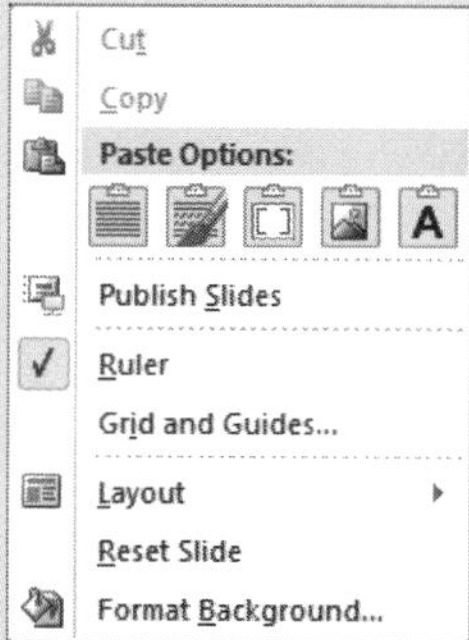

FIGURE 9–7
Paste Options in shortcut menu

TIP

When you use the Paste button to paste the copied table, a Paste Options button appears in the lower-right corner of the pasted table. If the Paste Options button does not appear, click the File tab, click Options, and then click Advanced. Under Cut, copy, and paste, enable the option Show Paste Options button when content is pasted.

6. In the shortcut menu, under Paste Options, click the **Use Destination Styles** button. The table is imported on the slide, and the presentation design theme is applied to the table. The copied data is inserted in a PowerPoint table, and the Table Tools tabs are available.
7. Drag a table corner handle to enlarge the table. Note that as the table gets bigger, the font size stays the same. If you adjust the font size, you will likely also need to adjust the column widths. Click **Undo** on the Quick Access Toolbar two times to remove the table from the slide.
8. In the Clipboard group, click the **Paste** button arrow and then click **Paste Special** to open the Paste Special dialog box. Enable the **Paste link** option. Under As, the option Microsoft Word Document Object is already selected. Click **OK**.
9. Drag a table corner handle to enlarge the table. Because the data is pasted as a picture, when you resize the object, the text also appears larger. Adjust the size of the picture to fit on the slide, and then reposition the picture as needed.
10. Switch to the Word window. Select the first column and then drag and drop the column so it is the second column. The first column is now *Cleaning Items*, the second column is *Food Items*, and the third column is *Hygiene Items*.
11. Select all the rows in the first column, except for the heading, and remove the bold format.
12. Switch to the PowerPoint window. The table is updated with the new data arrangement.
13. Save the changes to the presentation file, and leave the file open for the next Step-by-Step.
14. Switch to the Word window. Save the changes to the document and then close the document. Leave the Word application open.

Exporting Slide Information to a Word Outline

You have already seen how easily you can import information from a Word document into a PowerPoint presentation. You can just as easily export slide information to a Word document by converting the presentation information to an outline in Rich Text Format.

When you export PowerPoint data as an outline, the information appears in a new Word document with outline heading styles. Exported outlines contain no graphics, tables, or charts; the exported information includes only the slide text. In the Word document, you can modify the styles to reduce the font size and remove unnecessary font styles.

Step-by-Step 9.5

1. If necessary, open the **Revised Community Service 4.pptx** file. Save the presentation as **Revised Community Service 5**, followed by your initials.
2. Click the **File** tab, and then click **Save As** to open the Save as dialog box. If necessary, navigate to the drive and folder where you save your solution files.
3. In the File name text box, replace the existing text with **Community Service Outline**, followed by your initials.
4. Click the **Save as type** list arrow and select **Outline/RTF (*.rtf)**. Then click **Save**.
5. If necessary, launch Word. Open the **Community Service Outline.rtf** file from the drive and folder where you save your solution files. The outline document shows all the text content from the presentation slides. Note that many of the font colors are white, so the text doesn't show in the document.
6. Press **Ctrl+A** to select the entire document, and then change the font color to **Automatic** (black).
7. Note that the font sizes are quite large, because text on PowerPoint slides is formatted to appear much larger for easy reading. Press and hold **Ctrl**, and then press the left bracket key ([) about 20 times to shrink all the text by 20 points.
8. Scroll down through the document. Note that there are two levels of bulleted items.
9. Switch to Outline view. Note that there is no body text. All the content is formatted with a heading style.
10. Switch to Print Layout view.
11. Save the changes to the document and then exit Word.
12. Save the changes to the presentation and leave the presentation open for the next Step-by-Step.

Embedding Excel Worksheet Data in a Slide

If the data you need for a slide already exists in an Excel worksheet, you can import the information to the slide using the copy and paste, link, and embed options.

Copying and pasting information from Excel to a slide is very similar to copying and pasting information from a Word document, but there are some differences. When you copy worksheet data and use the default Paste command, the copied information is inserted on the slide as a table. To embed or link the data, you must use the Paste Special command. When the data is embedded, you can use Excel commands to edit the data. When the data is linked, changes to the data in the Excel application are automatically updated on the slide.

Step-by-Step 9.6

1. If necessary, open the **Revised Community Service 5.pptx** file, and when prompted, update the links. Save the presentation as **Revised Community Service 6**, followed by your initials.
2. Launch Excel. Open the **Donations.xlsx** file from the drive and folder where your Data Files are stored. Save the workbook as **Updated Donations**, followed by your initials.
3. Select the cell range **A1:E3** and copy the data to the Clipboard.
4. Switch to the PowerPoint window. Go to slide 4.
5. In the Clipboard group, click the **Paste** button. The worksheet data is imported in the slide in a table format. The table is quite small, and if you drag the table corner handles to enlarge the table, you'll need to adjust the font sizes and column widths. Click the **Undo** button on the Quick Access Toolbar to remove the table.
6. Right-click the Slide pane. In the shortcut menu, under Paste Options, click the **Embed** button. Because the slide background is black, the Excel data is not visible.
7. Double-click the table picture. The Ribbon changes to show Excel commands, and the worksheet data is now visible. The cell range A1:E3 is still selected.
8. On the Home tab, in the Font group, click the **Fill Color** button arrow and then select a dark orange color.
9. Click anywhere outside the Excel data to hide the Excel commands.
10. Drag the picture corner handles to enlarge the picture, and reposition the picture on the slide.
11. Switch to the Excel worksheet. Click cell **E3**, type **331**, and then press **Enter**. Save the changes and close the workbook. Leave Excel open.
12. Switch to the PowerPoint window. You cannot update the Excel data because no link was created. Double-click the picture to access the Excel commands.
13. Click cell **E3**, and then type **331**. Do not press Enter because that will create a new blank row. Instead, click outside the worksheet data to hide the Excel commands. The picture now reflects the new data for 2014.
14. Save the changes and leave the presentation open for the next Step-by-Step.

Linking an Excel Chart to a Slide

Linking chart data is similar to linking worksheet data. A linked chart appears on the slide surrounded by a border and selection handles. You can resize or move the chart on the slide the same way you would any other object. You also have access to most of the Chart Tools commands to modify the chart effects and elements, such as the chart title. The object on the slide maintains a link to the source document, but only changes to the chart data in the source document appear in the chart on the slide.

Step-by-Step 9.7

1. If necessary, open the **Revised Community Service 6.pptx** file, and when prompted, update the links. Save the presentation as **Revised Community Service 7**, followed by your initials.
2. If necessary, launch Excel. Open the **Participation.xlsx** file from the drive and folder where your Data Files are stored. Save the workbook as **Updated Participation**, followed by your initials.
3. Select the chart and copy it to the Clipboard.
4. Switch to the PowerPoint window. Go to slide 6, and then right-click the Slide pane. In the shortcut menu, under Paste Special, position the mouse pointer over each button to show a ScreenTip and a live preview of the pasted contents on the slide.
5. Click the **Use Destination Theme & Link Data** button. The chart is inserted on the slide and formatted for the current presentation design theme.
6. Enlarge and reposition the chart next to the bulleted list on the slide.
7. Select the legend *# employees* on the right and change the font size to **14** point.

8. Switch to the Excel window. Click cell **F3** and change the number to **42**.
9. Right-click the chart and, in the shortcut menu, click **Change Chart Type**. The Change Chart Type dialog box opens, as shown in **Figure 9–8**. In the right pane, under Line, click the fourth option **Line with Markers** and then click **OK**.

FIGURE 9–8
Change Chart Type dialog box

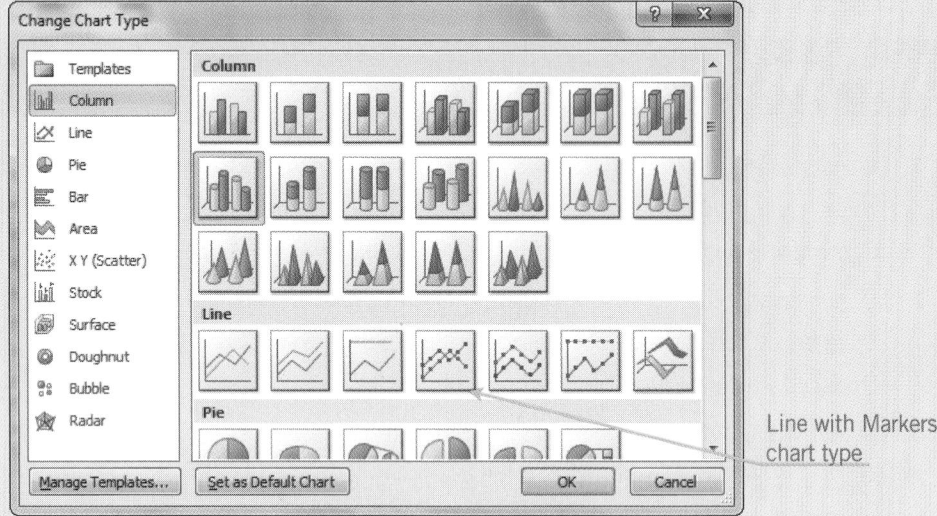

10. Save the changes to the worksheet and then exit Excel.
11. In the PowerPoint window, the data in the chart is already updated. The chart type did not change because only the underlying chart data is linked.
12. Save the changes to the presentation and leave the presentation open for the next Step-by-Step.

Copying Data from an Access Table

You cannot link or embed data from an Access table or form. However, you can copy the data and paste it into other Office applications. When copied data from an Access table is pasted onto a slide using the default Paste command, the data is formatted in a table. You can use the PowerPoint table commands to modify the table formats, reorder columns and rows, and arrange the table on the slide. When using the Paste Special command to paste copied data, you can choose to use the destination theme or keep the source formatting. You can also paste the copied data as text only.

Step-by-Step 9.8

1. If necessary, open the **Revised Community Service 7.pptx** file, and when prompted, update the links. Save the presentation as **Revised Community Service 8**, followed by your initials.
2. Insert a new slide at the end of the presentation using the Title Only layout. In the Title placeholder, type **PARTICIPATION IS GROWING!**.
3. Launch Access. Open the **Volunteer Participation.accdb** file from the drive and folder where your Data Files are stored.
4. In the left pane, if necessary, click any expand buttons to show all Access Objects, as shown in **Figure 9–9**. If necessary, click Enable Content in the yellow message bar.

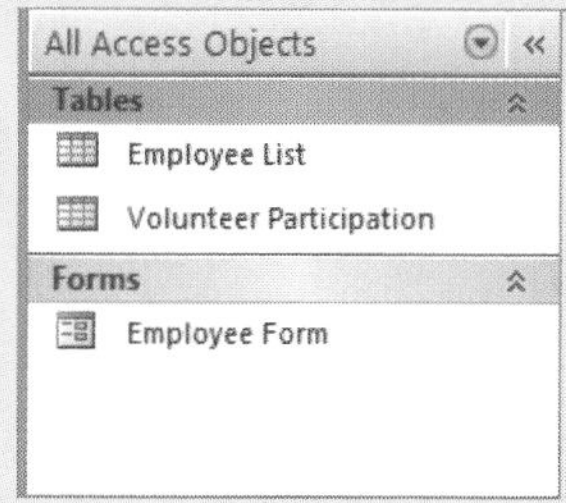

FIGURE 9–9
Access Objects pane

5. Under Tables, double-click **Volunteer Participation** to open the Volunteer Participation table.
6. The first cell in the Service column is selected. Press and hold **Shift**, and then click the last cell with data in the 2014 column (*65*). All the table data is selected. In the Clipboard group, click the **Copy** button.
7. Switch to the PowerPoint window. Go to slide 18. Right-click the slide and in the shortcut menu, under Paste Options, click **Use Destination Theme**. The copied data is inserted in a table, but because of the background colors, you cannot see the text.
8. Click the **Table Tools Design** tab. In the Table Styles group, click the **More** button and in the second row under Best Match for Document, select the **Themed Style 2 – Accent 2** style.
9. Select all the data in the table including the table title, and then use the Mini toolbar to change the font size to **24 point**.
10. Position the mouse pointer on the border between the *Service* and *2010* column headings. When the pointer changes to a double-headed arrow, double-click to AutoFit the column width for the contents. Then AutoFit each of the remaining five columns.
11. Position the insertion point anywhere within the row *County Park Cleanup*. Click the **Table Tools Layout** tab. In the Rows & Column group, click the **Insert Above** button. A new blank row is inserted in the table.

12. Select the last row in the table. Drag and drop the selected content to the new blank row. Then right-click the blank row at the bottom of the table, and in the shortcut menu, click **Delete Rows**.
13. On the Table Tools Layout tab, in the Arrange group, click the **Align** button and then click **Align Center**. Click the **Alig**n button again and then click **Align Middle**.
14. Save the changes and leave the presentation and the Access database open for the next Step-by-Step.

Saving a Slide as a Graphic File

Slides usually include graphics and design elements to draw attention and hold interest. You can save slides as individual graphic files, and then you can use the files to insert pictures in other applications.

Step-by-Step 9.9

1. If necessary, open the **Revised Community Service 8.pptx** file, and when prompted, update the links.
2. If necessary, launch Access and open the **Volunteer Participation.accdb** file from the drive and folder where your Data Files are stored. Save the database as **Revised Volunteer Participation**, followed by your initials.
3. In the PowerPoint window, select the first slide. Click the **File** tab, and then click **Save As**. Navigate to the drive and folder where you save your solution files.
4. In the File name text box, type **Title Slide**.
5. Click the **Save as type** list arrow, and then select **JPEG File Interchange Format (*.jpg)**. Click **Save**, and when prompted to export every slide or only the current slide, click **Current Slide Only**. (When you select the Every Slide option, each slide in the presentation is saved as an individual graphic slide.)
6. Switch to the Access window. If necessary, in the Objects pane, click the arrows to expand the list to show all objects.
7. Under Forms, double-click **Employee Form.** A form for entering employee data opens in the right pane, as shown in **Figure 9–10**.

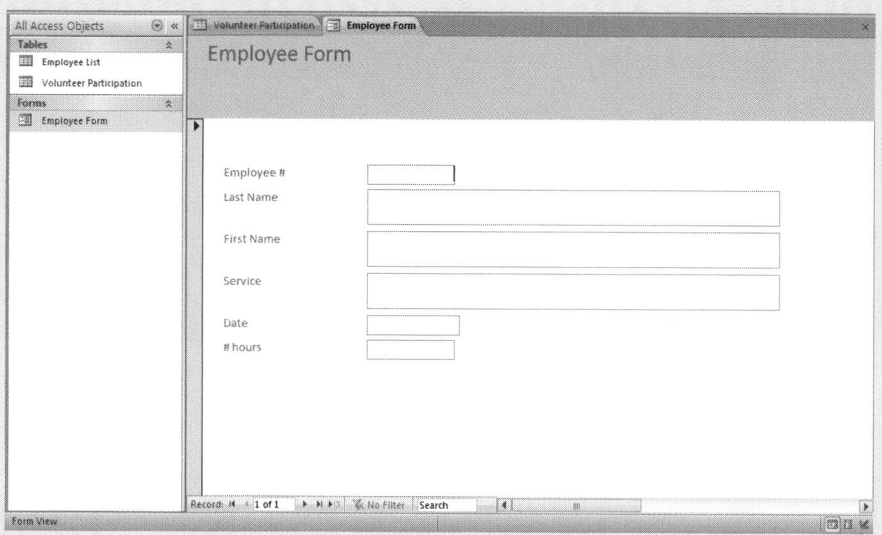

FIGURE 9–10
Employee Form

8. In the Views group, click the **View** button arrow and then click **Design View.**
9. If necessary, click the **Form Design Tools Design** tab. In the Controls group, click the **Insert Image** button. Click **Browse** and navigate to the drive and folder where you save your solution files.
10. Select the filename **Title Slide.jpg**, and then click **OK**. The mouse pointer changes to a crosshair with a picture icon. To the right of the form text boxes, drag the mouse pointer to create a shape to specify the image size, as shown in **Figure 9–11**.

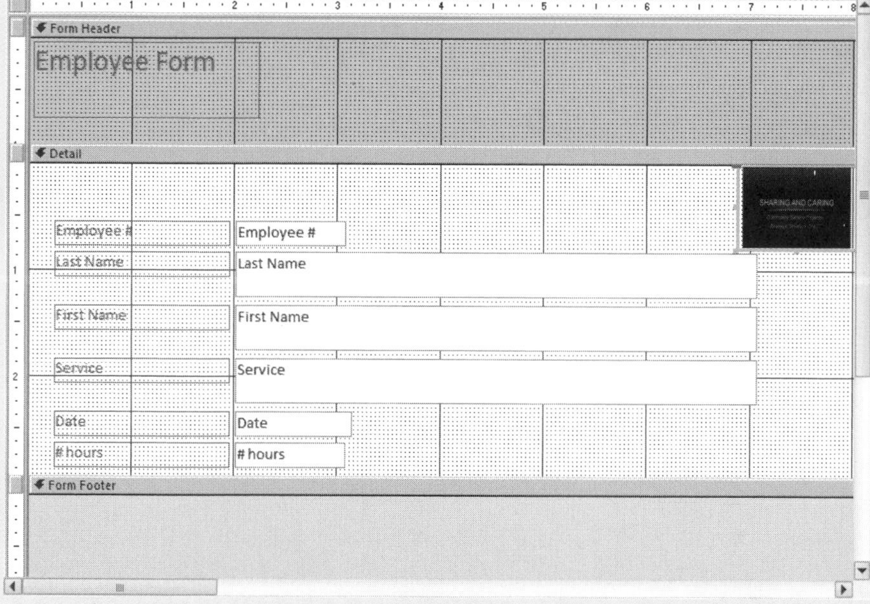

FIGURE 9–11
Inserted image in Design view

11. In the Views group, click the **View** button arrow and then click **Form View**. The slide picture now appears with the form.
12. Click the **Save** button on the Quick Access Toolbar to save the changes to the form. Then exit Access.
13. Close the presentation file without saving any changes.

SUMMARY

In this lesson, you learned:

- You can quickly access and reuse slides that have been created in another presentation.
- To share information among applications, you can copy and paste the information, link the data, embed the content, or convert the information to a different file format.
- When you paste a copied slide into Word or Excel, the copied slide is inserted as a picture.
- You can easily create slides from outlines already created in a Word document.
- When copying and pasting table data from Word into PowerPoint, there are several Paste Special options that enable you to control how the data on the slide can be edited.
- Content on slides can be exported to a Word document by converting the presentation content to a different file format.
- Excel worksheet data and charts can be copied and pasted onto slides with the options to link or embed the data. To embed or link the data, you must use the Paste Special command.
- Access table data can be copied and pasted onto slides, but the data cannot be linked or embedded.
- Slides can be saved as graphic files and then inserted as pictures in other applications.

VOCABULARY REVIEW

Define the following terms:

export
import
integration
slide library

REVIEW QUESTIONS

TRUE / FALSE

Circle T if the statement is true or F if the statement is false.

T F **1.** When a copied slide is pasted into a Word or Excel document, the slide is inserted as a picture.

T F **2.** When copying and pasting slides from one presentation to another, both presentations must be open.

T F **3.** When using the Reuse Slides command to import slides, you can only import one slide at a time.

T F **4.** An embedded document can be edited in the destination document.

T F **5.** A linked object on a PowerPoint slide is actually a picture of the object in the source application.

MULTIPLE CHOICE

Select the best response for the following statements.

1. To keep data current, when pasting copied table data you should choose to ______________ the data.

   A. copy and paste (default setting)

   B. link

   C. embed

   D. convert

2. An embedded object is stored in the ______________ document.
   A. source
   B. destination
   C. integrated
   D. exported
3. When importing slides from one presentation to another, ______________.
   A. the design template for the current presentation is applied to the imported slides by default
   B. you can choose to keep the source formatting of the imported slides
   C. you must reapply a design theme
   D. A and B
4. When Access table data is copied and pasted onto a slide, ______________.
   A. the copied data appears in a table on the slide
   B. the copied data is linked to the source file
   C. the copied data is embedded on the slide
   D. none of the above
5. When slide information is exported to a Word outline, ______________ are not included in the Word document.
   A. graphics
   B. tables
   C. charts
   D. all of the above

WRITTEN QUESTIONS

Write a brief answer to the following questions.

1. You use the Slides from Outline command to import information from a Word document to a presentation. What happens if none of the information in the Word document is formatted with heading styles?

2. When you change the chart type in the source document, why doesn't the change appear in the linked chart object?

3. What are the advantages to pasting copied data as a picture?

4. When presentation information is exported to an outline in a Word document, why are the font sizes so large?

5. What are the benefits of sharing information among applications?

PROJECTS

If you have a SAM 2010 user profile, your instructor may have assigned an autogradable version of the indicated project. If so, log into the SAM 2010 Web site at *www.cengage.com/sam2010* to download the instruction and start files.

PROJECT 9–1

1. Create a new blank presentation. Save the presentation as **Final Preserving Wetlands**, followed by your initials.
2. On the Title slide, in the title placeholder, type **Preserving Our Wetlands**. In the subtitle placeholder, type your first and last names.
3. Import slides from an outline created in Word. The **Wetlands Outline.docx** file is stored in the Data Files folder.
4. Apply a design theme. If desired, modify the slide master and layout masters and/or change the color scheme.
5. Reuse slides that were created in another presentation, the **Preserving Wetlands.pptx** file, which is stored in the Data Files folder. Reuse slides 7, 8, and 9, which all display charts and show the titles *Local Wetland Losses* and *Rate of Wetland Loss*. Position all three slides in the same sequence before the last slide in the presentation. Apply the destination formatting to the reused slides.
6. If necessary, modify the chart formats on the reused slides so that the data is clearly displayed.
7. Create a graphic file of slide 11. Save the file in JPEG format and name the file **Wetland Losses**, followed by your initials.
8. Save the changes and close the presentation.

SAM PROJECT 9–2

1. Open the **County Parks.pptx** file from the drive and folder where your Data Files are stored. Save the presentation as **Revised County Parks 1**, followed by your initials.
2. Launch Word and open the **Visitor Centers.docx** file from the drive and folder where your Data Files are stored. Copy the table and, in PowerPoint, paste it as a picture onto slide 6. Resize and reposition the table and modify the picture colors so the information fits well in the design theme and can be read easily. In Word, close the document without saving changes.
3. Launch Excel and open the **Park Visitors.xlsx** file from the drive and folder where your Data Files are stored. Save the worksheet as **Revised Park Visitors**, followed by your initials. Select and copy the worksheet data (*range A1:E9*) and then, in PowerPoint, link the data to slide 4. Resize and reposition the picture of the table to fill the blank area on the slide. If necessary, modify the picture colors. Leave the worksheet open.
4. Switch to Excel and, in the worksheet, click cell **E9** and type **1590**. Save the changes, and then confirm that the edit is updated in the presentation file. Leave the worksheet open.
5. In Excel, select and copy the chart in the worksheet. In PowerPoint, embed the chart on slide 5, using the destination theme. Resize and reposition the chart to fill the blank area on the slide. If necessary, modify the chart fonts so the legend and axis titles are easy to read. Exit Excel, saving any changes to the worksheet.
6. Save the changes to the presentation. Then save the slide information as an outline in Rich Text Format. Name the new file **County Parks Outline**, followed by your initials.
7. In Word, open the outline file **County Parks Outline**. If necessary, change the font color for all the text. Change the font size and paragraph alignments. Save the changes to the document and exit Word.
8. Leave the presentation open for the next Project.

PROJECT 9–3

1. If necessary, open the **Revised County Parks 1** file from the folder where you save your solution files and save the presentation as **Revised County Parks 2**, followed by your initials.
2. Launch Access and open the **Popular County Parks.accdb** file from the drive and folder where your Data Files are stored. Open the Park Information table.
3. Select all the table data except the ID values, and do not include the bottom blank row in the selection. Then copy the selected data to the Clipboard.
4. Switch to PowerPoint and paste the copied data as a table on slide 3, using the destination theme. Increase the font sizes and resize and reposition the table in the blank area on the slide. AutoFit each of the column widths in the table, and make any other adjustments so the table data is easy to read.
5. Exit Access without saving any changes to the database.
6. Save the changes to the presentation and then exit PowerPoint.

CRITICAL THINKING

ACTIVITY 9–1

When copying and pasting a table from a Word document to a slide, one of the Paste Special options is to Keep Text Only. Practice using this paste option to view the results. Write a brief paragraph explaining why you would or would not use this option to paste table data on a slide.

ACTIVITY 9–2

In this lesson, you learned several ways to integrate content between applications. Refer to **Table 9–1** and describe a scenario for using each of the four integration options. For example, you would use the copy and paste option to copy a URL in a Works Cited Page at the end of a report and then paste the information on a slide so that you can create a hyperlink on the slide.

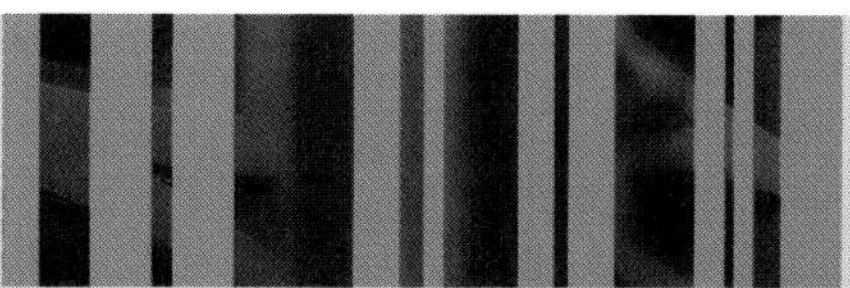

Estimated Time: 1.5 hours

LESSON 10

Sharing and Delivering Presentations

■ OBJECTIVES

Upon completion of this lesson, you should be able to:

- Add, edit, and delete comments.
- Compare and combine presentations.
- Rehearse timings and record narrations.
- Save and send presentations.
- Protect presentations and attach a digital signature.
- Annotate slides during the presentation.
- Set up a self-running slide show.
- Broadcast presentations.

■ VOCABULARY

broadcasting
case sensitive
comment
digital signature
document workspace site
encryption
kiosk
markup
Portable Document Format (PDF)
PowerPoint Viewer
XML Paper Specification (XPS)

The content and format of the slides for your presentation are almost completed. You are now ready to make some final edits and then explore options for sharing and delivering the presentation. In this lesson, you will learn about the final preparations before distributing a presentation and features you can use when delivering the presentation.

Collaborating on a Presentation

Team members commonly collaborate on creating a presentation. Often a presentation is reviewed by several individuals before the final version is completed. As team members review the presentation, they edit the content, add new content, change formats, and share their thoughts. PowerPoint offers several features for providing feedback and comparing changes.

Editing Slide Content

When you think about editing slide content, you probably first think about editing the words in the text boxes. You can, of course, also edit the text box formats. In the next Step-by-Step, you will apply colors to both text and text box borders and shape effects to enhance the appearance of the slides. You will also apply column and indentation formats to customize the text layout. You can personalize the edits you make by setting your own user name and initials in the PowerPoint Options dialog box. This helps reviewers to identify who made the changes in the presentation.

Step-by-Step 10.1

1. Open the **Festival** file from the drive and folder where your Data Files are stored.
2. Click the **File** tab, and then click **Options** to open the PowerPoint Options dialog box, as shown in **Figure 10–1**. Your settings will differ. Under Personalize your copy of Microsoft Office, make note of the User name and Initials text boxes. Then, if necessary, input your first and last name and your initials. Click **OK**.

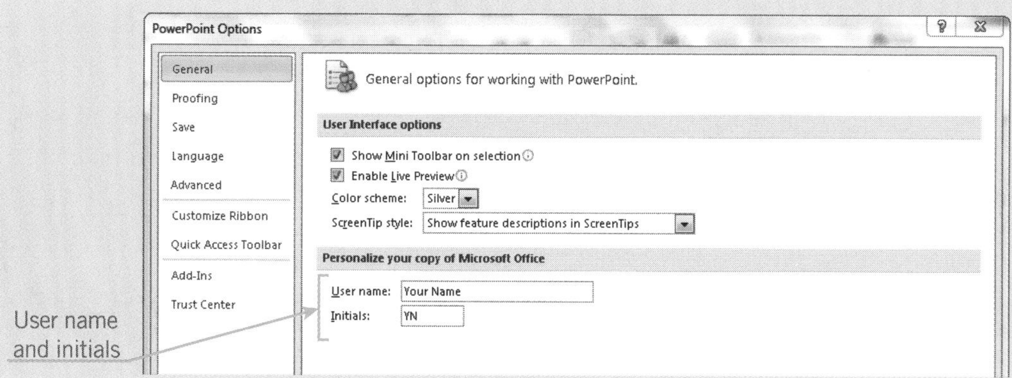

FIGURE 10–1 PowerPoint Options dialog box

3. Save the presentation as **Revised Festival 1**, followed by your initials.
4. Go to slide 7. Click anywhere in the paragraph to select the text box. On the Home tab in the Paragraph group, click the **Columns** button and then click **More Columns**. In the Number box, change the setting to **2**. In the Spacing box, if necessary, set the spacing at **0.5"**. Click **OK**. In the Paragraph group, click the **Justify** button.
5. The text box should still be selected. Format the text box shape fill and outline:
   a. Click the **Drawing Tools Format** tab. In the Shape Styles group, click the **Shape Fill** button arrow. In the submenu, click the **Red, Text 2, Darker 50%** theme color.
   b. In the Shape Styles group, click the **Shape Outline** button arrow. Point to **Weight**. In the submenu, click **More Lines**. The Format Shape dialog box opens.
   c. Under Line Style, in the Width box, enter the setting **6 pt**.
   d. Click the **Compound type** button arrow, and then select the third option, **Thick Thin**.
   e. In the left column, click **Line Color**. Then in the right column, click the **Color** list arrow. In the submenu, click the **Gray-50%, Accent 1** theme color.
   f. Close the Format Shape dialog box.
6. Triple-click the paragraph to select the entire paragraph. Click the **Home** tab. In the Font group, click the **Font Color** button arrow and then click the **White, Background 1** theme color.
7. Click the **Drawing Tools Format** tab, and in the Shape Styles group, click the **Shape Effects** button. Point to **Bevel**, and in the submenu under Bevel, click the first option, **Circle**.

8. Go to slide 2. Select all the paragraphs in the bulleted list. In the Paragraph group, click the **Dialog Box Launcher** to open the Paragraph dialog box.
9. Under Indentation, change the Before text setting to **.8** and then click **OK**. The bulleted items shift to the right.
10. Click the **Undo** button to restore the bulleted list to the default setting.
11. Go to slide 4. Insert a clip art image of a king or a crown. After inserting the clip art image, close the Clip Art pane. Resize, reposition, and recolor the image as needed.
12. Save the changes and leave the presentation open for the next Step-by-Step. (If you are ending your PowerPoint session, click the File tab and then click Options. Restore the user name and initials to the settings you noted in Step 2 above.)

Adding, Editing, and Deleting Comments

VOCABULARY
comment
markup

A ***comment*** is an annotation that is added within a document by the author or reviewer. Comments provide an easy way to share ideas and suggestions without changing the content of the presentation. PowerPoint automatically assigns numbers to comments as they are inserted in the presentation, and initials for the commenter's user name are included. The numbers are sequential, regardless of the user name. By default, comments appear in the upper-left corner of the slide, but you can drag and drop the comment icons to reposition them. You can easily navigate the comments by using the Previous Comment and Next Comment buttons, and you can delete one or all of the comments.

Comments inserted on slides are often referred to as ***markup***. Markup appears in Normal view, but it doesn't appear in Slide Show view. You can specify whether or not to include markup when you print slides or handouts. If you don't want the markup to appear as you work with slides in Normal view, you can toggle the feature off.

Step-by-Step 10.2

1. If necessary, open the **Revised Festival 1** file from your solution files. Save the presentation as **Revised Festival 2**, followed by your initials.
2. Go to slide 2. Click the **Review** tab. In the Comments group, click the **New Comment** button. A text box showing your user name and the current date appears in the upper-left corner of the slide. To the left of the text box is an icon showing your initials and the number 1. See **Figure 10–2**.

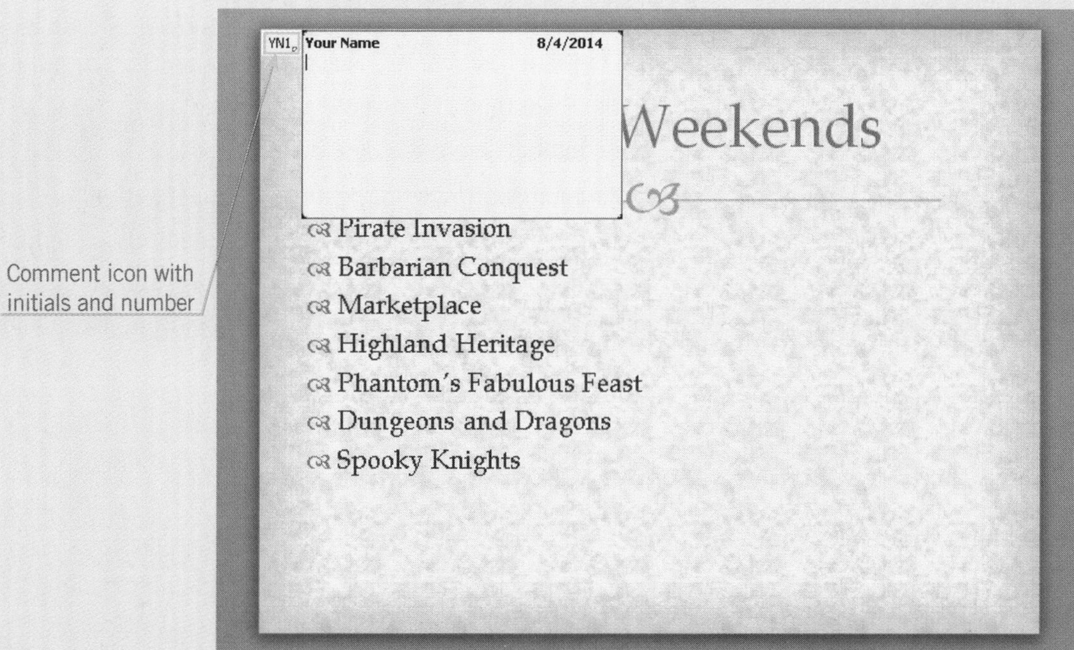

FIGURE 10–2 New comment text box

3. With the insertion point positioned in the comment text box, type **Add the dates for each of these themes.**. Click anywhere in the Slide pane outside the comment box, to collapse the text box. The comment icon still appears in the upper-left corner.
4. Double-click the **comment icon** to reopen the comment text box. (When you click the icon only once, the comment text appears, but you cannot edit the content.) Position the insertion point in front of the word *dates*, type **scheduled**, and then press the **spacebar**. The revised sentence should now read *Add the scheduled dates for each of these themes.*.
5. Click outside the comment text box to collapse it so that only the icon appears. In the Comments group, click the **Show Markup** button to toggle the Show Markup feature off. The comment icon no longer appears on the slide.
6. Go to slide 4. Click the **New Comment** button. The Show Markup feature is automatically toggled back on. Note that the comment box is labeled with your initials and the number 2. In the comment text box, type **Insert a photo of the Queen's Kitchen.**. Then click outside the text box to collapse it.
7. In the Comments group, click the **Previous Comment** button. The Comment 1 text box on slide 2 opens. Click the **New Comment** button. A new icon with the number 3 and a new text box overlays Comment 1. Although a new comment is inserted between Comments 1 and 2, the comment numbers are not adjusted. Type **Need to confirm that these theme titles are accurate.**. Collapse the comment text box.

TIP

You can also edit a comment by right-clicking the comment icon and then clicking Edit Comment in the shortcut menu.

8. Select the **Comment 1** icon, and then drag it to the bottom of the slide and position it in the lower-left corner. Leave the number 3 comment at the top of the slide. Even though the sequence of the comments on the slide changes, the numbers are not adjusted.
9. Click the **Next Comment** button to navigate to Comment 3 at the top of the slide. Even though the comment numbers are not in sequential order on the slides, the next comment is the number 3 comment on this same slide. Click the **Next Comment** button again to move to Comment 2 on slide 4.
10. Click the **Previous Comment** button twice to navigate to Comment 1 on slide 2. In the Comments group, click the **Delete Comment** button arrow and then click **Delete**. The comment is removed from the slide. However, the comment at the top of the slide still shows the number 3. When you delete a comment, the numbers of the remaining comments are not updated.
11. Click the **File** tab and then click **Print**. If you print the slides in a presentation, the comment icons will appear on the slides, as shown in **Figure 10–3**.

TIP

To delete a comment, you can also right-click the comment icon and then click Delete Comment in the shortcut menu.

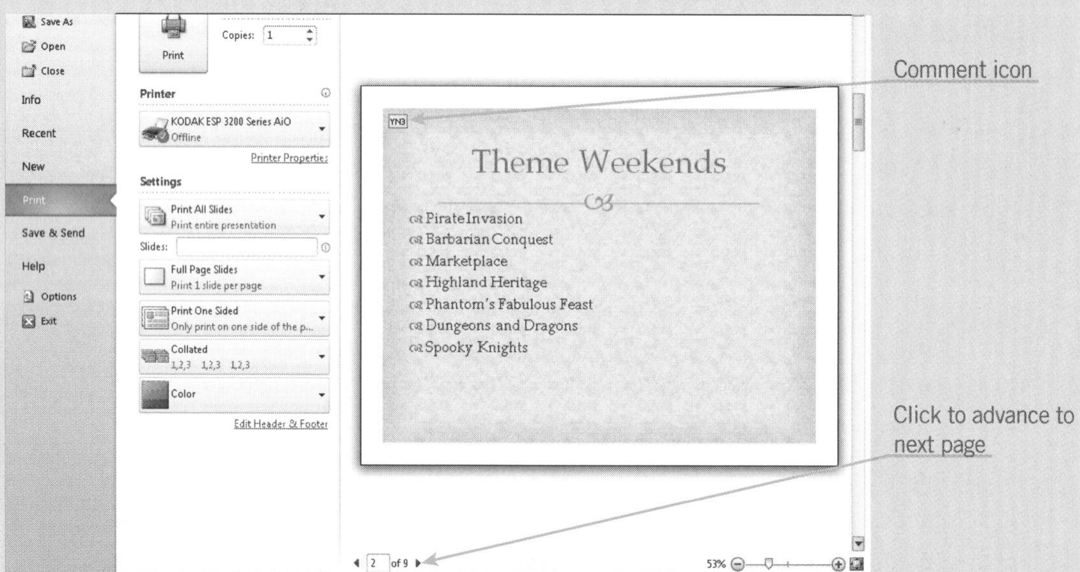

FIGURE 10–3 Print preview of a slide with a comment

12. In the preview pane, click the **Next Page** button. The comment text will print on a separate page, as shown in **Figure 10–4**. Advance to page 6 to view the comment for slide 4. Under Settings, click **Full Page Slides** to view the Print Layout settings. Disable the **Print Comments and Ink Markup** option. The comments no longer show in the preview pane.

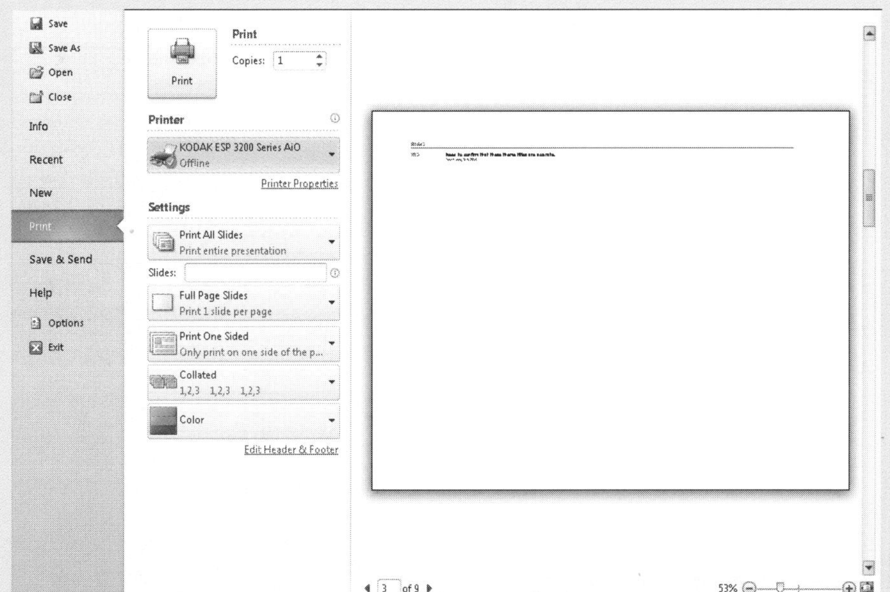

FIGURE 10–4
Print preview of comment text with a reference to slide number

13. Click the **Review** tab. In the Comments group, click the **Delete** button arrow and then click **Delete All Markup in this Presentation**. When prompted to delete all comments and ink annotations, click **Yes**.
14. Save the changes and leave the presentation open for the next Step-by-Step. (If you are ending your PowerPoint session, click the File tab and then click Options. Restore the user name and initials to the settings you noted earlier in Step-by-Step 10.1, Step 2, and then click OK.)

Comparing and Combining Presentations

To compare different versions of presentations, you can arrange slides on the screen to view more than one presentation at a time. Another option is to merge two presentations to compare the content. Once combined, differences between the two presentations are listed in the Reviewing pane. Differences can include inserted or deleted slides and new text, graphics, and formats. The user name associated with the saved presentation is shown, and you can choose which version of content you want to keep in the merged document.

Step-by-Step 10.3

1. If necessary, open the **Revised Festival 2** file from your solution files. Save the presentation as **Revised Festival 3**, followed by your initials. Then open the **Festival Reviewer A** file from the drive and folder where your Data Files are stored.
2. Click the **View** tab. In the Window group, click the **Cascade Windows** button. The windows are stacked.

3. In the Window group, click the **Arrange All** button to view the presentations side by side. As you scroll through the slides in each window and compare the two presentations, you'll find that it can be difficult to identify the differences. It is easier to compare the content using the Compare feature. Close the Festival Reviewer A window, and then maximize the Revised Festival 3 window.

4. Click the **Review** tab. In the Compare group, click the **Compare** button. If necessary, navigate to the drive and folder where your solution files are stored. Select the filename **Festival Reviewer A** and then click **Merge**. The Reviewing pane opens, as shown in **Figure 10–5**. Note that the Reviewing pane displays two sections on the Details tab: Slide changes and Presentation changes.

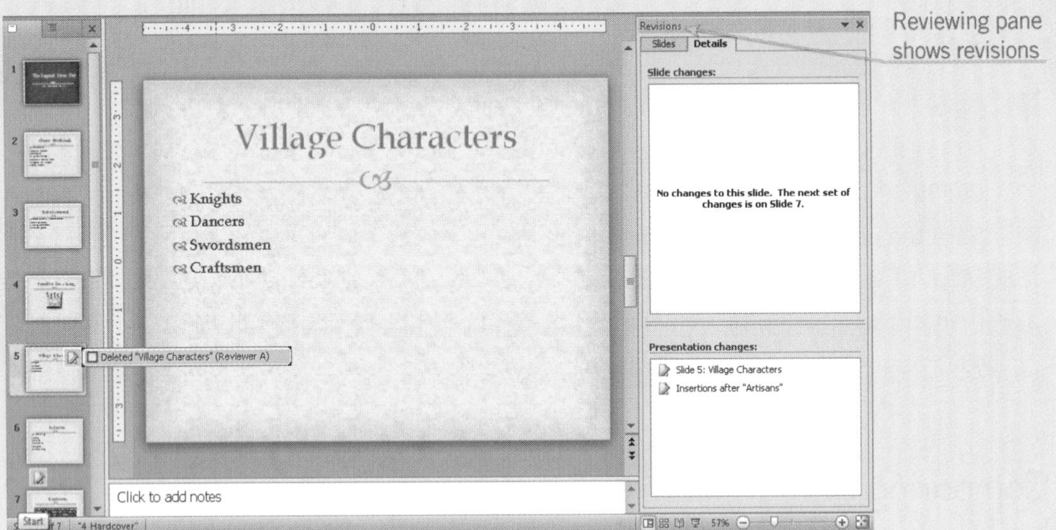

FIGURE 10–5 Reviewing pane for a merged presentation

5. On the Slides tab on the left, click the **slide 2** thumbnail. In the Reviewing pane on the right, under Slide changes, click **Content Placeholder 2: Pirate Invasion Ba....** A markup summary ScreenTip appears to the right of the content placeholder in the slide window indicating that the Reviewer A presentation includes *Oktoberfest*. See **Figure 10–6**.

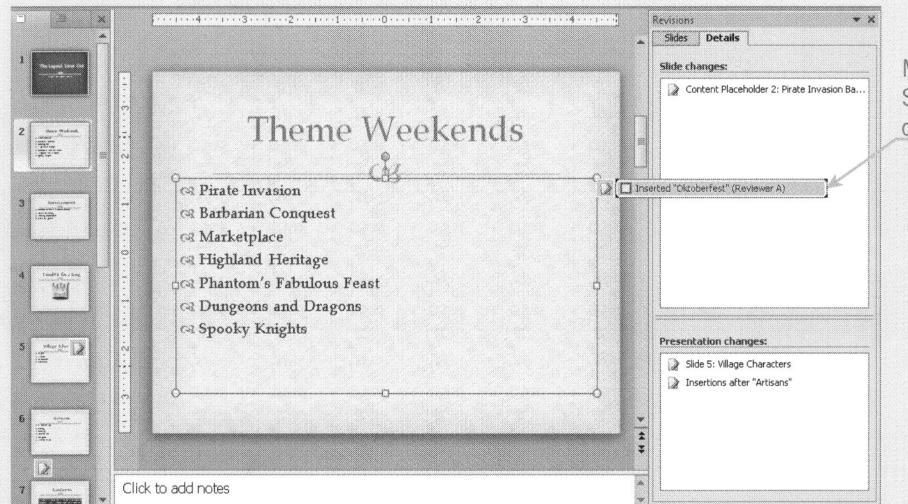

FIGURE 10–6 Markup indicating text inserted in the Reviewer A presentation

6. In the Reviewing pane, click the **Slides** tab to view the Theme Weekends slide as it appears in the Reviewer A presentation. See **Figure 10–7**. Click the blue check box above the slide thumbnail to accept all changes by Reviewer A. The bulleted item *Oktoberfest* is added to the list in the placeholder in the slide window.

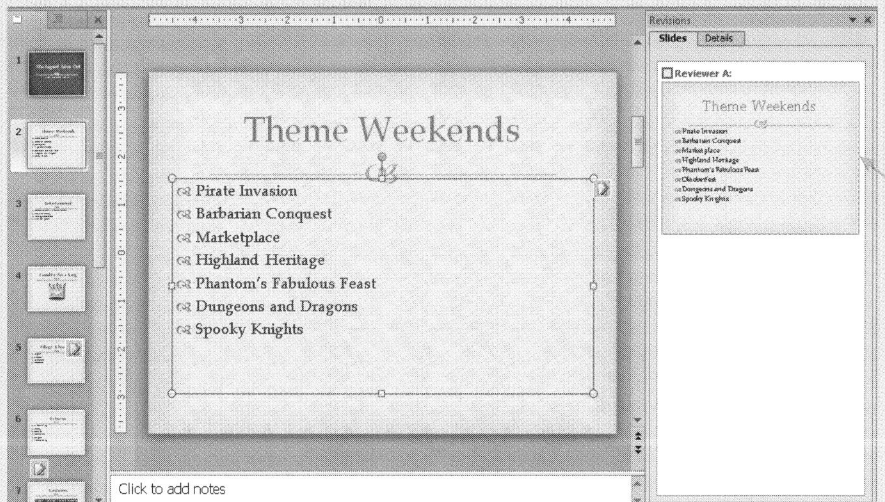

FIGURE 10–7 A thumbnail of the slide in the Reviewer A presentation

7. On the Slides tab on the left, click the **slide 4** thumbnail. In the Reviewing pane on the right, click the **Details** tab. Under Slide changes, click **Picture 2**. A markup summary ScreenTip to the right of the content placeholder in the Slide pane indicates that the Reviewer A presentation shows the canvas contents (in other words, the content holder is blank). Click anywhere in the slide window to collapse the markup without making any changes. The clip art you inserted on the slide will remain.

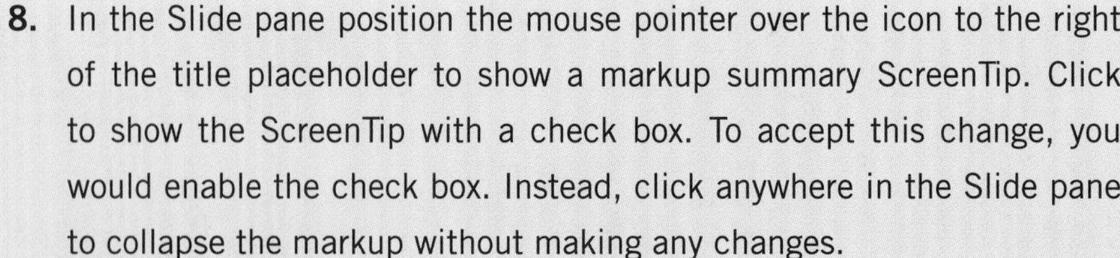

8. In the Slide pane position the mouse pointer over the icon to the right of the title placeholder to show a markup summary ScreenTip. Click to show the ScreenTip with a check box. To accept this change, you would enable the check box. Instead, click anywhere in the Slide pane to collapse the markup without making any changes.

9. In the Reviewing pane, under Presentation changes, click **Slide 5: Village Characters**. A markup summary ScreenTip appears next to the slide 5 thumbnail on the Slides tab, as shown in **Figure 10–8**. The markup indicates that the slide was deleted in the Reviewer A presentation. Click the blue check box on the markup summary ScreenTip to accept the change. Slide 5 is removed from the merged presentation.

TIP

You can also accept and reject changes by clicking the Accept Change and Reject Change buttons in the Compare group on the Review tab.

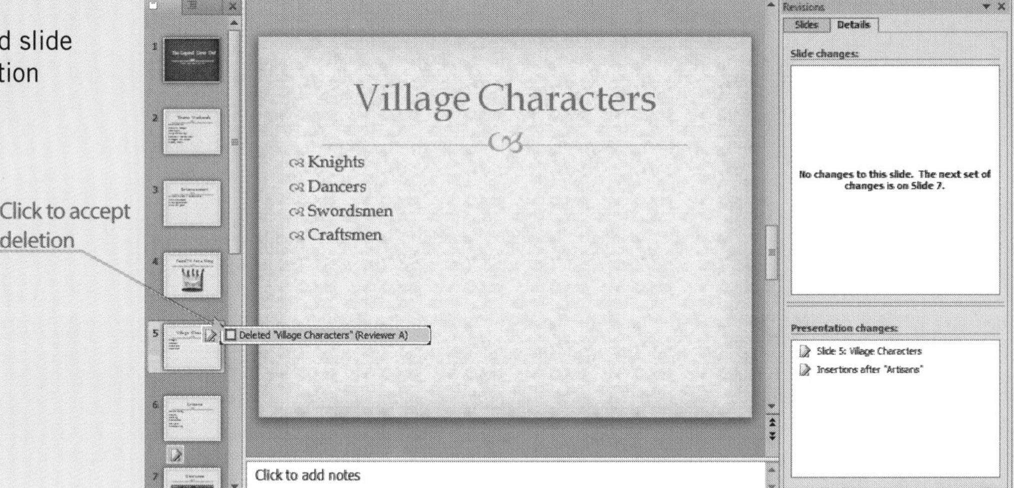

FIGURE 10–8
Markup indicating a deleted slide in the Reviewer A presentation

10. On the Slides tab, click the icon between the slide 5 and slide 6 thumbnails. The markup indicates that a slide with the title *Competitions* was inserted in the Reviewer A presentation. Click the blue check box to accept the change and add the new slide to the merged presentation. Note that a new thumbnail for slide 6 now shows an icon with a check mark. The ScreenTip for the icon indicates that the new slide from Reviewer A was added to the presentation.

11. Go to slide 7. Click the icon to the right of the content placeholder in the Slide pane. A list of several differences is displayed, as shown in **Figure 10–9**. Click the check box at the top of the list to accept all the differences as they appear in the Reviewer A document. Note that all the text box formats you applied are now removed. Uncheck the top check box to restore the text box settings.

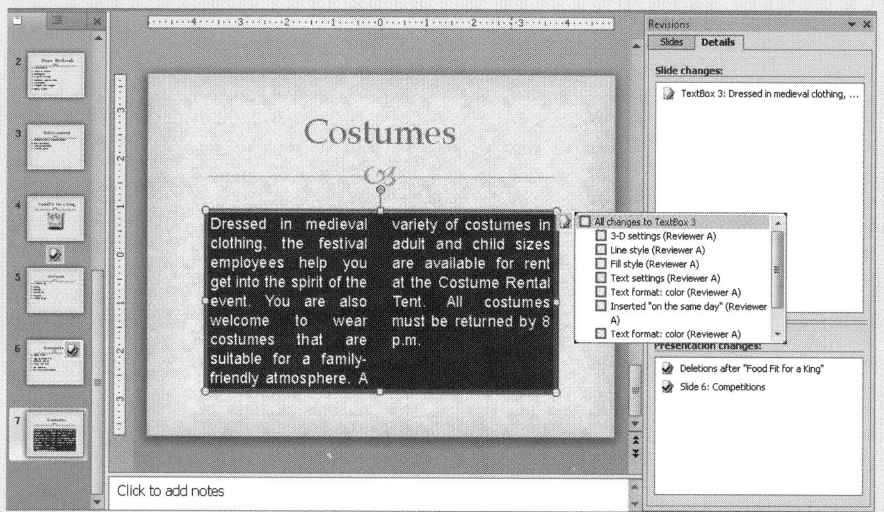

FIGURE 10–9
List of differences on slide 7

12. In the list, enable the change **Inserted "on the same day" (Reviewer A)**. Then click anywhere in the Slide pane to collapse the markup summary. Select the text in the text box and format the font color **White, Background 1**.
13. Close the Reviewing pane. Click the **Review** tab. In the Compare group, click the **End Review** button. When prompted to end the review for the current document, click **Yes**. All markup is removed from the presentation.
14. Click the **File** tab, and then click **Options**. Restore the user name and initials to the settings you noted earlier in Step-by-Step 10.1, Step 2. Click **OK**. Save the changes and leave the presentation open for the next Step-by-Step.

Coauthoring Presentations

Word features enable multiple users to work on the same presentation at the same time. You can upload presentations to a ***document workspace site***, which is a Web site that provides a central location for storing and sharing files. Files are stored in a library and can be password protected so that users must know the password to gain access or to open folders or files.

VOCABULARY
document workspace site

Microsoft SharePoint provides a document workspace site that enables a business to customize file storage and handling to suit its needs. Files can be stored and updated, file status information is provided, and employees can access the files remotely, enabling team members to collaborate and work together in real time. You need authorization to publish or access files at a SharePoint site, so introducing and showing SharePoint features is beyond the scope of this lesson.

Microsoft also offers SkyDrive, a free Windows Live service that provides password-protected online storage. You can assign passwords to control who has access to your files. To access SkyDrive, you must have a Windows Live account. If you use Hotmail, Live Messenger, or Xbox LIVE, you already have a Windows Live ID. If not, it only takes a minute to sign up. The following Step-by-Step will guide you in setting up a personal SkyDrive account.

Step-by-Step 10.3

1. If necessary, open the **Revised Festival 3** file from your solution files. Save the presentation as **Revised Festival 4**, followed by your initials.
2. Click the **File** tab, and then click **Save & Send**. In the center pane, click **Save to Web**.
3. If you have a Windows Live ID, click the **Sign In** button, enter your ID (e-mail address) and password, and then click **OK**. (If you do not have an account, click the link to sign up for Windows Live and follow the directions to create a new account.)
4. If necessary, under Personal Folders, click the **My Documents** folder to select it. Then click the **Save As** button. The Save As dialog box opens. There may be a slight delay before the dialog box opens. Note that the path where the file will be stored shows a Windows Live network address.
5. You do not need to change the filename, so leave everything as is and click **Save**.
6. Close the Revised Festival 4 document. The document has been uploaded to the server.
7. Using your browser, go to **www.windowslive.com**. If necessary, sign in. Click **Office**, and if necessary, open the Your documents folder and the My Documents folder, and then click the **Revised Festival 4** file. The presentation will open in the PowerPoint Web App. You will see options to open the file in PowerPoint, edit the file in your browser, share the file, and start the slide show.
8. If you want full access to the PowerPoint features to edit the presentation, you can open the presentation in PowerPoint. Above the slide window, click the option **Open in PowerPoint**. If a prompt appears asking if you trust the source, click **OK**. The presentation will open in PowerPoint on your computer. When prompted to enter your Windows Live ID credentials, type your password and click **OK**. Close the presentation.
9. Return to your browser, and if necessary, sign back into your Windows Live account. View your online files and open the **My Documents** folder. Point to the **Revised Festival 4.pptx** file, and then click the **Delete** button. When prompted, click **OK** to confirm the deletion.
10. In your browser, click **sign out** in the upper-right corner to sign out of Windows Live. Close your browser.

EXTRA FOR EXPERTS

When you click Edit in Browser, some of the Ribbon commands appear in the Web App and you can make common edits such as adding and deleting slides and changing font and paragraph formats. The file is saved automatically in the default folder on your computer.

Rehearsing Timings and Recording Narrations

If you have set automatic slide timings, you can use the Rehearse Timings button to find out if you have allowed enough time for each slide. This feature is also beneficial if you want to know how long it might take a person to go through the show slide by slide. When you choose Rehearse Timings on the Slide Show menu, the presentation immediately starts running. A toolbar containing a stopwatch box appears on the screen to show how much time you have spent viewing each slide and the presentation as a whole. After you have finished the presentation, PowerPoint reports how long it took you to progress through all the slides and prompts you to choose to use your rehearsal timings the next time you view the slides.

If your computer has a microphone, you can record narrations for your presentation. This is a useful option for a slide show that runs automatically on the Web. After selecting settings for recording narrations, PowerPoint starts the slide show. A narration is saved for each slide, and you can also save the slide timings to fit the narrations. If you have already rehearsed timings and saved them for the slides in the presentation, you can choose to save the new timings that are required for the recorded narrations. You do not need to record a narration for every slide. You can start recording narrations from the beginning of a slide show, or you can start recording from the current slide. Each slide that contains a narration displays a sound object in the lower-right corner. Voice narration takes precedence over any other kind of sound on your slides. If you have recorded narration, you will not hear other sounds you have inserted.

Step-by-Step 10.4

To complete Steps 9–13, you must have a microphone and a sound card installed in your computer.

1. Open the **Revised Festival 4** file from your solution files.
2. Click the **Slide Show** tab. In the Set Up group, click the **Rehearse Timings** button. The presentation opens in Slide Show view. The Recording toolbar, shown in **Figure 10–10**, appears in the upper-left corner of the screen.

FIGURE 10–10
Recording toolbar

3. Click the **Pause** button on the Recording toolbar to stop the clock. The dialog box shown in **Figure 10–11** appears.

FIGURE 10–11
Dialog box indicating recording is paused

4. Click **Resume Recording**, and then click the slide (or press Page Down or the down arrow key) to advance to the next slide. Wait at least four or five seconds for each slide, and then advance to the next slide. When you click the last slide, a prompt will appear asking if you want to keep the slide timings. Click **Yes**.
5. If necessary, switch to Slide Sorter view. The timings for each slide are displayed below the lower-left corner of each slide thumbnail.
6. Click the **slide 7** thumbnail. Click the **Transitions** tab. In the Timing group, under Advance Slide, change the setting in the After box to **00:15.00**. This will add more time to view slide 7.
7. Click the **Slide Show** tab. In the Start Slide Show group, click the **From Beginning** button. The slides will automatically advance based on the timings you rehearsed as well as the one timing you edited. When the slide show ends, click to exit Slide Show view.
8. Save the changes.
9. Go to slide 2. On the Slide Show tab, in the Set Up group, click the **Record Slide Show** button arrow and then click **Start Recording from Current Slide**. The Record Slide Show dialog box opens.
10. Make sure both options are enabled, as shown in **Figure 10–12**. By enabling the Slide and animation timings option, the rehearsed timings in the earlier steps will be replaced with the new timings needed for the recorded narrations.

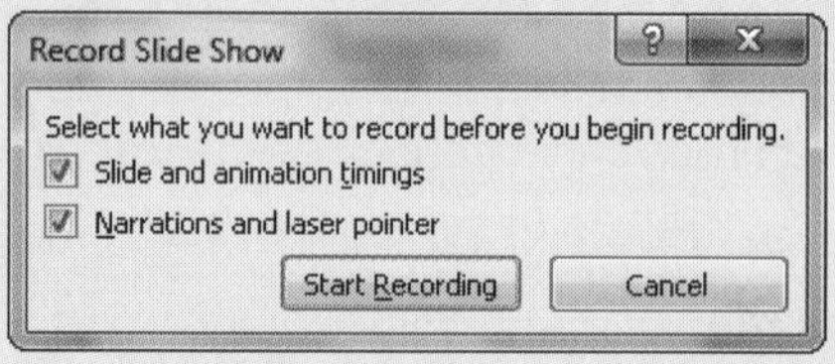

FIGURE 10–12
Record Slide Show dialog box

11. Click **Start Recording**. The Recording toolbar will appear in the upper-left corner. Start talking about the content on the slide. Say the following: "As you can see, there are several upcoming adventures. Special events are planned for each theme."
12. Wait a second or two, and then press the **down arrow** to advance to the next slide. Say the following: "Each weekend there are a variety of shows and activities that provide opportunities for people of all ages to learn and have fun." Press **Esc** to stop recording, and then switch to Slide Sorter view.

13. Note that the timing for slides 1, 4, 5, 6, and 7 did not change. Also note that there is an audio icon in the lower-right corner of slides 2 and 3. Start the slide show from the beginning. Allow the slides to advance automatically, and listen to the recordings for slides 2 and 3. (If you are not satisfied with the recording, you can delete the audio icon on the slide and re-record the narration.)
14. Save the changes and leave the presentation open for the next Step-by-Step.

Preparing Presentations for Distribution

After finalizing the presentation content, the next step is to prepare the presentation for distribution. PowerPoint provides several options for saving presentation files to share with others. Before distributing the files, you should consider protecting them so others cannot edit the content. Also, before distributing presentation files, you may want to verify your identity and confirm that the information in the file is valid.

Saving and Sending Presentations

To distribute presentation files, you can send the file via e-mail or in a fax message. Obviously, to send the file via e-mail, you must have a network or Internet connection, and you must have sufficient bandwidth (the speed of data transfer) for transferring the file. Publishing to a slide library or to a SharePoint site is another alternative so that others can access the slides.

Not all users have access to the PowerPoint application. If your audience only needs access to the presentation content, you can save the files in other formats. The ***Portable Document Format (PDF)*** was created by Adobe Systems in 1993. Microsoft first offered the ***XML Paper Specification (XPS)*** format in Office 2007. Both the PDF and XPS document formats are designed to preserve the visual appearance and layout of each page and enable fast viewing and printing.

VOCABULARY

Portable Document Format (PDF)

XML Paper Specification (XPS)

Table 10–1 lists some of the presentation file types and describes the benefits of using each file type.

TABLE 10–1 Presentation file types

PRESENTATION FILE TYPE	BENEFITS OF USE
Presentation (*.pptx)	This is the default PowerPoint 2010 presentation format; the file can be opened in PowerPoint 2007 and 2010.
PDF Document Format (*.pdf)	Preserves the document formatting and enables file sharing when users have the Adobe software that enables editing.
XPS Document Format (*.xps)	Preserves the document formatting in a final form.
OpenDocument Presentation (*.odp)	Files can be opened in presentation applications that use the OpenDocument format, which makes it possible to share and collaborate on documents across multiple systems and multiple platforms; formatting might be lost.
PowerPoint Show (*.ppsx)	Saves time because the file automatically opens in Slide Show view. To quickly access the file when giving a presentation, save the file to the Desktop.
PowerPoint 97-2003 Presentation (*.ppt)	The file can be opened using previous software versions from PowerPoint 97 to Office PowerPoint 2003.
Template (*.potx)	Use to format future presentations.
PowerPoint Picture Presentation (*.pptx)	Each slide is converted to a picture; the file size is reduced, and some information may be lost, such as narrations and audio. When you open the file, you will not be able to edit the content.
PNG Portable Network Graphics (*.png)	Prints quality image files of each slide.
JPEG File Interchange Format (*.jpg)	Produces Web-quality image files of each slide.

By default, presentations are created for on-screen viewing. This means that the slides you see on your screen have been sized to fit the proportions of a monitor screen. However, PowerPoint gives you a number of other standard slide sizes from which to choose, or you can set a custom size. You can also adjust the slide layout and change the page setup and orientation to fit other formats, such as the 16:9 aspect ratio of the widescreen format.

Step-by-Step 10.5

1. If necessary, open the **Revised Festival 4** file from your solution files.
2. Click the **File** tab, and then click **Save & Send**. The options for sending a presentation via e-mail appear in the right pane, as shown in **Figure 10–13**.

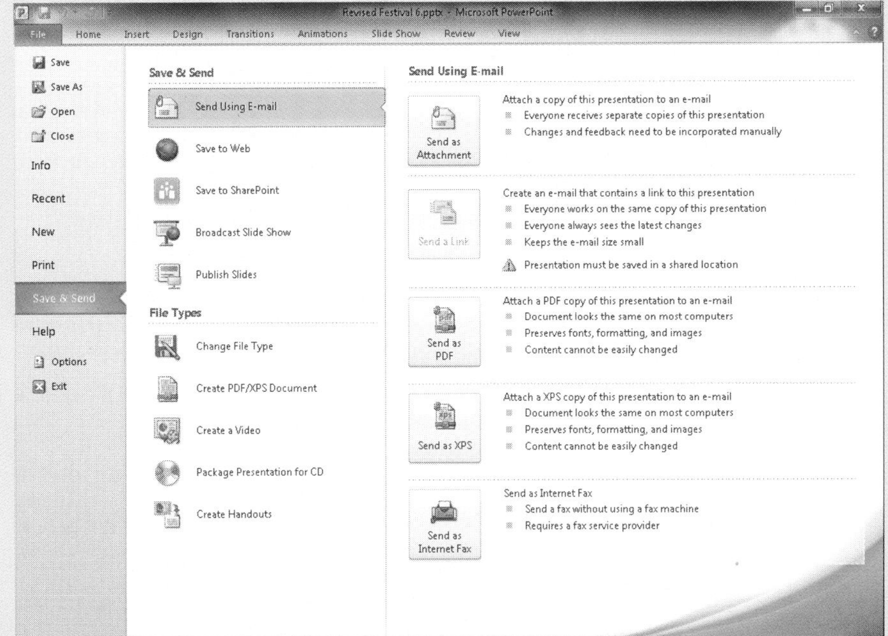

FIGURE 10–13
Send Using E-mail options

3. In the center pane, under File Types, click **Create PDF/XPS Document**. Then in the right pane, click the **Create PDF/XPS** button. The Publish as PDF or XPS dialog box opens. Click the Save as type list arrow and then click **PDF (*.pdf)**. If you have Adobe Reader installed on your computer, when you save the document using the PDF format, the document will open in the Adobe Reader application.
4. Navigate to the file and folder where you save your solution files. Click the **Save as type** list arrow, and then click **XPS Document (*.xps)**. You do not need to change the filename. Click **Publish**. The new presentation opens in XPS Viewer.
5. The XPS Viewer does not include automatic slide timings. Scroll down to view the slides. The audio icons still appear on the slides, but you cannot play the narrations. Close the XPS viewer.
6. Click the **File** tab, and then click **Save As**. Click the **Save as type** list arrow, and then click **PowerPoint Show (*.ppsx)**. Click **Save**.
7. Close the presentation and exit PowerPoint. Then navigate to the drive and folder where your solution files are stored. Double-click the filename **Revised Festival 4.ppsx**. Note that the file automatically opens in Slide Show view, and the slides start playing.
8. Press **Esc** to stop the slide show. Note that when you stop the slide show, the file closes and PowerPoint is not open.
9. Open the **Revised Festival 4.pptx** file from your solutions folder.

TIP

If you do not see the file extension (*.ppsx), open the Control Panel and then open Appearance and Personalization. Click Folder Options, and then click the View tab. Under Advanced settings, make sure the option Hide extensions for known file types is disabled.

10. Click the **Design** tab. In the Page Setup group, click the **Page Setup** button. The Page Setup dialog box opens, as shown in **Figure 10–14**. Note that you can use the Width and Height boxes to set a custom size.

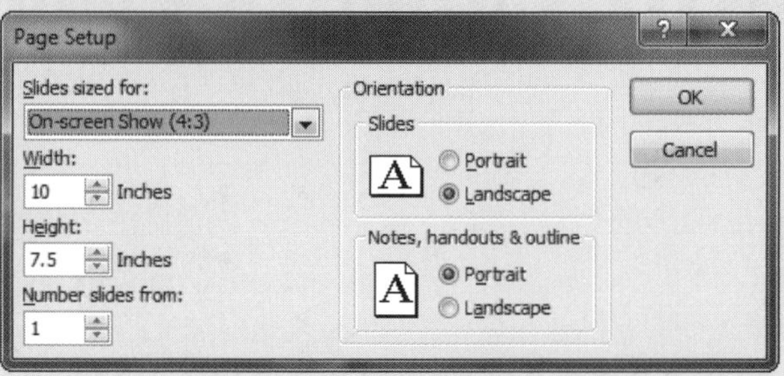

FIGURE 10–14
Page Setup dialog box

11. Change the height to **6.1** inches. Then click the **Slides sized for** list arrow, and then click the standard size **On-screen Show (16:10)**. In the Orientation section, under Slides, enable the **Portrait** option. Click **OK**. The slide layout changes are obvious in Slide Sorter view. In the Page Setup group, click the **Slide Orientation** button and then click **Landscape**.
12. Click **File**, and then click **Save As**. Click the **Save as type** list arrow, click **OpenDocument Presentation (*.odp)**, and then click **Save**. When prompted to continue to save in this format, click **Yes**. Close the presentation.
13. Open the **Revised Festival 4.pptx** file from your solution files. Click **File**, and then click **Save As**. In the File name box, change the filename to **Revised Festival Picture**, followed by your initials. Click the **Save as type** list arrow, and near the end of the list of formats, click **PowerPoint Picture Presentation (*.pptx)** and then click **Save**. When prompted that a copy has been saved, click **OK**. Close the presentation.
14. Open the **Revised Festival Picture** presentation. Note that you cannot make any edits. Switch to Slide Show view and review the presentation. Note that the audio icons on slides 2 and 3 do not play. Close the presentation.

EXTRA FOR EXPERTS

The default setting in PowerPoint is Unrestricted Access. You can use the Restrict Permission by People feature to grant designated people access to your presentations, yet they still cannot edit, copy, or print the files. To use the Restrict Permission by People feature, you must be able to authenticate the credentials of people by using an Information Rights Management (IRM) service.

Protecting Presentations

When sharing a presentation file, you may want to consider protecting the presentation so that others do not make changes to the file. When you use the Mark as Final command, you are indicating that the status of the document is final. PowerPoint saves the file as a read-only document, but this does not provide secure protection. If users want to make edits, they can easily toggle off the Mark as Final feature.

To restrict access to presentations, you can encrypt the files so they are not readable without a password. ***Encryption*** is a standard method for encoding data. When assigning passwords in PowerPoint, the characters can be any combination of letters, numerals, spaces, and symbols. A strong password includes a combination of text, numbers, and symbols and consists of at least eight characters. The password is ***case sensitive***, which means that when entering a password to open a file, the upper and lower casing of the letters must be identical to the casing of the letters in the assigned password. If the casing of the letters differs, the file will not open. Passwords can be changed or deleted using the Encrypt Document dialog box.

VOCABULARY
encryption
case sensitive

Step-by-Step 10.6

1. Open the **Revised Festival 4.pptx** file from your solution files. Save the presentation as **Revised Festival 5**, followed by your initials.
2. Click the **File** tab. In the center pane, click the **Protect Presentation** button and then click **Mark as Final**. When prompted to mark the presentation as final, click **OK**. Read the dialog box that explains the purpose of marking the document final, and then click **OK** to close it. The information in the center pane changes to show Permissions, as shown in **Figure 10–15**.

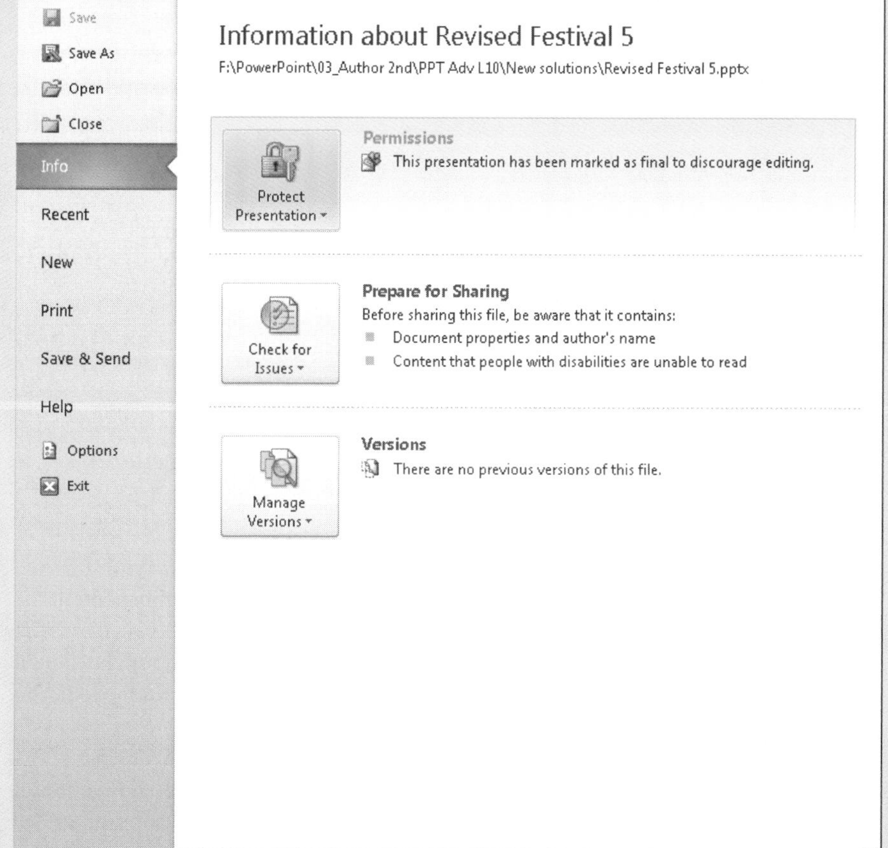

FIGURE 10–15
Backstage view with Permissions setting

3. Click the **Home** tab. Note the yellow message bar at the top of the document indicating that the presentation has been marked as final. Also note that the Marked as Final button appears in the status bar.
4. Click **Edit Anyway** in the yellow message bar at the top of the slide window. The presentation can now be edited.
5. Click the **File** tab and, in the center pane, click the **Protect Presentation** button. Click **Encrypt with Password**. The Encrypt Document dialog box opens, as shown in **Figure 10–16**.

FIGURE 10–16
Encrypt Document dialog box

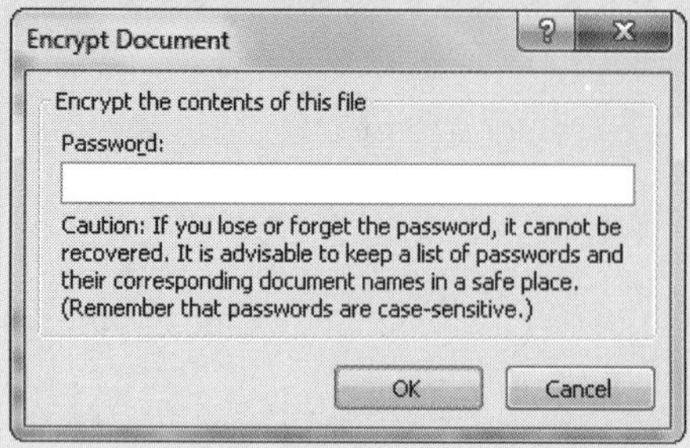

6. In the Password text box, type **RF2014!**. Click **OK**. The Confirm Password dialog box opens. In the Reenter password text box, type **RF2014!** and then click **OK**.
7. Save the changes to the presentation, and then close the file.
8. Reopen the **Revised Festival 5** presentation from your solution files. When prompted to enter the password, type **RF2014!** and then click **OK.**
9. Click the **File** tab, and then click the **Protect Presentation** button. Click **Encrypt with Password** to open the Encrypt Document dialog box. Delete the current password, and then type the new password **RF2014#1**. Then click **OK**. Then reenter the new password and click **OK**.
10. Save the changes and leave the presentation open for the next Step-by-Step.

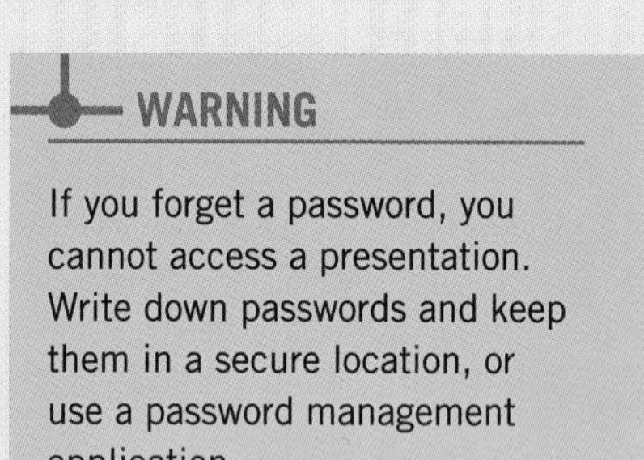

If you forget a password, you cannot access a presentation. Write down passwords and keep them in a secure location, or use a password management application.

Attaching a Digital Signature

VOCABULARY
digital signature

A ***digital signature*** is an attachment to a file or e-mail message certifying that the information in the file is authentic and safe. The digital signature is embedded in the presentation, and although it is not visible, recipients of the presentation can see that the file has been digitally signed. Signed files are marked as final and remain signed until the file is changed. If the presentation is edited, the signature is removed. You can embed multiple digital signatures in the same presentation.

Digital signatures are easy to create using the Digital Certificate for VBA Projects tool. However, when you use this feature, you create a self-signed digital certificate, which does not verify your identity and, therefore, is only appropriate for personal use. Furthermore, the digital certificate can only be used on the computer where it is created.

The Digital Certificate for VBA Projects tool is used in this lesson to demonstrate how to attach a digital signature to a document. If you need an authenticated certificate, you must secure a service from a third-party vendor; several commercial certification authority services are compatible with Office applications.

Step-by-Step 10.7

1. If necessary, open the **Revised Festival 5** file from your solution files. (To open the file, you will need to enter the password **RF2014#1**.) Save the presentation as **Revised Festival 6**, followed by your initials.
2. Click the **File** tab, and then click the **Protect Presentation** button. Click **Encrypt with Password**. Delete the current password, leave the text box blank, and then click **OK**. The file is no longer password protected.
3. View the digital signatures on your computer:
   a. Launch Internet Explorer.
   b. Click the **Tools** button, and then click **Internet Options**.
   c. In the Internet Options dialog box, click the **Content** tab. Under Certificates, click **Certificates**. A list of digital signatures available on your computer appears. Check to see if your digital signature appears in the list.
   d. Close both dialog boxes, and then close Internet Explorer.
   e. If your personal signature was not in the list, go to Step 4. If your personal signature was in the list, go to Step 5.
4. Create a new digital certificate:
   a. On the taskbar, click the **Start** button, click **All Programs**, click **Microsoft Office**, click **Microsoft Office 2010 Tools**, and then click **Digital Certificate for VBA Projects**.
   b. In the Create Digital Certificate dialog box, in the Your certificate's name box, type your first and last names. Click **OK**.
   c. A message box appears indicating that a new certificate has been successfully created. Click **OK** to close the dialog boxes.
5. If necessary, click the File tab. In the center pane, click the **Protect Presentation** button and then click **Add a Digital Signature**. A message box appears explaining that Microsoft does not warrant a digital signature's legal enforceability. Click **OK**.
6. In the Sign dialog box, under Purpose for signing this document, type **To confirm the validity of the information in this presentation.**. If your name does not appear in the Signing as: box, click Change, select your certificate, and then click OK.

7. In the Sign dialog box, click **Sign**. If a prompt appears saying that the signature cannot be verified, it is because your certificate is a self-signed certificate and the certificate was not issued by a trusted certificate authority (CA). If so, click Yes to use the certificate.
8. A message box opens confirming that the signature has been successfully saved with the document. If any changes are made to the document, the signature will be invalid. Click **OK**.
9. In the center pane, you may see a warning about an invalid signature. In the center pane, click the **View Signatures** button to open the Signatures pane.
10. Point to your signature in the pane, and then click the **down arrow** to the right of your signature. A menu of options for the selected signature opens, as shown in **Figure 10–17**. Your settings may look different.

FIGURE 10–17
Signatures pane showing options for signatures

11. Click **Signature Details**. If your certificate is not trusted, click the link Click here to trust this user's identity.
12. Click **View** to review the certificate information. Click **OK**, and then click **Close** to close the dialog box.

13. A yellow message bar at the top of the slide window shows that the document has been marked as final to discourage editing. The Signatures icon appears in the status bar, indicating that the document contains a signature.
14. The signature was automatically saved with the document. Close the Signatures pane. Leave the presentation open for the next Step-by-Step.

Package a Presentation

If you plan to show a presentation on a different computer, you can compress and save the file to a folder (such as a flash drive) or to a CD. You can choose to include linked files and/or to embed TrueType fonts. You can also restrict access by assigning passwords, and you can inspect the file.

If the destination computer does not have PowerPoint installed, you can use ***PowerPoint Viewer***, a Microsoft application that enables you to open PowerPoint presentations when the PowerPoint application is not installed on the computer. You will need to download and install the PowerPoint Viewer on the destination computer. When using the PowerPoint Viewer, you can view and print presentations, but you cannot edit the presentations.

VOCABULARY
PowerPoint Viewer

Step-by-Step 10.8

1. If necessary, open the **Revised Festival 6** presentation from your solution files. Save the presentation as **Revised Festival 7**, followed by your initials. When prompted about invalidating all the signatures, click **Yes**.
2. In the yellow message bar at the top of the slide window, click **Edit Anyway**. When prompted to continue, click **Yes**, and then when prompted to remove the signature and save the document, click **OK**.
3. Click the **File** tab, and then click **Save & Send**. In the center pane, under File Types, click **Package Presentation for CD**. Then in the right pane, click the **Package for CD** button. The Package for CD dialog box opens. Under Files to be copied, the current filename appears, as shown in **Figure 10–18**.

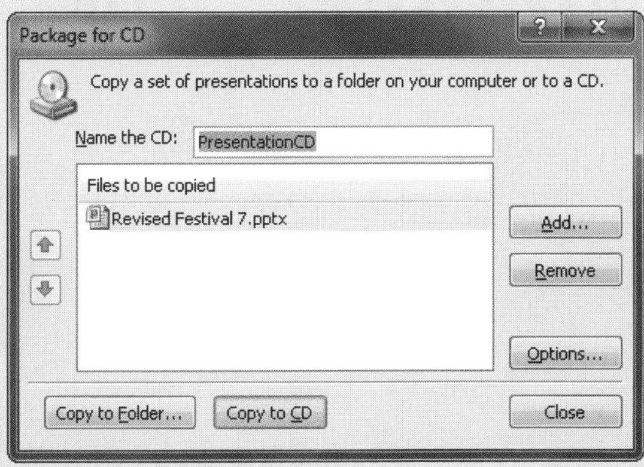

FIGURE 10–18
Package for CD dialog box

4. Replace the text in the Name the CD text box with **Festival CD**, followed by your initials.
5. Click **Options** to open the Options dialog box, as shown in **Figure 10–19**.

FIGURE 10–19
Options dialog box

6. Under Include these files, make sure the options Linked files and Embedded TrueType fonts are enabled. In the first password box, type the password **RF2014#1**. In the second password box, type **RF20114!** and then enable the option **Inspect presentations for inappropriate or private information**. Click **OK**.
7. When prompted to confirm the password to open each presentation, type **RF2014#1** and click **OK**. When prompted to confirm the password to modify each presentation, type **RF20114!** and then click **OK**.
8. If you were to click Copy to CD, the files would be burned to a CD using the CD/DVD drive on your computer. Instead of burning a CD, click **Copy to Folder**. The Copy to Folder dialog box opens.
9. Click **Browse**, navigate to the drive and folder where your solution files are saved, and then click **Select**. The path to your solutions folder appears in the Location box.
10. In the Copy to Folder dialog box, click **OK**. When prompted to include linked files in your package, click **Yes**.
11. The Document Inspector window opens. Click **Inspect**. When the inspection results appear, click **Remove All** to remove the document properties and personal information. Then close the Document Inspector dialog box.
12. A window showing the contents of the Final Festival folder opens. Double-click the **PresentationPackage** folder. Note that the folder contains seven files and all are related to the Revised Festival 7 file.
13. Close the window. Then close the Package for CD dialog box.
14. Leave the Revised Festival 7 presentation open for the next Step-by-Step.

Delivering Presentations

The most traditional way to deliver a presentation is for a presenter to stand up in front of the audience and control the slides. When delivering a presentation this way, you can use tools to underline or highlight text and objects on the slide. However, PowerPoint offers several other features that enable you to deliver the presentation to an audience in a remote location or to create a self-running presentation.

Annotating Slides during a Presentation

You might occasionally want to draw or write on your slides as you present them. PowerPoint has several options for writing new content and highlighting existing content. After adding annotations, you can erase them. If you don't erase the annotations, you have the option of keeping or discarding them when you exit the slide show.

You can also use the mouse pointer as a laser pointer and customize the color.

Step-by-Step 10.9

1. If necessary, open the **Revised Festival 7** presentation from your solution files.
2. Click the **Slide Show** tab. In the Set Up group, click the **Set Up Slide Show** button to open the Set Up Show dialog box, as shown in **Figure 10–20**.

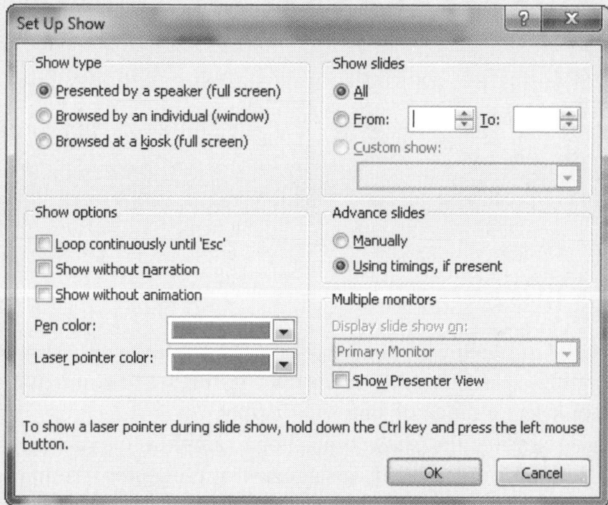

FIGURE 10–20
Set Up Show dialog box

3. Under Show type, the default option Presented by a speaker (full screen) should already be enabled. Under Show options, change the Pen color setting to blue and change the Laser pointer color setting to green.
4. Under Advance slides, enable the option **Manually**. Then click **OK**.
5. Select the **slide 5** thumbnail. Then switch to Slide Show view.

6. Hover the mouse pointer over the lower-left corner of the screen. Four transparent buttons will be displayed. Click the **Pen** button, and then in the shortcut menu, click **Pen**. The mouse pointer changes to a small blue dot.
7. Click and drag the mouse pointer to create a circle around the word *Pottery*. Then click and drag the mouse pointer to underline the word *Blacksmithing*.
8. Press **Esc** to toggle off the pen.
9. Press and hold the **Ctrl** key as you click and hold down the left mouse button and drag the mouse around to move the laser pointer on the screen.
10. Click the **Pen** button in the lower-left corner, and then click **Eraser**. The mouse pointer changes to an Eraser. Click the blue circle around the word *Pottery* to remove the annotation.
11. Right-click anywhere on the slide. In the shortcut menu, point to **Pointer Options** and then click **Highlighter**. The mouse pointer changes to a vertical yellow bar. Drag the mouse pointer over the word *Leatherwork* to highlight the text. Press **Esc** to toggle off the highlighter.
12. Because you are using the mouse for annotations, you cannot click to advance slides during a presentation. Press **PageDown** (or press the down arrow key) to advance to the next slide.
13. Advance to the end of the slide show and click to exit. A prompt will appear asking if you want to keep the ink annotations. Click **Keep**.
14. Save the changes and leave the presentation open for the next Step-by-Step.

Setting Up the Show

Before you present your slides, you should use the Set Up Show command to verify your current settings and to specify additional settings. For example, you can hide specific slides or select a range of slides to display.

You can also specify the show type. For example, you can prepare the slide show to be self-running for a ***kiosk,*** an interactive computer terminal available for public use. Or, you can set up the presentation so that an individual can view the slides and control when to advance them. You can also control whether the slides appear with or without narrations and animations.

The Show Set Up group also includes a feature to record the presentation. When you use this feature, PowerPoint records both the timings and narrations as you deliver the presentation. A recording of the presentation enables you to go back and listen to your narrations afterwards, and those who missed your presentation can review the slides and listen to your narration at a later point.

VOCABULARY
kiosk

EXTRA FOR EXPERTS

If you want to show only one of your custom shows, click the Custom show option and select the show. Additional options allow you to adjust the resolution of your presentation and to display it on multiple monitors.

Step-by-Step 10.10

1. If necessary, open the **Revised Festival 7** presentation from your solution files. Save the presentation as **Revised Festival 8**, followed by your initials.
2. If necessary, switch to Normal view. Go to slide 5. Point to the highlight annotation, click to select the object, and then press **Delete**. Then delete the blue underline.
3. On the Slides tab, click the **slide 4** thumbnail. Then, if necessary, click the **Slide Show** tab. In the Set Up group, click the **Hide Slide** button. Note that on the Slides tab, the number for the selected slide shows a diagonal line, indicating that it will not appear in the slide show.
4. In the Set Up group, click the **Set Up Slide Show** button to open the Set Up Show dialog box.
5. Under Show type, enable the **Browsed at a kiosk (full screen)** option. Under Show options, the Loop continuously until 'Esc' option is automatically enabled. The option is grayed out, so you cannot disable it. Under Advance slides, enable the **Using timings, if present** option. Click **OK**.
6. In the Start Slide Show group, click the **From Beginning** button and watch the presentation. The slides will advance using the timing settings, and the narrations will also play. The slide with the title *Food Fit for a King* will not appear in the slide show. When the last slide appears, the presentation will play again.
7. Press **Esc** to switch to Normal view. Save the changes to the presentation.
8. Save the presentation as **Revised Festival 9**, followed by your initials.
9. Create Action buttons:
   a. Go to slide 1. Click the **Insert** tab. In the Illustrations group, click the **Shapes** button. At the bottom of the menu, under Action Buttons, click **Action Button: Forward or Next**. The mouse pointer changes to a cross.
   b. Drag the mouse pointer in the lower-right corner of the slide to create a button approximately 1" wide by ½" high. When you release the mouse button, the Action Settings dialog box will open. Click **OK**. Select the action button and copy it to the Clipboard.
   c. Go to slide 2. Paste the forward action button copied from slide 1 to slide 2. Do not be concerned about the button overlaying the audio icon. Audio icons do not appear during a slide show.

d. Click the **Shapes** button. Under Action Buttons, click **Action Button: Back or Previous**. Draw a similar sized shape in the lower-left corner of slide 2, then click **OK**. Reposition and resize the two buttons as needed.

e. Select both action buttons and copy them to the Clipboard. Then copy the buttons to slides 3–7. You need to copy only a Back or Previous button on slide 7.

10. Go to slide 4. Click the **Slide Show** tab, and in the Set Up group, click the **Hide Slide** button to toggle the feature off. The diagonal line no longer appears on the slide number on the Slides tab.

11. In the Set Up group, click the **Set Up Slide Show** button. Under Show type, enable the **Browsed by an individual** option. Under Show options, make sure the Loop continuously until 'Esc' option is disabled.

12. Under Show slides, in the From box, enter **2**. In the To box, if necessary, enter **7**. Under Advance slides, enable the option **Manually**. Then click **OK**.

13. In the Start Slide Show group, click the **From Beginning** button and review the presentation. You will need to click the Forward or Next action button to advance to the next slide. When the last slide appears, you can click the Back or Previous action button.

14. Press **Esc** to switch to Normal view. Save the changes and leave the presentation open for the next Step-by-Step.

EXTRA FOR EXPERTS

You can also insert the Action Button: Beginning shape to create a hyperlink to the first slide in the presentation or the Action Button: End shape to create a hyperlink to the last slide in the presentation.

Broadcasting Presentations

VOCABULARY
broadcasting

Broadcasting is a way to present slides to an audience that cannot convene in one location for the presentation. If, for example, you work in a very large company or for a company that has branch offices located over a wide geographic area, broadcasting is a sensible way to reach all your potential viewers. A broadcast presentation is saved in HTML format, which means your viewers do not need PowerPoint to view the slides. Instead, they view the slides using their standard Web browser.

Using the Broadcast Slide Show command, you connect to the Microsoft PowerPoint Broadcast Service. You must first sign in with your Windows Live ID. Then you provide the URL link to those you want to invite to watch a synchronized view of your slide show. Up to 50 remote attendees may participate in the broadcast. When they access the Web page, they can view the presentation and see animations and transitions just as they would view the slide show on your computer. You can manually control the slide display, or you can set automatic timings.

Step-by-Step 10.11

You must have a Windows Live ID to complete these steps.

1. If necessary, open the **Revised Festival 9** presentation from your solution files.
2. If necessary, click the **Slide Show** tab. In the Start Slide Show group, click the **Broadcast Slide Show** button to open the Broadcast Slide Show dialog box.
3. Click **Start Broadcast**. When prompted, sign into your Windows Live account. The Broadcast Slide Show dialog box opens. Click **Send in Email**. A new e-mail message opens in Outlook. All you would need to enter is the recipient's e-mail address. The subject line and body of the message are already complete.
4. Close Outlook.
5. In the Broadcast Slide Show dialog box, click **Start Slide Show**. Remote viewers can now view the slide show online.
6. Press **Esc** to switch to Normal view. In the yellow message bar, click **End Broadcast**. When the prompt to disconnect all remote viewers appears, click **End Broadcast**.
7. Close the presentation.

TIP

If you do not have Outlook installed on your computer, you can click Copy Link and then create an e-mail message in your e-mail application and paste the link into the body of the message.

SUMMARY

In this lesson, you learned:

- When collaborating on a presentation, team members can use comments to provide feedback on slides. You can easily add, edit, and delete comments.
- You can view presentations side by side, but the Compare feature makes it easier to identify the differences between two presentations.
- To enable team members to collaborate and work together in real time, presentations can be stored and updated so that employees can access the file remotely.
- The Rehearse Timings button is beneficial in helping you estimate how much time you need to show the slides in the presentation.
- If you have access to a microphone, you can record narrations that will play during the slide show.
- PowerPoint provides several options for saving and sending presentations, including the Web, e-mail, and fax. There are also several options for file formats suitable for a variety of uses.
- You can protect presentations to ensure that others do not make changes to the file, and you can restrict access by assigning a password. You can also certify that the information in the file is authentic.
- As you present a slide show, you can use tools to annotate the slides, and then you can choose to keep or discard the annotations.
- Your audience does not need to be in the same room with you to view your presentation. PowerPoint provides several options for delivering presentations remotely.

VOCABULARY REVIEW

Define the following terms:

broadcasting
case sensitive
comment
digital signature
document workspace site
encryption
kiosk
markup
Portable Document Format (PDF)
PowerPoint Viewer
XML Paper Specification (XPS)

REVIEW QUESTIONS

TRUE / FALSE

Circle T if the statement is true or F if the statement is false.

T F 1. When comments are deleted from slides, the remaining comment numbers are automatically updated.

T F 2. Marking a document as final is one of the more secure ways to protect a document.

T F 3. Multiple users can work on the same presentation at the same time.

T F 4. When annotating slides during a slide show, the annotations are automatically saved with the slides.

T F 5. Voice narrations take precedence over any other kind of sound on your slides.

FILL IN THE BLANK

Complete the following sentences by writing the correct word or words in the blanks provided.

1. A(n) ________________ is a central location for storing and sharing documents.
2. A(n) ________________ is an attachment to a file or e-mail message certifying that the information in the file is authentic and safe.
3. ________________ is a way to present slides to an audience that cannot convene in one location for the presentation.
4. ________________ is a standard method for encoding data.
5. A(n) ________________ is an interactive computer terminal available for public use.

WRITTEN QUESTIONS

Write a brief answer to the following questions.

1. What are the benefits of saving a document in a PDF or XPS format?

2. Explain how you can print copies of the comments added to slides.

3. Explain how rehearsing timings helps you estimate how long it will take you to go through a presentation.

4. What are the advantages of packaging a presentation to a CD (or copying the presentation to a file folder)?

5. What are the advantages to using the Compare feature to review changes made in multiple versions of a presentation?

PROJECTS

If you have a SAM 2010 user profile, your instructor may have assigned an autogradable version of the indicated project. If so, log into the SAM 2010 Web site at *www.cengage.com/sam2010* to download the instruction and start files.

PROJECT 10–1

1. Open the file **Karate 1** from the drive and folder where your Data Files are stored. Save the presentation as **Revised Karate 1**, followed by your initials.
2. Note the current settings for the user name and initials. Change the user name to your name, and change the initials.
3. Go to slide 6. Add the comment **Do you think we should apply related font colors to the words in this list?**. Collapse the comment text box.
4. Edit the comment text by adding the following sentence at the beginning of the comment: **Are the colors in the correct sequence?**. Collapse the comment text box.
5. Save the changes to the presentation. Restore the user name settings.
6. Save the file as **Revised Karate 2**, followed by your initials.
7. Use the Compare feature to compare the **Revised Karate 2** presentation to the **Karate Reviewer A** file in the Data Files folder.
8. Accept the following changes from Reviewer A:
   a. Reordering of the bulleted items on slide 2. (*Hint*: Look at the Karate Reviewer A slide on the Slides tab of the Reviewing pane.)
   b. All font color changes on slide 6.
   c. The new slide at the end of the presentation.
9. Do not accept the changes on slide 5.
10. Delete all the comments in the presentation, and end the review.
11. Save the changes to the presentation.
12. Package the presentation to a CD (copy the file to a folder in your Solutions folder). Name the folder **Final Karate**, followed by your initials. Create a password to modify each presentation: **#1ETARAK**. Include linked files and inspect the files for private information. Remove all personal information.
13. Restore the user name settings noted in Step 2. Close all open files, folders, and dialog boxes.

SAM PROJECT 10–2

1. Open the file **Scarecrow 1** from the drive and folder where your Data Files are stored. Save the presentation as **Revised Scarecrow 1**, followed by your initials.
2. Rehearse the timings for all the slides. Animations have been applied throughout the slides, so be sure to click and advance to each item on a slide before moving on to the next slide.
3. Save the timings. Then set the time for slide 5 to **15**.
4. Save the changes to the presentation.
5. Save the presentation in the PDF format, using the same filename.
6. Protect the Revised Scarecrow 1.pptx file by encrypting it with a password. Use the password **014@FRCC#**.
7. Save the changes and close the file.

PROJECT 10–3

1. Open the file **Scarecrow 2** from the drive and folder where your Data Files are stored. Save the presentation as **Revised Scarecrow 2**, followed by your initials.
2. Go to slide 2. Apply an emphasis effect to the text box. (*Hint*: Use the More Emphasis Effects command to make sure you see all available effects.) Trigger the effect to start after the previous, and adjust the timing if necessary.
3. Beginning with the first slide, record the entire slide show. Record the slide and animation timings as well as narrations and laser pointer. Take your time advancing through the slides, and record narrations on at least two of the slides. (*Hint*: You can read the slide content, or you can add your own comments regarding the content.) Review the narrations, and re-record them if necessary.
4. Set the slide show up to run all slides at a kiosk. The show should include the narrations and animations.
5. Save the changes to the presentation.
6. Attach your digital signature to the presentation. The purpose of the signature is to confirm that the file is authentic and safe.
7. Close the file.

PROJECT 10–4

1. Open the **Karate 2** file from the drive and folder where your Data Files are stored. Save the presentation as **Revised Karate 3**, followed by your initials.
2. Add action buttons to slides 1–7 so the individual can navigate forward and backward through the slides.
3. Show the presentation from the beginning. When you get to slide 5, use the Pen tool to underline each of the bulleted terms. Discard all annotations.
4. In the Set Up Show options, change the show type to be browsed by an individual who can manually advance through the slides. Show all the slides.
5. Save the changes to the presentation.
6. Close the file.

CRITICAL THINKING

ACTIVITY 10–1

Ask a classmate or friend to partner with you so you can experience broadcasting a presentation. Then reflecting on the experience, answer the following questions: What did it feel like presenting without seeing your audience? Did your partner feel that it was a positive experience? Do you think you are likely to use the broadcasting feature anytime in the near future?

ACTIVITY 10–2

Describe a scenario for which you would create a self-running presentation to be browsed at a kiosk. Would you include narrations on some or all of the slides? Why or why not?

UNIT REVIEW

Advanced Microsoft PowerPoint

 REVIEW QUESTIONS

MATCHING

Match the correct term in Column 2 to its description in Column 1.

Column 1

_____ 1. An interactive computer terminal available for public use.

_____ 2. Provides an outline of topics and is useful for presentations with custom shows.

_____ 3. A list of coordinates related to a specific image.

_____ 4. Tiny colored dots that compose the image on a computer screen.

_____ 5. A standard method for encoding data.

_____ 6. An object that becomes part of the destination file and can be edited in the destination file.

_____ 7. A line bordering the chart plot area used as a frame of reference for measurement.

_____ 8. Reviews the topics in a presentation and can be used as an introduction to or a review of a presentation.

_____ 9. An object inserted as a static object that accesses data stored in the source file.

_____ 10. Related data points that are plotted in a chart.

Column 2

A. agenda slide
B. axis
C. bitmap
D. data series
E. embedded object
F. encryption
G. hot spot
H. image map
I. kiosk
J. legend
K. linked object
L. pixels
M. summary slide

MULTIPLE CHOICE

Select the best response for the following statements.

1. A ______________ image takes more time to open, but when you increase and decrease the image size, the clarity of the image will not change.
   A. dpi
   B. vector
   C. raster
   D. ppi
2. The PowerPoint proofing tools check ______________.
   A. spelling and grammar
   B. capitalization
   C. formats
   D. all of the above
3. The option to ______________ data is most useful when you want to keep the data current.
   A. convert
   B. embed
   C. link
   D. copy and paste
4. A ______________ chart is effective for showing how parts relate to a whole.
   A. column
   B. line
   C. pie
   D. radar
5. The ______________ controls the formatting for all the slides in the presentation.
   A. layout master
   B. custom design template
   C. main layout master
   D. slide master
6. To restrict access to a presentation file, you can ______________.
   A. encrypt the file
   B. attach a digital signature
   C. mark the presentation as final
   D. all of the above
7. PowerPoint's ______________ feature will automatically correct commonly misspelled words, without prompting you.
   A. AutoCorrect
   B. AutoComplete
   C. AutoType
   D. Custom Dictionary
8. To change column width in a table, you can use the ______________ command.
   A. AutoFit
   B. Distribute Columns
   C. Adjust Columns
   D. A or B

9. To add blank space around a graphic, you can ________________.
   A. drag the side handles of the graphic
   B. drag the corner handles of the graphic
   C. outcrop the graphic
   D. any of the above
10. Sizing a graphic to exact proportions is referred to as ________________.
   A. scaling
   B. nudging
   C. cropping
   D. aspect ratio

WRITTEN QUESTIONS

Write a brief answer to the following questions.

1. What two factors affect the size of a picture file?

2. Why is it important to select the right chart type?

3. What are the benefits of organizing slides into sections?

4. Why would you use Paste Special options when copying slides from one presentation to another?

5. How can you reduce the file size of a presentation that includes pictures, video clips, and audio clips?

6. What is progressive disclosure?

7. When would you use PowerPoint Viewer?

8. What formats does a table style provide?

9. How are slide masters useful?

10. When you export PowerPoint data to a Word document, what information appears in the Word outline?

PROJECTS

PROJECT 1

1. Open the **Fire Instructions** file from the drive and folder where your Data Files are stored. Save the presentation as **Revised Fire Instructions**, followed by your initials.
2. Go to slide 4. Remove the second-level bullet formats. Replace the first-level bullets with a custom bullet, using a symbol of your choice.
3. Insert a new Title and Content slide between slides 1 and 2. Create a bar chart using the data below. Add the slide title **Previous Year Fires**.

	ZONE 1	ZONE 2	ZONE 3
Cooking	33	21	28
Heating equipment	14	7	17
Arson	5	4	2
Other equipment	7	5	6
Electrical distribution	11	8	9

4. Go to slide 6. Select the list of terms in the content placeholder and convert the text to a vertical list SmartArt object. Apply a SmartArt style. Animate the objects with an entrance effect so that each level of the chart appears one by one.
5. Go to slide 8. Change the bulleted list to a numbered list. Change the number style to the 1) format, and change the number size to 125% of the text.
6. On slide 3, add a clip art image (illustrations or photographs) of a smoke alarm. On slide 8, add a clip art image of a fire extinguisher. Crop, resize, and reposition the graphics as needed. Also, recolor the graphics to fit the color scheme, or remove the picture background.

7. Apply entrance effect animations to the bulleted lists on slides 3 and 5 so that each bulleted item appears on click. Apply exit effect animations to the bulleted list on slide 8 so that each bulleted item disappears on click. (*Hint*: Be sure to use the More Entrance Effects and More Exit Effects commands so you can choose from all options available.) Also on slide 8, apply a custom motion path to move the image from left to right on the slide, and then from left to right again. Adjust the timing of the motion effect as needed, and format the motion animation to appear after the previous animation.
8. Go to slide 9. Select the list of terms in the content placeholder and convert the text to a Process SmartArt Object. Apply a SmartArt style. Animate the objects with an entrance effect so that each level of the chart appears one by one.
9. Go to slide 10. Format the two lists:
   a. Increase the font size in both lists to 44 pt.
   b. Click to the left of the first list to select the blank text box. In the text box, type **RACE**. Format the text direction with the **Stacked** option and center align the text. Change the font size to 44 pt and apply the bold format.
   c. Click to the left of the second list to select another blank text box. Type **PASS**, and then apply the same text formats as described in Step 9b.
10. Select all four text boxes. Using theme colors, apply a shape fill and a shape outline.
11. Change the slide background by using a solid, gradient, picture or texture, or pattern fill. Apply the new background format to all slides.
12. Save slide 10 as a picture in the JPEG format and using the filename **Guide**, followed by your initials.
13. Rehearse the timing for each of the slides, starting at the beginning of the presentation.
14. Save the changes with the timings and close the presentation.

PROJECT 2

1. Open the **Codes** file from the drive and folder where your Data Files are stored. Save the presentation as **Revised Codes**, followed by your initials.
2. Change the slide background to a gradient fill using the preset styles or by creating your own gradient style. Be sure to format a background that is compatible with the font colors on slides 3–7. It may be necessary to reapply the black font color on slide 4.
3. Insert a new Title and Content slide at the end of the presentation. Delete the blank title placeholder. Create a table using the data below.

CODE	ALERT
Blue	Emergency in the area designated; real emergencies such as cardiac arrest
Red	Fire discovered in designated area; "red code" used to avoid panic among patients
Black	A disaster has struck in the city, county, or area; the facility will accept the injured
Yellow	A bomb threat has been received; maintain the safety of patients, visitors, and personnel
A	Suspected abduction of an infant or child; follow protocol for unit shutdown
Gray	Security response is needed or anticipated; follow protocol for your unit

4. Remove the background graphic for slide 8. AutoFit the column widths and resize the table to fill the slide area. If desired, change the table style.
5. Apply an entrance effect animation for the table.
6. Go to slide 6 and add the following comment to the slide: **Be sure to mention that Code A used to be referred to as Code Purple.**
7. Use the slide master to format animations for the first-level bulleted lists. Choose an entrance effect triggered on click, and set the effect options to appear by first-level paragraphs.
8. On the slide master, format a transition for each of the slides. Then preview each slide to make sure the slide master formats are correct. Make any necessary corrections and save the file.

9. Inspect the presentation and remove document properties and personal information from the file, but do not remove comments and annotations.
10. Protect the presentation by encrypting the file using the password ***BLP/911**.
11. Save the changes and close the file.

PROJECT 3

1. Open the **Cabins** file from the drive and folder where your Data Files are stored. Save the file as **Revised Cabins**, followed by your initials.
2. Create a new custom dictionary named **WWCR** and save the dictionary in your solutions folder. Add the words *Whyspering* and *Michigamme* to the dictionary.
3. Create a slide background using a clip art image of a cabin, woods, or an outdoor scene to apply to all slides in the presentation. Adjust the transparency of the background image so you can easily read text on the slides. Apply the background to all slides.
4. If necessary, change the font color(s) on the slide master to complement the background image and also to make the text easier to read.
5. On the slide master, format a slide transition. Set up a duration of 3 seconds for the transition. Apply a sound to play with the transition, such as wind.
6. On the slide master, format entrance effects for the first- and second-level bulleted lists. Format the bulleted items to appear after previous, with a 2 second delay.
7. Go to slide 6. Set the transition to advance after 10 seconds.
8. Set up the show for self-running at a kiosk. Show all slides, using the timings.
9. Remove the custom dictionary from the dictionary list.
10. Save the changes and close the presentation.

PROJECT 4

1. Create a new photo album using the following picture files, which are stored in the drive and folder where your Data Files are stored.

   Buffalo.jpg

   Elephant.jpg

   Leopard.jpg

   Lion.jpg

   Rhinoceros.jpg
2. Choose the **1 picture** layout option, and apply the **Compound Frame, Black** frame shape. Add captions below all pictures, and format all the pictures black and white.
3. Arrange the pictures in the following sequence:

   Leopard

   Lion

   Buffalo

   Rhinoceros

   Elephant
4. Title the photo album **The Big 5!**, and if necessary, replace *Your Name* in the Subtitle placeholder with your first and last names.
5. Save the presentation as **Big 5a**, followed by your initials.
6. Reset all the pictures in the photo album.

7. Go to slide 2. To make it easier to locate the leopard in the photo, apply the **Glow Diffused** artistic effect.
8. Apply a different artistic effect to each of the remaining photos in the album, and if desired, change the picture colors.
9. Save the presentation as **Big 5b**, followed by your initials.
10. Reset all the pictures in the photo album. Edit the photo album as follows:
    a. Disable the caption option.
    b. Disable the black and white option.
    c. Apply a theme.
    d. Change the frame shape so that it complements the designated theme.
11. After applying the new photo album settings, make adjustments as necessary. Apply a transition to all slides, and change the setting to advance the slide after 5 seconds for all slides.
12. Use the Compress Pictures command on the Picture Tools Format tab, using the document resolution as the target output to compress all the pictures in the presentation. Then save the presentation as **Big5c**, followed by your initials.
13. Save the presentation as a video, using the portable device setting. Use the recorded timings. Assign the filename **Big5d**, followed by your initials, and use the .wmv format.
14. Close the Big5c presentation.

PROJECT 5

1. Open the **Diving** file from the drive and folder where your Data Files are stored. Save the presentation as **Diving Videos**, followed by your initials.
2. Go to slide 2. In the content placeholder, insert the **1 meter.avi** file from the drive and folder where your Data Files are stored.
3. Trim the video to not play the first 3 seconds, and stop playing the video before the cheer at the end of the clip.
4. Go to slide 3. In the content placeholder, insert the **3 meter.avi** file from the drive and folder where your Data Files are stored. Set the playback volume to **Low**.
5. Go to slide 4. In the content placeholder, insert the **10 meter.avi** file from the drive and folder where your Data Files are stored. Set the playback volume to **Low**.
6. Format the playback for each of the video objects on slides 2–4 as follows:
    a. Resize and reposition the video to fill the area below the slide title.
    b. Start the video automatically.
    c. Hide the video when it is not playing.
7. Apply video style formats, or borders and styles, to the video objects on slides 2–4.
8. If you have access to a microphone, record the narrations described below for slides 2–4. Hide the audio objects during the show, and format the audio clips to play automatically. In the Animations pane, rearrange the order of the animated objects so that the audio clips play before the videos.
    a. For slide 2, say **Dive 405c, inward 2 ½ somersaults in the tuck position.**
    b. For slide 3, say **Dive 107b, forward 3 ½ somersaults in the pike position.**
    c. For slide 4, say **Dive 614b, armstand forward 2 somersaults in the pike position.**
9. Apply a transition to all of the slides with a 3 second duration. Set the transition to automatically advance to the next slide after a 1 second delay. The animations should be arranged so that the audio clip plays before the video starts to play.
10. Set up the show so that the media controls do not appear when you position the mouse over a media object.
11. Compress the media files using the Presentation Quality setting, and save the presentation.

SIMULATION

You work for Santos-Pearce, an insurance company. Your supervisor will be speaking at an upcoming conference sponsored by the local Chamber of Commerce. Businesspeople and community residents will attend the session. Your supervisor has asked you to prepare a presentation to provide an overview of the types of insurance offered by the company.

JOB 1

The company offers several types of insurance. Fortunately, you have a file used for new employee orientation that outlines the various insurance types. A coworker recently prepared a similar presentation, so you can access information from that file, too. Then you can apply a design and customize the formats.

1. Open a new presentation and create new slides by inserting an outline from the document **Insurance Overview.docx** located in the drive and folder where your Data Files are stored. Save the new presentation as **Revised Insurance 1**, followed by your initials.
2. Delete slide 2. On slide 1, in the Title placeholder, Type **Santos-Pearce**. In the Subtitle placeholder, type **Protect Yourself and Your Loved Ones**.
3. Open the slide master and apply the following formats:
    a. Apply the **Newsprint** theme.
    b. Change the color theme to **Hardcover**.
    c. Customize the Hardcover theme colors by changing the Hyperlink color to **White, Text 1** and changing the Followed Hyperlink color to **Gold, Hyperlink**.
    d. Create a custom bullet.
    e. Change the font size for level 1 bullets to **32 pt.** Change the font size for level 2 bullets to **28 pt.**
    f. Create a footer using the company name Santos-Pearce. Do not show the footer on the title slide.
4. At the end of the presentation, reuse some slides from the presentation **New Insurance**, located in the drive and folder where your Data Files are stored. Select the slides with the titles *Farm Insurance* (second slide) and *Specialty Insurance* (last slide).
5. Divide the slides into sections and name the sections as indicated below.

    Slides 1 and 2: **Introduction**

    Slides 3–6: **Life and Health**

    Slides 7–9: **Vehicle**

    Slides 10–14: **Property**

    Slides 15–16: **Farm and Specialty**
6. Collapse the slides and rearrange the order so that the *Property* section appears after *Life and Health* and before *Vehicle*.
7. Save the changes and leave the presentation open for the next Job.

JOB 2

At the company Web site, clients can provide feedback about their satisfaction with the company products and services. The data is updated each week. The feedback has been very positive, and you decide that a chart showing the current results will add credibility to the presentation.

1. If necessary, open the **Revised Insurance 1** file from the drive and folder where your solution files are stored. Save the presentation as **Revised Insurance 2**, followed by your initials.
2. In Excel, open the **Client Survey.xlsx** file from the drive and folder where your Data Files are stored. Save the worksheet as **Current Client Survey**, followed by your initials.
3. Copy the chart to the Clipboard. Switch to the presentation window. Insert a new Title and Text layout slide at the end of the presentation. Paste the chart onto the slide, using the destination theme and linking the data.
4. In the Title placeholder, type **Customer Satisfaction**. Increase the chart area to fill the area on the slide, and enlarge the pie chart as much as possible.
5. Change the legend font size to **18 pt**. Format the layout for the data labels by enabling the option **Percentage** and disabling the option **Value**. Position the data labels in the center of the categories in the chart. Select the data labels and format the font size to **18 pt** and change the font color to white.
6. Animate the chart with an entrance effect, and format the animation so that the parts of the chart appear by category. Add a subtle sound (such as a click) to the animations.
7. Save the changes and leave the presentation open for the next Job.

JOB 3

You decide it will be easier for the audience to comprehend the differences between insurance types by including a table in the presentation. To introduce the table content in increments, you decide to format the table for progressive disclosure.

1. If necessary, open the **Revised Insurance 2** file from the drive and folder where your solution files are stored. Save the presentation as **Revised Insurance 3**, followed by your initials.
2. Go to slide 4. Insert a new Title and Content slide. In the Title placeholder, type **Comparison**. Insert a table with 5 columns and 6 rows. Enter the following data in the table. Use a symbol to create the check marks and, if necessary, increase the font size of the symbol.

	TERM	WHOLE	UNIVERSAL	VARIABLE
Death benefit	√	√	√	√
Flexible payments			√	√
Invested in market				√
Guaranteed cash value		√	√	
Tax advantages	√	√	√	√

3. Resize the table and make it as big as possible to fit on the slide. AutoFit the column widths to fit the content. Distribute the rows equally and center the text vertically in the cells. Modify the table style if desired.
4. Copy slide 5, and then paste the copied slide four times between slides 5 and 6. Remove table rows from the copied slides to create progressive disclosure of the table.
5. Save the changes and leave the presentation open for the next Job.

JOB 4

To enhance the presentation, you decide to add graphics to some of the slides. Providing a visual image for each type of insurance will help the audience relate to and remember the presentation content.

1. If necessary, open the **Revised Insurance 3** file from the drive and folder where your solution files are stored. Save the presentation as **Revised Insurance 4**, followed by your initials.
2. Insert a new Content with Caption layout slide at the beginning of the Life and Health section (before slide 3). In the Title placeholder, type **Life Insurance**. In the text box on the left, type **Relieve anxiety over life's uncertainties!**. Then insert a clip art image (an illustration or a photograph) of a family.
3. Insert a new Content with Caption layout slide between slides 10 and 11. In the Title placeholder, type **Health Insurance**. In the text box on the left, type **Live well!**. Then insert a clip art image (an illustration or a photograph) related to health, fitness, or the medical field.
4. Insert a new Content with Caption layout slide at the beginning of the Property section (before slide 14). In the Title placeholder, type **Property Insurance**. In the text box on the left, type **Protect your assets!**. Then insert a clip art image (an illustration or a photograph) of the interior or exterior of a home.
5. Insert a new Content with Caption layout slide at the beginning of the Vehicle section (before slide 20). In the Title placeholder, type **Vehicle Insurance!**. In the text box on the left, type **Ride safely!**. Then insert a clip art image (an illustration or a photograph) of a vehicle, such as an auto or a motorcycle.
6. Insert a new Content with Caption layout slide at the beginning of the Farm and Specialty section (before slide 24). In the Title placeholder, type **Farm Insurance**. In the text box on the left, type **Protection against perils!**. Then insert a clip art image (an illustration or a photograph) of a farm.
7. Insert a new Content with Caption layout slide between slides 25 and 26. In the Title placeholder, type **Specialty Insurance**. In the text box on the left, type **Avoid the risks!**. Then insert a clip art image (an illustration or a photograph) related to travel, pets, and so on.
8. Modify the clip art images you added to fit in with the color scheme and design. For example, recolor or remove the picture backgrounds, apply a picture style, modify the borders, make corrections, or change the color and add artistic effects.
9. Go to slide 2. Convert the text in the bulleted list to a SmartArt object, such as the Target List option.
10. Save the changes and leave the presentation open for the next Job.

JOB 5

The slide content is complete, so you can now create an agenda slide and add some transitions to the slides.

1. If necessary, open the **Revised Insurance 4** file from the drive and folder where your solution files are stored. Save the presentation as **Revised Insurance 5**, followed by your initials.
2. Create the following custom shows:

   Slides 3–10: **Life Insurance**

   Slides 11–13: **Health Insurance**

   Slides 14–19: **Property Insurance**

   Slides 20–23: **Vehicle Insurance**

   Slides 24–25: **Farm Insurance**

   Slides 26–27: **Specialty Insurance**

3. At the end of the Introduction section (after slide 2), insert a new Title and Content slide. Create an agenda slide:
   a. Insert a **Vertical Box List** SmartArt object, and add three additional shapes.
   b. Enter the custom show names in the shapes.
   c. Create hyperlinks to the custom shows, and enable the option to return to the agenda slide at the end of each custom show.
   d. Resize and reposition the SmartArt object so it fits on the slide.
4. Choose a transition format and apply the transition to all the slides. Set the transition to trigger on mouse click.
5. Preview all the slides and animations, and make any necessary corrections. Review the progressive disclosure on slides 7–11 and make any necessary adjustments.
6. Save the changes and leave the presentation open for the next Job.

JOB 6

Your supervisor is very pleased with your work and asks you to save the presentation in other formats to make it easy to share the information and design with others.

1. If necessary, open the **Revised Insurance 5** file from the drive and folder where your solution files are stored. Save the presentation as **Revised Insurance 6**, followed by your initials.
2. Inspect the document, and then remove all document properties and personal information.
3. Save the presentation as a video, using the same filename and the Portable Devices setting. Use the default setting to spend 5 seconds on each slide.
4. Save the presentation as an XPS document, using the same filename. Close the XPS viewer.
5. Add your digital signature to the presentation. The purpose for signing the document is to verify the integrity of the content.
6. Save the presentation as a template. Be sure to save the file in your solutions folder. Name the file **S-P Template**, followed by your initials, and change the file type to **PowerPoint Template (*.potx)**. When prompted about removing the digital signature and proceeding, click **Yes**.
7. Delete all slides except the first slide. Remove all sections.
8. Save the changes and close the presentation.

Estimated Time for Unit: 5.5 hours

ADVANCED

MICROSOFT OUTLOOK UNIT

LESSON 4 **2.0 HRS.**
Managing Messages

LESSON 5 **1.5 HRS.**
Managing Contacts

LESSON 6 **2.0 HRS.**
Managing Calendars and Tasks

Estimated Time: 2 hours

LESSON 4

Managing Messages

OBJECTIVES

Upon completion of this lesson, you should be able to:

- Change views.
- Use Quick Steps.
- Find messages and manage conversations.
- Categorize and flag messages, and add reminders.
- Create rules.
- Personalize and proof messages.
- Track messages.
- Apply security settings to messages.

VOCABULARY

branch
conversation
digital signature
encryption
private key
public key
rule
Search Folder

Microsoft Outlook is a powerful tool designed to help you organize your business and personal life. Outlook provides many options for managing and customizing settings when creating, sending, and receiving e-mail messages.

Many e-mail features are designed specifically for use with a Microsoft Exchange Server account, which is an e-mail-based collaborative communications server for businesses. Most home and personal accounts typically use a Web-based e-mail service such as MSN® Hotmail® or a POP3 e-mail account with an Internet service provider (ISP).

In this exercise, the figures will show folders and e-mail messages that do not exist on your computer. The figures are intended as a guide for you to correlate the steps to the folders and e-mail messages that appear on your screen. You will be working with e-mail messages you have exchanged with other students or the instructor.

Organizing Incoming Messages

If you have only a few messages in your Outlook folders, you probably won't have any difficulty organizing the messages. You might even be able to see them all on the screen at one time. In a real-world situation, however, you might have dozens of messages, with more arriving every hour. In this case, being able to categorize, condense, and even ignore messages will enable you to manage them efficiently.

Changing Views

To save time checking and managing your messages, you can customize the view to suit your needs. The information that appears on your screen varies depending on the view setting. Using default settings, the Navigation Pane appears in all views and the messages are organized within folders that appear in the Navigation Pane. You can minimize, expand, or hide the Navigation Pane. To increase the available space for the message list and the Reading Pane, you can switch from Normal view to Reading view.

The Favorites folder, which appears at the top of the Navigation Pane, contains shortcuts to folders that you frequently access. You can add shortcuts to the Favorites folder, and you can also remove shortcuts from the folder. To make more space available in the Navigation Pane, you can collapse the Favorites folder or you can hide it.

You can choose the information that is displayed for each message, such as the level of importance, the subject, and the file size. You can also choose the order of the messages. Using default settings, e-mail messages are arranged by date, with the most recent e-mail at the top of the list. But you can customize the settings to view the messages arranged by the sender name or by importance.

EXTRA FOR EXPERTS

To change the font style and size for the text that displays in the Navigation Pane, click the View tab. In the Layout group, click Navigation Pane, click Options, and then click Font.

Step-by-Step 4.1

1. Launch Outlook. Confirm the view settings for mail:
   a. If necessary, click the Mail button in the Navigation Pane.
   b. Click the **View** tab. In the Current View group, click the **Change View** button.

c. Enable the option **Compact**. (Note that if you have an IMAP e-mail account, you may see the option IMAP Messages instead of Compact, and you should enable that option.) If the option is already enabled, click the **Change View** button again to close the menu.

d. In the Conversations group, make sure the option Show as Conversations is disabled. If prompted to not show messages arranged by conversation, click **This folder**.

2. In the status bar (the lower-right corner of the window), click the **Reading view** button. As shown in **Figure 4–1**, the Navigation Pane on the left and the To-Do Bar on the right are minimized, which maximizes the available space in the Reading Pane. (Note that the folder names and messages on your screen will differ.) If a message is selected in the message list, a preview of the message will appear in the Reading Pane.

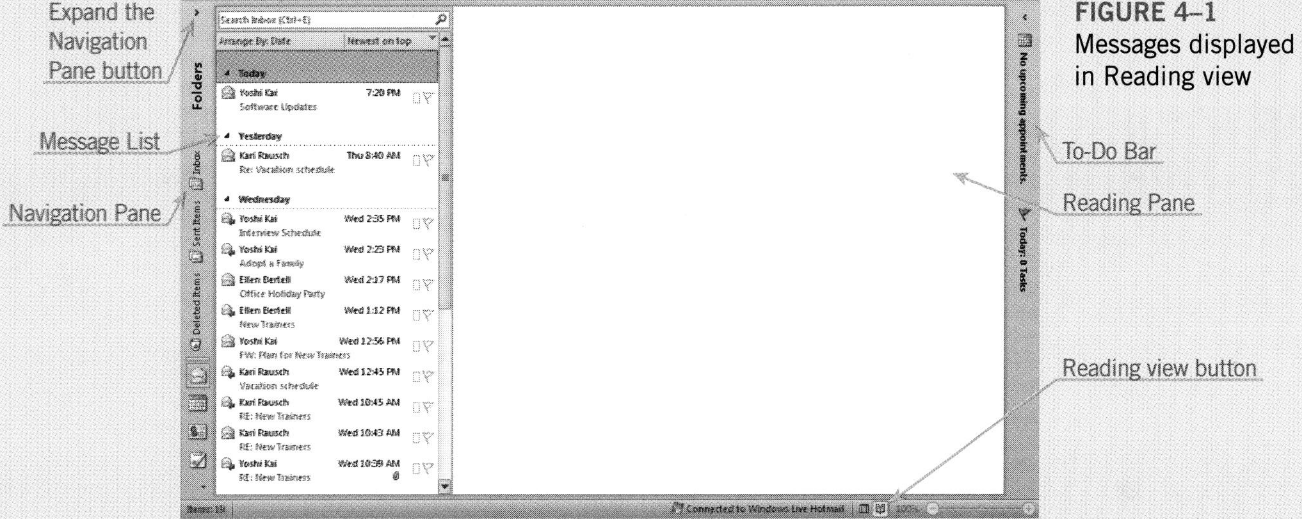

FIGURE 4–1 Messages displayed in Reading view

3. In the status bar, click the **Normal view** button to reset the view to the default settings.

4. In the Layout group, click the **Navigation Pane** button. Note that there are three display settings: Normal, Minimized, and Off. Click **Minimized**. The Navigation Pane is minimized, but the To-Do Bar on the right does not change.

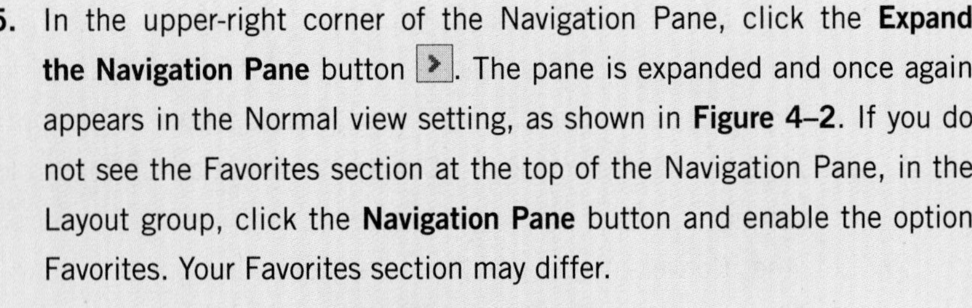

5. In the upper-right corner of the Navigation Pane, click the **Expand the Navigation Pane** button. The pane is expanded and once again appears in the Normal view setting, as shown in **Figure 4–2**. If you do not see the Favorites section at the top of the Navigation Pane, in the Layout group, click the **Navigation Pane** button and enable the option Favorites. Your Favorites section may differ.

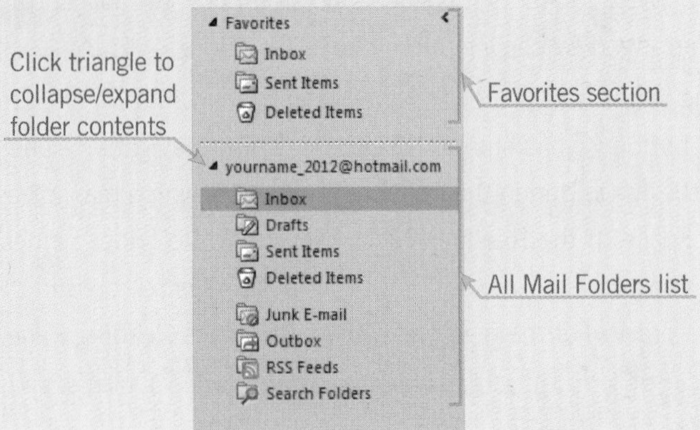

FIGURE 4–2
Navigation Pane in Normal view

TIP

You can also resize the Navigation Pane by dragging the right border to increase/decrease the width of the pane.

6. Click the **triangle** to the left the your mail folder to collapse the folder contents listing. The triangle now points to the right. Click the **triangle** again to expand the contents of the folder. When the contents are expanded, the triangle tilts downward and points to the lower-right corner.
7. To add a new shortcut to Favorites, point to and click a folder in the All Mail Folders list (for example, Outbox) and then drag and drop the folder into the Favorites section of the Navigation Pane. The folder contents are not moved, but a link to the folder is created within the Favorites folder.
8. In the Layout group, click the **Navigation Pane** button and then click **Favorites** to toggle the feature off. The Favorites folder no longer appears at the top of the Navigation Pane, but folders in the All Mail Folders list are not affected. Click the **Navigation Pane** button, and then click **Favorites** to toggle the feature back on. The same folders are displayed again.
9. To delete the link in the Favorites folder, right-click the **shortcut** you created in Step 7, and then click **Remove from Favorites**. The folders in the All Mail Folders list remain unchanged.
10. In the All Mail Folders list, select the **Inbox** folder. If necessary, in the message list, click the most recent message. On the View tab, in the Arrangement group, click the **From** button. (If you do not see the From button, you can click Arrange By at the top of the message list, and then click From.) The messages are rearranged in alphabetical order by the name of the sender. The most recent message is still selected, with the list scrolled to the appropriate point.

11. In the Arrangement group, click the **Reverse Sort** button. The messages are rearranged again by the sender name, in reverse alphabetical order, and the most recent message in the list is selected.
12. In the Arrangement group, click the **Expand/Collapse** button and then click **Collapse This Group**. All messages for the sender of the most recent message are collapsed. Click the **Expand/Collapse** button again, and then click **Collapse All Groups**. Now you can easily review the list of all senders, without viewing the messages from each sender.
13. In the Arrangement group, click the **Date** button. (If you do not see the Date button, at the top of the message list, click **Arrange By** and then click **Date**.) The messages are all expanded and rearranged in chronological order, with the most recent message at the top of the list.
14. Leave Outlook open for the next Step-by-Step.

Using Quick Steps

To simplify repetitive tasks, you can use Quick Steps, and with a single click, you can apply multiple actions to a message. For example, if you typically forward messages to your manager, you can create a Quick Step to complete the task. Outlook provides five default Quick Steps, and the first time you use one of those Quick Steps, you are prompted to enter the setup information. You can also create your own custom Quick Steps.

Step-by-Step 4.2

1. In the Navigation Pane, right-click the **Inbox** folder, and in the submenu, click **New Folder**. The Create New Folder dialog box opens. In the Name text box, type **Trainers** and then click **OK**. A new subfolder is added below the Inbox header in the Navigation Pane, as shown in **Figure 4–3**.

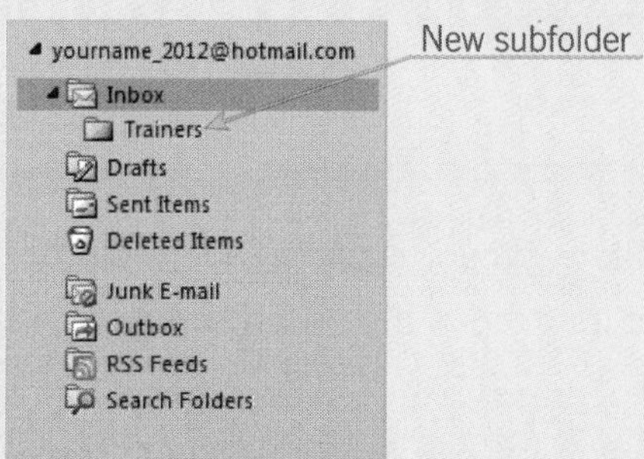

FIGURE 4–3
New subfolder added to Inbox

2. Click the **Home** tab. In the Quick Steps group, click the **More** button and then click **Manage Quick Steps** to open the dialog box shown in **Figure 4–4**.

FIGURE 4–4
Manage Quick Steps dialog box

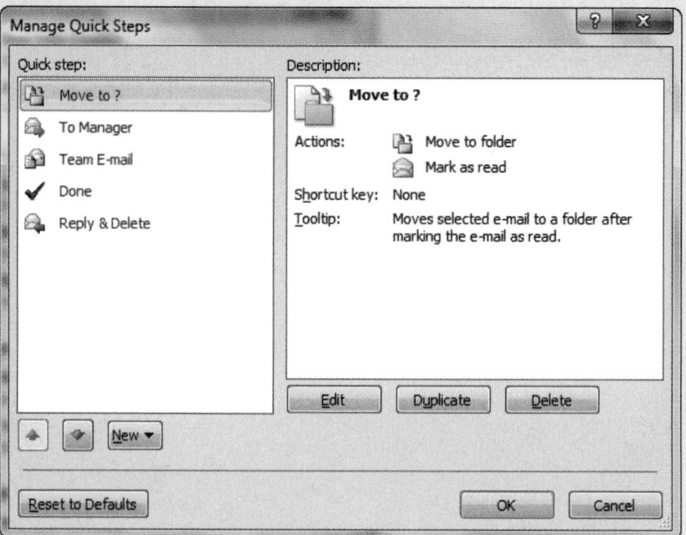

3. Click each option under Quick step, and review the description of each option. Then click **Cancel** to close the dialog box.
4. The first time you use one of the default Quick Steps, a First Time Setup dialog box will open, as shown in **Figure 4–5**. Then you can complete the settings to customize the Quick Step. Do not customize any of the Quick Steps at this time.

FIGURE 4–5
First Time Setup dialog box

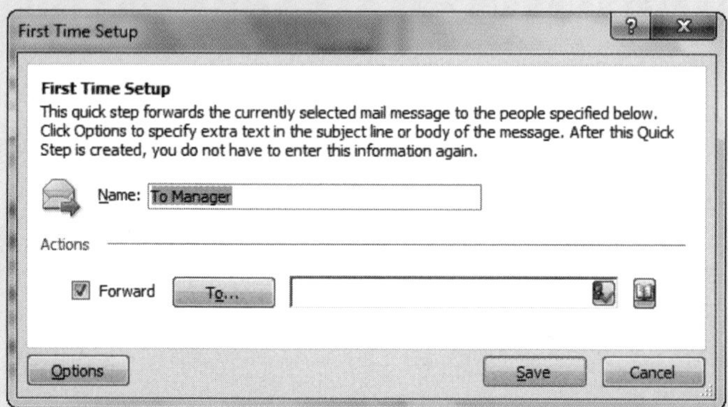

5. In the Quick Steps group, click the **More** button, and then click the **Create New** button to open the dialog box shown in **Figure 4–6**.

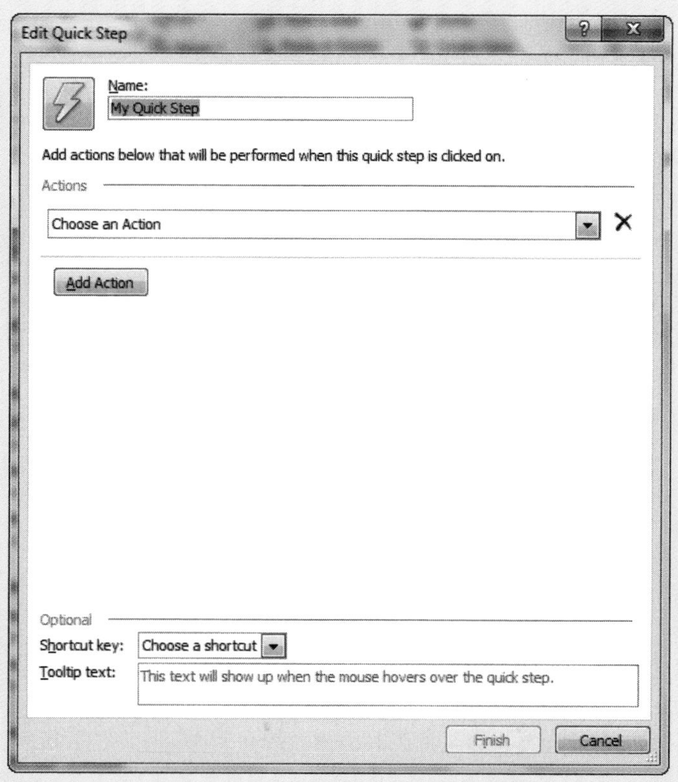

FIGURE 4–6
Edit Quick Step dialog box

6. Create a new Quick Step:
    a. Under Actions, click the **Choose an Action** list arrow, and then under Filing, click **Move to folder**. The dialog box shows the options for the selected action.
    b. In the Name text box, edit the existing text to read **Move to Trainers**.
    c. Under Actions, click the **Choose folder** list arrow and then click **Trainers**.
    d. Click **Finish**. The Quick Steps group is updated, and the new *Move to Trainers* button is displayed.
7. In the message list, select a message. In the Quick Steps group, click the **Move to Trainers** button.

8. In the Navigation Pane, click the **Trainers** folder. The message you moved will be displayed in the message list. Drag and drop the message from the message list to the Inbox folder in the Navigation Pane, as shown in **Figure 4–7**.

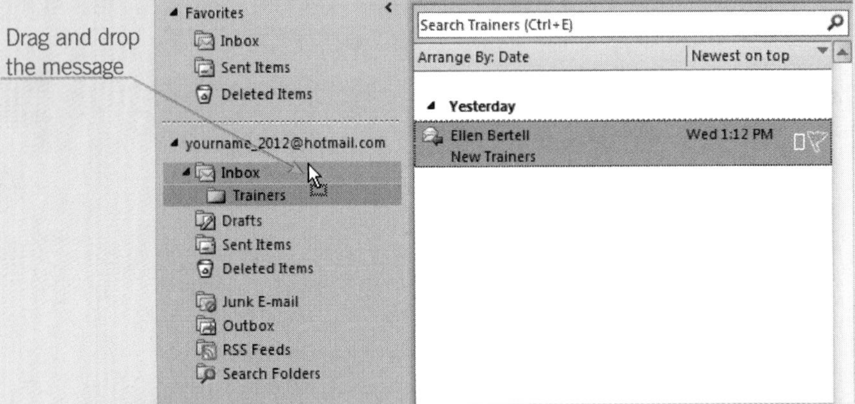

FIGURE 4–7
Drag and drop a message into a different folder

9. In the Navigation Pane, right-click the **Trainers** folder heading and then click **Delete Folder**. When prompted to move the folder and all of its contents into the Deleted Items folder, click **Yes**.
10. In the Quick Steps group, click the **Dialog Box Launcher**. The Manage Quick Steps dialog box opens. In the left pane, under Quick step, *Move to Trainers* is already selected. Under the right pane, click **Delete** and then click **OK**. The custom button is removed from the Quick Steps group.
11. Leave Outlook open for the next Step-by-Step.

Finding Messages

You can quickly locate a message by entering a keyword or phrase in the Search text box at the top of the message list. To further refine the search, you can use commands on the Search Tools Search tab, which enables you to specify many more search criteria, such as the sender's name, the subject, whether or not there is an attachment, when the message was received, and more. For example, if you are looking for a message with an attachment that you received this week, you can filter the messages using both criteria.

VOCABULARY
Search Folder

You might find that you frequently search for the same criteria. For example, you might search daily for schedule updates for a specific project. Rather than repeatedly using the Search feature and entering criteria to find related messages, you can create a ***Search Folder***, which is a virtual folder that contains a list of all e-mail messages that match specific search criteria. The messages are not actually stored in the Search Folder. Instead, the Search Folder contains a link to the messages that meet the defined search criteria, while the messages remain in the Inbox or another e-mail folder. Each time you open the Search Folder, the specified search is automatically performed and the list of messages meeting the search criteria is updated. Search Folders are only used to locate e-mail messages.

If you delete the Search Folder, the messages identified by the search criteria are not deleted because the messages are not stored in the Search Folder. The Search Folder only contains links. However, if you open the Search Folder and delete one of those links to a specific message, not only is the link removed from the Search Folder, but the message is also removed from its actual location. Therefore, be cautious when deleting links from a Search Folder.

Step-by-Step 4.3

1. If necessary, select your **Inbox** in the Navigation Pane. At the top of the message list, note that the Search text box changes based on which folder is selected, and it now reads *Search Inbox.* Click the **Search Inbox** text box, and then type the first name of a sender for one or more messages that are in your Inbox. In the example shown in **Figure 4–8**, the keyword *kari* has been entered in the search text box, and all messages containing the keyword are displayed in the message list.

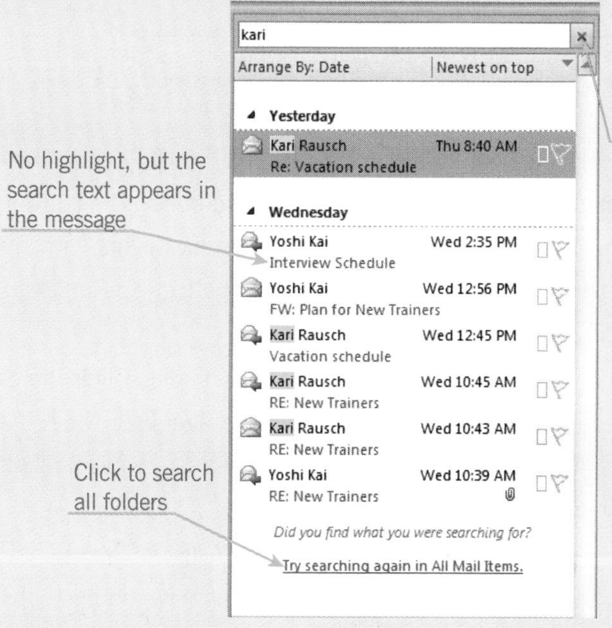

FIGURE 4–8
Search results for *kari*

2. Usually the sender's name is included in the From field in a message header (the area above the message body containing the To, From, and Cc fields), so many occurrences of the name are highlighted in the message list. However, the search text may also appear in other message header fields, or the search text may appear in the body of a message. Those messages are also included in the search results. If a message without a highlight appears in your list, select the message to preview the contents. All occurrences of the search text (in this case, a sender's name) will be highlighted in the message header and/or the body of the message.

TIP

If the Search Text box in your Navigation Pane does not show Search Inbox, click the File tab and then click Options. In the Outlook Options dialog box, click Search and under Results, enable the option Current folder. Click OK.

3. The current search results show only messages in the Inbox folder. Scroll to the bottom of the message list and click the link **Try searching again in All Mail Items**. The list of results will most likely expand to include messages from other folders shown in the Navigation Pane, including the Sent Items folder and the Deleted Items folder.

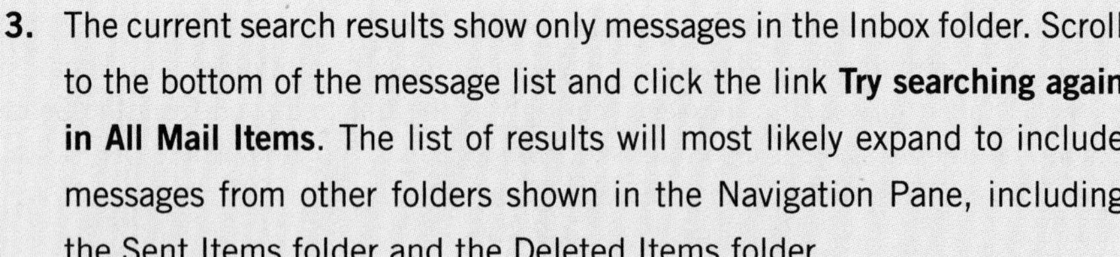

4. To restore the message list to the default view, click the **Close Search** button on the right side of the Search text box (or simply delete the text in the Search text box).
5. Click the **Search Inbox** text box. The Ribbon shows the Search Tools Search tab. In the Refine group, click the **Has Attachments** button. Only messages with attachments appear in the message list. Note that the search criteria *hasattachments:yes* appear in the Search text box. If you have several messages with attachments, the prompt shown in **Figure 4–9** may appear just below the Search text box. If this prompt appears, click it to view all messages with attachments.

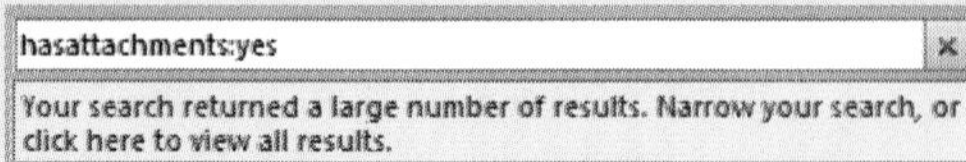

FIGURE 4–9
Prompt to show all messages with attachments

6. On the Search Tools Search tab, in the Refine group, click the **This Week** button. All messages with attachments received during the current week appear in the list. The default setting for a week begins with Sunday. The Search text box now displays criteria for both *has attachments:yes* and *received:this week*.
7. In the Navigation Pane, click the **Sent Items** folder. Click the **Search Sent Items** text box at the top of the message list. Note that the messages are arranged based on default settings, and no search criteria appear in the Search text box.
8. In the Refine group, click the **More** button. A list of additional criteria appears. Click **Cc**. A Cc search text box displays under the Search Sent Items text box, as shown in **Figure 4–10**. If you remember copying someone on a message, you can use this filter to help you find the message. Click the **Remove** button to the right of the Cc search text box.

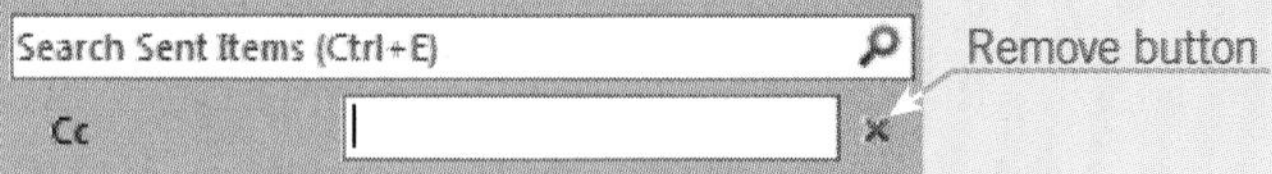

FIGURE 4–10
Search text box with Cc field

9. In the Navigation Pane, click the **Inbox** folder. Click the **Search Inbox** text box, and if necessary, click the Search Tools Search tab. In the Options group, click the **Recent Searches** button and then click **has attachments:yes**. The results again show only the messages with attachments.

10. Click the **Folder** tab. In the New group, click the **New Search Folder** button to open the dialog box shown in **Figure 4–11**.

FIGURE 4–11
New Search Folder dialog box

11. Scroll down and, under Organizing Mail, click **Large mail**. Under Customize Search Folder, click **Choose**. In the Mail Size dialog box, change the KB size to **110** and click **OK**. Then click **OK** to close the New Search Folder dialog box. In the Navigation Pane, the new search folder, labeled *Larger Than 110 KB*, appears as a subfolder below Search Folders.
12. The Larger Than 110 KB folder is selected in the Navigation Pane. All messages larger than 110 KB appear in the message list. Message size is often large because of embedded pictures or attached files. You can use this search folder to identify large messages, and then you can choose whether to delete the messages in order to conserve space in your Inbox.
13. In the Navigation Pane, right-click the **Larger Than 110 KB** folder, and then click **Delete Folder**. When prompted to permanently delete the Search Folder, click **Yes**.
14. Leave Outlook open for the next Step-by-Step.

WARNING

Be sure you select the Delete Folder command—not the Delete All command. Deleting the Search Folder will delete the links, but it will not remove the messages from the other folders.

Managing Conversations

It is common to exchange multiple e-mails with one or more colleagues or friends about a particular subject. In the process, you create a chain of related messages. Even using the handy search features, finding the messages in the chain can take time, and you might miss some of the messages. The solution is to group your messages by conversation. A ***conversation*** is a chain of messages from the first message through all responses. When a new message in the chain is received, the entire conversation moves to the top of the message list. A conversation is based on the subject line for the message, so if the subject line changes, a new conversation is created.

VOCABULARY
conversation

Arranging messages by conversations enables you to see the complete course of the message exchanges. You know who replied to the messages and when. You can respond to messages more efficiently because you can easily identify and view the most recent responses, and you can get a visual map of all the related messages before you act.

By default, conversations are collapsed in the message list. When conversations are collapsed, you can view the conversation heading, which is the subject line. A small white triangle is used to identify a conversation with multiple messages. A white triangle appears to the left of a conversation, even when the conversation is not selected, to indicate that at least two messages are included in the conversation. If a white triangle appears when you select a message, only one reply in the conversation is included. When you expand all the messages in a conversation, the triangle turns black and tilts downward. You can then view all the individual messages in the current folder as well as other folders.

VOCABULARY
branch

Lines and dots provide a visual map to illustrate the relationship between messages, including related messages in other folders. Big orange dots indicate the most recent messages in the conversation. Each big orange dot indicates a branch in the conversation. A ***branch*** is a split in a conversation. For example, if you send a message to two or more recipients, and each recipient responds, then each response creates a new branch in the conversation. The branch heading shows the From field for the message, and lines are used to help identify the branches. When you click one of the branch recipients, the latest message in the branch appears on top. Small orange or gray dots indicate earlier messages in the branch. Messages that are displayed in gray italics are located in another folder, such as the Sent Items folder. Even though the message is stored in a different folder, you can still view the content of that message in the Reading Pane.

The Clean Up command eliminates redundant messages and gets rid of extra copies of messages. You can clean up all folders at the same time. If you no longer want to view ongoing messages in the conversation, you can choose to ignore the conversation. When you ignore a conversation, all current and future messages in the conversation are moved directly to the Deleted Items folder.

Step-by-Step 4.4

A conversation is described and illustrated in this exercise, but you will not be able to view the same conversation on your computer screen. However, if you follow the steps below, you can compare the conversations in your Inbox to those illustrated in this Step-by-Step.

1. In the Navigation Pane, click your **Inbox** folder. Click the **View** tab. If necessary, in the Arrangement group, click the Date button to organize the messages by date, with the newest message at the top.
2. In the Conversations group, enable the command **Show as Conversations**. When prompted to show messages arranged by conversations, click **This folder**. Note that the Date button in the Arrangement group changed to *Date (Conversations)*, and at the top of the message list, the Arrange By setting is Date (Conversations).
3. In the Conversations group, click the **Conversation Settings** button, and if necessary, enable the option Show Messages from Other Folders.

4. Review the conversations in your message list. A small triangle to the left of a message subject line indicates that the conversation contains multiple messages. Stacked envelopes next to the conversation heading also indicate multiple messages. See **Figure 4–12**.

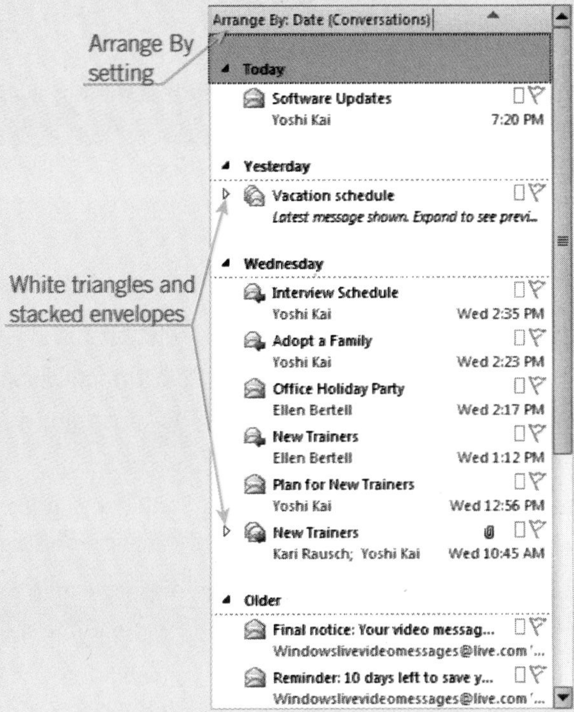

FIGURE 4–12
Messages arranged by Date (Conversations)

5. In your message list, find a conversation with multiple messages. (If you don't see any white triangles, select a message that you responded to, and then a triangle will be displayed to the left.)
6. Click the **white triangle** once. The conversation is expanded to show the most recent messages, as shown in **Figure 4–13**. The orange dots identify the most recent messages. In the example in Figure 4–13, the conversation has two branches: messages exchanged with both Kari and Yoshi and messages exchanged with just Kari. Note that the triangle is not tilted downward, so there are more messages in this conversation. The text below the conversation heading, *Split conversation. Expand to see all items.*, indicates that the conversation is split and has more than one branch.

TIP

If the conversation includes unread messages, the subject is bold and the number of unread messages appears to the right of the subject.

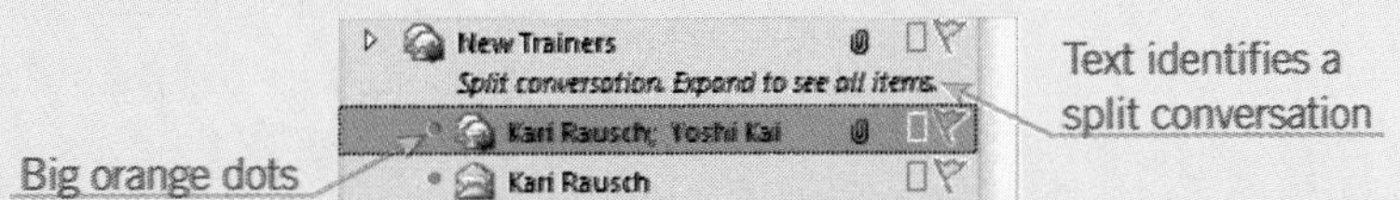

FIGURE 4–13
Most recent messages in a conversation

7. Click the **white triangle** again. The conversation is expanded to show all the messages, including those from the Sent Items folder, as shown in **Figure 4–14**. The gray italic fonts indicate the related messages are in a different folder. Note that the triangle turns black and is now tilted downward.

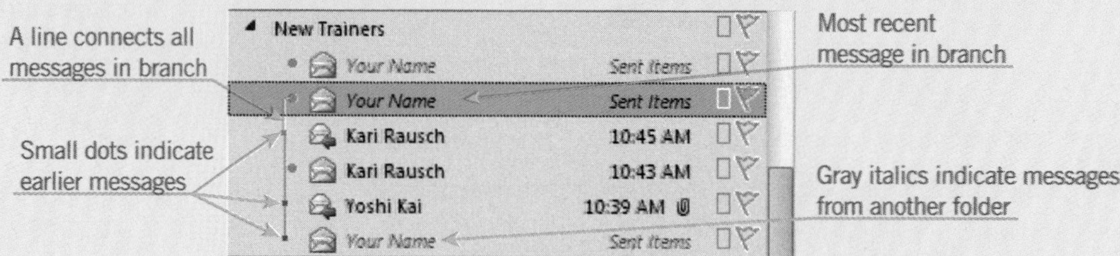

FIGURE 4–14 All the messages in a conversation

8. Review the conversation map to see the relationship of the messages. When you select a different message within the conversation, the line identifies related messages in a branch. To illustrate, in Figure 4–14, the lines and dots indicate the following:
   a. A message from Your Name, in the Sent Items folder, is the most recent message in the conversation.
   b. At 10:45 AM, Kari responded to the message that Yoshi sent. The small orange dot next to the selected message indicates that it is not the most recent message in the conversation.
   c. Yoshi's message, which was sent at 10:39 AM, was a response from a message sent by Your Name (at the bottom of the line, from the Sent Items folder).
   d. The message Kari sent at 10:43 AM was part of a different conversation branch; therefore, the line does not connect to that message.
9. If necessary, select a message with a small orange dot. Click the **Home** tab, and in the Respond group, click the **Reply** button. Note that a prompt appears at the top of the header: *You are not responding to the latest message in this conversation. Click here to open it.*
10. Click the note at the top of the heading, and then click **Open the Latest Message in This Conversation**. The most recent message is opened, and you can then reply or forward it. Close both messages without any action.

11. Click the **black triangle** to collapse the conversation. The conversation is still selected. On the Home tab, in the Delete group, click the **Clean Up** button and then click **Clean Up Conversation**. When prompted to move redundant messages to the Deleted Items folder, click **Clean Up**. When prompted to apply the action to all items in the selected conversation, click **OK**. If there are no redundant messages in the conversation, a prompt will appear explaining that, based on your Clean Up settings, no messages were moved to the Deleted Items folder.
12. On the Home tab, in the Delete group, click the **Ignore** button. If prompted to apply the action to all items in the selected conversation, click **OK**. When prompted to move the conversation to the Deleted Items folder, click **Cancel** to abort the action.
13. Click the **View** tab and, in the Conversations group, disable the **Show as Conversations** option. When prompted, click **This folder**.
14. Leave Outlook open for the next Step-by-Step.

TIP

If you ignore a conversation and then change your mind, you can move the messages back to a folder in your Navigation Pane. Open the Deleted Items folder, select the messages you want to restore, right-click the selection, point to Move, and then select a folder.

Assigning Categories to Messages

Tags make it easy for you to quickly identify messages and even group and sort the messages. You can tag a message by assigning a category. Outlook provides a list of color category names, such as Blue, Green, and Orange. You can rename these categories, or you create a new category, select a color, and assign a unique name. For example, you can create a new category for a project, and then you can tag e-mail messages that are related to that project. To simplify the process of categorizing several messages, you can set Quick Click options to repetitively assign a specified category. The Quick Click setting remains until you change it.

Step-by-Step 4.5

1. In the message list, select a message from the Inbox folder. Click the **Home** tab, and in the Tags group, click the **Categorize** button. The default categories are shown in **Figure 4–15**. Your list may differ.

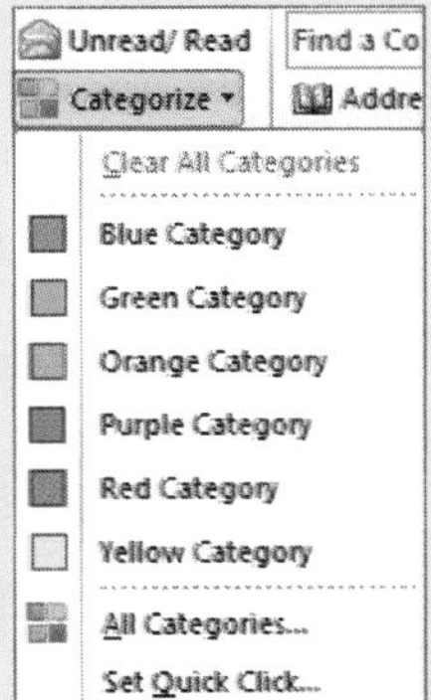

FIGURE 4–15
Default categories

2. Do not click any of the options. If you were assigning a category for the first time, you would be prompted to rename the category, as shown in **Figure 4–16**. And if desired, you could assign a shortcut key, which is not necessary for this exercise.

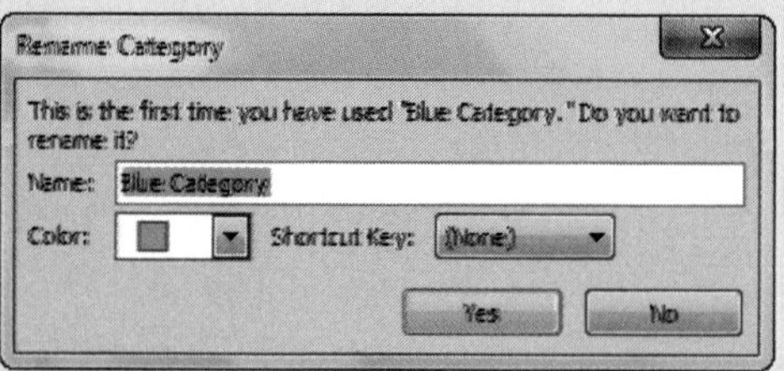

FIGURE 4–16
Prompt to rename a category

3. In the Categorize menu, click **All Categories** to open the dialog box shown in **Figure 4–17**. Note that you can add new categories, rename existing categories, or assign shortcut keys to categories.

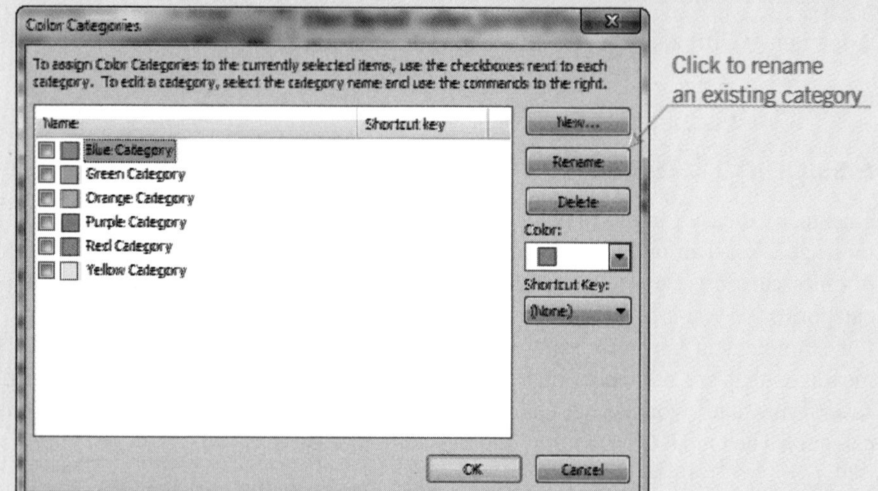

FIGURE 4–17
Color Categories dialog box

4. Click the **New** button to open the Add New Category dialog box. In the Name text box, type **Important**. Then click the **Color** list arrow and select the **Dark Red** category color. Click **OK** to create the new category. Note that in the Color Categories dialog box, the new category has been added at the bottom of the list. Click **OK** to close the Color Categories dialog box. Both the conversation and the selected message show a dark red box in the category column, as shown in **Figure 4–18**. In the Reading Pane, an *Important* category banner appears in the InfoBar, the area above the address fields.

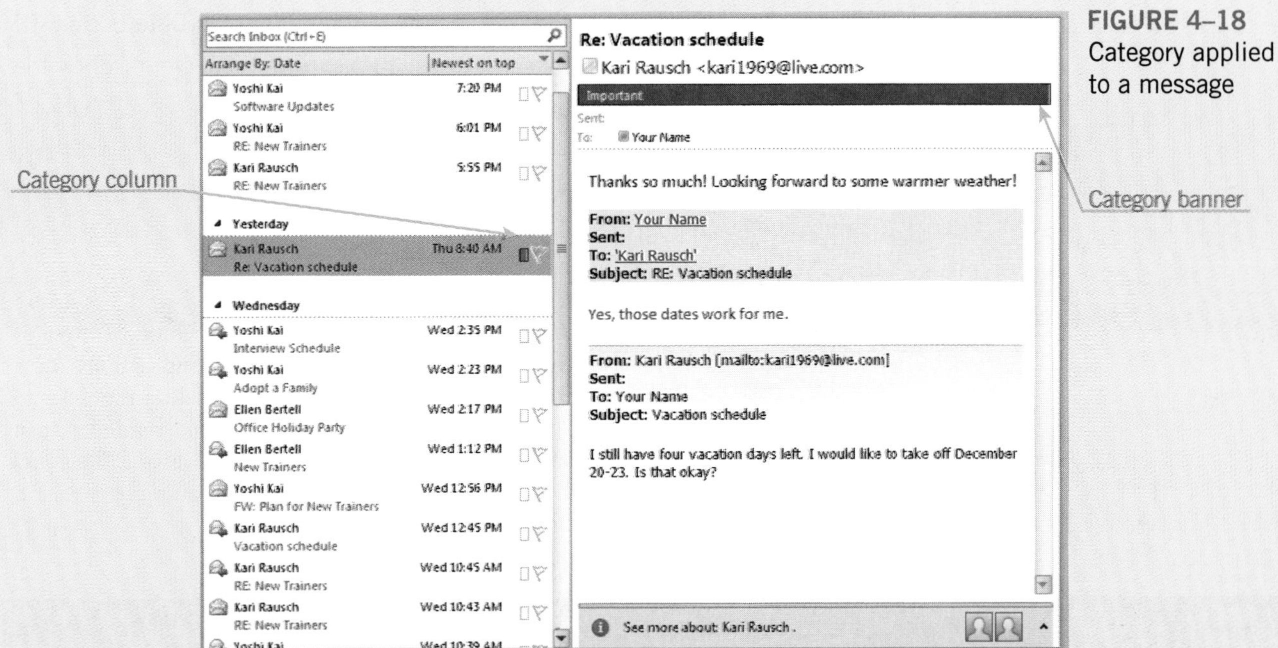

FIGURE 4–18
Category applied to a message

5. In the Tags group, click the **Categorize** button and then click **Set Quick Click**. In the Set Quick Click dialog box, click the **list arrow,** click **Important**, and then click **OK**. Now you can apply the Important category to multiple messages without opening the Categorize menu.
6. In the message list, click an empty category tag box; it will be filled with the dark red color. Click the category tag box for another message. Continue until you have at least three messages tagged for the Important category.
7. Click the **View** tab. In the Arrangement group, click the **Categories** button. All of your messages are arranged by category. If necessary, scroll to the bottom of the message list to view the Important group.
8. Click another empty category tag box in your message list. The categorized message is moved to the end of the list and now appears in the Important group.
9. The Quick Click setting is still set for the Important category. To remove the category assigned to one of the messages, in the Important group, click a dark red category tag box. The fill color is removed from the category tag box, and the message no longer appears in the Important group. The message is moved back to the default message list. Remove the category from the other messages in the Important group.
10. Click the **Home** tab. In the Tags group, click the **Categorize** button and then click **All Categories**. Under Name, select **Important**, and then click **Delete**. When prompted to delete the category, click **Yes**. Click **OK** to close the dialog box.

TIP

If you are viewing messages by Dated (Conversations), the flag is applied to all items in the conversation.

TIP

Note that if you want to apply a different category, you need to click the Categorize button and select a new category, or you need to change the Quick Click setting.

11. Click the **View** tab. In the Arrangement group, click the **Date** button. (If the Date button does not appear in the Arrangement group, click the **Arrange By** option at the top of the message list and then click **Date.**)
12. Leave Outlook open for the next Step-by-Step.

Flagging Messages for Follow Up

Many of us depend on notes to remind us to follow up on tasks. Outlook provides several different versions of a flag to help you identify follow-up actions for a message. If the message requires a response or action, you can add a reminder to your to-do list that specifies the start and/or due dates. Flags and reminders can be applied to both incoming and outgoing messages. Details about the flags and reminders appear above the address fields in the InfoBar in the Reading Pane and in an open message. Reminders also appear on the To-Do Bar.

Step-by-Step 4.6

1. Click the **View** tab. If necessary, in the Arrangement group, click the Date button to organize the messages with the newest message on top.
2. In the message list, a message should already be selected. Click the **Home** tab. In the Tags group, click the **Follow Up** button and then click **Today**. In the message list, a red flag appears in the Flag Status column next to the message, as shown in **Figure 4–19**. The bright red flag indicates that an action or response is a high priority for today. In the Reading Pane, you can see a note in the InfoBar that provides follow-up information. Because you flagged the message to follow up today, the start and due dates are the current date.

FIGURE 4–19
Red Flag tag in the message list

3. Click the **Follow Up** button, and then click **Set Quick Click**. In the Set Quick Click dialog box, click the **list arrow** and then click **Next Week**. Note that the flag color is lighter than the Today flag, which will indicate there is more time for the follow up. Click **OK** to close the dialog box.
4. In the Flag Status column, click a **flag icon** to tag the message with a Next Week flag. Click a couple more flag icons. Each time you click a flag icon, the Next Week flag appears. The Set Quick Click option enables you to apply the *Next Week* flag several times without opening the Follow Up menu.
5. In the Tags group, click the **Follow Up** button and then click **Add Reminder**. The Custom dialog box opens, as shown in **Figure 4–20**. Your settings will differ.

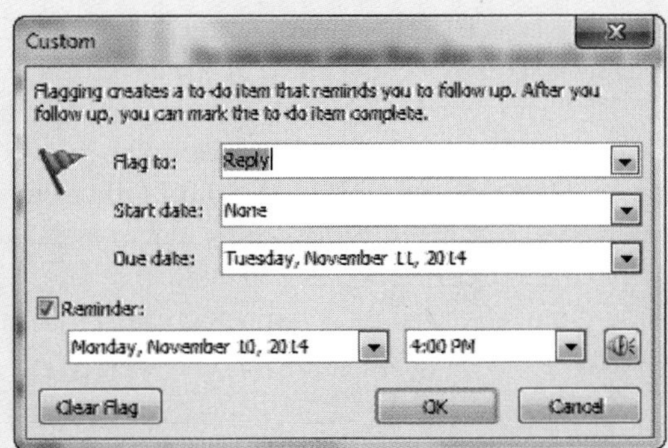

FIGURE 4–20
Custom dialog box

6. Apply custom settings for the flag and a reminder:
   a. Click the **Flag to** list arrow, and then click **Reply**.
   b. Click the **Start date** list arrow, and then click **None**.
   c. Click the **Due date** list arrow, and then select the date for next Tuesday.
   d. The Reminder option is already enabled. Under Reminder, click the **list arrow** and then select the date for next Monday.
   e. Click **OK**.
7. The Next Week flag appears in the Flag Status column. Also, the task appears on the To-Do Bar. Open the selected message. In the InfoBar, a note appears indicating that you need to reply by the specified date. The note also includes information about the reminder.
8. Note the subject line for the selected message. In the Navigation Pane, click the **Tasks** button. In the To-Do List, double-click the **subject line** for the message. The message opens. Close the message.
9. In the Navigation Pane, click the **Mail** button. Click one of the Next Week flag icons in the message list. The flag icon changes to a check mark to indicate that the task is complete. Right-click the check mark, and then click **Clear Flag**.
10. Right-click each of the other flag icons in the Flag Status column and clear the flag for each message.
11. Leave Outlook open for the next Step-by-Step.

Creating Rules

A ***rule*** is an action that Outlook automatically performs based on a condition. Rules are used to manage both incoming and outgoing messages. For example, you can create a rule to move all messages from a specific sender to a designated folder, or you can create a rule to add a tag to a message of high importance. Outlook provides a number of rule templates, and you can customize these rules.

VOCABULARY
rule

EXTRA FOR EXPERTS

If you use an Exchange Server account, an Automatic Reply feature in Backstage view would be available to simplify this process.

When customizing existing rules or creating new rules, you identify conditions for when to apply the rule, specify the action(s) to take, and include any exceptions to the rule. The rule is turned on by default and is ready to be used when a message is first received or sent. However, you can also run rules manually. When you no longer want to use a rule you created, you can disable or delete the rule.

In the next Step-by-Step, you will create an Out of Office rule to automatically reply to incoming messages. Automatic replies to incoming messages are commonly used in a business environment. Before establishing the rule, you will create a template with a standard message, and then you will create a rule to use the template file to reply to messages.

Step-by-Step 4.7

1. Create a message template:
   a. If necessary, click the **Home** tab. In the New group, click the **New E-mail** button.
   b. Click the **Format Text** tab. In the Format group, click the **Plain Text** button.
   c. In the message body, type the following:

      I will be out of the office November 12 and 13. If you need assistance, please call my assistant Darian at 419-555-2311.
   d. Click the **File** tab, and then click **Save As**.
   e. In the File name box, type **Out of Office**. Click the **Save as type** list arrow and select **Outlook Template (*.oft)**. Navigate to the drive and folder where you save your solution files. Click **Save**.
   f. Close the message. When prompted to save changes, click **No**.
2. If necessary, select a message in your Inbox. On the Home tab, in the Move group, click the **Rules** button and then click **Create Rule** to open a dialog box similar to the one shown in **Figure 4–21**. Your settings will differ because some of the options include information from the selected message. In the Create Rule dialog box, you can create simple rules such as playing a sound when a message is received from a specified contact. If you click the Advanced Options button, the Rules Wizard will open, but the proposed options will be based on the selected message. Close the dialog box.

FIGURE 4–21
Create Rule dialog box

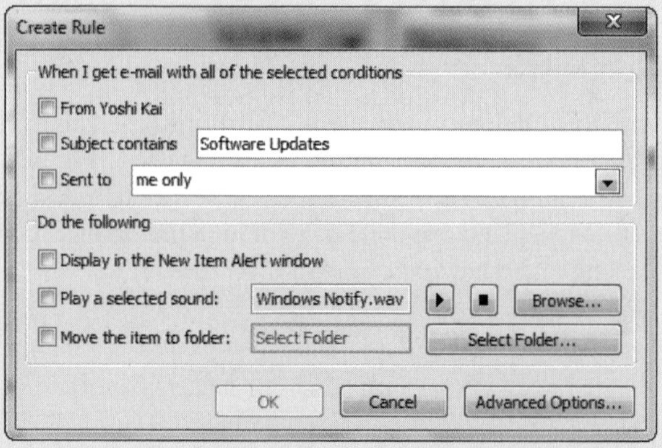

3. In the Move group, click the **Rules** button, and then click the **Manage Rules & Alerts** button to open the dialog box shown in **Figure 4–22**. Using this dialog box, you can begin the Rules Wizard by starting from a blank rule.

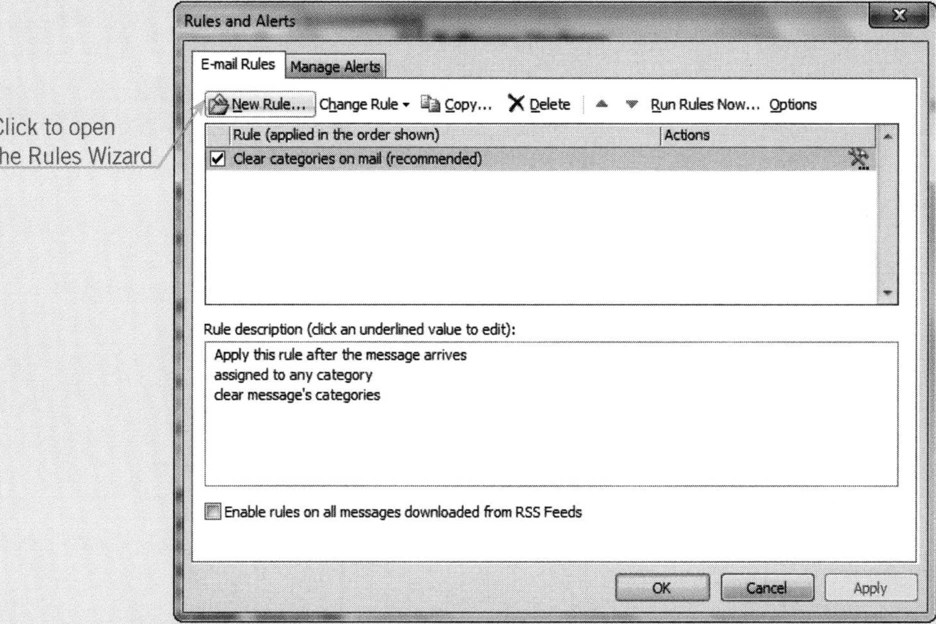

FIGURE 4–22
Rules and Alerts dialog box

4. Click **New Rule** to open the Rules Wizard dialog box. Under Start from a blank rule, select **Apply rule on messages I receive**, as shown in **Figure 4–23**.

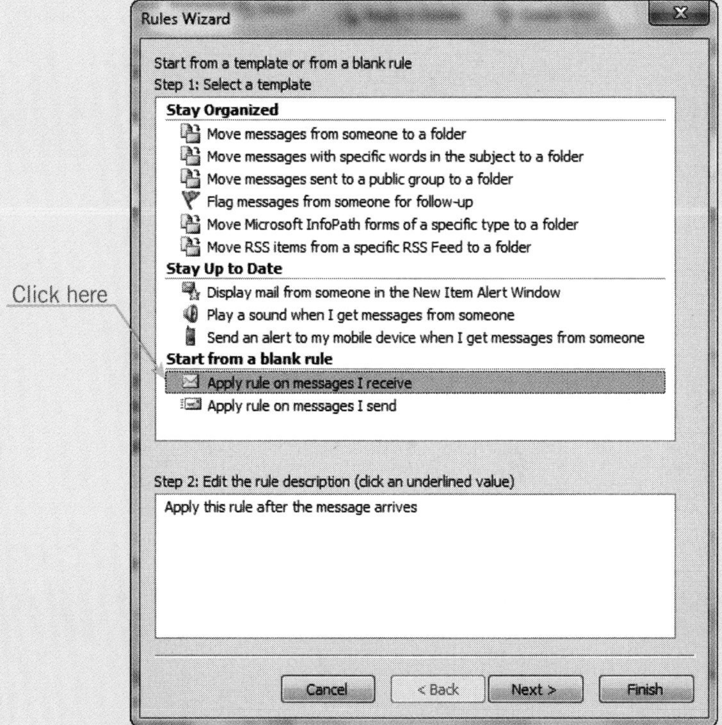

FIGURE 4–23
Rules Wizard dialog box

5. Click **Next** to show the options for conditions. Scroll down to review the list. You can select multiple options. Under Step 1, enable the options **sent only to me** and **where my name is in the To or Cc box**, as shown in **Figure 4–24**.

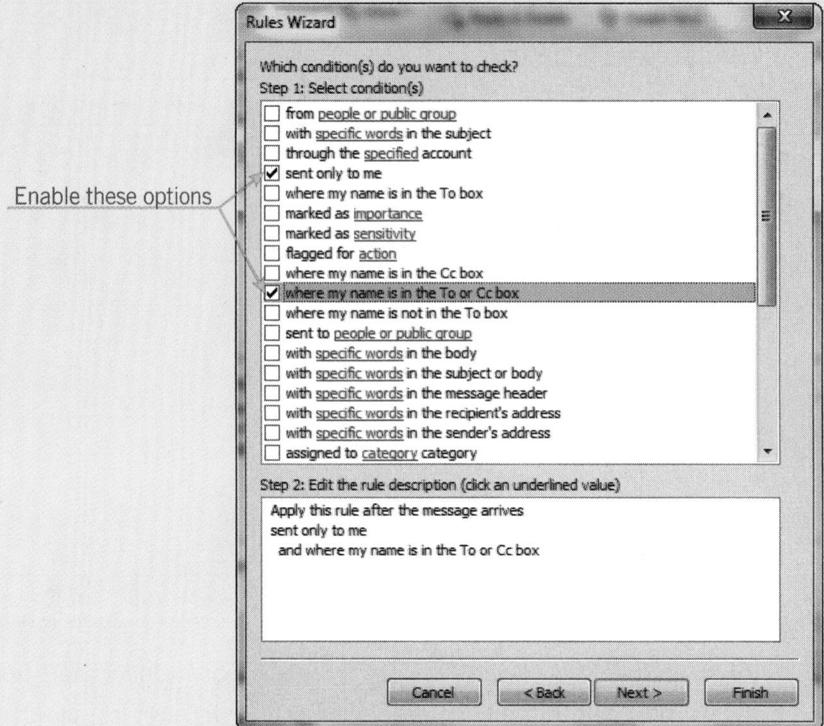

FIGURE 4–24
Conditions in the Rules Wizard dialog box

6. Click **Next** to show the action options. Review the options. Note that you can forward the message and you can play a sound. Under Step 1, enable the option **reply using a specific template**, as shown in **Figure 4–25**.

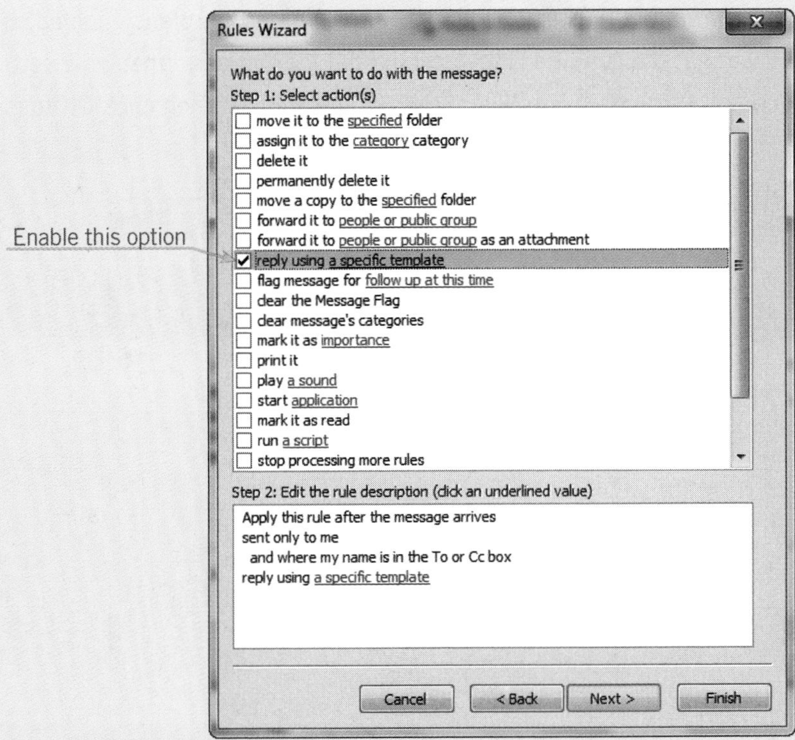

FIGURE 4–25
Actions in the Rules Wizard dialog box

7. Under Step 2, click the link **a specific template**. In the Select a Reply Template dialog box, click the **Look In** list arrow and then select **User Templates in File System**.
8. Click **Browse**, navigate to your solution files folder, and then click **OK**. Select the filename **Out of Office**, and then click **Open**.
9. Click **Next** to show the exception options. Scroll through the list to review the exceptions, but do not enable any exceptions. Click **Next** to show the last dialog box in the Rules Wizard. In the text box under Step 1, the existing text is already selected. Type **Out of Office**.

10. Note that under Step 2, the option to turn on the rule is enabled. Note also that the conditions are described under Step 3. When your settings match those shown in **Figure 4–26**, click **Finish**. Then click **OK** to close the Rules and Alerts dialog box.

FIGURE 4–26
Finish rule setup in the Rules Wizard dialog box

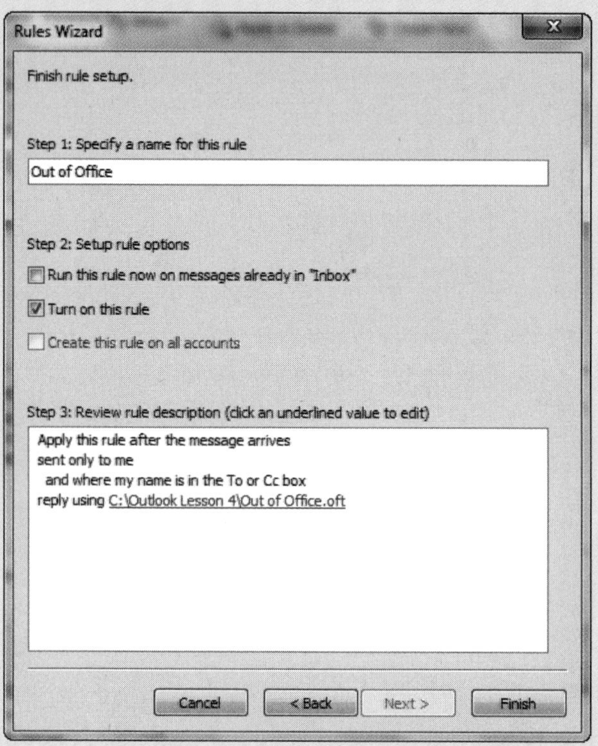

11. On the Home tab, in the Move group, click the **Rules** button and then click **Manage Rules & Alerts**. On the E-mail Rules tab, under Rule, disable the **Out of Office** rule by clicking the check box. The rule is disabled when the check box is blank.
12. The blue background indicates the Out of Office rule is selected. With the rule selected, click **Delete** in the toolbar just above Rule. When prompted to delete the rule, click **Yes**. Click **OK** to close the dialog box.
13. In the Navigation Pane, click the **Outbox** folder and then select the blank message you created in Step 1. In the Delete group, click the **Delete** button. Click the **Inbox** folder.
14. Leave Outlook open for the next Step-by-Step.

Preparing Outgoing Messages

When preparing outgoing messages, you should consider the appearance of the message, the sensitivity and importance of the message, the file sizes of attachments, and the accuracy of the content.

Personalizing and Proofing Messages

Outlook offers many features to help you create messages with a professional appearance. If you have chosen to send your e-mail messages in HTML format rather than as plain text, you can customize them using stationery backgrounds. You can apply Quick Styles or you can design your own formats by applying themes and changing font attributes, just as you would in other Office applications.

To avoid embarrassment, you can use the Spelling feature and the AutoCorrect Options to proofread, correct, and format message content.

You can create multiple signatures to be added at the end of each message. For example, you may want to create a signature for business e-mails and a second signature for personal e-mails. The signature can include both text and images. To add a signature at the end of a message, you use the Signature command in the Include group on the Message tab. You can change the settings so a signature is automatically inserted in every message you write.

Step-by-Step 4.8

1. If necessary, click the **Home** tab. In the New group, click the **New E-mail** button. In the message body, type **Outlook offers several backgrounds, font themes, and Quick Styles to format messages.**. Click the **Options** tab. In the Themes group, click the **Fonts** button. Position the mouse pointer over the menu options to see a live preview of the font themes. Click **Angles**. If a signature block appears in the e-mail message, the formatting for the signature block does not change.
2. Click the **Format Text** tab. In the Styles group, click the **Change Styles** button and then point to **Style Set**. A submenu displays several styles. Click **Simple**. Note that the font style, font color, and the message alignment all change.
3. Click the **File** tab, and then click **Options**. If necessary, click **Mail** in the left pane. Under Compose messages, note that you can enable the option to Always check spelling before sending. Click **Spelling and Autocorrect**. You can specify AutoCorrect Options and create custom dictionaries just as you can in other Office applications. Click **Cancel**.

4. In the right pane, under Compose messages, click **Stationery and Fonts**. The Personal Stationery tab in the Signatures and Stationery dialog box opens. The default settings are shown in **Figure 4–27**. Note that you can click Font to change the default font settings for creating new mail messages, replying or forwarding messages, and composing and reading plain text messages.

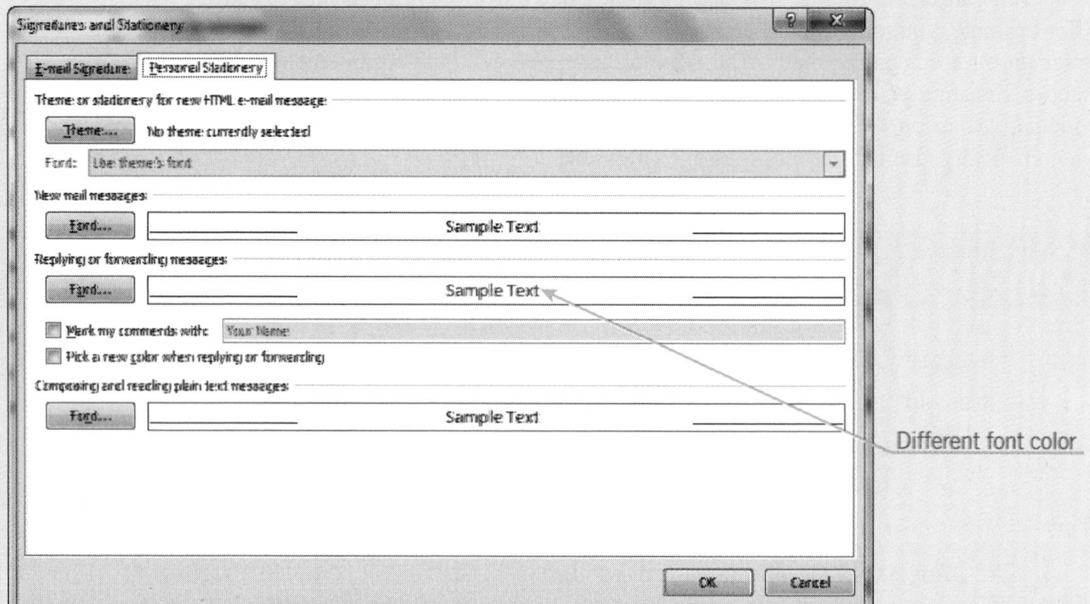

FIGURE 4–27 Default settings for Personal Stationery

5. Click **Theme** to open the Theme or Stationery dialog box. Under Choose a Theme, click several of the theme names to preview the preset font styles and backgrounds. Select **Quadrant**, and then click **OK**. Click **OK** to close the Signatures and Stationery dialog box. After changing the default settings for the personal stationery theme, the current message window will not show the new formats. You won't see the effects of the new settings until you open a new message window.
6. In the Outlook Options dialog box, under Compose messages, click **Signatures**. The E-mail Signature tab in the Signatures and Stationery dialog box opens, as shown in **Figure 4–28**. Your settings will differ.

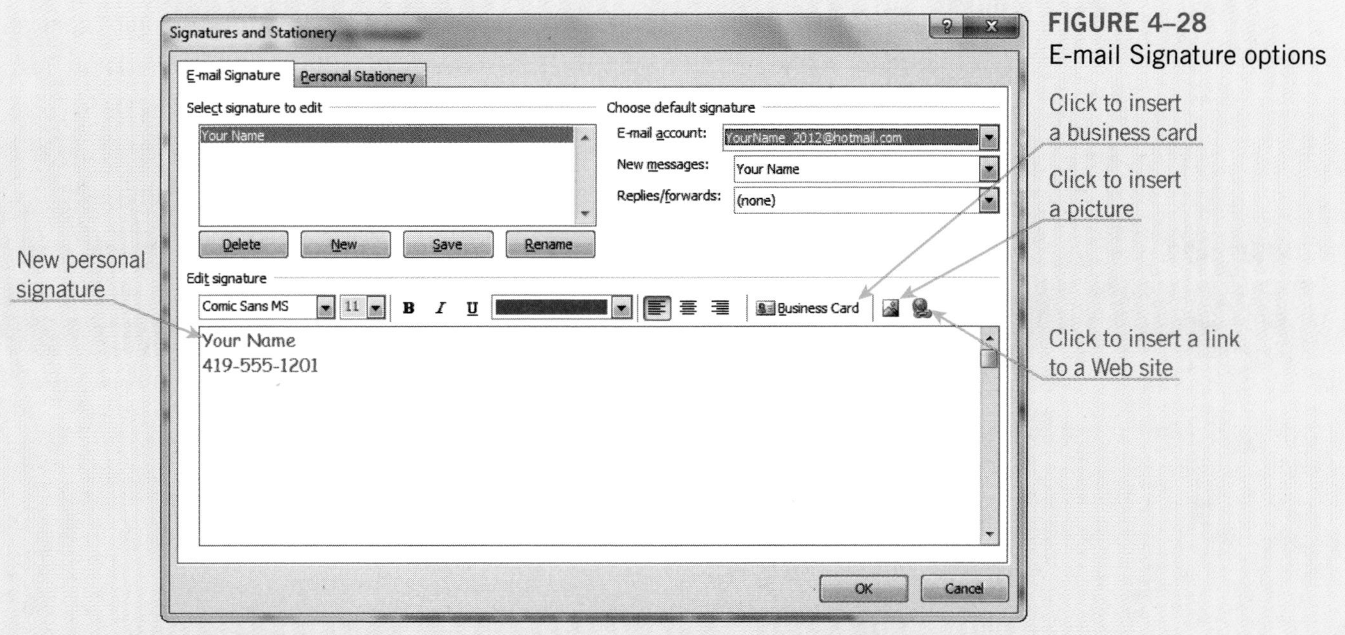

FIGURE 4–28
E-mail Signature options

7. Create a new signature and change the default settings for signatures:
   a. Under Select signature to edit, click **New**. In the New Signature dialog box, type your first and last names and then click **OK**.
   b. Under Edit signature, type your first and last names. Press **Enter** and then type your phone number.
   c. Format the signature text as desired, applying font styles, font colors, bold and/or italic formats, and text alignment.
   d. If you have created an electronic business card, you can include the business card in the signature; or, if you want to insert a photo, you can click the Picture button. You can also insert a hyperlink to a Web site.
   e. Under Choose default signature, click the **New messages** list arrow and then select your name.
   f. Click the **Replies/forwards** list arrow, and then select your name.
8. Click **OK** to close the Signatures and Stationery dialog box. Click **OK** again to close the Outlook Options dialog box. Close the message without saving the changes.
9. On the Home tab, in the New group, click the **New E-mail** button. Your custom signature is automatically inserted in the message body.
10. Click in the message body, above your signature. Click the **Insert** tab. In the Illustrations group, click the **Picture** button. If necessary, navigate to the Libraries folder, and then open the Pictures folder. Open the Sample Pictures folder. Select the **Koala** picture, and then click **Insert**.

11. The Picture Tools Format tab is displayed. In the Size group, change the picture height to **.7"**. In the Arrange group, click the **Wrap Text** button and then click **Top and Bottom**. Deselect the picture. The picture is positioned in the upper-left corner of the message body, and the insertion point appears below the picture, as shown in **Figure 4–29**.

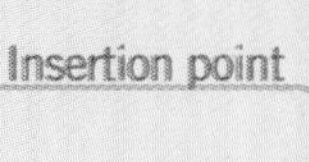

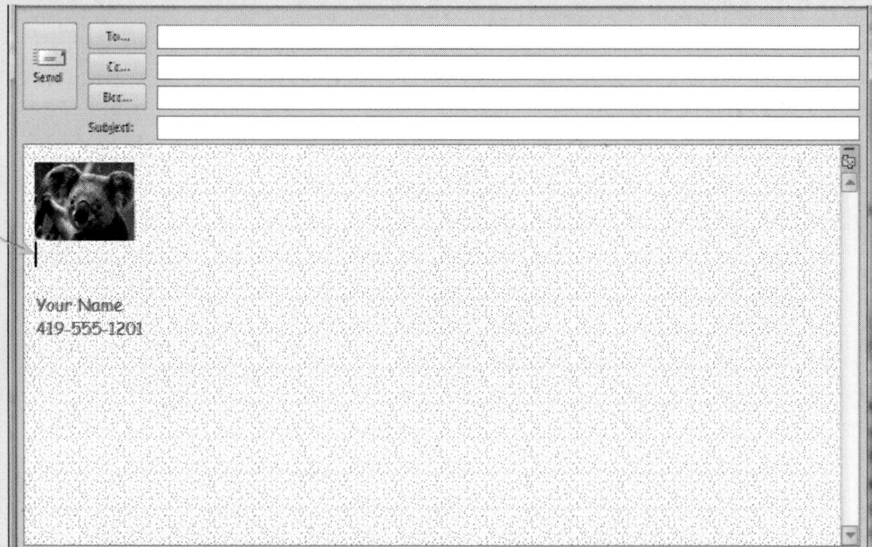

FIGURE 4–29
Personalized message with custom signature and stationery background

12. Restore the Signatures and Stationery settings to the default settings:
    a. Click the **File** tab and then click **Options**. If necessary, click Mail.
    b. Under Compose messages, click **Signatures**. Under Select signature to edit, select the signature you created and labeled with your name and then click **Delete**. When prompted to delete the signature, click **Yes**. Your signature is also removed from the settings for the default signature for new messages and for replies/forwards.
    c. Click the **Personal Stationery** tab. Click **Theme** to open the Theme or Stationery dialog box. Under Choose a Theme, at the top of the list, select **(No Theme)**. Then click **OK**.
13. Click **OK** to close the Signatures and Stationery dialog box, and then click **OK** to close the Outlook Options dialog box.
14. Close the message without saving the changes. Leave Outlook open for the next Step-by-Step.

TIP

Just as you can enhance graphics in other Office applications, you can apply corrections, color, and artistic effects and remove backgrounds from pictures and clip art inserted in the message body.

Inserting and Attaching Files to Outlook Messages

Inserting a picture is not the same as attaching a picture to a message. When a picture or clip art image is inserted in the body of a message, the recipient can see the image when they open the message. When a picture or clip art image is attached to the message, the recipient does not see the image, and they can choose whether or not to open the file and/or save the file on their computer.

When clip art images and pictures are inserted or copied into the body of a message, the content is embedded in the message body. You can resize and position the objects, and you can apply artistic effects, just as you would in other Office applications. Note that when you use plain text, all font formats are removed and you cannot insert graphics.

Outlook 2010 blocks attachments larger than 20 MB. The recipient's e-mail provider might have even lower limits. Furthermore, your message might cause your recipient's mailbox to exceed the storage quota. So, when attaching files or embedding content in a message, you must be aware of the file sizes. Outlook offers a feature for compressing the files. Note that artistic effects applied to graphics can be compromised by the compression.

TIP

You can also attach Outlook items to a message. For example, you can attach a contact, an appointment, or a task.

Step-by-Step 4.9

1. If necessary, click the Home tab. In the New group, click the **New E-mail** button.
2. In the Subject text box, type **Family Update**. Click in the message body and type **Kylie is now five years old.**.
3. Click the **Insert** tab. In the Illustrations group, click the **Picture** button. Navigate to the drive and folder where your Data Files are stored. Select the filename **Kylie.bmp** and then click **Insert**. The picture is inserted in the body of the message.
4. The Picture Tools Format tab will appear. Format the picture:
   a. In the Size group, change the height setting to **2"**. If necessary, change the width setting to **1.33"**.
   b. In the Arrange group, click the **Wrap Text** button and then click **Top and Bottom**. Then drag the picture and position it above the line of text.
   c. In the Adjust group, click the **Artistic Effects** button. In the second row, click the third option **Paint Brush**.
   d. The picture should still be selected. In the Adjust group, click the **Compress Pictures** button to open the dialog box, as shown in **Figure 4-30**. Your settings will differ.

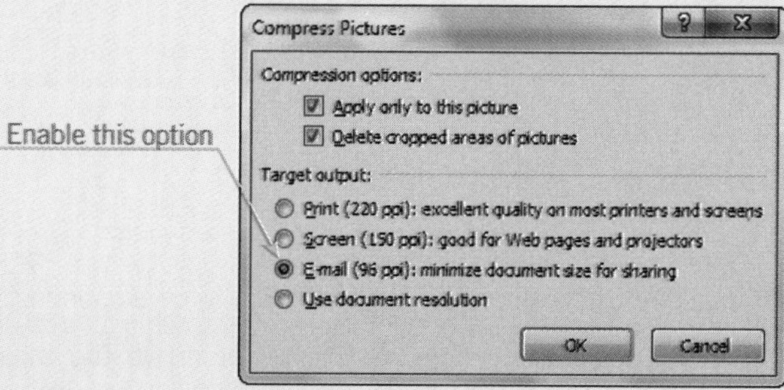

FIGURE 4–30
Compress Pictures dialog box

   e. Under Target output, enable the option **E-mail (96 ppi): minimize document size for sharing** and then click **OK**.

5. Click the **Save** button on the Quick Access Toolbar to save the message to the Drafts folder.
6. Click the **File** tab. Note that the Properties information shows the file size is approximately 80–95 KB.
7. Click the **Message** tab. If necessary, select the picture in the message body. Press **Delete**.
8. Click the **Insert** tab. In the Include group, click the **Attach File** button. Navigate to the drive and folder where your Data Files are stored. Select the filename **Kylie.bmp**, and then click **Insert**. The file is attached to the message.
9. Click the **Save** button on the Quick Access Toolbar.
10. Click the **File** tab. Note that the Properties information shows the file size is 1 MB. Also note that the top of the center pane shows an option to resize images when sending the message. See **Figure 4–31**. If you were to send this message, the size of the attached file would be reduced to 79 KB.

FIGURE 4–31
Backstage view for message with attached file

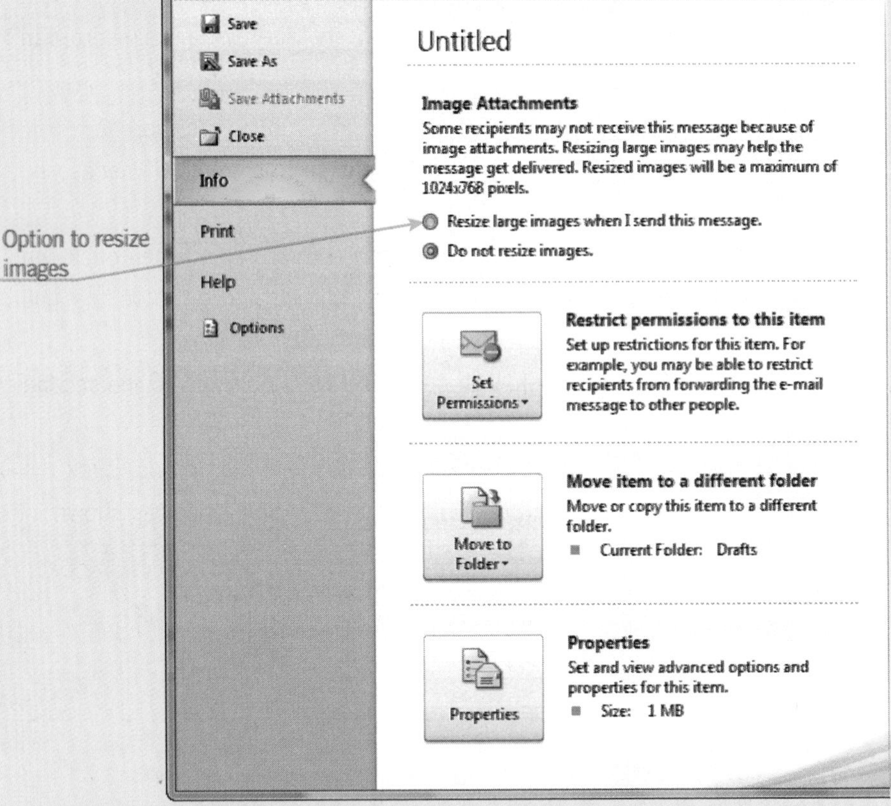

11. Click **Close** to close the message. If prompted to save changes, click **Yes**.
12. In the Navigation Pane, click the **Drafts** folder. In the message list, select and delete the message with the subject line *Family Update*.

13. In the Navigation Pane, click the **Deleted Items** folder. In the message list, review the deleted messages. If there are some messages you do not want to delete, move them to a different folder. Right-click the **Deleted Items** folder, and then click **Empty Folder**. When prompted to permanently delete all of the items and subfolders, click **Yes**.
14. Leave Outlook open for the next Step-by-Step.

Tagging and Tracking Messages

Setting a level of importance for a message not only gets the recipient's attention, it also provides a helpful visual indicator. The recipient can sort messages by importance without even opening them. Another way to draw attention to a message is to flag it. You can flag a message to remind the recipient to follow up, or, as you did in Step-by-Step 4.6, you can flag a message to remind yourself to follow up.

You can track a message to find out when it was delivered and when it was read. You can track selected messages, or you can track all messages. Recipients of your messages are notified that you have requested a receipt for the message. They can answer Yes or No to this request. If they respond with Yes, you will receive a report in your Inbox confirming the date and time your recipient received the message.

If a recipient tells you that they did not receive your message, you do not need to re-create the message—you can resend the message. If the original message was sent to multiple recipients, you can remove the other recipients' names from the To box. And, you can add new recipients who did not receive the original message.

You can apply a setting so that a message will expire after a specified date. When the message expires, it still remains in the folder and can still be opened, but in the message list, the message appears with a strikethrough.

If you send an e-mail within your organization, you may be able to stop delivery of the message. If the recipient has not already read the message or deleted it from their Inbox, you can recall the message. You can request notification of whether or not the recall is successful.

If you have some experience working with e-mails, then you've probably at some time made embarrassing errors. For example, you forgot to attach a file; or even worse, you sent the message to the wrong person. Be sure to proofread the header information and the message body before you click Send.

EXTRA FOR EXPERTS

If you use a Microsoft Exchange Server, you can use the MailTips feature to help you avoid embarrassing mistakes. The feature is enabled by default. Clicking Reply All to a large recipient list or sending messages to addresses outside the organization will trigger an alert.

Step-by-Step 4.10

1. Click the **Inbox** folder, and then open one of the messages. In the Respond group, click the **Forward** button.
2. In the Tags group, click the **High Importance** button. Although you don't see any changes in the message header, the red exclamation mark will appear in the message subject line in your Sent Items folder and in the recipient's Inbox.

3. In the Tags group, click the **Follow Up** button and then click **Add Reminder**. In the Custom dialog box, create a reminder for yourself and for the recipient:
   a. Click the **Flag to** list arrow, and then click **Reply to All**.
   b. Click the **Start date** list arrow, and then click **None**.
   c. Click the **Due date** list arrow, and then select next Wednesday's date.
   d. Make sure the Reminder option is enabled. Then click the **date** list arrow and select next Tuesday's date. Click the **time** list arrow and select **11:00 AM**.
   e. Enable the **Flag for Recipients** option. Click the **Flag to** list arrow, and then click **Reply**.
   f. Under Flag for Recipients, enable the **Reminder** option. Then click the **date** list arrow and select next Tuesday's date. Click the **time** list arrow and select **8:00 AM**. Then click **OK**.
4. Note that a note appears above the message header and describes the reminders that will be flagged for both the sender and the recipient.
5. Click the **Options** tab. In the Tracking group, click the **Dialog Box Launcher** to open the Properties dialog box, as shown in **Figure 4–32**.

FIGURE 4–32
Properties dialog box

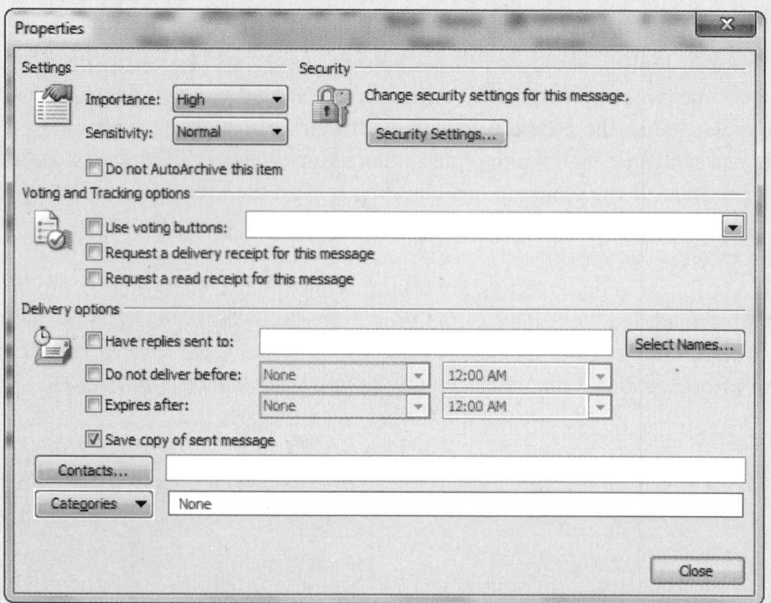

6. Under Voting and Tracking options, enable the option **Request a delivery receipt for this message**. Then enable the option **Request a read receipt for this message**.
7. Under Delivery options, enable the option **Have replies sent to**. Your e-mail address will automatically be displayed in the text box.

8. Click **Select Names**, and then double-click a contact in your Address Book. The selected contact's e-mail address is added to the Reply To box at the bottom of the dialog box. Click **OK**. When the recipient replies to the message, your e-mail address and your contact's e-mail address will automatically be added to the To box.
9. Enable the option **Do not deliver before**, click the adjacent **date** list arrow, and then select tomorrow's date. Enable the option **Expires after**, click the adjacent **date** list arrow, and then select the date one week from today. Click **Close**.
10. The Options tab is updated and includes descriptions of the new settings. Close the message without sending it and without saving the changes. Had you sent the message, a delivery receipt would eventually appear in your Inbox. Close the original message.
11. Open a message from your Sent Items folder. On the Message tab, in the Move group, click the **Actions** button and then click **Resend This Message**. The message is opened in a new window. You can edit the recipients, and you can edit the body of the message before you resend the message. Close the message without sending it or saving the changes. Close the original message.
12. Open another message in the Sent Items folder. To recall the message, on the Message tab, in the Move group, click the **Actions** button and then click **Recall This Message**. A dialog box similar to the one in **Figure 4–33** opens. A note may appear at the top of the dialog box indicating how many recipients may have already opened the message.

TIP

You can click Categories and assign a default or custom category to the message.

EXTRA FOR EXPERTS

You can also track a message by opening the message in the Sent Items folder. On the Message tab, in the Show group, click the Tracking button. Note that the Show group and the Tracking button will not appear until at least one receipt is received.

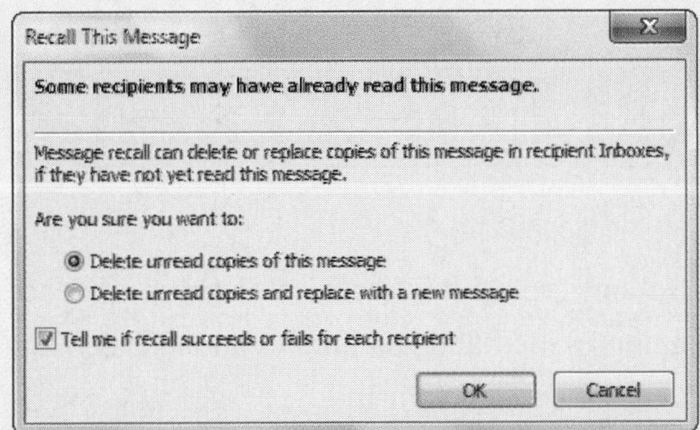

FIGURE 4–33
Recall This Message dialog box

13. Click **Cancel**. If you enable the option to receive feedback about success or failure and then click OK, after a few minutes, you will receive a notice in your Inbox indicating whether or not the recall was successful. Close the message.
14. Leave Outlook open for the next Step-by-Step.

Changing Security Settings

Often we don't stop to think about the personal information we are sharing in e-mail messages. For example, when we include multiple recipients in the To box, we are sharing those e-mail addresses with all the recipients. And, do we know who will see that information once we click the Send button? The message could get forwarded several times, to people we don't know and whom we will probably never meet. But if the information is sensitive, we want to make sure we control who gets to see it.

To avoid exposing e-mail addresses for recipients, instead of entering the addresses in the To box, enter the names in the Bcc box. Only the sender can see the names of the recipients.

Sensitivity settings are useful for advising recipients on how to take action on messages. For example, you can apply the Sensitivity setting Private to a message. Hopefully, the recipient would understand that you do not want the message shared with others. However, Sensitivity settings only suggest an action for the recipient, and they do not include any restrictions, so the recipient can still forward the message and share it with others.

Outlook does provide options for restricting permission to access a message. To use this feature, however, you must use the Information Rights Management (IRM) service, provided by Microsoft, which authenticates the credentials of people who create or receive the e-mail messages. IRM is outside the scope of this lesson. To learn more about the IRM service, search Outlook Help using the keywords *Information Rights Management.*

VOCABULARY
digital signature
private key
public key
encryption

A ***digital signature*** is an attachment to a file or e-mail message certifying that the information in the file is authentic and safe. Before you can digitally sign a message, you must obtain a digital ID. A digital ID contains a ***private key***, which is a key that stays on the sender's computer, and a certificate with a ***public key***, which is a key that a sender gives to a recipient. You can get a digital ID from your e-mail administrator or from a Certificate Authority.

Encryption is a standard method for encoding data. Sending and viewing encrypted e-mail messages requires that the sender and the recipient share their digital IDs. This means the sender and the recipient must send each other a digitally signed message, which enables you to add the other person's certificate to their Contacts.

Step-by-Step 4.11

1. Open a new message.
2. Click the **Options** tab. In the Show Fields group, if necessary, toggle on the **Bcc** button. A Bcc address field is added below the Cc field. Any e-mail addresses entered into the Bcc field will not be visible to the message recipients.
3. On the Options tab, in the Permission group, click the **Permission** button and then click **Do Not Forward**. If you have not authenticated user credentials, information about the Information Rights Management service is displayed. Click **Cancel**. A prompt indicates that you cannot use this feature without credentials. Click **OK**.
4. On the Options tab, in the More Options group, click the **Dialog Box Launcher**. Click **Security Settings** to open the Security Properties dialog box, as shown in **Figure 4–34**.

TIP

If the Permission button does not display in the Permission group on the Options tab, you can access the permission options in Backstage view. With the message window open, click the File tab, and then click Set Permissions.

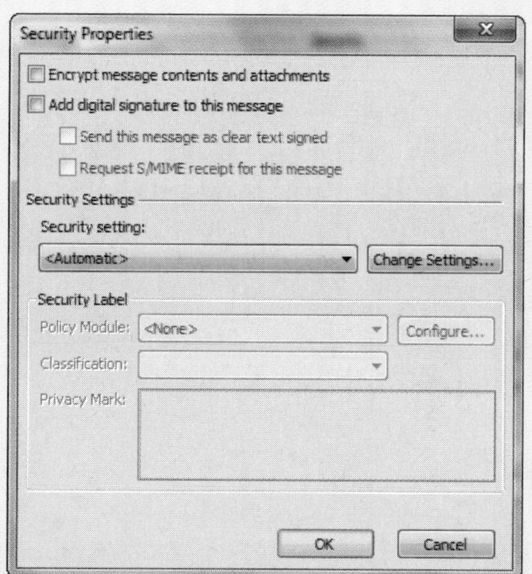

FIGURE 4–34
Security Properties dialog box

TIP

If you have a digital ID, the Sign Message button appears in the More Options group.

EXTRA FOR EXPERTS

To digitally sign all messages, click the File tab and then click Options. Click Trust Center, and then click Trust Center Settings. Click the E-mail Security tab. Under Encrypted e-mail, enable the option Add digital signature to outgoing messages. Then click OK twice.

5. Enable the **Encrypt message contents and attachments** option.
6. Enable the **Add digital signature to this message** option. Click **OK** to close the Security Properties dialog box. Then close the Properties dialog box.
7. Now that the security settings are applied, the message is ready to send. If you do not have a digital ID associated with the e-mail account, when you click Send, a prompt will indicate that there are no certificates. Close the message without saving any changes.

SUMMARY

In this lesson, you learned:

- Outlook offers many different ways to organize and view messages.
- You can use Quick Steps to simplify tasks and complete multiple actions with a single click.
- When looking for messages, you can use several Search features to filter messages based on several types of criteria.
- Arranging messages by conversations enables you to group related message exchanges for efficient handling.
- Tags make it easy for the sender to quickly identify messages and even categorize and sort the messages. Tagging messages with flags helps the sender prioritize messages with visual reminders, and the sender can also add reminders to their to-do list.
- Adding tags to messages provides a visual indicator for the recipient so they can determine the level of importance without even opening the message.
- Rules enable you to automatically apply actions based on specific conditions to manage your messages. Rules can be applied to both incoming and outgoing messages.
- Outlook offers several features for formatting and enhancing the appearance of your messages, including themes, font styles, backgrounds, and personalized signatures.
- You can track sent messages to find out when they were delivered and when they were read. You can also add reminders for both the sender and the recipient, and you can add vote buttons to get feedback from recipients.
- Several features are available to restrict access to the personal information in your messages. However, most of the security settings require authenticated credentials and digital IDs.

VOCABULARY REVIEW

Define the following terms:

branch
conversation
digital signature
encryption
private key
public key
rule
Search Folder

REVIEW QUESTIONS

TRUE / FALSE

Circle T if the statement is true or F if the statement is false.

T F 1. If you delete a Search Folder, messages identified by the search criteria are not deleted.

T F 2. Using default settings, the Navigation Pane appears in all views.

T F 3. You can receive notification that a message was delivered to the recipient's dialog box, but you cannot confirm if the recipient opened the message.

T F 4. When you no longer want to use a rule, you can disable it or delete it.

T F 5. Rules are used to manage both incoming and outgoing messages.

MULTIPLE CHOICE

Select the best response for the following statements.

1. You may be able to stop delivery of a sent message, if ________________.
   - A. the message was sent within your organization
   - B. the recipient has not already read the message
   - C. the recipient has not already deleted the message from their Inbox
   - D. all of the above
2. If you no longer want to view ongoing messages in a conversation, you should ________________.
   - A. clean up the subfolder
   - B. clean up all of the folders
   - C. choose to ignore the conversation
   - D. all of the above
3. Rules are created by defining ________________.
   - A. conditions
   - B. actions
   - C. exceptions
   - D. all of the above

4. The ______________ indicate the most recent message in a branch of the conversation.
   A. small orange dots
   B. big orange dots
   C. black triangles
   D. white triangles
5. Outlook 2010 blocks attachments larger than ______________.
   A. 110 KB
   B. 20 MB
   C. 10 MB
   D. 1 MB

WRITTEN QUESTIONS

Write a brief answer to the following questions.

1. Why is a Search Folder described as a virtual folder?

2. What is the quickest way to assign a category to several messages?

3. What are the benefits of arranging messages by conversations?

4. How do you know when all the messages in a conversation are visible?

5. How does tagging a message to show the level of importance help the recipient?

PROJECTS

PROJECT 4–1

1. Select your Inbox.
2. In the message list, assign categories to your messages. For example, assign different color categories for family members, friends, and coworkers. Be sure to use the Quick Click feature.
3. Review the messages and tag the messages for high or low importance.
4. Flag messages that require follow up. Be sure to choose an appropriate flag to indicate urgency for completing the follow up.
5. Add reminders to one or more messages and be sure to specify the type of action and the start and due dates. Also set reminders for yourself.
6. As you complete the necessary tasks in the next few days, update the Flag Status column by marking those messages complete.

PROJECT 4–2

1. Select your Inbox, and then select a message in the message list.
2. Use the Rules Wizard to create a new rule to play a special sound when messages from your manager (or a colleague or a friend) are downloaded to your Inbox:
   a. Start from a blank rule.
   b. For conditions, identify the person.
   c. For actions, play a sound of your choice.
   d. For exceptions, do not play the sound if it is an automatic reply.
   e. Assign a unique name to the new rule.
3. Test the rule. (*Hint*: Ask your manager, colleague, or friend to send you an e-mail message.) Make any necessary edits.
4. If you are using a public computer (in a classroom or lab), or if you don't want to continue using the rule, delete the rule.

PROJECT 4–3

1. Open a new message window.
2. Apply a new theme or stationery, using the HTML format. (*Hint*: Close the current message and open a new one so the new background settings are applied.)
3. Insert a clip art image or photo in the message body. Resize and reposition the image, and apply artistic effects or picture styles to enhance the image.
4. Compress the pictures in the message.
5. Create a new personal signature:
   a. Assign a unique name for the signature.
   b. Use font styles and colors to enhance the text.
   c. Consider adding a photo or a hyperlink to a personal Web site.
6. Save the message as a template in your solutions folder. If you have permission to save files on the computer you are using, and if you think you will use the personal signature in the future, also save the message as a template in the default templates folder so you can use it for future messages.
7. If you are using a public computer, open the Signatures and Stationery dialog box and restore the default setting for theme, which is (No Theme).

CRITICAL THINKING

ACTIVITY 4–1

You want to send three pictures to a friend via e-mail, but when you attach all three files to the message, the file size exceeds the server limits. What can you do to solve the problem?

ACTIVITY 4–2

You learned in this lesson that you can create multiple signatures for e-mail messages. What information would you include in a signature for business messages? What information would you include in a signature for personal messages?

Estimated Time: 1.5 hours

LESSON 5

Managing Contacts

OBJECTIVES

Upon completion of this lesson, you will be able to:

- Create new contacts.
- Edit existing contacts.
- Create a contact group.
- Assign categories to contacts.
- Find contacts.
- Forward contact information.
- Communicate with contacts.
- Create a mail merge.

VOCABULARY

contact group

distribution group

electronic business card

vCard

Outlook offers several features so you can keep your contacts up to date and organized. You can share your contact information with others, and you can use the features to initiate communication with your contacts.

Some Contacts features are designed specifically for use with a Microsoft Exchange Server account, which is an e-mail-based collaborative communications server for businesses. Most home and personal accounts typically use a Web-based e-mail service such as MSN® Hotmail® or a POP3 e-mail account with an Internet service provider (ISP).

In this lesson, many of the figures show contacts and messages that do not exist on your computer. The figures are intended as a guide for you to correlate the steps to the contacts and messages you have exchanged with other students or the instructor.

Updating Contacts

Keeping contact information up to date is an ongoing task. You often need to add new contacts and edit or remove existing contacts. Outlook offers several features to simplify these tasks.

Creating New Contacts

VOCABULARY
electronic business card

> **WARNING**
>
> Because Suggested Contacts is considered part of the Outlook Address Book, when you synchronize your contacts to other devices or applications, the Suggested Contacts may be included. To ensure that the Suggested Contacts are not included in the synchronization, in the Navigation Pane, select the Suggested Contacts folder. Click the Folder tab, and in the Properties group, click the Folder Properties button. On the Outlook Address Book tab, disable the Show this folder as an e-mail Address Book option.

Creating a new contact is simple and easy, but when you need to create several new contacts, the task can be tedious. Outlook provides shortcuts to create new contacts. When you send or receive messages, you can use the information in the To, From, Cc, and Bcc boxes to create new contacts. If the message includes an ***electronic business card***, a file that provides contact information in a business card format, you can use that information to create the new contact.

When you send an e-mail message to someone who is not in your Outlook Contacts list, Outlook automatically stores the e-mail information in the Suggested Contacts folder. You can then use that information to add a new contact to your Outlook Contacts list. There is no limit to the number of contacts that can be stored in the Suggested Contacts folder, but if desired, you can delete contacts from the folder.

Adding several new contacts for the same company is an easy process. After you create the first contact for a company, you base other new contacts on the first contact so that you don't need to re-enter all the similar information, such as company name, business address, and business phone. By default, your contacts are automatically added to the Safe Senders list, which is used to filter junk e-mail. Messages from safe senders are never moved to the Junk E-mail folder. You can change this setting in Backstage view.

If you have contact information stored on another computer or device, you can use the Import and Export command to avoid having to re-create the contacts. You will learn about importing and exporting Outlook data in Lesson 6.

Step-by-Step 5.1

1. Launch Outlook. If necessary, click the **Mail** button in the Navigation Pane to display your Inbox message list. Open any one of the e-mails in your Inbox.
2. In the From box in the message header, right-click the **sender's name** to display the shortcut menu shown in **Figure 5–1**.

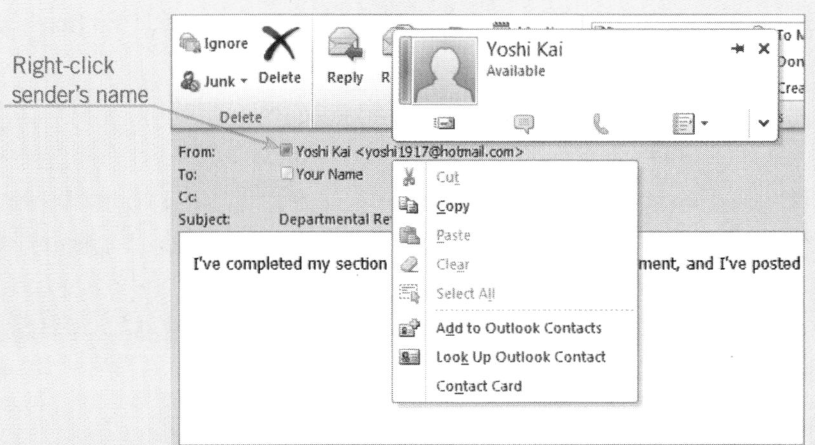

FIGURE 5–1
Shortcut menu after right-clicking sender's name

3. In the shortcut menu, click **Add to Outlook Contacts**. A Contact window, similar to the one shown in **Figure 5–2**, opens. The name shown in the Display as field in the Contact window is the name that will appear in the To, Cc, and Bcc boxes in a message header.

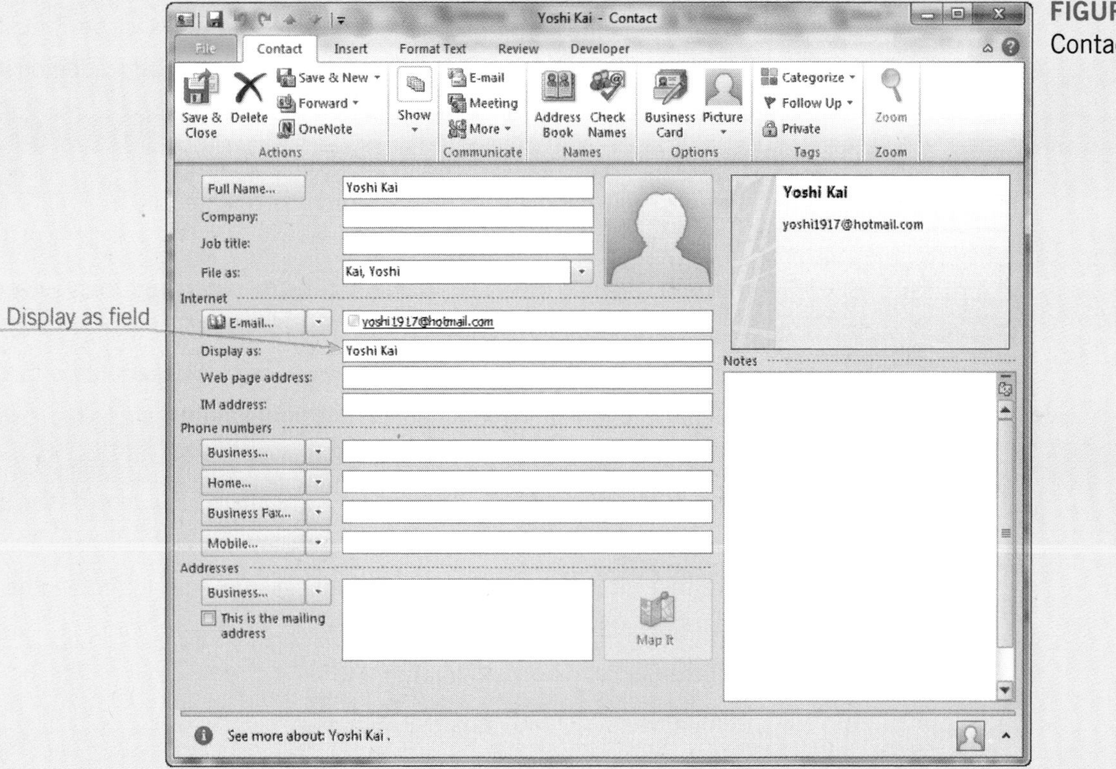

FIGURE 5–2
Contact window

4. Do not edit any of the information. Close the Contact window, and when prompted to save the changes, click **No**. Then close the Message window.

5. In the Navigation Pane, click the **Contacts** button. Click the **Home** tab. In the Current View group, explore the options for viewing your contacts. If necessary, click the More button to show all four layout options. Then, change to Business Card view.
6. If you see a Suggested Contacts folder in the Navigation Pane, as shown in **Figure 5–3**, click the folder to show the contents. Suggested new contacts appear on the right.

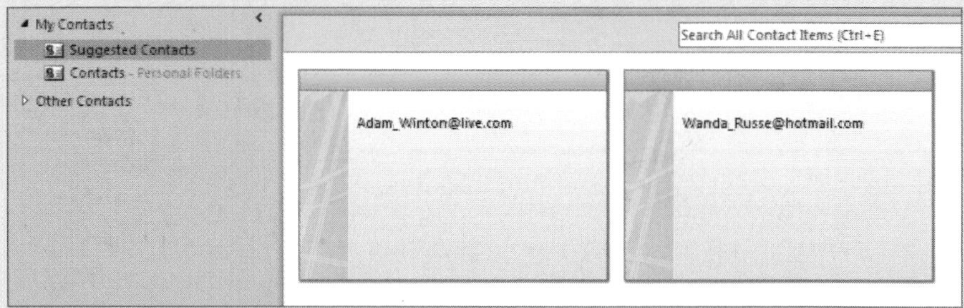

FIGURE 5–3
Suggested Contacts folder contents

7. If you have suggested contacts on your screen, double-click one of them. A new Contact window will open. The only data provided is the E-mail address and the Display as information. You can then add additional contact information. If you opened a new Contact window, close the window.
8. To create multiple contacts for the same company, enter the information for the first contact:
   a. In the Navigation Pane, select the **Contacts** folder, and then select your Contacts folder.
   b. On the Home tab, in the New group, click the **New Contact** button.
   c. Type the following information in the appropriate fields. You can advance to the next field by pressing Tab. Note that if you press Enter while navigating through the text boxes, a dialog box may open. If this happens, click Cancel to close the dialog box and proceed. Also note that after you type an e-mail address and advance to another field, text automatically appears in the Display as text box.

      Full Name: **Roland Elliott**
      Company: **Elliott Enterprises**
      Job title: **President**
      E-mail: **r_elliott@elliottenterprises.xyz**
      Web page address: **www.elliottenterprises.xyz**
      Business phone: **724-555-0020**
      Business fax: **724-555-0021**
      Mobile phone: **724-555-9071**
      Business address: **210 Lemon Hill Road, Prosperity, PA 15329**
   d. If necessary, enable the This is the mailing address option.

9. To create additional contacts for the same company:
   a. On the Contact tab, in the Actions group, click the **Save & New** button arrow and then click **Contact from the Same Company**. A new Contact window opens containing the company information (company name, Web page address, business and fax numbers, and business address).
   b. Type the following information in the appropriate fields. After typing the e-mail address, click the **Display as** text box to fill in the Display as field.

      Full Name: **Ellen Bertell**

      E-mail: **ellen_bertell@hotmail.com**
   c. Click the **Save & New** button arrow and then click **Contact from the Same Company**. A new Contact window opens. Type the following information in the appropriate fields. After typing the e-mail address, click the **Display as** text box to fill in the Display as field.

      Full Name: **Kari Rausch**

      E-mail: **Kari1969@hotmail.com**
   d. Click the **Save & New** list arrow, click **Contact from the Same Company**, and then type the following information in the appropriate fields. After typing the e-mail address, click the **Display as** text box to fill in the Display as field.

      Full Name: **Yoshi Kai**

      E-mail: **yoshi1917@hotmail.com**
   e. On the Contact tab, in the Actions group, click the **Save & Close** button. The Contact windows for the other new contacts you created are open. Click the **Save & Close** button in each window to close the contacts. All the new contacts now appear in your Contacts folder.
10. Leave Outlook open for the next Step-by-Step.

EXTRA FOR EXPERTS

When viewing contact information, if you have an Internet connection, you can click the Map It button in the Contact window to view a map of the contact's address. You can use this feature to get a visual of where the contact is located.

Editing Existing Contacts

The Contact window also includes fields for personal information about the contact. For example, you can enter the contact's nickname as well as information about their spouse, children, birthday, and much more.

To put a face or image with a name, you can add a photo of the contact person or a company logo to the contact information. When the sender and receiver both use Microsoft Outlook 2010 or 2007, the image appears in the message header of the open message (or the message when viewed in the Reading Pane). However, it is important to keep in mind that many individuals and businesses view messages in plain text, and the plain text format does not support graphics. Images for a contact form or an electronic business card can be in .jpg, .png, .gif, .bmp, or .tif format. When stored with the contact information, the files are automatically sized to 90 pixels by 90 pixels.

Step-by-Step 5.2

1. If necessary, click the **Contacts** button in the Navigation Pane, and select your **Contacts** folder.
2. Double-click the **Roland Elliott** contact to open the Contact window. If necessary, maximize the window.
3. Click the blank picture to the right of the Full Name field. Browse to the drive and folder where your Data Files are stored. Select the **Elliott Logo.jpg** picture, and then click **OK**. The company logo now appears in the Contact window, and the logo image will also appear on the electronic business card, as shown in **Figure 5–4**.

FIGURE 5–4 Contact information with an image

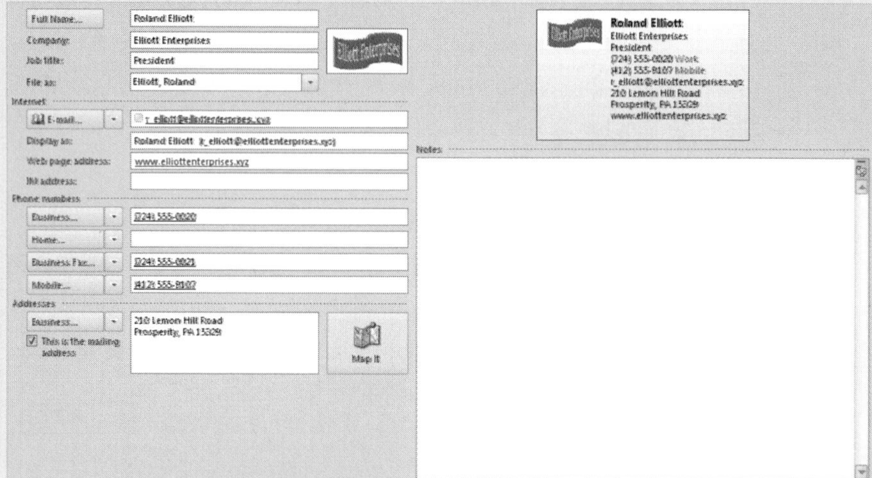

4. On the Contact tab, in the Options group, click the **Picture** button. Note that the menu shows the options Change Picture and Remove Picture. Click anywhere outside the menu to close it.
5. On the Contact tab, in the Show group, click the **Details** button. The Contact window changes to display more fields for the contact information, as shown in **Figure 5–5**.

FIGURE 5–5 More fields for contact information

Department: Manager's name:
Office: Assistant's name:
Profession:
Nickname: Spouse/Partner:
Title: Birthday: None
Suffix: Anniversary: None
Internet Free-Busy
Address:

6. Click the **Anniversary** list arrow and then select tomorrow's date. In the Show group, click the **General** button to show the standard fields in the form.

7. In the Actions group, click the **Save & Close** button. If you are prompted to add Roland Elliott's Anniversary to your personal calendar, click **Yes**.
8. Note that there is now a reminder under the Tomorrow heading in your To-Do Bar. When you enter dates in the Birthday and Anniversary fields, an appointment recurrence reminder is automatically applied. The default setting is for the reminder to appear 15 minutes before the start of the calendar day, and the reminder is set to appear yearly. If you want to set a reminder four or five days in advance so you have time to mail a card, add a reminder to your Outlook calendar.
9. In the To-Do Bar, right-click the reminder, point to **Delete**, and then click **Delete Series**. Deleting the series removes the reminder for the current year and all annual recurrences. If the new anniversary date does not display in the To-Do Bar, open your Outlook calendar, go to tomorrow's date, select the anniversary event for Roland Elliott, and delete the series.
10. Leave Outlook open for the next Step-by-Step.

TIP

You can flag a contact to create a visual reminder that appears in List view. For example, a sales representative would flag a contact to follow up with a client this week. The contact name and flag will appear in the To-Do Bar.

Managing Duplicate Contacts

By default, if you save a contact or an electronic business card with the same name or e-mail address as one that already exists, a prompt will appear indicating that you are creating a duplicate contact. You can then choose to replace or update the existing contact. Or, you can add a second e-mail address to the contact information. If you choose to update the contact information, all the content fields are compared and new or changed information from the new contact is added to the existing contact. Only one copy of the contact is saved. The original contact or copy information is moved to the Deleted Items folder. If you suspect you have some duplicate contacts, one of the best ways to identify them is to organize the contacts by phone number, because the phone number field is one of the most commonly used fields on a contact form.

Step-by-Step 5.3

1. If necessary, click the Contacts button in the Navigation Pane, and select your Contacts folder.
2. On the **Home** tab, in the New group, click the **New Contact** button. Type the following information in the appropriate fields. As you begin typing the e-mail address, if Roland's existing e-mail address displays in a ScreenTip, you can press Enter to use the AutoComplete feature.

   Full Name: **Roland Elliott**

   E-mail: **r_elliott@elliottenterprises.xyz**

   Mobile phone: **412-555-1791**

3. In the Notes pane, type **Roland established the company in 1995.**.
4. Under Internet, click the **E-mail** list arrow and then click **E-mail 2**. In the text box, type **roland@elliottenterprises.xyz**.
5. On the Contact tab, in the Actions group, click the **Save & Close** button. The dialog box opens to notify you that a contact for Roland Elliott already exists, as shown in **Figure 5–6**. You can drag the lower border of the dialog box down so that you can see all the fields displayed in Figure 5–6. Note that revision marks are used to show a difference in the mobile phone number, a new E-mail 2 address has been created, and the Notes field is updated.

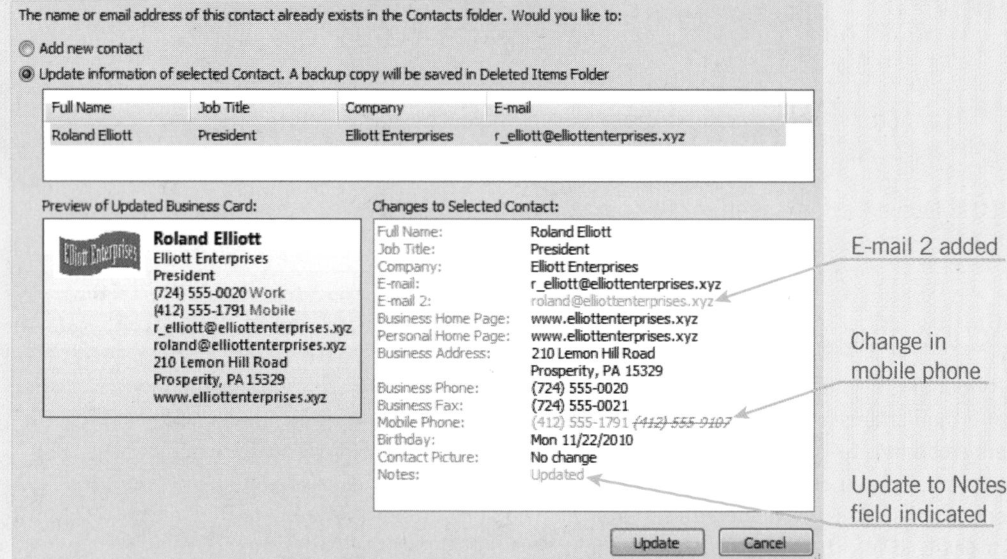

FIGURE 5–6
Alert about duplicate contact

6. Click **Update** to update the existing contact. Open the Contact window for Roland Elliott. Note that the mobile number has been updated, and the information has been added to the Notes pane, with a reference to date and time when the note was added. If you click the E-mail list arrow and select E-mail 2, you will see that the second e-mail address has been added. Close the Contact window.
7. On the **Home** tab, in the New group, click the **New Contact** button. Type the following information in the appropriate fields.

   Full Name: **Roland Elliott**

   E-mail: **r_elliott@elliottenterprises.xyz**

   Mobile phone: **412-555-1791**

8. On the Contact tab, in the Actions group, click the **Save & Close** button. This time, when the alert about the duplicate contact appears, enable the option **Add new contact** and then click **Add**.

9. On the Home tab, in the Current View group, click the **More** button and then click the **Phone** button. Your Contacts list is now arranged by phone numbers. Scroll down through the list. You will see two entries for Roland Elliott, and you may see other duplicate contacts.
10. Select the **Roland Elliott** contact that does not display a company name. On the Home tab, in the Delete group, click the **Delete** button.
11. In the Current View group, click the **More** button and then click the **Business Card** button to rearrange the Contacts list.
12. Leave Outlook open for the next Step-by-Step.

Organizing Contacts

As you have seen, fields in the Contact window allow you to store a lot of information about your contacts. However, the contact information is only useful if you can access the information when you need it. Therefore, organizing the contacts for quick and easy access is essential. You can organize contacts in groups, and you can use search tools to help you quickly access the contacts.

EXTRA FOR EXPERTS

If you are using Microsoft Exchange Server, you can create subfolders in the Contacts folder.

Creating a Contact Group

As you work with your contacts, you will no doubt find that you often have to deal with specific groups of contacts. For example, you might often need to send messages to all members of the Development Team or you might need to schedule a meeting with all support personnel. You can save yourself a lot of time by arranging your contacts into groups. A ***contact group***, often referred to as a ***distribution group***, is a grouping of contacts collected under one name. The group stores shortcuts to contacts in your Contacts folder. A message sent to a contact group goes to all members of the group. Contact groups can be used in messages, task requests, and meeting requests.

When you create a new contact group, it is saved in your Contacts folder and the new group is automatically added to the Address Book. If a group member is not already in your Address Book, you can create a new contact in the group and the contact will be added to the Address Book. You can drag and drop to move or copy a contact to a different group folder.

VOCABULARY

contact group

distribution group

Step-by-Step 5.4

1. If necessary, click the Contacts button in the Navigation Pane, and select your Contacts folder.
2. On the Home tab, in the New group, click the **New Contact Group** button. In the Name text box, type **Team Project**. In the Actions group, click the **Save & Close** button. The new group is added to your Contacts list.

3. On the Home tab, in the Current View group, click the **More** button and then click the **List** button. The Contacts list is rearranged, and the contact group is arranged in alphabetical order with the other contacts in the list. Also, note that contacts that include a company name are arranged by the company name at the bottom of the list. See **Figure 5–7**. Your list will differ.

FIGURE 5–7
Contacts arranged by List option

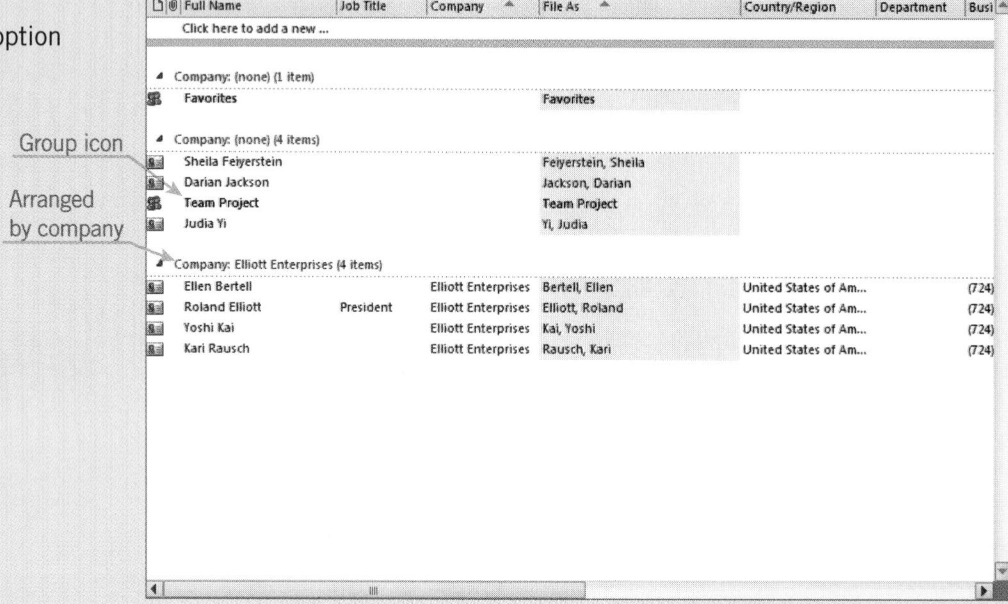

4. Double-click the **Team Project** group to open the Team Project Contact Group window. On the Contact Group tab, in the Members group, click the **Add Members** button and then click **From Outlook Contacts**. A dialog box similar to the one shown in **Figure 5–8** opens. Your contact names will differ, and some contacts may appear more than once.

FIGURE 5–8
Select Members Contacts dialog box

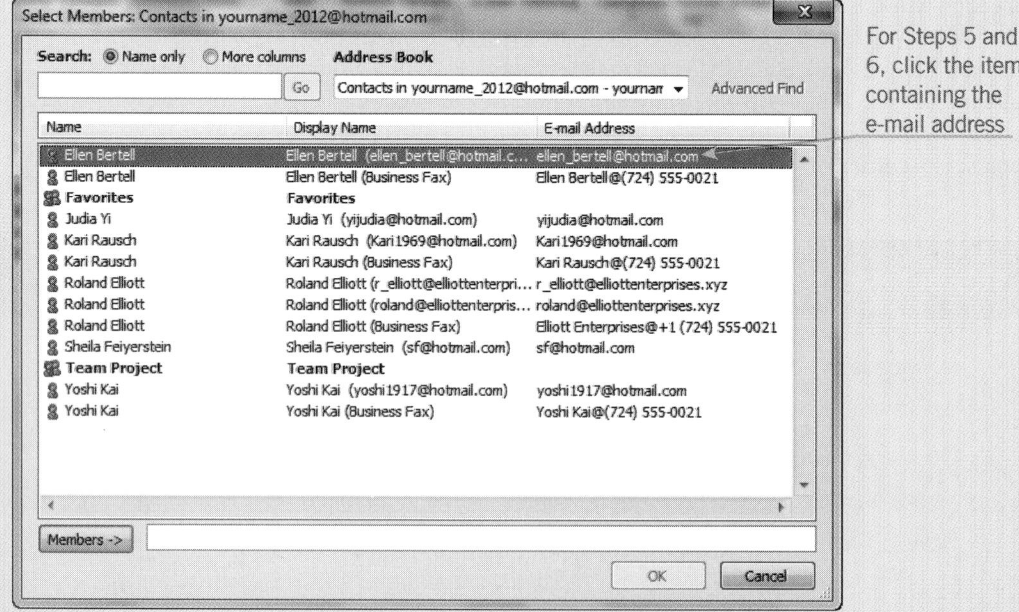

5. Double-click the **Ellen Bertell** contact. If you see two lines for Ellen Bertell, double-click the line with the e-mail address. The contact name and e-mail address appear in the Members box at the bottom of the dialog box.
6. Select the **Kari Rausch** contact. If you see two lines for the contact, select the line with the e-mail address. Press and hold **Ctrl** and then click the **Roland Elliott** (the r_elliott e-mail address) and **Yoshi Kai** contacts. Then click **Members ->**. The selected contacts are added to the Members box. Click **OK** to close the dialog box. The Team Project Contact Group window now displays four contacts, as shown in **Figure 5–9**.

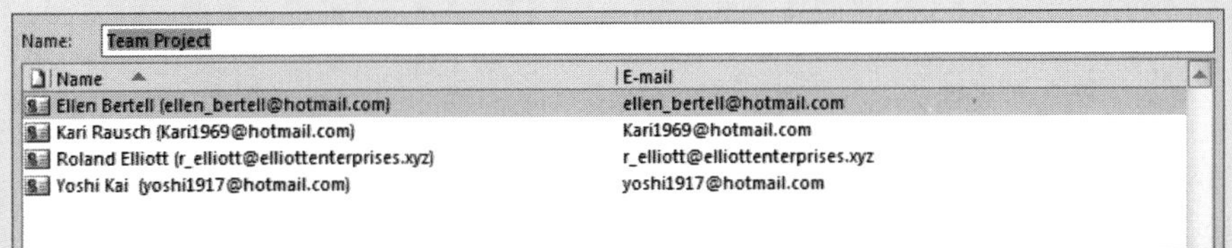

FIGURE 5–9
Team Project Contact Group members

7. Click the **Add Members** button and then click **New E-mail Contact**. The Add New Member dialog box opens. Confirm that the Add to Contacts option is enabled. Type the following information in the appropriate fields, and then click **OK**.

   Display name: **Rachel Sanders**

   E-mail address: **r_sanders@elliottenterprises.xyz**
8. In the Actions group, click the **Save & Close** button. (If your server has not processed the e-mail addresses provided for the contacts in the group and you cannot save the changes to the group, select the **Rachel Sanders** contact, and then in the Members group, click the **Remove Member** button, then click the **Save & Close** button before proceeding with Step 9.)
9. Review your Contacts list. Note that if you were able to successfully add the new contact in Step 8, Rachel Sanders was added to your Contacts list but does not appear under the Company: Elliott Enterprises section.
10. Double-click the **Rachel Sanders** contact to open the Contact window. In the Company field, type **Elliott Enterprises**. Click the **Save & Close** button. Rachel Sanders is moved to the Company: Elliott Enterprises section.
11. In the Navigation Pane, click the **Mail** button. On the Home tab, in the New group, click the **New E-mail** button. In the header, click **To** and then if necessary, in the Select Names: Contacts dialog box, navigate to your Contacts list. Under Name, double-click **Team Project**. The contact group appears in the To -> box at the bottom of the dialog box. Click **OK**.

12. Note that the group name appears in the To box in the message header, as shown in **Figure 5–10**. Adding the group is faster than adding each recipient individually.

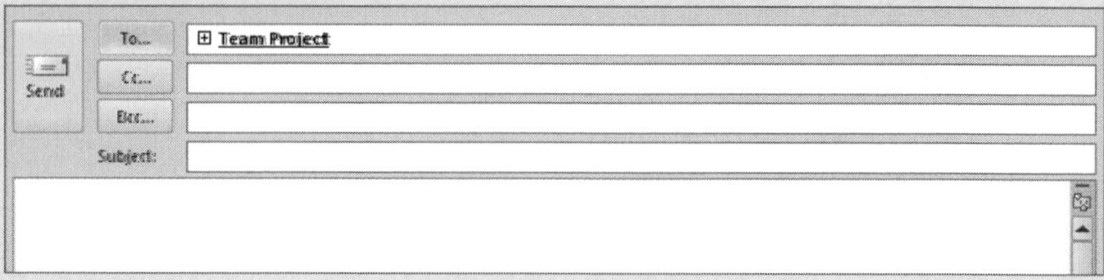

FIGURE 5–10
Contact group inserted in To box of message header

13. Close the message window without saving the changes. Leave Outlook open for the next Step-by-Step.

Assigning Categories to Contacts

In addition to creating groups, you can assign categories to help you identify and sort contacts. You may wonder why it's useful to assign categories to contacts if you've already organized them into groups. To illustrate, you may work with multiple groups, and within each group, the members assume various responsibilities. For example, the members of a Development Team include a team leader, a tester, two trainers, and two engineers. If you create categories to identify each of these responsibilities, you can easily sort your contacts when you need to send an e-mail to all team leaders.

Step-by-Step 5.5

1. Click the **Contacts** button in the Navigation Pane, and if necessary, select your **Contacts** folder.
2. Select the **Team Project** group. On the Home tab, in the Tags group, click the **Categorize** button, and then click **All Categories** to open the Color Categories dialog box. Click **New** to open the Add New Category dialog box.
3. In the Name text box, type **Team Leader**. A color is already assigned. Leave the color setting as is and click **OK**.
4. Create three more new categories:
   a. Click **New**, in the Name text box type **Engineer**, and then click **OK**.
   b. Click **New**, in the Name text box type **Trainer**, and then click **OK**.
   c. Click **New**, in the Name text box type **Tester**, and then click **OK**.
5. Click **OK** to close the Color Categories dialog box.
6. Double-click the **Ellen Bertell** contact. On the Contact tab, in the Tags group, click the **Categorize** button and then click **Team Leader**. A Category bar is added above the Full Name field.

7. Click the **Categorize** button again and then click **Trainer**. Two categories have been assigned to the contact. In the Actions group, click the **Save & Close** button.
8. Open the following contacts and assign the categories as indicated, then save and close the Contact windows.

   Roland Elliott: **Engineer**

   Yoshi Kai: **Engineer**

   Kari Rausch: **Trainer**

   Rachel Sanders: **Tester**
9. Open the **Team Project** group. Note that because you created the categories with the Team Project group selected, a Category bar appears just below the Ribbon. The bar shows all the categories that have been assigned to contacts in the group. See **Figure 5–11**; the colors in your category bar may differ. However, to view the category for each contact, you must open the Contact window.

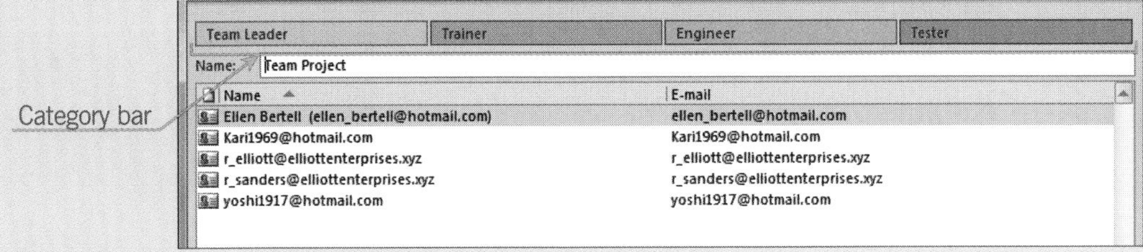

FIGURE 5–11
Categories assigned in the Team Project Contact Group

10. Close the Team Project Contact Group window.

11. Click the **View** tab. In the Arrangement group, click the **Categories** button. (If the buttons in the Arrangement group are dimmed, then in the Current View group, click the Change View button and click the List button.) All your contacts are arranged by category, as shown in **Figure 5–12**. Note that the Team Project group is included in the sort because the categories were assigned to the Team Project group.

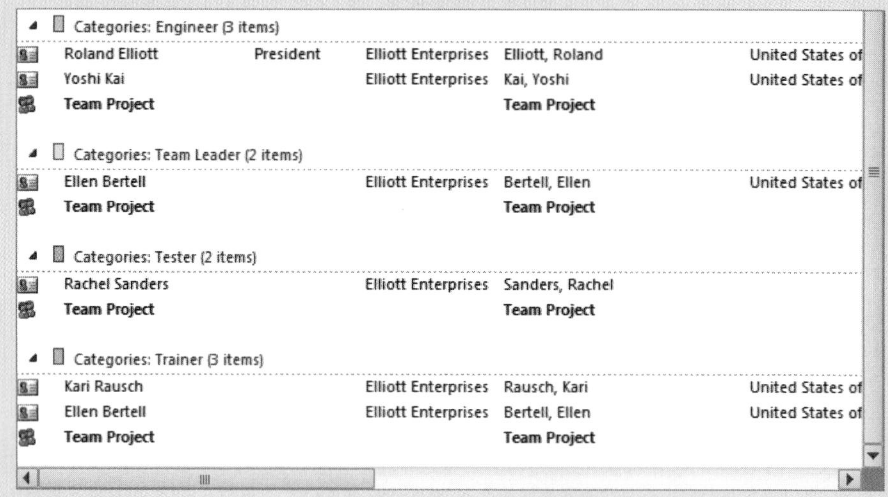

FIGURE 5–12
Contacts arranged by category

12. In the Current View group, click the **Change View** button and then click the **Business Card** button. Leave Outlook open for the next Step-by-Step.

Finding Contacts

To avoid having to scroll through many field names, you can use the search tools to quickly find contacts. You can choose to search a specific folder or all folders, and you can search for names or partial names. For example, if you can't remember the full company name or the individual's first and last names, you can type a portion of the name in the search box, and all contacts with matching text will appear in the results. You can narrow the search even more using the Advanced Find options.

Step-by-Step 5.6

1. If necessary, click the Contacts button in the Navigation Pane, and select your Contacts folder.
2. At the top of the Contacts list, click the **Search Contacts (Ctrl + E)** text box. Type **k**. At least two matches are found because the Yoshi Kai and the Kari Rausch contacts both contain the letter k. Depending on the entries in your Contacts list, you may see many more results. To the right of the Search Contacts text box, click the **Close Search** button.
3. Click the **Search All Contact Items** text box. On the Search Tools Search tab, in the Options group, click the **Search Tools** button and then click **Search Options** to open the Outlook Options dialog box. Note that under Results in the right pane, you can enable the option All folders. If you have multiple contact folders, this option ensures results that would show matches from all the folders. Click **Cancel**.
4. Click the **Search Tools** button again, and then click **Advanced Find**. The Advanced Find dialog box opens, as shown in **Figure 5–13**.

TIP

If the Search Text box in your Navigation Pane does not show Search Contacts (Ctrl + E), click the File tab, and then click Options. Click Search, and under Results, enable the option Current folder. Click OK.

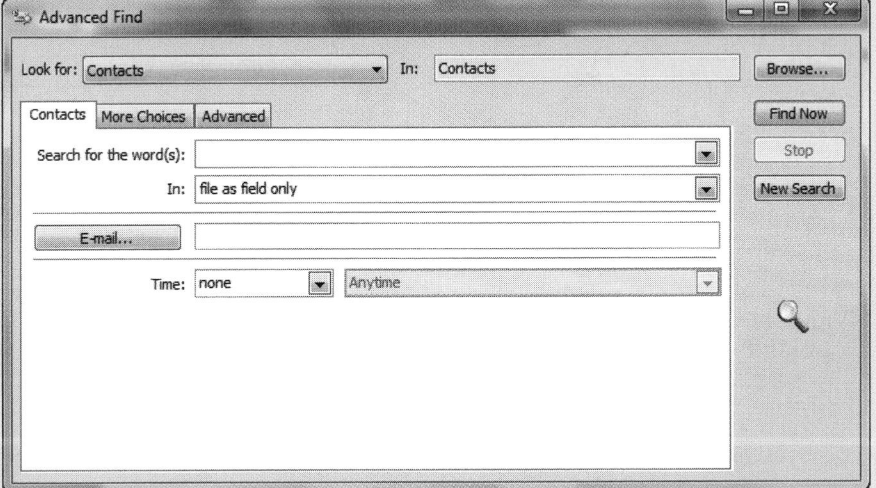

FIGURE 5–13
Advanced Find dialog box

5. In the Search for the word(s) text box, type **Elliott**. Click the **In** list arrow, and then click **company field only**.

6. Click the **More Choices** tab to display the options shown in **Figure 5–14**. Note that there are several options to further filter the search, including categories.

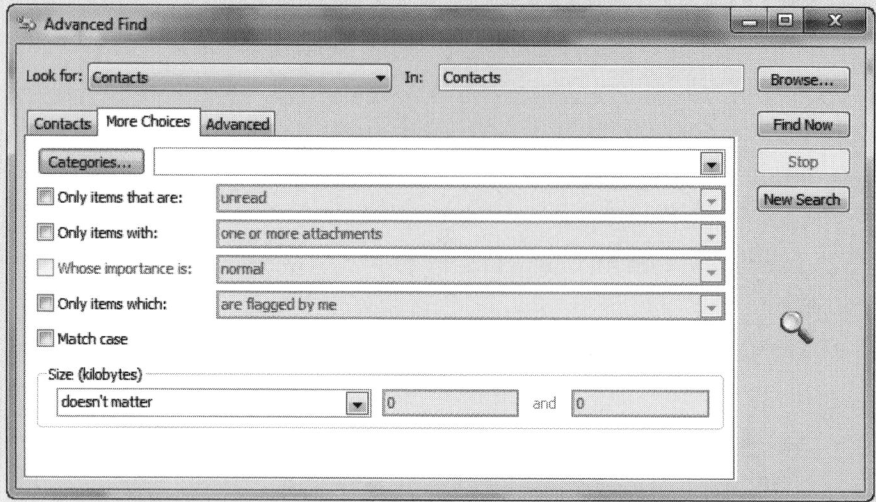

FIGURE 5–14
More Choices tab in the Advanced Find dialog box

7. Click the **Advanced** tab to display the options shown in **Figure 5–15**.

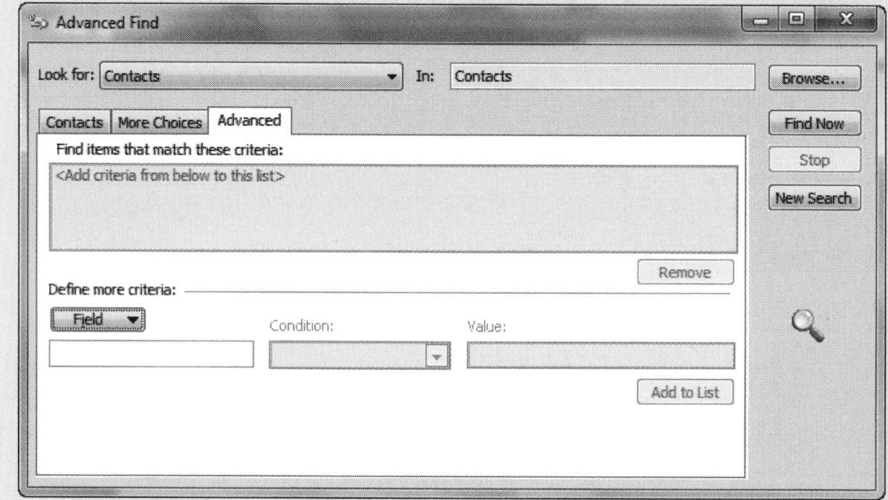

FIGURE 5–15
Advanced tab in the Advanced Find dialog box

8. Click **Find Now**. The results appear at the bottom of the dialog box, as shown in **Figure 5–16**.

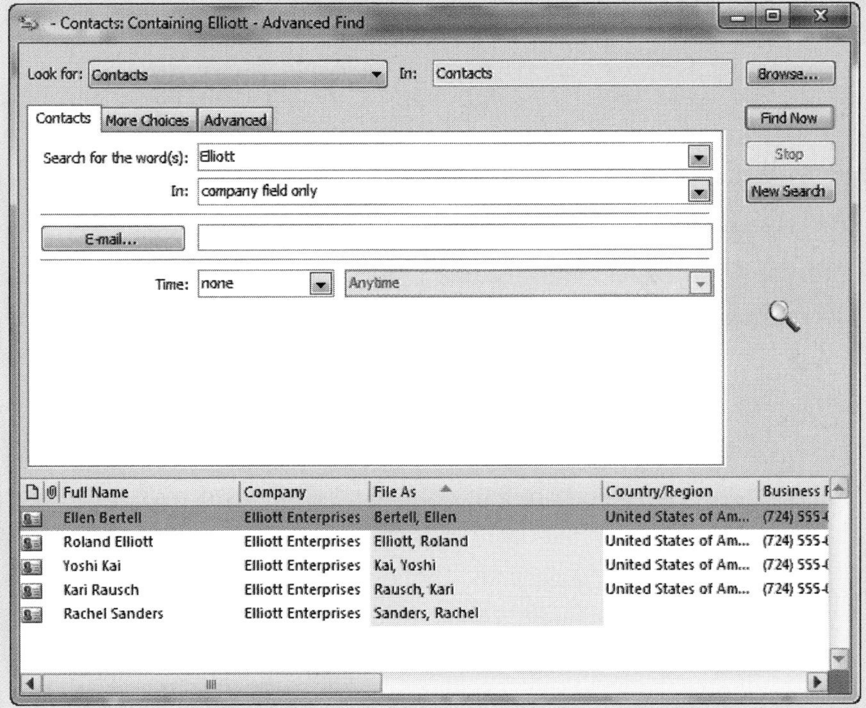

FIGURE 5–16
Results for contacts containing keyword *Elliott*

9. Double-click **Yoshi Kai** to open the Contact window. Then close the Contact window.
10. Close the dialog box. Leave Outlook open for the next Step-by-Step.

Forwarding Contacts

Outlook provides a command that makes it quick and easy to forward contacts and contact groups. You can choose to forward contact information as a business card, a vCard file, or an Outlook Contact. The ***vCard*** file format is a standard format used for sharing contact information on the Internet. The vCard file extension is .vcf.

VOCABULARY
vCard

When you receive a message with an electronic business card, a vCard file, or Outlook Contact attached, you can download the file to create a new contact or update an existing contact.

Keep in mind that how the electronic business card appears in an e-mail message depends on the e-mail application that is used. Recipients using Outlook 2010 or 2007 will see the message exactly as you see it. However, recipients using earlier versions of Outlook or other e-mail applications may not see the image. Furthermore, recipients who view their messages in plain text will not see an image. If you're not sure the recipient can view the business card in the message body, you can attach the electronic business card as a file. Then the recipient can open and save the information in their Contacts list.

Step-by-Step 5.7

> **TIP**
>
> You do not need to open the contact window to forward it. You can select the contact, and then on the Home tab, in the Share group, click the Forward Contact button and select an option.

1. If necessary, click the Contacts button in the Navigation Pane, and select your Contacts folder.
2. Double-click the **Ellen Bertell** contact to open the Contact window.
3. On the Contact tab, in the Actions group, click the **Forward** button, then click **As a Business Card**. The electronic business card is inserted in the message body, and the data file is attached to the message. Note that the attached file shows the .vcf file format. Close the message without saving the changes.
4. The Ellen Bertell Contact window is still open. Click the **Forward** button again and then click **In Internet Format (vCard)**. A new message window opens, and the contact data file is attached to the message. Note that the data file was converted to the vCard format (.vcf). The difference between this attachment and the business card attachment in Step 3 is that this attached file includes all the contact information and not just the business card information. Close the message without saving the changes.
5. Click the **Forward** button once again and then click **As an Outlook Contact**. When the new message window opens, you'll see an attachment. The attachment contains the contact information, but it has not been converted to the vCard format. The recipient can save the contact in their Outlook Contacts list. Close the message without saving the changes.
6. Close the Contact window. Leave Outlook open for the next Step-by-Step.

Communicating with Contacts

Outlook makes it easy for you to communicate with your contacts. Using your contact information, you can quickly open a new e-mail message window, open a meeting invitation window, and even place phone calls. You can also create merged documents and e-mail them to your contacts.

Initiating Communication

Contact features make it convenient for you to start communication with your contacts. With the Contact window open, a single click will open a new e-mail message window or a new meeting invitation window. If your computer has a connection to a phone line, you can click a button and let the computer dial the phone number and create the connection for you.

Step-by-Step 5.8

1. If necessary, click the Contacts button in the Navigation Pane, and select your Contacts folder.
2. In the Contacts list, select the **Roland Elliott** contact.
3. Click the **Home** tab, and in the Communicate group, click the **E-mail** button. A new message window opens, and the contact name and both e-mail addresses are already inserted in the To box. (When multiple e-mail addresses are stored in the Contact information, all the addresses are inserted in the To box. If you don't want to send the message to all the addresses, you can delete the addresses you do not want to include from the To box.) Close the message window without saving the changes.
4. The Elliott contact should still be selected in the Contacts list. In the Communicate group, click the **Meeting** button. A new meeting invitation window opens. In addition to showing the contact name and address in the To box, the header pane also includes settings to establish dates and start and end times for a meeting. When the recipient opens the message, they will see options to respond to the meeting invitation. Invitations for meetings will be discussed in more detail in Lesson 6. Close the message without saving changes.
5. In the Communicate group, click the **More** button and then point to **Call**. A menu opens with all the numbers you have entered for that contact (such as business, home, fax, mobile). If your computer is connected to a phone line, you can click one of the phone options to dial the number. Click anywhere outside the menu to close it.
6. Leave Outlook open for the next Step-by-Step.

EXTRA FOR EXPERTS

The Outlook Social Connector (OSC) connects you to the social and business networks you use and enables you to see more information about your contacts. For example, if you use Windows Live, when you set up a meeting with contacts, you can view information about those individuals who will be attending the meeting. To use the Outlook Social Connector, you may need to install an add-in. If your organization uses Outlook 2010 and Microsoft SharePoint 2010, the Outlook Social Connector can automatically connect without the add-in.

TIP

Before making a call, you can click Journal Entry in the More options to create an entry so that you can keep track of call time and duration.

Creating Mail Merges

You can use your Contacts list to prepare form letters, mailing labels, envelopes, or catalogs. You can merge the data to a new document, to a printer, or to an e-mail message. When you set up a mail merge in Outlook, you use the mail merge features in Word. Because mail merge was covered in the Word unit for this course, the mail merge features are not covered in detail in the next Step-by-Step. If you are not familiar with the Word mail merge features, you can use the Mail Merge Wizard to guide you through the process.

You can choose options for the merge, including how many contacts to use, what fields to use, and whether to start a new merge document or use an existing one. You can merge all contacts or only selected contacts. In the next Step-by-Step, you will explore using the merge features to create e-mail messages and mailing labels.

Step-by-Step 5.9

1. If necessary, click the Contacts button in the Navigation Pane, and select your Contacts folder.
2. Select the contacts that are to be included in the merge. In your Contacts list, click the **Ellen Bertell** contact. Press and hold **Ctrl** and click the **Yoshi Kai**, **Kari Rausch**, and **Rachel Sanders** contacts.
3. On the Home tab, in the Actions group, click the **Mail Merge** button. The Mail Merge Contacts dialog box opens, as shown in **Figure 5–17**.

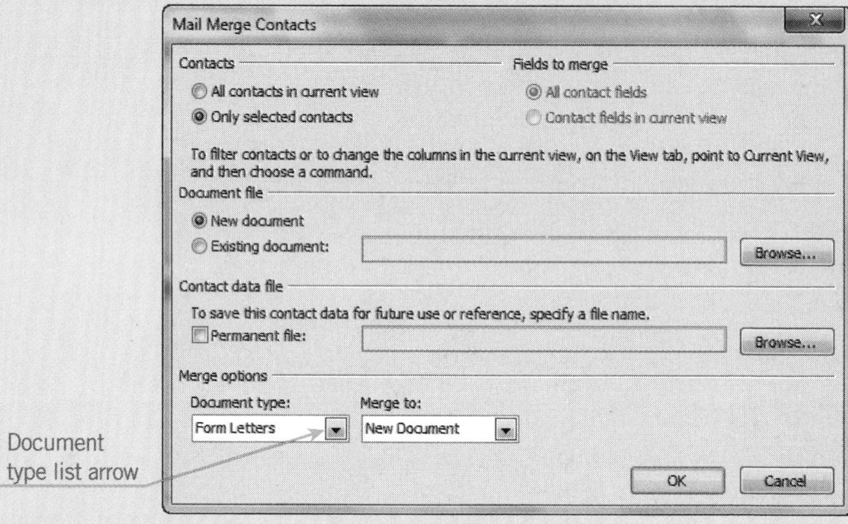

FIGURE 5–17
Mail Merge Contacts dialog box

4. Select the merge options:
   a. Under Contacts, note that the Only selected contacts option is already enabled.
   b. In the lower-left corner, under Merge options, click the **Document type** list arrow and then click **Form Letters**.
   c. Click the **Merge to** list arrow and then click **E-mail**.
   d. In the Message subject line text box, type **Departmental Review**. Then click **OK**. A new document window opens in Word. Note that the Ribbon shows the Mailings tab with the mail merge features.
5. In the document window, type the following:

   Each year we complete a departmental review. Next week I will be sending each of you forms so that you can provide feedback about our department status. The forms must be completed and submitted to our HR department by the end of the month.
6. You already selected the contacts before you began the merge process, so you are ready to complete the merge. On the Mailings tab, in the Finish group, click the **Finish & Merge** button.

TIP

Contacts stored within contact groups cannot be merged, because the group members are shortcuts to the contacts.

7. Note that there are three options. If you click Edit Individual Documents, the merged messages will open a new Word document. If you click Print Documents, the messages will be sent to the printer. Click **Send E-mail Messages**, and the Merge to E-mail dialog box opens, as shown in **Figure 5–18**. Note that under Send records, the All option is enabled. This refers to all the selected contacts, not all the contacts in your Contacts folder, so you can leave the setting as is.

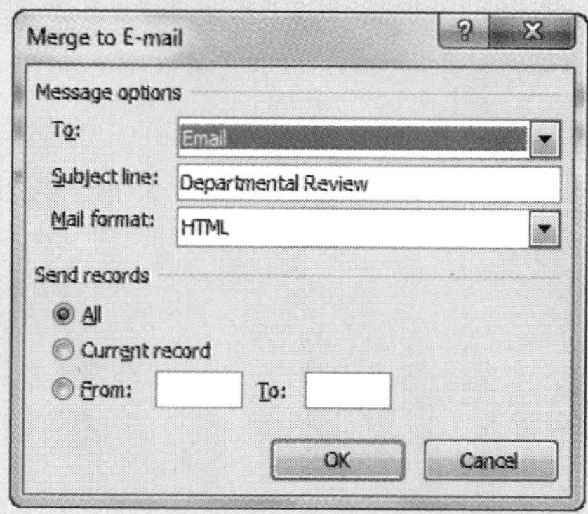

FIGURE 5–18
Merge to E-mail dialog box

8. If you click OK, the individual messages for each selected contact would be sent to your outbox. Do not click OK. Click **Cancel** to close the dialog box.
9. Exit Word without saving the changes to the document. Leave Outlook open for the next Step-by-Step.

Deleting Contacts and Categories

When you remove a member from a group, the contact still remains in your Contacts folder and your Address Book. Even when you remove an entire group, all the contacts remain intact. To remove a contact or a group, you must delete the item from your Contacts folder. Now that you have completed all the Step-by-Step exercises, you will remove all the new contacts and categories you created.

Step-by-Step 5.10

1. If necessary, click the Contacts button in the Navigation Pane, and select your Contacts folder. Select the **Team Project** group.
2. On the Home tab, in the Tags group, click the **Categorize** button and then click **All Categories**.
3. Click the **Engineer** category to select it, and then click **Delete**. When prompted to delete the category, click **Yes**.
4. Repeat the process described in Step 3 to delete the Team Leader, Tester, and Trainer categories.

EXTRA FOR EXPERTS

If you have access to a network that includes Microsoft Exchange Server, you can use public folders to share Outlook items with your coworkers who are also using Outlook. You can specify the coworkers with whom you want to share the folder's content by granting the individual permission to access the folder. Each user may be granted a different level of access. The permission levels are associated with roles. For example, the Reviewer role allows your coworker to read, but not to create, modify, or delete items. The Editor role allows a coworker to read, create, modify, and delete items, and the Reviewer role allows a coworker to only read items and files. To restrict access, select the folder, and on the Folder tab, in the Properties group, click the Folder Permissions button to access the Permission Level List and permission options.

5. Deselect the check boxes for the Engineer, Team Leader, Tester, and Trainer categories. Click **OK** to close the Color Categories dialog box.
6. Double-click the **Team Project** group to open the Team Project Contact Group window. Select the **Kari Rausch** contact. On the Contact Group tab, in the Members group, click the **Remove Member** button. Then close the window. When prompted to save the changes, click **Yes**. Note that the Kari Rausch contact is still in your Contacts folder.
7. The Team Project group should still be selected. On the Home tab, in the Delete group, click the **Delete** button. The group is removed from the Contacts list. However, all the contacts in the group, including Rachel Sanders, who was entered as a new contact in the group, still remain in your Contacts list.
8. In your Contacts list, click the **Ellen Bertell** contact. Press and hold **Ctrl**, and then click the **Roland Elliott**, **Yoshi Kai**, **Kari Rausch**, and **Rachel Sanders** contacts.
9. On the Home tab, in the Delete group, click the **Delete** button.

SUMMARY

In this lesson, you learned:

- Outlook features several shortcuts for creating new contacts. You can quickly create multiple contacts for the same company without re-entering the company information for each contact.
- The Contact window includes numerous fields for recording the contact's information. Personal information such as spouse's names and dates for special occasions are also available.
- Organizing contacts in groups can make it more convenient for you to access them. Groups also allow you to add multiple names to the To box of an e-mail message with a single click.
- Another way to organize contacts is to assign categories, which you can then use to arrange or search for contacts.
- Outlook includes several advanced features you can use to help you quickly locate contacts.
- You can also share contact information by forwarding it to others via e-mail. You can send the information as an Outlook Contact, or you can save the information in a standard format so the recipient can use it in other applications.
- Shortcuts in the Contact window enable you to quickly set up meetings, make phone calls to contacts, and send e-mails.
- Contact data can be merged into form letters, mailing labels, envelopes, or catalogs, and you can set up the mail merge process in Outlook.

VOCABULARY REVIEW

Define the following terms:

contact group
distribution group
electronic business card
vCard

REVIEW QUESTIONS

TRUE / FALSE

Circle T if the statement is true or F if the statement is false.

T F 1. A message sent to a contact group goes to selected recipients within the group.

T F 2. When you receive messages, you can use the information in the From box to create new contacts.

T F 3. The images for an electronic business card will display in all e-mail formats.

T F 4. When you send an e-mail message to a contact group, all the recipient names and addresses appear in the To box.

T F 5. When you search for contacts, Outlook does not show contacts saved within a group.

MULTIPLE CHOICE

Select the best response for the following statements.

1. When you create a new contact group, ________________.
   A. the group is saved in your Contacts folder
   B. you must add the new group to the Address Book
   C. all members in the group must also be in the Address Book
   D. all of the above
2. You can forward contact information as a(n) ________________.
   A. electronic business card
   B. vCard file
   C. Outlook Contact
   D. all of the above
3. Contact groups can be used in ________________.
   A. messages
   B. task requests
   C. meeting requests
   D. all of the above
4. When you update existing contact information with a new duplicate contact, ________________.
   A. both copies of the contact are saved
   B. only one copy of the contact is saved
   C. both contact copies are updated
   D. a new third contact is created and the other two contacts are automatically deleted

5. You can initiate a ______________ from an open contact.
   A. reply e-mail
   B. meeting confirmation
   C. phone call
   D. all of the above

WRITTEN QUESTIONS

Write a brief answer to the following questions.

1. What is the purpose of the Suggested Contacts folder?

2. When completing the mail merge process, what options are available for the merged document?

3. Why is sorting contacts by phone number a good way to find duplicate contacts?

4. What is the difference between attaching a business card or a vCard file to an e-mail message?

5. What Outlook features make it convenient for you to communicate with your contacts?

PROJECTS

PROJECT 5–1

1. Select a contact in your Contacts list. Send a meeting invitation to that individual. For example, if you plan to meet a friend for lunch next week, provide the information in an invitation message.
2. Send the message and wait for a response from the recipient. Hopefully, they will respond and accept your invitation!

PROJECT 5–2

1. Review your Contacts list and delete any duplicate contacts.
2. Update the contacts by adding personal information such as birthdays and anniversaries.
3. If you have a long list of contacts, organize them into groups. For example, create a group for friends and family and create another group for colleagues.

4. Create a new Contact group and name the group **Colleagues**. This will help you organize your business or academic contacts.
5. Add members to the new contact group using your Outlook Contacts list. If you can think of anyone else you would like to add to the group, create a new contact.
6. Create some new categories (such as instructor and classmate or the names of the departments within your organization) and assign the categories to some of your contacts.
7. In the future, when you want to contact everyone in the group (such as an out-of-office notice), you can send an e-mail message to the group.

PROJECT 5–3

Partner with a friend or colleague and practice sharing contact information. Ask your partner to forward the information for one of his/her contacts as a business card, a vCard file, and as an Outlook Contact. This way you can compare all three forms of sharing the contact information.

PROJECT 5–4

1. In your Contacts list, select multiple contacts you would like to invite to an upcoming event.
2. Set up a mail merge for a form letter to be merged to e-mail. Be sure to create a message subject line.
3. Create an e-mail message in the Word document. Proofread the message.
4. When you are satisfied with the message, send it to your selected contacts.

CRITICAL THINKING

ACTIVITY 5–1

Describe the groups and/or categories you would create to organize your personal contacts.

ACTIVITY 5–2

What are the advantages to adding images or photos to contact information?

Estimated Time: 2 hours

LESSON 6

Managing Calendars and Tasks

OBJECTIVES

Upon completion of this lesson, you should be able to:

- Customize calendar views and settings.
- Organize meetings.
- Respond to meeting invites.
- Share calendars.
- Organize and display tasks.
- Export Outlook data.
- Delete calendar items and tasks.

VOCABULARY

alternate calendar

iCalendar format

Outlook's calendar and task features help you organize your schedule and tasks. In this lesson, you will explore many features that will help you better manage your time.

Changing Calendar Views and Settings

Managing a business schedule, tracking project timelines, and juggling your personal commitments can be difficult. To avoid time conflicts and manage your time more efficiently, you can take advantage of several Outlook features and customize the settings and views for how you work.

> **TIP**
>
> If you want to start with a blank calendar, click the View tab. In the Current View group, click the Change View button and then click List. Select and delete all appointments or events scheduled for the next month. For example, if the current month is October, delete all items scheduled in November. The items are moved to the Deleted Items folder. When you complete the lesson, you can move the items back to the appropriate calendar folder.

Creating New Appointments and Events

Before you begin learning more about Outlook's Calendar features, you need to create some appointments and events in your calendar. The following Step-by-Step will provide a review of basic Outlook Calendar features using default settings, and you will create some appointments and events that you can then use for applying the more advanced features introduced in this lesson.

If you are using a classroom or lab computers, it's likely that the default Outlook calendar is blank. However, if you are using your own personal computer to complete the exercises in this lesson, there may already be appointments and events scheduled on your calendar. You can leave all of these items on your calendar. You will assign categories to the appointments and events that you create in the next Step-by-Step, which will make it easy to visually identify them as you work through the exercises in this lesson. At the end of this lesson, you will delete the new items you added to your calendar.

Step-by-Step 6.1

1. Launch Outlook and then click the **Calendar** button in the Navigation Pane. Confirm or, if necessary, change the settings as described below:
   - **a.** Click the **View** tab. In the Layout group, click the **Navigation Pane** button and then, if necessary, enable the **Normal** option to expand the Navigation Pane.
   - **b.** On the View tab, in the Layout group, click the **To-Do Bar** button and then, if necessary, enable the **Minimized** option. The To-Do Bar is minimized.
   - **c.** In the Current View group, click the **Change View** button and then, if necessary, click **Calendar**.
   - **d.** Click the **Home** tab. In the Arrange group, click the **Month** button. Your screen should look similar to **Figure 6–1**. If multiple calendars appear in the Navigation Pane, enable the default Calendar, as shown in the figure.

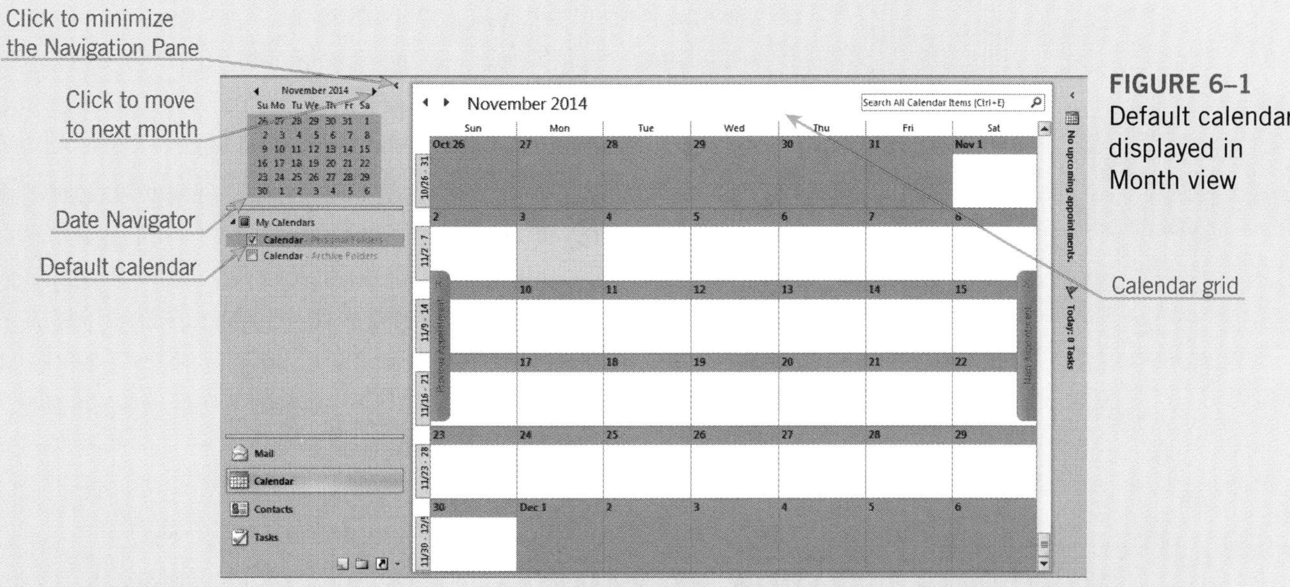

FIGURE 6–1 Default calendar displayed in Month view

2. At the top of the Date Navigator, click the **Next** arrow button to advance to the next month. In the Date Navigator, select the date for the first Monday of the next month. The calendar view will change to Day view. On the Home tab, in the New group, click the **New Appointment** button to open the appointment window. If necessary, disable the All day event option, as shown in **Figure 6–2**, and then type the following information in the appointment window:

Subject:	**Interview with training candidate**
Location:	**Conference Room B**
Start time:	**2:00 PM**
End time:	**3:30 PM**
Description:	**Candidate: Christina Jordan**

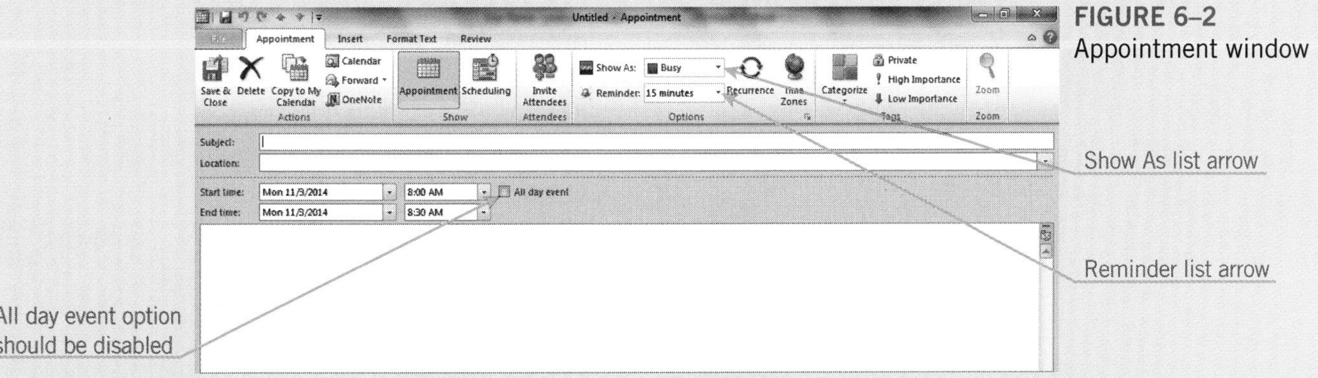

FIGURE 6–2 Appointment window

TIP

To quickly jump to a different month, click the month name at the top of the Date Navigator and then select one of the three previous months or one of the next three months.

EXTRA FOR EXPERTS

To change the default sound for reminders, click the File tab, click Options, and then click Advanced. Under Reminders, make sure the Play reminder sound option is enabled and then click Browse. Navigate to the drive and folder where the sound files are stored (for example: C:\Program Files\ Microsoft Office\MEDIA\CAGCAT10), and then select a .wav sound.

3. On the Appointment tab, in the Options group, click the **Reminder** list arrow and then click **1 hour**. In the Tags group, click the **Categorize** button and then click **Blue Category**. (If prompted to rename the category, click **No.**) In the Actions group, click the **Save & Close** button.
4. On the calendar grid, click the **Forward** button to advance to the following day (the first Tuesday of the next month). Create two more new appointments for training candidates. Both interviews will be in **Conference Room A**. The first appointment is from **10:00 AM** to **11:30 AM** with candidate **Juan Cortez**, and the second appointment is from **2:30 PM** to **4:00 PM** with **John Croix**. Set 1-hour reminders before each of the two new appointments. Use the **Categorize** button in the Tags group to apply the **Blue Category** to both calendar items. Save and close each appointment.
5. On the Date Navigator, select the last Friday in the next month. Create a new event:
   a. In the New group, click the **New Items** button and then click **All Day Event**.
   b. In the subject box, type **Vacation**.
   c. In the Options group, click the **Show As** list arrow and then click **Out of Office**.
   d. In the Tags group, click the **Categorize** button and apply the **Green Category**. (If prompted to rename the category, click **No.**) A green category bar appears above the Subject box. You do not need a reminder for this event.
   e. Save and close the event.
6. In the Date Navigator, select the second Saturday in the next month. In the calendar grid, click the **9:00 am** time block, then press **Shift** and click the **12:30 pm** time block to establish a time range of 9:00 AM to 1:00 PM, as shown in **Figure 6–3**.

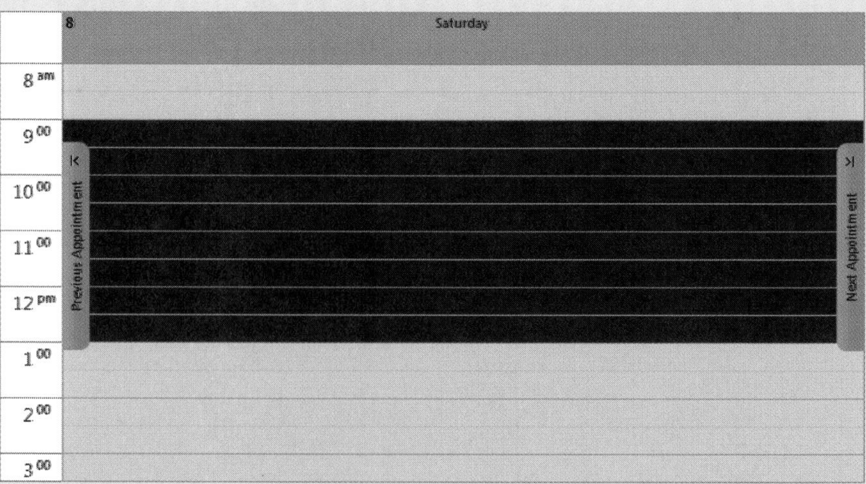

FIGURE 6–3
Selected range of time blocks

7. In the New group, click the **New Appointment** button. In the Subject text box, type **Bay Area Community Service**. In the Location text box, type **Food Bank**. Set a reminder **1 day** before the event. Apply the **Green Category**. Save and close the appointment. Click the day name on the calendar grid to deselect the time block.
8. Create a new appointment for the first Tuesday of the next month, using the following information. By default, the time blocks are set for 30 minutes, so you will need to type the 11:45 time setting. Set a reminder for 15 minutes before the appointment, and apply the **Blue Category**. Save and close the appointment.

Subject:	**Lunch with E.J.**
Location:	**Village Diner**
Start time:	**11:45 AM**
End time:	**1:00 PM**

9. Create a new recurring appointment for a staff meeting:
   a. Create a new appointment for the first Wednesday in the next month. Use the subject **Staff Meeting**. The meeting will be held in **Conference Room A**, beginning at **8:00 AM** and ending at **10:00 AM**. Apply the **Blue Category**.
   b. In the Options group, click the **Recurrence** button. In the Appointment Recurrence dialog box, under Recurrence pattern, enable the **Weekly** and **Wednesday** options, as shown in **Figure 6–4**. Under Range of recurrence, click the **End by** list arrow, and select the last Wednesday of the same month. Click **OK** to close the dialog box.

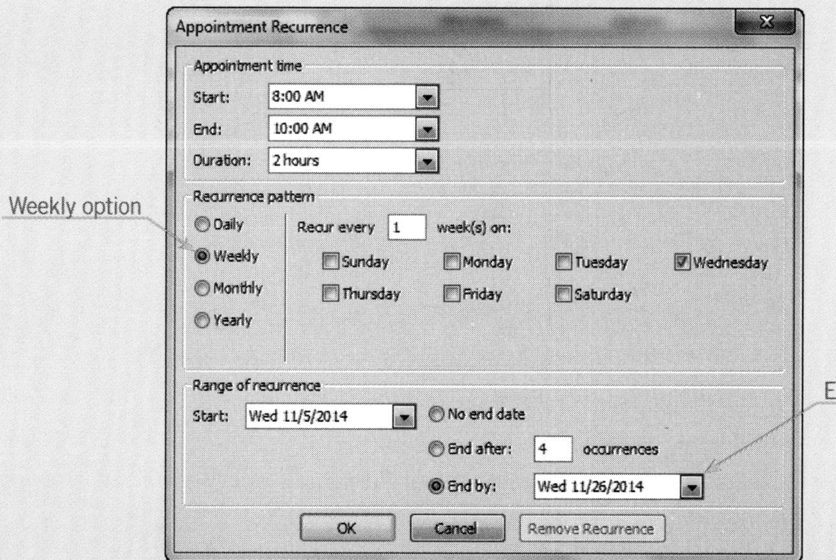

FIGURE 6–4 Appointment Recurrence dialog box

   c. Click the **Save & Close** button.

> **TIP**
>
> To quickly navigate to a specific date, on the Home tab, in the Go To group, click the Dialog Box Launcher and then select the destination date. If desired, change the view (Day, Week, Month, or Work Week), and then click OK.

10. Create a new appointment for the second Wednesday of the next month, using the subject **Alex Clark**. The meeting will be in **My Office** from **9:45 AM** to **1:45 PM**. A message appears above the Subject box indicating a conflict with another appointment. The issue will be addressed later. In the description area, type **Preview new software developments**. Apply the **Blue Category**. Save and close the appointment window.
11. On the Home tab, in the Arrange group, click the **Month** button to switch to Month view. Double-click the **Staff Meeting** item for the second Wednesday of the next month. When prompted to open the occurrence or the series, the Open this occurrence option should already be enabled. Click **OK**. Change the End time to **9:30 AM**. In the Actions group, click the **Save & Close** button.
12. Create new appointments for the third Monday in the next month, using the following information. You do not need to set reminders. Apply the **Blue Category** to each item, and then save and close. As you enter the second and third appointments, a message will appear indicating adjacent appointments.

    Subject: **Call Seth Warwick**
    Start time: **10:00 AM**
    End time: **10:10 AM**
    Description: **419-555-1099**

    Subject: **Call Alaina Chang**
    Start time: **10:10 AM**
    End time: **10:20 PM**
    Description: **419-555-4576**

    Subject: **Call Neyomi Young**
    Start time: **10:20 AM**
    End time: **10:30 AM**
    Description: **419-555-1002**
13. Click the **View** tab. In the Arrangement group, click the **Month** button. Double-click the **Bay Area Community Service** item for the second Saturday of the next month. To the right of the Start time fields, enable the **All day event** option. Because all-day events still show some time as free on the calendar, in the Options group, click the **Show As** list arrow and then click **Busy**. Then click the **Save & Close** button.
14. Leave Outlook open for the next Step-by-Step.

Customizing Calendar Views

As you've worked with Outlook, you've most likely used several different views to access your schedule. Changing the view enables you to focus on different time periods, such as one week or one month at a time. You can also select a range of days, or multiple noncontiguous days, to be displayed at the same time in Day view. For example, your manager announced three noncontiguous dates for upcoming employee training sessions. Attendance at the sessions is mandatory. You can display only those three dates in your calendar to see if there are any conflicts for those dates. You can also create custom views by filtering categories assigned to items in your calendar.

By default, the calendar shows 30-minute blocks of time for appointments. You can increase or decrease these periods by adjusting the Time Scale settings.

Step-by-Step 6.2

1. If necessary, click the **Calendar** button in the Navigation Pane. If necessary, expand the Navigation Pane and minimize the To-Do Bar.
2. In the Date Navigator, click the first day of the next month. Change the amount of detail that appears in the calendar:
   a. In the Arrange group, click the **Month** button arrow and then click **Show Low Detail**. Only the all-day events appear in the calendar.
   b. Click the **Month** button arrow and then click **Show Medium Detail**. Shaded areas indicate scheduled appointments, but no information about the appointments is displayed.
   c. Click the **Month** button arrow and then click **Show High Detail**. The appointment subjects are displayed.
3. In the Date Navigator, select the second Monday in the next month. Press and hold **Ctrl** and then, on the Date Navigator, click the Wednesday and Friday in that same week. The schedules for only those three days appear in the calendar grid, as shown in **Figure 6–5**.

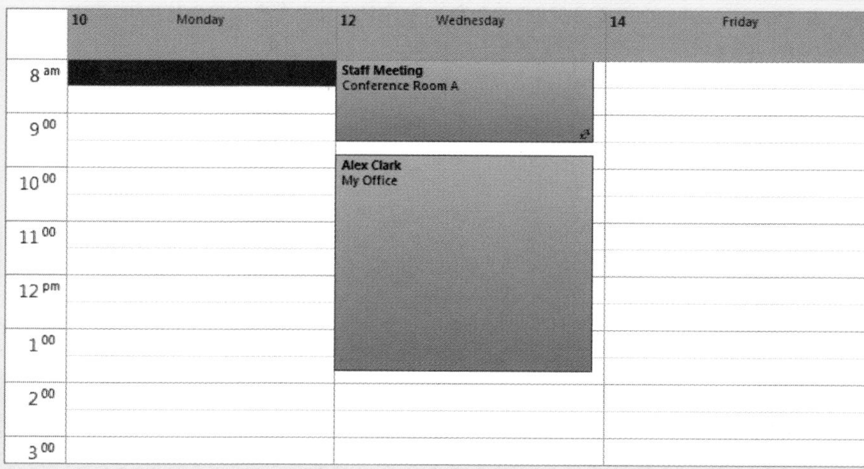

FIGURE 6–5
Multiple noncontiguous days displayed in Day view

4. In the Date Navigator, click the third Monday in the next month. Click the **View** tab. In the Arrangement group, click the **Time Scale** button and then click **30 Minutes**. This is the default Time Scale setting. Note that the three appointments all appear in the 30-minute time interval, as shown in **Figure 6–6**.

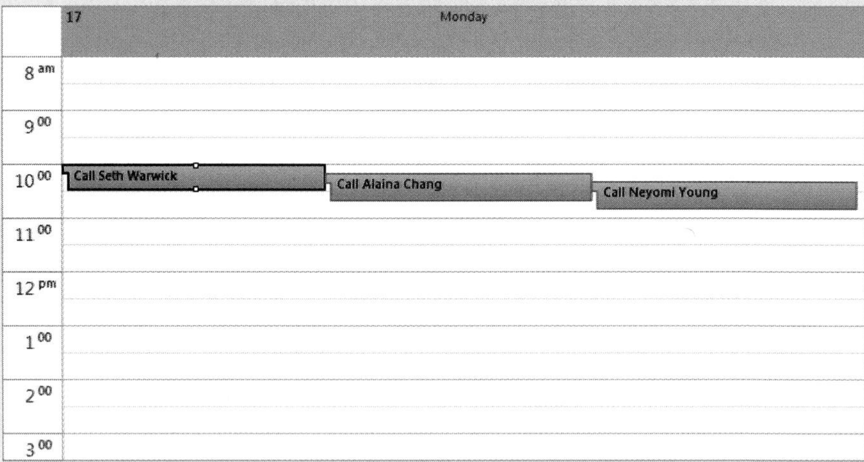

FIGURE 6–6
Three appointments within a 30-minute time block

5. In the Arrangement group, click the **Time Scale** button and then click **15 Minutes**. Scroll down to view the schedule beginning at 10:00 am. Note that the appointments now appear in two different time blocks, as shown in **Figure 6–7**. Even though more space is available for details about the appointment, you now see fewer blocks of time for the day's calendar.

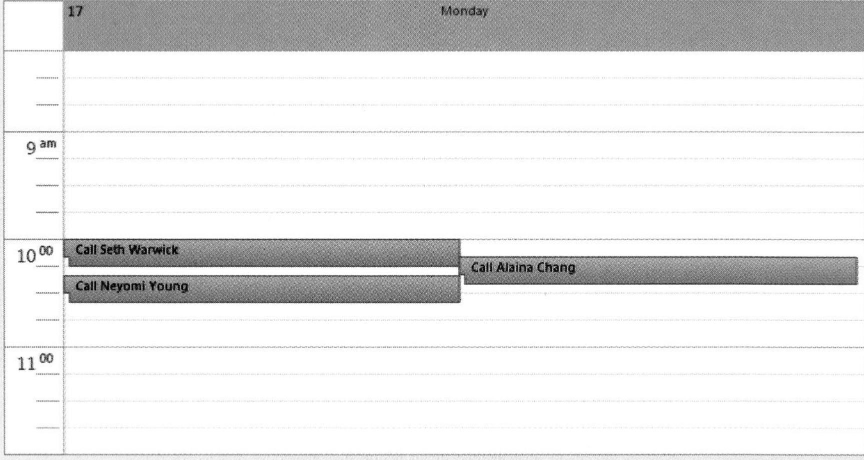

FIGURE 6–7
Three appointments within a 15-minute time block

6. Click the **Time Scale** button and then click **30 Minutes** to restore the default setting. Scroll up to show the appointments, if necessary.
7. In the Arrangement group, click the **Month** button. Note that both blue and green category items appear in the calendar.

8. In the Current View group, click the **View Settings** button. In the Advanced View Settings: Calendar dialog box, click **Filter** to open the Filter dialog box.
9. Click the **More Choices** tab, and then click **Categories** to open the Color Categories dialog box shown in **Figure 6–8**. Under Name, enable the **Blue Category** option.

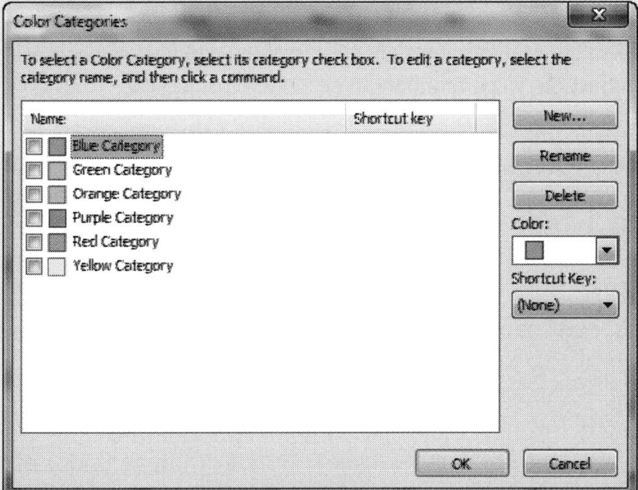

FIGURE 6–8
Color Categories dialog box

10. Click **OK** three times to apply the filter and close the dialog boxes. Now only the Blue Category items appear in the calendar.
11. Click the **View Settings** button and then click **Filter**. Click the **More Choices** tab and then click **Clear All**. Then click **OK** twice to accept the changes and close the dialog boxes. All the calendar items appear.
12. Leave Outlook open for the next Step-by-Step.

Customizing Calendar Settings

Your Outlook calendar is created based on several default settings. For example, using the default settings, the week begins on a Sunday and the work week is Monday through Friday. If you have a different work schedule, you can customize the calendar settings so that the Work Week view displays the days in your work week schedule.

When scheduling events or meetings that involve persons in different time zones, you can display a second time zone in Day view to help you keep track of the time differences. So that you can readily see the time for people in other time zones, you can display the contact's time zone close to your appointments.

Holidays affect our schedules, and Outlook provides options for automatically adding holidays to your calendar. If you interact with individuals in other countries, you can choose to show their holidays. For example, if you work with people in China, you may want to add Chinese holidays to your calendar. You can add multiple sets of holidays.

Your default calendar display is based on the language and date formats that are set in the regional and language options for your operating system. The Gregorian calendar is Outlook's standard English calendar. If you communicate with others around the world, you might find it useful to add an ***alternate calendar***, which is a second calendar that appears in the same view as the standard Outlook calendar. For example, if you collaborate with people in Japan, you can show the Gregorian and Lunar calendars at the same time.

VOCABULARY
alternate calendar

Outlook automatically assigns week numbers to every week in the calendar, but by default, these week numbers are not displayed. You can enable an option so that the week numbers appear on the left side of the Date Navigator. Outlook provides three choices for assigning the numbers: start on January 1, first four-day week, or first full week. The week numbers are standardized and always begin with number 1; you cannot adjust the week numbers to reflect the fiscal year.

Step-by-Step 6.3

1. If necessary, click the Calendar button in the Navigation Pane. If necessary, expand the Navigation Pane and minimize the To-Do Bar.
2. In the Date Navigator, click the first Monday of the next month. Click the **Home** tab and, in the Arrange group, click the **Work Week** button. By default, the calendar will show Monday through Friday of the current week. Click the **File** tab and then click **Options**. In the Outlook Options dialog box, in the left pane, click **Calendar**.
3. Under Work time, make note of the current settings. Then change the work week settings so that only the Mon, Tue, Wed, and Thu options are enabled. Click the **First day of week** list arrow and then click **Monday**.
4. Scroll down to the Time zones section. If the first Label box is blank, type **My Time**. If the first Label box already contains text, leave it as is. Note that your current time zone is displayed in the first Time zone box, as shown in **Figure 6–9**. Your settings may differ.

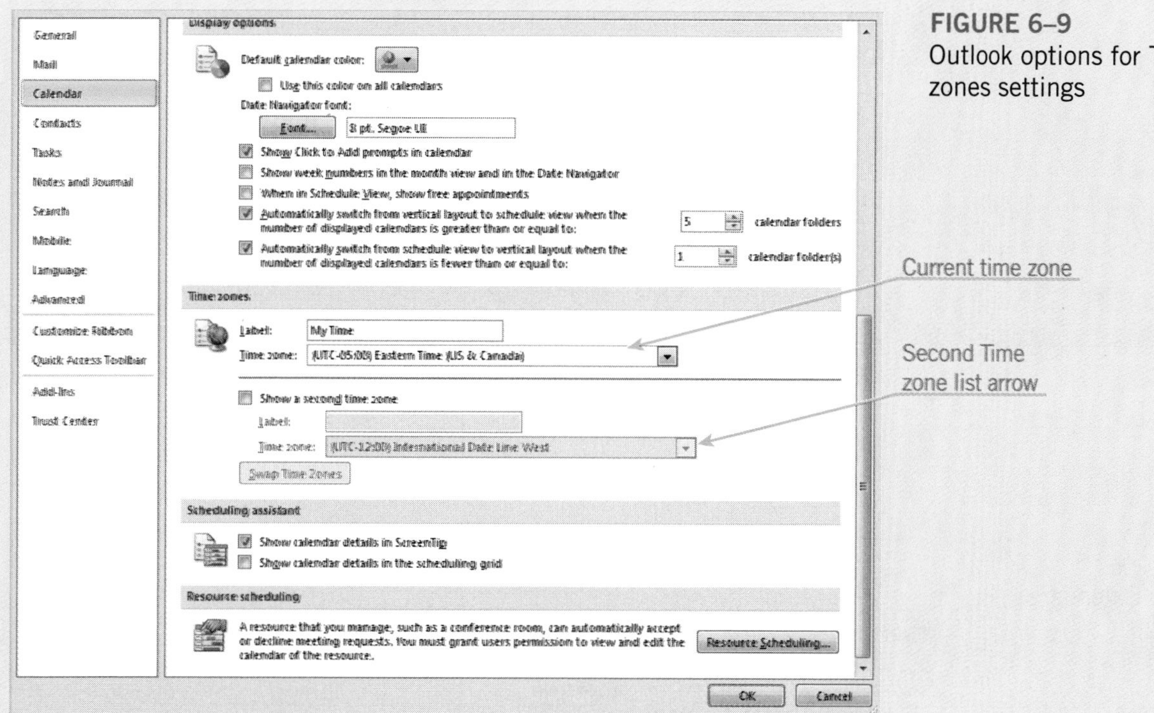

FIGURE 6–9
Outlook options for Time zones settings

5. Enable the option **Show a second time zone**. Click the second **Time zone** list arrow to show the available time zones. Scroll down and select a different time zone from your own. For example, if you live in the Eastern time zone, select (UTC-10:00) Hawaii.

6. In the Label box above the second Time zone box, type an appropriate name for the second time zone. In the example above, you would type Hawaii. Then click **OK**. As shown in **Figure 6–10**, the calendar grid now shows two different time zone columns.

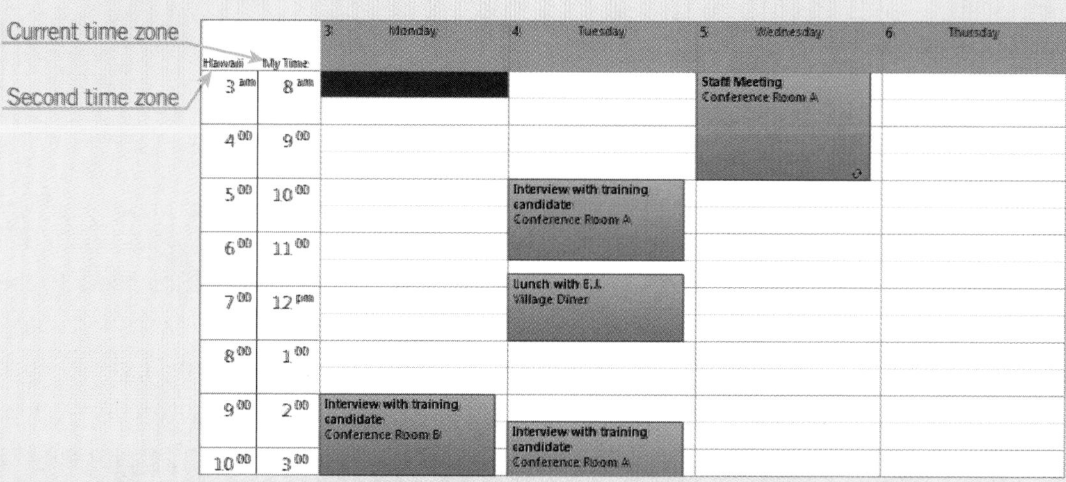

FIGURE 6–10
Calendar with two time zone settings

7. Click the **File** tab, and then click **Options**. In the Outlook Options dialog box, on the left pane, click **Calendar**. Under Work time, change the settings back to those noted in Step 3. (The default settings for the Work week are Mon, Tue, Wed, Thu, and Fri.)

8. Reset the setting for the First day of the week, as noted in Step 3. (The default setting is Sunday.)
9. Scroll down to the Time zones section. If the first Label box was blank in Step 4, delete the text you typed. Delete the text you typed in the second time zone label box, and then disable the option **Show a second time zone**.
10. Scroll up to the Calendar options section. Click **Add Holidays** to open the Add Holidays to Calendar dialog box, as shown in **Figure 6–11**. Note that the selected location is based on your region, but you can choose a different location. (When you click OK, the holidays for the selected location are added to the calendar as all-day events.) Click **Cancel** to close the dialog box without adding holidays to your calendar.

FIGURE 6–11
Add Holidays to Calendar dialog box

11. Under Calendar options, enable the option **Enable an alternate calendar**, as shown in **Figure 6–12**. In the first box under the option, click the **Alternate calendar language** list arrow and then click **Japanese**. In the Alternate calendar type box on the right, make sure Lunar is selected.

FIGURE 6–12
Calendar options

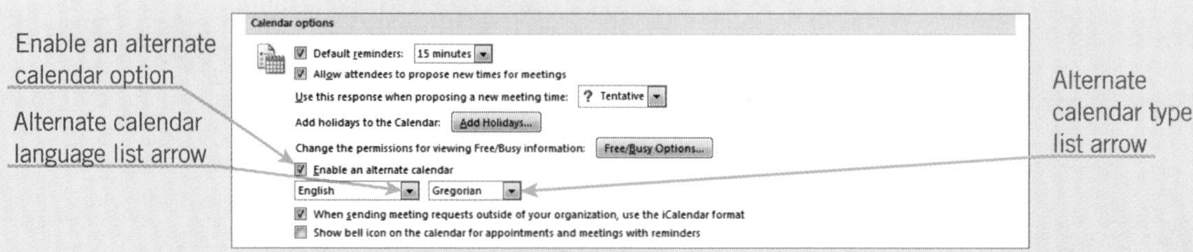

12. Under Display options, enable the option **Show week numbers in the month view and in the Date Navigator**. Then click **OK** to close the Outlook Options dialog box. On the View tab, in the Arrangement group, click the **Month** button. The calendar changes and shows more information, as shown in **Figure 6–13**. In the Date Navigator, the week numbers appear on the left. The week numbers are also visible in the calendar grid, and the dates in the calendar grid are shown in both English and Japanese.

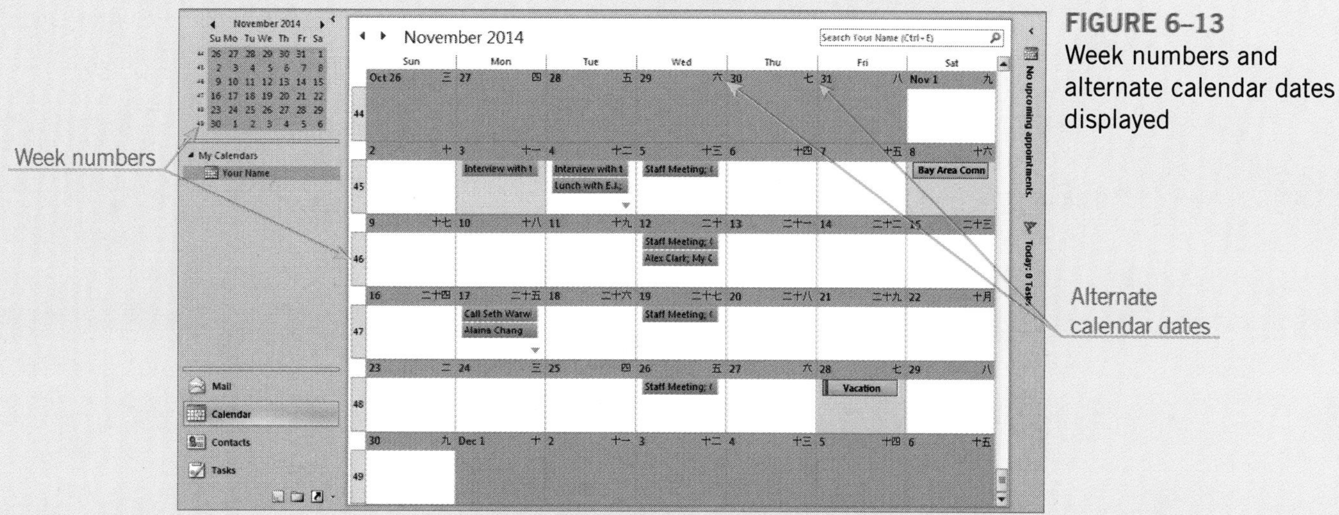

FIGURE 6–13
Week numbers and alternate calendar dates displayed

13. Click the **File** tab, and then click **Options**. In the Outlook Options dialog box, on the left pane, click **Calendar**. Under Calendar options, disable the option **Enable an alternate calendar**. Under Display options, disable the option **Show week numbers in the month view and in the Date Navigator**. Click **OK** to accept the changes.
14. Leave Outlook open for the next Step-by-Step.

Creating Multiple Calendars

Creating multiple calendars enables you to view different schedules, and you can create as many calendars as you need. If you have several calendars, you can organize them in groups.

When you select multiple calendars in the Navigation Pane, you can view the selected calendars side by side, and you can choose whether to show the calendars in Day view, Week view, Work Week view, or Month view. When calendars are displayed side by side, you can drag and drop calendar items to move and copy them from one calendar to another. Instead of comparing the calendars side by side, you can overlay the calendars, which means all the schedules from the selected calendars appear in one calendar grid. Then you can view all the appointments and events from all of the selected calendars at the same time. Since each calendar has an associated color, the colors on calendar items in the overlaid calendars help you distinguish the source calendar.

Step-by-Step 6.4

1. If necessary, click the **Calendar** button in the Navigation Pane. If necessary, expand the **Navigation Pane**, minimize the To-Do Bar, and show the calendar in **Day view**.

2. On the Home tab, in the Manage Calendars group, click the **Open Calendar** button, and then click **Create New Blank Calendar** to open the Create New Folder dialog box, as shown in **Figure 6–14**.

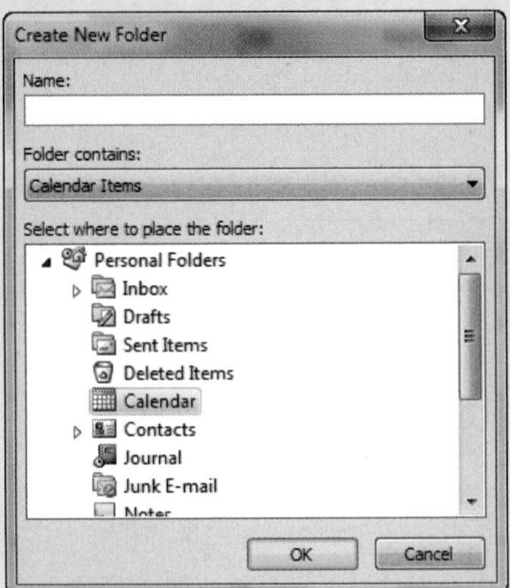

FIGURE 6–14
Create New Folder dialog box

3. Under Name, type **Classes**, then click **OK**. Under Select where to place the folder, select your personal folder, and then click **OK**. A new calendar appears in the My Calendar folder on the Navigation Pane. (If a prompt appears indicating that subfolders cannot be saved to a Web-based account, click OK. You may not be able to complete the remaining steps in this Step-by-Step. However, you can read the steps and look at the figures to learn about creating and organizing multiple calendars.)
4. In the Navigation Pane, right-click the **Classes** calendar and then click **New Calendar**. Under Select where to place the folder, select your personal folder and then click **OK**. In the Name box, type **Rehearsals** and then click **OK**. Repeat the process to create calendars titled **Volunteer Schedule**, **Meal Deliveries**, and **Birthdays**.
5. In the Navigation Pane, right-click **My Calendars** and then click **New Calendar Group**. A new group is added to the Navigation Pane. Type **Personal** and press **Enter** to create a name for the group. Repeat the process to create a calendar group named **Food Bank**. Your Navigation Pane should show the calendars and groups shown in **Figure 6–15**.

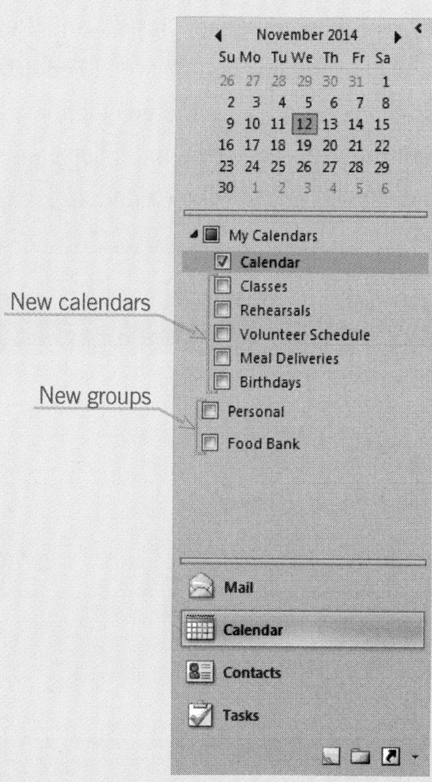

FIGURE 6–15
New calendars and groups

6. In the Navigation Pane, select the **Classes** calendar and drag it to the Personal calendar group. Drag and drop the Rehearsals and Birthdays calendars to the Personal calendar group. Drag and drop the Volunteer Schedule and Meal Deliveries calendars to the Food Bank calendar group. Your Navigation Pane should now look similar to **Figure 6–16**.

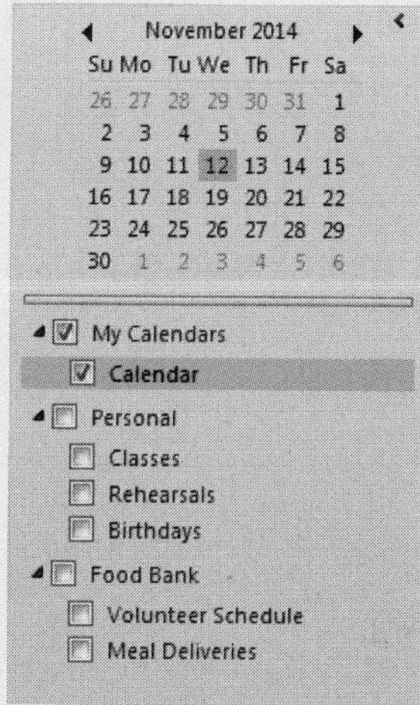

FIGURE 6–16
Calendars rearranged in groups

7. In the Personal group, enable the **Classes** and **Rehearsals** calendars. Disable the default **Calendar**. Then click the **Food Bank** group to enable both calendars in the group. The selected calendars appear side by side, as shown in **Figure 6–17**. Note that the color bands on the Navigation Pane correspond to the colors of the calendars.

FIGURE 6–17
Selected calendars displayed side by side

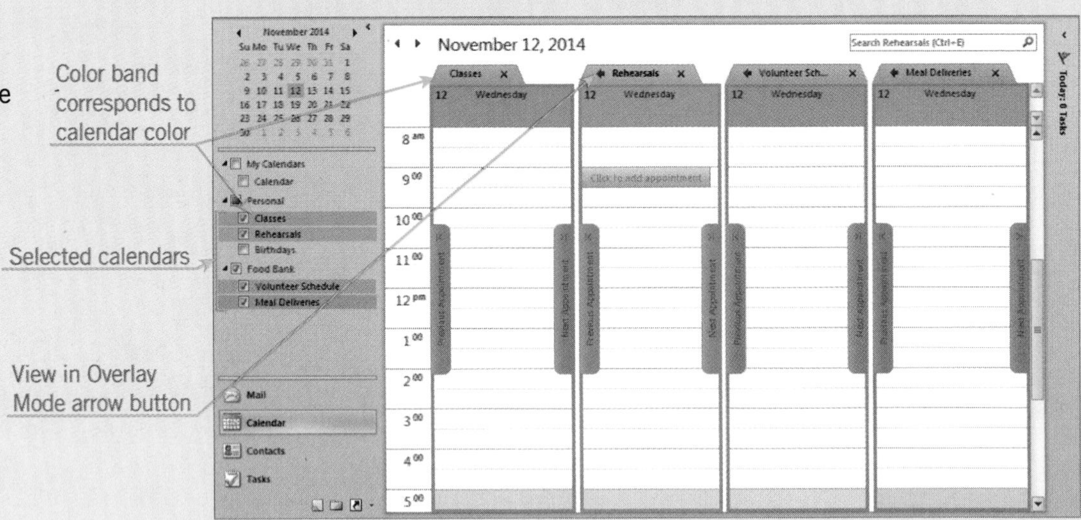

8. In Day view, add some appointments to the calendars:
   a. In the Classes calendar grid, select the **9:00 – 9:30 am** time block and type **Chemistry exam**. Then drag the bottom border of the time block down to select one more block so that the appointment is scheduled from 9:00 am to 10:00 am.
   b. In the Rehearsals calendar grid, select the **12:00 – 12:30 pm** time block and type **Lunch with director**. Then drag the bottom border of the time block down to select one more block so that the appointment is scheduled from 12:00 pm to 1:00 pm.
   c. In the Volunteer Schedule calendar grid, select the **2:00 – 2:30 pm** time block and type **Meet with coordinator**.
   d. Click and drag the **Meet with coordinato**r item to the 2:00 – 2:30 pm time block in the Meal Deliveries calendar grid. In the Meal Deliveries calendar grid, drag and drop the copied **Meet with coordinator** item down one block so the appointment is scheduled from 2:30 pm to 3:00 pm.
9. In the Arrange group, click the **Work Week**, **Week**, **Month**, and **Schedule View** buttons to display the calendars in different views. Then click the **Day** button to return to Day view.

10. In the upper-left corner of the Rehearsals calendar tab, click the **View in Overlay Mode** arrow button. The Rehearsals calendar items appear in a combined Classes and Rehearsals calendar. Click the **View in Overlay Mode** arrow button in the Volunteer Schedule calendar and the Meal Deliveries calendar to overlay all the items, as shown in **Figure 6–18**. Note that the colors for the calendar items help you identify the source calendar.

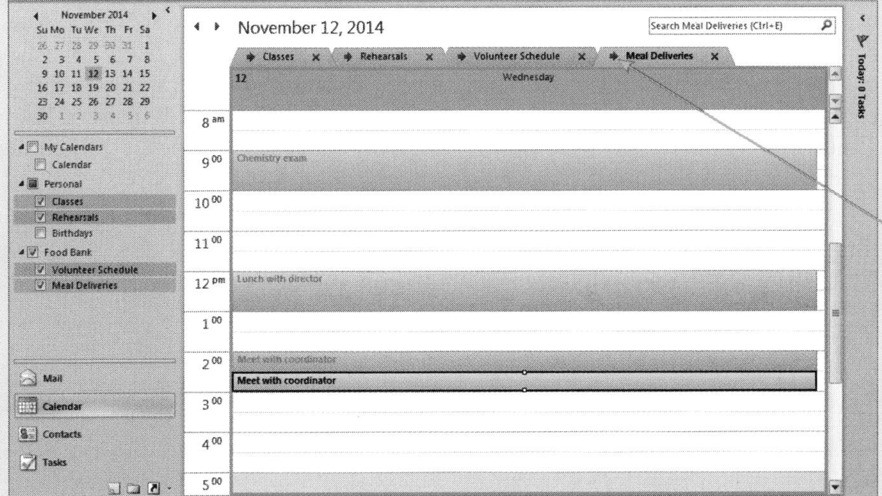

FIGURE 6–18
Four calendars overlaid in one calendar grid

11. To switch back to the side-by-side view, click the **View in Side-By-Side Mode** arrow button in the upper-left corner of the Rehearsals calendar tab, the Volunteer Schedule calendar tab, and the Meal Deliveries calendar tab.
12. To delete a calendar group, you must first delete the calendars in the group:
    a. In the Navigation Pane, right-click the **Meal Deliveries** calendar and then click **Delete Calendar**. When prompted to delete the folder, click **Yes**.
    b. In the Navigation Pane, right-click the **Volunteer Schedule** calendar and then click **Delete Calendar**. When prompted to delete the folder, click **Yes**.
    c. In the Navigation Pane, right-click the **Food Bank** group and then click **Delete Group**. When prompted to delete the group, click **Yes**.
13. Delete each of the calendars in the Personal group, and then delete the Personal group.
14. Leave Outlook open for the next Step-by-Step.

Managing Meetings

EXTRA FOR EXPERTS

When you have the ability to view others' calendars (using SharePoint or Exchange Server accounts), you can view the attendees' calendars before creating a meeting request. After selecting the calendars of those you want to invite, in the Arrange group on the Home tab, click the Schedule View command to display the selected calendars, which will be stacked vertically. You will see all of their schedules so you can determine the best time to schedule the meeting.

Meetings differ from appointments in that you must invite other people to join you for a meeting, and you must also let them know the time and location of the meeting. Instead of calling or faxing to invite people to attend a meeting, the meeting organizer can easily and quickly complete the task by creating a meeting request and sending the invitation via e-mail. When selecting participants for the meeting, the organizer can choose whether to notify the recipient that the meeting is required or optional. For meetings that are scheduled on a regular basis, such as weekly or monthly, the organizer can apply recurrence settings.

When attendees open a meeting request in their Outlook Inbox, a Quick View of their calendar appears so they can see if they are available for the suggested date and time. If the meeting request includes recurring dates, they can quickly navigate to other dates in their calendar. Attendees can respond to a meeting invitation by choosing one of the four options: Accept, Tentative, Decline, and Propose a New Time. The organizer can track the responses from all those who were invited to the meeting.

In the next Step-by-Step, you will learn how to send and accept a meeting invitation. If you are not able to send and receive messages, you will not be able to complete all of the steps, but you can refer to the figures to help you visualize the process of sending and responding to meeting invitations.

Step-by-Step 6.5

TIP

You can easily turn an appointment into a meeting by inviting attendees. Open the appointment and, in the Attendees group, click the Invite Attendees button and then complete and send the e-mail message.

1. If necessary, click the Calendar button in the Navigation Pane. If necessary, expand the Navigation Pane and minimize the To-Do Bar.
2. In the Date Navigator, select the first Friday in the next month, and drag and select the time span **1:00 pm – 2:00 pm**. In the New group, click the **New Meeting** button. A new e-mail message opens. Click the **To** button to open the Select Attendees and Resources dialog box, as shown in **Figure 6–19**.

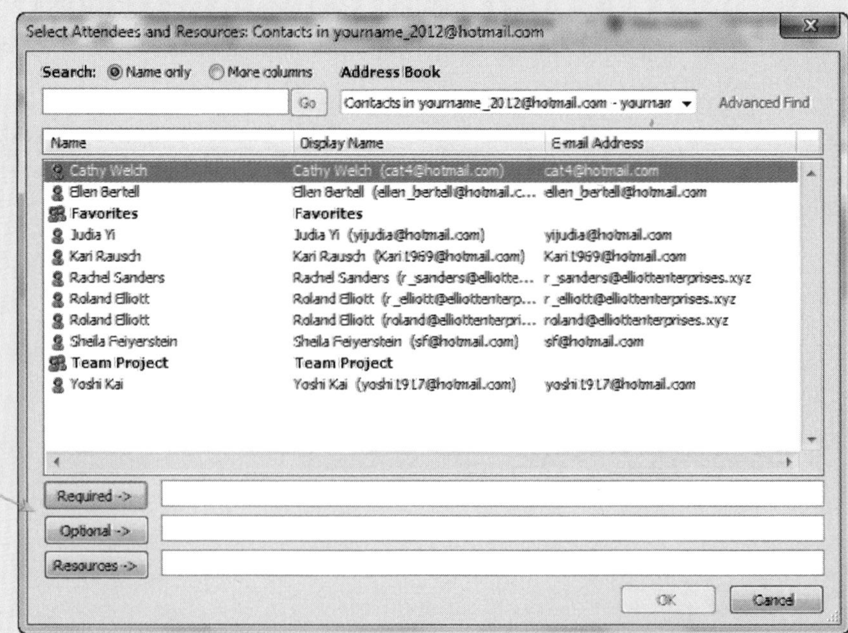

Required and Optional options

FIGURE 6–19 Select Attendees and Resources dialog box

3. Under Name, select a recipient name. If you are permitted to exchange e-mails with classmates, select a classmate name. Then click **Required** at the bottom of the dialog box, and the selected recipient's name is displayed in the Required box.
4. Under Name, select a second name, press and hold **Ctrl**, select a third name (preferably classmates), and then click **Optional**. The names of the selected recipients are displayed in the Optional box. Click **OK**.
5. In the Subject text box, type **Team Project Update**. In the Location text box, type **My Office**. Note that because you selected the date and time before opening the invitation message, the start and end times have already been set. In the message body, type **Review Team Project status**.
6. In the Options group, click the **Recurrence** button. Set a weekly pattern, and end the range after three occurrences. Click **OK**. In the Tags group, click the **Categorize** button and then click **Blue Category**. **Figure 6–20** shows an example of a completed meeting invitation.

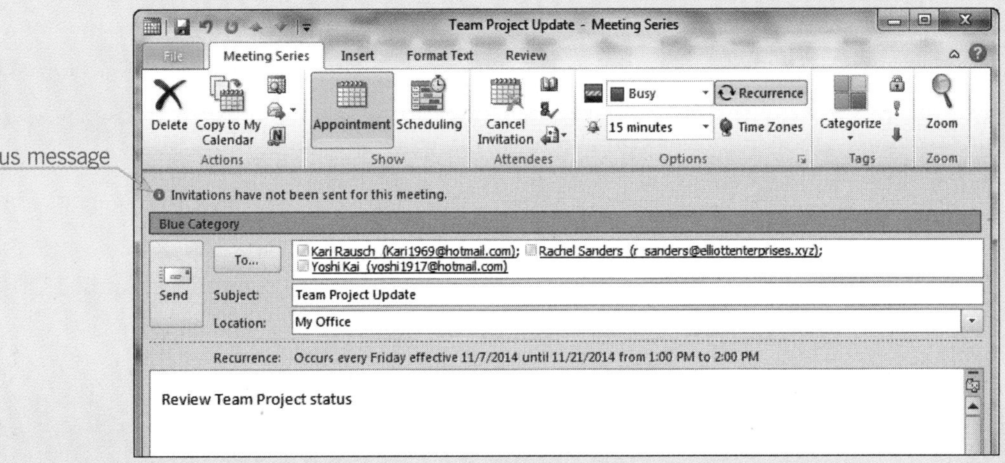

FIGURE 6–20
A meeting invitation before it is sent

7. If you selected classmates for meeting participants, click **Send**. If you cannot exchange e-mails with classmates, close the message window without saving the changes.

8. If you receive a meeting invitation from a classmate, open the message in your Inbox. **Figure 6–21** shows an example of the meeting invitation after it is opened in an Inbox. Note that a Quick View of the attendee's calendar appears in the invitation.

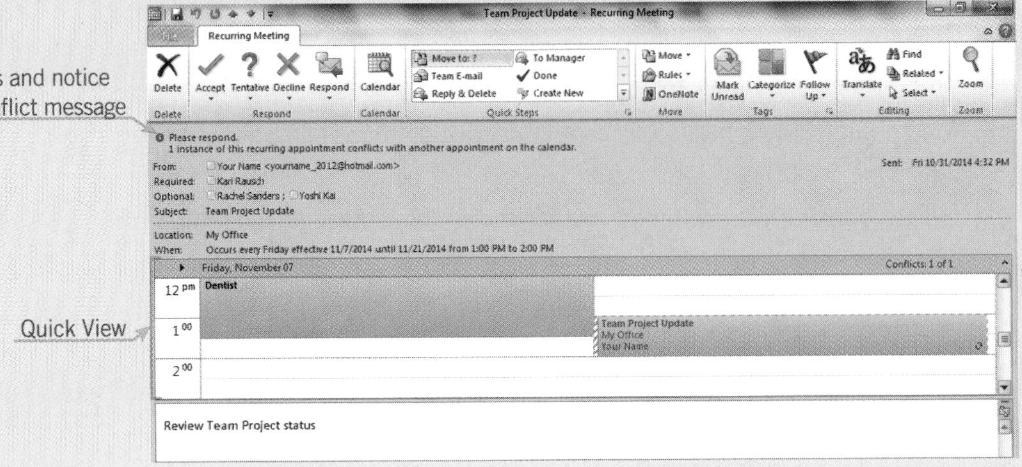

FIGURE 6–21
A meeting invitation when it is opened in an Inbox

TIP

When you click a response button and then select Send the Response Now, a reply message is automatically generated and sent to the organizer.

9. If you are able to respond to an invitation, complete the following steps using buttons in the Respond group. (*Note*: If you are not able to respond to an invitation, you can view a sample response message in Figure 6–22.)
   a. Click the **Tentative** button and then click **Edit the Response before Sending**. A new message window opens.
   b. In the note area, type **I already have a commitment until 1:30 p.m. next Friday, but I will try to change that appointment.**.
   c. When your message window looks similar to **Figure 6–22**, click **Send**.

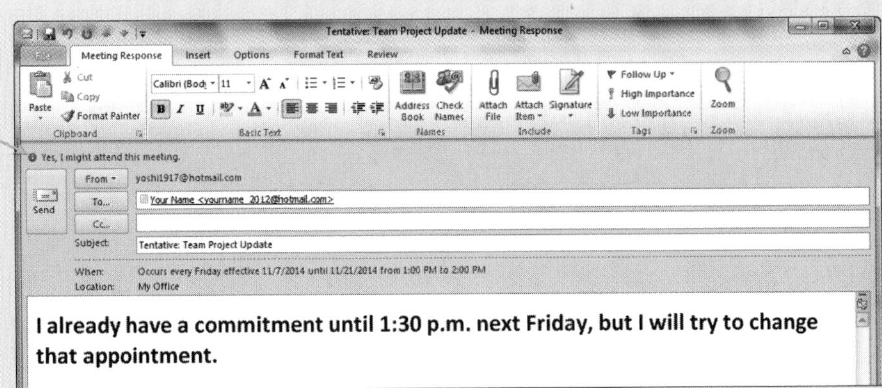

FIGURE 6–22
A message for response to a meeting invitation

10. If you responded to the meeting invitation, in the Navigation Pane, click the **Calendar** button. Switch to Month view, and advance to the next month. A sample of an updated calendar is shown in **Figure 6–23**. Note that the appointment is scheduled for three consecutive Fridays in the next month, and the appointment subject displays the Tentative border.

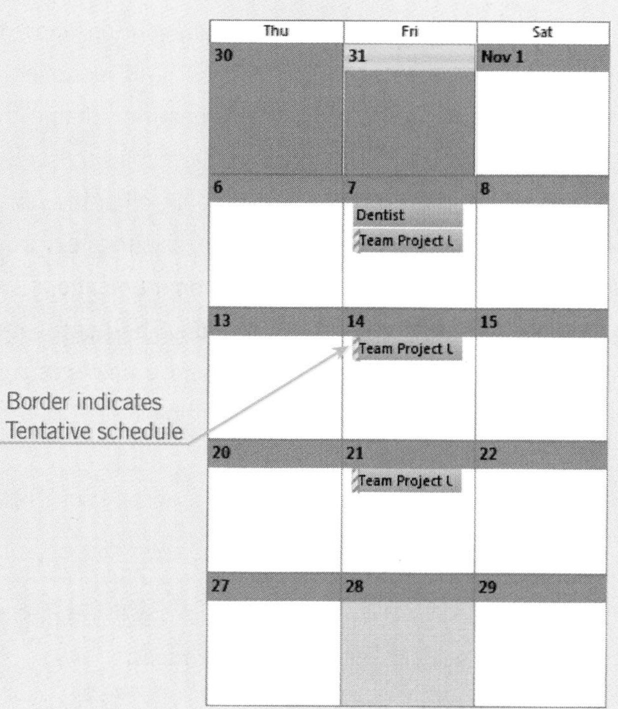

FIGURE 6–23
Recipient's calendar showing the new meeting in the schedule

11. If you sent a meeting invitation to classmates (Step 7 above) and received a response, click the **Mail** button in the Navigation Pane and then click the **Inbox Items** folder. Open the response you received from your classmates. As shown in **Figure 6–24**, the message window shows a status report for the responses. Close the message window. Click the **Inbox** folder.

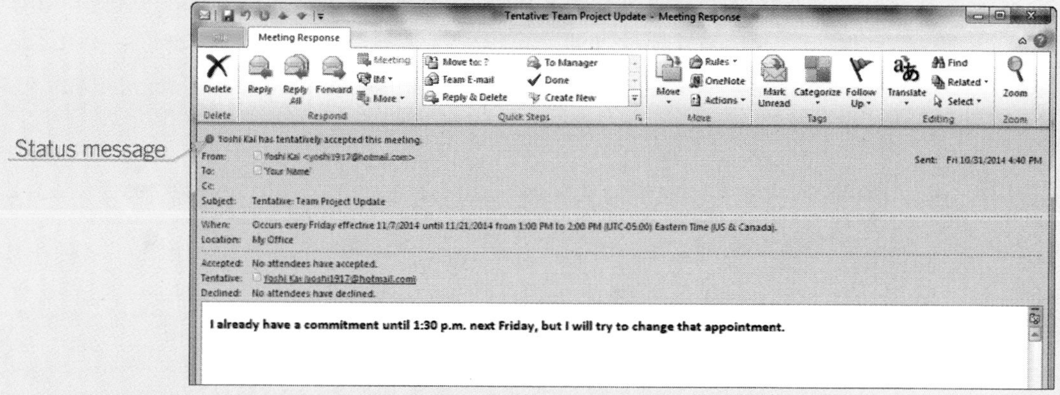

FIGURE 6–24
A response message in an Organizer's Inbox

12. In the Navigation Pane, click the **Calendar** button and, if necessary, advance to the next month. In the calendar grid, double-click the first occurrence of the Team Project Update meeting. Enable the **Open the series** option and click **OK**. The meeting invitation window is opened. On the Meeting Series tab, in the Actions group, click the **Cancel Meeting** button. In the message body, delete the existing text and then type **We will monitor the project with online communications.**, as shown in **Figure 6–25.** Then click **Send Cancellation**. The item is removed from your calendar (the organizer's calendar) and a new message is sent to the recipients originally invited to the meeting.

FIGURE 6–25
Cancellation message

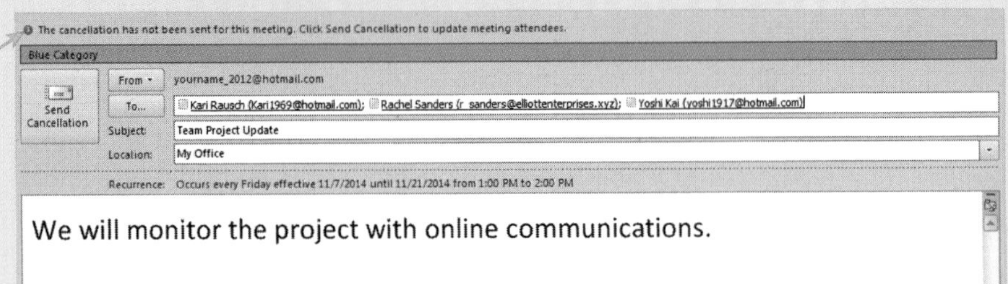

> **TIP**
>
> You can drag and drop the appointment or meeting to a different date or time on the calendar. You can also change the subject by clicking the text and making the necessary edits.

13. At this point, attendees will receive a new message about the meeting cancellation. When an attendee opens the cancellation message, the Quick View will display an update as shown in **Figure 6–26**, and the subject for the scheduled meeting will now show *Canceled: Team Project Update*. If you have been exchanging e-mails as an attendee, but not as the organizer, you will need to remove the item from the calendar. If so, click the **Mail** button on the Navigation Pane and then open the cancellation message. On the Recurring Meeting tab of the message window, in the Respond group, click the **Remove from Calendar** button. Close the message window.

FIGURE 6–26
Updated Quick View after meeting is canceled

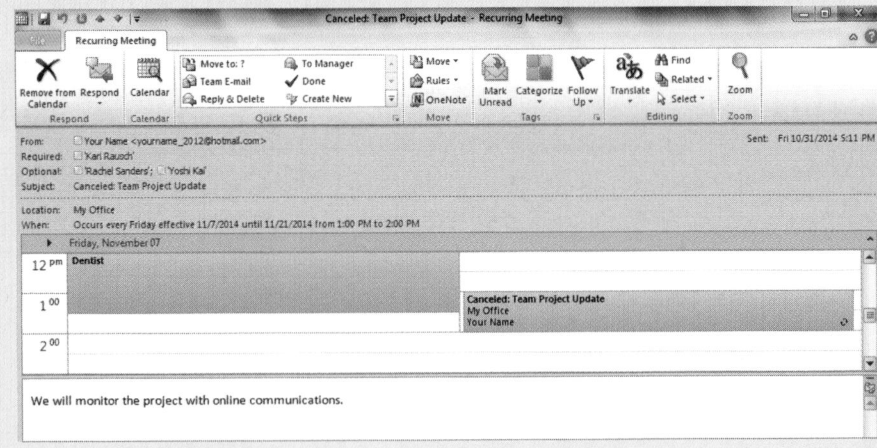

14. Leave Outlook open for the next Step-by-Step.

Sharing Calendars

Outlook provides several options for sharing your calendar information with others. You can specify the calendar dates you want to share, and then you can send your calendar to others via e-mail. The file is saved as an ***iCalendar***, which is an Internet calendar saved in a format that is compatible with Outlook and other calendar programs. The iCalendar file extension is .ics. The file is attached to the e-mail message, and when the recipient opens the attachment, a prompt asks the user if they want to add the Internet calendar to Outlook.

Another way to share a calendar is to print a hard copy. Outlook offers several print layouts, and you can select the dates you want to print.

If you want to make a calendar available to several people, you can publish it to the Internet. For example, you can publish a basketball team schedule so coaches, players, and spectators can all see it. When publishing a calendar to the Internet, it is saved in the iCalendar format. You can publish the calendar to Office.com. To use this service, you must sign in to your Windows Live ID account. Or, you can publish a calendar to a WebDAV Server. The server you are using must support the World Wide Web Distributed Authoring and Versioning (WebDAV) protocol, and you must know the WebDAV server address.

Additional calendar sharing features are available in Microsoft Exchange Server accounts, but they are beyond the scope of this lesson.

Before sharing your calendars with others, it's important to review the items and decide if you should mark some appointments or events as private. When an appointment, meeting, or event is marked private, people who receive your calendar online will be able to see the date and the start and end times for the item, but they will not see the subject, location, and other details. You cannot mark a single occurrence as private; you must mark the entire series as private.

VOCABULARY

iCalendar

EXTRA FOR EXPERTS

The iCalendar format provides an alternative method for sending a meeting request. The organizer can create an e-mail message and attach an iCalendar file (or create a link to an iCalendar file). When the recipient opens the iCalendar file, the event is automatically added to their calendar program. The recipient does not have the opportunity to click a button to accept or decline, so you will not receive a confirmation e-mail. However, the recipient can reply to the e-mail message.

Step-by-Step 6.6

1. If necessary, click the **Calendar** button in the Navigation Pane. If necessary, expand the Navigation Pane and minimize the To-Do Bar. If necessary, advance to the next month using the Date Navigator and switch to Month view.
2. In the calendar grid, select the **Bay Area Community Service** item scheduled for the second Saturday in the next month. Click the **View** tab and, in the Arrangement group, click the **Day** button.
3. On the Calendar Tools Appointment tab, in the Tags group, click the **Private** button. Note that when the calendar is displayed in Day view, a lock appears to the right of the subject indicating that the item has been marked private.

TIP

Organizing schedules in different calendars makes it easier to share particular activities with others without disclosing all your activities.

4. Click the **Home** tab. In the Share group, click the **E-mail Calendar** button. A new message window opens along with the Send a Calendar via E-mail dialog box shown in **Figure 6–27**. Your dialog box will differ.

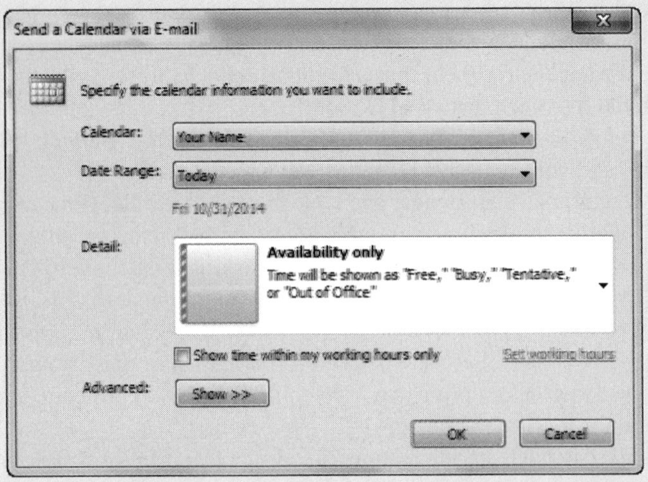

Send a Calendar via E-mail

Specify the calendar information you want to include.

Calendar: Your Name

Date Range: Today

Fri 10/31/2014

Detail: **Availability only** Time will be shown as "Free," "Busy," "Tentative," or "Out of Office"

Show time within my working hours only Set working hours

Advanced: Show >>

OK Cancel

FIGURE 6–27
Send a Calendar via E-mail dialog box

5. Click the **Date Range** list arrow and then select **Specify dates**. Click the **Start** list arrow and then select the first day of the next month. Click the **End** list arrow and then select the last day of the next month. Enable the option **Show time within my working hours only**. Click **OK**. A subject is added to the message window and the calendar file is already attached to the message.
6. The calendar also appears in the message body, as shown in the figures: **Figure 6–28** shows the date range for the calendar information, and **Figure 6–29** shows some of the calendar items. Scroll through the message body to view the calendar items. Note that no weekend appointments or events are included.

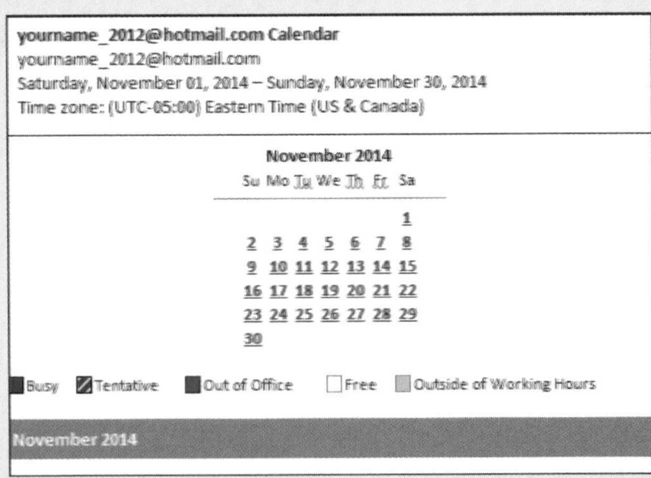

FIGURE 6–28
Calendar date range information embedded in the message body

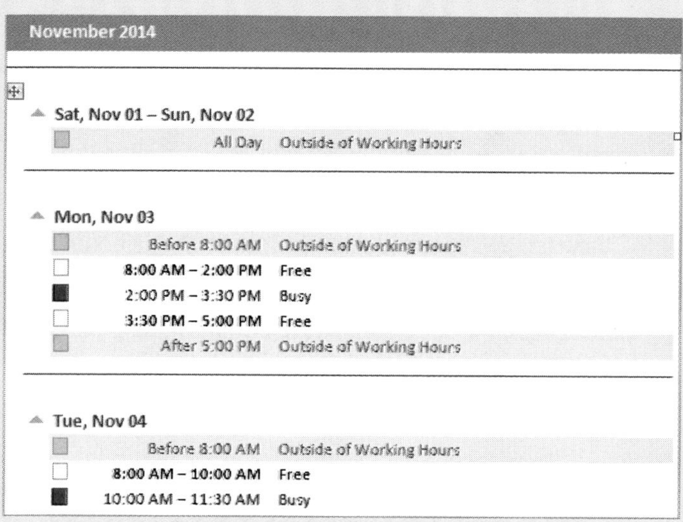

FIGURE 6–29
Calendar items embedded in the message body

7. Click the **File** tab and then click **Save As**. Navigate to the drive and folder where you save your solution files. In the File name box, type **My Calendar**, followed by your initials. Leave the Save as type setting as is. Click **Save**.
8. Scroll through the message and view the items. Note that the meeting details are not included, and the weekend events are also not presented. Close the message without saving the changes. When the recipient opens the attached .ics file, the items will automatically be added to the recipient's calendar.
9. Switch to Month view. In the calendar grid, double-click the **Interview with training candidate** item for the first Monday of the next month to open the appointment window.
10. On the Appointment tab, in the Actions group, click the **Forward** button arrow, and then click **Forward as iCalendar**. A new message window opens, and the appointment information is saved to an iCalendar file, which is already attached to the message. Close the message window without saving the changes. Then close the appointment window.
11. In the Date Navigator, select the first Monday in the next month. If necessary, switch to Day view. Click the **File** tab and then click **Print**. Under Settings, click each of the styles to preview the different styles. Then click the **Weekly Agenda Style**. Position the mouse pointer over the Preview Pane. The pointer changes to a magnifying glass. Click the first item for Saturday. Note that the Bay Area Community Service item includes a lock, but the subject and the location information *(Food Bank)* are both displayed.

EXTRA FOR EXPERTS

If your account is configured for text messaging, you can send your calendar information as a text message to a mobile phone.

12. Under Printer, click **Print Options**. At the bottom of the dialog box, under Print range, enable the option **Hide details of private appointments** and then click **Preview**. Scroll to Saturday. The preview now shows *Private Appointment*. Click **Print Options** and disable the **Hide details of private appointments** option. Then click **Preview**.
13. Click the **View** tab and switch to Month view. In the calendar grid, click the **Bay Area Community Service** item. On the Calendar Tools Appointment tab, in the Tags group, click the **Private** button to toggle off the feature.
14. Leave Outlook open for the next Step-by-Step.

Managing Tasks

Creating a list of tasks is easy, but organizing the tasks is what makes the list effective. Outlook offers many features to help you organize and view tasks.

Creating New Tasks

Before you begin learning about organizing tasks, you need to create some new tasks. The following Step-by-Step will provide a review of some basic Outlook Tasks features, and you will create several tasks that you can then use in other Step-by-Steps in this lesson. If you are using a classroom or lab computer, it's likely that the Task list is blank. However, if you are using your own personal computer to complete the exercises in this lesson, there may already be existing tasks in your Tasks folder. You can leave the existing tasks in the folder. At the end of the lesson, you will delete the new tasks created for this lesson.

Step-by-Step 6.7

1. In the Navigation Pane, click the **Tasks** button.
2. If necessary, click the **Home** tab. In the New group, click the **New Task** button. Maximize the task window and then enter the following information:

Subject:	**Update training manual**
Start date:	Select the second Wednesday of next month.
Due date:	Select the third Wednesday of next month.
Priority:	**High**
Reminder:	Enable the **Reminder** option, and select the day before the start date (the second Tuesday of next month). Set the reminder time to **3:00 PM**.
Category:	**Blue**

3. In the Actions group, click the **Save & Close** button.

4. Create a second task. Enter the following information in the task window. Then save and close the task window.

   Subject: **Set up meeting with Kari to review resumes**

   Start date: **Today**

   Priority: **High**

   Category: **Blue**

5. Create a third task. Enter the following information in the task window. Leave the window open for the next step.

   Subject: **Update expense report**

   Start date: Select the date for next Monday.

   Due date: Select the date for next Wednesday.

   Priority: **Normal**

   Category: **Blue**

6. On the Task tab, in the Recurrence group, click the **Recurrence** button. In the Task Recurrence dialog box, set the recurrence pattern for **Weekly** and to end after **8** occurrences. Click **OK** to save the recurrence settings.
7. In the Show group, click the **Details** button. In the Total work text box, type **45 minutes**. This is the amount of time you think you will need to complete the task. Note that after completing a task, you can display the Details options and enter the actual time spent for tracking purposes. Click the **Save & Close** button to save the task information.
8. Create a fourth task. Enter the following information in the task window. Then save and close the task window.

   Subject: **Pay the utility bill**

   Start date: Select the date for the next workday (M-F).

   Priority: **High**

   Category: **Green**

9. Create a fifth task. Type the following information in the task window. Then save and close the task window.

   Subject: **Set up an appointment with accountant**

   Due date: Select the date for next Wednesday.

   Priority: **Low**

   Category: **Green**

10. Leave Outlook open for the next Step-by-Step.

Organizing and Displaying Tasks

As you work with Outlook, you can see your tasks in many views. You can open the Tasks folder and see all the tasks in the To-Do List window. When you display your calendar in Day view, Work Week view, or Week view, you see tasks in the Daily Task List at the bottom of the calendar grid. By default, tasks also appear in the To-Do Bar. Outlook provides options for arranging the tasks in each of these views. For example, you can arrange the tasks by category, importance, or due dates.

The To-Do Bar displays the Date Navigator, appointments, and a list of tasks. You can resize or hide each part to customize the To-Do Bar to show the information most useful to you. For example, if you have a lot of tasks, you can reduce the space allocated for the appointments to allow more space to display the To-Do List. If you find the To Do-Bar takes up too much space, you can resize it or hide it.

Step-by-Step 6.8

1. If necessary, in the Navigation Pane, click the Tasks button. Confirm the following settings and make any necessary changes:
   a. Click the **View** tab. In the Layout group, click the **To-Do Bar** button. Enable the options **Normal**, **Date Navigator**, **Appointments**, and **Task List**. Note that you will need to click the To-Do Bar button multiple times if you have to reset more than one of the options.
   b. Click the **To-Do Bar** button, then click **Options** to open the To-Do Bar Options dialog box. If necessary, enable all options. Click **OK**.
   c. In the Current View group, click the **Change View** button and then click **To-Do List**.
2. Compare your screen to **Figure 6–30**. Your screen may differ, but note that some of the tasks are displayed at the bottom of the To-Do Bar, and they are arranged in order by Due Date.

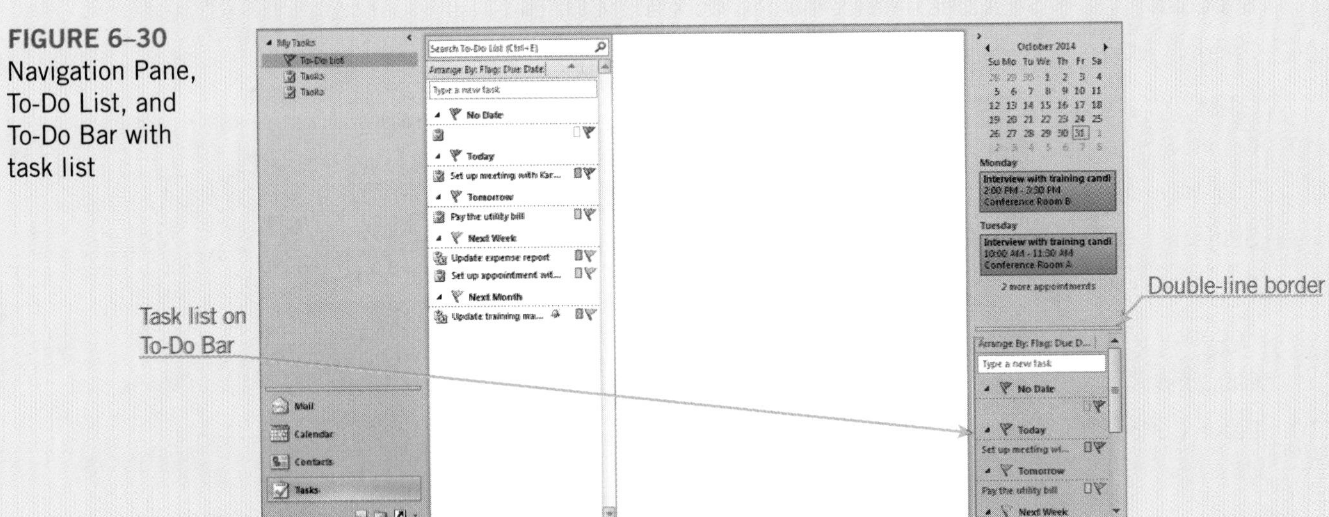

FIGURE 6–30 Navigation Pane, To-Do List, and To-Do Bar with task list

3. Note that in Figure 6–30, only two items appear in the Appointment section of the To-Do Bar, and a note indicates there are two more appointments. Position the mouse pointer over the double-line border that separates the appointments from the tasks. When the pointer changes to a double-headed arrow, drag the border up and down to show/hide the appointments.
4. Drag the double-line border up so that all the tasks are displayed in the To-Do Bar.
5. In the Layout group, click the **To-Do Bar** button and then click **Options**. In the Number of month rows text box, change the number to **2** and then click **OK**. Your To-Do Bar now shows two months in the Date Navigator. (Note that you can only show one calendar in the Navigation Pane.)
6. Drag the left border of the To-Do Bar to the left to expand the width and double the number of calendars in the Date Navigator. Then drag the left border of the To-Do Bar to the right to show only two calendars in the Date Navigator.
7. In the Layout group, click the **To-Do Bar** button, click **Options**, and then change the number of month rows to **1**. Click **OK**.
8. At the top of the task list in the To-Do Bar, click **Arrange By: Flag: Due Date** and then click **Importance**. The Ribbon displays the Task Tools Task List tab, which only applies to the task list in the To-Do Bar. The task list on the To-Do Bar is rearranged by priority level, but the To-Do List in the center of your screen does not change.
9. Click the **View** tab. In the Arrangement group, click the **Categories** button. The To-Do List in the center pane is rearranged by category. Note that the task list in the To-Do Bar does not change.
10. At the top of the Navigation Pane, under My Tasks, select the first Tasks folder. In the Current View group, click the **Change View** button and then click **Next 7 Days**. This view gives you a summary of the tasks you need to complete in the next seven days. In the Arrangement group, click the **Categories** button.
11. In the Navigation Pane, click the **Calendar** button. In the Date Navigator, select the next work day this month. Note that in Day view, tasks appear in the Daily Task List pane below the calendar grid. In the Arrange group, click the **Work Week** button. In the upper-left corner of the calendar grid, click the **Forward** button. Note that the Daily Task List shows tasks arranged by due date. Double-click a task subject in the Daily Task List pane to open the task window. Close the task window.

12. Click the **View** tab. In the Layout group, click the **Daily Task List** button, point to **Arrange By**, and then click **By Start Date**. This setting is useful when you need to be reminded to get started on a task. Click the **Daily Task List** button, point to **Arrange By**, and then click **By Due Date**.
13. In the upper-left corner of the To-Do Bar, click the **Minimize To-Do Bar** arrow [>]. The To-Do Bar is collapsed. Click the **Expand To-Do Bar** arrow [<] to restore the To-Do Bar to Normal view.
14. Leave Outlook open for the next Step-by-Step.

Exporting Outlook Data

If you don't have sharing options, such as those available in a Microsoft Exchange Server account, you can import and export Outlook items from computer to computer or from computer to mobile device. You can also export Outlook data that can be imported into other applications, such as an Excel spreadsheet. When you export Outlook items to be used on other computers using Outlook, you create an Outlook Data File with the .pst file extension. The file is similar to the file created when you archive items. During the export process, you have the opportunity to indicate which folder you want to export items from, and you can apply a filter to select specific items within the folder.

When importing data into Outlook, you must download a .pst file. Because you may not have permission to import files to a classroom or lab computer, you will not practice importing files in this lesson.

Synchronizing data enables you to keep your contact and calendar information the same in all locations. When you edit information in one location, you can upload or download files to another computer or a mobile device so that the information is the same in both locations. Most mobile devices and Web-based e-mail accounts provide applications that help you synchronize data with Outlook files, but because the features are specific to each application, synchronizing files is beyond the scope of this lesson.

TIP

When you archive your Outlook items, you create a backup of the calendar items in another Outlook data file. AutoArchive settings may already be set for your Outlook items; however, some businesses block this option. To check your archive settings, click the File tab, click Options, and then click Advanced. Under AutoArchive, click AutoArchive Settings.

Step-by-Step 6.9

1. Click the **File** tab and then click **Options**. In the Outlook Options dialog box, on the left pane, click **Advanced**. Under Export, click **Export** to open the Import and Export Wizard dialog box.
2. Under Choose an action to perform, select **Export to a file** and then click **Next**.
3. Under Create a file of type, click **Outlook Data File (.pst)** and then click **Next**.
4. Under Select the folder to export from, select **Tasks**. Then click **Filter**. The Filter dialog box opens.

5. Click the **More Choices** tab. Click **Categories** and then enable the option **Blue Category**. Click **OK** twice to close the dialog boxes and return to the wizard.
6. Click **Next** to advance to the next step in the wizard. Under Save exported file as, a path and filename are already displayed. Click **Browse** and navigate to the drive and folder where your solution files are stored.
7. In the File name text box, type **My Outlook** and then type your initials. Leave the Save as type setting .pst as is and click **OK**.
8. In the wizard, under Options, enable the **Do not export duplicate items** option. Click **Finish** to complete the wizard steps. When prompted to add an optional password, leave the text boxes blank and click **OK**. Then click **OK** to close the Outlook Options dialog box.
9. Leave Outlook open for the next Step-by-Step.

Deleting Calendar Items and Tasks

To remove a calendar or task, you must delete the items from your Calendar and Tasks folders. Now that you have completed all the Step-by-Step exercises, you will remove all the new calendars and tasks you created.

Step-by-Step 6.10

1. In the Navigation Pane, if necessary, click the **Calendar** button. If necessary, change the To-Do Bar setting to **Normal**.
2. If necessary, click the **View** tab. In the Current View group, click the **Change View** button, and then click **List**.
3. In the Arrangement group, if necessary, click the **Categories** button. The calendar items are grouped by categories, as shown in **Figure 6–31**. Your list may differ.

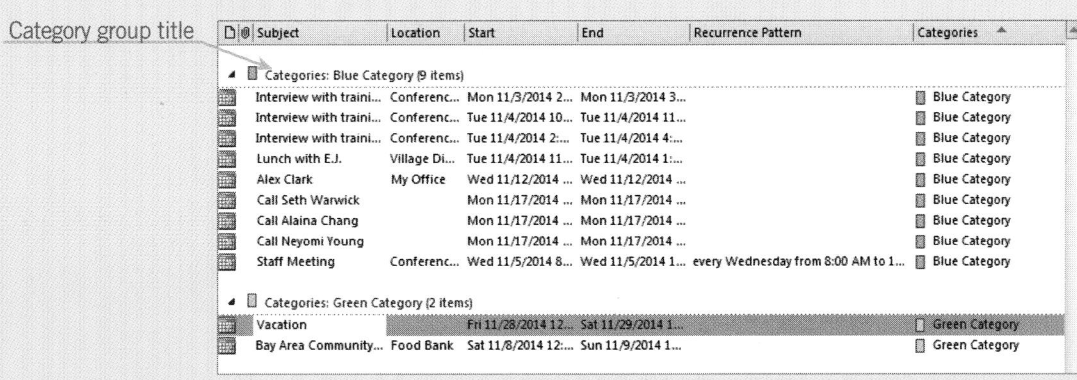

FIGURE 6–31 Calendar items grouped by category

4. Click the **Home** tab. Select the **Blue Category** group title and then, in the Actions group, click the **Delete** button. When prompted about applying the action to all items in the selected group, click **OK**. All the Blue Category items are removed from the calendar.
5. Select the **Green Category** group title and then press **Delete**. Then confirm the action by clicking **OK**.
6. In the Navigation Pane, click the **Tasks** button. The tasks are already arranged by category in the To-Do List, as shown in **Figure 6–32**. Your list may differ. The task list also appears in the To-Do Bar, but that list is arranged by Importance.

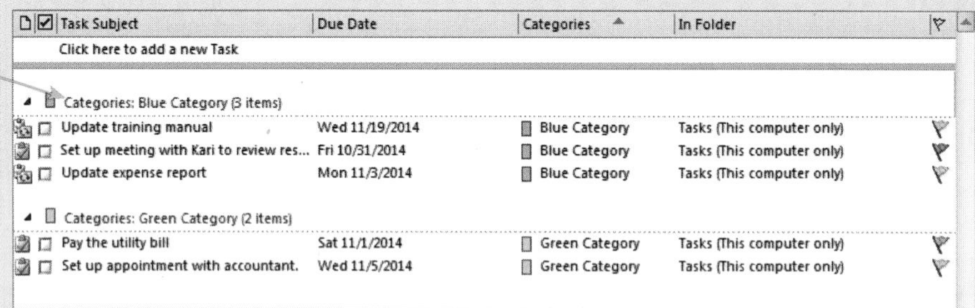

FIGURE 6–32
Task items grouped by category

7. Select the **Blue Category** group title and then press **Delete**. When prompted to apply the action to all items in the selected group, click **OK**. If prompted to delete associated e-mail messages and/or contacts, click **OK**. If prompted to delete just this or all future recurrences, select the Delete all option and click OK.
8. Select the **Green Category** and then click **Delete**. Then click **OK** as needed to confirm the deletions. If any tasks you created in this lesson still appear on the To-Do Bar, delete those tasks by right-clicking the task subject and then clicking Delete.

SUMMARY

In this lesson, you learned:

- Changing the calendar views enables you to focus on different time periods, such as one week or one month at a time.
- You can customize your calendar by adjusting the settings for holidays and showing an alternate calendar.
- You can create multiple calendars and organize them into groups.
- Outlook offers several features that make it easy to organize and track meeting invitations. You can easily respond to meeting invitations, and Outlook will automatically add the meeting to your schedule.
- You can share your calendar information with others via e-mail or by printing hard copies.
- Tasks are often visible as you work with Outlook, and you can arrange how the task information is displayed in the To-Do List, in the calendar, and in the To-Do Bar.
- You can filter data from an Outlook folder and then export the data to a file so the information can be opened on another computer using Outlook.

VOCABULARY REVIEW

Define the following terms:

alternate calendar

iCalendar

REVIEW QUESTIONS

TRUE / FALSE

Circle T if the statement is true or F if the statement is false.

T F 1. When sharing calendars, you can specify the calendar dates you want to share.

T F 2. Using the default calendar settings, the week begins on Monday.

T F 3. An iCalendar format is compatible with Outlook and other calendar programs.

T F 4. You can add multiple sets of holidays to a calendar.

T F 5. You can set up week numbers with custom numbers to display on the calendar.

MULTIPLE CHOICE

Select the best response for the following statements.

1. When you choose the option to display week numbers, the numbers display in the ________________.
   A. Date Navigator
   B. Calendar
   C. To-Do Bar
   D. A and B
2. By default, the calendar shows ________________ blocks of time.
   A. 60-minute
   B. 30-minute
   C. 15-minute
   D. 5-minute
3. When you export Outlook data to be used on other computers using Outlook, you create a(n) ________________ file.
   A. .ics
   B. .otl
   C. .msg
   D. .pst
4. The Daily Task List is displayed ________________.
   A. in the Task List window
   B. at the bottom of the calendar grid
   C. in the To-Do Bar
   D. in the Navigation Pane

5. To show more than one month in the Date Navigator, ______________.
   A. minimize the Navigation Pane
   B. reduce the amount of space for appointments and tasks to allow more space for the Date Navigator
   C. expand the width of the To-Do Bar
   D. A or C

WRITTEN QUESTIONS

Write a brief answer to the following questions.

1. How do you change the view to show multiple noncontiguous days?

2. How can you create more space for details about appointments in the calendar grid?

3. How do meetings differ from appointments?

4. How can you change the view to display only the all-day events in a calendar?

5. What happens when a recipient opens an iCalendar file attached to an e-mail message?

PROJECTS

PROJECT 6–1

1. Create a new calendar, and name the calendar **My Stuff**. Add U.S. holidays to the new calendar. (If you are not able to create a new calendar, use your default calendar to complete Steps 2 and 3.)
2. Add new appointments and events to your calendar for next month. For example, add recurring appointments for your classes and school-related activities, such as French Club. Also, create appointments for social events such as movies, football games, or dances. Apply priorities and categories, and add details and reminders as needed. (If you are using the default calendar, assign a category color as you create each item so you can easily identify the items that you add to the calendar.)
3. If desired, mark some of the items as Private.
4. E-mail the calendar, selecting the date range for the entire month. You do not need to limit the calendar to your working hours. Instead of sending the message to someone, save the message using the filename **Next Month Calendar 1**, followed by your initials and the Unicode (*.msg) file format. Close the message window without saving changes.
5. Display the calendar in Month view with high detail. Minimize the Navigation Pane.
6. In the To-Do Bar, show two months in the Date Navigator, stacked vertically.
7. Take a screen shot. (*Hint*: Press the PrintScreen button on your keyboard.) Then open a new Word document and paste the screen shot into the Word document. Change the page layout to landscape. Resize the screen shot image to fill the page.
8. Save the Word document as **Next Month Calendar 2**, followed by your initials, in your solutions folder. Then close the Word document.
9. Organize a meeting with at least two of your contacts for a two-hour study session sometime next week. Enter a subject and a location, and type a brief sentence in the message body.
10. Save the message as **Study Group Invite**, followed by your initials. Use the file type **Outlook Message Format – Unicode (*.msg)**. Then close the message without saving the changes.
11. If you are using a public computer and you have permission to print documents, print the calendar using the Monthly Style. If you want to keep the information for future use, leave the items in the calendar. Otherwise, delete the My Stuff calendar, or delete the items you added to the default calendar.
12. Expand the Navigation Pane, and change the To-Do Bar setting to display one calendar.

PROJECT 6–2

1. You may already have tasks in your To-Do List. Create some new tasks for things you need to do during the next month, such as write a report for a class assignment, prepare for an exam, or schedule a dentist appointment. Set priorities for each of your tasks, and also include due dates and details. Assign categories to each of your tasks. For example, use different category colors for class assignments, family events, or social activities.
2. In the To-Do Bar, organize the task list by due date. Customize the To-Do Bar to show as many of the tasks as possible.

3. In the To-Do List view, arrange the To-Do List by categories.
4. Take a screen shot. (*Hint*: Press the PrintScreen button on your keyboard.) Then open a new Word document and paste the screen shot into the Word document. Change the page layout to landscape. Resize the screen shot image to fill the page.
5. Save the Word document as **My Tasks**, followed by your initials, in your solutions folder. Then close the Word document.
6. If you are using a public computer and you have permission to print documents, print the To-Do List using the Table Style. If you want to keep the information for future use, leave the items in the To-Do List. Otherwise, delete the tasks you added.

CRITICAL THINKING

ACTIVITY 6–1

What types of appointments and events would you store in an additional calendar, and what would you name the calendar?

ACTIVITY 6–2

Describe an example of when it would be useful to add holidays for a different country to your calendar.

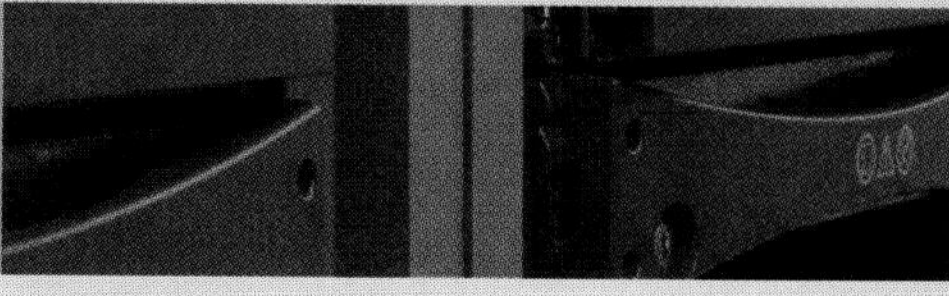

CAPSTONE SIMULATION

The Alexander Pharmaceutical Company

Introduction

For the past several months, Maria Garcia, the vice president of marketing for The Alexander Pharmaceutical Company, has spearheaded a project to recommend technology purchases and upgrades for the marketing staff. Maria's team includes you, Elaine, Donald, Louis, and Vincent. After much analysis and research, the team is prepared to present its recommendations to the company's board of directors. As a member of Maria's team, you will compile all the information and prepare final documents for the acquisition proposal.

JOB 1

Elaine drafted a proposal and then routed the document to Maria and Vincent, who each added comments and edited the document. All revisions were tracked. Your first task is to review these revisions and comments and then accept or reject the changes.

1. Start Word. Open **CS Job 1a** from the drive and folder where your Data Files are stored.
2. Combine the revisions from the data file **CS Job 1b**. Save the new document as **Proposal**, followed by your initials.
3. Accept all the revisions except Vincent's change of *should* to *will* under the *Results and Benefits* heading. Delete all the comments.
4. At the end of the third sentence, which begins, We are long overdue . . ., add the following autonumbered footnote: **A chief goal in the new fiscal year is to maximize the potential of the marketing staff.**. Format the footnote number as desired.
5. Open the data file **CS Job 1c** and copy the table to the Clipboard. Switch to the **Proposal** document. Paste the table after the heading *Results and Benefits*.
6. In the Proposal document, apply a table style and modify the formats as desired. Adjust the column widths and change font sizes and text alignment as needed to make the content easier to read.
7. Sort the table in ascending order by the *Benefit* column.
8. Check spelling and grammar and make any necessary corrections.
9. Save the changes. Close the Job 1c document and leave the Proposal document open.

JOB 2

To manage your work on the proposal, you will be scheduling and tracking various items. Use Outlook to complete the following tasks.

1. Open Outlook. Create a new contact group named **Proposal Team**, followed by your initials. Add the following members as new e-mail contacts using the following display names and e-mail addresses.

DISPLAY NAME	E-MAIL ADDRESS
Maria Garcia	M_Garcia@alexander.com
Elaine Estes	E_Estes@alexander.com
Donald Linebarger	D_Linebarger@alexander.com
Louis Moreno	L_Moreno@alexander.com
Vincent Ferrino	V_Ferrino@alexander.com

2. Plan a meeting on Monday of next week at 10 a.m. to discuss the status of the proposal. The meeting will probably take about an hour and should be scheduled for Conference Room A. Use the Proposal Team group list to send invitations to the meeting. You do not need a reminder for this meeting. Do not send the message. Instead, take a screen capture of the Message window and paste the capture in a Word document. Save the Word document as **Job 2 Message**, followed by your initials. Close the Message window without saving the changes.
3. Maria has asked you to provide proposal status reports. Create a recurring task starting next Monday to provide weekly status reports to Maria. This task is of high importance. Add a reminder for the Friday before. After creating the task, take a screen capture of the Task window and paste the capture in a Word document. Save the Word document as **Job 2 Task**, followed by your initials. Close the Task window without saving the changes.
4. Exit Outlook.

JOB 3

You decide to enhance the appearance of the Proposal document by applying a new style set and modifying some of the heading styles.

1. If necessary, open the **Proposal** document. Change the style to the **Distinctive** style set. Change the color theme to **Foundry**. You will only notice changes in the table colors.
2. To modify the document title, change the font size to **18**, format the text as **bold**, and apply a **center alignment**.
3. To modify all the Heading 2 styles in the document, open the Modify Style dialog box and make the following changes:
   a. Change the font size to **16 pt**.
   b. Apply the **bold** format.
   c. Make sure the changes in the style will apply only in this document.
4. Create a new paragraph style:
   a. Name the new style **Text**.
   b. Base the new style on the **Normal** style.
   c. The font should be **Calibri**, **11 pt**.
   d. The paragraph alignment should be **left**.
   e. Apply a special format for a first line indent of **0.25"**.
   f. Add **6 pt** spacing after the paragraph.
   g. Make sure the style changes apply only in this document.

5. Apply the new Text style to the following paragraphs:
   a. The paragraph after the document title
   b. The first paragraph after the heading *Needs*
   c. The first paragraph after the heading *Impact of Deferral*
   d. The first paragraph after the heading *Proposed Solution*
   e. The paragraph just before the heading *Results and Benefits*
   f. The paragraph after the heading *Proposed Capital Expenditures*
6. Create a new paragraph style for the bulleted lists:
   a Name the new style **Bullets**.
   b. Base the new style on the **Normal** style.
   c. The font should be **Calibri, 11 pt**.
   d. The paragraph alignment should be **left**.
   e. Apply a special format for a **hanging indent** of **0.25"**.
   f. Add **6 pt** spacing after the paragraph.
   g. Make sure the style changes apply only in this document.
7. Apply the new Bullets style to all the bulleted paragraphs in the document.
8. Under the heading *Proposed Solution*, two bulleted items have subentries. Remove the spacing after each of the bulleted items with subentries. To keep the subentries with the main bulleted items, apply the *Keep with next* text flow option to all but the last subentry in each group. Format the last subentry in each group to have a **6 pt** space after the paragraph.
9. Automatically hyphenate the entire document.
10. Save the changes.

JOB 4

Maria started an Excel worksheet to itemize the projected expenses for the technology acquisition. She has asked you to include the worksheet in the proposal document. Before you can do so, you need to complete and format the worksheet.

1. Start Excel. Open **CS Job4** from the drive and folder where your Data Files are stored. Save the workbook as **Technology Proposal Workbook**, followed by your initials.
2. The items listed in this worksheet are grouped into three general categories: Hardware (cells A5:D10), Application Software (cells A12:D13), and Other Costs (cells A15:D16). You need to create subtotals for these categories in the blank rows below each group of items. In cell A11, type **Hardware Total**. In cells **A14** and **A17**, type **Application Software Total** and **Additional Cost Total**, respectively. In cell **D18**, add a formula to sum the totals of cells **D11**, **D14**, and **D17**. Add **Bold** formatting to cells **A11**, **D11**, **A14**, **D14**, **A17**, **D17**, **A18**, and **D18**.
3. Select cells **A1:D4** and then add the Theme Fill Color **Red**, **Accent 2**, **Lighter 40%** to the cells. Select cells **A18:D18** and then add the same Fill Color.
4. Select the range **A5:D17** and then add the Theme Fill Color **Red**, **Accent 2**, **Lighter 80%** to these cells.
5. Increase the indention in cells **A11**, **A14**, and **A17** by one indention.
6. Create a **3-D Clustered Chart** using the cells **A4**, **D4**, **A11**, **D11**, **A14**, **D14**, **A17**, and **D17**.
7. Move the chart to its own worksheet named **Technology Upgrade Chart**. Save the workbook.
8. Switch to the **Technology Upgrade Estimates worksheet**. Select the range **A4:D18** and copy the content to the Clipboard.
9. Switch to the **Proposal** document. Position the insertion point at the end of the last paragraph at the end of the document. Press **Enter** once to insert a blank paragraph with the Text style. With the insertion point in the blank paragraph, use the Paste Special command to paste the unformatted text.
10. Convert the pasted text to a table. AutoFit the table contents and apply a table style. **Center-align** the column headings. **Center-align** the content in the *Quantity* column. **Right-align** the content in the *Costs* and *Total* columns. **Center** the table horizontally on the page.
11. Save the changes to the **Proposal** document.

JOB 5

The Proposal document is almost final, but as you read through it, you decide that some of the text needs to be rearranged and edited.

1. If necessary, open the **Proposal** document. Select the heading *Impact of Deferral* and all the text under the heading, and then move the selected content so it appears after the table and before the heading *Proposed Capital Expenditures*.
2. At the end of the paragraph just before the heading *Results and Benefits*, insert an autonumbered footnote: **Based on current fiscal year data**.
3. Search for the words *slump*, *disappointed*, and *discontented* and then use the Thesaurus to find synonyms to replace them.
4. Maria sends you an e-mail message telling you she is exploring lease options and might want to revise her worksheet figures. She suggests you add the following paragraph in Text style below the embedded worksheet object:

   Pursuing advantageous leasing options might reduce expenditures in the first year. Proposed leasing options could result in reduced bottom-line expenditures.
5. Save the changes to the Proposal document. Leave the Proposal document and the workbook open.

JOB 6

Maria asks that you prepare a draft of a slide presentation so she can present the proposal at the upcoming board meeting. She has already created a chart in the associated Excel workbook.

1. Launch PowerPoint. Apply an appropriate design theme. If desired, customize the color scheme and the background. Save the presentation as **Technology Proposal**, followed by your initials.
2. On the slide master, create a footer to show the text **The Alexander Pharmaceutical Company**. Be sure to open the Header and Footer dialog box and enable the Footer option so the company name will appear on each slide.
3. On the slide master, format the level 1 bullets with an entrance animation so that each bulleted item (paragraph) appears on click and by paragraph.
4. Create new slides from the outline provided in the **CS Job 6** data file.
5. Edit the slides as follows:
   a. Delete slide 1.
   b. Change the slide layout for what is now the new slide 1 to **Title Slide**.
   c. Enter the subtitle **Presentation by Maria Garcia**.
   d. Change the layout for slide 9 to **Title Only**.
6. Switch to the **Technology Proposal Workbook**. Copy the **Technology Upgrade Chart** to the Clipboard. Switch back to the presentation. On slide 9, use the Paste Special command to embed the chart using the destination theme.
7. Resize the chart to fit below the slide title. Change the legend and axis font sizes to **14 pt**.
8. Save your changes and close the presentation.

JOB 7

Maria decides that the board may want to visualize the data in another format, such as a PivotTable and PivotChart. You will create these objects in Excel.

1. If necessary, start Excel. Open the **CS Job 7** data file and then save the workbook as **Technology Proposal Workbook 2**, followed by your initials.
2. Select the range **A4:D14** and create a PivotChart in a new worksheet from this range. Use **Description** for the Axis Field and **Total** for the Values. If necessary, change the Total value to Sum.
3. Add **Accounting Number Format** to the PivotTable range **B2:B12** in Sheet1. Increase the column width to display the data and formatting.
4. Increase the size of the PivotChart to display the text and values.
5. Change the worksheet named Sheet1 to **PivotTable-PivotChart**. Save the changes to the workbook. Copy the chart to the Clipboard.
6. Switch to the **Technology Proposal presentation**. Insert a new slide at the end of the presentation, using the Blank layout. Use the Paste Special command to embed the chart using the destination theme.
7. If necessary, resize and reposition the chart so that it fills the slide.
8. Save the changes and then close the presentation.

JOB 8

You decide to bring the data in the Technology Upgrade Estimates worksheet into Access to analyze and store it.

1. If necessary, start Excel. Open the **Technology Proposal Workbook 2** and then, if necessary, start Access and open the **AlexanderPharm.accdb** database. Save the database as **AlexanderPharmaceutical**, followed by your initials.
2. In Access, import the data in the Technology Upgrade Estimates worksheet into a table.
3. In the Import Spreadsheet Wizard, change the field names to the column headings as they appear in the worksheet. (The field names will be Description, Quantity, and Costs). Do not import the Totals column and do not have Access create a Primary Key field. Name the table **tblTechnologyUpgrades**.
4. Open the table and delete the top four records that were the title, subtitle, a blank row, and column headings in the worksheet.
5. Switch to Design view and change the Data Type for the **Quantity** field to **Number** and the Data Type for the **Costs** field to **Currency**.
6. Add a **Calculated** field with the Field Name **Total**. Have the new field show the total for each record of data based on the quantity multiplied by cost. Change the Result Type to **Currency**.
7. Use the Report Wizard to create a report from the table. Use all the fields in the report and sort by the **Costs** field. Select the **Tabular** format and name the report **rptTechnologyUpgrades**.
8. Change the report title to **Technology Upgrades** and change the position of the **Description** and **Costs** fields so that the Description field appears to the left of the Costs field.
9. Add a Text Box control in the **Report Footer** that calculates the grand total for the report. Change the Label Name to **Grand Total**.
10. Save the report.
11. Export the report to **Word** and save the report as **Technology Upgrade Report**.
12. Open the report in Word and print the report.

JOB 9

Maria decides to use Navigation forms in the AlexanderPharmaceutical.accdb database to make the frequently used tables, reports, and queries easily accessible. By adding this feature, Maria will be able to increase the efficiency of the marketing effort.

1. If necessary, switch to the **AlexanderPharmaceutical.accdb** database.
2. Create a Navigation form with Horizontal Tabs. Place **rpt** and **rptCustomerList** in this form.
3. Save the Navigation form as **NavigationCustomerReports**.
4. Change the title in the Header to **Customer Reports**, and change the tabs for the reports in the Detail section to **Customer Report** and **Customer List**. If necessary, apply the bold format and a dark color for all the text in the report.
5. Save and close the form.
6. Create a Navigation form with Horizontal Tabs. Place **rptTechnologyUpgrades** and **rptMembers** in this form.
7. Save the Navigation form as **NavigationFrequentlyUsed**. Apply the bold format and a dark color for all the text in the report, if necessary.
8. Change the report title in the Report Header to **Frequently Used Reports** and change the tabs for the reports to **Technology Upgrades** and **Board Members**, respectively.
9. Save and close the form.
10. Leave the database open.

JOB 10

Currently, only a few members of the project team have access to the database, but you want to make it accessible to Maria and other team members. To accomplish this task, you will create a main Navigation form that opens when the database opens. The Navigation form will serve as a main menu; users will click a selection in the form to view data. The Navigation form will guide users and make it easy for them to access and export customer information into a Word document.

1. Create a Navigation form with Horizontal tabs. Place the **NavigationCustomerReports** and **NavigationFrequentlyUsed** forms in this Navigation form.
2. Use the Property Sheet to change the width of the form to **8"**, save this Navigation form as **Main Menu**, and then close the Navigation form.
3. Change the options in this database so that the Navigation pane and full menus will not be displayed.
4. Create an AutoExec macro that opens the Main Menu form when the database opens.
5. Close the database file.
6. Open the **AlexanderPharmaceutical.accdb** database to test the AutoExec macro.
7. Close the database and then exit Access.

JOB 11

You need to prepare a mail merge letter to accompany the proposal when it is mailed to board members. You will use data in the Alexander Pharmaceutical database as the data source for the merge.

1. Open the **CS Job 11** file from the drive and folder where your Data Files are stored. Save the document as **Proposal Letter Main Document**, followed by your initials.
2. Below the heading, insert a date field with the format ***MMMM d, yyyy***.
3. Start the mail merge process to create a letter and specify the current document as the main document. To select the recipients, open the **tblBoardMembers** table in the **AlexanderPharmaceutical** database from your solution files. Include all records in the table.
4. Set up the main document.
   a. Insert the address block using the *Joshua Randall Jr.* format. You will need to match the fields so that the First Name in the address block is associated with the field EmpFirst and the Last Name in the address block is associated with the field EmpLast.
   b. Insert a greeting line using the *Joshua* format and include a colon after the greeting line.
5. Preview the letters and make any necessary changes. You should have three form letters. Merge all the letters into a new document. Save the new document as **Alexander Merged Letters**, followed by your initials. Close the document.
6. Save your changes to the **Proposal Letter Main Document** and then close the document.

JOB 12

To finalize the Proposal document, you need to create a table of contents and a title page with a watermark.

1. If necessary, open the **Proposal** document. Insert a **Next Page section break** at the beginning of the document. Then insert a second **Next Page section break**.
2. On the first blank page, create a title page. Type **Technology Acquisition Proposal**. Apply the **Title** style and then center the text. Press **Enter** twice. Change the paragraph alignment to **Left**. Type the following information:

   Prepared by: The Technology Proposal Team

   Maria Garcia

   Elaine Estes

   Donald Linebarger

   Louis Moreno

   Vincent Ferrino

   [Your Name]
3. Create a custom text watermark **Alexander Pharmaceutical** to show on all pages in the document. Format the font style, size, color, and layout as desired.
4. Position the insertion point in front of the section break at the top of the second page. Insert a table of contents, applying a style of your choice.
5. On the table of contents page, insert a page number at the bottom of the page, using the **Plain Number 3** style. Change the page number format to ***i,ii,iii***, starting on the contents page I. Then format the page number on the next page to start at 1.
6. Update the fields in the table of contents to show the correct page numbers.
7. Insert a page break before the heading **Proposed Solution** so that the heading and introductory paragraph appear on the same page with the bulleted lists.
8. Preview the document, and make any other necessary changes. Save your changes and then close the document.

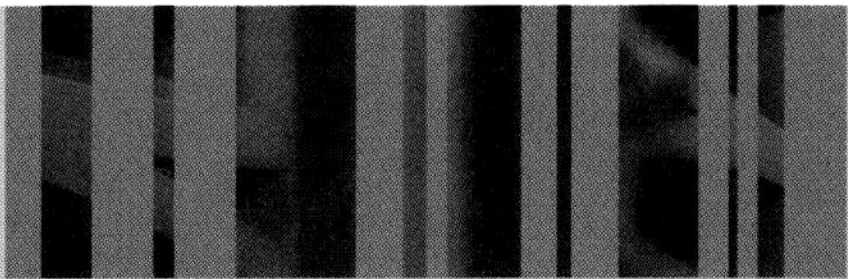

APPENDIX A

Computer Concepts

The Computer: An Overview

A computer is a machine that is used to store, retrieve, and manipulate data. A computer takes ***input***, uses instructions to ***process*** and ***store*** that data, and then produces ***output***. You enter the data into the computer through a variety of input devices, such as a keyboard or mouse. The processor processes the data to produce information. Information is output presented in many ways such as an image on a monitor, printed pages from a printer, or sound through speakers. Computer ***software*** is stored instructions or programming that runs the computer. ***Memory*** inside the computer stores the programs or instructions that run the computer as well as the data and information. Various ***storage devices*** are used to transfer or safely store the data and information on ***storage media***.

A ***computer system*** is made up of components that include the computer, input, and output devices. Computer systems come in many shapes, sizes, and configurations. The computer you use at home or in school is often called a ***personal computer***. ***Desktop computers*** often have a 'computer case' or a ***system unit***, which contains processing devices, memory, and some storage devices. **Figure A–1** shows a typical desktop computer. Input devices such as the mouse or pointing device, and keyboard are attached to the system unit by cables or wires. Output devices, such as the monitor (display device), speakers, and printer are also attached to the system unit by cables or wires. ***Wireless technology*** makes it possible to eliminate wires and use the airwaves to connect devices. ***Laptop*** or ***notebook*** computers have all the essential parts: the keyboard, pointing device, and display device all in one unit. See **Figure A–2** for a typical notebook computer.

FIGURE A–1 A desktop computer system

FIGURE A–2 A laptop computer

When learning about computers, it is helpful to organize the topics into a discussion about the hardware and the software, and then how the computer processes the data.

Computer Hardware

The physical components, devices, or parts of the computer are called ***hardware***. Computer hardware includes the essential components found on all computers such as the central processing unit (CPU), the monitor, the keyboard, and the mouse. Hardware can be divided into categories: Input devices, processors, storage devices, and output devices. ***Peripheral devices*** are additional components, such as printers, speakers, and scanners that enhance the computing experience. Peripherals are not essential to the computer, but provide additional functions for the computer.

Input Devices

There are many different types of input devices. You enter information into a computer by typing on a keyboard or by pointing, clicking, or dragging a mouse. A ***mouse*** is a handheld device used to move a pointer on the computer screen. Similar to a mouse, a ***trackball*** has a roller ball that turns to control a pointer on the screen. Tracking devices, such as a ***touchpad***, are an alternative to the trackball or mouse. Situated on the keyboard of a laptop computer, they allow you to simply move and tap your finger on a small electronic pad to control the pointer on the screen.

Tablet PCs allow you to input data by writing directly on the computer screen. Handwriting recognition technology converts handwritten writing to text. Many computers have a microphone or other ***sound input device*** which accepts speech or sounds as input and converts the speech to text or data. For example, when you telephone a company or bank for customer service, you often have the option to say your requests or account number. That is ***speech recognition technology*** at work!

Other input devices include scanners and bar code readers. You can use a ***scanner*** to convert text or graphics from a printed page into code that a computer can process. You have probably seen ***bar code readers*** being used in stores. These are used to read bar codes, such as the UPC (Universal Product Code), to track merchandise or other inventory in a store. See **Figure A–3**.

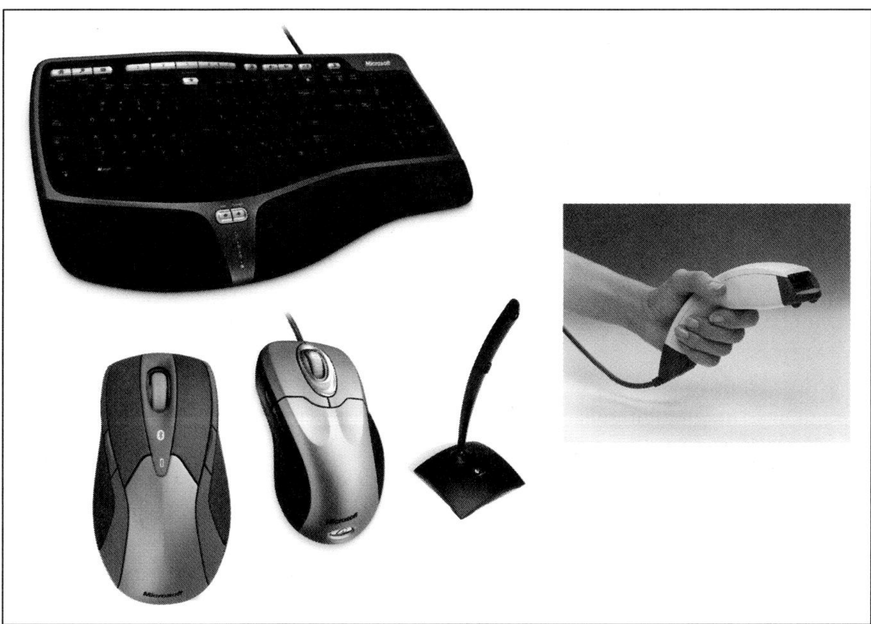

FIGURE A–3 Examples of input devices

Processing Devices

Processing devices are mounted inside the system unit of the computer. The ***motherboard*** is where the computer memory and other vital electronic parts are stored. See **Figure A–4**. The ***central processing unit*** **(CPU)** is a silicon chip that processes data and carries out instructions given to the computer. The CPU is stored on the motherboard of the computer. The ***data bus*** includes the wiring and pathways by which the CPU communicates with the peripherals and components of the computer.

FIGURE A–4 A motherboard

Storage Devices

Computers have to store and retrieve data for them to be of any use at all. Storage devices are both input and output devices. A ***storage medium*** holds data. Storage media include hard drives, tape, memory cards, solid state flash drives, CDs, and DVDs. A ***storage device*** is the hardware that stores and retrieves data from a storage medium. Storage devices include hard drives, card readers, tape drives, and CD and DVD drives.

Storage devices use magnetic, optical, or solid state technologies. Magnetic storage uses magnetic fields to store data and can be erased and used over and over again. Optical technology uses light to store data. Optical storage media use one of three technologies: read-only (ROM), recordable (R), or rewritable (RW). Solid state storage uses no moving parts and can be used over and over again. There are advantages and disadvantages to each technology.

Most computers have more than one type of storage device. The main storage device for a computer is the ***hard drive*** that is usually inside the system unit. Hard drives use magnetic storage. The hard drive reads and writes data to and from a round magnetic platter, or disk. **Figure A–5** shows a fixed storage unit. It is not removable from the computer.

EXTRA FOR EXPERTS

What does it mean when a computer advertisement refers to megabytes or gigabytes? Data is digitally encoded on a disk as a series of 1s and 0s. A **byte** stands for a single character of data. The prefix "mega" means a million. A megabyte is a million bytes. The prefix "giga" means a billion. A gigabyte (GB or Gbyte) is approximately one billion bytes. The term 'tera' means a trillion. A terabyte (TB or Tbyte) is one thousand gigabytes.

FIGURE A–5 An internal hard drive

External and removable hard drives that can plug into the USB port on the system unit are also available. External drives offer flexibility; allowing you to transfer data between computers easily. See **Figure A–6**. At the time this book was written, typical hard drives for a computer system that you might buy for your personal home use range from 500 gigabytes (GB) to 2 terabytes.

FIGURE A–6 An external hard drive

The ***floppy disk drive*** is older technology that is no longer available on new computers. Some older computers still have a floppy disk drive which is mounted in the system unit with access to the outside. A floppy disk is the medium that stores the data. You put the floppy disk into the floppy disk drive so the computer can read and write the data. The floppy disk's main advantage was portability. You can store data on a floppy disk and transport it for use on another computer. A floppy disk can hold up to 1.4MB (megabytes) of information. A Zip disk is similar to a floppy disk. A ***Zip disk*** is also an older portable disk technology that was contained in a plastic sleeve. Each disk held 100MB or 250MB of information. A special disk drive called a ***Zip drive*** is required to read and write data to a Zip disk.

Optical storage devices include the ***CD drive*** or ***DVD drive*** or *Blu-ray drive*. CDs, DVDs, and ***Blu-ray drive (BD)*** use optical storage technology. See **Figure A–7**.

FIGURE A–7 A CD/DVD/Blu-ray drive

These drives are typically mounted inside the system unit, although external versions of these devices are also available. Most new computers are equipped with CD/DVD burners. That means they have read and write capabilities. You use a CD/DVD drive to read and write CDs and DVDs. A ***CD*** is a compact disc, which is a form of optical storage. Compact discs can store 700 MB of data. These discs have a great advantage over other forms of removable storage as they can hold vast quantities of information—the entire contents of a small library, for instance. They are also fairly durable. Another advantage of CDs is their ability to hold graphic information, including moving pictures, with the highest quality stereo sound. A ***DVD*** is also an optical disc that looks like a CD. It is a high-capacity storage device that can contain up to 4.7GB of data, which is a seven-fold increase over a CD. There are two variations of DVDs that offer even more storage—a 2-layer version with 9.4GB capacity and double-sided discs with 17GB capacity. A DVD holds 133 minutes of data on each side, which means that two two-hour full-length feature movies can be stored on one disc. Information is encoded on the disk by a laser and read by a CD/DVD drive in the computer. ***Blu-ray discs (BD)*** offer even more storage capacity. These highest-capacity discs are designed to record full-length high-definition feature films. As of this writing, a BD can store upwards of 35GB of data. Special Blu-ray hardware, including disc players available in gaming systems and Blu-ray burners, are needed to read Blu-ray discs.

A CD drive only reads CDs, a DVD drive can read CDs and DVDs, a Blu-ray drive reads BDs, CDs, and DVDs. CD/DVD/BD drives look quite similar, as do the discs. See **Figure A–8**.

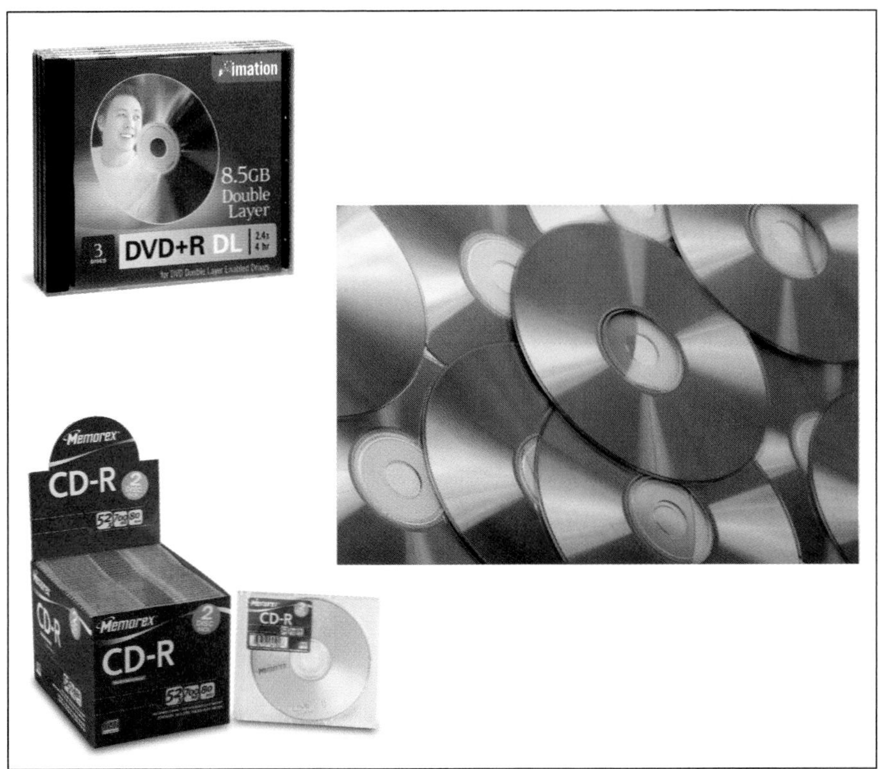

FIGURE A–8 CDs, DVDs, and Blu-rays look alike

Solid state storage is another popular storage technology. A ***USB flash drive*** is a very portable small store device that works both as a drive and medium. It plugs directly into a USB port on the computer system unit. You read and write data to the flash drive. See **Figure A–9**.

FIGURE A–9 A flash drive

Solid state card readers are devices that can read solid state cards. Solid state storage is often used in cameras. See **Figure A–10**.

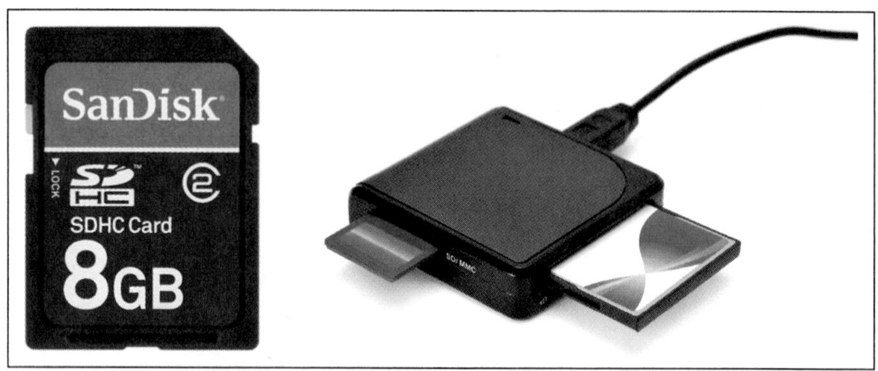

FIGURE A–10 Solid state card and card reader

Magnetic tape is a medium most commonly used for backing up a computer system, which means making a copy of files from a hard drive. Although it is relatively rare for data on a hard drive to be completely lost in a crash (that is, for the data or pointers to the data to be partially or totally destroyed), it can and does happen. Therefore, most businesses and some individuals routinely back up files on tape. If you have a small hard drive, you can use DVDs or CD-ROMs or solid state storage such as a flash drive or memory card to back up your system. **Figure A–11** shows a tape storage system.

FIGURE A–11 Tape storage system

Output Devices

The ***monitor*** on which you view your computer work is an output device. It provides a visual representation of the information stored in or produced by your computer. The typical monitor for today's system is a flat-screen monitor similar to a television. Computer monitors typically use ***LCD technology***. LCD stands for Liquid Crystal Display. See **Figure A–12**. LCD monitors provide a very sharp picture because of the large number of tiny dots, called ***pixels***, which make up the display as well as its ability to present the full spectrum of colors. ***Resolution*** is the term that tells you how clear an image will be on the screen. Resolution is measured in pixels. A typical resolution is 1024 × 768. A high-quality monitor may have a resolution of 1920 × 1080, or 2560 × 1440 or higher. Monitors come in different sizes. The size of a monitor is determined by measuring the diagonal of the screen. Laptops have smaller monitors than desktop computers. A laptop monitor may be 13", 15", or 17". Desktop monitors can be as large as 19"–27" or even larger.

FIGURE A–12 An LCD monitor

Printers are a type of output device. They let you produce a paper printout of information contained in the computer. Today, most printers use either inkjet or laser technology to produce high-quality print. Like a copy machine, a ***laser printer*** uses heat to fuse a powdery substance called ***toner*** to the page. ***Ink-jet printers*** use a spray of ink to print. Laser printers give the sharpest image and often print more pages per minute (ppm) than ink-jet printers. Ink-jet printers provide nearly as sharp an image, but the wet printouts can smear when they first are printed. Most color printers, or photo printers for printing photographs, are ink-jet printers. Color laser printers are more costly. These printers allow you to print information in a full array of colors, just as you see it on your monitor. See **Figure A–13**.

FIGURE A–13 Printers

Laptop or Notebook Computer

A ***laptop computer***, also called a ***notebook computer***, is a small folding computer that can literally fit in a person's lap or in a backpack. Within the fold-up case of a laptop is the CPU, data bus, monitor (built into the lid), hard drive (sometimes removable), USB ports, CD/DVD drive, and trackball or digital tracking device. The advantage of the laptop is its portability—you can work anywhere because you can use power either from an outlet or from the computer's internal, rechargeable batteries. Almost all laptops have wireless Internet access built into the system. The drawbacks are the smaller keyboard, smaller monitor, smaller capacity, and higher price, though some laptops offer full-sized keyboards and higher quality monitors. As technology allows, storage capacity on smaller devices is making it possible to offer laptops with as much power and storage as a full-sized computer. See **Figure A–14**.

FIGURE A–14 Laptop computers

Personal Digital Assistants (PDA) and Smartphones

A ***Personal Digital Assistant (PDA)*** is a pocket-sized electronic organizer that helps you to manage addresses, appointments, expenses, tasks, and memos. If you own a cell phone, chances are it is a ***Smartphone*** and it can do more than just make and receive phone calls. Today, many handheld devices, such as cell phones and Personal Digital Assistants include features such as a full keypad for text messaging and writing notes, e-mail, a browser for Web access, a calendar and address book to manage contacts and appointments, a digital camera, radio, and digital music player. Most handheld devices also include software for games, financial management, personal organizer, GPS, and maps. See **Figure A–15**.

FIGURE A–15 Smartphones

The common input devices for PDAs and some Smartphones include touch-sensitive screens that accept input through a stylus pen or small keyboards that are either built in to the device or available as software on the screen. Data and information can be shared with a Windows-based or Macintosh computer through a process called synchronization. By placing your handheld in a cradle or through a USB port attached to your computer, you can transfer data from your PDA's calendar, address book, or memo program into your computer's information manager program and vice versa. The information is updated on both sides, making your handheld device a portable extension of your computer.

How Computers Work

All input, processing, storage, and output devices function together to make the manipulation, storage, and distribution of data and information possible. Data is information entered into and manipulated or processed within a computer. Processing includes computation, such as adding, subtracting, multiplying, and dividing; analysis planning, such as sorting data; and reporting, such as presenting data for others in a chart or graph. This next section explains how computers work.

Memory

Computers have two types of memory—RAM and ROM. ***RAM***, or ***random access memory***, is the silicon chips in the system unit that temporarily store information when the computer is turned on. RAM is what keeps the software programs up and running and provides visuals that appear on your screen. You work with data in RAM up until you save it to a storage media such as a hard disk, CD, DVD, or solid state storage such as flash drive.

Computers have sophisticated application programs that include a lot of graphics, video, and data. In order to run these programs, computers require a lot of memory. Therefore, computers have a minimum of 512MB of RAM. Typical computers include between 2GB and 4GB of RAM to be able to run most programs. Most computer systems are expandable and you can add on RAM after you buy the computer. The more RAM available for the programs, the faster and more efficiently the machine will be able to operate. RAM chips are shown in **Figure A–16**.

FIGURE A–16 RAM chips

ROM, or ***read-only memory***, is the memory that stays in the computer when it is turned off. It is ROM that stores the programs that run the computer as it starts or "boots up." ROM holds the instructions that tell the computer how to begin to load its operating system software programs.

Speed

The speed of a computer is measured by how fast the computer processes each instruction. There are several factors that affect the performance of a computer: the speed of the processor, or the ***clock speed***, the ***front side bus speed***—the speed of the bus that connects the processor to main memory—the speed in which data is written and retrieved from the hard drive or other storage media, and the speed of the graphics card if you are working on programs that use a lot of graphic images. These all factor into a computer's performance.

The speed of a computer is measured in ***megahertz (MHz)*** and ***gigahertz (GHz)***. Processor speed is part of the specifications when you buy a computer. For example, to run Windows 7 on a computer, you need a processor that has 1 gigahertz (GHz) or faster 32-bit (x86) or 64-bit (x64) processor. Processors are sold by name and each brand or series has its own specifications. Processor manufacturers include AMD, Intel, and Motorola.

Networks

Computers have expanded the world of communications. A ***network*** is defined as two or more computers connected to share data. ***LANs (local area networks)*** connect computers within a small area such as a home, office, school, or building. Networks can be wired or wireless. The ***Internet*** is the largest network in the world connecting millions of computers across the globe. Using the Internet, people can communicate across the world instantly.

Networks require various communication devices and software. ***Modems*** allow computers to communicate with each other by telephone lines. Modem is an acronym that stands for "MOdulator/DEModulator." Modems convert data in bytes to sound media in order to send data over the phone lines and then convert it back to bytes after receiving data. Modems operate at various rates or speeds. ***Network cards*** in the system unit allow computers to access networks. A ***router*** is an electronic device that joins two or more networks. For example, a home network can use a router and a modem to connect the home's LAN to the Internet. A ***server*** is the computer hardware and software that "serves" the computers on a network. Network technology is sometimes called "client-server." A personal computer that requests data from a server is referred to as a ***client***. The computer that stores the data is the ***server***. On the Internet, the computer that stores Web pages is the ***Web server***. **Figure A–17** shows a network diagram.

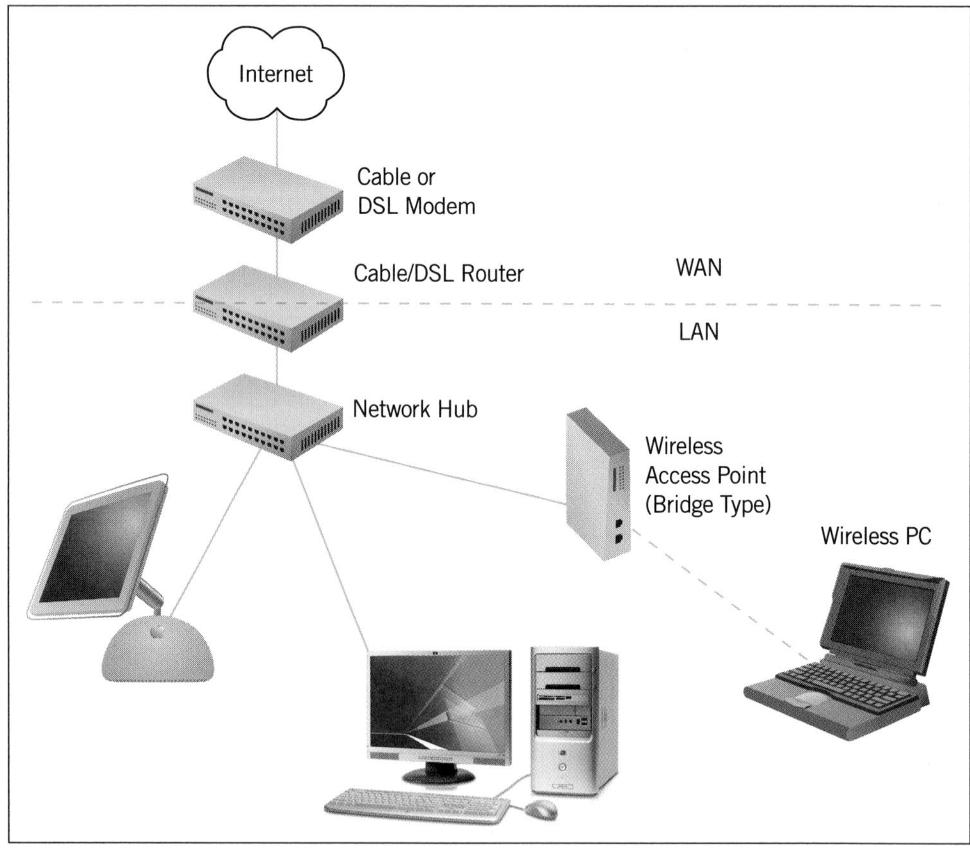

FIGURE A–17 Diagram of a network

Networks have certain advantages over stand-alone computers: they allow communication among the computers; they allow smaller capacity computers to access the larger capacity of the server computers on the network; they allow several computers to share peripherals, such as one printer; and they can make it possible for all computers on the network to have access to the Internet.

Connect to the Internet

To connect to the Internet you need to subscribe to an ***Internet Service Provider (ISP)***. There are several technologies available. Connection speeds are measured in bits per second. Upload speeds are slower than download speeds. ***Dial-up*** is the oldest, and the slowest Internet access technology that is offered by local telephone companies. To get access to the Internet, your computer has to dial out through a phone line. Many people have moved to ***always-on connection technologies***. The computer is always connected to the Internet if you turn the computer on, so you don't have to dial out. These always-on faster technologies, known as a ***Digital Subscriber Line (DSL)***, include cable connections, satellites, and fiber optic. They are offered by telephone and cable television companies, as well as satellite service providers. It can be noted that satellite Internet access is the most expensive and dialup is the cheapest. DSL is through phone lines. **Table A–1** shows a brief comparison of these technologies based on the time this book was written and average speed assessments.

TABLE A–1 Comparing average Internet access options

FEATURE	SATELLITE	DSL	CABLE	FIBER OPTIC
Max. High Speed	Download speeds ranging anywhere from 768 Kbps up to 5.0 Mbps	Download speed 10 Mbps/ upload speed 5 Mbps	Download speed 30 Mbps/ upload speed 10 Mbps	Download speed 50 Mbps/ upload speed 20 Mbps
Access is through	Satellite dish	Existing phone line	Existing TV cable	Fiber-optic phone lines
Availability	Available in all areas; note that satellite service is sensitive to weather conditions	Generally available in populated areas	Might not be available in rural areas	Might not be available in all areas as fiber-optic lines are still being installed in many areas

Software

A ***program*** is a set of instructions that the computer uses to operate. ***Software*** is the collection of programs and other data input that tells the computer how to run its devices, how to manipulate, store, and output information, and how to accept the input you give it. Software fits into two basic categories: systems software and applications software. A third category, network software, is really a type of application.

Systems Software

The ***operating system*** is the main software or ***system software*** that runs a computer and often defines the type of computer. There are two main types or platforms for personal computers. The Macintosh computer, or Mac, is produced by Apple Computer, Inc. and runs the Mac operating system. The PC is a Windows-based computer produced by many different companies, but which runs the Microsoft Windows operating system.

Systems software refers to the operating system of the computer. The operating system is a group of programs that is automatically copied in from the time the computer is turned on until the computer is turned off. Operating systems serve two functions: they control data flow among computer parts, and they provide the platform on which application and network software work—in effect, they allow the "space" for software and translate its commands to the computer. The most popular operating systems in use today are the Macintosh operating system, MAC OS X and several different versions of Microsoft Windows, such as Windows XP, Windows Vista, or Windows 7. See **Figure A–18** and **Figure A–19**.

FIGURE A–18 Windows 7 operating system

FIGURE A–19 Mac OS

Since its introduction in the mid-1970s, Macintosh has used its own operating system, a graphical user interface (GUI) system that has evolved over the years. The OS is designed so users "click" with a mouse on pictures, called icons, or on text to give commands to the system. Data is available to you in the WYSIWYG (what-you-see-is-what-you-get) format; that is, you can see on-screen what a document will look like when it is printed. Graphics and other kinds of data, such as spreadsheets, can be placed into text documents. However, GUIs take a great deal of RAM to keep all of the graphics and programs operating.

The original OS for IBM and IBM-compatible computers (machines made by other companies that operate similarly) was DOS (disk operating system). It did not have a graphical interface. The GUI system, Windows™, was developed to make using the IBM/IBM-compatible computer more "friendly." Today's Windows applications are the logical evolution of GUI for IBM and IBM-compatible machines. Windows is a point-and-click system that automatically configures hardware to work together. You should note, however, that with all of its abilities comes the need for more RAM, or a system running Windows will operate slowly.

Applications Software

When you use a computer program to perform a data manipulation or processing task, you are using applications software. Word processors, databases, spreadsheets, graphics programs, desktop publishers, fax systems, and Internet browsers are all applications software.

Network Software

A traditional network is a group of computers that are hardwired (connected together with cables) to communicate and operate together. Today, some computer networks use RF (radio frequency) wireless technology to communicate with each other. This is called a ***wireless network***, because you do not need to physically hook the network together with cables. In a typical network, one computer acts as the server, controlling the flow of data among the other computers, called nodes, or clients on the network. Network software manages this flow of information.

History of the Computer

Though various types of calculating machines were developed in the nineteenth century, the history of the modern computer begins about the middle of the last century. The strides made in developing today's personal computer have been truly astounding.

Early Development

The ENIAC, or Electronic Numerical Integrator and Computer, (see **Figure A–20**) was designed for military use in calculating ballistic trajectories and was the first electronic, digital computer to be developed in the United States. For its day, 1946, it was quite a marvel because it was able to accomplish a task in 20 seconds that normally would take a human three days to complete. However, it was an enormous machine that weighed more than 20 tons and contained thousands of vacuum tubes, which often failed. The tasks that it could accomplish were limited, as well.

FIGURE A–20 The ENIAC

From this awkward beginning, however, the seeds of an information revolution grew. The invention of the silicon chip in 1971, and the release of the first personal computer in 1974, launched the fast-paced information revolution in which we now all live and participate.

Significant dates in the history of computer development are listed in **Table A–2**.

TABLE A–2 Milestones in the development of computers

YEAR	DEVELOPMENT
1948	First electronically stored program
1951	First junction transistor
1953	Replacement of tubes with magnetic cores
1957	First high-level computer language
1961	First integrated circuit
1965	First minicomputer
1971	Invention of the microprocessor (the silicon chip) and floppy disk
1974	First personal computer (made possible by the microprocessor)

The Personal Computer

The PC, or personal computer, was mass marketed by Apple beginning in 1977, and by IBM in 1981. It is this desktop device with which people are so familiar and which, today, contains much more power and ability than did the original computer that took up an entire room. The PC is a small computer (desktop size or less) that uses a microprocessor to manipulate data. PCs may stand alone, be linked together in a network, or be attached to a large mainframe computer. See **Figure A–21**.

FIGURE A–21 An early IBM PC

Computer Utilities and System Maintenance

Computer operating systems let you run certain utilities and perform system maintenance to keep your computer running well. When you add hardware or software, you make changes in the way the system operates. With Plug and Play, most configuration changes are done automatically. The ***drivers***, software that runs the peripherals, are installed automatically when your computer identifies the new hardware. When you install new software, many changes are made to the system automatically that determine how the software starts and runs.

In addition, you might want to customize the way the new software or hardware works with your system. You use ***utility software*** to make changes to the way hardware and software works. For example, you can change the speed at which your mouse clicks, how quickly or slowly keys repeat on the keyboard, and the resolution of the screen display. Utilities are included with your operating system. If you are running Windows XP, Windows Vista, or Windows 7, the Windows Control Panel provides access to the many Windows operating system utilities. **Figure A–22** shows the System and Security utilities in the Control Panel for Windows 7.

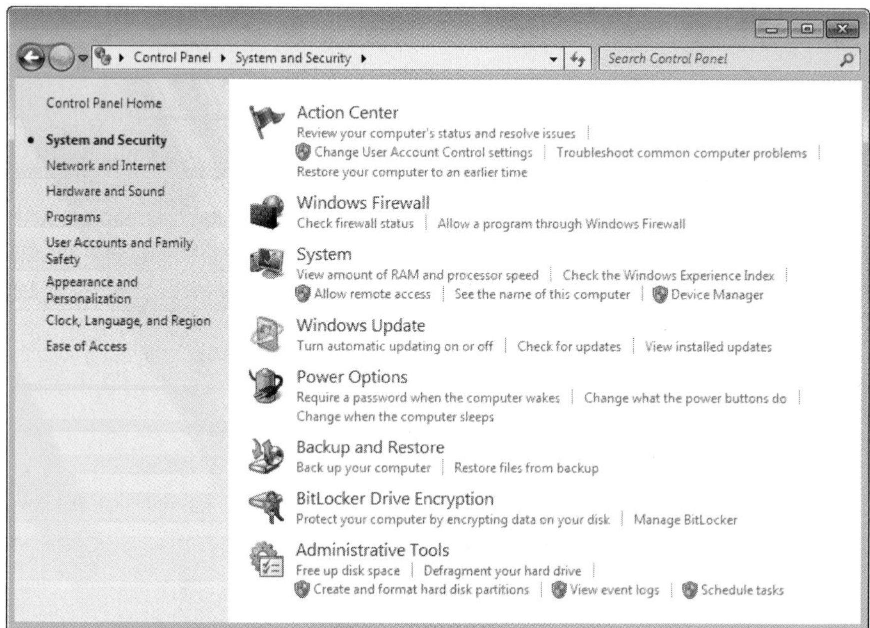

FIGURE A–22 Control Panel for Windows 7

Virus and Spyware Protection

Certain maintenance should be performed regularly on computers. ***Viruses*** are malicious software programs that can damage the programs on your computer causing the computer to either stop working or run slowly. These programs are created by people, called ***hackers***, who send the programs out solely to do harm to computers. Viruses are loaded onto your computer without your knowledge and run against your wishes. ***Spyware*** is also a form of a program that can harm your computer. There are utilities and programs called ***antispyware*** and ***antivirus*** programs that protect your computer from spyware and viruses.

You should install and update your antivirus and spyware protection software regularly, and scan all new disks and any incoming information from online sources for viruses. Some systems do this automatically; others require you to install software to do it.

Disk Maintenance

From time to time, you should run a program that scans or checks the hard drive to see that there are not bad sectors (areas) and look for corrupted files. Optimizing or defragmenting the hard disk is another way to keep your computer running at its best. Scanning and checking programs often offers the option of "fixing" the bad areas or problems, although you should be aware that this could result in data loss.

Society and Computers

The electronic information era has had global effects and influenced global change in all areas of people's lives including education, government, society, and commerce. With the changes of this era have come many new questions and responsibilities. There are issues of ethics, security, and privacy.

Ethics

When you access information—whether online, in the workplace, or via purchased software—you have a responsibility to respect the rights of the person or people who created that information. Digital information, text, images, and sound are very easy to copy and share, however, that does not make it right to do so. You have to treat electronic information with respect. Often images, text, and sound are copyrighted. ***Copyright*** is the legal method for protecting the intellectual property of the author—the same way as you would a book, article, or painting. For instance, you must give credit when you copy information from the Web or another person's document.

If you come across another person's personal information, you must treat it with respect. Do not share personal information unless you have that person's permission. For example, if you happen to pass a computer where a person left personal banking information software open on the computer or a personal calendar available, you should not share that information. If e-mail comes to you erroneously, you should delete it before reading it.

When you use equipment that belongs to your school, a company for which you work, or others, here are some rules you should follow:

1. Do not damage computer hardware.
2. Do not add or remove equipment without permission.
3. Do not use an access code or equipment without permission.
4. Do not read others' e-mail.
5. Do not alter data belonging to someone else without permission.
6. Do not use the computer for play during work hours or use it for personal profit.
7. Do not access the Internet for nonbusiness related activities during work hours.
8. Do not install or uninstall software without permission.
9. Do not make unauthorized copies of data or software or copy company files or procedures for personal use.
10. Do not copy software programs to use at home or at another site in the company without permission.

Security and Privacy

The Internet provides access to business and life-enhancing resources, such as distance learning, remote medical diagnostics, and the ability to work from home more effectively. Businesses, colleges and universities, and governments throughout the world depend on the Internet every day to get work done. Disruptions in the Internet can create havoc and dramatically decrease productivity.

With more and more financial transactions taking place online, ***identity theft*** is a growing problem, proving a person's online identity relies heavily upon their usernames and passwords. If you do online banking, there are several levels of security that you must pass through, verifying that you are who you claim to be, before gaining access to your accounts. If you divulge your usernames and passwords, someone can easily access your accounts online with devastating effects to your credit rating and to your accounts.

Phishing is a criminal activity that is used by people to fraudulently obtain your personal information, such as usernames, passwords, credit card details, and your Social Security information. Your Social Security number should never be given out online. Phishers send e-mails that look legitimate, but in fact are not. Phishing e-mails will often include fake information saying that your account needs your immediate attention because of unusual or suspected fraudulent activity. You are asked to click a link in the e-mail to access a Web site where you are then instructed to enter personal information. See **Figure A–23** and **Figure A–24**. Phishing e-mail might also come with a promise of winning some money or gifts. When you get mail from people you don't know, the rules to remember are "you never get something for nothing," and "if it looks too good to be true, it's most likely not true."

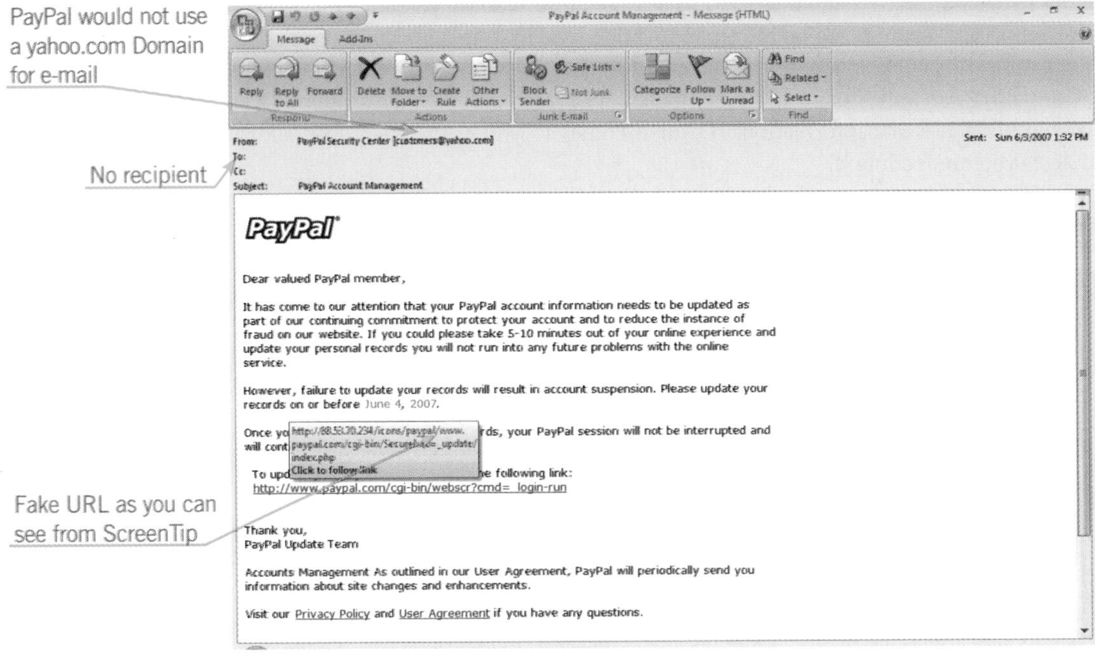

FIGURE A–23 Fake PayPal e-mail for phishing

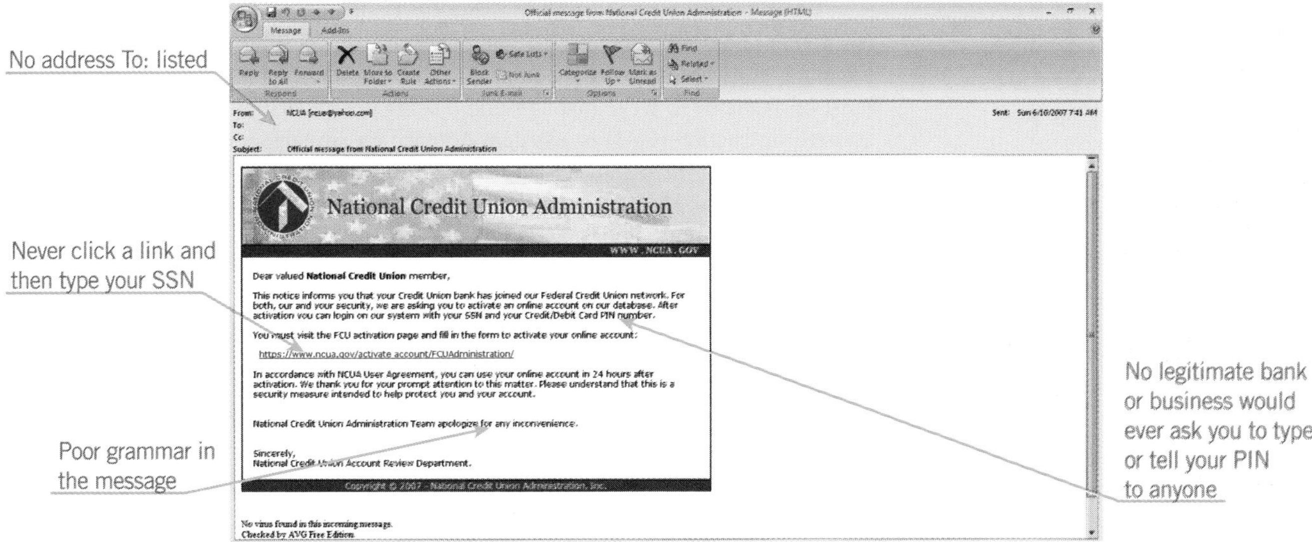

FIGURE A–24 Fake Credit Union e-mail for phishing

Whatever the ruse, when you click the link provided in the phishing e-mail, your browser will open a Web site that looks real, perhaps like your bank's site, eBay, or PayPal. But, in fact, this is a fake site set up to get you to give up your personal information. Phishing sites are growing. You should never click a link provided in an e-mail to get to sites such as your bank, eBay, or PayPal. Your bank or any other legitimate Web site will never ask you to type personal information on a page linked from an e-mail message. Always type the Web page address directly in the browser. Banks and Web sites have been trying to stop phishing sites through technology. Other attempts to reduce the growing number of reported phishing incidents include legislation and simply educating users about the practice.

Just as you would not open someone else's mail, you must respect the privacy of e-mail sent to others. When interacting with others online, you must keep confidential information confidential. Do not endanger your privacy, safety, or financial security by giving out personal information to someone you do not know.

EXTRA FOR EXPERTS

Ebay is an online auction Web site that provides people a way to buy and sell merchandise through the Internet. PayPal is a financial services Web site that provides a way to transfer funds between people who perform financial transactions on the Internet.

Career Opportunities

In one way or another, all careers involve the computer. Whether you are a grocery store clerk using a scanner to read the prices, a busy executive writing a report that includes charts, graphics, and detailed analysis on a laptop on an airplane, or a programmer writing new software—almost everyone uses computers in their jobs. Farmers use computers to optimize crops and order seeds and feed. Most scientific research is done using computers.

There are specific careers available if you want to work with computers in the computer industry. Schools offer degrees in computer programming, computer repair, computer engineering, and software design. The most popular jobs are systems analysts, computer operators, database managers, database specialists, and programmers. Analysts figure out ways to make computers work (or work better) for a particular business or type of business. Computer operators use the programs and devices to conduct business with computers. Programmers write the software for applications or new systems. There are degrees and jobs for people who want to create and maintain Web sites. Working for a company maintaining their Web site can be a very exciting career.

There are courses of study in using CAD (computer-aided design) and CAM (computer-aided manufacturing). There are positions available to instruct others in computer software use within companies and schools. Technical writers and editors must be available to write manuals about using computers and software. Computer-assisted instruction (CAI) is a system of teaching any given subject using the computer. Designing video games is another exciting and ever-growing field of computer work. And these are just a few of the possible career opportunities in an ever-changing work environment. See **Figure A–25**.

FIGURE A–25 Working in the computer field

What Does the Future Hold?

The possibilities for computer development and application are endless. Things that were dreams or science fiction only 10 or 20 years ago are now reality. New technologies are emerging constantly. Some new technologies are replacing old ways of doing things; others are merging with those older methods and devices. Some new technologies are creating new markets. The Internet (more specifically, the Web), cell phones, and DVD videos are just a few inventions of the past decades that did not have counterparts prior to their inventions. We are learning new ways to work and play because of the computer. It is definitely a device that has become part of our offices, our homes, and our lives.

Social networking has moved from the streets and onto the Web. People meet and greet through the Internet using sites such as MySpace, Facebook, and Twitter.

Emerging Technologies

Today the various technologies and systems are coming together to operate more efficiently. Convergence is the merging of these technologies. Telephone communication is being combined with computer e-mail and Web browsing so users can set a time to meet online and, with the addition of voice technology, actually speak to each other using one small portable device.

The Web, now an important part of commerce and education, began as a one-way vehicle where users visited to view Web pages and get information. It has evolved into sites where shopping and commerce takes place and is now evolving into a technology where users create the content. Web 2.0 and sites such as Facebook.com, flickr.com, LinkedIn.com, twitter.com, wikipedia.com, and youtube.com have content generated by the people that visit the Web sites. See **Figure A–26**.

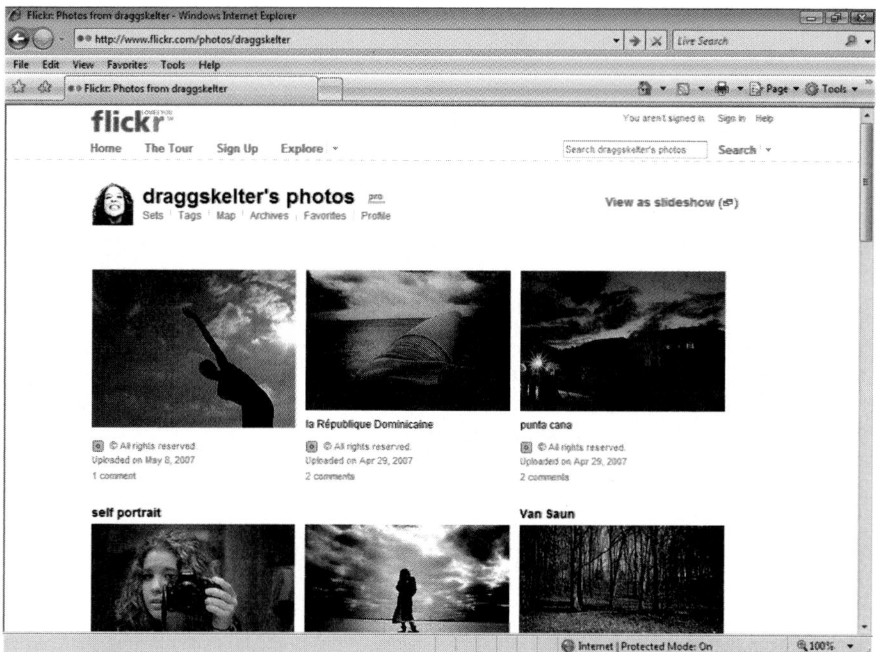

Used with permission: Emily C. Bunin

FIGURE A–26 User generated content

Computers have radically changed the way the medical profession delivers health care. Through the medical community, computers have enhanced medicine and healthcare throughout the world.

Trends

There are many trends that drive the computer industry. One trend is for larger and faster storage. From megabytes, to gigabytes, to terabytes, storage is becoming less an issue as the cost of storage is also dropping. RAM today is increasing exponentially. The trend is to sell larger blocks of RAM with every new personal computer. Newer processors also operate at speeds that are faster than the previous generation processors.

The actual size of computers is decreasing. Technology is allowing more powerful components to fit into smaller devices—laptops are lighter, monitors take up less space on the desktop, and flash drives can fit in your pocket and store gigabytes of data.

Home Offices

More and more frequently, people are working out of their homes—whether they are employees who are linked to their office in another location or individuals running their own businesses. ***Telecommuting*** meets the needs of many industries. Many companies allow workers to have a computer at home that is linked to their office and employees can use laptop computers to work both from home and on the road as they travel. A laptop computer, in combination with a wireless network, allows an employee to work from virtually anywhere and still keep in constant contact with her or his employer and customers.

Business communication is primarily by e-mail and telephone. It is very common for serious business transactions and communications to occur via e-mail rather than through the regular mail. Such an arrangement saves companies time and workspace and, thus, money.

Home Use

More and more households have personal computers. The statistics are constantly proving that a computer is an essential household appliance. Computers are used to access the Internet for shopping, education, and leisure. Computers are used to maintain financial records, manage household accounts, and record and manage personal information. More and more people are using electronic banking. Games and other computer applications offer another way to spend leisure dollars, and the convergence of television, the Internet, and the computer will find more households using their computers for media such as movies and music.

The future is computing. It's clear that this technology will continue to expand and provide us with new and exciting trends.

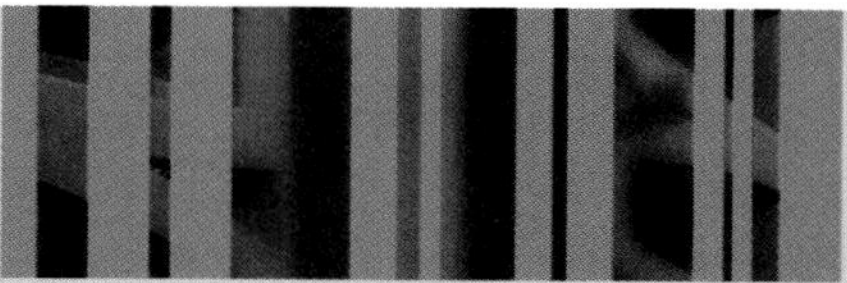

APPENDIX B

Keyboarding Touch System Improvement

Introduction

- *Your Goal—Improve your keyboarding skills using the touch system so you are able to type without looking at the keyboard.*

Why Improve Your Keyboarding Skills?

- To type faster and more accurately every time you use the computer
- To increase your enjoyment while using the computer

Instead of looking back and forth from the page to see the text you have to type and then turning back to the keyboard and pressing keys with one or two fingers, using the touch system you will type faster and more accurately.

> **WARNING**
>
> Using two fingers to type while looking at the keyboard is called the "hunt and peck" system and is not efficient when typing large documents.

Getting Ready to Build Skills

In order to get ready you should:

1. **Prepare your desk and computer area.**
   a. Clear your desk of all clutter, except your book, a pencil or pen, the keyboard, the mouse, and the monitor.
   b. Position your keyboard and book so that you are comfortable and able to move your hands and fingers freely on the keyboard and read the book at the same time.
   c. Keep your feet flat on the floor, sit with your back straight, and rest your arms slightly bent with your finger tips on the keyboard.
   d. Start a word-processing program, such as Microsoft Word, or any other text editor. You can also use any simple program such as the Microsoft Works word processor or WordPad that is part of the Windows operating system. Ask your teacher for assistance.

> **EXTRA FOR EXPERTS**
>
> There are two forms that you will complete as you work through this appendix to improve your typing skills: the **Timed Typing Progress Chart** and the **Keyboarding Technique Checklist**. Both forms are printed as the last two pages at the end of this Appendix.

2. Take a two-minute timed typing test according to your teacher's directions.
3. Calculate your words a minute (WAM) and errors a minute (EAM) using the instructions on the timed typing progress chart. This will be the base score you will compare to future timed typing.
4. Record today's Date, WAM, and EAM on the Base Score line of the writing progress chart.
5. Repeat the timed typing test many times to see improvements in your score.
6. Record each attempt on the Introduction line of the chart.

Getting Started

Keyboarding is an essential skill in today's workplace. No matter what your job, most likely you have to learn to be an effective typist. Follow the hints below to help you achieve this goal:

- Ignore errors.
- To complete the following exercises, you will type text that is bold and is not italicized and looks **like this**.
- If you have difficulty reaching for any key, for example the y key, practice by looking at the reach your fingertips make from the j key to the y key until the reach is visualized in your mind. The reach will become natural with very little practice.
- To start on a new line, press Enter.

Skill Builder 1

Your Goal—Use the touch system to type the letters j u y h n m and to learn to press the spacebar.

Keys

SPACEBAR

What to Do

1. Place your fingertips on the home row keys as shown in **Figure B–1**.

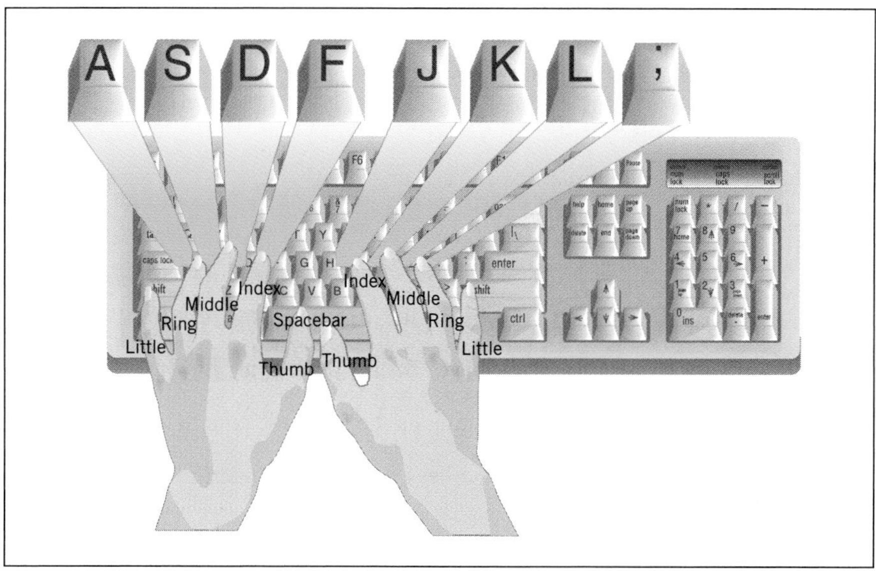

FIGURE B–1 Place your fingertips on the Home Row keys

2. Look at **Figure B–2**. In step 3, you will press the letter keys j u y h n m. To press these keys, you use your right index finger. You will press the spacebar after typing each letter three times. The spacebar is the long bar beneath the bottom row of letter keys. You will press the spacebar with your right thumb.

> **TIP**
>
> The home row keys are where you rest your fingertips when they are not typing. The index finger of your right hand rests on the J key. The index finger of your left hand rests on the F key. Feel the slight bump on these keys to help find the home row keys without looking at the keyboard.

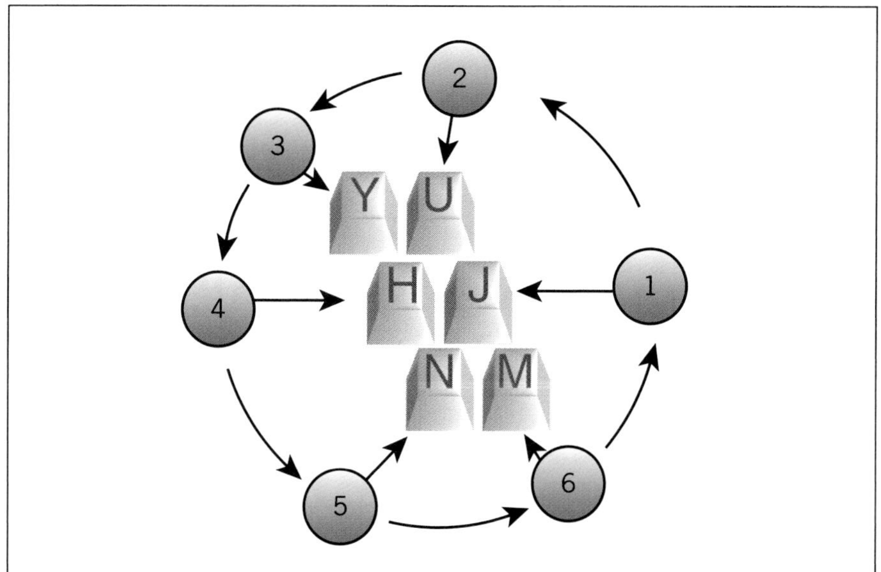

FIGURE B–2 Pressing the J U Y H N M keys

3. Look at your keyboard. Repeat the letters silently to yourself as you move your right index finger from the j key to press each key three times, and then press the spacebar. Start typing:

jjj uuu jjj yyy jjj hhh jjj nnn jjj mmm

jjj uuu jjj yyy jjj hhh jjj nnn jjj mmm jjj

4. Repeat the same drill as many times as it takes for you to reach your comfort level.

   jjj uuu jjj yyy jjj hhh jjj nnn jjj mmm

   jjj uuu jjj yyy jjj hhh jjj nnn jjj mmm jjj

5. Close your eyes and visualize each key under each finger as you repeat the drill in step 4.

6. Look at the following two lines and type:

   jjj jjj jjj juj juj juj jyj jyj jyj jhj jhj jhj jnj jnj jnj jmj jmj jmj

   jjj jjj jjj juj juj juj jyj jyj jyj jhj jhj jhj jnj jnj jnj jmj jmj jmj

7. Repeat step 6, this time concentrating on the rhythmic pattern of the keys.

8. Close your eyes and visualize the keys under your fingertips as you type the drill in step 4 from memory.

9. Look at the following two lines and type these groups of letters:

   j ju juj j jy jyj j jh jhj j jn jnj j jm jmj j ju juj j jy jyj j jh jhj j jn jnj j jm jmj

   jjj ju jhj jn jm ju jm jh jnj jm ju jmj jy ju jh j u ju juj jy jh jnj ju jm jmj jy

10. You may want to repeat Skill Builder 1, striving to improve typing letters that are most difficult for you.

Skill Builder 2

The left index finger is used to type the letters f r t g b v. Always return your left index finger to the f key on the home row after pressing the other keys.

Your Goal—Use the touch system to type f r t g b v .

What to Do

1. Place your fingertips on the home row keys as you did in Skill Builder 1, Figure B–1.

2. Look at **Figure B–3**. Notice how you will type the letters f r t g b v and then press the spacebar with your right thumb.

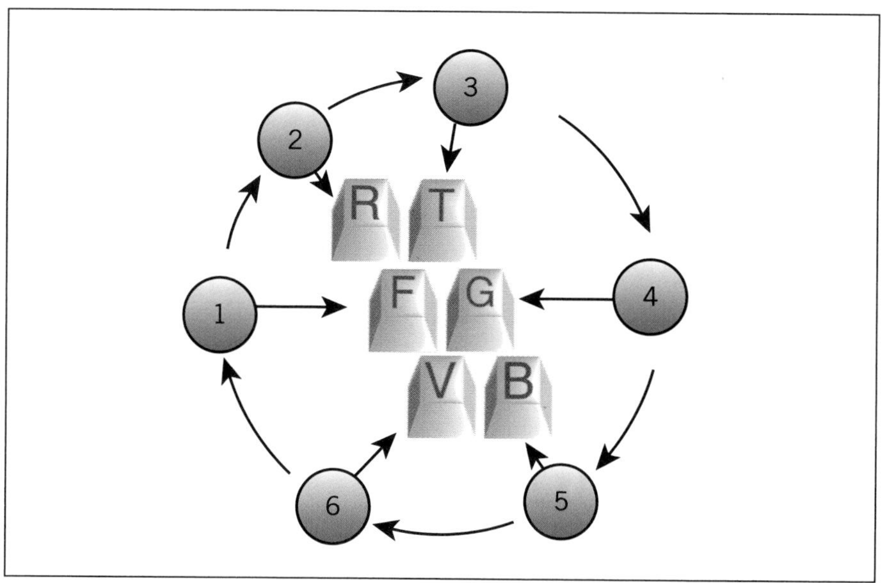

FIGURE B–3 Pressing the F R T G B V keys

3. Look at your keyboard. To press these keys, you use your left index finger. You will press the spacebar after typing each letter three times. The spacebar is the long bar beneath the bottom row of letter keys. You will press the spacebar with your right thumb.

   After pressing each letter in the circle, press the home key f three times as shown. Don't worry about errors. Ignore them.

   fff rrr fff ttt fff ggg fff bbb fff vvv

   fff rrr fff ttt fff ggg fff bbb fff vvv fff

4. Repeat the same drill two more times using a quicker, sharper stroke.

   fff rrr fff ttt fff ggg fff bbb fff vvv

   fff rrr fff ttt fff ggg fff bbb fff vvv fff

5. Close your eyes and visualize each key under each finger as you repeat the drill in step 4.

6. Look at the following two lines and key these groups of letters:

   fff fff fff frf frf frf ftf ftf ftf fgf fgf fgf fbf fbf fbf fvf fvf fvf

   fff fff fff frf frf frf ftf ftf ftf fgf fgf fgf fbf fbf fbf fvf fvf fvf

7. Repeat step 6, this time concentrating on a rhythmic pattern of the keys.

8. Close your eyes and visualize the keys under your fingertips as you type the drill in step 4 from memory.

9. Look at the following two lines and type these groups of letters:

   fr frf ft ftf fg fgf fb fbf fv fvf

   ft fgf fv frf ft fbf fv frf ft fgf

10. You are about ready to type your first words. Look at the following lines and type these groups of letters (remember to press the spacebar after each group):

jjj juj jug jug jug rrr rur rug rug rug

ttt tut tug tug tug rrr rur rub rub rub

ggg gug gum gum gum mmm mum

mug mug mug hhh huh hum hum hum

11. Complete the Keyboarding Technique Checklist.

Skill Builder 3

Your Goal—Use the touch system to type k i , d e c.

Keys K I , (comma)

TIP

Ask your classmate to call out the letters in random order as you type them with your eyes closed. Do the same for your classmate. Ask your classmate or your teacher to complete the Keyboarding Technique Checklist.

EXTRA FOR EXPERTS

The keyboard has letters, punctuation marks, and symbols. You can refer to these all as 'characters'.

What to Do

1. Place your fingertips on the home row keys. The home row key for the left middle finger is d. The home row key for the right middle finger is k. You use your left middle finger to type d, e, c. You use your right middle finger to type k, i, , as shown in **Figure B–4**.

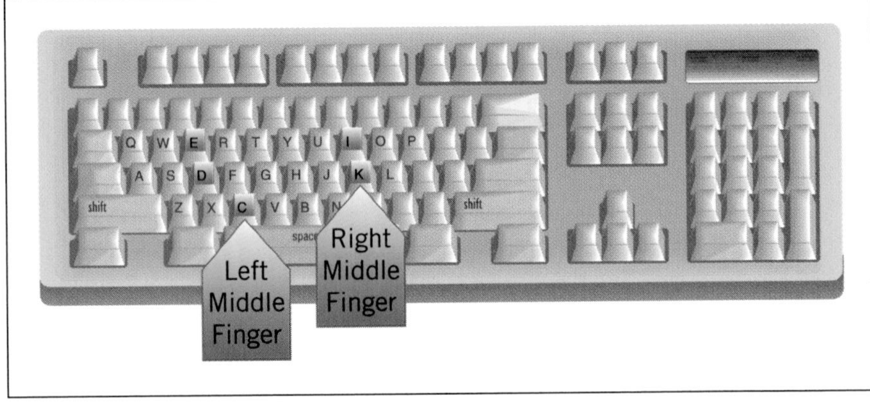

FIGURE B–4 Pressing the K I , D E C keys

2. Look at your keyboard and locate these keys: k i , (the letter k key, the letter i key, and the comma key).

3. Look at your keyboard. Repeat the letters silently to yourself as you press each key three times and put a space between each set of letters and the comma to type:

kkk iii kkk ,,, kkk iii kkk ,,, kkk iii kkk ,,, kkk iii kkk ,,, kkk iii kkk ,,, kkk

4. Look at the characters in step 3 and repeat the drill two more times using a quicker, sharper stroke.
5. Close your eyes and repeat the drill in step 3 as you visualize each key under each finger.
6. Repeat step 3, do not look at the keyboard, and concentrate on the rhythmic pattern of the keys.

What to Do

1. Place your fingertips on the home row keys.
2. Look at your keyboard and locate these keys: d e c (the letter d key, the letter e key, and the letter c key).
3. Look at your keyboard. Repeat the letters silently to yourself as you press each key three times and put a space between each set of letters to type:

   ddd eee ddd ccc ddd eee ddd ccc ddd eee ddd ccc ddd eee ddd ccc ddd

4. Look at the letters in step 3 and repeat the drill two more times using a quicker, sharper stroke.
5. Close your eyes and repeat the drill in step 3 as you visualize each key under each finger.
6. Repeat step 3, do not look at the keyboard, and concentrate on the rhythmic pattern of the keys.
7. Look at the following lines of letters and type these groups of letters and words:

   fff fuf fun fun fun ddd ded den den den

   ccc cuc cub cub cub vvv vev vet

   fff fuf fun fun fun ddd ded den den den

   ccc cuc cub cub cub vvv vev vet

8. Complete the Keyboarding Technique Checklist.

Skill Builder 4

Your Goal—Use the touch system to type l o . s w x and to press the left Shift key.

What to Do

1. Place your fingertips on the home row keys. The home row key for the left ring finger is s. The home row key for the right ring finger is l. You use your left ring finger to type s w x. You use your right ring finger to type l o . as shown in **Figure B–5**.

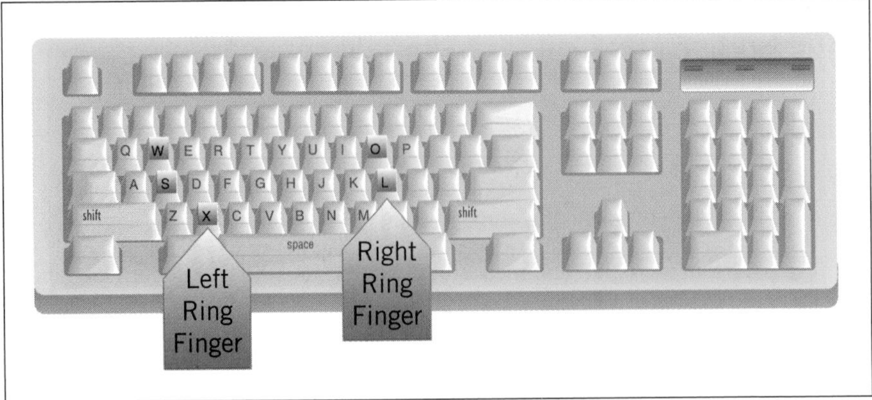

FIGURE B–5 Pressing the L O . S W X keys

2. Look at your keyboard and locate the following keys: l o . (the letter l key, the letter o key, and the period key).
3. Look at your keyboard. Repeat the letters silently to yourself as you press each key three times and put a space between each set of letters and the periods to type:

   lll ooo lll ... lll ooo lll ... lll ooo lll ... lll ooo lll ... lll ooo lll ... lll ooo lll ... lll

4. Look at the line in step 3 and repeat the drill two more times using a quicker, sharper stroke.
5. Close your eyes and repeat the drill in step 3 as you visualize each key under each finger.
6. Repeat step 3, do not look at the keyboard, and concentrate on the rhythmic pattern of the keys.

Keys S W X

1. Place your fingertips on the home row keys.
2. Look at your keyboard and locate the following letter keys: s w x
3. Look at your keyboard. Repeat the letters silently to yourself as you press each key three times and put a space between each set of letters to type:

   sss www sss xxx sss www sss xxx sss www sss xxx sss www sss xxx sss

4. Look at the line in step 3 and repeat the same drill two more times using a quicker, sharper stroke.

5. Close your eyes and repeat the drill in step 3 as you visualize each key under each finger.

6. Repeat step 3, do not look at the keyboard, and concentrate on the rhythmic pattern of the keys.

Key Shift SHIFT (Left Shift Key)

You press and hold the Shift key as you press a letter key to type a capital letter. You press and hold the Shift key to type the character that appears above the numbers in the top row of the keyboard and on a few other keys that show two characters.

Press and hold down the left Shift key with the little finger on your left hand while you press each letter to type capital letters for keys that are typed with the fingertips on your right hand. See **Figure B–6**.

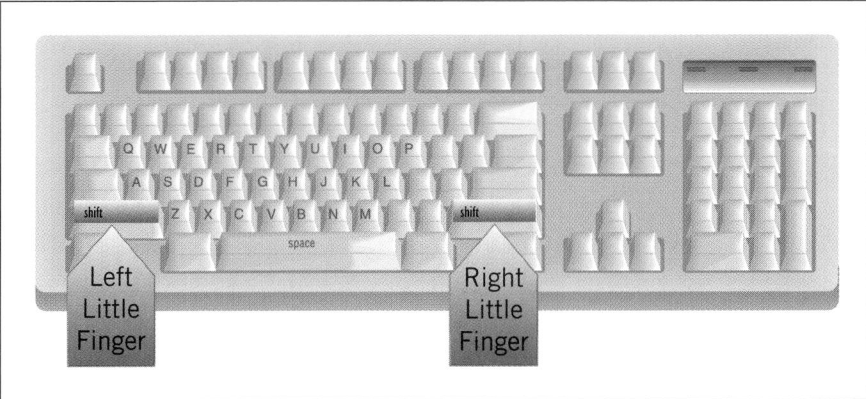

FIGURE B–6 Using the Shift keys

1. Type the following groups of letters and the sentence that follows.

   jjj JJJ jjj JJJ yyy YYY yyy YYY nnn NNN nnn NNN mmm MMM

   Just look in the book. You can see well.

2. Complete a column in the Keyboarding Technique Checklist.

Skill Builder 5

Your Goal—Use the touch system to type a q z ; p / and to press the right Shift key.

Keys ; (Semi-Colon) P /

What to Do

1. Place your fingertips on the home row keys. The home row key for the left little finger is a. The home row key for the right little finger is ;. You use your left little finger to type a q z. You use your right little finger to type ; p / as shown in **Figure B–7**.

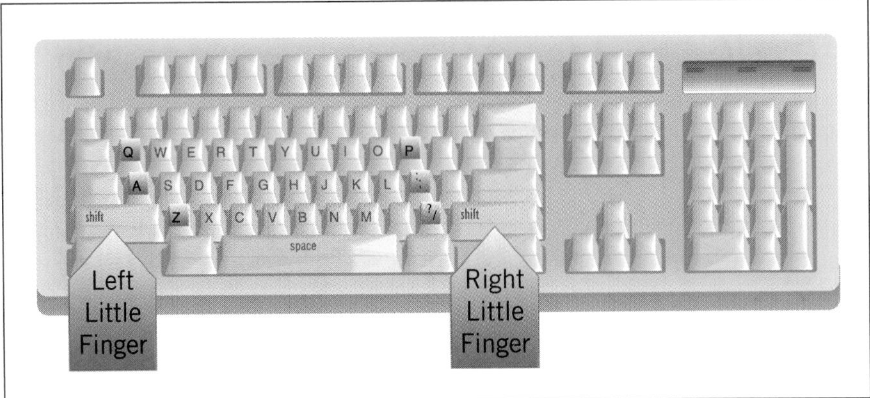

FIGURE B–7 Pressing the A Q Z ; P / and the right Shift key

2. Look at your keyboard and locate the following keys: ; p / (the semi-colon, the letter p, and the forward slash).
3. Repeat the letters silently to yourself as you press each key three times and put a space between each set of characters to type:

   ;;; ppp ;;; /// ;;; ppp ;;; /// ;;; ppp ;;; ///

   ;;; ppp ;;; /// ;;; ppp ;;; /// ;;; ppp ;;; /// ;;;

4. Look at the lines in step 3 and repeat the drill two more times using a quicker, sharper stroke.
5. Close your eyes and repeat the drill in step 3 as you visualize each key under each finger.
6. Repeat step 3, do not look at the keyboard, and concentrate on a rhythmic pattern of the keys.

Keys 

1. Place your fingertips on the home row keys.
2. Look at your keyboard and locate the following keys: a q z (the letter a, the letter q, and the letter z).
3. Look at your keyboard. Repeat the letters silently to yourself as you press each key three times and put a space between each set of letters and type:

   aaa qqq aaa zzz aaa qqq aaa zzz aaa qqq aaa zzz aaa qqq aaa zzz aaa

4. Look at the line in step 3 and repeat the same drill two more times using a quicker, sharper stroke.

5. Close your eyes and repeat the drill in step 3 as you visualize each key under each finger.

6. Repeat step 3, do not look at the keyboard, and concentrate on the rhythmic pattern of the keys.

Key Shift (SHIFT) (Right Shift Key)

Press and hold down the right Shift key with the little finger on your right hand while you press each letter to type capital letters for keys that are typed with the fingertips on your left hand.

1. Type the following lines. Press and hold down the right Shift key with the little finger of your right hand to make capitals of letters you type with the fingertips on your left hand.

   sss SSS rrr RRR

   Press each key quickly. Relax when you type.

2. Complete another column in the Keyboarding Technique Checklist.

Skill Builder 6

You will probably have to type slowly at first, but with practice you will learn to type faster and accurately.

Your Goal—Use the touch system to type all letters of the alphabet.

What to Do

1. Close your eyes. Do not look at the keyboard and type all letters of the alphabet in groups of three with a space between each set as shown:

   aaa bbb ccc ddd eee fff ggg hhh iii jjj

   kkk lll mmm nnn ooo ppp qqq rrr sss

   ttt uuu vvv www xxx yyy zzz

2. Repeat step 1, concentrating on a rhythmic pattern of the keys.

3. Repeat step 1, but faster than you did for step 2.

4. Type the following sets of letters, all letters of the alphabet in groups of two with a space between each set as shown:

   aa bb cc dd ee ff gg hh ii jj kk ll mm nn oo pp qq rr ss tt uu vv ww xx yy zz

5. Type the following letters, all letters of the alphabet with a space between each letter as shown:

   a b c d e f g h i j k l m n o p q r s t u v w x y z

6. Continue to look at this book. Do not look at the keyboard, and type all letters of the alphabet backwards in groups of three with a space between each set as shown:

   zzz yyy xxx www vvv uuu ttt sss rrr

   qqq ppp ooo nnn mmm lll kkk jjj iii

   hhh ggg fff eee ddd ccc bbb aaa

7. Repeat step 6, but faster than the last time.

8. Type each letter of the alphabet once backwards:

   z y x w v u t s r q p o n m l k j i h g f e d c b a

9. Think about the letters that took you the most amount of time to find the key on the keyboard. Go back to the Skill Builder for those letters, and repeat the drills until you are confident about their locations.

Timed Typing

Prepare to take the timed typing test, according to your teacher's directions.

1. **Prepare your desk and computer area.**
   a. Clear your desk of all clutter except your book, a pencil or pen, the keyboard, the mouse, the monitor, and the computer if it is located on the desk.
   b. Position your keyboard and book so that you are comfortable and able to move your hands and fingertips freely.
   c. Keep your feet flat on the floor, sitting with your back straight, resting your arms slightly bent with your fingertips on the keyboard.

2. Take a two-minute timed typing test according to your teacher's directions.

3. Calculate your words a minute (WAM) and errors a minute (EAM) scores using the instructions on the Timed Typing Progress Chart in this book.

4. Record the date, WAM, and EAM on the Skill Builder 6 line in the Timed Typing Progress Chart printed at the end of this appendix.

5. Repeat the timed typing test as many times as you can and record each attempt in the Timed Typing Progress Chart.

Skill Builder 7

Your Goal—Improve your typing techniques—which is the secret for improving your speed and accuracy.

What to Do

1. Rate yourself for each item on the Keyboarding Technique Checklist printed at the end of this appendix.

2. Do not time yourself as you concentrate on a single technique you marked with a "0." Type only the first paragraph of the timed typing.

3. Repeat step 2 as many times as possible for each of the items marked with an “0” that need improvement.

4. Take a two-minute timed typing test. Record your WAM and EAM on the Timed Typing Progress Chart as 1st Attempt on the Skill Builder 7 line. Compare this score with your base score.

5. Looking only at the book and using your best techniques, type the following technique sentence for one minute:

   . 2 . 4 . 6 . 8 . 10 . 12 . 14 . 16

   Now is the time for all good men and women to come to the aid of their country.

6. Record your WAM and EAM in the Timed Typing Progress Chart on the 7 Technique Sentence line.

7. Repeat steps 5 and 6 as many times as you can and record your scores in the Timed Typing Progress Chart.

Skill Builder 8

Your Goal—Increase your words a minute (WAM) score.

What to Do

You can now type letters in the speed line very well and with confidence. Practicing all of the other letters of the alphabet will further increase your skill and confidence in keyboarding.

1. Take a two-minute timed typing test.

2. Record your WAM and EAM scores as the 1st Attempt in the Timed Typing Progress Chart.

3. Type only the first paragraph only one time as fast as you can. Ignore errors.

4. Type only the first and second paragraphs only one time as fast as you can. Ignore errors.

5. Take a two-minute timed typing test again. Ignore errors.

6. Record only your WAM score as the 2nd Attempt in the Timed Typing Progress Chart. Compare only this WAM with your 1st Attempt WAM and your base score WAM.

Get Your Best WAM

1. To get your best WAM on easy text for 15 seconds, type the following speed line as fast as you can, as many times as you can. Ignore errors.

   . 2 . 4 . 6 . 8 . 10

   Now is the time, now is the time, now is the time,

2. Multiply the number of words typed by four to get your WAM (15 seconds × 4 = 1 minute). For example, if you type 12 words for 15 seconds, 12 × 4 = 48 WAM.

3. Record only your WAM in the 8 Speed Line box in the Timed Typing Progress Chart.

4. Repeat steps 1–3 as many times as you can to get your very best WAM. Ignore errors.

5. Record only your WAM for each attempt in the Timed Typing Progress Chart.

Skill Builder 9

Your Goal—Decrease errors a minute (EAM) score.

What to Do

TIP

How much you improve depends upon how much you want to improve.

1. Take a two-minute timed typing test.

2. Record your WAM and EAM as the 1st Attempt in the Timed Typing Progress Chart.

3. Type only the first paragraph only one time at a controlled rate of speed so you reduce errors. Ignore speed.

4. Type only the first and second paragraphs only one time at a controlled rate of speed so you reduce errors. Ignore speed.

5. Take a two-minute timed typing test again. Ignore speed.

6. Record only your EAM score as the 2nd Attempt in the Timed Typing Progress Chart. Compare only the EAM with your 1st Attempt EAM and your base score EAM.

Get Your Best EAM

1. To get your best EAM, type the following accuracy sentence (same as the technique sentence) for one minute. Ignore speed.

   Now is the time for all good men and women to come to the aid of their country.

2. Record only your EAM score on the Accuracy Sentence 9 line in the Timed Typing Progress Chart.

3. Repeat step 1 as many times as you can to get your best EAM. Ignore speed.

4. Record only your EAM score for each attempt in the Timed Typing Progress Chart.

Skill Builder 10

Your Goal—Use the touch system and your best techniques to type faster and more accurately than you have ever typed before.

What to Do

1. Take a one-minute timed typing test.
2. Record your WAM and EAM as the 1st Attempt on the Skill Builder 10 line in the Timed Typing Progress Chart.
3. Repeat the timed typing test for two minutes as many times as necessary to get your best ever WAM with no more than one EAM. Record your scores as 2nd, 3rd, and 4th Attempts.

TIP

You may want to get advice regarding which techniques you need to improve from a classmate or your instructor.

Assessing Your Improvement

1. Circle your best timed typing test for Skill Builders 6-10 in the Timed Typing Progress Chart.
2. Record your best score and your base score. Compare the two scores. Did you improve?

	WAM	EAM
Best Score	______	______
Base Score	______	______

3. Use the Keyboarding Technique Checklist to identify techniques you still need to improve. You may want to practice these techniques now to increase your WAM or decrease your EAM.

Timed Typing

Every five strokes in a timed typing test is a word, including punctuation marks and spaces. Use the scale above each line to tell you how many words you typed.

```
    .    2    .    4    .    6    .
If you learn how to key well now, it
  8    .   10    .   12    .   14    .   16
is a skill that will help you for the rest
    .    18   .    20   .    22   .    24
of your life. How you sit will help you key
.    26   .    28   .    30   .    32   .    34
with more speed and less errors.  Sit with your
   .    36   .    38   .    40   .    42   .
feet flat on the floor and your back erect.
    44   .    46   .    48   .    50
To key fast by touch, try to keep your
.    52   .    54   .    56   .    58   .
eyes on the copy and not on your hands or
   60   .    62   .    64   .    66   .    68
the screen.  Curve your fingers and make sharp,
 .    70   .
quick strokes.
 72   .    74   .    76   .    78   .
Work for speed first.  If you make more
  80   .    82   .    84   .    86   .    88
than two errors a minute, you are keying too
  .    90   .    92   .    94   .    96   .
fast. Slow down to get fewer errors. If you
   98   .   100   .   102   .   104   .
get fewer than two errors a minute, go for
106  .
speed.
```

Timed Typing Progress Chart

Timed Writing Progress Chart

Last Name: ______________________ *First Name:* ______________________

Instructions

Calculate your scores as shown in the following sample. Repeat timed writings as many times as you can and record your scores for each attempt.

Base Score	Date	WAM	EAM	Time

To calculate WAM: Divide words keyed by number of minutes to get WAM. For example: 44 words keyed in 2 minutes = 22 WAM [44/2=22]

To calculate EAM: Divide errors made by minutes of typing to get EAM

For example: 7 errors made in 2 minutes of typing = 3.5 EAM [7/2=3.5]

	1st Attempt			2nd Attempt		3rd Attempt		4th Attempt	
Skill Builder	**Date**	**(a) WAM**	**(b) EAM**	**WAM**	**EAM**	**WAM**	**EAM**	**WAM**	**EAM**
Sample	9/2	22	3.5	23	2.0	25	1.0	29	2.0
Introduction									
6									
7									
8					-----				
9				-----					
10									
7 Technique Sentence									
8 Speed Line			-----		-----		-----		-----
9 Accuracy Sentence		-----		-----		-----		-----	

Keyboarding Technique Checklist

Last Name: ______________________ *First Name:* ______________________

Instructions

1. Write the Skill Builder number, the date, and the initials of the evaluator in the proper spaces.
2. Place a check mark (✓) after a technique that is performed satisfactorily.
3. Place a large zero (0) after a technique that needs improvement.

Skill Builder Number:	Sample										
Date:	9/1										
Evaluator:	SL										
Technique											
Attitude											
1. Enthusiastic about learning	✓										
2. Optimistic about improving	✓										
3. Alert but relaxed	✓										
4. Sticks to the task; not distracted	✓										
Getting Ready											
1. Desk uncluttered	✓										
2. Properly positions keyboard and book	✓										
3. Feet flat on the floor	✓										
4. Body erect, but relaxed	0										
Keyboarding											
1. Curves fingers	0										
2. Keeps eyes on the book	✓										
3. Taps the keys lightly; does not "pound" them	0										
4. Makes quick, "bouncy," strokes	0										
5. Smooth rhythm	0										
6. Minimum pauses between strokes	✓										

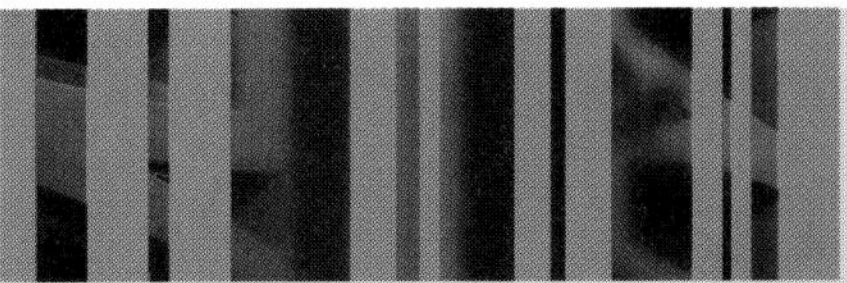

APPENDIX C

Differences between Windows 7, Windows Vista, and Windows XP

The Windows Experience

- Microsoft offers many new features in Windows 7 that are not available in Windows XP and Windows Vista.
- The overall Windows experience has been vastly improved from Windows XP to Windows 7. If you make the jump from XP to Windows 7, you will discover a great number of changes that are for the better. In addition, many of the new features introduced in Windows Vista were retained in this latest version of the popular operating system. Upgrading to Windows 7 is also an easier, more streamlined transition.

- With Windows 7, Microsoft has simplified everyday tasks and works more efficiently. This is all in response to issues users had with the Windows XP and Windows Vista experience. The major differences between Windows XP, Windows Vista, and Windows 7 are in the Start menu, dynamic navigation, desktop gadgets, improved security, search options, parental controls, and firewall, as well as improvements to the Windows Aero feature, see **Figure C–1**.

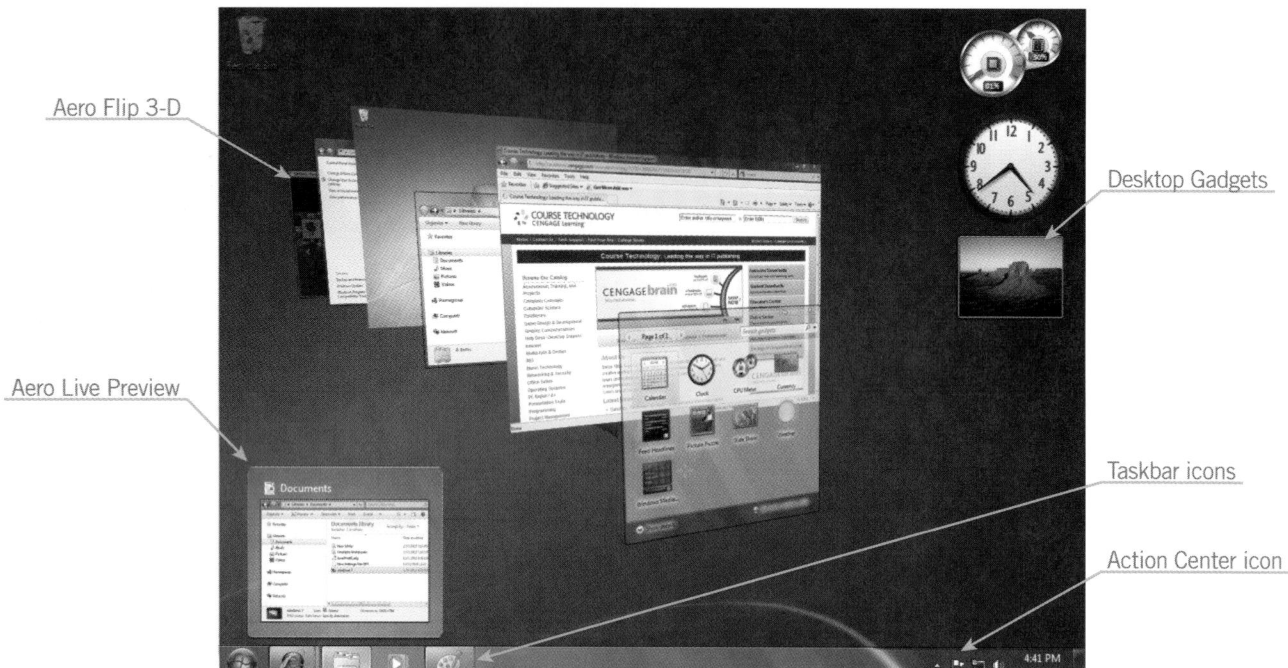

FIGURE C–1 Windows 7 Features

Windows Aero

- Windows Aero is a new graphic interface feature which gives a "transparent" quality to windows, dialog boxes, and other items in the Windows Vista and Windows 7 environment.
- Flip 3-D, or simply Flip, shows mini versions of windows and thumbnails in the Windows 7 environment when turned on.

Windows XP users had to download Windows Desktop Enhancements and PowerTools from the Microsoft Web site to change their Windows experience. Windows Vista and Windows 7 now have many different themes and options built into the operating system, making it easy to modify the Windows experience. One theme, introduced in Windows Vista is Aero.

Windows Aero is a feature which was first introduced in Windows Vista and is not available in the Windows XP operating system. Windows Aero, enabled by default in Windows 7, is a more aesthetically pleasing user interface to Windows Vista and Windows 7 systems. For example, Windows XP utilizes ScreenTips only when pointing to items on the Taskbar, Desktop, and Menus. The basic ScreenTips found in Windows XP have been enhanced to show live "sneak-previews" of windows with a simple point to the icon on the taskbar , as shown in **Figure C–2**.

Windows 7 made major improvements to the function of Aero. These new features include Aero Peek, Aero Shake, Aero Snap, Touch UI, and many other visual effects covered in this section. Compare the evolution of the Taskbar ScreenTip in Windows XP to Windows Vista and finally in Windows 7 in the figures below.

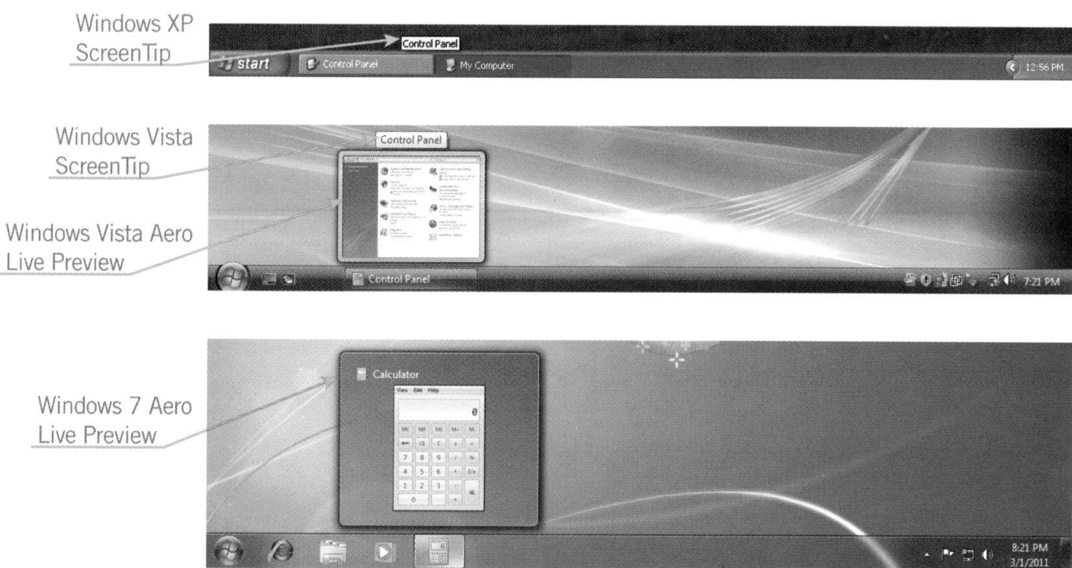

FIGURE C–2 Comparing Windows XP taskbar with Windows Vista and Windows 7

Understanding the Desktop

- Gadgets, introduced in Windows Vista, and Jump Lists, introduced in Windows 7, are two new desktop features.
- Windows 7 also includes multiple Aero themes to customize your desktop including the Desktop Background Slideshow.

At first glance, the Windows XP desktop only appears to differ slightly from that of Windows Vista, but the new features available with Windows 7 are substantial. The icons, shortcuts, folders, and files are generally the same; however, there are major aesthetic visual differences in this version. The most obvious addition from XP to Vista is the desktop gadget. Gadgets were not available in Windows XP. In **Figure C–4**, notice the appearance of three gadgets on the sidebar. Desktop gadgets are also available in Windows 7; however the sidebar function has been abandoned. Users simply add the gadget to the desktop.

The Taskbar in Windows XP includes the notification area, quick launch (when enabled), Start button, and icon(s) representing open programs. Beginning with Windows 7, you can now easily pin items to the Taskbar instead of using a quick launch feature. Jump lists, Aero themes and the Desktop Background Slideshow, explained in this chapter, are also new features to Windows 7.

FIGURE C–3 Windows XP Start menu and Desktop

The Start menu has been slightly enhanced from Windows XP to Windows 7. All Programs no longer appears on an additional menu, it has been merged with the Start menu. Windows Vista introduced a search function built into the Start menu, which allows users to search the computer easily for documents, applications, and help. Compare the evolution in desktops from Windows XP to Windows 7 in **Figures C–3, C–4,** and **C–5**.

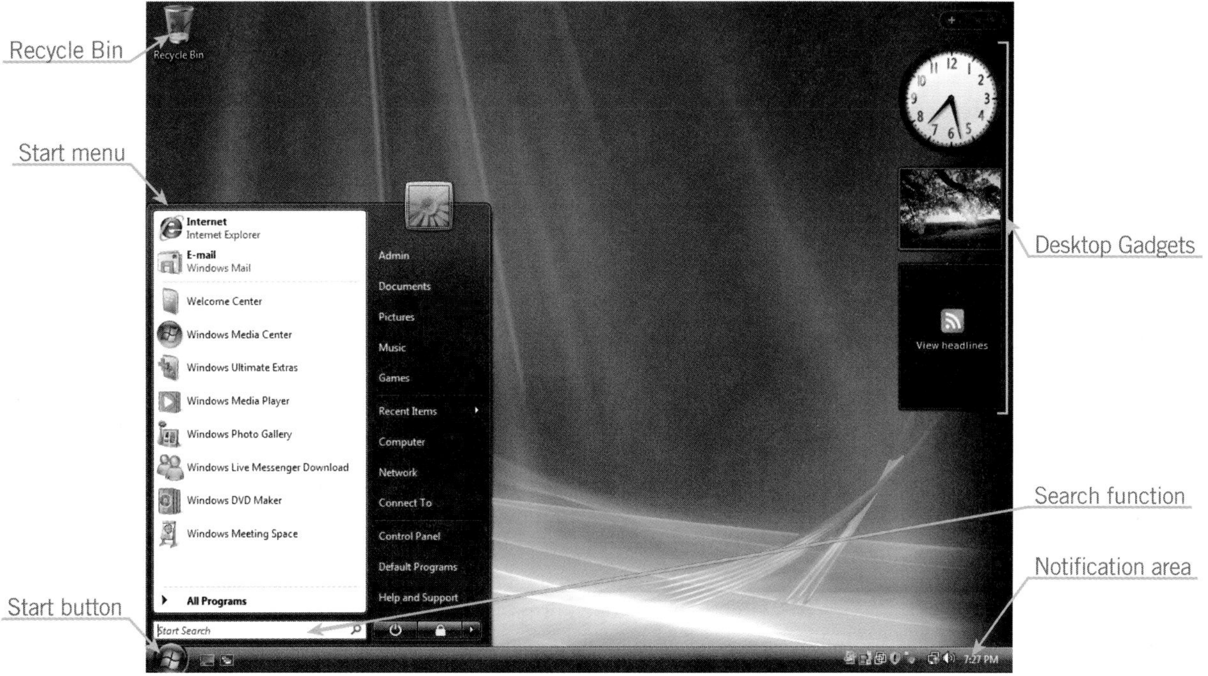

FIGURE C–4 Windows Vista Start menu and Desktop

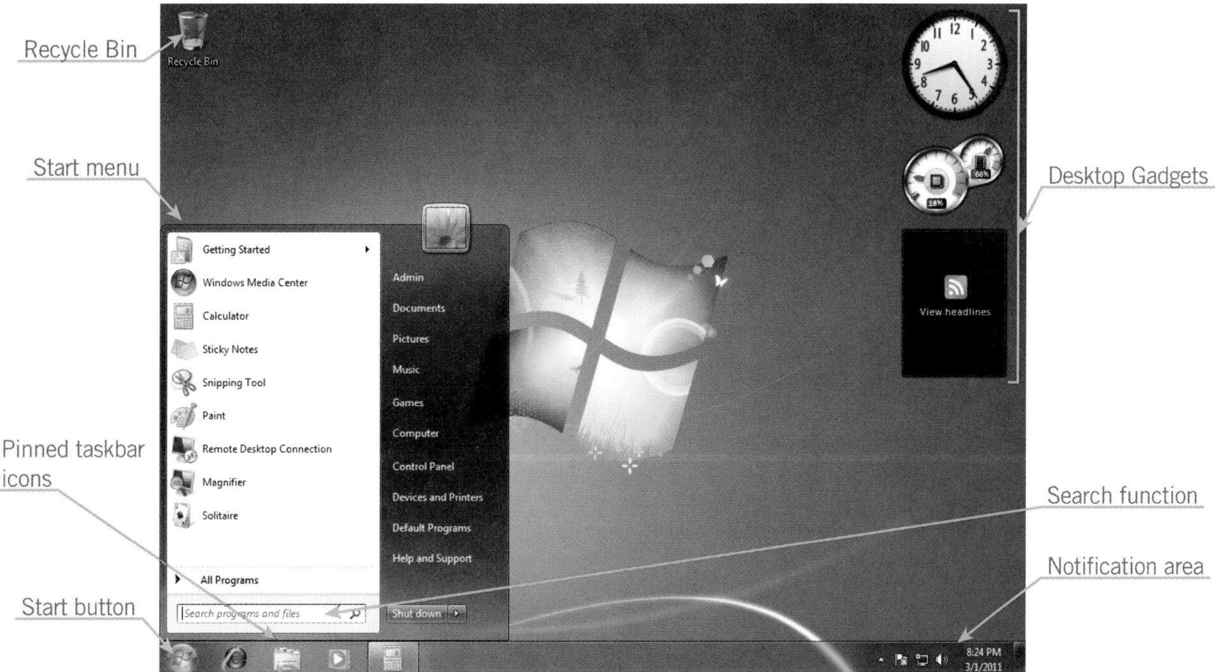

FIGURE C–5 Windows 7 Start menu and Desktop

Navigating in Windows

- The Address bar in Windows 7 now functions differently, with more direct navigation functions.
- Windows 7 now includes a comprehensive Navigation pane in Windows Explorer.

Windows Explorer provides the tools to navigate and locate items on your computer. The Address bar has been upgraded from Windows XP to allow for easier movement between folders. In Windows XP, the only available methods were the Back button and drop-down arrow. See **Figure C–6**. A big difference is in the function of the path. You may now click the folder in your path to move back. You may also begin a search directly from the Address bar, which is a new Windows 7 feature. Windows XP users' only option to search was to utilize the Search Companion.

The Navigation pane, which provides links to common or recently used folders, is dramatically different in Windows 7, compared to Windows XP, which only featured Favorites. "My Documents", the default user folder in Windows XP, is now a collection of folders grouped in Libraries in Windows 7. These folders, as well as Favorites, are easily found on the new Navigation pane and are easily customizable.

To switch between open programs easily, Windows XP's only option aside from clicking the icon on the Taskbar, was to tab through available programs, in a basic method with no preview of the program state. Windows Flip, introduced in Windows Vista, allows you to move to an open file, window or program by pressing the Alt+Tab keys, while showing a preview of the program's current state in Aero. The Windows Vista version of Flip was enhanced for Windows 7 users, although the function remains the same. See **Figures C–8** and **C-9** on the following pages.

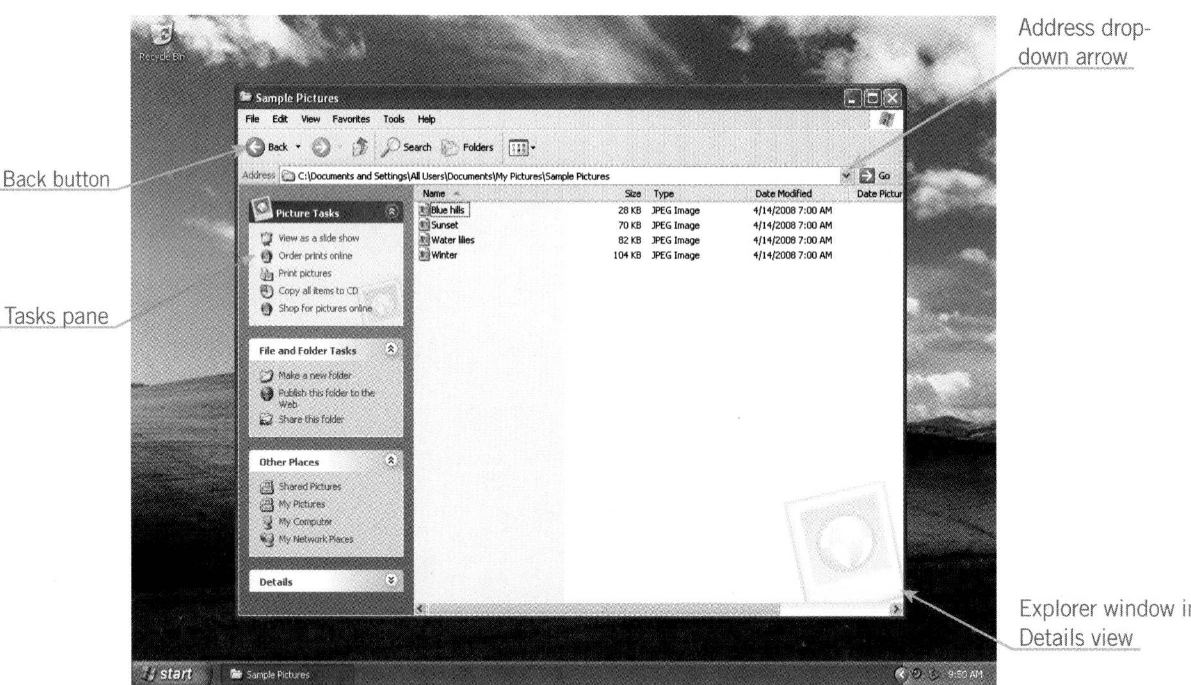

FIGURE C–6 Windows Explorer as seen in Windows XP

FIGURE C–7 Windows Explorer as seen in Windows Vista

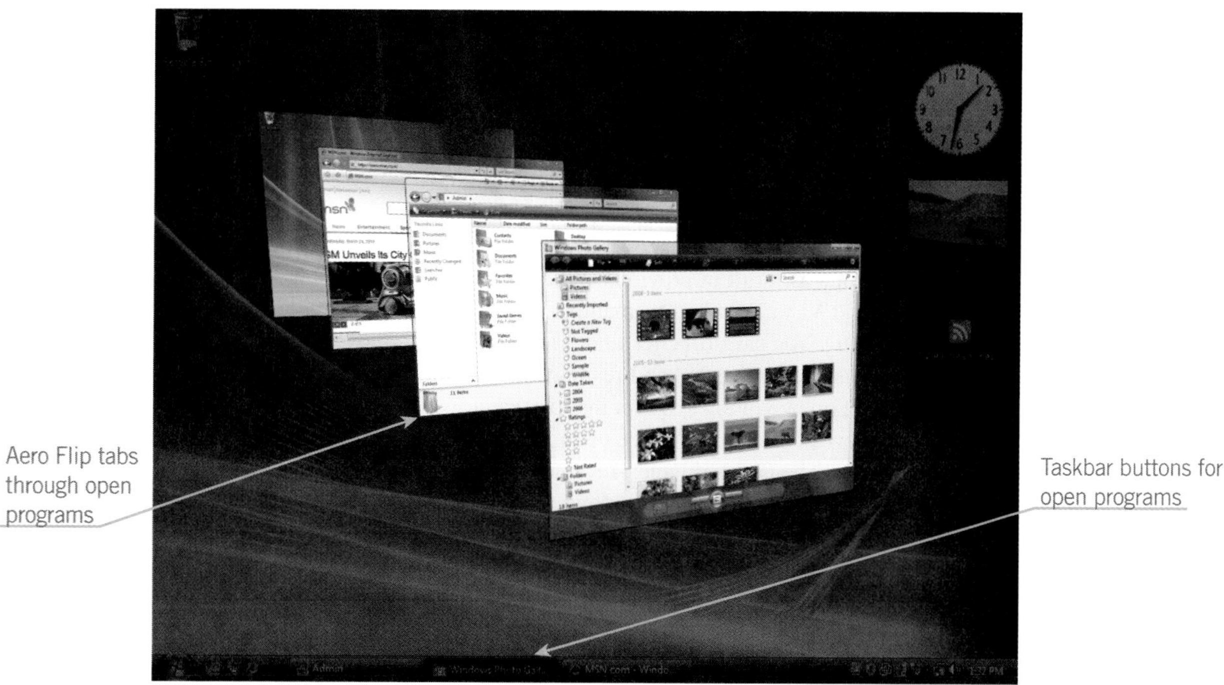

FIGURE C–8 Flip in Windows Vista

FIGURE C–9 Flip 3-D in Windows 7

Using Windows

- The new Aero Shake and Aero Snap allow you to easily move, resize, minimize and maximize open windows.
- The Control Panel now includes additional descriptive links, making it easy to find the item you are looking to modify.

Moving and resizing windows in Windows 7 provides the same essential functions as it did in previous Windows versions, with a few additions. In Windows XP and Vista, you had to manipulate each window individually, by clicking and dragging. You can still click and drag to resize and move windows; however this function has been upgraded and revamped in Windows 7. Aero Shake allows you to "shake" all open windows except that particular window to a minimized state. Aero Snap is a new way to easily resize open windows to expand vertically, or side-by-side.

The Control Panel, revamped in Windows Vista, has a new look in Windows 7, compared to that in Windows XP. The Search text box allows you to search for the Control Panel task you wish to perform. There are also descriptive linked items now replacing the "classic" icon format. **Figures C–10**, **C–11**, and **C–12**, which are shown on the following pages, illustrate the differences in the Control Panel from Windows XP to Windows 7.

FIGURE C–10 Windows XP Control Panel

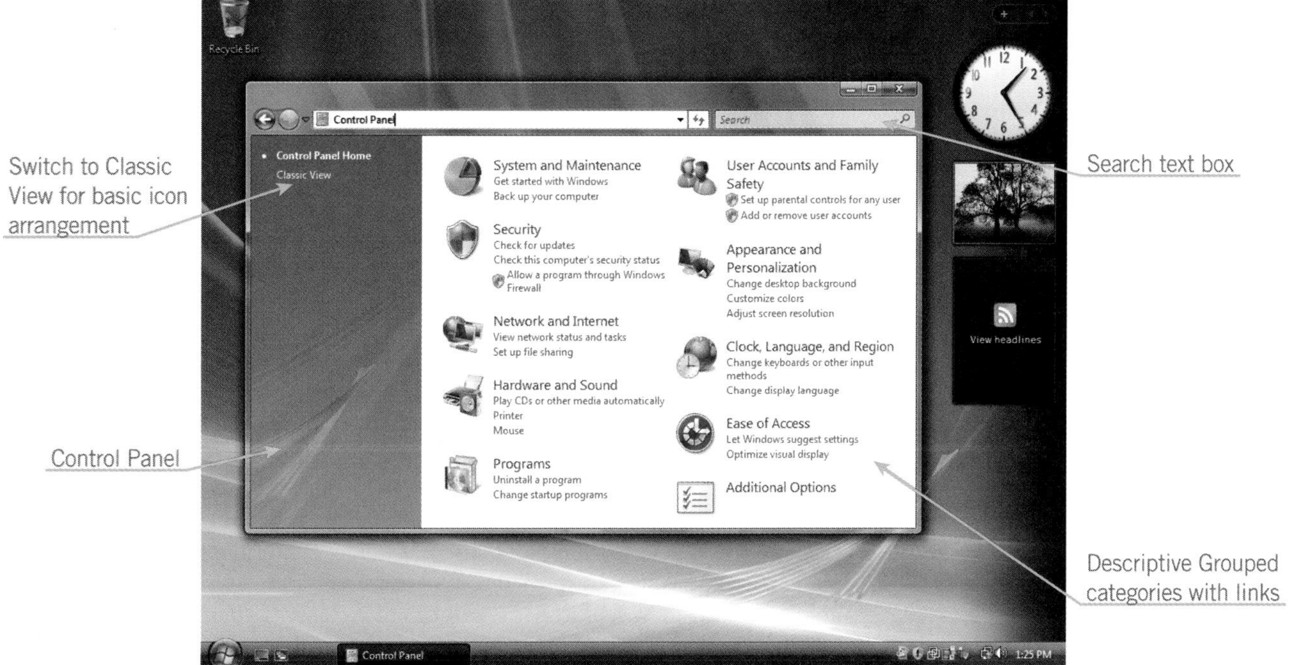

FIGURE C–11 Windows Vista Control Panel

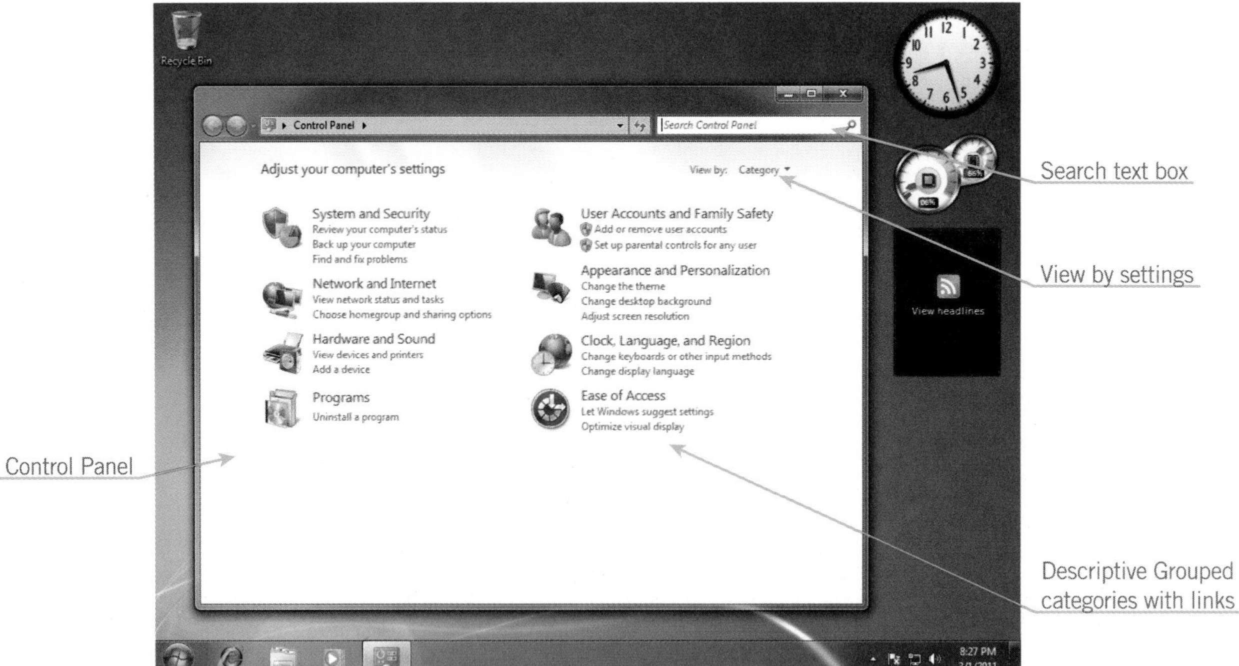

FIGURE C–12 Windows 7 Control Panel

Managing Your Computer

- The Action Center is a new feature in Windows 7 which consolidates message traffic from Windows maintenance and security features.
- Basic system utilities, such as Disk Cleanup and Disk Defragmenter, remain essentially the same from Windows XP to Windows 7.

Windows XP and Windows Vista's only method of receiving information on security and maintenance was the Security Center, available from the Control Panel. Windows 7 has improved this function, by creating a new Action Center, which communicates with the firewall, spyware protection, and antivirus software. Windows 7 users can now navigate to the Action Center by visiting the System and Security section of the Control Panel to view computer status and resolve issues. The Action Center is also pre-configured in Windows 7 to send important alerts to the Notification area of the taskbar.

One of the major upgrades in Windows 7 is in performance. Windows 7 was designed to run on less memory, shutting down services when not in use. In the Control Panel of Windows 7, there is a new Performance and Information Tools section. If you are a previous Windows XP user, you should familiarize yourself with this new feature. You will be able to assess your computer's performance, adjust settings, run disk cleanup, and launch advanced tools to manage your computer.

Windows Defender, introduced in Windows Vista is Microsoft's answer to spyware protection. This was not available for Windows XP users, pre Windows XP Service Pack 2. Windows XP Service Pack 2 users could download it from the Microsoft Web site and install it manually. Windows 7 also includes Windows Defender by default.

Windows Update, introduced in Windows XP has remained the same throughout the transitions through Windows Vista and Windows 7. Windows Update, which automatically downloads and installs important updates, was one of the only ways

Microsoft offered to maintain a secure PC with Windows XP. Now, in Windows 7, the Action Center, Performance Information and Tools, Windows Defender, and Windows Update work together to keep your computer secure. **Figures C–13**, **C–14**, and **C–15**, which are shown on the next few pages, compare Windows XP and Vista's Security Centers with Windows 7 Security Center and Action Center.

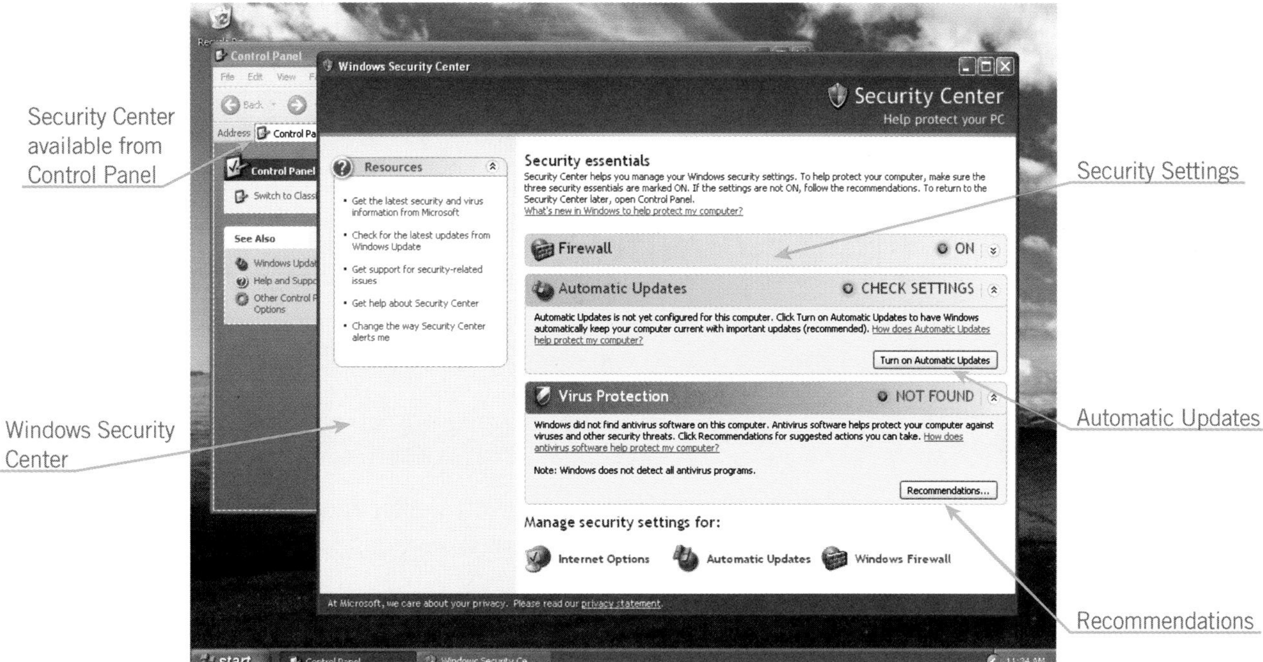

FIGURE C–13 Windows XP Security Center

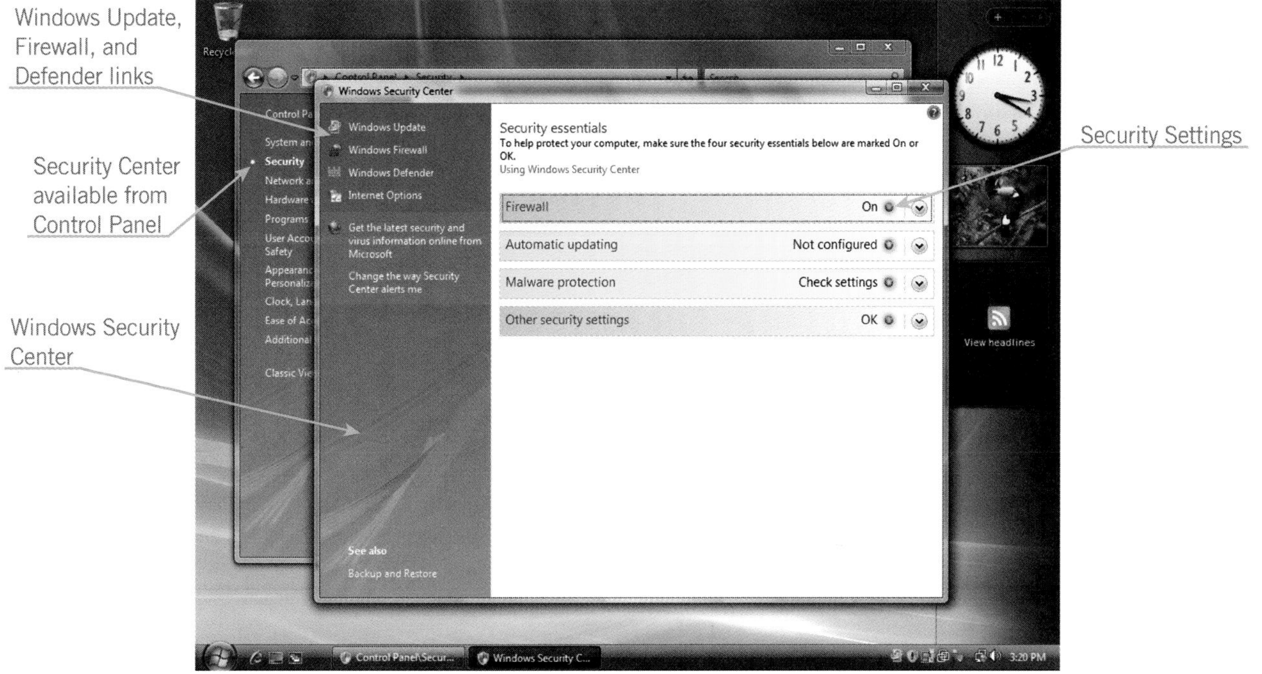

FIGURE C–14 Windows Vista Security Center

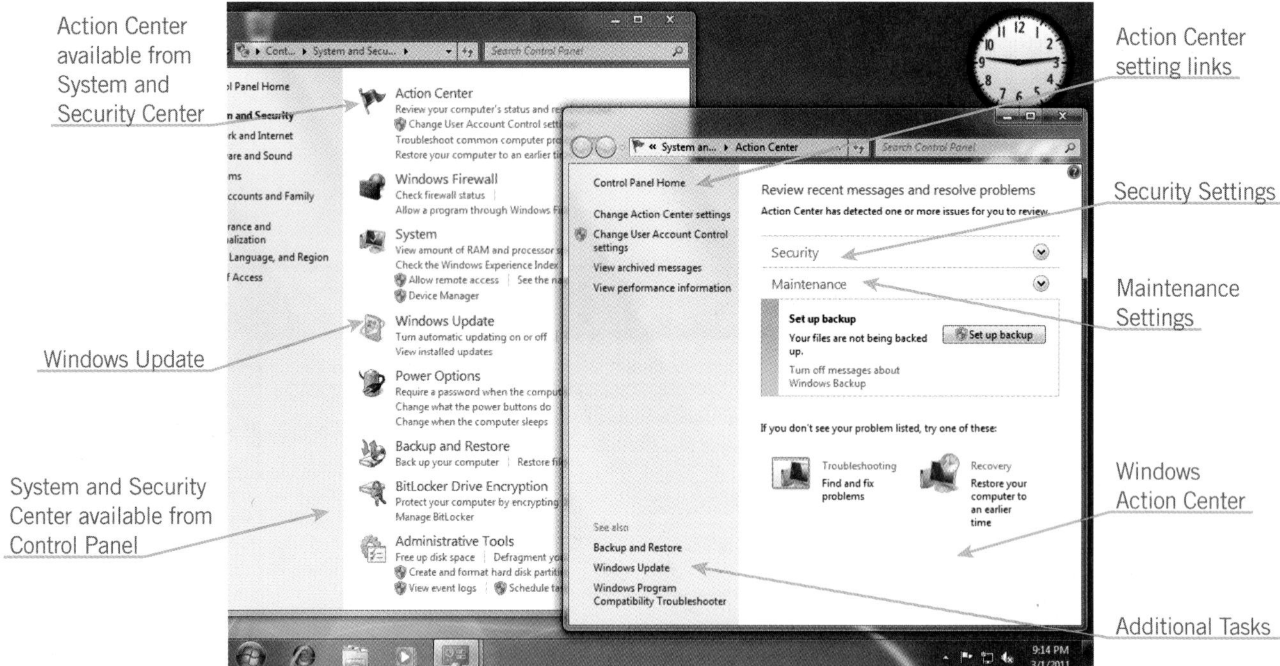

FIGURE C–15 Windows 7 Security Center and Action Center

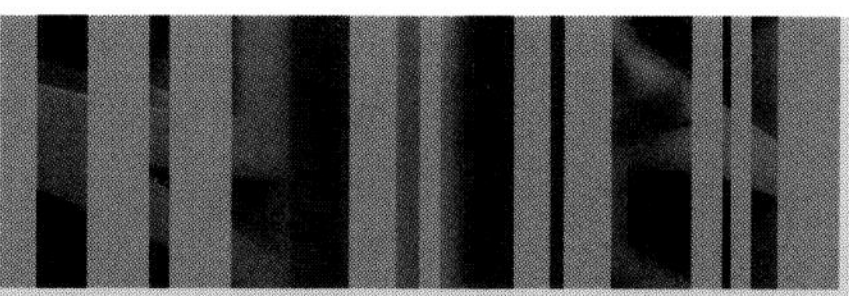

Estimated Time: .5 hour

APPENDIX D

Using SkyDrive and Office Web Apps

■ OBJECTIVES

Upon completion of this lesson, you should be able to:

- Explore cloud computing and Windows Live.
- Obtain a Windows Live ID and sign in to Windows Live.
- Upload files to SkyDrive.
- Use Office Web Apps View and Edit modes.
- Create folders on SkyDrive.
- Organize files on SkyDrive.
- Give permission for access to a folder on your SkyDrive.
- Co-author using the Excel Web App.

■ VOCABULARY

cloud computing
co-author
Office Web Apps
OneNote
SkyDrive
Windows Live

If the computer you are using has an active Internet connection, you can go to the Microsoft Windows Live Web site and use SkyDrive to store and share files. From SkyDrive, you can also use Office Web Apps to create and edit Word, PowerPoint, Excel, and OneNote files, even when you are using a computer that does not have Office 2010 installed. In this Appendix, you will learn how to obtain a Windows Live ID, how to share files with others on SkyDrive, and how to use the Word, Excel, and PowerPoint Web Apps, including co-authoring in the Excel Web App.

Understanding Cloud Computing and Windows Live

VOCABULARY

cloud computing

Windows Live

Cloud computing refers to data, applications, and even resources that are stored on servers that you access over the Internet rather than on your own computer. With cloud computing, you access only what you need when you need it. Many individuals and companies are moving towards "the cloud" for at least some of their needs. For example, some companies provide space and computing power to developers for a fee. Individuals might subscribe to an online backup service so that data is automatically backed up on a computer at the physical location of the companies that provide that service.

Windows Live is a collection of services and Web applications that you can use to help you be more productive both personally and professionally. For example, you can use Windows Live to send and receive email, chat with friends via instant messaging, share photos, create a blog, and store and edit files. Windows Live is a free service that you sign up for. When you sign up, you receive a Windows Live ID, which you use to sign into your Windows Live account. **Table D–1** describes the services available on Windows Live.

TABLE D–1 Services available via Windows Live

SERVICE	DESCRIPTION
Email	Send and receive e-mail using a Hotmail account
Instant Messaging	Use Messenger to chat with friends, share photos, and play games
SkyDrive	Store files, work on files using Web Apps, and share files with people in your network
Photos	Upload and share photos with friends
People	Develop a network of friends and coworkers and use it to distribute information and stay in touch
Downloads	Access a variety of free programs available for download to a PC
Mobile Device	Access applications for a mobile device: text messaging, using Hotmail, networking, and sharing photos

SkyDrive is an online storage and file sharing service. With a Windows Live account, you receive access to your own SkyDrive, which is your personal storage area on the Internet. You upload files to your SkyDrive so you can share the files with other people, access the files from another computer, or use SkyDrive's additional storage. On your SkyDrive, you are given space to store up to 25 GB of data online. Each file can be a maximum size of 50 MB. You can also use your SkyDrive to share files with friends and coworkers. After you upload a file to your SkyDrive, you can choose to make the file visible to the public, to anyone you invite to share your files, or only to yourself. You can also use SkyDrive to access Office Web Apps. When you save files to SkyDrive on Windows Live, you are saving your files to an online location. SkyDrive is like having a personal hard drive "in the cloud."

Office Web Apps are versions of Microsoft Word, Excel, PowerPoint, and ***OneNote***, an electronic notebook program included with Microsoft Office, that you can access online from your SkyDrive. Office Web Apps offer basic functionality, allowing you to create and edit files created in Word, PowerPoint, and Excel online in your Web browser. An Office Web App does not include all of the features and functions included with the full Office version of its associated application. However, you can use the Office Web Apps from any computer that is connected to the Internet, even if Microsoft Office 2010 is not installed on that computer.

VOCABULARY

SkyDrive

Office Web Apps

OneNote

Obtaining a Windows Live ID

To save files to SkyDrive or to use Office Web Apps, you need a Windows Live ID. You obtain a Windows Live ID by going to the Windows Live Web site and creating a new account.

Note: If you already have a Windows Live ID, you can skip Step-by-Step D.1.

Step-by-Step D.1

1. Start Internet Explorer. Click in the Address bar, type **www.windowslive.com**, and then press **Enter**. The page where you can sign into Windows Live opens.
2. Click the **Sign up** button. The Create your Windows Live ID page opens.
3. Follow the instructions on the screen to create an ID with a new, live.com email address or create an ID using an existing email address.
4. After completing the process, if you signed up with an existing email address, open your email program or go to your Web-based email home page, and open the email message automatically sent to you from the Windows Live site. Click the link to open the Sign In page again, sign in with your user name and password if necessary, and then click the **OK** button in the page that appears telling you that your email address is verified.
5. Exit Internet Explorer.

WARNING

If the URL doesn't bring you to the page where you can sign into Windows Live, use a search engine to search for *Windows Live*.

Uploading Files to SkyDrive

You can access your SkyDrive from the Windows Live page in your browser after you signed in with your Windows Live ID, or from Word, Excel, PowerPoint, or OneNote. Then you can upload a file to a private or public folder on your SkyDrive.

Uploading a File to SkyDrive from Backstage View

If you are working in a file in Word, Excel, or PowerPoint, you can save the file to your SkyDrive from Backstage view. To do this, you click the File tab, click Save & Send in the navigation bar, and then click Save to Web. After you do this, the right pane changes to display a Sign In button that you can use to sign in to your Windows Live account. See **Figure D–1**.

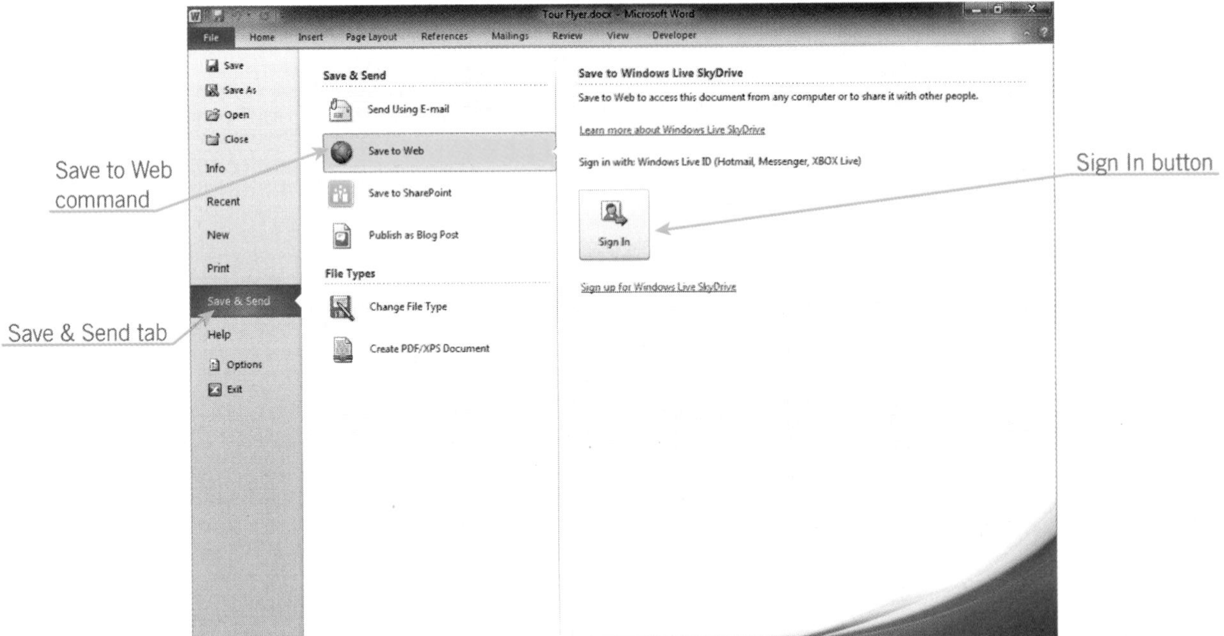

FIGURE D–1 Save & Send tab in Backstage view in Word after clicking Save to Web

Click the Sign In button to sign into Windows Live. After you enter your user name and password, the right pane in Backstage view changes to list the folders on your SkyDrive and a Save As button now appears in the right pane. See **Figure D–2**.

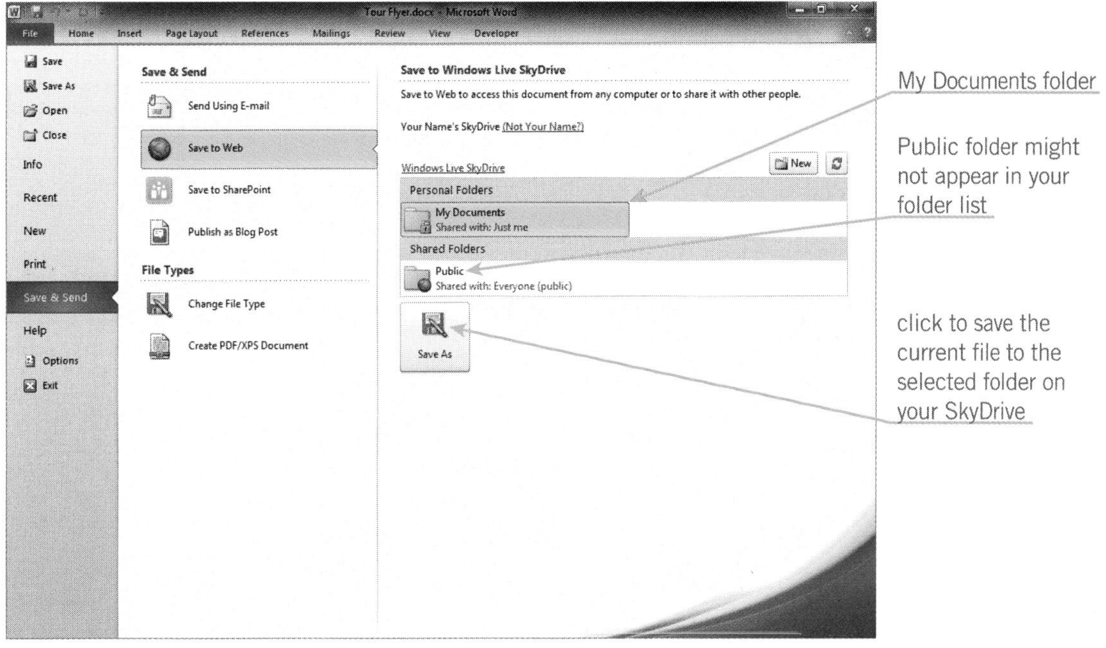

FIGURE D–2 Save & Send tab after connecting to Windows Live

To save the file, click the correct folder, and then click the Save As button.

Step-by-Step D.2

1. Start Word. Open the file named **Tour Flyer.docx** document from the drive and folder where your Data Files are stored.
2. Click the **File** tab, and then click **Save & Send** on the navigation bar. The Save & Send options appear in Backstage view as shown in Figure D–1.
3. Under Save & Send, click **Save to Web**.

4. Click the **Sign In** button. The Connecting to docs.live.net dialog box opens. See **Figure D–3**. If you are already signed into Windows Live, you will see the folders in your SkyDrive account listed instead of the Sign In button. Skip this step (Step 4) and Step 5.

FIGURE D–3
Connecting to docs.live.net dialog box

5. In the E-mail address box, type the email address associated with your Windows Live ID account. Press **Tab**, and then type the password associated with your Windows Live account in the Password box. Click the **OK** button. The dialog box closes, and another dialog box appears briefly while you connect to the Windows Live server. After you are connected, the folders on your SkyDrive appear in the right pane in Backstage view, as shown in Figure D–2.
6. In the right pane, click the **My Documents** folder, and then click the **Save As** button. Backstage view closes, and then after a few moments, the Save As dialog box opens. The path in the Address bar identifies the Public folder location on your SkyDrive.
7. Click the **Save** button. The dialog box closes and the Tour Flyer file is saved to the My Documents folder on your SkyDrive.
8. Exit Word.

Uploading a File to SkyDrive in a Browser

You can also add files to SkyDrive by starting from an Internet Explorer window. To do this, go to www.windowslive.com, and then log in to your Windows Live account. See **Figure D–4**.

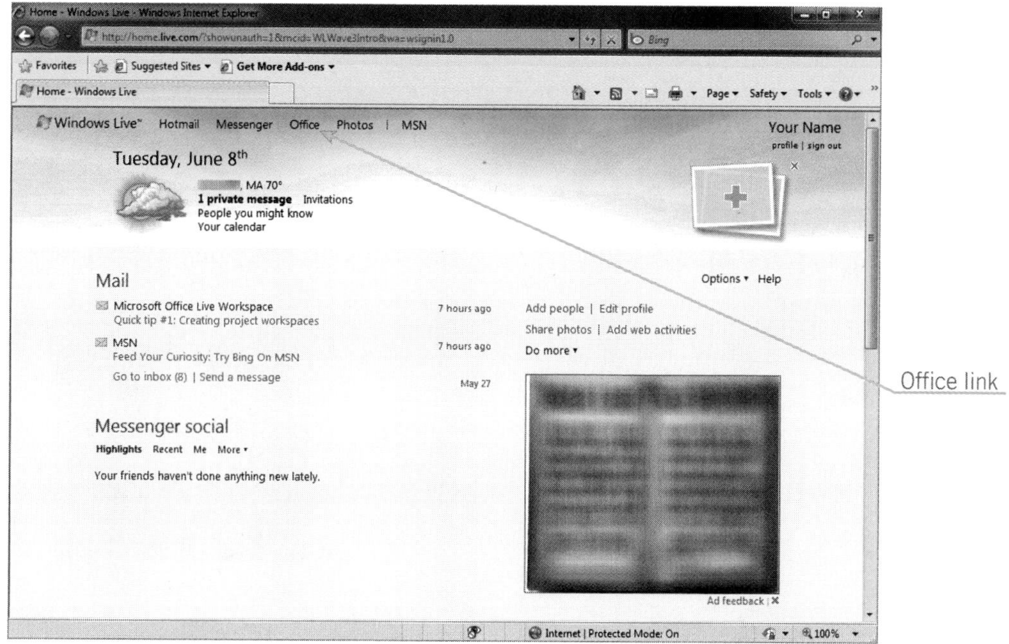

FIGURE D–4 Windows Live home page

To get to your SkyDrive, you click the Office link in the list of navigation links at the top of the window. To see all the folders on your SkyDrive, click View all in the Folders list on the left. See **Figure D–5**.

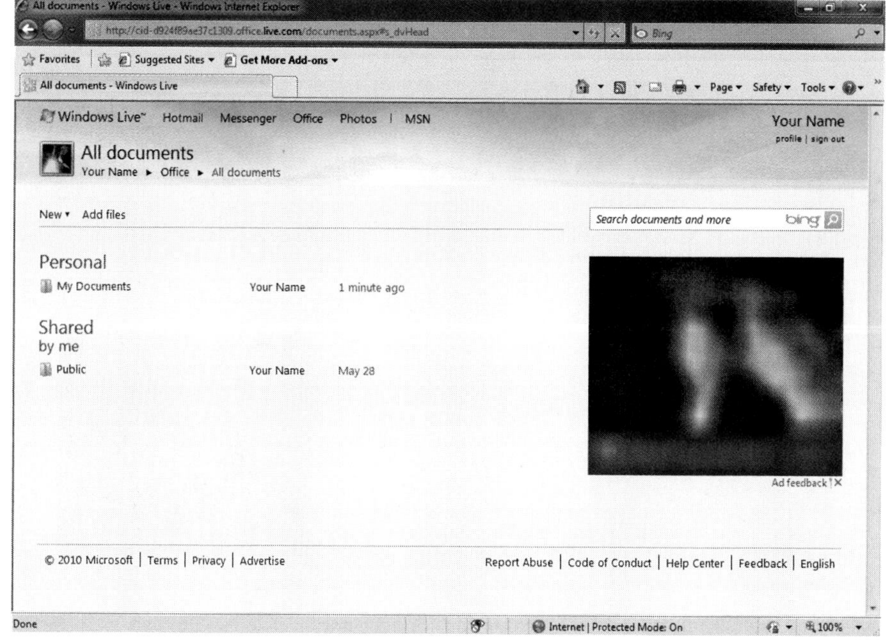

FIGURE D–5 Folders list on SkyDrive

Click the folder to which you want to add the file to open it. See **Figure D–6**.

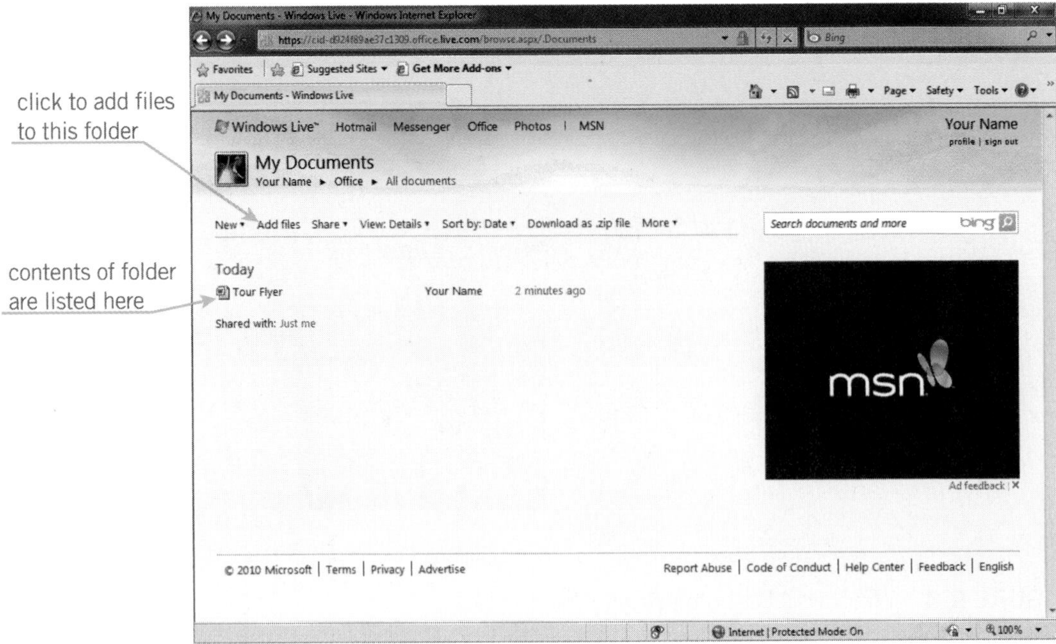

FIGURE D–6 My Documents folder page on SkyDrive

Click the Add files link to open the Add documents to *Folder Name* page; for example, if you click the Add files link in the My Documents folder, the Add documents to My Documents page appears. See **Figure D–7**.

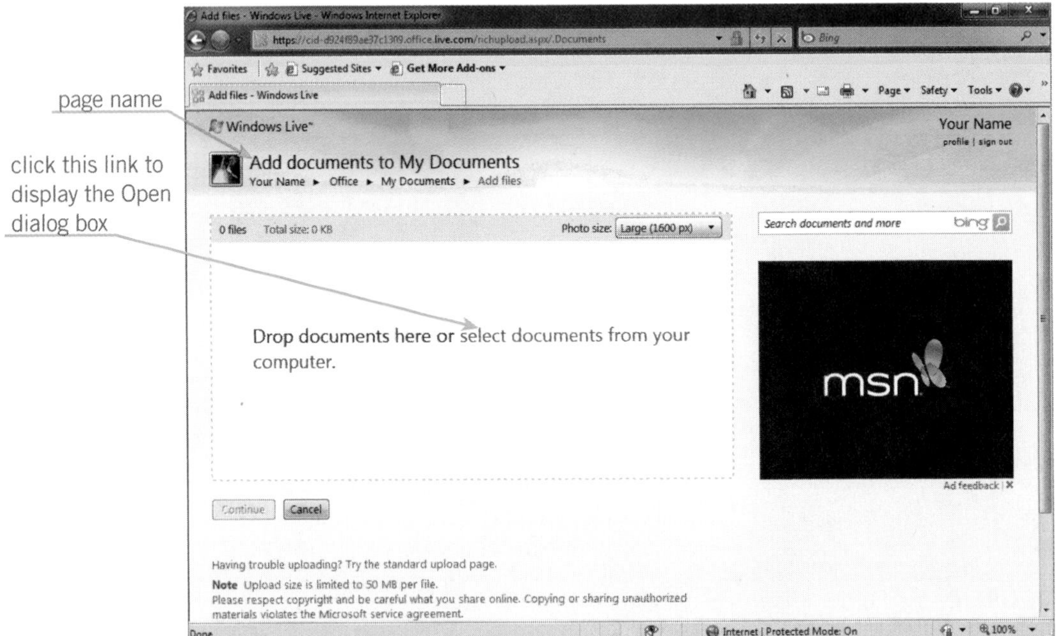

FIGURE D–7 Add documents to My Documents page on SkyDrive

Click the "select documents from your computer" link to display the Open dialog box. Locate the drive and folder where the file is stored, click it, and then click Open. The file uploads and is listed in the box. Click Continue to display the folder containing the files you uploaded to your SkyDrive.

Step-by-Step D.3

1. Start Internet Explorer. Click in the Address bar, type **www.windowslive.com**, and then press **Enter**.
2. If the Sign In page appears, type your Windows Live ID user name and password in the appropriate boxes, and then click **Sign in**. Your Windows Live home page appears similar to the one shown in Figure D–4.
3. In the list of command links at the top of the window, click **Office**. Your SkyDrive page appears.
4. In the list under Folders on the left, click **View all**. All the folders on your SkyDrive appear, similar to Figure D–5.
5. Click the **My Documents** folder. The My Documents page appears, similar to Figure D–6.
6. In the list of command links, click the **Add files** link. The Add documents to My Documents page appears, as shown in Figure D–7.
7. Click the **select documents from your computer** link, navigate to the drive and folder where your Data Files are stored, click **Tour Sales.pptx**, and then click the **Open** button. The file uploads and appears in the box on the Add documents to My Documents page.
8. At the bottom of the box, click the **select more documents from your computer** link. In the Open dialog box, click **Tour Data.xlsx**, and then click **Open**. The Excel file is listed in the box along with the PowerPoint file.
9. Below the box, click **Continue**. The My Documents folder page appears listing the files in that folder.
10. Keep the My Documents folder page displayed in Internet Explorer for the next Step-by-Step.

Using Office Web Apps

There are two ways to work with files using the Office Web Apps. You can view a file or you can edit it using its corresponding Office Web App. From your SkyDrive, you can also open the document directly in the full Office 2010 application if the application is installed on the computer you are using. You do not need to have Microsoft Office 2010 programs installed on the computer you use to access Office Web Apps.

Using a Web App in View Mode

To use a Web App in View mode, simply click its filename in the folder. This opens the file in View mode in the Web App. **Figure D–8** shows the Tour Flyer Word file open in the Word Web App in View mode.

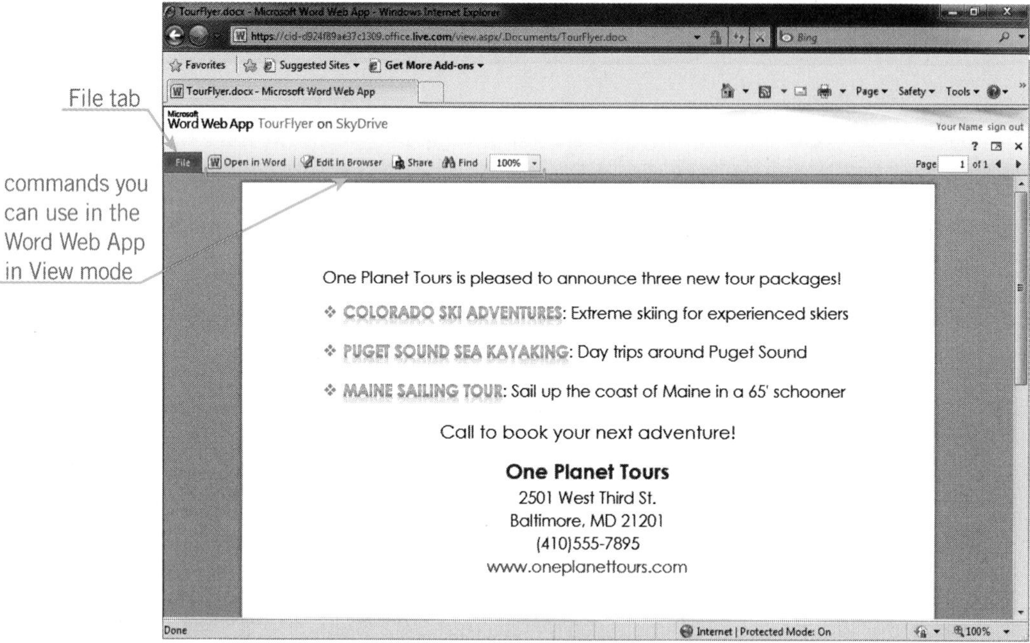

FIGURE D–8 Tour Flyer document open in View mode in Word Web App

Step-by-Step D.4

1. Click **Tour Flyer**. The Tour Flyer document opens in the Word Web App in View mode, as shown in Figure D–8.
2. Click anywhere in the document window, and then type any character. Nothing happens because you are allowed only to view the document in View mode.
3. Click the **File** tab. A list of commands opens. Note that you can print the document using the Print command on this menu.
4. Click **Close**. The document closes and the My Documents folder page appears again.
5. Leave the My Documents folder page open for the next Step-by-Step.

TIP

Position the mouse over a file icon to see the full filename and other details about the file.

Using a Web App in Edit Mode

You can also edit documents in the Office Web Apps. Although the interface for each Office Web App is similar to the interface of the full-featured program on your computer, a limited number of commands are available for editing documents using the Office Web App for each program. To edit a file in a Web App, point to the file in the folder page, and then click the Edit in browser link. You will see a Ribbon with a limited number of tabs and commands on the tabs. **Figure D–9** shows the file Tour Sales open in the PowerPoint Web App in Edit mode.

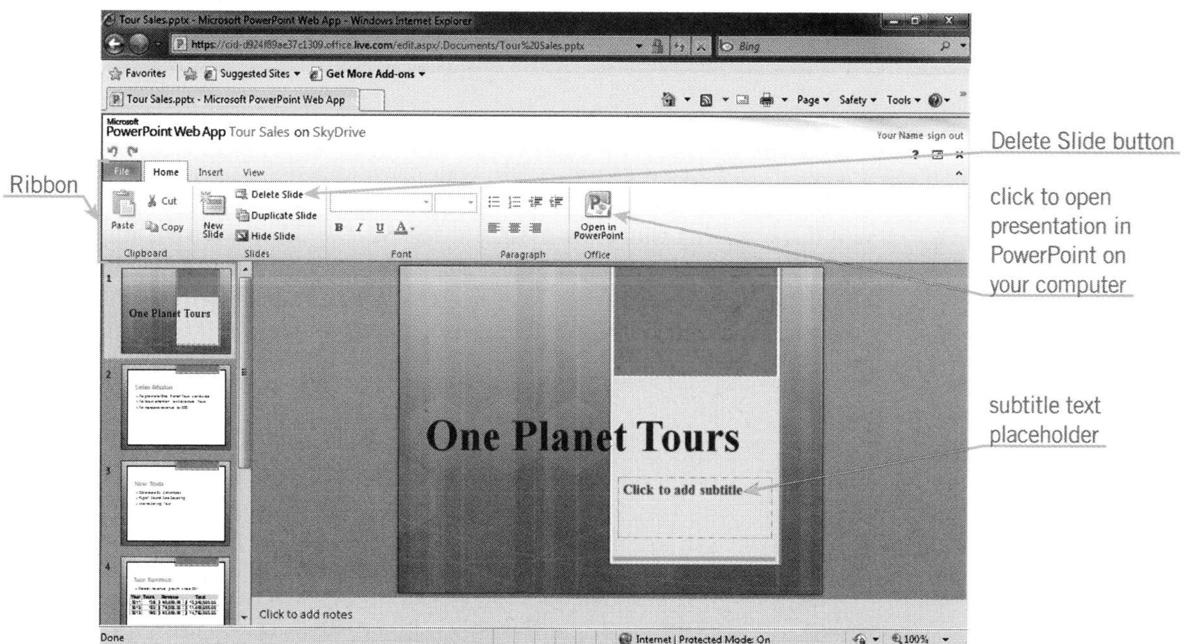

FIGURE D–9 Tour Sales presentation open in Edit mode in PowerPoint Web App

Step-by-Step D.5

TIP

To create a new file on SkyDrive using an Office Web App, open a folder, click the New link, and then select the appropriate Office Web App.

TIP

When you make changes to a file using a Web App, you do not need to save your changes before you close it because changes are saved automatically.

1. In the list of files in the My Documents folder, point to **Tour Sales**. A list of commands for working with the file appears.
2. In the list of commands, click the **Edit in browser** link. The Tour Sales presentation appears in the PowerPoint Web App in Edit mode, as shown in Figure D–9. In Edit mode, you see a version of the familiar Ribbon.
3. In the Slide pane, click in the subtitle text placeholder, and then type your name.
4. In the Slides tab, click **Slide 3** to display it in the Slide pane. The slide title is *New Tours.*
5. On the Home tab, in the Slides group, click the **Delete Slide** button. The *New Tours* slide is deleted from the presentation and the new Slide 3 (*Tour Revenue*) appears in the Slide pane. Now you will examine the other two tabs available to you in the PowerPoint Web App.
6. Click the **Insert** tab on the Ribbon. The only objects you can insert in a slide using the PowerPoint Web App in Edit mode are pictures and SmartArt. You can also create a hyperlink.
7. Click the View tab. Note that you cannot switch to Slide Master view in the PowerPoint Web App.
8. Leave the Tour Sales file open in the PowerPoint Web App for the next Step-by-Step.

Editing a File Stored on SkyDrive in the Program on Your Computer

If you are working with a file stored on your SkyDrive and you want to use a command that is available in the full-featured program on your computer but is not available in the Web App, you need to open the file in the full-featured program on your computer. You can do this from the corresponding Office Web App by clicking the Open in *Program Name* button on the Home tab on the Web App Ribbon.

Step-by-Step D.6

1. Click the **Home** tab. In the Office group, click the **Open in PowerPoint** button. The Open Document dialog box appears warning you that some files can harm your computer. This dialog box opens when you try to open a document stored on a Web site.
2. Click the **OK** button. PowerPoint starts on your computer and the revised version of the Tour Sales presentation opens on your computer. The presentation is in Protected view because it is not stored on the local computer you are using.
3. In the yellow Protected View bar, click the **Enable Editing** button. Now you can insert a footer on the slides.
4. Click the **Insert** tab, and then click the **Header & Footer** button in the Text group.
5. Click the **Footer** check box, type **2013 Sales Projections** in the Footer box, and then click the **Apply to All** button. When you use the full-featured version of a program, you do need to save the changes you made, even when it is stored in a folder on your SkyDrive.
6. On the Quick Access Toolbar, click the **Save** button. The modified file is saved to your SkyDrive.
7. In the PowerPoint window title bar, click the **Close** button. The PowerPoint program closes and you see your browser window listing the contents of the My Documents folder.
8. Click the **Tour Sales** file. Slide 1 of the Tour Sales file appears in the PowerPoint Web app in View mode.
9. At the bottom of the window, click the **Next Slide** button twice. Slide 3 (*Tour Revenue*) appears in the window. Remember that you deleted the original Slide 3, *New Tours*. Also note that the footer you added is on the slide.
10. Click the **File** tab, and then click **Close**. The PowerPoint Web App closes and the My Documents page appears.
11. Leave the My Documents page open for the next Step-by-Step.

WARNING

You can also open a document stored on your SkyDrive in the program stored on your computer from View mode in the corresponding Office Web App.

WARNING

If the Connecting to dialog box opens asking for your Windows Live ID credentials, type the email address associated with your Windows Live ID in the E-mail address box, type your password in the Password box, and then click the OK button.

Creating Folders on Your SkyDrive

You can keep your SkyDrive organized by using file management techniques, similar to the way you organize files on your computer's hard drive. You can create a folder in your SkyDrive in the Internet Explorer window or from Backstage view in the program on your computer.

To create a folder on your SkyDrive in Internet Explorer, click the New link in the list of commands, and then click Folder to open the Create a new folder page on your SkyDrive. See **Figure D–10**.

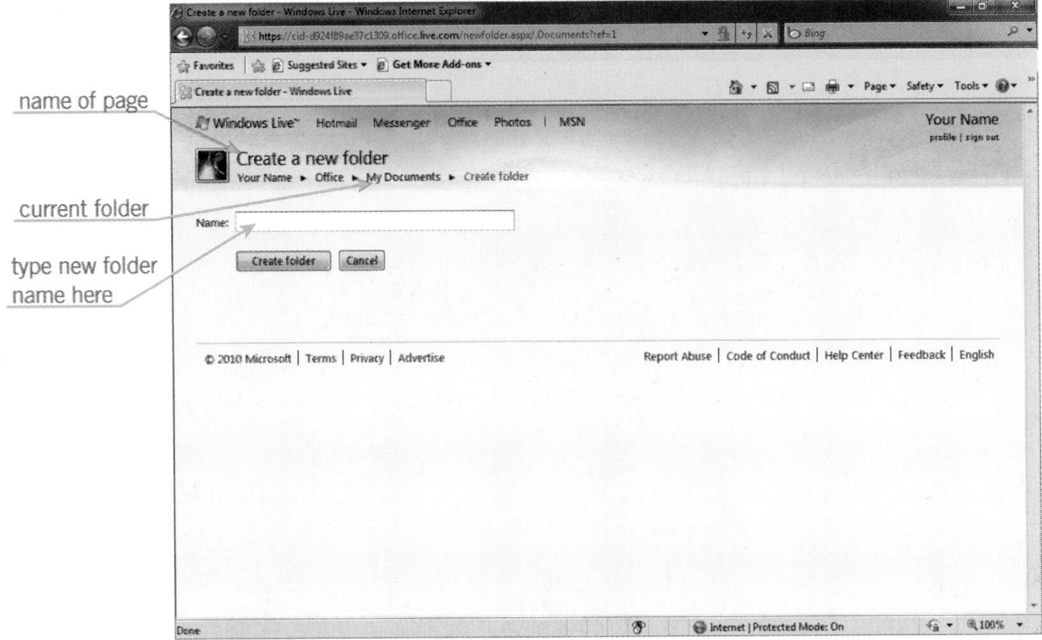

FIGURE D–10 Create a new folder page on SkyDrive

To create a new folder on your SkyDrive from the Save & Send tab in Backstage view in an application, click the New button in the upper-right. This opens the same Create a new folder page shown in Figure D–10.

Type the name for the new folder in the Name box, and then click Next. The Add files to *Folder Name* page that you saw earlier appears. If you want to upload a file to the new folder, you can do so at this point. If you don't, you can click the link for the new folder or click the SkyDrive link to return to your SkyDrive home page.

Step-by-Step D.7

1. In the list of command links, click the **New** link, and then click **Folder**. The Create a new folder page appears with the insertion point in the Name box.
2. In the Name box, type **Sales**, and then click **Create folder**. The new empty folder is displayed in the browser window. You can see that you are looking at the contents of the new folder by looking at the navigation links. See **Figure D–11**.

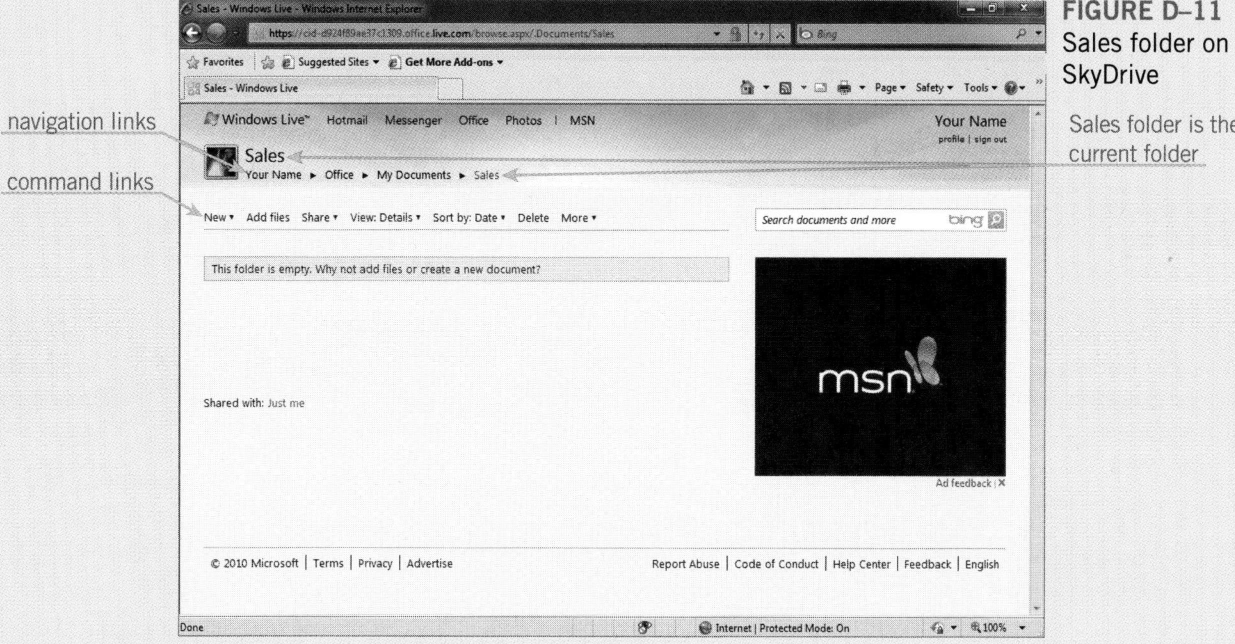

FIGURE D–11
Sales folder on SkyDrive

3. Leave the Sales folder page open for the next Step-by-Step.

Organizing Files on Your SkyDrive

As on your hard drive, you can move and delete files on your SkyDrive. To move or delete a file, first display the commands for working with the file by pointing to its name in the file list in the folder. To move a file, click the More link, and then click Move to open the "Where would you like to move *File Name*?" page. See **Figure D–12**.

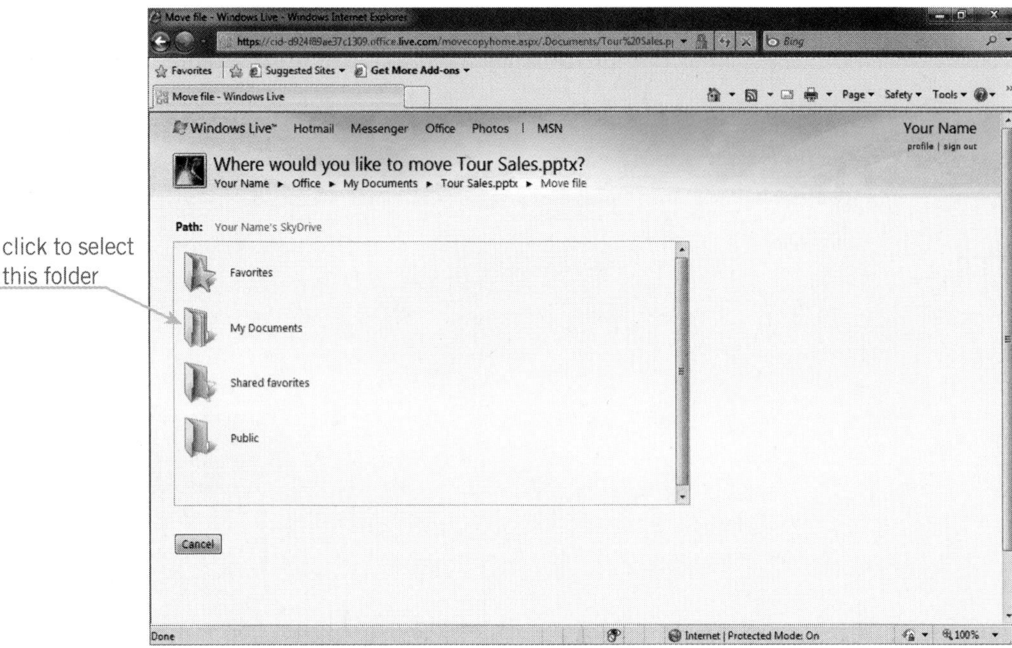

FIGURE D–12 Folder list that appears when moving a file

In the list of folders, click a folder. Then, at the top of the list, click the "Move this file into *Folder Name*" command. The folder into which you moved the file appears, along with a message telling you that the file was moved.

To delete a file, point to it to display the commands for working with the file, and then click the Delete button in the list of command links.

Step-by-Step D.8

1. In the list of navigation links, click the **My Documents** link. Point to **Tour Sales**. The commands for working with this file appear.
2. In the list of command links, click the **More** link, and then click **Move**. The "Where would you like to move Tour Sales.pptx?" page appears, and a list of folders on your SkyDrive appears.
3. In the list of folders, click the **My Documents** folder to display the list of folders located inside that folder. Click the **Sales** folder. The contents of the Sales folder appear in the list of folders. Because this folder does not contain any additional folders, you see only a command to create a New folder and the command to move the file.
4. In the list of folders, click **Move this file into Sales**. After a moment, the contents of the Sales folder appear, along with a message telling you that you have moved the Tour Sales file from the My Documents folder.
5. In the list of navigation links, click the **My Documents** link. The contents of the My Documents folder appear.
6. Point to **Tour Flyer**. In the list of command links, click the **Delete** button. A dialog box opens warning you that you are about to permanently delete the file.
7. Click **OK**. The dialog box closes, the file is deleted from the My Documents folder on your SkyDrive.
8. Leave the My Documents folder page open for the next Step-by-Step.

WARNING

Depending on the resolution of your computer, you might not need to click the More link to access the Move command.

Giving Permission for Access to a Folder on Your SkyDrive

If you upload a file to a private folder, you can grant permission to access the file to anyone else with a Windows Live ID. You can grant permission to folders located at the same level as the My Documents folder. You cannot grant permission to individual files or to folders located inside a locked folder. If you grant permission to someone to access a folder, that person will have access to all the files in that folder.

To grant permission to someone, click the folder to display its contents, click the Share link in the list of navigation links, and then click Edit permissions. The Edit permissions for *Folder Name* page appears. You can use the slider bar to make the contents of the new folder public by sharing it with everyone, your friends as listed on your Windows Live ID account and their friends, just your friends, or only some friends. You can also share it only with specific people that you list in the box in the Add Specific People section. When you type someone's name or email address associated with the person's Windows Live ID account in the box in the Add specific people section, and then press Enter, the person's name appears in a box below with a check box next to the name or email address. The box to the right of the person's name or email address indicates that the person can view files in the shared folder. You can then click the arrow to change this so that the person can view, edit, or delete files. See **Figure D–13**. Click Save at the bottom of the window to save the permissions you set.

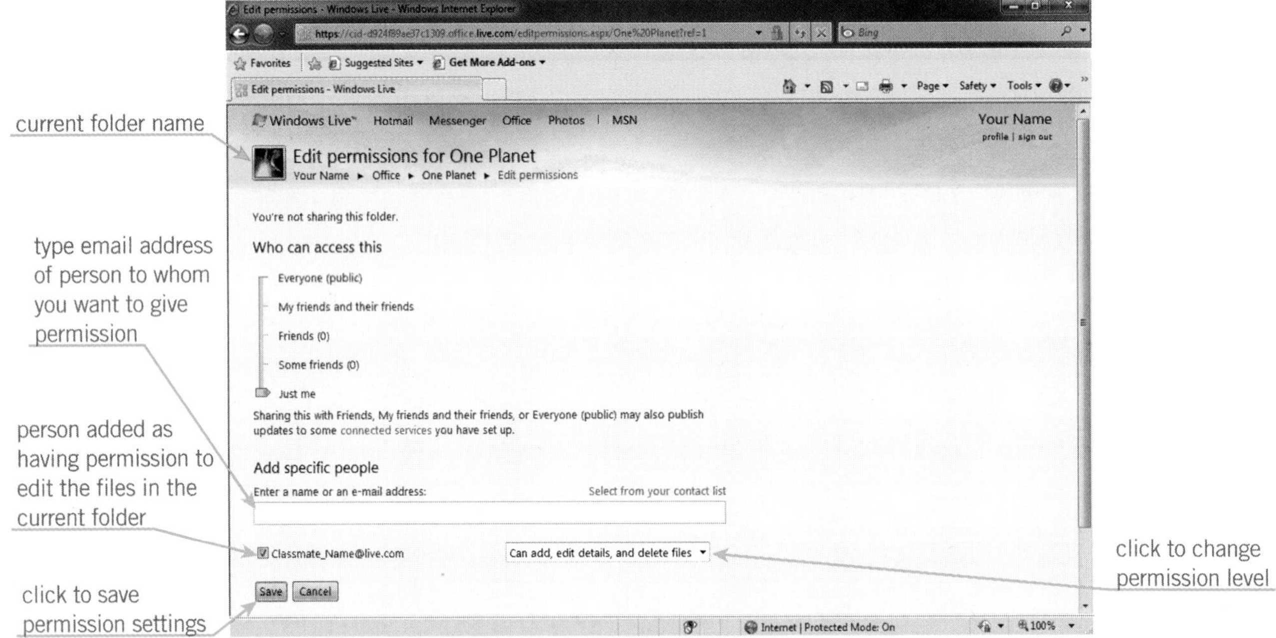

FIGURE D–13 Edit permissions for One Planet page on SkyDrive

To complete the next Step-by-Step, you need to work with a partner who also has a Windows Live ID account.

Step-by-Step D.9

1. In the list of navigation links, click the **Office** link, and then in the list of links on the left, click **View all**. The All documents page appears.
2. In the list of command links, click the **New** link, and the click **Folder**. The Create a folder page appears with a temporary folder name in the Name box. The temporary name is selected, so you can just type the new name.
3. In the Name box, type **One Planet**. Click **Next**. The One Planet folder page appears.
4. In the list of navigation links, click the **Office** link. In the list of folders on the left, click the **My Documents** link. The My Documents folder page appears.
5. In the file list, point to **Tour Data**, click the **More** link, and then click **Move**. The Where would you like to move Tour Data.xlsx? page appears.
6. In the list of folders, click **One Planet**. In the new list that appears, click the **Move this file into One Planet**. The One Planet page appears with the Tour Data file listed.
7. In the list of command links, click the **Share** link. Click **Edit permissions**. The Edit permissions for One Planet page appears.
8. Under Add specific people, click in the **Enter a name or an e-mail address** box, type the email address of your partner, and then press **Enter**. The email address you typed appears below the box. A check box next to the email address is selected, and a list box to the right identifies the level of access for this person. The default is Can add, edit details, and delete files, similar to Figure D–13. You want your partner to be able to edit the file, so you don't need to change this.
9. At the bottom of the window, click **Save**. The Send a notification for One Planet page appears. You can send a notification to each individual when you grant permission to access your files. This is a good idea so that each person will have the URL of your folder. Your partner's email address appears in the To box.

TIP

Because you are creating a folder at the same level as the My Documents folder, there is a Share with box below the Name box. You can set the permissions when you create the folder if you want.

TIP

To make the contents of the folder available to anyone, drag the slider up to the top so it is next to the Everyone (public).

> **WARNING**
>
> If you do not receive a message from Windows Live, make sure you are checking the email account associated with your Windows Live ID. If you created a new live.com or hotmail.com email address when you signed up with Windows Live, you need to use Hotmail to see the email message sent to you.

10. Click in the Include your own message box, type **You can now access the contents of the One Planet folder on my SkyDrive.**, and then click **Send**. Your partner will receive an email message from you advising him or her that you have shared your One Planet folder. If your partner is completing the steps at the same time, you will receive an email message from your partner.
11. Check your email for a message from your partner advising you that your partner has shared his or her Sales folder with you. The subject of the email message will be "*Your Partner's Name* has shared documents with you."
12. If you have received the email, click the **View folder** button in the email message, and then sign in to Windows Live if you are requested to do so. You are now able to access your partner's One Planet folder on his or her SkyDrive. See **Figure D–14**.

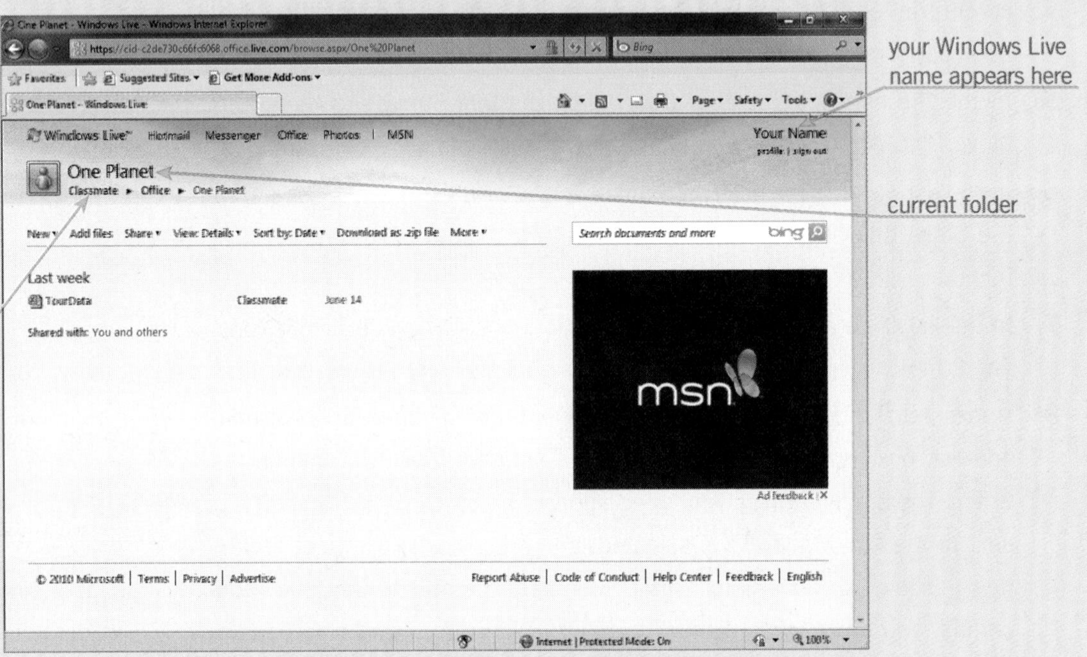

FIGURE D–14
One Planet folder on someone else's SkyDrive

13. Leave Internet Explorer open for the next Step-by-Step.

Co-Authoring with the Excel Web App

When you work with the Excel Web App, you can use its ***co-authoring*** feature to simultaneously edit an Excel workbook at the same time as a colleague. When you co-author a workbook, a list of the people currently co-authoring the workbook appears at the bottom of the window. Co-authoring is not available in the Word or PowerPoint Web Apps. When you open a file in the Excel Web App, a notification appears at the right end of the status bar notifying you that two people are editing the document. See **Figure D–15**. You can click this to see the email addresses of the people currently editing the workbook.

VOCABULARY
co-author

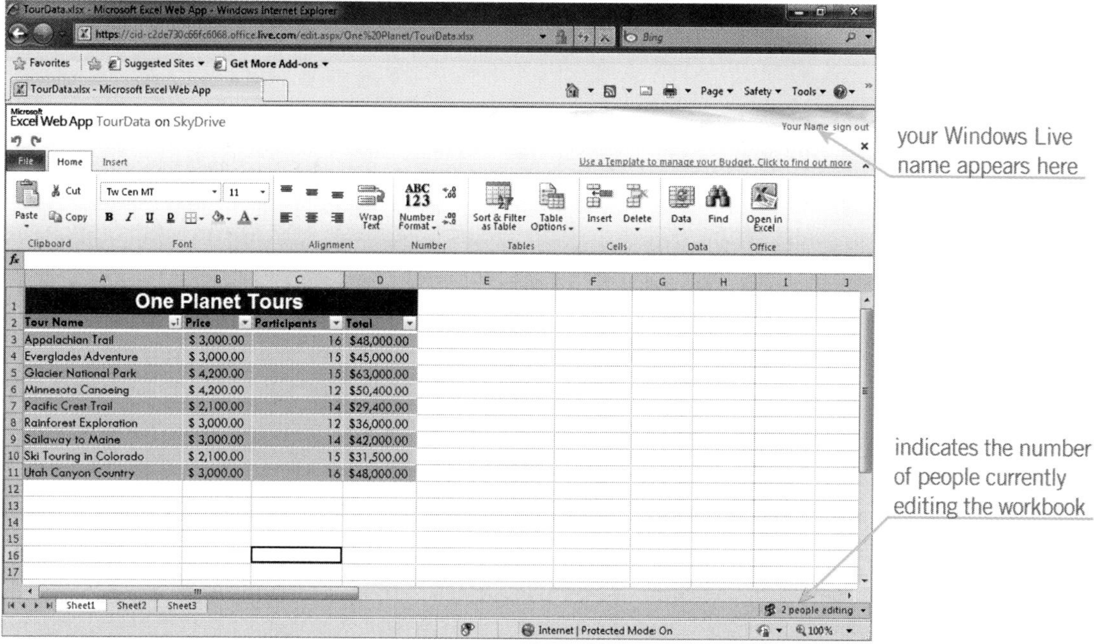

FIGURE D–15 Tour Data file open in Edit mode in Excel Web App with two people editing

To complete this next Step-by-Step, you need to continue working with the partner who has permission to access the One Planet folder on your SkyDrive and who gave you permission to access his or her One Planet folder.

Step-by-Step D.10

1. Decide with your partner whether you will modify the Tour Data file stored on your SkyDrive or on his or her SkyDrive. After you decide the SkyDrive account with which you are going to work, both of you display the contents of that One Planet folder.
2. Point to **Tour Data**, and then in the list of command links, click the **Edit in browser** link.
3. In the status bar, click the **2 people editing** button. A list pops up identifying you and your partner as the two people editing the document.

   Decide with your partner which one of you will execute Step 4. The other person will then execute Step 5.
4. Either you or your partner click cell **A12**, type **Gulf Islands Sailing**, press **Tab**, type **3000**, press **Tab**, type **10**, and then press **Tab**. The formula in the other cells in column D is copied automatically to cell D12 because the data in the original Excel file was created and formatted as an Excel table. Both you and your partner see the data entered in row 12.

   If you entered the data in row 12, you partner should execute Step 5; if your partner entered the data in row 12, you should execute Step 5.
5. Either you or your partner—the person who did not execute Step 4—click cell **B12**, type **3700**, and then press **Tab**. The data entered is reformatted in the Accounting number format, and the total in cell D12 is recalculated. Again, both you and your partner see the change executed.

   Both you and your partner should execute the rest of the steps in this section.
6. Click the **File** tab, and then click **Close**. The changes you made to the Excel workbook are saved automatically on the current SkyDrive account. You are finished working with the Office Web Apps, so you can sign out of Windows Live.

7. In the upper-right of the SkyDrive window, click the **sign out** link. You are signed out of Windows Live.
8. In the title bar of your Web browser window, click the **Close** button [X] to exit your Web browser.

OneNote Web App

The other Office Web App is OneNote. As with Word, Excel, and PowerPoint files, you can share OneNote files on SkyDrive directly from OneNote. Note that you need to click the Share tab in the navigation bar in Backstage view, and then click Web and specify Windows Live as the Web location. After you upload a OneNote file to SkyDrive, you can work with it in its corresponding Web App.

GLOSSARY

3-D reference A reference to the same cell or range in multiple worksheets that you use in a formula.

A

absolute cell reference A cell reference that does not change when copied or moved to a new cell.

action button An interactive button that performs instructions such as going to a specific slide or other object that you can create by drawing from the Shapes gallery.

action query An action query makes changes to the records in a table.

active cell The cell in the worksheet in which you can type data.

active worksheet The worksheet that is displayed in the work area.

adjacent range A range where all cells touch each other and form a rectangle.

adjustment handle A yellow diamond-shaped handle that appears on a selected object. Drag the handle to change the appearance of the object.

agenda slide A slide that provides an outline of topics for a presentation.

Align To arrange objects to line up with the other objects on a slide or place an object relative to other objects on a slide to specify how the contents of a cell are lined up horizontally and vertically within the cell. Align commands include: Left, Center, Right, Top, Middle, and Bottom.

alignment The position of text between the margins.

alphanumeric data Data that contains numbers, text, or a combination of numbers and text.

alternate calendar A second calendar that displays in the same view as the standard Outlook calendar.

and operator An operator used in a query that selects records that match all of two or more conditions in a query.

animation Adds motion to an object.

append Append means to add.

argument The value the function uses to perform a calculation, including a number, text, or a cell reference that acts as an operand; the additional information that Access needs based on the chosen action.

Ascending sort To arrange data with letters in alphabetical order (A to Z), data with numbers from lowest to highest, and data with dates from earliest to latest.

aspect ratio The ratio between the width and height of an graphic.

aspect ratio The relationship of an object's height to its width.

attribute A formatting feature that affects how a font looks, such as a style, the color, or an effect.

audit Check for accuracy.

AutoComplete A feature in Word that guesses names of calendar items, such as the days of the week and months, as you type them, and then suggests the complete word.

AutoCorrect A feature in Word that corrects errors as you type.

AutoExec macro An AutoExec macro allows you to have one or more actions automatically execute when the database is opened.

AutoFilter A menu that opens when you click the arrow on the right side of a field selector in a datasheet. The menu contains options for sorting data and for applying and clearing filters.

AutoFit An automatic determination of the best width for a column or the best height for a row, based on its contents.

AutoFormat As You Type A feature in Word that applies built-in formats as you type.

automatic grammar checking A feature in Word that checks your document for grammatical errors as you type, and flags them with a green, wavy underline.

automatic page break A page break Excel inserts whenever it runs out of room on a page.

automatic spell checking A feature in Word that checks your document for spelling errors as you type, and flags them with a red or blue wavy underline.

AutoNumber A data type that automatically adds a unique field value to each record in a table.

axis A horizontal or vertical line that establishes the relationship between data in a chart.

axis title A chart label that clarifies what is being measured, such as dollars, number of units, or time spans.

B

background The area behind the text and graphics on a slide.

backup A backup is a duplicate copy of your database created by using the Back Up Database option when you save the file.

banded columns When you create a table, the columns can appear with different formats. Typically, one column will have a lighter format and the adjacent column will have a darker format. This type of formatting is referred to as banding.

banded rows When you create a table, the rows can appear with different formats. Typically, one row will have a lighter format and the adjacent row will have a darker format. This type of formatting is referred to as banding.

best fit The term used when a column in a datasheet is resized to the best width for the data contained in the column.

bibliography A list of source materials that are used in the preparation of a work. (See also *works cited page*)

bitmap A file format that consists of rows of tiny colored dots called pixels that compose an image on a computer screen.

bits Tiny colored dots that compose an image on a computer screen. (See also *pixels*)

blank database template A template that creates a database that contains only an empty table.

blank presentation A new presentation that does not have theme elements, text, or objects.

boilerplate text Standard text that is reusable in documents, such as contracts and correspondence.

bookmark An item or a location in a document that you identify and name for future reference so you can jump quickly to a specific location within the same document.

border A line around the edges of a cell.

bound control A control in a form or report that is connected to a field in the record source and is used to display, enter, and update data.

branch A split in an Outlook mail conversation.

broadcast Placing a link to a presentation on the Web to allow others to watch your presentation as you give it from a remote location through a Web browser.

building block Document parts that you can store in Word and reuse.

bullet A small graphic symbol used to identify items in a list. Text in the content placeholder on a slide is usually preceded by a round or square bullet.

button Called a control because it controls the macro actions that are assigned to it.

C

calculated control A calculated control can be used to perform calculations on the values in other fields.

calculated field A field in a query, form, or report that displays a value that is calculated using a combination of operators, constants, and the values in other fields.

callout A special type of label in a drawing that consists of a text box with an attached line to point to something in the drawing.

caption A label that identifies or describes an illustration, a table, or a picture.

case-sensitive Refers to uppercase and lowercase characters in a password. Passwords must be entered in the same uppercase and lowercase letters in which they were created.

case sensitive When entering a password to open a file, the upper and lower-casing of the letters must be identical to the casing of the letters in the assigned password.

case-sensitive When entering a password, the upper- and lowercasing of the letters must be identical to the casing of the letters in the assigned password.

category axis The identifying labels listed on the horizontal axis in a chart.

cell The intersection of a column and a row in a table or worksheet.

cell reference A unique identifier for a cell that is formed by combining the cell's column letter and row number.

cell style A collection of formatting characteristics you apply to a cell or range of data.

center To position text so that it is centered between the left and right margins.

chain A series of links that let the story flow from one text box to the next, enabling you to continue a story elsewhere in the document.

chart A visual representation of numerical data; can be in the form of lines, bars, wedges in pies, or other graphics. Also called *a graph.*

chart area The entire chart and all other chart elements.

chart floor The foundation, or base, of a 3-D chart.

chart layout An arrangement that specifies which elements are included in a chart and where they are placed.

chart sheet A separate sheet in the workbook that stores a chart.

chart style Formatting applied to a chart based on the colors, fonts, and effects associated with the workbook's theme.

chart template A chart that you create and add unique formats and settings to, then you save the chart as a template. Chart templates are saved in the same default location as the preformatted chart templates.

child In a PivotTable, when there is more than one level, the main row heading is referred to as the parent and the level of detail below this level is the child.

citation A reference in a document that credits the source of information or other content, such as a picture or a chart, or references specific legal causes or statutes.

clear To remove all the formatting applied to a cell or range of cells.

clip art Graphics stored in the Clip Organizer or available online that you can insert in any presentation; the term clip art refers not only to drawn images, but also to photographs, movie clips, and sound files.

Clipboard A temporary storage place in the computer's memory, available to all the programs, which can hold only one selection at a time; to place items on the Clipboard, you use the Cut or Copy command. An item on the Clipboard can be pasted into the file. Also called *system Clipboard.*

code Macro actions formatted in easy-to-read sentences, just like text in a book; a set of instructions and data for a computer program.

color palette A coordinated set of colors available for use in a document.

color scheme A set of 12 coordinated colors associated with a built-in theme.

column Appears vertically in the worksheet; identified by letters at the top of the worksheet window.

column chart A chart that uses bars of varying heights to illustrate values in a worksheet.

column heading The column letter.

combination chart A chart that shows data on two y-axes for the purpose of showing different data in the same chart.

combo box A combo box displays a list of values and lets you select one from a list.

comma-separated values (CSV) A file format in which commas separate the field values of each record in the data source and paragraph marks separate individual records.

command button A command button is a button that users can click to perform common tasks, such as moving to the next record in a form or adding a record.

comment An annotation that is added within a document or presentation by the author or reviewer; explanatory text that you can add to a macro that does not affect the way the macro is executed; a note attached to a cell that explains or identifies information contained in the cell.

common field A field that appears in two or more tables in a database and that has the same data type and field values. A common field (also called a matching field) is used to relate tables and usually has the same field name in the related tables.

compacting A process that rearranges the way a database is stored on disk and optimizes the performance of the database.

concatenate A function that combines the text from two or more cells into one cell.

condition In a query, a condition (also called a criterion) specifies which data to display in the query results.

conditional formatting Formatting that changes the look of cells that meet a specified condition; allows you to add formatting features to the data based on criteria you specify.

consolidating Bringing data from several worksheets together into one worksheet.

contact group A grouping of contacts under one name.

content control A special placeholder designed to contain a specific type of text, such as a date or the page number.

contextual spell checking A feature in Word that checks your document for words that are spelled correctly, but that might be misused, and flags them with a blue, wavy underline.

control An object in a form or report, such as a label or text box, that displays data from the record source on which the form or report is based.

control layout A "container" that groups together the controls in a form or report so that you can change the formatting of and move these controls as a group.

conversation A chain of messages from the first message through all responses.

copy To place a copy of selected text on the Clipboard or the Office Clipboard; to duplicate a cell's contents without affecting the original cell.

criteria A term indicating that a query contains two or more conditions.

criterion Criterion refers to the specific information you are searching for.

crop To remove a portion of a graphic or adding white space around a graphic; to remove part of a picture.

cross-reference A reference from one part of a document to related material in another part of the document; an index reference; in an index, a cross-reference refers the reader to another index entry.

custom AutoFilter A feature that lets you display only cells that meet specific criteria.

custom show A feature that allows you to create presentations for different audiences by selecting specific slides from a presentation.

cut To remove selected text and place it on the Clipboard or the Office Clipboard; to move cell contents from the original location and place in a new location.

D

data label Text or numbers that provide additional information about a value or data marker in a data series.

data marker A symbol (such as a bar, line, dot, or slice) that represents a single data point or value from the corresponding worksheet cell.

data point The actual point in the chart that corresponds with the data in the worksheet.

data series A group of related information in a column or row of a worksheet that is plotted on the chart.

data source The file used in a mail merge that contains the information that varies in each document; the chart data stored in a range of cells in the worksheet; when used with a form letter, the term given to the file that contains the records to insert in the form letter. The data source might be a Word document, an Excel workbook, or an Access database.

data table A grid that displays the data plotted in the chart.

data type The property of a field that determines the type of data that you can enter into the field, such as numbers or text.

data validation A feature to ensure that the data is entered as accurately as possible.

database A collection of objects that work together to store, retrieve, display, and summarize data and also to automate tasks.

Database Documenter A feature in Access that is used to create a report that documents each selected object in a database.

database management system (DBMS) A program that you use to store, retrieve, analyze, and print information.

datasheet A worksheet that appears with a chart on the slide and contains the numbers for the chart; displays the data for a table or query in rows and columns, with records in rows and fields in columns.

datasheet selector The box in the upper-left corner of a datasheet that, when clicked, selects all fields and records in the datasheet.

datasheet tool An Access tool that creates a form that looks like a datasheet.

datasheet view The view of a database table that displays data in rows and columns.

date and time functions Functions that convert serial numbers to a month, a day, or a year, or that insert the current date or the current date and time.

Default Value property A field property that lets you specify the value to enter into that field for each record in a table.

delimited Data that is separated by a tab, semicolon, comma, or space.

delimiter A character, such as a comma, space, or a tab, used to separate data.

dependent The cell with a function that depends on other cells for the function results.

Descending sort To arrange data with letters from Z to A, data with numbers from highest to lowest, and data with dates from oldest to newest.

description property An optional field property that you can use to describe the data to store in the field.

design grid The top half of the Table window in Design view that displays the name, data type, and optional Description property for each field in a table.

Design view (table) The view of a table that lets you add, delete, and rearrange fields. You can also use Design view to make changes to the way that fields store data.

Destination The location where data will appear.

destination file The file to which you are transferring data when you move data between applications. See also *source file*.

Destination range The location in the worksheet where the result of a function will be placed.

detail query A query that shows every field in each record in the query results.

detail section The section in Design view for a form or report that contains the detail records from the record source.

diagram A visual representation of data to help readers better understand relationships among data.

digital signature An attachment to a file or e-mail message certifying that the information in the file is authentic and safe.

disable To make inactive, such as tracking changes.

distribution group See *contact group*.

Document Inspector A feature that enables you to check for hidden metadata or personal information in a presentation.

document properties Information about the presentation file including title, author, and keywords.

document template Template type containing document settings, content, and styles that are available only to documents based on that template.

document workspace site A central location for storing and sharing files.

draft view A way of viewing a document on screen that shows only the text of a document; you don't see headers and footers, margins, columns, or graphics.

drag To select text by positioning the I-beam pointer to the left of the first character of the text you want to select, holding down the left button on the mouse, dragging the pointer to the end of the text you want to select, and then releasing the button.

drag-and-drop To drag selected text from one place in a document to another.

drop cap A letter or word at the beginning of a paragraph that is larger than the rest of the text and used to draw attention to the content.

E

Effects options The Entrance, Exit, Emphasis, and Motion Path animation features such as pinwheel, diamond, and fly effects that you can use to animate objects.

electronic business card A file that provides contact information in a business card format.

embed To place an object that was created in another application such as Microsoft Word or Excel in a slide. When you select the object, the original program will open for editing.

embedded chart A chart is inserted in the center of the worksheet.

embedded macro An embedded macro is a macro that performs an action within an object, such as a macro that opens a form when you are already viewing another form.

embedded object An object that becomes part of the destination file; an embedded object can be edited in the destination file.

enable To make active, such as tracking changes.

encrypt When the information in the file is scrambled into illegible data.

encryption A standard method for encoding data.

endnote A note placed along with other notes at the end of a document to provide additional information to a document or cite the source of content.

exact match condition A condition in a query that specifies the exact condition that a record must satisfy to be displayed in the query results.

exploded pie chart A pie chart with one or more slices pulled away from the pie to distinguish them.

export To send information from one application to another application.

export A term used when data is saved into a different file format.

expression An arithmetic formula that performs a calculation.

Expression Builder The Expression Builder is where you type, or build, an expression.

F

field One or more characters that create a piece of information, such as a first name, a last name, or a telephone number.

Field List pane A pane in Design view for a form or report that displays the tables and other objects in the database and the fields they contain.

field name A label identifying a field in a data source.

Field Properties pane The bottom half of the Table window in Design view that displays properties for the selected field in a table.

field property An additional description of a field beyond the field's data type that specifies how to store data in the field, such as the number of characters the field can store.

field selector The top of a column in a datasheet that contains the field name. Clicking a field selector selects the column.

Field Size property The property that identifies the number of characters that a Text, a Number, or an AutoNumber field can store.

field value The specific data stored in a field for a record.

fill The background color of a cell.

fill handle The black square in the lower-right corner of the active cell or range that you drag over the cells you want to fill.

filling Copying a cell's contents and/or formatting into an adjacent cell or range.

filter A temporary rearrangement of the records in a table, query, form, or report based on one or more specified conditions.

filter A tool to screen records by identifying criteria that must be met before the records are included in a merge.

filter arrow An arrow that appears in a column heading cell that opens the AutoFilter menu.

Filter By Form A filter that you can apply to a datasheet or form that rearranges the records based on one or more field values that you select from a list.

Filter By Selection A filter that you can apply to a datasheet or form that rearranges the records based on a selected field value or part of a field value.

financial functions Functions that are used to analyze loans and investments.

find An Access command that lets you specify how to locate data in an object.

first-line indent A description of the indent in a paragraph when only the first line of text in the paragraph is indented.

fixed width Data that is separated at the same place in each cell, such as after 15 characters.

floating object An object in a document that acts as if it were sitting in a separate layer on the page and can be repositioned anywhere on the page.

font The design of text.

font effect See *text effect*.

font size The height of characters in points.

font style A formatting feature you can apply to a font to change its appearance; common font styles are bold, italic, and underlining.

footer Text that is printed at the bottom of each page.

footnote A note that appears at the bottom of the same page where it is referenced to provide additional information to a document or cite the source of content.

foreign key When two tables in a database are related, the common field in the related table is called a foreign key.

form A database object that displays data from one or more tables or queries in a format that has a similar appearance to a paper form.

Form Footer section The section in Design view for a form that contains the information that is displayed at the bottom of the form.

Form Header section The section in Design view for a form that contains the information that is displayed at the top of the form.

form letter A document that contains merge fields that indicate where to insert data from a data source, such as an Access database or an Excel workbook.

form tool An Access tool that creates a simple form that includes all the fields in the selected table or query.

form view A view of a form that displays the data in the record source in a form.

Form Wizard An Access wizard that creates a form based on a record source and using options that the user specifies to select the form's record source and layout.

format To change the appearance or look of text.

Format Painter A feature that copies format attributes such as colors, borders, and fill effects from an object, text, or cell to apply the same formatting to another object, text, or cell.

format property A property for a field that specifies how to display numbers, dates, times, and text.

formula An equation that calculates a value based on values currently entered in cells.

Formula AutoComplete A tool to help you enter a formula with a valid function name and arguments.

formula Bar The box to the right of the Name Box that displays a formula when the cell of a worksheet contains a calculated value (or the results of the formula).

freeze panes To keep selected rows and/or columns of the worksheet visible on the screen as the rest of the worksheet scrolls.

Full Screen Reading view A way of viewing a document on screen that shows text on the screen in a form that is easy to read; the Ribbon is replaced by a small bar called a toolbar that contains only a few relevant commands.

function A shorthand way to write an equation that performs a calculation; an action that can be defined in VBA code where you use statements to describe the action you want the function to perform.

function number A number that represents a calculation in the SUBTOTAL function.

G

gauge chart A chart that shows the amount of progress accomplished towards a goal. Also called a progress chart.

global template Template type containing document settings and styles that are available to all documents.

gradient fill A background fill composed of two or more colors that gradually blend from one color to another.

grand total The total for all the data in column(s) or row(s) in a worksheet.

graphic A picture that helps illustrate the meaning of the text and make the page more attractive; graphics include predefined shapes, diagrams, and charts, as well as photographs and drawings.

grid Vertical and horizontal lines that appear on the Slide pane and help you place text and objects.

gridlines The lines in a table that form the rows and columns.

grouping A feature that allows you to move, format, or resize several objects as if they were one object.

grouping level An option for reports that organizes data based on one or more fields into groups.

guidelines Vertical and horizontal lines that you can display on the Slide pane to help place objects on the slide.

gutter margin See *inside margin.*

H

handles Appear when an object is selected and are used to drag to resize the object.

handout master The master view for the audience handouts; includes placeholders for the slides, a header, footer, and the date and slide number.

handouts Printouts that include a small image of the slides and an area to take notes. Handouts can be formatted in several different ways using the Handout master formatting and Backstage view print options.

hanging indent A description of the indent in a paragraph when the first line of text is not indented but all of the following lines in the paragraph are.

header Text that is printed at the top of each page.

hierarchical Hierarchical refers to the different levels of automation in a form.

horizontal gridlines Lines that appear within the chart itself and are horizontal.

hot spot A hyperlink created for part of an image map.

hyperlink A reference that opens a Web page, a file, a new document, or an e-mail address when you click it.

hyphenation A setting that allows a word at the end of a line to split between syllables.

I

iCalendar An Internet calendar saved in a format that is compatible with Outlook and other calendar programs.

image map A graphic that contains multiple hyperlinks on various parts of the image without dividing the graphic into separate objects.

import A term used when data is copied from a file into a different location.

incremental search A search that returns matches for the string of characters in the document as you type; as the search text is augmented, the matches in the document change.

indent The space between text and the margin; to shift data within a cell and insert space between the cell border and its content.

index An alphabetic listing, usually at the end of a document, of pertinent words and phrases contained in a document, that references the page numbers where the related topics appear in the document.

inline object An object in a document that can be repositioned as if it were a character in the line of text.

input mask A pattern for common types of data entered in a field. Access includes several input mask formats, such as phone numbers, social security numbers, and ZIP codes.

insertion point A blinking vertical line that shows where text will appear when you begin typing.

inside margin The right margin on a left page and the left margin on the right page when a document is set up with mirrored margins. Also called *gutter margin*.

integration To share information among applications.

J

join line The line that connects tables that have a relationship; the join line connects the common fields and indicates the relationship type.

justify To format a paragraph so the text is distributed evenly across the page between the left and right margins and both the left and right edges of the paragraph are aligned at the margins.

K

keyword A word or phrase used in a search.

kiosk An interactive computer terminal available for public use.

L

Label Wizard An Access wizard that creates a report of standard or custom labels.

landscape orientation A page or worksheet rotated so it is wider than it is long.

layout The way content and text placeholders are placed on the slide.

layout master In the slide master, the individual layouts that determine the location of content and text placeholders for the slides.

layout view A view of a form or report that displays data from the record source and that lets you make certain types of changes to the form or report, such as increasing the size of a text box control.

leader A solid, dotted, or dashed line that fills the blank space before a tab stop.

left-align To position text so that it is aligned along the left margin.

legend A list in a chart that identifies the data series indicated by the colors, patterns, or symbols used in the chart.

Line chart A chart that uses points connected by a line to illustrate values in a worksheet.

line tool An Access tool that you can use to draw a line in a form or report.

link See *hyperlink*.

linked object A file, chart, table, or other object that is created in another application such as Excel, stored in a source file, and inserted into a destination file, such as a PowerPoint slide, while maintaining a connection between the two files.

list box A list box lets you select more than one value, and a combo box lets you enter a value or select a value from a list.

live preview A live preview occurs when you move your mouse pointer over a theme in the Themes gallery and it is temporarily applied to the form so that you can see how your form would look with that theme applied.

logical functions Functions that display text or values if certain conditions exist.

logo A logo is a graphic or picture that can be placed in a form.

lookup table The range of data you create in either a vertical or horizontal format that Excel will use to match against criteria in a LOOKUP function.

M

macro A group of sequential commands and actions combined as a single command to automatically complete a task.

mail merge A process that combines a document with information that personalizes it.

main document The term given to a form letter when it is used in a mail merge operation in Word.

main tabs Tabs that appear on the Ribbon when the application is launched.

manual calculation Lets you determine when Excel calculates formulas in the worksheet.

manual page break A page break you insert to start a new page.

MAPI (Messaging Application Programming Interface) A Windows programming interface that enables programs to send e-mails.

margin Blank space around the top, bottom, left, and right sides of a page.

markup Revision marks and annotations that appear in a document or presentation.

mathematical functions Functions that manipulate quantitative data in a worksheet.

merge To combine multiple cells into one cell.

merge field A placeholder in the main document in a mail merge that is replaced with data from the data source when you perform the merge.

metadata Data that describes other data.

mirrored margins Margins on left and right pages that are identical—"mirror" each other—when facing each other; usually used in books and magazines.

mixed cell reference A cell reference that contains both relative and absolute references.

motion path A way to animate an object by drawing the path on the slide. Allows you to make an object move along a specified path on the slide.

multilevel list A list with two or more levels of bullets or numbering. Also called *outline numbered list*.

Multiple Items tool An Access tool that creates a form that lists all the fields in the record source in a datasheet format.

multitable query A query that is based on the data in two or more tables.

N

Name Box The cell reference area located below the Ribbon that displays the cell reference of the active cell.

navigation form A navigation form is a special kind of form that has both a main form control and subform controls automatically built in.

Navigation Pane The pane in Access that displays the objects in a database.

negative indent A description of an indent in a paragraph in which the left indent marker is past the left margin. Also called *outdent*.

nonadjacent range A range that includes two or more adjacent ranges and selected cells.

nonbreaking hyphen A nonprinting special formatting character used to indicate hyphenated words that should not be split if the hyphen falls at the end of a line.

nonbreaking space A nonprinting special formatting character used to indicate words that should not be split between lines.

normal template Word's default global template.

Normal view The worksheet view best for entering and formatting data in a worksheet; the view in PowerPoint that includes the Slides/Outline tabs on the left, the Slide pane showing the selected slide in the center, and the Notes pane beneath the Slide pane; commonly used to place objects on the slide.

notes master The master view for the notes pages. Includes placeholders for the slide, notes, header, footer, date, and slide number.

Notes Page view A view in PowerPoint for working on the speaker notes page; includes placeholders for the slide notes.

notes pane The area below the Slide pane in which you can type speaker notes.

nudge To move an object vertically or horizontally in small increments.

number format Changes the way data looks in a cell.

O

object Anything that can be manipulated as a whole, such as clip art or another graphic you insert into a document; objects can be inserted, modified, resized, repositioned, and deleted.

Office Clipboard (or **Clipboard**) A temporary storage area for up to 24 selections you copy or cut.

one-to-many relationship A relationship between two tables in a database in which one record in the primary table can match many (zero, one, or many) records in the related table.

Open Exclusive mode In the Open Exclusive mode, only the person who opened the database can use and make changes to it; all other users are locked out from opening and using the database.

operand A constant (text or number) or cell reference used in a formula.

operator Operators are the mathematical characters—such as plus (+), minus (–), multiplication (*), and division (/)—that determine the type of calculation in the expression.

optional hyphen A nonprinting special formatting character used to indicate where a word can be divided if all the characters in the word do not fit on the same line.

order of evaluation The sequence used to calculate the value of a formula.

orientation Rotates cell contents to an angle or vertically.

or operator An operator used in a query that selects records that match at least one of two or more conditions in a query.

organization chart A SmartArt graphic used to show hierarchy and relationships of people or objects.

orphan The first line of a multi-line paragraph that is split from the other lines in the paragraph and appears at the bottom of a page or a column.

outdent See *negative indent.*

outcrop Add blank space around a graphic.

outline numbered list See *multilevel list.*

Outline tab A tab used to enter text in Normal view, located on the left side of the window in the same pane as the Slides tab.

Outline view A way of viewing a document on screen that displays headings and text in outline form so you can see the structure of your document and reorganize easily; headers and footers, page boundaries, graphics, and backgrounds do not appear.

outside margin The left margin on the left page and the right margin on the right page when a document is set up with mirrored margins.

P

Package for CD A feature that allows you to save a presentation to a CD to be viewed on a computer that does not have PowerPoint installed.

page break The place where one page ends and another begins.

Page Break Preview The worksheet view for adjusting page breaks in a worksheet.

Page Layout view The worksheet view that shows how the worksheet will appear on paper.

pagination The system by which text and objects are manipulated to create the page layout.

parameter Parameter means to vary. In Access, a parameter query will produce data that varies.

parent In a PivotTable, when there is more than one level, the main row heading is referred to as the parent and the level of detail below this level is the child.

passim A word used in annotations to indicate that terms, passages, or page references occur frequently in the work cited; in Word the default setting *Use passim* formats multiple page references on the same line in a table of authorities.

password A password is a collection of characters that a user types to gain access to a file.

paste To copy an item stored on the Clipboard or the Office Clipboard to a location in a file.

picture A digital photograph or other image file.

pie chart A chart that shows the relationship of a part to a whole.

PivotChart The data in a PivotTable can be rearranged and summarized in different ways so that you can view the data from various perspectives.

pixels Short for picture elements; tiny colored dots that compose an image on a computer screen. (See also *bits*)

placeholder A placeholder appears in a field before the value is entered; a boxed outline on a slide that can be used to insert text or an object when clicked.

plot area A rectangular border that encloses the two axes and the data series; depending on the chart formats, the plot area may also include category names, data labels, and axes titles.

point The unit of measurement for fonts.

point-and-click method In a formula, to click a cell rather than type its cell reference.

Portable Document Format (PDF) A format developed by Adobe Systems designed to preserve the visual appearance and layout of each page and enable fast viewing and printing.

portrait orientation A page or worksheet rotated so it is longer than it is wide.

PowerPoint presentation A computer slide show created in PowerPoint.

PowerPoint Viewer A Microsoft application that enables you to open PowerPoint presentations when the PowerPoint application is not installed on the computer.

precedent Cells that supply the values used in a function.

presenter view Offers a way for you to view your presentation with the speaker notes showing on one computer screen, while an audience views the presentation without viewing the speaker notes on another computer screen.

primary axis The y-axis on the left side of the chart.

primary key The field in a database table that contains a unique field value for each record in the table.

primary table In a one-to-many relationship, the table that contains the records on the "one" side of the relationship.

print area The cells and ranges designated for printing.

Print Layout view The most common way of viewing a document on screen; it shows how a document will look when it is printed, and you can work with headers and footers, margins, columns, and graphics, which are all displayed.

Print Preview The view of a table, query, form, or report in Access that shows how the object will appear when printed and that lets you make adjustments to the printer and print settings.

print titles Designated rows and/or columns in a worksheet that print on each page.

private key A key for a digital ID that stays on the sender's computer.

procedure A procedure is a group of statements written in VBA code that can include several functions.

progressive disclosure A technique that reveals slide content in increments.

property Identifying information about a file that is saved along with the file, such as the author's name and the date the file was created.

public A function in a module that is accessible throughout the database.

public key A key for a digital ID that a sender gives to a recipient.

publishing Placing a presentation in a format for others to use; published presentations include handouts, Package for CD, and presentations on a document management server, in a document workspace, and on the Web.

pull quote A line or phrase excerpted from the main text and used to draw attention in a document.

Q

query A database object that lets you ask the database about the data it contains.

Quick Access Toolbar A small customizable toolbar at the top of the screen with buttons for common commands such as Save and Print.

Quick Part A building block stored in the Quick Parts gallery and available when you click the Quick Parts button in the Text group on the Insert tab.

Quick Style A predefined format that you can apply by clicking a button in the Styles group on the Home tab.

R

range A group of selected cells.

range reference The unique identifier for a range, which is the cell in its upper-left corner and the cell in its lower-right corner, separated by a colon.

range-of-values condition A condition in a query that specifies a range of values that a record must satisfy to be displayed in the query results.

raster graphics Graphics created in a file format that consists of rows of tiny colored dots called pixels that compose an image on a computer screen.

read-only A term used to describe data that can be viewed but not changed.

read-only document A document users are able to open and read, but to which they are unable to make changes.

Reading view A PowerPoint view you can use to display your presentation; very much like Slide Show view, the slide does not quite fill the screen and you can use navigation buttons on the status bar beneath the slide.

record A group of related fields, or a single field, treated as a unit in a data source, such as all the contact information for one individual.

record selector The box to the left of a record in a datasheet that, when clicked, selects the entire record.

record source The tables or queries that contain the data used in a form or report.

reference marker A superscript number or custom character, such as an asterisk, inserted in the document to reference a footnote or endnote.

referential integrity A set of rules that a DBMS follows to ensure that there are matching values in the common field used to create the relationship between related tables and that protects the data in related tables to make sure that data is not accidentally deleted or changed.

related table In a one-to-many relationship, the table that contains the records on the "many" side of the relationship.

relationship The feature of a DBMS that lets you connect the data in the tables in the database so you can create queries and other objects using the data from two or more tables.

relative cell reference A cell reference that adjusts to its new location when copied or moved.

report A database object that displays data from one or more tables or queries in a format that has an appearance similar to a printed report.

report selector The box in the upper-left corner of a report where the horizontal and vertical rulers intersect that you can click to select the entire report.

report tool An Access tool that creates a simple report that includes all the fields in the selected table or query on which it is based, uses a columnar format, formats the report using a theme, and includes a title with the same name as the record source.

report Wizard An Access wizard that you can use to create a report by specifying a record source, layout, sort order, and grouping level.

required property A field property that specifies whether a value must be entered into the field.

research task pane A task pane that provides access to information typically found in references such as dictionaries, thesauruses, and encyclopedias.

revision bar A vertical line that appears in the left margin of a Word document, indicating that there is a tracked change or comment related to the paragraph.

Ribbon An area at the top of an Office program window that contains commands for working with the open file; the commands are organized under tabs.

right-align To position text so that it is aligned along the right margin.

rotate handle The green handle on a selected object that you can drag to turn the object clockwise or counterclockwise.

row Appears horizontally in the worksheet; identified by numbers on the left side of the worksheet window.

row heading The row number.

rule An action that Outlook automatically performs on both incoming and outgoing messages, based on certain conditions.

run The term given to the act of opening a query and displaying the query results.

S

sans serif fonts Fonts that do not include serifs.

scale To resize a worksheet to print on a specific number of pages.

scaling Sizing a graphic so that its proportions are precise.

scatter chart A chart that shows the relationship between two categories of data; sometimes called an XY chart.

Scenario Manager Performs a "what-if" analysis on several cells of data by changing the data in these cells.

screen clipping The area you choose to include in a screenshot.

screenshot A picture of all or part of something you see on your monitor, such as a Word document, an Excel workbook, a photograph, or a Web page.

Search Folder A virtual folder that contains views of all e-mails messages that match specific search criteria.

section A part of a document where you can apply a layout, headers and footers, page numbers, margins, orientation, and other formatting features different from the rest of the document.

section break A formatting code that used to divide a document into sections.

select To highlight a block of text.

selection rectangle The box that appears around an object when it is selected.

separator line A line that separates the body text from the footnote area.

serif A small line or curl at the end of a font character that embellishes the character.

serif fonts Fonts that have serifs.

secondary axis The y-axis on the right side of the chart.

shape Rectangles, circles, arrows, lines, flowchart symbols, or callouts that can help make a worksheet more informative.

shared workbook A file that can be accessed and changed by more than one person.

sheet tab The name of each worksheet at the bottom of the worksheet window.

sidebar Text set off from the main body of text in a text box that provides additional information for the reader.

signature line A security feature that you add to a workbook file so that someone else can sign, or verify, the information in the workbook.

Simple Query Wizard The wizard in Access that lets you create a query and indicate what you'd like to see in the query results by selecting options in dialog boxes.

sizing handle A square, circle, or set of three dots that appears on a selection rectangle around an object and that you can drag to resize the object.

SkyDrive A program that allows you to access and share files online with friends, family members, or co-workers on the Web.

slicer A visual control that looks like a notepad. The slicer lets you filter your data in a PivotTable.

slide layout The placement of placeholders or objects on a slide that determines how all of the objects on a slide are arranged.

slide library A special type of library used in SharePoint to store presentation slides.

slide master Determines the graphics and layout for the slides in a presentation. Each theme has a slide master, and slide masters include layout masters.

slide pane The main work area for the selected slide in Normal view.

Slide Show view A view in PowerPoint that shows the slides on the full screen with animations and transitions.

Slide Sorter view A view in PowerPoint that displays a thumbnail of each slide in the order in which they appear in the presentation; used to rearrange slides, check timings, and view slide transitions.

slide transition The animated way in which a slide appears and leaves the screen during a slide show.

slides tab In Normal view, the tab on the left slide of the PowerPoint window that displays thumbnails of each slide.

SmartArt A predesigned chart or diagram that visually illustrates text and includes formatted graphics.

SmartArt graphic A graphic diagram that visually illustrates text and includes formatted graphics.

snap to When an object is drawn to the guide or grid as though it were magnetic; used for exact placement of objects.

source The location that data is being transferred from.

source file The file in which a linked or embedded object is stored in a presentation.

source file The document file from which you are transferring data when you move data between applications.

sort To arrange a list of words or numbers in ascending or descending order.

sparkline A miniature chart that can be displayed in a single row or column of data.

spell checker A feature used to locate and correct spelling errors.

splash screen A splash screen is a form that appears when you open a database that welcomes the user to the database. A splash screen can contain information such as a company's name and the same themes used in the database.

split To divide the worksheet window into two or four panes that scroll independently.

Split Form tool An Access tool that creates a form using all the fields in the selected record source and splits the window into two panes, with one displaying the form in Form view and the other displaying the form in Datasheet view.

spreadsheet A grid of rows and columns in which you enter text, numbers, and the results of calculations.

statistical functions Functions that are used to describe large quantities of data.

startup options Startup options are options that Access performs when the database is opened.

status bar A bar at the bottom of the program window that provides information about the current file and process.

streaming video Media sent in a continuous stream of data that can be played from an online source without waiting to download the file.

story The text contained within a text box.

style A combination of formatting characteristics such as alignment, font, font size, font color, fill color, and borders that are applied simultaneously; a set of predefined formats you can apply to characters, paragraphs, tables, and numbered and bulleted lists.

style sheet A list of all styles that are used in a document or available in a template.

subdatasheet When two tables are related, the datasheet for the primary table contains expand indicators for each record. Clicking an expand indicator in the primary table displays the records in the related table in a subdatasheet.

subreport Subreports are reports you create and then embed in another report.

subtotal The total of only specific parts of the data.

Sum button Inserts the SUM function to add long columns or rows of numbers.

summary query A query that summarizes relevant data, such as adding the field values in a column that displays price data, in the query results.

summary slide A slide that reviews the topics in a presentation.

switch A special instruction that modifies a field result.

syntax Syntax is a name for the wording that is used in VBA (Visual Basic for Applications).

System Clipboard See *Clipboard.*

T

Tab A section of the Ribbon.

tab order Tab order is the order of movement in a record when you press the Tab key.

tab stop An indicator in a paragraph that marks the place where the insertion point will stop when you press the Tab key. Also called *tab.*

table An arrangement of text or numbers in rows and columns, similar to a spreadsheet.

table of authorities A summary of the references used in a legal document to cite cases, statutes, rules and other sources.

table of contents A sequential list of contents that provides an overview of the topics in a document.

table of figures A sequential list of all the figures (such as tables, equations, pictures, charts, graphs, and other illustrations) included in a document.

Taskbar The area at the bottom of the Windows screen that contains the Start button as well as program or window buttons for open programs.

template A file that already contains the basic elements of a document, workbook, presentation, or database, such as page and paragraph formatting, fonts, and text and from which you can create a new file.

text box A shape specifically designed to hold text.

text effect Formatting for text that is similar to font styles and can help enhance or clarify text. Also called *font effect.*

text functions Functions that are used to format and display cell contents.

theme A preset collection of design elements, including fonts, colors, and other effects.

thesaurus A feature used to find a synonym, or a word with a similar meaning.

Thesaurus A built-in reference for finding synonyms for words in a document.

thumbnail A small graphic image.

title bar The area at the top of the each window that contains information about the window as well as window controls such as the Minimize, Maximize, and Close buttons.

toggle To switch between two options or to turn a feature on or off.

toolbar A small bar that appears at the top or bottom of a window instead of the Ribbon; it displays buttons you can click to quickly choose a command.

tool tabs Contextual tabs that appear on the Ribbon when objects are selected in a document.

total row The optional row in a datasheet that counts of the number of values in a column. When a field contains numeric data, you can use the Total row to calculate the total, average, minimum, or maximum value in a column.

tracer arrow An arrow drawn from cells to show dependents or precedents.

Track Changes A tool in Word that keeps a record of any changes you or a reviewer makes in a document by formatting inserted text in a color and underlined, and deleted and moved text in a balloon in the right margin.

transition See *slide transition.*

trigonometric functions Functions that manipulate quantitative data in a worksheet.

truncate To hide text that does not fit in a cell.

U

unbound control A control in a form or report, such as a line, rectangle, or picture, that is not connected to the record source on which the form or report is based.

V

validation range The range of cells that you select to apply the validation rule.

validation rule Allows you to set parameters for worksheet cells where values will be entered.

validation rules Rules that need to be met before the data can be entered.

value axis The identifying numbers listed on the vertical axis in a chart.

variable name A variable name is simply a symbolic name that you assign to a value. Creating variable names that make functions easy to understand can help make your database more user-friendly

VBA (Visual Basic for Applications) A computer programming language and environment designed for use within Office and other Microsoft applications.

vCard A file format standard used for sharing contact information on the Internet.

vector graphics Graphics created in a file format that consist of lines, curves, and shapes.

vertical alignment The position of text on a page between the top and bottom margins.

vertical gridlines Lines that appear within the chart itself and are vertical.

view buttons In an Office program window, buttons that you can click to change views quickly.

virus A computer program designed to replicate itself; often causes damage to computer data, documents, and the computer operating system.

W

Watch Window Lets you view the data while working in another worksheet.

watermark A ghost image that appears behind the content of a document. A watermark image can also be created by impressing text or a graphic image in the paper when the paper is manufactured.

Web Layout view A way of viewing a document on screen that simulates the way a document will look when it is viewed as a Web page; text and graphics appear the way they would in a Web browser, and backgrounds are visible.

widow The last line of a multi-line paragraph that is split from the other lines in the paragraph and wraps to the next page or column.

wildcard character A wildcard character is a character, such as an asterisk, that you can use to represent incomplete or unknown information when performing a search.

word processing The use of a computer and software to enter and edit text and produce documents such as letters, memos, forms, and reports.

word wrap A feature in Word that automatically wraps words around to the next line when they will not fit on the current line.

WordArt Feature that displays text as a graphic; includes options for formatting, text fills, shapes, and effects.

workbook The file used to store worksheets; usually a collection of related worksheets.

workgroup collaboration The process of working together in teams, sharing comments, and exchanging ideas for a common purpose.

works cited page A list of source materials that are used in the preparation of a work. (See also *bibliography*)

worksheet A computerized spreadsheet in Excel.

worksheet range A group of adjacent worksheets.

wrap text To move data to a new line when the cell is not wide enough to display all the contents.

X

X-axis The horizontal axis in a chart.

XML Paper Specification (XPS) A format developed by Microsoft designed to preserve the visual appearance and layout of each page and enable fast viewing and printing.

XML Paper Specification (XPS) A format developed by Microsoft designed to preserve the visual appearance and layout of each page and to enable fast viewing and printing.

Y

Y-axis The vertical axis in a chart.

Z

zoom The percentage the file is magnified or reduced on the screen; 100% zoom represents the normal size; percentages higher than 100% mean the document appears larger on screen; percentages lower than 100% mean the document appears smaller on screen.

Zoom Slider A feature on the status bar that can be dragged to change the zoom percentage of the Slide pane in the PowerPoint window.

INDEX

B

C

E

F

G

J

K

N

O

Q

R

T

U

V

W

PHOTO CREDITS

Figure Number	Credit line
A-1	Courtesy of Hewlett-Packard Company
A-2	© Alex Roz/Shutterstock.com
A-3a	Courtesy of Microsoft Corporation
A-3b	Courtesy of Microsoft Corporation
A-3c	Photograph courtesy of Intermec Technologies
A-3d	Courtesy of Logitech
A-3e	Courtesy of Microsoft Corporation
A-4	Courtesy of Intel Corporation
A-5	Courtesy of Seagate Technology
A-6	© Inga Nielsen/Shutterstock.com
A-7	© Feng Yu/Shutterstock.com
A-8a	Courtesy of Imation Corp.
A-8b	Courtesy of Imation Corp.
A-8c	© sad/Shutterstock.com
A-9	Courtesy of SanDisk Corporation
A-10a	Courtesy of SanDisk Corporation
A-10b	© Serg64/Shutterstock.com
A-11	Courtesy of Hewlett-Packard Company
A-11	Courtesy of Hewlett-Packard Company
A-12	Courtesy of ViewSonic Corporation
A-13a	Courtesy of Hewlett-Packard Company
A-13b	Courtesy of Hewlett-Packard Company
A-14	©tatniz/Shutterstock.com
A-15a	Courtesy of Apple
A-15b	© iStockphoto
A-16	Courtesy of Kingston Technology Corporation
A-17	Courtesy of Hewlett-Packard Company
A-20	Courtesy of IBM Archives
A-21	Courtesy of IBM Archives
A-22	n/a
A-25a	© Jose Luis Pelaez, Inc./ Getty Images
A-25b	© Ryan McVay/ Getty Images